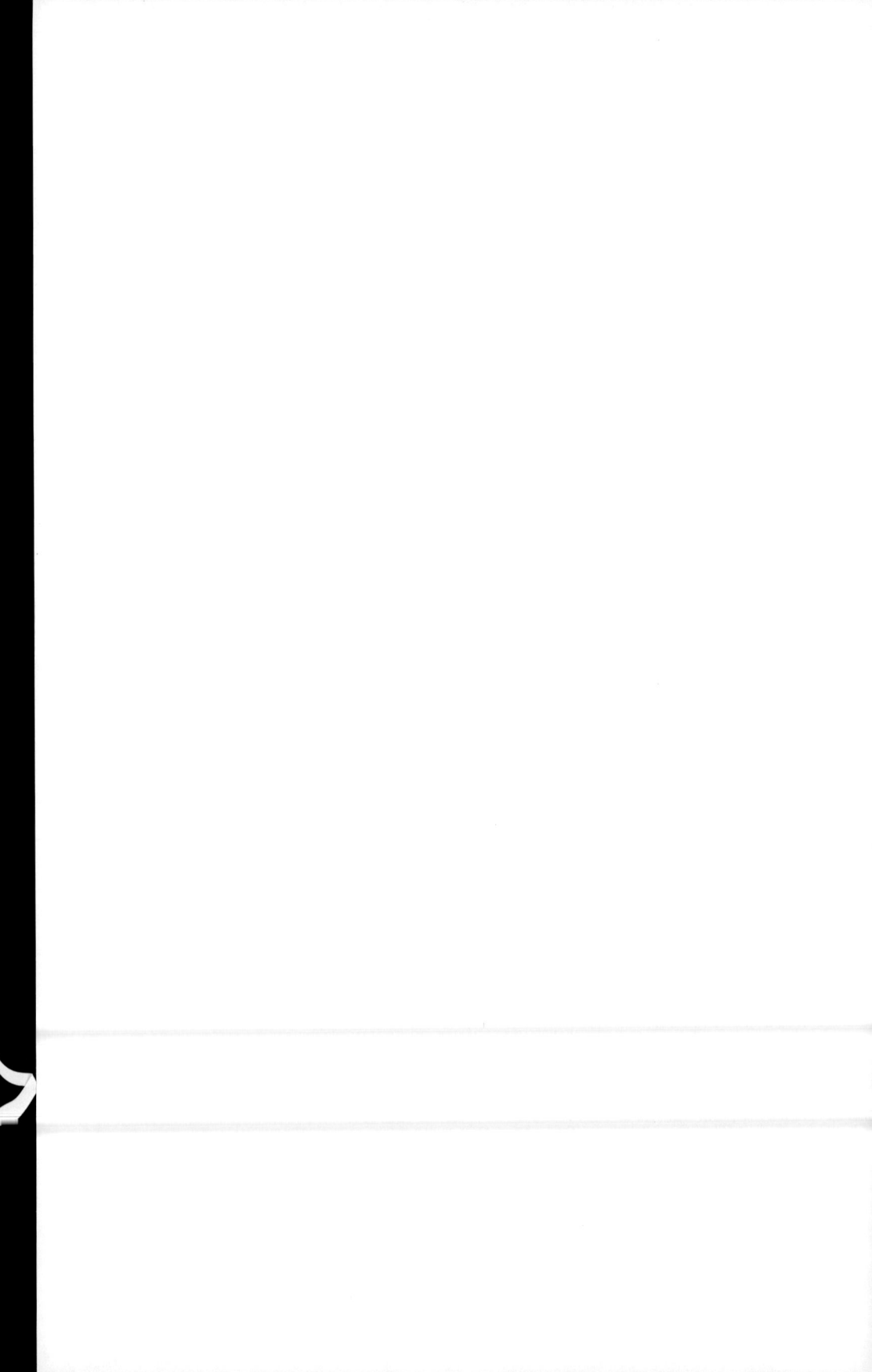

CONCERT LIFE

IN NINETEENTH-CENTURY

NEW ORLEANS

CONCERT LIFE
IN NINETEENTH-CENTURY
NEW ORLEANS

{ A Comprehensive Reference }

JOHN H. BARON

Louisiana State University Press
Baton Rouge

Publication of this book is made possible in part by the support of Adelaide Wisdom Benjamin, Marie-Jeanne Trauth, the Gustave Reese Endowment of the American Musicological Society, the New Orleans Jazz & Heritage Festival and Foundation Inc., and Tulane University.

Published by Louisiana State University Press
Copyright © 2013 by Louisiana State University Press
All rights reserved
Manufactured in the United States of America
First printing

Designer: Michelle A. Neustrom
Typeface: Vulpa
Printer and binder: Maple Press

Library of Congress Cataloging-in-Publication Data
Baron, John H.
  Concert life in nineteenth-century New Orleans : a comprehensive reference / John H. Baron.
      pages cm
  Includes bibliographical references and index.
  ISBN 978-0-8071-5082-5 (cloth : alk. paper) — ISBN 978-0-8071-5083-2 (pdf) — ISBN 978-0-8071-5084-9 (epub) — ISBN 978-0-8071-5085-6 (mobi)
  1. Music—Louisiana—New Orleans—19th century—History and criticism.
  2. Music—Social aspects—Louisiana—New Orleans—History—19th century.
  3. Concerts—Louisiana—New Orleans—History—19th century. 4. Musicians—Louisiana—New Orleans. I. Title. II. Title: Concert life in 19th-century New Orleans.
  ML200.8.N48B37 2013
  780.78'7633509034—dc23

2012049694

The paper in this book meets the guidelines for permanence and durability of the Committee on Production Guidelines for Book Longevity of the Council on Library Resources. ∞

To my New Orleans children,
Beth Seltzer, Daniel Seltzer, Jeffrey Baron,
and Miriam Baron, and to my grandchildren,
Edie, Teddy, and those who may follow.

CONTENTS

LIST OF ILLUSTRATIONS | *ix*

PREFACE | *xi*

ACKNOWLEDGMENTS | *xiii*

Introduction: New Orleans | *1*

BOOK I. A TOPICAL HISTORY

Part I. Musical Institutions and Genres

1. Concert Venues in New Orleans: 1805–1897 | *9*
   1805–1819 | *9*
   1819–1897 | *12*
   Churches, Parks, and Other Venues | *25*

2. Symphonic Music in Nineteenth-Century New Orleans | *31*
   Orchestral Music Prior to the Civil War | *32*
   The Civil War Period | *39*
   Recovery during the Post–Civil War Years | *44*
   The Final Years of the Century: 1880–1897 | *54*

3. The Concert Societies and Series | *68*
   The Philharmonic Societies | *68*
   Collignon's Classical Series | *76*
   L'Orphéon Français | *87*
   Frohsinn | *93*
   Other Societies | *95*

4. Music and Race in Nineteenth-Century New Orleans | *97*

5. Music Education | *105*
   Music Education to 1861 | *105*
   Music Education during and after the Civil War | *109*

6. Women in the Musical Life of the City in the Eighteenth and Nineteenth Centuries | *121*

Part II. Personalities

  1. Louis Hus Desforges: Pioneer Conductor and Violinist | *141*
  2. Gregorio Curto: Bass Singer, Church Musician, and Vocal Teacher | *146*
  3. Paul Emile Johns: Tycoon, Musician, and Friend of Chopin | *164*
  4. Ludovico Gabici: Violinist and Conductor | *169*
  5. Eugène Prévost: Eminent Conductor and Composer | *179*
  6. Theodore von La Hache: Prolific Composer, Organist, Teacher, and Choral Conductor | *184*
      Works of Theodore von La Hache | *192*
  7. Hubert Rolling: Pianist and Composer | *197*
      Works of Hubert Rolling | *203*
  8. Jeanne Franko: Famous Violinist in a Musical Family | *205*
  9. Marguerite Elie Samuel: Champion of Good Taste | *210*
  10. Mark Kaiser: Violinist, Teacher, and Proud Citizen | *223*
  11. Gustave D'Aquin: Flutist and Band Conductor | *233*
  12. Theodore Curant: Verdi's Violinist in New Orleans | *244*
  13. Henry Wehrman Jr.: Violinist and Collector of Creole Songs | *249*
  14. William Henry Pilcher's Conservatory of Music | *258*

BOOK II. A CHRONOLOGICAL HISTORY

  1. The Early Years: 1805–1835 | *269*
  2. The Musical Metropolis: 1836–1849 | *303*
  3. The Great Years: 1850–1860 | *349*
  4. Concert Music during the Civil War: 1861–1865 | *391*
  5. Recovery of the Postwar Years: 1865–1872 | *401*
  6. From the City to the Lake and the Great Exposition: 1872–1886 | *427*
  7. The Grand Old City: 1887–1897 | *481*

NOTES | *547*

BIBLIOGRAPHY | *657*

INDEX | *665*

ILLUSTRATIONS

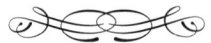

BUILDINGS AND PARKS
Following page 30

Théâtre d'Orléans, 1809–1813
Théâtre d'Orléans, 1819–1866
Camp Street Theatre, 1823–1880
Two views of the Washington Artillery Hall
Saint Charles Theatre, 1835–1842
New American Theatre, 1835–1840
Varieties Theater, 1854–present
Mechanics' Institute Hall
Old and New Odd Fellows' Hall
Academy of Music
Lyceum Hall
French Opera House, 1859–1919
French Opera House seating plans
German National Theater
Grunewald Hall, 1874–1892
Church of the Immaculate Conception, 1857–1928
Saint Louis Cathedral, 1794–present
Spanish Fort Concert Hall
Spanish Fort, typical crowd scene
Jockey Club in the City Fair Grounds

PORTRAITS
Following page 266

Jeanne Franko
Marguerite Samuel
Mark Kaiser

Theodore Curant
Henry Wehrmann Jr.
The Beethoven Quartet
William Henry Pilcher
Pilcher's Conservatory, Recital Hall
Julia Calvé Boudousquié
Ole Bull
Camillo Sivori
Charles Boudousquié
Louis Grunewald
Philip Werlein
Teresa Carreño
J. W. H. Eckert
David Bidwell
Florence Huberwald
Ovide Musin

MAPS

Map 1. New Orleans, 1838 | *2*
Map 2. New Orleans, 1874 | *3*

PREFACE

This is the first and only comprehensive history of classical concerts in New Orleans from 1805 to 1897.[1] During this period the musical scene in New Orleans was probably unrivaled by that in any other American city. There was regular repertory opera in New Orleans when the major cities on the East Coast and in the Midwest had none. There were professional and amateur orchestras, chamber music, and flourishing choral societies. Louis Moreau Gottschalk—arguably the most important musician in nineteenth-century America—was born and bred there, and so were Bazille Barès and Edmond Dédé, among other African American classical musicians. Henri Vieuxtemps, Henri Herz, Anton Rubinstein, Sigismond Thalberg, Henrietta Sontag, and many other European superstars loved the music scene in New Orleans in the nineteenth century. No important American artist, from Adelina Patti and her sisters on down, could escape its charm. It was a city unlike any other, in its architecture, its cuisine, its ethnically and socially diverse population, and its taste for classical music. It suffered war, epidemics, fires, and floods, none of which could curtail its citizens' thirst for great music.

This history is in two books. Book I is a topical history of the concerts and selected biographies of important musicians in New Orleans; Book II is a chronological history of the concerts.[2] Our major source for the concerts is newspaper advertisements and reviews. Almost all of these are from newspapers published in New Orleans during the nineteenth century, but some are from New York, Paris, and elsewhere. Furthermore, some diaries, autobiographies, and personal scrapbooks and unpublished papers have been consulted. Unless otherwise indicated, translations are my own. In addition, I have consulted numerous studies by musicologists and other historians and cited these in the notes and bibliography.

ACKNOWLEDGMENTS

This study would not have been possible without the assistance of generous friends and students, chief among whom are Jack Belsom and Sarah Borgatti. I also wish to thank the dedicated librarians at Tulane University, the Louisiana State Archives at the United States Mint in New Orleans, the Historic New Orleans Collection, Louisiana State University Library in Baton Rouge, and the New Orleans Public Library who provided me with microfilms, supporting volumes, archival material, illustrations, and crucial advice. I also wish to thank the librarians in the microfilm room of the East Jefferson Parish Library who helped me with newspaper films during the first year after Hurricane Katrina when other archives were closed. In 1972, Professor Robert Stevenson suggested that I look into the history of classical music in New Orleans and started me on my study of this particular subject. Subsequently, still many years ago, Mark McKnight discussed with me the possibility of our writing a history of the music of New Orleans from 1718 to the present, and I realized at that time that I was not prepared to do so. I decided, then, to concentrate on one aspect of that history over a confined period and thus make a contribution to that overall history; the present volume is the result. I am grateful for subventions from Gustave Reese Endowment of the American Musicological Society, the New Orleans Jazz and Heritage Foundation, the School of Liberal Arts of Tulane University, Mrs. Adelaide Benjamin, and Marie-Jeanne Trauth. Ultimately this work was made possible through the encouragement of my wife, Doris, who often made important suggestions.

CONCERT LIFE
IN NINETEENTH-CENTURY
NEW ORLEANS

INTRODUCTION

New Orleans

New Orleans was first inhabited by American Indians. Then, from 1718 on it was the haven for adventurers, refugees, slaves, soldiers, and do-gooders from Europe and the rest of the world. The French established it as a dumping ground for humans they regarded as antisocial, and a disregard for established rules and morals in the colony led to a society that relished lifestyles that were considered sinful in Anglo America. Thus, its musical culture, which was always central to its life, produced a multifaceted dimension that was different from the rest of continental America.[1] During the nineteenth century this unique musical society was remarkable not only for its contributions to the creation of the important American genres of ragtime and jazz, but also in its establishment in America of certain European art forms, most notably opera and public concerts. This last—public concerts in nineteenth-century New Orleans—is the focus of this volume.

By the beginning of the nineteenth century, the racial, religious, ethnic, social, political, and cultural diversity in New Orleans resulted in a unique blend of peoples that made the city probably the most fascinating city in America if not the world. The term "Creole" in 1803 was used to distinguish native-born Louisianans from those who were not native born. It was an all-encompassing term that applied to all native-born persons of any racial, religious, or ethnic background. It included Anglo-Saxons as well as those of French, Spanish, and other national backgrounds. Understood in New Orleans was that blacks were an underclass and whites ruled, but this distinction was not an issue with the term "Creole." During the eighteenth century, the intermingling of Africans (free as well as enslaved), Europeans, and Native Americans in New Orleans produced an array of mulattoes, quadroons, octoroons, and various in-between types, and their place within the political structure of the city was clearly below pure whites. How all of this affected the music of the city will be elaborated upon in part I, chapter 4.

MAP 1. New Orleans, 1838. Bradford, opposite 33.

The heart of New Orleans in 1800 consisted of a French sector (the French Quarter or Vieux Carré) and a fledging American sector. The French sector was shaped as a rectangle bounded on one side by the Mississippi River (considered the front side), by a swamp on the opposite (rear) side that was defined by North Rampart Street, on the left side by Canal Street (a proposed canal was never built), and on the right side by Esplanade Avenue; these boundaries exist today. (See map 1.)

The Americans settled on the other (uptown) side of Canal Street, and several French suburbs (fauxbourgs) extended below Esplanade Avenue. Huge plantations (farms) were carved outside New Orleans along the Mississippi River, many of which were absorbed by the Greater New Orleans urban setting during the nineteenth century. The swamp beyond Rampart Street—today extending from Tremé to Lake Pontchartrain—was called Congo Square at the edge nearest Rampart Street and, during the nineteenth-century, developed into what are known today as Mid-City, Lakeview, and the Lake Front. The lake and the river give shape to the city; its crescent design earned the city the nickname "Crescent City."

Most of these areas of New Orleans were French speaking in 1800 and English speaking in 1900. The white, black, and mulatto population intermingled in all sections. Germans, Irish, Italians, and other European groups had their own areas later in the nineteenth century, largely outside the French Quarter but also within that area. During the early nineteenth century the city was divided politically into three municipalities or districts: the French (I) and American (II) municipalities (the French Quarter and the areas uptown from Canal Street respectively) and a third municipality including the French suburbs below Esplanade Avenue. They were run as distinct governments from 1836 to 1852 since the ethnic groups had difficulty working together. Thereafter, New Orleans was unified as a single city divided into eleven wards, gradually expanded to seventeen by the 1870s. Wards 1–3 comprise the American sector, and wards 4–6 comprise the French sector; the other wards are the areas that were added later, including Algiers (Ward 15 on the other side of the Mississippi

MAP 2. New Orleans, 1874. "Plan of New Orleans" by S. Augustus Mitchell. Maps of New Orleans, 1874, Image File C5-D7-F4, Louisiana Research Collection, Tulane University.

River) and the Town of Carrollton (Ward 17 to the west of the First Ward). (See map 2.)

What made New Orleans into a world music capital was the establishment of opera from 1796 on, largely through the immigration of talented performers from Santo Domingo after 1791. During the second and third decades of the new century, opera performances reached an artistic level surpassed only by the best houses in Europe and nowhere equaled in America. With the presence of both professionals and enthusiastic, trained amateurs, a concert life emerged in 1805. The concerts usually were multidimensional with both vocal and instrumental performers performing solo, chamber, and large ensemble pieces. For most of the century these were termed "concerts vocal et instrumental," but they could also be called "soirées" with no apparent distinction. The term "recital" does not appear until later in the century. Rarely did an artist appear alone on a program. A special type of concert was termed "intermède," which was a performance usually by a soloist or small ensemble at one of the opera houses before, after, or during the intermission of a dramatic, operatic, or dance work. Orchestral concerts that were termed rehearsals were probably not like our modern open rehearsals where the conductor is prone to interrupt the music for suggestions to the players; rather they were actual concerts.

The venues for concerts could be indoors or outdoors. When indoors, they would typically be in various halls designed primarily for opera or spoken drama. The first opera house of significance—the Theater d'Orléans—became an important concert hall that was superseded by the famous French Opera House in 1859. By mid-century, concert halls were erected specifically for concerts, both in the French Quarter and in the American sector. Churches throughout the city provided space for concerts. Outdoor concerts in several of the parks and squares existed before the Civil War but became prominent right afterward and throughout the rest of the nineteenth century.

The musical environment in New Orleans was enhanced by various clubs and societies, often devoted to a particular kind of concert (orchestral, choral) or composer (Gounod, Mendelssohn). Ancillary musical activities—such as music stores, music publications, music education, instrument building—were necessary for the rich concert scene in nineteenth-century New Orleans.

BOOK I

{ A Topical History }

PART I

Musical Institutions and Genres

1

Concert Venues in New Orleans
1805–1897

The performance venues in New Orleans in the nineteenth century included both private and public locations. Concerts in private homes were occasionally mentioned, but it is difficult to reconstruct the specific rooms where the performances took place, even if we can locate today the actual home.[1] While the homes in the French Quarter in general would have had only modest space, seating perhaps a dozen or two listeners at most, the homes in the American sector were larger and in some cases could seat perhaps up to fifty or sixty listeners. Public concert halls and churches, however, can usually be identified, in some cases with a good deal of detail, and how performers and listeners regarded these places sometimes can also be ascertained. These usually sat hundreds and even thousands of persons. Some of them still exist. The word "salle" simply meant hall; it could be in a theater, a church, a school, or a private space. There were also outdoor venues and cafés.

1805–1819

Initially there was a distinction between the theaters in New Orleans, where plays, operas, vaudevilles, ballets, a few concerts, and the intermèdes were performed, and other venues where most concerts were performed followed by social dancing (balls). The theaters from 1805 to 1819 were usually well described, and their histories can be shown. The concert halls received less attention.

There were three early theaters in New Orleans where dramatic productions including operas took place. The first operas in New Orleans were performed in the Saint Peter Street Theater, the edifice of which still stands on Saint Peter Street between Royal and Bourbon streets. It served as a theater only from 1792 to 1810 and housed actors, such as those directed by Louis Tabary,[2] who had fled Santo Domingo (Haiti). In 1796 Grétry's *Silvain*[3] was performed there, and apparently also most operas from then until 1808. Louis Tabary was an actor in the Saint Peter Street Theater and was involved in intrigues to take over the theater (he became director in April 1806) and to create a rival theater.[4] Until 1807 there is no record of any concerts at the Saint Peter Street Theater, but a charitable concert was held there on January 31, 1807, in honor of Mr. Bourgeois from Santo Domingo, who was old and responsible for a large family.[5] Later that year, on December 29, a benefit concert for the violinist Desforges was also performed at the theater.[6] The Saint Peter Street Theater had its own orchestra and chorus, which were honored on August 20, 1807. There were intermèdes on May 10, 1807, and shortly after October 22, 1808.[7] Once the Saint Philip Street Theater opened and there was competition for dramatic productions, some concerts apparently were held in the Saint Peter Street Theater (for example, on March 11, 1809, October 11, 1810, and December 26, 1810). In December 1810 all the dramatic productions were followed by concerts and balls.

In the summer of 1806, Tabary, manager of the Saint Peter Street Theatre, started making efforts to build a what the *Moniteur de la Louisiana* called a "nouvelle salle de spectacle."[8] It was to be located on Bourbon Street between Orleans and Sainte Ann streets and was to be designed by the French architect Laciotte. The project fell through, however, and Tabary began negotiating with Bernardo Coquet, who owned a dance hall on Saint Philip Street, to convert the hall into a new theater. Coquet's dance hall, known as Salle Chinoise (it was famous as a hall where only free women of color and white men were admitted), opened briefly in 1807 as the Théâtre les Varietes Amusantes.[9] In 1808 it was rebuilt, enlarged, and renamed after the street on which it was located. At this point Tabary was ousted and returned to the Saint Peter Street Theater, where he acted and was again, for a short while, director.[10]

When the Saint Philip Street Theater opened in 1808, the competition with the Saint Peter Street Theater forced the latter by 1810 to cease activities as a theater. According to John Smith Kendall, the Saint Philip Street Theater seated "700 persons and had a large parquet and two tiers of boxes."[11] It seems that no time was wasted in performing concerts at this new theater; on April 5, 1808, there was an intermède concert featuring Gauthier on the clarinet.[12] But clearly this theater was not as popular for concerts as the Salle Accoutumée or even the Saint Peter Street Theater. Caldwell opened his American theater in the Saint Philip Street Theater building on December 24, 1817, which meant an English-speaking theater in the midst of the French Quarter, which led to considerable antagonism.[13] In 1820 Caldwell moved to the Théâtre d'Orléans, the main French opera stage in New Orleans, four nights per week and remained at the Saint Philip Street Theater for the other three nights,[14] but the French citizens did not appreciate an American theater in their midst. In 1823 Caldwell moved out of the French Quarter altogether. The Saint Philip Street Theater survived as a French theater until 1832 when it ceased to be a theater of any type.

The third early theater to open in New Orleans was ultimately the most important for concerts as well as operas. The Théâtre d'Orléans in one form or another served as the principal home of opera and many concerts from 1809 to 1866. The Théâtre d'Orléans was the result of efforts by impresario John Davis, another Haitian refugee, to present opera on a regular basis in a regular opera house. The first Théâtre d'Orléans was opened on December 5, 1809, and burned down in 1813. It was rebuilt in 1816–17 but again was destroyed by fire in 1819.[15] The first concert held in this second building was on December 9, 1817.

The third building was the most durable; it was constructed in 1819 and finally succumbed to fire only on December 7, 1866.[16] It was the home of the main opera troupe in New Orleans from 1819 until it was replaced by the larger, more modern French Opera House in December 1859. Once the third Théâtre d'Orléans building was erected, many of the most important concerts in the city were performed there. All three Théâtres d'Orléans were built on the same spot in the French Quarter, between Sainte Ann and Orleans streets, between Bourbon and Royal streets. Lacariere Latour was the architect for the first Théâtre d'Orléans. Albert A. Fossier described the second theater as Doric "and the hall as having a parquet, two rows of boxes, galleries and latticed boxes for people in mourning who did not wish to be seen by the audience."[17] This last feature was important enough that the new French Opera House in 1859 provided similar space. The third building was designed by Thibault, with Leriche for the stage and scenic arrangements. It underwent renovations, especially in the summer of 1837;[18] it is described below. What replaced it after 1866 was a dance hall, not a concert or opera house.[19]

Most concerts performed from 1805 to 1811 were not in the theaters but in venues designated as Salle Ordinaire or Salle Accoutumée.[20] Other designations were Salle Ordinaire de Bals (January 14, 1806; February 7, 1806) and Salle du Grand Bal (February 20, 1807; March 1810). It is possible all these designations were for one venue, but we have no descriptions of any of these places or their locations, so we cannot be sure. Since these concerts were inevitably followed by balls, which required proper space for dancing, we can assume that the concerts were held in ballrooms with the orchestra stationed for both a concert and a dance, or that the concert hall and dance hall were adjacent. We do not know where the first concert in 1805 was performed, and we also know nothing about the locations of some other early concerts (December 23, 26, 1808; February 17, 1809; November 26, 1810).

From January 27, 1812, to January 1, 1818, most concerts were performed in the Salle de Condé on Rue de Condé.[21] In each case the concert was followed by a ball in the same location. Then the primary concert hall moved over to the second Théâtre d'Orléans or Salle d'Orléâns, with the concert either in the theater or the salle and the dance in the salle.[22] Presumably a concert was held in the large theater of the Théâtre d'Orléans unless otherwise stated specifically as in the salle (dance hall as a separate room in the Théâtre d'Orléans). During this second decade of the nineteenth century the Saint Philip Street Theater continued to be used as an occasional concert hall and ballroom,[23] but it served primarily as a site for operas, vaudevilles, and plays. During some of those dramatic productions there were intermèdes.[24] When the Saint Philip Street Theater accepted Caldwell and his American troupe between 1817 and 1823, intermèdes occasionally were performed in the English productions as well.[25]

A number of early concerts were performed in specific, unique locations other than the ones mentioned so far. The site of the Salle de MM Lefaucheur & Comp., used for a concert on June 19, 1806, is presently unknown. A grand concert followed by a grand formal ball was held in the Salle Ordinaire des Grands Bals of M Ponton on March 7, 1808. There was no M Ponton in the French Quarter in 1808, but a M Patton had several properties including a tannery, and he could very well have provided space for such an event. On Saturday, September 24, 1808, there was a Créole comedy in two acts, with songs, performed at Théâtre de la Gaîté ci-devant de la Rue Saint Philippe as a benefit for Tessier. M Rifaux (author of the comedy, an excellent amateur), played the role of Joseph, a negre cultivateur, and between acts there was a musical intermède by the orchestra. It is possible that this was a theater especially for Creoles of color. The concerts and balls on November 30, 1810, and March 23, 1811, in the salle de Mr. Boniquet, were in the rooms owned by Joseph Antoine Boniquet, entrepreneur.[26] P. Maspero's Exchange Assembly Hall was the site of a concert and ball on February 17, 1817.

1819–1897

With the opening of the third Théâtre d'Orléans in December, 1819, nearly all public concerts moved over to this hall, and it remained the most important concert hall in New Orleans until the 1850s. Within its first few days, there were orchestral intermèdes. This theater had not only its main hall for drama, operas and concerts, but also its dance hall for balls, a café, and a billiard hall. *New-Orleans Directory for 1842* contains the following description.

It is in the lower story of the Roman Doric order; certainly not a pure specimen; and in the upper, of what may be called the Corinthian Composite. The interior and scenic arrangements of the house are excellent, for seeing and hearing—being a pit or parquet, quite elevated and commodious, with grated boxes at the side for persons in mourning. Two tiers of boxes, and one of galleries above, the whole being of such a shape as to afford satisfaction to the spectators.

In front and so far below the first tier of boxes, that the heads of those sitting are not above the front rail of the boxes, is a gallery wide enough for one row, which affords the most desirable seats in the house, and is generally occupied by amateurs—as the seats are distinct, and being numbered can be taken for the night. Nothing can exceed the decorum and quiet of the audience, except the brilliancy of the dress circle, which on certain occasions is completely filled with the beautiful ladies of our city, in full evening costume. The performances are in the French language, and the stock company [is] always at least respectable. The orchestra is excellent, and melodramas and operas are perfectly got up at this house. The strict adherence to nature and history, in costume and manners, will always please the man of taste, who visits the Théâtre d'Orléans.

Connected with this edifice, and forming part of the same structure of the building are large ball and supper rooms, in which hitherto most of the Terpsichorean gaieties of our city have had their scene—as society, military, and other balls have generally been given there. A communication exists between this suite of rooms and the Theatre: the pit having been repeatedly floored over, and the house occupied as a ball room, thus furnishing, when brilliantly lighted, in connexion with the suite adjoining, a coup d'oeil not to be surpassed for effect in America. The ball rooms, &tc. were built A.D. 1817 [sic], at a cost of about $100,000, and offer on Orleans street a striking facade. The lower story being Roman Doric in prolongation of that of the Theatre, and the upper story Ionic—although now, by the erection of the City Exchange ball rooms, about to be shorn of their glories, still Davis's Rooms will live in the memory of thousands who have first seen the humors of the place within these walls, and have been there often interrupted in their pleasures, by Sol's intrusive glare.[27]

After six years Caldwell found that he could no longer operate an American theater in a French theater building in the French Quarter, so he left both the Théâtre d'Orléans and the Saint Philip Street Theater and in 1822–23 built the

American Theatre in the American sector of the city: between Saint Charles Avenue and Camp Street, between Poydras and Gravier streets.[28] He hired the architect M Mondelli, who constructed an 1100-seat auditorium and a nice but small stage; there was a pit and parquet, three balustrades, a second gallery for Creoles of color, and an upper gallery where "the mob and women of the town sit."[29] It was the first theater in New Orleans to install gas lanterns. For many years this theater, also known as either the Camp Street Theatre or Hall, presented all kinds of dramatic and musical events primarily for the English-speaking populace of the city. In 1833 Caldwell decided to leave the theater to go into business as the exclusive seller of gas in New Orleans, so the theater was taken over by Noah Ludlow and Sol Smith. In 1839 they transformed the building into a ballroom on the upper story, an auction house on the bottom.

After 1842 Ludlow and Smith, who were no longer interested in having dramatic productions in the hall, leased it to nontheatrical people to prevent competition with the New American Theatre (see page 15), which they now owned; "many singers of note gave concerts there." According to Kendall, "After the Civil War, some brothers named Montgomery, well-known New Orleans businessmen, rented the whole building; but when they relinquished it, as they did in a year or two, the place was divided between a local militia organization—the Washington Artillery—and the Young Men's Christian Association. The former was domiciled on the upper floor, and the latter took possession of the lower floor. From this time onward, the place was known no longer as the Camp or as the American or as a theater, but as Armory Hall."[30] It was used for various purposes and torn down in 1881. Apparently in 1880 the Washington Artillery moved into its own quarters on Saint Charles between Girod and Julia streets—into a building that was constructed in 1872 and that from 1880 on was known as Washington Artillery Hall. Concerts were held at the American/Camp/Armory no matter what the hall was named, and they continued to be held at Washington Artillery Hall.

Meanwhile, Caldwell tried to re-enter show business in 1835 by building his own new theater at 432 Saint Charles Avenue, which opened on November 30, 1835.[31] Seating 4,100 persons, the Saint Charles Theatre was the largest hall in America and was surpassed in size by only three halls in Europe. The outside frontage was 132 feet, with a depth of 175 feet. The grand salon was 129 feet by 26 feet. The theater had four tiers of boxes, surrounded by enormous galleries; at the back of forty-seven boxes were boudoirs or retiring rooms. The huge chandelier had 176 gas lights. The stage was much larger than that at the American Theatre; the proscenium was fifty feet with an opening of forty-four feet.

From pit floor to ceiling was fifty-four feet, and from the stage to the roof was sixty-two feet. The scenery was forty-four feet high and forty-eight feet wide, with the wings, and overall the stage was ninety-six feet wide and seventy-eight feet deep. After it was destroyed by fire in 1842, Ludlow and Smith took over what was left of it and rebuilt it as it had been. The Saint Charles Theatre soon became the most important English-language theater in the city and the site for many operas and concerts.[32]

Ludlow/Smith and Caldwell were now serious enemies. To counteract Caldwell's Saint Charles Theatre, Ludlow and Smith built the New American Theatre on the corner of Poydras and Camp streets, bounded by Saint Francis Street. Kendall notes, "The stage was fine and large, and admirably equipped. The auditorium was spacious, with three tiers of seats above the parquet, accommodating twelve hundred persons. The parquet seats were so arranged that they could be removed in two hours and replaced in three or four hours, so that whenever it became desirable to utilize the space as an arena for the exhibition of those circus features which were just then so popular both in the United States and England, it was possible to do so in the minimum of time."[33] It burned down in 1842, shortly after the Saint Charles burned down. Caldwell then seized the property on which the New American Theatre stood, while Ludlow and Smith grabbed his damaged Saint Charles Theatre. They each rebuilt their newly acquired theater, but while Ludlow and Smith flourished at the Saint Charles, Caldwell failed and the New American went dark in January 1843. It struggled under various managers and companies, sputtered, and closed permanently on January 24, 1855.[34]

Occasionally concerts were held at the Merchants Exchange. The *New Orleans Directory for 1842* states: "Fronting on Royal Street and Exchange Place, [it] was erected by a joint stock company in the years 1835–6, from the designs and under the superintendence of C. B. Dakin, Esq., architect. Both fronts are of white marble, in a plain and bold style of design. The grand Exchange room is extremely beautiful in plan and designs, and is of the Corinthian order, from the exquisite little monument of Lysicrates, at Athens. The cost of its erection was $100,000."[35]

Another location for concerts in the early 1840s was Exchange Hall. This was actually the City Exchange on Saint Louis Street, between Chartres and Royal streets. The following description appears in the *New Orleans Directory for 1842*.

> The building occupies a front of about 300 feet on Saint Louis Street, by 120 feet each, on Royal and Chartres. The principal facade on Saint Louis street,

may be generally described as being composed of the Tuscan and Doric orders. The main entrance to the Exchange, is formed by six columns of the composite Doric order. Through this portico you enter into the vestibule of the Exchange, a handsome, though simple hall, 127 feet long by 40 in width. This room is used for general business, and is constantly open during waking hours. You pass through it into one of the most beautiful rotundas in America, which is devoted exclusively to business, and is open only from noon to three o'clock, P.M. This fine room is surrounded by arcades and galleries always open to the public, (Sundays excepted,) and its general effect cannot fail to impress the visitor. By a side entrance on Saint Louis Street, access is had to the second story, the front of which on this street is occupied by a suite of ball rooms and their dependencies. The great ball room is magnificent in its size and decorations. The painted ceiling particularly is of beauty unsurpassed in America.

The building includes within its walls, an hotel for families, calculated to accommodate 200 persons, at the corner of Royal Street, the Exchange Ball Rooms, &c., as also the Improvement Bank at the corner of Chartres Street, stores, public baths and other establishments.[36]

In 1849 the Association Variété constructed the Varieties Theater, which was destined for burlesque, vaudeville, and farces. It burned down in 1854 and was replaced by a second theater named Gaiety. A third theater, known as the Grand Opera House, was built in 1882 and remained in service until it was demolished in 1906. All three buildings were used at times for concerts, though classical concerts were not their main fare. During the Civil War, the theater valiantly tried to keep up the cultural life of the city. It presented a Shakespeare season from November 1863 to spring 1864 (*Hamlet, Richard III, Merchant of Venice, Much Ado About Nothing,* and others), and it even attempted opera, such as the second act of *Il Trovatore* and the third act of *Robert le Diable* on March 23, 1863.[37] But with money scarce and the directors of the theater concerned about filling the hall, serious music could not be its main attraction.

The Mechanics Institute of New Orleans had a performance hall in its building between Baronne and Dryades streets and between Canal and Common streets. It was constructed by 1852 when the first concerts took place there. After the Civil War, the building was used for the 1866 Louisiana Constitutional Convention and continued still in 1873 as the location of the state legislature. Gottschalk played a concert there in 1865, and there was a single concert in November 1865, and a rehearsal in the basement in 1867. In July 1866, the hall received international attention as the scene of notorious race riots that led to many deaths.[38] Later the Fisk Free and Public Library of New Orleans was situated there;[39] Tulane University purchased it in 1883 and sold it to Grunewald in 1903, who incorporated it into his new Grunewald Hotel (today, the Roosevelt Hotel).

With the growth of concert life in New Orleans in the 1840s and 1850s, new halls had to be built with concerts rather than dramas or circuses as their main purpose. The most important was Odd Fellows' Hall. The first such hall was built in 1852 in Lafayette Square in the American sector.[40] It was defiled by Union soldiers during the Union occupation of the city and then rebuilt at the end of 1865 with the architect Henry Howard.[41] It was destroyed by fire on July 4, 1866. Two years later a reporter in the *Picayune* recounted the grandeur of this hall:

> The cost of the old Hall, which was situated on the corner of Camp and Lafayette streets, 104 feet on the former and 171 on the latter street, was $180,000; the ground, which is now a most valuable piece of real estate, having only cost $15,000. The style of the old Hall was from the temple of Diana, and the interior finished in a style to correspond with the character of the building, the whole presenting to the eye a most chaste and beautiful effect. It was the pride of our city, and in its concert and ball-rooms were wont to gather, during the years that it stood, the elite and beauty not only of New Orleans but of the whole Mississippi valley. It was with its grand dome one of the few landmarks of the city which first caught the eye of the stranger, and there was many a sad face, outside of the members of the order in the crowds which gathered around to view the tottering walls and smoking ruins of the once magnificent edifice.[42]

The second Odd Fellows' Hall was built in 1868 with the designs of James Gallier, the leading architect of the city, and it remained in use as a main concert venue until the end of the century when it was occupied by Van Horns Tool Company; it was razed around 1910. The new hall was not built on the same site as the old one but was in close proximity: at 600 Camp Street between Lafayette and Poydras streets. According to the *Picayune*:

> The dimensions of the new building, which is complete in every particular, and which was yesterday dedicated, is fifty feet front, by one hundred and seventy feet in depth. The main portion of the building is over four stories in height, with a side building two stories high, through which the entrance is made to the concert hall and ball-room. The architecture of the new Hall

is of the order known as the Renaissance, which came into vogue in France about one hundred and fifty years ago, the front of white stucco, the whole presenting a most finished and handsome appearance.

The corner stone of the new hall was laid on the 4th of February last. . . . The visitor, in entering the new Hall in order to reach the ballroom, passes through the spacious doorway of the side building into the vestibule, which is lighted up by a large chandelier, suspended from the ceiling, and thence up a broad flight of stairs to the first landing, where are located the masking and cloak rooms. Thence up another short flight, and he finds himself in a vestibule which opens upon the right by large doorways directly into the ball-room. This vestibule is also brilliantly lighted up at night, and with the walls adorned with elegant fresco work, presents a most inviting appearance. The ball-room is a glorious one, and if anything, more attractive than the spacious ball-room of the old Hall although somewhat smaller in its dimensions, the latter having been 133 feet by 50 feet, while the former is only 100 by 50 feet. This room is beautifully finished, and the wall adorned with fresco work of the most artistic designs. The bronzed gas brackets on either side are in fine keeping with the other appointments, and with the immense centre chandelier, which has not yet been erected, will pour down such a flood of light that it will be hard to tell when the daylight steels in, as it often will, in the carnival season, upon the "dancers, dancing in tune. . . ."

Directly in the rear of the ball-room is the supper-room, a spacious affair, 70 by 50 feet, lighted by some thirteen bronze brackets and a couple of handsome chandeliers.[43]

Not everyone was pleased with the acoustics of the second Odd Fellows' Hall. In his review of Florence Huberwald and Marguerite Samuel's recital there on February 10, 1894, the reviewer in *L'Abeille* wrote,[44] "The acoustics there are bad, detestable, and it is impossible to judge how the voice carries. In order for a singer such as Mlle Huberwald to be able to sound pleasant, it is necessary for her to be especially soft. . . . Mme Samuel was nice and gave a second concert, which she called a recital, in the back hall of Odd Fellows,' poorly constructed and less elegant, but where the acoustics are better than in the large hall which is better suited to a ball than to a musical soiree. We remember the charming concerts, recitals and lectures that were given some time ago in the elegant foyer of the Opera House and which were so successful."

The Academy of Music, on Saint Charles Avenue between Commercial Alley and Poydras Street, dates from 1853.[45] It was built by the impresario David

Bidwell for Dan Rice's appearances in New Orleans and was used mostly for circuses. The architect was George C. Lawrence. It had about two thousand seats.[46] At the end of 1854 it was converted into a playhouse by Tom Placide and was known briefly as the Pelican Theater. The Academy of Music switched from circuses to minstrel shows for the 1860–61 season. While it served these principal entertainments, it was also a popular concert venue for the years 1857 to 1897. During the Civil War there were only a few serious concerts, such as on April 9, 1862, when the Queen Sisters from Charleston, South Carolina, began a week's run of original plays with orchestral music,[47] and on April 18, 1864, when the Italian opera singer Teresa Conioli performed "favorite selections from popular operas."[48] After the war, there were occasional concerts, culminating at the beginning of 1896 when Paderewksi performed there.[49]

Inside the city hall in Lafayette Square in the second municipality (American sector) there was a lecture hall that also sometimes served as a concert hall. It was called Lyceum Hall. The earliest mention of this hall is at the beginning of 1850 when the actor William L. Fleming gave a series of readings of the plays of Shakespeare (*Hamlet* and *The Merchant of Venice;* January 5ff.). Alternating with his lectures were some concerts by Maurice Strakosch (January 11ff.). Apparently in 1853 P. T. Barnum lectured there, and he described the hall: "At New-Orleans, I lectured in the great Lyceum Hall in Saint Charles Street, a new building just completed by the Second Municipality. I did so on the invitation of Mayor Crossman, and several other influential gentlemen. The immense Hall contained more than three thousand auditors, including the most respectable portion of the New-Orleans public. I was in capital humor, and had warmed myself into a pleasant state of excitement, feeling that the audience was with me."[50]

Along with the Odd Fellows' halls, the most significant concert hall built in the 1850s was the new French Opera House in 1859 on the corner of Toulouse and Bourbon streets. Although designed as a hall for the spectacle of opera, it was especially noted for its fine acoustics and served well for major concerts. On opening night, December 1, 1859, the *Picayune* reporter was mesmerized by the new auditorium.

> Of course, the opening of the new Opera House was the great event of the evening; and it was not a surprise to any one, we imagine, to find it as full as it could hold, from the first row of the parquette to the very ceiling. The coup d'oeil presented by the auditorium, when viewed from the centre of the parquette, was superb indeed. The house is constructed so as to afford a full view of the audience from almost every point, and its gracefully curved tiers

of boxes, rising one above the other, each gradually receding from the line of the other, and then filled, in a great degree, with ladies, in grand toilette, presented a spectacle that was richly worth viewing. The private boxes on each side of the proscenium are elegantly draped with crimson damask, and are all occupied by families for the season. The whole house is painted white, and the decorations of the fronts of the boxes are in gold; the first circle, with rich festoons, and those above it with panel work. A magnificent mirror in a gold frame, on the wall on each side of the proscenium, adds greatly to the picturesque effect of the auditorium. The entrances to the house are numerous, spacious and commodious, and the crush room, ladies' retiring rooms, &c., are constructed upon a scale of great elegance and convenience.[51]

He marveled that it took just seven months to construct the theater under the leadership of architect Gallier and builder Esterbrook.[52] *The Bee* critic was just as ecstatic: "Manager Boudousquié's new theatre—the Opera—was opened last night, and its inauguration was a triumphant success. The theatre was crowded to overflowing, and the boxes were very fashionably filled. The audience seemed in the best possible humor, pleased with the appearance of the house and pleased with the new troupe. The auditorium, from its form, is beautiful, and when the decorations are completed it will be one of the handsomest theatres in the United States. As far as we could judge last night, the acoustic properties of the hall were perfect, and an important feature is that every seat is near to and commands a full view of the stage."[53] For the *Bee* critic it was wonderful that everyone in the audience had a good view of the stage rather than that everyone (on stage or in the audience?) had a full view of the audience. Fifteen years later a voice was raised questioning the comfort of the hall,[54] and over the years the hall was renovated many times.[55] Many concerts were held in what was initially called the Opera Theater (Théâtre d'Opéra) and then simply the French Opera. Although in the French Quarter and initially built for French-language theater and opera, when the hall burned down in 1919, the entire city went into mourning. It had become the symbol of the best European culture transplanted to America.

Lorelle Bender has given a detailed description of the building.

The French Opera House was an imposing brick[56] building of the Italian style of architecture. It extended one hundred sixty-six feet on Bourbon Street and one hundred eighty-seven feet on Toulouse Street. A gallery six feet wide and sixty feet long projected over the main entrance, which was on

Bourbon Street, to protect the women entering and leaving the theater in bad weather. The actor's entrance was on Toulouse Street.

In the basement were seven shops: two on Toulouse Street, one at each corner and one on Bourbon Street. . . .

Two broad and high flights of steps on the main entrance on Bourbon Street led to the first and second dress circles, parquettes, and boxes. There was a broad lobby entrance extending all around the dress circle. A corridor led from the lobby to the spacious and beautiful auditorium. The interior decorative schemes were subdued: faded reds contrasted with creamy whites; some use of gold, but no gaudy or bizarre effects.

The stage, which projected in a curve, was eighty-five feet wide and sixty feet deep. The arch was supported on either side by two Corinthian Columns, thirty-two feet high, on square pedestals. On either side of the columns were three tiers of boxes, two in either tier, making twelve stage boxes in all. There was a spacious orchestra pit in front of the stage.

The parquette seats were arranged in a curve to correspond with the stage. There were five latticed boxes on either side of the parquettes. The open boxes, or bagnoirs, were around the pit.

There were four tiers. The first was a dress circle, containing two rows of "stalls," fifty-two in all, and twenty latticed boxes. The second tier was also a dress circle, containing sixty chairs and twenty latticed boxes. The third tier was plainly furnished and the admission was a little cheaper than the admission to the pit. The fourth tier was for negroes.

The latticed boxes were made for ladies in mourning, although they were often occupied by timid, retiring young ladies or by reserved older women. All of the boxes had private parlors.

On either side of the stage were large property rooms for the expensive and beautiful stage equipment. Behind the stage were large racks for the scenery not in use.

On the second floor was a group of luxurious lounge rooms, where the elite of the South gathered between acts of operas or on gala special occasions. The main salon called the "crush room," sixty feet long, twenty-six feet wide, and twenty-eight feet high, opened on the gallery that projected over the Bourbon Street entrance. Adjoining this salon at its lower end (Toulouse Street corner) were club rooms for the stockholders of the theatre, a parlor, and a general meeting room. Connecting with the main salon at the upper end were rooms for ladies, a large parlor, a cloak room, and a boudoir. These rooms were the most luxurious theater parlors in America at that time.

Over the central salon was a small theater that was used for rehearsals.

The building was well ventilated. On either side of the auditorium was [an] open yard, inclosed within the building. The entrances on Bourbon Street and Toulouse also provided ventilation. There was a net work of halls, and corridors that led to every part of the building in such a way that the house could have been emptied in a short time.[57]

After the Civil War several new venues appeared, including the German National Theater in 1867 and Grunewald Hall in 1874. The German community in New Orleans had grown before the war and by the 1850s had its own regular newspaper and cultural events. After the war it claimed some property on Poydras Street not far from Lee Circle (today the site of Le Pavillon Hotel) and in 1866 opened the German National Theater.[58] In the 1870s the theater was renamed Werlein Hall after Philip Werlein, who owned the property. The building was destroyed by fire in 1889. The hall seated up to 1,600 persons and was the site of German dramas and operas. According to the *New Orleans Times,* in 1868 it was available for concerts, soirees, balls, meetings on all nights except Wednesdays and Saturdays when there was dancing.[59]

An important concert venue was built by Louis Grunewald in 1873–74. Referred to as Grunewald Hall or, sometimes, as Grunewald Opera House, it was designed by the architect Hillyer and was located on Baronne Street between Canal and Common streets. It fronted Baronne with a length of 103 feet by a depth of 160 feet. J. Curtis Waldo described it in 1879: "the principal hall, the concert room, [is] a spacious apartment 100 x 54 feet, being superbly frescoed, and decorated with portraits of the ancient and modern leading musicians of the world. It has a seating capacity of 1000, and has been pronounced by De Murska, Wilhelmj, Hans von Bulow, and others competent to give an opinion, to have the most perfect acoustics of any hall in America. . . . The extensive lower floors, Nos. 18, 20 and 22 Baronne street, are occupied by the proprietor as a music store, and show rooms for his very large stock of pianos, organs, and wind and string musical instruments."[60] This hall, which was the preferred concert venue for Marguerite Samuel and many other local chamber musicians, was destroyed by fire in 1892. It was replaced by the Grunewald Hotel (later named Roosevelt and Fairmont hotels).

Harmonie Hall, at the corner of Bienville Street and Exchange Alley (Passage de la Bourse), was the site for a concert on February 4, 1874.[61] There seem to have been no other concerts there. During the early 1870s the hall was part of the Harmony Club, a Jewish bachelors club founded in 1862. By 1876 the

Harmony Club moved elsewhere and the hall, at 55–57 Bienville, was renamed Screwman's Hall. Two decades later, on October 25, 1895, George O'Connell performed at the Harmonie Hall of the Young Men's Gymnastic Club at 222 North Rampart Street.[62] The gym was founded in 1872, and from the beginning it had musical ensembles that performed concerts at Odd Fellows' Hall and elsewhere. By 1894 it had its own hall entitled "Harmonie Salle" in which it performed frequently in the last years of this history (1894–97). Numerous photographs and drawings of the club do not allow for a separate hall for concerts, so the presumption is that the concerts were performed on the gymnasium floor. There probably is no connection with the earlier Harmonie Hall. A new, large, and impressive Harmony Club Hall was built in 1896 on the corner of Jackson and Saint Charles Avenue.

There was a concert on April 22, 1857, at a Union Hall on Jackson Street. This was in the American sector. Otherwise, from January 17, 1869, on, concerts at "Union Hall" meant the French Union Hall (Union Française) on North Rampart Street just outside the French Quarter. Built by 1869 but probably much earlier, it was renovated in 1872 by architect James Freret.[63] It was used frequently for concerts after 1881, but there were isolated concerts in 1869 and 1876.[64] It was described in 1884 as a perfect venue for the final recital of the year for a piano studio:

> The French Union Hall is very much in vogue. One sometimes forgets that it is chosen frequently for festivals, balls, concerts, spectacles, and with good reason. It is good, it is fair that such enterprises be seriously encouraged; it is useful that the public contributes, as far as it can, to the success of the enterprise which brings support and relief to the poor; that it gives children their first source of satisfaction and success: education. Not only for the French colony, this hall is for the entire Louisiana population since it is conveniently situated. Furthermore it has a garden secured by a brick wall and gets breezes from all sides. Now, in the season we are in, this is not something to be disregarded. And this is a convenient locale without being too vast, yet it can accommodate a sizeable crowd where a voice can be heard without losing its tone and its delights, the nuances of a piano or other instrument will not be lost there.[65]

An important part of the Cotton Exposition in 1884–85 were the concerts, most of which were held in the Music Hall on the Exposition grounds in what is today Audubon Park. "Grand concerts, vocal and instrumental, are given regularly in what is known as Music Hall, which has a seating capacity for 11,000 people and six hundred musicians, and a mammoth organ."[66] The organ was built by the Pilcher family and at the time was the largest in America. After the fair the hall and most of the buildings were destroyed; the organ was donated to the Jesuit Church.

The three most important halls built in the 1890s were the hall for the national meeting of the German singing societies, the Athenaeum, and the hall in the Y.M.C.A.[67] The first was a temporary building, while the latter two remained well into the twentieth century as major concert venues. The North American Sängerbund Festival scheduled its 1890 convention in New Orleans, and a special Sängersfesthalle was then constructed out of wood. It accommodated two thousand singers and an orchestra with five thousand seats for the audience. The massive hall was 150 feet on Saint Charles Avenue, 200 feet deep, with a 90-foot stage. The hall opened on February 12, 1890, and the audience was not only the largest ever to attend an indoor concert in New Orleans but, except for the outdoor extravagances of Patrick Gilmore in 1864, the largest until then to attend any musical event in the city.

The Atheneum was built in 1896 as a large hall in the Young Men's Hebrew Association building located on Saint Charles and Clio streets at Lee Circle (Uptown Lakeside, where the Katz and Besthoff Building now stands). It was just about in the same location as the Sängersfesthalle. A *Picayune* reporter suggested the first-time visitor

> pause and observe the theatre hall a moment. When it is full of people there is no suggestion of emptiness or of vastness about it. It is like all other well filled halls. There was no vast roominess, out of all proportion to the human mites. If one sees this room with throngs present, the effect is the same. And yet its floor dimensions are 58 by 98 feet. He might be puzzled, unless he is an architect, to know how this result is brought about; how the room, so vast, looks snug whether there are one or one thousand people in it. At this point the reflective person pauses to observe the height. It is then the 24 feet of wall shows the wisdom of giving to this hall a height occupying almost that of two stories of the building.[68]

In addition to the Athenaeum and Sängersfesthalle, another hall built in the 1890s was that at the Y.M.C.A. at 815 Saint Charles Avenue near Julia Street. It was named the Helme Memorial Hall and featured a few concerts during the final year of this survey: on Tuesday, December 3, 1895, the inaugural concert under the direction of Mrs. Robert Abbott;[69] on Thursday, January 30, 1896, Signorina Moreska and Signor Gore, with Hernandez' Mexican Orchestra, performing opera selections; on March 19, 1896, Marguerite Samuel in a joint recital, and similar programs were there during the ensuing months. The hall was built in 1895 and replaced an earlier structure at 15 Camp Street.

CHURCHES, PARKS, AND OTHER VENUES

Other important venues for concerts included the churches. Most of the churches in the city were Roman Catholic and were spread about the entire New Orleans area. In some cases concerts were separate events performed in the church sanctuary; in other cases the concerts were in adjoining school, social, or meeting halls. On special occasions regular liturgical services were enhanced with concert-like music by local composers as well as by famous European ones (Rossini, Beethoven, Mozart, Schubert, and others). For example, Collignon, then master of the Chapel of the Jesuit Church of the Immaculate Conception, conducted Weber's Mass in E Minor on Monday, November 22, 1864, at the church;[70] Mr. Dubos, chapel master of Saint Louis Cathedral, directed a charity concert at Saint Alphonse's Hall (on Saint Andrew Street near Magazine Market) on January 10, 1865; and Gregorio Curto directed a grand sacred concert, vocal and instrumental, at Sainte Anne's Church (on Saint Philip Street, between Roman and Prieur streets) on February 23, 1865.[71] Collignon used a large number of professionals and amateurs, while Dubos was assisted by La Hache, Charles Mayer, Henri Page (a violinist newly arrived in the city), Mr. Bremer, and others, with a full choir. Dubos's program included Neukomm's "Hymn of the Night" (words by Lamartine).[72] Curto's concert was accompanied by Louis Grunewald on the organ, and the concert's aim was to raise money for a new organ.

The central church of the Catholics in New Orleans was in the nineteenth century, as it is today, Saint Louis Cathedral in Jackson Square, the main, front square of the French Quarter facing the Mississippi River. Throughout the nineteenth century it was often referred to simply as "the Cathedral." The present building was started in 1792 after a fire destroyed its predecessor, and it is a significant hall in size, though with an echo typical of large churches. The first concert of which we have record occurred on Wednesday, November 22, 1837, when Curto conducted a new mass of his to celebrate Sainte Cecilia's Day.[73] There were solo singers, choir, and professional orchestral musicians. After a renovation in 1851, Curto conducted another new mass of his, performed by fifty young people of both sexes.[74] A number of other new religious pieces by local composers were premiered at the cathedral during the next forty-five years. For example, Hubert Rolling Sr.'s "Piu Pelicane" was premiered there on Sunday, March 24, 1872, and was repeated the following week at High Mass at the moment of elevation;[75] Mlle Octavie Romey's Grand Mass was performed there on or about December 19, 1875, by the Bouquet Musical Club under her direction;[76] Hubert Rolling Jr.'s "Ave Maria" was sung on October 22, 1882, for the Offertory.[77] Of course some of the classics were performed there as well. For example, Mozart's Mass in C on Easter Sunday, April 2, 1876;[78] Rossini's Solemn Mass on May 12, 1877;[79] Haydn's Mass No. 2 on December 25, 1882;[80] an unspecified mass by Haydn on December 7, 1884;[81] Haydn's Mass No. 1 in B flat and Adolphe Adam's "Noël" at High Mass on Christmas, 1889;[82] Mozart's Mass No. 12 on March 20, 1892;[83] and Haydn's Mass No. 1 on December 25, 1896.[84]

In addition, however, there were concerts that were only partially religious or not religious at all. On March 25, 1877, for example, there was a grand sacred concert directed by J. Cartier of sacred vocal works with organ, piano, and a few other instruments accompanying but also Wieniawski's *Legende* and Sivori's *Romance sans Parole*.[85] J. Cartier conducted another concert at the cathedral on April 12, 1878, which mixed opera arias and sacred music.[86] Another mixture occurred on March 22, 1884, whereas on March 16, 1885, and April 17, 1886, a visiting Mexican orchestra gave completely secular concerts. Soloists and instrumentalists from the French Opera sometimes performed a solo or two in a regular Sunday Mass, and in general the performance level in the cathedral concerts seems to have been very high.

One church social hall popular for its music was Saint Patrick's newly constructed Hall (Camp Street in Lafayette Square, the largest hall in the city in 1874). The church dates to 1840, and for some time during the nineteenth century was erroneously referred to as a cathedral. The parish was established in 1833, the first parish outside the boundaries of the original city. The first structure was a small wooden building at the site the church occupies today. At the time of its construction the neighborhood consisted of fine mansions. The Irish hired noted architects Charles and James Dakin to plan it. Construction began around the existing wooden church which was dismantled and carried out when the new edifice was completed. The new church was of Gothic style in elegant details, with a ceiling imitating Exeter Cathedral. The tower is 185 feet high, the vestibule 40 feet, the nave 85 feet. It was a triumph in Gothic comparable to any parochial structure of its kind in Europe. But there were construction problems in the swampy area. The foundation was found to be defective in part.

So the church hired James Gallier, an Irish architect who came to New Orleans in 1834, to complete the building. The walls of the tower were settling at one side. Gallier accomplished a remarkable feat of engineering skill. He removed the old foundation, replacing it with a new one, without pulling down the walls. The Church of the Immaculate Conception (the Jesuit Church) was built in 1857 and survived intact until 1928 when it was rebuilt on the same site. Both structures were located at 130 Baronne Street near Canal Street, opposite the Grunewald/Roosevelt Hotel. Father John Cambiaso designed the Immaculate Conception Church based on Moorish models, which distinguished this church from all others in the city. After the Cotton Exposition of 1884–85, the huge Pilcher organ in the Music Hall was transferred to the Jesuit Church.

Coliseum Square was one of the most attractive squares in the American sector, and there were numerous churches of various denominations around it where concerts and special musical services were held. Saint Paul's Episcopal Church was located at the corner of Erato and Camp streets. The first Saint Paul's Church was built in 1836 and burned in 1891; it was replaced by the second building in 1893. The Steele Chapel (white Methodist Church), 1218 Felicity Street, was destroyed by fire in 1887 and replaced by Felicity United Methodist Church the next year. This Gothic Revival masonry church may have been the first church in New Orleans to have had electric lighting, installed in 1888. Saint Alphonse's Catholic Church, 2045 Constance Street, was constructed in 1855 by the Redemptorist Fathers who came to New Orleans in 1840 from Baltimore. After establishing a church for the German Catholics at St Mary's Assumption across the street, they built this church for the Irish and other English-speaking Catholics. Sainte Theresa of Avila Catholic Church was built in 1848–49 at 1145 Coliseum Street by the architect T. E. Giraud.

Sainte Anna's Hall, at 186 Esplanade between Tremé and Marais streets, was attached to an Episcopal Church and has no connection with Sainte Anna's Asylum near Coliseum Square. The Episcopal church hosted concerts and special musical services from the late 1880s into the 1890s.

There were a number of other halls or venues which were only rarely used for concerts. These include Mr. Vigule's hall on the corner of Orleans and Royal streets, which hosted a single concert on April 9, 1837, and the hall of M Faivre, piano manufacturer, at 56 Royal Street between Bienville and Douane streets, which hosted two concerts on November 22, 1851, and March 2, 1853. The Masonic Hall, on Saint Charles Avenue at Perdido Street, was the occasional site of concerts from the 1860s to the 1880s. The Globe Hall (Theater) was actually a dance hall where a good amount of drinking and smoking took place. It was used for a series of concerts by female visitors from Austria, however, in October 1875.

Café concerts also became popular over time. One of the earliest occurred on May 13, 1855, at Vauxhall Gardens. On May 3, 5, and 9, 1863, a group of the most distinguished players formed a light orchestra á la Strauss at the saloon of M Guth on Conti Street between Royal and Bourbon.[87] Philip Greuling was the chef d'orchestre, Oliveira was the solo violinist, and the others included A. Dantonnet, L. Mayer, C. Dantonnet, Bastloul, F. Eberhardt, T. Flemings, J. Charlton, C. Hopf, G. Monteri, and F. Keckel. The idea of chamber music during the spring and summer in coffee shops or restaurants came first before the war and is found again afterwards, and it gave financially strapped musicians during the war another source of income.

One must be careful not to confuse concert halls with "concert saloons" that became popular after the war.[88] It is altogether possible that people gathered at Guth's saloon to listen to the music, but concert saloons in general were not places for concerts in the normal sense. These were meeting places for loose women and men of all classes who desired to escort the women to nearby hotels. The music was at best background, and Tivoli Gardens and Wenger's were not where one went to hear good classical music

By 1880 summer concerts at Spanish Fort and West End, both on Lake Pontchartrain north of the city, were well established. While the earliest concerts there were probably held entirely outdoors or in makeshift band shells, both resorts eventually built substantial halls to house their many concerts. The first one at Spanish Fort on May 1, 1880, was a promenade concert, where people walked around to the sound of the orchestra. By April 1, 1882, there was a concert hall, and two months later it was a grand pavilion. An opera house opened in February 1884. West End also had promenades and a pavilion which was destroyed by fire in May 1894. They worked rapidly, however, and by the end of May there was already a new pavilion which, it was hoped, would have better acoustics than the old one.[89]

In the city itself there were concerts at the public Lafayette Square and at the private Jockey Club in the City Fair Grounds (horse race track). Lafayette Square, which had several halls available for indoor concerts (Lyceum Hall and the churches) also hosted several outdoor concerts before the Civil War (for example, on Thursday, October 20, 1853, when the Philharmonic Society performed a grand instrumental concert for the benefit of the orphans of the Third District), during the war (with Patrick Gilmore's multi-wind-percussion band orgies), and afterwards (on May 30, 1884; June 13, 1884; June 1, 1886; and May

3, 1892, for example). The Jockey Club was a highly exclusive place where an elite group held promenade concerts in the gardens yearly from May 4, 1880, to at least June 15, 1892.

Several local societies had their own performance venues, where they also rehearsed. The Frohsinn rehearsed at their rooms on Bourbon Street before they moved into the German National Theater. The Orphéon Français and the Aeolian Harp Circle, both under the direction of George O'Connell, had small concert rooms; the latter gave a concert in their hall on Royal Street on March 15, 1885, while the former opened up its hall to a group of singers and instrumentalists on June 5, 1887. Both groups, however, usually performed elsewhere and reserved their own rooms for rehearsals.

Mention must also be made of halls that were exclusively designed for black or "colored" audiences. The social realities of nineteenth-century New Orleans included segregation in various guises. In most halls Creoles of color (mulattoes) were able to attend concerts by sitting in special areas designated for them, while black slaves or domestics were sometimes permitted, sometimes barred from concerts. A few halls founded by Creoles of color (most notably, at the beginning of the century, Saint Peters Street Theater) apparently had no such discriminatory seating for whites. Later black benevolent societies formed a few halls for concerts, of which Economy Hall in the Tremé neighborhood was the most important. The Economy Benevolent Society was founded in 1836, and in the year 1875 it had a concert hall which enjoyed numerous concerts.[90] On Sunday, May 9, 1875, there was a benefit concert for M Paulin Dardignac, baritone of the opera; he was accompanied on piano by Basile Barès.[91] A second concert at Economy Hall by Mademoiselle le Liugier and M Miral, with M Dardignac, took place on May 16.[92] A week later there was a spectacle concert to benefit the society.[93] At the end of the year, on December 20, 1875, there was another benefit grand concert at the hall.[94] In the 1890s, when the distinguished violinist Dédé returned to New Orleans, his native city, he may have given concerts there as well; Barès was his accompanist.

The Amis de l'Esperance, a society of colored persons in the 1890s, had a hall at 922 North Liberty Street between Saint Philip and Dumaine streets, in the Tremé District. The hall was two stories high, of frame construction, with a frontage of about 35 feet and a depth of about 125 feet. Apparently it had bad acoustics but, because of ever-present racial prejudice, Dédé had to perform there on December 10, 1893, and January 21, 1894. Even worse, perhaps, was the hall of La Société des Francs Amis at 1820 North Robertson Street between Saint Anthony and Bourbon (Bons-Enfants or Pauger) streets. This society was the principle one for Creoles of color. The lot was purchased by the group in 1861, and the hall is still standing.[95] It is a one-story building of frame construction, set off from the street about 25 feet, with a frontage of 35 feet and a depth of 95 feet.

For his concert on January 8, Dédé performed at the Union Chapel on Bienville Street, between Villere and Marais streets. Union Chapel, whose congregation was founded in 1846, was a black Methodist church which could seat six hundred persons on a regular basis. Alecia P. Long reports: "According to one source the Union Chapel's commodious facility was one of the largest and finest African American church buildings, surpassing most other churches of color in the state in size and beauty."[96] Unfortunately, when the Red Light District of New Orleans was created around it in 1897—the so-called Storyville—the church was forced to move into a better neighborhood. The congregation survives today as the Grace United Methodist Church. Two days later, on January 10, Dédé performed at the Saint John Berchman Asylum, on the corner of Orleans and Bourbon streets. The asylum was created for black female orphans by the Sisters of the Holy Family, a black order of nuns established in New Orleans in 1842.[97] In 1881 the sisters moved into a building on Orleans and Sainte Ann, between Royal and Bourbon streets, which had been built as the Orleans Dance Hall; in 1889 the Saint John Berchman Asylum was built on an adjacent lot that in 1811 had been the site of the first Théâtre d'Orléans.

The variety of venues utilized by the musicians in New Orleans during the nineteenth century corresponds to the variety of programs and kinds of performances. From very elitist sophisticated concerts to popular concerts for the common person the needs of the musicians and audience were accommodated by suitable halls and other spaces. There were options that gave the concert life of the city a richness that could appeal to a wide audience.

Théâtre d'Orléans, 1809–1813. Tanesse Map. Courtesy of the Library of Congress.

Théâtre d'Orléans, 1819–1866. Gibson, opposite 312.

Camp Street Theatre, 1823–1880. Painting by August Norieri, ca. 1890, after a drawing by H. Reinagle, 1830. Courtesy of the Collections of the Louisiana State Museum.

Two views of the Washington Artillery Hall. Military and Naval Buildings folder, Image File, Louisiana Research Collection, Tulane University.

Saint Charles Theatre, 1835–1842. Exterior (*above*), interior (*below*).
Theatres and Opera Houses folder, Image File, Louisiana Research Collection,
Tulane University. Cf. Fossier, 368.

St. Charles Theatre. Jewell, 76.

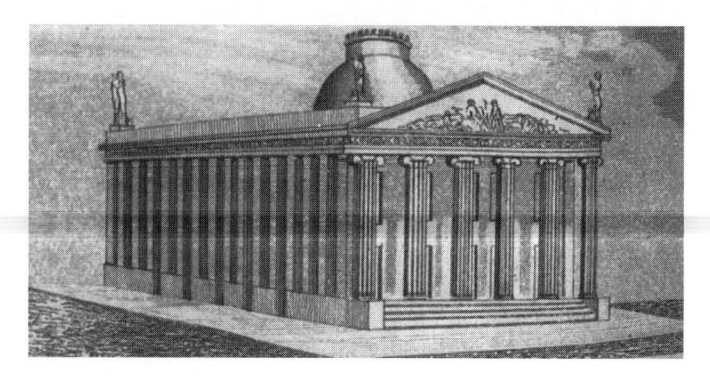

New American Theatre, 1835–1840. Gibson, opposite 312.

Varieties Theater, 1854–present. Jewell, 44.

Mechanics' Institute Hall, 1852ff. Jewell, 88.

Old Odd Fellows' Hall, 1852–1866. Hammond, unnumbered introductory advertisements.

New Odd Fellows' Hall 2, 1868–ca. 1910. Jewell, 47.

Academy of Music, 1853ff. Waldo, 48.

Lyceum Hall, 1853ff. Waldo, 36.

French Opera House, 1859–1919. *Above,* view of the exterior (Waldo, 50). *Below*, interior view from the stage. Music folder, Ephemera Collection, Louisiana Research Collection, Tulane University.

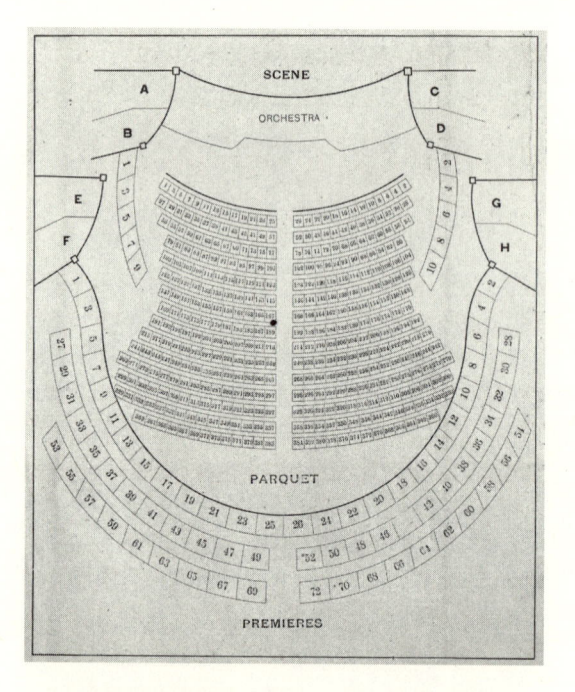

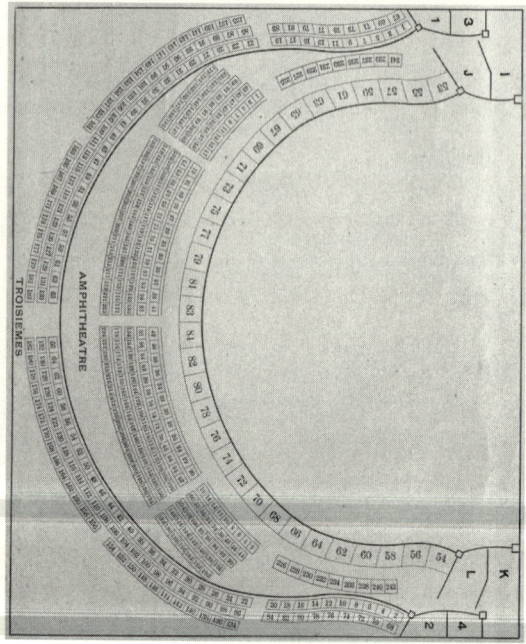

French Opera House seating plans. *Above,* downstairs and first balcony. *Below,* upper balconies. Tulane Vertical Files. Music folder, Ephemera Collection, Louisiana Research Collection, Tulane University.

German National Theater, later Werlein Hall. Jewell, 119.

Grunewald Hall, 1874–1892. Waldo, 38.

Church of the Immaculate Conception (Jesuits' Church), 1857–1928. Jewell, 53.

Saint Louis Cathedral, 1794–present. Jewell, 115.

Spanish Fort Concert Hall. Spanish Fort folder, Image File, Louisiana Research Collection, Tulane University.

Spanish Fort, typical crowd scene. Spanish Fort folder, Image File, Louisiana Research Collection, Tulane University.

Jockey Club in the City Fair Grounds. Jewell, 113.

2

Symphonic Music in Nineteenth-Century New Orleans

The history of orchestral music in New Orleans begins at the end of the eighteenth century when the first theater orchestra was established. During the nineteenth century it was the theater orchestras that provided the main impetus for the development of orchestral music in the city. The unique strength of the city's theater orchestras vis-à-vis those of theaters in most other cities of the United States, especially during the first sixty years of that century, gave the Crescent City its reputation for the highest standard in instrumental performance. Most important was the Orchestra of the French Opera that operated in the Théâtre d'Orléans from 1819 to 1859 and in the Théâtre d'Opéra (known later as the French Opera House) from 1859 to 1919. Its members were recruited from the conservatories of Europe, some came to New Orleans via Santo Domingo, and, after a while, many were trained by older members of the local orchestra in the best discipline of the Paris Conservatoire. Excellent orchestral musicians were found in other theaters in New Orleans as well.

The musical century is divided by the Civil War (1861–65). Until 1861 New Orleans had fine orchestras, within and outside the opera, whereas afterwards orchestral music struggled along with the financially strapped opera. Before the war the economic and political stability of the city, coupled with a huge growth in the population, allowed musical activities to flourish. During this time opera was a mainstay of the cultural life, and no other city in America could boast as outstanding opera as New Orleans. Not only one, but sometimes two or three operas could be heard and seen nightly. At first, the theater orchestras were busy enough with the fare in the theaters themselves. Besides accompanying opera and operettas, they assisted in vaudeville and dance performances and even in dramas where they would supply background for melodramatic pieces, music during intermission, and overtures.[1] During the second and third decades of the century they became more identifiable as orchestras per se by performing apart from the theatrical productions in benefit concerts, in concerts of visiting artists, in balls, and in café concerts. By the 1850s an orchestra appeared that was to be the first to concentrate on orchestral literature and not function as accompaniment.

The economic and political instability during and after the Civil War led to uncertainty in the opera houses, especially in the French Opera House. Often there were complete, exciting seasons of French opera, but too often there were bankruptcies, incomplete seasons, or no seasons at all. Impresarios came and went with amazing frequency, as compared to the long-tenured residency of impresarios before the war. This had a disruptive effect on the orchestral musicians in the theaters, though other activities outside the theaters sometimes kept them busy. But now and then, an orchestra appeared in concert, usually through the efforts of individual local musicians who fought for symphonic music, or with the arrival of a visiting ensemble. A nucleus of highly skilled instrumentalists who lived in New Orleans provided the basis for the formation of orchestras and provided the city with at least a modicum of the basic symphonic repertory. After 1880 the city maintained considerable orchestral activity through the end of the century.

ORCHESTRAL MUSIC PRIOR TO THE CIVIL WAR

Before the Civil War each of the theaters boasted an orchestra. From 1819 to 1859 the orchestra of the Théâtre d'Orléans was the best in town, with leaders such as Adolphe Elie and Eugène Prévost. Its purpose was to accompany operas, whatever their origins, in the French language for the French-speaking citizens of New Orleans. The equally venerable Saint Charles Theatre also had an orchestra, and from time to time we read about its activities. This theater sometimes presented opera in German, Italian, or English, but it mainly served the English-speaking population with dramas and comedies. Intermèdes occurred between acts of plays early in the century, and the first of these, in 1807, already included an orchestra accompanying in a concerto.[2] The practice continued unabated until the war. In November 1856, the function of the theater orchestra to entertain between acts of a play is clearly mentioned in print: "the orchestra will play *I Lombardi*" (November 14); "airs from *La Sonnambula* by the orchestra" (November 18); "airs from *Lucia di Lamermoor* [sic] by the orchestra" (November 20).[3]

One of the last theaters to open before the war was the Gaiety, which served primarily the Creoles of color. When the theater opened on Thursday evening,

November 6, 1856, it presented operas, but there is no designation of an orchestra.[4] There probably was one, however. A month later an orchestra is clearly described in print: "During the evening the orchestra will perform the *Camille Polka and Mazurka,* composed by R. Stopel, and dedicated to Miss Matilda Heron. Also, the popular *Gaiety Offering Waltz,* composed by R. Meyer."[5]

The very last theater to open before the war was the new French Opera House (officially designated simply Théâtre de l'Opéra). Initial reviews concentrated on the beauty of the hall and the fine singers who were assembled for the opening in December 1859. But the critic of the *Picayune* was quick to pick up on the importance of the orchestra and its conductor, Eugène Prévost. "A word for the chorus and orchestra. . . . We have been delighted to note the delicate and discriminating manner in which the piano [soft] passages are rendered, and to find in the performances of M. Prévost's orchestra a refutation of the old fling, that operatic bands in this country do not understand the meaning of *pianissimo.*"[6]

The 1850s witnessed an increase in the number of guest performers who found the audiences in New Orleans both eager to listen and willing to pay. One of the best orchestras to reach New Orleans at this time was that of Louis Jullien, who was touring America in 1853–54. Jullien announced a series of twelve orchestral concerts in February and March 1854, at Odd Fellows' Hall. The programs were mixed with serious concert music, opera arias, patriotic marches, ballads, and light dances. For the opening concert on February 18, for example, the orchestra performed the Overture to Auber's *Masaniello,* the Allegretto in B flat from the Symphony No. 8 in F by Beethoven, quadrilles, a waltz, a polka, and a galop by Jullien himself, while the singers performed excerpts from Meyerbeer's *Les Huguenots* arranged by Jullien and arias from *Lucia di Lammermoor* and *Sonnambula.*[7] One of the quadrilles, based on numerous American hymns ("Hail Columbia," "Star Spangled Banner," "Our Flag Is There," "The Land of Washington," "Hail to the Chief," and "Yankee Doodle" are cited), included twenty solo musicians from the orchestra. In addition there was a clarinet solo, a violin duet, and a solo singer singing "Where the Bee Sucks" from Arne's *The Tempest.*

During the ensuing month's programs, the orchestra gave further selections from Beethoven's symphonies (Allegro and *Storm* [movement 4] from the Symphony No. 6 and Andante in A [movement 2] from the Symphony No. 2), all recurring on subsequent programs, and included numerous overtures such as those to *Zampa, Der Freischütz, Fra Diavolo, The Magic Flute, Euryanthe, Oberon,* and *Fidelio.* There were also excerpts from symphonies by Schubert and

Haydn, and on March 8 the orchestra performed the entire Symphony No. 3 by Mendelssohn. Jullien also performed unscheduled "pops" concerts without the serious and vocal music of his scheduled appearances. Upon request and since it was Carnival season, he led his orchestra in "the most popular dance music" to accompany masked balls.[8] The orchestra achieved considerable popularity while in New Orleans and possibly could have continued to perform for the rest of the season there, but the tour had already been booked elsewhere. The orchestra was scheduled for Mobile on March 13 and Montgomery on March 18. Jullien showed that orchestral concerts could draw an audience in New Orleans, though he mixed them with lighter music and vocal music to bring in people who might not otherwise have tried to sit through a serious orchestral concert. It was now up to the local musicians to see if there was ample interest in serious orchestral concerts without the sugar coating.

A high point was reached in the history of instrumental music in New Orleans when Gustave Collignon founded his Classic Music Society in 1856. For four seasons before the Civil War and again in the season 1871 to 1872, this organization presented to a select audience the basics of chamber and orchestral music of the time. The first year was mostly chamber music, but by the second season the focus had switched from chamber to orchestral music. While concentrating on the symphonies and overtures of Beethoven and Mendelssohn, Collignon mixed in works by Weber, Schubert, Haydn, Gluck, Rossini, Robert Schumann, and others. His aim was to present the best classical music with as high caliber musicians as he could assemble from the ranks of professional and amateur players in the city. If the reviewers in the local press are to be taken seriously, he achieved his goal many times over. The orchestra that emerged during the first season and came to be the essence of the Classic Music Society by the second season was the city's first full symphony orchestra, apart from those associated with opera houses and dance halls.

Collignon was born in Rennes, France, in 1818, and at the very young age of six entered the Paris Conservatoire.[9] There he studied piano with Pierre-Joseph-Guillaume Zimmerman (1785–1853) and harmony and composition with Mathurin-Auguste-Balthasar Barbereau (1799–1879). He graduated from the conservatory in 1837 with the first prize. Pierre Davis (son of John Davis) of the Théâtre d'Orléans brought him to New Orleans in 1848, though in what capacity is uncertain. He was a pianist, which means he could have been used as a rehearsal accompanist at Davis's theater. He appears in the city directories only from 1853 on as a music teacher, and after the war his title was professor of music. He married the daughter of his teacher Barbereau, and one of their daughters, Madame Comès, with her extraordinary voice, became his most distinguished pupil. At some point he became musical director and organist at the Jesuit Church of the Immaculate Conception on Baronne Street.

The first season of the Classic Music Society consisted of six concerts, mostly devoted to chamber music. (See chapter 3 for the programs of all the concerts of the Classic Music Society.) In fact, there are only two specific indications that an orchestra was present. On the second program an orchestra accompanied a Weber piano concerto,[10] and in the last concert it accompanied a performance of one of Mendelssohn's piano concertos and possibly also Weber's *Concertstück*.[11] No mention is made of the pianist, but Collignon himself may have been the soloist since on the fifth program he is listed as playing the Mendelssohn Piano Concerto No. 1 in G Minor (where, however, no mention is made of an orchestral accompaniment).[12] The chamber music is predominantly by Beethoven, Mozart, and Mendelssohn, with Haydn, Hummel, Weber, and Joseph Mayseder (1789–1861) also represented. Collignon played the piano in those chamber works calling for the instrument, and Ludovico Gabici was the principal violinist. Violoncellists Oertl and Rudolph Meyer and clarinetist G. Kuffner—highly regarded local musicians—also participated. Singers from the opera were heard on all six programs.

The following fall another group of musicians attempted to preempt the Classic Music Society. As early as December 20, a concert of the Sainte Cecilia Musical Society was announced for Odd Fellows' Hall, where Beethoven's Symphony No. 5 was to be performed. The announced aims of the society sound similar to those of the Classic Music Society. The *Daily Creole* reported: "The Cecilia Musical Society is composed of the first musical artists of this city, and is organized on a plan similar to the Philharmonic Society of New York. Its members propose, during the season, to give four grand concerts, and on each occasion the programme will embrace much of the music of the old masters, interspersed with selections from patriotic and national airs of our own country."[13] This was to be a nonprofit organization, and the conditions of subscription were close to those of the Classic Music Society. "They therefore ask the public to come forward and subscribe to the proposed concerts, upon terms which they deem most liberal, viz: five tickets for each concert, ten dollars; two tickets for each concert, five dollars; with the privilege of attending the rehearsals twice in each month." Rehearsals were to be held every first and third Saturday of each month in Odd Fellows' Hall, from 11 a.m. to 1 o'clock.[14] The actual date for the first concert was more than a month later than originally announced: on Thursday, January 31, 1857. Mr. Hoeffner was the conductor.[15] However, whatever the reason, no further concerts were announced that season, and the way was clear for Collignon to resume his series in the fall of 1857. The Cecilia Society continued to exist, but under different conditions.

The second season of the Classic Music Society was devoted almost exclusively to orchestral music, without any chamber music, but a basso also performed two arias on the third concert (January 20, 1858),[16] and a chorus joined the orchestra for performances of Kreutzer's *The Chapel* and Mendelssohn's *Adieux to the Forest* on the fourth concert (February 19, 1858).[17] Although we do not know the programs for two of the six concerts, the four remaining programs give a good picture of what Collignon intended. Beethoven's Symphonies Nos. 2, 4, and 5 were played in their entirety, and excerpts were heard from the Symphony No. 7. The *Fidelio* Overture was also performed. Mozart was represented by *The Magic Flute* Overture and two movements from the *Jupiter* Symphony. Collignon conducted, as well, Weber's *Jubilee, Oberon,* and *Euryanthe* Overtures and Berlioz's arrangement of Weber's *Invitation to the Dance.* Mendelssohn's Overture to *A Mid-Summer Night's Dream* and another unnamed overture were on the first and third concerts respectively. After the regular season concluded, Collignon and the society performed a benefit concert on May 5, 1858, for Sainte Mary's Orphan Boys' Asylum. The program repeated some excerpts from earlier programs and added some lighter music, including the Andante from Haydn's *Surprise* Symphony No. 94 and overtures by Hérold and Auber that would have been well known to the opera-going public of New Orleans at that time. No doubt the inclusion of these works as well as some vocal arias was aimed at securing a larger audience than that which normally attended the society's concerts in order to raise more money for the orphanage.

Beethoven's Symphonies Nos. 2, 3, 5, and 6 were the featured works during the third season. Mendelssohn's *A Mid-Summer Night's Dream, Calm Sea, Ruy Blas,* and *Fingal's Cave* Overtures proved to be staples of the repertory, and works by Spohr and Schubert were added to it. A complete Haydn Symphony (No. 46 in B Minor) was highlighted on the first concert on December 8, 1858, and this may be the first time a complete Haydn symphony was performed publicly in New Orleans. Rossini's *William Tell* Overture had its first performance at a society concert on March 30, 1859, and favorite overtures by Weber were repeated from the previous season. The Mozart *Don Giovanni* Overture was heard on March 30. Collignon brought back a solo voice for the third concert on February 2, 1859, and for the first time a work by Clara Schumann, her *Andante and Variations for Two Pianos,* was performed at a society concert—here by MM G. Paulsackel and T. Wohlein on the March 30 program.[18]

Beethoven continued to be the featured composer during the fourth season when his Symphonies Nos. 3, 4, and 5 were heard in their entirety and part of the Symphony No. 1 was played on the third program (February 3, 1860). Every one of the six concerts had something by Beethoven; the *Egmont* and *Leonore* (probably No. 3) Overtures were on programs when the symphonies were not heard. Clearly, Collignon's aim was not just to perform the works once and be done with them but rather to play them again and again so that the audience would come to know them intimately. Mendelssohn, too, appeared on every program, with complete performances of his *Scottish* and *Italian* Symphonies Nos. 3 and 4, the *Ruy Blas, A Mid-Summer Night's Dream* (twice), and *Fingal's Cave* Overtures, and the wedding march from *A Mid-Summer Night's Dream*. Mozart, as well, received attention with his Overtures to *Don Giovanni* and *The Magic Flute* and the complete *Jupiter* Symphony No. 41. Three of the concerts included vocalists singing opera arias, and overtures to well-known operas by Rossini, Weber, Auber, and Hérold seem to have been added to the repertory in order to increase the size of the audience. As at the end of the second season, there was an additional charity concert that followed the final concert of the fourth season. On May 16, 1860, the society performed a popular concert for the benefit of Sainte Mary's Orphan Boys Asylum. Two unusual works were added to the potpourri of popular movements and overtures: a march performed by the (wind?) band of the orphanage, and Romberg's *Song of the Bell*, an oratorio with singers and full orchestra.[19]

Collignon obviously had both the entrepreneurial ability to organize the Classic Music Society and the musical talent to guide it along musical lines that catered to the most sophisticated tastes. Raising money—the bane of any musical organization—became important, and he was able to find the means to keep it going until, as the war approached, the financial collapse of the city made it impossible for him to continue. The orchestra consisted of both professionals and amateurs, and while the latter might perform without pay, the former certainly needed to be compensated. Therefore, the concerts were open to subscribers only, who the first season (spring 1856) paid $20 for three tickets for each concert.[20] The initial concert was in the Lyceum Hall, which was too small to accommodate the size audience that Collignon anticipated. Therefore, all the remaining prewar concerts were held in the much larger Odd Fellows' Hall. By the end of the second season (April 1858) there were 217 subscribers,[21] each paying now $35 per season, for a total income of $7,595.[22] The orchestra consisted of from sixty to seventy performers, and each concert cost $1,100. Thus, after this season, there was a net profit of $995, and Collignon felt assured that he need not raise the price of the subscription for the next season (1858–59). As lagniappe, he provided each subscriber with four rather than three tickets for each concert, and all the rehearsals—each Sunday at noon at Odd Fellows' Hall—would be open to subscribers.[23] He anticipated additional costs, but these he hoped would be offset by an increase in the number of subscribers. By the opening of the fourth season (1859–60), the price of the subscription remained $35 and the number of subscribers was greatly increased.[24] Now each subscriber could count on five tickets for each concert as well as admission to the rehearsals. If his aim was for 300 subscribers, the size of the audience for each concert would maximize at 1,500 persons.

A fifth season was planned for 1860–61, but it never materialized. On November 18, 1860, the *Picayune* announced that the first rehearsal of the society was to take place that day at Odd Fellows' Hall.[25] As the reporter stated, "We are rejoiced to find that the fears we had begun to entertain that this society was not to give us any concerts this winter were groundless. We are to have the usual series of six, and we earnestly counsel the lovers of fine music to come forward in goodly number, and add their names to the subscription list." The program chosen for this rehearsal was Beethoven's Symphony No. 6, Rossini's Overture to *The Siege of Corinth,* and Mendelssohn's *Calm Sea* Overture.[26] But the original fears were, unfortunately, well founded, and, after some rehearsals and much delay, the first concert never took place. On Sunday, December 23, 1860, the *Picayune* ran an obituary for the fifth season: "The stringency of the times we have fallen upon has been considered a sufficient apology, by the gentlemen of the Classic Music Society, for withdrawing their announcement of a series of concerts, the present season."[27] The society planned one more concert, originally scheduled for January 23, 1861, but finally performed on February 5 at Odd Fellows' Hall.[28] This was a benefit for the orphanage of Saint Vincent, and the program was Mozart's Mass No. 12. The chorus consisted of fifty women and men and was accompanied by a large orchestra composed of the best musicians of the city.

During the period of the Classic Concerts, Maurice Strakosch revisited New Orleans. On March 12, 1858, he conducted an orchestra in a concert with his wife and other singers at Odd Fellows' Hall, and the next day he gave a second concert.[29] It is uncertain if this was an orchestra he was traveling with or one he picked up when he reached the city. But there is no doubt that another orchestra that performed in Odd Fellows' Hall on Wednesday, February 23, 1859, was a visiting ensemble. Ullman's New York Academy of Music Concerts at Odd Fellows' Hall included an orchestra from New York conducted by Carl Anschutz.[30]

Every piece on the program was accompanied by the full orchestra. The fare consisted of various arias from *Don Giovanni, Norma, La Traviata, Il Trovatore, The Barber of Seville,* and *The Marriage of Figaro,* some solo piano pieces, and two overtures for orchestra: Flotow's *Martha* and Nicolai's *The Merry Wives of Windsor.* Likewise, M Musard seems to have brought his own soloists and orchestra from France to perform at Odd Fellows' Hall on February 25–26, 1859.[31]

THE CIVIL WAR PERIOD

The impending political decisions to secede from the Union and join the Confederacy caused a demoralization of the social and cultural life of the city during 1860, and the cultural crisis reached a head when these events became a reality between January and March of 1861. War broke out on April 12, 1861, and one week later President Lincoln ordered a blockade of all southern ports. For one year New Orleans was under a Union siege, which was ended on April 28, 1862, with the peaceful surrender of the city to Union Admiral David Farragut. For the next three years New Orleans was occupied by Union soldiers, who seemingly took no interest in fostering the arts that had made New Orleans one of America's proudest cities. During the siege and occupation, the citizens of New Orleans themselves were primarily concerned with the basics of survival, including where food was coming from and how their men were faring in the battles. Music, however, was not abandoned entirely.

Already during the late 1850s some of the important Creoles of color in the city's musical life had left—the Tio family for Mexico and Dédé and Lambert for France. The Classical Music Society was an immediate victim when it could not raise enough subscriptions to start its 1860–61 season. The French Opera continued through this, its first full season at its new house, the French Opera House, buoyed on by the appearance of the sparkling soprano Adelina Patti from December 1860 through April 1861, but an attempted second season, 1861 to 1862, folded after a performance of Meyerbeer's popular *Robert le Diable* on January 25, 1862. Once the blockade of the city was lifted and the citizens had a modicum of security, there was a chance that the French Opera House could reopen. The famous conductor of the French Opera, Eugène Prévost, had hoped to recruit a troupe of singers and instrumentalists for a full winter season for 1862–63, but, as *L'Abeille* reported, "the continuation of the War delayed indefinitely the engagement of a new troup," and he returned to France.[32] He took his temporary leave of the city after a benefit in his honor on Saturday, July 27, 1862,[33] and did not return until after the war.

Basically the new Opera House was closed for the duration of the Civil War, and for New Orleanians used to seeing and hearing operas sprinkled with dramas, comedies, and vaudevilles nearly every day for seven months a year, this was a cultural disaster. The house was open only for a handful of benefit concerts or operas—for the victims of the burning of Charleston on January 4, 1862,[34] for the singer E. Glatigny on June 22, 1862,[35] for the conductor Predigam on July 6, 1862,[36] for Prévost on July 27, 1862,[37] for the singer Madame De Latournerie on February 12, 1863,[38] and again on February 28,[39] for Isidore Nenning on March 23, 1863,[40] for the aspiring young Creole singer Emma Bournos on May 7, 1863, who was on her way to Paris,[41] for Mlle Maillet on October 4, 1863, upon her departure from New Orleans,[42] for M Octave on April 2, 1864,[43] for M John on April 9, 1864,[44] for Minnie Hauk on April 15, 1864, before her departure for Europe,[45] and for M Durieu on April 24, 1864.[46]

On those occasions during the siege and occupation when complete operas were performed, clearly enough singers and the orchestra remained in the city so that such performances were feasible. During the siege, it was difficult for anyone to leave the city, but once the Union conquered New Orleans, travel to other places in the North, like New York, and to Europe was possible again. A small exodus began—at least of some of the singers, and Prévost, did leave. But many were still in the city for the *La Favorite, The Barber of Seville,* and *Lucia* performances the winter of 1862–63 and remained for the various excerpts performed over the next two years.[47]

A climax was reached on July 18, 1864, when the mostly empty French Opera House, the ground upon which it stood, "all its stage properties, furniture and appurtenances of every description" were put up for sale in order to pay off creditors.[48] An auction was set for August 19, but nothing transpired on that date. Charles Boudousquié, who was the leader of the original stockholders, was a Confederate soldier and not available to respond.[49] Oliveira, discussed below, scheduled a concert in the hall for September 15, but the sheriff, who seized the building, refused to allow the event. On October 1 the property was sold to the Union Insurance Company, who had sued the owners for unpaid bills.[50] The most magnificent opera house in America, which had been built at a cost of $250,000, was picked up for a mere $80,000.

Fortunately, Union Insurance Company, in order to justify its purchase, sought to make the hall available for performances, and within days concerts were once again scheduled. If not operating at full capacity, at least there was a semblance of activity. Professor G. M. Loening directed Haydn's oratorio *Creation* on October 11, 27, and 31, 1864, at the Opera House with a large chorus drawn from different churches and with a "complete orchestra composed of the most distinguished professionals and amateurs of the city."[51] Other concerts involving orchestras, however, were absent.[52] By the following February, a German theater was installed in the French Opera House, which returned in October for a regular season of mostly German plays.[53]

The French Opera House, then, was not the focal point of music with orchestras during the Civil War years. Nor was the still new, architecturally beautiful Odd Fellows' Hall, which had served as the venue not only of the Classic Concert Society but also of many visiting artists. It was the preferred hall for chamber and orchestral concerts, but these were now impossible. Right at the beginning of the occupation, the Union troops were billeted in the building, which had a chilling effect on the presentation of such concerts not only in this hall but throughout the city.[54]

Instead, four other venues were opened on a regular basis for entertainment and retained orchestras. The Academy of Music was the home of circuses and popular shows, but occasionally there would be serious concerts, such as on April 9, 1862, when the Queen Sisters from Charleston, South Carolina, began a week's run of original plays with orchestral music,[55] and on April 18, 1864, when the Italian opera singer Teresa Conioli performed "favorite selections from popular operas."[56] Sanford's Opera Troupe played there, but opera in the traditional sense was not its fare. For almost twelve months a year, the Academy of Music was open, and by 1864 it was the only hall that could still draw a crowd.

The Varieties Theater tried more successfully to be more sophisticated. It presented drama, including a Shakespeare season from November 1863 to spring 1864 (*Hamlet*, *Richard III*, *Merchant of Venice*, *Much Ado about Nothing*, and others), and it even attempted opera, such as the second act of *Il Trovatore* and the third act of *Robert le Diable* on March 23, 1863.[57] But with money scarce and the directors of the theater concerned about filling the hall, serious music could not be its main attraction.

Without competition from the French Opera House, the old Théâtre d'Orléans presented some opera, but productions there were less and less frequent (it was finally destroyed by fire late in 1866). Predigam, who was the conductor of the fourth act of *La Favorite* at the French Opera on February 12, 1863, for the benefit of Mme De Latournerie[58] and on April 6, 1863, when they produced *Norma*,[59] was conductor of the Varieties Theater on March 12, 1863, when he conducted the interlude during a benefit for Mrs. W. C. Galdsane, and was conductor of the orchestra and chorus at the Théâtre d'Orléans in November, 1863 where he "obtained an excellent ensemble."[60] Before Prévost left for Europe, Predigam was conductor of the Théâtre d'Orléans, where a benefit was held in his honor on July 6, 1862 (he also conducted the orchestra on this occasion).[61] When the Théâtre d'Orléans produced *Lucia* on March 23, 1863, with an "increased orchestra,"[62] presumably with Predigam conducting, it was remarked that this was the first complete opera performance of the season.[63]

The old Saint Charles Theatre was used only rarely at first and then, by the end of 1862, had regular seasons of pantomimes and plays. Perhaps the high point of the theater's attractions during the occupation came in the winter-spring season of 1863 when John Wilkes Booth appeared in Shakespearean plays such as *Richard III* and plays by other authors.[64] The theater was old, however, and during the late summer of 1864 it underwent renovations in preparation for the coming season.

A few other theaters were used for an occasional play or concert that may have involved orchestras. For example, the Ambigu Comique Theater, on the corner of Grands Hommes Street and Champs Elysées, presented a play on September 13, 1863.[65] Concerts were also held at some of the churches. Collignon, then master of the Chapel of the Jesuit Church of the Immaculate Conception, conducted Weber's Mass in E Minor on Monday, November 22, 1864, at the church;[66] other church concerts which may have used orchestral accompaniment occurred on January 10, 1865, and on February 23, 1865.[67]

The orchestras associated with the Academy of Music, the Varieties Theater, the Théâtre d'Orléans, and the Saint Charles Theatre were thus able to survive, though the economy of the city was so bad that survival must have been at the subsistence level. The musicians in the French Opera Orchestra, however, had to find other employment for most of the time. Because of their superior skills, many were no doubt welcomed in the four open theaters. Predigam was apparently the regular conductor of the Varieties Theater, but when Prévost moved back to Europe in the summer of 1862, Predigam moved over to both the French Opera House and the Théâtre d'Orléans without surrendering his position at the Varieties Theater.[68] The Academy of Music, hardly the venue for fine music, nonetheless had as its orchestral director the finest violinist in the city: Jacques Oliveira.[69]

In addition, the dance halls remained open with their orchestras actively participating. On May 3, 5, and 9, 1863, a group of the most distinguished players formed a light orchestra à la Strauss at the saloon of M Guth on Conti Street between Royal and Bourbon streets.[70] Philip Greuling was the chef d'orchestre, Oliveira was the solo violinist, and the others included A. Dantonnet, L. Mayer, C. Dantonnet, Bastloul, F. Eberhardt, T. Flemings, J. Charlton, C. Hopf,

G. Monteri, and F. Keckel. The idea of chamber music during the spring and summer in coffee shops or restaurants came first before the war and is found again afterwards, and it gave financially strapped musicians during the war another source of income.

Whenever there was a benefit concert or a special church performance, the best local instrumentalists would be hired to accompany. The only possible instance of a Beethoven work with orchestra being performed during the occupation occurred on March 26, 1865, when Curto led a complete performance of Beethoven's oratorio *Christ on the Mount of Olives* at the French Opera House.[71] One hundred and twenty persons participated in this concert, which also included the Overture to Rossini's *Stabat Mater* and the first two parts of Curto's own *Stabat Mater*. There is no indication of the nature of the accompaniment, whether orchestral or not, but with the inclusion of both professional and amateur musicians and the large number of performers an orchestra may have been involved.

Into this abysmal scene stepped the violinist Jacques Oliveira, whose public performances from 1862 to 1865 assured New Orleanians the chance to hear top professional artists and kept chamber music alive.[72] Sometimes he was accompanied by piano, but on at least a few occasions he could have performed with orchestra. For example, on March 18, 1863, Oliveira "has kindly consented to perform at the Varieties Theater a grand solo on the violin; the orchestra will perform a new march under the leadership of Mr. P. Gruelling."[73] It is possible that Greuling moved over to the piano to accompany Oliveira, but it is just as possible that the orchestra was used. A similar situation occurred at the French Opera House five days later when Oliveira played an intermède between acts of *Lucia*. The orchestra was under the direction of M Reiter and Mme Boudre played the piano,[74] but did Mme Boudre or M Reiter with his orchestra accompany him?

Besides Oliveira, other violinists were in front of the New Orleans public during this time. Probably the most important was Henri Page, who had arrived in New Orleans by 1865 and gave a recital at the Saint Charles Theatre on April 17 that year. A newspaper reported that he was "assisted by [the pianist] Mlle Charpeaux, [the singer] A. Flandry, and a number of distinguished amateurs of New Orleans. The programme comprise[d] a number of judicious selections from De Bériot, Thalberg, Donizetti and other composers."[75] Among the works played was a waltz by Page himself, which was executed by the orchestra. Mr. (Robert?) Meyer was director of the orchestra of the National Theater on the corner of Saint Peter and Saint Claude streets, opposite Congo Square, when on January 15, 1863, he conducted the orchestra in a concert of arias and duets that also included the Overture to Auber's *Fra Diavolo*.[76]

Another kind of orchestra is evident during the occupation: the wind band. A grand concert of the Bande de cuivre under the direction of Charles Jeager occurred on Saturday, June 6, 1863, at 8 p.m., at the Globe Hall, corner of Saint Claude and Saint Pierre streets.[77] They played excerpts from operas, potpourris, overtures, and arias. A dance followed. Jaeger's band remained popular after the war.

RECOVERY DURING THE POST–CIVIL WAR YEARS

Robert E. Lee surrendered his army to Ulysses S. Grant on April 9, 1865, though the fighting continued for a few more weeks elsewhere. New Orleans survived the war with relatively little physical damage but with great harm to its economy and its morale. The entire occupation was hard on its people, especially the last year, and numerous citizens had fled to avoid the deprivations. War, conscription, the end of slavery, a new Louisiana constitution, the assassination of Lincoln, and, simply, the insecurity of rapidly changing political conditions took precedence over music unless it was a benefit for charity or a musician in need. Everything had to be approved by the military authorities, even the concert of sacred music in honor of Saint Joseph's Day at the French Opera House directed by Robert Meyer and Curto mentioned above. This was a charity concert that grossed $2,242, all but $500 of which was available for distribution to over seven hundred families impoverished by the war. It took weeks to figure out how to divide such a small sum for so many people.[78]

Within days of the end of the war, a pall was lifted off the musical life of the city. The French Opera House, the center of the classical musical scene, had barely witnessed any concerts and no operas during the final year of the war. By the end of April and beginning of May, however, musical activity increased significantly. Leon Prévost, son of Eugène,[79] announced on May 1 that he was back to conduct the Orchestra of the French Opera House in a special farewell concert on Saturday, May 6, 1865,[80] and he conducted an orchestra in another grand concert on May 24, 1865.[81]

Nonetheless, it would take a few years for the city to fully recover its prewar eminence as a major center of classical music. While many local musicians, both professionals and amateurs, either stayed in the city throughout the war or returned shortly thereafter, the steady flow of fresh musicians from Europe and the rest of America and the European education of many native children had been greatly curtailed. It would take some time to restore this flow, but by the return of the Classic Music Series in 1871, the musical life of New Orleans approached its prewar status.

As will be shown in Book II, the opera's return after the war was shaky. This inevitably impacted concert life in New Orleans. But benefit concerts involving orchestras continued after the end of the war since this was a type of concert that had proven useful for musicians for well over a hundred years throughout Europe as well as America. The city was full of needy people—orphans and widows, injured soldiers, musicians who had not had full employment, among others—and benefits were a major source for raising money for charities to aid these people. Perhaps the first after the fall of the Confederacy was when a full orchestra accompanied Eva Brent at the French Opera House on April 17, 1865, which was a benefit for "poor families of this city."[82] Luccia Bordesi sang opera excerpts during a benefit for Fannie Melmes at the Saint Charles Opera House on May 4, 1865.[83] Many of these concerts included orchestras or chamber music, such as the benefit for Jewish widows and orphans that took place on May 22, 1865, in the French Opera House.[84] On this occasion a choir of fifty men and women, directed by Mr. S. Mosche of the Rampart Street Synagogue, were joined by a "splendid orchestra" conducted by Robert Meyer. The musical part of the program was followed by a dramatic part.[85] Benefits continued for years afterwards; for example, two years later Collignon directed sixty of the "best instrumental performers," in support of Carlo Patti.[86]

Only a handful of concerts with orchestra were not benefits. On Monday, April 29, 1867, Henri Page, first violinist of the French Opera House Orchestra, gave a recital at the house to a small audience.[87] He was an excellent violinist but apparently did not have the charm of Oliveira and received an indifferent response from the audience. The program, accompanied by "tous les artistes de l'orchestre,"[88] included opera excerpts performed on the violin, songs sung by M Fernando, a duo for flutes (performed by the pupils of Leopold Carrière, also a member of the house orchestra), a piece for two pianos from *Norma*, and so forth. The orchestra played the Overture to *Les Diamants de la Couronne* and the waltz *Les Soeurs de Charité* composed by Page. The concert had good parts, but some pieces dragged. A much more auspicious concert occurred eight months later. Eleven-year-old Mark Kaiser, a native of New Orleans, made his debut in the National Theater on December 19, 1867; he played a Giovanni Battista Viotti violin concerto with full orchestra. The orchestra also performed overtures.[89]

Besides the orchestras at the main opera houses (French Opera House, National Theater, Saint Charles Theatre) some of the other theatres maintained orchestras as they had during the war years. This was especially true of the Varieties Theater and the Academy of Music, where Professor Younkers was chef d'orchestre during the 1867–68 season.[90] The number of concerts in churches also grew after the war, and in some cases orchestras were involved.

Balls continued to be a major source of income for orchestras, and the number of balls increased considerably. All the venues were used, and when the Théâtre d'Orléans was destroyed, it was replaced shortly thereafter not by a theater but by a dance hall.[91] While the balls were open to paying members year round, during Carnival season (from the beginning of January through Mardi Gras, the Tuesday before Ash Wednesday) the balls were limited to invited members of a social society or Krewe. A novel feature was introduced for Carnival in 1868 when four masked balls were planned at the French Opera House which were open for a fifteen-dollar subscription fee. The music for the balls was performed by the excellent Orchestra of the Opera House featuring the newest and most brilliant quadrilles. The conductors of the orchestra were gentlemen associated with the best theater orchestras in the city: MM Isai and Carlo Patti.[92] After Carnival came Saint Joseph's Day in March, when again—but for a shorter period of time—the city would enjoy fancier-than-usual balls. On Saint Joseph's Day, March 19, 1866, an orchestra performed four Promenade Concerts at Odd Fellows' Hall during the masked balls.[93] An excellent orchestra of musicians was assembled, including a wind band led by Charles Jaeger and a string orchestra led by Leonard Bayersdorffer. Besides the dances, they played excerpts from operas and the *Grand Polonaise Promenade* by Mayseder.

By the conclusion of the war, Charles Jaeger emerged as the leading conductor of wind orchestral music. He continued with his own concerts, such as in the Cedre Magnolia Garden, next to the Bayou Bridge. The concert on Sunday, June 4, "un grand concert sacré," began at 5 p.m. and cost twenty-five cents. But increasingly he participated with string orchestras in order to perform works requiring the combination of these two sonorities. For example, on Friday, November 23, 1866, he played four excerpts from the Mass No. 12 by Mozart at the Mechanic's Institute at 3:30 p.m. This performance was directed by La Hache (vocal director), Collignon (orchestral director), Gustave Smith (accompanist), and Jaeger (head of the band).[94] The following Sunday at 2:30 p.m. he joined the same group at the Société Agricole et Industrielle at the Fair Grounds for a larger Grand Concert Sacre.[95] The concert was performed by "a grand orchestra and the celebrated brass band of Jaeger, with a large chorus of amateurs." The program consisted of choral, symphonic, and wind band music. The symphonic pieces were Gluck's Overture to *Iphigénie,* Andante from the

Surprise Symphony No. 94 of Haydn, orchestral excerpts from Mozart's *The Magic Flute,* The *Jublié* Overture by Weber, and Meyerbeer's *Marche au Flambeau* (for double orchestra). The orchestral program was typical of the concert programs of the Classic Music Society that Collignon had conducted before the war, and clearly he was ready to resume that series. The solo wind band pieces were excerpts from Rossini's *Stabat Mater,* Schubert's *Serenade,* and Kreutzer's *La Chapelle.* Additional choral works were by Kreutzer, L. H. (La Hache?), Mendelssohn, and Becker.

It was not until the season of 1871–72, however, that the orchestral life of the city at last returned to the glory days of the late 1850s. At this time the Classic Music Society was reborn with Collignon at the helm. At the first open rehearsal on Sunday, October 8, 1871, at half past noon, thirty-six of the best instrumental performers of the city presented Beethoven's Symphony No. 6 and the Overture to Weber's *Oberon.*[96] The event took place in the foyer of the National Theater and was highly successful. Nearly three hundred subscribers were reported, though this large number of patrons was barely able to underwrite the expense of such a large and professional ensemble.[97] In all, fourteen such performance/rehearsals took place from October 8 to the following April 28. Although these were billed usually as rehearsals, they nonetheless provided New Orleanians the opportunity to hear the finest orchestral music by the great masters played by professionals. By the third concert the orchestra had been enlarged to a "complete orchestra."[98] The season included Beethoven's Symphonies Nos. 1, 2, 3, 6, and 7; Mozart's *Jupiter* Symphony No. 41; Mendelssohn's *Scottish* Symphony No. 3; Haydn's *Surprise* Symphony No. 94 (some of these more than once); overtures by Beethoven (*Egmont*), Weber (*Der Freischütz, Oberon, Euryanthe, Jubel*), Mendelssohn (*Fingal's Cave, Ruy Blas*), Rossini (*William Tell*), Gluck (*Iphegénie en Aulide*), Auber (*La Muette de Portici*); and an assortment of other works (Meyerbeer's "Marche aux Flambeaux," Robert Schumann's *Rêverie,* the Weber/Berlioz *Invitation to the Dance*), and numerous individual movements of symphonies. No concertos were performed.

To add to the delight of the lovers of symphonic music, the season 1871–72 also brought to the city America's most famous traveling orchestra: the Theodore Thomas Orchestra. This ensemble of fifty to sixty musicians, led by Thomas, was assisted by a solo pianist (in Chopin and Mendelssohn concertos), a solo violinist (Paganini's Violin Concerto No. 1), and a solo "corniste."[99] They performed five grand concerts in Odd Fellows' Hall, but their last concert was at the Varieties Theater. A local critic ranked Thomas's ensemble among the best in the world and, in comparison with the Orchestra of the Classic Music

Society, it had better precision of attack and perfect ensemble performance that came because Thomas had worked with the same musicians for six years.[100] The same critic rated the string section of the Thomas Orchestra very high, but the winds were inferior. Among the works performed were Beethoven's Symphony No. 5, the overtures to *Lohengrin* and *Tannhäuser* by Wagner, *Der Freischütz* by Weber, *A Mid-Summer Night's Dream* by Mendelssohn, and *Prometheus* by Beethoven, the concertos mentioned above, and other pieces.

The resurgence of great symphonic music in New Orleans was coupled with a new enthusiasm for chamber music at the beginning of 1872. For the first time an attempt was made to establish a resident string quartet. Three members of the French Opera Orchestra—MM Auber, Comtat, and Raoul—were joined by a "distinguished amateur," M Wapler, to inaugurate a new series devoted to the string quartets of Haydn, Mozart, Beethoven, and Mendelssohn.[101] As the critic of *L'Abeille* saw it, chamber music is often misunderstood, even by many performers, but "this kind of music is in its essence poetic." All four musicians mentioned above, he continued, studied this music and understood it. Concerts were to take place at noon on Sundays.

Unfortunately, the classical music scene took a nosedive the following season, and most rest of the 1870s was largely a disappointment. The economy of the city remained bad, and the creditors once again stalked the Opera House and put a damper on all performances. The Opera House opened the 1872–73 season without grand opera, and few concerts were given. From then until 1880 the city was often without its own grand opera company, and without a resident opera company there was no need to maintain a high-quality orchestra. When the orchestra was allowed to disintegrate, the number of chamber concerts as well as orchestral concerts outside the opera declined noticeably. There would be visiting opera companies so that New Orleanians would on occasion be able to enjoy their favorite pastime, and these would usually be at venues other than the French Opera House—such as at the Varieties Theater or the Saint Charles Theatre. Those theaters, as well as the more popular ones (especially the Academy of Music) maintained their own orchestras to play for vaudevilles, opéra comiques, circuses, and minstrel shows, but the level of playing there was apparently less rigorous than at the French Opera.

When the opera staged a brief comeback in the fall of 1873, a critic in *L'Abeille* stated, on November 9, 1873, how much the orchestra and its conductor Eugene Momas were treasured by the people of the city. In reviewing a performance of *Les Huguenots* on November 1, A.M. states:

There was another grand voice of which we should not fail to speak, and it is about it that we terminate this musical discourse. This voice is that of the orchestra; for the orchestra is a composite voice composed of all the instruments, and it is everywhere the mother voice, so to speak, which allows the singers to group and seek their place. Monsieur Momas, charged with directing the movements of all these tonal forces into a harmonious whole, takes his task with as much skill as conscience. He is currently one of the best conductors in France; we honestly believe that he draws the best possible sounds from the personnel at his disposal. These instrumentalists are of different nationalities, and some of them were entirely unknown to him before his arrival in New Orleans, and yet he has brought them together so that, after a few rehearsals, he has left little to be desired. He has done much in a short time, and we are sincerely grateful for that.[102]

Thus, it was not only operagoers who were to be disappointed at the fall of the opera, but also anyone who valued orchestral music, and New Orleans had both audiences.

The vicissitudes of the French Opera in the 1870s must have been difficult for the members of the orchestra. Although the opera was revived by the fall of 1873, between 1876 and the middle of 1880 there was a four-year hiatus in which only visiting troupes performed full-scale opera. The orchestra was used for vaudeville, ballet, operettas, and an occasional concert, but the infrequency of full-scale operas with visiting conductors and singers would have inhibited the preservation of the quality of performance that a steady conductor and singers would have brought about. There apparently was much more turnover in the personnel of the orchestra at this time, for something new appears in the newspapers at the end of the spring 1874 season: advertisements for positions in the orchestra.[103]

In spring 1874, Louis Grunewald saw the position of the musicians as desperate and so, in order to save them, he created a spring festival of twelve concerts in his store on Baronne Street. Thirty members of the orchestra were hired.[104] These spring concerts, entitled Concerts Populaires, were given on Mondays, Wednesdays, and Fridays, and Robert Meyer was conductor. To ensure maximum returns for the players, musician/businessman Grunewald would earn something only if the musicians were fully paid. Admission was by subscription only, and it cost five dollars for tickets to all twelve concerts. The concerts extended from May 18 to June 13. The restaurant that abutted the concert hall was transformed into a parlor of ice creams and refreshments.

Smoking was permitted (for gentlemen only) in a room leading to the gallery. There were ten- to fifteen-minute intermissions for promenades, conversation, and refreshments. The programs, which were supposed to be different on each occasion, consisted of overtures and potpourris from operas, parts of classical masterpieces, dances (including the latest Strauss waltzes from Vienna), some instrumental solos with the accompaniment of piano or orchestra, and some vocal solos. A typical program was that on May 22: Wagner (*Tannhäuser* march), Hérold (Overture to *Zampa*), Rossini (excerpts from *William Tell*), Kalliwoda (Adagio and Scherzo from Symphony in A Minor), Strauss (*Wiener Woods*), Lindpaintner (Overture to *Jocko*), Robert Schumann (*Träumerei*), Meyerbeer (air from *Robert le Diable*), waltzes, and a polka. On May 27 the program was the *Freischütz* Overture, different Strauss waltzes, Auber's Overture to *La Sirène*, and so forth, but they did repeat Robert Schumann's *Träumerei* owing to popular demand, and the full Kalliwoda symphony.

The situation at the French Opera House continued to deteriorate the following fall. By January 4, 1875, the Opera House closed down and its director, Canonge, resigned (he thereupon launched a new career as the city's foremost music critic).[105] To support the musicians of the orchestra there were some performances outside the French Opera House—a practice that continued from before. Only rarely could anyone devise a scheme such as that by Grunewald to keep the core of the orchestra active, and few solo performers could afford to hire them en masse to accompany a recital. There was one such concert in the spring of 1874, on Thursday, April 17, however, when M D. Delcroix, Louisiana pianist, played at Grunewald Hall with the assistance of the French Opera Orchestra under Momas and several singers (Devoyod-Acs and Van Hufflen).[106]

Rather, dancing and marching seemed to be a more workable situation since organizations sponsoring those events were in a better position than individuals to afford the orchestra. During the years from 1874 to 1879 there were many such events. On April 9–10, 1874, for example, there was a Promenade and Concert at Odd Fellows' Hall, given by the women of the Church of New Jerusalem and performed by one of the best bands (orchestras?) of musicians in the city. "Following the English model," people came in at 7 and the dancing started at 8:30 p.m.[107] On December 5, 1874, there were two separate balls for which orchestral musicians were needed, one at the French Opera House and another at Grunewald Hall. Despite bad weather (wind and rain), everyone had a good time. As reported in *L'Abeille,* "The men and women dancers have flown into the swirl of the dance as defined by the orchestral chords and have shown themselves to be fearless."[108]

A "brilliant orchestra of wind instruments" served for the fancy, masked Mardi Gras ball at the French Opera House on February 14, 1877,[109] and the fourth annual grand ball of the Saint Maurice Mutual Aid Society in Grunewald Hall on March 9, 1877, was serenaded by the "excellent music of A. Cunniot."[110] Whether or not any or all the members of the bands were from the Opera House Orchestra is not known, but at least an opportunity to utilize the best (wind?) performers in town was there. A marching occasion occurred on January 17, 1875, at the annual session of the District Grand Lodge No. 7 of B'nai B'rith. Accompanied by Robert Meyer's orchestral (wind?) band, the members of the lodge adjourned in a body to attend the twentieth anniversary celebration of the Jewish Widows and Orphans Home. They marched in the street, ultimately arriving at the home on Jackson and Chippewa streets.[111]

In addition there were church concerts with the potential to utilize at least some of the Opera House Orchestra. Once again Collignon was involved in some of these. For a concert at the Church of the Immaculate Conception on Friday, December 12, 1873, many professionals and amateurs participated, and on March 29, 1874, at the same church Gounod's Grand Mass was performed.[112] In a special concert on April 22, 1874, at the same church, honoring Collignon, he conducted among other works Berlioz's *The Flight to Egypt* (from *L'Enfance du Christ*), for solo, chorus and orchestra.[113]

The next few years were in glaring contrast to those that preceded them. The intense activity of concerts and operas during the years 1871 to 1874 gave way to a void by the fall of 1875 as hopes for a strong opera faded. Some orchestral musicians must have left town to find jobs where the economy was not so bad. Those who stayed turned to teaching or became amateur musicians while working in other occupations. Plays in French continued to be performed, and sometimes the house orchestra would entertain between acts, as on April 2, 1880, when the orchestra performed a musical intermède consisting of a romance (ballad) from Thomas's *Mignon* and an excerpt from Donizetti's *The Daughter of the Regiment*.[114]

When Max Strakosch brought his opera troupe back to New Orleans on November 24, 1879, he advertised in advance, through his local agent Canonge, that he still needed first and second violins, violas, and a second trumpet for the orchestra. If these were not forthcoming within four or five days, Canonge was to inform Strakosch, who would then hire these musicians in Cincinnati and/or Saint Louis to come to New Orleans.[115] No doubt some players from the French Opera took advantage of a few weeks' employment, though we have no records of how this advertisement was received by them. The critic in *L'Abeille* was clear even if not wholly accurate. Strakosch was bringing opera to New Orleans for the first time since 1876, he said, and therefore deserved support.[116] This city was renowned for opera before the war, and yet for only seven or eight years between the end of the war and 1879 was there opera; Reconstruction destroyed the ability of New Orleans to pay for opera. He suggested that maybe New Orleans should join one or two other cities in creating a company that would have a permanent orchestra, chorus and ensemble.[117] In any case, Strakosch was to give the city a month of great opera again, opening with *Il Trovatore,* and his orchestra "acquitted itself with great success."[118] Not only did the orchestra accompany the singers, but also it performed between acts. Especially significant was the evening of December 31, 1879, when at the French Opera House during a Strakosch performance of *Il Trovatore,* "between the second and third acts the orchestra will play for the first time *Harmonies de la Nature,* a suite for orchestra, composed by M Hubert Rolling of New Orleans." The conductor was S. Behrens.[119]

The city was not without opera at the other theaters, though the French population was happy only when opera was performed in French at the French Opera House. These other theaters and their visiting opera troupes also had orchestras which were part of the orchestral ambiance of the city. For example, there was un orchestre nombreux at the Varieties Theater on March 5, 1879, when the Gilbert and Sullivan operetta *H.M.S. Pinafore* had its New Orleans premier; there was un grand orchestre at the Grand Opera House on Canal Street on January 6, 1880, when the Maurice Grau Company began several weeks of performances of operas; there was a grand chorus and orchestra at the Grand Opera House on February 9, 1880, when the Emma Abbott Opera Company opened its several week stand with Balfé's *Bohemian Girl*; and there was an orchestra that accompanied the D'Oyle Carte Company presentation on March 24, 1880, of *The Pirates of Penzance.*[120] There was even an orchestra at the Saint Charles Theatre on March 15, 1880, when the Colville Burlesque Company began a series of spoofs on serious opera.[121]

All through the struggles of the French Opera, the other theaters in New Orleans managed to stay afloat by presenting operettas, vaudevilles, and comedies that required less money to put on and were appealing to a wider audience. Although in musical circles the orchestras at these establishments were held in less esteem, they nonetheless were there night after night and provided employment for a large number of professionals. They accompanied the dramatic or vaudeville routines and at times played for the breaks between acts.[122] The spring of 1880 was a popular time for Gilbert and Sullivan, as shown above, and it continued with another performance of *H.M.S. Pinafore* on April 5, 1880, at the Academie de Musique by the Haverly Opera Company from New York.[123] All during this time and well into the 1880s, Wenger Gardens, at 11 and 13 Bourbon Street, boasted "the grandest orchestra in the world" executing airs from 11 a.m. to midnight.[124] Beginning on January 1, 1881, and every evening and on Sunday afternoons thereafter, Wenger Gardens had a grand concert of the celebrated orchestra of women from Berlin under the direction of Mlle Kate Liebold,[125] and in January 1883, a female orchestra from Vienna started performing every evening.[126]

In 1876 and 1880 there were some concerts where orchestras were used, but rarely did an orchestra appear in such a capacity in the intervening years. Advertisements appeared between December 15 and 17, 1876, seeking sponsorship of a concert under the auspices of the Athenaeum at either Grunewald Hall or the French Opera House, with full orchestra, featuring and promoting D'Aquin. There is no evidence that such sponsorship was ever found.[127] Possibly an orchestra was used on February 18, 1877, during a grand concert at Grunewald Hall featuring Mlle Louise Dorel of the Comedie Française of Paris and New York, which featured two vaudevilles and an opera bouffe by Offenbach, though it is uncertain if this was a concert performance of those works or a staged version.[128] Only in 1879 were there concerts again featuring orchestras. On April 15, 1879, Thédore Curant gave a concert at Grunewald Hall with Lena Little, H. E. Lehmann, Livain, Kitziger, Cartier, Mueller, Eckert, and an orchestra of thirty of the best musicians conducted by Livain. Included were the Overture to Wallace's *Maritana*; Weber's *Jubel* Overture (both played by orchestra); a Haydn string quartet with Curant, Kitziger, Cartier, and Mueller; the Beethoven Violin Concerto with Curant accompanied by Samuel; the Mendelssohn Piano Concerto in G Minor No. 1 performed by Samuel and orchestra; a flute piece; and other works.[129] On May 14, Marguerite Samuel repeated the Mendelssohn concerto and played solo piano works, while the orchestra, under the direction of Greuling, played Reissiger's *Felsenmühle* Overture.[130]

At a promenade concert on June 29, 1879, at Magnolia Gardens, as part of the sixth annual festival of the musicians' benevolent society and union, Eckert directed an orchestra of fifty musicians in symphonies, marches, and other pieces, and dancing followed the formal concert.[131] There was a preliminary concert at 3 p.m. and the grand concert at 5 p.m. in the batisse principale. On Monday, Robert Meyer led a program "for the gourmets of good music" with an elite orchestra. The program included Meyer's *Grande Marche*, Caraffa's Overture to *La Violetta*, Wagner's Overture to *Tannhäuser*, a *Capriccio* by Collignon, a potpourri from Rossini's *William Tell,* a Strauss waltz, the Overture to Weber's *Freischütz,* a violin solo by Léonard performed by Curant, a potpourri from Halévy's *La Juive,* selections from Gounod's *Faust,* a flute solo by Gervartes performed by Livain, and another Strauss waltz, *Wein, Weib und Gesang.*[132] By 1880, however, orchestras were once again used at public events. On Saturday, January 3, 1880, when the Louisiana Athenaeum Club presented literary prizes to young competitors at the Opera House, the orchestra participated with a fanfare, then the Priests' March from Meyerbeer's *Le Prophète*; in the second half the orchestra played an andante and then concluded the affair with Hubert Rolling's *Marche Triomphale* (Rolling was a member of the Athenaeum Club). The rest of the program was speeches.[133] A full concert with "complete orchestra of forty of the best musicians in the city" was directed by Theodore Curant at Grunewald Hall on March 30, 1880, and included Alice Schwarz, Annie Seawell, F. Bremer, D. Delcroix, and Eckert.[134]

Bands were also employed for classical concerts. On June 5, 1877, when Mlle Bouligny, assisted by Mme Schwartz and others, offered a charity concert at Grunewald Hall to benefit the Lady Servants of the Poor, a military band played an overture and a march.[135] On November 18, 1877, a German military band led by Carl Beyer began performing at Grunewald Hall. Along with the Theodore Thomas (orchestra), it was considered one of the two best large instrumental ensembles in the United States.[136]

THE FINAL YEARS OF THE CENTURY: 1880–1897

Many of the old-guard musicians were gone by 1880. Oliveira died in 1867, Gabici died during the war, Curto was an old man, Eugène Prévost died in 1872, and even the indefatigable Collignon conducted his last concert in 1879 and was living with his daughter, the soprano Comès, in Paris by 1880.[137] During the 1870s several new musical leaders emerged who had an impact on the concert scene in New Orleans. Chief among these were Eckert, Rolling, Caulier, and Cartier. Furthermore, a new group of younger musicians came into their own during the last two decades of the nineteenth century. They were led by natives Mark Kaiser, Marguerite Elie Samuel, Henri Joubert, and Gustave D'Aquin. They were instrumentalists (violin, piano, violin, and flute, respectively), and they all had studied in Paris. They were committed to the performance of the best classical music that Europe had to offer, and they resuscitated both orchestral and chamber music, which had all but died at the end of the 1870s with the old generation.

There were two major events that spurred the cultivation of orchestral music during the last two decades of the nineteenth century. These were the opening of summer resorts on Lake Pontchartrain to the north of the city, and the two-year Cotton Exposition that was held on what is now Audubon Park in Uptown New Orleans.

In 1879 orchestral concerts began to appear regularly at resorts on Lake Pontchartrain. The first of these to open for concerts seems to have been Spanish Fort, which had concerts nightly from mid-July through August of that year. The longstanding problem that orchestral musicians had with regard to summer employment seemed to have found a solution, and for the next few years many of them could count on steady income during the months when the theaters were dark. In turn, New Orleanians, sweltering in the summer heat and humidity, were encouraged to take the train from the Rampart Street Station and spend at least the evening by the lake with its cooling breezes. In the summer of 1879, the first train left the city at 5:30 p.m. each day and continued every twenty minutes, and the last train back from the lake left there at 11:10 p.m. The next spring, on May 1, 1880, Mr. Moses conducted an orchestral program at Spanish Fort featuring a cornet solo by Mr. R. Gewert, which began a popular tradition of cornet solos during these concerts.[138]

But it was the season of 1881 that was the high point of orchestral music at Spanish Fort. Beginning on May 10 and continuing until October 5, there were special classical orchestral concerts every few nights that complemented the regular nightly semiclassical concerts; these special concerts were entitled Grand Concerts Promenade.[139] The orchestra, with forty players, was conducted usually by W. Borchet and featured Rudolphe Gewert (cornetist), Gustave D'Aquin (solo flute), O. John (solo clarinet), and Professor Weifenbach (tambour major) on each program.[140] Theodore Curant conducted on May 27, 1881.[141]

The special nights usually consisted of three performances: (1) an early semiclassical orchestral concert at 5:30 or 6:30 p.m. in the garden, (2) the featured special classical concert, after a ten-minute intermission, in the concert hall, and (3) a final semiclassical orchestral concert in the garden. The garden concerts were generally lighter in content but not without some serious classical music. For example, on June 3 the first garden concert consisted of Pilfe's *March en Avant,* Waldteufel's *Vales Pluie d'Or,* Donizetti's *Fantasie La Favorite,* and Gast's *Polka Les Délices d'Interlaken* featuring R. Gewert on cornet; stuck in the middle of this first garden concert was Beethoven's *Fidelio* Overture.[142] The second garden concert was lighter with Sarasate's *Dansées Espagnoles,* Faust's *Quadrille de l'Empereur,* and Eduard Strauss's *Polka (Schnell) Unter der Eme.* The special concert in between the two garden concerts, however, was more pretentious. It began with Rossini's *William Tell* Overture, featured the young violinist Maurice Dengremont performing two works by Hubert Léonard (his teacher in Paris), and ended with Keler Bela's *Grand Galop Infernal,* a six-part work of demonical character ("Choeur des Esprits Infernaux," "Combat des Furies," "Danse des Démons, Minuit," "Pluton Parait," and "Réception de Pluton"). In the middle of the serious concert the esteemed Jeanne Franko performed Liszt's Polonaise No. 2 for solo piano. Dengremont and Franko were regulars at Spanish Fort that spring.[143] During the summer Henri Joubert, Marguerite Samuel, and Gustave D'Aquin were featured with the orchestra on several occasions, Madame D'Aquin and Alice Schwartz sang with Borchert's group, and Jeanne Franko continued to appear.[144]

The following year the concerts at Spanish Fort began on May 11, 1882. There was music every night of the season, provided by "the celebrated orchestra of M Borchert, consisting of 23 musicians who executed choice pieces of music."[145] Herr Theodore Hoch, horn player, was featured on many concerts.[146]

By 1881 West End also had its own orchestral concerts, in direct competition to those at Spanish Fort. They lasted from May 1 to October 1. A large orchestra was featured with Mr. Moses as conductor and William Rickel as cornet soloist.[147] A separate train schedule was set up to accommodate those preferring West End, and a new phenomenon was employed to draw crowds: the use of electric lights. Until 1883 the West End concerts were overshadowed by the talent at Spanish Fort, so the entrepreneurs at West End staged a coup. They fired Moses, hired D'Aquin away from Spanish Fort, and put him at the head of the West End Orchestra, "carefully chosen from the best professionals who live in New Orleans during the summer."[148] Largely through D'Aquin's skills the concerts in West End surpassed those in Spanish Fort in importance in 1883. The season opened on April 1 with Sunday concerts, and from May 3 until mid-September there were concerts every evening from 4:00 to 7:00. The celebrated cornetist Signor A. Liberati was featured from May 15 to 29, and the cornetist Fred C. Bryant, the saxophonist A. Lefebre, and the xylophonist Charles Lowe also appeared. In 1884, whenever there were operettas performed at the Pavillon in West End, D'Aquin's orchestra of eighteen to twenty musicians performed before and afterwards.[149]

Spanish Fort, however, did not simply give up in 1883. Instead they hired Borchert to continue the grand orchestral concerts there. He had twenty-five musicians every evening and in addition gave extra concerts on Tuesdays, Thursdays, and Saturdays.[150] A typical concert, that of June 9, included music by Strassy, Auber, Strauss, Suppé, Keler-Bela, Gounod, and Faust.[151] During the off-season there also were concerts there. On March 23, 1884, for example, there was a three-part performance at Spanish Fort: a concert of eight works, an operetta by Offenbach (*Les Deux Aveugles*), and a ballet comique by Mmes Gossi and Watson. The concert began at 1:30, the spectacle at 4:30.[152] On Wednesday, April 23, 1884, three singers from New Orleans—Mmes Sholia and Roux and M Puget—gave a concert at Spanish Fort, on behalf of the Dames Servantes des Pauvres for the benefit of those who needed to return to France. There were three parts: the operetta *Lischen et Fritzchen* (Offenbach), a concert of monologues, romances (ballads), and chansonettes with Greuling accompanying on the piano, and a one-act comedy, *Le Piano de Berthe*.[153] The fifteenth annual July 4 festival at Spanish Fort, with fireworks, occurred in 1884 with Professor Borchert conducting the orchestra in a concert from 5:00 to 11:00 p.m.[154] A grand ball followed in the concert hall. As late as September 27, 1884, there was a grand ball and concert at Spanish Fort.

Milneburg, the third resort on the lake, also had concerts in 1884. The season started with a grand evening of amusements featuring the Grande Compagnie de Vaudeville. Professor J. B. Vogel's orchestra played before and after a display of balloons. On July 7 the Milneburg Opera House had a Grand Orchestre of winds and strings led by Vogel.[155]

Meanwhile, summer outdoor orchestral concerts occurred in the city as well. On May 30, 1884, there was a concert at Jackson Square at 7:00 p.m. directed by M Moses who formerly conducted the concerts at West End. The series continued every Friday until the beginning of winter. The orchestra played dances and overtures to operas.[156] A typical concert at Jackson Square conducted by Borchert, on June 13, 1884, included the Overtures to *Poet and Peasant* (Suppé) and *Martha* (Flotow).[157]

While prior to 1879 professional orchestral musicians struggled to survive, they were now assured of a full summer's employment—something rare for them even in the best years of the 1850s. With the revival of opera at the French Opera House in 1880, the winter season, too, was once again viable. The economic situation had improved so that the Orchestra of the French Opera House was back in form.[158] In the budget for the 1880–81 season, in addition to the singers and choristers, actors, dancers, and administrators, plans were for an orchestra of forty persons.[159] The reinstitution of French opera occurred without cutting out the performances of operas in the other theaters, which maintained their orchestras.[160]

In January 1881, the performances of opera at the French Opera House were in high gear. Momas was again chief conductor of the orchestra, and De Lestrac was his principal assistant.[161] The orchestra was highly regarded and was not limited to accompanying. When Momas conducted the complete opera *William Tell* at the French Opera House on February 8, 1881, critic Canonge singled out the overture as performed in a brilliant manner.[162] So good was the Momas rendition of the overture that it was repeated on February 13, 1881, at a concert given by De Beauplan, head of the opera troupe at the French Opera House, to benefit flood victims.[163] On February 1 the orchestra performed a symphony between the first and second acts of Victor Massé's opera *Paul et Virginie*.[164] Individual members of the orchestra were recognized, such as M Clayette (trumpet soloist), Oscar Reine (oboist), and M Tournié (violoncellist).[165] At the conclusion of the season the troupe left for tours of Cincinnati and Chicago, and entrepreneurs in Chicago and New York wanted to create a three-city company with New Orleans so that they could share in the glories of the New Orleans French Opera.[166]

With the orchestra now up to full strength, symphonic concerts were more prevalent. On January 13, for example, D'Aquin conducted some musicians from the French Opera House in a performance of his own Symphony in F in the salon of M le Dr. Bayon. The piece, which received its world premier in Paris on March 11, 1880, was dedicated to Mme Bayon.[167] On April 27, 1881, there was a grand concert at Grunewald Hall, presented by Theodore Curant and assisted by Alice Schwarz, Jeanne Franko, Robert Meyer, J. W. Eckert and his complete orchestra of forty musicians. Curant played the Beethoven Violin Concerto with orchestra, and Franko played the Mendelssohn Piano Concerto No. 2 in F Minor with orchestra.[168] On May 15, 1881, D'Aquin led a grand vocal and instrumental concert at Grunewald Hall; the second half of the concert was devoted to D'Aquin's Symphony in F Major, for which a grand orchestra was hired.[169] Three years later D'Aquin again conducted members of the French Opera House orchestra at Grunewald Hall, featuring four of the city's best violinists: Joubert, Kaiser, Curant, and Bayon.[170] On December 17, 1881, the restaurant waiters' association of the city had a grand concert at Odd Fellows' Hall, performed by the band of Professor W. Borchert.[171]

The 1881–82 opera season was taken over from De Beauplan by Max Strakosch.[172] Even if it was to last only a few months instead of half a year, it was a significant one. Strakosch recruited his singers in New York and France.[173] Initially he wanted Momas to conduct, but the revered conductor refused to return without increased salaries and tenure for the orchestra.[174] Therefore Strakosch hired S. Behrens and Sig. De Novellis, two new conductors from Europe, to replace Momas.[175] The opening took place on December 12, 1881, and the season included *The Tales of Hoffman, Tribute de Zamora, La Sonnambula, Lucia, Rigoletto, Les Puritains, The Magic Flute, Dinorah, Faust, Linda, Martha, Don*

Pasquale, Aïda, Trovatore, La Favorite, Carmen, Mefistofele, and other works.[176] The orchestra was enlarged and "complete."[177] The director of the 1882–83 and 1883–84 seasons was M Défossez.

Orchestras were often hired to entertain during festivals at various parks. On May 15–16, 1881, for example, the Grand German Folk Festival at the Fair Grounds was inaugurated by a concert at noon.[178] The program was composed of operatic pieces executed by a double orchestra, with a Liedertafel and with speeches. A charity festival with a symphony executed by forty amateur instrumentalists, under the auspices of the Louisiana Field Artillery and Louisiana Women, was held in April 1883.[179] The Jockey Club had regular parties for invited guests at its gardens, and there were two orchestras: one accompanying a promenade and another in the dance hall.[180] The Orphéon Français threw its evening festival on June 17, 1882—a concert and a ball—at the Grand Pavillon at Spanish Fort.[181] It included a full orchestra. On March 31, 1883, the French Orpheons gave a grand concert and ball at Grunewald Hall, again with orchestra.[182] On April 1, 1883, the Liedertafel of New Orleans gave a grand vocal and instrumental concert at the Grand Opera House to benefit Charity Hospital.[183] An orchestra played Gluck's Overture to *Iphigenia in Aulis,* the Andante from Beethoven's Symphony No. 5, the *Swedish Wedding March* by Soedermann, and the *Bacchanal* from *Philomène et Baucis* by Gounod; Alice Schwarz sang an aria by Auber, Mlles Marie Wannack and Cécile Marx played Alard's *Fantaisie de Concert* on *Faust,* and, for the second half of the program, the grand chorus joined the orchestra in Romberg's setting of *Das Lied von der Blocke* by Schiller.

But the 1883–84 opera season was not financially successful, so in the middle of the season—after the January 23, 1884, performance of *Les Huguenots*—the French Opera closed and many of its performers were left without means to support themselves.[184] The company, reformed under the directorship of Maurice Grau with Défossez as assistant, then moved to Havana, which, with Grau in charge, was probably a good thing for the company, though for the musicians left behind in New Orleans it was of little consequence.[185] A number of benefits for these poor instrumentalists and choristers occurred during the next weeks, such as on February 3 at the French Opera House (another performance of *Les Huguenots*),[186] and two others at Werlein Hall and Spanish Fort a week later.[187] Mr. Charles Amstutz, one of the violinists in the orchestra of Défossez's troupe, proposed giving a concert to raise money for his return to France. Nine other musicians from the troupe were destitute.[188] As late as March 22 forty members of the chorus and orchestra were still in dire need, and another benefit for them was held at the French Opera House: a special matinee performance of *La Belle*

Hélène and an evening one of *Orphée aux Enfers*.[189] It is for this aborted season that we have specifics on the makeup of the orchestra: six first violins, four second violins, three violas, three violoncellos, three basses, two flutes, a first clarinet (doubling on bass clarinet), a second clarinet, a first oboe (doubling on English horn), a second oboe, two bassoons, four horns, two cornets á piston, three trombones, an ophicleide, timpani, a bass drum, and a piano—in total thirty-nine musicians.[190]

An interesting performing group entitled Etudiants Espagnols also performed for the benefit of the stranded musicians on February 13. This group had come to New Orleans to perform six concerts from February 14 to 24, 1884, at Spanish Fort.[191] It was supposed to leave New Orleans for Cuba and various places in Central America, but it became so attached to the city that it cancelled its tour and decided to stay.[192] In March it performed at least twice. The first concert occurred at the French Opera House in the intermissions of a performance of Offenbach's *La Grande Duchesse de Gérolstein* where it played orchestral works by Rossini, Granados, and Waldteufel between the first and second acts, works by Arditi, Wagner, and Schubert between the second and third acts, and more orchestral music by Gounod, Verdi, and an anonymous composer after the third act.[193] The second concert was a Grand Concert Sacré at Saint Louis Cathedral where it performed sacred and secular works by Verdi, Schubert, Arditi, Gounod, Suppé, Mozart, Flotow, and anonymous.[194] And when the Spanish Choral Society of New Orleans held its first anniversary meeting on April 6, 1884, one of the members of the orchestra of La Estudiantina, Mr. Ramiro Martinez, decided to stay in New Orleans and played some guitar pieces.[195]

Private orchestral concerts continued during the winter and spring of 1884. In January 1884, the Pavillon Faranta, corner of Bourbon and Orléans streets, provided dime entertainment, including "the best orchestra in New Orleans."[196] It was only a brass band of fourteen musicians that played at M Antoine Chastel's home at the corner of Saint Peter and Royal streets in the French Quarter on February 23, 1884, to raise money for the ball of the French Benevolent and Mutual Aid Society of New Orleans to take place at a later date at the French Opera House.[197] Two concert-promenades were held on May 2 and 15, 1884, at the Jockey Club by an orchestra "of our best musicians"; a second orchestra played for dancing.[198] Also on May 2, 1884, there was a communion ball for little children with an orchestral accompaniment.[199] An orchestra performed for the concert and ball given by the French Orphéon Society at Grunewald Hall on May 23, 1884.[200]

Preparations for a full opera season for 1884–85 at first went smoothly.[201] Mr. Le Chevallier Vianesi was hired as first conductor (from the Italian orchestra at Covent Garden and from the Metropolitan in New York and the Saint Petersburg). The orchestra had forty-four players.[202] Two Massenet operas were planned, and the composer was invited to New Orleans for their openings; the famous composer, however, refused to come.[203] In anticipation of the French Opera, on November 2, 1884, the Vraie Troupe d'Opéra Comique season opened at Grunewald Hall with a performance of Lecocq's *Le Petit Duc*. For this performance there was "un orchestre complete, sous la direction de Philip Greuling."[204]

Into this situation of frequent summer orchestral concerts and a halting winter season, New Orleans experienced its second catalyst for an orchestral revival. At the Louisiana Exposition of 1884–86 in what today is Audubon Park, orchestras and bands played major roles in entertainment and in ceremonies. During the first season, from December 1, 1884, to June 1, 1885, Mexico provided the main orchestras for the exposition. There were two of them, one primarily a string ensemble of eighteen or twenty players, and the other a wind ensemble (band). The former is usually referred to as the Typical Mexican Orchestra (Orchestra Typique Mexicain), while the latter was the Eighth Cavalry Band (Mexican Eighth Regiment Orchestra).[205] Sometimes, in the sources, it is unclear which group was actually performing. The director of the cavalry band was Encarnacion Payen, and the director of the typical Mexican orchestra was Carlos Curti, but often the group playing was simply called the Mexican musicians, usually with Payen conducting. The Eighth Cavalry Band under Encarnacion Payen gave its first concert at the Music Hall in the Exposition on Sunday, January 18. The band had sixty-six performers, all excellent. The program included the *Tannhäuser* March (Wagner), *La Preciosa Fantasie* (Weber), *Schottish Rosas y Abroyos* (Videnqué), *Le Carnaval de Venise* (variations by Bont), *Nos Danza* (by N.), *Der Freischütz* Overture (Weber), *Souriens-toi Waltz* (Waldteufel), *Potpourri on La Fatinitza* (Suppé), Hymn, March, and Ballet from *Aïda* (Verdi), *A Media Noche Minuet* (Avilos), plus "Dixie's Land," "Himno de Riego," and "Yankee Doodle."[206] The first concert of the "Mexican Orchestra of the 8th Cavalry" occurred on March 1, 1885, in the Music Hall in the Exposition.[207] Just two days later, on March 3, the "Mexican Orchestra" performed a free concert at Spanish Fort, and from March 7 to 13 the "Mexican Imperial Orchestra," composed of twenty musicians, performed every evening at the Spanish Fort Opera House.[208] It is difficult to assess which group performed on which occasion, but probably on March 1 it was the band, and the rest of the time it was just the string orchestra. Meanwhile, during the day the Mexican musicians also performed at the exposition. On March 8, for example, at a 2:30 p.m. performance, the program included works by Suppé, Wagner (*Tannhäuser* selection), Videngué, Verdi, a *Serenade de Boccaccio,* Waldteufel, Flotow, L. Rentier, Baron Mary, and García. The concert also offered solo piano pieces.[209] On March 11 the Orchestra Typique Mexicain, directed by Carlos Curti, performed at the Exposition works by Suppé, Curti, Waldteufel, A. Figueroa (solo violin), Curti again (solo xylophone), Rossini (*William Tell*), Schubert, and "N,"[210] and on March 14 the Mexican Eighth Regiment Orchestra played at the exposition pieces by Auber (Overture to *Zanetta*), Villaprado (*Amour et Joie* and *La Danse de l'Orgie*), Bizet (*Fantasie* on *Carmen*), pieces by "N" and "X," Verdi (*La Belle Andalouse* and the *Overture de Violetta* [*La Traviata?*]), Donizetti (*Lucia*), Thompson (*La Cloche de la Liberté*), and three Mexican pieces.[211] The Mexicans continued to perform at the exposition through May 31, when the first year's fair came to an end.[212]

On March 15, 1885, the Mexican Eighth Regiment Orchestra joined forces with local performers from New Orleans for a concert at the exposition. The program included works by Wagner (Overture to *Tannhäuser*), Beethoven (*Louanges aux Cleux,* chorus with orchestra), Bach (*Grande Fantasia and Fugue in B Minor,* played on the organ by William Pilcher), Reichard (chorus with orchestra), Knoll (*Polka du Fort Espagnol,* played by the New Orleans Orchestra, H. Knoll trumpet soloist), Wagner (*Rienzi* Grand March), Moehring (chorus with orchestra), Handel (*Alleluia,* Pilcher on organ), Schulhof (solo piano by Ricardo Castro, a young student at the Mexican Conservatory), "The Star Spangled Banner" (chorus with orchestra), and Schubert (German serenade, performed by the Mexican Military: woodwinds and brass).[213] Ten days later there was another concert by Payen at the Exposition Music Hall with another New Orleanian. The program included a *Fantasie Indienne* by Mlle Léona Queyrouze written for and dedicated to Payen and played by the Mexican military band. Other works were by Auber, Donizetti, Viderigue, Rossini, Suppé, Gounod, and Martin. The concert also included a *Grande Fantasie* on *La Traviata,* played by M Adrian V. Galarza, first clarinetist of the ensemble, and here accompanied by Marguerite Samuel. Mrs. Samuel, whom Canonge raved about, should have played Gottschalk, the critic exclaims, to show all these foreign visitors what Louisiana music has to offer.[214]

When there were special occasions at the exposition, the Mexicans were called upon to add to the ceremonies. On March 12, for example, at the opening of the Nebraska exhibit, the twenty string players of the Typical Mexican Orchestra performed with the assistance of two canaries in a cage which the orchestra then imitated.[215] Six weeks later, on April 28, at the opening of the Arkansas exhibit, the Mexican orchestra played some national hymns. Then, musicians led by Encarnacion Payen, playing *Les Gardes de Paris* by Sellenick, led a procession from Government Hall to the central Music Hall of the Principal Palace, where the musicians sat down without stopping to play. After this there was a ceremony in which the Mexican musicians played intermittently.

The Mexicans made a deep impression on New Orleanians both in the precision of their performances and in the nationalist Mexican music they played. Immediately upon their arrival in the city they did more than play at the exhibition; they played wherever concerts could attract an audience. On December 7, 1884, the military band under Payen performed a Haydn mass at Saint Louis Cathedral,[216] and on December 9 the same ensemble performed a concert-promenade at the Washington Artillery Hall.[217] On Monday, March 16, the Typical Mexican Orchestra played an evening concert at Saint Louis Cathedral with Carlos Curti as conductor.[218] The program included the Overture to A. Thomas's *Raymond*; Curti's *Minuet*; Schubert's *Serenade*; Francis Thomé's *Andante Religieux* for solo violin (performed by A. Figueroa); the Overture to Flotow's *Martha*; Gounod's "Ave Maria"; Beethoven's Romance in F (played by Figueroa); and the Overture to Rossini's *William Tell*. No applause or calls were allowed in the church. In addition to several Spanish Fort concerts, the orchestra also played at West End on March 19.[219]

By the time the exposition closed, the orchestra and/or band, under Payen and his assistant Lt. Paris, had been in New Orleans for six months and had played not only for the exhibition but also for benefits for charities, sometimes as many as three concerts a day, without showing any signs of weariness.[220] The very generous Mexicans remained for another ten days in New Orleans and continued to entertain the local residents. A benefit for Charity Hospital at the end of May at the French Opera House was followed on June 2, 1885, with a concert at Carrollton Gardens to help raise money for a school for the poor.[221] Three days later they gave a free concert on the Exhibition Grounds. On June 7, they gave two final concerts at the Exhibition Grounds, and the next day the Jockey Club honored M Eduardo E. Zarate, Mexican commissioner general, with a promenade and dance; the Mexican Orchestra provided the music.[222] The Mexicans left New Orleans on June 9 for Saint Louis and a tour of the United States.[223]

But their influence remained for years in the new sounds that New Orleans performers and composers kept in their ears and in the new compositions by local composers that these sounds engendered. As early as May 17, 1885,

Grunewald announced the publication of some Mexican pieces, and Werlein announced a new piece by Marguerite Samuel, *Serenade Boccaccio,* which she adapted from a piece she heard performed by the Mexican orchestra.[224]

After the Mexicans left, there was a return to normal musical activities in the city. The music at West End opened for the season on May 24, 1885. The wind orchestra, under the direction of D'Aquin, consisted of fifty professionals, featuring the cornetists A. H. Knoll and O. Schuchardt, the trombonist G. Sontag, D'Aquin himself as flutist, and clarinetist A. Renz. The concerts began at 5 p.m. on Sundays and at 6 p.m. on other days. The reviewers stated that not only were the soloists excellent, but also the ensemble.[225]

With the Mexicans gone, a new orchestra had to be contracted for the second season of the exposition. During the fall of 1885, a festival orchestra was created to perform regularly. Professor Gustave D'Aquin, whose orchestral concerts at West End had become popular the previous summer, formed the orchestra and was its conductor. Was this a band or an orchestra? Sometimes it is referred to as a military orchestra, which might imply an all-wind ensemble, while at other times it is designated ambiguously just as "orchestra." Usually four concerts were given in the afternoons, four or five days per week, starting in November and running to February. The two principal venues were the Music Hall in the Main Building and the Palais du Gouvernement. Each concert lasted about forty-five minutes and consisted of four works: an opening overture followed by one or two dances, a march, and/or a potpourri of opera tunes. The most popular composers were Waldteufel, Suppé, Auber, Adam, Flotow, Rossini, Verdi, Gounod, and Mendelssohn. Among the opera excerpts were Sullivan's *The Mikado* and *Patience,* Bizet's *Carmen,* Offenbach's *La Belle Hélène,* Balfé's *The Bohemian Girl,* Halévy's *Charles VI,* Donizetti's *Lucia,* and Wagner's *Tannhäuser.* D'Aquin contributed his own works occasionally, such as his *Grande Marche Finale* at the 5:00 p.m. performance on November 29, 1885, and the 5:15 p.m. performance on December 17, 1885.[226] About half the composers were minor figures, popular in the 1880s but now forgotten: Michaelis, Navarro, Beyer, Bousquet, Williers, Gung'l, Keler Bela, Coote, Farbach, Leutner, and others. Where D'Aquin recruited his performers is uncertain, but since his concerts were finished by 6:00 or 6:15 p.m., it would have been possible for theater musicians—if such they were—to appear in the evenings at the various theaters in time for their regular jobs.

D'Aquin took his orchestra (wind band?) into the city for additional concerts. On Monday, November 16, 1885, for example, D'Aquin and his orchestra joined the Shakespeare Club in a soiree at the French Opera House. The orchestra played Weber's *Der Freischütz* Overture, a transcription of themes from *Faust,* Weber's *Invitation to the Dance,* Boccherini's Minuet, a Waldteufel *Polka de Minuet,* and at the end Meyerbeer's "Marche aux Flambeaux." The concert was under the auspices of the ladies' committee of the American Exposition.[227]

Meanwhile, on special occasions at the exhibition, D'Aquin and his ensemble added luster to the events. On January 1, 1886, at the grande fete populaire, jour de l'Emancipation, the official program began with the Overture to *William Tell,* music by the Orchestra D'Aquin, some songs, and lots of speeches. This was followed later in the day by three concerts in the Music Hall, with such works as Weber's *Invitation to the Dance,* Boccherini's *Minuet,* a Waldteufel *Polka de Minuet,* and at the end Meyerbeer.[228] A week later, on January 8, 1886, for the opening of the Creole exhibit, the program began with the Overture to *Sémiramide,* a *Gloria in Excelsis* by D'Aquin (choir of two hundred voices), Creole songs, Curto's solo and choir *Le Reveil de la Louisiane* with words by Canonge, Handel's "Hallelujah" Chorus, and a plethora of speeches. At the end of the program announcement on January 5, D'Aquin invited all inhabitants of New Orleans to meet at the Washington Armory to rehearse the choral pieces.[229]

During much of the month of January, however, D'Aquin stepped aside and John Strauss (also spelt "Stross" and "Stoss") led the band with similar programs. Strauss was the former conductor of the Imperial German Military Orchestra.[230] There were other orchestras in the city, all connected with opera productions or dances,[231] but otherwise attention was focused on the larger instrumental ensembles—bands as well as orchestras—at the exhibition. When the entertainment centers at the lake opened in late spring, D'Aquin's name was missing and a new set of conductors appeared. In fact, D'Aquin had pulled up his New Orleans roots and moved permanently to New York.

After the exposition closed and for the next decade, the lake concerts provided the main orchestral music performed in the city. Particularly noteworthy was the summer season at Spanish Fort in 1887. It began earlier, on March 13, and with a major new ensemble: a full symphony orchestra: the New Orleans Symphony Orchestra (sixty-five musicians) under the direction of G. Borchert.[232] The orchestra was not a nightly affair, such as were the bands, and its concerts subsequently moved to different locations. On April 18, 1887, for example, it performed at the Grand Opera House,[233] and so successful was it that it returned on April 29. As observed by the Daily *Picayune* critic, this was, in his estimation, the first time since the Thomas concerts that New Orleanians heard such a good program.[234] The program consisted of Mendelssohn's *Ruy Blas* Overture, Svendsen's *Concert Andante,* the introduction to Wagner's *Lohengrin,*

Beethoven's *Namensfeuer* Overture, the Overture to Mozart's *Don Giovanni*, *Träumerei* by Robert Schumann, Weber's *Oberon* Overture, and selections by Johann Strauss. It was a fine audience. Other concerts by the orchestra in the future were to include the *Danse Macabre* of Saint-Saëns, Beethoven's Symphony No. 7, and the Overture to Wagner's *Tannhäuser*. But in May, Borchert moved his orchestra of sixty-five onto steamboats—first the Oliver Beirne on May 10 and then the E. J. Gay on May 19. On the first cruise the orchestra was specifically referred to as the New Orleans Symphony Orchestra, while on the second it was simply called Borchert's Symphony Orchestra.[235] On May 22 and 24 the same ensemble appeared on the same two steamers, and Borchert announced that he would be conducting his orchestra every Tuesday, Thursday, and Sunday onboard cruises leaving from Canal Street and landing at Jackson Street.[236] He took out time on June 15 to conduct a promenade concert for the Louisiana Jockey Club, where he conducted his Military Orchestra of thirty musicians in a program of music by Verdi, Andran, Bugalossi, Berger, Keler Bela, Meyerbeer, Strauss, Suppé, Missud, Gounod, Christian Bach, Sousa, and Parlow.[237] A month earlier Sontag conducted his wind band at the Jockey Club's promenade and received lavish support from the *Picayune* critic,[238] but by June, Sontag was preoccupied by concerts at West End which opened on May 22, 1887, and Sontag with his band of forty musicians performed there nightly.[239]

While visiting orchestras only occasionally appeared in New Orleans during the century—most notably the Julien Orchestra of the 1850s and the Thomas Orchestra of the early 1870s, they did add luster to the musical scene. During the last two decades of the nineteenth century, additional orchestras came. When Adelina Patti returned to New Orleans on December 20, 1886, for a grand concert at the Saint Charles Theatre, she included a "large orchestra of fifty select musicians, under the direction of Signor Luigi Arditi."[240]

Among the visiting ensembles was the newly formed Boston Symphony Orchestral Club which came to Grunewald Hall in 1889 and again in 1892.[241] The orchestra came on the first occasion in a benefit for Miss Florence Huberwald and performed five light works: Arnhold Krug's *Serenade,* Boccherini's *Minuet,* Langey's *Mandolina,* Moszkowski's *Serenade,* and a Brahms Hungarian Dance. Inserted among these were works for voice, flute, viola d'amour, and violoncello; Huberwald also sang Fauré's *Sancta Maria*. On the second occasion the orchestra did only slightly better with a movement from a Haydn symphony, intermezzi by Delibes and Mascagni, Bach's *Air* and Bizet's *Slumber Song*. A violinist added a De Bériot concerto. These somewhat trivial works enlivened the orchestral life of the city, but they did little to satisfy those of more demanding orchestral tastes. For such sophisticated audiences in New Orleans, local musicians provided more attractive music. For example, Mark Kaiser played not only a De Bériot concerto with the French Opera House orchestra (led by Curant) on April 25, 1889, but also the much more significant Mendelssohn Violin Concerto. As the critic stated, "The orchestral numbers throughout were as skillful and as finished as the high standard of the selections would lead one to expect. The leaders acquitted themselves gloriously."[242]

In February 1890, there were three orchestral concerts as part of the North American Saenger Festival held at a new building designed specifically for the festival on Saint Charles and Howard avenues. The programs were far more substantial than those by the Boston Club. There were symphonies by Schubert (the *Unfinished*), Beethoven (No. 5), and Haydn (Haydn, Symphony in G Major No. 6), overtures by J. C. Bach, Goldmark, Weber, and Wagner (*Rienzi* and *Tannhäuser*), and miscellaneous works for orchestra by Berlioz (from the *Damnation of Faust*), Wagner, Moszkowski, Anton Rubinstein, Hugo Kaun, and Liszt. Marguerite Samuel played Liszt's Hungarian Fantasy. The concerts also included, as befitting the occasion, works for solo voices and choruses.

New Orleans possessed a history of orchestral and chamber music throughout the nineteenth century that has been little recognized by musicians and musicologists. That the city housed a highly trained cadre of instrumentalists and maintained a high standard of instrumental performance not only assured the musical prominence of the city in the nineteenth century but also explains, in some measure, why, when new styles of performance emerged at the beginning of the twentieth century, New Orleans produced so many outstanding instrumental performers.

3

The Concert Societies and Series

During the nineteenth century, several musical societies were organized to promote concerts of classical music. Some were vehicles for amateurs to perform in while others presented musicians at the highest professional level. Some were primarily choral societies and on occasion included instrumental music as well; others were orchestral societies; still others were band ensembles.

THE PHILHARMONIC SOCIETIES

Perhaps the best-known name for a society—Philharmonic Society—was actually a name adopted in New Orleans by at least eleven different societies during the nineteenth century.[1] Inevitably there has been some confusion as to the nature of these societies, their personnel, and the types of concerts that they were involved in. The earliest reference to a Philharmonic Society in New Orleans is for a concert at the Théâtre d'Orléans on February 5, 1825, performed as a benefit for Mr. P. Lewis.[2] The program was the usual mixture of piano, vocal, and violin works, but the unusual feature was the presence of Mr. Lewis's three children playing piano: June (age eight), Miss S. Lewis (age four), and James (age thirteen). The local violinist, Mr. C. Herz, performed a Viotti violin concerto as well. An orchestra opened each half of the program with an overture (Etienne-Nicolas Méhul's [1763–1817] Overture to *Joseph* and C. Bochsa's "Ouverture Militaire"). After the concert there was a dressy ball in the ballrooms of Mr. Davis on Orleans Street. The Philharmonic Society at this juncture was an informal union of local artists who joined to present their collective talents at a single concert. Both amateurs and professionals performed on the same program, which took place on the most important and largest stage in the city, and the ostensible purpose of the concert was to raise money for the Lewis family. The designation "Philharmonic Society" might have been an advertising ploy to lend prestige to an event that, with the appearance of children, might have been construed as somewhat less than a high artistic performance. In any case, it seems to have been an isolated event, not part of a series sponsored by an ongoing organization.

Two years later another Philharmonic Society took on a more specific character, though again it was not a formally organized group. It was clearly a performing organization, both of instrumental and vocal music, and it featured local musicians. Although it seems not to have lasted more than a year, this society differed from that of two years earlier by performing in more than one concert. On Thursday, May 24, 1827, this Philharmonic Society took part in a benefit for the Male Orphan Asylum.[3] The varied program at the Théâtre d'Orléans consisted of Nicolo's opera *Cinderella* (a fairy opera in three acts), a recitation by an amateur on the death of Lord Byron, Barré and Desfontaines's vaudeville *Two Edmonds* (in two acts), Mr. Segura's performance of two violin pieces, and "choice pieces of music" played by the Philharmonic Society. At this point it was an instrumental group that participated in a concert but did not run its own program. A month later, on Wednesday, June 20, there was a soiree and concert to benefit the girls' orphanage, at Mr. Rash's gardens on Chartres Street. As the *Courier de la Louisiane* reported, "The Philharmonic Society will perform, during the evenings, many choice pieces, and M Johns will play the piano."[4] Here the society ran its own program, though it was assisted by the most important pianist in the city at the time. More ambitious was the concert of vocal and instrumental music by the society on December 14, 1827, at the home of Madame Herries, Chartres Street.[5] Aside from six songs sung by Mme Depass, the Philharmonic Society performed an overture (Rossini's *L'Italien à Alger*), a dance, a march, a chorus and duet (from François-Adrien Boieldieu's [1775–1834] *La Dame Blanche*), and two harmony pieces.[6] This second Philharmonic Society, then, was apparently on its way to becoming a major organization for the performance of concerts in the city, but then nothing further is known of a Philharmonic Society for the next eight years.

The growth of the city's population by the mid-1830s and the establishment of a much larger coterie of professional and gifted amateur musicians resulted in an expanded concert life. By December 1835, there was a call for the creation of a new (third) Philharmonic Society, one with a set of bylaws and officers. Just as in 1825 and 1827, the new Philharmonic Society was a union of local musicians from different theaters and from different walks of life into a single performing body.[7] Business meetings were held regularly in order to determine when, where, and what to perform as well as social activities accompanying concerts.[8] By November 12, 1836, the new society was a fact, though it was another year before this Philharmonic Society gave its first concert. Most of the members had been part of the 1827 group, and drawing on both the positive and negative experiences of that venture, they were forming a better society.[9]

Of particular importance for the group was the celebration of Sainte Cecilia's Day on November 22 in honor of the patron saint of music. The celebration in 1837, at Saint Louis Cathedral, involved a new mass by Curto with top singers and professional orchestral musicians; the Philharmonic Society probably provided the chorus and sponsored a banquet. Proceeds from the concert went to orphans.[10] The following year the philharmonic repeated the event,[11] by which time the society had an orchestra that was led by M Lehmann.[12] H. E. Lehmann (Berlin, 1805–New Orleans, 1866) was a prominent conductor; horn, cornet, and trumpet player; composer; and teacher in New Orleans from 1834 until his death. The Sainte Cecilia concert in 1838 elicited from the critic: "the orchestra of a society in large part composed of amateurs cannot pretend to perfection, and some small blemishes serve sometimes to bring forth the beauty of an ensemble d'un tableau." Taking everything into account, the execution was good and satisfying and did honor to the gentlemen of the philharmonic. Of special note was the excellent playing of Cioffi, solo trombonist of the French Opera Orchestra.[13] The critic objected to the policy of the Philharmonic Society not to admit strangers to membership in what was an important asset to the city, but members of the society denied that its membership was secret or closed.[14] It was, however, understood to be a French organization.

In addition to commemorating Sainte Cecilia's Day, the Philharmonic Society performed on other occasions as well. On March 3, 1839, it took part in a Grand Vocal and Instrumental Concert "for the benefit of the exiles from Mexico, who have taken refuge in New Orleans." Performed at the City Exchange ballroom on Saint Louis Street, the concert included a number of local professional instrumentalists such as Miolan (violinist), Henings (clarinetist), Sy (Syr) (bassoonist), and Cioffi (trombonist), an unnamed amateur singer and a professional singer (Mr. E. Chazotto), a husband-wife violoncello-piano duo (Bamberger) and two overtures presumably performed by the philharmonic (Overture to *Le Dieu et La Bayadère* and Rossini's *William Tell* Overture).[15] On November 6, 1839, the philharmonic performed at a 6 p.m. séance which was then repeated the following day as part of the Sainte Cecilia's Day celebrations.[16] On April 9, 1840, the Philharmonic Society Orchestra, directed by M Constantin, executed several overtures between acts of dramas and vaudevilles at the Théâtre de la Renaissance.[17]

On Sunday, February 1, 1846, la Société Philharmonique de l'Union gave a performance in the Salle Washington (Saint Philip Street) during a benefit dramatic performance of Voltaire's tragedy *Oedipus* and a vaudeville in one act. The affair ended with a Grand Bal Paré, all to benefit an unfortunate one.[18] What this particular Philharmonic Society was is impossible to ascertain since we know nothing of the performers or the type of performances that they gave.

In the fall of 1847, Lehmann, who was director of the Philharmonic Orchestra in 1838, led the Philharmonic Society of New Orleans in three benefit concerts for the Howard Association (October 13, October 20, and November 9).[19] By 1847, however, the society seems to be something other than what it was in 1837–39. This time the orchestra is specifically referred to as an "accomplished association of amateurs,"[20] The first concert took place at Armory Hall and the others at the Théâtre d'Orléans. The third was in honor of Lehmann, whose own, somewhat bizarre compositions received readings on all three evenings.[21] Since there is a gap of seven years between these performances and the ones by the third philharmonic, it is possible that this was a new organization, a fourth Philharmonic Society. It is also possible that the term "philharmonic" was simply an alternate title for the orchestra for soirees founded by Cobini and Lehmann in 1836 (see page 340).

In 1844 another Philharmonic Society apparently had its own hall, which was above the restaurant of M Canonge.[22] Presumably the philharmonic's hall would be used for rehearsals and even meetings, but also it was available for others to rent. The orchestra itself, consisting of "the best and most numerous professional musicians," under the direction of F. Cobini, was also available for hire "by responsible persons." There seems to be no relation between this philharmonic and the ones of 1837–39 or 1847 other than the involvement of cornet-player H. E. Lehmann, who was working with Canonge on lists of members; rather, the ensemble appears to be a dance orchestra of professional players. In his numerous publications from 1853 to 1858, Lehmann titles himself "Chef d'Orchestre des Soirées et Artiste du Théâtre d'Orléans";[23] he does not mention a philharmonic society.

The philharmonic societies discussed heretofore were French organizations. In 1846 another Philharmonic Society was organized by the German community in New Orleans. Its emphasis was on its own performance of German orchestral music. Thus on March 30, 1846, at the Armory Hall, the German Philharmonic Society Grand Concert featured Beethoven's *Egmont* Overture, Weber's *Der Freischütz* and *Oberon* overtures, and Beethoven's Symphony No. 5. Also on the program was a violin concerto by the non-German De Bériot played by Mr. A. Waldauer, and two airs sung by Mr. R. Santini. The orchestra consisted of "36 musicians, who have for several months been assiduously engaged in studying and practicing." The orchestra was under the direction of William Furst and Theodore Schoenheit.[24] The critic felt that, "although the ensemble was not perfect and things were not always precise, nonetheless it was a stirring concert and a triumph for the Philharmonic Society."[25]

Up to the middle of the century there were probably six different philharmonic societies that had existed in New Orleans: the first one (1825), the second (1827), the third (1835–39), the fourth (1844), the fifth (1847), and the German one (1846). Three more such societies appear in the 1850s. The first of these was organized by Curto and La Hache in 1852, the second by Syr in 1853, and the other was organized by the Creoles of color sometime before the outbreak of the Civil War. The one led by Curto and La Hache was primarily a choral society that utilized members of the French Opera Orchestra to accompany the voices. In 1852 the chorus consisted of fifty amateur men and women, all members of the New Orleans Philharmonic Society. The *Picayune* reported: "The two successful sacred concerts recently given under the direction of MM Curto and La Hache [presumably December 3 and 7, 1851] afforded sufficient proof that we possess ample amateur musical talent of good quality, and that our citizens know how to appreciate it." Therefore, "we are pleased to learn that a number of the amateurs of our city in musical matters are about to form a philharmonic society on a wide and permanent basis. New Orleans certainly possesses plentiful material for the successful organization of such a society, and we have often wondered that one has not long ere this been formed."[26] By February 15 the new society had a constitution and bylaws, and a concert was being prepared for Saint Patrick's Cathedral.[27]

A concert by this seventh Philharmonic Society took place on May 19, 1852, not at Saint Patrick's Cathedral but at the Lyceum Hall of Professor Leroy. It may have been preceded by other concerts, though we have no information about them. The concert on May 19 included choral, vocal solo, and chamber music, but no orchestra. Curto conducted many men and women of the Société Philharmonique de la Nouvelle Orléans in choruses by Mozart, Rossini, and Hammel (Hummel?). Also on the program were the violinist Jahn (concertmaster of the French Opera) who played a solo, Fourmestreau (first oboe of the French Opera), La Hache (organist of the Société Philharmonique), and M Trust (harpist of the French Opera) who played a trio, and several amateur singers. La Hache and an amateur woman opened the concert with Czerny's four-hand piano arrangement of Rossini's Overture to *Sémiramide*.[28] The very next week Curto led the society chorus (now almost sixty voices) in another concert, this time accompanied by the complete Orchestra of the Théâtre d'Orléans. The program included (among other things) Auber's overtures to the *Cheval de Bronze* and *Masaniello* (played by full orchestra), and it ended with the "Hallelujah" Chorus from Handel's *Messiah*.[29] This Philharmonic Society reappeared after the war with a new name: the Harmonic Society (see below).

The following year another (eighth) Philharmonic Society of the Friends of Art, founded and directed by the bassoonist Mr. C. Syr, gave two benefit instrumental concerts for the orphans whose parents died in the plague that had recently struck the city. Titled a "soirée musicale," each was given outdoors in Lafayette Square. During the first concert on October 6, 1853, the orchestra raised $183.55 which was handed to the director of the German girls' orphan asylum.[30] The second concert, which began at 6:30 p.m. on Thursday, October 20, was to benefit the orphans of the city's Third District.[31] Syr's society clearly had its own organization, consisting of an arrangements committee of six amateurs, a secretary (Mr. Charles Ammel—possibly the Hammel on the program of May 19, 1852), and a president (Syr himself).[32]

The most often cited Philharmonic Society of the 1850s is that mentioned by Trotter in his classic book *Music and Some Highly Musical People* (1878). There he states that "the Creoles of color formed a [ninth] Philharmonic Society sometime before the outbreak of the Civil War. They loved art but refused to sit in 'black'-designated areas of the white theatres. Constantin Deberque and Richard Lambert were at times conductors of these concerts." The only year that Deberque and Lambert lived in New Orleans at the same time was 1853; Deberque was in New Orleans in 1852, and Lambert was there from 1853 to 1857. We know from the *City Directory* of 1857 that Lambert was a "free man of color," but we know nothing about the racial background of Deberque. We also do not know if Richard Lambert had any family ties to Charles Lambert, the most prominent professional musician among the Creoles of color in the city.[33] However, it is possible that Deberque was the Constantin who conducted la Société Philharmonique in several overtures during intermèdes at the new Théâtre de la Renaissance on April 9, 1840,[34] and it is, therefore, also possible that this philharmonic group dates back to 1840. Earlier, Trotter states that in 1853 the (white) Philharmonic Society was a small string orchestra, with French, German and Italian musicians;[35] since, as we have seen, Curto and La Hache's Philharmonic was a choral group, Trotter must be referring to Sy's group of 1853. Since he is accurate with the description of the latter (though we have no proof that only string players were in Sy's orchestra), we can assume that Trotter was probably accurate in his brief description of the Philharmonic Society of the Creoles of color.

During and for a decade after the Civil War there is no mention of a Philharmonic Society. The ruined economy and the need to regroup the musical forces of the city no doubt prevented an immediate revival. Yet the city had many musicians, and the love of European classical music was prevalent, so inevitably a philharmonic-like society would reappear. In 1866 Theodore von La Hache re-formed a Harmonic Association, which like his Philharmonic Society of prewar days, was comprised of amateur singers. Six soirees were given.[36] (See the discussion of La Hache on page 184.)

From 1876 to 1894 a tenth New Orleans Philharmonic Society existed as a choral group, but a number of prominent instrumentalists considered themselves members as well. Among these was the revered clarinetist François Kroll (ca. 1807–85), who had belonged to one of the philharmonics before the war,[37] and the younger Marguerite Samuel and Mark Kaiser. The professional musicians from the French Opera—solo singers and orchestral musicians—frequently participated in the society's concerts.

The first concert by this tenth Philharmonic Society, of which we have a record, occurred in cooperation with the Germania Quartette Club on February 14, 1876, at Grunewald Hall.[38] Mr. Edward Groenevelt (name also appears as Groenvelt and Gruenevelt), who now was the musical director of the Philharmonic Society, led a choir in three choruses from Mendelssohn's oratorio *Elijah,* which were sung well, and great applause greeted vocal solos, a duet, and a trio.[39] Shortly afterward, "an organizational meeting was held of the New Orleans Philharmonic Society, whose president [was] Louis Grunewald. There [were] active members (all singers) and passive members (who attend[ed] rehearsals and performances); both sexes [were] represented. There ha[d] already been one concert and another [was] soon to come."[40] By the next fall this Philharmonic Society was presenting regular concerts, which were termed "public rehearsals." The fifth in its series occurred on Wednesday, February 28, 1877, at Grunewald Hall. It had come to symbolize the best in classical taste in the city.[41] The following season the concerts continued. On October 21, 1877, Mark Kaiser and Marguerite Elie Samuel—the best violinist and the best pianist in the city at the time—joined the society in the concert.[42] On December 22, 1877, the Philharmonic Society with the Fryer Opera Troupe performed Mendelssohn's *Elijah* at the French Opera House, with star members of the troupe, Eugénie Pappenheim, Charles Adams, Adelaide Phillips, and Alouin Blum, in the solo parts. It was conducted by Groenevelt. This was the first time this famous oratorio was performed in New Orleans with full chorus (the Philharmonic Society) and full orchestra (Fryer's opera orchestra whose regular conductor was Max Maretzek).[43] On April 8, 1878, Groenevelt led more choruses from Mendelssohn's *Elijah* and Verdi's opera *Ernani* at Grunewald Hall, and various other vocal works and one piano piece (Liszt's Hungarian Rhapsody No. 1, performed by Miss Marie Herr) rounded out the program.[44]

Unlike all the preceding philharmonic societies, this tenth incarnation—both a choral society and an orchestra—became a relatively long-time fixture in New Orleans. For at least eighteen years it maintained its stature and performed regular classical concerts. Among the concerts was that of February 17, 1881, when the Philharmonic Society under Groenevelt gave a concert at Grunewald Hall to benefit flood victims. J. W. H. Eckert was the accompanist in the choral works, while Samuel played Chopin, Mendelssohn, and Henri Ketten. Mendelssohn's choral pieces still figured prominently.[45] There were additional concerts on April 5, 1882, with orchestra,[46] and on December 15, 1882.[47] On March 21, 1883, the concert of sacred music by the Philharmonic Society at Grunewald Hall was its twenty-seventh "rehearsal."[48]

On January 6, 1890, Marguerite Samuel, Mark Kaiser, and others performed at a Philharmonic Society concert to benefit the Home of the Convalescents with the "enlarged Opera House Orchestra under the leadership of Sig. Julius A. Bona of Her Majesty's Opera, London." The orchestra had forty players, most from the French Opera. Samuel played solo (Liszt's Hungarian Fantasy and two encores), but Kaiser played the second and third movements from Mendelssohn's Violin Concerto with the orchestra.[49] The program also featured the first performance in the city of Wotan's "Farewell and Magic Fire Scene" from *Die Walküre* by Wagner, and included Mendelssohn's "Wedding March" from *A Midsummer Night's Dream,* the Overture to *Mignon* by Ambroise Thomas, the Adagio Assai and Allegro Molto from Beethoven's Symphony No. 3, the Prelude to Wagner's *Lohengrin,* ballet music to *Le Cid* by Massenet, and arias by Ponchielli and Flotow with Mr. A. Guillé, tenor of the French Opera. The critic of the *Times-Democrat* reported: "Sig. Bona appears to be a masterful leader, wielding his baton with authority, and controlling and directing the orchestra with skill and judgment. The admirable manner in which the orchestral portion of the entertainment was accomplished is the best evidence of his efficiency. Embarrassed by the richness of the programme it is difficult to signalize among the pieces played by the orchestra, particular ones as pre-eminently worthy of mention, yet may be designated the selections from Beethoven and from Wagner's 'Walküre'; and also the music from 'Le Cid,' which was of delightful Spanish type."[50]

The Philharmonic Society continued to give concerts as late as 1894. On Monday, December 17, 1894, it presented its first grand concert of the season, with magnificent choruses by the best masters with over a hundred voices and a large orchestral accompaniment, at Odd Fellows' Hall. The program contained a chorus from *Cavalleria Rusticana,* an organ fantasia by Liszt, a baritone solo and chorus from Anton Rubinstein's oratorio *The Tower of Babel,* a solo sung by Mr. Jules Braunfeld, an alto solo by Robert Schumann, selections from Haydn's *Creation,* a song sung by Mme S. Duquesne, and other pieces.[51]

By the mid-1890s the New Orleans Mendelssohn Club was regarded as a successor to the Société Philharmonique.[52] But in 1896 a new Philharmonic Society was founded.[53] This eleventh such society, unlike any of its predecessors, was primarily an organization for the presentation of concerts by others, especially world-famous nonresident artists such as Alma Gluck (ca. 1914), Eddy Brown (December 3, 1917), Jascha Heifetz (February 19, 1919), the Flonzaly String Quartet (March 24, 1919), and the Saint Louis Symphony (May 9, 1914). It ran seasons of concerts, often at the Athenaeum, later at the Municipal Auditorium. But locals sometimes participated, as when Eugénie Wehrmann-Schaffner and the Newcomb String Quartet performed at Grunewald Hall on April 13, 1915, or when it collaborated with the Symphony Orchestra Association of New Orleans during the 1917–18 season.[54] This last collaboration set a precedent, so that when, in December 1957, the Philharmonic Society and the new New Orleans Symphony Orchestra merged, it was a natural cooperation that lasted until 1991. The history of the New Orleans Philharmonic Symphony Orchestra and its successor, the Louisiana Philharmonic Orchestra, however, belongs primarily to an era beyond the confines of this book.

The overall story of the New Orleans Philharmonic Society, then, is a complicated one, but it is a major segment in the history of concert music in the nineteenth century. There probably were eleven such societies, though some of these were later reincarnations of earlier ones, and although most were choral societies, they were also promoters of music and wind and orchestral ensembles. The members were highly trained and esteemed professionals as well as talented and enthusiastic amateurs.

COLLIGNON'S CLASSICAL SERIES

There were many other societies and series of classical concerts in New Orleans in the nineteenth century besides those labeled "philharmonic." The two most important were the series set up by Collignon both before and after the Civil War and the Orphéon Française during the last two decades of the century.

Beside the various concerts given by the philharmonic societies before the Civil War, the concert series developed by Collignon in the 1850s were towering colossuses of great art. Through the efforts of this one man, New Orleans experienced its first independent symphony orchestra, its first regular chamber and orchestral concert series, and its first systematic hearing of the greatest European instrumental works. Much emulated then and since, Collignon's work remains virtually unique in its high standards and comprehensiveness.

Gustave Collignon and his wife arrived in New Orleans in November 1848, after fleeing Paris as a result of the 1848 Revolution. He was regarded as an eminent pianist[55] and made his debut as a pianist in New Orleans on December 4, 1848, in a grand concert that included Curto and other distinguished professionals.[56] He quickly established himself as a teacher as well.[57] He also composed a piano fantasy in the form of a Spanish waltz which was orchestrated by Gabici and performed at a grand concert at Lyceum Hall on April 23, 1851.[58]

Collignon's main achievement began on January 16, 1856, with the first of the Collignon concerts at Odd Fellows' Hall. He established a series of classical concerts which in the first year consisted of chamber works and then, by the second year, gave New Orleans its first regular seasons of symphonic music. The impetus for this probably was the visit to the city of Jullien's orchestra from February 18 to March 11, 1854. At these concerts fragments of Beethoven symphonies and other major classical works were performed successfully and demonstrated that there was an audience eager for such pieces.[59]

Collignon began his series of six concerts in 1856 with chamber pieces performed by the best instrumentalists in New Orleans. (See the list of Collignon's concerts prior to the Civil War on pages 79–83.) From the start Gabici was the leading violinist, with members of the other theater orchestras also contributing. Robert Meyer was probably the best violoncellist at the time, and Kuffner the finest clarinetist. Collignon himself played the piano both as chamber participant and as soloist in concertos by Mendelssohn and Weber. At the second concert he brought in an orchestra which also played on the fifth and sixth concerts. Opera arias were performed by leading singers of the Théâtre d'Orléans. The first concert was at the Lyceum Hall, but afterwards all concerts were in the larger Odd Fellows' Hall. From the start the composers featured were Europe's most distinguished, beginning with Mozart, Haydn, Beethoven, Spohr, Mendelssohn, Hummel, and Weber.

After the first season Collignon waited a year and a half before starting his second season. This hiatus in regular programming of the Classical Series enabled Collignon to regroup and reformulate his intentions. He decided that from this point forward his classical concerts would be devoted to symphonic music with virtually no chamber music; when a pianist appeared, he or she would be confined to a single piece or two rather than dominating a program as happened in so many other concerts.[60] In addition there were only a few vocal performances which were sandwiched between the main attraction, which was symphonic music. Surprisingly concertos, which were part of the first season, disappeared during the remaining seasons. To test his new approach to orchestral concerts, he presented one concert during the spring of 1857, on April 29, at Odd Fellows' Hall.[61] It was billed as presented by the Society for the Cultivation of Classical Music. The program included works by Weber, the second movement of Mendelssohn's Symphony No. 4, and Beethoven's complete Symphony No. 6. It became the prototype for the Classical Series for the next few years.

The six performances each season now took place at noon on Sundays when all the theater musicians would be free from their full-time jobs. With a good core of professional orchestral players Collignon could present to New Orleanians the Beethoven symphonies (except Nos. 8 and 9), almost always in complete rather than truncated versions and not once but two or three times (the Symphony No. 6 four times). It is possible the Symphony No. 8 was played on one of the three concerts for which we have no program. The overtures, performed as concert works, were limited to the *Egmont, Fidelio,* and *Leonore* (presumably no. 3). Peppered in between were important works by Mendelssohn (symphonies, concertos, overtures), Mozart (symphonies, overtures), Haydn (symphonies), and other classicists. Schubert's and Robert Schumann's symphonies were neglected, as were the works of Berlioz (except for the ever-popular arrangement of Weber's *Invitation to the Dance*).[62] Indeed, the German composers were favored over the French, whose representation was limited to opera overtures. At the end of the second and fourth seasons, Collignon and his orchestra were asked to perform an extra benefit concert for orphans, when some of the music from that season would be repeated and when larger choral works would be appropriate.

From 1856 to 1860 the Classical Concert Series of Collignon presented regular subscription concerts. Advertisements in the newspapers were sparse because apparently there was an enthusiastic and full audience that did not need to be reminded of each performance. Over three hundred subscribers were known for the second season, and only subscribers and their friends were admitted.[63] A fifth season was planned for 1860–61, and the initial concert was to be held on December 12, 1860, with Beethoven's Symphony No. 6 as the highlight and works by Mendelssohn, Rossini, and others; it never took place. A "second" concert was scheduled for January 23, 1861, but was postponed to February 5. In it Collignon conducted Mozart's Mass No. 12 with a chorus of fifty men and women and his orchestra comprised of the best musicians of the city, to benefit the younger orphans at Saint Vincent's.[64] By April 19, 1861, the Union blockade of the city had officially begun, however, and after November, further concerts were virtually impossible. Many musicians and other citizens had fled, food and other supplies were scarce, and cultural entertainment was not in people's plans. In May another concert was scheduled to benefit the orphans, and thereafter the Classical Concerts ceased operation. For a little over four years, however, Collignon had created a concert environment that was the crowning achievement of his life and which established regular symphonic concerts by a local orchestra as a phenomenon in the history of the music of New Orleans. For the next century and a half other orchestras would appear and would prove that New Orleans was indeed receptive to such a repertory.

Collignon's Concerts Prior to the Civil War

FIRST YEAR

January 16, 1856. First concert. Mozart, Andante and Allegro from Quartet No. 1 for piano, violin, viola, and violoncello (Collignon, Gabici, Buccholz, and Oertl). Haydn, Andante, Scherzo, and Finale from Quartet from Opus 76. Hummel, Septet for piano, oboe, viola, flute, violoncello, horn, and double bass, spread out over the two parts of the concert. Arias by Madam Pretti and Taccani Tasca. Lyceum Hall. (*The Bee,* Jan. 15, 1856, p. 1, col. 10.)

February 8, 1856. Second concert. Beethoven, Quartet. Beethoven, Trio for violin, violoncello, and piano. Portion of another Beethoven trio. Beethoven, Sonata for piano and violin (Collignon and Gabici), Mendelssohn, Quartet. Weber, Concerto for piano and orchestra. Also arias by Junca and Taccani Tasca (newly arrived prima donna).[65] (*Picayune,* Feb. 8, 1856, p. 2, col. 1.)

February 20, 1856. Third concert. Hummel, Septet. Mayseder, Sextet. Beethoven, Trio. Junca ("La Calunnia" from *The Barber of Seville*) and Delagrave vocalists. (*Picayune,* Feb. 20, 1856, p. 6, col. 1.)

February 29, 1856. Fourth concert. Beethoven, Septet. Arias by Taccani Tasca and Laget. Works by Mozart and Mendelssohn. (*L'Abeille,* February 29, 1856, p. 2, col. 2; *Picayune,* Feb. 28, 1856, afternoon ed., p. 3, col. 1.)

March 7, 1856. Fifth concert. Junca (basso) and Tasca (soprano) sing arias. Rudolph Meyer plays a solo on the violoncello. Adagio from Beethoven, Septet for violin, clarinet, viola, horn, bassoon, violoncello, and double bass. Mendelssohn, Piano Concerto in G Minor No. 1, performed by Collignon. First Allegro from Weber, Quartet for piano, violin viola, and violoncello. Beethoven, Trio for piano, clarinet, and violoncello. *La Romanesca,* a dance of the sixteenth century. (*Picayune,* Mar. 7, 1856, p. 4, col. 1; *The Bee,* March 7, 1856, p. 1, col. 1.)

April 4, 1856. Sixth and last concert of season. Hummel, first Allegro from Septet in D Minor. March and Finale from Weber, Concertstück. Mendelssohn, Piano Concerto in G Minor No. 1 with orchestra. Weber, Duo with Kuffner (clarinet) and Collignon (piano). Also arias: Auber, *Cheval de Bronze,* and Hölzel, *La Tyrolienne,* both sung by Mme Colson, prima donna of the opera. Ambroise Thomas, Romance sung by Delagrave (tenor). Another aria sung by Louise Puget. Rossini, "La Calunnia" from *The Barber of Seville,* sung by Junca (basso of the opera). Delserte, a song. (*Picayune,* Apr. 4, 1856, p. 4, col. 1; *L'Abeille,* Apr. 4, 1856, p. 1, col. 1.)

SECOND YEAR (FALL 1857–SPRING 1858)

November 26, 1857. First concert. Mozart, Overture to *The Magic Flute.* Beethoven, Symphony No. 2. Mendelssohn, Overture to *A Midsummer Night's Dream.* Allegretto and Scherzo from Beethoven, Symphony No. 7. Weber, Overture to *Oberon.* (*Picayune,* Nov. 26, 1857, p. 4, col. 1.)

December 6, 1857. Second concert. Orchestral concert. Program lost. (*The Bee,* Dec. 5, 1857, p. 1, col. 2.)

January 20, 1858. Third concert. Weber, *Jubel* Overture. Mendelssohn, overture. Two movements from Mozart, Symphony No. 41 (*Jupiter*). Beethoven, Symphony No. 5. Arias sung by Junca "La Calunnia" (*The Barber of Seville*) and "Pro Peccatis" (*Stabat Mater*). (*Picayune,* Jan. 17, 1858, afternoon ed., p. 1, col. 4.)

February 19, 1858. Fourth concert. Gluck, Overture to *Iphigenia.* Weber's Overture to *Euryanthe.* Weber, *Invitation to the Dance* orchestrated by Berlioz. Choral works: Kreutzer's *The Chapel,* Mendelssohn's *Adieux to the Forest.* (*Picayune,* Feb. 28, 1858, p. 4, col. 1; *L'Abeille,* Feb. 19, 1858, p. 1, col. 2.)

March 31, 1858. Fifth concert. Beethoven, Symphony No. 4. Beethoven, *Fidelio* Overture. Works by Mozart, Haydn, Rossini, Mendelssohn, and Weber. (*Picayune,* Mar. 31, 1858, p. 1, col. 4; *L'Abeille,* Mar. 31, 1858, p. 2, col. 2.)

April 28, 1858. Sixth concert. Program lost. (*Picayune,* May 1, 1858, afternoon edition, p. 2, col. 2.)

May 5, 1858. Charity Concert for Sainte Mary's Orphan Boys' Asylum. Andante from Haydn, *Surprise* Symphony No. 94. A movement from Beethoven, Symphony No. 4. Auber's Overture to *Masaniello.* Weber's *Jubel* Overture. Hérold's Overture to *Zampa.* Berlioz's arrangement of Weber, *Invitation to the Waltz.*

Men's chorus from Weber, *Euryanthe*. Delagrave and Janes in several pieces. (*Picayune,* May 2, 1858, p. 3, col. 1.)

THIRD YEAR (FALL 1858–SPRING 1859)

December 8, 1858. First concert. Haydn, Symphony No. 8 in B Minor. Beethoven, Symphony No. 3. Mozart, Overture to *Don Giovanni*. Weber, Overture to *Euryanthe*. Spohr, Overture to *Jessonda*. (*Picayune,* Dec. 9, 1858, afternoon ed., p. 1, col. 5.)

January 5, 1859. Second concert. Gluck, Overture to *Iphigenia*. Weber, *Concertstück,* performed by G. Collignon. Haydn, andante from unnamed symphony. Mendelssohn, *Ruy Blas* Overture. Beethoven, Symphony No. 7 in A. (*Picayune,* January 5, 1859, p. 1, col. 3.)

February 2, 1859. Third concert. Mendelssohn, *Fingal's Cave*. Beethoven, Symphony No. 2 in D. Beethoven, Overture to *Leonore*. Scherzo from a symphony by Schubert. Weber, Overture to *Der Freischütz*. An aria from Verdi's *Jérusalem*. Two additional arias sung by a woman. (*Picayune,* Feb. 1, 1859, p. 1, col. 4; Feb. 5, 1859, p. 2, col. 1; and Feb. 6, 1859, p. 6, col. 1.)

March 23, 1859. Fourth concert. Program lost. (*Picayune,* Mar. 22, 1859, p. 1, col. 3.)

March 30, 1859. Fifth concert. Mozart, Overture to *The Magic Flute*. Beethoven, Symphony No. 5. Mendelssohn, *Calm Sea* Overture. Andante from Haydn, *Surprise* Symphony No. 94. Clara Schumann, *Andante and Variations for Two Pianos,* performed by M. G. Paulsackel and T. Wohlein. Rossini, Overture to *William Tell*. (*Picayune,* Apr. 3, 1859, p. 6, col. 1.)

April 27, 1859. Sixth concert. Beethoven, Symphony No. 6. Mendelssohn, Overtures to *Ruy Blas* and *A Midsummer Night's Dream*. Weber, *Jubel* Overture. Beethoven, Movement 2 from Symphony No. 3. Two movements from Haydn, Symphony No. 3. (*Picayune,* Mar. 26, 1859, p. 2, col. 1; May 1, 1959, p. 7, col. 1.)

FOURTH YEAR (FALL 1859–SPRING 1860)

December 7, 1859. First concert. Mendelssohn, Symphony No. 3. Méhul, Overture to *Chasse de Jeune Henri*. Bellini, "Casta Diva," sung by Mme P. Ruhl. Beethoven, *Leonore* Overture. F. Abt, aria "When I Am Near Thee." Meyerbeer, "Torchlight March" ("Marche aux Flambeaux"). (*Picayune,* Dec. 7, 1859, p. 1, col. 2.)

January 6, 1860. Second concert. Mozart, Overture to *Don Giovanni*. Beethoven, Symphony No. 4. Mendelssohn, *Roy Blas* Overture. Works by Rossini, Verdi, Weber/Berlioz. (*L'Abeille,* Jan. 6, 1860.)

February 1, 1860. Third Grand Concert. Gluck, Overture to *Iphigenia;* Mozart, *Jupiter* Symphony. Weber, Overture to *Oberon.* Mendelssohn, *Fingal's Cave.* Weber, grand scene from *Der Freischütz,* sung by Mme Dalmont-Messmaker. Andante from Beethoven, Symphony No. 1. L. Venzano, *La Venzano Grand Waltz,* sung by Messmaker. Auber, Overture to *La Muette. (Picayune,* Feb. 1, 1860, p. 1, col. 3; Feb. 5, 1860, p. 13, col. 1.)

February 29, 1860. Fourth concert. Mozart, Overture to *The Magic Flute.* Mendelssohn, *Italian* Symphony No. 4. Weber, Overture to *Euryanthe.* Beethoven, *Egmont* Overture. Auber, Grand Aria from *La Muette,* sung by Messmaker. Andante from Haydn, *Surprise* Symphony No. 94. Flotow, "The Last Rose of Summer" from *Martha.* Herold, Overture to *Zampa. (Picayune,* Mar. 5, 1860, p. 6, col. 1.)

March 21, 1860. Fifth concert. Beethoven, Symphony No. 3. Weber, Overture to *Der Freischütz.* Rossini, Overture to *William Tell.* An andante by Haydn. "Wedding March" from Mendelssohn's *A Midsummer Night's Dream. (Picayune,* Mar. 18, 1860, p. 2, col. 2.)

April 25, 1860. Sixth concert. Spohr, Overture to *Jessonda.* Beethoven, Symphony No. 5. Mendelssohn, Overture to *A Midsummer Night's Dream.* Andante by Haydn. Meyerbeer, "Torchlight March" ("Marche aux Flambeaux"). Weber, Overture to *Juliet. (Picayune,* Apr. 14, 1860, afternoon ed., p. 1, col. 5; Apr. 18, 1860, p. 1, col. 3; Apr. 22, 1860, p. 2, col. 3.)

May 16, 1860. Grand vocal and instrumental concert for the benefit of Sainte Mary's Orphan Boys' Asylum. Mendelssohn, Overture to *Ruy Blas.* Andante from Haydn, *Surprise* Symphony No. 94. March by the Orphans Brass Band. Weber, *Invitation to the Dance.* Mendelssohn *Calm Sea* for chorus and orchestra. Weber's *Der Freischütz* Overture. Romberg's *Song of the Bell,* oratorio with singers and full orchestra. Hérold's Overture to *Zampa. (Picayune,* May 12, 1860, p. 1, col. 4; May 17, 1860, p. 1, col. 3.)

FIFTH YEAR (FALL 1860–SPRING 1861)

November 18, 1860. Announced rehearsals and refuted a rumor that the new season was not going to take place. (*Picayune,* Nov. 18, 1860, p. 6, col. 1.)

November 25, 1860. Plans for fifth year. (*Picayune,* November 25, 1860, p. 8, col. 1)

December 12, 1860. Scheduled first concert. Beethoven, Symphony No. 6. Mendelssohn, *Calm Sea* Overture. Rossini, Overture to *Le Siége de Corinth.* Other pieces. (*Picayune,* Nov. 20, 1860, p. 2, col. 4; Nov. 25, 1860, p. 8, col. 1.)

December 23, 1860. Official announcement that there would be no concerts during the fifth year. (*Picayune,* Dec. 23, 1860, p. 6, col. 1.)

February 5, 1861. Second concert (?), originally scheduled for Jan. 23, 1861. Mozart's Mass No. 12, performed at Odd Fellows' Hall by fifty men and women plus an orchestra of the best musicians of the city. To benefit the younger Asile de Saint Vincent orphans. (*The Bee,* Feb. 4, 1861, p. 1, col. 3.)

May 15, 1861. Grand concert conducted by Collignon at Odd Fellows' Hall, for the Orphelin d'Asile de Sainte Marie. (*L'Abeille, May 15, 1861, p. 1, col. 7.*)

During the Civil War, Collignon apparently remained in New Orleans, where he was master of music at the Jesuit Church of the Immaculate Conception. On November 22, 1864, he conducted Weber's Mass in E-Flat at this church to benefit the poor of the Saint Vincent de Paul Society.[66] After the war it took several years before the economy of the city was such that more concert series could be developed. Meanwhile, Collignon continued to conduct individual concerts in New Orleans both at the church and in secular surroundings. For example, on November 18 and 21, 1866, he performed a Mozart mass as part of the opening of a fair at the Fair Grounds.[67] A few days later, he participated in a grand concert sacré at the Fair Grounds, where he was assisted by La Hache, Gustave Smith (accompanist), and Jaeger. The program included excerpts from Mozart's *The Magic Flute* and works by Mendelssohn, Weber, Schubert, Becker, Kreutzer, Meyerbeer, Gluck, Haydn, and Rossini.[68] On Tuesday, May 7, 1867, he assisted in a grand concert vocal et instrumental at the National Theater to benefit Carlo Patti (Adelina's brother), chef d'orchestre of the Variety Theatre. He conducted an orchestra of sixty of the best players in the city.[69] The very next day he conducted a mixed choir in a grand concert at the French Opera to benefit flood victims. Works on the program were by Mendelssohn, Verdi, Schank, Marliani, Hayes, Gottschalk, Aubry, Wely, and Gounod.[70] Some other concerts directed by Collignon occurred on May 24, 1867;[71] March 15, 1868;[72] March 19, 1869, with an orchestra of forty-five players;[73] September 25, 1869, with a mixed choir of seventeen, mostly from the German community, doing Cherubini's Mass and Mozart's *Ave Verum Corpus*;[74] November 7, 1869, doing a Haydn mass;[75] and November 14, 1869, when Collignon conducted and played the organ.[76]

In the fall of 1871 Collignon re-established his Classical Concert Series, though apparently for only one season. (See the list of Collignon's concerts after the Civil War on pages 84–85.) The repertory and the performing forces were much the same as that developed before the war. Beethoven symphonies in their entirety were featured, along with Weber and Gluck overtures, excerpts from Mozart and Haydn symphonies, and Mendelssohn's popular Symphony

No. 3. There were six concerts presented in the fall and four more in the spring of 1872. After the last concert one critic was so enthusiastic that he hoped Collignon would continue conducting during the summer. Noting that his orchestra is composed almost entirely of French Opera orchestral players, the critic continued, "After having heard the admirable Scottish Symphony [No. 3] by Mendelssohn so perfectly performed, everyone is saying how unwise it would be not to keep in New Orleans the large majority of musicians who have just come together for this interpretation." If Collignon would organize something for the summer, it would be of great good fortune for the people of New Orleans.[77]

Collignon's Concerts after the Civil War

FALL 1871 SERIES

October 8, 1871. First concert. Beethoven, Symphony No. 6. Weber, Overture to *Oberon*. (*L'Abeille*, Oct. 6, 1971, p. 1, col. 6.)

October 22, 1871. Second concert. Mendelssohn, *Scottish* Symphony No. 3. Weber, *Der Freischütz* Overture. (*L'Abeille*, Oct. 21, 1871, p. 1, col. 6.)

November 5, 1871. Third concert. National Theater. Gluck, Overture to *Iphigénie en Aulide*. Beethoven, Symphony No. 2. Andante to Mozart, Symphony in C (probably No. 41). Meyerbeer, "Marche aux Flambeaux." (*L'Abeille*, Nov. 3, 1871, p. 1, col. 6.)

November 16, 1871. Fourth concert. National Theater. Mendelssohn, *Scottish* Symphony No. 3. Andante from Haydn, *Surprise* Symphony No. 94. Weber, *Jubel* Overture. (*L'Abeille*, Nov. 25, 1871, p. 1, col. 6.)

December 10, 1871. Fifth concert, National Theater. Beethoven, Symphony No. 7. Adagio from Haydn, Symphony No. 3. Berlioz/Weber, *Invitation to the Dance*. (*L'Abeille*, Dec. 10, 1871, p. 1, col. 6.)

December 24, 1871. Sixth concert, National Theater. Beethoven, Symphony No. 6. Andante from Haydn, Symphony No. 3. Weber, Overture to *Der Freischütz*. (*L'Abeille*, Dec. 23, 1871, p. 1, col. 6.)

SPRING 1872 SERIES

March 3, 1872. First séance for large orchestra directed by G. Collignon. Mendelssohn, *Ruy Blas* Overture. Beethoven, Symphony No. 3. Andante from Schubert, Symphony in C. Rossini, Overture to *William Tell*. (*L'Abeille*, Mar. 1, 1872, p. 1, col. 3; Mar. 2, 1872, p. 1, col. 6.)

March 17, 1872. Second séance for large orchestra under G. Collignon. Beethoven, *Egmont* Overture. Mozart, *Jupiter* Symphony No. 41. Mendelssohn, Andante from the *Italian* Symphony No. 4. Weber. Overture to *Euryanthe*. (*L'Abeille,* Mar. 15, 1872, p. 1, col. 2; Mar. 16, 1872, p. 1, col. 7.)

April 14, 1872, Sunday. Third concert of Collignon's Société de Musique Classique. Weber, *Euryanthe* Overture. Beethoven, Symphony No. 6. Robert Schumann, *Reverie.* Auber, Overture to *La Muette de Portici.* (*L'Abeille,* Apr. 5, 1872, p. 1, col. 6; Apr. 13, 1872, p. 1, col. 3 and 6; concert postponed from Apr. 7, 1872; see *L'Abeille,* Apr. 7, 1872, p. 2, col. 3.)

May 12, 1872, Sunday. Fourth and last classical concert of the season by Collignon. Mendelssohn, *Scottish* Symphony No. 3. (*L'Abeille,* Apr. 27, 1872, p. 1, col. 3, May 5, 1872, p. 2, col. 1.)

Works Performed in Collignon's Orchestral Series, 1857–1871
(The number before the decimal is the year; the number after the decimal is the concert number that year.)

Abt, *When I Am Near Thee* (1860.1)

Auber, *La Muette,* Grand Aria (1860.4)

Auber, Overture to *La Muette de Portici (Masaniello)* (1858.7) (1860.3) (1872.3)

Beethoven, *Funeral March on the Death of a Hero* (1859.6)

Beethoven, Overture to *Egmont* (1860.4) (1872.2)

Beethoven, Overture to *Fidelio* (1858.5)

Beethoven, Overture to *Leonore* No. 3 [?] (1859.3) (1860.1)

Beethoven, Symphony No. 1, Andante (1860.3)

Beethoven, Symphony No. 2 (1858.1) (1859.3) (1871.3)

Beethoven, Symphony No. 3 (1859.1) (1860.5) (1872.1)

Beethoven, Symphony No. 4 (1858.5) (1860.2)

Beethoven, Symphony No. 4, a movement (1858.7)

Beethoven, Symphony No. 5 (1858.3) (1859.5) (1860.6)

Beethoven, Symphony No. 6 (1859.6) (1861.1) (1871.1) (1871.6) (1872.3)

Beethoven, Symphony No. 7 (1859.2) (1871.5)

Beethoven, Symphony No. 7, Allegretto and Scherzo (1858.1)

Bellini, *Norma,* "Casta Diva" (1860.1)

Flotow, *Martha,* Last Rose of Summer (1860.4)

Gluck, Overture to *Iphigénie en Aulide* (1871.3)

Gluck, Overture to *Iphigénie* [*Aulide* or *Tauride*?] (1858.4) (1859.2) (1860.3)

Haydn (1858.5)
Haydn, Andante (1859.2) (1860.5) (1860.6)
Haydn, Symphony No. 3, two movements (1859.6)
Haydn, Symphony No. 3 [?] Adagio (1871.5)
Haydn, Symphony No. 3 [?] Andante (1871.6)
Haydn, Symphony No. 8 (B Minor) (1859.1)
Haydn, Symphony No. 94, Andante (1858.7) (1859.5) (1860.7) (1871.4) (1860.4)
Hérold, Overture to *Zampa* (1858.7) (1860.4) (1860.7)
Kreutzer, *The Chapel* (1858.4)
Méhul, Overture to *Chasse de Jeune Henri* (1860.1)
Mendelssohn (1858.5)
Mendelssohn, *Adieux to the Forest* (1858.4)
Mendelssohn, *Calm Sea* Overture (1859.5) (1861.1)
Mendelssohn, *Fingal's Cave* Overture (1859.3) (1860.3)
Mendelssohn, Overture (1858.3)
Mendelssohn, Overture and Chorus, *Calm Sea* (1860.7)
Mendelssohn, Overture to *Midsummer Night's Dream* (1858.1) (1859.6) (1860.6)
Mendelssohn, *Roy Blas* Overture (1859.2) (1859.6) (1860.2) (1860.7) (1872.1)
Mendelssohn, *Scottish* Symphony No. 3 (1860.1) (1871.2) (1871.4) (1872.4)
Mendelssohn, *Italian* Symphony No. 4 (1860.4)
Mendelssohn, *Italian* Symphony No. 4, Andante (1872.2)
Mendelssohn, Wedding March from *Midsummer Night's Dream* (1860.5)
Meyerbeer, "Marche aux Flambeaux" ("Torchlight March") (1860.1) (1860.6) (1871.3)
Mozart (1858.5)
Mozart, Mass No. 12 (1861.2)
Mozart, Overture to *Don Giovanni* (1859.1) (1860.2)
Mozart, Overture to *The Magic Flute* (1858.1) (1859.5) (1860.4)
Mozart, *Jupiter* Symphony No. 41 (1860.3) (1872.2)
Mozart, *Jupiter* Symphony No. 41, Andante (1871.3)
Mozart, *Jupiter* Symphony No. 41, two movements (1858.3)
Romberg, *Song of the Bell* (1860.7)
Rossini (1858.5)
Rossini, unnamed work (1860.2)
Rossini, *The Barber of Seville,* aria (1858.3)
Rossini, Overture to *The Siege of Corinth* (1861.1)
Rossini, Overture to *William Tell* (1959.5) (1860.5) (1872.1)
Rossini, *Stabat Mater,* "Pro Peccatis" (1858.3)
Schubert, Symphony in C, Andante (1872.1)

Schubert, Symphony, Scherzo (1859.3)
Schumann, Clara, *Andante and Variations for Two Pianos* (1859.5)
Schumann, Robert, *Reverie* (1872.3)
Spohr, Overture to *Jessonda* (1859.1) (1860.6)
Verdi (1860.2)
Verdi, *Jérusalem,* aria (1859.3)
Venzano, *La Venzano Grand Waltz* (1860.3)
Weber (1858.5)
Weber, Concertstück (1859.2)
Weber, *Euryanthe,* chorus (1858.7)
Weber, *Der Freischütz,* grand scene (1860.3)
Weber, *Jubel* Overture (1858.3) (1858.7) (1859.6) (1871.4)
Weber, Overture to *Euryanthe* (1858.4) (1859.1) (1860.4) (1872.2) (1872.3)
Weber, Overture to *Der Freischütz* (1859.3) (1860.5) (1871.2) (1871.6)
Weber, Overture to *Juliet* (1860.6)
Weber, Overture to *Oberon* (1858.1) (1860.3) (1871.1)
Weber/Berlioz, *Invitation to the Dance* (1858.4) (1858.7) (1860.2) (1860.7) (1871.5)

Although Collignon continued to conduct concerts until June 1879, he did not resume his series. On at least one occasion, he accompanied a visiting artist with an orchestra,[78] but most of the concerts were at the Church of the Immaculate Conception, with his daughter, Mme Henriette Comès, singing solo parts, or at Saint Patrick's Church in Lafayette Square.[79] On May 27, 1876, the Drama Club of Louisiana gave a benefit for the Union Française at the Opera House, and there was a musical intermède directed by Collignon, with seven pieces (Adam, Maillard, Adam, Massé, Gounod, Verdi and Meyerbeer). The singers included Comès, Pérat, Van Hufflen, Météyé, Claiborne, and Stutz (?).[80] Collignon also composed music.[81] He was often honored and received the dedication of a work by Frederick Kitziger.[82] By 1880 Collignon had returned to France with his daughter,[83] and he died sometime before September 13, 1884, when his widow died at age fifty-nine.[84]

L'ORPHÉON FRANÇAIS

On December 8, 1867, Eugène Prévost, the former conductor of the French Opera, announced the creation of the Orphéon Louisianais, which would hold its first meeting on January 14, 1868. The main purpose of this society was to provide classroom musical instruction for men, young men, and boys from seven to fourteen years old, with the purposes of contributing to the development of musical taste among young people and helping nurture instrumentalists and singers.[85] There is no further record of the society.

The society known as Orphéon Français was organized in December 1881, with thirty members and a board of directors, and from this date to the end of the century its presence was felt continuously throughout the city.[86] There is no evidence that this was a descendent of the Orphéon Louisianais, but it may have been, particularly since there was a school associated with it at the French Union.[87] In any case, it was a new organization on Sunday, March 26, 1882, when the French literary organization Athénée Louisianais held its annual public meeting at Grunewald Hall with various musical numbers interspersed with literary readings. The main purpose of the meeting was to announce prizes for winners of writing contests in the French language, which was to help perpetuate the French language in a city that was increasingly becoming English-speaking. The Orphéon Français under MM Rossi and Vulliet opened with a piece by Curto to words by Canonge.[88] A few weeks later the Orphéon Français gave a vocal and instrumental concert of its own at the French Union Hall on Rampart Street. Works performed were almost exclusively by French or Belgian composers (A. Lamotte, Vieuxtemps, Gounod, Auber [piano, four hands], L. de Rillé, Wekerlin, and Halévy), with Donizetti and Verdi as adopted foreigners. There were several choruses, several arias and duets, a piano duet, and two violin solos performed by the former New Orleanian Jeanne Franko.[89] That spring, on June 17, 1882, the Orphéon Français threw an evening festival—a concert and a ball—at the grand pavilion at Spanish Fort on Lake Pontchartrain. A full orchestra accompanied the society in choruses by A. Thomas and L. de Rillé and also contributed an overture and excerpts from operas by Mercadante and Offenbach.[90] In October 1882, M Defossez, head of the French Opera, signed a contract with the chorus of the French Union [Orphéon Français] to reinforce the opera chorus by thirty-five to forty voices to a total of eighty or eighty-five voices.[91] Participation in the French Opera may have limited the number of separate concerts by the society but did not end them. Thus on October 18, 1882, there was a vocal concert by the Orphéon Français,[92] and the following March 31, 1883, it gave a grand concert and ball at Grunewald Hall.[93]

Various conductors led the programs, but two were the most important. Vulliet, first musical director of Orphéon Français, conducted the first concert in 1882, and, although he is rarely mentioned, he continued as leader at least through September 1886.[94] Under him the membership in the society grew from an original thirty to almost two hundred by the second year.[95] There is no indication of who was in charge when the society participated in the grand entertainment at the Opera House for the benefit of the Mount Carmel Asylum on October 27, 1883,[96] but for the concert and ball given by the French Orphéon Society at Grunewald Hall on May 23, 1884, the conductor was Mme Mandevilla Prévost.[97] By October 1887, the new conductor of Orphéon Français was George L. O'Connell. Unlike his predecessor's relative obscurity, O'Connell—from this time through the end of the century—had his name posted everywhere that the ensembles of Orphéon Français appeared and in many other concerts as well.[98]

The principal hall for the concerts was either Grunewald Hall or the French Union Hall, which apparently was renovated by the end of 1885.[99] Not all concerts were choral, as on June 5, 1887, when at the society's hall a concert *en famille* (that is, a chamber concert) was given by Eugene Medal, Paul Brunet, William Auglade, and August Vidondez, assisted by several friends. There were several duets for violin and piano played by Medal and Brunet. Misses A. and R. Bihli played solos and duets on the piano. Also a trio for violin, cornet, and piano was played by Medal, Auglade, and Brunet. Vidondez sang comic songs.[100] Orchestral concerts also were common.

Concerts of the Orphéon Français, 1888–1896

March 12, 1888. Grunewald Hall. Orchestra of the Cercle Gounod and the Orphéon Français, directed by Mr. George O'Connell. Overture. Cercle Gounod was a string quintet in one piece, a group of string instruments in another, and an orchestra in a third.[101]

September 2, 1888. The Orphéon Français gave a matinee concert at the Gouthier Hotel in Covington under George O'Connell. Performers included E. Médal, H. Wehrman *fils*, J. Voorhies, H. Vallé, E. Dussé, L. H. Barbey, O. Legendre, A. Brunet, and P. E. Carrière (member of the Camera Club).[102]

September 21, 1888, Friday. The Orphéon Français had a public rehearsal at its location on Royal and Orleans streets, limited to the number of listeners. George O'Connell, director. Pieces by Suppé, Planquette, Spirti (G. Ricci), Bruant, Verdi, Tito Mattei (S. Cohen), Coen (orchestra), Massé, De Bériot (G. Ricci), Paulus (G. Oliver), Lecocq, Bumbert, and Waldteufel.[103]

October 7, 1888. The Orphéon Français performed again a musical matinee at the Gontheir Hotel in Covington. George L. O'Connell, director. Ricci, Wehrman, L. H. Barbey (cornet), and the orchestra played.[104]

October 25, 1888. Soirée musicale by the Orphéon Français under Geo. L. O'Connell. Included a children's ensemble. This was a society of amateurs, but H. Wehrman, Ricci, M S. Cohen, Alex. Lazare, and other professionals also performed.[105]

November 5, 1888, Monday. A concert sponsored by the Democratic French Club, which featured members of the Orphéon Français. It also included a conference by the French literary scholar Alcée Fortier.[106]

May 31, 1889. Public rehearsal of the Orphéon Français at the hall corner of Royal and Orleans streets. The orchestra of the society played Hasselmann's march, the choir sang choruses by Gounod, Rupes, Ladombe, and Waldteuffel, and soloists sang songs. Ricci was the musical director, and Mr. M. Heichelheim was the accompanist.[107]

September 2, 1889. Concert at Milneburg by the Silver Cornet Brass Band (afternoon) and Orphéon Français (evening). All sorts of instrumental music during the day, and the evening concert was followed by fireworks and a ball.[108]

September 8, 1889, Sunday. The outdoor Orphéon Français's concert from the previous Sunday at Milneburg was rained out, so they played this Sunday at the Washington Hotel in Milneburg. It consisted of singers and an orchestra.[109]

October 25, 1889. Rehearsal by the Orphéon Français on Orleans and Royal streets. The Orpheon Orchestra performed an Overture *Promotion,* Mr. H. Wehrman performed on the violin; in addition there were songs, chorus of L'Orpheon, etc.[110]

November 20, 1889. Entertainment by the Camera Club and Grunewald Hall. According to the *Picayune,* "The Orphéon Français Orchestra, under the direction of Professor Albert Heichelheim, volunteered its valuable services and opened the programme with a selection beautifully rendered." In addition to songs, "Mr. H. Wehrman, a very clever young violinist, played a charming polonaise." There was also a violin obbligato by Mr. C. W. Vogel and a duet with Wehrman and Mr. George W. Weingart, accompanied by Mr. Paul Brunet.[111]

February 7, 1890. A benefit concert at Grunewald Hall for George L. O'Connell. In two parts, the program consisted of the West End Orchestra directed by M Lenfant, different choral groups (including a children's chorus), some piano pieces, some songs, the Orchestra and Chorus of the Orphéon Français, Gustave Joubert, etc.[112]

March 28, 1890. Concert by the Orphéon Français circle, under the direction of M George L. O'Connell. Included performances by twenty students, accompanied by MM O'Connell and Paul Brunet. In addition there was a sextet by Fauconier performed by H. Wehrman (violin 1), J. Voorhies (violin 2), J. Wiegel (viola), J. Wortmann (string bass), F. Ramos (flute), and P. Brunet, piano.[113]

April 7 and 8, 1890 (Monday and Tuesday). Two concerts vocal and instrumental by amateurs of the city to benefit Saint Louis Cathedral, performed at the French Opera House. Also children danced a Farandole. April 7: works by Schlepegreli, Enfanta, Meyerbeer (March from *Le Prophète*), Faure, Massenet, and V. Massé. Several works performed by the Orphéon Orchestra. April 8: works by Gounod, Granier, etc., assisted by Mark Kaiser (solo violin), the Orpheon Orchestra, and singer Mme E. Lejeune.[114]

May 7, 1890. Soirée complimentaire by Geo. L. O'Connell, assisted by the new Orchestra of West End directed by M Lenfant and managed by M Victor Nippert. Also the Orphéon Français, the Choral Society of New Orleans, the New Orleans Quartette Club, and various church choirs performed. Included Mme F. Bourgeois, a pupil of Curto.[115]

May 15, 1890, Thursday. Concert and ball at Grunewald Hall by Orphéon Français. Orchestral, choral, solo instrumental, and vocal works, including the solfege class. Conducted by George L. O'Connell.[116]

May 21, 1890. Grand concert vocal et instrumental to benefit Professor Eckert, at Grunewald Hall. There is a contradiction in dates; announced for May 27, too. Accompanied by the Orphéon Français Orchestra conducted by George O'Connell. Chamber music (trio: harp, violin, and violoncello). Kaiser, Wehrman, Armand Veasey, and Grisai performed.[117]

October 24, 1890, Friday. Performance of the Orphéon Français at their headquarters, Orléans at Royale.[118]

November 29ff, 1890. George O'Connell advertised that he was teaching solfege, chant, and piano, and that he was director of the Orphéon Français, director of the Aeoleon Harp Circle, director of the Gounod Circle, and piano accompanist of the New Orleans Amateur Opera Company. He was residing at 171 North Derbigny Street.[119]

December 14, 1890. A list of officers and committees of Orphéon Français.[120]

January 23, 1891, Friday. Grand vocal and instrumental concert by the Orphéon Français at Grunewald Hall.[121]

April 11, 1891. Concert and ball by l'Orphéon Français at Grunewald Hall. Orchestral and choral music, vocal solos, and M Charles Maillet violin. Composers included Schubert, Bizet, etc.[122]

May 28, 1892, Saturday. Concert of the Orphéon Français reviewed at length by Canonge. They used to give two series of concerts: in their own hall and in Grunewald Hall, but now they relinquished the latter for good reason. They were too small a group for the large Grunewald Hall, so this concert was performed in the much smaller French Union Hall. The orchestra had a dozen players: strings, woodwinds, and brass. The orchestra was directed by Professeur P. A. Borge, and the ensemble was improved; especially effective was the piece by Léo Delibes. Henri Wehrman Jr. was exceptional in Sarasate's *Souvenirs de Faust*. Also the choir did well.[123]

April 20, 1893. Farewell concert offered to Professor Borge by L'Orphéon Française, at the French Union Hall. Included two young violinists, Charles Maillet and Paul Tosso; M Raybaud (clarinet); singers, etc.[124]

May 7, 1893. Concert at City Park given by L'Orphéon Français under Professor Bergé [Borge].[125]

October 14, 1893, Saturday. Grand concert gratuit by L'Orphéon Française. The French Consul was there, and it was a great success. Program included Wehrman Jr. in a solo and in a duo with O. Aubert Jr. Each of the two halves began with an orchestral overture.[126]

April 18, 1894. General annual meeting of L'Orphéon Français at its hall on the corner of Royale and Orleans.[127]

April 24, 1894. At the installation of new officers of L'Orphéon Français, there was a vocal concert by MM Fonteynes, Maumus, and Alex. Lazare.[128]

October 18, 1894. A concert by Léon Fonteynes, ex-baritone of the French Opera, at the French Union Hall, assisted by numerous amateurs and artists and some from the Orphéon (Massé, Lazare, Gaillard, and Rutily), and M Renaud, well known from the French Opera and Saint Louis Cathedral. Also Grisai, Chèvre (piccolo both at the French Opera and West End) and M H. Wehrman.[129]

January 12, 1895. Report on the last meeting of L'Orphéon Français and its supporters and officers.[130]

May 5, 1895, Sunday. Vocal and instrumental concert by the Orchestre Euterpe, directed by M Octave Aubert Jr. and L' Orphéon Français directed by Professor H. Richard. At Jackson Barracks Park, for the benefit of Saint Maurice Church.[131]

September 8, 1895, Sunday. A festival given by the French Women's Society at Southern Park. Assisted by L'Orphéon Français. Included songs and choruses.[132]

March 22, 1896. Various new pieces of music announced by the publishers Werlein (Voges, Veasey), Dunning-Medine Co. (Carrie J. Hackney), J. A. Fourrier of Baton Rouge, Junius Hart (Gomes, W. T. Francis, H. C. Blackmar), and James S. McCabe. "The Picayune has received from the composer, Professor Hans Richard, the talented musician and leader of L'Orphéon Français, one of his 'Decollete Waltzes,' for the piano, published by the L. Grunewald Company, Limited."[133]

April 5, 1896. L'Orphéon Français performed a concert and ball at Tulane Hall. Well-known local singers participated.[134]

FROHSINN

The Germans, who were a sizeable minority in New Orleans by the early nineteenth century, had their own cultural societies, chief among which were the choruses.[135] The first was der Deutsche Liederkranz, founded in 1838, which existed for a number of years.[136] The principal singing clubs from the second half of the nineteenth century were the Turn-Verein (founded in 1851), the Deutsche Männergesangverein (founded in 1873), the Liedertafel (founded in 1878), the New Orleans Quartette Club (founded in 1882), Frohsinn (founded in 1885), and the Liederkranz (resurrected in 1889). Frohsinn, which had counterparts in other cities such as Mobile, was organized in New Orleans to specialize in German-language events.[137] It was very successful in presenting concerts, plays, and other cultural attractions to those who spoke German in New Orleans. It differed from the other German societies in that women, too, were members.

A central component of Frohsinn was its dramatic wing, which frequently presented dramas and farces with musical accompaniment. For example, on November 29, 1891, the club presented two comedies in German, which may have included songs since the reviewer praised especially the performers' voices.[138] That instruments may also have been present on such occasions is made clear for the performance on March 31, 1895, when Frohsinn presented a play at Washington Artillery Hall. In the *Picayune* the next day, the critic stated that "the orchestra played some excellent music during the evening."[139] Frohsinn even presented an opera in April 1892.[140] On the other hand, some dramatic events show no evidence of any music, such as when the comedy *Aufgeschoben ist nicht Aufgehoben* was performed on October 30, 1892.[141] The policy, however, was to offer dramas and musicales alternately a month apart, so that the latter occurred about three or four times a season.

The other important wing of Frohsinn was the Choral Society, which often appeared in its own concerts as well as at concerts in which others participated. On November 23, 1888, for example, the chorus, with soloists, presented, on its own, a concert at Odd Fellows' Hall,[142] whereas on Thursday, March 5, 1891, at Grunewald Hall, it joined others in a grand complimentary benefit offered to Mlle Jeanne Faure by her pupils.[143] Also on this latter program, besides the pupils, were Marguerite Samuel, Heinrich Kraus (violoncellist), and Joseph Durel (baritone). Professor Carl Weiss was director of the Frohsinn chorus on this occasion. A year later, there was a concert by the Frohsinn Verein at Grunewald Hall House, when members of the French Opera Orchestra assisted.[144] Performers included Mme Elizabeth Abt, Xavier Saetens, Charles Ludwig, Julius

Maier, and Louis Grunewald. An original composition by Mr. Wilhelm Leps, musical director of the Frohsinn, was premiered.[145] Two weeks later, on February 18, 1892, there was the fifth annual concert at Grunewald Hall to benefit the German Protestant Home for the aged and infirm.[146] There were vocal and instrumental solos by a number of persons, including Cesar Grisai, Henry Wehrmann, and Xavier Saetens, and members of the Frohsinn assisted. On May 18, 1892, Frohsinn dedicated the proceeds from its musicale, at Grunewald Hall, to benefit the Louisiana Society for the Prevention of Cruelty to Animals; the event was sponsored by Louis Grunewald.[147]

When Grunewald Hall was destroyed by fire in 1892, the music library of Frohsinn—then valued at three thousand dollars—was also destroyed.[148] That did not deter the club from putting on a concert, on December 9, 1892, at Odd Fellows' Hall, in which Pomero, Grisai, and Van Den Daelen—all professionals from the French Opera—volunteered their services. The male chorus and a mixed chorus from Frohsinn were featured. Leps wrote a vocal quartet that was premiered on this evening's fare, and then he accompanied Pomero in some music by De Bériot. The evening ended with dancing, which apparently was a common occurrence. Earlier that year, on February 25, for example, Frohsinn held a masked ball at Grunewald Hall which started with a musical program but was primarily dancing.[149] Because even the performers were masked, no one ever found out who the performers were. In subsequent years, other such Carnival balls were held.[150]

In addition to dramatic and musical evenings, Frohsinn also offered frequent musical, literary, and soirees dramatiques, during which there would be a few musical numbers interspersed with readings and skits. Sometimes these would not be announced until the performance, such as on April 5, 1891, at Grunewald Hall,[151] on August 5, 1891, at Lake View Park,[152] on January 28, 1894, at Washington Artillery Hall,[153] and March 25, 1894, at Washington Artillery Hall.[154] In 1894, Frohsinn announced that it would give an oratorio concert in honor of Leps the following November, and that J. W. H. Eckert offered his aid for the event.[155] The only composition mentioned was Anton Rubinstein's *Tower of Babel*. Political events within Frohsinn, however, seemed to have curtailed this concert.

The most successful years for Frohsinn were from 1892 to 1894, when Leps was the musical director. He even took his chorus to Cleveland in 1893 for the Sängerfest, where it "scored a grand success,"[156] and the following year to the Chicago Exposition.[157] Perhaps foreshadowing the function of many music societies after 1897, Frohsinn also sponsored at least one concert by an outside group. On Friday, March 20, 1891, Frohsinn sponsored a concert by the Mendelssohn Quintette Club of Boston at Grunewald Hall.[158] If it had continued to do so, Frohsinn might have survived, but, owing to pecuniary difficulties, Frohsinn died in 1900.

OTHER SOCIETIES

Among other musical societies was the Society of the Friends of Arts, which gave a concert at the cathedral on Sunday, November 22, 1840, in honor of Saint Cecelia's Day.[159] The society was composed of amateurs. The 1840 concert consisted of some music by Meyerbeer and Rossini.

Another society was the Société de Musique Sacrée de la Nouvelle Orléans. Its fourth concert, on November 16, 1842, contained religious works of Haydn, Handel, Pergolesi, Beethoven, Rossini, and Mercadante.[160] The following January 20, the society gave its sixth concert at Mr. Clapp's Church. "The selections are very choice and beautiful, comprising some of the finest conceptions of the great masters."[161] The program included works by Haydn, Handel, Mozart, and Rink, and a piece by William Furst dedicated to the firemen of New Orleans. The chorus was accompanied by an orchestra that also played an overture.

Cobini and Lehmann announced on November 20, 1836, and following, that they had formed an organization to present music for public and private serenades, military music, and banquets, and other occasions.[162] They hired fifty of the best professional musicians in the city, including a pianist (see page 340).

Half a century later there was La Lyre d'Orphée, a choral group composed exclusively of young women and girls who sang only in French. It was organized on April 7, 1891, at the home of Mme J. Mailhas, corner of Royal and Saint Louis streets.[163] The purpose of the club was the cultivation of an appreciation of "higher" classical music and developing such vocal and instrumental talent as was found among the members. The initial concert took place at the Union Française Hall on Wednesday, October 28, 1891.[164] The group consisted of fifty women, and the concert included also solo songs and an instrumental quartet. Nearly a year later, on October 19, 1892, it gave another concert (soiree musicale), conducted by Professor George O'Connell, at Grunewald Hall.[165] Closely allied with the Lyre d'Orphée was Le Luth, an organization of gentlemen having the same objectives. In time, it was hoped, the organization would grow until New Orleans would have a grand choral oratorio society such as existed in Boston, Saint Louis, Cincinnati, and other cities. "The members [were] very enthusiastic." A joint concert by Le Luth and La Lyre d'Orphée, in honor of their conductor O'Connell, took place at the Washington Artillery Hall on December 12, 1892.[166] They gave the local premier of Gounod's cantata *Gallia*. Also on the program, among other things, were Mozart's Overture to *The Abduction from the Seraglio*, vocal music by Mendelssohn, a violin piece by Alard played by Wehrman, and the quartet from *Rigoletto*. A week later, on December 19, 1892, the Lyre d'Orphée gave a grand musicale at Grunewald Hall.[167]

By the late 1880s and 1890s there was a plethora of musical clubs and societies in New Orleans. George O'Connell was involved in a number of these besides the Orphéon Français, La Lyre d'Orphée, and Le Luth: the Aeoleon Harp Circle, the Gounod Circle, and the New Orleans Amateur Opera Company.[168] About these clubs only a few aspects are known. The Aeoleon Harp Circle gave an instrumental and vocal concert (with J. J. Sarrazin and Bayon, violinists, playing a duo and solos) at the French Union Hall on February 15, 1884,[169] and it was still in existence at the end of November 1890 when O'Connell advertised that he was the director of this club. The Gounod Circle seems to have been a more substantial organization, with its own orchestra and a series of concerts. It gave its third soiree musicale on Wednesday, December 14, 1887, in the salons of Dr. Henri Bayon, 125 Bourbon Street, between Toulouse and Saint Peter.[170] The following April 3, 1888, the Orchestra of the Gounod Circle, at Grunewald Hall, performed several orchestral works on a program that featured the young pianist Miss Helena Augustin.[171] She played solo works by Rubinstein, Chopin, Bach, and, with orchestra, the Allegro from Hummel's Concerto No. 2. At the end of November, O'Connell advertised that he was also the director of the Gounod Circle. We know nothing of the New Orleans Amateur Opera Company other than O'Connell's comment that he was the director, again at the end of November 1890. The New Orleans Mendelssohn Club was active from at least 1869 when, on April 17 of that year, a quartet of male singers was announced as "the Mendelssohn Club."[172] There is an undated reference to the Mendelssohn Club of New Orleans in a scrapbook that belonged to Mark Kaiser; it probably comes from the 1880s.[173] In this instance the Mendelssohn Club was referred to as the successor to one of the Sociétés Philharmoniques. In the fall of 1887, J. W. H. Eckert auditioned singers,[174] and on March 1, 1888, the Mendelssohn Society of New Orleans gave its second free concert of the season;[175] as opposed to the more famous Boston Mendelssohn Club, the New Orleans organization was a vocal group. At this concert it sang three choral works (two choruses from Mendelssohn's *Saint Paul* and a Latin drinking song for male chorus), and the rest of the program was sung by members of the French Opera Troupe; there were also violin solos by Theodore Curant, accompanied by Ella Grunewald.

4

Music and Race in Nineteenth-Century New Orleans

At the beginning of the nineteenth century, the French-speaking community ruled a polyglot population that differed greatly from any other American community. As the nineteenth century progressed, the predominant French-speakers felt threatened. Anglo-Saxons poured in, as well as many persons of other ancestries, and when the French in New Orleans needed to emphasize their supposed rights as original landowners and clarify their cultural distinctions from the newcomers (especially Americans), the word "Creole" took on new meaning. In addition, by the time of the Civil War, some in the French community were so scared of being confused with African Americans that they redefined the term and established the myth that Creoles were aristocratic, French-Spanish-cultured native New Orleanians and exclusively white. By the end of the nineteenth century, any one of the groups of native-born persons with mixed white and nonwhite ancestry—anyone not 100 percent white—was termed "Creoles of color" or "persons of color."[1]

The social status of individuals, however, also depended, in 1800, on the relative wealth of some as well as the individual's educational level. Some persons of color had advanced education, and some excelled in classical music, literature, and other arts. Some persons of color owned slaves, and some whites owned none. The cultures of Africans, Native Americans, and Europeans fused. These cultures were not monolithic; there were differences among German, Anglo-Saxon, French, and Spanish Europeans, among the various Native American tribes (Chickasaws and Choctaws), and among Africans coming directly from Africa and those arriving via Santo Domingo (Haiti) or Cuba.[2]

All these differences and mixtures faced a new cultural injection after 1803 when, in the wake of the Louisiana Purchase, English-speaking Americans began to settle in large numbers in New Orleans. Differences in language, culture, religion, politics, and education caused tension between the well-educated, business-oriented English-speakers and the plantation French-speakers. Mainly, the French felt threatened. The clash between the attitudes of the older settlers and the newer ones eventually intensified whatever racial discrimination existed in 1800. In the first decade of the nineteenth century this was not a major factor since the American invasion, was, in part, balanced by the resettlement from Haiti of a few thousand French-speaking Creoles—whites, blacks, and persons of color, and simultaneously immigration directly from France continued unabated. Many of these were well-educated, European-oriented individuals who immediately made a positive economic and cultural impact on the city, keeping it French.[3] Yet, lest one assume there was no discrimination, in 1807 slaves and persons of color had separate seating areas apart from themselves and whites (see page 272), and in 1820 Davis barred all slaves from his Théâtre d'Orléans (see page 602).

But Anglos were pouring in, so the French made alliances. Technically, since the term "Creole" included any native-born Louisianan, the few English-speaking natives and the many nonwhite natives were also Creoles. The profitable intermarriage of French speakers and English speakers and the union of some of them in business began to weaken the hold of the former on the entire fabric of New Orleans society, but this influx of foreign French kept the French speakers on top at least into the 1830s.[4] With the French apparently there was more tolerance of nonwhites, most of whom in those years spoke French. In addition, women of color, in the first few decades of the nineteenth century, were much prized by white men, and special balls were held just for some of these women so that white gentlemen could meet them. In November 1805, for example, there appeared in a newspaper the following advertisement: "August Tessier has the honor of informing the public that, since the first of November, he is the proprietor of the city building and the corresponding dance hall belonging to M Bernard Coquet. He will present balls every Wednesday and Saturday for free women of color, as he has announced, and he dares to flatter himself that those who were satisfied at the first ball will be even more so at the rest. One will find all sorts of refreshments, soups, wines, etc., and even suppers and dinners. His house is and will continue to be open to all kinds of persons who wish during the day to take refreshments and to gamble."[5] Many liaisons were established that resulted in further French-speaking mixtures of whites and persons of color.

Two decades later, however, there were clear signs that discrimination against these persons of color was getting worse. For example, on Sunday, July 4, 1830, there was a concert and dance for young Creole amateurs from age seven to fifteen. The cost of entry was fifty cents for whites, twenty-five cents persons of color, and half-price for children.[6] Presumably "children" were under seven. What is clear is that, while children of both races danced at the same party, a cheaper price for blacks infers that they were regarded as lesser persons. There was tolerance in that the races mixed, but not without some racial divide. By 1847 the dances were separate. At the Salle de Bal, reached by the Pontchartrain Rail Road, a bal paré et masque was held every Wednesday and Sunday (understood: for whites only), and for "quarteronnes" every Tuesday, Thursday, and Saturday. *L'Abeille* noted, "Un superbe orchestre a été engage, et il y aura un excellent restaurant et une buvette bien garnie."[7] This separateness continued in 1853 when Madam L. Dumagene advertised a school at 54 Bourbon Street between Bienville and Douane [Dumaine] streets, where she taught various subjects including music "pour les jeunes personnes de couleur."[8] Separate black schools reflected the fact that many other schools were for whites only. Prominent Creole families who looked white but had a taint of black ancestry sometimes tried to hide the latter, but, as Joseph Beaumont (1820–70) wrote in his song *Toucoutou,* they were better off to accept it and be happy with it.[9]

Meanwhile, slaves and servants often were barred entirely from white places of entertainment. On January 5, 1829, for example, regulations of the society balls at the Orleans Ball-Room (Salle d'Orléâns) were published, and the ninth (last) rule stated: "No servant will be allowed to be introduced by the subscribers, lest they should encumber the room. The door-keeper will refuse them entrance."[10] Two years later, the newspapers carried the announcement of a children's ball, with the statement, "After the children's ball, servants will not be permitted to remain in the ball room."[11] On January 10, 1835, in an advertisement for a mimic, "trestigiator," and "angostemith" at the Theatre of Mr. Saubert on Camp and Gravier streets, Faubourg Sainte Mary (today's Central Business District), "People of colour [are] not admitted."[12] When the circus came to town in March 1836, the newspaper made clear that "Slaves [are] not admitted without a pass from their masters";[13] they were admitted, however, with such a pass.

When the renowned concert pianist Henri Herz came to New Orleans in 1847, he witnessed cruelty by his landlady to a young black servant and demanded that she stop or he would leave. It worked, at least for the moment. Herz at the time taught several talented young persons in the city, and he was dumbfounded by the inability of his young New Orleans female student from attending his concerts because she was partially black.[14] He offered to perform a concert just for African Americans, but his manager, on the urgings of the local officials, prevented this since it would greatly alienate his white audience.

Trotter notes that, a decade later, sometime before the outbreak of the Civil War, Creoles of color formed a Philharmonic Society. They loved art but refused to sit in "black"-designated areas of the white theaters.[15] Constantin Deberque and Richard Lambert, both Creoles of color, were at times conductors of these concerts. These men were free and therefore, unlike slaves or servants, enjoyed a number of musical opportunities, including employment in orchestras (for ballroom dances and theater music, perhaps even opera), chamber ensembles (for small entertainments and dances), and military bands (for parades and other outdoor events). Both Tio and Doublet worked during the day as cigar makers (according to the 1850 census), but evenings and on weekends they were successful musicians.[16] When Lambert left New Orleans permanently and made his debut in Paris on March 21, 1854, the newspapers in New Orleans were sufficiently proud of him to advertise the event.

During the Civil War and Reconstruction, persons of color established themselves in positions of power and influence, but not without some struggle. They established their own newspapers, which appealed to radical whites as well as Creoles of color, and they assumed leadership positions in the new state government. They took upon themselves the responsibility of assisting the former slaves who came to New Orleans, often without the means for succeeding in an urban environment, and established benevolent societies to aid them. They opened schools at all levels and three colleges, where music was part of the curriculum. There was always some racial prejudice during Reconstruction, but there were also major signs of the unique integration and assimilation that separated New Orleans from the rest of the country. Once the Union army took over New Orleans and the city was under the watchful eye of the federal government, blacks achieved an integration unknown elsewhere in the South.

Before the Union troops entered New Orleans, during the siege of the city, old policies of discrimination continued. For example, on Sunday, December 15, 1861, at the opening of the Théâtre d'Orléans, several light works were performed, including Offenbach's one-act operetta *La Nuit Blanche*. First parquets, loges and baignoires grilles, second parterres and baignoires decouvertes were reserved for whites; loges grilles de secondes for families of color; third level for slaves.[17] But not all white citizens were happy with this, and when given a chance, they worked directly with black musicians in an integrated setting. The young white piano prodigy Marguerite Elie, for example, who was stranded in Paris during the war, found no problem playing a violin-piano sonata with the negro violinist José White at a matinee concert directed by M Lebouc on January 11, 1864.[18] She could not have performed with him in New Orleans until

1862. Just after the war ended, on May 10, 1865, Samuel Snaër Jr. (1835–1900) led a soiree musicale at the "white" Théâtre d'Orléans to benefit the Colored Orphans' Home at Soule House; the orchestra received much praise, especially for its performance of Edmond Dédé's *Quasimodo* Symphony.[19] Snaër, a Creole of color, was an outspoken integrationist; at the time he was a highly regarded musician, as were other participants, such as Victor Eugene McCarty, a mulatto artiste. That the Théâtre d'Orléans was now open to black concerts and that it received notice in the white press shows that, at least to some degree, the two groups were more accepting of each other than before the war and than what was to come a decade and a half later.

An announcement in the *New Orleans Daily Crescent* of April 13, 1866, suggests that, under the façade of better racial relationships, old stereotypes of Africans remained firm.

> The habitues of the Academy of Music will regret to learn that Billy Emerson and Dick Parker, as they are familiarly known to the public, are about to depart for Europe. Their negro performances, it is generally conceded, have never been excelled, and have very rarely been equaled, and, when they leave, the manager of the Academy must find some remarkable attraction to fill their part of the bills. These gentlemen, upon the invitation of a number of influential citizens, have been tendered a benefit at the Academy, which will come off this evening. Let them have a bumper. The managers of the Academy, showing a generous appreciation of the merits of the beneficiaries, have thrown the full strength of the company into a series of brilliant entertainments.[20]

MM Emerson, Parker, and others (Hart, Gorman, Rushton, and Franklin) performed, with "their comic Ethiopian assistants," routines labeled "Ethiopic eccentricities." These occurred "sandwiched" between pantomimes, gymnastics, "vocalizes," and the fairy ballet *Telemachus*.[21] If Emerson and Parker had been black performers, then their "negro" acts were treated with equality by the management of the theater. But it is more likely that they were black-faced whites. As for the audience, an 1869 Louisiana law forbade "discrimination in places of public resort. Many Negroes tried to end discrimination by suing the businessmen who refused them service. They filed at least fourteen suits against soda shops, saloons, theaters, and the opera in New Orleans between 1869 and 1875."[22]

The most notorious civil rights suit came in 1869 when McCarty refused to sit in a colored area of the French Opera.[23] He accused the director of the Opera House, M Calabrési, of denying him access to the white seats. Calabrési, for his part, was worried that whites would stay away from the financially strapped theater if McCarty were allowed next to them. To answer this, Alderman Camp organized the radicals who promised large donations for subscriptions for blacks. Nothing seems to have come of the suit, and blacks continued to sit in black-designated areas of the theater.[24] This continued until the 1874–75 season when the White League prevailed upon the leadership of the French Opera to exclude blacks despite the significant financial loss of donations from the wealthy black community that ensued.[25]

After Reconstruction, segregation became much more virulent and rigid. Yet here, too, there were signs of mixing, such as in 1879 at Spanish Fort, where African Americans were urged to visit since there 'there is no distinction.'"[26] There was resistance to blacks at first, but in the second summer blacks enjoyed all the amenities.[27] Still, suppression of blacks in all areas of public life increased during the 1880s, including in the concert halls.

White and black performers intermingled at concerts more readily than white and black audiences. On Sunday, May 9, 1875, there was a benefit concert in Economie Hall for M Paulin Dardignac, baritone of the French Opera.[28] The pianist was M Basile Barès, the former slave, composer, and for many years the owner of a piano store.[29] Most of the performers were amateurs. A week later there was a second concert, with Dardignac joined by Mlle Liogier and M Miral, the latter two white performers; a third concert at the predominantly black Economie Hall was held on May 23, and another on December 20.[30]

In the face of lingering racial prejudice, however, some blacks preferred to remain separate. A number entered all-black colleges, of which there were three in the 1870s. New Orleans University, a college for black students sponsored by the African Methodist Episcopal Church, offered music as one of the main courses of study.[31] The school, which opened in 1873 and closed in 1934, "was most noted for the quality of musical training it provided. It began early trying to preserve Negro spirituals, and by 1880 its 'Original New Orleans University Singers' were famous for their renditions."[32] All three black colleges in the city considered music an important part of the curriculum. According to John W. Blassingame, "The three Negro colleges also added significantly to the intellectual and cultural life of New Orleans. A number of Negro musicians, artists, poets, and writers studied at these schools."[33]

An outcome of this separateness, during the 1870s, was that many African Americans had a prominent role in the classical musical life of the city as a whole. Chief among these were Snaër, McCarty, Arthur P. Williams, Charles Vêque, and J. A. Davies. There was also one small Negro symphony orchestra in the city.

Organized by Louis Martin, the orchestra began playing at concerts in 1877. The black *New Orleans Louisianian* newspaper boasted that "the twenty-man orchestra's playing of several difficult overtures, symphonies, etc., evidenced careful training, and reflected credit upon their accomplished leader, Professor Louis Martin."[34] Blassingame notes: "The most notable operatic event in the Negro community occurred in 1875 when a French opera troupe was stranded in New Orleans. The Creole Negroes organized several concerts in May to raise money for the troupe and even took roles in some of the scenes from the operas which the troupe performed. Led by Aristide Mary and other opera fans, large crowds attended the performances and requested that the company include on the program selections from 'La Traviata,' 'Rigoletto,' 'La Muette de Portici,' 'La Juive,' 'La Favorite,' 'La Reine de Chypre,' and "Guillaume Tell.""[35]

But by the 1880s the racial divide was stricter than at any time before. It is true that more liberal-minded white New Orleanians occasionally opened their concerts to black performers, such as on February 15, 1889, at Grunewald Hall to benefit the German Protestant Home for the Aged. Performers included Misses Emily and Katie Kundert, Minerva Adams, Etta Roehl, Mrs. Ida Riemann Kaiser, MM Louis Fuhr and O. G. Keller, the Sixth District Singing Society under Professor J. Engel, the Oak City Quartette, the colored songsters from North Carolina, accompanied by Eckert, and the Evangelical Singing Society of Carrollton under Mr. H. Haverkamp.[36] As Dale A. Somers notes, at the Cotton Exposition from 1884 to 1886, when the eyes of the entire world were on New Orleans, "there is no color line, and that is a great feature of the Exposition. The colored people are treated like the whites, and there certainly can be no complaint that discrimination is shown."[37] But by 1888, racist white propaganda, fueled by contempt for the Negro persona, refused to let blacks into concert halls.[38] White audiences relished such blatantly anti-black compositions as *Negromania, Pay day on the Plantation,* by Puerner, which was performed on June 1, 1890.[39] Another such work was the piece *Nigger in the Barnyard* by Lovenberg, described as a "descriptive conglomeration."[40] It was performed in a concert at West End by the Washington Artillery and Continental Guards Military Band under Professor Wunch, on April 24, 1897. The *Picayune* snidely praised Negroes for their melodies but noted that Negro music was devoid of art.[41] Once the federal government acquiesced in the racists' policies and the world looked the other way (in the 1890s), blacks were systematically denied equal and fair treatment.

When the distinguished black violinist Edmond Dédé returned one last time to his home city and gave a series of concerts (December 10 and 17, 1893, and

January 21, 1894),[42] he could not perform in a white hall or with white performers, but that did not stop white audiences from joining blacks in thronging to his concerts. Indeed, when Dédé published new music in New Orleans to coincide with his visit, it was the white engraver Henri Wehrmann Sr. who prepared the edition and the black Barés who sold it in his store.[43] Dédé, a free black of Haitian origins, was born in New Orleans in 1827, studied there with Gabici and Prévost, and was taught at the Paris Conservatoire by Halévy in composition and Alard on violin. He also studied with the elder Lambert. He died in Paris in 1903.[44] The citizens of Paris and Bordeaux welcomed him. He had a distinguished fifty-year career on the violin and as conductor in both cities. In New Orleans, however, he played in such acoustically bad halls as the Salle des Amis de l'Esperance or the Salle des France-Amis. His accompanist was Basile Barés. He played a lot of his own works and received rave reviews.

The racial bigotry that affected the musical life of the city continued in many guises. In fall 1896 the New Orleans Glee Club sponsored train excursions to Baton Rouge, Thibodaux, and Donaldsonville. Blacks and whites could not ride together, so there were special cars for colored persons.[45] Despite protests by leaders of the black community, Jim Crow had taken over New Orleans. The great days of concert life in New Orleans were over, and it would take more than a half-century before blacks and whites would once again participate equally in its classical concerts.

Thus, the social situation in New Orleans during the nineteenth century was so complicated by race, language, national origin, historical location, and wealth that concert life was itself unusual and inconsistent. Who performed at concerts and who attended them crossed cultural lines despite all the social barriers, and the result was, during much of the nineteenth century, a musical scene that was unusually rich.

5

Music Education

A healthy musical environment requires the musical training of performers from beginners to advanced professionals, of composers, and of the audience. From the beginning of the nineteenth century, New Orleans was fortunate to have music teachers who imparted those skills to pupils who, in turn, conveyed them to the next generation.

The kinds of music education that occurred in the city grew from that of a single tutor instructing a pupil to that of a large music faculty instructing a large number of students. The one-on-one practice, where a single teacher taught a single student, continued throughout the century, but by mid-century two or more teachers sometimes worked in tandem, and by the end of the century there was a significant conservatory of music.

MUSIC EDUCATION TO 1861

The first music teacher that we know about in the nineteenth century was Le Sieur D'Hébécourt, who announced on December 4, 1802, that he was prepared to teach beginning reading, writing, and arithmetic to young children in his home, and to teach French and English to more advanced children. He also was ready to teach history, geography, and mathematics and to instruct talented students in music, design, and dance.[1] Thus music was part of good breeding, but not yet separated from other facets of education. One can only surmise that Le Sieur D'Hébécourt was modestly conversant in the rudiments of elementary music and that his pupils were at the start of their musical education. The case was a little different with M Douvillier, who on February 5, 1803, offered to teach guitar at his home on Royal Street "opposite the printer."[2] There is no evidence that he was a virtuoso or even a professional guitarist, and his students presumably could be older children or adults. The skill of playing the guitar required somewhat more than the mere rudiments of music, however, though not necessarily much more.

The title "professor" usually meant that a person was skilled as an instrumentalist or singer and taught music. A "professor" had much more musical skill than either Le Sieur D'Hébécourt or M Douvillier and made a living as a professional musician. Such seems to have been the cases with Professor Brun, a "professeur de forté-piano," who gave a concert on Tuesday, December 17, 1805,[3] and Remondet, "professeur de forté-piano," who gave his concert on Saturday, October 10 or 17, 1807.[4]

Some of the professionals taught their own children with the hope that they might follow in their parents' footsteps, but this rarely worked out well. For example, M Minière, a professional pianist, taught one daughter the piano and another voice;[5] they were never heard of again. And Desforges taught the violin to his eldest son who gave one public performance at age nine and retired forever.[6] Only Ernest Guiraud, Marguerite Elie, and Léon Prévost, children of local professionals, went on to distinguished professional careers.

Most of the students, however, were not immediate family members, and when they were good enough, they performed publicly. For example, a female student of Minière performed piano in a Pleyel sonata for pianoforte accompanied by violin and bass, on December 6, 1810,[7] and the following March 9, 1811, a young female pupil of Nicolai played a pianoforte concerto by Lachnilh accompanied by orchestra.[8] Nicolai was the leading clarinetist in the city, but clearly he also taught piano. M Chéry, a violinist, presented two young pupils of his at a concert on February 20, 1813. M Chéry was also a dancing master, and after the concert, Chéry himself and one of his pupils danced.[9]

The most frequently met music pedagogues at the time taught piano and voice. Brun, Minière, and Nicolai—the earliest "professors" of piano—have already been mentioned. Nicolai continued to teach piano as well as clarinet.[10] A new name is that of Charles Gilfert, whose student, Mme Labadie, performed on a number of programs before 1820.[11] In November 1820, Mr. Le Roy announced his presence in the city as a teacher of vocal music and pianoforte, harp, guitar, and lyre.[12] Mr. Emile Johns, who had a distinguished career in the city as pianist, composer, and music businessman, also taught piano throughout the 1820s. Mr. A. Julia, "maitre de piano," appeared in March 1824 and was "available to give piano lessons. He accompanie[d] his students with the violin and provide[d] their instruments free."[13] Ignacio Pena advertised in November 1830 that he was a voice and piano teacher.[14] J. Norès, who is frequently encountered as an accompanist in concerts of the 1830s, made his first appearance as a teacher of piano in December 1830.[15] Mme Zimmer,[16] Miss Russell,[17] M Trust,[18] and Mme G. Boyer were other piano teachers during the 1830s. Trust was director of choruses of the Italian Opera at the Saint Charles Theatre and offered lessons during his leisure hours. Boyer was a skilled harpist.[19] And then there was an unnamed "young lady who has for ten years past taught the piano in this city, [and who now] desires a situation in a private family, or in a young women's boarding school, as a teacher of music."[20] Other professional musicians skilled in keyboard music also taught but did not advertise. The most famous such situation was that of F. J. Narcisse Letellier, a singer, who was the piano teacher of the young Louis Moreau Gottschalk.[21]

As the city grew exponentially during the 1840s and 1850s, so the number of music teachers grew, and the quality of instruction improved greatly at the upper end. By the 1840s private piano instruction was offered by most professional musicians living in the city. To be sure, there continued to be those who specialized in beginners, and the tradition of teachers going from home to home to teach continued. In November 1843, for example, Mme Gabi, professor of harp, piano, and voice, offered her services to the women and families of New Orleans.[22] Increasingly boarding and public schools offered piano instruction along with general subjects, such as at Mme Charpeaux's Institution and Mrs. Desrayaux's Institution.[23] Mme Nay combined music and literary education for private students in March 1855.[24] But increasingly the outstanding pupils had teachers they could turn to. Henri Herz, the famous French pianist, taught advanced piano students when he resided briefly in New Orleans in 1847. The important conductor Gustave Collignon was also a concert pianist and taught that instrument in 1850.[25] For the top students, there was an exceptional situation when Gottschalk returned home for an extended stay in March 1855. He suggested he would teach advanced students.[26]

Vocal teachers were as plentiful as piano teachers. Not surprisingly, owing to the grandeur of the opera throughout the century, several of these teachers were outstanding singers. The two most famous were Gregorio Curto and Julie Calvé Boudousquié, both of whom are discussed at length elsewhere in this book. Both were important singers at the French Opera in the 1830s. Both began their teaching careers before the Civil War, and afterwards they continued for several decades. Vocal instruction at the other end of the spectrum, for children and other beginners, began in the 1720s at the Ursuline Convent School, and was widespread by the beginning of the nineteenth century. Mr. Rochefort[27] and Mr. and Miss Laporte[28] were private voice teachers in 1814 and 1816. The latter couple taught piano and guitar as well; they had recently arrived from Paris and were teaching according to the methods of the Paris Conservatoire. Some of the other piano teachers also taught voice, such as Ignacio Pena and Mr. Montilly in the 1830s. Montilly, a professor of the pianoforte, taught at the Academy for Young Ladies, of which he and his wife were in charge.[29] The academy was in Mr. Leprutre's buildings, No. 82 Saint Louis Street, between Royal and Bourbon streets. The practice of combining vocal and piano instruction continued in the following decades. In 1856 Eugène Chassaignac, for example, was a professor of singing and piano.[30] Vocal instruction combined with instruments other than piano was common enough. Mr. Charles Milon, for example, was a teacher of voice and guitar in 1832.[31] It was a rare situation when M and Mme Letelliox gave only voice lessons in New Orleans in 1830.[32] Vocal instruction continued in the schools, such as at Mme Parent's Institution for Young Ladies (corner of Dumaine and Rampart streets), where Mr. Curto taught vocal music to the girls.[33] Solfège was frequently mentioned as part of the musical curriculum of schools and individual music lessons.

Many of the important professional violinists in the city taught their instrument. The first, Desforges, had a series of pupils besides his son. On Tuesday, March 9, 1813, he and one of his best pupils performed Blache's Symphonie Concertante for grand orchestra,[34] and a year later, on Monday, April 11, 1814, Desforges and three of his students—MM Morand, Brosset, and Beauregard—played Viotti's Simphonie Concertante.[35] An otherwise unknown violinist, Mr. Destroup, advertised on November 15, 1817, that he was a

> teacher of the violin, guitar, forte-piano and vocal music, lately from France, [and] has the honour of informing the inhabitants of New-Orleans, that he intends residing in this city, and giving lessons. He will do everything in his power to accelerate the progress of the pupils confided to his care. He has brought out with him violins made by the best makers, which he will dispose of to amateurs, on very reasonable terms; as also guitars, sonatas for the violin, by the celebrated Viotti, & Kreutzer, concertos by Rhodes & Kreutzer. He has also new romances with accompaniment of the guitar, and derived pieces from newest operas, &c. &c. He will be found at Mr. Sie. Geme, on the levee near the garrison barracks.[36]

Destroup was smart enough to realize that his students would need instruments and printed music from which to play. As his selection of sheet music shows, he anticipated advanced enough students who could play some of the more difficult new pieces.

Desforges's successor, C. Herz, continued the practice of performing publicly with his best students. Two of Herz's pupils performed a symphony for two violins and full orchestra in a benefit for Herz on February 21, 1824, at which time Herz also played a Viotti concerto.[37] In 1830 he published an invitation for pupils on violin and piano accompaniment to come to his home at 120 Sainte Ann Street.[38] Adolphe Elie, trained at the Paris Conservatoire, was a violinist in the French Opera Orchestra when young Louis Moreau Gottschalk studied violin with him.[39] When New Orleans reached its golden period of the 1840s and 1850s, its most significant violinist, Gabici, was also one of its most significant teachers (see part II, chapter 5). His first known student was Adolphe Bounivard, who at the age of ten performed a set of variations composed by Gabici. This took place at the Théâtre d'Orléans on May 23, 1843, and Gabici conducted the orchestra.[40] His favorite student of the 1840s was Victor Gerber, with whom he performed publically at least three times between November 13, 1847, and May 2, 1849.[41] Gabici is credited with ignoring the color barrier in New Orleans at the time when he included among his pupils the Creoles of color Edmond Dédé and Charles Lambert (see page 104).

There were harp and guitar teachers from the start of the century. Mme Zimmer taught harp in 1834, Mr. Trust in 1836, Mme Boyer in 1838, and Mme Gabi in 1843. M Douvillier was the first to advertise that he would teach at his home: on February 5, 1803.[42] Others over the next few decades included Mr. and Miss Laporte, Mr. Destroup, Mr. Lepage, Mr. Charles Milon, Mr. Trust, and Mr. F. Kroll—most of whom we have already encountered in other capacities. Lepage was the first clarinet teacher to be mentioned.[43] Other woodwind teachers included Mr. Bell (first clarinet of the French Opera, 1820s), Mr. Kroll (oboist and flutist of the French Opera, 1821–40s), Jandot father and son (clarinetists at the French Opera, 1820s onward), Signor Ribas (oboist of the Saint Charles Theatre, 1843), Leopold Charles Augustin Carrière (flutist of the French Opera, 1842–73), and M L. Fourmestreau (first oboe of the French Opera, 1843–69). Cioffi, who was a popular trombonist in the French Opera Orchestra during the late 1830s, taught his instrument in New Orleans.[44]

MUSIC EDUCATION DURING AND AFTER THE CIVIL WAR

During the war many musicians left the city, but Mme Boyer remained. In March and April 1863, she advertised that she was available to teach music, especially solfège.[45] Curto, too, remained and taught both amateurs and at least one who became professional (his most famous student, Minnie Hauk).[46] Julie

Calvé (Mrs. Charles) Boudousquié returned just after the war was over and announced "to her former students and to those families who know her reputation, that she is again teaching voice."[47] The Institute Saint Charles was open during the war, and on July 29, 1865, the music students of Mlle Laudumiez on piano and Mme Cambier on voice gave their final concert there.[48] Most of the musicians in the French Opera Orchestra left after the siege, and it was only in 1867 that the orchestra was again at full strength; and so the lessons by those members who taught would have been curtailed during the years 1862 to 1867.

By 1867 musical life in New Orleans was beginning to return to normal, though only seldom would the city experience the grandeur that existed before the war. Some new teachers appeared. Among them was M A. Duquesnay (Le Mercier du Quesnay), who was active from 1867 to at least 1879.[49] Some of his vocal students were church choristers, though he taught other facets of music as well. There were returnees, as well, most notably Eugène Prévost, the former conductor of the French Opera. Instead of returning as a conductor, however, he returned as a teacher.[50] He created the Orphéon Louisianais, which had its first meeting on January 14, 1868. This was both a school and a performing organization. He opened classes for adult men, young men, and boys from seven to fourteen years old. The aim of the Orphéon Louisianais was to contribute to the development of musical taste among young people and help nurture instrumentalists and singers. There is no evidence that this organization lasted past Eugene Prévost's death in 1872, but the idea persisted when the new Orphéon Français opened in 1881.

After the war, both Curto and Boudousquié continued as the preeminent vocal teachers in the city. In November 1869, Curto was professor of music in the normal and high schools of New Orleans.[51] He also taught the students at Saint Patrick's Church,[52] and he may have taught as well at the Ursuline Convent.[53] His pupils, seemingly all girls and women, were abundant and often performed in choirs and choruses in concerts throughout the city.[54] The best sang solos; such were Mlle Mamie G. Preis, who gave a vocal and instrumental concert at Werlein Hall on May 2, 1885,[55] and Mlle Baumann, who gave her vocal and instrumental concert at the French Opera House three days later.[56] Curto was much admired by his students, who took care of him in his old age.[57] When someone accused him of begging for money from his former students, Curto explained that he never asked for money from them, even from those who became famous, such as Minnie Hauk.[58]

Julie Calvé (Mrs. Boudousquié) returned to New Orleans in 1865 and quickly became the breadwinner in the family. Her husband was not rehired as director of the French Opera, and, after he died on August 24, 1866, she devoted much of the rest of her life to teaching. Her spectacular singing career had earned her a huge following in the city, so she was able to attract many gifted young female singers. For a few years she was associated with the Institute Saint Louis, Dauphine Street, where she teamed up with Lavillebeuvre as a music teacher.[59] The concerts performed by her pupils in private homes and in large concert halls were major events in the city for twenty-five years.[60] In some of the earlier concerts she performed on the programs along with her students;[61] later her students did her honor by the quality of their singing. As Placide Canonge stated, "after conquering even Paris with her singing, [she] has now conquered as a professor."[62] Just as Curto sent some of his pupils to fame in New York and Europe, so did Boudousquié. Mme Anita Kinen, a native of New Orleans, a pupil of Mme Boudousquié, and an amateur singer, scored a success in Paris in 1889 as an interpreter of the music of Widor.[63] The best tribute to her success as a vocal teacher came from the critic L. Placide Canonge: "Among different events, we spoke to you of the recital (annual audition) of the pupils of Mme Charles Boudousquié, which will take place at Grunewald Hall tomorrow. We said that the remarkable pupils are of a good number in this class, and that these bright students, so excellently directed in the delicate study of singing, are possessed by some voices of true value."[64]

> Mrs. Boudousquié, after such a distinguished career on the stages of Paris and New Orleans—she has never sung in provincial houses, which is a distinct advantage—has acquired profound experience in teaching. She does not rush the students; she trains the ear by her method. "Polish without cease and repolish" goes the expression. She applies this maxim to singing. At the risk of abandoning her own preferences, she does not praise. She knows the danger of too much praise, too much exaggeration. The student whose musical education is in her hands finds invariably in her the loving care that assures us the good (vocal) effects, indisputably, which I discussed in an article that I published yesterday.[65]
>
> Once the student is studying a particular piece, the very judicious and authoritative teacher does not allow the student to leave one page until the correct effect, as much as possible, has been obtained. To remain fixed on the same spot in the same composition may seem monotonous, or too fastidious, if you wish a more accented word; but soon the student recognizes the truth in this way of proceeding, and the step once cut, one will realize that tomorrow's work is that much easier, simpler.
>
> Finding again the same difficulties, she knows how to conquer them; the horizon is enlarged, the path is smoother without always having to find a

guide to show the way. The passage that always plagued you and made you nervous, that you pondered too long, you now can resolve quickly. This conscientious fidelity to a reasonable, logical method can sometimes alienate a student who is impatient to reach the results, but such has not been the case with the artist with whom we are concerned.

Madame Boudousquié's class always increases in size and we do not believe that we deceive anyone that she sometimes refuses some students. When she produces those who appear in public, they show that they have made serious progress; it is with some pleasure to hear them. That is not a risky statement by us; it will be proven correct once again tomorrow. See you there.

Besides Curto and Boudousquié, the most significant voice teachers in New Orleans during the 1870s and 1880s were M Van Hufflen and Mrs. James (Corinne) Nott. Van Hufflen, a singer in the French Opera, was active in New Orleans during the 1870s. His pupils performed in at least one concert, on April 20, 1876, at Grunewald Hall,[66] and his most successful student was Miss Kate Thayer, who was the daughter of New Orleanian Fred N. Thayer; by 1878 she was singing "with great success" in New York and Baltimore.[67]

Mrs. James Nott first appeared in New Orleans in the mid-1880s when she was teaching at the Locquet-Leroy Institute. On February 28, 1885, her pupils gave a concert there, and the critic of *L'Abeille* was ecstatic: "une brillante inauguration."[68] She remained a powerful teacher until May 1892, when she appears to have left the city. During those seven years she presented her students in more concerts than did any other individual teacher, and she herself often sang a song or two.[69] After the initial recital in 1885, she seems to have taught without further association with the Locquet-Leroy Institute; she may have taught at the Picard Institute or on her own.[70] Among her students was Miss Jeanne Faure, who spent the years 1885 to 1887 in Dresden, Germany, studying voice, and then returned for a grand concert at Grunewald Hall on Wednesday, November 30, 1887.[71] By the fall of 1889, Faure was herself a professor of voice in New Orleans.[72]

Although there were many piano teachers in New Orleans during the last quarter of the nineteenth century, none could compare to Marguerite Elie Samuel (see part II, chapter 9). She returned from her studies at the Paris Conservatoire briefly in 1865–66, but then went back to Paris to marry and bear three children. After the marriage failed, she returned to New Orleans permanently in the fall of 1877 and immediately began to teach and concertize.[73] She continued to teach until the beginning of the twentieth century, and many of her concerts included some of her best students.[74] Her tastes in music had been formed in

France and Germany, where she mingled with some of the greatest musicians of the age, and she imparted these tastes to her students. She was a good citizen and participated in various local societies and organizations, including the Musicians' Guild and the Women's Committee for the Chicago Exposition of 1893.

A pair of outstanding piano teachers were Hubert Rolling and later his son, William. Although Hubert was active before the war, he reached his high stature as a teacher afterwards.[75] On Saturday, May 14, 1881, William Rolling joined his father in presenting their pupils in concert,[76] and thereafter most of their student recitals were joint.

There were several excellent violin teachers in New Orleans during the last quarter of the nineteenth century. Chief among them were Mark Kaiser (see part II, chapter 10) and Theodore Curant (part II, chapter 12). Both appeared in recitals with their students and often had joint recitals. Among Kaiser's favored students was Joe Leopoldo,[77] while one of Curant's was Horace Peters, a graduate of the Leipzig Conservatory.[78] Henry Wehrman Jr. began his career as a teacher of violin and mandolin in the 1890s.

Léon Prévost, son of Eugène, returned to New Orleans from France in the fall of 1873 and announced to his friends and former students that he was again "teaching solfège, harmony, piano, etc., either privately or in class."[79] Mme M. Prévost, who was Léon's sister, taught young female vocal and piano pupils during the 1880s.[80]

A partial list of piano teachers in New Orleans during the last quarter of the century includes Professor F. Pothonier, Professor M. Delcroix, Mme Pauline Blache, Miss Louise Malie, Mme H. H. Wulff, and Miss Grace Kellogg. All seem to have taught beginners and intermediates. Blache and Malie taught at Grunewald's and Werlein's, respectively. Vocal teachers included Mme Pauline Blache, Professor L. Emile Richard, Professor Jules Cartier, Mlle Varelli Jauquet (formerly of the French Opera), Mme Devrient, Miss Kate Dykers, Mrs. A. T. Vaurigaud, M Emmanuel Lafarge (tenor of the French Opera), Mrs. E. Chaillot, and Miss Florence Huberwald. Some taught at schools or music stores, but most taught privately in their homes. Among the flute teachers were A. Livain and Leopold Carrière. A few other teachers who taught music without specifying a particular instrument were Madame Uranie Cambier, Mrs. Widow J. D. Murr, Mme Buck, Mlle Marie Roubion, Mrs. J. L. Vincent, and Miss Delphine Points. Mr. Wells taught mandolin and guitar.

Before the war Mme J. F. Locquet had her own studio where she taught music.[81] Her studio was taken over by Ms. Burr and continued to offer music lessons for many years. In September 1872, Locquet joined with Ms. Leroy to establish a new institute.[82] Located on Prytania Street, the Locquet-LeRoy Institute continued through the 1880s. It offered to young women studies in English, French, and music. Several distinguished teachers, whom we have already mentioned, taught there; among these were Julie Boudousquié and Corinne Nott.[83]

Besides the Locquet-LeRoy Institute, several conservatories were started in New Orleans after the war. Theophilus Masac was president of the New Orleans Conservatory (Conservatoire de la Nouvelle-Orleans) when it was founded in September 1871, and it was located at 90 Baronne Street.[84] M A. Miari boasts that he was a professeur at the conservatory when he gave a concert on Friday, May 3, 1872, at the German Company Hall. Miari was assisted at the concert by M Van Hufflen and many talented professionals and amateurs, at least some of whom were also associated with this conservatory.[85] The following September, Mrs. William R. Evans was director, and it was now located at 207 Canal Street. Instruction was offered in piano, voice, solfège, harmony, violin, violoncello, parlor organ, and other instruments. Room and board were provided for out-of-towners.[86] Much later, in 1889, the New Orleans Opera Association proposed starting a conservatory, and from 1891 to at least 1895 there was such an institution directed by Emile Malmquist.

The most successful conservatory in New Orleans in the nineteenth century was the Pilcher Conservatory. Founded by William Henry Pilcher in 1885, the conservatory had a large curriculum taught by some of the best teachers in the city. Pilcher himself taught piano and organ, and other members of his family taught there over the ensuing twenty-five years.[87] When William Henry went on tour, his wife ran the conservatory. Wehrman and other leading violinists were on the faculty. The conservatory had a student orchestra and choirs with weekly rehearsals.[88] Concerts were presented on a regular basis featuring students and faculty. Most of the concerts were at the conservatory itself, and a few were at local churches and other venues. The press quickly noted the high quality of the performances as a result of the high standards of education.[89] Eventually there were hundreds of students who attended and who came not only from New Orleans but from other places in Louisiana and outside the state. (For details on this conservatory see part II, chapter 14.)

The most significant competitor to the Pilcher Conservatory was the Orphéon Français. This was not a conservatory but rather a society that included an educational component. George L. O'Connell was in charge and conducted numerous concerts during the late 1880s and 1890s. A typical concert including students occurred on March 28, 1890.[90] The student orchestra had twenty students (four violin 1, four violin 2, one viola, one string bass, two flutes, two clarinets, three cornets á piston, one saxophone, one trombone, and piano), accompanied by MM O'Connell and Paul Brunet; it played two pieces. In addition, members of the faculty (H. Wehrman, violin 1; J. Voorhies, violin 2; J. Wiegel, viola; J. Wortmann, string bass; F. Ramos, flute; and P. Brunet, piano) performed a sextet by Fauconier.

While the more musically inclined students sought private lessons with a single teacher or in a music school, the vast majority of young people in New Orleans learned music in their regular schools. Usually we learn about them when they performed at graduations and other special school events.[91] Occasionally they performed full concerts, such as on March 19, 1870, when female students of Professor Sipp at Mrs. Stamps's Academy at 404 Carondelet Street sang "difficult" choruses from Mozart's Mass No. 12 and Haydn's *Creation*.[92] Another occurred on June 28, 1872, when the (black) Gravier School Glee Club gave a concert at Lyceum Hall. There were solos, duets, and choruses: ballads and comic songs, accompanied by Professor A. P. Williams.[93] On March 8, 1873, Mme Romey (pianist), who was supervisor of the Haute-Ecole of the Central District, brought her students to a grand concert at the Exposition Hall on Saint Charles for the benefit of fire victims. Mme Zeiss-Denis, M Van Hufflen and M Caulier (violinist) appeared with a choir of a hundred young girls.[94] There were sporadic concerts of students at the Carnatz Institute (corner of Washington and Coliseum, January 6, 1876); the pupils of the Saint Charles Institute (January 26, 1876); pupils of the Saint Louis Institute, Mme Mathey, director (March 29, 1879); and students at the Matthey-Ricard Institute (April 22, 1896).[95]

Brass bands were also a feature of many Catholic schools during the late 1860s and 1870s, and this tradition continues to the present day. The nineteenth-century bands did not perform at football games but rather at various school functions such as fairs, exhibitions of the students (which showed their rhetorical and musical training), and graduations. They also played at church benefits. A typical occasion occurred on Monday, December 21, 1868, when a (wind?) band made up of boys from Christian Brothers Parochial School played at a fair to benefit the new Saint Joseph's Church.[96] Another such occasion was on Sunday, January 24, 1870, when the boys of Sainte Mary's Orphan Boys Asylum played in a band led by Charles Bothe at Saint Louis Cathedral to raise money for their asylum.[97] John Eckert led a school band at Saint Joseph's School graduation at the National Theater on June 2–3, 1872,[98] and he followed it on June 3–7, 1872, with the College Band at Sainte Mary's graduation at the Varieties Theater.[99] The opening of the Algiers Fair on July 7, 1872, included boys from Sainte Mary's Jefferson College and their brass band.[100]

Sometime in the 1890s the teaching of music in the public schools of New Orleans was mandated by the School Board. The rule did not go unchallenged, but it stuck anyway. In 1896, a young teacher in a boys' public school originally objected to the introduction of musical studies in the classroom, but changed his or her mind.

> I must confess that we teachers as a general rule looked dubiously at the regulation to introduce the study of music in the public schools when it was first agitated by the board. We began the work with many misgivings, and dreaded the increase of duties, and such a duty as that of teaching sight reading in music to large classes. But what a help the new order of things has become to us. Music touches the little child as we have found out few things can; the children have taken up the study with a zest that lends a charm to all other studies, and, instead of our burdens being made heavier, they have been lightened so much that we look forward to the half hour devoted to singing and music as not only a relaxation and pleasure, but a wonderful means of brightening up the children and helping them to take up the remaining duties of the day when their interest begins to flag. Now I teach boys; we teachers in boys' schools especially dreaded the introduction of music; but instead of disturbing the discipline, it has induced better order, and proved a noble refining influence. The wisdom of the school board in adding music to the curriculum has been fully demonstrated.[101]

After many years of operating independently, the individual music teachers decided, in January 1889, to band together in an umbrella organization entitled the New Orleans Music Teachers' Guild. The *Picayune* reported:

> The purpose of the organization will be to encourage a taste for music among the people, which will not only be a benefit to the teachers themselves, but may eventually lead to the establishment of a conservatory of music, which is very much to be desired. New Orleans is admitted to be a music-loving city, the only place in this country where the love of the art is sufficiently intense to support a regular opera. It is therefore desirable that every possible effort should be made to foster and encourage this predilection, and no better way could have been thought of than the organization in question.
>
> It is intended to give grand concerts periodically, in which the best talent of the city will be called into service, so that not only will the existing enthusiasm be maintained but further increased.[102]

Initially the Musicians' Guild, as it became known, attracted only women teachers, but men soon joined as well. The idea of a conservatory was soon dropped for financial reasons, though the existence of the Pilcher Conservatory may have contributed to the squelching of this idea. Rather, it was decided by the membership that it "should be confined, for the present, to developing and cultivating musical talent and taste by meeting once a week either for rehearsal or for the enjoyment of perfected music work, concerted or solo, contributed by the members of the association under the superior direction of the musical leader; the aim being to bring the best talent of the city together, to make teachers of ability known to the public, further develop their natural talent, and knowledge of music—most especially classical music—and to do the same for students." As reported in the *Picayune*:

> The guild struggled along bravely through the long, weary summer months, meeting twice a week at the room so kindly lent them. As the first fall month inaugurating the busy season approached, the membership having surprisingly and encouragingly increased until it counted between seventy-five and eighty members; the treasury enriched by a liberal donation from Mr. D. H. Holmes, besides the dues of members; and the necessity of serious work being realized, it was unanimously voted that a suitable room be taken and that the musical director be paid a salary, the only salaried officer of the guild.
>
> A handsome room at No. 240 Baronne street was engaged; Mr. Werlein generously loaned the guild four pianos for three months, and the members set to work earnestly and enthusiastically, in addition to their private guild concerts, which occur once a month, to prepare for a grand concert to be given at Grunewald Hall on the 11th of December, which, while it gives the public the opportunity of supporting the association, will afford them the privilege of hearing some of the best talent of the guild.
>
> This plucky young organization is nobly endeavoring to firmly establish here an institution which is both charitable and for the cultivation of art.
>
> Following are the names of members composing the officers of the guild, the board of directors and the standing committees:
>
> Officers—Miss Mary Wilson, president; Miss Mary Abbott, vice-president; Mrs. Margaret C. Bisland, secretary; Miss Mary Scott, treasurer; Miss Amelia Cammack, librarian; Mme Marguerite E. Samuel, musical director.
>
> Board of Directors—Mrs. Luela Chapman, Mrs. Pinekney Smith, Mrs. T. S. Kennedy, Miss B. McCoard, Mrs. Kate Shaw, Mrs. M. Whitfield, Miss C.

Durrivé, Mrs. M. S. Gallegher, Mrs. Gruenevelt, Mrs. Schubey, Miss A. Bradford, Mrs. Ike Scott, Mrs. R. L. Macmurdo, Mrs. Yuille. . . .

The names of new members wishing to join the guild must be indorsed by two members already belonging to the association.[103]

Except for Samuel, none of the officers were leading musicians in the city. Yet their names and their cause attest to a vigorous musical education scene in New Orleans at the end of the century. At least one prominent teacher, Mrs. Charles Boudousquié, was not an officer but belonged. Her students participated in the concert on December 11, 1889, which took place despite the death of Jefferson Davis a few days before.[104] The guild prospered over the next decade and became an important vehicle for music education and concerts in New Orleans.

Since the purpose of the guild was music education, the president, Mary Wilson, decided that the members needed to hear from one of America's leading musicologists about the history and present state of music in the world. From January 17 to 19, 1890, the famous Professor Louis C. Elson of Boston lectured to the members of the guild on "The Geneology [sic] of Music," "German Music," "English Music," and "Scottish Music."[105]

At its first annual meeting, on Saturday, February 1, 1890, the guild decided that it needed a vocal and an instrumental instructor, and Samuel, McMurdo [sic], and Scott were appointed to find one.[106] By April, Professor Carl Weiss was selected for that position.[107] That fall, Weiss organized a singing class of fifty pupils, mostly women, who "were carried through several difficult vocal exercises, after which the pupils were allowed to sing their favorite selections."[108] From the *Picayune*:

> The ladies and gentlemen will be trained together this season, receiving instructions in vocal music on Monday evening and instrumental on Wednesday.
>
> Once a month the guild will give a concert, charging as low admission as possible, in order to encourage the patronage of concerts and thus advance the cause of musical progress in this city.

Eventually the vocal class met on Wednesday and the instrumental class on Monday. In the fall of 1890, Weiss replaced Samuel as musical director, which by the beginning of the guild's second season numbered 120 members and by January 1891 had grown to 133. Mark Kaiser joined and performed on its November 26, 1890, concert, which also included selections by the choir and several other music teachers.[109] The guild expanded its operations to include important visiting artists in performances in New Orleans; the first of these was Miss Nealy Stevens, "distinguished pianist and pupil of Muskowski, Kullak and Listz [sic]," who performed on January 19.[110] A month later, on February 25, 1891, there was a typical monthly concert:[111]

> The soiree musicale given last night by the Musicians' Guild at its rooms, No. 135 Canal street, was well attended and proved to be a most enjoyable affair. The programme, though short, was varied and interesting throughout. Mrs. and Miss Whitfield and Misses Trapolin played the sixth symphony of Haydn. The choral class rendered Rubinstein's "Night," a two part song. Mrs. Bengnot displayed her skill as a pianist in one of Chopin's nocturnes. Mrs. Wirth sang Liszt's "Loreli" with good effect. Mr. Mark Kaiser and Mrs. Gallagher, violin and piano, favored the audience with "Barcarolle," by Bohm, and "Introduction et Gavotte." Miss Henderson played Brahm's [sic] "Rhapsodie." The soft, melodious voices of Mrs. Yuille and Miss Socola blended most harmoniously in the duo "Breezes of Light," by Gounod. Miss Mayer, an accomplished pianist, played a selection from Schubert-Liszt, most delightfully. The "Marche Funebre," third symphony of Beethoven, was given with deep feeling and exceptional delicacy. The exquisitely shaded playing merited unlimited praise, and the hearty applause which followed it was well deserved. Professor Weiss was the musical director of the evening.

On April 8 the program consisted only of the works of Mozart, while on June 17 the varied program included works by Beethoven, Weber, Grieg, and Raff, as well as Mozart.[112] These concerts were held at Werlein's Music Store on Canal Street, but by January 1894 the guild's concerts were being held at the new Sophie Newcomb College in the Garden District. At a "rehearsal" there on January 27, 1894, the guild's performers were divided into junior and senior groups.[113] The former (four young women) played the "allegro movement of Haydn's first symphony" on two pianos and the latter (four adult women) performed Mendelssohn's *Fingal's Cave* Overture on two pianos. Other works included the "Intermezzo" from *Cavalleria Rusticana,* a Mendelssohn concerto, and Robert Schumann's Symphony No. 1. Weiss had left his position by January 1893, when the guild sought another musical director,[114] and by the concert on January 27, 1894, Professor Frank Simms was in charge. Simms was also the organist of Saint Paul's Church. According to the *Picayune,* "almost every musician of note and lover of music in this music-loving city" was a member of the guild.[115] A concert on January 27, 1895, again at Sophie Newcomb Memorial Hall and under Simms's direction, included works by Mendelssohn, Gade, Spohr, Sullivan, and Beethoven; and a concert the following April 20 included works by Schubert, Mozart, Vieuxtemps, Cowen, and Beethoven.[116] There were more concerts in 1896 and 1897 and beyond.

The guild had succeeded in its original aims, and with the Pilcher Conservatory provided institutional umbrellas for the furtherance of music education in New Orleans. With the abundance of music teachers, the youth as well as the adults of the city were assured a continuance of the classical music tradition that during the nineteenth century had made New Orleans a leading center for music—concert music and not just opera.

6

Women in the Musical Life of the City in the Eighteenth and Nineteenth Centuries

Women have always played an important role in the musical life of New Orleans, so much so that to write a separate chapter on women in the music of New Orleans seems almost superfluous or redundant. Yet there is a sexual bias towards men both in the sources of nineteenth-century music history and in the general conception of gender roles in the commercial world of music. If women instrumental performers, for example, perform like men, it is an uncanny feat that becomes the focus of attention, and the implication is that women are supposed to perform like women (less vigorously) and that that is their place. It is men alone who were pictured as engaged in the commerce of music. These are, of course, false images, and musical activities beyond the home were indeed often performed by women in New Orleans, even in the eighteenth and nineteenth centuries. And some women, of course, achieved an excellence that merits their inclusion in any history of the musical life of the city. Therefore, in addition to pointing out some of the general roles of women in music, it may be useful to highlight the careers of some of the most interesting women in the history of the music of the city.

From the beginning of European settlement, the role of music was highlighted in the education of women. One of the first notable achievements of the women of New Orleans in the field of music was the creation, in 1727, of the oldest school of music in America still to exist.[1] In that year a small group of Ursuline nuns came to New Orleans and founded a convent school for the education of the young girls now beginning to populate the new colony. Singing hymns and moralistic songs was part of the curriculum. In 1754 the nuns received a gift of a songbook that provided 294 such songs, giving us an ear into the music sung at the convent school. Entitled *Nouvelles Poésies Spirituelles et Morales sur les plus Beaux Airs de la Musique Français et Italienne avec la Bas,* it was originally copied by someone with the initials "C.D." in 1736, and it is drawn from a larger choir book printed in France in 1737.[2] The songs are by various composers famous in Italy and France during the seventeenth and eighteenth centuries, including André Campra, François Couperin, Louis-Nicolas Clérambault, Henry Desmarest, Michel Lambert, Jean-Baptiste Lully, Marin Marais, and Louis Marchand.

The songs range from easy to moderately difficult, and there are some ornaments, typical of French song of the first half of the eighteenth century, to challenge the vocally more dexterous. Each song is accompanied by a basso continuo. Many are strophic, some with strophic variations. The hauntingly beautiful "La Solitude" by Marin Marais, for example, uses a short ostinato bass over which a soloist (teacher) presents simple, varied phrases, each echoed by a group (students); this is ideal for the beginners. On the other hand, Henry Desmarest's "Grandeur de Dieu" and "Sa Puissance, Sa Bonté" are short dramatic songs with wide ranges, leaps, and ornaments that would be more suitable for intermediate students. All the songs are attractive and would have inspired the young women not only to endorse the morality preached in the text but also to continue to sing them for aesthetic enjoyment for the rest of their lives.

Other Catholic schools for women, in the nineteenth century, followed the pattern of the Ursuline School.[3] One of them, Curto's school for orphan young girls, has been discussed elsewhere in this book. This means that the vast majority of women in New Orleans during the nineteenth century—a city where the Catholic religion was dominant—were musically literate and trained to appreciate the great art music that they themselves perpetuated. This music was brought from the church into the home and into everyday life. And it affected not just Catholics.

The stereotypical image of the wealthy white or mulatto woman who runs the household on the plantations in and around New Orleans in the eighteenth and much of the nineteenth century is not entirely unfounded. Such women had a lot to do with the managing of the household, education of the children, and entertainment for family and friends. Many of the elite young girls traveled from the outlying plantations to the Vieux Carré—the old center of New Orleans—for instruction at the Ursuline School, but some young girls on these estates had to be educated at home. Music was part of this education and an important part of the entertainment. The mother or aunt or some other mature woman would start the young person off with basic musical knowledge; then private music instructors were brought in to teach more advanced skills, especially if the pupil showed some talent. Members of the family participated in home musicales, and proper young women were expected to sing or play such instruments as the piano, the harp, or the flute. These were family activities, but girls were also expected to entertain with music when guests arrived. When a young woman was advanced enough in her instrument to have a favorite group of compositions which she liked to perform, she traveled to one of the music stores in the Vieux Carré and had those compositions bound in albums, hundreds of which survive today in New Orleans. The music could be Mozart or Mendelssohn or the latest arrangements of opera tunes or schottisches (popular dances) for piano; or they could be Creole songs, French romances, German Lieder, or popular English ditties.

The Ursuline School and other Catholic schools in the nineteenth century often provided education for young girls who were abandoned or orphaned, and presumably music was part of the education.[4] For those women—white, black, or mulatto—who were not in charge of the households on the plantations or who did not manage large homes in the Vieux Carré or Garden District and for whom education in the Catholic schools was not an option, music was also a part of everyday life. From the lullabies that they sang to their infants to the dances for all ages that they accompanied by singing, handclapping, and drumming, they provided a steady spate of music for education and entertainment. They did not necessarily learn their music from music tutors or conservatory-trained professors of music, and they probably could not read music, but they learned orally from their families and their peers. And while the women on the plantations and in fine homes kept the musical traditions of European art music alive, the poorer women cultivated various ethnic and folk traditions as their inheritance. The greatness of the music of New Orleans depended on these diverse musical cultures and their eventual interaction and fusion, and there is no doubt that the wealth of musical talent that this city has produced is an outgrowth of the home environments that for nearly three hundred years women nurtured privately among their families.

But besides the important environment of home music, which was largely directed by women, we find women outside the home as well. They were composers, stage performers, conductors, publishers, engravers, professional teachers, entrepreneurs, and business dealers. They worked with and competed successfully against their male counterparts. Their patronage was as large as that of the men, and they worked hard to maintain high levels of professionalism in all aspects of music even if, in many cases, maintaining amateur status.

Once opera was established in New Orleans in 1796, there was a steady stream of women singing on the stages of the city. This continued throughout the nineteenth century and until well into the twentieth. Some of them were world famous, and their appearances in New Orleans were only brief. Jenny Lind (1820–87), for example, perhaps the most heralded soprano of the nineteenth century, gave thirteen concerts in the city from February 10 to March 8, 1851. These were not opera performances, though much of the music performed was from operas and was greatly appealing to this particular audience. That New Orleanians were experts in opera comes from the city having regular repertory opera companies from the beginning of the century, and on the very nights that Lind performed in the English Saint Charles Theatre, competing performances of complete operas were staged as usual in the rival French Théâtre d'Orléans.

On the first program, for example, Lind sang an aria from Bellini's *Sonnambula* and another from Mozart's *The Magic Flute* and joined her baritone singing partner Signor Belleti in a duet from Rossini's *Il Turco in Italia*. Belleti sang two Rossini arias from *The Siege of Corinth* and *The Barber of Seville* ("Largo al Factotum"). For the rest of the program, Lind sang a Swedish folk song and an unusual song by Meyerbeer for soprano and two flutes; the orchestra performed two overtures by Auber, and violinist Joseph Burke performed *Rondo Russe* by Charles De Bériot. The other concert programs were much the same, and frequently arias and songs from one event would recur on a later program. While in New Orleans, Lind found time to visit the girls' orphanage and tell the occupants that they were lucky to be so well taken care of after the tragedy of losing their parents.[5] She also devoted the proceeds (over $4,500) from her February 26 concert to various local charities.[6] She had to postpone two concerts because of a cold, but rather than canceling them, she rescheduled them. It was announced that she was to leave New Orleans for Natchez and Saint Louis via the steamship *Magnolia* on March 8, but when the boat was delayed for a day, she agreed to give one unscheduled concert on that evening since the demand to hear her was so great in the city.[7] Of course, one never is sure whether these delays and extra concerts following the "absolutely final" performance were honestly come by or the result of Barnum's uncanny sense of viable publicity stunts.

Many other prominent female singers visited the city, including Henrietta Sontag (1806–54), who was supposed to start her residency on February 6, 1854, but wisely postponed it until a week later. Had she performed on the sixth she would have come just three days after native son and superstar Louis Moreau Gottschalk (1829–69) had thrilled the audience in New Orleans with one of his spectacular concerts, and that was a very hard act to follow. Gottschalk performed his second concert on February 3 when he led ten pianos in a patriotic show and performed his own works, including a premier. Sontag gave seven concerts between February 13 and March 18, 1854, together with the young violinist Camille Urso. She also appeared with the Italian Opera Company during the month of March at the Saint Charles Theatre, singing Zerlina in *Don Giovanni* and the title role in *Lucrezia Borgia*. Furthermore, she found time to sing in a program of sacred music, including excerpts from *Messiah* and *The Creation*, as well as the complete *Stabat Mater* of Rossini. In anticipation of her fourth recital on February 17, the critic for *The Bee* wrote, "Thus far her career amongst us has been brilliantly successful. To-night should crown and consumate [sic] her triumphe [sic]."[8] Sontag then went on to Mexico, where she triumphed in *Lucrezia Borgia* as part of the Italian Opera Company, but suddenly she was stricken with cholera and died on June 16. As Nicolas Slonimsky reports, "her beautiful voice[,] . . . her striking physical appearance, and her natural acting abilities led to her reputation as the equal or superior to all other divas of the age."[9]

The situation with Adelina Patti (1843–1919) was different. Her career was not cut short, like Lind's and Sontag's, and she appeared and reappeared in New Orleans over a half century. Adelina first came to New Orleans as a child in the company of her older sister Amalia Patti (1831–1915) and Amalia's husband, pianist and impresario Maurice Strakosch (1825–87). Amalia and Strakosch made their debuts in the city during three concerts beginning on April 21, 1851, together with soprano Theresa Parodi who, as one of the world's foremost interpreters of the roles of Norma and Lucrezia Borgia at the time, was the main feature, and Amalia stayed long enough to perform in opera performances from May 14 to 26. The group came back in April of the following year. Then on February 26, 1853, Amalia returned to the city with Strakosch, the famous violinist Ole Bull, and her nine-year-old sister, Adelina. According to Adelina's own testimony, she was a very difficult child and made life for her sister and brother-in-law impossible,[10] yet the New Orleans public who heard her for the first time fell in love with her immediately. She performed in all six concerts between February 16 and March 22. As one reviewer said, "the young Adeline Patti marched this evening from one success to another and conquered the sympathy of her audience."[11] When Strakosch brought Bull and Adelina back to New Orleans the following year, her love affair with the city was cemented. Beginning on February 14, 1854, Bull, Strakosch, and Adelina performed in Mechanics' Hall. Daring to compete that night with another star singer—Henrietta Sontag—the trio proved that the city had enough patrons of music to fill two halls simultaneously. Adelina, *L'Abeille* reported, "was received with all the honors. The lovely *soprano* of this gifted child—so clear, limpid, bell-like and easy in its range—seems to have gathered strength and to have acquired increased flexibility since we last heard her."[12] Amalia did not appear on the programs of 1854. In turn, Adelina did not perform with her sister, Strakosch, and Parodi when they returned for twelve concerts from January 3 to February 23, 1856, but she did team up with the young New York violinist Paul Julien for three concerts in New Orleans on March 29 and April 1 and 4, 1856. Mostly she sang the same arias on all three programs, substituting one piece in each case.

Adelina did not appear again in New Orleans until the end of 1860.[13] She came to sing concerts but was asked to join the opera company at the newly built French Opera House (then called Théâtre de l'Opéra). For four months she was the prima donna of the company. Her roles included the title role in *Lucia* (Donizetti), Leonore in *Il Trovatore* (Verdi), Lady Harriet in *Martha* (Flotow), Dinorah in *Le Pardon de Ploërmel* (Meyerbeer), Valentine in *Les Huguenots* (Meyerbeer), and leading parts in *The Barber of Seville* (Rossini) and *Rigoletto* (Verdi). For special occasions (benefit performances for her colleagues) she also sang segments from *La Sonnambula* (Bellini), *La Traviata* (Verdi), *Ernani* (Verdi), and on two occasions the "Mad Scene" from *Lucia*. In between she found time to give concerts in Baton Rouge, Natchez, Vicksburg, and Jackson.

It was twenty-one years before Adelina returned to New Orleans, this time as a world-famous diva, but she had lost none of her popularity. The Saint Charles Theatre was packed beyond capacity on January 15, 1882, when she sang in *Faust* and *La Traviata* and on January 19 when she sang the fourth act of *Il Trovatore* with chorus and orchestra. In between, on January 17, she gave a concert where she sang "Ah! Fors' e loi" (*La Traviata*) and "Home Sweet Home" on the printed program and ended with two encores: "Coming thru the Rye" and the French romance "Si vous n'avez rien à me dire." Patti ended her visit with a Grand Farewell Concert on January 26 at noon; she sang arias from *Lucia* and the second act of *The Barber of Seville*. Adelina was back in February 1885 singing concert excerpts from *Martha, Linda di Chamounix* (Donizetti), *Faust,* and *Crispino e la Comare* (Luigi and Federico Ricci) and appearing in Her Majesty's Opera Company on January 27 as Violetta (*La Traviata*) and on January 30 in the title role of Rossini's *Sémiramide*. On December 20, 1886 she appeared with Sofia Scalchi in various operas directed by Luigi Arditi (1822–1903).

Adelina returned to New Orleans for the last time on February 6, 1904, fifty years after she made her debut as a nine-year-old. The *Picayune* critic noted that she had lost her upper register, and though she took good care of her voice and still had her natural stage presence, she had to transpose "The Jewel Song" from *Faust* down to a lower register so that she could get through the aria.[14] She also sang "Voi che Sapete" (*The Marriage of Figaro*), which she could still bring off. Coloratura and ornaments, however, were now for her a thing of the past.

Throughout the nineteenth century and into the beginning of the twentieth, New Orleans continued to host many of the leading prima donnas. To name just a few in the nineteenth century, there was soprano Adelaide Phillips (1833–82), adopted daughter of Jenny Lind, whose performance of "Una Voce poco Fa" (Rossini) on January 17, 1871, was received with favor. Carlotta Patti (1835–89), sister of Amalia and Adelina Patti, performed three grand concerts on December 17, 18, and 19, 1872, at Exposition Hall. Ilma de Murska (1836–89), Hungarian soprano who was known as the "Croatian Nightingale," sang at the Opera House on March 1 and 3, 1875, then gave concerts on March 5 and 6 at Grunewald Hall, returned to sing opera scenes on March 10, performed more concerts on March 12 and 13, sang Gilda in *Rigoletto* at the Opera House on March 13 and Lucia in *Lucia de Lammermoor* on March 17, and concluded with an Easter day concert (March 28) at Grunewald Hall. After leaving the city for a short spell to fulfil previous commitments, she returned on April 7 for more concerts.

The well-known Swedish soprano Christine Nilsson (1843–1921) was not well received when she sang on January 9 and 11, 1883. Emma Nevada (1859–1940), née Wixom, from the gold-rush city Nevada City, California, came with Her Majesty's Opera Company in January 1885 and sang in various operas, including *La Sonnambula*. She studied with Mathilde Marchesi in Vienna and became a favorite of Verdi's at La Scala in Milan. She returned on January 12, 1902, to perform at the Tulane Theatre with several instrumentalists, including Pablo Casals. The distinguished American soprano Clara Louise Kellogg (1842–91) gave a recital on Ash Wednesday, March 10, 1886, at the French Opera House, where she sang works from *Faust* ("The Jewel Song"), *Mefistofele* (Boito), and *Martha* (Flotow). Emma Romeldi gave a Grand Testimonial Operatic Concert on January 31, 1886, assisted by local artists. Miss Florence Huberwald came to Grunewald Hall on February 25, 1889, to sing an excerpt from *Charles VI* (Halévy) and another from Fauré's *Sancta Maria*. Mathilde Bruguière came on April 27, 1893. Ellen Beach Yaw (1869–1947), nicknamed "Lark Ellen," came first on December 26 and 29, 1894, and returned on March 15 and 16, 1897. Yaw was noted for a very high range, and her singing inspired Sir Arthur Sullivan to write the role of Sultana Zubedyah in *The Rose of Persia* (1899) specifically for her. The great Wagnerian soprano Lillian Nordica (1857–1914) sang seven works, including "Dich teure Halle" from *Tannhäuser,* on November 20, 1896 in the Athenaeum; she returned on January 22, 1907, for a performance of *La Gioconda.*

While Lind, Sontag, the Patti sisters, and all of the above were visitors to New Orleans, some women stars of the opera companies in New Orleans remained in the city, even after they no longer sang, and became honored citizens. Most were recruited initially by John Davis and other New Orleans opera impresarios from the best talent that Europe had to offer.[15] Davis and Caldwell went to Europe during the summers, sought out new young singers, signed them to contracts for at least a season, and brought them via boat from France to New Orleans.[16] Some left after a season and either returned to Europe or sought success in another American city. Others stayed, sang for years in the opera, and taught.

Probably the best soprano to have been brought to New Orleans and to have remained there for the rest of her life was Julie Calvé. Julie Calvé (apparently no relative of Emma Calvé, 1858–1942) was one of the most celebrated singers in nineteenth-century New Orleans. She was born in Rennes, France, in May 1815, and received her vocal training in France.[17] In 1837 John Davis of the Théâtre d'Orléans hired Calvé to be his prima donna for the upcoming season, and she made her debut in New Orleans on November 21, 1837, as Rosina in Rossini's *The Barber of Seville*. For nine seasons her lyrical soprano voice thrilled audiences not only in New Orleans but also in New York during the French Opera's tours there in 1843 and 1845.[18] She retired after the 1845–46 season. On May 29, 1858, she married Charles Boudousquié, who was soon to become director of the new opera house on Bourbon and Toulouse streets that opened at the end of 1859 (the French Opera House). At the outbreak of the Civil War, Julie and Charles left the city and did not return until a few weeks after hostilities ended (April 9, 1865). At that point she advertised in the newspapers that she was back in New Orleans and ready to teach voice, while Charles, never able to regain his position at the French Opera House, started to work at an auction house. For many years she taught in New Orleans (see pages 110–112), and she died there on December 30, 1898.

Vera Brodsky Lawrence, in her *Strong on Music,* waxes eloquently on the powerful impression that Calvé made on New Yorkers in the summer of 1843 and 1845.[19] She was "the enchanting young French actress/singer," "the latest toast of the town," "displaying [her] fascinating singing and acting gifts," "superb," "powerfully charming." She appeared in an amazingly large number of operas in 1843, all of which were in her New Orleans repertory: *L'Ambassadrice* (Auber), *Le Domino Noir* (Auber), *L'Éclair* (Halévy), *Le Pré aux Clercs* (Hérold), *Le Chalet* (Adam), *Les Diamants de la Couronne* (Auber), *The Daughter of the Regiment* (Donizetti), *Cosimo* (Eugène Prévost), *Anna Bolena* (Donizetti), *Le Postillon de Longjumeau* (Adam), *Les Rendez-vous Bourgeois* (Nicolo Isouard), and *Le Rossignol* (Lebrun). Lawrence cites specifically a review of the New York premier of *The Daughter of the Regiment* in the *Herald* on July 21, 1843: "Never had [Calvé] been so severely 'tested,' or so triumphant. 'Applause is an inadequate term,' declared the reviewer, nothing less than 'vehement cheering rewarded this truly talented Prima Donna.'" In 1845 she added to some of the above operas *La Favorite* (Donizetti), *La Juive* (Halévy), and *Robert le Diable* (Meyerbeer).[20]

Calvé was, of course, equally appreciated in New Orleans itself. That she rose quickly to the top position as prima donna by her second season in New Orleans is shown by the rancor with which the previous prima donna regarded her. Madame Ellermann was furious at the administration of the opera because she had come to be regarded as inferior to Calvé.[21] Ellermann was not a bad singer and had thrilled New Orleanians with her performances in the title role of *Norma*, but she was not as effective in the role of Alice in *Robert le Diable* as Calvé.

On the occasion of Calvé's benefit concert in the Salle d'Orléans on April 21, 1840, the reviewer in *L'Abeille* was swept away by the greatness of her singing:

> Yes, the performance on Tuesday was a great triumph for Miss Calvé, and, dare we say it, never has a triumph been better earned. Doesn't this delicious singer have the right to it, who has so often ravished us with the melodious accents of her voice, simultaneously both so clean and light? Doesn't this intelligent actress have the right to it, she who has grown each day with a singular success in the most diverse roles? Henriette, Rosine, Isabelle, Valentine, Angèle, Effy, Anne de Bouleyn, all these so very different women which our great composers have brought to life in their marvelous inspirations, has she not caused them to come to life under our eyes with incontestable superiority? It is our duty to take stock of all the pleasures that she has had us taste, and this duty everyone has enjoyed. Never has the public sympathy for an artist manifested itself so energetically: after the third act of Anne de Bouleyn where Miss Calvé exhibited her dramatic qualities so preciously and which seems so little compatible with her talent distinguished above all by grace and finesse, the bravas and the most frenetic clapping were heard, and when the artist reappeared, she was covered with a rain of flowers and bouquets, and the cheers, the thunder of hands began again. The enthusiasm that filled the entire hall was so energetic that it moved deeply the one for whom it was addressed; Miss Calvé was visibly moved: she said without doubt, in this instance so sweet and so glorious, that one should not forget the efforts and the work that was imposed on a public that had so generously thanked her. Can one pay too dearly for such witnesses of sympathy and admiration?[22]

On April 5, 1841, Calvé participated in a Grand Concert Spirituel given by M Eugene Prévost, then conductor of the Orchestra at the Théâtre d'Orléans. It was a spectacular event featuring orchestral music, a two-violin Symphonie Concertante by Rodolph Kreutzer performed by MM Elie and Milan (premiers violons du Théâtre d'Orléans), a clarinet solo, an oboe solo, various arias and ensembles by Rossini, Prévost, and Donizetti performed by Calvé and other members of the opera company at Théâtre d'Orléans, and a "Fantasia sur le Piano" by an unknown composer "exécutée par le jeune Gottschack [sic], élève de M Letellier." Over the next few years she was in demand to sing at benefits, no doubt because her presence on a program would guarantee a large audience.[23]

Very little is known about Kate Thayer, who appeared with her Grand Concert Company at Grunewald Hall on December 26–27, 1879.[24] Thayer was a native New Orleanian who had formed her own touring group, including several singers, a cornetist, an accompanist, and a virtuoso pianist, Theresa Carreño (see below). Thayer's father was a local "négociant" (wine merchant),[25] and Kate's singing career seems to have started very much as a part of the social life of the city, where she often performed for charities.[26] In 1879 "la jeune cantatrice orléanaise" was now risking her career on the success of this extensive tour, of which she was not only the star but also the manager, and the two concerts in New Orleans were the seventieth and seventy-first on her busy schedule.[27] On the first program she sang an aria from Verdi's *Nabucco,* Luigi Ardita's "Il Bacio" (waltz song), and Schubert's "Serenade" accompanied by cornet and piano.[28] Her encores included, among others, Foster's "Swanee River" and "Home Sweet Home." According to *L'Abeille*'s reviewer, "She has a soprano voice that she modulates with an ease that indicates that she has been well trained. A little emotional at the beginning, the young virtuoso quickly showed that she possesses power and sang as a true artist her grand air bristling with difficulties. Miss Thayer has a pearl-like voice comparable to a magic flute."[29]

Many of Thayer's friends were in the audience, and she was showered with bouquets of flowers at the end. But the hall was not full. Partly this may have been owing to the competition. It was Christmas season, and Max Strakosch was in town with his opera company performing *Mephistophe* (Boito), *Norma, Aida, Les Huguenots, Sonnambula, Carmen,* and *Martha* and featuring Teresina Singer,[30] Maria Litta (1856–83),[31] and another singer with strong ties to New Orleans: Gaston Gottschalk.[32] Furthermore, there was nonmusical theater and, toughest rival of all, Buffalo Bill. But partly the small audience may have been owing to the fact that Thayer, though very good, was not a world-class soprano and could not attract a major audience in a city used to the best singers.

In addition to singers there were numerous women who performed instruments before the New Orleans public. One such was the young violinist Camille Urso (1842–1902). Urso was born in France and studied with Lambert Massart at the Paris Conservatoire. By 1852 she had moved to America, where she first appeared in many concerts in Boston.[33] Later her family moved to Nashville, but by then she was concertizing extensively. In 1853 she toured much of the country with the Germania Musical Society,[34] and in 1854 she toured with Henrietta Sontag. She first performed in New Orleans in four concerts with Sontag at Odd Fellows' Hall on February 13, 14, 16, and 17, 1854. Mostly she played fantasias on opera airs from *La Favorite, Daughter of the Regiment* (arranged by Alard), *Lucrezia Borgia,* and so on, while Sontag performed arias by Donizetti, Rossini, and Meyerbeer. She also performed Vieuxtemps's *Souvenir des Pyrenees* and *Souvenir de Venice.* After the first concert, the English critic of *The Bee* stated: "part of this tribute [to the success of Sontag's concert] ought in fairness to be claimed by CAMELLA URSO. This young girl whose age cannot exceed 13 years, is a miracle of talent. Her performances on the violin display astonishing mastery of that difficult instrument, intense and glowing feeling, and a ripeness of artistic knowledge as rare as it is admirable. With patient study there is scarcely a limit to the excellence she may attain."[35]

Urso also performed in a series of Combination Concerts, as they were called, when Sontag and/or members of the Italian Opera Company under Luigi Arditi performed excerpts from operas; these were held on March 10, 13, 18, and 21, 1854. On April 18 Urso performed during the intermission of opera performances at the Théâtre d'Orléans, which elicited the following from *L'Abeille:* "Miss Camille Urso, the young artist whose triumph was experienced at Miss Sontag's concerts, will be heard this evening at the Théâtre d'Orléans. She will play a grand fantasy from *Norma,* reminiscences of Bellini, and variations on an air from *Lucrezia Borgia.* The event will occur during the breaks between the charming opera *L'Eau Marveilleuse* by Grisar and two wonderful vaudevilles: *Edgar et sa Bonne* and *La Ninise de St. Flour.*"[36] Urso's final appearance in New Orleans in 1854 seems to have been on May 3 at a private benefit for Mme Deron's Young Ladies Seminary, when "this charming artist will play some favorite pieces with the talent that we have come to know as hers."[37] The concert was originally scheduled for April 28 but had to be postponed owing to the indisposition of the soloist. Urso returned to New Orleans in November 1878 for three additional concerts.[38]

Besides Urso a number of female violinists appeared in concert during the nineteenth century. Madam De Vernay, violinist, gave a grand concert on January 11, 1860, playing a work by Dancla, a *Grand Fantasia sur la Sonnambule,* and an arrangement of a Bach piece for quintet. The fifteen-year-old Chilean pianist and violinist Josefina Filomeno gave an intimate soiree at Collignon's home so that local music patrons would be interested in her giving public concerts.[39] She was fresh from studying in Paris. On February 6, 1868, she gave her first public concert in the German Hall. She performed both on the piano and on the violin works by Liszt, Gottschalk, Vieuxtemps, and Alard. Her colleagues on the program were Auguste Davis, Gustave Smith, and Météyé. The review was ecstatic: "She plays the violin in a really remarkable way with delicate expression and a musical taste that denotes in her a special organization as well as an excellent musical education. The public of connoisseurs at the concert applauded her enthusiastically."[40] She returned to the National Theater on February 21, where she played the Mendelssohn Violin Concerto and violin pieces by Paganini and Vieuxtemps and piano works Liszt, Gottschalk, Thalberg, and others.[41] One review noted, "While she is very strong on the piano, she sings on the violin."[42] Before leaving New Orleans and returning to her native Valparaiso, Chile, she gave two more concerts. On March 7, she offered one more concert at the National Theater. The piano pieces were Thalberg's *Grande Fantasie "Moise,"* Gottschalk's *Concert de Weber* and *Dernier Espoir,* and Liszt's *Sextuor de Lucie;* the violin pieces were Vieuxtemps's *Grand Caprice,* Miska Hanser's *Théme et Variations* from *Lucrèce,* and Alard's *Fantasie La Muette.*[43] And on March 27, her farewell concert was at the Lyceum Hall of City Hall at 8 p.m. She was assisted by A. Graff (baritone of the German Opera), August Coudere (first oboist of the French Opera), and Greuling (accompanist).[44]

The most interesting family of musicians was the Franko family. On February 3, 1870, Selma and Jeanette Franko performed both on the violin and on the piano at Odd Fellows' Hall in the company of their younger sister Rachel (singer), and their brothers Nathan and Sam (both violinists). Frequently, when singers performed concerts, they included violinists in the program. When Adelina Patti gave her 1882 concerts in New Orleans, for example, she included the "pretty but not remarkabl[y] talented" violinist Mlle T. Castellan in the programs.[45] Whatever the critic thought, "Mlle Castellan's violin solo, 'Scene de Ballet,' (De Bériot) was encored, as the audience was pleased with her admirable performance."[46] For her last concert in 1904, Adelina had Roza Zamila play the violin. When Emma Romeldi gave her concert in 1886, Miss Lillie Romeldi, "celebrated violin soloist," participated. When the violinist was the main attraction, as in the cases when Ole Bull performed, singers were there to assist as well. The most brilliant American violinist of the age, Maud Powell, played at the Atheneum on December 23, 1896.[47]

Some of the great female pianists of the nineteenth century also performed in New Orleans. Perhaps the most famous of these was the Venezuelan Teresa Carreño (1853–1917), who performed three times in December 1872 as part of Max Strakosch's presentation of Carlotta Patti in the great hall of the Exposition Building,[48] and returned as a backup to Kate Thayer on December 26–27, 1879, in Grunewald Hall.[49] Her performance on December 17, 1872, was received with great acclaim, though the sexist bias of the reviewer in the *Picayune* shone through clearly: "In M'lle Teresa Carreno, the audience recognized, at once, a pianist who is thoroughly mistress of her instrument. She combines the delicacy and taste of the finished female player, with a strength, brilliancy and power that are expected only of one of the opposite sex; and is equally at home in Gottschalk's romantic, or in Mendelssohn's classic scores. Add to this, the beauty and grace of youth, and it is not to be wondered at that M'lle Carreno at once became a most decided favorite."[50] For her performance on December 16, 1879, Carreño performed Liszt's Polonaise in E "with the brilliancy and finish that has characterized her as the most accomplished lady pianist before the public."[51] The reviewer was enthusiastically praising Carreño and meant no insult to her; the reviewer's astonishment that a woman could perform like a man was not his or her personal prejudice alone against female performers but a deeply ingrained attitude of many of that time.

Another pianist, though much less well known, was Miss Hedwige Brzowskia, who performed a grand concert on January 27, 1860. On the first part of the program she performed the Allegro from Chopin's Concerto in E Minor No. 1, and on the second part of the program she performed the rest of the concerto. Inserted in between were works by Weber, Thalberg, and Rubinstein, and a "Grand Fantasia from Sonnambula."[52] Originally from Poland, Brzowskia stayed in New Orleans long enough to become a teacher in the New Orleans Institute of Music. Fannie Bloomfield Zeisler (1863–1927), one of the great pianists of the same generation as Carreño, performed at the Atheneum on March 14, 1908.[53] A woman who was the equal of Carreño and Zeisler was Marguerite Elie Samuel (discussed in part II, chapter 9), a native New Orleanian who spent most of her life in the city. Probably the most gifted nineteenth-century pianist from New Orleans after Gottschalk, she was a champion of chamber music and upheld the highest standards of classical art music. Another distinguished woman pianist was Octavie Romey, who was also an accomplished composer.

Apparently she was born in France around 1824, and her early compositions were highly praised by Parisian musicians in 1842 when she was just eighteen years old.[54] She probably came to New Orleans around 1864 and remained active there as a performer until 1876.[55] She taught piano at the Girls High School. Romey is last mentioned in the *City Directory* of 1880, and her whereabouts after that date are unknown.[56] Her lavish setting of "Le Marseillaise" is a virtuoso piece of the first order; it was published by Blackmar in New Orleans in 1864, and she performed it publicly in New Orleans in 1870.[57] In 1875 a mass of hers was performed in the Jesuit Church.[58]

One other woman instrumentalist must be mentioned. The harp was one of the popular household instruments in the nineteenth century, and occasionally harpists performed publicly in New Orleans. One such concert occurred on Tuesday, March 14, 1893, at the French Opera House.[59] Isabelle Bressler, who is referred to as a "Wonderful Child Harpist" and "that little girl harpist," performed with the assistance of "the artists of the French Opera Orchestra." The *Picayune* reviewer found that the musical talent of "Miss Bressler, the fair laureate of the Conservatory of Music of Paris . . . borders on genius itself."[60] Her program consisted of a ballad and a march by A. Hasselmens (Bressler's teacher at the conservatory), a concerto by Carl von Oberthur (accompanied by piano), a trio for harp, violin, and violoncello, also by Oberthur, and variations on "Carnival de Venice" by Godefroid. Not only the reviewer found her "charming" and "brilliant" and playing "with exquisite grace of manner," but the audience, made up of many devotees of the harp, found her equally so. "All her numbers were encored, and she generously responded with some quaint selections."

Theresa Cannon (1859?–1930) was probably the most important woman in church music in New Orleans in the nineteenth century. After studying piano with Hubert Rolling and voice with Gregorio Curto, she began her professional career in 1870 at age eleven as a mezzo soprano in sacred music performances and as organist and musical director of the choir at Sainte Anne's Church—a position she retained until at least 1893.[61] During the 1870s there were few church concerts that did not include her. Cannon, who devoted her career exclusively to church music, was compared favorably to some of the best opera singers in town, and as for her directorship, the *Morning Star* felt "confident that under her control [the choir at Sainte Anne's] will be equal to any other in New Orleans." Her regular playing and singing during weekly concerts at Sainte Anne's in May 1872 elicited a description as "touching and brilliant performances."[62]

She often brought to Sainte Anne's the best professional and amateur musicians in the city to perform important concerts featuring works by Rossini,

Mozart, Adam, Stradella, Meyerbeer, La Hache, Verdi, Curto, Lambillotte, Palaoni, Donizetti, and Cherubini, and she was invited to bring her choir to other churches in the city, including Saint Louis Cathedral. Many of these were benefits for orphanages, churches, and schools. When Grunewald Hall opened in January 1874, Cannon's concert on Sunday, January 11—one among many inaugurating the new hall—was the only one to attract a large audience. It was a grand vocal and instrumental concert for the benefit of the Orphan Boys of Saint Vincent's Home, and besides Cannon it included many well-known amateurs of the city under her leadership.[63] In 1876 she married Denis Henry Buckley.[64] She continued her singing career at least until the end of the century. She sang at a benefit concert for Trinity Church on November 20, 1891; at a soiree in Pass Christian in August 1895; and at the graduation of McDonogh School No. 10 in May 1899.[65] Her younger sister, Mary Cannon, was also an accomplished singer who sang in the Sainte Anne's Choir but died in 1894 at the age of thirty-two.[66] In 1886 and 1887 both Theresa and Mary were among the choir soloists at Temple Sinai for the Yom Kippur services.[67] About 1895 Theresa became organist of Saint John the Baptist Church. As a tribute to her talents as the most gifted musical director of Catholic Church music in New Orleans, she was also named organist of Saint Louis Cathedral in 1898, a post she held together with that at Saint John the Baptist until a few weeks before her death on June 10, 1930.

In addition to professional women performing in New Orleans, there were also concerts performed by amateur women. Since the custom of the time was not to publicize the names of amateur women, their names are generally not known; sometimes their initials were given in programs. One of these, Mrs. Josephine Schreiber Beugnot (died 1879), was described by her daughter as an excellent pianist who assisted Collignon in his charity concert of December 18, 1861, when a group of amateurs sang Rossini's *Stabat Mater* with an orchestra.[68] Another may have been Coralie Leblond, a native of New Orleans, who, according to her granddaughter, was a concert pianist at fourteen and a composer; she may have been a pupil of Hubert Rolling.[69] Immediately after the Civil War there were many charities that called on amateur women to raise money. By giving concerts they were able to contribute the take at the gate to the particular needy group. On May 8, 1867, for example, there was a "concert de dames, au Théâtre de l'Opera . . . au benefice des inondes [flood victims]."[70] Men joined the women under whose auspices the concert took place. The chorus was led by Collignon in Mendelssohn and Gounod. Besides songs and choruses, there was instrumental music: two trios for piano, organ, and violin by Wely (the piano was played by Mme H., organ by Gustave Smith, and violin by Henri Page), a trio for piano, organ, and violoncello (Mme H., Gustave Smith, and Mr. Oertl, respectively), and a piece from *Il Trovatore* for two pianos, violin, and violoncello (performed by two amateurs, Henri Page and Mr. Oertl). Blackmar donated pianos, Paul Alhaiza provided the hall for free, and the gas company provided lighting free. Gottschalk's music was on the program.

On Saturday, November 17, 1866, an instrumental and vocal concert for charity included various "chamber" pieces for violin and piano (performed by Henri Page and Mme Locquet), for piano four hands, and for flute and piano (Vender Gucht and Norès). Among the vocal pieces, the cavatina from *The Barber of Seville* was sung by the baritone Fernando accompanied by Auguste Davis on the piano.[71] Another concert by women took place at the National Theater on January 16, 1868, for the benefit of widows and orphans of Confederate soldiers. The director was Octavie Romey.[72] The women sang and played the piano. Romey herself was represented on the program as both a pianist and a composer. Among the pieces were one for twelve pianos and twenty-four female pianists, another for violin played by the young Mark Kaiser, and many songs.[73]

Another scheme to raise money for charity was announced by some women of New Orleans on December 6, 1866. In order to underwrite a hospital for widows and orphans of soldiers killed in the War, the women opened a café in the Hotel Saint Louis and, to attract people to it, they obtained the voluntary performances of some of the city's best artists: Fernando (baritone), Henri Page (violinist), Gustave Smith (organist at Saint Alphonse's), and Mme Fleury-Urban.[74]

While the many contributions of women to the concert life of New Orleans have been amply demonstrated, their role as teachers is just as important. The tradition of women teaching music in New Orleans goes back at least to 1727. In the nineteenth century there are numerous women whose names appear in advertisements in the newspapers or are listed under "Music Teachers" in the city directories. Madame Letellier, for example, and her husband announced in 1830 that they offered voice lessons to whoever was interested,[75] and a decade later Mary de A. Santangelo was prepared to teach voice, guitar, and other educational subjects.[76] Hedwige Brzowskia was teaching in the New Orleans Institute of Music in 1860. In 1869, Carla Patti announced herself as "Second Musical Director French Opera, Professor Music, Lessons given on the Violin and Accompaniment, 39 Liberty Street."[77] Calvé taught when her career as an opera diva was over and after her husband died.[78] Marguerite Samuel taught while her career was in full bloom. In addition to these top performers, however, there were also women whose careers centered entirely on their teaching since they had no notable careers as concert performers. Boyer and Locquet were the leading music teachers in New Orleans during the mid-nineteenth century and survived the Civil War. A particularly noteworthy case is that of Isabelle Pilcher (1865–1935), who ran the Pilcher Conservatory from at least 1896 to 1904 in lieu of her absent and perhaps unfaithful husband William Henry Pilcher (see part II, chapter 14).

Besides the persons actively engaged in the composition, performance, and teaching of music, there were those whose business acumen was necessary in order for the art to flourish. We have already cited the case of Kate Thayer, who was manager as well as performer in her own tour. Women were also directors of opera companies that visited New Orleans. For example, within two months in the 1876–77 season, three different companies, with women in charge, came to the city. On December 14, 1876, Caroline Riching-Bernard's opera troupe opened at the French Opera House with *Maritana* and followed with *Il Trovatore, Martha,* and, on the Saturday matinee, *The Bohemian Girl.*[79] It had fifty artists. Immediately afterward (December 24, 1876), the Aimée Operetta Troupe, after performances in Havana, debuted at the Varieties Theater with Offenbach's *Jolie Perfumeuse.*[80] The director of this company was Mlle Marie Aimee. Among other opéra comiques that she performed in New Orleans were Lecocq's *La Fille de Madame Angot, Giroflé-Girofla* (Lecocq), *La Grande Duchesse* (Offenbach), *La Timbale d'Argent* (Léon Vasseur), *La Vie Parisienne* (Offenbach), *La Boulangere a des Ecus* (Offenbach), and *La Périchole* (Offenbach). The originally intended half-week stay with four performances was extended into the middle of January with several dozen performances. Finally, Miss Soldene, with her new and complete English Comic Opera Company, opened with "the comical and very dramatic cantata, entitled *Trial by Jury*" on January 29 and 30, 1877, at Bidwell's Academy of Music.[81] This is the first known performance of a Gilbert and Sullivan operetta in New Orleans, and it came less than two years after its March 25, 1875, premier in London. Soldene advertised that hers was "with the original London cast." Also in her repertory were *La Fille de Madame Angot,* Florimond Herve's *Chilperic* and *Poulet et Poulette,* and Offenbach's *Madame L'Archiduc.* The Alice Oates Comic Opera Company was also in town at this time, but Oates did not manage the company.[82] Beginning in February 1880, the Emma Abbott Opera Company, which was another company managed by a woman, made numerous appearances in the city.

Women were also involved in the managing of music stores that provided the hard material musicians needed in the practice of their art. For instance, Mrs. Maria Elie, Marguerite's mother, ran a music store on Canal Street.

As for publishing, the name of Madame Henri Wehrmann appears on the printed editions of much of the music published in New Orleans in the nineteenth century and on some music published elsewhere. She was born Charlotte Marie Clementine Bohne in Paris in 1830.[83] While growing up in the French capital she learned how to engrave music and became very skilled in that endeavor. On October 22, 1848, she married Henri Wehrmann from Prussia, and a year later M and Mme Wehrmann and their oldest child emigrated from Europe to America where they settled in New Orleans. Charlotte's father had come over to New Orleans about a year before the Wehrmanns and set up a music business. Henri set himself up as a music printer, and both he and his wife engraved music. It is possible that she did all the engraving, though her name appears only on a third of the printings that they did. At first they worked for Werlein's, which was the leading publisher of music in New Orleans during the nineteenth century, but before long they were engraving and printing music for other publishers such as Louis Grunewald, Junius Hart, and others. During the period from 1849 to 1888, Mrs. Wehrmann engraved first editions of some of the works of Louis Moreau Gottschalk, the most famous musician from New Orleans, as well as other local composers Curto and La Hache. She engraved the first printed edition of *Dixie* that was published by Werlein's. She engraved the piano arrangements of the music played by the Mexican bands that so greatly influenced the music of New Orleans during the 1885 Cotton Exposition.[84] Henri Wehrmann, who was born in 1827, died in New Orleans in 1903, and Mrs. Wehrmann died in New Orleans in 1910 at the age of eighty. She was survived by three of her four children, one of whom was Henry Wehrman Jr., a well-known violinist and composer in New Orleans (see chapter 14). The daughter of her deceased son Valentine was Eugénie Wehrmann-Schaffner, a pupil of Marguerite Elie Samuel and a distinguished concert pianist in New Orleans.

To single out only women in discussing the music of New Orleans is as unbalanced as to single out only men. We have done so here only in an attempt to right an unbalance that has been apparent in music histories until recently. The history of music in New Orleans is the continual interplay and often fusion of diverse musical traditions and roles, and this interplay and fusion are not only among people of different races, religions, social and economic backgrounds, and national origins but also between sexes. The influence of individuals on other individuals is what has led to the creation of the music of New Orleans, and ultimately it is irrelevant whether the person is male or female.

PART II

Personalities

1

Louis Hus Desforges
Pioneer Conductor and Violinist

Louis Hus Desforges is among the earliest professional musicians to have made a career performing in concerts in New Orleans. He was born about 1776 in La Rochelle, France,[1] and was in New Orleans by August 7, 1799, when he married Isavel Victoria Dupre. The following year, on June 12, 1800, Isavel gave birth to a son, Louis Hus Desforges Jr.[2]

Desforges first appeared in concert, as an arranger, on Tuesday, December 17, 1805, in a program benefitting M B. Brun. Here his arrangement for grand orchestra of the "President's March" opened the program. Given the fact that he is known later as a conductor, it is possible that Desforges also conducted the orchestra throughout the concert, which included several overtures, two concertos, and additional works.[3] We can only speculate as to why he was in New Orleans at this time, but it is probable that Desforges was one of the few professional musicians hired to play in and even lead the orchestra at the Salle Accoutumée for plays, operas, and dances.

A year later, the press began to report on Desforges's seemingly increased activity as a professional musician. Desforges himself had his first known benefit concert on January 19, 1807,[4] and, two weeks later, he performed as a violinist in a concert featuring his own Violin Concerto.[5] He repeated the concerto on or about February 18.[6] The following fall his *Allemande à Grand Orchestra* was on a benefit program for M Remondet.[7] He performed a violin concerto by the amateur M Blache, with orchestra, on December 29, 1807.[8] That Desforges was earning his living as a professional violinist is evinced by his having regular benefit concerts and his name never carrying the rubric "amateur" as in the case of M Blache. On March 7, 1808, he performed a violin concerto by Fodor in a benefit concert for Mme Nicolai,[9] and the following week he participated in a trio by Pleyel in a benefit for Mme Labat. His arrangement of "President's March" (now entitled "Hail Columbia") was also on the program.[10] On September 24,

1808, he was clearly listed as a conductor for the first time. He conducted his own two *Valses* for grand orchestra during an intermède between two comedies at the Théâtre de la Gaîté.[11] On December 23, 1808, he conducted one of his most popular works, *La Querelle Musicale,* at the Saint Louis Theater in a benefit for himself and clarinetist Philip Laroque; he also played a violin concerto by Pleyel.[12] The following January 3 and 13 he performed his own Symphonie Concertante for violin and violoncello, with Mr. Minière on the latter instrument,[13] and his *La Querelle musicale* was repeated on February 18 in the Salle Accoutumée.[14]

During the next year, Desforges continued as a regular at concerts in New Orleans. He performed Blache's Violin Concerto again, on March 9, 1809, at the Saint Peter Street Theater in a benefit for Mlle Laurette Fleury.[15] Another benefit concert for Desforges occurred on November 2 that year, when he played a Viotti concerto and had two of his own compositions performed: a march dedicated to President Madison and *Le Querelle M Sigale,* for large orchestra.[16] On February 14, 1810, he participated in two works: a *Sextuor Concertant* by M Laroque for clarinet (Fortier), violin (Desforges), horn (Labat), and bass (Minière),[17] and the Viotti Symphonie Concertante for two violins (with the amateur Amat).[18] On February 28, at the Salle Accoutumée, Desforges switched to the viola and joined with violoncellist Minière in a duet sonata by the German violoncellist Christophe Schetky (1740–73).[19] The following November 14, Desforges played an anonymous violin concerto and heard his arrangement of the arietta "Céleste Mélodie" for singer (Mr. Rochefort) with both guitar and orchestral accompaniment; he also introduced his son Louis Hus Jr., age nine, performing in a trio for two violins and bass (the son performed the first violin part).[20]

Whatever the reason, we do not find Desforges in another concert for over a year. On January 16, 1812, he reappeared at the Saint Philip Street Theater in a benefit for the widow of M Bayon; he played a concerto by Viotti.[21] Then there is another year before we see him again, this time on March 9, 1813, in a concert for his own benefit. On the program he performed a Rode concerto and a symphonie concertante apparently for three violin solos (Desforges with MM Blache and a pupil of Desforges) accompanied by grand orchestra.[22] Ten days later Desforges played a trio concertante for viola d'amore (Fortier), violin (Desforges), and clarinet (Laroque), at a benefit for Laroque in the Salle de Condé. Desforges also concluded the program with a set of his own variations on "L'Anglaise."[23] At the end of the year, on December 20, there was another benefit for Desforges during which he performed his own Violin Concerto and directed the orchestra in his "President's March," Variations on *L'Anglaise,*

March for General Harrison, and, "after the concert," a new *Créole Waltz* dedicated to Major General Villeré.[24]

It is clear that Desforges was also busy as a violin teacher. That his son was good enough to appear in public in 1809 and that one of his pupils did so in 1813 attest to an interest among the residents of New Orleans in studying with him and to his success in preparing them for the task. It is possible that some of his students, who remained amateurs, filled the ranks of the theater orchestras during the first two decades of the nineteenth century. Some appeared in concerts with their teacher.

On April 10, 1814, Desforges again appeared in public as a violist in a once-popular concerto by Bernard Lorenziti (ca. 1764–after 1813). This was another benefit for himself and featured, in addition, his pupils Morand, Brosset, and Beauregard, among others.[25] Two years later, on February 5, 1816, Desforges performed with M Girault the *Symphonie Concertant* of Viotti for two violins; this was a benefit for A. Girault and took place at the Salle de Condé.[26] At the end of this year, on December 30, there was another benefit for Desforges, in which he performed Rode's Violin Concerto No. 7 and conducted several of his own works: a *Chasse* for full orchestra, dedicated to Governor Villère, and a march for full orchestra dedicated to General Lefebvre Desnoueties.[27] On February 23, 1817, Desforges performed his own variations on *La Joie des Maçons,* again at the Salle de Condé,[28] and, on December 9, he joined Mr. Maurise in variations on two airs for violin and the new instrument, the bassette horn, at the Salle d'Orléâns.[29] On January 17, 1818, he joined Laroque (clarinet) and an amateur violoncellist in Laroque's Trio as part of a benefit concert for Laroque.[30]

There was a benefit given to Desforges in the Salle d'Orléâns on November 25, 1818. He performed, with an amateur, his variations concertantes for two violins, and his Variations on *L'Anglaise* was also played.[31] At a benefit concert for Paul Emile Johns on December 4, Desforges played his own Violin Concerto,[32] and the following February 17, 1819, in a benefit concert for Laroque, he played his variations on an air from *Vive Henry IV.*[33] Another benefit concert for Desforges was held on February 7, 1820, at the new Théâtre d'Orléans. It opened with his *Governor Villère March* and ended with his *Marche Militaire.* In between he performed the Viotti Symphonie Concertante for two violins with C. Herz (a young violinist who basically had replaced Desforges by 1820). *L'Anglaise Variations* was also on the program; Mr. Aimé sang two numbers, and Johns played Dussek's *Military* Concerto.[34] For reasons given below, following this concert we hear nothing about Desforges as a public performer for seven years, until we encounter his last benefit concert, on Wednesday, April 25, 1827, at the

Théâtre d'Orléans.[35] Here he performed a Pleyel violin concerto, but perhaps the anonymous military march performed by the full orchestra was one of his compositions.

When the city was bombarded during the War of 1812, Desforges "joined the battalion of volunteers under Major Plauché."[36] At the end of December 1814, "he was wounded in the head by a rocket" and lost part of his hearing. While he continued to perform and conduct, and as late as 1838 was still a member of the orchestra at the Saint Charles Theatre,[37] the results proved less than satisfactory. Henry Castellanos described witnessing Desforges conduct the Overture to *La Dame Blanche* at the Camp Street Theatre in the 1830s. He referred to him as "an old, almost deaf Frenchman."

> An incident which occurred in the Camp street theatre may be worth recording. It is certainly characteristic of the times.
>
> It was the Fourth of July night, a holiday then celebrated with greater *éclat* and outward manifestations of patriotism than at the present day, that this temple of Thespis was filled to repletion with a crowd, the majority of whom were backwoodsmen from the Western country. Great preparations had been set on foot by the manager to make the performance an acceptable and *recherché* affair, particularly to our musical *dilettanti*.
>
> The leader of the orchestra was an old Frenchman, whom I remember well. He was afflicted with almost complete deafness, occasioned by the explosion of a caisson at the battle of New Orleans, and how he managed to direct his artists with such ability has ever been to me an unfathomable mystery. For several weeks he had had his musicians rehearsing the overture of the opera of "La Dame Blanche"—a novelty then—and when, after many wearisome efforts to attain perfection, he saw the acme of his ambition about to be crowned with success, visions of entranced audiences, tumults of applause and salvos of *encore* filled his imagination with rapture. At last, the long desired occasion, fraught with such pleasing anticipations, finally arrived.
>
> As I have already said, the house was jammed. It was a hilarious, promiscuous and uproarious audience. They had come to have fun, and fun they were determined to have.
>
> Seated in front of the footlights, with waving *baton* in hand, the bent form of old man Desforges was to be seen, giving the three consecrated raps. The magnificent symphony began. Never had the music of Boieldieu been interpreted with such effects of pathos and sweetness, when, all of a sudden, a call for "Yankee Doodle" was heard from the galleries. Heedless of the interrup-

tion, the orchestra proceeded with the music, when the cry of "Yankee Doodle" was taken up again, and began to resound from dome to pit. The deafening noise reached old Desforges' ears like the murmur of a gentle breeze, wafting upon its wings faint echoes of applause. Mistaking the cause of the uproar, the musical leader was delighted. He had attained, as he imagined, the goal of his ambition, and, throwing his whole soul into a supreme effort, was about to give additional language and expression to his charmed violin, when crashes following crashes gave notice that the work of demolition of benches and chairs had commenced, amid angry shouts of "Yankee Doodle."

At this stage of pandemonium the curtain was pushed aside, and Mr. Caldwell made his appearance. Turning to Mr. Desforges he shouted to him to stop. "The people don't want that," he said, "they want Yankee Doodle."

The old man realized the situation. He stood up in a stupor, and only had time to gasp out, "Yankee Dude!" Then, stung to the quick by the affront put on him by the populace, he shrieked out in quick, piping tones: "You want Yankee Dude? Well, you no have Yankee Dude! Because why? Because not necessair."

At this outburst of rage and pluck, the audience broke out into plaudits and shouts of laughter, and the overture *was* finished without further interruption. They had had more fun than they had bargained for.[38]

Desforges's career was apparently over by the time of this incident. There is no more record of his having appeared in public as performer or conductor and no further mention of any of his compositions or arrangements. He had been for many years a conductor of theater orchestras and first violinist in the Opera Orchestra; as such he moved over to the Théâtre d'Orléans in 1819 but could not have remained there for very long if his hearing was as bad as Castellanos states.[39] The violinist Herz was already the first violinist of the French Opera in 1820. Desforges lived to a decent old age, dying on November 18, 1862, at the age of eighty-six. His residence was 275 Royal Street, in the French Quarter. Since he was predeceased by his son Louis Hus Desforges Jr. (1800–1860), and since his other children apparently were not musical,[40] his musical heir was his grandson-in-law Hubert Rolling (see part II, chapter 7), the husband of Louis, Junior's daughter Marie Louise Willamine Irma Desforges.

2

Gregorio Curto

Bass Singer, Church Musician, and Vocal Teacher

One of the most distinguished musicians in New Orleans during the nineteenth century was Gregorio Curto. At first a leading member of the opera troupe at the Théâtre d'Orléans, he later became one of the more successful composers of opera in America, a conductor, a church musician, and a teacher of voice. His continued presence in the city ensured the respect that the musical life of New Orleans garnered among professional musicians and music lovers throughout America.

Curto was born in the old Spanish city of Tortoso, about 1805.[1] His parents were very poor peasants, and it was by chance that a soldier with some musical background and stationed near his village heard him singing and decided to help him achieve some musical education.[2] His earliest musical studies must have proven him to be gifted, so that by the age of twelve or thirteen he was already advanced enough to be in Paris studying with the renowned pedagogue Alexandre Choron (1771–1834). Choron had served as director of the Paris Conservatoire from about 1816 to 1817, and in that latter year—forcefully removed from that great institution—founded his own singing school where Curto became one of his first students. About 1819, when Curto was not yet fourteen, he was sufficiently proficient in music that he served for one year as organist of the cathedral in Soissons, France. But by 1820 he was back in Paris working closely with Choron in voice and composition. To support himself during the next ten apprentice years, Curto was maître de chapelle at the church of the Sorbonne, and at the same time he became a voice teacher at Choron's school.[3] Despite a strong education in composition and professional experience in church music, Curto was heading toward a career as an opera singer. In 1830, when he was twenty-five, he made his Paris debut at the Italian Opera in Rossini's *La Gazza Ladra*. With backgrounds in religious music, opera, and singing as well as composition, his future seemed very bright.

Shortly after his debut, in the summer of 1830, he came to the attention of John Davis, who was in Europe recruiting singers for the upcoming season at the Théâtre d'Orléans. Davis's opera troupe was the most important not only in New Orleans but throughout America at that time, and he offered enough incentives for Curto to join up. Davis and his entourage with Curto arrived in New Orleans via Baltimore on November 11, 1830,[4] and three days later they opened the new season at the Théâtre d'Orléans with François-Adrien Boieldieu's popular *La Dame Blanche*. Composed just five years before, this opera was frequently performed in New Orleans during the nineteenth century. Curto sang the part of Gaveston and, according to one reviewer, he demonstrated a strong voice, but apparently he was not much of an actor. "M. Curto—he has a sonorous voice, harmonious . . . but as for his gestures, we can't yet say, let's give him some time."[5] Four days later Curto sang the role of Ferdinand Villebell in Rossini's *La Pie Voleuse* (*La Gazza Ladra*, or *The Thieving Magpie*), but he is not mentioned in the review, nor is he mentioned in the review of Rossini's *The Barber of Seville*, performed on November 21, when he sang the role of Don Basilio.[6] For two seasons Curto was one of the main figures at the Théâtre d'Orléans. He sang leading parts in Rossini's *L'Italiana in Algieri* and Donizetti's *Anna Bolena*, in addition to *La Dame Blanche*, *La Gazza Ladra*, and *The Barber of Seville*. By 1832, however, Curto retired from the active opera stage, though he may have continued on occasion to sing there, such as in Meyerbeer's *Les Huguenots* after 1836.[7] Instead, he earned his livelihood by serving as a church musician, and he began to cultivate those other occupations for which he then became locally best known: composition, conducting, and teaching.

In addition to singing at Théâtre d'Orléans from 1830 to 1832, Curto also performed in dramas. Davis featured not only operas but also vaudevilles (we might term these "operettas"), classical dramas (by French masters from Corneille in the seventeenth century to Dumas in the nineteenth), ballets, and recitals. Sometimes an opera would be performed side by side on the same evening with a drama and/or a vaudeville. Despite his poor review as an actor, Curto is reputed to have acted in classical works by Racine and Corneille.[8] The most significant aspect of his short acting career, however, is that while doing so at Théâtre d'Orléans in 1830 he met his future wife, Delphine Clozel, and by 1834 they were living together, presumably as husband and wife.

Delphine was born in Basle, Switzerland, about 1795. She had been married previously to Jean Joseph Eduard Clozel and had borne him a son who died in infancy (Modeste Henri Clozel, June 2, 1825–June 21, 1825).[9] Since there is no record of their marriage in New Orleans and they are not listed in any directory before 1830, it is likely they were married before coming to New Orleans. When Jean Joseph, her first husband, died is uncertain, but he left her a widow by 1830.[10] In addition to Modeste she probably had another son by her first husband when she was young. This son was probably the Mr. Clozel who made his debut at the Théâtre d'Orléans on November 29, 1832,[11] in plays *Joseph* and *Rabelais*, and who also appeared on the same stage on December 4, 1836 in the vaudeville *L'Héritière* and on May 25, 1838, in M Bouchardy's *Gaspardo le Pêcheur* (a drama in four acts) for the benefit of Monsieur Clozel and Monsieur Welch. On April 11, 1840, there was another benefit for Monsieur Clozel at the theater when he appeared in a reprise of *Il y a Seize Ans,* a three-act drama by Victor Ducange. M Clozel the actor retired in 1842. It is unlikely that the J. M. Clozel who was living in New Orleans in 1860 was Delphine's actor son since in 1832 he would have been only eight years old, but since the name is rare throughout the nineteenth century in the New Orleans area, he may have been another son. The 1860 census points to his birthplace as South Carolina, and since we have no knowledge of the Clozels in New Orleans before 1824, the family may have come from there.[12] These two Clozels, then, would have been Curto's stepsons.

Delphine was a successful actress in New Orleans, appearing in many productions during the 1830s. Even after she married Curto, she continued to act. During the fall of 1835 alone she had leading roles in all the dramas at the Théâtre d'Orléans: as Catherine de Médici in Alexander Dumas's *Henri III et sa Cour,* as Amélie in Victor Ducange's *Trente Ans ou la Vie d'un Jouer,* as Dona Lucrezia Borgia in Hugo's *Lucrèce Borgia,* as Marguerite in Gaillardet and Dumas's *La Tour de Nesle,* and an unknown role in Hugo's *Marie Tudor.* In 1836 (December 8) she appeared in a vaudeville, *Les Gants Jeunes.* Her next known appearance at the Théâtre d'Orléans was in a new five-act play by Placide Canonge entitled *Gaston de Saint Elme,* performed on May 17, 1840, for the benefit of Orphelins, the local orphans' home.[13] She also had occasional parts in the operas. For example, at the New Orleans premier of *Robert le Diable* by Meyerbeer on May 12, 1835, Mme Clozel is a dame d'honneur d'Isabelle. At least until 1844, as long as she was on the stage, Mrs. Curto kept her previous name of Clozel or Closel, but in the city directories she now accepted her new married name. On May 20, 1842, Mme Clozel appeared at the Théâtre d'Orléans in *Le Marquis en Cage.* By May of 1844, however, she was no longer a regular at the theater, but she continued to perform occasionally that year, as on May 14 when she played the title role in Racine's *Athalie* and the part of Jocaste in Voltaire's *Oedipe.* Thereafter, Delphine retired and served out her remaining years as Madame Curto. She died on December 19, 1870, at the age of seventy-five.[14] Sometime thereafter Curto married Eugénie, who survived him.[15] She ran a school at their residence at 299 Saint Philip Street near the corner of Prieur. Is she the same Eugénie who performed in the 1840s at the Théâtre d'Orléans?

While Curto was occupied from 1832 on as a church musician, on a few occasions he continued to sing publicly at the Théâtre d'Orléans. For example, he appeared at a grand concert for the benefit of MM Vallière and Norès on February 27, 1836, and at a benefit for himself on June 4, 1839, he probably sang in a concert version of the second act of Rossini's *Italienne à Alger*. On the first occasion Curto performed a trio from *William Tell* with MM Heymann and Bailly, regulars then at Théâtre d'Orléans. The 1836 concert occurred in the Salle d'Orléâns followed by a ball—it was, after all, Carnival season. There were other benefits for singers in the spring of 1836, but Curto did not perform in them while Haymann and Bailey did. On June 3, 1843, Curto again appeared in a concert at the Théâtre d'Orléans singing one of his own works, the *Grand Duo*, together with the tenor M Varnay; the two also sang the *Duo de Masaniello*. The concert was organized by M Lehmann. Curto sang again in public to open the second half of Henri Herz's second grand concert on February 24, 1847, at Armory Hall; he chose an "Air from the Opera *L'Esule di Roma*." A particularly impressive grand concert was scheduled for December 6, 1848, but after several delays finally occurred on December 13. On this occasion Curto sang with M Munios in a duo from Donizetti's *Marino Faliero* and a duo with Mlle "N" from his own *Quido et Matilde*.[16] The concert took place at the Salle Saint-Louis and had the support of a large reception committee made of citizens from the first, second, and third municipalities. After 1848, however, we find only one more notice of Curto singing solo in front of a public audience: on October 12, 1864, he sang the role of Raphael in Haydn's *Creation* at the French Opera House.[17]

With his knowledge of the opera stage and with his skills as a composer learned from Choron, Curto inevitably turned to writing his own operas after 1832.[18] The first of these was his three-act opera *Le Nouvel Hermite* which was premiered at the Théâtre d'Orléans on the evening of Tuesday, May 6, 1834. It was part of a benefit performance for Madame Clozel, who was the librettist of the opera. Also on the program was a performance of *Madam Gregoire ou Le Cabaret de la Pomme de Pin* (a chanson in two parts by MM Rochefort, Dapeuty, and Charles); between the two acts of this piece, Mme Clozel and Mme Guardot played a scene from the tragedy of *Phedre*.[19] The ensuing newspaper review was more excited that *Le Nouvel Hermite* was written "by a lady of this city" whose great talent had always been admired in the most exacting roles, than that the composer was Curto.[20]

Curto's next "opera" seems to have been rather a single scene from the story *Le Lépreux*; it was premiered on May 10, 1845, at the Théâtre d'Orléans on a benefit concert by members of the Italian Opera who had performed since March 3 that year at the American Theatre. The benefit concert included, besides Curto's scene, the second act of *L'Elisir d'Amore* and the third act of *Sémiramide*. The critic in *L'Abeille* wrote that the experts in the city had predicted great success for the work.[21] On May 17, 1845, there was another benefit concert at the Théâtre d'Orléans for MM Arnaud, Douvry, and Garry, during which excerpts from various operas by Donizetti (*La Favorite*), Halévy (*La Juive*), Rossini (*William Tell*) and Curto (*Le Lépreux*) were performed. The three singers were regulars at the opera in New Orleans, and Mlle Caroline who joined Douvry in the apotheosis of Curto's opera was Douvry's daughter. A chorus performing the "grande scène" from the "opera" preceded the duet. A writer for *L'Abeille* on the day of this performance was looking forward to "*Le Lépreux* by Curto whose second hearing so well confirmed its success and in which Mr. Douvry and his daughter rivaled one another in voice and in feeling."[22] There is no evidence that more than the chorus and duet were ever written for this tragic story.

Curto's second full opera, *Agathe ou Le Testament,* was premiered at the Théâtre d'Orléans on May 2, 1846, on a program that also featured a benefit to M Arnaud and excerpts from *Zampa* (Hérold), *La Sirene* (Auber), *Lucie de Lammermoor* (Donizetti), and *L'Aumonier du Régiment* (author unknown). Curto's opera, which is based on Scribe's popular vaudeville *L'Héritière,* is in two acts, three scenes, and was translated from Italian. Unfortunately the reviewer in *L'Abeille* two days later found fault with Curto's work.[23] While he recognized the merits of Curto's music and the many fine airs and duets, he faulted the piece as an opera. The original story, which was played frequently at Théâtre d'Orléans during the 1830s in Scribe's version, is too light hearted to be set as a serious opera, and Curto tried to make big, serious roles out of what were light-weight characters in the original. Surrounded as it was on May 2 by major works with heavy roles, Curto's misunderstanding of the personages in his opera were made all the more glaring.

Curto fared better with his next opera, *La Mort de Sardanapale,* which was premiered at the Théâtre d'Orléans on May 7, 1849. A two-act grand opera based on a work of Lord Byron, it was the featured event on a benefit performance for M Fiot, the scenic designer of the opera company, and was preceded by a performance of the new one-act vaudeville *Le Chatenu de la Roche Noire.* This time the anonymous reviewer in *L'Abeille* considered Curto's work a success and found it worthy of the bravos and "felicitations" from the audience.

[T]he overture seemed to us in a vague style and perhaps a little too labored to be able to be judged fairly at the first hearing. It always has a powerful effect and was played with that superiority that distinguishes our musicians of the Théâtre d'Orléans Orchestra. We do not wish to analyze the whole piece because of lack of space here; we say only that the first act is of great beauty and the highlight of the act, a magnificent trio, is rendered in a grand and truly magisterial manner. Beside the trio, performed by Duluc, Valet and Mrs. Berton, we must cite also the previous duet performed by Duluc and Mrs. Berton, and in the second act the charming couplets: "Effacez Vous, Souvenirs Superflus[.]" The choruses are perfectly suited and dominate the orchestra, a quality too rare in our day; we cite among them the chorus of the vow, in spite of reminiscences of *Les Huguenots*, which ends the first act, and the final chorus of the sealing which is well written: nevertheless, a major defect is the recall of the romance: "La Voilà, la Voilà, Cette France Chérie," &c. In sum, the music of Curto is beautiful and proved unquestionably the progress that this composer makes and the taste of the public which understood the score completely and applauded it accordingly. We do not speak of the poem, which is a translation of Byron, nor of the costumes which seem to have been very exact. We are forever thankful to Duluc, who, not to deprive us of this performance, did not hold back and who sang his part while suffering from a fever and risked damaging his magnificent voice.[24]

Curto may have written an opera, *Tancrède*, that probably would have been completed before May 1852, when a cavatina from the work was performed in public and published. The text was by Placide Canonge. More likely, however, Curto may have written only this cavatina, specifically for the soprano A. Wiedemann, to be inserted in performances of Rossini's *Tancrède* at Théâtre d'Orléans in which Wiedemann was the leading lady. It was common practice in the nineteenth century, in New Orleans as well as in Europe, to insert newly composed arias into established operatic masterpieces in order to enable a specific singer to show off or to cater to local popular tastes. Mozart's operas in particular were so mutilated.

Even though he is still listed as a comedian in 1832,[25] when he stopped singing regularly at the opera, Curto most likely was professionally a church musician from this year forward. His intense training and background in Paris had been in church music, and he had all the qualifications to be one of the leading church musicians in New Orleans. The first recorded evidence of his working for the church comes on May 2, 1832. A certain "A. Curto" was appointed organist at Saint Louis Cathedral on this date. Alfred Lemmon convincingly demonstrates that this A. Curto and a Mr. Curtaud who appears shortly thereafter must be the same as Gregorio Curto.[26] Two years later Curto, who was living on Sainte Ann Street between Villeré and Robertson, was listed in the *City Directory* as parish organist at a church, and he continued to be known as the organist at Saint Louis Cathedral at least until 1841. During this time the famous episode involving seven-year-old Louis Moreau Gottschalk is reputed to have taken place, when the young prodigy played the organ at a service in the cathedral. This would suggest that Curto knew the child Gottschalk and may even have taught him, but as Alfred Lemmon and Frederick Starr have pointed out, there is no other evidence of such a relationship which, if it were a fact, would certainly have led Curto and his supporters to boast about it.[27]

Probably in 1848 Curto was appointed maître de la chapelle at the new Sainte Theresa Church on Camp Street, a short distance uptown from the Vieux Carré.[28] He held this position for only a few years, but while he was there he dedicated some of his compositions to this small but charming church. Directly across the street from the church was the Sainte Thérèse Girls Orphan Asylum, and a block away was the Sainte Thérèsa school, in both of which he seems to have been involved as musician and music teacher. He conducted concerts for the benefit of the orphanage, and the young women provided Curto with a steady flow of music students and choristers. In 1855 Curto moved over to the older and much larger Saint Patrick's Church where he held the same post as maître de chapelle, and his successor at Sainte Theresa was the renowned local composer and organist Théodore von La Hache.[29] In 1870 he apparently was still maitre de chapelle de Nouvelle Orleans (that is, at Saint Patrick's), but by 1877, when he was elderly and probably had stepped back from his earlier active role at Saint Patrick's, Curto was the organist of Sainte Anne's Church on Saint Philip Street near his home.

As befits many church musicians, he supplemented his church duties by conducting, composing, and teaching. On June 29, 1841, Curto directed a grand spiritual concert at Saint Patrick's Church. There were a choir, soloists from the French Opera, and the Opera Orchestra. On the second half of the program Curto conducted his *Grande Symphonie* for orchestra, and Nourrit and Bernadet from the French Opera also performed a fragment from Curto's *Requiem*. This is the first citation of a performance of a sacred work by Curto, who later was a prolific composer of church music, and it is the only reference we have to a nonvocal work of his.[30] Curto continued to conduct occasional public concerts with sacred music. On April 14, 1847, for example, he conducted a *Grand Ora-*

torio de David at the new Church of Christ on Canal Street. This performance was to inaugurate a new organ at the church and to help pay for it. The organist for the concert and probably the regular organist there was F. F. Mueller. A decade after he apparently left Saint Louis Cathedral, "Mr. Curto [was] in charge of music for the dedication of the extensively renovated cathedral,"[31] and "for that special occasion Curto composed a Mass sung by an amateur chorus comprised of fifty women and fifty men."[32]

In early 1851 Curto conducted a concert at Armory Hall in the second municipal district for the benefit of the Orphelins, a female orphan asylum. The choir of twenty-four women and twenty-six men and the orchestra were well rehearsed.[33] The program was a potpourri of operatic excerpts; it began with the Overture to *Sémiramide,* the duet from *Lucia,* the prayer from *Joseph,* the sextet from *Lucia,* and the grand air from *Robert de Diable* on the first half, and the Overture to *William Tell,* the chorus and grand aria from Verdi's *Jérusalem,* the duet from *Anna Bolena,* and the sermon from *Athalie* by Curto himself. There is no other mention of this work by Curto, but given the nature of the other works on the program, we can surmise that it was from another opera that he had composed or was in the process of writing (or perhaps, like *Tancrède,* it was a newly composed scene to be inserted in another composer's *Athalie* when performed at the Théâtre d'Orléans). At the end of the concert there was a heavy rain, and the newspaper reporter was more concerned how the orphan girls who attended the concert were escorted back to their asylum outside the Vieux Carré than with the music. A local citizen got horses from his stable, brought carriages, and took them home.[34]

Later that same year, on November 20 and December 3, 1851, La Hache and Curto joined forces in two grand sacred concerts. On the first of these, at the Lyceum Hall, Curto's *Psalm 84* for solo and choir was performed, as was La Hache's *The Grave,* for solo and choir. They also performed works by Kuhlau, Spohr, Gluck, Novello, Méhul, Hummel, Adams, Rossini, Haydn, Weigl, Fesca, and Mozart. On the second concert, which Curto conducted, they were joined by the violinist Fred Meyer and the pianist Panisack (a pupil of Aloise Schindler) and performed works by Mozart, Haydn, Hummel, and others. The overwhelming success of these two events led the two musicians to a new project.

On January 9, 1852, Curto and La Hache decided to organize a Philharmonic Society in New Orleans with themselves as co-directors. The fine reception by the public that the two concerts of sacred music had had a few weeks before demonstrated that New Orleans had the talent necessary for such a society.[35] The first concert of the Philharmonic Society, conducted by Curto, took place on Wednesday, May 19, at the lycée, for the benefit of the singer, Professeur Leroy. La Hache appeared as official organist of the Philharmonic and was joined by M Jahn (conductor of the French Opera, who had several violin solos), M Fourmestreau (first oboist of the French Opera), M Trust (harpist of the French Opera), M Leroy and his wife (singers), and several unnamed vocalists. Apparently Curto conducted the orchestra and the choir in two large choruses by "Hammel" (Hummel?) and Mozart, and probably he also led the orchestra in accompanying the singers in various opera arias by Méhul, Rossini, and Donizetti.[36] M LeRoy sang an encore.[37] The second concert of the Philharmonic Society was just a week later, on May 26, 1852, at Armory Hall. It was performed in honor of Curto. With the consent of Davis, director of the opera at the Théâtre d'Orléans, four of the leading singers at the French Opera donated their talents: Madames A. Wiedeman and Fleury Jolly and Messieurs Diguet and Génibrel. There was a mixed choir of sixty voices—the Philharmonic Society choir, accompanied by the Orchestra of the French Opera. In addition, several unnamed soloists are listed as members of the Philharmonic. Besides the usual opera works by Auber, Meyerbeer, Rossini, Donizetti, and Hummel, and choral works by Bishop (his ever-popular "Home Sweet Home") and Handel (the program ended with the "Hallelujah" Chorus from *Messiah*), Curto's cavatina from the opera *Tancredi* was sung by Madame Wiedemann. (The music businesses of H. D. Hewitt and W. T. Mayo had a hand in making the concert possible. They both sold tickets, and Hewitt's firm provided the William Hall and Society of New York piano. In addition, Hewitt signed the advertisement in the newspaper as "Secretary," presumably of the Philharmonic Society.)

The short life of the Philharmonic Society was over by the end of its first year. There may have been several reasons, but certainly contributing to it was the flood of concerts in New Orleans by famous world-class musicians of the time. A new venue that had opened in 1851, Odd Fellows' Hall, apparently had acoustics comparable to the Théâtre d'Orléans and much better than those of the lycée and armory, so that now events could take place without displacing the opera at the Théâtre d'Orléans. Native son Louis Moreau Gottschalk returned home in the spring of 1853 and gave at least nine recitals (in addition to performing on the debut recital of Marguerite Elie on May 16, 1853), which he then repeated the following year.[38] Famed violinist Ole Bull, who had made his New Orleans debut nearly a decade before, returned to the city in 1851 in the company of the soprano Theresa Parodi, the pianist Maurice Strakosch[39] and Strakosch's wife, the soprano Amalia Patti. Their concerts and the concerts including the Patti sisters during the 1850s are discussed above. Meanwhile, two other famous singers came for several concerts each: Jenny Lind for thirteen concerts from February to March 1851 and Henrietta Sontag in 1854.[40] On February 18, 1854, Paul Julien arrived from New York and began a series of twelve concerts that lasted until March 2; Julien also teamed up with Adelina Patti for a concert on March 29, 1856. Encouraged by the success of Julien's mixed concert series in 1854, M Gustave Collignon created his Société de Musique Classique, which enabled audiences in New Orleans to hear complete symphonies by Beethoven and Mendelssohn, as well as overtures and tone poems by the likes of Weber and Berlioz, from 1856 to 1860. The wonderful young violinist Camille Urso appeared in several recitals between April 18 and May 3, 1854. There was only so much attention that local patrons could give to concert music outside the opera, and with such heady competition the local talent, of which Curto and La Hache were so proud in 1851 and 1852, could not contend. Collignon, for whatever reason, was able to compete, but Curto was not.

There does not seem to be another public concert by Curto until May 12, 1858, when he once again conducted a choir, orchestra, and soloists in a benefit in Odd Fellows' Hall, this time for the Jewish Widows and Orphans Home.[41] The first half began with the Overture to Weber's *Der Freischütz* and the second half with the Overture to Rossini's *La Gazza Ladra*. The rest of the program consisted of choruses, airs, a duet and a trio from operas by Weber, Rossini, Auber, Meyerbeer, Halévy, and Donizetti, and a poem and chorus from Curto's own *Jeanne d'Arc*. This opera, which is listed by Louis Panzeri as *La Mort de Jeanne d'Arc* in two acts, is not known to have been performed in its entirety in New Orleans. In any case, if completed, it probably was written in the 1850s.

November 12, 1866, was an important date for Curto, for on that occasion he was honored with an entire evening of his compositions. It was a huge "grand concert dramatique" with full orchestra in the French Opera House conducted by Robert Meyer. The program was in three parts: (1) the first part of Curto's opera *Le Lepreux,* (2) the first 4 sections of Curto's *Stabat Mater,* a grande scene lyrique by Curto, and two vocal selections by Auber, and (3) the grand lyric scene by Curto, *La Mort d'Abel* sung with costumes.[42] Among the singers was Mlle Emma Fairex, his pupil.[43]

With his public performing career virtually at a standstill by 1853, Curto concentrated on his church duties, composition, and teaching. Suddenly there appeared many editions of works by Curto, perhaps composed earlier but in any case not published until the performing career was at a standstill. We have already noted the public performances in New Orleans of four full operas and separate scenes that Curto composed by 1853 and a symphonic work. None were published. Aside from the last, all the surviving music by this composer includes voices. There are many secular songs—mostly solos but also one duet for two sopranos—published between 1853 and 1885, that seem to have been composed for pupils. There are also twelve masses for choirs of three, four, or five voices published between 1855 and 1876, one oratorio (*La Mort d'Abel*) from 1866, and a number of other sacred settings published from 1857 to 1883. Thus, the composition and publication of music took over Curto's life as his public performance career ended and, initially, as the Civil War approached. When he did appear in public after 1853, it was largely with his students and for the benefit of his students.

Curto claimed to have written fifteen polyphonic masses, but only fourteen have been ascertained. In 1855 he published a set of seven masses which were to be followed by eight more. According to the title page, all these masses were regularly sung at Curto's own church, Sainte Theresa of New Orleans. By 1870, however, only four more were published. These eleven masses are as follows:

1. Sainte Elizabeth
2. Saint Louis
3. Sainte Anne
4. Saint Augustin*
5. Saint Vincent de Paul*
6. Sainte Thésèse*
7. Notre Dame,* dedicated to the church Notre Dame in Bay Saint Louis, Mississippi
8. Saint Philomène
9. Sainte Cécile (1856),* dedicated to Curto's friend "mon ami E. Prévost"
10. *L'Immaculée Conception* (1869)* dedicated to Monsieur l'Abbé Simon, "cure de St Eustache"
11. Sainte Trinité (ca. 1870)* dedicated to Father Halbedl[44]

Those with the asterisk (*) have been located. The tenth mass, *L'Immaculée Conception,* differs in printed format from the others (published in New York, not New Orleans) and is dedicated not to a New Orleanian but to a colleague in Paris.[45] A twelfth mass, dedicated to Sainte Eugénie, for three-voice choir (soprano, tenor, and bass) with organ was published by Louis Grunewald in New

Orleans in 1876 and survives today at the archive of Louisiana State University in Baton Rouge; it is listed as Curto's twenty-fifth mass, but more likely it is number 15. Two additional masses—*La Messe de Dumont* for five voices and *La Messe Imperiale* for four voices—are listed on the covers of his other masses but have not been located. Whether these constitute two of the missing numbers 12 to 14 is uncertain.

Curto sets the usual Ordinary texts of the masses: Kyrie, Gloria, Credo, Sanctus, and Agnus Dei. How he relates these movements harmonically to each other shows his gift at harmonic juxtaposition and the sophistication that the composer achieved through his experiences with excellent masters in France. In general the masses are well written by a professional church musician with considerable skills as a singer, choir director, and teacher. There is nothing amateurish about them, except that any ordinary church choir of amateurs could perform them successfully. They range from three- to four-voice choirs, with a few solo passages interspersed and with the accompaniment of organ. There is also an array of styles and textures, including a few fugues.

In addition to the regular masses, Curto set a *Requiem Mass* together with the Office for dead children. They were published in New Orleans in 1855, the same year as the first seven masses. These are strikingly different from the others in that Curto has preserved the standard Gregorian chant that was used at Sainte Theresa's Church. The Office movements are in modern notation and with an organ accompaniment provided by Curto. Seven of the eight movements of the *Requiem Mass* (Introit, Kyrie, Absolve, Dies Irae, Sanctus, Pie Jesu, and Agnus Dei) are scored for three voices (soprano or tenor, alto or baritone, and bass) and organ and utilize the chant as a cantus firmus in the alto or baritone voice, while the Offertory (following the Dies Irae) is, like the Office, set in simple monophonic plainsong with organ accompaniment.[46]

Besides full-scale services, Curto also set smaller liturgical passages and non-liturgical sacred texts. The most pretentious of these is his *Stabat Mater* No. 2 (the whereabouts of No. 1 is unknown). Published in Paris in 1869, it was first performed on June 4, 1868, in New Orleans for the benefit of the Society of Saint Vincent de Paul. The published score is dedicated to "La Confrérie de la bonne Mort et de Notre-Dame des Sept Douleurs Paroisse Saint Eustache de Paris."[47] The original performance had a full orchestra accompanying the voices, but the published version gives only a piano part. There are eleven movements, each with a different vocal scoring. The four-voice choir (two sopranos, tenor, and bass) participates in six of them, while solos, duets, and trios perform in the rest. The "Cujus Animam" is a solo trio followed by the choir, the "Inflammatus" is a solo quartet followed by the choir—the whole movement performed a cappella—and "Juxta Crucem" is a bass solo followed by the choir.

There is a *Te Deum* for four voices mentioned on the cover of the 1855 *Requiem* score, but it has not been found. In 1857 Curto began a series of publications entitled *25 Motets a Une, Deux, Trois, et Quatre Voix* printed in New Orleans and apparently used by Curto at Sainte Theresa's. They are Latin works, of which only four have been located. They are bound together in the original publication: "O Salutaris" (no. 1); "Monstra te esse matrem" (no. 2), a motet to the Holy Virgin; "Offertoire: Da Pacem Domine" (no. 3); and another "O Salutaris" (no. 5). The first "O Salutaris" is incomplete; it is scored for solo voice and organ. The other setting (no. 5) is a duet for soprano or tenor and bass with organ accompaniment. "Monstra Te Esse Matrem" is set for soprano or tenor with organ, and the "Offertoire" is a duet for two sopranos with organ. These are functional pieces without any concert-hall intentions.

Quite different is another Latin motet which Curto published later. "Ave Maria," for soprano or tenor with organ, published by Grunewald in New Orleans in 1870 and dedicated to his friend L. Heichelheim, is a much more significant composition. Fifty-four measures long (in 12/8 meter), it is in four sections, with a coda for organ alone. While the singing technique is not difficult, it is as dramatic as any aria in an opera, and the harmony reinforces the operatic nature of the piece.

In addition to these works is a series of sacred songs—in French, English, or Latin—which Curto seems to have written for his students or other amateurs. Most are simple, but "Deux Voix" is a significant work. A setting of a text by L. Placide Canonge and translated by K. R. Shaw, it was written for the benefit of the Orphanage Sainte Thérése, dedicated to Mme E. Ambre, and published in New Orleans around 1880–81.[48] It is set for voice and piano and is much more advanced vocally, harmonically, and melodically than nearly all other works by Curto. It contrasts the despairing voice of an orphan with the voice of the artist who is lending a helping hand.

The other sacred songs are much simpler. Curto's *The Lord's Prayer for Three Voices* follows both a French version and an English translation by Miss E. C. Wingate and seems designed for a class of high-school girls. Indeed, Curto calls himself a "professor of music in the normal and high schools [of] New Orleans" on the title page. Published in 1869, the work is dedicated to George Peabody Esq., who may very well be the head of the Peabody High School with which Curto was associated in the 1880s. The Latin and English song "Ingemisco" for mezzo soprano with piano or organ was published two years later in 1871 by

Grunewald and is dedicated to the mezzo Mlle Ph. de Edelsberg, who was at the French Opera at that time. It is a song to instruct the young person in correct moral behavior; one will have hope of being forgiven for his wrongs if he himself has forgiven a dying thief. The rhythm is uncomplicated, the phraseology is unvaryingly regular, the vocal range is an octave and a fifth (a sixth if an alternate high note is taken), and the harmony is virtually static. "The Guardian Angel" is another easy song published earlier, in 1857 in New Orleans, dedicated to Miss Amedie Macarty, and translated from the French by E. M. Allison. Like "Deux Voix," it was published for the benefit of the Camp Street Orphan Asylum (Sainte Theresa's). For voice and piano, it is a plea for one's guardian angel to take care of oneself. The strophic solo song "Merci Mon Dieu, Reward Thou Lord" (Grunewald 1876)[49] and the late "O Mother, Dear Jerusalem" (New Orleans, 1883) are similarly simple.[50]

Mostly for the benefit of his students Curto wrote a number of secular songs, all intended for those private students of whom he expected much more than of the high school or orphanage students. Reasonably difficult is "Amour e Foi, Melodie," whose French text was by the physician Dr. Alfred Mercier, secretary of the Athenée Louisianais, and dedicated to Madame J. Pike. It was printed in New Orleans at the end of Curto's life, in 1885. It tells one to have faith in one's lover, and this faith will bring one out of despair. It is slightly more difficult than "Mo Aimé Toué," Curto's only song in the New Orleans Creole dialect. Subtitled "a Chasonette Créole," it has four strophes sung to a simple tune. Basically the singer cannot resist her love, and there are ample references to popular Afro-Creole dances like the calinda. "Inès" is another simple song, a rondo with text by Placide Canonge and dedicated to Mlle E. Pinparé. Pedro follows Inès in a dance, but she does not love him. She tells him to guard his forests and prairies while she guards her heart. In "To My Sweetheart" (published by Grunewald in 1875) Curto sets words by Mrs. C. Edmonston and dedicates the piece to Miss Cora A. Townsend, who may have been one of his pupils. In a very simple setting Curto sneaks in a few small chromatics and an augmented sixth.

In 1860 Curto published *Les Etoiles,* a set of eight songs of which six survive. These are more challenging than his other secular songs, and several are of great dramatic worth. "Myrrha" (no. 4) is actually drawn from Curto's opera *La Mort de Sardanapale* (1849) and consists of an introduction, a recitative, an arioso, a strophic aria (two strophes) and a coda. It is a very expressive piece, as are the much simpler "Mourir d'Amour" (no. 7) and "Père et Ro" (no. 3). The first is a song of fear of unrequited love that can be sung by a singer who is not very advanced, while the second is a dramatic romance where a king does not regret his losses except for that of his main treasure, his son. "Minuit Sérénade" (no. 1), "Je ne le Dis pas" (no. 2), and "L'Orphelin" (no. 8) are also very simple strophic songs with texts that enable the singer to develop modes of expression: the first is a basic love song; the second is sung by someone in love with a black-eyed, blond-headed girl—a demon, but he can't really help it; and the third describes an orphan child weeping on his mother's gravestone.

Another excerpt from an opera survives—a cavatina from the opera *Tancrède*. Dedicated to Mme Wiedemann, star of the Théâtre d'Orléans, the words are by Canonge. It was published by Manouvrier in New Orleans in 1852. The aria begins on an augmented sixth, but otherwise the harmony is not very complicated. The vocal technique is ostensibly not difficult, yet it is a piece that requires a professional voice. This work, like the excerpt from *La Mort de Sardanapale*, was intended not for students but for the best singers that New Orleans had to offer, the professionals whom Davis brought over from France and who, like Curto himself, were used to the highest standards that Europe boasted at the time. Only the best of Curto's students, such as Alice Fleury, were encouraged to sing them. This is a major work, and like the simpler dramatic songs in *Les Etoiles*, they demonstrate why Curto was held in such high esteem by his contemporaries and why his music is worthy of revival.

Of special interest is Curto's one song of the Civil War. "Ne m'Oubliez pas" was published in 1861 and is dedicated to Mme E. R. Magner. While all of Curto's other songs sing of others' travails, love, and sorrows, this song hits home. "Vous me quittez pour marcher à la gloire" (You leave me to march to glory) was a text that reached the heart of every parent or wife or child as he or she watched a loved one leave the city in that initial year of the war and held fears that that person would never return. Until 1861 such thoughts in a civilized city like New Orleans were abstract, but with the outbreak of hostilities closely monitored by the local citizenry, fear and the ugly reality of war superseded operatic drama. Curto, a dramatic composer, was compelled to express the drama of the moment in his music.

It remains to consider Curto as a renowned teacher of voice. While he did start as a professor at Choron's school in Paris and became associated with several schools during his later years in New Orleans, notably Peabody High School during the early 1880s and then at the end of his life at the Mrs. Gregorio Curto [Eugénie] School,[51] the bulk of his teaching career was private lessons.

His best-known student was Minnie Hauk (1851–1929).[52] Hauk was born in New York and in about 1860 arrived in New Orleans as a young girl of nine with her parents. It was a difficult time as the Civil War approached, as it then raged, and as the port of New Orleans was blockaded by the Union forces. A northern family could not safely return to the north. In Hauk's own words many years later,

> It was there that I attracted the attention of the well-known French singing-master, M Curto. He had been a contemporary of Duprez, the great tenor of the Paris Opera, but he had lost his basso voice, and had settled in New Orleans—then far more "Frenchy" than it is now—to give singing lessons. He was a French gentleman of the old school. He took a cordial interest in me, gave me lessons twice a week, and predicted a great future for me as a singer.... When, soon afterwards, a charity concert was arranged to take place at the Grand Opera House, for the wounded of both Federals and Confederates, *Maître* Curto thought I might take part in it.... I was then about nine years old.[53]

She sang the difficult aria "Casta Diva" from Bellini's *Norma,* as well as some other works. Hauk was a big success. But then, on May 1, 1862, the Union Army took the city, and Hauk's family could at last travel unimpeded back home to New York. She left New Orleans for New York where she then sang for Max Maretzek. She chose to sing "Casta Diva." "After the training my dear old *Maître* Curto had given me, I felt sure I could do it."[54] Maretzek, however, was not entirely impressed, and as any good singing teacher would have said, he told her she should start at the beginning, not the top. He referred her to another teacher in New York, who then prepared her for her Brooklyn debut in 1866.

Besides Minnie Hauk, two other students of Curto's were Fleury Urban and Marie Durand Hitchcock.[55] In 1873 Jewell refers to Fleury Urban as already famous and Hitchcock as one who will be famous, yet there is very little information about the latter and none about the former. Marie-Louise Durand, a native of Brooklyn, made her Chicago debut as Zerlina on October 2, 1868, and she sang in *Lucia* in Brignoli's Italian Opera Company in Chicago on July 9, 1869.[56] The only newspaper reference to Marie Durand Hickinson [sic] at the time is to a young, inexperienced singer. Curto dedicated to Alice Fleury his song "Myrrha" which was published as no. 4 of his song series *Les Etoiles* in 1860. "Myrrha" is actually a "scène et romance" from Curto's opera *La Mort de Sardanapale* (1849) and is clearly the most expressive and difficult song in the collection. Curto must have thought very highly of her as both singer and musician to have dedicated this work to her. It is possible she was the Mlle Fleury Jolly who appeared with Curto in his concert at Armory Hall on May 26, 1852.

Curto seems to have taken great care to nurture his students. When he directed a concert in Odd Fellows' Hall on October 29, 1861, in the midst of war and great anxiety, his "amateur" singers were protected both in the advertisements and in the review by anonymity. The arias, duets, and trios were demanding, including hits from the operas that had been popular at both the old opera house (Théâtre d'Orléans) and the new one (Théâtre d'Opéra): *La Dame Blanche* (Boieldieu), *Il Trovatore* (Verdi), *Sémiramide* (Rossini), *Montechi e Capuletti* (Bellini), *L'Étoile du Nord* (Meyerbeer), *Robert le Diable* (Meyerbeer), *The Barber of Seville* (Rossini), *Cheval de Bronce* (Aubert), *La Gazza Ladra* (Rossini), and *Roi d'Yvetot* (Adam). The program, dedicated to the Artillerie Crescent, was deemed a great success.[57] Individual singers, without being named, were applauded for their great talent: "A young girl, who sang here yesterday for the first time in public and who is endowed with a magnificent organ and a happy musical sense, admirably sang two romances, one from *Robert le Diable* and the other from *Il Trovatore*. Once again we had the pleasure of hearing two other singers, whom we heard on a previous occasion and of whom we have already spoken, who were also applauded with enthusiasm." All acquitted their roles in a remarkable manner. On another occasion, after the war was over and concert life was just beginning to return to normal, Curto joined his pupil "Mlle J. R." in the grand farewell concert for Marguerite Elie before her return to Paris and marriage there.[58] Once again, he felt obliged to hide the identity of a performer who was at a precarious point of her career.

After a productive life as a singer, composer, conductor, church musician, and teacher, Curto died on November 19, 1887, age eighty-two and a resident of New Orleans for fifty-seven years.[59] He was survived by his wife, Eugénie; no one else is mentioned in his obituary. His funeral took place at his home on the corner of Saint Philip and Prieur streets at 4 p.m. on Tuesday, November 21. Members of the musical and literary societies of the city were invited to attend.

Years after Curto died, there appeared an article about him in a newspaper in New Orleans. Though full of historical inaccuracies, it reflects the respect in which Curto was held even after he was gone.

> In a way-back little directory of New Orleans of 1820 occurs the name A. Curto, comedian.[60] Whether this Curto was any relation to Gregorio Curto is not known. Gregorio came here when quite young, but we have no knowledge of his forbears. Wherever he received his musical education deponent sayeth not, but he was an efficient teacher and a talented musician. In a notice of him given by a contemporary it is said that during his residence in New Orleans "he made a generation of singers." Many of those he taught went on to the operatic stage and achieved name and fame, Minnie Hanck [sic] and

Marie Dumont [Durand] Hitchcock among others. In the directory of 1861 he modestly calls himself "G. Curto, Professor of Music, 299 Saint Philip Street," but he was much more than that. He was a composer of strength and merit, his specialty being masses. It is remembered of him that when he found a promising voice, the lack of money on the part of its possessor to remunerate him never stood in his way. To train that voice was a luxury he never denied himself. He died in 1884 [*sic*], and "none of the older musicians of New Orleans is embalmed in kinder memories."[61]

3

Paul Emile Johns

Tycoon, Musician, and Friend of Chopin

In 1832 Chopin dedicated his famous Mazurkas Opus 7 to M Johns de Nouvelle Orléans. No other American was ever so honored by the Polish émigré. Why did this seemingly obscure American cotton magnate deserve Chopin's admiration? Who was this gentleman from one of the leading cultural centers of nineteenth-century America?

Paul Emile Johns or simply Emile Johns as he was known in New Orleans, was born in Cracow, Poland, about 1798.[1] It is probable, however, that he grew up in Vienna, since he sometimes gives Vienna as his birthplace on official documents. By 1820, when he was already active in New Orleans, his mother Barbara Tcheszka was dead and his father Frederic Johns was living in Vienna, apparently remarried.[2] For over forty years Emile Johns lived in New Orleans, though he made frequent trips abroad.[3] He was married three times and sired at least five daughters and possibly two sons.[4] His first wife Anna may have been an actress.[5]

It is not known when or where Johns received his musical training, but when he arrived in New Orleans about 1818 he was already an accomplished pianist. For on February 10, 1819, he is first listed in New Orleans as a concert artist and performed a Beethoven concerto with an orchestra (we do not know which one). It just so happens that this is the earliest known performance of any of the Beethoven piano concertos in the United States[6] (see page 283).

In 1822 Johns is listed in New Orleans as "teacher on the pianoforte" and in early 1823 as "pianiste."[7] For the next six years he was an active member of the growing musical life of New Orleans, and, along with several other pianists, Johns appears most often in concert programs as accompanying other artists. A typical such concert occurred at the Théâtre d'Orléans on Monday, January 28,

---

This chapter was originally published in *Report of the Eleventh Congress* (of the International Musicological Society), *Copenhagen 1972*.

1828.[8] Advertised as a "grand concert vocal et instrumental, suivi d'un grand bal," it starred M Jandot, flutist in the Opera Orchestra and son of the principal clarinetist at the theater in Bordeaux, France. The program began with the usual Rossini overture (this time to *L'Italienne à Alger*). It continued with a series of opera arias by Rossini and Mozart sung by members of the French Opera Company, and flute and clarinet concertos by Tolou and Gauthier performed by Jandot and Gauthier accompanied by the Opera Orchestra. The program concluded with a *Fantasie pour la Flûte sur le Rossignol et Tancrède* by Jandot performed by Jandot accompanied on the piano by Mr. Johns.

Johns's role in the concerts was usually secondary, but in February 1824 he had his opportunity to demonstrate all his talent. On Monday, February 2, he and Mr. Chéret, a singer at the local opera, put on a benefit concert at the Théâtre d"Orléans.[9] The program featured J. L. Dussek's Piano Concerto No. 2 performed by Johns and the Opera Orchestra. Two evenings later the same artists gave another concert in the same hall, this time not only featuring Johns as pianist—in Steibelt's Piano Concerto No. 3 and in Mayseder's *Third Grand Poland Air*—but also featuring Johns as composer.[10] The program concluded with a *Grand Military March*, "lately composed by Mr. Johns, executed with full orchestra." Two other works by Johns were premiered within the next two weeks. Another benefit concert—this time "for the benefit of a needy family"— on February 9 featured Johns in his dual role as pianist and composer.[11] He accompanied the clarinetist Le Page in a nocturne by Bochsa, and the concert ended with *A Warlike Symphony*, "composed for the occasion by Mr. Johns, and executed by all the orchestra." The crowning achievement, however, came on the evening of Tuesday, February 17, when "for the benefit of Mr. Johns" the French Opera gave the first and apparently last performance of his *Séjour Militaire, ou La Double Mistification,* an opéra comique in one act.[12] The program also included a French comedy in one act and a vaudeville féerie entitled *The Sleeping Beauty* in two acts with a grand spectacle by Barré and Radet. The principal music reviewer in New Orleans at the time could find little to say about all Johns's efforts except to criticize on moral and aesthetic grounds the conclusion of each of the three benefit concerts with Mardi Gras *bals* (Mardi Gras fell on March 2 in 1824).[13] Despite this rebuke, the custom continued for many years, though never again was Johns so prolific.

Johns's name appears in another concert as both a composer and a pianist. On May 30, 1827, at a concert "for the benefit of Mr. Segura, leader of the orchestra and first violinist of the Havana Theatre," Johns improvised a piece on the piano.[14] The reviewer of the time does not mention this but speaks of Segura as the "greatest violinist that ever visited New Orleans." Perhaps discouraged by such neglect, Johns seems to have ended his career as pianist in 1828, for although his name is prominent in New Orleans for a long time thereafter, there is only one further mention of his piano playing. On June 27, 1850, he performed his *Mazurka de Concert* at a grand concert in the Lyceum.[15] He did supplement his earnings, however, by playing the organ in church; from at least October 1, 1842, until at least February 1844, he was organist at Saint Louis Cathedral.[16]

Sometime during the musically active years of the 1820s Johns may have composed his *Album Louisianais: Hommage aux Dames de La Nouvelle Orléans,* the most significant music of his to survive.[17] Published by Pleyel in Paris sometime between 1831 and 1834, this elegant collection contains six strophic songs and two pieces for piano alone. Each piece is dedicated to a different Creole woman of the city. The songs, with sentimental French verses by an unidentified "J.L.," are clearly under the influence of Rossini and may be accompanied by piano or harp. The second song is a bolero, and the fifth and sixth are romances. Each song is preceded by an appropriate and attractive engraving. The two piano pieces are a Valse in E-flat Major and a Polonaise Héroïque in F Minor. The two are forceful pieces which are technically not difficult to perform and which suggest the virtuosity of a Dussek or Hummel. They are not unpleasant and bear some superficial resemblance to Chopin's waltzes and polonaises.

Johns was first involved with the publication of music in 1830 when, jointly with George Willig of Philadelphia, he produced W. W. Waddel's *Governor Gilmer's Grand March.* There is no indication that Johns actually printed the piece; that was assuredly left to Willig. But most of the music sold by Johns during the 1830s, even composed by local New Orleanians, was not published by him. This includes works by G. P. Manouvrier, such as his "Les Magnolias" ("Valse Louisianaises à la Strauss," dedicated to Madam E. Johns),[18] which was published by Wittig in 1838, and "Haste, Boatman, Haste-Barcarolle" (words by Miss Castello) printed in New York by Hewitt and Jacque also in 1838. Only in 1839 did Johns publish by himself his own song "Romance," with text by Dominique Rouquette, which was produced solely by him in New Orleans without a co-publisher.[19]

In January 1826, Johns advertised in the local newspapers that he had new music from Paris to sell at his home or at the store of a friend.[20] This apparently is the beginning of his second career in the city. On December 14, 1830, he officially announced the establishment of E. Johns and Company, music sellers and stationers. Just returned from London, Paris, Vienna,[21] and the principal cities of Germany, where he entered into agreement with the principal "music venders and editors," he began a dealership that lasted for him until 1846. The store was at first primarily a music store, selling the latest European albums, sheet music, and musical instruments. At least one piano survives today with the plaque "made by Pleyel and Sons exclusively for Mr. E. Johns."[22] Johns had competitors, and seemingly treated one of them, a woman, a bit roughly.[23] Because of this competition, he was forced to include other items besides musical ones, and before long his advertisements announced for sale political biographies, art prints, sewing needles, scissors, furniture, pen-knives, and saddles. By 1837, when his store burned down and he was forced to relocate, he was also active as a printer of books, and in November 1839 he and his partner Manouvrier began publishing the first German-language newspaper in the city: *Der Deutsche*.[24]

It is during this period that Johns made frequent trips to Europe to find new instruments to sell back home. His relationship with Pleyel and Sons seems to have started before 1830 when he first sold music in New Orleans, and it was only natural, then, that in the summer of 1832 while in Paris, Johns was in touch with Pleyel. While negotiating with the American for sale of his pianos, Camille Pleyel probably introduced Johns and Chopin, two Polish emigrants, to each other. Chopin and his Polish friends in Paris may have been considering coming to America, and they would have had a lot of questions to ask Johns. Particularly Chopin, who had his career as well as his patriotism to consider, would have had much to learn from his American colleague. New Orleans was an attractive location for young performers and composers of opera, and the audiences were eager to hear music. But Johns had failed in his career as pianist and composer in the New World. The city of New Orleans could not maintain so many pianists, at least not with the financial returns Johns apparently sought. The dazzling piano career of Louis Moreau Gottschalk, the greatest pianist from nineteenth-century New Orleans, was carried on largely away from the city, and in any case his example was several decades into the future.[25] Johns's view of America that he presented to Chopin would have been colored by his own frustrations, and Chopin may have decided against leaving for the United States because of Johns's position.

Johns obviously made a strong impression on Chopin, for the latter then dedicated his Opus 7 to him and gave Johns a letter of introduction to Ferdinand Hiller in August 1832. The letter is lost, but Niecks reports that Chopin introduced Johns as "a distinguished amateur of New Orleans" and warmly recommended him.[26] No further communication between Chopin and Johns is known.

E. Johns and Company flourished as the chief representative of Pleyel in New Orleans. For a time G. P. Manouvrier was a partner. This gentleman was also a local composer who wrote pieces for the women of New Orleans; one such work is dedicated to the first Mrs. Johns (see above).[27] In 1846 Johns sold his store to W. T. Mayo who in 1852 resold the store to Philip Werlein. Werlein's remained the largest music store in New Orleans until 2002, and survived until 2005 as the most important piano store in the Greater New Orleans area.

When Johns sold his store, he seems to have left music entirely. Perhaps through the influence of his second and third wives, both of whom came from the same wealthy plantation family, Johns went into the more prestigious business of cotton. From 1850 to 1860 he is known as a dealer and merchant in cotton, although in 1851, at least, he tried his hand also in wholesale groceries, especially wines and liquors.[28] He held the post of Russian consul in New Orleans from at least 1848 until 1860, and he was a knight in the order of Sainte Anne of Russia.[29]

On April 20, 1860, Johns attended the wedding in New Orleans of his daughter Mathilde to Mr. Leopold Christ, originally of Baden, Germany.[30] After the wedding Johns sailed for Europe, and on August 10 he suddenly died in Paris after an operation.[31] He is buried there in the Montmartre Cemetery, not far from such notables as Berlioz, Stendhal, and Delibes. Whatever the reasons, Johns's great promise as composer and pianist, like that of so many, was not realized, and his claim to a footnote in history lies with his momentary contact and perhaps influence on a far greater man.

4

Ludovico Gabici
Violinist and Conductor

Ludovico Gabici was born in Ravenna, Italy, about 1813.[1] We know nothing about his early life or his education. When we first meet him in 1837, he is the twenty-four-year-old chef d'orchestra or conductor of the Italian Opera in Havana. He was married to Caroline Deninger (ca. 1813–83), a native of Stuttgart, Germany, who bore him a son, Charles L. Gabici, and a daughter, Louise Amélie.[2] Whether he married her before or after his arrival in the Crescent City is also not known.

Gabici first appeared in New Orleans as conductor of the visiting Italian Company from the Grand Opera of Havana. He arrived in New Orleans about April 1, 1837, and during the next week led performances of Bellini's *I Capuleti e i Montecchi*.[3] Whether he stayed in New Orleans from this point on or returned a year later is uncertain, but we next meet him in New Orleans in June 1838, as an instrumental performer at the Vauxhall in the Saint Charles Theatre.[4] Concerts were given nightly in conjunction with other, usually dramatic entertainment. Later that year he was the intended manager and conductor of a new Italian opera company that was being formed in the city.[5] The patrons intended to erect an opera house, but nothing seems to have come of that. For the next few years, however, the Italian singers from Havana came to New Orleans, and Gabici conducted them with a local orchestra in favorite Italian operas. In April 1840 he was once again associated as a violinist with the Italian opera of Havana,[6] but it is not yet certain whether he was commuting from Havana or living full time in New Orleans. Although he is first listed in the *New Orleans City Directory* only in 1842 when he was residing on Philippa Street, he was already living in New Orleans full time by October 1840, when he announced that he would give Italian language, singing, violin, and guitar lessons at Harby's Day and Boarding Academy, No. 256 Common Street.[7] In May 1841, he was active in the concert life of the city. He performed two solo works at Mr. Trust's

Concerts at the Verandah Hotel on Wednesday, May 12, and again on Monday, May 17, where he played one of his own works as well as Mayseder's *Thema with Variations.*[8]

Gabici was next heard from as a composer. Early in February 1842, his composition based on the *Idylle of Göethe* [sic] was performed at the Théâtre d'Orléans by its orchestra under Eugène Prévost and with the assistance of the German Glee Club.[9] As the critic stated, "This is a splendid effort Gabici has made with the Idylle of Göethe, and the Glee Club rendered it in a manner every way worthy of so brilliant a composition. Gabici has every encouragement to indulge his favorite passion, and the refined taste of the day will doubtless yet award him a name that shall live honorably with posterity." Another composition by Gabici was heard on Friday, April 29, 1842, when Mr. Dantonnet, violoncellist, performed his *Fantasia for the Violincello* [sic], *with Accompaniments by the Orchestra, from [Meyerbeer's]* The Huguenots.[10] Eugène Prévost once again conducted the orchestra of the Théâtre d'Orléans at that theater. On the same program Gabici also played the violin in a duet with harp, the latter performed by Mr. A. J. Trust.

On Wednesday evening, May 18, 1842, Gabici was leader of the orchestra at a concert of the Sacred Music Society at Rev. Mr. Clapp's Church under the direction of Trust.[11] The vocal concert included works by Haydn, Mozart, Beethoven, Handel, Arne, Bellini, Reghini, and C. Keller. A few weeks later, on June 7, nearly the identical program was repeated, but this time the pianist, Mr. Wallace, joined in.[12] Wallace had already performed in the city on June 2 with Gabici, Cioffi, and Fourmestreau participating.[13]

Later in 1843 Gabici is referred to as a "Keeper of the Conti Street Hotel."[14] It might seem strange that Gabici was working in the Conti Hotel, but actually there is a strong possibility that he had a very important position there. Every Tuesday, Thursday, and Saturday the Salle Conti, in the hotel, featured grand balls, and in the fall of 1842 these balls were listed just under the advertisements of the Théâtre d'Orléans in *L'Abeille* as among the most important "amusements" in the city. Modestly the advertisements stated, "The orchestra, comprised of numerous talented musicians, is unquestionably the best in the city. It will execute all waltzes and new contradances, many of which were composed by members of the orchestra." Gabici may have been a violinist in that orchestra, a contributor to the new compositions by the artists of the orchestra, or even its conductor.

Gabici was mentioned as a musician in an advertisement in *L'Abeille* for a grand concert to take place on Saturday evening, December 3, 1842, in the ballroom of the Saint Louis Hotel, and there he is announced as the conductor of the orchestra. The featured soloist was W. V. Wallace, now titled "the violinist," who was assisted by singers Mlle Celine Douce, Mr. Varnay, and Mr. E. Sheppard. Besides accompanying these artists, Gabici began both halves of the program conducting (unnamed) overtures.

In April 1843, Gabici was again conducting the Italian Opera Company of Havana in two weeks of Italian operas at the New American Theatre.[15] The orchestra consisted of thirty of the best artists of New Orleans, while the singers came from Havana. Among the operas performed were *I Puritani* (Bellini), *Gemma de Vergy* (Donizetti), *Norma* (Bellini), and *Lucia di Lammermoor* (Donizetti). Shortly after the departure of these singers, Gabici led an orchestra at the New American Theatre in a benefit for the singer Mrs. Castellan; the complete *Norma* was sung with Castellan in the title role.[16] Then on May 23 he conducted a grand vocal and instrumental concert at the Théâtre d'Orléans that included a violin solo by his pupil Adolphe Bounivard in a new piece written especially for the occasion by Gabici.[17]

During the summer of 1844 Gabici seems to have spent time in nearby Bay Saint Louis, Mississippi. He was director of a dance orchestra that, according to the *Picayune,* made a sensation: "The music was most excellent—of this you can judge when I tell you that Gabici led the band, and those that 'played second fiddle' and other instruments, all knew their business well."[18] He next appeared as a violinist in a performance of a piano trio by Reissiger at the Salle Saint Louis on December 30, 1844.[19]

During the spring of 1845, Gabici was once again a member of the orchestra of the Italian Opera Company that was appearing at the American Theatre on Poydras Street. The Italian Company began a series of twenty-four full-length performances of standard Italian operas on March 3 and ended early in May. On April 25 a series of benefit concerts dove-tailing the opera performances began for various members of the troupe. The one for Gabici, "the well-known Violinist, who has been attached to the Orchestra of the Italian Company during the present season,"[20] took place on May 1. It was a substantial program that included Ole Bull's arrangement of "Casta Diva" from Bellini's opera *Norma,* the Violin Concerto No. 1 of Charles De Bériot, and a *Tremola* by De Bériot. He was accompanied by members of the Italian Company's Orchestra, "who wished to testify to this excellent violinist its gratitude for the services which it has received."[21] On May 5 a benefit concert was held for the conductor of the orchestra, Signor La Manna, this time at the Washington Battalion Armory; the Orchestra of the American Theatre accompanied him. Two days later the Italian Company crossed over to the rival Théâtre d'Orléans for a benefit concert to aid the Italian Benevolent Society of New Orleans; the program consisted of three acts from three separate operas. And on May 10 the Italian Company performed at the Théâtre d'Orléans the second act of Donizetti's *L'Elisir d'Amore,* the third act of Rossini's *Sémiramide,* and the world premier of Gregorio Curto's *Le Lepreux.* Since he was a prominent member of the Italian Company's Orchestra (probably its concertmaster), Gabici likely performed in all these benefit concerts.

The following spring Gabici was again conductor of the Italian opera troupe that performed in the American Theatre on Poydras Street.[22] He led the ensemble in Bellini's *I Capuleti e i Montecchi* on May 19 and 21, 1846; Donizetti's *Lucia* on May 23 and May 25; and Bellini's *Norma* on May 27 and May 28. Perhaps Gabici and his company realized from the previous season that it could not compete with the well-established French opera at Théâtre d'Orléans, so instead of having the performances during the other's season, Gabici waited until the French Opera's season had concluded. As long as singers came in from Havana, he had to wait until the season there was over, too. While the critic of *L'Abeille* found the singing excellent at the first performance of *I Capuleti,* he was not so complementary of the orchestra under Gabici: "In sum, when the relations between public and artist are well established, when the orchestra has achieved an ensemble stronger than any nuance of disagreement, between the harps, for example, and the other instruments, the dilettantes of our city could have some very pleasant evenings: which is what we wish for them with all our hearts." He either did not attend any of the remaining performances, or he considered them not worthy of review. News concerning the Mexican War dominated the pages of the newspapers, and the papers' readers probably were less concerned with the merits of opera performances than with General Taylor's victories. After all, all three of these operas had been performed at the Théâtre d'Orléans numerous times and two of them previously by Gabici himself with earlier Italian companies, so yet another set of performances was not particularly newsworthy. On the other hand, at the last performance on May 28, Gabici led the entire musical ensemble in "a Grand Patriotic Cantata in honor of the GLORIOUS VICTORY of the 8th and 9th inst, by the American Army under Command of Gen. TAYLOR, composed expressly for the occasion by Sig. L. GABICI."[23] Since the music has not been found, it would have been nice to have a review so as to judge how the audience in New Orleans at the time reacted to Gabici as a composer.

By the end of 1846 Gabici was leader of the orchestra at the Saint Charles Theatre,[24] which given its only sporadic programming of concerts and operas gave Gabici time to perform elsewhere. On November 13, 1847, for example, he conducted an orchestra in the ballroom of the Market Exchange on Saint Louis Street that was a grand concert for the benefit of an orphanage.[25] The featured soloist was the flutist Carrière, originally from the Royal Conservatory of Music in Paris and now an honored member of the French Opera Orchestra. One of the soloists was the eleven-year-old prodigy Victor Gerber, pupil of Gabici, in an unnamed piece. When Major General Zachary Taylor visited the Saint Charles Theatre on December 3, 1847, Gabici was ready to honor him with his *Grand Triumphal March*.[26] Mayo published the piece a few weeks later. Two months after that, on February 1, 1848, Gerber appeared again, this time at the age of fourteen![27] It was the second concert of the soprano Madame Ablamowicz at Armory Hall.

Gerber, Gabici's pupil, performed again at a concert at Armory Hall on March 14, 1849. Gregorio Curto was also on the program, which was primarily a showcase for Mme T. Cailly from Paris.[28] Gabici scored a particular triumph on May 2, 1849, in a concert at the ballroom of the Saint Louis Hotel.[29] Once again young Gerber (back at eleven years) performed, this time in a concerto by De Bériot. In addition he joined his teacher in a *Grande Fantaisie* for two violins concertantes by L. Maurer. Gabici performed alone his own work based on music of Bellini's *Norma*, and conducted a symphony by Beethoven. Several singers from the Théâtre d'Orléans also participated. The reviewer in *L'Abeille* anticipated an exciting concert: "Mr. Gabici's concert takes place this evening. The tickets have sold with great speed since people know that the proceeds will support the young Gerber.[30] This pupil of Gabici is going to continue his musical education in Europe. His precocious talent has won him the sympathies of the New Orleans public, and they will have proof of it this evening. It is impossible for a large audience not to respond to the call of Gabici. Beethoven, De Bériot and Donizetti will be the fare of the soirée, and these names exercise a powerful influence on those of musical taste. We will hear also a charming composition of Mr. Chassignac and a Rêverie de M Gabici."[31] Two days later the reviewer gave his rave review: "Gabici's concert was one of the most beautiful of the season: the Saint Louis Hall was mobbed, Wednesday evening, with a large crowd who came to hear young Gerber. He proved once again that he has the stuff of a great artist: he will go far. Mr. Gabici seconded his student. Mr. Chassaignac and Mrs. Cailly sang with taste."[32] On May 4, 1849, Gabici, together with several other musicians including Mr. H. C. Page and Eugène Chassaignac performed for the Firemen's Charitable Association at the American Theatre.[33]

Whether or not he retained his post at the Saint Charles Theatre is uncertain; his last dated appearance there was as conductor for a special concert in honor of General Zachary Taylor on December 3, 1847.[34] In addition to the concerts in 1847, 1848, and spring 1849, at other venues, he next appears as the house conductor at the Théâtre des Variétés on Gravier Street as Chef d'Orchestre.[35] Opening its doors for the first time on December 8, 1849, under the management of J. Placide, this new venue featured dancers and singers as part of its troupe. By 1860, however, the Théâtre des Variétés had a new chef d'orchestra, Eugène Fenellen.

Gabici appeared as the composer of a special ballet on a program at Placide's Variétés on April 10, 1850.[36] It was a benefit for the dancer Mademoiselle Antonio Hilariet and included among the other dancers Elizabeth Baron, H. Valles, Señor Vegas, Mr. Magin and Mr. Bourary. The second divertissement was signaled: "Grand new Pas THE NATIONAL FLAG by Mlle A. Hilariet, assisted by the Corps de Ballet, composed expressly for this occasion, by Mr. Maugin, and the music by Signor Cabici [sic]." There is no indication whether Gabici performed or conducted. At the end of the year he was still the leader of the orchestra.[37]

On March 21, 1851, Gabici conducted an orchestra at the Lyceum Hall on Lafayette Square that featured Charles Wynen on violin and on his own homemade instrument called the yerowa y soloma (made of wood and straw).[38] As usual Gabici began both halves of the program with unnamed overtures, and then accompanied the soloist in works by De Bériot and Wynen himself. The pianist E. Groenevelt also played two solo works. The program concluded with the one work for yerowa y soloma, a set of variations by Wynen on motives from Rossini's *La Cenerentola* and Donizetti's *Lucrezia Borgia*. The following month Gabici was again scheduled to conduct at the Lyceum, which now seems to have been his musical home. The Grand Concert Tombola as advertised on April 23, 1851, seems never to have taken place, however, owing to the illness of one of the soloists.[39] On this occasion Gabici was to have led an orchestra of fifty musicians in overtures to Rossini's *La Pie Voleuse* and Auber's *La Muette de Portici,* and accompanied several singers. He also was to have conducted *La Morena, Grande Fantasie Caprice sous Forme de Valse Espagnole,* originally composed for piano by Collignon and arranged for orchestra by Gabici, and a new work *Grant Port Pourri on National Airs* [sic], composed for the yerowa y soloma and orchestra by Gabici. The sick soloist was Charles Wynen, who was to have performed a version of *Le Carnaval de Venise* by himself and also to have joined Gabici and two other, unnamed violinists in De Bériot's Le Trémolo for four violins in its American premier.

The number of concerts in which Gabici participated dwindled beginning in the fall of 1851. On Wednesday evening, September 24, 1851, he conducted fifty musicians in a grand vocal and instrumental concert at Armory Hall to benefit a Kentucky Regiment that had invaded Cuba the previous year.[40] Amateurs also participated. Then on October 28, 1852, Gabici conducted an orchestra "of some thirty musicians in various pieces of instrumental music" during the opening ceremonies of the new Mechanics' Institute on Philippa Street near Canal Street.[41] The program began with the Overture to Weber's *Oberon*. When Louis Moreau Gottschalk returned to his native city and gave a series of concerts, he included Gabici in the third one on April 13, 1853.[42] Gottschalk (piano) and Gabici (violin) performed together a duet by Gottschalk. Beginning on June 20, 1853, Gabici conducted a series of instrumental concerts at Tivoli Garden on Carondelet Walk.[43] The musicians were drawn from the French Opera, the Saint Charles Theatre, and Variety Theater orchestras. The first program included lighter classics by J. Gung'l, Lanuer, Auber, Furatenan, Proch, Flotow, and Massach. It cost twenty-five cents for men while women went for free.

When Gustave Collignon began his Classic Concert Series, Gabici was involved. There is no evidence he performed in most of the concerts, but he did so as violinist on the first concert on Wednesday, January 16, 1856, at the Lyceum Hall, when he joined Collignon, Buccholz, and Certel in the Andante and Allegro from Quartet No. 3 by Mozart for piano, violin, viola, and violoncello.

Gabici made a decisive career change in 1856 when he opened up a music store called Southern Musical Emporium or Depot.[44] There were two locations: 172 rue Royale in the French Quarter (later changed to 86 rue Chartres) and 39 Camp Street in the American sector.[45] During the rest of 1856 he continued to list his music store as a place where one could purchase all the scores for the pieces performed at the concerts, but after the collaboration with Collignon, there were no more known concerts in which Gabici participated. From then until 1860, he advertised himself as "L. Gabici, professor of music, Importer and Dealer in Pianos and Music. Piano Fortes tuned. He is prepared to recommend professors and teachers of music either for city or country instruction, 39 Camp and 86 Chartres."[46]

Gabici was the sole agent in New Orleans for Steinway and Sons and for the Melodeons of Mason and Hamlin but also sold Pleyel and Erard pianos imported from France and other brands as well. In addition he carried harps, guitars, violins, accordions, flutes, brass instruments, and "musical merchandise of every description."[47] He turned to business in order to try to make a better living than what the career as a violinist and conductor enabled him to earn. Although quite able and popular, he was not the most successful conductor in the city, for that position would have been the conductor of the Théâtre d'Orléans

Orchestra until 1859 and thereafter the conductor of the orchestra at the new French Opera House. Eugène Prévost had those positions locked up. There probably was at least a subsistence living that could be earned from playing in or leading dance orchestras. But was he any more successful in business? He had considerable competition from Werlein's, Grunewald's, Elie's, and other music stores, and there were at least five other major importers of pianos in the city. He moved the store frequently, according to the yearly city directories, with locations both in the French Quarter and in the American Sector, which is some indication of instability. By 1860, however, there are no more advertisements in the newspapers, and it is only the *City Directory* for that year that tells us that he had a store. In the following year, 1861, he is listed only as a professor of music. This evidence, coupled with the virtual disappearance of his name from concert bills after 1856, suggests that Gabici had virtually retired from public life. He was still young, but to account for this withdrawal from his very active career, he may have been ill, and his death at the beginning of 1862 at the age of forty-nine may have been the result of a steady physical decline after 1856 ("general debility" in the burial record) rather than owing to the outbreak of war and the blockade of the city by the Union Army.

Gabici's importance in New Orleans was not only as a conductor and violinist but also, as we have already seen, as a teacher. Aside from Gerber, who at least for the moment gained considerable notoriety in New Orleans, Gabici's most famous pupil was Edmond Dédé (1827–1903).[48] Dédé, whose father was a military band member, studied violin with Gabici before 1848, when he left New Orleans for the first time to go to Mexico to escape the increasing prejudice against Creoles of color. He returned in 1853 and worked primarily as a cigar maker. In 1857, with the Civil War looming and conditions for anyone of color in New Orleans deteriorating, Dédé moved to France, where he became a celebrated violinist in Bordeaux. He returned to his native city briefly in 1893, long after Gabici's death, but left soon again for France to escape the humiliation heaped on all blacks at that time. He died in France, where he was honored and respected. Gabici and his colleague La Hache bear important testimony to the special creed among many musicians in New Orleans that continued into the jazz era: in New Orleans talent and musicianship are color blind, and the love of music superseded intolerance.

Another free Creole of color who studied violin with Gabici was John B. Doublet (1828–83).[49] Doublet lived next door to Gabici, a phenomenon that was common in New Orleans, where whites and free blacks mingled far more than in other cities, and it was no surprise that, eager to learn the violin well,

Doublet would take advantage of the friendly neighborhood atmosphere and learn from the best that the city had to offer. Although at first he earned his living in the cigar business—common among musicians of color before the Civil War, after the war Doublet was one of the leading violinists in the city and likely made his living playing in dance orchestras. His two sons Anthony (or Joseph E.) and Charles Doublet were musicians as well, and during the late 1880s they teamed up with their cousins, Louis and Lorenzo Tio Sr., to form the Tio and Doublet String Band (orchestra).[50]

From his surviving compositions we learn the names of several other students of Gabici. Since these are songs or piano works, it seems likely that he taught not only violin but piano and voice. From his song "Stand By Our Flag," dedicated to a woman from Attakapas (now Vermilion Parish, Louisiana), we see that his pupils came not only from the city but from the country as well. It seems ironic that Gabici, who championed musicians who were Creoles of color, would also have had white pupils from Attakapas where simultaneously some of the most vicious pre–Civil War atrocities against African Americans took place.

A handful of compositions by Gabici survive in the Louisiana Collection of Tulane University's Library:

1. Again We Meet in all our Pride: Hymn, Solo and Chorus, as sung by Mrs. Howard, Miss Melville, Mrs. Duffield, McKeon and Spear, at Placides Varieties, on the occasion of the laying of the corner stone of the New Odd Fellows' Hall, written by Bro George W. Christy, music composed and respectfully dedicated to the U.O.O.F. of Louisiana by Bro L. Gabici, New Orleans—W. T. Mayo, 1850. Title + 5 pages. Piano and voice. Strophic with refrain.

2. The Beauty of Esplanade Street, Schottisch, composed and dedicated to Miss Rebecca Rodriguez by L. Gabici. New Orleans, published by L. Gabici, 1856. Sold @ L. Gabici, 39 Camp Street. For piano solo. Title + 5 pages.

3. Ethelvida's Wedding Polka for the piano, composed and respectfully dedicated to Mrs. S. Covas Late Miss E. Tremoulet by L. Gabici. New Orleans: F. Hartel and Co., 1856. Title + 5 pages. Piano solo. Wehrmann engraver.

4. Grand Triumphal March composed and respectfully dedicated to Maj. Gen. Zach. Taylor. L. Gabici, leader of the orchestra of the Saint

Charles Theatre, performed on the occasion of the general's visit to that establishment, December 3, 1847. New Orleans: Mayo, n.d. Xerox copy. Title + 4 pages. Piano solo.

5. Marietta Polka composée et Dediée a Melle Marie Benachi par L. Gabici. New Orleans: L. Gabici, 39 Camp Street, 1856. Title + 5 pages. Piano solo.

6. Stand By Our Flag, A National Song written for and dedicated to his pupil Miss Ernestine Labau of Attakapas, by J. B. Menny, music by L. Gabici. New Orleans: L. Gabici, 1857. Wehrmann engraver. Strophic song with piano. Title + 3 pages.

During his twenty-year residency in New Orleans Gabici made a strong impact and helped raise standards, particularly in playing the violin. His generosity as a teacher extended to any talented youngster, and as a result his knowledge of the technique of the violin was passed on to new players of different races.

5

Eugène Prévost
Eminent Conductor and Composer

Eugène-Prosper Prévost was one of the most important musicians to have lived and worked in New Orleans in the nineteenth century. He had significant careers as conductor and composer both in Paris and in New Orleans, and his influence on the music in New Orleans lasted well beyond his death through his many students.

He was born in Paris on April 23, 1809, and attended the Paris Conservatoire from 1827 to 1831.[1] Like Berlioz he studied with Le Sueur, and before he graduated he wrote two opéra comiques which were performed in Paris in 1831. Having won the coveted Prix de Rome in 1831, he traveled to Italy, where he lived until 1835 when his opéra bouffe *Cosimo* was staged at the Opéra Comique in Paris. The *Picayune* reported that, for the next few years, he was "the conductor of the theatre in Le Havre, where his wife, Eléonore Colon, was a singer." In 1838 he emigrated to New Orleans, where he became conductor of the French Opera at the Théâtre d'Orléans.[2]

The first opera by Prévost performed in New Orleans was *Cosimo* on January 4, 1839.[3] Then followed his one-act *Le Bon Garçon* at the Théâtre d'Orléans on April 30 and May 8, 1840.[4] *Esmeralda* was given on March 2, 1842;[5] *La Chaste Suzanne* was performed on April 15, 1845;[6] and *The Battle of Buena Vista* on May 25, 1847. The latter was described as "a great lyric and historical scene—not a simple *cantata,* but a complete opera with recitative, solo, chorus, and performed in costume by the entire operatic choir."[7] He may have rewritten his old opera *Cosimo,* for when it was performed on May 11, 1854, it was billed as "a new and original opera."[8] This "very pretty little opera" was on a typical dual slate with *Der Freischütz*. Prévost's "accomplished daughter, M'lle Aimée Prévost" was featured in *Cosimo*.[9] The opera or "operetta"[10] met with success and was repeated on May 23, this time coupled with a vaudeville.[11] The following year, on May 17, 1855, Prévost conducted his opera *La Chaste Suzanne*.[12]

Other compositions of his which he conducted himself while in New Orleans include the *Grand Patriotic Overture* on January 8, 1842, in a concert at the Théâtre d'Orléans; it was written in "Memory of the Battle fought Jan. 8, 1815."[13] He repeated the same overture for the same anniversary on January 8, 1845.[14] His Overture and "Grand Valse" from *Cosimo* were performed on February 28, 1844.[15] Local publishers were eager to print his works. William T. Mayo published his *Gen. Taylor's March* and Song *"Departure of the Volunteers,"* composed and dedicated to the "Army on the Rio Grand" in 1846,[16] and the local music dealer Mr. Horst had for sale Prévost's "elaborate musical composition . . . entitled 'Palo Alto and Resaca de la Palma, a military and historical composition, dedicated to General Taylor and his army.'"[17] At the outbreak of the Civil War he published yet an additional military piece, the two *Pas Redoublé*, for the battalion of the Orleans Guards.[18]

But however significant his compositions, Prévost's chief activity was as conductor. By 1844 his conducting was so prized that the *Picayune* could make the following statement: "To remind the lovers of music who frequent the Orleans theatre, how much of the pleasure they there enjoy is due to the skill of Mr. Prevost, would be superfluous. He is entitled to the palm of being the best leader of an orchestra in the country, and he enjoys this distinction not more with us, where he is best known, than in the Northern capitals."[19] Throughout the 1840s and 1850s his conducting at the Théâtre d'Orléans was extolled by the local critics. One went so far as to state, in 1859: "The Opera, at the Orleans theatre, to-morrow evening, will be the "Pré aux Clercs" of Hérold, which was so admirably sung last evening, on the occasion of the fair Cordier's benefit. The overture of this opera, as performed by the fine band of Mr. Prevost, is of itself sufficient to compensate one for the trouble and expense of a visit to the theatre."[20] When the orchestra moved from the Théâtre d'Orléans to the new French Opera House at the end of 1859, it had "forty-five efficient performers, embracing the best of the orchestra of the old Orleans when under the management of M Boudousquié, with many first-rate musicians culled from the best in Paris and New York . . . under the leadership of M Prevost, an old favorite and an acknowledged *artiste*."[21]

His conducting was not limited to the Théâtre d'Orléans and the French Opera House; on May 6, 1844, he conducted the first part of Haydn's *Creation*, along with Curto's "The Oath of the Priest" from *Athalie, Sweet Peace* by the local tenor A. Varnay, and Rossini's *Stabat Mater* at Saint Louis Church. The chorus was "sung by the Ladies and Gentlemen, members of the Musical Athenaeum, and accompanied by a full Orchestra, under the direction of Mr. E. Prevost."[22] Before a benefit concert on April 28, 1847, the critic of the *Picayune* wrote:

"M Prévost has become identified with the French theatre, as its musical director and the efficient leader of the orchestra. To his sustained exertions, his abilities as a leader, and his professional enthusiasm, we are indebted for an orchestra unrivalled in this country, and almost in the same measure for the admirable manner in which operas have been given at the Orleans theatre. It becomes us to cherish such an *artiste,* and to-morrow evening the opportunity will be presented."[23] Three years later the same newspaper iterated its praise of the maestro: "*Farewell Benefit of Mons. Prevost.*—To-morrow evening will be represented at this fashionable house, for the first time this season, Donizetti's grand opera of 'Lucretia Borgia,' being for the farewell benefit of Mons. Prevost, leader of the orchestra. . . . The beneficiary is an accomplished musician, and has many claims on the patronage of the frequenters of the opera, for the able manner in which he has for years led the orchestra at the Orleans theatre. We trust he will have a full house."[24]

A farewell benefit did not necessarily mean that Prévost was leaving New Orleans. Rather it meant that the season was coming to an end and, to help the conductor make ends meet during the summer, he could take the gate for himself. There were similar benefits for Prévost nearly every year.[25] He also participated in many benefits for other musicians and causes. On April 2, 1856, to honor Mozart on his hundredth birthday, Prévost and Théodore de la Hache conducted an all-Mozart program of both operatic and sacred works at Odd Fellows' Hall.[26] The program benefited the German Orphan Asylum. A few days later, on April 11, he conducted the French Opera Orchestra in a grand vocal and instrumental concert for Désiré Delcroix at Odd Fellows' Hall.[27] On April 24, 1861, as one of the final concerts before the city was blockaded, Prévost led "a full orchestra and numerous chorus" in La Hache's cantata that had been premiered at the dedication of Odd Fellows' Hall in 1852 and in Mozart's Mass No. 12.[28] The occasion was a benefit for Prévost's friend and colleague Théodore de La Hache.

After enduring the blockade for a year and the many privations it no doubt presented, especially when operas and concerts were almost entirely suspended, Prévost decided to return to Paris. He conducted one last concert at the French Opera House, on July 26, 1862,[29] and then he, his wife, and a son sailed for Liverpool on August 16.[30] Once in Paris he quickly found employment as a conductor for Jacques Offenbach's light-opera theater Les Bouffes Parisiens,[31] and he continued to conduct the Grand Imperial Concerts through the fall of 1866.[32] When he finally returned to New Orleans at the end of summer 1867, he was no longer primarily a conductor but rather a teacher.[33] He did conduct a few concerts during the next few years, such as in a grand musical and literary entertainment at the National Theater on April 24, 1868, at a benefit for the Saint Vincent's Infant Orphan Asylum during the week of March 30, 1869, and at a grand vocal and instrumental concert for his own benefit performed by his pupils at Odd Fellows' Hall on October 23, 1869.[34] Now his musicians were principally amateurs rather than professionals. On February 4, 1872, he accompanied a group of amateur singers and the professional Mr. Jules Méteyé in a vocal concert at Odd Fellows' Hall, but this time he "presided at the piano with that vivacity and skill for which he has long been remarkable."[35] Prévost's last known public concert occurred on April 6, 1872, at a grand vocal and instrumental concert at Odd Fellows' Hall "for the benefit of the orphans and education of poor young girls."[36] The performers were amateurs, and it is uncertain whether Prévost conducted an orchestra or simply accompanied on the piano.

The first official notice of this career as a teacher was on May 15, 1855, when he was listed as a member of the faculty of the Day and Boarding School for Young Ladies, "founded in 1833 by M'me Lairis and conducted since 1840 by M'me Desrayaux."[37] Along with Julie Calvé he taught singing and solfège there, and he remained on the faculty until he left for France in 1862. During the regular musical season (October to May) the school was located in the French Quarter, on Burgundy Street between Customhouse and Bienville streets, and during the summer it moved to Pass Christian, Mississippi. Prévost moved to Pass Christian as well, where he not only taught at the school but also took on private lessons. Even after he moved to France, he is listed on the faculty of Mme Desrayaux's school. When Prévost returned to New Orleans in 1867, he again joined Julie Calvé Boudousquié in teaching, this time at the Locquet Institute, a young women's boarding school, Nos. 212 and 214 Saint Charles Street and No. 201 Camp Street.

Eugène Prévost died at his home in New Orleans on August 19, 1872, at 11:00 p.m., at the age of sixty-four.[38] The cause of death was given as hepatitis and hemateuna.[39] Just a month earlier, L. Placide Canonge, then manager of the French Opera, was pleading for a renewed grand opera troupe for the upcoming season, and "should there be a Grand Opera Troupe, the orchestra will be under the direction of Mr. Eugene Prévost."[40] Neither the troupe nor its intended conductor appeared that fall. When news of his death reached Paris, the famous composer Ambroise Thomas, who had known Prévost since their student days at the Paris Conservatoire, sent to Canonge "a letter expressive of his deep regret, and his sympathy with the family and other friends of the deceased artist."[41]

Prévost had at least four children. Besides his daughter Aimée, he had three sons. Eugène *fils,* who died at seventeen on April 9, 1856, of a gun accident,[42] and Léon, who succeeded his father as conductor at the French Opera. Another son accompanied his parents to Europe in 1862 since Léon remained in New Orleans during the war. Léon served in the infantry of the Louisiana Legion.[43] He was active in the city from 1865, first as a teacher and then as a conductor.[44] He died in 1877 at age forty-five.

6

Theodore von La Hache
Prolific Composer, Organist, Teacher, and Choral Conductor

Theodore von La Hache was born in Dresden, Germany, in 1822 and received a thorough musical education there from Karl Gottlieb Reissinger.[1] He came to New Orleans probably in 1842,[2] but the first public record of him in the city was on February 19, 1846, when he married Maria Emilia Johnston in Saint Patrick's Church (then a cathedral). His musical career in the city began about that time when he was first known as a successful professor (teacher).[3] Also in 1846 he published his first important work, Fantasia and Variations on the Ethiopian Air "The Rose of Alabama," Opus 2 (Philadelphia: A. Fiot, 1846). On February 3, 1847, he participated in a grand concert at Armory Hall given by the pianist Leopold de Meyer and the American violinist Joseph Burke.[4] La Hache's piano work *Souvenir de Leop. de Meyer, Valse de Bravours,* was probably composed at this time. His role in the concert was as piano accompanist for the singer Mme Emilie Hammarskold, who had minor billing,[5] and when he played in public, it was usually in this role as accompanist. The following November 9 his composition *Matainoros* (grand pas redouble) was part of the third concert by the Howard Society and the Philharmonic Society of New Orleans at the Théâtre d'Orléans, in honor of "Mr. Lehmann, who has worked so hard to popularize music in the city." The orchestra, consisting of fifty wind players, sandwiched La Hache's piece between works of Auber and Donizetti.[6]

During the next twenty years La Hache's name is found on the programs of many concerts. Sometimes he was only assisting other artists, such as on March 2, 1848, for the concert by Mr. Wall, the blind Irish Harper, at Armory Hall, which also featured a comedian. According to *The Bee,* "In announcing this [concert, Wall] also desires to observe that he will be assisted by the most distinguished Amateurs in Music, both Ladies and Gentlemen on the occasion. . . . Also, Professors Miller and La Hache, advantageously known to the community for their eminent musical attainments, in conjunction with several amateurs of both sexes, whose musical powers never fail to captivate and enthrall the congregated assemblage, gratuitously consented to throw their mite into the scale."[7]

La Hache played the piano on Saturday, January 4, 1862, at a grand military concert, vocal and instrumental, at Odd Fellows' Hall.[8] The two-part program was mostly orchestral, performed by the orchestra of the Crescent Cadets, under M Hoeffner with marches and other pieces by well-known composers as well as by Hoeffner and La Hache themselves (the latter's *Grande Marche de la 5e Compagnie du Washington Artillery*). In addition, Mme Dupeire (with unnamed associates) sang arias, duets, and trios by Rossini, La Hache, Verdi, and Donizetti apparently with La Hache at the piano. Many years later, on Friday, March 6, 1868, La Hache arranged a concert for the fifteen-year-old Josefina Filomeno, pianist and violinist.[9] La Hache, Herman Braun, Dubos, and at least one amateur participated.

La Hache was music director of Saint Patrick's Church until 1855, at which time Gregorio Curto succeeded him, but he was still conducting the choir there in 1857. By that time, however, he had already been organist at Sainte Theresa's Church since 1850, and remained in that position until his death. Thus, he made his career that of a church musician, for which he has been largely known ever since. He was both a director of church choirs and an organist, and as a result he wrote a large body of music for the church.

While he earned his living as a church musician, piano teacher, and accompanist, after 1851 his fame locally rested much more on his conducting and his compositions.[10] As a conductor he was primarily a leader of choirs, and apparently when orchestras were involved, one of the city's orchestral conductors often did the actual conducting at the concert with La Hache preparing the chorus in advance. Seemingly La Hache began his public conducting career on Thursday, November 20, 1851, at a grand sacred concert at Lyceum Hall. Curto was the principal conductor, but the program was arranged by La Hache, which probably meant that he prepared the chorus. The program consisted mostly of choral works, plus a few solo songs, by Fr. Kuhlau, Curto, Spohr, Gluck, Novello, Méhul, Hummel, A. Adam, Rossini, Haydn, J. Weigl, La Hache, Fesca, and Mozart. Each ticket entitled the purchaser not only to entrance to the concert but also to a published book of the pieces with the names of the subscribers printed therein.[11] The event was so successful that it was repeated on December 3.[12] Because choruses consisted primarily of amateurs, we find the professional La Hache performing much more with nonprofessionals than with professional singers, a trait not true with most of the other leading professional musicians of the city. This continual and intimate contact with the lay public secured him a wide and warm reputation among the citizens of New Orleans.[13]

There were a few more concerts during the 1850s, such as on January 16, 1854, when he conducted a grand vocal and instrumental concert at Odd Fellows' Hall to benefit the Protestant Orphans Home, Fourth District, whose sixty-seven children had been made homeless by the yellow fever epidemic of 1853. He was assisted by several amateur women and men, accompanied by the "unrivaled" Odd Fellows' Hall Orchestra.[14] Another was an oratorio concert at Lyceum Hall, to benefit the conductor of the choir of Saint Patrick's Church (La Hache) and its organist (A. Trust).[15] This took place on February 11, 1857, and featured Dr. F. Schneider's grand oratorio *Le Jugement Dernier*. Jenny Lind's violoncellist, M H. Braun, also participated.

During the occupation of New Orleans by federal troops and immediately following the Civil War, La Hache emerged as one of the most important musical personalities to remain in the city and as a significant conductor. On Sunday, October 19, 1862, he conducted an adaptation of Donizetti's *Les Martyrs* at Sainte Theresa's Church, where he was now the regular organist. The performance was for the benefit of the female orphan asylum on Camp Street, and, according to *The Bee*, "on the whole, Mr. Von La Hache . . . must have been satisfied with his success."[16] On June 16, 1864, La Hache directed Oliveira, Greuling, and numerous artists and amateurs in a grande soiree musicale at Saint Alphonse's Hall. Most of the program consisted of choruses and vocal ensembles from operas, including, again, Donizetti's *Les Martyrs*.[17] He conducted another benefit for the female orphan asylum on January 8, 1865, this time at Sainte Theresa's Church, where the program was a solemn high mass (a Mass for Peace, for chorus and orchestra, of his own composition).[18] A few months later, on May 17, 1865, with the war over and life beginning to return to normal, he directed a program by his pupils in a grand concert at Saint Alphonse's Hall, and once again included excerpts from Donizetti's *Les Martyrs*, as well as various German, French, and English romances.[19] Six months later, on Thursday, December 7, 1865, the fall season of concerts opened with a vocal and instrumental concert at Odd Fellows' Hall conducted by La Hache to benefit Trinity Church.[20] On February 16, 1866, he conducted the musical parts of a Stonewall Jackson ceremony at Odd Fellows' Hall, which had been postponed from a week earlier.[21]

The Civil War may have been over by then, but the aftermath would be felt for years to come. The war brought to the city all sorts of new challenges, for which the musicians responded with fundraisers. Chief among La Hache's contributions was the benefit concert for the Louisiana widows and orphans of the war on Monday, April 30, 1866, at Odd Fellows' Hall. Octavie Romey was the musical director; La Hache was the conductor of choruses. The program included four grand-opera overtures played on twelve pianos by twenty-four women; two violin pieces played by Oliveira (in one case accompanied by Greuling); various vocal pieces, including one by Miss Annie McLean (who sang every Sunday at Trinity Church); and Romey herself played a few piano solos.[22]

In early May 1866, La Hache was involved with the German Volksfest at the Fair Grounds, including Charles Jaeger's twenty-piece brass band, with impresario Gustave Ostermann (manager, at times, of the new French Opera House and the German National Theater). A vocal concert of choruses for the outdoor event was arranged by La Hache, J. M. Loening, E. Grau, and L. Krebs, for the first day of the Volksfest on May 6.[23] He was back at the Fair Grounds the next November 18 and 25 for two grand sacred concerts, with Collignon, Gustave Smith (accompanist), and Jaeger. Featured on the program were Mozart's Mass No. 12 as well as excerpts from *The Magic Flute* (Mozart) and works by Mendelssohn, Weber, Schubert, Becker, Kreutzer, Meyerbeer, Gluck, Haydn, and Rossini.[24] On Wednesday, February 6, 1867, La Hache directed a concert at the Moresque Building on Camp and Poydras streets.[25] He was assisted by Charles Schramm, Oliveira, Charles Mayer (pianist), Louis Mayer (violoncellist), Gustav Smith (pianist), Miss Emma Fairex, Miss L. Guion, and gentlemen amateurs. The following March 24 he directed a sacred concert in the new Church of Saint Vincent de Paul,[26] and two months after that a solennité musicale at the Cathedral to benefit the victims of a flood.[27] At the last, La Hache was assisted by Collignon, Gustave Smith, and "many artists and amateurs of talent." The Opera Orchestra probably accompanied. The chorus was made up of anyone who wished to sing, and La Hache rehearsed this motley group on May 21 at La Hache's piano store.

Over the next two years La Hache continued to conduct choruses for an occasional concert; again most were sacred concerts to raise money for charities or churches. On Wednesday, February 5, 1868, he led a concert at the German Company Hall for the benefit of Mount Olivet Episcopal Church in Algiers. Performers were H. Braun, Mrs. Roach (formerly Annie McLean), her sister Ms. McLean, Romey, Mrs. Prudhomme, Mr. Cheeler, Mr. Meytier, and the young master of the violin Mark Kaiser. Since not enough money was raised, another concert was given on February 24.[28] La Hache's last known concert, however, on Friday, May 7, 1869, at the Théâtre des Variétés, was different both for the venue (a secular one) and in nature (it was simply a vocal and instrumental concert).[29] He was assisted by M Sipp (piano), Carlo Patti, and Hermann Broun.

As a composer La Hache published music regularly not only in New Orleans but also in New York and Boston, which gained him fame throughout the United States. His earliest published works from at least 1846 to 1860 were piano pieces for the parlor, often written with his students as dedicatees. For special events he wrote marches for (wind) band to honor dignitaries, such as former presidents and generals, who came to New Orleans for brief visits, and he then arranged the marches for piano. On a few occasions he arranged the popular songs of others for piano. There also were a few songs of his own composition. Not surprisingly, from 1850 on he began to write sacred music, no doubt for practical performance at the two churches where he worked but also for concerts. These included about thirteen masses, some of which were published long after La Hache's death and edited by others. Among the sacred choral music was his last published work, a collection of liturgical music for the whole Catholic year as set by classical composers. During the war he wrote a number of patriotic Confederate songs and piano works; among the latter were a series of *Improvisations* on various southern songs. The song "The Conquered Banner," Opus 643, published in 1866, was his most famous wartime song. Announcements appeared regularly in the press that Grunewald and occasionally other publishers had just issued his pieces.[30]

On Friday, March 6, 1857, he performed his *Elegie Dramatique* on the fourth and last concert by LaGrange at Odd Fellows' Hall.[31] Especially important works received major reviews. For example, on May 25, 1862, the critics found his *Grand Dedication Cantata,* sung at the dedication of Odd Fellows' Hall, very good. "We have our doubts whether this cantata has been surpassed in merit by any composition yet written in America."[32] After his death his music was not forgotten in New Orleans. It appeared, for example, in a service and a concert at Saint Louis Church on Sunday, March 10, 1872,[33] and at another at Saint John the Baptist Church on Dryades Street on April 8, 1888.[34]

Aside from his regular duties in New Orleans, La Hache was anxious to develop musical forums or concert series where the best music would be heard on a regular basis. The success of his and Curto's concerts at the end of 1851 led the two of them to create a new Philharmonic Society, whose formation was announced on January 9, 1852 (see page 72): "The two successful sacred concerts recently given under the direction of MM Curto and La Hache afforded sufficient proof that we possess ample amateur musical talent of good quality, and that our citizens know how to appreciate it. The two gentlemen we have named will be at the head of the [new] society. Their professional talent and experience in such matters are a guarantee that the objects of the association will be thoroughly carried out. The election for officers of the society will take place on Monday evening next, at Mr. Hewitt's music store, No. 39 Camp street, when all gentlemen wishing to become members can attend."[35]

This Philharmonic Society, not to be confused with the many other similarly named organizations in New Orleans in the nineteenth century, was short lived. Probably it was a cultural victim of the great yellow fever epidemic of 1853. But it did have at least one grand vocal and instrumental concert, on May 18, 1852, at the Salle du Lycée.[36] Curto conducted many men and women of the Société Philharmonie de la Nouvelle Orleans, with M Jahn (chef d'orchestre de l'Opéra Français), M Fourmestreau (first oboe of the French Opera), M La Hache (organist of the Société Philharmonic), and M Trust (harpist of the French Opera). There was no symphonic music per se; only vocal music accompanied by orchestra, with some chamber music.

In the next few years Collignon established his classical music series, which was largely orchestral, but La Hache still saw a need for major choral concerts. Therefore he collaborated with Eugène Prévost in a number of concerts in which Prévost conducted and La Hache prepared the chorus. One such event, a grand concert for the orphans at Odd Fellows' Hall, took place on April 2, 1856.[37] It was billed as "The Grand Mozart Festival given for the benefit of the German Orphan Asylum, Fourth District," one of La Hache's favorite charities. The "exceedingly attractive" program included "gems from the sacred and operatic works of Mozart."

Immediately after the war, La Hache was instrumental in establishing a new society, the Harmonic Association of New Orleans, and kept it going for possibly two seasons. The *Times* published the announcement of the society.

> THE HARMONIC ASSOCIATION. Having before us a notice from the Secretary announcing that the rehearsals for the second season will be resumed next Tuesday evening, and sharing the general pride in the success of this excellent musical society, we embrace this occasion to give our readers some information as to its character and objects. In November last [1865] a number of ladies and gentlemen amateurs met, and adopted the following preamble: "Being desirous of cultivating a taste for classic and modern music, and associating the music talent of New Orleans together for mutual improvement, we have formed ourselves into an association, called the Harmonic Association of New Orleans, etc."
>
> A constitution and by-laws were adopted, and officers elected. The members had a social gathering once a week, and in a month after a musical soiree

was given at Odd Fellows' Hall, at the expense of the gentlemen members. About fifteen hundred invitation cards were extended to heads of families, with the view to obtain subscribers at the following rates: Those paying ten dollars a year to receive twelve tickets for six concerts, and those paying twenty dollars a year receiving twenty-four tickets for six concerts. Very many of our best citizens subscribed, and the association gave three concerts up to last July. The musical director, Mr. T. Von La Hache was untiring in his efforts, and we may say without hesitation, that the concerts of the first season, given under his direction have never been excelled by those of any similar association.

In another column [of this newspaper] the active members are called together again next Tuesday evening, and our citizens are invited to come forward and subscribe. What more delightful gratification than for the head of a family occasionally to take the dear ones at home to hear sublime works of the great masters? We would advise all ladies and gentlemen amateurs, who are not yet members, to join at once. Let all who understand music and have good voices—and there are as many fine singers here as in any other city on the globe—let them, we repeat, contribute their talents by becoming active members, and let our music-loving community open their purses and help the association to bear the expenses. They will be richly rewarded by attending the concerts.[38]

Once again, it was largely the amateurs with whom La Hache worked, while Collignon worked primarily with professionals. There were six concerts of the Harmonic Association planned, but only four took place between February 8 and July 19, 1866.[39] The program of the first soiree, on February 8, "embraced vocal and instrumental selections—solos and concerted pieces—from the works of Donizetti, F. Paer, Weber, Verdi, Mozart, Winter, Perry, Adam, Thalberg and Mendelssohn." Most of the performers were amateurs, but La Hache was joined by Marguerite Elie, fresh home from her studies at the Paris Conservatoire and about to return to Paris to marry. About fifteen hundred persons attended, by invitation, and the atmosphere was reminiscent of that of the prewar Classic Music Society of Collignon.[40] The second soiree, at Odd Fellows' Hall on April 12, elicited this review:

THE HARMONIC SOCIETY CONCERT.—The concert at Odd Fellows' Hall, last evening, was a great triumph for the musical genius and proficiency of the Crescent City. The immense hall was as full as it could hold, and as might be expected, made a magnificent display of beauty and tasteful toilets. Of course the "Gloria in Excelsis" from Lindpaintner's "Coronation Mass," and Ernani's "Pardon" were the pieces of the occasion, and "The Last Rose of Summer," with flute and piano accompaniment, was given by Miss R., with exquisite taste and beauty. The baritone in "The Pardon" was superb, and the chorus, under Professor La Hache's direction, beyond all praise. And, indeed, every piece was given with wonderful beauty and correctness, and held the very large and cultivated audience charmed throughout the evening. It was incomparably the best musical entertainment of the season, and reflects great credit upon the Harmonic Association.[41]

After the fire at Odd Fellows' Hall, another concert of the association occurred on July 19, 1866, at Mechanics Institute.[42] Two additional ones were to be held that fall, but aside from the call to rehearsal on October 7, nothing further is known of the association. Rather, La Hache prepared the chorus for the concerts at the Fair Grounds in November (which could have been with the Harmonic Association chorus, though no such designation is given).

Toward the end of his life La Hache suffered from lead poisoning, which curtailed his career as a keyboard performer.[43] He was nominally still organist at Sainte Theresa's Church, but his son Theodore Jr. did the actual playing.[44] His last two concerts were on May 27 and June 29, 1868, when he conducted Mozart's Mass No. 12; he led all the church choirs of the city combined, with many others, totaling one hundred, and members of the French Opera Orchestra.[45] Fortunately, by then he had another source of income. In 1866 he entered business with the piano importer and music publisher George W. Doll[46] and went to New York to purchase pianos. By 1867 he had started publishing music, and he took advantage of being at a publishing firm to oversee the publication of his own *Morning Service* (arrangements "from classical sources [of] the music of the whole Roman year"),[47] perhaps his most functional sacred composition. After only a few months, however, Doll left the business, and La Hache and one of his sons ran it for the next several years. But whatever success he had with the business, La Hache died poor, on November 21, 1869, at the age of forty-seven years and eight months,[48] and therefore there were at least two benefit concerts for the widow of Theodore von La Hache and their blind daughter. The first was on Friday, June 28, 1872, at Sainte Theresa's Hall,[49] and the second was held at Grunewald Hall on February 6, 1874. Louis Grunewald himself, out of respect for the man, supplied gratis two Steinway grand pianos for this second piano and vocal recital.[50]

Works of Theodore von La Hache

Fields discusses many of the works of La Hache. Below is an overview of his compositions, not a complete catalogue. Most published works are found in libraries in New York City, Boston, Johns Hopkins University (Lester Levy Collection), Duke University, the Library of Congress, The New Orleans Public Library, Tulane University Library, and Louisiana State University in Baton Rouge. The list of opus numbers makes sense until the early 1850s, but after that date the opus numbers seem to be fantastical (such as 538 and 644). If indeed La Hache wrote that many works, nearly all are lost.

ANTHOLOGIES

The Musical Album for 1855. Contains a collection of choice songs, waltzes, polkas, etc. New York: Firth, Pond & Co.; New Orleans: P. P. Werlein, 1854.

Album for 1857. Contains the latest and most favorite piano compositions; also the eight prize songs of the New York Musical Review. Boston: Oliver Ditson, 1856.

PIANO WORKS

The Bohemian Glass Blower (Le Verrier de Boheme); Polka de Salon. New Orleans: Louis Grunewald, 1860. 2nd ed. New Orleans: Blackmar & Co., 1860.

Le Carnival de Venice: Variations de Salon. New Orleans: P. P. Werlein, 1854.

Les Charmes of New York, Grand Valse Sentimentale. Opus 26. New York: C. G. Christman, 1848.

Confederates' Polka March. New Orleans: A.E. Blackmar & Bro., 1862. As performed by Jaeger's Brass Band.

Deux Polkas Brillantes. Opus 24, nos. 1 and 2. *La Belle Americaine* and *La Belle Creole.* New York: William Hall and Son, 1848.

L'echo. Opus 8. New York: Firth, Hall, and Pond, 1847.

Emilia, Valse d'Etude.

E Pluribus Unum, or The Confederates Waltzes. New York: Firth, Pond & Co., 1854. The southern states. No. 11 Tennessee; No. 12 Virginia; No. 13 North Carolina; No. 14 South Carolina; No. 15 Georgia; No. 16 Florida; No. 17 Alabama; No. 18 Mississippi; No. 19 Louisiana; No. 20 Texas.

Ever of Thee Quickstep. By Foley Hall, arr. La Hache. Opus 499. New Orleans: P. P. Werlein & Halsey, 1861.

Fantasia and Variations on the Ethiopian Air "The Rose of Alabama." Opus 2. Philadelphia: A. Fiot, 1846.

La fleur de lis [The lily]. Valse Characterisque. Opus 7. Philadelphia: A. Fiot, 1846.

Freedom's Tear. New Orleans: P. P. Werlein, 1861.

Funeral March in Memory of Major Ringgold.

Genl. Taylor's Victory March [and] Gen Worth's Quick Step. Opus 4. New York: Firth, Hall, and Pond, 1847.

Grand Etude de Salon pour Piano. 1858.

Grand Fantasie on "I've Fallen in the Battle." Opus 620. New Orleans: Louis Grunewald, 1865.

Grand Parade March; Parade March and Quick Step. New Orleans: P. P. Werlein & Halsey, 1861.

Grand Procession March of the Firemen in New Orleans. Opus 2, no. 1. New York: Firth, Hall, and Pond, 1847.

Grand Triumphant March. Opus 10. New York: Firth, Hall, and Pond, 1847.

Improvisation on "My Southern Sunny Home." New Orleans: Blackmar & Co., 1865.

Improvisation on "The Bonnie Blue Flag." Opus 537. New Orleans: A. E. Blackmar & Bro., 1862. New York, Saint Louis, New York, Missouri: John L. Peters, 1866.

Improvisation on the Favorite Air "My Maryland." Opus 546 d.

Improvisation on the Favorite Melody "Her Bright Smile Haunts Me Still." Morceau de Salon. Opus 503. New Orleans: A. E. Blackmar & Bro., 1862.

Jenny Lind, Grand Valse de Caprice. Opus 16. New York: Firth, Hall, and Pond, 1847.

Locomotive Polka. New York: Wm. Hall and Son, 1849.

Mon Espoir: Mazurka. New Orleans, 1872.

The New Orleans Fireman's Funeral March. New Orleans, Werlein, n.d.

Parade Polka March of the 5th Company, Washington Artillery. New Orleans: Louis Grunewald, 1861.

Picnic Polka. Opus 102. Boston: Oliver Ditson, 1854.

La Plage de la Mer: Variations sur le Theme Favori "Shells of Ocean." Morceau de Salon. Opus 497. New Orleans: P. P. Werlein & Halsey, 1861.

Poésie de la Valse. Opus 6. Philadelphia: A. Fiot, 1846.

La Rosalia; Nouvelle Musique pour les Quadrilles Lanciers. By Pedro de Herrera, arr. La Hache. New Orleans: Blackmar & Cie., 1863.

La Sicilienne. New York: Firth, Pond and Co., 1853.

Six Select Ballads, Composed for the Piano. New Orleans: Blackmar; Baltimore: George Willig, H. McCaffrey, 186?.

Souvenir de Leop. de Meyer, Valse de Bravours.

Souvenir de Nouvelle Orleans, Polka de Salon ded. To Strakosch.

"Sweet Bye and Bye" [and] "Take Me Home." San Francisco: Blackmar & Co., 1880.

The Temptation Polka, Morceaux de Salon. New York: William Hall and Son, 1851.

Time to Go, a Favorite Waltz. New Orleans: Grunewald, 1857.

United States Polka Quadrilles. New York: William Hall and Son, 1848.

Victory Polka. New York: J. L. Peters, 1870.

Winter, Grand Waltz. New York: Firth, Hall, and Pond, 1847. (Fields gives 1846.) Published as part of the *Four Seasons,* with the other three months written by William Scharfenberg, Henry C. Timm, and Herman S. Saroni.

"Woodman Spare That Tree" Polka. New York: Firth, Pond, and Co., 1850. (Fields gives 1846.)

SACRED WORKS

Besides these well-known publications, a few minor unpublished religious works have been preserved from the inheritance of Mr. Henri Fourrier and can be found at the Department of Archives at the Library of the Louisiana State University in Baton Rouge. This collection contains handwritten copies of four short hymns, a benediction, and two anthems.

Masses

Corpus Christi Mass for soprano, alto, tenor, and bass; arranged for four voices by B. Hamma. New York: J. Fischer & Brothers, 1897.

Grand Jubilee Mass. Dedicated to the Handel and Haydn Society of Boston.[51] 1851.

Mass for Double Choir. Performed at Sainte Theresa's Church in 1852.

Mass in Honor of Saint Louis. Revised and arranged for 4 voices by B. Hamma. New York: J. Fischer & Brothers, 1892.

Mass in F for one or two voices with tenor and bass ad lib, edited and arranged to conform with the motu proprio of his holiness Pope Pius X by Eduardo Marzo.

Mass in G for one or two voices with tenor and bass ad lib, edited and arranged to conform with the motu proprio of his holiness Pope Pius X by Eduardo Marzo.

Mass of Saint Anthony. 1855.

Mass of Saint Peter. Opus 141. 1855.

Mass of Sainte Theresa. 1855. Edited and arranged for mixed voices by James A. Reilly. Boston: McLaughlin & Reilly, Co., 1925.

Union Mass. 1858.

Unison Mass in F; Messe en Fa, pour Choeur à l'Unisson avec Soli. Mayence, B. Schott's Söhne, 1866? Revised by Tito Tedesco. New York: J. Fischer & Bro., 1903. Revised edition by Eduardo Marzo. Philadelphia: Oliver Ditson Co., 1915.

Unison Mass in G with alto, tenor, and bass, edited by B. Hamma. New York: J. Fischer & Brothers, 1896. Revised by Eduardo Marzo. Philadelphia: Oliver Ditson Co., [1915].

La Celebre Missa pro Pace Complete. Opus 644, for solo voices (STB), chorus (SATB) and organ. Boston: Henry Tolman & Co., 1867; reprint New York: S. T. Gordon, 1869; second reprint New York: Gordon, 1895.[52]

Other Sacred Works

The New Collection of Sacred Choruses, Quatuors, Trios, Duos & Solos, Selected from the Works of Adam, Rossini, Winter, Mozart, Haydn, Cimarosa, Hummel, Gluck, Spohr, etc., and Carefully Adapted to English Words for the Use of Sacred Music Societies, Church Choirs, and the Parlor / by Theodore La Hache, Organist in New Orleans. New York, William Hall & Son, 1853.

SECULAR VOCAL WORKS

Songs and Choruses

"Alone." Opus 31. New York: Wm. Hall and Son, 1848.
"Carrie Bell." Augusta, Georgia: Blackmar & Brothers, 1861.
"The Conquered Banner." Opus 643. New Orleans: A. E. Blackmar, 1866.[53]
"Freedoms Tear Reverie."
"Genevieve's doves: Reverie." New Orleans: La Hache, 1862.
"I am Dying, Egypt, Dying." Opus 632. 3rd ed. New Orleans: A. E. Blackmar, 1865.
"The Invitation, a Serenade." New York: Wm. Hall and Son, 1848.
"I Wish You Would Propose, or, The Leap Year." New York: Wm. Hall and Son, 1848.
"I Would Like to Change My Name; A Favorite Encore Song." Opus 538. New Orleans: Louis Grunewald, 1862. 4th ed. Augusta, Georgia: Blackmar & Bro., 1862. 5th ed. Augusta, Georgia: Blackmar & Bro., 1862.
"Keep Step to the Music; a National Song." Boston: Oliver Ditson; C. C. Clapp & Co., 1856.
"McNairy." Dedicatee: Miss Sue V. McNairy of Nashville, Tennessee.
"My Gentle Spirit-Bride." Opus 334. New Orleans: Philip Werlein, 1860.
"Near the Banks of That Lone River." Augusta, Georgia: Blackmar & Bro., 186?. Voice and piano.
"Near the Banks of That Lone River." Boston: Ditson, Oliver, 1882. Mixed voices, four parts with piano.
"O All Ye Lands—O Censure Not the Heart That Loves—Barcarole Rondiletta." New York: Dyer and Willis, 1853.
"The Orphan's Appeal," from *Grand Dedication Cantata.* 1852.
"Popping the Question; Risquer la Demande." New Orleans: Blackmar, 1864.
"Rosey Thorn Reverie." New Orleans: P. P. Werlein & Halsey, 1862.

"Sweet Bye and Bye [and] Take Me Home."

"The Volunteers Farewell, or Farewell My Dearest Katie." 1862.

"We're Coming Again to the Dear Ones at Home!" By G. M. Wickliffe, arr. La Hache. New Orleans: Louis Grunewald, 1865. Voice, piano, chorus (SATB)

"The White Man's banner; Seymour and Blair's Campaign Song." New Orleans: A. E. Blackmar, 1868.

Cantatas

Grand Dedication Cantata. For the opening of Odd Fellows' Hall, November 22, 1852.

Schiller Cantata, Grand Chorus for Male Voices. For the centenary of the birth of Friedrich Schiller, celebrated at Odd Fellows' Hall, November 10, 1859.

7

Hubert Rolling
Pianist and Composer

William Hubert Rolling was born in Alsace in 1824 and studied music in Strasbourg and Paris.[1] He immigrated to New Orleans with his parents in 1841 and was a resident of the city until he died in 1898.[2] During his fifty-seven years in New Orleans he was recognized as one of the best pianists, organists, composers, and teachers in the city.

Rolling's first wife was Marie Louise Willamine Irma Desforges, granddaughter of Louis Hus Desforges, the first important classical musician in New Orleans (see part II, chapter 1). After her death he married Miss Tarrut, and when she too died, he married Miss Jacquet. Rolling and his first wife sired a son, William Hubert Rolling Jr. (1857–1943), who joined his father as musician and who is often confused with him. In this discussion, I refer to the father as Hubert Rolling and the son as William H. Rolling.

Hubert Rolling made his debut in New Orleans on March 25, 1843, at the Saint Louis Exchange Hall.[3] He performed his own *Grand Fantasia for the Piano*. The featured performers on the program were William Wallace, piano, and the German Glee Club, and Rolling was an add-on near the end of the evening. This set a pattern: there seem to be no public concerts featuring Rolling, but he often participated as accompanist, either on piano or organ. For example, on Saturday, April 5, 1873, he took part in a grand religious concert at Saint Louis Cathedral. The program included M Cartier, Mme Comès, other singers, Joubert on violin, and, in a minor role, M Hubert Rolling.[4] He apparently spent some time at the nearby Mississippi Gulf Coast, where he performed. On September 10, 1881, in Bay Saint Louis, Rolling played a Chopin polonaise and one of his own works.[5] At a concert sponsored by the French Union in honor of Mlle Regina Fremaux (mezzo soprano), at Grunewald Hall on April 1, 1883, Rolling joined D'Aquin and Joubert as instrumentalists accompanying a group of singers.[6]

At the end of his career, on March 29, 1896, in the afternoon, Hubert Rolling held a private, select gathering at his home (Bourbon and Hospital streets). The purpose was to hear Henri Dubos, one of the editors of *The Bee*, talk about Wagner. However, Rolling was prevailed upon to play some of his own works, in one case with his son (on organ). "Professor H. Rolling, who is one of the most eminent pianists of the city and a composer of much merit, was prevailed upon to play one of his own creations. He gave two of them, "Plaintes des Flots" and a military march, both of which are descriptive pieces. The professor and his son, who is also an excellent musician, gave Rossini's 'Stabat Mater,' on the piano and organ, in an admirable manner."[7] Clearly Rolling was not a great virtuoso pianist and was not regarded in the same light as Marguerite Samuel or Gustave Collignon. His playing was "admirable," which one can interpret as adequate, competent, professional, even skillful, but not exciting and not superior.

The reactions to his best compositions, on the other hand, often led to ecstatic reviews that placed Rolling among the best composers in the history of New Orleans. The first time we meet Hubert Rolling the composer is on May 20, 1853, when a new work by him is announced in *L'Abeille*. The newspaper described this piece, Polka Aérienne, as follows: "Mr. Rolling just published a polka which we have heard performed and which we believe will be very popular in the salon. This piece, original in structure and with a sustained rhythm, stands out for its fresh melodies and nice cadences. It is striking in its second reprise for a clever modulation. The charm that this piece effects makes it easily remembered. We see with pleasure that the composer has indicated all nuances to make it easy for the amateur to show its sparkle. As for its accompaniment, it contrasts by its variety of harmony that is, unhappily, too often neglected in polkas. One discovers immediately that the composer is also an accomplished performer."[8] Rolling published this work in 1853 as Opus 15; we do not know anything about the first nine opera of his, or the dates of opera 10 to 14. The five surviving early works are all for piano and are typical salon works of the time.

When we next encounter Rolling as composer, his compositions are much more pithy and serious. No doubt this was the result of living through the Civil War in a besieged and occupied city. The first of these postwar works, *Harmonie Religieuse*, a piece in memory of the victims of the Civil War, was composed in New Orleans in the summer of 1866 and was published in Paris in 1867. It was reviewed in the Parisian *Journal des Pianistes:*

> An eminent artist from New Orleans, Mr. Hubert Rolling, greatly appreciated in Louisiana as a pianist and composer, moved by a delicate sense of

patriotism, just threw a crown of the sweetiest [sic] melody on the tombs of the victims of the Civil War that has desolated his country. Wishing to share the public expression of grief with us, Mr. Rolling has promised to give our readers the premier of his work. *L'Harmonie Religieuse* dramatizes the different mishaps of the grand drama of which Europe has felt the grievous repercussion. A solemn march in C minor pathetically begins the chant of remembrance; then the temple is opened and the organ prepares us, by solemn chords, for the prayer the people address to the god of armies. Written in B-flat major, this prayer is a smooth melodic inspiration. By an ingenious enharmonic modulation the composer sounds again a raw carillon, followed by a bursting Hymn of the Glorification of the Martyrs, in an uplifting and sublime style. One can say of Mr. H. Rolling that he orchestrates rather than composes, and we have the conviction that in France as well as in the United States, the *Appel à Dieu* will obtain a true artistic success. Mr. Rolling waits now in Paris for the examples of his compositions which he will sell for the benefit of l'Hôpital du Sud.[9]

Rolling's next major work was *Harmonie de la Nature,* originally for piano. It was composed in New Orleans in 1868 and published in Paris. Antoine-Élie Elwart, professor of composition at the Paris Conservatoire, wrote of this new piece in the Parisian *Moniteur de l'Orphéon:* "*L'Harmonie de la Nature* embraces, under the skilled and melodic pen of the master from New Orleans, all the voices which concur to the grand concert which each day is raised to the Creator."[10]

In 1879 Rolling orchestrated *Harmonie de la Nature,* and this version received its premiere on December 31, 1879, during an intermède between the second and third acts of *Il Trovatore* at the French Opera House. Strakosch was conducting the opera but seems to have handed over the baton to Chef d'Orchestre S. Behrens, who led the French Opera Orchestra in *Harmonies de la Nature, Suite, pour l'Orchestre.*[11] When it was performed again on March 2, 1890, under the baton of Mr. Lenfant, before a performance of Verdi's *Jérusalem,* it was so successful that it was encored and then repeated on March 8 at an intermède at the French Opera, this time between acts of *La Traviata.*[12] Canonge wrote several reviews of these performances,[13] one of which is this:

> Mr. Rolling performed, the other day, at the benefit for Mr. Guille, one of his compositions: "Harmonie of Nature"; the audience from every corner of the hall spontaneously called for an encore. This piece was written first for piano,

and many among you, no doubt, have heard it performed by the professor or perhaps by one of his students. It was first heard in New Orleans, then in Paris, and as its success reached every temperament of the artist, Mr. Rolling decided to give more weight to his piece by orchestrating it. In this latter form the audience at the Opera heard the premier on Sunday, March 2. The effect was so favorable that the orchestral musicians had the good idea to repeat the piece on the occasion of their benefit concert Saturday evening. This piece, which had given so much pleasure in the piano version, gained a lot through the orchestral transcription.[14]

A review also appeared in Paris in 1890, which was copied by *L'Abeille*.[15] On March 15, 1891, on the occasion of the publication of *Harmonie de la Nature* in Philadelphia, a brief notice of the earlier performances appeared: "One recalls the success which *L'Harmonie de la Nature* obtained under the direction of Maugé when it was performed by the Opera orchestra, just as when Mr. Lenfant conducted it with the same orchestra. Although it has lengthy developments, it was played entirely a second time."[16]

Rolling followed *Harmonie de la Nature* with an arrangement of an earlier piano piece for wind band. It was entitled *Marche Triomphale* and was dedicated to General Beauregard. It was announced on November 26, 1869, and its premiere was by the Charles Jaeger Band on February 9, 1870. *L'Abeille* reported:

> We heard with extreme pleasure yesterday evening the *Marche Triomphale* composed by Mr. Hubert Rolling and dedicated by him to General Beauregard, and performed by that famous band of musicians so nicely directed by Jaeger. We need not say that the performance was perfect despite the fact that the work was brand new. Our colleagues on Camp Street[17] were as impressed as we were, and like us, were pleasantly surprised, for the skilled compositions of Mr. Rolling are not those which we often hear on the streets and in our public places. This time our great composer wanted to prove that he, just as they, knows how to write popular music, and the success, his brilliant success, justified his endeavor. The *Marche Triomphale* is inspiring; the accompagnment is rich and varied; and the movements proceed with an irresistible verve. It seems to us that this composition is destined to be heard in all the salons of New Orleans, which has the honor of possessing good pianists and, let us add, good pianos (something rare enough). The *Marche Triomphale* is for sale at all the music stores and will be quickly sold out.[18]

The *March* was indeed the most popular of Rolling's compositions and was played often not only by the Jaeger Band and others in concert but also by bands marching up and down the streets of New Orleans.[19] Over the next few years Rolling wrote two other works with the same title. The first of these, *Marche Triomphale* No. 2, was dedicated to Governor Francis P. Nichols. It, too, was originally written for piano and later transcribed for wind band. On May 5, 1877, it was performed as a fanfare by J. Sporer and J. Walcher in a public ceremony. "The new work by Mr. Rolling has a lively and sparkling allure; the melodic character of the first part is elevated, and in the trio of the second part we note especially the gracious opposition of highs and lows," noted *L'Abeille*.[20] The third *Marche Triomphale*, *Marche Triomphale de l'Exposition des Amériques 1885–1886*, Opus 28, was dedicated to the women of Louisiana and was published in New Orleans by Grunewald in 1885. The use of the same title for three different pieces leads to confusion when we try to determine, after 1876, which piece was actually performed. For example, on Saturday, January 3, 1880, at the award ceremony for the literary prizes awarded by the Louisiana Atheneum Club at the French Opera House, a participating orchestra concluded the affair with Hubert Rolling's *Marche Triomphale* (Rolling was a member of the Atheneum Club).[21] It could have been either of the first two marches.

Although Rolling performed regularly in churches, only one piece of his seems to be liturgical. Rolling's "Piu Pelicane," Opus 22, was premiered at Saint Louis Cathedral on Sunday, March 24, 1872. It was repeated the following week at High Mass at the moment of elevation. The performers were among the best in the city: Mmes Dubos and Uberwall, MM Berton and Van Hufflen.[22] But he did write religious music not intended for liturgical use. *Harmonie de la Nature* falls into this category. In fall of 1875 *L'Abeille* reported the success in Paris of a new work by Rolling entitled *Rêve des Concerts du Ciel*. It was published in New Orleans as Opus 23, and was dedicated to M Ambroise Thomas, director of the Conservatoire in Paris. The work merited a review in the Parisian journal *Moniteur de l'Orphéon* by Elwart, who a few years earlier had reviewed *Harmonie de la Nature* in the same journal. It is a religious work for piano in six movements. Mlle Guitry, pianist and first-prize winner at the conservatory, performed the work many times in Paris during the 1875–76 season.[23] The piece had its New Orleans premiere on Sunday, April 9, 1876, in a private concert given by Hubert Rolling at his home, corner of Bourbon and Hospital streets. Any profits from the sale of the work were to benefit the Société des Servantes des Pauvres.[24]

While the larger orchestral, choral, and band pieces drew high praise from the critics on both sides of the Atlantic Ocean, the smaller, usually less pretentious piano works were not neglected. On December 5, 1880, there was a sympathetic review of his piano works in *Moniteur de l'Orphéon,* which was then reprinted in *L'Abeille.*

> Hubert Rolling is not only a composer for his instrument but also a poet, a searcher, an artist in the highest meaning of the word. He sings only when inspiration serves him, and that happens often enough; but if his thought is high, he has the rare gift to remain the master and not get carried away by it. We know his descriptive, imitative symphony for grand orchestra, very somber and correct, but, what is not common (the genre and the model being given) is that we can call it an oeuvre. Our old friend Elwart, who in the course of teaching harmony had finally known this, held in great esteem the Harmonies de la nature, often performed in the United States. By its color, its verve, its concentrated elan, recalls the Marche Triomphale without imitating it, always in the manner of Gottschalk, apart from its profundity. The bass march of the trio and the song which follows allows the performer to prove his qualities of power and agility. The piece presents no real difficulty for the pianist of average ability: it demands dexterity and then even more dexterity. Much effect. The cold solemn machine grabs its public, like players of whist in the salon.[25]

Much of Rolling's time was taken up with teaching. Among his earlier students was Mlle Mouton, who performed in a concert on April 7, 1875, in Grunewald Hall.[26] From 1880 on his students' recitals were regularly mentioned in the newspapers.[27] By May 14, 1881, Hubert Rolling's most successful pupil, his son William H. Rolling, was giving joint student recitals with him.[28] On April 14, 1883, the recital was a grand soiree and was significant enough to be reviewed by Canonge.[29] From this point on Canonge, who was the principal music critic of *L'Abeille,* covered all the recitals by both Rollings' students. The recital on May 16, 1885, showed the young Rolling taking after his father as composer as well as pianist.[30] The program included a new piece by W. H. Rolling and works by Saint-Saëns, Ravina, Mendelssohn, G. Satter, Jaël, Henri Herz, Chopin, Goria, Strakosch, de Vilbac, H. Rolling, and Rossini. Of the May 2, 1890, joint recital, Canonge wrote: "We will speak again of this concert in the next number of L'Abeille. It suffices for us today to write that this performance marks an excellent end to the year. It proves again the intelligent care, the high practical value in the teaching of the two Mr. Rollings."[31] Usually the recitals were public and at the large Grunewald Hall. At other times, however, the recitals were private, such as in March 1882, when father and son and their pupils performed at the Rollings' home.[32] Eighty guests were invited. On May 14, 1886, there appeared the name of Mme Henry Rolling at a soiree musicale by the pupils of M H. Rolling at Grunewald Hall.[33] There is no other Mme Henry Rolling mentioned and there is the probability that it was, instead, Mme Hubert Rolling, who at this date was probably Mme Jacquet Rolling. Sometimes other professional artists joined in on the students' recitals, such as Theodore Curant on May 2, 1888; this was common practice in New Orleans during the nineteenth century.

While William Hubert Rolling did not receive as much acclaim as his father, he was nonetheless a significant musical figure in New Orleans at the end of the nineteenth century. As a pupil not only of his father but also of Curto, he first appeared in a concert by Curto and his pupils in New Orleans on April 21, 1875, at Grunewald Hall.[34] The following year he received the dedication of a new composition by his father's friend Professor Elwart of Paris.[35] His own earliest composition was probably Danse de Pluton, dedicated to Antoine-François Marmontel, the leading piano professor at the Paris Conservatoire, who acknowledged it with flattering words; it was published in 1880.[36] At a literary and musical meeting at Grunewald Hall on January 18, 1879, William Rolling played Mozart.[37] His new composition, "Ave Maria," was premiered at Saint Louis Cathedral for the Offertory on Sunday, October 22, 1882.[38] Since he was an instructor's aide at the Young Men's Gymnastic Club, he was also a frequent participant in the concerts given by the organization.[39] In 1881 he was the organist in Bay Saint Louis, Mississippi, for Easter services,[40] and the following September he accompanied his father there for concerts.[41] He remained at his father's side as a teacher into the 1890s and continued to teach in New Orleans after his father's death.

Works of Hubert Rolling

Clematite. Polka Mazurka. Opus 14. Piano. Dedicated to Aminthe Desforges, n.d.
"La Creole." Tenor or Soprano and Piano. Dedicated to Mme Vve Charles Boudousquié (Julie Calvé), 1876.
The Cuckoo. German Waltz, as Played in Tivoli Gardens. Opus 12. New Orleans: Lithographed by X. Magny, n.d.

Une Fleur. Valse pour le piano. Opus 10. Dedicated to Mlle Willamine Desforges. New Orleans: Lithographed by X. Magny, n.d.

General G. T. Beauregard Triumphal March. Charles Jaegers Band, 1869.

Harmonie de la Nature. Opus 19. Piano. Dedicated to Elwart. Paris. See 1891, 1868.

Harmonie de la Nature. Opus 19. Piano. Dedicated to Elwart. New Orleans: Werlein. Apparently a second edition, 1891.

Harmonie Religieuse. Piano. Paris: chez G. Brandus et S. Dufour, n.d. (1866 is date from newspaper ad).

Marche Triomphale. Band arrangement. New Orleans: Lithograph X. Magny, 1869.

March Triumphal de l'Exposition des Amériques 1885–1886. Opus 28. Dedicated to the ladies of Louisiana. New Orleans: Grunewald, 1885.

"Piu Pelicane." Opus 22. Four voices and piano, 1872.

Plaintes des Flots, sur la Plage de la Grande-Ile. Hymne à l'Océan. Opus 25. Piano. Paris: Crevel, 1895.

Polka Aërienne. Opus 15. Piano. New Orleans: Lith. X. Magny, 1853.

Un Rêve des Concert du Ciel. Opus 23. Paris: Petit Aîné, 1875.

"La Reveil." Chant Patriotique. Song. Dedicated to Club d'Orléans, 1877.

Tivolienne. Polka allemande. Opus 13. Piano. Dedicated to Mme Julia Bonnabel. New Orleans: Lithographed by X. Magny, n.d.

Triumphal March [of] Governor Francis P. Nichols. Piano. Executed by the Silver Cornet Band, 1877.

Voix de la Nuit. Rêverie. Opus 27. Piano. Paris: Petit Aîné, 1880.

WORKS BY ROLLING WITH NO DATE AND NO OPUS NUMBER
All of these works were in Hubert W. Rolling Jr.'s possession in 1998.

"Appel a Dieu."

Grand Caprice pour la Main Gauche.

Grande Fantaisie sur le Motifs Originaux.

Grande Fantaisie Poetique.

"Hymne Patriotique sur le Motif de la Marsellaise."

"Hymne a Pie IX."

Valse Characteristique pour le Piano. Dedicated to P. Abat. New Orleans: Lithographed by X. Magny.

Valse de Tivoli. Dedicated to Mlle Rosella Roussel. New Orleans: Lithographed by X. Magny.

8

Jeanne Franko
Famous Violinist in a Musical Family

Jeanne Franko (New Orleans, 1855–New York, 1940) was the second oldest of at least eight children of Hamman and Helene Bergman Franko, German Jews who had immigrated to New Orleans before their marriage in 1849.[1] Hamman's family name originally was Holländer—a distinguished German Jewish family of musicians that included the violinist Gustav and the composer Victor Holländer.[2] At least five of Hamman and Helene Franko's children were significant musicians.

Hamman was a successful jeweler in New Orleans. However, when the Union Army occupied the city in 1862, he was forced to flee New Orleans and moved to Breslau, Germany, with his young family. Years later he recounted how he was robbed by General Butler and the U.S. Army.[3] Hamman remained loyal to the Confederacy. Upon returning to his native Germany, he immediately provided for the musical education of his children, and Jeanne received thorough training. She studied violin with the greatest master of the time, Henri Vieuxtemps, who had played numerous concerts in New Orleans in the 1840s and 1850s; she also studied with Heinrich De Ahna (1815–92), soon to become concertmaster of the Berlin Royal Orchestra. She made her debut in Paris before the age of fourteen.

Upon returning to America in 1869, Jeanne, Selma (1853–1932), Sam (1857–1937), Rachel (1860–?), and Nahan Franko (1861–1930) caused a sensation by performing as a family in New York's Steinway Hall on September 17—a concert repeated on October 24 at a Terrace Garden Concert in New York and in various other cities including Washington, D.C., where the child Sousa heard them and later recalled his amazement at their feat. While all five children

---

This chapter was originally published in *Jewish Women in America: An Historical Encyclopedia*, ed. Paula Hyman and Deborah Dash Moore (New York: Carlson Publishers, Inc., 1997), 472–73.

played the violin, Jeanne, Selma, and Sam also played the piano. Jeanne and her family had a triumphal return to New Orleans in February 1870. They gave two concerts in Odd Fellows' Hall. On February 3, Nahan (seven), Rachel (nine), Sam (ten), Jeanne (twelve, here called Jeannette) and Selma (fourteen) gave the following program:

I

1. *Il Trovatore, Fantaisie Brillante* (Alard): Sam (violin), Jeannette (piano accompaniment)
2. *L'Invitation à la Dance, Ronde Brilliant* (Weber, arranged for two pianos): Selma and Jeannette
3. "Ave Maria" (Gounod): Nahan, Rachel, Sam, and Jeannette (violins), Selma (piano)
4. *Heimatslange,* for two violins (Gung'l): Selma and Jeannette (violins), Sam (piano)
5. *L'Oiseau sur l'Arbre, Grand Caprice, Burlesque pour Violon* (Hauser): Sam (violin), Selma (piano)

II

1. *Souvenir de Bellini, Fantaisie Brillante* (Artôt): Jeannette (violin), Sam (piano)
2. *Solo de Piano, Joyful [sic] & Sorrowful* (Wilmers): Selma (piano left hand)
3. *Tarentella, Morceau de Salon* (Vieuxtemps): Sam (violin), Jeannette (piano)
4. *Variations pour Quatre Violons,* on "God Save the Queen" (Sam Franko): Nahan, Rachel, Sam, and Jeannette (violins), Selma (piano)[4]

The subsequent concert, on February 9, 1870, was equally challenging.[5]

During the ensuing seventeen years the siblings frequently performed together throughout the country, usually with Jeanne as pianist and Rachel as soprano vocalist. In 1881 and 1882, Jeanne and some of her siblings sojourned in New Orleans, no doubt to spend time with their aging parents. Once in their native city, they could not resist giving family concerts. On February 23, 1881, Sam, Jeanne, Rachel, and Nahan performed at Grunewald Hall.

The concert organized to benefit [an] unfortunate family took place last night in Grunewald Hall, before, we are happy to say, a brilliant gathering. So cruel proof of the shipwreck of the Joséphine, the presence of such a large audience in their musical concert was such a witness of the sympathy that their misfortunes inspired in our population. The persons who took part in this good work had double reasons to celebrate, for it gave them satisfaction to assist in a true solemn event which was also a concert given by serious artists of merit. Miss Rachel Franko has a very nice voice which she modulates with grace and ease which one acquires only after long study in a good school. She sang very coyly the aria from the Barber of Seville, which she repeated owing to the frenzied applause of the public. Her sister, Miss Jeanne, is a pianist; she played the Chopin Ballade in B Minor, and she, too, experienced excessive applause. Mr. Sam and Mr. Nahan Franko, both violinists, contributed greatly to the success of the concert: for the public, a good deed and an evening passed agreeably; for the beneficiaries, witness of the sympathies of the audience and a fruitful income.[6]

On March 6, 1881, the four Franko children played a Sunday matinee.[7]

Other professional musicians in New Orleans sought Jeanne Franko's assistance when they presented their own concerts. She was a drawing card for them and assured that there would be a good audience. For example, on April 27, 1881, the leading New Orleans violinist Théodore Curant gave a grand concert at Grunewald Hall.[8] He was assisted by Alice Schwartz, Jeanne Franko, Robert Meyer, J. W. H. Eckert, and "a complete orchestra of 40 musicians." Curant played the Beethoven Violin Concerto with orchestra, Franko played the Mendelssohn Piano Concerto No. 2 in F Minor with orchestra, and they jointly played the Andante from Rubinstein's Sonata Opus 13 in G Major. The orchestra performed by itself Leutner's *Festival Overture,* the *Tannhäuser* March, and a few small works; there was also a Robert Schumann quartet on the program. Three weeks later the important local flutist Gustave D'Aquin gave a concert at Grunewald Hall and, once again, Jeanne Franko assisted in the concert by performing Chopin's B Minor Scherzo.[9] Once the spring-summer season began at Spanish Fort, Jeanne was a frequent participant. On May 27 she performed Liszt's Hungarian Fantasy and Chopin's *Valse,* Opus 42, at a concert featuring Dengremont and conducted by Curant.[10] Two days later, at a matinee on Sunday May 29 at Spanish Fort, Jeanne repeated the Chopin scherzo and also played Godard's gavotte and etude. This time Rachel sang two solos.[11] On May 31, at Spanish Fort, Jeanne performed Liszt's Hungarian Fantasy and an arrangement by Liszt of Mendelssohn's *A Midsummer Night's Dream*;[12] on June 3 she performed a polonaise by Liszt;[13] and on June 6 a Liszt Hungarian Rhapsody.[14] After a vacation she reappeared at Spanish Fort on September 6, 1881, in a special concert that also featured D'Aquin and the violinist Henry Joubert. She performed *Wiener Bonbons, a Grande Fantasy,* by Rive King.[15] She also performed on September 13.[16]

Jeanne may have left New Orleans from October 1881 to March 1882 since she is not on any programs during that time. She is back on the stage in New Orleans on Thursday, March 30, 1882, when she is the featured soloist in a concert at Grunewald Hall. But this time she appeared not as a pianist but as a violinist. This was no surprise to New Orleanians. According to *L'Abeille,* "Everyone knows how good a violinist she is. She conquered here, made her claim, a just fame, and she is esteemed and loved among all the good families."[17] She was assisted by some of the most distinguished musicians in the city: Mme Bayon, Mme D'Aquin, Mme M. Zuberier, M Curant, M Bremer, and M Eckert. With Curant she performed a concerto for two violins, and Eckert was the piano accompanist throughout the evening. She appeared in one more concert, on April 15, 1882, as part of a performance by the Orphéon Français, at the French Union Hall on Rampart Street. She performed Vieuxtemps's *Fantaisie-Caprice* for solo violin and an anonymous *Grande Fantaisie pour Violon*).[18] The reviewer reported that she stole the show: "It is Miss Jeanne Franko who had the honors of the soirée. Her performance of Vieuxtemps' Fantaisie Caprice on the violin earned her two bows."[19]

Jeanne's final concert in New Orleans in 1882 occurred on November 2, at Grunewald Hall. As pianist she took part in a performance of the Robert Schumann Piano Quintet, with the distinguished New Orleans string quartet of Curant, Kaiser, Mullen, and Emil Seifert. The *Picayune* reported, "The quintette was played with a great deal of vim and in a most correct manner, but lacked the delicacy and pure intonation which are so necessary in the performance of chamber music. Insufficient rehearsal was probably the cause of this."[20] Seifert replaced Mr. Joubert at the last minute because of Joubert's illness.

After November 2, 1882, there are no more known concerts by Jeanne Franko in New Orleans until after the turn of the century. Her move to New York was permanent, and she quickly established herself as an important musician there. Among the siblings only Sam Franko returned for one more concert. On Tuesday, June 14, 1887, Sam gave a violin recital at Grunewald Hall.[21] He played works by Corelli, B. Godard, and Sarasate. Assisted by Mark Kaiser and Théodore Curant, he also performed a *Capriccio* by T. Hermann for three violins.

New Orleanians learned of Jeanne's concert in New York on January 12, 1884, when she performed with Sam and Nahan.[22] The biggest event for Jeanne came two months later, on March 22, 1884, when she performed a concert at Steinway Hall in New York in which she played virtuoso piano works by Liszt and Chopin and just as difficult violin works by Wieniawski and Vieuxtemps. She repeated this feat over the years.[23] The other siblings also settled in New York. Sam later was highly regarded not only as violinist but as conductor and composer. Nahan was concertmaster and conductor of the Metropolitan Opera Orchestra, and he played viola in the New York String Quartet whose other members were Sam Franko and Charles P. Schmidt, violins, and Victor Herbert, violoncello. Selma married David Goldman, her first cousin and a fine amateur violinist, and their second son, Edwin, was the famous American bandmaster; later Selma was Jerome Kern's teacher. In 1888 another sister, Rose (Franko) Burden, accompanied Jeanne on the piano and in 1895 performed with Sam Franko.

After 1886 Jeanne rarely performed with her family. She appeared as violin soloist with orchestras led by Theodore Thomas, Anton Seidl, John Philip Sousa, and others, and in 1895 she founded the Jeanne Franko Trio with Celia Schiller (piano) and Hans Kronold (violoncello), which played many public concerts during the next few years. During her professional career she toured California, Texas, Chicago, Saint Louis, New Orleans, as well as Baltimore and Washington, D.C. She was a member (perhaps leader) of the Woman's String Orchestra of New York (founded in 1896 by Carl V. Lachmund), and she probably was also a member of the all-women's orchestra of the Women's Philharmonic Society of New York (founded in 1899 by Amy Fay's sister). But many of Jeanne's concerts were private musicales in homes or hotels, usually to raise money for charity. She spent the summer of 1907 in Germany where she and Sam together performed privately for a noble family and where Sam discovered baroque music for his New York early music ensemble.

Meanwhile Jeanne was recognized as a significant teacher of music in New York. As early as April 24, 1888, eleven of her pupils gave a concert in Steinway Hall,[24] and similar events occurred during the next thirty years.[25] In a 1910 interview in *Musical America* she attributed her success as a teacher to her emphasis on thorough musicianship and hard work. Jeanne died on December 3, 1940, in New York.[26] She was married to Hugo Kraemer, who predeceased her. They had no children.

9

Marguerite Elie Samuel
Champion of Good Taste

In the midst of the highly successful musical life of old New Orleans, it is perhaps surprising to read that some residents of the Crescent City considered the popular taste not to be as high as it should be. After all, for most of the nineteenth century New Orleans was the envy of all other American cities for its exquisite music. There were hundreds of opera performances each year, usually performed by excellent professionals from Paris and other French cities. Concerts were relatively frequent by local and international soloists. Yet there was always an undercurrent of discontent by those whose tastes went beyond the enjoyment of popular opera tunes. In Paris, too, there were challenges to the popularity of L'Opéra by those who preferred symphony and chamber music.[1] At the end of the nineteenth century there appeared a brilliant pianist in New Orleans who became the leader of those who wanted more intimate music; her name was Marguerite Elie Samuel. Her struggle for the acceptance of what she regarded as the best classical music actually began in the 1860s.

Marguerite Elie was born in New Orleans on May 17, 1847.[2] Her father was the well-known local violinist Paul Adolphe Elie (1804–84), and her mother, Marie Waller (1826–1912), was apparently also a musician.[3] She had a younger sister Louise (1850–1921), who is not known for any musical gifts.[4] As a child Marguerite showed great talent on the piano and was especially noted for her abilities at improvisation. She made her debut in New Orleans on April 25, 1856.[5] A few months later, when she was nine years old, her parents sent her to Paris to get further training in music. It was customary for children from New Orleans, both boys and girls, to go to France to complete their education, and Marguerite's immediate predecessors were Louis Moreau Gottschalk (1829–69) and Ernest Guiraud (1837–92). She entered the Royal Conservatory of Music and Declamation where she studied under such men as Daniel-François-Esprit Auber, Gioachino Rossini, Ambroise Thomas, Fromenthal (Jacques) Halévy,[6] and

Victor Tasse. Her father's contacts allowed her personal entrée also to Guiraud and Georges Bizet, who nurtured her career outside the conservatory, and to Camille Pleyel and his family, who introduced her to many of the most distinguished artists of Paris. Her piano playing must have been extraordinary, and when she was fifteen she played a Mendelssohn trio with Jean-Delphin Alard (1815–88), one of the most important French violinists of the century, a professor at the conservatory, and a senior chamber musician at the time. At one point in her studies at the conservatory she beat all her fellow students in a contest, winning both first and second prizes in front of an audience of three thousand. An anonymous writer described her as follows: "She had a marvelous gift of memory along with her brilliancy of execution and rare powers of expression and a touch of thistle down lightness."[7]

When the Civil War broke out in 1861 and New Orleans was occupied by the Union Army the following year, Marguerite found it prudent to remain in Paris rather than return to the turmoil of her native city. Upon graduation from the conservatory, she continued her piano and other music studies in Paris with Camille-Marie Stamaty (1811–70, who had been Gottschalk's teacher), Julius Schulhof (1825–98), Rossini, and Henri Herz (1803–88). Her public career in Paris included accompanying the celebrated violinist José Silvestre White in Ad. Blanc's Sonata in A on January 11, 1864,[8] and at the end of April that year she played in a concert by the best students of Stamaty in the salons Pleyel-Wolff.[9] Just prior to leaving Paris she appeared in the third of a monumental series of piano concerts in Paris on September 6, 1865, performing numerous works by Stamaty, including his first and second book of four-hand etudes *Les Concertantes* with the composer on the other piano.[10]

After the war, when she was eighteen (winter season 1865–66), she returned to New Orleans for six months and performed in concerts before appreciative audiences. Her initial concert "just after her arrival from Paris" was a private one, "which satisfied the accomplished and experienced judges, who were invited to hear her, that she really possessed ability to maintain the elevated and arduo[u]s position she deigned assuming."[11] The public concerts took place on December 19, 1865, and April 9, 1866, in the new, huge French Opera House in the Vieux Carré (seating capacity 2,300), and on January 4 and January 11, 1866, in the Odd Fellows' Hall (seating capacity 500).[12] In the first three public concerts, she was joined by the singer Miss P. Lafargue and the violinist Jacques Oliveira, who were accompanied by Philip Greuling. The violoncellist Herr Meyers (Louis Mayer) joined them on the second concert. Her return to New Orleans was heralded in the local press:

> We are pleased to learn that much interest is felt by our citizens in the first [public] concert of M'lle Marguerite Elie, which is only natural, from the fact of her being a native of New Orleans; that her father has long been a resident of our city, deservedly esteemed by all who know him, and especially so among the musical circles, professional and amateur; and that, from an early age, his daughter exhibited a talent for the piano, which induced her friends to predict for her a bright, artistic career when she should grow to womanhood, and have finished her musical education under the best masters Europe could furnish.
>
> We naturally look forward to her debut among us, after so many years absence and study, with great interest; but we feel no doubt [a]s to her success in the difficult career she has chosen.[13]

Clearly Marguerite was a well-trained virtuoso pianist, and the program was a demanding one. It included a Carl Maria von Weber concerto for piano, Chopin's *Valse* in A-flat Major (presumably either Opus 34, no. 1, or Opus 42), Stamaty's *Barcarole* from Weber's *Oberon,* Schulhof's *Chanson Solace,* and Thalberg's *Fantasia* on tunes from Auber's opera *La Muette de Portici.*[14] The English reviewer of *L'Abeille* extolled her playing: "M'lle Elie's style shows in an eminent degree cultivation, facility, accuracy, and, above all, exquisite delicacy. Nor does she lack vigor, but this she has too fine a taste to display in bold and garish specimens of musical gymnastics and pyrotechnics."[15] The highlight of the evening was her performance of Thalberg's *Fantasie,* to which the French reviewer of *L'Abeille* responded: "The cup is full between her and the public, and the verdict sews up the opinion that we already formulated of the talent of Mdemoiselle Elie."[16] The reviewer in the *Picayune* was equally enthralled:

> The brilliant assemblage at the Opera House last night, whilst reminding one pleasingly of the days of yore [that is, the prewar lavishness of New Orleans's concert life], was a gratifying testimonial to the *debutante,* who showed, during the course of the evening, that she fully merited this tribute offered by wealth, beauty and fashion, to youth, elegance and talent, under the aegis of modest maidenhood. We have not space for an elaborate notice, and content ourselves with saying that the concert was a complete success. The warmth of the reception seemed to inspire each of the artists, and so excellently did they execute their parts that each was called out after each performance, by the unanimous and persistent applause of the audience. We congratulate M'lle Elie on the remarkable success of her artistic début in her native city.[17]

This reviewer was less excited at her second public concert. He was perfectly satisfied that Marguerite played more Thalberg—his "Home Sweet Home," in addition to the finale of Liszt's arrangement of three operatic fantasies on themes from the opera *Lucia di Lammermoor* by Donizetti, and two works by her teacher Schulhof (*Caprice* and *Chanson Slave*): "M'lle Elie plays with remarkable lightness, delicacy and taste; with artistic understanding of expression and modulation; with perfect ease and thorough accuracy. She does honor in these respects to her celebrated masters, Stamaty and Schuloff." He could not fault her taste and technique, but he thought she was too young to be the brilliant showman such music needed if it was to be sold to the American audience: "She lacks passion, force and power, which are scarcely to be expected from one of her youth and inexperience in public performances."[18]

The reviewer, perhaps a bit cynically, saw the American public as more interested in loud, blatant, unsophisticated music, and was worried that Marguerite's delicate taste would be rejected by this public. As Gottschalk had discovered a little over a decade earlier, Americans in general wanted to hear variations on "Yankee Doodle" or sentimental works that made them cry, and they had little patience for the great works of art that were coming from Europe. Bravura and unsubtle showmanship (which is what the *Picayune* reviewer meant by "passion, force and power") were what Marguerite lacked—a common trait that she was unlikely to learn in Paris or in French-speaking New Orleans. The large crowd that filled the Opera House for the first concert and even the more modest-sized audience for this second concert in Odd Fellows' Hall no doubt included not only connoisseurs of music but many of the city's curiosity-seekers who were drawn by the lure of a young, charming woman so highly regarded in the press and by the musical experts.

Very specifically, the reviewer continued with this advice: "We would again suggest to her that classic music will not do except for small and select audiences of professional and amateur musicians. The "paying" public in this country would rather hear her play arrangements of popular airs, selections from well known operas, favorite waltzes, marches, etc, than Mendelssohn, Beethoven, and the great geniuses of that class." This is in reference to the final piece on the program, which she, Oliveira, and Mayer played together: Mendelssohn's Trio No. 2, which launched her career as the preeminent New Orleans chamber pianist of the late nineteenth century. This particular piece she had learned with Alard in Paris, and while the audience for such music is never as large as that for a circus, there was a definite audience for this music of "the great geniuses" both in Paris and in New Orleans. Fortunately for the connoisseurs in New Orleans, she paid scant heed to the reviewer's suggestions about chamber music. Indeed, perhaps as a reaction to this review, Marguerite Elie made the performance in New Orleans of chamber music and the piano music of the greatest European masters her passion and mission in life—even in front of "the 'paying' public." Ultimately, however, she succumbed to the inevitable realities of concert life in America as claimed by the critic and aimed her art at "the small and select audiences of professional and amateur musicians" rather than playing cheap music for the mass audience.

At the third concert, she did prove to the *Picayune* writer that she could perform with "passion, force and power": "The Odd Fellows' Hall concert last evening was a decided success. The audience was very fair as to numbers, and certainly seemed to enjoy the entertainment thoroughly. M'lle Lafargue's vocal efforts added to her reputation; Oliveira was himself, a master of the violin, and more and more popular; and M'lle Elie, being accustomed to her audience, as the French critics say, played with more brilliancy and expression than has been her wont. Schuloff's *Airs Bohémiens,* as played by her, drew a well merited encore." The audience was not large ("some two hundred and fifty ladies and gentlemen . . . quite a fashionably cultivated, and appreciative assemblage"),[19] owing to competition from the newly reopened opera and other theaters. Yet the performance "was a decided success and more than realized the brightest anticipations of her many friends and admirers."[20]

On April 2 the *Daily Crescent* announced that "this charming *pianiste* will give a farewell concert at the New Opera House next Monday, the 9th, in commemoration of her coming departure from her native city to prosecute [sic] her studies to final perfection under the great European masters."[21] Here she once again appeared in the largest concert hall in the city, this time performing as part of a concert featuring students of Curto. Although the concert on January 11 was billed as Marguerite's farewell concert, the actual farewell concert was the one on April 9 (also advertised as Mlle Elie's Farewell Concert). Here, for the first time I have ascertained, she performed a work of Gottschalk (*La Jota Argonessa*); she played only two other pieces on the program (Jean-Henri Ravina's *Le Brindisi* and a piece by Louis Niedermeyer).[22]

Having conquered[23] the music-loving audience in New Orleans, Marguerite returned to Paris in 1866 with the intention of living there permanently.[24] She had become engaged to Leopold Samuel before her visit to New Orleans, and when she went back to Paris she married him and started her family. She withdrew from public performance and devoted herself to her growing family. She had two daughters who grew to adulthood, and a third child about whom we know nothing except that he died young.[25] When she married Leopold Samuel, he apparently was well to do and, typically for sons of prosperous parents, he became an investor in the Paris stock exchange. About the year 1876, however, he made some bad investments and lost everything. When informed of this, Adolphe Elie urged his daughter to move back to New Orleans with her children, where she could return to her career as a concert artist and have the support of her parents. Marguerite took her father's advice and left her husband in Paris. There is no evidence he ever visited her in New Orleans, but when he died on March 19, 1898, in Paris, the local New Orleans newspapers carried his obituary the next day with Marguerite mentioned as his widow.[26] She retained his name for the rest of her life.

Upon her resettlement in New Orleans in 1876 or 1877, she went to live with her parents, who together now ran a music store on Canal Street, the main thoroughfare in the city. In October 1878, the newspaper *L'Abeille* ran advertisements for the first time announcing Marguerite's availability as a piano teacher: "Reprises des cours et des leçons de piano de Mme L. Samuel, a partir du 11 Novembre. S'adresser: 145 rue du Canal, chez M Élie."

For the next decade she continued to teach privately, and then, beginning in 1889, she became a faculty member of the Southern Academic Institute, 216 Coliseum Street, in the American sector of the city. Among her pupils were her daughter, Margot, Edna Flotte Ricau (long-time piano instructor at Sophie Newcomb College), Anita Socola Sprecht, Helena Augustin, and Eugénie Wehrmann Schaffner. Helena, daughter of Major Augustin, music editor of the New Orleans *Times-Democrat,* was the most celebrated of her pupils; she "received her early piano training from Mme Samuel of New Orleans, then with Scholtz of Dresden, Barth in Berlin, Schulhoff in Dresden, and Moritz Moszkowski (1854–1925) in Berlin."[27] She later was a pupil of Maria Teresa Carreño (1853–1917) in Berlin.[28] Before leaving for Europe, Helena Augustin made her New Orleans debut on April 3, 1888; she is listed on the program as "Mrs. Samuel's Pupil" and was joined by her teacher in a performance of Saint-Saëns's *Danse Macabre* arranged for two pianos.[29] Eugénie Wehrmann was a member of one of the most distinguished music families in New Orleans[30] who thought enough of Marguerite to send Eugénie to her rather than to one of the many other fine piano teachers in the city. Eugénie followed Marguerite at the end of the century as a specialist in playing the piano in chamber music, and then went to Paris, where she was for a time accompanist of France's premier violinist, Jacques Thibaut (1880–1953).

Marguerite's name appears at once in the concert life of New Orleans. She attempted to give two concerts on consecutive nights on April 14 and 15, 1879, including Beethoven's *Moonlight* Sonata and Chopin's *Grande Polonaise*

Brillante, Opus 3 in C, on the first evening and Mendelssohn's Piano Concerto No. 1 in G Minor, Georges Mathias's *Fantasie Valse,* and Henri Ketten's *Basquaise* on the second. She also agreed to accompany Theodore Curant in the Beethoven Violin Concerto on the second program. As it turned out, she was "indisposed" for both events, but on May 14, 1879, she performed almost all the pieces scheduled for April 14 and 15 on one program (only the Beethoven Violin Concerto was omitted).[31] For the next two years there is only one report of a concert—on March 20, 1880 at Grunewald Hall. Busy raising two young daughters and teaching piano, she possibly found little time to practice the long hours necessary to be ready to appear on stage. Rather, composing seems to have occupied her time.

Among her compositions during these early years of resettlement was "a nice musical composition based on the well-known sonnet by Arvers, "Ma vie a son secret," the publication of which was announced in *L'Abeille* on March 30, 1879.[32] It was performed (premiered?) by Mlle E. Lehmann, probably accompanied by Marguerite, on the May 14, 1879, recital mentioned above. It is a poignant song about love for a woman that can never be revealed; set for mezzo soprano in B major, it is a small masterpiece and reveals Marguerite's lofty artistic sensibility. Her piano work *Vers le Soir [Twilight] Poésie musicale,* Opus 1 (engraved by Mrs. Henri Wehrmann and published in 1878 by Marguerite's mother Marie Elie),[33] is dedicated to her cousin Eugénie Fould. It is a virtuoso composition in five flats (D-flat major) with bravura runs and hand crossing that rules out amateur performances; it shows that Marguerite had considerable professional technique. A third work by Marguerite is her *Serenade Boccaccio,* based on music of Franz von Suppé and dedicated to her pupil Helena Augustin.[34] Marguerite and Helena, like many other New Orleanians, had enjoyed the concerts by the Mexican Military Band that played during the Cotton Exposition in New Orleans in 1884 to 1885, so Marguerite arranged for piano the von Suppé piece that she heard the band play. The three-page piece is moderately difficult. A fourth work, the song "Heart and Tears," is announced in *Werlein's Musical Journal* on June 1, 1884, about which the critic of the *New Orleans Times Democrat* (probably Major Augustin himself) wrote, it "reveals the talent as a composer of our most accomplished pianist."[35]

During the 1880s Marguerite's activities as a concert performer continued. She resumed concerts from February to May of 1881, playing compositions by Mendelssohn, Chopin, and others. That summer she made an appearance at Spanish Fort. The entertainment at Spanish Fort consisted usually of light classics played by an orchestra or dance music played by a dance band. On Thursday evening, June 23, 1881, at 6:30 p.m., there was a "Grand Concert" in three parts.[36] Parts one and three were performed in the outside garden and consisted of orchestral renditions of some well-known works by Waldteufel, Nicolai, Carl Maria von Weber, Von Suppé, and Johann Strauss, and a few less-known works by Piefke,[37] Hoch, Doering, and Daniels. Part two of the concert, beginning at 8 p.m., was held in the inside hall, and here, after the Overture to *William Tell* by Rossini, there were solo performances by Henri Joubert (violin), Gustave D'Aquin (flute), and Mme Elie-Samuel (piano). She was not intimidated at all by the location of her performances sandwiched between light works at a resort; she played the Ballade No. 3 of Chopin and later the Liszt arrangement of the septet from Donizetti's *Lucia*. The nonchalant review in the *Picayune* the next day might infer that she had played before in the same setting.[38]

Sometime during the 1880s a New Orleans newspaper stated that Marguerite circulated an announcement that she was organizing "a series of musical recitals, and to that effect secured some of the best instrumental talent in the city for the execution of concerted music."[39] Her intentions were to play only "the choicest compositions of Haydn, Mozart, Beethoven, Mendelssohn, Schumann, Spo[h]r, Chopin, Raff, Bra[h]ms, etc." The newspaper commentator was sure that Mme Samuel could carry off this new plan since her "talent as a pianiste is unsurpassed in this country, and [she] joins to virtuosity and taste a thorough acquaintance with traditions and great musical intelligence." He or she notes that in every other American city this kind of music is standard because opera is lacking, but because opera is so prevalent in New Orleans, the local musicians have tended to neglect serious chamber and recital music. That this was not entirely the case in New Orleans, however, is evident from the large number of concerts that were frequently heard in the city during the nineteenth century alongside the abundant opera seasons. Yet, in comparison with the number of opera performances, chamber music was not as widely heard. In any case, Marguerite's intention was to perform such works frequently enough so that they would become as familiar to the New Orleans audience as their beloved opera arias. Marguerite's concerts were to take place at the thousand-seat Grunewald concert hall, but no printed programs have yet been found.

Later in the 1880s, on Monday, March 12, 1888, Marguerite and a number of other local female musicians "tendered" a concert for the violinist Guillaume Ricci at Grunewald Hall.[40] She performed a Gavotte by Bach, a Chopin Ballade, and "Romance Daylle" by "W. Masson."[41] She continued to be active as a teacher, as revealed a month earlier on the program of the "soiree musicale given by Mrs. M. Samuel for her pupils, with the kind assistance of Miss Jeanne

Faure [soprano], and Mr. Ricci" at Grunewald Hall on Monday, February 6, 1888. The April 3, 1888, concert debut of her pupil Helena Augustin has already been cited.

On December 19, 1887, Mrs. Samuel performed Rubinstein's *Kamenoi Ostrow* and Liszt's *Campanella* for a Mendelssohn Society concert at Grunewald Opera House.[42] The Mendelssohn Society, an intimate chamber music club, was formed by the leading violinist in New Orleans at that time, Mark Kaiser, with other gentlemen of New Orleans as the successor to the Société Philharmonique.[43] From now on she often performed with her close friend Mark Kaiser. On April 25, 1889, she took part in a Grand Orchestra Concert at Grunewald Opera House that was produced by Kaiser who also played some violin pieces (including the Mendelssohn Violin Concerto). The *Picayune* reported: "Mme Marguerite Samuel gave an andante Spianato et Polonaise by Chopin, with orchestra accompaniment under the direction of Mr. Bernard Bruenn. She displayed many good qualities, especially in the direction of execution, brilliancy and sustaining power. She has also a complete mastery of the keys, while her musical instinct and memorizing qualities are excellent. She has acquired a perfection of polish which makes her excel in works of Chopin."[44] A week later she took part in a benefit concert in honor of Mrs. James Nott, a local singer and voice teacher.[45] Marguerite's contribution was the Liszt arrangement of Mendelssohn's *A Midsummer's Night Dream*. The *Picayune* critic referred to her as "the great pianist."[46]

In the 1890s Marguerite was once again very active as a performer. Reviews were always ecstatic. "Mme Marguerite Samuel . . . deftly charms the ears and hearts of New Orleans music-lovers with her finished performances on the pianoforte,"[47] raved one critic. "Mme Samuel entranced the assembly by the rare ability with which she executed the Hungarian Fantasia [Liszt]—her touch being bold and brilliant, delicate and light as occasion required,"[48] claimed another. On this second evening she was called back for two encores: part of the Liszt and a Chopin mazurka. On yet a third occasion the critic stated, "Mme M. Samuel, one of the most brilliant of southern pianists, a pupil of Listz [sic], played the 'Midsummer's Night Dream,' composed by her old teacher. This introduced an adaptation of Mendelssohn's wedding march and the effect was grand. As an encore Mrs. Samuel played 'Campanella,' also by Listz."[49] Despite the reviewer's enthusiasm (and consistent misspelling of Liszt's name), there is no evidence that Marguerite ever studied with Liszt.

Marguerite was involved in two concerts on March 18 and 19, 1890. On the first occasion she did not perform herself but rather had her new song "Cooling" premiered by Miss Jeanne Faure, a local voice teacher. The program was in honor of Faure's student Miss Annie Lee Fitch and was held at Grunewald's Opera House. The song, a four-stanza poem by Pearl Rivers, is a love song and was described by the *Picayune* critic as "delightful music."[50] On the second occasion Marguerite joined the visiting Belgian violinist Ovide Musin (1854–1929) in a performance of Beethoven's Sonata for Violin and Piano No. 7 in C-Minor. She also played a Chopin Nocturne and *Valse des Dames* by Rafael Joseffy (1852–1915). The program included numerous other works performed by Musin and his team, but as the critics of the local papers exclaimed, "It can scarcely be doubted that the appearance of Mme Marguerite Samuel to play Beethoven's Sonata in C Minor with Mr. Musin was the feature of the evening. The sonata was given with all four movements. After following the triumph of the two artists in Beethoven's masterpiece, the palm was awarded their matchless rendition of the allegro-vivace. Rarely indeed does one hear music blended so fairly. Mme Samuel surpassed herself in the brilliancy, expression and delicacy of her execution, and the ensemble of the instruments was beyond criticism."[51] Another review stated, "The chief interest was centred [*sic*] in Mr. Musin and Madame Samuel, two artists of the first rank, whose many sided talents had ample opportunity to reveal themselves in the varied numbers assigned them. . . . Never, within the recollection of the writer, has so superb a work [the Beethoven sonata] been so superbly rendered in New Orleans. The two performers seemed imbued with the spirit of the great master, and the two instruments blended their tones as if controlled by one mind."[52]

When the Musin Troupe returned to the Grunewald Opera House two nights later, March 20, Marguerite did not participate. Instead the group relied on its staff pianist, Mr. Eduard Scharf, and one critic was harsh in his criticism of the choice of works and the pianist: "The programme, as a whole, was far inferior to the one given on Tuesday. There was no Beethoven, no Mozart, no Wagner and no Chopin among the composers; no Madame Samuel among the performers. Mr. Scharf is a good pianist, but he cannot replace our own great artist to whom he is greatly inferior in delicacy and clearness."[53]

On March 9, 1891, Marguerite Samuel assisted in a concert dedicated to Marguerite Martini at Grunewald Hall.[54] She played Chopin's "Funeral March" and Mendelssohn's Prelude No. 1. She performed three recitals in the winter of 1893, each featuring a Beethoven piano sonata (Opus 26 on January 14, Opus 58 on February 18, and the *Moonlight* on March 11). Once again she challenged the conventional wisdom and tastes of the *Picayune* reporter of twenty-five years earlier in making her programs of the highest order and not catering to the lowest common denominator of popular expectation. Other composers emphasized were Chopin, Liszt, Mendelssohn, Bach, Saint-Saëns, and Stamaty, with single works by Robert Schumann, Raff, Hiller, A. Rubinstein, and Heller.[55] The following February 12, 1894, she gave another solo recital at Odd Fellows' Hall with works by Raff, Weber, Liebling, Guilmant, Leshytiski (Leschetizky), Rubinstein, Chopin, and Henselt. She also played her own arrangement of Guilmant's "Song of the Séraphs," and the program ended with Mendelssohn's Caprice No. 22 with her former pupil Miss Socola on the second piano.

Marguerite repeated two of the Beethoven piano sonatas in recitals on March 13, 1897 (Opus 58) and March 12, 1898 (Opus 27).[56] The earlier performance took place at Dunning-Medine's Music Store on Camp Street; she also played Robert Schumann's *Papillons,* Grieg's Piano Concerto, *Impromptus* by Schubert and Chopin, and others. The later performance, at the nine-hundred-seat Athenaeum,[57] included besides the Beethoven sonata a repetition of the Grieg Concerto, works by Bach, Handel, Scarlatti, Chopin, Liszt, and Pugno, and Chabrier's *España* arranged for two pianos by Raoul Pugno, who joined Marguerite in this rendition.

Always eager to improve the quality of music in her native city, Marguerite helped form the New Orleans Musicians' Guild. Article 2 of the organization's state charter, dated November 6, 1889, reads as follows: "The objects and purposes of said corporation shall be the cultivation and development of correct musical taste in New Orleans, for co-operation and mutual assistance among musicians and students of music, for the advancement of musical education in all its branches, intellectual and practical, and for the purpose of stimulating the young to the appreciation of the higher order of music."[58] Mrs. Marguerite (Samuel) was named musical director of the guild, which was to hold meetings every Wednesday evening to keep members informed of the current state of music in the city. The charter mentions that the musical director was to make a weekly report. Monthly dues for members was fifty cents.

She collaborated with the best local chamber instrumentalists at other locations. On November 26, 1894, Marguerite joined the Mark Kaiser String Quartet in a concert of chamber music at the Odd Fellows' Hall. The members of the ensemble were Mark Kaiser and Henry Wehrman, violins, Emile Malmquist, viola, and Cesar Grisi, violoncello. After the quartet played Beethoven's Opus 18, no. 4, and Carl Schuberth's Quartet Opus 34, Marguerite joined them in the Robert Schumann Piano Quintet. The collaboration continued on the next March 9; members of Mark Kaiser's quartet joined Marguerite in a Mozart piano quartet. She also played Liszt's *Liebestraum* and *Tarentella* and accompanied Kaiser alone in Raff's Piano-Violin Sonata, Opus 78. The quartet played by itself a single movement from a Haydn quartet.

There were other occasions when Marguerite performed in conjunction with other musicians. Besides his quartet recitals, Kaiser also organized small orchestral concerts, largely to give his pupils a chance to perform publicly. On one such occasion Marguerite Samuel played works by Chopin accompanied by the orchestra under the baton of Bernard Bruenn.[59] On March 11, 1899, Marguerite accompanied Miss Lydia Eustis in a song recital.[60] Included were songs by Rubinstein, Ambroise Thomas, Fauré, Robert Schumann, Grieg, McDowell, and others, and piano solos by Chopin (Waltz No. 1), Yenssen (*Murmuring Breezes*), and Guiraud (*Allegro de Concert*).

Marguerite Samuel's career seems to have ended early in the new century. There are no more concert programs that have survived, and the last newspaper account of her performances appears in the *Picayune* on Sunday, March 17, 1901. On this occasion she performed in her own parlors rather than in a regular concert hall.[61] It is uncertain whether these parlors were at the address given on her calling card (corner of Third and Prytania streets) or at the address on Baronne Street where she held her student concerts. Depending on the size of her home, there would have been two, three, or even four large rooms joined by wide, tall doorways, and she probably had her piano centrally located so that persons sitting in any one of the parlors could hear if not see her. The *Picayune* covered the event.

MRS. SAMUEL'S RECITAL
A Delightful Audience Greets the Distinguished Local Artist

Mrs. Marguerite Samuel gave another one of her delightful musicales yesterday afternoon. During the winter season Mrs. Samuel gave two recitals, in which her pupils took part. Yesterday afternoon's recital was by Mrs. Samuel herself, and was attended by many of the most accomplished musicians in a music-loving metropolis, as well as many persons of culture and refinement in New Orleans society. Mrs. Samuel's handsome parlors were quite filled yesterday, and the audience showed its appreciation by frequent and continuous applause. Mrs. Samuel is one of the best musicians and professors in this city, and counts among her former pupils many persons who have since made their mark in the musical world. Mrs. Samuel played selections from the most famous masters, and her touch was never more true nor her expression finer.[62]

There is no indication of what she performed, but once again, as in her New Orleans debut thirty-six years earlier, she was uncompromising in her art. Even if the audience was small (her parlors, wherever they were, could hardly accommodate an audience the size of which normally would fill the old Odd Fellows' Hall, the Athenaeum, Grunewald's Opera House and Hall, let alone the French Opera House), she continued to play only works by the "most famous masters" rather than popular ditties.

Marguerite's name continued to appear in the city directories through 1911, where she is described as a music teacher residing at 837 Baronne Street (the building had been razed by the 1930s). Reports of her students' recitals continued in the newspapers, as on March 8, 1903: "Yesterday afternoon the pupils of Mme Marguerite Samuel gave an attractive entertainment at 837 Baronne Street. The large parlors of the residence were crowded, and the programme presented was decidedly interesting."[63] The students were not only pianists but vocalists as well.

Perhaps the reason for her withdrawal from the public stage was that her health was failing. By 1912 she had moved to Florence, Italy, to stay with her married daughter, Mrs. Charles Abnon De Lima, "in the hopes of repairing her shattered health."[64] She died there on October 27, 1912, and was buried in Florence.

Marguerite Elie Samuel's efforts on behalf of chamber music and the classics of European piano music in New Orleans did not fail.[65] The Kaiser and Wehrman quartets continued into the 1930s, and these two violinists trained ensembles that continued after they themselves ceased playing. Audiences were cultivated that kept the appreciation of chamber music alive in New Orleans to the present. Marguerite's piano students such as Eugénie Wehrmann kept playing the best chamber and solo works, and the music lovers of New Orleans were prepared for the next generation of outstanding local players led by Giuseppe Ferrata (1864–1928). Had she remained in Paris and resumed her career there, perhaps her name would have been a household one. As it is, her influence on the musical life of one major American city was lasting.

10

Mark Kaiser
Violinist, Teacher, and Proud Citizen

The finest violinist to have been born in New Orleans and to have lived there most of his life was Mark Kaiser. A child prodigy in New Orleans, he perfected his technique and style in Paris and began his career at age eighteen back in America. After a decade of dazzling audiences from Dubuque and Saint Louis to Boston and New York and of residing as a concertizing violinist in Baltimore and Chicago, he returned to New Orleans late in 1882 where he performed, taught, and conducted for the remainder of his life. He was one of the most highly respected musicians in the city not only for his artistry but for his humanity.

Kaiser was born on February 22, 1855, at his family residence at 80 Chartres Street. His father, Samuel Kaiser (ca. 1823–85), a native of Prussia, was a partner in L. & S. Kaiser, wholesale dealers in German, French, and English goods, which opened around 1851. By 1857 the brothers Samuel and Louis Kaiser each had his own store at 69 Chartres and 48 Chartres respectively. Mark's mother was Maria Kaiser (ca. 1823–1909).

When he was a child, Mark heard the violinist Jacques Oliveira, who thrilled audiences in the city during the Civil War, and this virtuoso inspired him to study the instrument. His teacher in New Orleans was Michael Hoeffner, a Viennese native and a professor of music in the Crescent City from at least 1843 to 1889. Kaiser progressed rapidly, and while still a small child he made his local debut in a recital at the "Red Church" in Saint Charles Parish. When he was twelve, on December 19, 1867, he was the featured soloist in a grand concert "for the benefit of the young and accomplished violinist Mark Kaiser, eleven years of age [*sic*], . . . when he will be kindly assisted by the first musical talent of the city, and the orchestra and artists of the National Theatre." He played demanding works: Viotti's Grand Concerto No. 5 with full orchestra, an arrangement for violin and piano of airs from Donizetti's *The Daughter of the Regiment*, and Paganini's *Le Carnival de Venise*.[1] The purpose of the concert was "to defray the expenses of a trip to Europe, where [Kaiser] hopes to perfect himself in his art."[2] The writer for a local newspaper was already well aware of the boy's talents when he wrote, "All lovers of music, for Mark wields the bow of a master already, and all those who would encourage true worth and genius, should go to the National this evening to hear him play. The theatre has kindly been placed at his disposal, and the whole orchestra have volunteered their services for the occasion.... We can promise all a rich musical treat, for we have listened to the sweet notes of this youthful prodigy's violin."

That so many professional musicians would volunteer their time for a child demonstrates the high regard in which the discerning musicians of the city held Kaiser. Two days later the reviewer ran ecstatic:

> Young Mark Kaiser, the youthful musical prodigy, made his debut before a crowded and brilliant audience last evening, at the National Theatre, the use of which was kindly tendered for the purpose by the management. Mark may consider himself especially favored by the very flattering ovation which was given him, for it is rare that genius, however great, meets with such proofs of appreciation, without having previously received the approbation of the general public. He may be said to have won renown by a single effort. We have no desire to give the young aspirant more credit than we think he justly deserves, but if he have not the soul of a musician, and if he do not prove himself hereafter worthy of the praise we have accorded him, then we shall never trust our judgment more. There was a perceptible tremulousness in the boy's manner when he stood, for the first time, before the garish foot lights, the sight of the large audience, the loud murmer [sic] of expectancy which sounded in his ears, was calculated to abash an older person, but he soon forgot the presence of every one, and seemed to be perfectly wrapped up in the music—the aria from "La Fille du Régiment"—which his bow drew from the violin with such marvelous skill and sweetness.
>
> To see this child of eleven rendering the most difficult airs with perfect ease and accuracy, and with his puny arm handling the bow with the confidence of a master, excited the special wonder of every one present. In response to the prolonged encore which greeted his execution of "The Carnival of Venice," Mark gave a gem from "Trovatore" with such exquisite pathos as to elicit the heartiest outbursts of applause from the assembled multitude. We understand that it is the intention of Mr. Kaiser to take his talented son to Europe at an early day to study his art. The best wishes of the community will

attend him, and we trust at some future day to listen to the strains of his violin when time and study shall have placed him among the first of the world's great musicians.[3]

Despite the artistic success of the concert, Kaiser needed additional help to afford to go to Europe. This he got from John Slidell (1793–1871), the former Louisiana politician and Confederate sympathizer, who spent the Civil War years in France and remained there afterwards in fear of returning to face possible arrest for treason and other scandalous acts. Slidell helped Kaiser both financially and socially when he reached Paris in 1868. Slidell's daughter Mathilde had married Emile von Erlanger, also living in Paris and a prominent member of society, so he arranged for Kaiser to make his debut in Paris by playing in a private soiree at the home of Baroness Erlanger.[4] There he impressed one witness who fully expected him one day to rival "Ernest, Vieuxtemps, Joachim and his other predecessors."[5]

At first Kaiser studied with Jules Garcin (1830–96), solo violinist of the French Opera orchestra and of the Société des Concerts, composer, and a conductor at the Paris Conservatoire.[6] Then he was admitted to the conservatory, where he studied violin with the famous pedagogue Charles Dancla (1817–1907), whose American pupils also included Maud Powell (1868–1920). Years later Kaiser was still in touch with his former teacher and referred one of his own students to his master.[7] Kaiser made such a good name for himself at the conservatory that its director, the opera composer Ambroise Thomas (1811–96), recommended to the American ambassador in Paris in 1873 that the young student be allowed to compete for the annual prize of the conservatory.[8] Kaiser did not take up the offer, however, and a few months after Thomas's letter he ended his five-year sojourn in the French capital and returned to America.

Kaiser's motivation for leaving Paris and coming back to the United States may have been an offer to tour the country with the renowned English pianist Arabella Goddard (1836–1922). From 1873 to 1876 she traveled to various American cities, and in many of her recitals Kaiser played a solo or two. The reviews were outstanding.[9] In Wheeling he was referred to as "already an established favorite and we believe it impossible for him to make a poor note on his violin." "Mr. Mark Kaiser, as a violinist, has but one successful rival now before the American public," says a Richmond reviewer who does not tell us who that "rival" was. In Boston the program announced Mark Keiser's [sic] violin solo as Alard's setting of an aria from Verdi's *La Traviata*, but instead he played an opera excerpt from Auber's *Masaniello* (better known as *La Muette de Portici*), "and did it so remarkably well that the audience would not rest content until it was given more. In compliance with the demands of the clapping hands and stamping feet, he played the 'Cradle Song' from Roemer. Mr. Keiser's fineness and delicacy of touch prove him to be a master of the violin." The *Toledo Commercial* remarked that "Mr. Kaiser proved himself to be an artist of the first rank. The solos he gave were of the French school, and required great dexterity both of bow and fingers."

Just before he joined Goddard's tour, Kaiser came to back to New Orleans and gave a recital. On December 17, 1873, he performed at Grunewald Hall accompanied by Philip Greuling[10] and Mr. Pothonier. Two young women—the singer Mme Zeiss-Denis and the pianist Mlle Le Blanc—also participated in the program.[11] This gave the New Orleans audience, who had witnessed the achievements of the thirteen-year-old violinist before his Parisian studies, a chance to see just how far he had matured in five years under the guidance of Garcin and Dancla. The reviewer A.M. (Alfred Mercier), writing in *The Bee*, noted that he showed intelligence, displayed a fine bow arm, and conveyed "his remembrances, his aspirations toward the ideal beauty, his dreams of love, of glory, of success, etc." to a remarkable degree for one still so young.[12]

When the distinguished soprano Therese Tietjens (Titiens; 1831–77)[13] came to America in autumn 1875, under the aegis of Max Strakosch, she included both Goddard and Kaiser in her concerts.[14] She opened on September 18, 1875, in New York and gave her farewell performance there on April 10, 1876. Kaiser does not appear to have performed with the group in the New York concerts where several other violinists had solos, but in Boston (December 6),[15] Hartford (December 30), Pittsburgh (January 6), Buffalo (January 20) and also Baltimore, Troy, Utica, Rochester, Columbus, and Cincinnati he collected very strong reviews of his solo appearances. In Rochester the newspaper extolled Mark Kaiser, the violin virtuoso, who "in his violin solo, 'Fantasia on Muette de Portici,' first awakened the audience to any degree of warmth, and his efforts elicited hearty applause." The Troy reviewer was just as enthusiastic: "Mr. Kaiser's violin solos, a fantasia by Alard and a romance by Dancla, were delightful. He is a musician of great promise, and we have no hesitation in saying that if he continues on the road on which he seems to have started, glory is sure to await him. His tone is round and pearly and very sympathetic, and his bowing is splendid, both as to style and effect." At the Opera House in Columbus, Ohio, "Mr. Mark Kaiser [showed that], although quite a young man, [he] is already an artist of ability," and another reviewer stated, "The first encore was given to the violinist Mark Kaiser. The Fantasia he played was an exceedingly sweet and attractive one, as expressive as the tones of one we love and was played with a delicacy and taste that caught the audience completely. His concluding piece was of a similar character and merits similar encomiums."

At the conclusion of Tietjens's tour, Kaiser returned to New Orleans, possibly with the intention of settling down. On April 21, 1876, he performed in a concert in Saint Patrick's Hall. It was a benefit for the Royal Guards and included various solo and ensemble singers, a flutist, and Kaiser accompanying "a young lady who appeared for the first time before so large an audience" and, by himself, playing a solo.[16] For the next two years Kaiser was living with his parents on Terpsichore Street, giving occasional concerts. For example, on February 7, 1877, Kaiser performed together with the local flutist Livain and several others for "a large and fashionable audience" at Grunewald Hall. He played Vieuxtemps's *Ballade et Polonaise de Concert*, Alard's *Fantasie sur le Trouvère*, and Reissiger's Grand Trio, in this last assisted by Jules Cartier, pianist, and Obéron. According to the *Picayune*: "To say that the music was fine, would be doing poor justice to the accomplished artists who regaled the critical ears of the hundreds who listened intently to each note. As the magnificent strains of harmony from Mr. Kaiser's violin echoed through the spacious hall, the audience became enraptured, and at the conclusion of this solo on the violin, 'Ballade et Polonaise de Concert,' burst into loud and continued applause."[17]

After two years in New Orleans, however, the opportunity for another road trip could not be resisted. This time Kaiser joined the Roze-Mapleson group that toured the East and Midwest from late November 1878 to February 1879. Marie Roze (1846–1926), French soprano, was originally intended for the premier role of Bizet's *Carmen* but was replaced before the first performance; she was the first Manon in London. With the help of Mapleson, she was active in America from 1877 to 1879.[18] On tour with her, Kaiser frequently played a solo and received as enthusiastic reviews as earlier. In Detroit on November 24, 1878, they played the Whitney Opera House, where Kaiser performed the *Fantasie* on *La Muette de Portici* by Alard and the andante movement from a concerto by Bazzini, plus several encores. As the *Detroit Free Press* reported: "Though a very young man, he is an artist who knows the possibilities of his instrument; whose perceptions of the beautiful in tone are obviously clear, and whose execution, especially his bowing, indicates immense practice, by which he has attained a high degree of technical skill. His exquisite taste was shown in his performance of a lullaby, the which his instrument sang with such tenderness and pathos of expression as made the notes seem almost vocal."[19]

In Dubuque he scored an especial triumph: "The violin solo by Mark Kaiser was something to live in one's memory forever. He drew forth the sweetest and most delicious strains with his magic bow that ever mortal ears listened to. The romanza he executed for an encore brought tears to many eyes, for the violin seemed almost to wail in agony."[20] On December 3, 1878, the *Chicago Tribune* reported: "The novelty of the concert was the debut in this city of Mr. Mark Kaiser, a young violinist, originally from New Orleans, we believe, who has been studying in Paris, and an artist of excellent promise. His numbers were Alard's fantasia on "Masaniello," and the Andante movement from a concerto by Ba[z]zini, both of which were encored. In the former he displayed a very spirited style and facile execution, but his best effect was made in the latter, in which he played with fine feeling and excellent tone. His success with the audience was unmistakable, and was in reality the most emphatic feature of the evening." The same sort of reviews appeared in newspapers in Rochester (November 13, 1878), Buffalo (November 14), Montreal (November 16), Toronto (November 21), Minneapolis (December 7), Boston (January 2, 1878), Potsdam, New York (January 3–4), as well as in Cleveland, Milwaukee, Indianapolis, Saint Louis, Cincinnati, and New York City.[21]

The tour ended in Potsdam, following which he moved to Baltimore, where he became "first violinist of the Peabody Conservatory [Orchestra], under the leadership of Oscar Hamerick [Asger Hamerik], who was director there. . . . While in Baltimore, he organized the Beethoven [String] Quartet."[22]

About 1881 or 1882 Kaiser possibly went to Chicago to live.[23] He had made a strong impression there as a performer in 1878, and the city was just beginning to provide the musical atmosphere that would nurture a talent such as his, but his heart was in New Orleans, and he soon returned home. A few years later he was offered a major position in Chicago but turned it down. It was reported that "Mr. Marks[24] Kaiser, the favorite violinist of this city [New Orleans], has returned after an extended absence in the West and will resume his duties as a professor of the violin. Mr. Kaiser had a flattering offer from the Lyric School to remain in Chicago, but declined [in order] to remain in New Orleans."[25] Apparently the guiding force beyond the establishment of the Lyric School in 1886 was the baritone Gaston Gottschalk (1847–1912), younger brother of Louis Moreau Gottschalk.[26] Gaston had spent very little time in New Orleans and did not know Kaiser from there. Rather, he probably knew Kaiser from the latter's concertizing in the Roze-Mapleson tours and from the strong reputation that the violinist had throughout the eastern half of the country. In 1886 Kaiser's playing was still fresh in the memory of others in Chicago.

When Kaiser returned to New Orleans from Chicago in 1882, however, he was not retiring to a cultural backwater. In 1882 New Orleans still had its opera, and there were also a number of other gifted instrumentalists living there, such as

Marguerite Samuel and Hubert Rolling. At that time, it appeared to be ahead of Chicago in musical establishments, and of course it had the added lure of family.

Right away he appeared in concert. On November 2, 1882, he played to a packed audience at Grunewald Hall.[27] The program opened with the Robert Schumann's Piano Quintet, with Jeanne Franko as pianist and with Mullen,[28] Theodore Curant, and Emil Seifert[29] assisting. As usual, this concert was a mixture of performers and types of music, but the main event was Kaiser in the last two movements of the Mendelssohn Violin Concerto, which was so highly received that he played an encore, Bach's *Andante* (*Air*?) for the G String. Later in the program he played the virtuosic Fantasie on *Faust* by Alard and Reber's *Berceuse*. After Liszt's Polonaise No. 2 performed by Franko, "the concert ended with two string quartettes." The *Picayune* reviewer praised the technical aspects of the concert but saw the young artists as not yet grasping the phrasing and expression called for in the pieces. There were intonation problems in the quintet, but these were attributed to a lack of practice together as an ensemble (the violoncellist was called upon at the last moment to replace the originally scheduled one who was ill).

This concert signaled the gradual change in Kaiser's efforts from a concertizing virtuoso to a chamber musician. His interest in chamber music was already revealed in Baltimore with his formation of a quartet there. Over the next two decades, as he settled into a comfortable position as the most important violinist in New Orleans, he found less need to show off his amazing technique and more concern with raising the standards of listening among the public. In the 1880s he still performed occasionally as a soloist, such as on April 29, 1889, when he and some other distinguished New Orleans artists (Marguerite Samuel, Theodore Curant, and W. Hubert Rolling) honored Mrs. James Nott; Kaiser played a ballad by Moszkowski.[30] On another occasion Kaiser supervised a concert at Grunewald's Opera House, where Curant led the orchestra, Samuel played Chopin, and Kaiser himself played a De Bériot concerto and the Mendelssohn.[31] His sister-in-law, Mrs. Ida Rieman-Kaiser, a contralto, sang Anton Rubinstein's "Der Asr" on the same occasion.[32] And on January 6, 1890, he performed the second and third movements of the Mendelssohn Violin Concerto for a small audience at the French Opera House in a benefit for the (Jewish) Home of the Convalescents.[33] The accompanying orchestra was led by Signor Julius A. Bona, of Her Majesty's Opera House, London. Marguerite Samuel was also on the program, performing Liszt's Hungarian Fantasy.

But from the formation of a chamber music society with Mrs. Samuel in 1890, until 1909 when he went into partial retirement, he is the premier chamber musician of the city. In 1890 a newspaper carried Mrs. Samuel's announcement of the establishment of a permanent chamber group that would bring the outstanding chamber music repertory to the New Orleans public. She was particularly complimented on her choice of Kaiser as associate: "We hear that among the musicians who will take part in these recitals is Mr. Marks Kaiser, whose talent as a musician and a violinist is recognized here as foremost. Mrs. Samuel could not have secured a better auxiliary, for his German nature has inclined him to the study of the sort of music, which he knows well and plays with all the ardor of a lover and the correctness of a scientist."[34]

In 1891 Kaiser organized two string quartet ensembles. At the inaugural concert of the New Symphony Quartette in his home on Saint Charles Avenue, Kaiser was joined by second violinist Henry Wehrman Jr., violoncellist Cesar Grisai, and violist Emile Malmquist in Beethoven's Opus 18, no. 4; Carl Schuberth's Opus 34; and a few other works. This was to be the first of a season of concerts, though no evidence survives of others. That same year the Beethoven String Quartet, consisting of Kaiser as first violin, René Salomon as second violin, Henry Wehrman Jr. as violist, and T. R. Watts as violoncellist, started a series of concerts in the parlor of Harry T. Howard on Saint Charles Avenue.[35]

In the summer of 1893 Kaiser joined other New Orleanians in at least two concerts in the north. On Monday evening, July 24, he performed at the Fountain Springs House, a fancy resort in Waukesha, Wisconsin, about a hundred miles north of Chicago. Many Chicagoans traveled to Waukesha for the spring waters that were near the resort; it was a popular venue to escape the midsummer heat of the city. The program featured an orchestra (works by Von Suppe and Sousa), recitations, solo singing, a trombone solo, and Mr. Mark Kaiser, violin solo, playing Caprice No. 1 by Musin. On Thursday, August 10, Kaiser and Margarite Samuel were featured soloists for Louisiana Day at the Columbian Exposition in Chicago. While the main attractions on that day at the fair were Indian dancing and Patrick Gilmore's band, the Louisiana concert was "a big success."[36] Marguerite Samuel played Saint-Saëns's *Allegro Appassionato* and two works by Louis Gottschalk: *Ricordatti* and *Jota Aragonesa*. Mark Kaiser repeated the Caprice No. 1 by Musin. In addition, Kaiser's sister-in-law, Mrs. Ida R. Kaiser, sang Gounod's "Entreat Me Not to Leave Thee" and, with two others, the trio "Lift Thine Eyes" from Elijah by Mendelssohn.

By 1894 Kaiser had renamed his New Symphony Quartette the Mark Kaiser String Quartet.[37] It gave a concert on November 26, 1894, at Odd Fellows' Hall with Marguerite Samuel, pianist, and Mme Marie Malmquist, soprano. The program was much the same as that in 1891, including Beethoven's Opus

18, no. 4, and Schuberth's Opus 34, but it also included the Robert Schumann Piano Quintet, Pierné's Serenade, Beethoven's *Andante and Variations,* a Haydn serenade, and DeSeve's *Berceuse*.[38] The following March 9 the Kaiser Quartet teamed up with Mrs. Samuel once again at Odd Fellows' Hall for a performance of a Mozart piano quartet (Wehrman sat out), Joachim Raff's Sonata, Opus 78 (Kaiser and Samuel), and a Haydn quartet movement.[39]

In 1909 Henry Wehrman replaced Kaiser as the first violinist in these quartets. From this point he took the role that Kaiser had enjoyed until then. Almost a generation younger than Kaiser, he and René Salomon shared the first violin spot in the next decade, and Wehrman continued as well to be the violist in some performances.[40]

By this time, teaching had become Kaiser's main occupation. When he returned to New Orleans at the end of 1882, he announced that he was available to teach music, and he is listed in the *City Directory* of 1883 as a music teacher living at 471 Saint Charles Avenue. While he apparently taught mostly at home, during the ensuing decades he was associated with some of the city's music schools. He was a faculty member of the Pilcher Conservatory in 1889 and 1894–95, he taught at the Locquet-Leroy Institute at 200 Camp Street in 1890, and in 1919–20 he was part of the New Orleans Conservatory of Music and Dramatic Art, Felicity and Coliseum streets.[41] He was associated with the Music School of Sophie Newcomb College where in 1927 he established the Mark Kaiser Medal for the outstanding music student.[42] As late as 1927 and until just prior to his death a year later, Kaiser coached an all-female string quartet which bore his name: the Mark Kaiser Quartet. This is not to be confused with the Mark Kaiser Quartet of 1894 in which Kaiser, Malmquist, Grisai, and Wehrman performed. The artists of this second Mark Kaiser Quartet were apparently his former students at the college.[43] He held orchestra classes every Wednesday evening from at least 1909 to 1928 at the Grunewald Hotel; it consisted of his present and former pupils. Of special concern for Kaiser were blind students, and he conducted an orchestra of the blind from at least 1915 until his death.

Kaiser and his wife were involved in several important musical organizations in the city. He was on the Board of the Philharmonic Society from its founding in 1906 until 1913, and in 1923–24 he served on the Program Committee of that organization. He had married Miss Hattie Caspar, "a pretty and talented young lady," at Touro Synagogue on Thursday, December 15, 1887, and she served on the board as well, from 1906 until her death in 1952. She also was on the Board of the Symphony Orchestra Association of New Orleans from 1917 to 1919. Mark was also a Mason.

There were a number of important musicians who considered Kaiser their friend. The famous Belgian violinist Eugene Ysaye came to New Orleans for a concert on March 25, 1905, and the first thing he did when he arrived in town a few days before the concert was to go on a fishing and hunting trip with his dear friend Mark Kaiser.[44] More than two decades later the distinguished New Orleans composer Giuseppe Ferrata dedicated his tone poem *Come Luce d'Incante Vole Aurora, di Te la Visione a Me Parve* (from a poem by L. Croce) to Kaiser. The piece was premiered by the Minneapolis Symphony Orchestra conducted by Ysaye's pupil Henri Verbrugghen at the New Orleans Athenaeum on February 5, 1926. Ferrata's dedication reads, "Homage of the composer to the eminent artist, Mark Kaiser." The year before, on the occasion of Kaiser's seventieth birthday celebrations, Ysaye telegraphed his greetings to Kaiser and sent a bouquet of flowers in the shape of a violin, while Ferrata wrote in the guest book: "To you, my dear friend Profr Kaiser for whom I have always had a deep admiration for your qualities as a perfect gentleman and eminent artist and teacher. I wish many many returns of your birthday. Affectionately your brother in art, G. Ferrata."

By the time he died on May 15, 1928, New Orleans bore little resemblance to the city where Kaiser was born seventy-three years earlier. The French Opera was gone, the city was in deep recession, and jazz had replaced opera as the music for which New Orleans was famous. Through his teaching and chamber performances, however, he had prepared several generations of New Orleanians for the kind of music that was important for him and thereby kept that music alive in the Crescent City. The formation of the New Orleans Symphony in 1936, the continuance of regular chamber concerts provided by the Philharmonic Society, the rebirth of a limited opera company in 1943, and the formation of a new chamber music society, the New Orleans Friends of Music, in 1955 show that the kind of music which Kaiser and Marguerite Samuel championed and taught has survived.

11

Gustave D'Aquin
Flutist and Band Conductor

Gustave D'Aquin was born in New Orleans about 1857. By the time he was a teenager he was studying flute with the leading flutist in the city, Leopold Carrière, who was a graduate of the Paris Conservatoire and had been first flutist in the French Opera Orchestra since at least 1841. D'Aquin debuted on November 28, 1872, in the second of two concerts led by Gustave Collignon and featuring the young violinist Camille Urso. The reviewer in *L'Abeille* felt that D'Aquin did honor to his teacher.[1] D'Aquin's debut was so successful that Carrière presented his prize student in a separate concert at Lyceum Hall on December 11.[2] The *Abeille* writer described D'Aquin as a Creole, and this term referred to his French background. The ulterior reason for this concert was to raise funds so that D'Aquin could go to Paris to study at the Paris Conservatoire. Also on the program was the young violinist, Henri Joubert, who was a pupil of Vieter Caulier and who was D'Aquin's closest friend. The following April 16, 1873, D'Aquin and Joubert performed together a trio for flute, violin, and piano by Godfrey at a grand vocal and instrumental concert given by Mlle Helene le Roux at Harmony Hall.[3] The violinist and flutist each played several solos as well, accompanied at the piano by M Cartier of the French Opera.

The two were not yet ready to go to Paris, so they continued to work with their local teachers and gave concerts in New Orleans into the spring of 1874. On November 4, 1873, for the opening of the new Grunewald Hall, Professor Van Hufflen presented a concert featuring Mme Nelville Mercier-Bier as vocal soloist.[4] D'Aquin played Tulou's *Fantasie* on themes from *Domino Noir* "with correctness and sentiment." Joubert played an air by Vieuxtemps "with a sentiment and style that indicated much improvement since his last public performance." The following spring the two were very busy. On Friday, May 1, 1874, there was a concert at Grunewald Hall for the benefit of Saint Augustin Church featuring the singers Mercier-Bier, Le Blanc, and Van Hufflen and the instrumentalists G. D'Aquin, H. Joubert, and Cartier.[5] Joubert played *Elegie* by Page and *Romance without Words* by Sivori. Exactly what D'Aquin played is uncertain; the reviewer in *L'Abeille* states that Joubert, D'Aquin, and Schaffer played a trio for piano, violin, and organ which was an arrangement of a Christmas song, but he probably meant flute, violin, and organ. A week later, on May 8, 1874, there was a concert of amateurs at Grunewald Hall for the benefit of the first Baptist Church (Magazine and Second streets). D'Aquin played a *Fantaisie sur un Air Russe* by Heinmeyer, while Joubert played Sivori's *Solo sans les Paroles* and the obbligato of a song sung by Mlle Grüneberg, the only singer on the program not of the French Opera.[6]

Before their farewell concert on May 11, 1874, the critic of *L'Abeille* paid special homage to the two promising musicians:

> The two young Louisianians . . . have been honorably assured a place in the orchestra of our Opera. There is not any attentive listener who has not remarked that all their practice, preceded by serious work, has helped them on their way to progress, since the beginning of the theatrical season. But these young virtuosi have not ignored the fact that they still have very much to do to achieve the summit of art, and it is in their intention to find a way to study with the great masters in Paris that they propose to give a concert whose profit will facilitate their trip.
>
> Our entire population, we are convinced, will find pleasure in assisting our two compatriots in executing their project. New Orleans has the noble ambition to become the first lyrical city in the United States, and to justify this pretention which will give it great honor, it ought to second all young artists like Mr. Gustave D'Aquin and Mr. Henri Joubert who give proof to the talents which are not lacking, to give them all flight as encouragement and necessary resources for the continuation of their work.[7]

Joubert and D'Aquin had the support of their fellow musicians, some of whom helped put up the money for the concert.[8] One of them, Momas, the conductor of the French Opera Orchestra, led the orchestra at the concert which took place not at one of the smaller theaters but at the French Opera House itself.[9] The orchestra played overtures by Adam (*Si J'tais Roi*) and Hérold (*Zampa*) and single pieces by Hansett and Schubert. Joubert played Sivori's Romance and Vieuxtemps's *Grand Air Varié,* and D'Aquin performed two flute solos: Guillon's *Mélodie Ecossaise* and Tulou's *Fantaisie du Domino Noir.* They did not play together. As *L'Abeille* reported: "Mr. D'Aquin charmed his listeners by the grace and sweetness of his song and by his ease at executing the very brilliant parts of these two pieces. The sound is clean, pure, and the scales and passages were done with great lightness. Mr. D'Aquin is already a very nice talent which will be perfected more by his work, and his artistic future has been announced under the most favorable circumstances."

Later that summer D'Aquin and Joubert sailed for Europe, and by November 29, 1874, they had auditioned for the Paris Conservatoire and been admitted.[10] The following May, D'Aquin sent a new composition of his—*Lamentation et Prière*—to New Orleans to be performed to commemorate a catastrophe that his uncle and aunt, Dr. and Mrs. Henri Bayon, had experienced the previous January with the loss of a child.[11] It was performed at Saint Louis Cathedral on May 16, 1875 by Cartier (organist), Hayen (violinist), and Livain (who had succeeded Carrière as first flutist of the French Opera). Alfred Mercier of *L'Abeille* extolled its beauties, and the following year, on April 20, 1876, the work was repeated with the same artists at a vocal and instrumental concert at Grunewald Hall.[12]

Apparently by the end of 1876 D'Aquin was back in New Orleans, where he was struggling financially as he launched his career. Some of his backers in New Orleans tried to raise money for him by promoting a concert to take place sometime between December 15 and 17 at either the Opera House or Grunewald Hall, when his new symphony would be performed.[13] Nothing seems to have come of this, and the next we hear of D'Aquin is on Tuesday, October 2, 1877, when he and Joubert are honored, at Grunewald Hall, in a vocal and instrumental concert offered by the women of New Orleans. D'Aquin performed Boehm's *Air Allemande* and Tulou's *Sixième Solo de Flute,* and together with Joubert and Mme Wulff he performed a flute, violin, and piano trio by Berr.[14] The following day, October 3, D'Aquin's *Requiem* was performed at Saint Augustin Church.

D'Aquin may have returned to Paris at this time to continue his lessons since there is no sign of him in New Orleans until the second half of 1880. Earlier that year, on March 11, his composition *Prière* and his Symphony in F were premiered in Paris. The reviewer in the Parisian *Gazette des Etrangers* wrote a review that was quoted in *L'Abeille*:

> It is with great interest that we heard the *Prière* and the Symphony in F by M Gustave D'Aquin. Courage, young man, you will arrive! Don't be scared of the task. We find that the *Prière* is a melody from one end to the other. The young lady sitting next to me said that this music carried her to the middle of the ocean at sunset and raised her soul to the sky. Happy composer who has the talent to cause charming young women to dream when they hear the

Prière. This piece is very well orchestrated; the grand homogeneity of the piece shows that the author is secure in his orchestration.

Without displeasing our charming neighbor, we prefer the Symphony in F to the Prière. Each to his own tastes. In the first part of the moderato we noticed a very successful fugue: the subject of the fugue is attacked from the start and returns each time ingeniously by each instrument; but it is the Andante that is the most satisfying. The composer, always master of his subject, was most inspired here. What we find most pleasing is that the composer attacks each moment without hesitation. He mounts each assault of his subject with the swagger and the ease of a true gentleman [zouave].[15]

But by October 22, 1880, both D'Aquin and Joubert had returned from France and assumed front positions in the orchestra of the French Opera.[16] Apparently Joubert preceded his friend back to the city prior to 1880, and D'Aquin had to be recruited to return during the summer of 1880.

From 1881 to 1886 D'Aquin was intimately connected to the musical life of New Orleans and before long took a leadership role. On January 9, 1881, Italian pianist Ernesto Pacini, with the assistance of Joubert and D'Aquin, gave a grand concert at Grunewald Hall. Joubert played *Souvenir* by D'Hayn, and D'Aquin played two flute solos by unnamed composers: *Berceuse* and *Légende*. Pacini played pieces by A. Fumagalli, Liszt, and Gottschalk.[17] Nine days later D'Aquin made what is apparently his conducting debut, which is significant because in the coming years he was much better known as a conductor than as a flutist. It was not a public debut, however; D'Aquin conducted some musicians from the French Opera in a performance of his Symphony in F in the private salon of his uncle, M le Dr. Bayon. The piece was dedicated to Mme Bayon. Alfred Mercier was one of the invited guests and later reported: "The Symphony in F is new proof of the hopes that the first productions of this young Louisianean gave to us a few years ago. There is remarkable progress. Mr. D'Aquin has been endowed by nature with musical faculties in which we sense a solid and potent basis which only demands hard work to produce fruits of the most beautiful kind. He has a lot of spirit, and he knows that we have a too great interest in him to merely compliment him with platitudes that are exaggerated. The symphony of our young friend elevates the level of what we hear and carries it far, very far into the enchanted regions of melody and harmony."[18]

On Sunday, March 27, 1881, the Athenaeum Club of Louisiana presented literary awards to various young people, and during the awards ceremony there was a concert interspersed with orations.[19] D'Aquin performed a flute solo accompanied by his aunt Mme Bayon. Interestingly, a thirteen-year-old pianist by the name of George Paoletti played Gottschalk's *Miserere du Trovatore*; Paoletti eventually succeeded D'Aquin as an important band conductor at the lake resorts. Nearly two months later D'Aquin finally had his Symphony in F performed publicly in New Orleans. On Sunday, May 15, 1881, at Grunewald Hall, he led a grand vocal and instrumental concert in which his wife sang, his aunt played the piano, and he himself played the Sixth Solo for Flute by Demersemann and the adagio and finale from the Grand Sonata by Hulhan (accompanied by Mme Bayon).[20] Jeanne Franko, Theodore Curant, Mme Dessommes, Mme Pauline Blache, and D'Aquin's pupil René Murphy were also on the first half of the program, which included his song "Le Dieu Mai." The second half of the program was the four-movement symphony, scored for piano and orchestra, with Mme Bayon playing the piano part and D'Aquin conducting.

D'Aquin made his first appearance at Spanish Fort on May 28, 1881, playing Desmersemann's Grand Solo de Flûte.[21] W. Borchert conducted the band. A few weeks later there was a concert at Grunewald Hall featuring Pauline Blache.[22] Mme D'Aquin sang a solo and a duet with Mme Dessommes, and "Jules" D'Aquin played an unnamed flute solo. This probably was Gustave D'Aquin. Back at Spanish Fort on June 21, Gustave D'Aquin, with his friends Henri Joubert and Marguerite Samuel and accompanied by an orchestra under Borchert, played the second concert of the evening, at 8 p.m., inside the concert hall.[23] At the end of the summer D'Aquin and Joubert, this time with Jeanne Franko, were back at Spanish Fort for another concert. On September 6, 1881, D'Aquin performed Doppler's Grand Hungarian Fantasia, accompanied by Mr. Edouard Déjan.[24] His final solo appearance for 1881 was at the French Union Hall on November 13 when he played Desmersemann's flute solo based on airs from La Juive.[25] Once again Mme D'Aquin was also on the program.

D'Aquin continued his very active schedule during the spring of 1882. On Sunday, February 19, 1882, he played Doppler's piece at a grand concert for charity at the Opera House.[26] He and his wife played during portions of the year's Athénée awards ceremony on March 26 at Grunewald Hall, and four days later he assisted in a concert in the same location for Jeanne Franko.[27] Mme D'Aquin took part in a Grand Concert Sacré by the Cathedral Choir directed by Frederick Kitziger at the cathedral, on Saturday, April 1, 1882,[28] and the next day D'Aquin performed at Spanish Fort to benefit flood victims.[29] In a concert offered to Mme Boudousquié by her numerous pupils on Wednesday, April 12, 1882, at the Opera House, G. D'Aquin performed J. Demersemann's *Le Trémolo Grande: Fantasia pour Flute,* and his wife sang the prison song from

Verdi's *Trouvère*.[30] L. Placide Canonge wrote that "Mr. D'Aquin . . . played as the true artist Le Trémolo of Demersemann. The whole piece was of the highest order, but above all the last part—a tour de force of execution where the artist, doubling so to speak bass and song, presents a veritable duet. This shock of sound, the one very distinct from the other, was very clearly and very happily performed." And about Mme D'Aquin, Canonge wrote, "I regretted only one thing in hearing Madame D'Aquin, that is that the piece, or rather the fragment of the piece chosen by her, was so short. Why tantalize the audience with food and then count their mouthfuls? She has a limpid, fresh, sympathetic, penetrating voice, full of soul and poetry—an impressionable nature that knows how to communicate its impressions."

On the evening of April 15, D'Aquin husband and wife, along with Joubert, participated in a theatrical presentation and concert at Spanish Fort to aid the Bienville School.[31] D'Aquin played the same *Le Trémolo,* Mrs. D'Aquin sang "Va, Dit-Elle" from Meyerbeer's *Robert le Diable,* and Joubert performed Vieuxtemps's *Fantaisie-Caprice.* Later that fall, on Wednesday, November 22, 1882, D'Aquin conducted his new Mass for Sainte Cecilia's Day for chorus and orchestra at Saint Louis Cathedral.[32] This was his second setting of the mass, and assisting him in its performance were the French Opera Orchestra and the singers Mme Bernardi and MM Tournié and Delrat. On Christmas Day at Saint Louis Cathedral, Delrat and other singers and instrumentalists from the French Opera performed Haydn's Mass No. 2, and M Reine, first oboist of the Opera Orchestra, played a pastoral by D'Aquin.[33]

During the spring of 1883, D'Aquin participated in a vocal and instrumental concert in honor of Oscar Reine at Grunewald Hall,[34] and in a concert sponsored by the French Union in honor of Mlle Regina Fremaux (mezzo soprano), at Grunewald Hall.[35] But what is most significant is the announcement on Sunday, April 1, that on that day West End opened its season of Sunday concerts, from 4 to 7 p.m., with its new orchestral conductor, Gustave D'Aquin, conducting its new orchestra, carefully chosen from the best professionals who live in New Orleans during the summer.[36] These Sunday concerts were not part of the regular series at West End that were to begin on May 3 but were in addition to them. D'Aquin thus launched a new career that was to be his for the remainder of his professional life. This first concert attracted a throng of people and made "an excellent impression." Beginning May 3 the West End concerts were held every evening, under the direction of D'Aquin, with the engagement of the soloists.[37] The week of August 26, there were performances of Gilbert and Sullivan and other operettas at West End, and "the celebrated orchestra of Professor G. D'Aquin" played many pieces before and after each opera.[38] Meanwhile D'Aquin continued to perform flute solos at concerts in the city, such as at the matinee concert at Grunewald Hall on April 29 to benefit the Southern Silk Industrial Association.[39] Henri Bayon and Mme D'Aquin also performed. Another event was the benefit matinee concert for Mme D'Aquin at Grunewald Hall on May 6, 1883.[40] The program included arias and instrumental music performed by Joubert, Bayon, C. Ziegler, Mlles L. Rouan and E. Parra, and Gustave D'Aquin. Joubert played Wieniawski's *Légende*.

In fall 1883, D'Aquin continued his dual roles as flutist and conductor. On October 27–28, for the grand entertainments at the Opera House for the benefit of the Mount Carmel Asylum, he led the orchestra, with the cooperation of numerous groups including the Orphéon Français.[41] He also was among the soloists. Then on Thursday, November 8, he joined Van Hufflen, the Aeoleon Harp Circle, Marguerite Samuel, Mme E. D'Aquin, Joubert, and E. Déjan at a concert in Grunewald Hall.[42] His flute solo was not named in the program. Meanwhile, through all this time, he retained his position as flutist of the French Opera Orchestra, which then had forty-six musicians.[43] During the intermède between acts of *Les Huguenots* at the Opera House on November 19, he and Joubert played solos and, according to Canonge, received "warm and long bravos."[44] On New Years Day, 1884, between a performance of *The Barber of Seville* and a ballet at the French Opera House to benefit the families of shipwrecked sailors and the French Union, there was a concert of arias, songs, and a trio by François Beer performed by Mme Joubert, Joubert, and D'Aquin.[45] As a composer D'Aquin was also represented this fall by a performance of his solemn mass to celebrate Sainte Cécile's Day at the Cathedral on Thursday, November 22, 1883.[46] The critic of *L'Abeille* had a few reservations about the piece; he found that D'Aquin wrote too much of the accompaniment for the winds rather than the strings. A month later D'Aquin was represented as both flutist and composer at the first two Christmas masses at the Saint Augustin Church with the choir directed by J. Hanno Deiler, organist.[47]

D'Aquin returned on May 11, 1884, to West End for a concert promenade. He conducted an excellent orchestra of eighteen to twenty persons which he formed from "the most popular musicians who had proven themselves a thousand times over." As in the previous summer, an operetta troupe had been formed from New York singers. *L'Abeille* reported: "Before and after the operetta, the orchestra, conducted by Mr. D'Aquin, performed at the pavilion an entire program so that those who did not attend the spectacle could have their share of pleasure. . . . The orchestra under the baton of Professor D'Aquin played overtures from the principal operas before and after each representation."[48] From July 27 through the rest of the summer M Fred C. Bryant, cornetist, joined the famous West End Band under the direction of D'Aquin.[49] On September 14, the band under D'Aquin was called a military band, no doubt because on at least this occasion it was a wind, not string band.[50] In fall he returned to the French Opera where, in addition to his regular duties in opera performances, he and Joubert put on a benefit for themselves. The concert took place on December 22, and, besides the two friends and their wives, the participants were Mme Pemberton-Hincks, Mlle Pemberton; MM Lefebvre, Henri Bayon, and August Dofilho.[51] The concert was a success.

As in the past year, D'Aquin and his associates were in a routine whereby their orchestral duties were coupled with occasional solo concerts. On January 22, 1885, they gave a concert at Werlein Hall to benefit the "Woman's Department of the World's Exposition" featuring Mmes Hincks and D'Aquin, Mlle Pemberton, Mmes Bayon et Lejeune; MM D'Aquin, Joubert, Bayon, Knoll, and Siebrant.[52] This was their contribution to the Cotton Exposition that highlighted the Mexican Military Band and that left the local musicians on the side. From Thursday to Sunday, April 4 to 7, D'Aquin and his wife had minor parts in the music at Saint Augustin Church.[53] She sang on Thursday evening, after the sermon, with the accompaniment of organ, violin, and flute performed by MM Deiler, Joubert, and D'Aquin. Sunday, at the grand mass at 10 a.m., the choir performed a mass by Weber; at the Offertory, Mme D'Aquin sang "Ave Maria" by Fauré with the accompaniment of organ, violin, and flute. A month later, Mme H. Bayon directed a charity concert for the diocese of New Orleans at Washington Artillery Hall. It took place on Wednesday and Thursday, May 6–7, 1885, and while Mme D'Aquin performed, it seems her husband did not.[54]

The music at West End opened for the season on May 24, 1885. The orchestra, under the direction of D'Aquin, consisted of fifty professionals, featuring the celebrated cornetists A. H. Knoll and O. Schuchardt, G. Sontag, trombonist, G. D'Aquin, flutist, and A. Renz, clarinetist. Concerts took place at 5 p.m. on Sundays and at 6 p.m. other days. Not only were the soloists excellent, but also the ensemble was deemed so.[55] The "orchestra" was clearly a concert band since bowed string instruments are never mentioned.

D'Aquin was more involved with the Cotton Exposition in the 1885–86 season than he had been the previous year. His ties with the Opera Orchestra seem to have been severed so that he could conduct more often elsewhere. During the fall D'Aquin organized a choir of all ages and both sexes for a performance at the opening of the exposition that year on October 11, 1885. The critics believed that it was probably the largest choir ever to perform in New Orleans.[56] Throughout November, he led concerts by a new orchestra at the exposition. On Monday, November 16, he and his orchestra joined the Shakespeare Club in a soiree at the French Opera House under the auspices of the ladies' committee of the American Exposition. The orchestra played the overture to Weber's *Der Freischütz,* a transcription of themes from Gounod's *Faust,* Weber's *Invitation to the Dance,* Boccherini's *Minuet,* a Waldteufel *Polka de Minuet,* and at the end Meyerbeer's "Marche aux Flambeaux."[57] On November 21, 1885, he began a series of four afternoon concerts each day at the fair; the concerts began at 1:00, 2:15, 4:00, and 5:00 p.m.[58] For this first four-concert day he performed music by Auber, Meissler, Donizetti, Navoro, Boieldieu, Waldteufel, Offenbach, Sonderman, Adam, Sullivan, Weiss, Flotow, Faust, Luigi Schneider (the clarinetist), and D'Aquin himself. This hectic schedule of quadruple concerts continued into the following January.[59] In addition, D'Aquin directed special concerts at the exposition, such as on January 1, 1886, for the "grande fête populaire, jour de l'Emancipation," and on January 8, for the opening of the Creole exhibit at the exhibition. For this latter concert D'Aquin invited all the inhabitants of New Orleans to meet at the Washington Armory to rehearse the choral pieces.[60]

Then suddenly D'Aquin left New Orleans for Paris. We do not know why he turned his back on New Orleans, but the critics surmised that he was torn between sentiment for his native city and the exciting musical life of Paris.[61] Perhaps he sensed that the declining economy of New Orleans meant that the musical life, which had been so active and rich during his youth, was ebbing into insignificance or at least turning in a new, unfamiliar direction. He returned to New Orleans by April 21, 1886, probably just to pack, but instead of moving to Paris, he relocated to New York, where he remained for the rest of his life. He returned only once, in 1913, for just a short visit.[62]

D'Aquin made his debut in New York's Chickering Hall on September 29, 1886. *The New York Times* critic thought highly of him: "A French flautist, M d'Aquin by name, was applauded for one of Doppler's fantasias—on Wallachian airs—which he interpreted with considerable virtuosity. Mme d'Aquin was overtasked in her air from Gounod, 'Reine de Saba.'"[63] It is uncertain what he and his wife did for the next few years. He was active at Central Congregational Church, Fifty-seventh Street west of Eighth Avenue, where his compositions were played by organist Signor Paolo F. Campiglio.[64] The earliest performance of D'Aquin's composition "Noël" was on December 27, 1890, at that church. He had built a reputation as a composer by 1891 when a handwriting expert, in discussing the handwriting of America's leading composers, wrote:

"Gustav d'Aquin's writing shows him to be a man of strong likes and dislikes. It is too bad that he encircles his entire signature with a flourish. He has a fair amount of ability and genius, much of which is apparently latent. There seems to be a natural element of reverence in his compositions."[65] In September 1892, he was the back-up conductor of the orchestra at New York's Casino Theater; Gustav Kerker conducted ballets, and "G. d'Aquin [took] his place during 'variety' portions of the show."[66]

By May 1893, D'Aquin assumed directorship of the Madison Square Garden Band, and he immediately became involved in numerous activities within and outside the venue. Madison Square Garden was a place for major conventions and rallies, and these events required a band to set the festive spirit of the occasion. One of his first shows was for a flower show.

> The concerts given every day and evening by the selected orchestra directed by Professor Gustav D'Aquin have been performances worthy of the audience's attention, even without the flowers. Most of the musicians in this orchestra are Seidl's men.
>
> The second concert by the musicians in this orchestra, opening with Gounod's "Ave Maria," with organ accompaniment, will probably serve as a good drawing attraction at the show today.[67]

Another of many such events was for the convention of the Sportsmen's Association in May 1895. "An auxiliary to the exposition [of the Sportsmen's Association] is a stage in the north gallery, and Gustave d'Aquin's orchestra. Every afternoon and evening there will be music and specialties by the variety actors and actresses and woman sharpshooters."[68] On October 28, 1895, he not only conducted his band for the Garden Food Show but premiered his most famous work, the "New York Times March."[69] At the opening of the House Furnishing Goods Exhibition on August 6, 1910, "D'Aquin's Military Band, stationed in the music loft over the main entrance to the Garden, played 'The House Furnishing Goods Exhibition March' and the doors were thrown open."[70]

In addition to these indoor performances, however, D'Aquin was also leading his band in rooftop concerts at Madison Square Garden. On May 26, 1893, he accompanied Mr. Reuben R. Brooks at such a rooftop concert; he then added pieces without Brooks.[71] The popularity of these concerts over the next few years made D'Aquin a musical celebrity among the unsophisticated musical audiences of the time. In 1895 a critic wrote,[72] "The present warm wave is regarded as a blessed relief by the managers of the roof gardens, and the Madison Square

Roof has received more than its ordinary portion of the increased patronage. The audiences have been very large for this season of the year, and the excellent specialties offered are applauded vigorously. Gustave d'Aquin's enlarged orchestra furnishes music of an unusually high order of merit." On one occasion the audience was offered a consolation ticket in case of rain: to go downstairs into the Garden and receive a free ticket to a concert band concert directed by Sousa.

Outside Madison Square Garden, D'Aquin was expected to lead his band in park concerts. In 1915 he was appointed leader for concerts for the West Side District of Manhattan. He was appointed because he was well known and had given concerts there the year before.[73] In 1914 he was in Central Park with his band.[74] The *New York Times* reported that "Park Commissioner Cabot Ward will open the municipal music season in Central Park today at 4 o'clock. A band of forty-seven men, conducted by Gustave d'Aquin, will furnish the music. Mr. d'Aquin was for a number of years conductor of French opera at New Orleans, and was leader of the Madison Square Garden Band for many years thereafter." The implication in this statement is that by 1914 he was no longer working for Madison Square Garden. The summer of 1916 he was again doing outside events: "The first of a series of four band concerts to be given by the West Side Municipal Band of the Department of Parks, under the leadership of Gustave D'Aquin, will take place tonight [July 19, 1916] in Colonial Park. The program, which will be made up of popular and classical selections, with 'The Star-Spangled Banner' as the opening and 'America' as the closing number, will be repeated Friday night in Abingdon Square Park, Sunday afternoon at 4 o'clock in Battery Park, and Sunday night in Washington Square Park. The concerts will be given under the auspices of the Department of Parks of the Boroughs of Richmond and Manhattan."[75] On July 14, 1918, he conducted Planquette's *Sambre et Meuse* and works of Gounod, Delibes, and Saint-Saëns on the Central Park Mall,[76] and on August 3, 1918, he led his band again in Central Park.[77]

During the 1920s D'Aquin continued his band concerts. His last known performances were on radio station WNYC on Sunday, August 29, 1926, at 8:30 p.m.[78] His composition "Noel" was repeatedly on concerts by organists.[79] D'Aquin died on December 17, 1932, and was survived by his wife, Eugénie, and his two daughters, Jeanette and Yvonne.[80] His importance for the music of New Orleans lies in his furthering the band music of West End, which in a short time after his departure from the city would be a major catalyst in the emerging new style of jazz. He departed just a little early and left the field to George Paoletti.

12

Theodore Curant
Verdi's Violinist in New Orleans

By the time Theodore Curant was born in Austrian Silesia in 1846, many Jewish musicians had already been able to enter the mainstream of European musical life from which they had been systematically excluded until the early nineteenth century. Curant showed musical promise as a child and received initial instruction on the violin in his native village. Later he studied at the Imperial Conservatory in Vienna, where one of his classmates was the noted conductor Hans Richter. Upon graduation with honors, Curant began a distinguished career as a violinist. The *Picayune* reported:

> After years, during which Professor Curant was numbered as a prominent member of some of the leading symphony and operatic orchestras, principally at Vienna,[1] he became connected with various musical enterprises, both French and Italian, and was first violin of the orchestra of the Grand Opera of the khedive of Egypt at Cairo in 1871, when Verdi's "Aïda" received its initial presentation under the leadership of the inimitable Bottesini. From thence a short period was passed in Alexandria, Egypt, after which, the love of adventure being strong and the inclination for variation of surroundings perfectly natural, Professor Curant, after visiting most of the prominent European centers, and even devoting a season at Havana, finally found himself in 1873 at New York City.[2]

From 1873 until the beginning of 1878 Curant was a front member of the first violin section of the Theodore Thomas Orchestra, based in New York. But Curant was not a healthy person, and therefore he sought a better climate in which to live. This brought him to New Orleans where he remained—with one short exception[3]—for the remainder of his life.

From February 26, 1878, until May 3, 1889, Curant performed and conducted many concerts in New Orleans. His first appearance was at a vocal and instrumental concert at Grunewald Hall on February 26, 1878, given by Mme Alice Schwarz.[4] It is uncertain what he did at that concert since the printed program, which proclaims his participation prominently at the top, does not indicate any specific piece performed by him. Likewise, while he is listed as a participant in an intermède at the German National Theatre on March 8, 1878, we have no idea what he actually performed.[5] On April 22, 1878, on the other hand, he performed Viotti's A Minor Concerto No. 22 and A. Bazzini's *Military Concerto,* Opus 42, with Cartier on piano.[6] This was part of a concert featuring Miss Kate Thayer, a native of New Orleans, who was trained in New Orleans but was now singing regularly in New York and Baltimore. The concert took place at Grunewald Hall. Three weeks later, on May 6, 1878, Curant performed pieces by Artôt and Kreuger at a concert in honor of Miss Corinne Bouligny at the French Opera House.[7] Curant also participated in chamber music on this occasion.

It is not until ten months later, on February 4, 1879, that we again hear of Curant performing in public.[8] It was a benefit for Curto at Grunewald Hall. On that occasion he performed a solo which the program does not name. Finally it was on April 15, 1879, that Curant at last presented his own concert.[9] As was customary at the time, he had the assistance of the best musicians in the city, including Kitziger, Cartier, Mueller, and Eckert. He performed Léonard's *Fantaisie Militaire* accompanied by an orchestra of thirty musicians and the Beethoven Violin Concerto with Eckert on piano.[10] He executed the former, a piece full of difficulties, "avec une grande correction," and "dans le concerto de Beethoven . . . il a déployé de sérieuses qualités d'exécution et de style." He also was first violinist in a Haydn string quartet, with the others being Kitziger, Cartier, and Mueller.

By March 30, 1880, we find Curant also as a conductor. He led an orchestra at a concert at Grunewald Hall with singers Alice Schwarz, Annie Seawell, F. Bremer, D. Delcroix, and Eckert.[11] A year later, on April 21, 1881, he appeared as both conductor and violin soloist.[12] He performed the Beethoven concerto again, this time with orchestra, and he also conducted the accompanying orchestra in the Mendelssohn F Minor Piano Concerto No. 2 with Jeanne Franko as soloist. In addition, Franko and Curant jointly performed the andante from Anton Rubinstein's Sonata Opus 13 in G Major—all on the same program with the Beethoven and Mendelssohn. The review in *L'Abeille* was glowing.

Above everything else we give double justice to Mr. Theodore Currant: first that he is a very serious musician, and that is rare among us. And what is equally rare, he performs only serious music. This genre of concert is not very lucrative, it demands a huge group of artists, the costs of the orchestra almost always absorb the receipts at the door; and we can only thank the beneficiary for sacrificing so his interests to the cult of true art. . . . But the greatest part of the concert was the great violin concerto in D Major by Beethoven, in which Mr. Currant deployed a mastery that we have not previously known. The compositions of this type are very difficult, and it takes an artist of the first order to play it convincingly. Mr. Currant showed a rare ability and was strongly applauded.[13]

Later that same spring Curant performed on a concert conducted by Gustave D'Aquin. It took place on May 15 at Grunewald Hall, and Curant played "with his usual superior ability" Wieniawski's *Légende* accompanied on the piano by Mme Henri Bayon.[14] On May 27, 1881, Curant led an orchestra at Spanish Fort but did not himself perform.[15] Rather he accompanied the young violinist Dengremont in De Bériot's Concerto No. 7 and Vieuxtemps's *Fantasie Caprice*.

Curant continued to appear on programs in 1882. He assisted Jeanne Franko once again in a concert at Grunewald Hall on March 30 where he played an unknown concerto for two violins with her.[16] Jeanne Franko, who was equally gifted on the violin and piano, devoted her energy on this occasion to the violin. On November 2 of that year he was first violinist in a performance of the Robert Schumann Piano Quintet, with Jeanne Franko as pianist, Kaiser as second violinist, Mullen as violist, and Emil Seifert as violoncellist.[17]

Curant participated in many benefit concerts for other artists. For example, on March 17, 1883, four violinists assisted Oscar Reine, oboist in the French Opera Orchestra, in a vocal and instrumental concert in his honor at Grunewald Hall.[18] The four—Joubert, Kaiser, Curant, and Bayon—performed together Alard's *Le Carnaval de Venise*. Later that fall Curant participated in a concert at Grunewald Hall to benefit Saint Stephen's Church. It took place on Wednesday, October 10, 1883.[19] Mrs. Pauline Le Blanc directed the Sainte Agnes Club, made up of amateur performers, assisted by some professionals such as Curant. In the first half, Curant, accompanied by pianist Le Blanc, performed excerpts arranged for violin and piano from Rossini's *William Tell*, and in the second half he performed a fantasia on Gounod's *Faust* and an anonymous trio for violin, piano, and organ with Mrs. Le Blanc and Mrs. Fournier.

On December 11, 1884, Curant performed the De Bériot Violin Concerto

No. 7 and some Wieniawski pieces with J. W. H. Eckert as accompanist.[20] At this concert some of Curant's pupils also performed. After his return from Mexico City, Curant gave a concert at Grunewald Opera House, on November 2, 1886, where he was joined by Kaiser, Van Hufflen, Salomon, Ida Riemann, and others.[21] We do not know the exact program, but probably Curant performed pieces by Rust and Vieuxtemps. Curant was ecumenical in offering his services to different religious groups. Along with Hincks, Sumner, Yuille, Berthe Pemberton, and the Continental Quartette he participated in a concert on November 18, 1886, to raise money for Christ Church,[22] and on May 30, 1887, at the confirmation service at Touro Synagogue, Kitziger got Kaiser, Curant, Moses, and others to assist with the music.[23] Alice Schwartz and Ida Riemann-Kaiser sang at the service. On February 3, 1888, at a concert for the benefit of Saint Joseph's new church, "Theodore Curant, the skillful violinist, played a pretty solo."[24]

Meanwhile, on April 20, 1887, he played a violin solo in a concert tendered to Miss Berthe Pemberton at Grunewald Hall;[25] "the first number on the program . . . was a violin solo, by Rust, played exquisitely by Professor Curant." Less than a week later, on April 26, 1887, he was part of a concert for Mark Kaiser;[26] he played in an arrangement of *Sancta Maria* by Fauré with violin, piano, and organ obbligato. At Sam Franko's violin recital at Grunewald Hall on June 14, 1887, Kaiser and Curant also participated in a performance of a capriccio by T. Hermann for three violins.[27]

In February 1888, Curant was the local New Orleans producer for a pair of chamber concerts performed by the Mendelssohn Club of Boston.[28] On April 10, 1888, at Grunewald Opera House, Curant played Godard's *Concerto Romantique* for violin solo and orchestra. On the same program he also conducted a grand orchestral concert with forty of the best players. The program was a formidable one: Beethoven's *Egmont* Overture, Robert Schumann's *Träumerei*, Weber's *Jubel* Overture, and "prière d'une Vierge" from Massenet's oratorio *Marie Madeleine*—all orchestral works. In addition, Pilcher played the Beethoven C Minor Piano Concerto No. 3 with full orchestral accompaniment under Curant.[29] Several weeks later, on May 1, Pilcher gave a grand orchestral concert at Grunewald Opera House and included Curant on the program.[30] Pilcher performed with orchestra the Mendelssohn G Minor Piano Concerto No. 1, a new work of his own composition, *Unique Marche di Bravoura,* Opus 8, dedicated to Eckert, and Beethoven's E-flat Piano Concerto No. 5. Curant, in turn, played Bazzini's *Concerto Militaire* for violin and orchestra, and the grand march and chorus from Tannhäuser. Just one evening later, on May 2, Hubert Rolling and his pupils gave a recital at Grunewald Hall. Curant, with W. Eckert accompanying, played an unnamed piece, and "last on the programme and a fitting climax to the musicale was the rendition of Beethoven's sonato [sic], andante, by Misses A. Socola, E. Noll and Professor Curant."[31] What piece by Beethoven the newspaper is referring to remains a mystery.

The following year, on April 25, 1889, Curant conducted thirty musicians in an orchestra accompanying Kaiser, who performed both a concerto by De Bériot and the Mendelssohn Violin Concerto.[32] Every seat was taken, and the reviewer concluded that under Curant "the orchestral numbers throughout were as skillful and as finished as the high standard of the selections would lead one to expect."

The last concert in which Curant is known to have participated occurred on May 3, 1889. It was a concert by Mrs. James Nott's pupils at Grunewald Hall. "Kaiser, the big, handsome violinist, played a ballad from Moskowski." Mrs. Samuel, "a pupil of Listz [sic]," was also on the stage. Gounod's "Ave Maria" was sung by twenty voice pupils with ten violins, organ, and piano; the violinists were Curant, Kaiser, Guillaume Ricci, Becker, Thomson, Burke, Gonsenheim, C. and L. Hase, and Specht.[33]

Curant died on August 23, 1889, from the disease that had brought him to New Orleans twelve years earlier.[34] He was extolled in an unusually long obituary in the Picayune "as truly one of nature's noblemen." Distinguished citizens Rabbi I. L. Leucht, Louis Grunewald, and Bernard Bruenn met two weeks later to organize a fitting concert in tribute to Curant and to benefit his family. The memorial concert for Theodore Curant at the Grunewald Opera House was held on October 29, 1889.[35] Performers included Mrs. Samuel, Mme James Nott, and Mark Kaiser, with M Rossi and Mr. J. W. H. Eckert as accompanists. Also on the program was Horace Peters, former student of Curant and recent graduate of the Leipzig Conservatory. Only the finest works were on the program: pieces by Mendelssohn, Beethoven, Ernst, Bizet, Gounod, and so forth. The *Picayune* reported: "The cosy little opera house was full of kindly and intelligent people. The entertainment had been well advertised, and it was the best gotten up and managed concert that has taken place in this city for a long time past. No overambitious and tiresome people were asked or allowed to sing or play, and no weak pupils of dizzy teachers were permitted to exhibit their show pieces for the advertisement, as frequently happens at benefit entertainments. Only useful and talented artists—the best that could be procured—were allowed a place on the programme, and the result was a delightful musical evening."[36]

13

Henry Wehrman Jr.
Violinist and Collector of Creole Songs

Henry P. Wehrman, one of the most distinguished violinists and composers in New Orleans at the end of the nineteenth century, spent most of his career in the twentieth century. Nonetheless, he figures so prominently in the last decade covered by this book that he deserves to be included here. While mention is made briefly of his later career, we will concentrate on his early career prior to 1898.

Henry P. Wehrman is usually referred to as Henry Wehrman Jr. His parents, Henri Wehrmann Sr. (1827–1903) and Charlotte Wehrmann (1830–1910), were among the most prominent engravers of music in America from 1849 to 1888, and their home was a center of music in New Orleans. Henry Jr. was born in New Orleans in 1870, the fourth and last child of Henri Sr. and Charlotte. He received musical training at a very early age on both piano and violin, and several times he went to Paris to further his violin studies. He wrote his first song, "Smiling Beauty," in 1883.

By the year 1888 Wehrman had achieved considerable local attention, both as a violinist and as a composer. The earliest known public performance by Wehrman on the violin is at a concert in Covington, Louisiana, at the Hotel Gonthier, on September 2, 1888. It was put on by the Orphéon Française of New Orleans under the direction of George L. O'Connell. Wehrman had a special connection to the Orphéon Français and frequently performed with them. It is possible that he studied in the student wing of the Orphéon Française. On this occasion he performed a violin solo arranged by Jean-Baptiste Singelée on motives from the opera *Norma,* and Henri Wieniawski's *Kaïawak*; in addition he was a member of the dance orchestra, consisting of eight musicians that accompanied a ball at the end of the concert. He is referred to as a virtuoso and composer.[1] This concert was followed on October 7 by another at the Hotel Gonthier in Covington where Wehrman performed Singelée's *Fantasie* on motives from *Rigoletto,* a duet with Mr. M. G. Ricci—"Au Clair de la Lune" by Faucheux, and, in the orchestra, *Souvenirs* from Flotow's *Stradella* and *Martha.*[2] Ricci and Wehrman repeated their duet at a soiree musicale of the Orphéon Française on October 25, this time back in New Orleans, at Grunewald Hall.[3] Ricci was the star instrumentalist on this occasion, and Wehrman is not even mentioned in the review.

Over the next few years Wehrman often played solo pieces and joined others in ensembles. Frequently he did so at special events, such as on November 20, 1889, when, once again under the aegis of the Orphéon Française (but this time under the direction of Professor Albert Heichelheim), he was part of the entertainment by the Camera Club at Grunewald Opera House. "Mr. H. Wehrmann, a very clever young violinist, played a charming polonaise, and with Mr. George W. Weingart executed a violin duet, the piano accompaniment being by Mr. Paul Brunet."[4] This followed a presentation of and a lecture on "lantern views of the Paris exposition, Johnstown disaster and English slides sent by the London Camera Club."

Subsequently Wehrman appeared on many programs with the Orphéon Français, often at Grunewald Hall with O'Connell as conductor.[5] Sometimes he was both composer and performer; sometimes he was soloist and other times a participant in chamber music.[6] He was not adverse to performing with students, his own and those at the Orphéon Français.[7] On May 21, 1890, he participated in a concert in honor of J. W. H. Eckert at Grunewald Hall.[8] Besides playing in the orchestra of the Orphéon Française, he played an obbligato violin in a song by Rebandi sung by Joseph Durel. His popular *Polka Marche* opened the second half of the concert.

In advance of Wehrman's April 3, 1891, concert at Grunewald Hall, the reviewer of *L'Abeille* had this to say about the young violinist: "Mr. Wehrmann is a Louisianian, still very young—probably 19 or 20—who is highly disciplined and who as violinist and composer progresses step by step to advance his artistic career. A man of sentiment and self criticism in his playing and in his writing, he has already written many pages worthy of attention."[9] The critic was ill and could not attend the concert but wrote, on April 4, that he found Wehrman a rare artist who combined modesty and merit.[10] He had heard that the house was full, despite serious competition from the French Opera and other entertainments in the city. Wehrman participated in various benefit concerts, such as that on May 7, 1891, at Werlein Hall given by the pupils and artist friends of the pianist, Mme Devrient, widow of the "well known eminent musician" Désiré Delcroix.[11] The same season, Wehrman took part in a benefit for MM G. Monna and J. Rossi, who had been faithful members of the French Opera since 1873.[12] Monna was a violoncellist in the orchestra who also had a brilliant career in Paris, and Rossi was one of the leading singers.

In December 1891, a new musical organization, called the Elite Parlor Orchestra, was established with Professor George L. O'Connell as leader and Wehrman as assistant leader.[13] We have no evidence of a concert by this orchestra until nearly a year later. According to the *Picayune,* in the third week of November 1892, "the Elite Parlor Orchestra under G. L. O'Connell and H. Wehrman, Jr., gave a delightful impromptu musicale at the residence of H. Wehrman, 127 Saint Peter Street. The latest new dance music and operettes were rendered, to the satisfaction of the many present."[14]

During the spring of 1892 Wehrman continued to be one of the busiest artists in New Orleans. On March 16, there was a complimentary musicale for pupils and friends of Mrs. J. L. Vincent at Grunewald Hall. Various amateur performers and Henry Wehrman rendered "difficult instrumental pieces . . . ably."[15] Clearly Wehrman, unlike many other professional musicians, had no problem appearing on the stage with students since his earlier days with O'Connell and the Orphéon Française. Two days later he participated in a concert at Grunewald Hall given by Signor Angelo Patricola and Mr. Hector Gorjux, with the accompaniment of a small orchestra; the audience was small because of unseasonably cold weather.[16] At the end of April the Carmelite fair at Grunewald Hall mixed recitations and musical numbers, among which were solos by Miss Fuqua with a violin obbligato by Wehrman. Also on the program he "gave a series of mandolin solos in true artistic style."[17] This side of Wehrman came out at the Pilcher Conservatory where he taught mandolin and later at the Music School of Newcomb College where he was responsible for the popularity of the Mandolin Society for several decades into the twentieth century. There would be other appearances by Wehrman on the mandolin. On one last occasion that spring, Saturday, May 28, there was a concert of the Orphéon Française conducted by Professeur P. A. Borge. Of all those on the program, Henri Wehrman Jr. was deemed exceptional in Sarasate's *Souvenirs de Faust.*[18]

In the fall of 1892 O'Connell conducted the initial concert of the Lyre d'Orphée at Grunewald Hall.[19] This was a group of fifty women along with an instrumental quartet and was the women's equivalent of another of O'Connell's creations, the Luth, an organization of men. It is possible that Wehrman was part of the instrumental quartet; in any case he is listed on the reception committee at the concert. On December 12, 1892, the two choral groups gave another concert at the Washington Artillery Hall.[20] The program was in honor of their conductor O'Connell, and this time "Mr. Henry Wehrmann, Jr., the talented young violinist, played Alard's fantasie concertante on Trovatore." The orchestra consisted of members of the French Opera Orchestra. Meanwhile, on November 28, there was a grand concert to benefit the Church of Saint John the Baptist, given at Odd Fellows' Hall.[21] The Orphéon Française provided the main attraction. Wehrman played the andante from De Bériot's Concerto No. 7, about which the *Picayune* critic stated: "Mr. H. Wehrmann, Jr., the well-known violinist and composer, was next on the programme. He had selected the Andante of De Bériot's seventh concerto. While of technical difficulties, the Andante in question is not a display piece, and in the selection, as well as in the rendition, Mr. Wehrmann showed himself a true artist. His fingering in the seventh position and his delicate phrasing of the minor passages won him a well-deserved encore. His second piece was a fantasy of his own composition."[22]

The next spring was a typically busy one. On March 15, 1893, Marguerite Samuel's student Mlle Léonice Vincent gave a recital at Odd Fellows' Hall. Wehrman joined Eckert and Vincent in a trio for violin, organ, and piano based on themes from Saint-Saëns's *Samson et Dalila,* and also seems to have performed a solo, which elicited praise and advice from the *Picayune* reviewer. He found that Wehrman had dexterity as well as finesse and grace in his left hand, plus energy and power in his bowing, and that he should go to Europe to one of the best conservatories to perfect his talent under one of the great European artists.[23] Less than a week later, on March 21, there was a concert by the Luth Society, directed by O'Connell, at Odd Fellows' Hall. The varied program included choruses from operas (among them the "Pilgrim's Chorus" from *Tannhäuser*), opera arias, and a bolero composed and played by Wehrman.[24] A month later, on Thursday, April 27, there was a benefit concert at Odd Fellows' Hall for the contralto Mlle Mathilde Bruguière, who was chosen by the leaders of the French Opera to represent Louisiana at the Chicago Exposition. While Wehrman did not perform at the concert, he apparently was one of the judges who chose Bruguière for this honor.[25]

On Monday, December 18, 1893, there was a free grand concert offered to Mlle Anita Lassen, the Danish singer, at Odd Fellows' Hall. Wehrman performed Dancla's Trio Concerto for two violins and piano with his niece Eugénie Wehrmann (piano) and Duvigneaud (violin), and he soloed in Wieniawski's *Légende.*[26] Wehrman must have been quick on his feet, for simultaneously he participated with a violin obbligato in one song during a sacred concert of songs and duets given by the altar guild of Saint George's Church.[27] The following evening, December 19, he took part in a monthly concert at the Y.M.C.A. by members.[28] Wehrman, Duvigneaud, Rayner, and one other performed a violin quartet, and both Henry and Eugénie Wehrmann with P. Duvigneaud performed a piano trio. On April 15, 1894, Wehrman played a piece during the Offertory at Saint Augustine's Church as part of a mass celebrating its patron saint's day.[29]

Wehrman was always busy, and he enjoyed performing in a variety of venues under different circumstances. He participated in a concert by Léon Fonteynes, ex-baritone of the French Opera, at the French Union Hall, assisted by numerous amateurs and artists and some from the Orphéon Française (Maumus, Lazare, Gaillard, and Rutily), and M Renaud, well known from the Opera House and Saint Louis Cathedral. This occurred on October 18, 1894, and Wehrman's role was to accompany his eleven-year-old niece.[30] He was too old to be a member of the new Orchestre d'Euterpe under the direction of Grisai that gave a concert at the same French Union Hall on Wednesday, October 24, 1894, but he managed to perform a mandolin solo.[31] This orchestra of some thirty-five to forty amateur musicians, consisted primarily of sixteen- and seventeen-year-olds. On November 21, at a grand concert by the friends of M le Professor Joseph Durel for his benefit, in the new Perseverance Hall at the intersection of Saint Claude and Dumaine streets, Wehrman was one of the featured participants.[32]

In spring he continued his activity as one of the most popular musicians in New Orleans. He performed a Grand Air for Violin at the grand entertainment for the benefit of the poor under the patronage of the Ladies' Auxiliary of Saint Vincent de Paul Society (Saint Augustin Parish) at French Union Hall, on April 15, 1895.[33] He is mentioned as a performer on Wednesday, April 24, during a grand concert and dramatic performance at the Academy of Music to benefit the waifs' home of the Louisiana Society for the Prevention of Cruelty to Animals.[34] The musical society of the Young Men's Gymnastic Club gave a concert at the club's salons on Rampart Street on May 16; the orchestra was conducted by O'Connell, and Wehrman and Grisai each had a solo.[35]

Wehrman played *Berceuse* and *La Sevillana* by Alard in a concert at Odd Fellows' Hall on January 20, 1896, for the benefit of the Cuban cause. The *Picayune* reviewer described the performance: "the same passionate playing and delicacy of conception which has made his name synonymous with excellent interpretation and fervid delivery, won him again last night round after round of applause. As an encore he played one of Ovide Musin's favorite compositions, and he did so in a manner that would have borne favorable comparison with the composer."[36] At a musicale on Monday, March 16, in Mrs. Nixon's School Hall, 2722 Saint Charles Avenue, for the benefit of the Society for the Prevention of

Cruelty to Animals, "the audience was charmed with Mr. Henri Wehrman's 'Romanza,' which was beautifully played on the violin."[37]

Wehrman took part at a grand vocal and instrumental concert at Odd Fellows' Hall by Miss Florence Huberwald, with her pupils, on Wednesday, April 8. The *Picayune* reported: "Mr. Henry Wehrmann, with his usual suavity and clearness, rendered his 'Romanza' and 'Gavotte Nugnotte,' and as an encore a 'Bolero' by himself. He played in his customary manner on his violin, giving his numbers all the intensity of his passionate nature, and as the compositions were of his own making, he expressed and hung over them like a tender and loving father. The Romanza, of the three, was the sweetest, and the one which would be more liked by the public, being a combination of a Chopin nocturne and a Liszt rhapsodie, such being the peculiar affect it produced on the audience, holding them enthralled until the last note ceased vibrating."[38] Wehrman again lent his talent to a concert at the Y.M.C.A. auditorium, this time to raise money for the Sailor's Bethel. On April 14 he played several solos on the violin.[39]

The next fall Wehrman was again participating in the musical life of the city. For a concert at the opening of the newly rebuilt concert hall of the Union Français on October 12, he participated as a comedian rather than as a musician.[40] Later in the twentieth century, he occasionally acted in theatrical productions. He was back on the violin a few days later, on October 22, 1896, for the first concert of that fall of the Orphéon Française at French Union Hall, directed by George L. O'Connell. With Eugénie he played a duo based on melodies from *William Tell,* and as an encore Raff's *Cavatina.*[41] In spring, on March 27, 1897, he again participated in the performance at Odd Fellows' Hall by Florence Huberwald.[42] On April 22, he assisted in a concert tendered to Mrs. James Nott by her pupils at the Athenaeum. The *Times-Democrat* critic extolled Wehrman's performance: "Mr. Wehrmann possibly never played in better style than he did while interpreting Allard's 'Rigoletta [sic].' The attainments of the talented young artist upon the violin have now become a matter of public recognition. Last night the clear tones of his instrument welled forth with a remarkable degree of vibration, and the technique of the player was made all the more prominent by the difficult selection. The delicacy of handling in the several positions was particularly noticeable, and the entire number was a model of skill and musical excellence. Mr. Wehrmann was loudly encored and responded, playing a catchy composition of his own."[43]

Wehrman's performances continued unabated after 1897 and well into the twentieth century. On several occasions he appeared as a violist, such as on April 21, 1932, in a recital at Dixon Hall, the music building of Newcomb College of Tulane University.[44] On that occasion he played works by Beethoven, Sammartini, Bruch, Brahms, Lalo, Popper, Saint-Saëns, and Robert Schumann, and his accompanist was his niece, Eugénie. Wehrman also played in the French Opera Orchestra as concertmaster in 1913–14 and in 1919; in 1917–18, René Salomon and Wehrman occupied the first desk of the first violin section of the Symphony Orchestra Association of New Orleans under the baton of Ernest E. Schuyten. His career as a conductor was more prominent after 1900. In 1910, for example, he was concertmaster of the New Orleans Symphony under Frank and conducted parts of the concerts.[45] From 1920 to 1934 Wehrman was conductor of the Tulane University Glee Club.

Early in the 1890s Wehrman became part of a string quartet, and for many years thereafter he was associated with this medium. Perhaps the first such ensemble he joined was the New Symphony Quartette, organized to perform all season, around 1891.[46] It gave its initial concert, informally, at Mark Kaiser's home on Saint Charles Avenue. Kaiser and Wehrman played violins, Grisai the violoncello, and Emile Malmquist the viola. The ensemble changed its name to the Mark Kaiser Quartet about 1894, and it performed a quartet by Carl Schuberth at Sainte Mary's Dominican Sisters on Saint Charles Avenue to a cloistered audience.[47] They also gave an informal recital for a limited number of friends. On November 26, 1894, the Kaiser Quartet performed at Odd Fellows' Hall Beethoven's Opus 18, no. 4; Carl Schuberth's Opus 34, and the Robert Schumann Piano Quintet with Marguerite Samuel; there were also some arias on the program.[48] The reviewer of this concert in *L'Abeille* was amazed that so many New Orleanians came to hear such esoteric music and that the concert was such a resounding success: "Our compliments and thanks to Misters Kaiser, Wehrmann, Malmquist and Grissi, the four excellent instrumentalists who have the mission to spread among us taste for this admirable music which is too little known here and which must be held in honor."[49]

By the end of 1896 Wehrman formed his own string quartet with J. Voorheis (second violin), J. Pomero (viola), and Cesar Grisai (violoncello).[50] This Wehrman did while remaining in the Kaiser Quartet. In early November 1903, Wehrman had another ensemble called the Beethoven Quartet, which gave its first program with works by Beethoven, Rubinstein (Opus 17, no. 2), D'Erlanger, Saint-Saëns, and one of his own pieces.[51] In 1909 Wehrman officially replaced the Kaiser Quartet with the Beethoven Quartet, whose members in 1909 were Wehrman, René Salomon, violins; G. Castillon, viola; and Grisai, violoncello.[52] On April 27, 1911, the Beethoven String Quartet gave a concert including works by Robert Schumann (Piano Quintet with Giuseppe Ferrata), Beethoven (Opus 18, no. 1), Bach, Mozart (a quartet minuet), Tchaikovsky (a quartet andante), and Bizet (an adagio), and three modern works by Pierné, Zarzycki, and Coleridge-Taylor.[53] In 1915 Wehrman had another string quartet ensemble, this one at the new school where he was now on the faculty, Newcomb College School of Music. The Newcomb String Quartet, consisting of René Salomon and Adrian Freische, violins; H. Wehrman, viola; and Otto Finck, violoncello, performed a concert at Tulane University's Gibson Hall; they played Mozart's K. 387 Quartet and the first movement of Schubert's A Minor Quartet.

In addition to string quartets, Wehrman often performed piano trios with his young niece Eugénie Wehrmann on piano and Grisai on violoncello. From 1895 on this was an important part of his public performance schedule. On May 4, 1895, at a Saturday matinee musicale at Odd Fellows' Hall on Camp Street, the Wehrman Trio, assisted by Theodore Hochart, baritone, and P. Duvigneaud, violin, performed Haydn's "last trio," and other music by Beethoven, Mendelssohn, Servain Rolla, and Fauré.[54] Wehrman himself performed Beethoven's Romance in F, about which the critic of *L'Abeille* stated that Wehrman "provoked great applause. Still a young person, he is accustomed to study music which is rarely heard, and he excels in certain productions which only the most experimental violinists dare to try. Proof of that, last Saturday, was in his performance of Beethoven's Romance in F at the first concert given by his new Trio."

Eight days later, on Sunday, May 12, 1895, the Wehrman Trio opened the first Conférence des Heroines Françaises, at the French Union Hall, assisted by many amateurs and artists.[55] There is no indication of what they performed. On Saturday, June 15, 1895, the Wehrman Trio was back at Odd Fellows' Hall for an evening concert. Once again we do not know the program.[56] Two years later the Wehrman Trio was still together, this time performing two concerts at the Y.M.C.A. to benefit that organization.[57] Wehrman directed these two events, on April 6 and 20, 1897, to highlight young, talented musicians in New Orleans. On the second program two movements of a Haydn piano trio were performed by his trio, which also accompanied several vocal pieces. On April 29, in a concert at the Y.M.C.A. to benefit the German Protestant Home, the trio played Haydn and Beethoven.[58] On February 16, 1905, the Wehrman Trio performed a complimentary musical recital in the banquet hall of the Saint Charles Hotel, but for this occasion it was not a piano trio. Eugénie and Henry played a number of works together, Eugénie played some solo piano pieces, and Mrs. Wehrmann-Moore sang songs.

Wehrman's activities as a teacher had definitely begun by December 17, 1893, when he was just twenty-three years old. In an advertisement by the New Orleans College of Music, Mrs. Samuel was director, Miss F. Huberwald, secretary, and the faculty is listed as Samuel, Kaiser, Bressler, Mr. E. Henderson,

Huberwald, Mr. A. Deiler, Mr. H. Wehrman, Mr. C. Weiss, and Mrs. Annie Shields.[59] Wehrman continued his teaching at the Pilcher Conservatory and at Tulane University, where his subjects went beyond the violin to include chamber music, mandolin, and choir. Years later he also taught at Louisiana State University and published works for students.

Henry Wehrman Jr. was a prolific composer who by the age of eighteen had already published a large number of piano works and songs. His entrée into the publishing world was made easy through the connections of his parents, who engraved and printed the music, but the continual performance of his music by amateurs and professionals justified those publications. In 1888, when he published the *Moonlight Waltz*, he already had twenty-seven pieces in print: *Parisiana Waltz*, *Nippy Polka*, *Pepita Mazurka*, *Queen of the South Schottische*, *Stella Waltz*, *Smiling Beauty Mazurka* (his first known composition), *Angel's Dream Waltz*, *Cotton Palace Polka*, *Newport Waltz*, *Glide Mazurka*, *Dudine's March*, *Moonlight Waltz*, *Latest Yorke*, *Fantastic Galop* (4 hands), *Beatrice Waltz*, *Souvenir Polka-March*, *Bohemia Waltz*, *Lydia Mazurka*, *Pleasant Memories Waltz*, "Forget-Me-Not" (song), *Sweet Love Polka*, *Dreamy Eyes Waltz*, *Favorite Yorke*, *Lilian Waltz*, *Friendship March*, *Young Soldiers' Patrol*, and *Gavotte*.

As was the custom among many composers in New Orleans, he often dedicated his works to particular persons or institutions with which he was connected. For example, in 1891 he published *Nelita*, "a Spanish dance, a graceful and tuneful measure, and has dedicated the work to Miss Nellie Pitkin, the accomplished daughter of Minister J. R. G. Pitkin."[60] Why he wrote *Hoo Hoo* in 1894 is unknown, but this simple, humorous piano piece suggests that there was an inside story to it.[61] Later that year he published a new waltz, *Souvenir*, "which is quite catchy."[62] In 1895 he published his *Fourth Battalion March* for piano.[63] And this is nowhere near a complete list of his compositions written before 1898. After the turn of the century Wehrman continued to publish songs and piano works, as well as some violin music. Among Wehrman's most important publications are his arrangements of twenty Creole folk songs in *Creole Songs of the Deep South* (New Orleans: Werlein, 1946).

Wehrman's association with George O'Connell was very close, and when the older conductor died in 1921, it was Henry Wehrman who directed the memorial service performed by O'Connell's Le Cercle Lyrique on November 25, 1921. In his last years Wehrman led a retired life. He was honored in 1949 for more than half a century of work for his church, the Presbyterian Church in Lafayette Square. Wehrman died in 1956 at the age of eighty-six.

14

William Henry Pilcher's Conservatory of Music

William Henry Pilcher was responsible for the establishment of the second conservatory of music in New Orleans. The Pilcher Conservatory of Music flourished in the Crescent City from 1885 to 1910, a period when New Orleans was changing from a city renowned for opera to a city renowned for jazz. It became the standard-bearer of the classical tradition of music in New Orleans, and its pupils—many from leading socialite families—were to be the arbiters of music of European origins for the next several generations of New Orleanians. Perhaps one of the reasons jazz originated in this particular city and so many great performers of jazz emerged from New Orleans is that New Orleans was a center for the performance and teaching of classical European music, and standards of excellence were high.[1]

That there was only one, short-lived conservatory in New Orleans before 1885 is understandable.[2] Nearly all New Orleanians who showed musical talent while studying elementary music in New Orleans went to Europe to study at the advanced level. The most famous case was Louis Moreau Gottschalk; other significant cases include Ernest Guiraud, Marguerite Elie, and the various members of the Franko family.[3] Meanwhile, at the elementary level, local teachers taught in their own homes or studios or visited the homes of their pupils. There was no one who was motivated to change the system until Pilcher, and he did so probably because other major cities in the United States were beginning to organize such music schools and he saw a way to capitalize on it. Pilcher's success led eventually to the opening of rival conservatories and music schools in the city and to a new concept of music education in New Orleans: that of the collective school where students are exposed to students in other musical disciplines than their own—instead of the insular private studio where the student had access, at best, to other students only in his or her own discipline.

Before studying the history of the Pilcher Conservatory, it would be useful to know something about the person who saw fit to create it. William Henry

Pilcher came from a very distinguished family of organ builders. (See the abbreviated family tree below.)[*] This gave him a secure background in music as a profession, and a number of his relatives were also involved in the conservatory. Since there is confusion by scholars as to the members of this family, the following is described in somewhat more detail than would otherwise be necessary.[5]

Henry Pilcher Sr. (1798–1880), William Henry's grandfather, was a distinguished organ builder who left Dover, England, in 1832 to come to New York.[6] There he opened an organ business that proved to be very successful.

His two sons, Henry Jr. (1828–90) and William (1830–1912), were just four and two years old when they were brought from Dover to New York. They were both destined to continue the family trade. The two young brothers went to Saint Louis in 1852 to open their own organ business, known as H. & W. Pilcher; their father joined them in Saint Louis in 1857 and retired in 1859.

Pilcher Family Tree

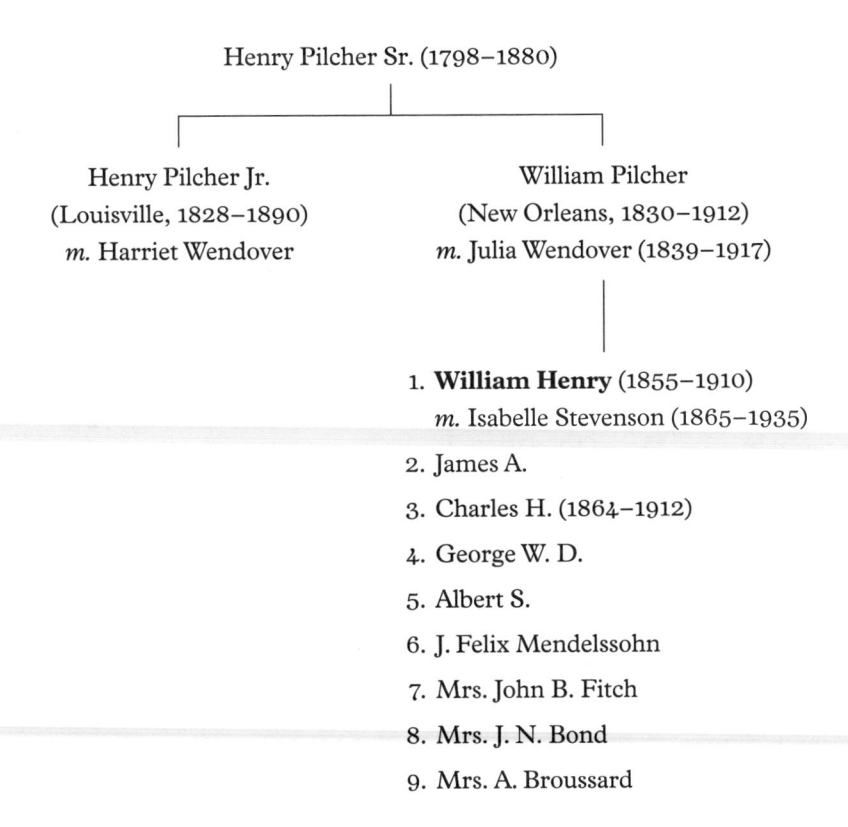

Henry Pilcher Sr. (1798–1880)

Henry Pilcher Jr.	William Pilcher
(Louisville, 1828–1890)	(New Orleans, 1830–1912)
m. Harriet Wendover	*m.* Julia Wendover (1839–1917)

1. **William Henry** (1855–1910)
   m. Isabelle Stevenson (1865–1935)
2. James A.
3. Charles H. (1864–1912)
4. George W. D.
5. Albert S.
6. J. Felix Mendelssohn
7. Mrs. John B. Fitch
8. Mrs. J. N. Bond
9. Mrs. A. Broussard

They were forced to close in 1861, however, with the beginning of the Civil War. In Saint Louis Henry Jr. and William married the Wendover sisters—William marrying Julia (1839–1917) and Henry Jr. marrying Harriet. On December 29, 1855, William and Julia had their first child of nine who would survive: William Henry Pilcher.[7]

When they closed their Saint Louis operation, the brothers moved to Chicago and opened yet another organ business in 1863. The anonymous author of the article on the Pilchers in the 1926 *Grove's Dictionary of Music and Musicians, American Supplement* says that the Chicago firm was destroyed by the great Chicago fire in 1871.[8] Sometime shortly after that, Henry Jr. moved to Louisville and established the Pilcher Organ Company that built most of the famous American Pilcher organs. His numerous sons and their heirs continued the firm until 1944 when shortages due to World War II made it impossible to acquire materials needed for organ building.

William, the younger brother, meanwhile, moved to Robin's Nest, Illinois, and opened an organ factory in Chicago with one of his sons which they operated from 1871 to 1873 (which son is uncertain, but William Henry would not be the likely candidate).[9] About 1878 William and Julia Pilcher relocated to New Orleans, where he established the New Orleans Pilcher Organ Company.[10] In the late nineteenth and early twentieth centuries William Henry's younger brothers Albert and Charles ran their father's factory, while another brother George was a "Pipe Organ Builder and Piano Expert" with Philip Werlein Ltd., one of the city's leading general music stores and publishers.[11] Charles also worked for Werlein.

The New Orleans Pilcher and Sons Organ Company built many organs, a few of which are still in use. Their most spectacular and famous organ was built for the Exposition Music Hall at the World's Industrial and Cotton Centennial Exposition in the city in 1884–85.[12] It won a gold medal at the exposition for its thirty-two-foot pedals patented by William Pilcher. At the conclusion of the exposition it was placed in the Jesuit Church of the Immaculate Conception, 130 Baronne Street in downtown New Orleans, where it survived in disrepair at least to 1992.[13] Other organs by the New Orleans family were at Saint Stephen's Roman Catholic Church on Napoleon Avenue in New Orleans[14] and in the Saint Augustine Catholic Cathedral in Saint Augustine, Florida. Two William Pilcher organs were recorded on a CD entitled *Historic Organs of New Orleans* in 1992 by the Organ Historical Society (OHS-89). One is the William Pilcher Organ built in 1890 for Trinity Lutheran Church in New Orleans, now in Our Redeemer Lutheran Church in Lafayette, Louisiana. It is much smaller than the

Cotton Exposition organ, but it was probably more typical of the organs built by Pilcher Brothers in New Orleans. The other organ was built around 1895 for Saint Bernard's Catholic Church in Breaux Bridge Louisiana, and after an intermediary stop in Lafayette, it has been in Saint Martin de Tours Catholic Church, Saint Martinsville, Louisiana, since 1977.

With the musical background that he got from his family and probably with some financial security that a successful organ business gave to the Pilchers, William Henry could embark on that precarious career of a concert artist. He began, however, as a chorister in the Chicago Episcopal Cathedral while his parents were living in Chicago. At one time he was even considering entering the ministry, but his musical instincts proved stronger. When he was eleven, he already was organist at Calvary Anglican Church in Chicago, and when he was thirteen (1868) he made a concert tour of the northern states and Canada. He later claimed to have more than nine thousand pieces in his repertory, playing over one hundred concerts per year, and when he bragged on November 23, 1906, that he was giving his 3,811th recital, it was no exaggeration.

William Henry served as organist at the Episcopal Church of the Epiphany and the Anglican Church of the Annunciation in Chicago before 1873, when, at age eighteen, he was hired as organist at Saint John's Catholic Church in Saint Louis, his native city. According to his anonymous biographer, he resigned the Saint Louis job after seven years with the intention of following his parents to New Orleans, but because there was a yellow fever epidemic in the Crescent City, he went instead to Galveston, Texas, where he was in charge of the music at Trinity Episcopal Church and where he established a music school. The chronology at this point is uncertain. He seems to have gone to Germany where, again according to his anonymous biographer, he studied with a Dr. Goldbeck, Franz Liszt, and Hans von Bülow and received a doctorate in music in 1880.[15] The same source indicates that he also studied organ with Antoine Edouard Batiste in Paris and William Thomas Best in Liverpool and London, but since Batiste died in 1876, William Henry must have been in Europe for a few years before 1880 and during his supposed tenure in Saint Louis. A possible explanation is that his church allowed him to go to Europe in or before 1876 to further his musical education, and instead of returning to Saint Louis, he went to Galveston.

When he finally arrived in New Orleans in 1881, William Henry quickly became one of the most important musicians in the city. Above all, his fame lay with his abilities as an organist. Reviews of his performances reiterate his exceptional pedaling technique and his consummate musicality. His piano playing was equally professional; on April 10, 1888, for example, he performed the Beethoven Piano Concerto No. 3 with a professional orchestra at the Grunewald Opera House and got a good review.[16] With his artistry, however, also came a certain degree of instability. His restlessness is evident in his continual shift in his duties as organist. He moved from church to church, from denomination to denomination, even from church to synagogue. In June 1881, William Henry was appointed organist at Trinity Episcopal Church in New Orleans. He kept that position until August 15, 1885, when he became organist at the Jesuit Church of the Immaculate Conception, so that he could play regularly on the famous large and powerful organ that his family had built. He resigned the post in 1890 and a few years later took a position at another Jesuit church, Holy Name of Jesus on Saint Charles Avenue, at that time some distance from the hub of New Orleans but not far from his family's organ factory. He resigned in 1896. Meanwhile, he was also music director at Temple Sinai (Reform) from 1890 to 1892.[17]

William Henry remained in New Orleans uninterruptedly until 1896, when he moved to New York to become organist at the Episcopal Church of the Nativity and also the Episcopal Church of the Epiphany. He returned to New Orleans in 1904 and lived there for the next five years. In 1909 he assumed a post at the Warren Avenue Congregational Church in Chicago. In September 1910 he was on a concert tour when, in Rosedale, Kansas, he suddenly took sick and died. He was survived by his wife, the former Isabella Mamie Stevenson (1865–1935, who had been his pupil); his parents; his five brothers, James A., Charles Hobart (1864–1912), George Washington Doan, Albert Snyder, and Joseph Felix Mendelssohn Pilcher; and his three sisters, Rosa (or Rosie, Mrs. John B. Fitch), Elizabeth (Mrs. J. N. Bond), and Carrie (Mrs. Albiades W. Broussard) of New Iberia (in the Cajun area of Southern Louisiana).[18]

William Henry was a prolific composer of keyboard and other kinds of music. He had over 109 works published in his lifetime, which included organ works, piano pieces, songs, and at least one large mass for choir and organ or orchestra.[19] It has been difficult to locate any of Pilcher's music, but four works survive in the Tulane University library.[20] One is a *Grande Valse de Concert,* Opus 7, no. 3, dedicated to Miss Belle T. Tilden of Mobile, Alabama. It was printed in 1880, the year before Pilcher arrived in New Orleans, and is engraved by the local New Orleans engraver Mrs. Henri Wehrmann and probably published by Louis Grunewald in New Orleans. It is somewhat flamboyant without undue variation from the key of B-flat major or from the necessary triple waltz meter. A little less flamboyant is Pilcher's *Galop Brillant,* Opus 24, engraved again by

Mrs. Wehrmann and printed by Grunewald in 1887. The work is dedicated to one of Pilcher's students from Bayou Sara, Louisiana, and to accommodate the student's ability at the keyboard, the work is labeled a composition "of moderate difficulty." Rhythmically it is strictly in two beats, reflecting the galop meter and clearly uninfluenced by local New Orleans African or other non-Western European rhythms. It is a nice, catchy piece and well worth revival.

The same year as the galop, Pilcher published his song "The Idyll of the Violet No. 4" with words by George Macdonald, Pilcher's English contemporary.[21] It was published by Standard Music and Photo Litho Company. The music is actually much better than the text, which is in a dated sentimental style common in the nineteenth century. The fourth piece in the Tulane Library is another song, "If So: Valse Song," dedicated to "my friend and pupil Miss E. C. Keller." The engraver is unknown, but it was published by Philip Werlein in 1890.[22] It is similar to "The Idyll."

Thus, when William Henry Pilcher decided to open his conservatory in 1885, he was a musician of various skills: composer, pianist, and organist. The aim of the school was to teach music in its broadest sense, that is, to teach performance skills, theory, and music history. He claimed that he taught music in all its branches, but clearly piano, organ, and voice predominated in the curriculum. Serious students were required to take some music history and music theory. His conception was new for New Orleans; William Henry opened not a studio limited to one discipline but a multifaceted conservatory. Other top musicians such as Frederick Kitziger (ca. 1845–1903), Marguerite Elie Samuel, and Hubert Rolling had studios, but they did not offer certified conservatory degrees like those offered by Pilcher.

The school was very popular. In its second year (1886–87) it had 85 students, mostly from New Orleans but also 6 from Saint Louis and 3 from elsewhere in Louisiana.[23] One year later, 1887–88, it had grown to 108 students, with 5 from Saint Louis, 3 from Texas, 1 from Mississippi, and a number from Louisiana but outside the New Orleans area (Shreveport, Baton Rouge, Ruston, Bayou Sara). Among the students were William Henry's brothers Charles, George, Albert, and J.F.M., and his sister Carrie. The 1887–88 catalogue lists 64 piano students, 48 vocal students, 8 organ students, and 11 taking history and theory.

The faculty expanded as the number of students increased. In 1888 Professor Theodore Curant was in charge of violin studies and had several assistants; he was succeeded the next year by the most important violinist in the city, Mark Kaiser. In 1892 Henry Wehrman taught mandolin. Isabella, William Henry's wife, taught piano, guitar, and banjo while Henry C. Blackmar (brother of A. E.

Blackmar, the well-known publisher of music in New Orleans and elsewhere)[24] taught "orchestral instruments." The Beethoven Musical Society was established as an ensemble for instrumental students at no additional fee so that they would gain experience with instrumental works of ancient and modern masters; there were weekly rehearsals. A Handel and Haydn Choral Society was organized, also with weekly rehearsals and without additional fees for the students; no outsiders were allowed to join them. Piano students paid twelve dollars for twelve weeks of class lessons, twenty-four dollars for lower-level private lessons, and thirty-six dollars per twelve-week session for upper-level private lessons. Organ and voice lessons were roughly equivalent, though organ students were required to pay an additional ten cents per hour for the bellows blower. Recitals were given each week, concerts with invited guests once a month. Each graduating student was required to give a solo recital during his or her last year of study.

On August 16, 1887 the *Daily New Orleans Item* (p. 29) commented, "Too much praise can not be bestowed upon Professor Pilcher for the manner in which he manages the studio, which is considered one of the best in the country. His pupils are taken from the representative families of this city and number about one hundred and fifty."

By 1892 the conservatory had moved to very prestigious quarters at 169 Saint Charles Avenue (next to the Washington Artillery Hall, where many concerts and balls were held). To be situated on Saint Charles Avenue meant that the school was now on the same street where the city's most elegant socialites lived. By 1904, however, the school had moved much further uptown. Pilcher moved the conservatory away from its downtown location on Saint Charles to the somewhat less prestigious but still attractive site on Milan Street because many English-speaking residents were moving away from downtown to the more spacious uptown neighborhoods. And since the school clearly catered to those citizens, this third and final location for the conservatory was convenient for the students.

In 1892 the curriculum expanded to include Italian, Latin, and Greek, and the name changed to "College of Music." Students came from many more states, including Iowa, Illinois, Georgia, Florida, Missouri, Texas, and Kentucky, as well as Mexico and Ireland. The new building on Saint Charles was able to house studios and a small recital venue, but for the major commencement concerts, various large community halls were used, such as Grunewald's Opera House for the sixth graduation in 1891 and the First Baptist Church for the ninth commencement on October 23, 1894. "Pilcher's Conservatory, Recital

Hall" shows the interior of the recital hall on Saint Charles Avenue; prominent in the foreground are a bust of Beethoven and a portrait of Mozart—clearly William Henry's musical icons.

What transpired in the years 1896 to 1904 is open to speculation. Isabella, Mrs. William Henry Pilcher, seems to have remained at the College of Music running things while her husband was in New York, and the school seems to have flourished even if the marriage seems to have failed. The college was renamed again the New Orleans Conservatory of Music, with Isabella as nominal head in the absence of the president, William Henry. His father, William Pilcher, was vice-president; his mother, Julia, was matron; and his sister Carrie was secretary. Isabella also taught from her home at 2115 Carondelet Street, or later 254 Burdette Street—both in the Uptown section. An Eveline Pilcher was also a music teacher in New Orleans during these years (at 2024 Saint Andrew Street), but it is uncertain if she was related to the others.

When William Henry returned to New Orleans in 1904, he first lived at 1215 Milan Street, where the conservatory had recently moved, but shortly thereafter he moved in with his parents and his brother Charles at 6022 Laurel Street near the organ factory. There is no sign that he returned to Isabella, though they continued to work together at the school.[25] It is there, on November 23, 1906, that William Henry gave his 3,811th recital, probably on the two-manual Pilcher organ that his family built for his original studio at the downtown Carondelet location.

By 1910, there was plenty of competition for the Pilcher Conservatory, and when William Henry died that year, there was little incentive to keep his school going. His heirs quickly closed it. Another New Orleans Conservatory of Music was set up by Emile Malmquist in 1898 at 1420 Prytania Street, not far from Pilcher's, and it was still on Prytania in 1911 after Pilcher's Conservatory was gone. Another conservatory that emerged about 1910 was the Southern College of Music, with Mrs. Arthur J. Schoenfeld, president, at nearby 1216 Felicity Street. Across town on the other side of the Vieux Carré (French Quarter) was Miss D. Points's Musical Institute and School of Oratory and Elocution, started in 1894 at 930 Elysian Fields Avenue, near North Rampart Street, which advertised "Music taught in all its branches; higher training a specialty." Studios limited to one particular aspect of music still flourished, such as Professor Julius Braunfeld's New Orleans School of Voice Training from 1899 on, at 1503 Carondelet Street near Pilcher's original location, and individual teachers, as elsewhere in the country, continued having private studios. But conservatories were here to stay. Most significantly, the Music School of Sophie Newcomb

College was opened at 1224 Seventh Street in 1909 by Giuseppe Ferrata, and of all the studios and conservatories in the city in 1910, it is the only one to survive to the present day, though now located on the Tulane University campus.[26] Several of Pilcher's teachers, notably Mark Kaiser and Henry Wehrman Jr., moved over to Newcomb College, and newly arrived Leon Maxwell, a transplant from Medford, Massachusetts, directed the music school from 1910 to 1952. Ferrata (1865–1928), a piano virtuoso and a pupil of Liszt, was in fact the founder of the Newcomb Music School and was easily the equal of or better than William Henry Pilcher.

Without William Henry's dynamism to guide Pilcher's school, which was powerful enough even while he was in New York, Pilcher's conservatory could not continue against so much competition. But nonetheless, Pilcher's lasting achievement was to create a type of institution that the city needed in 1885 and which paved the way for future such institutions of the twentieth and twenty-first centuries. The music departments and schools of music of Tulane University, Loyola University, Xavier University, Southern University, the University of New Orleans—today's successors to the Pilcher Conservatory—and even those of Louisiana State University in Baton Rouge and Southeastern Louisiana State University across Lake Pontchartrain in Hammond, Louisiana—owe Pilcher a debt of gratitude. In the context of American musical history, Pilcher did for New Orleans what others were doing from the 1850s to the end of the nineteenth century in other musical centers. Baltimore (Peabody, 1857), Oberlin (1865), Cincinnati (1867), Chicago (1867), Boston (New England, 1867), Philadelphia (1870), Detroit (1874), Milwaukee (1874), New York (1878), and Cleveland (1884) established conservatories, and if New Orleans was to remain a musical center, it, too, needed a comparable institution.[27] This Pilcher achieved, and no doubt whatever styles of music came after 1885, the skills and sensibilities taught at this conservatory and those of its heirs have had a lasting effect on the music of New Orleans through the talents, skills, and tastes of their graduates.

Jeanne Franko. Singer scrapbook.

Marguerite Samuel. Mount, 147.

Mark Kaiser. Gift of Philip Werlein, Ltd.
Courtesy of The Historic New Orleans Collection, Acc. No. 2005.0154.1.

Theodore Curant. *Daily Picayune,* Nov. 11, 1888, p. 10, col. 3.

Henry Wehrmann Jr. Mount, opposite 88.

The Beethoven Quartet (*Left to right:* Henry Wehrmann Jr., René Salomon, Léon Barzin, and César Grisai). Singer scrapbook.

William Henry Pilcher. Music folder, Pilcher's Studio of Music, Ephemera Collection, Louisiana Research Collection, Tulane University.

Pilcher's Conservatory, Recital Hall. Music folder, Ephemera Collection, Louisiana Research Collection, Tulane University.

Julia Calvé Boudousquié. Courtesy of Joan D'Arc Boudousquié Garvey.

Ole Bull. Lahee, frontispiece.

Camillo Sivori. Lahee, opposite 154.

Charles Boudousquié. Courtesy of Joan D'Arc Boudousquié Garvey.

Louis Grunewald. Waldo, 115.

Philip Werlein. The Historic New Orleans Collection, Acc. No. 1996.24.1.

Teresa Carreño. Cooke, opposite 108.

J. W. H. Eckert. *Daily Picayune,* June 24, 1908, p. 6, col. 5.

David Bidwell. *The Industries of New Orleans*, 110.

Florence Huberwald. Mount, opposite 143.

Ovide Musin. Singer scrapbook.

BOOK II

{ A Chronological History }

1

The Early Years
1805–1835

The first public concert known to have taken place in New Orleans in the nineteenth century occurred on Tuesday, December 17, 1805.[1] It was a vocal and instrumental program that was typical throughout the century in that it combined different performing bodies and a varied repertoire; it followed a pattern found in concerts in Haiti from 1769 to 1791.[2] There were in this case orchestral music, vocal music, and concertos for two different solo instruments with orchestral accompaniment. Amateurs and professionals performed together, in solos, in chamber ensembles, and in the orchestra. As was often the case, one performer was highlighted: Professor Brun on the pianoforte. The concert was followed by a ball. We do not know where this concert was performed. The concert was in two halves: part I: *President's March,* arranged for grand orchestra by Hus Desforges (a violinist and leader of the opera orchestra; see book I, part II, chapter 1); the Overture to *Démophon* for grand orchestra; an ariette sung by Mlle Fleury Sr. (leading soprano of the opera which, since the beginning of November, had been performing at least twice a week); a clarinet concerto performed by M Nicolai; a duo for two sopranos sung by the two Fleurys (mother and daughter)[3] with piano accompaniment; part II: the Overture to André–Ernest–Modeste Grétry's *Panurge* for grand orchestra, an ariette from *Armide* sung by the young Mlle Fleury, a piano concerto performed by Mr. B. Brun, Laroque's[4] *Pastorale* for grand orchestra, and a duo from Christoph Willibald Gluck's *Orphée et Eurydice* sung by the Fleurys.

What this first concert demonstrates is that, by December 1805, the city had an opera company, an orchestra with a conductor, a group of solo instrumentalists and singers, at least one local composer, and an audience that was willing to pay to hear the concert. The first opera known to have been performed in the city was Grétry's *Sylvain* on May 22, 1796,[5] and with the influx of musical persons from Santo Domingo as well as Europe during that decade and the one following, the city had the personnel for concerts as well as operas.[6] It was, perhaps, inevitable that such musicians would want to give concerts and that New Orleanians would want to enjoy the talents of their musicians outside as well as inside the opera theater.

This first concert must have been very successful because immediately thereafter two more concerts were held and the vogue was established. On January 14, 1806, the second *concert vocal et instrumental et bal* in New Orleans for the benefit of the clarinetist Nicolai, took place "in the ordinary ball room."[7] It cost one piastre per person. Mozart dominated the concert. Once again the program was in two halves: part I: a repetition of Desforges's arrangement of the *President's March;* an ariette from Mozart's *The Magic Flute* performed by Mme Nicolai; a piano concerto performed by M Julia; an ariette from Grétry's *L'Amant Jaloux* performed by Mme Nicolai; and a clarinet concerto by Joseph Willibald Michel (1745–1816) performed by M Nicolai; part II: a Mozart symphony for large orchestra; a duo from Nicolas Etienne Framery's (1745–1810) opéra comique *L'Infante de Zamor* sung by M Remondet and Mme Nicolai; Soler's Symphonie Concertante for two clarinets performed by MM Anderson and Nicolai; and the Overture to Mozart's *The Magic Flute.*

Four weeks later, on February 7, 1806, the third concert took place, once again in the New Orleans ordinary ballroom. This time the clarinetist, Mr. Anderson, was the driving force behind a vocal and instrumental concert in which he performed the Clarinet Concerto by Michel; his claim that this was the New Orleans premier of Michel's work does not take into account Nicolai's performance on January 14 and perhaps suggests a rivalry between the two clarinetists.[8]

There is no record of any more concerts until the next year, but in 1807 there were six concerts, four at the beginning of the year and two at the end. On January 10, 1807, a grand concert and ball were moved to the hall of MM Lefaucheur and Company to benefit Desforges. M Gauthier, amateur, performed his own Clarinet Concerto, and M Loss, artist (that is, professional), played a pianoforte concerto.[9] Nine days later amateurs and professionals joined in another concert, once again to benefit Desforges. As was now the custom, the vocal and instrumental concert was followed by a grand ball, once again in the hall of MM Lefaucheur and Company. The program was in two "acts": I. the Overture to Démophon;[10] a sonata by Muzio Clementi on the pianoforte, performed "par une Demoiselle Amateur"; "Ariette d'une Folle," performed "par un dame amateur"; a concerto by Jarnovick (Adalbert Gyrowetz, 1763–1850), performed by Desforges; and II: a sonata by Daniel Steibelt (1765–1823), performed by a "demoiselle amateur"; a romance, performed by "une dame amateur"; and a clarinet concerto, composed and executed by Mr. Gauthier.[11] Twelve days later, the third concert of the season was performed by musicians and amateurs for the benefit of Mr. Bourgeois (no. 9 Saint Peter Street), consisting of two acts: the Overture to Nicolas Dalayrac's (1753–1809) *Raoul Sire de Créqui*; an ariette sung by Mlle Fleury Sr.; Desforges playing his own Violin Concerto; the Overture to *Panurge*; an ariette sung by Mlle Fleury Jr.; and Gauthier playing his own Clarinet Concerto again.[12] And three weeks later, on February 20, 1807, there were the fourth concert and ball. The program consisted of I: the Overture to *Souterrain* by Laroque; a romance for harp accompanied by a woman; a sonata for piano by M Brun; a violin concerto by Desforges; and II: a duet for harp and piano performed by Brun and a woman; a scene from Steibelt's *Romeo et Juliette* performed by a woman with piano accompaniment; and a clarinet concerto.[13] This program included the earliest known use of the harp in a concert in the city. Note that usually when an amateur woman performed on a concert, her name was not given or only the initial of her last name appeared; this suggests that it was not yet fully socially acceptable for women to perform publicly or to be written up in a newspaper for public display of talent unless she was considered a professional, as were the cases of the two Fleurys, mother and daughter.

In addition to regular concerts, a trend started in 1807 for some mini-concerts—called intermèdes—to take place during an evening of dramatic performances. The first of these occurred on February 16, 1807, between a three-act comedy *L'Amant Bourru* and Dalayrac's opera *Isabelle et Rosalvo*, when M Gauthier played his own Clarinet Concerto.[14] This was so successful that he repeated the concerto between the same two dramatic performances six times that February and March, and the following year (April 6, 1808) he played the concerto again at the Saint Philip Street Theatre, this time during the first act of the pantomime *Mirza and Lindor*.[15] Others copied the idea. On May 10 and 19, 1807, Mr. Labadie performed a violin concerto by Jarnovick (Gyrowetz) between Grétry's *Sylvain* and Cimanosa's [sic] *Le Directeur dans l'Embarras*.[16] Even dancers liked the idea, so the next fall a dancer performed an intermède between a comedy and a ballet pantomime,[17] and on August 29, 1808, between the performances of two comedies a trio of dancers did a brief ballet.[18]

For the first time we also encounter a cabaret-like setting in New Orleans on April 23, 1807. The Nouveau Theatre opened, with various entertainments in the Chinese Room (La Salle Chinoise). These events were repeated every Wednesday and Saturday without interruption. "The entrepreneurs have neglected nothing in order to make the event agreeable. Above all, they have procured a good orchestra."[19] This provided a new venue of employment for musicians and enabled the city to lure professional players from abroad with added incentives. While the music was performed probably to accompany dancing or as background music, it did allow for individuals to play in front of an audience and set the stage for more concerts.

The next season (September 1807 to June 1808) began with the final two concerts of the year 1807. On Saturday, October 10 or 17, 1807, there was a vocal and instrumental concert to benefit M Remondet, a music professor; it was given by both amateurs and professionals ("musicians"), followed by a ball. For the first time there is mention of the racial divide in the audience: "Free persons of color who desire to attend are advised that the gallery, in which they usually come, has been arranged in a more confortable manner; no slaves can be admitted there. There is a special place for domestics."[20] This notice is both mean and demeaning, but it does convey to us the fact that the concerts were not designed for an exclusively white audience.

The Creoles of color newly arrived from Santo Domingo, certainly, were as interested in the best music from Europe as the whites who had come directly from Europe, and their attitude toward their slaves and domestics was no different from that of the whites: these slaves and domestics could, of course, witness the concert, but just don't let them sit nearby. The program consisted of a First Intermède (first half): an overture for grand orchestra, an aria sung by Mr. Remondet, an aria sung by Mlle Fleury, and Desforges's Allemande for orchestra; a Second Intermède: a chasse for grand orchestra, an ariette sung by an amateur, a duet sung by the two Fleurys, and another overture. This use of the word "intermède" to represent "half a concert" occurred only twice (see also March 8, 1808); the word otherwise was used exclusively to refer to the "mini concert" separating parts of a dramatic presentation.

The rest of the concerts during the 1807–8 season followed a familiar pattern. Desforges, Nicolai, and the Fleurys established themselves as regulars, but alongside the earlier group of musicians a few new ones appeared, such as Mme J. Gautrot Labat.[21] The repertory gradually expanded, but the programs remained composites of vocal, orchestral, and solo music from the famous composers of the time. On Tuesday, December 29, 1807, for example, there was another benefit concert and ball for the benefit of Desforges. The program contained an overture by Mozart, an ariette, a Clementi piano sonata performed by M Néveu, a duet sung by Mlle Fleury and M Chavenet, a violin concerto written by the amateur M Blache and performed by Desforges, variations on an air for piano performed by Néveu, and an overture for grand orchestra.[22] A month later, on January 28, 1808, there was a concert by the pianist Mme

Labat who, along with her husband, a horn player, dominated the program: an overture for grand orchestra; a pianoforte concerto and various airs by Cramer performed by Madame Labat; "Ariette des Visitandines" sung by Fleury Jr. and accompanied by obbligato horn performed by Mr. Labat; a Quatant de clarinet performed by M Fortier Jr., an amateur; a Porpera aria sung by M Godefroy accompanied by pianoforte performed by Mme Labat; Desforges performing his own Violin Concerto; and the Fandango of Steibelt performed by Mme Labat. A grand bal paré followed.[23]

Then on Monday, March 7, 1808, it was the turn of clarinetist Nicolai. This concert introduced a concept that was common during the first half of the nineteenth century, namely the presentation of talented children on programs that usually featured adults, both amateur and professional. This was a good chance for the young persons to gain poise performing before a sophisticated audience and at the same time allowed potential patrons the chance to find gifted young persons in whom to invest. The youngsters often were not beginners but advanced students who were about to launch careers or further their education abroad. The first intermède of the program contained the Overture to Gluck's *Iphegénie en Aulide*; an ariette from one of the operas entitled *Le Sorcier*; a pianoforte sonata performed by a young girl of eight years; the Michel Clarinet Concerto performed by Nicolai; *Les Folies d'Espagne* (the Spanish *La Folia*) with variations for pianoforte, executed by a young girl of eight years who had studied for seven months; and "Le Grande Ariette" from Méhul's *Euphrosine* sung by Mme Nicolai. The second intermède contained another pianoforte sonata performed by another young girl of seven; the Fodor Violin Concerto[24] performed by Desforges; a duet from Grétry's *Sylvain* sung by M Chavenet and Mme Nicolai; a pianoforte sonata for four hands performed by two young female amateurs; and a symphonie concertante for two clarinets by Devienne, performed by MM Fortier and Nicolai.[25]

The final two concerts of the season, on March 15 and 29, were no different. The first was the second concert by Mme Labat in the Salle Ordinaire and included her daughter, age nine, in a piece of chamber music. The full program was "Hail Columbia," arranged for grand orchestra by Desforges; followed by *La Marche Favorite du General Moreau,* orchestrated by M Laroque; Trio and Air by Pleyel for pianoforte, violin, and bass, performed by Mlle Labat, age nine, MM Desforges and Miniere; an air from the opera *Alexis* sung by Fleury Sr.; a new pianoforte concerto by Johann Ladislaus Dussek (1760–1812), followed by an air varié performed by Mme Labat; a new overture for grand orchestra composed by M Laroque; an opera duet accompanied by Mme Labat; and *L'Orage* for pianoforte by Steibelt, performed by Mme Labat.[26] The last concert and ball, on March 29, was given by Gauthier for the benefit of a respectable woman and her large family.[27]

The next season, 1808–9, began with five concerts. By now regular "seasons" were becoming established. Technically a season lasted from September to June of the following year, but because of the extreme heat and humidity (often accompanied by epidemics), it was rarely practical to begin a season before mid-October or early November, and to keep it going past mid-May of the following year.[28] As we shall see, this led to employment problems for the instrumentalists during the summer, and several attempts at summer concerts were made before 1879, when the Lake Pontchartrain concerts were established. The concert season paralleled the opera season and, eventually, the theater season as well, especially since many of the opera musicians and theater-hall musicians were involved in concerts as well. The first concert of the 1808–9 season, then, did not occur until November 18, 1808. It was a grand vocal and instrumental concert in the Salle Accoutumée to benefit the opera singer M Valois (or Vallois). This is the first concert in which a visiting artist performed, alongside local musicians; Mr. Jean Goez, maître of the English cathedral in Havana, was both a singer and a violinist. As was often the case during the early nineteenth century, however, a visitor to the city would remain for months, and in this case Goez was in New Orleans during the entire season or returned frequently. The first program began with a symphony for grand orchestra by Wranitsky,[29] a Grand Air and *Recitatif* by de Tote sung in Italian by Goez, an Italian duet by Cimarosa sung by Valois and Goez, and a violin concerto performed by Goez. The second part consisted of an Italian trio sung by Mlle Laurette Fleury, Valois, and Goez; a Spanish air sung by Goez; "El Maestro de Capell," an air bouffon with recitative accompanied by a grand orchestra; some boleros sung in Spanish by Goez, accompanied by a mouth organ;[30] and a grand rondeau by Wranizky with the accompaniment of a grand orchestra.[31]

The second concert and ball were on Friday, December 23, 1808, for the benefit of MM Desforges and Laroque. The program began with *La Chaconne de Floquet* for grand orchestra; a bouffon aria sung in Italian by Goez; a sextet concertant for violin, clarinet, horn, and bass, with the accompaniment of a second violin and a second horn, composed by M P. Laroque; Mme Labat playing the *Rondeau Pastoral* by Steibelt on the pianoforte; a Pleyel concerto performed by Desforges; a vocal trio performed by Goez, Mlle Laurette Fleury, and Valois; and the *Musical Quarrel* for grand orchestra arranged by Desforges.[32] A concert with the same program was scheduled for December 26, 1808, but was either a second performance of the December 23 one or else the earlier one had been postponed for three days.[33] On Tuesday, January 3, 1809, the next concert and bal paré took place in the Salle Accoutumée, to benefit the violoncellist Mr. Miniere.[34] The full program consisted of a Grand March by Cramer for orchestra, accompanied by harp played by Mr. de Brueys; a trio by Ignace Pleyel (1757–1831) for pianoforte, violin, and bass, the piano played by Mlle Miniere, age ten; a symphonie concertante by Desforges for violin and violoncello played by Desforges and Miniere; a romance accompanied on the piano by Mlle Miniere; a clarinet concerto performed by an amateur; and Jean-Louis Duport's (1749–1819) *Air and Variations* for violoncello performed by M Miniere.[35]

The fourth concert brought the first performance of a work by Haydn, who had only a few more months to live. The grand vocal and instrumental concert to benefit M Valois occurred on Friday, February 18, 1809. Once again Goez dominated. Besides the unnamed Haydn symphony,[36] the program consisted of an Italian aria sung by Goez; an Italian duet with Goez and Mlle Laurette Fleury; another aria sung by Goez; a trio with Mlle Laurette Fleury, Goez and Valois; an English air sung by Goez; a Steibelt fantasia on the pianoforte played by Mr. Néveu, followed by a theme and variations by himself; Goez singing an Italian song, an air, "Guerrier de Roland," arranged for orchestra by Mr. Néveu, sung in different languages by Goez; and another performance of the *Musical Quarrel* arranged for orchestra by Desforges (at popular request).[37] The fifth and last concert of the season fell on Saturday, March 11, and was for the benefit of the young Laurette Fleury. Fleury was joined by Goez in a duet from *Romeo and Juliette* by Antonio Sacchini and in an Italian buffa aria with recitative sung by Goez. Also on the program were two works by Wranizky (a symphony and *La Chasse*); a violin concerto by the amateur M Blache performed by Desforges; and a grand Italian aria by Domenico Cimarosa with clarinet, sung by Fleury.[38]

In addition to the regular concerts there were two important intermèdes in the fall of 1808. The first, on Saturday, September 24, 1808, occurred at the Théâtre de la Gaîté opposite St-Philippe Street. Between the two acts of a Creole comedy *Commerce de Nuit* in prose, which already was mixed with extra songs and ornamented with all sorts of spectacles, Desforges played *Two Valses* for grand orchestra of his own composition.[39] Then on Sunday, October 23, 1808, at the Theatre de la Rue Saint-Pierre, during a performance of the new opera *Maris Garçons* by Henri-Montan Berton, there was a quartet performed by harp, piano, horn, and violin.[40] Thus, though they were not separate concerts, both were significant concert occasions with what may have been a world premier of two new waltzes and a rare public performance at this time of chamber music. We have no record of concerts during the spring of 1809.

The 1809–10 season consisted of five concerts. The first was on November 2 and the last the following March 31. We do not have the complete programs, but apparently the programs and performers were much the same as before. Desforges performed his own concerto and a Viotti Symphonie Concertante for two violins in which the other violinist was an amateur. Ursule Labat (now eleven and a half years old) performed piano works by Steibelt, Dussek, and J. B. Cramer, and the child Miniere (now eleven) played a Cramer sonata for piano. There were chamber works, orchestral works (an overture by Dalayrac [1753–1809], again an unnamed Haydn symphony), excerpts from Haydn's *Creation* and from other vocal works, songs, and solo piano pieces.[41] What is also important in 1809 was the opening of the first Théâtre d'Orléans on December 5, 1809. This theater—destroyed twice by fire in 1813 and in 1816—and especially its third reincarnation built in 1819 were the sites for many future concerts.

The 1810–11 season was more substantial with ten concerts; the performers, again, were the same. Most concerts were performed at the Salle Accoutumée, but the concert on Saturday, March 9, 1811, was at the Saint Philip Street Theatre, and the final concert on March 21 was at the Salle de Mr. Boniquet. Desforges played his violin works, amateurs played clarinet concertos, M de Brueys played a harp concerto, the orchestra played more Haydn and overtures by Méhul, Gluck, and Mozart, and the girls Labat and Miniere (in a Muzio Clementi pianoforte sonata) were joined by another child, Desforges's nine-year-old son, on violin.[42] Besides concerts there were numerous balls this spring, which utilized a variety of orchestras or bands. Military ensembles of amateur musicians were frequent during Carnival.[43] These were not concerts, but they employed musicians who would have been available for concerts.

There were no concerts in the fall of 1811 and the fall of 1812, though there were occasional theatrical productions during this time. Yellow Fever raged especially in late summer of 1811, which would account for the absence of public events that fall.[44] The 1811–12 season, then, as far as we now know, consisted only of two concerts on Friday, January 16, and Monday, January 27, 1812. What is novel on the first of these programs was the appearance of a dancer, Mr. Chéry, who danced his own dance on the *Bacanal* by Steibelt.[45] The rest of the program consisted of a symphony for orchestra, an air by Méhul sung by an amateur singer with piano accompaniment, a Viotti concerto performed by Desforges, a Steibelt vocal romance accompanied by piano, a vocal ariette from the opera *Kondous* or *Les Chinois* by Dalayrac with orchestral accompaniment, and a Lefebvre clarinet concerto performed by Nicolai. The concert was a benefit for the widow Bayon, and it took place at the salle of the Saint Philip Street Theatre.[46] The second concert was for the benefit of Madame Juré, a pianist and harpist, and was in the Salle de Condé. The program consisted of a Méhul opera overture; a harp sonata by Jean-Baptiste Cardon (1760–1803) performed by Juré, followed by a romance; a new ariette; a rondeau variations for piano performed by Juré; a rondeau for grand orchestra; harp pieces performed by Juré accompanied by Desforges; and a clarinet concerto performed by an amateur.[47]

The next season fared a little better, with three concerts from February 20 to March 19, 1813. The one on February 20, at Théâtre Saint-Philippe, was the first concert in over a year and was a benefit for Chéry, the dancer, who was also a violinist. The program opened with the Overture to *Joseph* for grand orchestra, a duet from Gluck's *Armide* sung by Rochefort and Mlle Laurette (Fleury), a symphonie concertante for violin performed by two young pupils of M Chéry, and an opera air by Jean-Baptiste Lully sung by Rochefort; the second half contained a new violin concerto by Rhodes (Pierre Rode, 1774–1830) performed by Chéry, an arietta from *Le Traité Nul* by Pierre Gaveaux, a flute concerto performed by an amateur, and a new romance sung by an amateur. After the concert Chéry and one of his pupils danced.[48]

The second concert, on Tuesday, March 9, 1813, was a benefit for Desforges in the Salle des Grands Bals, Condé Street. The program was a new opera overture by Françoise de Fotz; a symphonie concertante for grand orchestra, performed by Blache, Desforges, and a pupil of his; a work of Steibelt performed by a young amateur pupil of Néveu; a quintetto d'harmonie performed on bassoon, horn, clarinet, oboe, and flute; a Rode (Rhodes) violin concerto performed by Desforges; and some caprices for violin composed and performed by an amateur newly arrived from France. The frequently encountered word "harmonie" meant music that was performed by a wind ensemble. Afterwards there came a concert of La Musique des Carabiniers (military music) and many waltzes for grand orchestra for the ball.[49] The last concert was on Friday, March 19, 1813, at the Salle de Condé to benefit M Laroque. The program started with the Overture to Méhul's *Le Jeune Henry* for grand orchestra; Rondeau and Variations on an Air by Michel for clarinet performed by M Fortier Jr., amateur; a vocal trio by Méhul; a trio concertante for viole d'amour, clarinet, and violin by Laroque, performed by Fortier, Desforges, and Laroque; a scene from Haydn's *Armide* arranged for grand orchestra by Laroque and sung by Laurette Fleury (New Orleans premier); and a dance with variations performed by Desforges.[50]

There was an upsurge in concerts during the 1813–14 season with eight performances. The first vocal and instrumental concert was on Tuesday, December 7, 1813, for the benefit of M Nicolai. The seven pieces on the program were played without pause. Featured were the Overture to Grétry's *Pierre le Grand;* an ariette for grand orchestra from Anacreon[51] sung by Madame Nicolai; a Steibelt sonata for pianoforte performed by six-year-old Julienne Meitzel, a pupil of M Nicolai; another ariette for grand orchestra sung by Madame Nicolai; a symphonie concertante for two flutes and grand orchestra by Fränzl performed by two amateurs;[52] a Méhul ariette for grand orchestra with Madame Nicolai; and a clarinet concerto by Hostie, performed by Nicolai.[53] The Salle Condé was now the concert hall of preference. The identical concert was also announced for December 10, which suggests either a repetition of the December 7 concert or a postponement from December 7 to 10. It cost one piaster[54] for "grandes personnes, quatre escalins[55] pour les enfans, & quatre escalins pour les personnes de couleur." This price list remained standard for the next forty years or so.

A special concert with ball was held on Monday, December 20, 1813, to commemorate the tenth anniversary of the Louisiana Purchase and to benefit Desforges. It began with the patriotic hymn "President's March" ("Hail Columbia") for full orchestra; an ariette for a female amateur accompanied by full orchestra; Steibelt's piano sonata performed by Mlle Eugénie Fleury, amateur; a vocal bolero for voice and full orchestra; a violin sonata composed and performed by Desforges; and a march for General Harrison for his victories in Canada, for full orchestra. After the concert a grand orchestra performed the "Creole Waltz" by Desforges dedicated to Major General Villeré.[56] This concert was followed by another patriotic one in the Salle de Saint Philippe on Monday, January 10, 1814, which was unusual. After the concert and before the ball, there was some sort of recreation of the naval battle between the American frigate *The United States* and the English frigate *The Macedonian* that had resulted in the American victory of December 9, 1813. The so-called War of 1812, after all, was in process. We do not know what was on the concert program.[57]

The remaining four concerts had no patriotic purposes and were more in line with earlier concerts. The program of the concert on February 10, 1814, in the Salle de Condé, is only partially known. It included the Overture to *Démophon* for full orchestra, a song sung by a female amateur, and concluded with a romance sung by an amateur woman accompanied by a guitar.[58] M Webster and M Labadie presented the next concert and ball on Saturday, March 5, 1814, at the Saint Philip Street Theatre. The program consisted of the Overture to

Boieldieu's *Calife de Bagdad*; an ariette for grand orchestra sung by Webster; the Pleyel Violin Concerto No. 1 performed by M Labadie; a romance sung by Webster; and Haydn's Symphony No. 85, *La Reine*.[59] A week later, on March 12, 1814, there was a concert in the Salle de Condé to benefit Mr. Rochefort's young vocal student Théodore Rion. It began with an overture for grand orchestra; then a vocal duet sung by an amateur and Mr. Rochefort; Rion, with the accompaniment of lyre and violin, sang "Polonaise du Concert Interrompa"; MM Fortier and Coeur de Roi performed a symphonie concertante de Vienne for two clarinets; and Rion sang a new romance with lyre accompaniment.[60] The final concert of the season occurred in the Salle de Condé on Monday, April 11, 1814, given by and to benefit Desforges. Desforges's three violin pupils MM Morand, Brosset, and Beauregard performed Viotti's Simphonie Concertante; Rion sang a polonaise (the same one as on March 12?); M Fortier (amateur) performed a clarinet concerto; Rion sang "Le Troubadour"; Desforges performed on "alto viola" an Italian concerto by Sr. Lorenzia; and M Tosso (amateur) performed a rondeau.[61]

From the summer of 1814 until January 1816, there were no concerts of which we have evidence. To what extent this may have been the result of the War of 1812 (which came to New Orleans at this time) we can only speculate. The next season which we can identify begins on Friday, January 26, 1816, with a vocal and instrumental concert, followed by a grand ball, at Salle de Condé, to benefit Coeur de Roi. It had been postponed several times owing to the weather. The program consisted of the Overture to Henri Montan Berton's *Montano et Stéphanie* by the "full band" (the whole orchestra); an aria from Paris's *Judgment* sung by Miss Lise; a flute concerto performed by an amateur; an aria from Nicolo Isouard's *Intrigues aux Fenêtres*; and *The Battle of Austerlitz* for full orchestra, "composed at Paris by one of the first compositors of France."[62] This was immediately followed on January 31, 1816, by a concert and ball at the Salle de Condé for the benefit of Mr. Laroque. It was originally scheduled for January 10. The featured selection was Laroque's *Battle of the 8th January 1815* ("composed according to historical facts" and dedicated to General Jackson) for full orchestra. The rest of the program consisted of the Overture to *Le Jeune Henri*; an aria from *Zoraïme and Zulnar* by "Berton,"[63] sung by Rochefort; a grand sonata by Bontempo performed on the pianoforte by Eugénie Fleury; and "The Bolero of Cendrillon" sung by Laurette Fleury.[64] This concert began a tradition of annual concerts commemorating the Battle of New Orleans.

Four more concerts were held during the next few months. On Wednesday, February 5, 1816, there was a vocal and instrumental concert, followed by a ball, at Salle de Condé, for the benefit of the violinist Mr. A. Girault. Featured were the Violin Concerto composed and performed by Girault and the Viotti Symphonie Concertante performed by Girault and Desforges. The "grand orchestra" played the Overture to Pierre Gaveaux's (1760–1825) *Traité Nul*; Rion sang an ariette, accompanied on the guitar, and a romance; and a Haydn symphony completed the evening.[65] The second vocal and instrumental concert, followed by a grand bal paré, happened at Salle de Condé on Friday, February 9, 1816, for the benefit of M and Mme Labadie. Mr. Labadie played Viotti's Violin Concerto No. 17, and Mme Labadie played a piano concerto by Dussek, both accompanied by full orchestra. Mme Labadie, a pupil of Mr. Charles Gilfert, and her husband also performed together a duo concertante for piano and lyre or guitar of six strings. The rest of the program was the Overture to *Médecin Turc* by Nicolo Bonart, a romance sung by an amateur, and the finale from a Haydn symphony.[66] The third concert of the season was on February 15, 1816, at the Salle de Condé, to benefit the clarinetist Maurise. Mr. Maurise played Michel's Clarinet Concerto. Also featured was a repetition of Laroque's *Battle of the 8th January 1815* ("*La Bataille du Huit Janvier dans laquelle On Jouera la Marche du General Jackson*"). The orchestra began with the Overture to Spontini's *Milton*; Hermilie Fleury sang an aria, "La Belle Arsenne";[67] an amateur sang a romance with guitar; and Mlle Laurette sang an aria by Benicwsky.[68] The fourth and last concert was originally scheduled for May 7 but not actually performed until May 11, 1816. It was a grand concert and ball given at Salle de Condé by Mr. and Miss Laporte, professors of music recently arrived from France. They taught piano, voice, and guitar, and Mr. Laporte was also a piano tuner and repairer. No program survives, but the announcement stated that it would include vocal and instrumental music.[69]

Although the next opera season began on October 31, 1816,[70] it was two months later before the first independent concert of the 1816–17 season got underway. However, on Thursday, December 19, 1816, between the three acts of a tragedy, *The Monks of La Trappe* by Arnaud, the orchestra of the Saint Philip Street Theatre—"composed of the amateurs and artists of this city"—executed the overtures to *Joseph*, *Romeo and Juliette*, the *Delirium*, and *Euphrosine* as an intermède.[71] There was also a dance after the tragedy and before the performance of the one-act folly *Jocrisse Sent Out of Service* by Charles-Augustin de Bassompierre Sewrin (1771–1853).[72]

On December 30, 1816, the regular concert season began with a concert and ball for Mr. Desforges's benefit, at Salle de Condé. The distinguished violinist performed Rode's Violin Concerto No. 7 and was himself the composer of three works for full band: a chasse dedicated to General Ripley, and two marches, one dedicated to Governor Villeré and the other to General Lefebvre Desnouetires. Also on the program were François Devienne's (1759–1803) Concerto No. 8 for German flute and Soler's Concerto No. 2 for clarinet, performed by amateurs lately from France; and a Haydn symphony.[73] After the New Year there were five additional concerts. The one on Tuesday, January 21, 1817, was a benefit for Laroque at Salle de Condé and once again featured his *La Bataille du Janvier 1815*. Also on the program were the Overture to Boieldieu's *Jean de Paris*; a duet from LeSueur's opera *La Caverne* performed by Mlle Laurette Fleury and an amateur; a symphonie concertante for flute and clarinet; and a vocal trio performed by Laurette, Mr. Rochefort, and the same amateur.[74] On Tuesday, February 4, 1817, the next concert and ball were for the benefit of Mlle Laporte, maitresse de piano, at Salle de Condé. Laporte played a Concerto Arabe for piano, and a theme and variations for piano of her own composition; and Laporte and an amateur performed two airs for piano and clarinet. An unnamed Haydn symphony for full orchestra was heard; and an amateur sang a Mozart air and a "Rondeaux de Bouffet."[75] Then Signor Pucci came to New Orleans and put on three concerts February 8, February 17, and February 23. This is the first instance of an outsider coming to the city for a short time (a little over two weeks in this case) and staging a series of concerts. Although he had an orchestra available for his concerts that played overtures and accompanied concertos, Pucci preferred the pedal harp when he sang, and he also gave the harpist solo opportunities. He presented one of his own compositions, and he brought in Italian, Welsh, and American airs. The first and third concerts were at the Salle de Condé, while the second was at Maspero's Exchange Assembly Hall. The third concert was designed to benefit the clarinetist Maurise, who played a concerto and his own Marche Militaire dedicated to Commodore Daniel Todd Patterson; and Desforges, as usual, was well represented on the program as both performer and composer.[76]

Before the next season began, Mr. Cargill, in a benefit at the American Theatre on November 4, sang many songs in the intermèdes between the performances of a comedy, *La Manière de Mourir d'Amour*; a play, *L'Intrigue*; and a farce, *Le Mal aux Dents*.[77] The 1817–18 season had six regular concerts and two intermèdes, beginning on December 9, 1817, with a vocal and instrumental concert given by Maurise, followed by a grand bal paré, at Salle d'Orléâns. Maurise performed Michel's Clarinet Concerto and, playing the basset horn, two sets of variations for violin and basset horn with Desforges on violin. The orchestra performed the Overture to Gaspare Spontini's *Milton;* Rochefort sang the Grand Rondo from *Joconde;* and Mlle Laurette (Fleury) sang a grande arietta brillante from the opera *Rossignol.* The practice of hawking the music was clearly established here; the newspaper announcement states that the songs in this concert were from a collection recently arrived from France and, presumably, would be available for amateurs in local stores.[78]

The second concert, on Wednesday, December 31, 1817, at Salle d'Orléans, introduced to the city Mr. Destroup, another professional violinist who was the first violinist of the Toulouse Theatre; it was a benefit for him. He performed a concerto by Rode. The program was in two halves, each begun by an orchestral overture—to *Calife de Bagdad* and *Montano et Stéphanie.* The rest was vocal music sung by Mlle Laurette (Fleury), Mr. Fortier Jr., and gentlemen amateurs of the city.[79] The next day, January 1, 1818, there was an unusual concert by Robert Ferguson on the Scottish bagpipes at Mr. T. Kenedy's, next door to Winn's Hotel, between Royal and Bourbon streets. He performed chiefly Scottish and Irish airs.[80] The three remaining concerts were more traditional. This year's concert to benefit Laroque was originally scheduled for January 14 and eventually performed on Monday January 17, 1818. *La Bataille du 8 Janvier 1815,* of course, was on the program, as well as Laroque's Trio for viola, clarinet, and violin performed by himself, Desforges, and an amateur. The concert began with the Overture to *Joseph* and included a piece from *Calife de Bagdad* performed in "harmonie" by artists and amateurs on wind instruments, and a rondo sung by an amateur woman, newly arrived from France, accompanied by orchestra.[81]

For the first time the Orleans Ball Room (Salle d'Orléâns) was the site for a concert; it was on Tuesday, February 10, 1818, for the benefit of Mr. C. A. Valois. The program included the Overture to *Félicie* by Gioseffo Catrufo (1771–1851); a vocal ariette from the same opera sung by Mlle Lisé Placide; a Viotti violin concerto performed by Destroup; a comic song, "Paddy Carey," sung by Mr. King; and a Méhul clarinet concerto performed by Maurise.[82] Shortly afterwards there was another intermède concert, on February 19, at the Circus, where Cargill again sang English songs between a melodrama, *Timour le Tartare,* and a comedy, *Le Magnetisme Animal.*[83] The last regular concert of the season was on Tuesday, April 7, 1818, at the Orleans Ball Room, with both professionals and amateurs. It was a lengthy program in two halves: part I: the Overture to *Bataille de Gemmappe* for full orchestra; a song sung by King; another song sung by an amateur and accompanied by piano; a grande ariette sung by Mlle Laurette (Fleury); a duet sung by King and an amateur, accompanied by piano; and a symphony for full orchestra; part II: rondeau for full orchestra; a song sung by King; a song sung by an amateur and accompanied by a guitar;

a duet sung by King and an amateur accompanied by a piano; and the Overture to *La Famille Suisse,* for full orchestra.[84] Later that month, on April 23, Maurise played a theme with variations for clarinet during an intermède at the Saint Philip Street Theater, in a benefit for him; he was a member of that theater's orchestra.[85] In addition, Mme Ludlow danced *L'Anglaise,* Mr. Vaughan sang an English song, MM Bainbridge and Ludlow sang a duet, and Mr. Morgan sang a comic song.

Before the 1818–19 season was over, the audiences of New Orleans were introduced to a new composer: Beethoven, who was then still composing in Vienna. The new season now had ten concerts, which made this the most substantial season so far. It opened on Wednesday, November 25, 1818, at Salle d'Orléans, with the annual concert and ball to benefit Mr. Desforges. Desforges performed two of his own compositions, both variations on different tunes. The first of these, *L'Anglaise en Variations,* was variations on "L'Anglaise" or, as it is now better known, "The Star Spangled Banner"; the second set of variations was for two violins, and Desforges was joined by an amateur. This probably was the amateur who also performed Rode's Violin Concerto No. 6. Of special interest is the first public appearance in New Orleans of the recently arrived Polish pianist Paul Emile Johns, who was to be an important musical figure in the city until his death in 1860; he played an unnamed solo piano piece. The program also included the Overture to *Joseph* for full orchestra; and songs sung by Mr. Chambers.[86]

Johns was now becoming a major attraction in the city. The next concert, on Friday, December 4, 1818, was a concert and ball at the Salle d'Orléans for his benefit. He played Dussek's *Military* Concerto and performed on piano his own *Eight Variations* for piano accompanied by violin and "basse," probably with Desforges, who was also represented playing his Violin Concerto.[87] Johns was not on the next two programs (January 18 and February 3), the first of which was devoted to the Labat family and the second to the bassoonist Mr. L. Even, recently arrived from France.[88] Nor was he part of the intermède at the Saint Philip Street Theatre on February 8 when several overtures were performed.[89] His appearance on the program of Wednesday, February 10, 1819, however, was a historical occasion for the city of New Orleans and for North America. During the concert and ball in the Orleans Ball Room, Johns performed a grand concerto for piano by Beethoven. We do not know which of the five concertos he played, but it is the first time that we have record of a Beethoven work performed in New Orleans and the first time that any Beethoven piano concerto was performed in North America.[90] One wonders if Beethoven, who was then living in Austria, was aware of this performance and how far his music had traveled. The rest of the program was also substantial and included the Overture to Vincente Martin y Soler's (1754–1806) opera *Una Cosa Rara* for full orchestra; a fragment of a concerto for bassoon played by Mr. Even; a vocal duet sung by Rochefort and Laurette (Fleury); an air sung by Laurette accompanied by Mr. Pilié on the flute; and *A Fancy Impromptu* executed by Mr. Johns. Johns sold the piano after the concert at Mr. Millaudon's; it was an unusual piano with seven pedals.

Already a remarkable season, there were five more concerts to come. On Wednesday, February 17, 1819, there was the annual concert and ball to benefit Laroque, in the Orleans Ball Room. The program consisted of a Boieldieu overture for full orchestra, Frédéric Kalkbrenner's (1785–1849) *Fancy* for piano performed by Ursule Labat, an arietta by Lebrun[91] sung by Laurette (Fleury) and accompanied by Mr. Pilié on flute, Variations on the "Air of Vive Henry 4th" for violin performed by Desforges, and a vocal duet sung by Rochefort and Laurette.[92] The next four concerts centered on Mme Knittel, a clarinetist. On Saturday, February 27, 1819, Knittel was assisted by amateurs and gentlemen of the orchestra, at the Saint Philip Street Theatre. The program included the Overture to the *Battle of Ivry* for full orchestra; the Bernhard Henrik Crusell (1775–1838) Clarinet Concerto; a song by an amateur; Joseph Kuffner's (1776–1856) Quartet for clarinet obbligato, violin, viola, and bass; a song imitating a woodpecker by whistling; and variations on a Tyrolese air for clarinet.[93] The second concert on Tuesday, March 9, 1819, was much the same. This time Knittel performed one of the Jean Xavier Lefèvre (1763–1829) clarinet concertos and Isaac-Franco Dacosta's (1778–after 1861) variations for clarinet; she also repeated the Tyrolese variations.[94] The programs did not vary much, and on April 1, 1819, she repeated the Lefèvre concerto and the Tyrolese variations and added some more variations by the otherwise unknown Agost.[95] For her final concert on Thursday, May 6, 1819, she followed a play at the Saint Philip Street Theatre with an intermède, after which there was a one-act opéra comique. This abbreviated program included an overture for full orchestra; a quartet for violin, viola, bass, and clarinet (Knittel on clarinet); and one more time, the variations on a Tyrolean air.[96] The entire evening was a benefit for Mme Knittel.

During the summer of 1819 there was an early instance of employment for the professional musicians between the end of the spring season and the beginning of the fall one. When all the theaters were closed, the musicians faced unemployment and possibly starvation. Even those who taught or ran music stores experienced cessation or cutbacks of work. Some returned to Europe. But this time a new type of venue existed that enabled the professionals to keep playing and earning a living. Starting on Saturday, August 28, 1819, performances of vaudeville were to be found in the Théâtre des Variétés Amusantes at Café de l'Harmonie. Entrance to the performance included four bons de consummation, which assured the proprietors of the cafe sufficient income as well.[97]

Only four regular concerts are known for the 1819–20 season. On Saturday, December 11, 1819, two new artists appear. The concert's beneficiary, Mr. Lepage, was a clarinet and guitar teacher and one of the musicians of the Théâtre d'Orléans, which had just opened and which would dominate the concert venues for the next forty years.[98] He appeared in a set of variations for clarinet and orchestra by Bochsa[99] and in a quartet for guitar, violin, viola, and bass by Leonhard von Call (1767–1815) where he was assisted by MM C. Herz, Paradol, and Brun. The orchestra played an overture, and after the concert Herz led the dance orchestra in the ball. There were also a few vocal works performed by Mr. Aimé (the song "Le Point de Jour") and by Mme Gaussin (an ariette from Berton's *Montano et Stéphanie*).[100] C. Herz was another new name on the concert programs; this Herz is not to be confused with Henri Herz, the famous French pianist, who did concertize in New Orleans in 1847. C. Herz, who lived in New Orleans for a long time, was a violinist and conductor. He gave his own benefit on Monday, January 3, 1820, when he performed a Rode concerto and a set of variations. The orchestra played the Overture to Méhul's *Jeune Henry* (a work which they also played as an intermède at the new Théâtre d'Orléans on Christmas day in 1819),[101] Laurette (Fleury) sang a song from *Rossignol,* the multifaceted Chéret sang a song from *Chaperon Rouge* (Boieldieu's take on *Little Red Riding Hood*), and Laurette, Chéret, and Rochefort sang a trio from Felix.[102]

The cultural divide between the French and American sectors of the city was especially strong at this time. In December of 1819 a French citizen of New Orleans decided to watch the American Theatre company which was occupying the Saint Philip Street Theatre.[103] Instead of the artistic, subtle sounds of famous French operas, he heard "Yankee Doodle" and other trifles. He found a few laudable things to say, but basically he looked down on the Americans in the audience who seemed to him to thoroughly enjoy the base entertainment. At the same time an American went to the same theater—the opening of the American Theatre in New Orleans—and critiqued it. He was much more sympathetic to the Americans and was basically opposed to the sneering view of the French citizen.[104] This discussion lasted for at least fifteen more years, when an editorial in *The Bee* found the orchestra at the American Theatre awful and the orchestra at the Théâtre d'Orléans great.[105] The singers in the American production of *Robert le Diable* in April 1835 were good, but in another review in the French press, "the orchestra seemed the only drawback, altho it was better than we apprehended; but it never can be effective under its present leader—who is an incubus on the establishment."[106]

Old names still appeared, however. The Labat women (Mme J. Gautrot, and her two daughters, Ursule and Constance) continued to give concerts, such as for their benefit on January 31, 1820, at the Théâtre d'Orléans. Ursule Labat, horn player (daughter of the horn player J. Gautrot Labat), and her mother performed a nocturne for French horn and piano, and then Ursule played some Woelfl variations alone on the piano and accompanied the violinist Herz with variations on a Russian air by Ferdinand Ries. Constance Labat, singer and pianist, sang a duet from Gioseffo Catrufo's *Félice* (with Mr. Aimé and accompanied on the piano by her mother), then played Johann Baptist Cramer's (1771–1858) *Concerto da Camera* on the piano, and returned to sing Lebrun's "Nightingale" song (once again accompanied by her mother). The orchestra opened the concert with the Overture to Dalayrac's *Camille*; and the evening ended with a serenade for two clarinets, two French horns, and two bassoons, performed by Mr. Bell, an amateur, and MM Even, Lepage, Buck, and Labat.[107] The fourth concert, on Monday, February 7, was the annual benefit for Desforges, who as first violinist had moved to the new Théâtre d'Orléans. The program was dominated by his playing and his compositions. He introduced his Violin Concerto No. 2 and two military marches, one dedicated to Governor Jacques Villeré and the other to the Louisiana Legion. In addition he performed Viotti's Symphonie Concertante with Herz and his variations on "L'Anglaise." Johns played Dussek's *Military Concerto*.[108]

Continuing theatrical performances during the summer was a purely economic matter for the musicians. For several summers in the early 1820s such performances were tried, but no concerts seem to have been held.[109]

The 1820–21 season consisted of ten concerts all performed in 1821. The Labats had another benefit on January 3, 1821, at the Théâtre d'Orléans featuring again the two daughters, Constance and Ursule. The theater orchestra performed an overture and accompanied a few of the arias. Herz, Aimé, and an unnamed flutist also performed, and the composers represented included Ries, Fränzl, Kalkbrenner, Steibelt, Paër, and Boieldieu.[110] Next, on Friday, January 25, 1821, at the Théâtre d'Orléans came Herz's benefit, assisted by artists of the orchestra of that theater. C. Herz performed Rode's Violin Concerto No. 9 and his own variations. Mr. Traub played a theme and variations for flute, and Mr. Bell of the Théâtre d'Orléans Orchestra played *Russian Rondeau* and Romance for clarinet. Pianist Ursule Labat played Joseph Woelfl's (1772–1812) *Rondeau* and a piece by Henri Herz of Paris, and Constance Labat sang with Aimé. The orchestra, as usual, began with an overture.[111] This is the first concert in New Orleans to have received a review.

> FRIDAY—Mr. Herz' concert—This esteemed artist has fully justified the good opinion that we had of his talents. Softness, rigor, lightness: all are found in his bowing. He effortlessly executes the most difficult passages, and if the Rode concerto itself is not full of gracefulness, Mr. Herz knows how to give this in all that he plays. The happy duet from *My Aunt Aurora* was sung very well by Miss Constance Labat and Mr. Aimé. One regrets only that, because of illness, Mr. Bell could not play his clarinet and that Mr. Chéret did not sing his air; but, on the other hand, we enjoyed Mr. Traub's playing of variations on a theme. SCRUTATOR.[112]

Although reviews of concerts are relatively rare until the mid-1830s, the need to publish them, starting in 1821, shows that by this time the city was reaching a high level of cultural sophistication. With published criticism, the performers were now scrutinized and held to ever higher standards of technique and musicality.

Concerts continued unabated for the next several months. The concert and ball on Monday, January 29, 1821, was a benefit for Lepage, professional clarinetist with the Théâtre d'Orléans Orchestra. He performed a clarinet concerto and a polonaise by Dacosta. He also enlisted the services of the entire orchestra for the overture, and both professional and amateur members of that ensemble for an adagio and polonaise for cor obligé, three clarinets, a flute, oboe, and two bassoons. Aimé and Chéret sang airs accompanied by the orchestra, while Johns performed the Turkish Rondo for piano by Galine.[113] Johns, in turn, was the beneficiary of the concert and ball at the Salle d'Orléans on Friday, February 2, 1821. He repeated the Turkish Rondo and added a piano concerto by Franz Xaver Gebel (1787–1843). Just as in the previous concert, the orchestra played an overture and then two chamber pieces: a Haydn quartet for clarinet principale, violin, viola, and bass, and a symphonie concertante for clarinets, oboes, horns, and trumpets. There was only one aria, sung by Aimé.[114] Then, on Monday, February 5, 1821, came the concert and ball to benefit Mr. L. Even, bassoonist in the Orléans orchestra, who performed a bassoon concerto by Etienne d'Ozy (1754–1813). This is the first known solo appearance of the bassoon in a concert in New Orleans. Other wind performers on the program included a Creole amateur bassoonist who was a pupil of Even and hailed from Louisiana, Mr. Buch and an amateur pupil of his who played a symphonie concertante for two horns, and François Kroll performing a set of variations for clarinet. This is the first known solo performance of Kroll, who soon became and for many years was the most popular clarinetist in New Orleans. As was now customary, Chéret and Aimé sang solos.[115] The violinist Paradol made his New Orleans debut on the next concert on Monday, February 12, 1821, at the Salle d'Orléans, by playing *"Variations sur une Barcarole Française, de Mozar"* (Mozart?) and in a symphonie concertante (probably by Viotti) for two violins with Herz. It was a short program that began with an unnamed overture and ended with an unnamed military symphony. Aimé sang an air midway through.[116]

The concert on Thursday, March 15, 1821, at Saint Philip Street Theatre, was another first. It was a concert entirely of songs, each accompanied by Mr. Johns. No singer or singers' names are given. All sung in English, the songs were by John Braham (1774–1856), Rossini, Doyle, and Sir Henry Rowley Bishop (1786–1855), and many anonymous songs were of Scottish and Irish origins. The last piece, by Bishop, was also accompanied by an obbligato flute.[117] The next two concerts are sparsely documented. Both took place at the Hall of the Principal, the first by Mrs. French on Thursday evening, April 5, 1821, and the second by Mr. Taylor with the assistance of Mrs. French, on Thursday, April 10.[118] A special concert followed by a ball occurred on Thursday, April 26, 1821, in la Salle d'Orléans to honor General Andrew Jackson, who was in attendance. It was given by Mme Burke, a singer, who sang seven numbers interspersed with orchestral pieces. Among her selections were light airs and serious opera arias, including one from *Montano et Stéphanie* and another, "O Dolce Concento," by Mozart with variations as sung by Catalani. Mr. Le Roi conducted the orchestra in two overtures, a symphony, a rondo, and a "finale."[119]

There is little documentation for concerts in the season 1821–22. The only one on record is the grand vocal and instrumental concert at Salle d'Orléans, to benefit Mr. Paradol, which took place on January 2, 1822. It is a significant one, however, since it is the first time (apparently) that a complete, unarranged string quartet by Haydn was performed in a public concert in New Orleans. It is announced as his twenty-second quartet (which at that time probably meant Opus 9, no. 4) and was performed by Paradol, Brun, "etc." The rest of the program consisted of an overture for full orchestra in which Mr. Bayle performed a clarinet solo; an air sung by Chéret; an air for bassoon performed by Mr. Even; and an "Apotheos a Trois Voix" in honor of Napoleon the Great.[120]

The 1822–23 season had at least five concerts. The first, featuring the violinist Mr. Volanges, took place on December 20, 1822, at the Théâtre d'Orléans. He performed a Viotti concerto, a polonaise by Viotti, and a Russian Rondo.

MM Alexis and Chéret each had a vocal solo, and the orchestra opened the first half of the concert with an overture.[121] On the following March 6, 1823, Mr. Lewis and his five children (ages four to twelve) came to town and gave an "Extraordinary Concert" at Hotel de Beale. It opened with a Mozart overture arranged for piano four hands. Then came three sets of harp variations; two sets of pianoforte variations; two pieces for one piano *six* hands, one of which also had violin accompaniment; a violin air; a duet for harp and pianoforte accompanied by violin; a violin duet; and a piano rondo.[122] Over the next few days the Lewis family gave two more concerts with the same general program: on March 13 and March 17. This last performance included an overture by Beethoven arranged for piano duet and Josef Gelinek's (1758–1825) piano variations on a waltz by Mozart.[123] The Lewis family returned in March and April 1824, when they played during intermèdes at the Théâtre d'Orléans.[124]

The final concert of this season took place on Monday, May 5, 1823, and was a vocal and instrumental concert by Mr. Christiani in the Orleans Ball Room. According to the *Courier de la Louisiane,* "Mrs. Gray, Mr. Aimé, and the gentlemen of the orchestra, will, by their talents contribute to render this Concert worthy of those who will honor it with their presence." Christiani was a composer, and not only were some of his works featured on this program, but a month later, on June 8, his musical-theater work *L'Habit du Chevalier de Grammont* was performed at the Théâtre d'Orléans with Christiani conducting from the piano.[125] On July 22 he sang in an opéra comique, *The Italian Singer and the Taylor,* and during the intermèdes sang with piano accompaniment some of his own songs. The orchestra was still a mixture of local amateurs and professionals, but an effort was beginning to take place to professionalize the entire ensemble. A call went out during this summer to encourage professionals—"artistes musiciens"—to present themselves to the directors of the theater.[126] The importance of this professionalization had immense consequences for the concert life of the city, since it meant that the pool of expert performers was increased and the incentives for adding to their incomes in concerts would be increased as well.

The first two concerts of the 1823–24 season occurred on February 2 and 4, 1824. Mr. Chéret and Mr. Johns gave two benefits for themselves at the Théâtre d'Orléans, in each case followed by a "dressed" ball.[127] Since Mardi Gras fell on March 2 that year, the Carnival season was already in high gear, and the custom to follow the concerts with costumed balls was well established and would continue at least until the Civil War.[128] But that did not mean that everyone in New Orleans liked the custom, and indeed a writer for one local newspaper attacked the concept as immoral.[129] The performers, however, were "charming, each in his own way." The first program began with a grand overture; Chéret sang a grand air; Herz performed François-Antoine Habeneck's (1781–1849) variations on the air "Clair de la Lune"; Mistress Alexis sang the cavatina "Pensieri Funesti" by Saverio Mercadante; Johns, accompanied by the orchestra, performed Dussek's Piano Concerto No. 2; and the orchestra ended the concert with a symphony. On March 4 the concert was similar: it opened with an overture; Johns, accompanied by the orchestra, performed Steibelt's Piano Concerto No. 3; Mr. and Mrs. Chéret sang an Italian duet by Farinelli; Johns played Mayseder's Third Grand Polish Air; Mr. Victor sang a comic song; and the program ended with the "Grand Military March" for full orchestra "lately composed by Mr. Johns."

New Orleanians have always been generous in times of need, and on Monday, February 9, 1824, was one such occasion: the artists and amateurs of the city raised money for the benefit of an unfortunate family by giving a vocal and instrumental concert in the Théâtre d'Orléans to be succeeded by a ball in the adjacent Ball Room. The theater orchestra started with the Overture to *Don Giovanni* "by the immortal Mozart," and gave the world premier of Johns's *A Warlike Symphony,* composed for the occasion and performed by the entire orchestra.[130] Herz performed Rode's Violin Concerto No. 8; Johns and Lepage performed Bochsa's *Nocturne* for piano and clarinet; an ensemble of clarinet, violin, two violas, and a bass violin (the last played by an amateur pupil of Mr. Bell) performed Kuffner's quintet; Chéret sang an aria accompanied by violin; and Mr. Victor sang another aria.

Subsequent concerts during this spring season were much the same as before, consisting mostly of benefits for individual musicians. Herz's benefit was held at the Théâtre d'Orléans on February 21 when he played a Viotti concerto with orchestra. Two of his pupils also played a symphony for two violins; Lepage performed Gambaro's[131] clarinet variations on an aria by Boieldieu with piano accompaniment; Christiani sang his own comic song; Mrs. Alexis sang a romance written by Chéret; Mr. and Mrs. Chéret sang a duet; and six singers including Mr. and Mrs. Alexis, Mr. and Mrs. Chéret, Pauline, Laurette (Fleury), and Saint Estéve sang "L'Enseignement Mutuel" by Boieldieu. The concert ended with Haydn's *Adieu* (Symphony No. 45).[132] The clarinetist Gauthier had his benefit on Wednesday, March 31, 1824, at the Théâtre d'Orléans. He played his own Clarinet Concerto and variations on *La Tyrolienne.* The orchestra began each half of the program with an overture (Johann Christoph Vogel's *Démophon* and Dalayrac's *Camille*). Mme Chéret sang an aria from Rossini's *The Barber of Seville* and then joined her husband for a duet from the same opera. Aimé and Mr. Chéret sang further arias.[133] These benefits were essential for the professional musician whose salaries from their jobs at the Opera House or other theaters alone were insufficient.

When Mr. and Mrs. Vincenzo Zapucci (or Zappucci) came to New Orleans, they were sandwiched between a comedy and an opéra comique by Solié on May 13, 1824, at the Théâtre d'Orléans. Since both were regarded as important musical personages—he was part of the Portuguese Royal Theatre, and they were both professors of Italian music—their intermède was called a grand vocal and instrumental concert. The program was indeed more substantial than customary for such a setting: a symphony for full orchestra by Rossini; a Rossini aria sung by Mr. Zappucci; a serious aria by Ferdinando Paër sung by Mrs. Zappucci; and a grand duo by Pietro Générali.[134] It was also imperative that they be featured on a full concert at the Théâtre d'Orléans for their own benefit. This occurred on May 23, 1824, with a two-part program consisting of two Rossini overtures by the entire orchestra; two songs and a duet by Générali; an aria by Rossini; a concerto composed and performed by Mr. Gauthier; a comic solo song by Paër; and a grand comic duet by Paër, "executed by Mr. & Mrs. Zappucci, who will do their best to satisfy the public."[135]

Another intermède was performed on Wednesday, June 2, 1824, when Miss Mongin sang a romance between two plays at the American Theatre.[136] Then the final concert and ball of the season were arranged by Gauthier for Sunday, June 20, 1824, at the Théâtre d'Orléans. For this he gathered, in his words, "All the most distinguished local professional and amateur musicians, . . . and there has rarely been such a complete and select orchestra in this city."[137] The ambitious program included, in part I: the Overture to Rossini's *Italiana in Algiers*; an air by Paër sung by Mr. Zapucci; Gauthier playing his own *La Tyrolienne* for clarinet; an aria from Mozart's *The Marriage of Figaro* sung by Constance Labat; another air for clarinet composed and performed by Gauthier; and in part II: the Overture to *The Barber of Seville*; a Rossini aria sung by Mr. Zapucci; Ignaz Moscheles's (1794–1870) *Clair de la Lune* piano variations performed by Ursule Labat; another aria by Paër sung by Constance Labat; and Scène et Rondeau for clarinet composed and performed by Gauthier.

A freak show started the 1824–25 concert season. Mr. Ellene (Hellene), an Italian troubadour, gave a concert with military music at the Saint Philip Street Theatre, on Sunday, December 12, 1824. He claimed to have performed in New Orleans four years before, though no record of the event has yet been found. He was his own orchestra, playing at the same time a hurdy-gurdy of his own invention, an Italian flute, Turkish cymbals, Chinese parasol, the bass drum, and the triangle. The program, in two parts, included a waltz by Mozart, two Mexican pieces, a Swiss march, an Italian march, and so forth. Not surprisingly, special half-price tickets were available for children under ten years.[138] Two weeks later he proposed another concert, which seems not to have taken place.[139]

Then, on February 5, 1825, we have for the first time a Philharmonic Society concert (see book I, part I, chapter 3). This was a concert and ball for the benefit of Mr. Lewis. On this occasion Lewis combined with some of the professionals in New Orleans, which gave his performance more stature. The Théâtre d'Orléans Orchestra performed the Overture to Méhul's *Joseph* and a military overture, and Herz played a Viotti concerto. The Lewis children filled in the rest of the concert. The ball took place in the usual ballrooms of Mr. Davis on Orleans Street.[140] The last known concert of the season was on Wednesday, February 9, 1825, at the Théâtre d'Orléans; it was a vocal and instrumental concert to benefit Mr. Louis Bayon, pupil of Mr. Bell, first clarinet of the Théâtre d'Orléans Orchestra. The program featured Michel's Concerto No. 12 for clarinet, performed by Mr. Bayon; a French air with variations composed and performed by Mr. Gauthier; two overtures; and several vocal selections.[141]

Our sources lack reference to any regular concerts performed after February 9, 1825, and before January 31, 1827. There was a performance of Mr. Chéret's Grand Cantate at the Théâtre d'Orléans upon the visit of General Marie Jean Paul Rochyves Gilbert Motier, Marquis de Lafayette, to New Orleans on April 11, 1825, but it was part of a regular theater program and was followed by a comedy.[142] The opera season opened at the Théâtre d'Orléans on December 3, 1826, with *The Barber of Seville*,[143] but in the first few weeks of the new opera season, four of the six operas did not make money. Probably the tickets were too expensive. Instead of three opera performances a week, performances of opera only on Sundays and Thursdays would suffice and give the singers more time to learn their parts. However, this did not speak to quality. The *Courier* critic compared the New Orleans troupe to the best of the second tier of French opera houses.[144]

When the sources again give us specifics on concerts, it is for four regular concerts during the spring part of the 1826–27 season. A new name appears on this first vocal and instrumental program of Wednesday, January 31, 1827, which is a benefit at the Théâtre d'Orléans for Mr. Elie, first violinist of the orchestra. Elie was a graduate of the Paris Conservatoire and was for the rest of his life to make New Orleans his home. He was active as a violinist and music entrepreneur and the father of one of the most important New Orleans pianists of the entire nineteenth century, Marguerite Elie Samuel. On this occasion he performed a Rodolph Kreutzer violin concerto. The rest of the program consisted of Rossini's Overture to *Les Folies Amoureuses* for full orchestra, a set of clarinet variations performed by Bayon, an air sung by Mme Fleury, flute variations performed by Lucien Herman, a vocal duet, the piano *Rondo Brillant* by Hummel performed by Mme Fleury; and a vocal quartet from *Irato* by Méhul.[145] The second concert, on April 25, 1827, at the Théâtre d'Orléans, was the annual benefit for Desforges, who this time played a Pleyel violin concerto. Besides the orchestra, which played the Overture to *La Dame Blanche,* another overture, and a grand military march, Gauthier played a set of clarinet variations on a Rossini air, and a whole new group of singers sang arias: Mr. Gonthier, Mme Milon, and Mr. Alexandre.[146]

Before the third regular concert there was another but highly unusual intermède at the Théâtre d'Orléans. On Thursday, May 3, 1827, after performance of the then famous three-act opera *Jeannot and Colin* by Nicolo Isouard, Mr. Robertson performed a waltz and march on the automaton trumpeter[147] accompanied by full orchestra. This was followed by a military symphony entitled *The Battle of Austerliz, or the Day of the Three Emperors,* by Beauvarlet-Charpentier with the whole orchestra (and automaton trumpeter[?]), and finally by hydraulic experiments. Robertson continued with further such concerts over the next few days.[148] The third regular concert—a grand concert of vocal and instrumental music by amateurs and professionals for the benefit of the singer Capt. Ramati—was held on Friday, May 18, 1827. Capt. Ramati performed four Rossini arias with Johns on piano, and a romance by Giovanni Pacini (1796–1867) with guitar accompaniment. He also performed a buffa song in Italian, Spanish, French, Polish, Turkish, and English with guitar. Buck and Evan performed a "Symphony and Concerto" by Jacques Widerkehr (1759–1823) for horn and bassoon; Johns, Even, and Lepage did an arrangement of an opera duet for clarinet, bassoon, and piano; and Elie played a Viotti violin concerto. Milon, Alexandre, and M Richard also sang, and the orchestra played overtures to begin each half (a Spanish overture and the Overture to Rossini's *Tancrède*).[149] About the fourth concert we know nothing other than that it was scheduled for May 30.[150]

Two special benefit concerts were held in the spring of 1827. The first of these, on May 24, 1827, was at the Théâtre d'Orléans as an intermède between Nicolo Isouard's opera *Cinderella* and Barré and Desfontaines's vaudeville *Two Edmonds.* It was a benefit for the boys' orphanage. Mr. Segura, leader of the visiting Havana Theater Orchestra, which was then performing at the Théâtre d'Orléans, played a fantasia and a Spanish bolero by Messa, and the "the Philharmonic Society will contribute to the pleasures of the evening by playing several choice pieces of Music."[151] A month later a special benefit soiree was held on

Wednesday, June 20, 1827, to raise money for the girls' orphanage. This time it was at a private garden owned by Mr. Rash on Chartres Street, and "only persons properly dressed will be admitted." The performers were once again, however, members of La Société Philharmonique with Johns playing the piano. They performed several choice pieces.[152] The opera season did not close this year until June 11,[153] very late, so a concert late in June was not out of the question. Segura, meanwhile, continued to give instrumental concerts as intermèdes during performances by the Havana troupe at the Théâtre d'Orléans.[154]

We have record of four concerts during the 1827–28 season. The first of these is another private concert in the home of Madame Herries, Chartres Street, with the assistance of the Philharmonic Society. It took place on December 14, 1827. This was not a simple soiree, however; rather it was a full vocal and instrumental concert. Mme Herries's home was apparently more than adequate for concerts, and in the next few years others were held there. The first part began with the Overture to *Italiana in Algiers* performed by the Philharmonic, but it is never made clear if this is a full orchestra or a small ensemble of amateur musicians. The only name of a performer cited is that of Mme Depass, who sang six arias. Other instrumental and vocal pieces were performed by the Philharmonic Society, including "Marche Militaire" by Gambaro, two pieces of harmonie (wind music), and several solo and choral pieces from *La Dame Blanche*.[155]

The next concert was more in line with earlier concerts. It was a grand vocal and instrumental concert at the Théâtre d'Orléans on January 28, 1828, given by the younger Jandot, pupil of his father, who was formerly first clarinetist at the theater in Bordeaux. The senior Jandot played Gauthier's Clarinet Concerto, and the junior Jandot played parts of the Flute Concerto No. 4 by Jean-Louis Tulou (1786–1865) and, with Johns on piano, Johns's Fantaisie pour la Flute with piano accompaniment on themes from Rossignol and Tancrède. The theater orchestra played the Overture to *Italienne à Alger*; Mr. Richard sang Mozart's "Non Piu Andrai" from *The Marriage of Figaro;* Milon sang the Cavatina from *The Barber of Seville*; Richard and Milon sang Rossini's *Pie Voleuse*; and Alexandre sang an air. The concert was followed by a ball.[156] The Labats held their annual concert and grand bal paré on Tuesday, February 5, 1828. Constance, who had studied with Ferdinand Paër, sang French and Italian songs, while her sister Ursule played the piano. Also featured were members of the orchestra, though we have no details on what they performed.[157] We have more information on the next concert, on Tuesday, February 26, 1828, which was a grand vocal and instrumental concert to benefit the orchestra of the Théâtre d'Orléans. It was also an intermède since it was preceded and followed by theater pieces. Constance Labat participated, as did Herz, performing variations for violin by Habenek; Herz and Elie played Kreutzer's Symphonie Concertante for two violins. The orchestra played the Overture to *Le Maître de Chapelle* by Paër and the Overture to *Le Jeune Prude* by Dalayrac.[158] In the meantime, on February 14 at the dance hall on the corner of Bourbon and Orléans streets, there was a dance recital by Nicolas Barabino which also included some purely instrumental works: a symphonie concertante, a military march, and more.[159]

There is nearly a year's hiatus before we have the next series of concerts at the beginning of 1829. These were not usual fare, however. The series started on Saturday, January 7, 1829, when M and Mme Candereen from Brussels played the first of several announced recitals at Salle d'Orléâns with the assistance of its director, Mr. Davis. (We have no record of a second recital.) The unusual factor in this recital was the instruments, including harp, flageolet, and double flageolet, along with voice, French horn, and violin; there was no orchestra or piano. It began with a grand symphonie on harp by Mrs. Candereen, who then sang a romance accompanied by Mr. Candereen. Next Mrs. Candereen performed a polonaise on harp which was followed by "La Chasse de Robin de Bois," which she sang. Mr. Candereen played a piece for flageolet and double flageolet and performed *La Grande Chasse de Henri IV* on French horn; he then did imitations of various types of singers (but it is uncertain how he imitated them). The program ended with the grande marche, a favorite of Napoleon, with Mrs. Candereen on harp and her husband on violin.[160] On Monday, January 27, 1829, Mr. Hélène, the Italian troubadour, returned to New Orleans with an outdoor concert extraordinaire on the corner of Bourbon and Orleans streets. His act approached that of a circus when he imitated the sounds of birds and when his accomplice, Jean Icard, performed tricks. He demonstrated some unusual instruments and played what probably were insignificant works, but near the end he played a waltz by Mozart for five instruments. His "concerts" continued through the week of February 7.[161]

The first regular concert of 1829 occurred at the Théâtre d'Orléans on Monday, February 2, 1829, with a grand vocal and instrumental concert, followed by a ball, to benefit the orchestra's first clarinetist, Bayon. The orchestra began the first half with the Overture to *La Forêt de Sénast,* a local concoction with music by Weber and Beethoven(!) and the second half with the Overture to *Le Jeune Henry* by Méhul. Bayon performed Michel's Clarinet Concerto No. 10, M Dits a set of variations for bassoon, M Prascheil a horn *Rondeau Pastoral,* and M Dantonnet a concerto for violoncello by Bernard Romberg (1767–1841). M Privat, Mlle Mariage, and M Deschamps sang arias and duets.[162] The second grand concert and ball, on Monday, February 9, 1929, was a benefit for Mr. Jandot fils, at the Théâtre d'Orléans. Mr. Jardot performed Tulou's Flute Concerto No. 2, a set of variations for flute on "Robin Adair" by Louis François-Philippe Drouet (1792–1873), with his father *Un Morceau d'Harmonie* for clarinet and piccolo, and a series of variations; and, again with his father but also including Pruschell (a conservatoire student) and Dits, A. Melchior's grand quarette for clarinet, flute, horn, and bassoon. In addition M Dantonnet, a student at the Conservatoire, played a potpourri for bass by Bernard Romberg. The Overture to Rossini's *Cendrillon* was put in harmonie by Sorriano, which means that it was arranged for wind ensemble. The wind ensemble was a mixture of professionals from the Théâtre d'Orléans orchestra and members of the Philharmonic Society. MM Alfred, Milon, Privat, and Mariage sang airs from Rodolph Kreutzer's *Lodoïska,* Rossini's *The Barber of Seville,* and Auber's *Duo de la Neige.*[163]

The third regular concert and ball occurred on Wednesday, February 18, 1829, to benefit Mr. Elie at the Théâtre d'Orléans. The highlight of the event was a symphonie concertante for four violins performed by Herz, Paradol, Elie, and an amateur; Elie also played a set of unnamed variations. Dits and Jandot repeated the flute and bassoon variations from the previous concert, while M Walsh, an artist newly arrived from England, played variations for piano by the Parisian Henri Herz. The concert opened with the Overture to Paër's *Maitre de Chapelle,* and the orchestra opened the second half with the Overture to *Léceister* by Auber. Privat and Mariage also sang works by Méhul.[164] The fourth concert of the season was the annual Labat concert and ball at the Théâtre d'Orléans on Wednesday, February 25, 1829. Ursule performed a piano duo by Henri Herz and C. P. Lafont, with C. Herz as second pianist, who also played the violin with her in duets. The orchestra played the usual two overtures (by Paër and Auber); Praechelt performed the same horn piece he did on February 2, and Constance sang airs by Meyerbeer, Rode, and others. The piano was a Pleyel newly arrived from Paris which was to be sold after the concert.[165] Herz had his benefit on Friday, March 6, 1829. He played *Variations Concertantes* for piano and violin accompanied by Ursule Labat, Mayseder's *Rondino,* and with Elie a set of variations for two violins by Ludwig Maurer (1789–1878). Dits performed a bassoon piece by F. Guébauer, the orchestra two overtures (one by Rossini), and Constance Labat, Deschamps, and Privat sang arias and romances.[166] The final concert of the season was by Mme Knight, a singer, before her departure from the city. She was joined, on Monday, March 30, 1829, by her husband accompanying on piano, and by Privat; Paradol directed the orchestra. Mme Knight sang airs by Cimarosa, Bishop ("Home! Sweet Home!"), Arne and an Irish air, and M Knight played a solo rondo by his teacher, Ferdinand Ries. The orchestra played overtures by Berton and Daleyrac.[167]

There is again a hiatus until the next series of concerts in 1830. The 1829–30 opera season opened at the Théâtre d'Orléans on November 22, 1829. On January 21, 1830, they performed an unusual opera in three acts entitled *La Forêt de Sénast,* arranged by Castil Blaze from the music of Mozart, Beethoven, Meyerbeer, Rossini, and others.[168] The concert season began on February 1, 1830, when Jandot fils gave another of his concerts followed by a grand, full-dress ball. There were a number of soloists on the program, including Jules Norès, a gifted pianist whom we will meet frequently from now on, whose debut consisted of the first movement of a piano concerto by Field. Gauthier played his Clarinet Concerto, Elie played a set of violin variations by De Bériot, and Jandot himself played Drouet's Flute Concerto No. 3 and a set of flute variations by the same composer. Jandot on the flute accompanied Mariage in *Le Rossignol.* There was only one overture, by Onslow, which opened the first half.[169] On Thursday, April 22, 1830, there was an intermède at the Théâtre d'Orléans entitled "grande soirée musicale" by Madame Feron, Mariage, Milon, and Privat, which was stuck between an opera *Bouffe et le Tailleur* by Gaveaux and a vaudeville *Angeline* by Théaulon and Dumersan. It consisted of two arias by Meyer and Fioravante and a duet by Rossini.[170] Sometime during the next month the husband-and-wife singing team of M and Mme Pearman gave the first of their three grand concerts at the home of Mme Herries. Their second vocal and instrumental concert was on Tuesday, May 25, 1830, and the third was on Friday, June 4. Besides arias and songs by popular composers of the time (Rossini, Mozart ["Crudel Perche Finora" from *The Marriage of Figaro*], Weber, Bochsa, Bishop, Barnett, and Braham), the programs included a piano fantasia performed by Mme Norès and chamber music—a quartet for two violins, viola, and flute by Gebauer, a quartet for two violins, viola and bass by Rossini (performed three times), and an instrumental quartet by Weber.[171] An unusually late concert occurred on Independence Day, Sunday, July 4, 1830.

From the mid-point of 1830 until the spring of 1833 all the known concerts in New Orleans were intermèdes. There was a farewell benefit concert on Wednesday, May 18, 1831, for Mrs. Cramer-Plumer (who in April had sung Susanna in the Théâtre d'Orléans performance of *The Marriage of Figaro*). She was joined by Mr. and Mrs. Pearman, Mr. Caldwell, and Mr. Cramer-Plumer in six songs, for duets, and one quartet. The performance was an intermède coming after Goldsmith's comedy *The Road to Ruin* and before the "laughable farce" of *Sevens the Main* in which Mrs. Plumer sang eight different characters.[172] Two other intermèdes occurred in a row to benefit Mme Feron of the Théâtre d'Orléans Opera Troupe. On Sunday, June 5, 1831, Mme Feron performed four works before the opera of the day started. These works included an aria of Mayer, a duet by Mercadante with Saint-Clair, variations by Paccini (Pacini), and the second act of Spontini's *La Vestale*.[173] Two days later, on June 7, she returned with three songs following an opera by Auber and before a vaudeville by Merle and Brazier. During the Auber opera *Le Concert a la Cour*, she inserted variations on the air "O Dolce Concento" (probably Catalani's variations on a Mozart aria from *The Magic Flute*) with Jandot fils playing an obbligato flute.[174] Yet another intermède, just by the orchestra, occurred on Wednesday, February 29, 1832, at the Camp Street Theatre. Master Burke (a jack of all trades) conducted the orchestra in the Overture to *Guy Mannering* and then starred in six different roles in the ensuing farce.[175] He repeated this feat on subsequent evenings, and even performed Barton's Violin Concerto at an intermède on March 13.[176] Then on Saturday, May 19, 1832, during a benefit theatrical performance for John Caldwell, Mr. Harris of the American Theatre Orchestra executed some variations on "that difficult instrument" the frauclaude, accompanied by the whole orchestra, which was augmented for that occasion.[177]

One other intermède that must be mentioned is that of Mme Guiraud, fresh from Paris with her husband, who gave a grand vocal and instrumental concert on December 11, 1832, at the Théâtre d'Orléans. This concert came between two comic vaudevilles, each in one act. The intermède program consisted of a horn solo by Lebeman, Guiraud playing her own *Grandes Variations Brillantes* for piano and a set of variations, a romance sung by Mme Saint Clair accompanied on the horn by Lebeman, an aria from *The Marriage of Figaro* by Mozart, and the Overture to Rossini's *Cenerentola* played by the theater orchestra.[178] Mme Guiraud's son, Ernest, a composer and brilliant teacher, would later bring fame to the family when he moved to Paris, was Bizet's roommate and colleague, and was a teacher of Debussy.

New Orleans also had a famous visitor who arrived in 1832 and who was not a musician but an inventor. On December 27, 1832, Johann Nepomuk Maelzel (1772–1838) was in the city performing on his various mechanical instruments at the Hotel des Planteurs, Canal Street No. 19. He continued until mid-February 1833. This is the same Maelzel who invented the metronome some twenty years earlier and who had even tried to help Beethoven recover his hearing.[179] He returned in January 1837 and exhibited his melodium and other mechanical instruments on the street, on the corner of Camp and Poydras.[180]

There were two concerts in the spring of 1833. The first, on April 27, was an unusual grand vocal and instrumental concert at the American Theatre in that it combined members of both the Théâtre d'Orléans and American Theatre orchestras. The concert came after a performance of the opera *Cinderella* (probably Rossini's *La Cenerentola*). The orchestra played the overtures to *Young Henry* by Méhul, *The Falconer's Bride* by Marschner, and *Der Freischütz* by Weber. Among the instrumental pieces was a clarinet concerto played by Mr. Henings; a flute solo played by Jandot fils; and a trio for piano, oboe, and violin performed by MM Norès, Vallière (Valler), and Dantonel (Dantonnet?). This concert also marked the first time that Gregorio Curto's name appeared on a surviving concert program (see book I, part II, chapter 2); he sang the aria "Ecco Miavio" and a duet with the baritone Mr. Thorne whose benefit the concert served. Curto had come to New Orleans in 1830 to sing opera, but within three years he had become more involved in church music and was a frequent participant in concerts apart from operas in New Orleans until the 1880s. On June 10, 1832, he sang during an intermède a setting of the "Raven and the Fox" by Lafontaine, with Norès as piano accompanist,[181] but the 1833 appearance—though he was still a member of the opera company—was the beginning of his new life.[182] A similar concert, this time a benefit concert for Mme Brichta, occurred at the American Theatre on Tuesday, May 21, 1833. "The orchestra . . . will be increased for the occasion, and will perform the fine Overture to Tancredi." The program otherwise was various vocal arias from operas.[183]

There is only one known concert in 1834, a grand concert on Monday, March 17, at the Salle de Bal performed by MM Vallière (Valler), Norès, Larseur, Danton (Dantonnet?), Léon Amédée, Lehmann, Hurteaux, and Mme Saint Clair.[184] In addition there were several intermède concerts during the year. On Tuesday, February 25, several singers sang between a comedy, a vaudeville, and a drama at the Théâtre d'Orléans.[185] A fancier intermède occurred on Tuesday, March 11, 1834, at a benefit performance at the Théâtre d'Orléans for the pianist Mme Saint Clair. Following the five-act *Lucrèce Borgia,* there was a soiree musicale which included the Overture to *William Tell*; a Mercadante duet; an aria from *Ivanhoe* by Rossini; and a piece for oboe and piano performed by Vallière and Saint Clair.[186] On May 21 at the American Theatre the opera *Music and Prejudice* was interrupted for "several pieces of music."[187] And finally Mr. A. F. Keene sang his own songs at dramatic presentations at the American Theatre on December 12 and 13, 1834.[188]

We have concentrated on public concerts because these were advertised in the newspapers and thus are documented. Private concerts in persons' homes are usually not reported, but occasionally we have some documentation. On

November 8, 1834, for example, Dr. Antommarchi, a friend of Napoleon, arrived in New Orleans, and in the evening several artists of the Théâtre d'Orléans repaired to the residence of Dr. Formento and serenaded him. Some popular airs were played. According to *The Bee*, "Ils ont exécuté, avec leur talent accoutumé, l'ouverture de Guillaume Tell, de Dieu and la Bayadère, la Marseillaise, et plusieurs autres airs."[189]

At the beginning of 1835 there were two concerts, one at the Orleans Ball Room and another at the Théâtre d'Orléans. The first, on Wednesday, January 21, 1835, was a grand vocal and musical concert, followed by a dress ball, for the benefit of Vallière, oboist. He played a varied air on oboe by Henri Brod (1799–1839), accompanied on the oboe a romance sung by Miss Dupuis, and joined Tobey and Norès in a trio for oboe, bassoon, and piano by Brod. The orchestra executed two grand overtures, the second by Fétis; Dantonnet played a violoncello solo; and Norès played an air for piano by H. Herz. There were also several vocal solos and a duet.[190] The second concert was a benefit for Kroll, the renowned clarinetist at the Théâtre d'Orléans. It took place on February 11, 1835. Kroll played an air by F. Beër (Friedrich Berr, 1794–1838), and some variations from Donizetti's opera *Le Comte d'Ory* with Norès on the piano. Mme Zimmer and Lehmann performed a serenade for harp and horn; Elie played a violin air and variations by De Bériot; and Vallière played an oboe air. The rest of the program was vocal arias and romances (sung by Curto and others), with the orchestra introducing the concert by playing the Overture to Rossini's *La Gazza Ladra*.[191]

In addition to these concerts there were two intermèdes. The first was a trumpet á piston solo by M Loffing of the Théâtre d'Orléans orchestra between two vaudeville comedies on Thursday, January 8, 1835.[192] The second, on Tuesday, February 24, between a drama and a comedy at the Théâtre d'Orléans to benefit M Perrin, consisted of three pieces: (1) duet for voice and horn performed by MM Heymann and Lehmann, with piano accompaniment by Larseneur; (2) variations on an air for oboe performed by Vallière; and (3) a grand vocal air sung by Mlle Dupuis.[193]

In March 1835, Mr. Keene of the American Theatre held numerous soirees at Banks' Arcade before and after some light dramatic works.[194] These were, in fact, intermèdes. The programs for Keene's soirees included no arias but Irish and Scottish ballads. After all, the audience at the American Theatre was not accustomed to opera but rather to circuses and such popular entertainment.[195] On May 13, 1835, Keene sang and played the piano at Vauxhall Gardens.[196]

The new Jardin du Vauxhall opened on May 6, 1835. It was a venue for dancing on Sundays, Mondays, Wednesdays, and Saturdays, on which occasions there was a band in the salon. On other days, when there was no dancing, an outdoor military band accompanied promenades.[197] A few concert musicians could count on this venue for summer income.

There were numerous intermèdes in December 1835. On Monday, December 7, for example, Signor Cioffi performed a concerto on the trombone amidst several dramatic performances at the brand new Saint Charles Theatre.[198] Two days later he repeated the concerto and, in addition, Kendall played a clarinet concerto.[199] At the same venue on December 11, Norton played on the chromatic trumpet between two dramas.[200] The next day, during a benefit performance at the Saint Charles Theatre of Shakespeare's *As You Like It,* Mr. Downes played a concerto on the flute. The evening began with a new overture performed by the house orchestra.[201]

The final regular concert in 1835, on December 7, was a performance at the Camp Street Theatre by Gambatti on the valve trumpet and Cuddy on flute.[202] Both Cuddy and Gambatti were the stars of this theater.[203] What is almost unique up to this point in the history of concert music in New Orleans is that there is a critique of it in the paper.[204] Gambatti is excellent, but the critic castigates Cuddy's flute playing that, he claims, often produced discordant and disagreeable sounds. Also his choice of repertoire was low class. There were occasional and important reviews of operas prior to this time,[205] and even rare reviews of concerts as early as 1821 and in 1824. This critique, however, is a long one, and it ushers in a new era in the concert life of the city. The leading French newspaper of the city—*L'Abeille* in its French version and *The Bee* in its English version—now had regular music critics, and from this time forth many musical events in the city were well covered. Criticism was intelligent and musically informed, and the readers of *The Bee* could use this criticism as a point from which to understand the growing musical life of the city. The critic had very specific recommendations for concerts: "We would also state that public opinion is against any instrumental performer exhibiting himself on the stage; and that though the performances of Norton on the trumpet, Cioffi on the trombone, Kendall on the clarinet or Downes on the flute may be excellent and please once in order to give the public a correct impression of their professional attainments—yet a repetition must cloy and offend. Their place is the orchestra, and ne sulor aultra crepidam."[206]

In the eighteenth century and before, it was commonly viewed in much of Europe that instrumental music had no place unless it accompanied voices or dance. New Orleans had fine instrumental musicians in the pit of the opera, and it boasted numerous dance orchestras.[207] Although opera performances formed the thrust of these reviews, there were—despite the old-fashioned view by the above critic that instrumental concerts were inappropriate—ample reviews of concerts. Beyond aiding us in uncovering the concert life of the city and demonstrating that in New Orleans instrumental music by itself was as valid as vocal music, the advent of regular music criticism in New Orleans is a sign of the evolution of the city from a provincial musical venue to a major musical center.

2

The Musical Metropolis
1836–1849

The change in the nature of the concert life in New Orleans by the latter part of the 1830s was considerable. Whereas previously a season normally consisted of four or five concerts, soon there was that number in one month alone. Before 1836 almost all concerts were by local musicians, but afterward the number of guest performers, often world-class stars, increased manifold—though the visitors were still outnumbered by the locals. Several new kinds of concerts emerged: sacred concerts mostly in churches, student recitals, and even full symphony-orchestra seasons. Sometimes more than one concert would be held at the same time. The number and quality of local musicians increased steadily with new settlers arriving from Europe or Havana (the singers Calvé, Devries, and Curto; the violinists Gabici and Cobini; the wind players Gambatti, Kroll, Carrière, Vallière, Cioffi; the pianists Norès, Guiraud, La Hache; the conductors Prévost and Collignon—to name just a few), and with the birth in the city of the likes of Gottschalk, Ernest Guiraud, Lambert, Dédé, and Barès, the city was practically self-sufficient in furthering its own musical ends. Couple with all this the increase in operatic performances, and New Orleans emerged from a provincial city to a musical mecca not surpassed at the time by any other American metropolis.

At the beginning of 1836 the editor of *The Bee/L'Abeille* made a bold move that had an abiding effect on the musical life of New Orleans. He hired a full-time music critic.[1] From this point forward the musical events of the city were well documented, which may account for the increased number of concerts of which we are aware. On the other hand, the increased number of concerts might have contributed to the need for a regular critic. Whatever the cause and effect, the bustling musical scene in New Orleans is attested to by the unnamed critic who in June 1838, stated: "Really we live in a musical atmosphere, and breathe nothing but the echo of sweet sounds. Concert upon concert presents its irresistible fascinations, and every species of entertainment is employed to refine, purify and elevate that taste for the most delightful of the arts, already so prevalent in our city."[2] Opinions did not change over the next two decades. On February 15, 1853, an editorial mused on the large number of events going on in New Orleans at this time. While most are plebian events, there are those of extraordinary merit: "In anticipation, there are GOTTSCHALK, OLE BULL and ADELINA PATTI, Mrs. Bostwick and her concert troup, and some other musical celebrities. It will be hard indeed, if the idler, or the temporary sojourner in New Orleans should be at a loss where to pass a pleasant evening. The only embarrassment he can possibly experience is that of effecting a choice amidst such a variety of interesting objects."[3]

The first regular concert in 1836 was on Monday, January 18, 1836, with a vocal and instrumental concert at the Salle d'Orléâns followed by a ball, given by Mr. F. Kroll, first clarinetist at the French Theatre.[4] *The Bee* reported, "The concert to be given this afternoon by Kroll will from its novelty and attractive matter, draw a full, fair and fashionable auditory of both classes of our population. A children's and dress ball are to follow in the same room." What does the critic mean by "both classes"? White and black, or French and American, or rich and poor, or male and female, or young and old? The program, in two halves, was, in part I: Overture to Mozart's *The Magic Flute* (house orchestra); Frédéric Berr, variations (Kroll); a vocal duet, arranged from *La Dame Blanche* for harp and oboe by Labavre and Wogt (Zimmer and Vallière); a Rossini duet; a Grand Caprice by Romberg for violoncello (Alfred Boucher); in part II: an Auber overture, a Rossini cavatina, trumpet variations on Rossini's *La Cenerentola* (Gambatti), a song, a piano and clarinet duet based on a tune from Rossini's *Comte Ory* (Mme Norès and M F. Kroll), and a romance for two voices accompanied by horn and piano (piano by Mme Norès).

The first concert of sacred music to be held in the city about which we have some information was on February 14, 1836. The performance of parts of both Handel's *Messiah* and Haydn's *Creation* was by singers from the American and Saint Charles theaters and was apparently geared to an English-speaking audience. The reviewer in *The Bee* asserts that he was nurtured in the tradition of oratorio in England and that therefore he was in a position to state that this performance in New Orleans was not yet up to English standards. While the orchestra was very good, the instruments drowned out the voices and the organist was mediocre. But what was important for him was "that the attempt [to perform oratorios in New Orleans] was an experiment to test the taste of the public" and that "it is to be trusted that oratorios will [now] be given every Sunday during Lent; and [I] hope that the errors of yesterday's display can easily be rectified."[5] Indeed, as time went on, the performance of sacred music became more frequent and popular.

The second regular concert was on Saturday, February 27, 1836. It was again a grand vocal and instrumental concert at the Salle d'Orléâns followed by a grand dress ball, for the benefit of MM Vallière and Norès. The two halves consisted of part I: the Overture to *Sémiramide* (Orleans Theater Orchestra), a vocal duet from *William Tell* (Heyman and the bass Bailly), a set of violoncello variations (Alfred Boucher), a vocal nocturne (Heyman and Mme Barthélemy), Cavatina from *Il Pirata* by Bellini performed on the valve trumpet by Gambatti; part II: Henri Herz's piano variations (Mr. Norès), an aria from *The Barber of Seville* (Barthélemy), variations on a Swiss air performed on clarinet by Kroll, a vocal trio from *William Tell* (Heyman, Curto and Bailly), and oboe variations on *Savoyard* (Vallière). Mr. Norès "presided at the Piano forte."[6] Three days prior to the concert, *L'Abeille* began what today is called a media blitz by publishing laudatory articles on both Vallière and Norès.[7] No doubt this kind of advertisement generated interest in the concert among New Orleanians and added to the box office receipts.

New arrivals were still trickling into the city. On or about March 4, 1836, Miss Russell performed, and occasionally thereafter she was heard in concerts. As a pianist, *The Bee* asserted, "she has few equals; and there are not many ladies who excel her in musical proficiency." She was an untrained singer, however, and needed lessons.[8]

On April 9, 1836, there was another grand vocal and instrumental concert, this one featuring the trumpeter Gambatti at the Théâtre d'Orléans. Joining Gambatti were various singers from the French Opera (Bailly, Hodges, de Rosa, Ravaglia, Sapignoli, Saint Clair, and Depuis) and the leading wind players in the theater orchestra: Cioffi (trombone), Kroll (clarinet), Vallière (oboe), Loffing (trumpet), and so forth. The orchestra was conducted by M Paradol; M Norès accompanied solos.[9] This time the newspaper added hype by giving an account of a verbal and physical battle between fans of Gambatti and Norton in Niblo's Garden in New York, which Cioffi ended by playing "Yankee Doodle" on his trombone in order to drown out the uproar and restore peace to the audience. On the day of the concert in New Orleans the critic added, "Gambatti's concert this evening will be the best this season; and is likely to command a full, fair and fashionable auditory."[10] Who would not want to be there?

Benefit concerts for specific musicians were well established prior to 1836 and continued as a major vehicle for the artists to earn a living. The popularity of a particular opera singer or theater orchestra member was hard to gauge during an opera performance, but in a benefit concert the size of the audience was a sure sign of the popularity of the performer. When the performer was the most popular basso at the Théâtre d'Orléans Opera, then a full house was expected, as on April 12, 1836, when Bailly sang. The whole city rejoiced when he was Bertram, l'Hôtelier in *Le Pré aux Clercs*; Figaro; the sergeant in *Le Chalet*, and so forth, and so the whole city owed it to Bailly to appear at his benefit.[11]

Two weeks later, on Thursday, April 28, 1836, it was the turn of the first trombonist of the orchestra to enjoy a benefit. As reported in *The Bee*, "The citizens of New Orleans seem to be better pleased with any species of musical entertainment as a public amusement than any other, and with concerts in preference to operas. We therefore remind all amateurs of good vocal and instrumental music that a concert will this evening be given by Signor Cioffi, at Davis' theatre in Orleans Street. It is expected to be attended by the elite of the fashionables and amateurs of the city."[12] The program was, in part I: an overture for full orchestra, an air sung by Mr. Bailly, a Bellini cavatina, two opera arias by Rossini and Bellini arranged and performed by Gambatti, a vocal duet, and variations on an opera aria from *La Dame Blanche* performed on trombone by Cioffi; part II: a vocal aria, variations performed on clarinet by Mr. Kendall, two opera arias, and the Cavatina from *The Barber of Seville* performed on trombone by Cioffi.[13]

Before the next benefit concert, there was a concert by a traveling virtuoso. On May 3, 1836, M Downes, professor of flute and a member of the Italian Opera Orchestra then in residence at the Saint Charles Theatre, gave a concert in New Orleans at the American Theatre accompanied by local musicians. This was a flutist who had recently given concerts in London, and he was in New Orleans as a temporary member of the Italian Opera.[14] This concert was followed on May 11 by a benefit for Gambatti before a performance of *La Juive* at the American Theatre. Technically an intermède, this concert was described as a "Musical Olio" consisting of the Overture to *Sémiramide* for full orchestra, the cavatina from *The Barber of Seville* for valve trumpet (Gambatti), a sung ballad (Mrs. Kappell), a duet for two valve trumpets (Gambatti and Loffing), a vocal aria (Mr. Wills), and another duet by Rossini for two valve trumpets (Loffing and Gambatti).[15] Within the next few days there were more benefits. On Tuesday, May 17, there was one for MM Guiraud and Saint Amand at the Théâtre d'Orléans,[16] and the very next evening there was another intermède benefit at the Saint Charles Theatre for Mr. H. Willis, "the able and attentive leader of the orchestra." The program included Willis performing a violin solo and Gambatti a solo on the trumpet.[17] Between the first and second acts of the Bellini opera *La Straniera,* M Boucher played a grand solo on the viola.[18]

While the number of concerts in general increased, the number of intermèdes skyrocketed at all the theaters of the city. It became a feature of dramatic presentations of all kinds to insert solos into intermissions whereby the star members of the theater orchestra could show their skills. On the same night (January 8, 1836) that M Guiraud's music was performed at the Théâtre d'Orléans (a drama *Episode Louisianaise* in two acts with music by Guiraud, followed by a cantata and an apotéose by Guiraud), Gambatti performed a patriotic air at the American Theatre, to commemorate the Glorious Eighth of January 1814.[19] On Tuesday, January 12, and on subsequent evenings a grand overture was performed at the Saint Charles Theatre between a comedy and a farce,[20] while at the American Theatre Gambatti continued to perform airs on the trumpet between dramas.[21] Later, on Thursday, February 18, 1836, at the Saint Charles Theatre, in the course of the evening two grand overtures were played,[22] and on March 17 we find Gambatti still playing his valve trumpet at the American Theatre in the middle of plays.[23] In April there was an intermède musical at the Théâtre d'Orléans between two dramatic presentations (a tragedy and a vaudeville). The performance was a benefit for M Perrin. The musical interlude, which had nothing to do with Perrin, consisted of a fantasia for clarinet and piano (Kroll and Norès), a vocal duet, and a trio by Brod for oboe, bassoon, and piano (Vallière, Tobey, and Norès).[24]

Although intermèdes were common at all the theaters, they were especially popular at the English-speaking Saint Charles. On Wednesday, May 11, 1836, during the entr'acte of a Bellini opera at the Saint Charles Theatre, Alfred Boucher played a violoncello solo and Cioffi played a trombone solo. The reviewer panned the opera but praised the "jolis morceaux" performed by Cioffi and Boucher.[25] The two men were not regular members of that theater's orchestra and apparently crossed over from the Théâtre d'Orléans as a special favor to the Italian opera troupe that was visiting in the Saint Charles. Back in February the Saint Charles Theatre advertised that it "[w]anted in addition to the Saint Charles Orchestra, twenty-five Musicians, for the Italian Opera. Application to be made to James G. Meader, at the Theatre."[26] The visiting Italian opera troupe came later in March, sponsored by Caldwell, the manager of the Saint Charles.[27] Performances of Italian operas were apparently not financially successful, though it introduced two works to New Orleans that had not been heard before: Bellini's *Il Pirate* and Rossini's *Otello.*[28] It was speculated that, had he put his theater below Canal Street, in the French Quarter, Caldwell would not have been subject to the prejudice of those living below Canal. (In other words, the French were not about to attend American opera, and there were not enough interested Americans to support that theater by themselves.) The orchestra, on the other hand, was great.[29]

In one review the critic found that Caldwell was not so successful financially but was so artistically "for giving [the citizens of New Orleans] the most splendid theatre in this country. . . . Caldwell's main-stay during the season was his orchestra, which was the best in this country—the French perhaps excepted. The violin of Willis the leader; the trombone of Cioffi, the clarinet of Kendall, the flute of Downes, the violoncello of Boucher, the bass viol of Cassolani, have made favorable and almost indelible impressions on the auditory nerves of the frequenters of that theatre. We regret to hear that many of these will be lost to our community next season."[30] Where all these extra musicians came from is unclear, but from what we have seen a number came over from the Théâtre d'Orléans and at least one, the flutist Downes, was acquired from elsewhere.

The clarinetist Kendall, likewise a member of the Théâtre d'Orléans orchestra, performed intermèdes at the Saint Charles for special occasions. On May 12, 1836, he even enjoyed a benefit concert of vocal and instrumental music at the Saint Charles after a presentation of Shakespeare's *The Tempest* "with the original music" and before a farce.[31] Two days later, between performances of *Lucrèce Borgia* by Victor Hugo and another play, both Cioffi and Kendall performed, according to *L'Abeille,* "a new overture, composed by Professor Comi, leader of the Italian Opera. . . . These gentlemen have had the great desire to offer their services for this benefit."[32] Two days after that there were two grand overtures performed between two plays at the Saint Charles, and on May 21 Boucher played a violoncello solo between two plays at the same theater.[33] Later, on Wednesday, May 25, 1836, a performance of John Howard Payne's drama *Clari, the Maid of Milan,* was followed by "a Grand Miscellaneous Concert, in which Signors Montressor, Ravaglia, de Rosa, Sapignoli, Lathan, Cioffi, and Signora Marozzi will appear."[34]

Through all this time New Orleans retained its bicultural atmosphere. While on the one hand it had now achieved a lofty artistic life with many well-trained musicians and even some of extraordinary talent, it also was the site of some of the raunchiest activities of lowlife people. In May it was noted that the beautiful Théâtre d'Orléans unfortunately had surrounding it a number of gambling saloons. The legislature passed a bill prohibiting such gaming places at the theater, but this by no means ended these activities there. One and a half years later an editorial lambasted the many cabarets in New Orleans as dens of iniquity:

places of free flowing liquor and violence.[35] Side by side, high art and low culture thrived, and this admixture has been a trademark of the French Quarter to the present time.

The theaters in New Orleans reopened in November, the American Theatre with *Hamlet* on November 22, 1836, and the Théâtre d'Orléans with a one-act play, a two-act drama, and a one-act vaudeville on November 24, 1836.[36] Caldwell was so sure of the success of his next opera season at the Saint Charles Theatre that he "has paid the Troupe all summer—he has made great increase in the orchestra, and no doubt every thing will accord—even the fullness of the house itself!"[37] Thus, even before the other theaters opened, the Saint Charles Theatre began its season on November 14 with a grand overture sandwiched between a spectacle and a comedy. The intermèdes continued, especially at the American and Saint Charles theaters. For example, on December 5, 1836, at the American Theatre, after a drama, Gambatti gave a trumpet solo and a dancer danced, after which came a farce.[38] On December 9, 1836, at the Saint Charles Theatre in a benefit for Mr. Barton, a drama was followed by a medley solo by Cioffi on the trombone, followed by scenes from *The Merchant of Venice,* which in turn were succeeded by a duet by Trust (harp) and Krakamp (flute). The program ended with the Overture to *Der Freischütz* and a farce.[39]

The highlight of the early part of the opera season was a performance of Mozart's *The Marriage of Figaro* at the American Theatre on Friday, December 23, 1836.[40] The opera season, then, was well along when on Monday, December 26, 1836, the first grand vocal and instrumental concert of the season occurred. Mme A. Guiraud was in charge, and the program consisted of, in part I: the Overture to *La Muette* (orchestra of the French Theatre), a trumpet fantasia (M Lehmann), an air (Bailly), Grand Fantasy by Kalkbrenner (Mme Guiraud), a vocal duet from Rossini's *Moses* (Krakamp and Heymann), an oboe fantasia (M Vallière); part II: the Overture to *Sémiramide,* romance from Les Huguenots (Heyman), piano variations on *Anna Bolena* by Henri Herz (Mme Guiraud), an aria from Rossini's *Sigismondo* (Orhman), another aria by Varney from *The Return from Exile* (Heymann), and a fantasia for clarinet (Kroll).[41] The second vocal and instrumental concert of the season was on Saturday, January 14, 1837, by the "reunited" artists of the Théâtre d'Orléans.[42] We do not know the program.

During Carnival season there were no regular concerts, but intermèdes continued at the theaters. At the American Theatre on Camp Street on January 24 a ballad, dances, and the Overture to *Der Freischütz* were scattered throughout two dramas and a farce;[43] on the same evening at the Saint Charles Theatre, the Grand Overture to *Bayadère* followed Sheridan's comedy *The Rivals,* after which came another theatrical work. On Monday, February 13, 1837, at the Saint Charles Theatre, Cioffi performed a trombone solo in the first intermission and, during the second intermission, a new, unpublished overture describing the Battle of New Orleans.[44]

Then followed a spate of concerts (or soirees musicales) in the grand salon of the Exchange Hotel, the first three led by Mr. C. E. Horn, vocalist and composer, assisted by M T. Bishop (singer) and M Trust (harp). The first program on Wednesday, March 1, included an introduction for piano and harp by Bochsa; other duets for harp and piano; various songs, including an arrangement by Horn of Beethoven's "Adelaide"; and harp solos. The second took place on Monday, March 6, and the third on Friday, March 10 (this last added Miss Horton), for neither of which do we have programs.[45] A final soiree musicale at the Exchange Hotel, with different performers, occurred on Wednesday, March 29, 1837, with Bishop, Trust, Mme Giraud (piano), Gambatti, Ravaglia, Lehmann, Kroll, Morley, and an amateur of the city. The program again included harp pieces; clarinet works; horn solos; and songs by Rossini, Braham, Bishop, and others.[46] The final regular concert of the season was held on Sunday, April 9, at 1 p.m. Alfred Boucher gave a concert at Mr. Vigule's hall, corner of Orleans and Royal streets. He was assisted by Mme Guiraud, MM Vallière, Elie, Kroll, Bishop, and so forth.[47] Once again we do not know the program.

This spring, when Caldwell decided to bring an Italian opera company to New Orleans, he did not go to Italy but rather to the Grand Opera in Havana, Cuba. Among the orchestral musicians who came from Havana to New Orleans was its chef d'orchestre, Ludovico Gabici, a superb violinist, who liked New Orleans so much that he decided to immigrate. Besides Gabici, distinguished Italians who came with him were V. Paini (primo contra basso), G. Burecci (primo violoncello), and F. Vay (primo viola). On Wednesday, April 4, 1837, the troupe opened at the Saint Charles Theatre with Bellini's *Montechi e Capuletti,* which was followed by operas by Rossini, Ricci, Donizetti, Mercadante, and Coppola.[48] Intermèdes were frequently a part of these evenings, such as on April 13 when the Overture to *La Dame Blanche* was performed between two dramas.[49] Perhaps inspired by the variety and relief that intermèdes provided during an evening of opera, Caldwell went one step further by pasting together on one evening scenes and even whole acts from different operas. J.B., in a letter to the editor in *The Bee,* blasted Caldwell and the Italian opera for doing this.[50]

Before the opening of the regular fall season of concerts there was another concert of sacred music, on Wednesday, November 22, 1837. This was the celebration of Sainte Cecilia's Day at Saint Louis Cathedral, and it was a benefit for orphans. Performed was a new mass by Curto, who had become the chapel master at the cathedral. He had at his disposal some of the top singers (Fornasari, Heymann, Bailly, and Welch) and professional orchestral musicians (including Cioffi with a trombone solo in the *Ite Missa Est*). After the performance, the Philharmonic Society threw a banquet.[51]

The season of 1837–38 saw the resumption of regular concerts, altogether fifteen of them: a record number at that time. It began on December 11, 1837, with a benefit concert for Mme Meyreto of the French Opera, "accompanied by the artistes professeurs of the orchestra of our theatre."[52] That was followed on Wednesday, January 10, 1838, with a soiree musicale by Bishop and Trust in the grand dining room of the Saint Charles Hotel. On this occasion the program consisted of part I: a trio for harp, piano, and oboe on *Norma* (Norès, Vallière and H. Trust); an aria; a violin solo (Cobini);[53] a harp solo (Trust); an opera aria (T. Bishop, accompanied on oboe by Vallière); and a pianoforte solo (Mme Guiraud); and part II: a duet for two harps (MM A. and H. Trust), an air (T. Bishop), an oboe solo on "Casta Diva" (Vallière), a grand march for harp (H. Trust), a song (Bishop), and a duet for harp and piano (Mme Guiraud and H. Trust).[54] The third grand vocal and instrumental concert, on Wednesday, January 17, was given by MM Vallière and Cobini in the drawing room of the Saint Charles Hotel; the most distinguished artists in the city performed. The program was, in part I: valve trumpet variations on *I Puritani* (Prévost), a violoncello air (Dantoner), a vocal romance (Mr. Bishop), a duet arranged from *Norma* for oboe and small bassoon (MM Tubey and Vallière), violin variations (Cobini), and a song (Bishop); part II: *Introduction and Polonaise* for piano by H. Hertz (Norès), an oboe piece by Brod (Vallière), variations for harp (Trust), concerted fantasia for clarinet and piano (Knoll and Norès), and a romance (Bishop).[55] The fourth concert, on January 22, 1838, was an elaborate vocal and instrumental concert for full orchestra at the Orleans Ball Room. The program was, in part I: the Overture to Norma, two arias, two opera duets; part II: the Overture to Rossini's *Otello,* two opera arias, a trombone solo with variations (Cioffi), and another opera duet. *The Bee* reported: "All the pieces will be accompanied by a full orchestra, directed by Mr. Gabici."[56]

Back on December 20, 1837, Fornasari announced that he and many other distinguished artists in the city had established four soirees musicales to be given in the Orleans Ball Room. He mentioned only one such artist at the time: Mme Albina Stella. He sought more subscriptions, particularly among the women of the city, and this became possibly the first organized concert series in the city.[57] We do not know the date or program of the first, third, and fourth concerts, but the second was held on Monday, January 29, 1838. The program was initially to be, part I: a Rossini overture, two opera duets, an aria, and a cavatina; part II: a Mercadante overture, a cavatina, an aria, De Bériot's variations on an air performed by violin (Gabici), and another aria. The changed program still featured Stella and Gabici. "The admirably organized orchestra of the French Theatre will likewise contribute to the entertainments of the evening," predicted *The Bee*.[58] This marked the first concert in which Gabici took part as soloist.

Meanwhile, a group of nine musicians from Germany came to the city and remained for several weeks. This was the first extended stay in New Orleans by a non-resident instrumental ensemble orchestra not associated with an opera company, and it began a trend that continued through the rest of the century. The group, which called itself the Prague Company, consisted of two first and one second violins, a viola, a clarinet, a flute, and two horns or trumpets (á piston), led by a conductor. How they sounded without a bass instrument is impossible to imagine. They also performed in New York, Boston, Baltimore, and Philadelphia. The first concert, on January 15 at the Théâtre d'Orléans, included solos, concertos, potpourris, waltzes, and overtures that were performed with extraordinary precision, remarkable talent, and vigor.[59] It was not well attended, so the second concert on Saturday, January 20, was held at the much smaller Saint Charles Hotel. This change in locale was not simply one of accommodation to a new theater, but changed the venue from the French side to the American side of town. As the French critic called it, the French citizens of the city should cross the Rubicon—that is, Canal Street—in order to attend.[60] Whatever the taunt, this concert was much better attended, and the locals appreciated again the precision of ensemble which Germans in general and this group in particular demonstrated. The third and final concert by the Prague Company was scheduled again at the Saint Charles Hotel for Thursday, January 25, but because of bad weather it was moved to January 27 in the Orleans Ball Room. We know next to nothing about the programs, but on this concert the group played the Overture to *Der Freischütz* and waltzes by Strauss.[61]

The next regular concert was again under the aegis of Bishop and Trust and featured the ballad singer Mrs. Strauss. It was a soiree musicale at the Saint Charles Hotel on February 10, 1838.[62] The hotel was again the site of a grand soiree musicale on February 28, featuring Mrs. Bailey, H. Trust, Mrs. Watson (pianoforte), Bishop, and a Mr. Dempster,[63] and on Friday, March 2, 1838, yet another concert was held there, this time to benefit Cioffi. Also participating were the singers Watson, Plumer, Conduit, Sapignoli, and George Holland, Watson also as pianist, and the harpist Trust with Cioffi on trombone or piano.

The program, mostly of vocal numbers, included a guitar solo as well, performed by Barbiere.[64] On Monday, March 12, there was another soiree musicale at the hotel with performances by Mrs. Bailey, Dempster, and Trust.[65] Sometime in the middle of March, Master Saint Luke, an eleven-year-old violinist, performed several concerts at the Saint Charles Theatre. He was on tour and was considered amazing.[66]

The next major sacred concert of the season took place on March 7 at Christ Church on Canal Street to benefit destitute orphan boys. It was billed as a "grand oratorio," but in fact no oratorio was performed; it was, rather, a concert of sacred music, under the direction of Mr. and Mrs. Watson. He was the musical director of the church, while she was the same Mrs. Watson who was performing regularly at the Saint Charles Hotel. Mr. Watson was apparently initiating the new organ, recently built in New York. Cioffi performed a trombone solo; Trust performed a harp solo; Mr. Cripps played on the double drum and cymbals; and the rest of the program consisted of vocal works by Handel, Haydn, Kent, Watson, Luther, Lowel Mason, and Moore. The singers included Mrs. Watson, Dempster, and Archer.[67]

Another New Orleans tradition may have begun on Sunday morning, April 22, 1838. Mme Boyer, who was a highly regarded teacher of harp and piano, led her student concert. Other student concerts probably occurred earlier, but this was the first of many to be reported in the newspapers. The critic enthusiastically praised Boyer's pupil Elodie Anoris, who was very talented on the piano. Mme Boyer's daughter Caroline sang, and the critic said that only at the French Opera could one experience better singing.[68]

There is plenty of evidence that guitar playing was popular in New Orleans before 1838, but with the concert of master guitarist Martinez on May 2, 1838, the level of guitar performance in the city reached an important height. It was a vocal and instrumental concert at the Orleans Hotel to benefit orphans.[69] The critic was ecstatic in advance that such an artist was to perform. The orchestral accompaniment was led by Gabici, and on the program were Bishop, Miss De Bar, Cioffi, Vallière, and Señor Reines (trumpet).

This concert was followed by four soirees to benefit important local musicians. The first was for Kroll on May 5, 1838, in the rotunda of the Bourse with an orchestra of thirty-five musicians directed by Kroll himself; they played overtures and different orchestral pieces. Norès accompanied the solo pieces on piano. The program, in two halves, consisted of, part I: the Overture to Auber's *Dieu et de la Bayadère,* a duo from Norma arranged for oboe and bassoon (Vallière and Tobey), clarinet variations by Frédéric Berr (Kroll), a ballad (Bishop), a trumpet piece arranged from *Der Freischütz* and played by M Lehmann, an orchestral waltz by Beër; part II: another Auber overture (to *Le Philtre*), Cioffi playing a trombone solo, a song by Brod (Bishop, accompanied on clarinet by Kroll), another waltz for orchestra, an oboe solo (Vallière), and yet another waltz for orchestra.[70]

The second soiree musicale, on Monday, May 14, 1838, was given by the singer Mlle Albina Stella in the salon of the Saint Charles Hotel. She was assisted by de Rosa and Sapignoli (singers), Norès (piano), Cioffi (trombone), Martinez (guitar), Lehmann (cornet à piston), and Trust (harp).[71] Two nights later, on May 16, 1838, a benefit soiree musicale was given by and for Vallière in the rotunda of the Bourse, with some of the same artists participating. The complete orchestra of the Théâtre Français conducted by M Varney played two Rossini overtures (from *La Pie Voleuse* and *Sémiramide*). Among the performers were Heymann, Kroll, Cioffi, Fallon (chef of the Saint Charles Theatre Orchestra, solo violin), Lehmann, Tobey (bassoon), Norès, and Vallière, and the composers represented were Rossini, De Bériot, Lehmann, Caraffa, Halévy, Kalkbrenner, and Vallière.[72] Only a month later was the last of the season's soirees: on June 15, 1838, for Fallon, in the grande salle of the Saint Charles Hotel. It was a grand wrap-up to the season in that so many musicians, representing different theaters in the city, participated. The grand French orchestra and many other professionals in music, vocal and instrumental, were there, including Gabici, Trust, Vallière, Kroll, Lehmann, Bayon, Buch, Evan, Barthet, Loffing, Selanit, Schneici, Jandot, Letellier, Dantonnet, Sansor, Gilles, Martinez, and Bailly.[73]

The number of intermèdes increased during the 1837–38 season. In most cases overtures began an evening of dramas or were inserted between two different dramas on the same evening. The 1837–38 season at the Théâtre d'Orléans opened on Thursday, November 9, with a drama, a vaudeville, and the orchestra playing a grand overture in between. The theater had been improved over the summer, and the new company was choice—especially its leading lady, the renowned soprano Julie Calvé.[74] A few days later, on November 13, the orchestra at the Saint Charles Theatre played the Overture to *The Miller and His Men* between plays and, though the "solos might have [been] better executed, we owe them something for the effort to please."[75]

Six days later the orchestra at the Théâtre d'Orléans played the *William Tell* Overture between two theatrical works. On Friday, April 27, 1838, at the same theater, before the performance of a Dumas drama and a vaudeville (not between), the grand orchestra played the Overture to *Der Freischütz* (*Robin des*

Bois).[76] Intermèdes were also performed on special benefit evenings, such as on May 8 (for Mlle Maria at the Théâtre d'Orléans) and May 22 (for Mme Néveu at Théâtre d'Orléans).[77] On the latter occasion Tobey played the bassoon while Calvé sang a Scottish air, and Lehmann played the cornet à piston in a solo of his own composition accompanied by the whole orchestra. On Tuesday, May 29 Lehmann again performed his solo for cor (cornet?) á piston accompanied by grand orchestra, this time followed by the *William Tell* Overture.[78]

The benefit evening for Calvé at the Théâtre d'Orléans on Friday, May 4, was much more elaborate than most benefits, probably because Calvé had become the greatest soprano yet to star at the French Opera in New Orleans.[79] Not only did she sing the lead in an entire three-act opera by Auber (*L'Ambassadrice*) in which she added a new aria, she also sang the third act of *Marie Stuart* and some romances. The orchestra played the Overture to Rossini's *Tancrède,* and somehow there was also time for a one-act vaudeville in which Mlle Eugénie performed six roles.[80]

The next season opened not with concerts but with arguments published in the newspapers about different aspects of music. The most important argument raged about the establishment of an Italian opera theater in New Orleans under the directorship of Gabici.[81] The question was about where the performances were to be held (the Théâtre d'Orléans closed its doors to the company), how much it would cost, and who would attend.[82] This led enthusiasts for the Italian opera to criticize the French Opera, and when the 1838–39 opera season opened at the Théâtre d'Orléans with *The Barber of Seville* on November 6, 1838, barbs flew in all directions.[83] In turn this gave one critic the chance to chastise the French for their snobbery against any English-speaking or at least non-French-speaking entertainment. In a three-column argument on November 14, 1838, he called for French speakers to go to the Saint Charles and Camp Street theaters since much of beauty went on there. Besides, nearly everyone (including slaves and free persons of color) in New Orleans was bilingual.[84] Having more than one opera company would make the cultural life of New Orleans, indeed, far more attractive to the cultured people of the entire country and would attract tourists. "The establishment of this company will form a new era in our rapidly progressing city, and will show to the north that we are advancing as well in the graces and refinements of social life as in the application of our boundless natural resources to the advancement of our commercial importance."[85] Despite considerable efforts on behalf of the Italian opera, nothing came of it. In January Gabici proposed to bring the Havana Italian opera back to the Saint Charles Theatre in April and June for three performances per week. He sought subscriptions, but apparently he didn't get enough, for there is no record of the opera coming to New Orleans during those two months.[86]

Before the regular concert season began there was a concert of sacred music. In what was becoming an annual event, the Philharmonic Society celebrated Sainte Cecilia's Day at the cathedral for the benefit of orphans on Thursday, November 22, 1838.[87] Meanwhile, from October through December the orchestra at the Saint Charles Theatre performed one or two overtures during each intermède.

By mid-December the 1838–39 concert season began. On December 17, 1838, there was a novelty benefit performance for George Holland at the Saint Charles Theatre. In the course of the evening Don Gustano performed a theme on the small "Hophclide," Holland's Toy Band performed Haydn's *Toy Symphony* (actually composed by Leopold Mozart), and the juvenile Toy Band concluded the performance with "Yankee Doodle." This was an intermède because the drama *Flying Dutchman* was also performed.[88] On Thursday, December 20, at the City Exchange Ball Room there was a grand concert of Mme Garcia Ruíz and several other artists formerly of the Italian company. It had originally been scheduled for December 17. The program consisted of, part I: arias by Donizetti, Meyerbeer, Bellini, and a violin solo by Berisi; part II: arias by Meyerbeer, Donizetti, Rossini, and Bellini.[89] The critic on *The Bee* took advantage of the concert to plead further for an Italian company in New Orleans. Since the city already had a group of Italian singers living there—including Ruíz, Geresini, de Rosa, and Albina Stella—it would be easy to form a company around them.[90] The next regular concert was on Monday, Christmas Eve. At City Exchange Ball Room a grand vocal and instrumental concert was followed by a grand dress ball. The large orchestra of sixty musicians was under the direction of MM Prévost, Cobini, and L. Herman and executed several overtures, quadrilles, and waltzes: part I: the Overture to Rossini's *La Gazza Ladra*; the Overture to George Rodwell's *Cheval de Bronze*, arranged by Beër; a quadrille by Musard; a duet from *Norma* (Vallière and Tobey); Strauss's "Grand Treble Time"; the Overture to *Gustavus* arranged by Beër; part II: a fantasia on two themes from *Les Huguenots* arranged and performed by Mr. L. Herman on piano and another on horn á piston; a cavatina from *La Juive* (Mathiron); an air with variations on the violin from De Bériot, performed by Mr. Miaulan, pupil of Bailliot; another Musard quadrille; and the Overture to *Sémiramide*.[91]

Intermèdes continued without interruption at the main theaters in January and February 1839, usually consisting of one or two overtures in the standard repertory (usually by Rossini or Auber). Sometimes the overtures were named, for example *Sémiramide* and *Maseniello* (January 7), *Freischütz* and *Sémiramide* (January 23), *Oberon* and *Le Philtre* (January 26), *Scipio* and *La Bayadère* (January 28).[92] Solos also occurred between acts of a play at the Saint Charles Theatre, for example on February 27, 1839, when Cioffi played a trombone solo.[93] The first regular concert for 1839 took place on Saturday, March 2, at the Saint Louis Hotel. It had originally been scheduled for February 27. Mme Caradori Allan gave her first of four soirees musicales by performing various arias (Bellini, Donizetti, and Rossini) and ballads.[94] Her second soiree was on Wednesday, March 6, at the Saint Louis Exchange Ball Room, which was larger than the venue for her first concert.[95] Subsequent concerts were on March 13 and April 5.[96] Mme Caradori Allan had been invited to New Orleans a year and a half earlier so that she could experience a much more sophisticated audience than that she would find elsewhere in the country. As *The Bee* put it, "The little musical enthusiasm prevailing in the United States is nearly entirely concentrated in New Orleans, and could the accomplished artist be persuaded to come among us—she should not pour her mellow strains on inattentive ears."[97]

A much more substantial concert took place on March 3. It was a grand vocal and instrumental concert to raise money to aid French refugees from Mexico. The French citizens of New Orleans had a duty to attend because they were French but more importantly because they were humans. The members of the Philharmonic were behind this concert as they often were when humanitarian issues were at hand. The concert was held in the ballroom of the City Exchange on Saint Louis Street "by a number of the most distinguished artists in the city, and the Philharmonic society." The program was, part I: the Overture to *Le Dieu et La Bayadère,* a clarinet solo by Mr. Henings, an aria from Joseph (E. Chazotto), a solo on the violin (Miolan), G. P. Manouvrier's "Grand Triumphal March of the Louisiana Legion Dedicated to the Governor A. B. Roman"; part II: a concerted duet for violoncello and piano performed by Mr. and Mrs. Bamberger, a bassoon solo (C. Sy), a vocal duet from Masauritto (Mr. Chozotte and an amateur), a trombone solo (Cioffi), and the Overture to *William Tell.* According to *The Bee,* "The object of the concert being entirely for the interest of humanity, the price of admission is left to the generosity of the public."[98]

Another fundraiser occurred on Saturday, March 9, at the Saint Louis Ball Room. A grand vocal and instrumental concert for the benefit of orphans was directed by Mr. J. J. Jandot with several distinguished artists of the city. The program consisted of, part I: a "Grand Patriotic Overture" by Eugène Prévost performed by orchestra, a trumpet air by H. Ducatel, a Rossini aria sung by a basso from Havana, a Ricci aria, a concerted duet by De Bériot for violin and piano performed by MM A. Marquis and Norès; part II: a quartet for four flutes by Walkiers (performed by MM Jandot, Morphy, Kohn, and Ordy), a Mayseder solo bassoon piece (Sy), a fantasia on various well known airs composed and performed by Mr. Jandot accompanied on the harp by Trust, a Rossini vocal duet, and the Overture to Auber's *Domino Noir*. Mr. Norès provided pianoforte accompaniment.[99] Before the month of March was out there was another concert of sacred music. On Sunday March 31, 1839, Prévost's Mass for Easter received its premier. The reviewer for *L'Abeille* found much of it dull, and questioned the propriety of some orchestral effects in a church.[100]

Over the next eight weeks there were a number of important concerts to benefit local performers, some of whom were about to depart permanently from the city.[101] The first was the soiree musicale by Mme Guiraud at the Salle Saint Louis on Monday, April 1. The program, which included a great many of the best musicians of the city, consisted of, part I: a fantasia for piano and violin on *William Tell* by De Bériot and Osborne (Mme Guiraud and Miolan), De Bériot's variations performed on the trombone (Cioffi), a Donizetti aria (Santini), Berr's *Fantaisie* for clarinet (Kroll), Moscheles's piano variations (Mme Guiraud); part II: an oboe solo composed and performed by Vallière, a vocal duet by Mr.(?) Guiraud (Varney and Santini), Meyseder's violin variations (Miolan), a trombone solo by Rossini (Cioffi), and Grande Fantaisie on Russian Airs by Thalberg (Mme Guiraud).[102] A similar program was given on April 8 at the Saint Louis Exchange to benefit Kroll (it had originally been scheduled for April 6). Mme Guiraud, Vallière, Sy, Miolan, Santini, Varney, and Norès performed some of the same pieces as before and some new ones.[103] On the other hand the grand vocal et instrumental concert at the Salle d'Orléans on Monday, April 22 (originally scheduled for April 20 but postponed owing to bad weather), was a benefit for Mr. Moreno, a guitarist. Thus, the program favored that instrument: part I: the Overture to Rossini's *Tancredi* performed on two guitars by Moreno and Escarraguell, a Rossini aria accompanied by guitar, variations performed by Moreno, a Bellini aria accompanied on piano by Brugriera; part II: Rossini's *Sémiramide* Overture arranged for two guitars, a Rossini aria accompanied by Moreno on guitar, variations on Rossini arranged for flute (Corral) and guitar (Moreno), and a duo and potpourri of opera pieces arranged by Moreno and performed by two guitars. Santini (singer) repeated the Bellini aria, which he had sung at Mme Guiraud's concert, because of popular demand.[104]

The next two concerts were especially emotional since they signaled the departure of two popular personalities. The first, on Saturday, May 4, 1839, was a soiree musicale given by Albina Stella before her departure for the North. The program was, part I: a trombone solo (Cioffi), a Donizetti aria (Santini), "Casta Diva" (Stella), a piano fantasia (Guiraud), a duet from *Elixir of Love* (Stella and Santini); part II: fantasia for bassoon (Sy), a vocal duet, a Bellini aria (Stella), trombone variations (Cioffi), and a vocal trio (Stella, Varney, and Santini). Mr. Norès played the piano.[105] Then on Saturday, May 25, Cioffi, who was returning to Europe, gave a farewell concert at the Saint Louis Hotel. *L'Abeille* published a farewell letter to him in Italian.[106] Fortunately, Cioffi was back in New Orleans by the end of the following season. The program was, part I: an Auber overture (full orchestra); a trombone trio (Cioffi and two of his pupils), arranged by Cioffi; a Berr clarinet solo (Henings); trombone variations by De Bério (Cioffi); part II: a Rossini overture (full orchestra), a key trumpet solo on Rossini tunes (Sig'r Roda), flute variations by Nicholson (Mr. Patterson), and trombone variations on "Home Sweet Home" (Cioffi).[107]

The very long 1838–39 opera season closed with Halévy's *L'Éclair* on June 30, 1839. Yet New Orleanians could hardly wait for the fall 1839 reopening of the theaters. The American Theatre announced the opening of its upcoming season for October 5, 1839. This would end the monotony of the past three months when there had been no theater in the city.[108] The same day there was a performance by the German Theatre, 106 New Levee Street, Third Municipality, although the regular season of the German Theatre started only on Sunday evening, December 22.[109] The Théâtre d'Orléans opened with Calvé, Clozel, and others a month later, on November 7, 1839.[110] When the full season of the German Theatre began on December 22, there was a large crowd to witness plays and two overtures played during the intermède. According to *The Bee*, "The overtures to *La Dame Blanche* and *Masaniello* were splendidly executed. The orchestra is quite large, and uncommonly effective, performing with the perfect *ensemble* and attention to harmony which characterize artists of that school."[111] Meanwhile, although efforts to build an Italian opera house in New Orleans had thus far failed, a new joint stock company was proposed to purchase and use the Camp Street Theatre for Italian opera.[112] The foundations were now set for the amazing events of the next two decades, when New Orleans would sometimes have as many as four different opera houses operating on the same evening.

Despite this exciting theater opening, the concert season 1839–40 was one of the worst in the city's history. There were no regular concerts that fall, probably because the instrumental musicians and professional singers were fully occupied at the four active theaters (d'Orléans, Camp Street, American, and German). The shortage of instrumentalists was implied by the frenzied appeal of the Camp Street Theatre for more musicians immediately on December 16, 1839.[113] Intermèdes continued since the musicians were already there, as at the Wednesday, December 25, concert at the German Theatre when two overtures (Rossini's *Tancrède* and Mozart's *The Abduction from the Serail*) were played between two plays.[114] The intermèdes at the Théâtre d'Orléans were mostly ballets. And there was one religious concert, that for Sainte Cecilia's Day by the Philharmonic Society on Wednesday, November 6, 1839.[115]

In January, a patriotic cantata dedicated to General Jackson by Prévost was performed at the Théâtre d'Orléans, along with an overture by Prévost.[116] In March the new Théâtre de la Renaissance featured many wind pieces during the entr'actes in the featured play, Beaumarchais's *The Barber of Seville*, and in a subsequent vaudeville *M Jovial*.[117] On April 8, Kroll played one of his own pieces at the Théâtre d'Orléans after a performance of Auber's three-act opera *Le Cheval de Bronze,* and the following night at the Théâtre de la Renaissance, during several intermèdes, "The orchestra of the Philharmonic Society, directed by M Constantin, will perform many overtures."[118] Gabici performed in concerts on April 20 and April 27.[119]

The 1840–41 concert season was even worse, possibly because some of the best instrumentalists had left the city. The orchestra of the American Theatre was thought to be very powerful, but the critic of *The Bee/L'Abeille* had nothing good to say about the orchestra of the Théâtre d'Orléans, and the singers of the latter simply did not understand Italian opera.[120] The most notable event at the Théâtre d'Orléans was the local debut on December 1 of Auguste Nourrit as Robert le Diable. He was the brother of the famous Adolphe Nourrit who had committed suicide on March 8, 1839, in Naples. F. Kroll, together with his brother, Mrs. Dantonnet, and Miolan, tried to revive the concert life of New Orleans by announcing a series of soirees to run during the winter. His repertory, however, including the latest waltzes and cotillions by Strauss for orchestra or quintet, was not very elevated.[121] The Misses Mary and Rosina Shaw of Philadelphia, accompanied by their father and a professor of the pianoforte, announced that they would be giving a series of concerts during the winter on Monday, Wednesday, Friday, and Sunday evenings at the Louisiana Ball Room opposite the Saint Louis Exchange. Each evening there was to be a "fresh" program. On the evenings when they were not singing, there would be balls. We know nothing more about these women and their performances.[122]

The number of intermèdes, however, grew to new record numbers. During November and December 1840, at the Saint Charles Theatre there were two overtures performed by the house orchestra nearly every evening spread among the evening's dramatic entertainment. The American Theatre, which opened its new hall in fall and had a good orchestra under the direction of C. M. Mueller (with violinists Croce, Martinez, and Braunfels, violoncellist Weber, contrabassist Robyn, flutist Hoseler, clarinetists Espeinhelm and Teltow, hornist Marchat, trumpeter Myner, trombonist Schnell, and drummer Meyers), consistently performed overtures during dramatic presentations and even during an equestrian ballet.[123] Among the overtures played were those to *The Magic Flute* (November 24 and December 4), Beethoven's *Fidelio* (December 10) and *Prometheus* (December 11), Louise Bertin's *Guy Mannering* (December 12), Hérold's *Pre aux Clercs* (December 29), and Rossini's *Tancredi* (December 29).

There were three concerts of sacred music during the season. On Sunday, November 22, 1840, the Society of the Friends of Arts performed at the Cathedral some music by Meyerbeer and Rossini in honor of Sainte Cecelia's Day. The society was composed of amateurs; it is uncertain what connection if any this group had with the Philharmonic Society that had been performing on Sainte Cecelia's Day the previous two years. The writer in *The Bee* "heard a choral swell on Sainte Cecilia's Day, productive of as much delight as the perfect execution of an Italian opera."[124]

The next concert of sacred music was on April 6, 1841. Eugène Prévost conducted a three-part grand concert spirituel, including original pieces and pieces by others. It was an extravaganza that included stars from the French Opera and the future star Gottschalk. The program consisted of, part I: Overture from *The Death of Ajax,* parts of an oratorio, the grand duet of *Evelina,* and the "Dies Irae" from a *Requiem*—all these by Prévost and sung by Bernadet and others, plus a bassoon fantasia based on the music of Halévy (Molet) and a "Fantasie sur le Piano, exécute par le jeune Gottschalk, éléve de M Letellier"; part II: "Bianca Capello," lyric duet (Nourrit and Calvé) by Prévost; Symphonie Concertante for two violins by Kreutzer (Elie and Miolan); "Degli Capuletti" (Calvé); a clarinet fantasia by Kroll (Kroll); and the Grand Trio from *William Tell* (Nourrit, Cossas, and Bernadet); part III: the Overture to *Quentin Durward* by Prévost; Moses's "Prayer" (Bernadet, Nourrit, and Calvé), oboe variations by Vogt (Fourmestreau), "Stances à l'Eternité" (Bernadet), and a trio by Donizetti (Bernadet, Nourrit, and Calvé).[125]

The third concert, on June 29, 1841, was also billed as a spiritual concert, this time given at Saint Patrick's Church. The program was not much different from that of Prévost except it was only in two parts and had Curto's compositions rather than Prévost's. The orchestra of the Théâtre d'Orléans was conducted by Curto, who chose an air and a trio from Méhul's *Joseph* (Nourrit, Bernadet, and Calvé), Meyerbeer's "Ave Regina" (Calvé), the "Hymne à l'Éternité" (Bernadet), a fragment of his own *Requiem* (Curto, Nourrit, and Bernadet), and instrumental music (Lehmann and Cioffi). There were also two grand symphonies, one by Curto.[126]

Yet another year of few concerts began in the autumn of 1841. In fact, the only concerts in the fall occurred on two successive days: November 22 and 23. In the first case, there was the annual Grand Mass for Sainte Cecilia's Day, with French and Italian scores, performed in the dance hall of the Saint-Louis Bourse at 9:30 a.m. by the amateur Société de Gymnase Musical led by Kroll.[127] The other concert was an exotic event: the Chinese drummer Hai-Hanan-Bal Hakan performed in the Washington and American Ball Room. He was accompanied by an orchestra made up of a large array of drums.[128] The city was full of musicians, however, but they were once again preoccupied with duties other than concerts. Productions of dramatic works other than operas opened on Sunday evening, November 7, 1841, at the Théâtre d'Orléans. The audience was small but enthusiastic for two vaudevilles. According to *The Bee,* "As soon as the Opera commences, the musical propensities of our population will assert their sway, and the bright eyed beauties of Louisiana will again throng the dress circle."[129] The performances at the Saint Charles Theatre were bolstered by "a first rate band led by Cioffi."[130] The American Theatre opened its season with a comedy on Saturday, November 20, 1841, with a full and effective orchestra led by Mueller.[131]

The first opera of the season, *The Barber of Seville,* was performed, on December 18, with full orchestra at the American Theatre.[132] Dance orchestras were also in abundance, such as the anonymous one advertising on November 29, 1841: "An orchestra for balls announces its availability. It consists of artists [professionals] and is available for society balls and family balls."[133] The band led by Cobini at the Saint Louis Ball Room, had an advertisement that ran: "Mr. H. E. Lehmann, no. 146 St. Louis Street, Manager of the St. Louis Ball Room Orchestra and other establishments, engaged Mr. Cobini as Leader and undertakes to furnish musicians for Soireés [sic] and Private Balls, piano alone or accompanied with violin and valve trumpet. He will also furnish music for serenades and banquets."[134]

There was a handful of concerts in spring 1842. On January 21, M Nagel gave a "Grand Farewell Concert" with the orchestra of the Théâtre d'Orléans. Nagel was the first violinist to the king of Sweden and a pupil of Paganini. The program contained the Overture to Cherubini's *Les Deux Journées* and Weber's *Der Freischütz* (theater orchestra); a concerto dedicated to the American public (Nagel); opera arias and duets by Labarre (Bernadet), Boieldieu (Nourrit), Grisar (Nourrit), Marliani (Calvé), and Spontini (Bernadet and Nourrit); Schubert's "Marguerite" (Mme Bamberger); a fantasia by Paganini (Nagel); and a *Burlesque Musicale* in four movements: Movement 1 on four strings, Movement 2 on three, Movement 3 on two, and Movement 4 on one, by Nagel (Nagel). The evening opened with a vaudeville in one act.[135] There was also a matinee musicale on Sunday, January 23, at noon in the Salle Saint Louis, with members of the Théâtre d'Orléans orchestra led by Prévost. Fourmestreau (Fourmestreau) was the featured soloist.

On February 14 there was a grand vocal and instrumental concert for the benefit of Gabici. The German Glee Club performed a setting by Gabici of an idyll by Goethe and a chorus from Romberg's *Le Pouvoir des Sons*. The program also held a cantata from Donizetti's opera *Torquato Tasso*, a song by Bishop (with obbligato flute played by Carrière), a fantasia for violoncello on melodies from *Lucia de Lammermoor* (Dantonet), and Panoska's fantasia for violin on themes from *Les Huguenots* (Gabici). The Théâtre d'Orléans orchestra accompanied everything and also played the Overture to Rossini's *Otello*.[136] Two months later, on April 29, there was another benefit grand concert, this one for Carrière, who before coming to New Orleans was a graduate of the Paris Conservatoire and first solo flute of the Théâtre Royal de l'Opéra Comique. The orchestra, conducted by Prévost, performed two overtures by Rossini and Auber. Dantonet played a fantasia for violoncello; Gabici and Trust played a duet for violin and harp; Carrière and Norès performed a grande fantasie concertante for flute and piano; Fourmestreau and Sy did a duet for oboe and bassoon; Mme Bamberger sang a melody by Schubert; Hubert Rolling played his own grande fantasie; and Carrière ended the program with some flute variations. This program marks the debut of Rolling, who figured as one of the most successful composers and pianists in New Orleans in the second half of the century.[137]

One event during the summer of 1842 caused a disruption in the lives of some of the musicians in New Orleans. On July 30, Caldwell's American Theatre was destroyed by fire. Caldwell immediately made plans to rebuild and hired an orchestra, singers, and others, but because of lease problems, everyone was thrown out on the street.[138] A number of musicians were in jeopardy, especially Gabici, who was quickly becoming a mainstay of the concert life of the city. Finally, on January 14, 1843, James H. Caldwell, who had done so much for the city, announced that he was severing his ties with the American Theatre permanently after thirty years involvement in New Orleans. He had lost

$100,000.¹³⁹ The Saint Charles Theatre also had trouble that fall and did not open until January 18, 1843.¹⁴⁰ Meanwhile Prévost was in France and was hiring his new troupe, including singers, chorus, and the following instrumentalists: a contrabass (named Romanie), a bassoon player (unnamed), and the répétiteur who was also third conductor of the orchestra (Grosdidier).¹⁴¹ The opera season opened at the Théâtre d'Orléans on November 13,¹⁴² but its major premier of the season—Rossini's complete opera *William Tell*—was apparently a flop. Not the instrumentalists and chorus, who were admirable, but the soloists disappointed.¹⁴³ In addition to the orchestra at the Théâtre d'Orléans, the dance orchestras were flourishing as usual, which gave employment to other good musicians.¹⁴⁴ There was plenty of talent in the city for concerts to resume, if only the likes of Gabici could find a place to earn a living.

There were two sacred concerts that fall. The first, on October 26, was held at Saint Patrick's Church with a chorus of fifty voices (women and men from New Orleans, who were members of the Athénée Musical) and an orchestra of forty excellent professional musicians. William Furst, regular organist of the church, conducted the orchestra and composed some of the music. The program consisted of the allegro from a symphony in "si minor" by Beethoven (?), music by Rossini and Furst, then the rest of the symphony by Beethoven, then music by the local musician Varney, more Furst and Rossini, Auber, and the Kyrie and Gloria of the Mass No. 12 of Mozart. Altogether the concert "gave general and unmingled satisfaction. . . . [T]he orchestra [was] tolerably complete."¹⁴⁵ The second sacred concert, on November 16, was conducted by the Société de Musique Sacrée de la Nouvelle Orléans. The group performed religious works of Haydn, Handel, Pergolesi, Beethoven, Rossini, and Mercadante. It claimed this was its fourth concert, but we have no record of previous ones.¹⁴⁶

One person dominated the concert season that fall and winter: William Vincent Wallace (1814–65). He was originally a violinist but on occasion also played the piano. On Saturday, December 3, 1842, he gave a vocal and instrumental concert at the Saint Louis Ball Room, assisted by Celine Douce(t), Mr. Varney, and Mr. E. Sheppard. The orchestra was directed by Gabici. The program included pieces by Paganini, Donizetti, Wallace, De Bériot, and Russell Sheppard. The orchestra accompanied most of the works and in addition rendered two unnamed overtures.¹⁴⁷ Wallace gave a second concert in the Théâtre d'Orléans on Wednesday, February 1, 1843, with a similar program: Wallace played the violin in his own Violin Concerto and also played the piano in other works of his own composition; there were also several singers on the program, and the whole concert was preceded by a vaudeville.¹⁴⁸ Then on Thursday, March 22, Wallace had a farewell concert at the Saint Louis Exchange Ball Room, assisted by several other artists and the German Glee Club. Once again he performed his own music and performed on both the violin and the piano. There was no orchestra this time, and the accompaniment was piano. He was joined by Cioffi (trombone) and Fourmestreau (oboe). Wallace left New Orleans for Charleston, South Carolina, by way of Mobile.[149]

After Caldwell retired, the American Theatre was reopened under new management, but the members of the orchestra walked out before a performance on February 8 in a dispute with the management.[150] Meanwhile, Gabici, the former leader of the orchestra, had taken another job as director of the dance establishment at Conti Street Ball Room. Balls were held every Sunday, Tuesday, Thursday, and Saturday. To help support Gabici, a benefit concert was arranged for February 9, right after the strike at the American Theatre.[151] This may have been the catalyst for his return to the American Theatre as leader, and whatever the dispute between the musicians and management, things were resolved so that, on April 15, a two-week run (twelve performances) of Italian opera at the American Theatre took place. The Italian Opera was fresh from Havana, which was where Gabici was leader before he came to New Orleans. The orchestra was composed of thirty of the best musicians in the country. The first performance was of *I Puritani.*

The sudden revival of both the American Theatre and Italian opera there was the result of Gabici's efforts. According to *The Bee,* "The orchestra was really fine, and reflects great credit on Mr. GABICI, the leader."[152] But the rapprochement between Gabici and the American Theatre was short lived. On May 8, Gabici conducted the Italian Opera performance with Madame Castellan and then resigned over a dispute with the managers of the opera company. "It will be found no easy matter to replace him," noted *The Bee.*[153] Indeed, the orchestra was in shambles, as reported the following week: "The artists should be more sure of themselves, and the orchestra should take the time to look over the score that they are not familiar with, if one judges from the poor ensemble of this performance. This fault is deplorable; it troubles the singers and turns off the audience. It hinders especially the appreciation of the music itself, some of which is without doubt very beautiful. At certain times the trouble that reigns in the orchestra is felt on the stage, and in the middle of all these discords Mme Castellan had a lot of trouble to find the inspiration that escaped her usual aplomb."[154] By May 23 Gabici, not to be put down, was conducting the orchestra of the Théâtre d'Orléans in concerts.

Concert life in New Orleans picked up considerably in the spring of 1843. The first concert was on March 29 at the Saint Charles Exchange. It was a vocal concert by Mr. Brough of the French Opera. Cioffi also performed a piece on the trombone.[155] Then came a series of concerts by a visitor, Max Bohrer, master of the Royal Chapel and violoncellist to the king of Würtemberg; he was assisted by Mr. L. Rakemann, a German pianist. The first concert, on April 8, 1843, at the Saint Louis Exchange Ball Room, included works by Bohrer, Bellini, Thalberg, Romberg, Meyerbeer, and H. Herz. Mme Bamberger also sang, with Furst at the piano.[156] The reviewer in *L'Abeille* found Bohrer's playing to have finesse, elegance, lightness, grace, and a delicacy that heretofore was unimaginable on the violoncello and thought only to be the style of violinists. The only regret is that he did not sufficiently emphasize the beautifully rich sound of his instrument, which did come forth, however, in an adagio by Romberg. Rakemann, in turn, was wonderful to hear because, rather than furiously pounding at his instrument, he calmly and tastefully pursued the musicality of the pieces played. And Mme Bamberger, in singing a cavatina from *Roméo et Juliette,* showed great progress since she left the theater. The second grand concert was on April 18 and included music by Bohrer, Rossini, Thalberg, Marliani, and Herz.[157] The third and farewell concert was on May 4, with Bohrer playing mostly his own compositions.[158] Once again the critic was impressed not only with the violoncellist but with Rakeman, whose performance alone of Thalberg's variations on the prayer of Moses demonstrated finesse of playing, a wide range of nuances, a powerful sound, and a depth of expression.

Another series of four concerts was given by Mme Anais Castellan Giampietro in the Saint Louis Ball Room on April 21 and 27 and May 12 and 23. Castellan was starring at the American theater in Italian opera, made her debut there on May 4 as Lucia in *Lucia de Lammermoor,* and was to score a big hit on May 16 when she sang the title role of Norma. According to the reviewer in *The Bee*:

> Her voice is a mellow, full soprano of astonishing compass, and considerable power. On the lower register its tones are wonderously rich and sonorous; its medium notes are replete with volume and expression, and on the upper range, they maintain their strength and fullness, except at the very highest limits of vocal exertion, where they naturally lose somewhat of roundness and vibration. . . . Her intonation is exquisitely pure and melodious; the flexibility of her organ is such as to permit her with the utmost ease to execute chromatic cadences; and her style and method are evidently those of the best Italian schools. Her transitions, which in one of the pieces on Thursday evening, were more than two octaves, are astonishingly accurate. Her execution is likewise marked by infinite expression. She feels the melody of the great masters of music, and throws her soul into the performance. Hence her sing-

ing is highly effective. In short Madame CASTELLAN is an artist in every sense of the term.[159]

For the first two concerts she was accompanied on piano by Mr. Norès and performed various arias (including "Casta Diva" from *Norma*) and other operatic scenes. She was joined by Cioffi on April 21 and by Miolan on April 27.[160] On May 12 she sang only one aria, the cavatina from Bellini's *Beatrice di Tenda*. She was joined by the singers Allard, Victor, and Fleury in other operatic parts, by the bassoonist Lacroix, who was in charge of the concert, in arrangements from operas, and by Miolan in an anonymous violin solo. No mention is made of accompanists.[161] On May 23 the concert was at the Théâtre d'Orléans and was accompanied by an orchestra led by Gabici, which, by itself, played the overtures to Auber's *Cheval de Bronze* and Donizetti's *Anna Bolena*. Gabici's pupil Adolphe Bounivard, age ten, played an air for violin by Gabici; Miolan performed several works; and Fourmestreau played an oboe work. Castellan sang two Bellini arias (one of which was, once again, "Casta Diva").[162]

The final concert in the spring of 1843 was on June 2 at the Théâtre d'Orléans, with the orchestra conducted by Gabici. It featured Lehmann on his cornet à piston and included works by Curto (a duet sung by Varney and Curto), De Bériot (Miolan soloist), Bochsa (a clarinet concerto performed by Henings), Rossini (overture), Méhul (overture), Lehmann (a grand march dedicated to the Louisiana Legion, for which thirty wind instrumentalists were brought in), and another duet by Caraffa (Varney and Curto).[163]

Meanwhile, the first half of 1843 witnessed a small number of sacred concerts. The Sacred Music Society put on its sixth concert at Mr. Clapp's Church on January 20. "The selections are very choice and beautiful, comprising some of the finest conceptions of the great masters." Works were by Haydn, Handel, Mozart, and Rink, and a piece by William Furst was dedicated to the firemen of New Orleans. The program was accompanied by an orchestra that also played an overture.[164] Rossini's *Stabat Mater* was performed twice at Saint Patrick's Church to benefit two different orphan asylums—on February 13 and March 7. It was performed by members of the Athénée Musical with an orchestra of the most celebrated musicians of the city, under the direction of A. Varney.[165]

The fall of 1843 was again a time for reorganization. After earning rave reviews in *The Philadelphia Inquirer* and *National Gazette* for her performances in Philadelphia, Calvé rejoined the French Opera Troupe, newly assembled in Europe, and arrived back in New Orleans on November 9. The renovation of the Saint Charles Theatre was finished by mid-November, and it opened with a new orchestra "composed of the following musical artists: MM Miolan (leader), G. Taylor, Verron, Hessing, Guasdingi, Curei, Charleton, Coastes, Brawn, Nyers, Kost, Warren, Ede, G. Holland, Jr., Clement, and Johnson. Signor Ribas, Professor of the oboe, will be added in a few weeks." At the beginning of December the English-language opera started a run at the American Theatre. There one heard English translations of *Norma, La Gazza Ladra, Sonnambula, Fra Diavolo, Zampa, Cinderella, Moïse, The Barber of Seville, Der Freischütz, Don Giovanni* (Mozart), *Elisir d'Amore,* and *Postillon de Longjumeau* (Adolphe Adam). One assessment read, "L'orchestre du Theatre Americain a singulierement gagne dans ces dernieres annees; il sera plus complet que jamais"; the English version in the *Bee* read, "The orchestra of the American is full and efficient. It ranks among its members a number of accomplished artists."[166]

The theaters were in place, the musicians were working, the audience was ready, but there were no concerts during the fall of 1843. What began as a dull concert season for 1843–44 exploded after the New Year into one of the most exciting and important concert seasons in the history of New Orleans. It started on January 15, 1844, when Henri Vieuxtemps (1820–81) arrived in the Crescent City. Vieuxtemps, then twenty-three years old and already recognized as one of the two or three greatest violinists of the time, had just appeared in New York and other eastern cities and was about to conquer New Orleans. Coincidentally, another of the greatest violinists of the age, Ole Bull (1810–80) had also just arrived in New Orleans with the same intention. Both gave their initial performances on January 17, 1844, at 7 p.m., Vieuxtemps in the French Théâtre d'Orléans and Bull in the American Saint Charles Theatre. "Vieuxtemps performed [seven] times during January: with full orchestra on January 17, 22, 27, and [31] in the Théâtre d'Orléans, and with a small group of instrumentalist[s] on January 20 and 24 in the smaller Salle du Bataillon Washington, and again with full orchestra on January 29 in the Saint Charles Theatre. Bull performed his six concerts with full orchestra, first at the Saint Charles Theatre (January 17, 19, 22, and 23) and then at the Théâtre d'Orléans (February 5 and 7)."[167] Or in summary, thirteen magnificent violin concerts were held in just three weeks.

But that was not all. As *L'Abeille* reported, "On February 28 the Belgian violinist Joseph Artôt (1815–45) began a nearly two-month stand in the city in conjunction with the famous French soprano Mme Laure Cinti-Damoreau." Before arriving in the city he had toured on the East Coast and was popular in New York.[168] He played both alone and with Mme Damoreau at the Théâtre d'Orléans in orchestral concerts and in intermèdes. He performed at the Washington Armory on March 4, at the Salle Saint Louis on April 8, and in a benefit concert for Prévost on April 13 at the Théâtre d'Orléans, where his and Damoreau's farewell concert took place on April 19. They left the city for the North on April 23. The critic of *L'Abeille* was charmed by Artôt, who "sings to us (on his violin) delicious inspirations which the human voice could not render better." Before Artôt was finished, however, on March 29 Vieuxtemps returned to New Orleans for yet one more concert at the Théâtre d'Orléans in the following program: De Bériot's *Le Trémolo* and his own Grand Concerto in Three Parts, *Souvenirs de Moscow,* and Grandes Variations on a Theme from *Norma* for One String—a piece just composed.

Programs of the Bull, Vieuxtemps and Artôt Concerts
New Orleans, 1844

Wednesday, January 17, 1844, Théâtre d'Orléans
   Mon Ami Pierrot, vaudeville in one act
   Overture to *Zanette,* by Auber (orchestra)
   L'Ange Déchulde de Rogel (Bauce)
   Grand Concerto in Three Parts, by Vieuxtemps (Vieuxtemps)
   "Romance of Guido and Ginevra" (Grosseth)
   Le Trémolo, by De Bériot (Vieuxtemps)
   Overture to *Gustave,* by Auber (orchestra)
   Air from *The Barber of Seville,* by Rossini (Fleury-Jolly)
   Carnival of Venice, by Paganini (Vieuxtemps)

Wednesday, January 17, 1844, Saint Charles Theatre
   Concerto in Three Parts: Allegro Maestoso; Adagio Sentimental; Rondo Pastorale, by Bull (Bull)
   Adagio Religioso, by Bull (Bull)
   Carnival of Venice, by Paganini (Bull)
   Polacca Guerriera, by Bull (Bull)

Friday, January 19, 1844, Saint Charles Theatre
   [Bull's concert program unknown]
   Gabrielle, a drama
   Concert part 1
   Vermonte, a play
   Concert part 2

Saturday, January 20, 1844, Armory
    Violin Concerto No. 4, Allegro, by De Bériot (Vieuxtemps)
    Piano Solo (Miss Vieuxtemps)
    Variations on a Theme of *Il Pirata,* by Vieuxtemps (Vieuxtemps)
    Duo Concertant on a theme from *Sonnambula,* by De Bériot (Vieuxtemps + Miss Vieuxtemps)
    Carnival of Venice, by Paganini (Vieuxtemps)

Monday, January 22, 1844, Saint Charles Theatre
    Largo Posato e Rondo Capricioso, by Bull (Bull)
    Quartetto, on one violin, by Bull (Bull)
    Adagio, by Mozart (Bull)
    Polacca Guerriera, by Bull (Bull)

Monday, January 22, 1844, Théâtre d'Orléans
    Un Val du Grand Monde, vaudeville in one act
    Overture to *Cheval de Bronze,* by Auber (orchestra)
    Concerto in E, Allegro, by Vieuxtemps (Vieuxtemps)
    "Grand Air of Sénéchal," from *Jean de Paris* (Bauce)
    Capricio, by Paganini (Vieuxtemps)
    Overture to *Zampa,* by Hérold (orchestra)
    Grand Air, *La Dame Blanche,* first act (Grosseth)
    Le Tremlolo, fantasia on a theme of Beethoven, by De Bériot (Vieuxtemps)

Tuesday, January 23, 1844, Saint Charles Theatre
    Concerto in Three Parts, by Bull (Bull)
    Adagio Religioso, by Bull (Bull)
    Variaziani di Bravura, on a Bellini theme, by Bull (Bull)
    Carnival of Venice, by Paganini (Bull)

Wednesday, January 24, 1844, Armory Hall
    Adagio and Rondo, by De Bériot (Vieuxtemps)
    Fantasia on Themes from *Don Juan,* by Thalberg (Miss Vieuxtemps)
    Fantasia Caprice, by Vieuxtemps (Vieuxtemps)
    Grand Duo upon themes from *Fra Diavolo,* by Herz and Lafont (Vieuxtemps and Miss Vieuxtemps)
    "Yankee Doodle," Grand Caprice, by Vieuxtemps (Vieuxtemps)

Saturday, January 27, 1844, Théâtre d'Orléans
    Un Mari Charmant, a vaudeville in one act
    Overture to *La Dame Blanche,* by Boïeldieu (orchestra)
    Concerto No. 2, First Movement, by De Bériot (Vieuxtemps)
    Romance (Bauce)
    Caprice, Paganini (Vieuxtemps)
    Overture to *Sémiramide,* by Rossini (orchestra)
    Concerto in E, Adagio and Rondo, by Vieuxtemps (Vieuxtemps)
    "Air de la Calomnie," from *The Barber of Seville,* by Rossini (Blès)
    Carnival of Venice, by Paganini (Vieuxtemps)

Monday, January 29, 1844, Saint Charles Theatre
    Variations on an Air from *Il Pirata* (Vieuxtemps)
    Le Trémolo, by De Bériot (Vieuxtemps)
    Carnival of Venice, by Paganini (Vieuxtemps)
    Caprice on "Yankee Doodle," enlarged with "Hail Columbia," by Vieuxtemps (Vieuxtemps)

Wednesday, January 31, 1844, Théâtre d'Orléans
    Une Passion, vaudeville in one act
    Overture to *Der Freischütz* by Weber (orchestra)
    Fantaisie-Caprice by Vieuxtemps (Vieuxtemps)
    La Demence de Charles VI (Bauce)
    Grand Duo Concertant, based on *Les Huguenots,* violin and piano, by Thalberg (Vieuxtemps + Mlle Vieuxtemps)
    L'Air du Gouverneur de Comte Ory, by Rossini (Bles)
    Les Arpeges, Caprice pour Violon et Violoncello Oblige (Vieuxtemps)
    Overture to *Gustave* by Auber (orchestra)
    Grand Duo Concertant, based on *Sonnambula,* by De Bériot (Vieuxtemps + Mlle Vieuxtemps)
    Air (Grosseth)
    Le Trémolo (Vieuxtemps)

Monday, February 5, 1844, Théâtre d'Orléans
    Overture to *The Barber of Seville,* by Rossini (orchestra)
    Duet from *Comte Ory,* by Rossini (Lecourt + Grosseth)
    Grand Concert in three parts, by Bull (Bull)

Air, from *Joseph,* by Méhul (Grosseth)
Adagio Religioso, by Bull (Bull)
Overture to *La Pie Voleuse,* by Rossini (orchestra)
The Carnival of Venice, by Paganini (Bull)
Air, from *Le Pie Voleuse,* by Rossini (Bauce)
Polacca Guerriera, by Bull (Bull)

Wednesday, February 7, 1844, at Théâtre d'Orléans
Overture (orchestra)
Largo e Rondo Capriccioso, by Bull (Bull)
A piece to be chosen
Quartet for four violins, by Bull (Bull)
Overture (orchestra)
Nocturne Amerique, by Bull (Bull)
A piece to be chosen
Rainala et Variazoni de Grayara, by Bull (Bull)

Monday, March 4, 1844, Armory
Introduction (piano)
Air, from *Sémiramide,* by Rossini (Damoreau)
Souvenirs de Bellini, Caprice Brilliant, by Artôt (Artôt)
The Deep, Deep Sea, French Romance, by Horn and Pujet (Damoreau)
Le Trémolo, by De Bériot (Artôt)
Fantasia (piano)
Cavatina from *The Barber of Seville,* by Rossini (Damoreau)
Grand Fantasia, on *Robert Le Diable* (Artôt)
Variations Concertantes, for voice and violin, on "The Last Rose of Summer" (Damoreau + Artôt)

Friday, March 15, 1844, Théâtre d'Orléans
The Barber of Seville, second and third acts
Grand Air from *Serment* (Cinti-Damoreau)
Le Rossignol, the Reprieve, by Lebrun (Cinti-Damoreau)
Andante Expressivo and *Rondo La Clochette,* by Paganini (Artôt)
Overture (orchestra)
Fantasie on a Theme from Norma, by Artôt (Artôt)
Une Passion, vaudeville in one act

Friday, March 29, 1844, Théâtre d'Orléans
　　Overture (orchestra)
　　Grand Concerto in thee parts, by Vieuxtemps (Vieuxtemps)
　　Air (Bauce)
　　Variations on a Theme of *Norma,* on a Single String, by Vieuxtemps (premiere performance by Vieuxtemps)
　　Overture (orchestra)
　　Variations on a Russian Theme, by Vieuxtemps (Vieuxtemps)
　　Grand Waltz, by Strauss (orchestra)
　　Fantasia for oboe (Fourmestreau)
　　Le Trémolo, by De Bériot (Vieuxtemps)

Monday, April 8, 1844, Saint Louis Hall
　　Overture to *Cosimo,* by E. Prévost (orchestra conducted by E. Prévost)
　　Duet from *Chateau d'Avanel* (Varney and Curto)
　　Grand Air from *La Muette de Portici,* by Auber (Cinti-Damoreau)
　　Hommage â Rubini, by Artôt (Artôt)
　　Grand Duet from *William Tell,* by Rossini (Cinti-Damoreau and Grosseth)
　　Overture, to *William Tell,* by Rossini (orchestra)
　　Variations, Rode (Cinti-Damoreau)
　　Le Rêve, by Artôt (Artôt)
　　Duo Concertant for voice and violin, newly composed by Artôt (Artôt and Cinti-Damoreau)

Saturday, April 13, 1844, Théâtre d'Orléans
　　Le Concert á la Cour, an opera in one act *(Cinti-Damoreau)*
　　Fantasia and Variations for the Violin, by Artôt (Artôt)
　　The Italian Singer and the Tailor, opera in one act (Cinti-Damoreau)

Wednesday, April 17, 1844, American Theatre
　　One Hour, comedy
　　Overture to *Oberon,* by Weber (orchestra)
　　Variation de Bravura, by Artôt (Artôt)
　　Variations, by Rode (Cinti-Damoreau)
　　Le Trémolo, by De Bériot (Artôt)
　　Concertante Variations for voice and violin, on "The Last Rose of Summer," by Cinti-Damoreau (Cinti-Damoreau)

Scene, Cavatina, from *The Barber of Seville,* by Rossini (Cinti-Damoreau)
Ballet
Grand Scena from *Le Serment,* by Auber (Cinti-Damoreau)

Friday, April 19, 1844, Théâtre d'Orléans
La Permission de Dix Heures, a vaudeville in one act
L'Ambassadrice, opera (Cinti-Damoreau)
Souvenirs of Bellini, by Artôt (Artôt)
Grand Aria from *Le Serment,* by Auber (Cinti-Damoreau)
Fantasia from *Robert le Diable,* Artôt (Artôt)
Three Romances (Cinti-Damoreau)
Le Domino Noir, one act (Cinti-Damoreau)

With the overwhelming interest by New Orleanians in the music of the famous visiting superstars, it is not surprising that there were few concerts by locals at this time. There was one, nonetheless, on February 1, 1844, at the Washington Arsenal on Camp Street. It was a grand concert of Mme de Goni and Mr. G. G. E. Knoop. Knoop played the violoncello, Mme de Goni played the guitar, and they were joined by J. M. Messmer, who played the cornet à piston, in duets and solos. It was only after the three violinists had gone, however, that we again find regular concerts by the resident musicians. M Grosseth, tenor at the French Opera, had a benefit concert on April 30 where he sang the fourth act of Donizetti's *La Favorite* and the grand duet from Halévy's *Reine de Chypre* with Mme Fleury-Jolly. On May 2 the Sacred Music Society of New Orleans performed a spiritual concert—Haydn's *Creation*—at Rev. Clapp's church, with William Furst, director and F. F. Mueller, organist, and on May 8 the Athenée Musical performed excerpts from Haydn's *Creation,* Varney's "O Douce Paix" (a trio), and Rossini's *Stabat Mater* at the Saint Louis Cathedral to benefit orphans. The singers of the latter musical organization were accompanied by a large orchestra directed by Prévost.[169]

Then on May 21 Mordand and Miolan shared a joint benefit intermède concert at the Théâtre d'Orléans, where the latter dared to perform *Le Trémolo* that both Artôt and Vieuxtemps played so well; this showed that a local artist could stand tall in comparison with the world's best. In the intermède Miolan also played an air by De Bériot and the orchestra played an overture.[170] The local critic was proud that Miolan of New Orleans was so good.[171] Two days later a charity concert was held for a family that had lost all its possessions in the sinking of the steamboat Buck Eye. It was a grand vocal and instrumental concert held at the Salle Saint Louis, with an orchestra conducted by Varney. The orchestra played the overtures to *Sémiramide* and *La Gazza Ladra*; Miolan played *Le Trémolo* and another work by De Bériot; and Bauce sang several arias. A wind harmonie performed arrangements of two arias by Auber and Donizetti.[172] Unfortunately, attendance was not good so the aim of the concert—to raise money for the indigent family—was unsuccessful.

There was one more concert in 1844, at the very end of the year. On December 30 a grand concert was given by the violoncellist M Adrien Garreau at the Salle Saint Louis. It included a trio for piano, violin, and violoncello by Reissiger (Gabici violin, Garreau violoncello, M Norès piano) and a *Sérénade* by Durutti (Hegeland, Buci, and Garreau).[173] On the same evening Cobini conducted a large orchestra of the best local musicians in a costumed ball held in the Philharmonique above the restaurant of M L. Canonge.[174]

The first half of 1845 was particularly robust with concerts. Haydn's *Creation* was again performed at Clapp's Church at the end of January, and at the Washington Armory Henry Phillips gave a concert of songs, accompanying himself on a Chickering piano as part of a promotion of that instrument at the store of Mr. Casey.[175] Ole Bull, fresh from his successes the previous year, returned in February for additional concerts. The first two concerts were with full orchestra conducted by William Furst. On the first (February 12) Bull played his own Concerto in A and other original works, plus Paganini's *Carnival of Venice*. The orchestra performed two overtures by Kalliwoda and Rossini (unnamed), and Mr. O'Guilmotte sang some songs.[176] The second concert (February 17) was similar to the first but with different pieces, such as Bull's *Cantabile Doloroso* and *Psaume de David*; Guilmotto sang two airs.[177] The third concert (February 19) featured Bull's *Niagara*; the fourth took place at the Washington Armory on February 21 with piano accompaniment by Furst. Bull alternated with Mrs. Emilie Hammarskold, the soprano and pianist. He played his own *Scotch Melodies, Fantasia upon Irish Melodies, Variazioni di Bravura* on a theme by Bellini, and Paganini's *La Campanella* and *Carnival of Venice*. She sang songs and played one unnamed piano work.[178] The next concert by these two featured Hammarskold with Bull assisting. It was on February 26 at Armory Hall. Hammarskold played piano music by Weber and Thalberg, and sang several songs, including an aria from Mozart's *The Marriage of Figaro*. An unusual piece on the program presented a new invention combining (somehow) the piano and Aeolian harp, with both Trust and Hammarskold involved. Bull repeated a few pieces from his earlier programs,[179] as he did in his two farewell concerts for this visit, on March

11 at the American Theatre and on March 13 at the Théâtre d'Orléans. He was assisted by the singer Candi and by a full orchestra on the first and by the singers Cassini and Garry and full orchestra on the second.[180]

Flutist Mr. Barton played on February 24 at Armory Hall and on February 26 at the Saint Louis Hotel, with some Swiss bell ringers known as the Campanologiens and Furst at the piano. Among the works was an arrangement of the second movement of Haydn's *Surprise* Symphony No. 94 (labeled No. 3).[181] The Campanologiens, without Barton, gave their farewell concert at the armory on March 17 before leaving for Havana.[182] They then returned for one more concert on April 16 before departing for Saint Louis. On March 28, M Ibañez (pupil of Thalberg) and the flutist M Davis gave a joint recital at the Saint Louis Hotel.[183] The former played fantasies on opera themes; the latter played some variations by Boehm; and they joined for additional opera variations. Since Ibañez and Davis were unknown to the public, to help attract an audience they were joined by local celebrities Varney and Saint Rose.[184]

The arrival of April meant more benefits for the performers. The benefit for William Furst was given on April 4 at Rev. Theodore Clapp's Church by the Society of Sacred Music. Among the many men and women participating were pupils of Furst and members of the Athénée Musical. The main work was Rossini's *Stabat Mater,* but the program also included two vocal works by Furst ("Patriotic Hymn to Washington," words by P. Canonge, and "Prayer and Bass Solo" from an unpublished opera, words by G. Calcaterra) and the Overture to Weber's *Oberon* (Théâtre d'Orléans Orchestra).[185] Mlle Eugénie's benefit at the Théâtre d'Orléans on April 22 included an orchestral intermède, of which we do not know the program. On the next night occurred the benefit for the singer Signorina Eufrasia Borghèse at the American Theatre. It was a full concert—the second and third acts of *Sémiramide,* an oboe piece by Bauer, two songs sung by Borghèse, and a duet from *Norma* (Borghèse and Amelia Ricci)—followed incredibly by the finale of the second act of *Lucia di Lamermoor.*[186]

On April 25 was the corresponding benefit for Ricci with a similar program,[187] and the leading tenor Perozzi had his benefit on April 28. At the benefit for M Dessonville on April 29 at the Théâtre d'Orléans there was an intermède that featured Arnaud, Garry, and Cassini in songs.[188] There was a benefit on May 1 for Gabici accompanied by the principal artists of the Italian Opera company with its orchestra. It included an aria from Norma arranged for violin in the style of Ole Bull, De Bériot's Concerto No. 1 performed by Wallace, and *Le Trémolo* by De Bériot in the style of Artôt and Vieuxtemps (whether performed by Wallace or Gabici is not mentioned).[189] The benefit concerts continued on May 5, at the Armory of the Washington Battalion, with a concert for C. La Manna, leader of the Italian Opera Orchestra.[190]

Throughout this spring, intermèdes continued as usual. One such musical interlude occurred on May 16, 1845, at the opera (Théâtre d'Orléans), including an aria from *The Barber of Seville* accompanied by a grand orchestra.[191]

The fall 1845 season was more active than usual. While the Théâtre d'Orléans was being renovated under its manager, Pierre Davis, with gas lamps in time for its November opening with *La Favorite*—the first time opera was performed in New Orleans with gas lighting,[192] entertainment came from outside the local establishment. An Italian troupe en route from New York to Havana via New Orleans decided, as long as it was in town, to present a grand vocal and instrumental concert in the Saint Louis Dance Hall. Featured were Rosina Picco (or Pico), Amalia Majocchi-Valtellina, Cerillo Antognini, and Atillio Valtellina. The reviewer rapped Signora Pico, yet he hoped that, since Pico and her troupe would be in New Orleans for a few more days, she would sing again and redeem herself.[193] Meanwhile the Saint Charles Theatre was scoring a theatrical triumph by presenting Junius Brutus Booth, the father of the famous Booth family of actors. Intermèdes still occurred in the theaters, such as at the American Theatre on November 10, 1845.[194]

The renovated Théâtre d'Orléans finally opened on November 23, with drama, but there were the inevitable intermèdes: *Marches Patrioques* by Prévost and the overtures to Rossini's *Sémiramide* and Weber's *Obéron*.[195] The reviewer in *L'Abeille* raved about the orchestral musicians in the overtures "executed with the perfection common in an orchestra where artists of talent rub elbows."[196] Later, on December 27, he added another fine tribute to the orchestra of the Théâtre d'Orléans, which was to perform another intermède between two vaudevilles: "There is an established empathy between the orchestra of the Théâtre d'Orléans and the public, and artists from outside who wish to be heard, would be wrong to believe this is something easily obtained."[197]

On Monday, December 8, the sisters Roneberg from Braunschweig performed a harp concert in the dancing room of Mr. Lavenant, 116 Chartres Street.[198] The Orphenan Family, a vocal quartet, gave its first concert at Armory Hall on Camp Street on December 10. During a Masonic funeral at the Methodist Church on Poydras Street, in honor of the late General Andrew Jackson and a number of late grandmasters of Louisiana, Curto's *Requiem* was sung by the choir.[199] Further concerts were on December 12, 16, 17, and 24.[200] M Miguel (accordion) and M Palagiz (violoncello) presented their unusual concert about December 4 at 200 Tchoupitoulas Street, Second Municipality, and it was enthusiastically received.[201]

The old cultural divide between French-speaking and English-speaking residents was still prevalent enough for the critic to state, "If the English-speaking New Orleanians are now coming to hear the lyric masterpieces in the Théâtre d'Orléans, so the French-speaking New Orleanians should cross Canal Street and go to the Saint Charles Theatre to witness great acting by Henry Placide."[202] The growth of the French Opera into a national cultural treasure did not mean that the English-speaking world in New Orleans was illiterate musically, and the snobbery of the French was not that apparent to visitors to the city who thoroughly enjoyed the depth of the artistic life there. The rich presentations at the Saint Charles and at the American theaters, as well as at the fast-developing German Theatre, enabled anyone in the city to experience a rewarding time. In the first half of 1846 the city had everything. While on January 10 at the Saint Charles Theatre Mr. and Mrs. Field enacted *Foreign and Native* and *Nicolas Nickleby,* with an intermède by the Ethiopian Harmonists, ten days later, at the Saint Charles Theatre, during a performance of Shakespeare's *Comedy of Errors,* "Miss Wilhelmina Roseberger, the celebrated German harpist, [played] a march with variations."[203] On February 1, *The Bee* informed, "The members of the New Orleans Brass Band will make their first appearance in their new uniform . . . at noon in the Saint Louis Ball Room, on which occasion they will perform several pieces of Music. This band [one of the first if not the very first concert band in New Orleans] is well organized and so deservedly popular, that they have obtained a remarkable celebrity."[204] Mr. Templeton presented his popular entertainment of Irish songs at Armory Hall on February 27 and March 4. His voice was not too good, perhaps because of a cold.[205]

During March the German Philharmonic Society prepared its first regular symphonic concert, which was given on March 30 at Armory Hall. There had been orchestral concerts in the city before this, but the seriousness of this particular enterprise sowed the seeds of what was to become, nearly a decade later, the first full orchestral season in New Orleans. The orchestra was under the direction of William Furst, whose activities so far had been mostly with choral music, and also Theodore Schoenheit. There were thirty-six musicians "who have for several months been assiduously engaged in studying and practicing." Furst sought out the best musicians, regardless of whether they were German. The music on the program was mostly German. It consisted of Beethoven's *Egmont* Overture (which had been performed before in intermèdes) and a complete Symphony No. 5 (probably the first time in New Orleans), Weber's overtures to *Der Freischütz* and *Oberon* (old favorites), a De Bériot violin concerto performed by Mr. A. Waldauer, and two airs sung by Mr. R. Santini—one of the airs composed by Furst. Although the ensemble was not perfect and things were not always precise, nonetheless it was a stirring concert and a triumph for the German Philharmonic Society.[206]

Other concerts in spring began with a vocal recital by James Valentine on March 18, 1846, at Armory Hall. He "has a powerful, pure and melodious voice." The concert was well attended.[207] On April 7, English pianist Leopold de Meyer arrived in New Orleans with the intention of giving a series of concerts. He had made a sensation everywhere else in America, and now he set out to conquer New Orleans. His first grand concert was on April 16 at Armory Hall with the singer Orlando Guilmette. Guilmette, first baritone of the Philharmonic Society of New York and Philadelphia, had made his New Orleans debut a week earlier, on April 9, in a grand vocal and instrumental concert at Armory Hall.[208] On April 16, among other things, Meyer improvised on various melodies on two Erard pianos, and he assaulted the audience with his loud, vigorous playing.[209] The second concert, April 20, again with Guilmette, was at the Saint Louis Exchange Concert Room. It had the same kind of program as on April 16.[210] The three remaining programs moved from the Saint Louis Ball Room (April 20) to Armory Hall (April 27) and to the Saint Charles Theatre (May 9), all again with Guilmette. The programs were much the same, except that on the last one Guilmette sang Henry Russell's "The Maniac" and "The Inch Cape Bell." The fifth concert had been scheduled for May 6, but since the Mexican War broke out, it was postponed three days and the proceeds from the concert went to the Louisiana soldiers who had been sent to Texas. Unfortunately, war fever made the attendance poor.[211] The only other known concert in the month was on April 12 when a mass by Guiraud was chanted at Saint Patrick's Church.[212] It was performed by both amateurs and professionals and was pleasing to the layperson's ear.

On May 2 at the Théâtre d'Orléans there was a benefit for the singer M Arnaud, but the main event was the world premier of a new opera—*Agatha*—by Curto.[213] From May 18 to 22 the Sloman family presented three concerts at the Saint Charles Theatre. The family consisted of Miss Anne Sloman (piano), Miss E. Sloman (harp), and Mr. Sloman (voice). They performed works of Rossini, Weber, Mozart, Bellini, Bishop, and Balfé. Sadly, the girls were not appreciated by New Orleans audiences.[214] From May 15 to 28, however, most attention in the city was focused on the Italian Opera at the American Theatre, where Gabici was conducting "an excellent orchestra" accompanying singers and a chorus. The repertory included *I Capuleti e i Montecchi* and *Norma*. At the last performance (*Norma*) on May 28, Gabici's *Grande Cantate Patriotique, en l'Honneur de la Glorieuse Victoire Remportée le 8 et le 9 de ce Mois par l'Armée Américaine Commandée par le Général Taylor . . . Chantée par Tous les Membres de la Compagnie Italienne* had its premiere.[215]

The primary activity in the fall was dancing, and there were several orchestras that were especially good. From October to May, M H. E. Lehmann, artist of the Théâtre d'Orléans, together with M Cobini, well-known conductor, provided small or large orchestras or military bands as the occasion dictated.[216] Likewise, for the dances every Tuesday, Thursday, and Saturday at the Globe Ball Room (Saint Claude and Saint Peter streets) from October to May, *The Bee* reported, "The Orchestra will be composed of the most superior artists in the city."[217] M F.A. Legendre, chef d'orchestra of the Salle Saint Louis and of the Washington Bataillon was available for soirees, balls, weddings, reunions, and other events. At the Salle de Bal, reached by the Pontchartrain Railroad, a bal paré et masque was held every Wednesday and Sunday for whites, and for quarteronnes every Tuesday, Thursday, and Saturday. According to *L'Abeille*, "A superb orchestra has been engaged, and there will be an excellent restaurant and a well-garnished buffet."[218] While Davis was in France rounding up his troupe for the upcoming French Opera season, the ballet season opened on November 4 at the Théâtre d'Orléans. The orchestra was involved not only in accompanying the ballet but also in playing two overtures between the sections of the ballet as intermèdes.[219] Of course, intermèdes continued at the Saint Charles Theatre, where Gabici was now in charge.[220]

The concert season for the first half of 1847 began on February 3 with the return of Leopold de Meyer, pianist, joined by Joseph Burke, the American violinist, at Armory Hall. It was reported that "Burke [was] a violinist of infinite skill, sweetness and artistic merit . . . [t]hough he has not an Italian name." They were also assisted by Hammarskold and Theodore de la Hache.[221] Featured was the Grand Duo from *William Tell*. Despite the advertisement that this was to be the first of a series of concerts, de Meyer's audience must have disappeared when, nineteen days later, a pianist of much greater fame started his series of concerts in New Orleans.

This was Henri Herz (1803–88), who arrived in New Orleans on February 8 with the violinist Camillo Sivori (1815–94) after appearing in Columbus, Charleston, and Savannah.[222] Sivori sometimes played without Herz, sometimes with him. While Herz lingered in Mobile on February 10, Sivori gave his first grand concert at the Théâtre d'Orléans, accompanied by the orchestra. He played his own Concerto in A Major, Paganini's Variations on *The Prayer from Moses,* and Paganini's *Carnaval de Venise.* The orchestra played the Overture to Auber's *Cheval de Bronze* and to Rossini's *La Pie Voleuse.* The two local opera singers Cassini and Dubreuil also took part. As an added feature, Sivori, Paganini's only pupil, was playing on Paganini's own violin.[223] The critic thought Sivori greater by far than Ole Bull, and second, perhaps, only to Vieuxtemps. For his second concert, on February 13, Sivori performed Paganini's Grand Concerto Fantastique in B Minor, the *Prayer of Moses* on one string, and Paganini's *Molenara,* a duet played on one violin. The orchestra performed two overtures (to *Gustave* by Auber and the other unnamed). Dubreuil, Cassini, and Olivier sang airs. Before the concert the one-act vaudeville *Le Caporal et la Payse* was performed.[224]

Henri Herz made his New Orleans debut on Monday, February 22, 1847, at the Saint Louis Hotel Concert Room. He appeared with orchestral accompaniment, assisted by Cassini and Fourmestreau (oboist), with Norès accompanying, presumably, the latter two. Herz played several of his own works with orchestra (Concerto No. 2, *La Violette,* and Fantaisie and Variations on a Trio from the *Le Pré aux Clercs)* and one piano solo (*Fantaisie Brillante* on airs from *Lucia di Lammermoor*).[225] His second grand concert, on February 24, was at Armory Hall, but apparently without orchestral accompaniment. This time he was assisted by the singers Cassini, August Brocard, and Curto, with Norès accompanying on the piano. Herz played more of his own compositions.[226] Once Sivori and Herz had each given one "solo" concert, they began to dovetail their concerts. Sivori's third, fourth, and fifth concerts were on February 26, March 3, and March 6, while Herz's third concert was on March 1 and the fourth on March 5.[227] Herz originally planned to give only two concerts in New Orleans, but probably because he was so warmly and knowingly received by an audience that far exceeded his expectations on his American tour, he agreed to play more. He was very happy in New Orleans, where he could again speak French: "I believed myself almost in France itself when I was in the French quarter of New Orleans. Indeed that quarter is like a portion of France which has succeeded in avoiding being swallowed up in the rushing torrent of American civilization."[228]

Finally on March 12 and 17, Sivori and Herz gave two joint recitals, at Armory hall and the Saint Louis Hotel, with Hammarskold singing and Norès accompanying on March 12 and the amateur Mme L. in a duet with Herz on March 17.[229] Mme L.'s appearance broke social taboos for amateur instrumentalists in that she performed on a public stage with a man; which was worse, that she appeared on the stage at all or that she appeared there with a man, is impossible to tell.[230] The two visiting artists were not finished, however. They played a few selections together in an intermède after a performance of Auber's opera *La Sirene* at the Théâtre d'Orléans on March 21, and on the following Wednesday, March 24, they performed a full concert at the armory with Hammarskold and Norès. The program ended with the Overture to *William Tell* performed by sixteen pianists (Herz, Norès, and fourteen men and women from New Orleans) on eight pianos.[231] Yet this was only a warm-up. They gave another dual concert on March 30—a grand concert spiritual—and after returning from some concerts in Mobile, they appeared together on three more occasions: April 8, 9, and 12.[232] All told, Sivori and Herz performed in New Orleans on seventeen concerts in about six weeks.

There were other concerts this spring. Rossini's *Stabat Mater* with orchestra was the feature in a concert on March 30, 1847, at the Théâtre d'Orléans. The program also included the Overture to *Oberon*.[233] On April 14, there was a concert dedicating a new organ at Christ Church on Canal Street. The organist was F. F. Mueller and the orchestral leader Curto.[234] Two days later Neukomm's *Oratorio of David* was performed by the women of Christ Church and amateurs to raise money for the organ. Once again Curto led an orchestra, and F. F. Mueller played the organ.[235] Neukomm's oratorio was repeated on Monday, May 10, at Rev. Clapp's Church by the Society of Sacred Music, Curto as leader and Mueller organist. No orchestra was mentioned.[236] The benefit for Eugene Prévost at the Théâtre d'Orléans on April 29 included works by Prévost dedicated to General Zachary Taylor, which he conducted in a mini-concert between the second and third acts of a performance of *Les Huguenots,* and at the end of May at Théâtre d'Orléans, Fourmestreau played an oboe solo during a performance of his new opera *Le Capitaine May et le General La Vega*.[237]

Eighteen forty-seven was, so far, the worst year in the history of yellow fever in New Orleans. Nearly three thousand persons died, more than in any other epidemic in the city until then. The summer and early fall were the high periods for the disease because of the heat and humidity. As a result, ordinary concerts were out of the question. Instead, concerts were organized largely around the Howard Association, an organization designed to give aid to victims of epidemics. On September 9, 1847, C. Hopf led the Yagers Allemands in a concert to raise money for the Société Allemande and the Howard Association.[238] On October 13 and 20 and November 9, the Philharmonic Society of New Orleans under the direction of M Lehmann gave benefit concerts for the Howard Association. On the first one, at Armory Hall, the program consisted of overtures by Rossini (*William Tell*) and Auber (*La Sirene*); excerpts from operas by Halévy, Donizetti, and Auber; national airs by De Lille; choruses; and the *Grand Danse Infernale* by Lehmann (with the accompaniment of pistols, raras, hootings, gongs, tamtams, chains, castanets, whistlings, rattles, six bells, and so forth). The second concert, at the Théâtre d'Orléans, was longer but otherwise similar to the first, including *Grand Danse Infernale* by Lehmann (but with a light show: fires of red, white, and so forth). The third concert by the Howard Society and the Philharmonic Society of New Orleans, again at the Théâtre d'Orléans, was in honor of Lehmann, who worked so hard to popularize music in the city. The ensemble had fifty wind players and had music by Prévost and La Hache as well as much of what was in the other two programs, including the *Grande Danse Infernale,* dedicated to members of the Howard Association.[239]

By November the pestilence had subsided, and a concert season as well as the opera began.[240] On November 13 the flutist Carrière organized a grand vocal and instrumental concert at the Salle de Bal de la Bourse Saint-Louis to benefit the orphans, including many whose parents had died in the epidemic. Carrière, a graduate of the Paris Conservatoire and now a member of the Théâtre d'Orléans Orchestra, was accompanied by an orchestra under Gabici. The orchestra played two overtures and accompanied Carrière, in Mayseder's Opus 40, as well as Gabici's eleven-year-old pupil Gerber. Also, an amateur pianist, Madame D., accompanied Carrière and played a solo, and an amateur woman sang an aria and a romance accompanied by Norès.[241] On December 3, in honor of the arrival of General Zachary Taylor in New Orleans, there was a special spectacle at the Théâtre d'Orléans featuring patriotic airs, *Marche du Gen. Taylor* (E. Prévost), another work by Prévost, a cantata by "M . . ." (citizen of New Orleans), and the first act of *La Dame Blanche.* The theater orchestra at this point had a new first violinist, M Gilles. The evening began with a two-act vaudeville.[242]

The first half of 1848 witnessed again a visitor whose concerts were important events for the city. In this case it was the mezzo soprano Madame Ablamowicz, whose first of five concerts was on January 27 at Armory Hall. She sang Italian cavatinas (Bellini, Donizetti, Verdi, and so forth) and Irish and Scottish ballads with the assistance of Carrière, Krollman (violinist), and Mueller (pianist). The critic of *The Bee/L'Abeille* found her voice sweeter, purer, and more exquisite than that of anyone else heard in New Orleans except Cinti-Damoreau and Caradori Allan.[243] Her second concert, with the assistance of Carrière, young Gerber (Gabici's student, now age fourteen), and Mueller, was on February 1 and the third on February 4 before her advertised departure for

Mobile and Havana. However, she did not leave New Orleans, for she sang two additional concerts in the Saint Louis Ball Room on February 8 and 10 and cancelled a third because of the illness of one of her children. The programs were much the same.[244]

There were two other concerts in January. On January 13 at Armory Hall, Mlle Brighta gave a vocal concert with Ottilie Wolf, Mlle C. M. Hitchcock, Signor Brighta Jr., and Signor Bibera, accompanied by Norès on the piano. On January 30 at noon, the Société Musicale of Armory Hall presented a wind band of thirty-six instruments in a benefit. The best composers were represented: Bellini, Donizetti, Weber, Mozart, and so forth.[245] In February there was one additional concert, that by P. Kroll in a concert of valses, quadrilles, galops, and marches composed by himself. It took place on Sunday, January 27, at the Saint Louis Ball Room and involved Kroll's Catalan Company Band, "one of the finest and most complete we have ever heard," according to *L'Abeille*.[246] Just before Mardi Gras (which fell on March 7, 1848), Mr. Wall, the blind Irish harpist, gave a concert at Armory Hall, assisted by a number of artists (Mueller and La Hache) and a comedian. A week after Mardi Gras he gave a second concert.[247]

In April, however, there were many concerts, most provided by just two groups. The first was the Orchester de Steyermarkische (more properly, Steyermarkische Orchester), composed of nineteen performers, which gave six concerts on April 4, 6, 8, 10, 11, and 12 at Armory Hall. Refugees from the German Revolution of 1848, many of the orchestra's members remained in the United States where they joined various musical societies, including the Mendelssohn Club of Boston. They mixed serious compositions with lighter ones by Auber, Aubert, Beethoven (*Egmont* Overture), Curant, Czepek, Donizetti, Fischer, Gung'l, Halévy, Hérold, Kallewoda, Labitzky, Lanner, Lands, Liszt, Meyerbeer, Morrelli, Strauss, E. Titl, Walther, and Weber.[248] The second group centered on the violinist Arditi with the pianist Desvernine and the string bassist Botesini. They arrived in New Orleans on April 5 and gave concerts on April 12, 17, and 28. There was a small turnout for the first concert at Théâtre d'Orléans, possibly because the critic stated that Arditi was not as good as Vieuxtemps and Sivori, but still played well. The other two concerts were moved to Saint Louis Hall.[249] The first concert included an orchestra, while in the other two the three artists performed chamber music, mostly arrangements from opera themes. Desvernine performed solo piano works by Thalberg and Liszt as well. The only other event in April was the premiere of a three-part oratorio, *Josué ou la Prise de Jéricho* by Prévost, at the Théâtre d'Orléans on April 6 as part of a benefit for Prévost, the much-admired conductor at that theater.[250]

The main attractions in May 1848 were the two concerts by Anna Bishop (of San Carlo, Naples) at Armory Hall on May 2 and 9. She was supposed to sing in New Orleans in March, but her appearances had to be postponed because she was in Mobile and made such a hit there that they demanded she stay longer. She sang some opera arias and songs and was assisted by Signor Roclisa, harpist.[251] Operas continued to the end of the month. During the summer there was a new venue for musicians to earn a living. "The ice cream parlor at Armory Hall has hired a splendid band, who will perform all the latest music—and being prepared with the richest and best favored CREAMS, SHERBERTS, etc."[252]

The fall of 1848 was again a time for dancing and reorganization of the French Opera. By October 5, Davis, in France, had completed hiring the troupe for the opera. He arrived back in New Orleans with the group on November 7, and the French Opera season opened with *La Favorite* on Tuesday, November 14.[253] It was a national election year, and on November 4, there was a parade for Zachary Taylor and Millard Fillmore in New Orleans, with clubs participating and each club supplying its own music.[254] Later, on November 21, there was a benefit at Armory Hall for Mr. Pope Oldham, president of the Glee Club, apparently a collection of separate singing clubs that helped in the Taylor presidential campaign.

The most significant event for the concert life of New Orleans this fall, however, passed almost unnoticed and was certainly not recognized at the time as such an important event. On November 16, 1848, it was reported in *L'Abeille* that "Mr. and Mrs. Collignon arrived several days ago in New Orleans. He is an eminent pianist, but he had to flee Paris after the 1848 revolution. Mrs. Collignon is equally talented."[255] Over the next three decades Gustave Collignon and his family would dominate all aspects of concert life in New Orleans and bring the city to a quality level that it has rarely equaled since. The first appearance of Collignon on a concert program in New Orleans occurred on December 4, 1848, when he performed with Curto and others. The program included duets: piano four hands, flute plus piano, and harp plus piano.[256]

The first half of 1849 began inauspiciously with only one known concert. On January 28, the Philharmonic Society gave a concert at Salle Washington to benefit orphans. The program has not been found. Then in March the season began in earnest with a great many concerts. Apparently the Steyermarkische Orchester was back in town and gave a concert at the Commercial Exchange on March 6. Francis Eziha, violinist, performed a De Bériot concerto and several other works, and the violoncellist Jungnickel performed a piece by Lee.[257]

That very day Maurice Strakosch (1825–87), billed as pianist to the emperor of Russia, arrived in New Orleans to begin a series of concerts. His debut at

Armory Hall on March 9 was the first of many performances which Strakosch was to give in the city over the next several decades, including not only playing piano but also featuring his conducting and playing in conjunction with other performers. During his first visit to the city he gave five concerts. On March 9 he was assisted by Cassini and M Thiedepape, and M Norès accompanied on the piano. The following Monday, March 12, he gave his second concert, this time at Saint Louis Hall. On this second program he was alone and performed only his own compositions: *Souvenir de Jenny Lind* based on airs from *Sonnambula, La Sylphide,* Grand Caprice from *Lucrèce Borgia, La Nayade* Etude, followed by *The Flirtation Polka* (composed for this concert), and Grande Fantaisie Dramatique on motifs from *Lucia di Lammermoor*.[258] Strakosch's reputation was not yet established, so attendance was small, but the critic placed him among the most renowned of the time. For his remaining three concerts Strakosch was back at the armory, where he was joined not only by Cassini and Faby but also, on the fourth concert on March 23, by Mme T. Cailly, who was in the city giving her own series of concerts, and on the fourth and fifth concerts (the last on March 30) by an orchestra of fifty musicians. On March 30 he played his spectacular composition *Vesuvius* (in four tableaux) for the first time in New Orleans. As far as we can tell, Strakosch played only his own compositions.[259]

Meanwhile, Mme Cailly gave her first concert in Armory Hall on Wednesday, March 14, to a large and appreciative audience. In his review *The Bee* critic described her voice as "a soprano of fair, average power, considerable compass, moderate flexibility, pure intonation and remarkable even in its range. It is a voice that will enable a tasteful singer to execute any music within the reach of a soprano, but that cannot attain the very highest qualities of excellence, because it is deficient in metallic resonance and in fullness of volume. Mad. T. Cailly manages her vocal powers with consummate skill, and has attained a facility of execution we have rarely seen equaled."[260]

She was a learned singer, a graduate of the Paris Conservatoire, but with some faults. Schmidt was the piano accompanist, and Cailly was assisted on the program by Carrière and the young violinist Gerber (Gabici's pupil). Strakosch and Cailly teamed up for her second appearance, on March 23, at Armory Hall; the program is unknown. A few weeks later, on April 13, Cailly gave her third concert, a grande soiree musicale, at the Saint Louis Hotel. Her associates were Mme Faby, Eugène Chassaignac, V. Gerber, and Norès. She sang solos by Meyerbeer, Auber, Grisar, and Donizetti, and the others joined her in duets and had their own solos; Gerber played a piece by De Bériot.[261] Cailly returned to Armory Hall on April 25 for her fourth concert and to the Saint Louis Hotel for her fifth concert on May 2, and her final performance, on Friday, May 4, was at the American Theatre with J. Messmer, Mr. and Mrs. J. S. Charles, Henry C. Page, Gabici, Chassaignac, and a large orchestra to raise money for the Firemen's Charitable Association.[262]

There were several other concerts that spring as well. Mr. Wilson of London performed four concerts of Scottish songs and ballads at Armory Hall. The first was on Tuesday, March 20, the second on Thursday, March 22, the third on Tuesday, March 27, and the fourth on Wednesday, March 28, in which he expanded his repertory to include English, Irish, and opera tunes as well.[263] On May 2, Gabici's concert for himself and his fifteen-year-old pupil V. Gerber was shared with Cailly (her fifth concert). The program included among various pieces "one of the prettiest symphonies of Beethoven" played by the orchestra.[264]

The fall of 1849 was devoted primarily to dance, both ballet at the Théâtre d'Orléans and social dancing at the various local halls. Davis was in Europe recruiting for the opera and arrived back in New Orleans for the opening in November. The German Theatre opened on November 18 for a few performances of German dramas. Meanwhile there was a new theater, Théâtre des Variété de Placide, Gravier Street, which opened on December 7, with Gabici as leader of the orchestra and composer of an overture for orchestra.[265] Aside from three evenings of Alpine songs sung by a family of Tyrolese singers who performed for the German community (December 9, 13, and 16), there were only two concerts during the fall of 1849. The first was a grand concert at the Saint Louis Ball Room on Friday evening, November 9. The performers were Mr. Reisinger accompanied by the Théâtre d'Orléans Orchestra. The program was in three parts: an overture by Weber (orchestra), *Prière* by Paganini (Reisinger), *Der Traum* by Reisinger (Reisinger), the Overture to *Norma* by Bellini (orchestra), *Souvenir de Suisse* by Reisinger (Reisinger), the finale from *Lucia di Lammermoor* (orchestra), *Souvenir de Bellini* by Artôt (Reisinger), *Souvenir de l'Amerique* by Vieuxtemps (Reisinger), *Grand Potpouri* (orchestra), and *Grand Carnival de Milan* by Reisinger (Reisinger).[266] The second fall concert was by Fräulein Amalie Schönbrunner, a pianist from the conservatory in Vienna, who performed at Armory Hall on Friday evening, December 21, in a grand instrumental and vocal concert aimed at the German-speaking population. She was assisted by a select orchestra of German residents in New Orleans, a male and female singer, the latter of whom was a native of New Orleans, a clarinetist, and a violoncellist. Prior to her public concert she played privately for some very knowledgeable musicians, who were so enthusiastic that they let the public know that they would be hearing someone destined to become famous.[267] A large audience turned out.

The decade ended with a concert and ball by the German Male Song Society (Deutsche Männer-Gesang-Verein) on Monday, December 31, at 8 p.m. at the Théâtre d'Orléans. It probably was a concert of very light music, since the main attraction was the dancing by members of the German community. The only artistic activity that exceeded concert music and opera in popularity was their sister art, ballroom dancing, yet even here, the music for the dance now was performed by an ever-increasing population of professional musicians who were there in New Orleans because of the opera and the concert life.

The city was now ready for its most successful decade in concert music. Its musical establishments had been built, its professional musicians were better and more numerous, and the audience was enthusiastic for the best that musical art could provide.

3

The Great Years
1850–1860

The 1850s were the most impressive years in the history of concert music in New Orleans. Not only were there more concerts than heretofore, but the quality of the concerts was, in most instances, very high. Local musicians spearheaded the concert life, but stimuli came from the outside as well, including new young virtuosi and returning masters. All this came at a time when the city had great opera seasons not only at the Théâtre d'Orléans, usually in French, but substantial English, German, and Italian opera companies as well.

The first concert of 1850 took place on Friday evening, January 4, at Exchange Hall. It was a joint recital by Eliza Biscaccianti, an American soprano who had sung in Naples, Milan, New York, Boston, and Philadelphia, and Maurice Strakosch, who had recently appeared as a concert pianist in New Orleans. They were joined by the local opera singer Cassini and the violoncellist Mr. Biscaccianti. The program consisted of Italian and English songs, duets, works by Strakosch, and so on (including an aria from *Giovanni d'Arco* by Verdi sung by Biscaccianti and one from *I Puritani* by Bellini sung by Cassini).[1] They gave their second and third concerts on January 7 and 9 with the same associates and in a similar program,[2] and continued in a similar vein in their fourth and fifth concerts on January 11 and 14 but with the singer Mr. T. Bishop joining in on the last one.[3]

Other concerts continued during the rest of the month. There was a grand concert at Lyceum Hall on January 16 to benefit the libraries of the public schools. A complete orchestra accompanied the singers, Miss Malone, Mr. T. Bishop, Mrs. C. Howard, and Miss Schoenbrunner.[4] On January 19 Miss Augusta Victoria and Miss Appolinie gave a concert at Lyceum Hall, together with eminent artists.[5] In the middle of the next month (Wednesday, February 20) the New York Italian Opera Company, en route to Mexico, stopped in New

Orleans long enough to give a concert at Lyceum Hall. They sang opera selections from works by Verdi, Rossini, Bellini, Mercadante, and Donizetti.[6] After the Carnival break, two other traveling opera stars, Mr. and Mrs. Leati, gave a concert in the city on March 14 at Histrionic Hall. It was billed as a grand operatic soiree, with costumes and an orchestra, and they were assisted by "vocal and instrumental members of the Histrionic Association, who have kindly tendered their valuable services."[7] They sang some songs and then selections from *Lucia di Lammermoor.*

There was a grand vocal and instrumental concert on April 9, given by the young Désiré Delcroix, a pianist born in Louisiana. This was a benefit before he went to Paris to study. The program consisted of the Overture to *Cheval de Bronze* by Auber (orchestra), the first movement of a piano concerto by Hummel (Delcroix, accompanied by orchestra), a vocal duet, the Overture to *Fra Diavolo* by Auber (orchestra), and a grand air du concert (Delcroix accompanied by orchestra).[8] The next evening Delcroix was back, at Lyceum Hall, Lafayette Square, assisted by the band of the French Theatre (Orchestra of the Théâtre d'Orléans) led by Mr. Berton, formerly of the French Opera. This time he was joined by Carrière, first flutist of the Théâtre d'Orléans, and the eminent artists Chassaignac, Gerber, and Norès.[9] In addition, on April 19 the pianist-violinist-composer William Vincent Wallace returned to the city to give a concert at Lyceum Hall. He performed on the piano his Grande Fantasie to Maritana, the nocturne *Zephyr,* a *Tarantelle di Bravoura,* and on the violin Variations on Opera Themes by Bellini and a new *Fantasie de Concert* on the Irish melody "'Tis the Last Rose of Summer" (composed just for this concert). He was assisted by vocalists and a strong orchestra.[10]

Strakosch either remained in New Orleans the entire spring or returned in time to perform several concerts in May. He teamed up with Wallace at Lyceum Hall on May 1 in a program that included the singer Mme Cassini (singing arias and "The Pearl of Andalousia") and Norès as piano accompanist.[11] Strakosch played some of his own works and with Wallace two grand duos (one by Strakosch based on music by Halévy and the other by Thalberg on airs from *Norma*). Next, both Strakosch and Wallace announced a "final" concert on Friday, May 10, 1850, in Lyceum Hall. As usual each played his own works; in addition, by popular request, the two performed together the Grand Duo for two pianos by Wallace. Strakosch's Grand Overture based on tunes from *Zampa,* executed by sixteen of the most distinguished men and women and amateur artists of New Orleans, concluded the program.[12] As so often happened, however, Strakosch and Wallace continued to perform after their announced "final" concert, no doubt owing to the enthusiastic reception they had by the people of the city. So on May 17 they performed again at Lyceum Hall. Strakosch played not only his own pieces but also Thalberg's Grande Fantasie on Airs of *La Muette*, a Chopin nocturne, and some of Mendelssohn's *Songs Without Words*. Wallace, in turn, played both violin and piano. Cassini sang "Casta Diva" and other works.[13] On Monday, May 20, they participated in a farewell concert for Eugène Prévost at the Théâtre d'Orléans, along with Rosa Dévries, Bessin, Duluc, Corradi, Graat, Carrière, Menehand, Léon Prévost (son of Eugène), and the theater orchestra. The orchestra played overtures by both Eugène and Léon Prévost. Wallace performed a fantasia for violin on airs of Bellini, and Strakosch played his fantasia on themes from *Lucia di Lammermoor*. The singers sang arias by Labarre, Donizetti, Meyerbeer, Weber, and others.[14] In between Carrière played a flute solo. The concert ended with a performance of Beethoven's *Coriolan* Overture. And on May 25 Strakosch performed three of his own works during an intermède at the Saint Charles Theatre—a grand intermède which was primarily devoted to romances (one by Chassaignac on words by Placide Canonge) sung by Mme Galinier.[15]

Yet another farewell concert was on Thursday, May 23, by Mmes Dévries and Bessin and M Bessin, who were also about to leave for Europe. It was held in Lyceum Hall and included Strakosch, the great Hungarian violinist Eduard Remenyi, and Bianchi as well as Léon Prévost. This time there was no orchestra, so Léon Prévost accompanied everyone on the piano. The singers sang arias by Verdi, Meyerbeer, Grétry, Auber, and Bellini, while Bianchi played a bassoon arrangement, Remenyi played Adagio Spianato by Ernst (with his own cadenza), and Strakosch played his own fantasia (which one is not indicated).[16] For his part, Remenyi gave a grand concert the next evening, May 24, at Commercial Hall, where he played a Vieuxtemps violin concerto, an arrangement of "Casta Diva" for one string, his own *Cradle Song, Carnival de Venice* by Paganini, and his own Grand Variations de Bravoure on National Airs.[17] The orchestra, conducted by Mr. Hoeffner, played two unnamed overtures, a potpourri on arias from *The Daughter of the Regiment*, and another fantasia. There were no other soloists.

The season lingered on into July with a series of grand subscription concerts at the Commercial Hall. There the orchestra under Hoeffner, which had accompanied Remenyi, played every Thursday from late April to July 6. There is no indication of who played in the orchestra or what the programs were, but probably the musicians were drawn from the theater orchestras. Another orchestra—the Amateur Orchestra of the Louisiana Histrionic Association—gave two concerts, one on June 14 at the Saint Louis Ball Room to benefit the

Firemen's Charitable Association, the other at the Histrionic Association building at 81 Gravier on July 6. In the first case some notable local professionals participated: Carrière, Chassaignac, Mrs. Howard, and Mr. and Mrs. Duclos. Among the unnamed amateurs was one who tackled a violin work of De Bériot. The orchestra accompanied and played two overtures and an arrangement by Mr. Meyer of arias from the opera *Delisario*.[18] During the second concert the orchestra performed the Overture to Auber's *Les Diamants de la Couronne*, the *William Tell* Overture, and the March from *Le Prophète* by Meyerbeer. Mr. H. P——a played a grand concerto of De Bériot, Mr. S——r and C——n played a grand duet by C. Herz and Lafont for piano and violin, and the last two were joined by Mr. A——l in the first part of Reissiger's Grand Trio for piano, violin, and violoncello. The only name given was that of Miss Petrie, singer; there were other, unnamed singers and also a flutist.[19]

The fall 1850 season was slow to start up, but the theatrical season was in full bloom. The Booth family was in town during October, including the sixteen-year-old Edwin Booth. Musical events from the East Coast filled the papers in New Orleans. They reported that Dévries, "our distinguished Prima Donna of the Théâtre d'Orléans, made her debut at New York . . . in the character of Norma." The *Evening Post* was lavish in its praise. The papers were continually reporting on Jenny Lind and her concerts in Boston, New York, Philadelphia, and so forth. Efforts were being made to bring her to New Orleans—in February. Mlle Parodi arrived in New York on October 27 and was engaged by Max Maretzek to sing at his New York opera that winter.[20] She made her debut on November 14 in New York and was called the rival of Jenny Lind. She would eventually sing concerts in New Orleans. Slowly the important members of the city's concert life were returning from spending the hot months up north. Collignon, for example, returned to New Orleans on October 17 and resumed teaching music to his many students.[21]

The earliest concert this fall seems to have been on Sunday, October 20. In a benefit for orphans at Sainte Theresa's Church, Curto sang along with his choristers his own mass. Some did not like his singing, but the reviewer (Jacques de R) was particularly pleased with his rendition of the Gloria, and thought the Benedictus the strongest part of the composition.[22] Another sacred concert was given on Friday, November 15, with the performance of Rossini's *Stabat Mater* at Saint Patrick's Church to raise money for a "public school" (actually, Catholic school).[23] The performance was repeated on November 20, this time to assist the orphans of the Third Municipality. In an unusual sign of cooperation between performing institutions, M Placide, the director of the Varieties Theater, delayed the start of his production on November 20 so that his concertmaster, Gabici, would have time to conduct the Rossini work at Saint Patrick's Church and then hurry over to his theater.[24] Meanwhile dances were occurring on a regular basis with orchestras made up of leading professional performers, and intermèdes were a part of many theatrical evenings. The Théâtre des Variétés featured an intermède musical between two other performances on November 27 and 30. Finally, on Friday, November 29, the opera season at the Théâtre d'Orléans began a week late.[25]

The spring season of 1851 was as exciting as the fall was dull. It began on January 8 with a benefit for orphans at Armory Hall. There were twenty-four women and twenty-six men in an amateur chorus which had rehearsed for two months. The chorus and accompanying orchestra were conducted by Curto. The program consisted of the Overture to *Sémiramide* (orchestra), a duet from *Lucia di Lammermoor*, the "Prayer" from Méhul's *Joseph*, the sextet from *Lucia*, the grand aria from *Robert le Diable*, the Overture to *William Tell*, the chorus and grand aria from *Jérusalem*, the duet from *Anna Bolena*, and the "Sermon" from *Athalie* by Curto.[26]

Then Jenny Lind came to New Orleans and made an impression that was to remain imprinted on the minds of opera fans for the rest of the century and beyond. She gave thirteen concerts over the span of four weeks, from February 10 to March 8, all in the Saint Charles Theatre. For the series Lind brought the nucleus of an orchestra from New York and relied on professional players from New Orleans to fill it out.[27] The conductor was usually M Benedict, but Joseph Burke also conducted. While Lind included many opera arias on her programs, she also included some lighter pieces, among which was the extraordinarily popular "Home Sweet Home" by Bishop on five programs (the third, fifth, sixth, eleventh, and thirteenth). She also sang segments from the oratorios *Creation* (Haydn) and *Messiah* (Handel), and a sprinkling of Swedish folk songs. Included on the first program were the overtures to Auber's *Masaniello* and *Les Diamants de la Couronne*, Burke playing *Rondo Russe* by De Bériot, and the orchestra playing Mendelssohn's Wedding March from *A Midsummer Night's Dream*. This concert lasted until very late in the evening, but that did not dampen the enthusiasm of the more than four thousand persons who crowded in to hear her.[28] Subsequent performances were on February 12, 14, 15, 17, 19, 21, 22, and 28, March 3, 5, 7, and 8. During the series the orchestra played two overtures per concert by Rossini (*La Gazza Ladra, Cheval de Bronze, William Tell, L'Italiana in Algeri*), Auber (*Masaniello, Les Diamants de la Couronne, Gustave, Fra Diavolo, Le Domino Noir, Zanetta, Le Serment, La Fiancée,* and *Le Dieu et la Bayadère*),

Beethoven (*Egmont, Creatures of Prometheus*), Boieldieu (*La Dame Blanche, Jean de Paris*), Benedict, Mozart (*The Magic Flute, Don Giovanni*), Weber (*Oberon*), Donizetti (*The Daughter of the Regiment*), and Hérold (*Zampa*), and the Mendelssohn *Wedding March* and a march by Benedict. Dresher performed the Berr Clarinet Concerto on February 22, and a flutist and a horn soloist replaced the violin and clarinet with appropriate works on some occasions.

The spring season was not yet over. Maurice Strakosch returned to the city with his new wife, the soprano Amalia Patti (1831–1915), and with the soprano Theresa Parodi,[29] who, as one of the world's foremost interpreters of the roles of *Norma* and *Lucrezia Borgia* at the time, was the main feature of their concerts beginning on April 25, 1851. Parodi and her entourage arrived in New Orleans around April 21. They stayed at the Saint Louis Hotel, and at 11:00 on the night of their arrival, a group of Italians serenaded her.[30] Parodi's first concert, with Amalia, Maurice Strakosch, Miska Hauser (violinist), Signor Avignone, and a full, "carefully selected orchestra," took place at Lyceum Hall.[31] Parodi sang "Casta Diva" from *Norma*, "Tanti Palpiti" from *Tancredi*, an andante and cabaletta from *Don Giovanni*, and a duet from *Norma* with Amalia. Amalia sang a romance from Donizetti's *Roberto Devereux* and the "Drinking Song" from *Lucrezia Borgia*. Avignone sang a romance from *Ernani*, and Hauser played a fantasia on tunes from *Lucia* and a piece entitled "L'Oiseau sur l'Arbre." The second and third concerts took place on Wednesday, April 30, and Friday, May 2, but now at the larger Saint Charles Theatre. The second concert was similar to the first, but the third dropped Avignone, and Hauser played Bull's Grand Concerto and *Rondo Pastorale* and his own piece.[32] Originally only three concerts were planned, but inevitably, succumbing to the enthusiasm of the audiences in New Orleans, the Parodi–Strakosch–Amalia Patti group gave a fourth concert on May 5.[33] Both Parodi and Amalie stayed long enough for opera performances at the Théâtre d'Orléans from May 14 to 26.[34] They would return several times in the next few years to give more concerts.

There was one concert in spring featuring the violinist Charles Wynen. On March 21, 1851, he gave a grand vocal and instrumental concert at Lyceum Hall with an orchestra conducted by Gabici. Not only did Wynen play the violin; he also played on a strange instrument called the yerowa y soloma (wood and straw instruments).[35] The orchestra played two overtures, Wynen played works by De Bériot, and Groenevelt played his own piano works. For the next two months Wynen was a part of many concerts in the city. Among these was the first of several concerts advertised as Grand Prize Concerts which were associated with an art exhibition at Union Gallery. On Friday, April 4, Mr. Francis Pothonier, a pianist from London, made his debut in New Orleans at a Grand Prize Concert at Armory Hall. He was assisted by Mrs. C. Howard and Mr. Reeves, singers, and Wynen on violin; Mr. M. Hoeffner led "a powerful orchestra of fifty performers." The orchestra played Marschner's Festival Overture and Beethoven's Symphony No. 6 ("never before performed in this city").[36] Another Grand Prize Concert, scheduled for April 23, was cancelled because Wynen was sick.[37] M Galvani of the Galerie de l'Union tried hard to replace the April 23 concert and finally decided on concerts with orchestra at the Saint Charles Theatre from May 5 to 15, 1851.[38]

Usually early May was the end of the concert season in New Orleans owing to the extreme heat and humidity that made playing instruments difficult and sitting in crowded theaters unbearable. But in 1851 the concerts continued into June. On Tuesday, May 27, 1851, Mme and Mr. Leati gave a complimentary concert with Pothonier, Signor Bianchi, and Wynen, at Armory Hall. The couple sang the duet "La Ci Darem" from *Don Giovanni* by Mozart. Wynen played a fantaisie brilliante on the violin and grand variations on the yerowa y soloma. Mrs. Leati sang, among various arias and songs, Gabici's pastoral melody "Il Retorno alla Montagna" with clarinet obbligato, composed expressly for Jenny Lind and sung for the first time in public by Mrs. Leati. Also on the program was a duo concertante for flute and pianoforte performed by an amateur of this city and Signor Bianchi.[39]

The following Friday, May 30, there was a "Great Musical Attraction!" at the Théâtre d'Orléans, subtitled "Grand Festival Concert Vocal and Instrumental, in the Paris, London, Berlin, Vienna Style," for the benefit of M H. E. Lehmann, artist of the Théâtre d'Orléans orchestra and conductor of his own private soirees.[40] Assisted by an orchestra of eighty musicians and all the vocalists of the French Theater, with soloists Mmes Dévries and Fleury-Jolly, and MM Duluc, Génibrel, Scott, Wynen, and Leopold Carrière. Jahn and Lehmann alternated as conductors of the "band." "Mr. Lehmann has taken the greatest care in the choice of all the pieces [of] which his concert is composed, variety, quantity, quality, and he promises to the public of New Orleans an unprecedented soiree. ... N.B. Under no pretext whatever, the Concert will be postponed." Perhaps a concert in the style of the major musical centers of Europe meant a concert that gave more attention to the orchestra than was customary. Usually the orchestra, when present at all, performed an opera overture at the beginning of each half of a concert and then either accompanied a soloist in one or two pieces or vanished altogether. On Lehmann's program, however, the orchestra not only played the customary opening overture of the evening (*Chasse du Jeune Henri* featuring all the horns of the orchestra) but included an overture to a *Stabat Mater* arranged by Mercadante, a grand waltz from *Le Prophète,* a new festival dance (mazurka and ecossaise, composed by Lehmann), a Grand Quadrille National Romain by Musard, and *Le Grand Choeur des Chasseurs,* from *Songe d'une Nuit d'Ete,* by Thomas, arranged for sixty wind instruments by Thomas Schoenheit—all the winds playing on the stage, not in the pit.

The grand vocal and instrumental concert on Monday, June 2, 1851, was given by Carrière, first flute of the Théâtre d'Orléans, at Armory Hall. On this occasion his associates were Dévries and Fleury-Jolly, Génibrel, Graat, Jahn, Wynen, Gilles, and the Théâtre d'Orléans Orchestra.[41] Violinist Jahn performed Vieuxtemps's *Souvenir d'Amerique,* variations on "Yankee Doodle." Génibrel sang the world premiere of *La Derniere Heure d'un Condamne, Scene Lyrique,* with words by Placide Canonge and music by a Creole woman. Carrière played a *Fantaisie et Variations* by Tulou and "The Last Rose of Summer." Wynen played only on his yerowa i soloma. Jahn conducted the orchestra, and Norès played the piano. The singers sang various opera arias and songs. Especially noteworthy on this program was the young Ernest Guiraud fils. According to *L'Abeille*: "The dominant qualities of this young artist are, in our opinion, a very pure taste, nice execution, and good rhythm. He played many difficult passages of his piece in a very brilliant manner."[42] While his parents had performed earlier on concerts in the city, this was probably the first public appearance of Ernest Guiraud, who would later become a musical celebrity in Paris.

The last regular concert of the season was on June 4, 1851, at the Théâtre d'Orléans, with many of the same artists encountered throughout the spring: Dévries, Fleury-Jolly, Génibrel, Wynen, Pothonier, Jahn, Graat, and the orchestra of the Théâtre d'Orléans under Jahn. Wynen played Paganini's *Carnival of Venice* with new variations by himself, Pothonier performed Herz's Grand Concerto in A Major, Fleury-Jolly sang Grand Arias Variations from Auber's *Les Diamants de la Couronne,* with orchestral accompaniment; and Fleury-Jolly and Dévries sang the Grand Duet from *Norma* with orchestral accompaniment. There were other songs and arias as well.[43] Since the opera season, too, was carried into June, intermède concerts were also occurring that late. For example, on Sunday, June 8, *Robert Macaire* in four acts and five tableaux was performed by artists and amateurs at the Théâtre d'Orléans, followed by the vaudeville Elle est Folle. Between the two was an intermède musical.[44]

There were several concerts during the fall 1851 season. On November 8 Carrière inaugurated the season with a vocal and instrumental concert at 124 Saint Louis Street in the Vieux Carré, at the hall of M Faivre, piano manufacturer. He was assisted by Laudumley, Frigerio (harmonium), Fourmestreau, Bachholtz (violinist), and an amateur.[45] On November 22, Fourmestreau gave his own concert, once again in the large hall of M Faivre, piano manufacturer. There was an orchestra of fifty musicians directed by M Jahn, conductor of the Théâtre d'Orléans Orchestra. The orchestra played the overtures to *William Tell* (Rossini) and *Domino Noir* (Auber). Also assisting were singers Graat and amateurs and instrumentalists Grasi, Mayer (in De Bériot's *Le Trémolo*), and Carrière.[46] La Hache gave two performances of the same concert, the second—at the request of certain women—on December 3 (we have no record of the first).[47] The opera season began on December 1, and although the chorus and orchestra were a little shaky, within a week or two they proved to be very precise and a good ensemble.[48] On Sunday, December 7, at the dedication of the newly renovated cathedral, a new mass by Curto had its premier.[49] At the Christmas service on December 25, Fourmestreau conducted a performance of Mozart's Mass No. 12 at Saint Patrick's Church with organ accompaniment by Trust.[50] On Friday, December 26, there was a soiree musicale at the school of Mme Charpeaux, where amateur students performed the Overture from *Jeune Henri*; a duet from *Muette de Portici* for violin and piano; a duet from *Robert le Diable* for violin and piano; a duet from *William Tell* for violin and piano; and a chorus of three parts, *L'Esperance* by Rossini. By the end of the month Edouard Boulanger, a pupil of Chopin, was in New Orleans and was preparing to give concerts in the city.[51]

The first concert of 1852 was a grand vocal and instrumental concert on January 21 at Armory Hall for the benefit of Mr. G. Kuffner, former member of the Théâtre d'Orléans Orchestra who had lost his right hand while shooting a pistol. The theater orchestra, under Jahn, performed the overtures to *Oberon* and *Der Freischütz* by Weber. Charles Bothe (ca. 1821–1902)[52] played a clarinet solo; Jahn played his own Grand Fantasia for violin; E. Guiraud played a grand fantasia on the piano; Fourmestreau played some oboe variations; and the singers Pilot, Génibrel, and Diguet sang arias, a song, and a duet.[53]

One of the most important musical events immediately following the New Year was not a concert but the creation of a new Philharmonic Society headed by Curto and La Hache.[54] Referring to the concerts of Curto on December 7 and La Hache on December 3, the writer for the *Picayune* felt that the city possessed "ample amateur musical talent of good quality, and that our citizens know how to appreciate it." As professionals, Curto and La Hache would be well qualified to direct the society. A month later the society had a constitution and bylaws and was ready to give a concert at Saint Patrick's Cathedral.[55] It was but one of several philharmonic societies that existed during the 1850s in the city (see book I, part I, chapter 3). In May, the Curto–La Hache organization gave three concerts, the first at Lyceum Hall on May 18, the second at Armory Hall on May 20, and the third on May 24, again at the armory. In the first case, the Philharmonic Society under Curto was the chorus in a grand vocal and instrumental concert that also had as participants Jahn (chef d'orchestre of the French Opera), Fourmestreau (first oboe of the French Opera), P. La Hache (organist of the Société Philharmonique), and Trust (harpist of the French Opera). There was no symphonic music but rather, alongside choral music, chamber music, including a trio for oboe, harp, and piano.[56] The chorus consisted of many men and women. Two days later, on May 20, Curto conducted a concert of the Société Philharmonique de la Nouvelle-Orleans at Armory Hall with chorus, soloists, and orchestra. The orchestra was the entire Théâtre d'Orléans Orchestra.[57] The third concert was titled a Grand Complimentary Concert given by the New Orleans Philharmonic Society to their leader, G. Curto. The choruses were executed by sixty men and women, members of the New Orleans Philharmonic Society. The program included (among other things) the overtures to the *Cheval de Bronze* and *Masaniello* by Auber (full orchestra), and it ended with the "Hallelujah" Chorus from Handel's *Messiah*.[58]

Meanwhile, on Friday, February 6, E. Boulanger's long-awaited debut in New Orleans took place in Armory Hall. Boulanger, official pianist to the queen of England, played the first two nocturnes and Étude de Grand Concert (Thalbert), *Le Bananier* (Gottschalk), his own *Polka di Bravura,* a duet on themes from *William Tell* with Jahn on violin (Osborne and De Bériot), and a novelty piece of his own (wherein he put a cloth over the piano keys and played without being able to see the keys). The orchestra, under Jahn, performed the overtures to *Gustave III ou le Bal Masque* by Auber and *Der Freischütz*, as well as the March from Meyerbeer's *Le Prophète*. Fourmestreau and Carrière also had solos.[59] Then on Wednesday, February 11, Signor P. Luciani gave a concert in Lyceum Hall with members of the Théâtre d'Orléans, both vocalists and instrumentalists. It was to benefit the Charitable Association of Pompiers. The orchestra featured a grand concerto by Luciani. Trust played piano accompaniment for various singers of opera arias by Adam, Verdi, Donizetti, and Luciani. There were several amateurs among the singers, plus the professionals Wideman, Graat, Génibrel, Howard, and Paola Baquerti. Fourmestreau and Jahn performed as instrumentalists.[60]

A few days afterward, Catherine Hayes came to town and began a series of six or seven concerts in New Orleans. She had had success singing in northern cities and was accompanied by several German artists as well as by Boulanger in two of her concerts.

Theresa Parodi arrived in New Orleans on April 4, 1852, accompanied by Amalia Patti, Maurice Strakosch, and Miska Hauser (violinist). Since Holy Week was coming up, they were unable to schedule concerts in New Orleans immediately, so they traveled to Mobile for two weeks.[61] Upon their return, Parodi and Patti starred on April 23 in a performance of *Norma* at the Théâtre d'Orléans, with Parodi in the title role and Patti singing Adalgisa. Following that, on April 28 and 30, Parodi and her entire group gave two concerts at the Théâtre d'Orléans, assisted by Signor Arnoldi, tenor of the French Opera. Unusually, each concert was in three parts, with each artist (except Arnoldi) having equal participation. Most of the music was drawn directly from operas or, in the case of the instrumentalists, was based on opera melodies. Hauser and Strakosch played mostly their own works; Hauser also performed a piece by Ernst, a piece by Bull, and the ever-popular *Carnival de Venise* by Paganini.[62]

During this time the Italian Opera Troupe of Max Maretzek was performing at the Varieties Theater, and on Saturday, April 9, they took note of the holiday season by preceding a full operatic performance of Donizetti's *La Favorite* by a performance of a grand chant sacré. With opera singers, chorus, and full orchestra they performed Rossini's *Stabat Mater*.[63] On April 21 an extraordinary concert took place at the New Commercial Exchange on Saint Charles Avenue. It was a vocal and instrumental concert by blind amateurs, who performed solo and in duets. Although the audience inevitably felt pity for the "infirmity" of the performers, the critic hoped that it would recognize their real artistic merits as well.[64] The 1851–52 season came to a close with a single dramatic concert by Mme Anna Bishop. On Friday, May 7, she gave a concert at the Théâtre d'Orléans, with the assistance of Siede (flute) and Braun (violoncello). At first she sang a recitative and aria from *Sonnambula* and a series of popular songs ("The Harp That Once through Tara's Halls," "Comin' thru the Rye," "Gratisa Agimus" by Catani, and "Home Sweet Home"); then she put on costumes and sang a scene from *Norma* and two Mexican pieces.[65]

The fall of 1852 began a year's season that was among the most remarkable in the history of the city. It began on October 19 with a concert given by pianist C. Paulsackel and organist Wohlien in the Salle du Lycée. Billed as a sacred concert, it was really a serious concert of chamber music, including, in part I: a septet (J. N. Hummel), Quartet in C Minor (Beethoven, Opus 18, no. 4); part II: a quintet (Robert Schumann), an octet (Mendelssohn).[66] This was a program of works that were becoming standards in chamber concerts during the middle of the century both in Europe and America, and except for the Hummel they are still today among the most cherished pieces of chamber music. The first orchestral concert occurred nine days later with the dedication of a new performance venue at the Mechanics' Institute. Mechanics' Institute Hall was advertised as a "Concert Hall and Lecture Room," on Phillippa Street between Canal and Common streets. Gabici led the orchestra in at least four works, but no titles or composers are given. There were also speeches and glees.[67] Another new venue—Odd Fellows' Hall—opened a month later, on November 22, 1852, and it soon became the preferred concert hall in the city.[68] That same evening the opera season began at Théâtre d'Orléans with a work by Halévy.[69]

The spring season of 1853 was arguably one of the greatest musical springs that the city of New Orleans has ever experienced. Among a plethora of concert events, it heard its most famous native son returning in glory after conquering Europe, and it heard several singers, among whom was a child destined to be the most famous opera singer ever to have performed in nineteenth-century New Orleans.

The new year began inauspiciously with animal shows at the Variety Theatre and the American Theatre. Lola Montes (or Montez) performed at the American Theatre throughout the month: "Well formed, horrible voice, no actrice," according to *The Bee*.[70] Balls leading to Mardi Gras were now held at Odd Fellows' Hall, with a grand orchestra led by M Ruffier.[71] The most baffling music occurred on February 23 at Dan Rice's Museum with concerts of Chinese songs and instrumental pieces, which the reviewer in *The Bee* simply could not fathom.[72] High culture was served, as usual, by the opera. But late in February things changed. On January 31 newspapers began to announce that Ole Bull was returning to New Orleans in February with Mr. Strakosch playing the piano and Mrs. Strakosch (who had appeared before under her maiden name, Amalia Patti), a singer. Also on the programs was Amalia Patti's very spoiled nine-year-old sister, Adelina Patti. The entourage arrived in the city on February 21 and gave the first of six concerts on February 26.[73] This was to be the first of many performances in the city by Adelina, who soon became the city's most highly regarded concert and opera singer.

All the concerts were at Odd Fellows' Hall and were part of a series billed as "Ole Bull's Farewell Concerts in America." As so often happens in musical history, "farewell" was a bit premature. The program as originally announced did not include Adelina: part I: the *William Tell* Overture on piano (Strakosch), the Cavatina from *The Barber of Seville* (Mrs. Strakosch), Paganini's *Witches Dance* (Bull), "Home Sweet Home" (Mrs. Strakosch), a violin work by Bull (Bull); part

II: *The Banjo* by Maurice Strakosch[74] (Strakosch), "Drinking Song" from *Lucrezia Borgia* (Mrs. Strakosch), Grand National Fantasia for violin alone (Bull), "Comin' thru the Rye" (Mrs. Strakosch), and *Carnival of Venice* by Paganini (Bull).[75] But a feud arose between the two sisters, and Amalia stayed off the stage for the first two concerts and Adelina replaced her. According to Adelina's own testimony, she was a very difficult child and made life for her sister and brother-in-law impossible.[76] The program as given was: part I: a fantasia on *Lucia di Lammermoor* (Strakosch), Cavatina from *Linda di Chamounix* (Adelina Patti), Violin Concerto No. 1 (Bull), an aria from *Sonnambula* (Adelina Patti), Paganini's *Dance des Sorciers* (Bull); part II: *The Banjo* by Maurice Strakosch (Strakosch), "Comin' thru the Rye" (Adelina Patti), Grand Fantaisie Nationale (Bull), "Chant de l'Echo" (Adelina Patti), and *Le Carnaval de Venise* (Bull).[77] The New Orleans public who heard Adelina for the first time fell in love with her immediately. As one reviewer said, "the young Adeline [sic] Patti marched this evening from one success to another and conquered the sympathy of her audience."[78] And one must remember: she was only nine!

The second concert was on Wednesday, March 2, and consisted of: part I: Grande Fantaisie on *The Daughter of the Regiment* (Strakosch), a cavatina from Verdi's *Ernani* (Adelina Patti), variations on an aria from Bellini's *Romeo et Juliette* (Bull), "Home Sweet Home" (Adelina Patti), Paganini variations (Bull); part II: *La Sylphide* by Strakosch (Strakosch), a romance (Adelina Patti), *Notturno Amoroso* (Bull), "Chant de l'Echo" (Adelina Patti), and *Le Carnaval de Venise* (Bull).[79] The third concert was on Friday, March 4, and this time Mrs. Strakosch took her place—but only on the second half of the program. The program was: part I: a piano work by Strakosch (Strakosch), an aria from *Sonnambula* (Adelina Patti), *Polacca Guerriera* by Bull (Bull), the Cavatina from *The Barber of Seville* (Adelina Patti), Grande Fantaisie Nationale (Bull); part II: *Le Rossignol* by Strakosch (Strakosch), romance from Meyerbeer's *Le Prophète* (Mrs. Strakosch), *Prayer* by Bull (Bull), "Chant de l'Echo" (Adelina Patti), the "Drinking Song" from *Lucrezia Borgia* (Mrs. Strakosch), and Paganini's *Danse des Sorcières* (Bull). The concert was billed as the final concert for this group in New Orleans, but since the first three had been so successful, more concerts were announced.[80]

The fourth concert was held on Wednesday, March 9, 1853, again at Odd Fellows' Hall. As in the first two concerts, Mrs. Strakosch was absent, and indeed she did not appear again on the series. The program was: part I: Dramatic Fantaisie from *Lucia* (Strakosch), a cavatina from *Ernani* (Adelina Patti), variations on an aria from Bellini's *Romeo et Juliette* (Bull), a song (Adelina Patti),

Paganini's *Introduction and Capriccio on Paisiello* (Bull); part II: *Le Banjo* (Strakosch), another song (Adelina Patti), a world premier of a piece for violin from *La Sonnambula* and *La Favorite* (Bull), "Chant d'Echo" (Adelina Patti), and the ubiquitous *Carnaval de Venise* (Bull).[81] The fifth concert was scheduled for Friday, March 11, but due to bad weather was postponed until the next evening. The proceeds from the concert were donated to a charity. The program was much the same as the previous one: part I: *Souvenir of Bellini* (Strakosch), opera aria (Adelina Patti), Paganini's *Dance des Sorcières* (Bull), "Home Sweet Home" (Adelina Patti), *Fantaisie Passionnée* by Bull (Bull); part II: *La Cloche Magique* (Strakosch), "Comin' thru the Rye" (Adelina Patti), *Prayer* (Bull), "Chant de l'Echo" (Adelina Patti), and *Le Carnaval de Venise* (Bull).[82] After the fifth concert, Bull's party left for Mobile,[83] but it returned to New Orleans for one more concert on Tuesday, March 22. The program was: part I: Grand Fantasie on *Lucia* (Strakosch), aria by Donizetti (Adelina Patti), Paganini's *Danse des Sorcières* (Bull), "Home Sweet Home" (Adelina Patti), Grande Fantaisie Passionnée (Bull); part II: *Le Rossignol* (Strakosch), Paganini's *Introduction and Capriccio on Paisiello* (Bull), "Comin' thru the Rye" (Adelina Patti), *Le Banjo* (Strakosch), and *Le Carnaval de Venise* (Bull).[84] The next day Bull, the Strakosches and Adelina Patti left New Orleans for Natchez.[85]

Meanwhile, there was another series of concerts in New Orleans that began on Monday, February 21, 1853, and overlapped with the Bull-Strakosch-Patti series. This series, of five programs, was led by Mrs. Emma G. Bostwick (soprano) of New York, assisted by Herr Henry Appy (violinist) from Holland, Julius Siede (flutist) from Leipzig, Miss Annie Oliver (nine-year-old concertina player) from Montreal, and Herr Thilow (pianist) from Coburg.[86] On February 18 members of the press attended a rehearsal by Bostwick and were impressed, not only with her but with Siede, who they thought was "the best flutist we ever heard." Siede also played on Jenny Lind's recitals and with Anna Bishop the previous year.[87] The first three concerts were at Armory Hall on February 21, 23, and 25, and were all that were originally intended, but a letter appeared in *The Bee* by a group of local citizens requesting Mrs. Bostwick to give more concerts. She responded that she would when she got back from Mobile.[88] True to her word, she gave two more concerts, the first at Odd Fellows' Hall on March 7 and the second at Mechanics' Institute Hall on March 11.[89] The programs were similar to those of Bull-Strakosch-Patti. On Monday, February 21, for example, the program was, part I: piano solo (Thilow), Donizetti cavatina (Bostwick), violin solo (Appy), concertina solo (Oliver), chanson (Bostwick), variations brillantes for flute (Siede); part II: Alard violin solo (Appy), voice and flute piece (Bostwick and Siede), ballade (Bostwick), Grande Fantaisie et Variations from *Norma* for flute (Siede), and chanson (Bostwick). On Wednesday it was, part I: piano solo (Thilow), *Ernani* cavatina (Bostwick), Artôt fantasia on *Norma* (Appy), "The Last Rose of Summer" (Bostwick and Siede), concertina solo (Oliver); part II: piano solo (Thilow), duo concertante for voice and violin (Bostwick and Appy), solo flute selections from Donizetti's operas (Siede), song (Bostwick), solo violin (Appy), and "Home, Sweet Home" (Bostwick).

Bostwick's third concert, on Friday, February 25, included two new artists, Charles de Martellini (piano) and Mr. H. Braun (solo violoncello): part I: Grand Fantaise (Martellini), Bellini cavatina (Bostwick), De Bériot Violin Concerto No. 6 (Appy), *Sacred Bravura* (Siede and Bostwick), solo concertina with dancer (Oliver and Lucy Neal); part II: flute solo from *Lucrezia Borgia* (Siede), Meyerbeer song (Bostwick), Vieuxtemps's *Souvenir d'Amerique* (Apey), Scottish ballad (Bostwick), solo violoncello on Bellini (Braun), and "Home Sweet Home" (Bostwick). After the return from Mobile, Bostwick's fourth concert (at the request of citizens of New Orleans) consisted of, part I: piano solo (Martellini), Grand Cavatina from *I Puritani* (Bostwick), Hausman violin solo (Appy), songs with flute (Bostwick and Siede), solo concertina (Oliver); part II: Bricinidi flute concerto (Siede), Scottish ballad (Bostwick), Vieuxtemps's *Souvenir d'Amerique* (Appy), Scottish ballad (Bostwick), violoncello solo (Braun), and Rode's celebrated variations (Bostwick). The final concert, postponed from March 9 to March 11, included, part I: solo piano (Martellini), a Handel song (Bostwick), a solo flute from *Lucia* and *Lucrezia* (Wiede), "Casta Diva" from *Norma* (Bostwick), and solo concertina (Oliver); part II: Wallace's Concerto No. 2, *Polka* (Thilow), a song by Wallace (Bostwick and Siede), Alard's Grand Fantasia (Appy), a ballad (Bostwick), a violoncello solo (Braun), and finally "Home Sweet Home" (Bostwick).

Local musicians continued to perform this spring. Of course the opera was in full production. Its esteemed conductor, Prévost, had his benefit on March 7 at the Théâtre d'Orléans.[90] On April 14 there was a notable premier of an opera by the young Ernest Guiraud at the Théâtre d'Orléans.[91] Mozart's *Don Juan* (*Don Giovanni*), a "grand opera in four acts [sic]," was performed on May 9 and 21 to much acclaim.[92] A new child prodigy appeared: the drummer Master English, who gave performances on March 8 and 9 at Armory Hall and later in the month every noon and in the evening at the Institut des Artisans assisted by Mme El Dora Lonie.[93] He also performed both an evening and a daytime concert at 3:30 p.m. on March 25 at Mechanics' Institute, assisted by a grand orchestra under the direction of Mr. G. G. Menol and other instrumental talent. There was a full military representation.[94] Amateur concerts, no longer so prominent in the city, continued nonetheless. On March 2, a soiree littéraire et musicale took place in the rooms of M Faivre, 56 Royale Street. "There will be," *L'Abeille* reported, "as we have already said, a musical intermède" between readings of French and Italian poems.[95] There were yet two more benefit concerts in May. The first, on Friday, May 13, featured Mr. W. F. Brough at Odd Fellows' Hall. Brough and his colleague at the opera Mrs. C. Howard sang various opera arias and songs; the orchestra played two overtures; and there was a piano soloist.[96] The second benefit, on Monday, May 23, was a grand vocal and instrumental concert at Odd Fellows' Hall, given by Leopold Carrière, first flutist of the Théâtre d'Orléans orchestra, assisted by Wideman, Paola, Paquetti, Bordas, Génibrel, Diguet, and Esembau. The orchestra was conducted by Prévost, and Melle Laudumiey played the piano. Leopold Carrière was "one of the oldest and most accomplished members of the orchestra attached to the French opera."[97]

However eventful and fulfilling all these concerts were, the spring 1853 concert season was highlighted by a much more momentous musical phenomenon: the return to the city of its most famous native musician, Louis Moreau Gottschalk (1829–69). The newspapers announced that Gottschalk had landed in early January in New York, where he caused a furor.[98] On March 29, 1853, he returned to New Orleans after an absence of twelve years.[99] Gottschalk had made his formal debut in New Orleans on April 5, 1841, and immediately sailed to France to continue his musical education. Over the next few years, as he established his reputation in Europe as one of the foremost pianists of his time; reports in the local papers kept track of his career. On April 22, 1847, for example, *The Bee* announced the publication of his *Polka de Salon* and that, still very young (eighteen), he was studying in Paris.[100] The next year *L'Abeille* quoted a tribute to the young Gottschalk from Paris newspapers,[101] and reported on his successful concert tour of Spain.[102] In 1850 news reached New Orleans of Gottschalk in Switzerland, Spain, and England, and there were rumors that he would return to New Orleans that fall.[103] Now it was 1853, he was back in the United States, and finally he had indeed returned home.

Gottschalk's first concert was private for the press and took place on Saturday, April 2.[104] Private press concerts were held frequently so that the critics would have a chance to write previews of concerts and inform the public of the special merits of an unknown or unproven artist. This was unnecessary in Gottschalk's case since his fame was enough to secure full houses at his performances and since the newspapers were already full of accolades for him—Gottschalk's name appeared in the papers almost daily during February, March, and April. Yet it was a courtesy that no doubt was greatly appreciated by the critics.

Gottschalk's first of eight regular concerts was at Odd Fellows' Hall on Wednesday, April 6, 1853. Naturally he performed mostly his own music: *The Chase of Young Henry, Duet Jerusalem* with Paulsackel, *National Glory from Bunker Hill, Le Bannier,* and *Le Carnival of Venice.* Also on the program was Wideman, who sang an aria from *Sémiramide,* a romance, and with the baritone Feitlinger two duets by Donizetti; Feitlinger himself sang a Donizetti aria, a Tyrolyse air, and a German melody.[105] The remaining concerts were on April 8, 13, 18, 25, 29, May 4 and 11—all at Odd Fellows' Hall except those on April 25 and 29 which were at the Théâtre d'Orléans.[106] Besides Gottschalk and the guests on the first program, he included on subsequent programs Fourmestreau (oboist), Herman Braun (violoncellist), Gabici, Mr. Juette (singer), Mme Paola (singer), Mr. Génibrel (singer), Esembau (violinist),[107] Miss Appotina Ludlam (guitarist), and an unnamed amateur (tenor). The fifth and sixth concerts were at the Théâtre d'Orléans so that Gottschalk could utilize its orchestra; he performed Prudent's *Les Bois* for piano and orchestra on both programs and a Weber concerto on the sixth. The orchestra by itself played an overture by Auber and Rossini's *William Tell* Overture. In addition to those compositions of his which he performed on the first concert, he played *La Moissonneuse, Gallop di Bravura, Waltz di Bravura* for two pianos, *Bamboula, Souvenirs de Bellini, National Glory* arranged for one piano, *Ossianic Dance, Dance of the Sylphs, Reminiscences of Spain,* and *National Poetic Caprices.* Besides several two-piano pieces, Gottschalk performed chamber music, especially on the seventh program, which included a Meyseder trio for piano, violin, and violoncello (Gottschalk, Esembau, and Braun), and the Andante and Finale of the Sonata in C of Beethoven for violin and piano (Esembau and Gottschalk). On his eighth program he gave the audience a list of twenty compositions of his and played intermittently works randomly selected from the list. Tickets for these concerts must have been scarce, so he announced that the fourth concert was given for his many friends who could not get a ticket to his first three concerts. The eighth concert was a benefit.

During his eight-concert stand in New Orleans, Gottschalk took a detour to Mobile between April 19 and 24. After his regular series was over he continued to perform in New Orleans. He took a big part in the benefit concert for Brough on May 13 by performing his *Poetic Caprices, National Glory,* and *Carnival of Venice.* Three days later he joined the veteran Mme Fleury-Jolly in an intermède at the Théâtre d'Orléans during a performance of Rossini's *Moses in Egypt* (which was substituted at the last minute for Mozart's *Don Giovanni* because of the illness of a singer).[108] His final concert this spring was a concert at

Mechanics' Institute Hall whose program is not entirely known. He was joined by Esembau (violin), Feitlinger (singer), and Miss A. Ludlum (guitar).[109] He left New Orleans for Natchez, Memphis, and New York on May 18, not to return until December.[110]

Never had the city of New Orleans had such an active concert season as that during the first five months of 1853, and it was not over yet. Despite the inevitable heat and humidity, for only the second time regular concerts spilled over into June. First, on Friday, June 3, there was a novelty concert at Mechanics' Institute Hall on Philippa Street, with mime, songs, Miss Ludlum on guitar, Mr. Meyer on violin, and other eminent artists, vocal and instrumental.[111] Then, to keep the theater musicians employed, a series of concerts began on June 20 at Tivoli Garden, with an orchestra drawn from musicians from the Théâtre d'Orléans, Saint Charles Theatre, and Varieties Theater, conducted by Gabici. Works by Auber, Gung'l, Lanner, Proch, Flotow, and Massach were given. Seven concerts in all were held: June 20 and 27, July 4 and 18, and August 1, 8, and 15. The intention was to have concerts every Monday evening, though bad weather forced some postponements.[112] Admission was twenty-five cents; dancing was free. Other composers represented after the first evening included Reisiger, Fiersteman, Verdi, Boeschhorn, Rossini, Bellini, Hérold, Jacob, Labitzky, J. Strauss, Groschoff, Gabici, Lumbye, Kalliwoda, Herzog, and Hasse. Of special interest was the first performance of a work by Richard Wagner, the *Rienzi* Overture, on August 8, 1853.[113] Mlle Ludlum gave one more concert at the Institut des Artisans on June 22, assisted by several eminent artists.[114] Others escaped to nearby Gulf Coast cities; the pianist Paulsackel and the oboist Fourmestreau gave a concert at Hotel Montgomery in Passe Christian by the charitable Association Howard on August 29.[115]

At this point in its history New Orleans was a major center for classical concerts as well as opera, and it seemed destined to grow even more important. However, fate challenged its exploding cultural life and caused it to turn aside to more important matters—but only temporarily. During the late summer and fall of 1853 New Orleans suffered its biggest yellow fever epidemic ever. A few persons had died from the disease every year, and there were bad years in 1819, 1822, 1833, 1841, and 1847 when a thousand or more were carried away by it. But in August of 1853 alone, 4,844 people died out of a population of 120,000. The epidemic caused many to leave New Orleans—some 25,000 fled the city in the summer of 1853.[116] By the end of the year, 8,400 persons had died from yellow fever. On September 1, 1853, a benefit concert for the relief of victims of the epidemic in New Orleans was held in New York City by Adelina Patti, Strakosch, and Ole Bull.[117] The impetus from the wonderful spring season, however, was an incentive for the citizens of the city to recover as quickly as possible, and, with the return of cooler weather, the epidemic began to recede. On September 22, Boudousquié, now the manager of the opera at the Théâtre d'Orléans, reported that he had signed all but two of the needed singers for the upcoming season.[118] Opening night was on November 15 with *The Barber of Seville*. Armory Hall opened on November 7 with the Campbell Minstrels, who included Edward Kendall, "the greatest bugler in the world and head of the Boston Orchestra," and George Kendall, the celebrated cornet à piston solo performer.[119] Five nights later the Saint Charles Theatre opened with *School for Scandal* and another play; its orchestral conductor, Gabici, conducted the house orchestra in an overture between the plays.[120] A minstrel show opened Odd Fellows' Hall, too, on November 14.[121] By October 6, 1853, concerts resumed. The Philharmonic Society gave a concert in Lafayette Square to benefit the Camp Street Orphanage.[122]

At the end of the year something new was afoot: the creation of a classical concert series. A call went out for a large number of families to subscribe to a series of twelve orchestral concerts to be given in Odd Fellows' Hall by the excellent house orchestra.[123] The orchestra performed at balls in the hall, especially during January and February, and in mid-January "the splendid Orchestra of Odd Fellows' Hall have volunteered their performances in aid of the" fair to benefit the orphans of the Third District.[124] Nothing is known further of this particular local attempt at an orchestral concert season, and it was not until 1856 that the idea finally came to fruition. The advertisements continued in the papers until mid-January. The arrival of Jullien and his orchestra the following February and his intention of giving twelve orchestral concerts may have been compensation for the temporary failure of the city's musicians in putting together a symphonic concert season of their own. Another explanation may be that, during Jullien's stay in the city, he absorbed the orchestra of Odd Fellows' Hall into his own troupe, though there is no specific evidence to this effect.

The major events for the spring 1854 concert season were the appearances of Gottschalk, of Ole Bull with Strakosch and Adelina Patti, of the Jullien orchestra, and of the two famous singers Sontag and Dévries. This was a season to rival that of 1853. Gottschalk returned to New Orleans at the end of 1853 and remained sequestered for almost the whole of January. But the pleas of his townsfolk were too much for him to resist, so he planned two concerts: on February 1 at the Mechanic's Institute and on February 3 at Odd Fellows' Hall. The highlight of both concerts was the performance of his new work, *Bunker

Hill, the Grand Symphony for Ten Pianos, a work which apparently is lost. He enlisted the help of nine other local pianists, including Paulsackel, Mr. and Mrs. Braun, his own teenage brother Edward, and several amateurs. Prior to the first concert, both the French and English newspapers wrote detailed descriptions of the piece.[125] In addition, he performed several other compositions of his, and he was assisted on the first program by Braun on violoncello, by the opera singers Borghèse and Betout from the Théâtre d'Orléans, and, on the second program, on February 3, by the soprano Mme Bertini and by M Braun on both violin and violoncello.

The Bull-Strakosch-Patti group performed two concerts at the Salle de l'Institut des Artisans (Mechanics' Institute Hall) on February 14 and 15.[126] Interestingly enough, Amalia was not on the programs. Strakosch once again performed only his own works, while Bull—who was the featured performer in these concerts—performed mostly his own pieces but also works by Paganini. Yet it was the ten-year-old Adelina Patti whom the audience now adored and who attracted the most attention. In the advance billing she was referred to as the "musical phenomenon who caused an immense sensation last year," and the reviewer this time found her growing in poise, musicality, and tone. She "was received with all the honors. The lovely *soprano* of this gifted child—so clear, limpid, bell-like and easy in its range—seems to have gathered strength and to have acquired increased flexibility since we last heard her."[127] On these two concerts she sang arias from Verdi's *Ernani,* Bellini's *Sonnambula* (twice), Donizetti's *Linda di Chamounix,* and the popular songs "Home Sweet Home," "Comin' thru the Rye," and Jennie Lind's "Chant de l'Echo" (twice).

For nearly a year New Orleanians had been reading of Jullien's tour of North America,[128] and the hype in the papers had prepared the people to expect great music when the first grand concert took place on Monday evening, February 20, 1854, in Odd Fellows' Hall. According to the critic of *The Bee,* "we expect to have instrumental music on a gigantic scale. The great leader has assembled together a perfect host of artists, composing an orchestra of colossal strength, and of rare individual excellence. When such artists as Koenig, Lavigne, Wjille, the brothers Mollenhauer, Botesini, Hughes and the like are performers in an orchestra, conducted by Jullien, something magnificent and delightful may not unreasonably be anticipated. Add to this Mad. Anna Zerr, whose reputation as a vocalist is of the highest order, and the New Orleans public will enjoy such a musical banquet as is offered once in a lifetime in America."[129] Jullien announced a series of twelve orchestral concerts to be given in February and March, but it actually came to thirteen. The programs were mixed with serious concert music, opera arias, patriotic marches, ballads, and light dances. The first concert had been scheduled for February 18, but Jullien did not arrive in the city in time so it was performed two nights later. The program on this occasion was typical for Jullien.[130]

Piece	Composer
Overture to *La Muette*	Auber
Quadrille California	Jullien
Allegretto from Symphony No. 3	Beethoven
Grand Air from *Lucia* (Mlle Anna Zerr)	Donizetti
Valse: La Prima Donna (solo coronet by Herr Koenig)	Jullien
Solo from *La Sonnambula* (solo Bottesini)	Bellini, arr. Bottesini
Quadrille National	Jullien
Three Pieces from *Les Huguenots*	Meyerbeer, arr. Jullien
Chanson (Mlle Anna Zerr)	Arne
Duet for two violins (brothers Mollenhauer)	Jullien
Clarinet Solo (M Wuille)	Wuille
Galop: *The Target*	Jullien

The Quadrille National, based on numerous American hymns, included twenty solo musicians from the orchestra. On subsequent programs—February 21, 23, 24, 25, 26, 27 (?), March 2, 4, 6, 8, 10, and 11—there would be additional token classical works, such as isolated movements from Beethoven's Symphonies Nos. 2, 4, 6, and 8, a movement from Haydn's *Surprise* Symphony No. 94, a Schubert-Beethoven symphonic concoction arranged by Roch Albert, and overtures by Beethoven (*Fidelio*, which Jullien claimed was the "premier," but where?), Mozart, Weber, Auber, Meyerbeer, and others. The only complete performance of a symphony was Mendelssohn's *Scottish* No. 3 on March 8. The programs, then, would be called "pops" concerts today, and while there was a large audience for such music in New Orleans, many serious local musicians—who knew they could do better than Jullien within a strictly classical framework—began to envision what would become the Classic Music Series beginning in 1856.

Upon request and since it was Carnival season, Jullien led his orchestra in "the most popular dance music" to accompany masked balls.[131] The orchestra achieved considerable popularity while in New Orleans and possibly could have continued to perform for the rest of the season there, had the tour not already been booked elsewhere. The orchestra was scheduled for Mobile on March 13 and Montgomery on March 18, and was then, after its arrival in the North, returning to Europe.[132] Jullien showed that orchestral concerts could draw an audience in New Orleans, though he mixed them with lighter music and vocal music to bring in people who might not otherwise have tried to sit through a serious orchestral concert. It was now up to the local musicians to see if there was ample interest in serious orchestral concerts without the sugar coating.

Two other prominent female singers visited the city this spring and performed concerts. The first was Henriette Sontag (1806–54) who was supposed to start her residency on February 6, 1854, but postponed it until a week later. Sontag gave, in all, nine concerts between February 13 and March 30, 1854, mostly together with the young American violinist Camille Urso. The final concert, on March 30, was a benefit for Urso whose repertory was limited to two fantasias whenever she played. In most of the later concerts Sontag sang with Rosa Dévries, whose connection with New Orleans was much longer—she had sung several seasons with the opera at the Théâtre d'Orléans and would return later. Both Sontag and Dévries also appeared with the Italian Opera Company during the month of March at the Saint Charles Theatre; Sontag sang Zerlina in *Don Giovanni,* Rosina in *The Barber of Seville,* Maria in *The Daughter of the Regiment,* and the title role in *Lucrezia Borgia,* while Dévries sang the title role in *Norma* and Donna Anna in *Don Giovanni.* Mlle Seidenburg (name also appears as Siedenburg, Siedenberg, and Seidenberg), Sigr. Arnoldi, and Sigr. Rocco joined the two sopranos in both opera and concert performances. The opera orchestra was led by Arditi.

Furthermore, Sontag found time to sing in a program of sacred music on March 23 in Odd Fellows' Hall, including excerpts from *Messiah* and *The Creation* as well as the complete *Stabat Mater* of Rossini.[133] In anticipation of her fourth recital, on February 17, the critic of *The Bee* wrote, "Thus far her career amongst us has been brilliantly successful. To-night should crown and consumate [*sic*] her triumphe."[134] The day after this concert the critic went on to state, "There are no bounds to our admiration of the consummate sweetness, flexibility and purity of Mad. SONTAG's voice; of her wondrous ease and brilliancy; of her faultless style; her perfect taste. Beyond all doubt she is the most accomplished vocalist ever heard in New Orleans."[135] There were complaints that Sontag and Lind charged too much for concert tickets—in excess of one dollar—which only the most famous could do (but even Gottschalk kept his ticket prices at a dollar), so she reduced the ticket price to one dollar for her later appearances.[136] Sontag then went on to Mexico, where she triumphed in *Lucre-*

zia Borgia as part of the Italian Opera Company, but suddenly she was stricken with cholera and died on June 16. As Nicolas Slonimsky reports, "her beautiful voice[,] . . . her striking physical appearance, and her natural acting abilities led to her reputation as the equal or superior to all other divas of the age."[137]

Local musicians were very busy at the theaters and had little time for concerts, especially since the big visiting stars were dominating the concert halls. On February 17, however, the violinist Victor Gerber gave a grand vocal and instrumental recital at Mechanics' Institute Hall. He was assisted by Betout, Paulsackel, Kuffner, and members of the Théâtre d'Orléans Orchestra under Prévost. Gerber, Gabici's pupil who was now a mature twenty-year-old, played Ferdinand David's *Fantasie, L'Elégie* by Ernst, and De Bériot's *Il Tesoro*. Paulsackel played a Weber piano concerto with orchestra, Betout sang an aria and a romance, Kuffner played a clarinet solo, and the orchestra performed two overtures by Auber.[138] Gerber got a warm reception "by a discriminating and attentive audience," *The Bee* reported. "His style is irreproachable, his method formed in the best schools of art, his training complete, his bowing careful and nice rather than bold and vigorous, his playing characterized by marked sensibility, feeling and soul."[139] On the very same evening Urso, too, performed at Armory Hall with the Sontag entourage and drew an equally enthusiastic review: "M'lle. URSO as usual gave the highest satisfaction. This little girl has a soul replete with musical inspiration. She is a genius of no ordinary character."[140] How active the concert life in New Orleans was when important concerts could be held simultaneously, and with the opera at the Théâtre d'Orléans competing! These were reminiscences of the first Bull-Vieuxtemps competing concerts.

The concert season, which was nearly the equal of that of 1853, concluded with two concerts by the singer Isidora Clark on May 3 and 8 at Odd Fellows' Hall. She was assisted by Mr. E. R. Hansen of Denmark (violin), C. Michel (tenor), Braun (violoncello), and a complete orchestra conducted by M Hoeffner. The orchestra played two overtures per concert (Weber and Auber, Auber and Kalliwoda), Hansen played two of his own works and a fantasie brillante by De Bériot, Braun played one of his own pieces, and the two singers took turns with opera arias (Bellini, Donizetti, Meyerbeer, and Verdi) and popular songs. About Miss Clark *The Bee* critic found a beautiful natural voice that needed polishing: "We heard Signora CLARK in one of VERDI's brilliant arias, in which she displayed her vocal powers to great advantage; and in the *Casta Diva* of Bellini, which she executed with perfect ease, and much brilliancy. Nature has evidently endowed this lady with extreme lavishness, but art and study are still requisite to render her all that she should be. Let her aim at expression and style, and trust herself fearlessly to the natural powers of her really beautiful voice, and she will undoubtedly become one of the most distinguished vocalists in America."[141]

The fall of 1854 was uneventful in terms of concerts. The opera season opened at the Théâtre d'Orléans in mid-November with a performance of *La Favorite*. The prima donna Mme Cambier was good but not without some serious weaknesses. On the other hand, according to *The Bee*, "Since last year, the orchestra has been enlarged and is now composed of a great number of skillful musicians. Its execution was remarkably exact, smooth and perfect. Indeed, we do not remember ever having heard the instrumentation of La Favorite rendered with more ensemble, vigor and precision."[142] The presence in the city of more instrumentalists of high caliber would inevitably mean the concerts in which they participated would reach higher standards than before. The intermèdes performed by these musicians were important, though truncated, concerts like the one at the Théâtre d'Orléans on Monday, December 17, between an opéra comique and two English vaudevilles.[143]

The spring 1855 season in New Orleans was not as spectacular as the two previous ones, but it was not without interest. Mme Valery Gomez gave a concert at Odd Fellows' Hall on Wednesday, February 14, less than a week before Mardi Gras.[144] Famous in Europe, she surrendered engagements at leading opera houses there in order to travel under Max Maretzek's auspices throughout America. She was assisted by the eminent pianist and composer Ferdinand Musard, the violoncellist Hermann Brown, and the pianist J. Luther. The Peak Family had a week's engagement at Armory Hall starting on February 23. During their six concerts they performed on bells, harps, guitars, and the cromonar. Meanwhile the Théâtre d'Orléans opera was in full gear (there would be several performances of *Don Giovanni* in April), including intermèdes, and a new theater, the Théatre Pélican,[145] presented English vaudevilles and operas such as *The Bohemian Girl* and scenes from standard Italian operas, also with intermèdes.

But the main event of the spring 1855 season was the third annual series by Gottschalk. He arrived back in New Orleans on February 27 and planned to stay three or four weeks.[146] He arranged to give lessons to worthy students and, of course, to give concerts.[147] The first recital occurred on March 13, on which occasion he played a special work—*American Sketches*—dedicated to the firemen of New Orleans, whom he invited to the concert. Of particular consequence for him was the world premier of one of his most popular compositions, *The Last Hope*.[148] He also performed *Mara la ho* (*Maria de la O*), *Gloires Italiennes* for two pianos, *Esquissez Américaines* in imitation of the banjo and an alarm clock, and *Carnaval de Venise*. He was joined by the singers Génibrel and Laget-Planterre and the local pianist Groenevelt (in *Gloires Italiennes*). His next appearance was at an intermède in honor of M John H. Lamothe, whose benefit performance was held at the Théâtre d'Orléans before a performance of Rossini's *Moses*. Laget-Planterre and Génibrel also sang during the intermède.[149]

Gottschalk's second recital, originally scheduled for March 21, was performed on Wednesday, March 28, at Odd Fellows' Hall. The program was partially a repetition of the first recital: part I: *American Reminiscences* (Gottschalk), a romance (sung by Mr. Lacroix), *Le Bannier* and *Bunker Hill* (Gottschalk), a Donizetti air (Madame Cambier), *Italian Glories* for two pianos (Gottschalk and Groenevelt); part II: *Bamboula* (Gottschalk), a song (Lacroix), Spanish pieces (Gottschalk), two songs (Cambier), *Mara La Ho* and the American premier of *Le Gocouyé*, an African dance from Cuba (Gottschalk). Ever attuned to the business aspects of music, Gottschalk listed in the advertisements those pieces of his available the following week in the music stores in New Orleans.[150] Gottschalk remained in the city until early May and scheduled just one more concert, on Monday, May 7.[151] Here he played his own *La Danse des Sylphes, Grande Fantasie Triomphale on Jérusalem* for three pianos (assisted by Pauer and Marshall), *Souvenirs d'Andalousie, Le Gocouyé, Symphonie de Guillaume Tell* for four pianos (assisted by Marshall, Trastour, and Fastman), and *Exquizes Américaines*. The singers Lacroix, Cambier, Duluc, and Laget-Planterre were also on the program. He was not entirely finished, however. On May 10 and 11 he performed "at intervals" during a fair at Odd Fellows' Hall to benefit an orphan home on the corner of Live Oak and Seventh streets.[152]

In March, Mme Rosa Dévries, who used to sing in the Théâtre d'Orléans Opera and had appeared the previous year with Sontag, returned with her own entourage for three concerts at Odd Fellows' Hall. She was now on a North American farewell tour prior to her departure for Europe. The first concert was on Friday, March 9: part I: a piano piece (Martin Lazare), an aria (Sr. Morino of the Italian Paris Opera), "Casta Diva" (Dévries), a violin fantasia (Sr. Pazarelli, first violinist at La Scala), Mozart's "Là Ci Darem la Mano" (Dévries and Morino); part II: a song (Dévries), another fantasia (Lazare), a Lucia aria (Morino), a Meyerbeer arioso (Dévries), Artôt's *Souvenir de Bellini* (Pazarelli), a Donizetti duet (Dévries and Morino), a waltz (Lazare), and the aria finale from *La Sonnambula* (Dévries).[153] The second concert was the following Monday, March 12, with the same assistants: part I: a piano work (Lazare), a Bellini aria (Morino), a Donizetti aria (Dévries), a De Bériot concerto (Pazarelli), a Donizetti duet (Dévries and Morino); part II: a recitative from an opera by Lazare (Dévries), Alkan's *Air de Ballet* (Lazare), a romanza (Morino), Vieuxtemps's

Souvenirs de l'Amerique (Pazarelli), Eckert's "Swiss Echo" (Dévries), a fantasia (Lazare), and an aria from Mozart's *The Magic Flute* (Dévries).[154] The third Dévries recital at Odd Fellows' Hall, on Friday, March 16, 1855, was a one-part program: a piano fantasia (Lazare), an aria from *Stabat Mater* (Morino), an air from *La Sonnambula* (?), a Paganini fantasia (Pazarelli), a *Lucia* duet (Dévries and Morino), an *Ernani* aria (Dévries), a fantasia on his own opera (Lazare), Rossini's "Tarentelle" (Morino), an aria from Rossini's *Stabat Mater* (Dévries), variations (Pazarelli), a Meyerbeer aria (Dévries), fantasia (Lazare), and Rondo from Verdi's *Jérusalem* (Dévries).[155] On March 24, the Dévries Troupe left for Natchez.[156]

Also this spring there appeared the Polish violinist Mr. L. Poznanski in just one concert, on Wednesday, April 11, at Odd Fellows' Hall, with singers from the Théâtre d'Orléans. Previously he had performed at a private soiree where the press was invited to witness his "admirable style and method, marked by perfect purity and chasteness of execution, great taste and expression." He had been a pupil of De Bériot, whose works were performed by nearly every violin soloist who had appeared in New Orleans to date, and thus his credentials were considerable. At the soiree he also performed on the viola d'amore and guitar but it appears that he did not do so at the public recital. He was accompanied by MM Pothonier and Trust on piano, and the singers Pretti Baille (soprano), Duluc (tenor), Lacroix (baritone) and Isidore (bass) were also on the program. *The Bee* critic found him "a violinist of superior merit," "without the pretension of being a rival of Ernest [sic] and Vieuxtemps."[157]

Before the season ended there were several benefits. At the Théâtre d'Orléans on May 17 there was the benefit for its conductor, Prévost, revered throughout the city for his conducting and his compositions. Then on Wednesday, May 23, in Odd Fellows' Hall, there was the benefit concert for Fourmestreau, first oboist at the Théâtre d'Orléans. He was assisted by Mme Laget-Planterre, Mme Cambier, and M Laget (singers), M Vanloo (first bassoonist of the theater in Brussels), M Gerber (Louisiana violoncellist?), M V. Gasmann (piano), and two other amateurs (unnamed).[158] After the concert season was over, the musicians kept busy with summer concerts in the gardens of the Washington Hotel at Lake Pontchartrain. The first was on Tuesday, May 22, 1855. M Lehmann, popular musician and proprietor and director of the hotel, began each concert at 6:30 p.m. and concluded the evening with fireworks.[159] These concerts were the precursors of the famous Lake Pontchartrain concerts that began in 1879 and continued into the twentieth century.

There were no significant concerts during the fall of 1855, but a major milestone in the history of concert life in New Orleans was reached in January 1856.[160] On January 15, Gustave Collignon gave the first of six Classic Series concerts whose performers were entirely local musicians. During this first season there were mostly chamber works on the programs, with a few orchestral pieces. There were few singers and they not on every program. The thrust was clearly to perform on a regular basis the top masterpieces of European instrumental music and to take advantage of the fact that the city of New Orleans possessed instrumental musicians who were capable of performing the most challenging music at the highest level of interpretation. Most of these musicians were performers in the local theater orchestras and had been trained in Europe at the best conservatories.

The first concert took place at Lyceum Hall, with Gabici and other local artists assisting. The program featured works by Mozart (the Andante and Allegro movements from his Piano Quartet No. 1 for piano, violin, viola, and violoncello, performed by Collignon, Gabici, Buccholz, and Oertl), Haydn (the Andante, Scherzo and Finale movements from one of the Opus 76 quartets), and Hummel (the complete septet for piano, oboe, viola, flute, violoncello, horn, and double bass, Opus 74, spread out over the two parts of the concert). There were also arias sung by Mme Pretti and Taccani Tasca. Evidently Lyceum Hall was too small for the large numbers of New Orleanians who wanted to experience such important concerts, so all subsequent concerts took place in the larger Odd Fellows' Hall. In order to know the music in advance of the concert and to play through the pieces on the program when one returned home after the concert, M Gabici's store, 172 Royal Street, had the scores available for purchase.[161]

Subsequent concerts took place on February 8, 20, 29, March 7, and April 4. A Beethoven string quartet and piano-violin sonata were on the second program, with Collignon and Gabici performing the latter. There was also a string quartet by Mendelssohn, and Collignon performed a Weber piano concerto with the accompaniment of a full orchestra.[162] Junca and Taccani Tasca sang a few songs. The third program featured a Beethoven trio, a sextet by Mayseder, and a repeat of the Hummel septet.[163] Junca sang again and was joined by Delagrave. On the fourth program Tacani Tasca and Laget sang arias, but most of the program was chamber music by Beethoven (septet), Mozart, and Mendelssohn.[164] Probably an orchestra was used for part of the fifth program on March 7 when Collignon performed the Mendelssohn G Minor Piano Concerto No. 1.[165] The rest of the program consisted of a few arias sung by Junca (basso) and

Tasca (soprano) and chamber music: Rudolph Meyer playing a solo on the violoncello, the Adagio and Presto from Beethoven's septet (violin, clarinet, viola, horn, bassoon, violoncello, and double bass), the first allegro of a piano quartet by Weber for piano, violin, viola, and violoncello, and Beethoven's trio for piano, clarinet, and violoncello. For the sixth and last concert of the season, on April 4, Collignon repeated the Mendelssohn concerto, this time unquestionably with orchestral accompaniment; he also played with orchestra the March and Finale of Weber's *Concertstück*.[166] The chamber pieces were the first Allegro from the Hummel Septet in D Minor, and the Weber duet for clarinet and piano with Kuffner (clarinet) and Collignon (piano). More arias than usual were on this program: one each from Auber's *Cheval de Bronze* and Hölzel's *La Tyrolienne*, both sung by Mme Colson, prima donna of the opera; a romance of Ambroise Thomas sung by Delagrave (tenor); another aria by Louise Puget; Junca (basso of the opera) sang "La Calunnia" from *The Barber of Seville*; and a song sung by Delserte.

The formation of a classical series would have been enough to make the spring of 1856 notable. But there were additional concerts as well. Theresa Parodi, traveling with Maurice Strakosch and Amalia Patti, was also active in the city. They came by boat from Memphis down the Mississippi and arrived in New Orleans on New Year's Day; they stayed at the Saint Louis Hotel.[167] Apparently they originally intended to give just three concerts, but before the end of the season the number of concerts was twelve. The first concert was planned for January 3 but was postponed one day because, according to the newspaper, January 3 was Thanksgiving Day.[168] Subsequent concerts were on January 7, 14 (postponed from January 11), 17, 19, February 11, 13, 15, 18, 19, 21, and 23—all at Odd Fellows' Hall.[169] They were scheduled to perform in Vicksburg, Natchez, Baton Rouge, and Jackson at the end of January, but as soon as these obligations were fulfilled, they went back to New Orleans, where they responded to the exceptional warmth and appreciation of the audiences.[170] The programs were typical, with Strakosch playing many of his own works, and Amalia, Parodi, and the baritone Leonardi singing arias and popular songs. The biggest novelty was the singing of "La Marseillaise" on nearly every program, replaced by "The Star Spangled Banner" on some. The critic of the *Picayune* was amazed that Parodi's voice was even stronger than in 1852, and "Amalia Patti-Strakosch has wonderfully improved since we last heard her here."[171] Strakosch "charmed" his audience, but Leonardi received a mixed review (fine in "Là Ci Darem" from *Don Giovanni* but not strong in "Gran Dio" from *Ernani*).

Adelina did not perform with her sister, Strakosch, and Parodi when they were in the city in January and February, but she did team up with the young New York violinist Paul Julien for three concerts in New Orleans on March 29 and April 1 and 4, 1856. Mostly she sang the same arias on all three programs, substituting one piece in each case. Julien and Adelina were joined by Ettore Barili (baritone) and August Gockel (pianist).[172] The reviewer was charmed by it all: "PAUL JULIEN is a violinist of extraordinary brilliancy, fire, purity and taste. His style is chaste and beautiful; his performance vigorous, easy and remarkable for sustained power. Little Miss PATTI our readers well remember. Her voice is an exquisite soprano, light, flexible, and of charming intonation, while her execution is wonderfully accurate and fine. She bids fair to become a vocalist of very superior attraction. Signor BARILI is a clever baritone, with a rich and cultivated voice, and Herr GOCKEL is certainly one of the most skillful pianists we have ever heard."[173] When Adelina appeared again in New Orleans at the end of 1860, she was a mature opera singer of seventeen.

Both Julien and Adelina had competition. Ole Bull was scheduled to perform in New Orleans on March 31, 1856, but the concert was postponed until April 3. His second and final performance was two days later. Instead of Strakosch and a Patti, Bull traveled this time with the cornet player Louis Schreiber, the pianist and composer Franz Roth, and two young singers Anna Spinola and S. Anna Vail.[174] As usual, Bull played either his own works or pieces by Paganini; there were no works by the French school. Meanwhile an eight-year-old girl became the new child sensation of the city. Her name was Marguerite Elie, daughter of the violinist M Elie of the Théâtre d'Orléans Orchestra, and she was destined to become the most distinguished classical concert pianist in the city during the last third of the century. Her debut was on April 25, 1856, in a benefit for her at the Théâtre d'Orléans.[175] She played Beyer's *Recollections of Milanelio,* Herz's *The Last Rose of Summer,* Jael's *Carnival of Venice,* and accompanied Deluc in Chassaignac's romance "Tell Me." Also on the program were the singers Colson, Junca, Laget, Delagrave, and Camillier. Prévost conducted two Rossini overtures: *La Gazza Ladra* and *The Siege of Corinth.*

There were other concerts as well. Theodore Von la Hache organized the Harmonic Association of New Orleans in a program composed of choice pieces, most by Mozart.[176] Prévost conducted the Théâtre d'Orléans Orchestra at Odd Fellows' Hall, and the proceeds went to the Orphan Asylum of the Fourth District. It took place on April 2, 1856, and cost seventy-five cents. La Hache intended to give six soirees in all, but there is no evidence of the other five. On

April 12 there was a benefit vocal and instrumental concert for the pianist Désiré Delcroix with the assistance of Colson, Delagrave, Junca, and the entire Orchestra of the Théâtre d'Orléans under Prévost.[177] M Delcroix performed Schulhof's *The Carnival of Venice,* Thalberg's Brillante Tarantelle, a Grand Concert Galop by Wely, and some variations on opera tunes from Donizetti's *Maria Stuarda.* The orchestra played the usual overtures by Rossini and Hérold, and the singers sang their arias and songs. Also on the program was violoncellist Rudolph Meyer, who played Beethoven's Variations on "Les Desirs." Mme Boudro provided piano accompaniment. A Mexican opera troupe interrupted its evenings of full operas to give a grand concert at the Gaiety Theater on April 23. The singers performed operatic selections by Mercadante, Rossini, Donizetti, and Verdi, followed by the fourth act of *Ernani* and the second act of *Jérusalem.* The orchestra was conducted by Mr. R. Stopel.[178] The season ended with a special intermède performance of Prévost's cantata *Henry Clay* with words by Rouquette. It was performed on May 12 at the Théâtre d'Orléans by members of the opera troupe during a performance of Donizetti's *Les Martyrs.*[179]

The summer seems to have been void of concerts, and the fall season was built primarily around opera and theater. During November the Gaiety Theater had a range of operas from Balfé's *The Bohemian Girl* to *Der Freischütz* and *Fra Diavolo.*[180] Its orchestra was conducted by Rudolph Meyer. When the troupe from the Gaiety Theater left on December 12 for a tour to Memphis and Saint Louis, attention was focused on another troupe at the same theater, now referred to as Crisp's Gaiety Theater, "the most elegant theater in the United States."[181] This theater, along with the Théâtre d'Orléans, continued to present operas at least through May.[182] As advertised, the orchestra played intermèdes which included pieces by R. Stopel and Meyer. The Saint Charles Theatre, too, throughout November and December, presented numerous intermèdes of overtures and arias played by the theater orchestra led by Gabici.

The only major concert was by the newly formed Sainte Cecilia Musical Society at Odd Fellows' Hall on December 20, 1856 (see page 35). The featured work on the first program was Beethoven's Symphony No. 5. Starting in January the society gave open rehearsals to subscribers the first and third Saturdays of each month from 11 a.m. to 1 p.m. in Odd Fellows' Hall. The first concert of the New Year was originally scheduled for January 14, 1857, but actually took place on Saturday, January 30, at 12:30 p.m. in Odd Fellows' Hall. Hoeffner was the conductor.[183] No further concerts by the Sainte Cecilia Society seem to have taken place this spring.

Indeed, the spring concert season of 1857 was less active than in the preceding four years, though two opera companies kept performing. On Saturday, February 7, there was a grand spectacle at the Musée de Vannuchi, with dancing, minstrels, and M Joseph Whitaker of the Kunkel Opera Troupe who sang romances.[184] The following Wednesday, February 11, the choir of Saint Patrick's Church, assisted by fifty distinguished men and women, sang Dr. F. Schneider's *Le Jugement Dernier,* a grand oratorio, at Lyceum Hall. It was a benefit for the church's organist, A. Trust, and music director, T. La Hache.[185]

Then on Thursday, February 26, Anna De LaGrange, assisted by Mme Siedenburg, Signor Ceresa, and Signor Taffanelli, performed the first of four grand concerts at Odd Fellows' Hall. The troupe sang arias and ensembles by Donizetti, Rossini, Verdi, and Bellini and a Lied by Gumbert.[186] Before the performance, the critic in the African American newspaper *L'Union* was upset that this concert was in the American Quarter of New Orleans; the singers, he affirmed, were French (in fact, only LaGrange was French and the repertory decidedly was not), and their grace and finesse could only be appreciated by the French in New Orleans. Yet it was hoped that the residents of the French Quarter would make the trip over to Odd Fellows' Hall since one could not expect the crude Americans to come to such a concert, let alone appreciate it. The critic also lamented that Maretzek had this spring put his concerts in New York and Havana and not in New Orleans, whose French citizens were much more sophisticated than the Americans or Spanish, wherever they were.[187]

Three days later, however, in his review the critic admitted he was wrong; the Americans were enthusiastic with LaGrange's performance, and she responded warmly to their reception of her art.[188] The second concert, on February 28, was much the same. LaGrange sang "Casta Diva" from *Norma,* "Rondo" from *Sonnambula,* "Batti Batti" from *Don Giovanni,* the "La Grange Polka," and various ensembles with the others, each of whom had a few solos.[189] At the third concert, on March 2, however, the repertory shifted a bit. This time Herman Braun was added to the program and played various pieces for violoncello. While Donizetti was represented by one aria and two duets, the other Italians gave way to Mozart, now represented by a duet from *Don Giovanni* and an aria from *The Magic Flute,* and Meyerbeer, Rode, and Fesca. In addition Seidenburg sang the "Serenade" by Schubert and Mme de LaGrange sang her own "Valse."[190] The final regular concert on March 6 was similar to the third concert, with Braun also on this program. Seidenburg sang Schubert's "Ave Maria" and an aria by Spohr. The unusual moment in the program came when La Hache performed his own

Elegie Dramatique in memory of the Arctic explorer Dr. E. K. Kane.[191] After these four concerts, however, LaGrange and her troupe were far from finished. She and her entourage performed in an intermède at the Théâtre d'Orléans on March 12 during a benefit for M Debrinay, second tenor of the opera troupe there.[192] On Monday, April 6, 1857, LaGrange and her troupe sang a concours (?) to benefit M John Lamothe, agent of the Théâtre d'Orléans. They sang fragments from *Norma, The Barber of Seville,* and *Amours du Diable*.[193] Meanwhile, LaGrange was brought over to the Théâtre d'Orléans to sing major roles. She was supposed to sing Lucia on March 11 but was indisposed. On March 13 she sang Fidès in *Le Prophète.* Subsequently she sang Norma in *Norma,* Rosina in *The Barber of Seville,* and other roles.[194]

Two minor concerts were held later that spring. In the first, there was an amateur grand concert for the benefit of the new Church of Our Lady of Good Help, given at Union Hall, Jackson Street, on Monday, April 22.[195] The second was very late in the season, on June 22 at Crisp's Gaiety Theater; it was a special benefit for the widow and children of Mr. Joseph Brenan. It consisted of two plays (John Howard Payne's *Charles the Second* and Thomas Haynes Bailey's farce *Perfection, or the Maid of Munster*), "besides a favorite song and recitation, with popular overtures during the performances."[196]

A major concert, however, was held at Odd Fellows' Hall on April 29, 1857. It was an isolated orchestral concert that stemmed both from the ill-fated Sainte Cecilia Musical Society concerts led by Hoeffner and the Classic Music Series led by Collignon. Hoeffner charged exorbitant prices for his concerts and was unable to provide the leadership necessary to carry out his series. Collignon, a pianist and not an orchestral musician, had the skills necessary to run a series successfully and also had the insight to see what kind of concerts the city most wanted to hear. This was the age of great European orchestral music, and while chamber music was strongly appealing to a limited audience of connoisseurs, orchestral music—equally chic at the time—had the potential for a much greater audience. Perhaps as a trial balloon, then, Gustave Collignon led an orchestra of about forty highly skilled professionals in a concert of the best orchestral music of the time: Beethoven's Symphony No. 6, the Scherzo and Finale from Beethoven's Symphony No. 5, the second movement of Mendelssohn's Symphony No. 4, and the overtures to Weber's *Oberon* and *Der Freischütz.* Three singers were supposed to sing arias on the program, but Junca and Cambier did not show up, so Delagrave sang alone a scene from *Der Freischütz*. The concert was a huge success. "The hall," *The Bee* reported, "was densely crowded."[197] Now Collignon was ready to make his great move: to establish a regular symphony orchestra for the city of New Orleans.

Fall was usually a dead period for concerts in New Orleans, but for Collignon it was the perfect time to establish his Classic Music Series. The first concert of the first season occurred on November 26, 1857. (See the list of Collignon's concerts prior to the Civil War, page 79, and the list of his concerts after the Civil War, page 84.) There were over three hundred subscribers; the concerts were limited to subscribers, their families, and their friends. The orchestral players were the best professionals who were in the city, mostly the first-desk players of the local theater orchestras. Since those players were obligated to play in the theaters during regular evening hours and at matinees, Collignon chose a perfect, non-conflicting time for his rehearsals and concerts: noon on Sundays.[198] In all, this was a consistent series with one concert every month from November to April and with a repertory heavy on the four most highly regarded orchestral composers known to that date: Beethoven, Mozart, Haydn, and Mendelssohn. Their works had been only rarely heard heretofore, and Collignon would now make sure that they would become familiar to New Orleanians. Added to these four were composers whose operas were well known and whose overtures were frequently heard at intermèdes and grand instrumental concerts: Rossini, Weber, Auber, and Hérold. The thrust was orchestral music; solo voices and choruses were simply adjuncts to the programs, if tolerated at all.

Having established his orchestra by the end of the first season, Collignon took advantage of extra events where his musicians could perform. On May 5, 1858, the orchestra performed a special charity concert for Sainte Mary's Orphan Boys' Asylum. This was not a subscription-only concert, so the assumption was that there were persons in the audience who had not heard Collignon's regular concerts, and thus the orchestra could repeat some pieces from the past season.

While the firm establishment of an orchestral concert series by a local orchestra was the main achievement of the spring 1858 season, there were other important concerts as well. Henri Vieuxtemps returned for three concerts in February, and shortly afterwards the famous piano virtuoso Sigismond Thalberg appeared in the Crescent City.[199] Vieuxtemps appeared separately until Thalberg arrived, and then they performed together. Vieuxtemps's concerts were on February 11, 13, and 16, and he was assisted by two singers: Mme Johansen and Miss Kemp. Their first joint concert was on Wednesday, January 24, at Odd Fellows' Hall.[200] In a few of the pieces Mme Vieuxtemps accompanied, and she accompanied the singers as well. Nearly everything on the program was related to opera arias, whether sung by M Ardavani or played as a fantasia by the instrumentalists. On February 23 Vieuxtemps and Thalberg gave free concerts for public-school children at the Gaiety Theater. On February 25, 27, and March 4 they gave three matinee musicales for three hundred subscribers; they played alone without any other performers. These concerts included some serious, non-virtuosic music, such as Beethoven's D Minor and A Minor violin-piano sonatas, Mayseder's trio (the violoncellist is not named), and single works by Mendelssohn and Chopin. Most of the programs, however, were pieces to show off the brilliant techniques of these two superior artists. The critic of *L'Abeille* could think of only one word to describe the appearance at one time of these two maestros: sublime.[201]

Overshadowed by the Vieuxtemps-Thalberg concerts were two given by the Russian Carlo Chenal; the second was at Odd Fellows' Hall on Tuesday, February 2, 1858, and included also the local singer Guillaume Manalmi and the local violinist M Wittriz.[202] Chenal played clarinet, piano, and an instrument called "le roseau magique." In mid-March the prima donna Erminie Frezzolini performed three concerts in New Orleans at Odd Fellows' Hall. She was accompanied by an orchestra led by Maurice Strakosch and assisted by Amalia Patti Strakosch, M White, and M Cherbuliez. At her first concert, on March 12, Frezzolini sang works by Bellini and Rossini; Amalia sang works by Meyerbeer, Balfé, Donizetti, and duets with Frezzolini; White and Cherbuliez each sang a single piece; and Strakosch performed one of his own compositions. Strakosch apologized that he had to charge $1.50 for tickets, but he needed the money.[203]

The second concert was on March 15, 1858, with much the same kind of program.[204] Boudousquié, manager of the Théâtre d'Orléans, decided to take advantage of the presence of Frezzolini and Amalia and arranged for three performances by these two singers with men he hired from Havana, to sing Italian opera at his theater beginning on Easter Monday.[205] On May 12, 1858, there was a benefit grand concert for the Jewish Widows and Orphans Home led by Curto at Odd Fellows' Hall. Besides the overtures to *Der Freischütz* and *La Gazza Ladra,* a few amateur women joined Curto's choir and members of the Théâtre d'Orléans Opera Troupe in various opera excerpts by Méhul, Auber, Meyerbeer, Donizetti, Halévy, Weber, and Curto himself.[206] The concert season ended two days later with Mlle Vestvali's farewell concert at Odd Fellows' Hall.[207] She was assisted by Signor Gariboldi (basso profundo), Signor Macchi (clarinetist), Herr Braun (violoncellist), Miss Jessi McLean (American contralto), Mr. Rouseau Delagrave, and Mr. Junca. Mr. Flandry "will preside at the piano." Vestvali sang three opera arias, Braun and Macchi each performed two solos, and the others sang one piece each.

The fall, as usual, was not the main season for concerts, but the third classical series of Collignon did get underway on December 8, 1858. It was a program to thrill the most sophisticated audience of the time: Haydn's Symphony no. 8 [sic] in B Minor, Beethoven's Symphony No. 3, Mozart's Overture to *Don Giovanni,* Weber's Overture to *Euryanthe,* and Spohr's Overture to *Jessonda.* Collignon conducted.[208] As in all the concerts, the performance began at noon on Sunday in Odd Fellows' Hall.

The spring 1859 season had several distinguished visitors. Musard of Paris, celebrated proprietor and chef d'orchestre of the Concerts and Bals Musard at the Hôtel d'Osmond in Paris, arrived in New Orleans for the purpose of giving a series of his popular concerts, bals parés, fancy dress balls, and bals masques. He had with him "upwards of twenty of his own principal soloists" from Paris "and the celebrated Orchestra of the New York Academy of Music, to which [was] added thirty of the best professors of New Orleans."[209] He also gave a bal masque in Mobile and Natchez. Mr. Brough, his manager, "is ready to make arrangements for Mr. Musard to conduct one or two private Balls, to be given by societies or clubs of the first respectability." At the same time that Musard came to the city, a number of singers currently associated with the New York Academy of Music arrived in New Orleans to present concerts, the first of which was at Odd Fellows' Hall on Wednesday, February 23. The singers were led by Mlle Poinsof and Mme Laborde, principal singers of the Paris Opera, and Carl Formes, basso from the Royal Opera in London; others were Mlle Berkal, Signor Florenza, and Gustave Satter. Every piece on the program was accompanied by a full orchestra, conducted by Carl Anschutz. The orchestra played overtures to Flotow's *Martha* and Nicolai's *The Merry Wives of Windsor*; the singers sang mostly opera arias, Mme Laborde played or sang (!?) Paganini's *Carnival of Venice* with Variations, and Formes sang one buffo aria from *Don Giovanni* and another from *The Marriage of Figaro.*[210]

On the following Friday and Saturday, February 25 and 26, Musard and the singing entourage joined in what was billed as two grand double concerts at Armory Hall.[211] In both concerts Musard played in part 1; the New York Academy group performed in parts 2 and 3. On February 25 Formes sang another Mozart aria from *The Marriage of Figaro.* The next day Musard performed dances with his orchestra in part 1. In part 2 Satter played a piano fantasia on *Ernani,* followed by excerpts from Haydn's *Creation* sung by Laborde, Poinsot, and Formes. In part 3 the not yet famous Theodore Thomas played a violin solo,

Formes sang Schubert's "Der Wanderer," Florenz and LaBorde sang a romance and some variations di bravura respectively, and Poinsot sang "Pollacca, Jerusalem." The concert ended with the New York Academy Orchestra in a march by Mendelssohn.

That was the last performance by the New York Academy group as a whole, but Musard continued performing concerts and accompanying dances past Mardi Gras. On Mardi Gras itself (March 8 in 1859), Musard conducted his orchestra in a grand concert promenade at Odd Fellows' Hall as part of a grand bal by the Society of Young Persons,[212] and on Friday, March 18, 1859, from 8 to 10 p.m., he gave a second grand bal masque at Odd Fellows' Hall for the same group.[213] In between, on Thursday, March 10, Musard gave a farewell concert at Odd Fellows' Hall. Also on the program were the last appearance in New Orleans of Mme Poinsot and the first appearances of Mlle Ghidni and Signor Maggiobotti, all of the New York Academy. On the same occasion there appeared Mlle Berkal, Signor Domenico, Mr. Perring, Mr. Fiedler (solo flute), Mr. Schmitz (French horn), and the orchestra, with M Legendre on cornet à piston in his farewell performance. The orchestra played the Overture to *Martha* and an *Il Trovatore* fantasia to begin each half, and the "Champagne Galop" and the "Express Train Galop" to end each half. In the middle were other dances ("Cecila Polka" played by Legendre and a Spanish quadrille), a solo for French horn, and several arias and ballads.[214]

In March another distinguished soprano arrived in the city. Her name was Piccolomini, and she was scheduled to perform the lead role in *La Traviata* at the Théâtre d'Orléans three times from March 11 to 14. Since she and her associates were brought all the way from London, costs associated with these appearances mandated that the price of tickets be three dollars (two to three times the usual price) with boxes sold at auction and the third gallery seventy-five cents (it was usually fifty cents).[215] On March 12, 1859, however, Piccolomini gave a grand concert and opéra comique de salon in full costume at Armory Hall. The first part of the program probably consisted of select arias (we do not have the program), and the second half consisted of a performance of Pergolesi's *La Serva Padrona* especially arranged for Piccolomini. Piccolomini was assisted by all the artists and a grand orchestra.[216]

After several postponements the young pianist Arthur Napoleon gave his first concert at Odd Fellows' Hall on Tuesday, April 19, 1859. He was assisted by Signorina Cairoli (New York Academy of Music), Miss Heywood (Drury Lane Theater, London), and Doehler Osborn (solo violinist of the New York Philharmonic). Siegfried Behrens was musical director, but there was no orchestra.

Napoleon played his own Grand Fantasia on *Les Huguenots,* a Grand Caprice (Mendelssohn's *A Midsummer Night's Dream*) by Liszt, his own Fantasia on *The Bohemian Girl,* and, with Doehler Osborn, De Bériot's Grand Duo on *William Tell.* Osborn also played Alard's *Solo Violin Fantasia on Anna Bolena* and the Adagio and Rondo from Ferdinand David's Violin Concerto No. 3. Heywood and Cairoli sang arias by Bellini, Verdi, Donizetti, and Meyerbeer and several English ballads.[217]

The critic of *The Bee* was enthusiastic about Napoleon: "He is certainly a musical prodigy, whose every touch awakens new melody, and whose rapid movements flash magic harmony, and leave lingering sweetness over the keys of the piano." And: "We have listened with great attention to his performances, and declare unhesitatingly that, with perhaps the single exception of THALBERG, young NAPOLEON is the greatest pianist who has ever visited America. In style and method, in precision and power, in the use of the left hand, in exquisite purity of modulation, in the faculty of prolonging the sound and of destroying the sharp staccato character, which is the great drawback of the instrument; in short, in all the qualities of an artist, this beardless boy leaves nothing to be desired." He performed another grand concert on April 25 at Odd Fellows' Hall, and then performed a grand matinee musicale at 12:15 p.m. on Wednesday, April 27, for "school pupils and children" at the small price of fifty cents a ticket. His fourth and final concert in New Orleans was at Odd Fellows' Hall, on April 29, with the other performers from his first concert. There were some repetitions and some new pieces.[218]

Local musicians also gave concerts during the spring of 1859. On Thursday, March 3, a grand vocal and instrumental concert took place at Lyceum Hall for the benefit of the Rev. Mr. Hedge's Church. According to the *Picayune,* it was "under the direction of Mssrs. LaHache and Cripps, assisted by members of the Academy of Music and other Amateurs of well-known ability."[219] Six weeks later two charity concerts were scheduled, but one was, probably when its organizers realized the conflict, postponed for five days. The first was on Friday, April 15, again under the leadership of La Hache, this time assisted by Pothonier, Hoeffner, Mr. Schroeder, and several men and women amateurs. It was labeled a grand musical entertainment and was held at Odd Fellows' Hall to benefit the Orphans Home. There was no orchestra. The program did begin with an overture (to *Zampa*) but played by Pothonier and La Hache in an arrangement for two pianos or one piano four hands. The violinist Hoeffner played N. Louis's *Concert Variations,* with La Hache on piano, and another grand violin solo. Some arias were sung in English, including works by Verdi and Adam. La Hache's "Veni" for soprano, tenor, and baritone was performed by three amateurs, as was the Trio from Onslow's *Le Colporteur*.[220] The postponed concert, which was actually performed on April 20, was a grand vocal and instrumental concert to benefit an artist's widow, under the patronage of the Artists of the Théâtre d'Orléans. Since the deceased was a professional member of the theater, a number of professional musicians from the theater participated: Lafranque, Angèle Cordier, Delagrave, Taste, Lucien Bourgeois, Bauce, and A. Jobert. They were joined by the celebrated pianist Mlle Hedwig Browska, who played Mendelssohn's *Rondo Capricioso* and Thalberg's Grand Fantasia from *La Sonnambula*. The orchestra, led by Prévost, opened each half with the overtures to *La Muette* and *William Tell*. Jobert played an oboe solo, and the others sang arias.[221] Finally, on April 25, there was a fourth grand vocal and instrumental concert at Lyceum Hall, once again conducted by La Hache and for the benefit of the Orphans Home.[222]

The most significant musical event of the fall 1859 season was not a concert or opera performance but the opening of a new hall which came to be known as the French Opera House. This sumptuous building was the most lavish theater in North America and became the symbol of the greatness of opera in New Orleans. Coming at the very end of a decade of supreme musical performances in the city, it showed the opulence of the city, the health of its musical life, and the importance of this art to the people of the city. Operas were the main fare there, but concerts and other entertainments occurred, too. On February 22, 1859, a meeting was held to decide to build a new opera house. A suitable location had not yet been determined.[223] On April 25, a report indicated that the new opera house's grounds at Toulouse and Bourbon were being prepared for the erection of the building. By then subscribers were already starting to choose their seats in the new hall, which was to replace the Théâtre d'Orléans.[224] The new theater officially opened on December 1, 1859, with a performance of the complete *William Tell*. The proprietors of the Théâtre d'Orléans, however, were not ready to quit, so for the entire spring of 1860 New Orleans had two French opera companies performing simultaneously. This led to *The Barber of Seville* and *Les Huguenots* both being performed on January 5, for example, and in an extreme case, *Lucia di Lammermoor* at both theaters on January 23!

The first concert in the French Opera House seems to have been a grand concert by violinist Mme De Vernay on January 11, 1860.[225] The house orchestra opened each half with the customary overtures, to *Les Diamants de la Couronne* (Auber) and *William Tell* (Rossini). Vernay played Charles Dancla's *Romance et Bolero*, a grande fantasia on *La Sonnambula*, and—with Mlle Saint-Urbain,

M Delcroix, and M Flandry—a quartet on "Ave Maria" by Bach. There were various songs and arias sung by Ecarlat, Melchisedec, Génibrel, Chol, Désiré Delcroix, Saint-Urbain, and Marie Pretti. Mme Vernay (De Vernay) made her debut in New Orleans on November 30, 1859, at Odd Fellows' Hall, where she elicited an extremely sexist review by the *Picayune:*

> We listened to the performance, at Odd Fellows' Hall, of a fantasia on airs in the "Lucia," on violin, by M'me De Vernay, who lately arrived here from Cadiz. The lady plays wonderfully well—for a lady; but we confess we are no very great lovers of that sort of performance. A woman does not look gracefully with a violin under her ear, and there is something incongruous to our thinking, in the idea of fair arms drawing a long bow, and fair fingers pinching fiddle strings. M'me Preti, formerly of the Orleans theatre, sang two operatic morceaux admirably, and Mr. De Montfort played on the harmonicorde, and showed himself an artist. There was a very slim attendance at this concert.[226]

Montfort was a Spanish composer and the leader of the group including Vernay.[227]

Most concerts continued to be performed at Odd Fellows' Hall. The fourth year of Collignon's Classic Music Series began on December 7, 1859, with Beethoven represented by the *Leonore* Overture (presumably No. 3) and Mendelssohn by his Symphony No. 3. Mme P. Ruhl sang "Casta Diva" and another aria by F. Abt.[228] The orchestra also played the Overture to *Chasse de Jeune Henri* and Meyerbeer's "Torchlight March" ("Marche aux Flambeaux"). Subsequent concerts were on January 6, February 1, February 29, March 21, and April 25. After the series was officially finished, Collignon conducted his orchestra in a seventh grand vocal and instrumental concert for the benefit of Sainte Mary's Orphan Boys Asylum on May 16, 1860.

Besides the Collignon series, there were other concerts in the spring of 1860. On January 27, there was a piano recital by Hedwige Browska at Odd Fellows' Hall, with an orchestra from the French Opera House under Eugène Prévost. The program included overtures to Boieldieu's *La Dame Blanche* and Mozart's *Don Giovanni.* Browska played works by Chopin, Weber, Thalberg, Rubinstein, and Liszt. De Vernay played De Bériot's *Scene de Ballet*—Fantaisie pour le Violon, Génibrel sang "Romance de Beatrice de Tenda" by Bellini, and Feitlinger and Melchisedec sang lighter works.[229] Then in February the American tenor Henry Squires, from the Academy of Music in New York, appeared in six concerts at Odd Fellows' Hall (February 7, 9, 10, 13, 15, and 17). He was assisted by "la petite Mary McVicker," musical genius, and the pianist Edward Hoffman. His tour was under the aegis of Strakosch. Like Napoleon just before him, Squires gave a grande matinee musicale on Wednesday, February 15, for women and children, for only fifty cents. The repertory was primarily English, Irish, and American songs.[230]

In March the singer Mme Anna Bishop returned to New Orleans and gave three concerts between March 7 and 12, all in Odd Fellows' Hall. Assisting her were the pianist Harry Sanderson and the baritone F. Rudophson.[231] At the same time the young African American pianist "Blind Tom"[232] started performing at Spaulding and Rogers' Museum. Tom was ten years of age and a slave. He was able to play by ear over eleven hundred pieces, including works by Bach, Beethoven, Chopin, Mendelssohn, and Liszt as well as his own works. He played long hours daily, from 11 a.m. to 10 p.m., and improvised a great deal. Although he is referred to as a prodigy, he was treated more as a curiosity than as an artist.[233] On March 22 the new violinist Henri Page made his concert debut in the city in an intermède at the German Theatre.[234] He had become a violinist in the new Théâtre d'Orléans orchestra (conducted by M Predigam) after the entire old orchestra of that theater (conducted by Prévost) moved over to the new French Opera House. Struggling to keep the Théâtre d'Orléans alive and at the same time to survive themselves, a group of singers from the Théâtre d'Orléans banded together to give three vocal concerts at Odd Fellows' Hall, the first on Monday, March 26. Various French chansons and opera arias in French were sung by Mme and M Messmaker, Mme and M Philippe, Dobbels, and Sotto.[235] The second concert was on March 31 and was similar to the first. The third was on April 11 and, besides the same five singers, included the amateur singer Gilbert Freghe in a comic chansonette and Henri Page playing some variations for violin.

At the very end of March, Marietta Gazzaniga (1824–84)[236] started a series of six concerts in the city and was assisted by Sanderson (who had come earlier in the month with Bishop), the Spanish tenor Tamaro, the local baritone Berthal, and the director of the program, Lucianao Albites (who later married Gazzaniga). The program of the first concert is missing, but at the second concert, on March 31, Gazzaniga sang arias by Donizetti and Meyerbeer, duets from Verdi's *I Masnadieri* and *La Traviata* and Mozart's *The Marriage of Figaro* with Tamaro, a trio from Verdi's *Attila* with Tamaro and Berthal, and she ended the concert with a Spanish song, "La Naranjera." Berthal sang a romance and "De Provenza" from *La Traviata*; Tamaro sang an aria from Donizetti's *Don Pasquale*. Sanderson played his own works and Thalberg's Grande Fantaisie sur *Les Huguenots*.[237] In her third and fourth concerts, on April 2 and 4, Gazzaniga and her entourage included, besides sacred and secular songs and arias, the fourth act of *La Traviata*.[238] On April 9 Gazzaniga sang the role of Leonore in *Il Trovatore* at the Théâtre d'Orléans[239] and the next day sang another concert, this time at the Lyceum Hall with the young violinist Charles Elliot, a pupil of De Bériot.[240] Sanderson, Tamaro, and Albites assisted Gazzaniga, together with a new singer, Miss Grace Willoughby, known for her ballad singing. Gazzaniga and Tamaro also sang in an intermède on April 10 at the Théâtre d'Orléans in a benefit for the artists of that venerable hall; it is uncertain how they could have managed a concert and an intermède at two different halls on the same evening, so it is possible that either the concert or the intermède was an afternoon event. In any case the singers had an extraordinarily heavy schedule, which continued with their sixth concert at the Théâtre d'Orléans on April 13. The program consisted of entire single acts from *Lucrezia Borgia, Il Trovatore,* and *La Favorite*.[241] In mid-April the artists from the Théâtre d'Orléans traveled to Donaldsonville for two "délicieuses soirées."[242]

The end of April and beginning of May brought just as exciting musical events to the city with the return of Parodi and her Italian Opera Troupe. Since operas were being performed nearly every evening at both the Théâtre d'Orléans and the French Opera House, Parodi's group performed in a lesser hall, the Amphitheater of Spalding and Rogers' Museum. Her associates were Signora Alaimo and Signuori Sbriglia and Gnone. The list of operas in a two-week period is breathtaking: from April 23 to May 6 they performed *Ernani, La Traviata, Norma* (twice), *Lucia di Lammermoor, La Sonnambula, Il Trovatore* (twice), *Don Giovanni, Rigoletto, Lucrezia Borgia, La Favorite, The Barber of Seville,* and *Poliuto*—all in Italian.[243] Simultaneously the French Opera House was performing, among other pieces, Halévy's *Les Mousquetaires de la Reine* and various comedies, and the Théâtre d'Orléans was doing, among many other works, *The Daughter of the Regiment* as well as lighter works. On Saturday, April 28, Parodi's group put on a matinee musicale at the amphitheater, which featured selections by Rossini, Mozart, Donizetti, Verdi, and good English composers.[244] Admission was seventy-five cents for adults and twenty-five cents for children.

The fall 1860 season began normally, and it looked like there would be another spectacular concert season just as there had been for the past decade. Fate, however, would intervene, and the city would never be the same again. Collignon made plans for his fifth year, and, although he held rehearsals in November, the first concert, which was to be presented on December 12, never took place.[245] On the program were scheduled Beethoven's Symphony No. 6, Mendelssohn's *Meerstille* Overture, the Overture to Rossini's *Le Siége de Corinth*; and other pieces.[246]

Meanwhile, the theaters reopened. The Variétés Théâtre announced that its chef d'orchestra was Eugene Fenellen.[247] The French Opera House reopened with a new, very significant prima donna. Adelina Patti, now a ripe seventeen, did not appear in New Orleans until the end of 1860, but when she did find herself again in the city, she came not to sing concerts but to join the opera company at the newly built French Opera House (then called Théâtre de l'Opéra). For four months she was the leading soprano of the company. Her roles included the title role in *Lucia* (Donizetti), Leonore in *Il Trovatore* (Verdi), Lady Harriet in *Martha* (Flotow), Dinorah in *Le Pardon de Ploermel* (Meyerbeer), Valentine in *Les Huguenots* (Meyerbeer), and leading parts in *The Barber of Seville* (Rossini) and *Rigoletto* (Verdi). For special occasions (benefit performances for her colleagues) she also sang segments from *La Sonnambula* (Bellini), *La Traviata* (Verdi), *Ernani* (Verdi), and on two occasions the "Mad Scene" from *Lucia*. In between she found time to give concerts in Baton Rouge, Natchez, Vicksburg, and Jackson. When she left in 1861, it was twenty-one years before Adelina returned to New Orleans, then as a world-famous diva.[248]

The musical accomplishments of the years up to this point were unsurpassed by any other city in America. The cornerstone of these accomplishments was the opera, which was not only the main French opera but also various competing operas that often gave a New Orleanian choices on a given evening as to which opera to attend. The concert life was supported by the opera musicians, many local amateurs, and important visitors from Europe and elsewhere in America, who came usually to stay for a month or more. The momentum was there to continue with even a greater concert life, but that was not to be.

4

Concert Music during the Civil War
1861–1865

From April 1861, New Orleans was under siege, and then from April 1862 until 1865 it was occupied by Union troops. The last concert before the blockade was on February 5, 1861, at Odd Fellows' Hall. It had been postponed from January 23. It was a benefit for the younger Asile de Saint Vincent orphans and featured Mozart's Mass No. 12, performed by fifty men and women, plus an orchestra of the best musicians of the city.[1] Another concert, during the blockade, was conducted by Collignon on May 15 for the same charity.[2] In addition, on May 2, there was a grand vocal and instrumental benefit concert for the "brave volunteers," conducted by La Hache and Cripps, at Odd Fellows' Hall and performed by amateur men and women. Included were several opera duos and trios, several opera choruses, two grand duos for two pianos (one by Thalberg and the other by Weber) played by Creole women, and some popular songs ("The Last Rose of Summer," "La Marseillaise" with chorus, and others).[3]

There was a brave attempt to keep concert life alive during the fall of 1861. Usually the fall was a dull time for concerts because the main attention was focused on the beginning of the opera season. The Opera House was open for reviews, comedies, and vaudevilles, not for operas, though an occasional intermède allowed the orchestra to play overtures and some opera singers to sing arias or scenes. Such was the case on October 27, 1861, for example, when, between a series of comedies, the orchestra played an overture, a scene from the fourth act of Halévy's *Charles VI* was performed, and Mme Delatournerie sang a patriotic song.[4] Subsequently, at every theatrical production at the Opera House, she sang the Confederate song "Guerre aux Yankees" (words by Col. A. Gérard and music by Capt. A. Chassaignac) with chorus and orchestra. The few concerts that did take place from October to December were mainly to raise funds and show support for the Confederate Army. On October 29, there was a grand vocal concert at Odd Fellows' Hall under the direction of Curto to benefit the Crescent Artillery. He and a number of amateur singers sang twelve opera arias by Boieldieu, Verdi, Meyerbeer, Rossini, Auber, Bellini, and Adam.[5] The critic in *L'Abeille* called the concert a complete musical success.

A similar concert, at Odd Fellows' Hall on November 7, was to benefit the Third Regiment of Louisiana in Chalmette. It differed from the earlier concert in that it included vocal ensembles from various operas by Verdi, Rossini, Adam, and Donizetti and instrumental music by Beethoven (violin-piano sonata) and Meyerbeer (a piano arrangement from *Les Huguenots*) and obbligato parts.[6] Mmes C. Fisher, Dimitry, and Caldwell organized a soiree patriotique or concert at Odd Fellows' Hall on December 9 to benefit the Edmonston Bataillon of Volunteers.[7] Rossini's *Stabat Mater* was performed on December 18 at the Opera House conducted by Collignon with a complete orchestra and a mixed chorus of eighty-nine singers, and at the end he had the orchestra perform Meyerbeer's popular "Marche aux Flambeaux." The concert, under the patronage of the regimental guards of Orleans, benefited the army of the west.[8] On December 23, Mme Mace's young girl students performed a concert at the Saint Charles Institute, Greenville, near Carrollton, for the benefit of the Louisiana volunteers in Missouri.[9] Seemingly the only concert not dedicated to the military was the performance of a mass written by Curto and performed by him on Christmas Day at Saint Patrick's Church.[10]

A concert season continued during the first part of 1862, but international stars were entirely absent. They had no way to get to New Orleans. On Saturday, January 4, there was a grand military, vocal, and instrumental concert at Odd Fellows' Hall, given by Mme Dupeire, seconded by amateurs and a grand orchestra under the direction of M Hoeffner, with Theodore von la Hache at the piano. The two-part program consisted of marches (by Hoeffner himself) and arias and duets by Rossini, La Hache, Verdi, and Donizetti. Furthermore, the orchestra played Weber's *The Battle of Waterloo*.[11] Later in the month there were two benefit concerts to assist the volunteer soldiers who were absent from the city.[12] The city was able to remain loyal to the Confederacy until the Union forces occupied it. Just two-and-a-half weeks before that, on April 9, the Queen Sisters from Charleston, South Carolina, began a two-week engagement at the Academy of Music. In the midst of dancing and singing with "music by their first class orchestra," they performed a "Grand Patriotic Song" in honor of the southern cause.[13] Such songs were impossible after April 28.

Once the Union forces entered the city, the theater that was used the most for concerts was the old Théâtre d'Orléans. Indeed, five of the six concerts or intermèdes during the late spring and summer of 1862 were at that hall, and the only music at the new French Opera House was one concert on August 14 and one opera, another performance of *La Dame Blanche,* on Sunday, August 17, conducted by Predigan.[14] The extreme heat of summer must have made the performances almost unbearable, yet they went on, perhaps in defiance of the new rulers of the city, who probably could not understand a word of the French spoken and sung in the hall. On Sunday, June 1, during a benefit for the actress Madame Reiter, there was a musical intermède composed of a grand air from *Charles VI* performed by Madame Delatournerie, a romance by M Devisme, two chansonnettes by M Charles, and solos d'harmonicorde by M Reiter.[15]

A week later there was a farewell benefit for M Génibrel, basso of the French Opera, at the Théâtre d'Orléans, including acts from *Robert le Diable* (the third), *Les Huguenots* (third), and an operetta, and an intermède musical.[16] Another musical intermède occurred on Sunday, June 22, with the popular zouave-artiste E. Glatigny who sang among other pieces the "Chant des Zouaves." The advertisements emphasized that the hall would be cooled as much as possible.[17] The two conductors of the opera were honored in July: Predigam on July 6, with excerpts from *Norma* and two new works,[18] and Prévost on July 26 in a varied program that featured Jacques Oliveira in De Bériot's Violin Concerto No. 7 (but not with orchestra: Philip Greuling accompanied on the piano) and with orchestra playing overtures.[19] These are the first known appearances of Oliveira (1836–67), who starred during the war in New Orleans, and of Greuling (ca. 1828–91), who soon became a fixture of concert life in the city. The final concert of the summer was on August 14, 1862, in the foyer of the Opera House, by Oliveira, A. Dantonnet, L. Mayer, and Greuling, with several female and male amateurs. The program consisted of two violin solos, a quartet with two violins, viola, and violoncello, a young amateur tenor singing several select pieces, and two female amateurs also singing.[20]

During the subsequent fall, La Hache, Oliveira, and Greuling spearheaded attempts to keep concert life alive. On Sunday, October 19, 1862, La Hache conducted an adaptation of Donizetti's *Martyrs* at Sainte Theresa's Church, where he was the regular organist. It was for the benefit of the female orphan asylum on Camp Street.[21] Two weeks later, on November 2, Oliveira played in an intermède during the drama *La Grace de Dieu* at the French Opera,[22] and he played in an intermède there again on November 16.[23] On December 1, Greuling directed the orchestra at the Varieties Theater,[24] and, on the 21st, Oliveira and Greuling played several pieces for violin and piano during yet another intermède.[25] The fall 1862 season ended with a soiree musicale at Mme Deron's Institute on December 29.[26]

The spring 1863 season saw a number of concerts, once again mostly by La Hache, Oliveira, Greuling, and Predigam. In January there were two at the old German or National Theater (corner of Saint Peter and Saint Claude streets, opposite Congo Square). The first, on January 15, was a grand vocal and instrumental concert featuring twelve of the best musicians of New Orleans, with M H. Haffner, the opéra comique singer straight from Italy. The orchestra played the overture to *Fra Diavolo* by Auber, a grand potpourri from Donizetti's *Daughter of the Regiment,* and some other works; the rest of the concert consisted of arias and duets.[27] Two weeks later, on January 29, there was a benefit for M Julian, the comic actor, who was about to leave the city. Several singers performed excerpts from operas, opéra comiques, comedies, vaudevilles, and a chansonnette. Predigam conducted the orchestra, while Oliveira, Carrière, and Hearn played solos. Oliveira played *Carnival de Venise* by Vieuxtemps, accompanied by Predigam on the piano.[28]

Besides an occasional concert, there were balls especially leading up to Mardi Gras. For these, the theater musicians of the city were employed, which kept them busy when they had too little at the theaters to keep them occupied.[29] Even after Mardi Gras, the balls needed orchestral musicians. For example, on April 4, 1863, there was a grand bal paré et masque at the Théâtre d'Orléans, where the orchestra was "composed of the best artists of the city."[30]

Two benefits took place on Thursday, February 12. One, for the departure of Mme Delatournerie, was at the Opera House and included a new opéra comique, the fourth act of *La Favorite,* and another comedie. The orchestra was directed by Predigam.[31] The other, for the Shakespearean actor George Ryer, was at the Varieties Theater, during which Oliveira, accompanied by Greuling, performed *The Carnival of Venice* and a fantasia on the opera *Il Pirata*.[32] On February 16, the Opera House opened for a grand vocal and instrumental concert to benefit the poor, as *The Bee* put it, "under the auspices of a few musical dilettanti of our city, whose talents form the charms of the social circle, and it required a circumstance like the present to give the public the rare and esteemed privilege of sharing the delights which are devoted to the edification of the parlor and the home circle alone." The critic hoped this would give respite from the dreariness of an occupied city during war. The program included opera arias, Jacques Oliveira, and piano duets by unnamed women.[33]

There were two benefits for actors during March at the Varieties Theater. The first, on Thursday, March 12, 1863, was for Mrs. W. C. Gladstane, with a musical interlude (pieces by Felicien David and Rossini) sung by Madame Delatournerie with Predigam conducting.[34] The second, on March 18, was for Vining Bowers; the complete program included a comedy, following which Oliveira played the violin and the orchestra played a grand march conducted by Greuling, after which there was a romantic drama in four acts.[35] Then, on Monday, March 23, there were competing musical events at the Opera House and the Varieties Theater. At the former was an "extraordinary" representation to benefit Isidore Nenning, with the assistance of various singers and Oliveira: *Lucia di Lammermoor*, in four acts, with an intermède by Oliveira. This was heralded as the first complete opera performance of the season, though a complete performance of *The Barber of Seville* took place on February 28 (the first complete opera heard in New Orleans, laments the writer in *L'Abeille*, for nearly two years).[36] The orchestra was directed by M Reiter; Mme Boudro played the piano.[37]

Simultaneously, at the Varieties Theater there was a grand operatic entertainment that featured the second act of *Il Trovatore*, the third act of *Robert le Diable*, and the commedietta *Morning Call*. There was an "efficient" chorus of both male and female voices and an increased orchestra.[38] Opera continued to sneak into the occupied city, with a complete performance of *Norma* at the Théâtre de l'Opéra (Opera House) on Monday, April 6; the orchestra was conducted by Predigam.[39] Trying to keep up, the Varieties Theater staged *Norma* without the music three days later.[40] On April 30, at a benefit performance for M Dubos, artist, at the Opera House, Reiter directed a fully staged performance of *Daughter of the Regiment*, along with two vaudevilles.[41]

Concerts continued occasionally in April and early May. There was a grand vocal and instrumental concert at the Opera House on Monday, April 13, 1863, consisting of choruses by Rossini and Cherubini sung by twenty-five female voices, a fantasia for two pianos by Thalberg, duets, and the Adagio and Rondo from the Concerto No. 7 by De Bériot; the concert was to benefit the local Creole singer Emma Bournos so that she could go to Paris to study with Duprez and attend the Paris Conservatoire. The newspaper critic pointed out that New Orleans was "the greatest music-loving city on this continent." On the program were a quintet for flute and strings performed by Oliveira, Dantonnet, Mayer, Heph, and one other, and a quartet with Oliveira, Dantonnet, Greuling, and Mayer.[42] Meanwhile, Oliveira and Greuling (of the orchestra of the Varieties Theater) gave three concerts at Guth's Saloon on Conti Street, between Royal and Bourbon streets, on May 3, 5, and 9. The performances were billed as "grands concerts à la Strauss," modeled after Johann Strauss's concerts in Vienna, and the selection of music was grand operatic overtures, potpourris, solos, and so forth.[43] There were just two concerts in June 1863. The first, on June 6, was a grand concert and dance at Globe Hall, with a wind band conducted by Charles Jaeger. The program included opera tunes, potpourris, overtures, and arias.[44] Over the next few years, Jaeger became a dominant figure in wind music in New Orleans. A second concert was held on Wednesday, June 10. It was a grand concert at the Théâtre de l'Opéra by Minnie Howe (Minnie Hauk?) and included a grand trio by De Bériot and another trio by Mayseder played by Oliveira, Greuling, and Meyer, a piece by Artôt and Carnival played by Oliveira, the Concertant de *La Favorite* by De Bériot performed by Oliveira and Greuling, national airs, and songs.[45] The hot months of July and August were without concerts.

The fall 1863 season began auspiciously enough on Sunday, September 13, with a new Grand Mass by Theodore von La Hache, performed at Sainte Theresa's Church where La Hache was organist.[46] During performances of vaudevilles at the Théâtre d'Orléans on September 27, Oliveira played in the musical intermède.[47] Several singers performed there on October 4 during another intermède.[48] The Academy of Music opened on October 7 with Sanford's opera troupe, which continued into November; here, too, there were frequent musical intermèdes.[49] A morale booster occurred on Sunday, October 18, with the first performance of Flotow's famous opera *Martha* at the Théâtre d'Orléans. The vocalists and instrumentalists of the orchestra felt a special bond as they were reunited in a rare performance of opera during the occupation.[50] A week later, Oliveira, Greuling, and Meyer gave a concert at the Théâtre de l'Opéra.[51] Although the Théâtre d'Orléans opened only on November 15, there was a performance there a week before of Adolphe Adam's *Postillon de Longjumeau,* with Predigam conducting the orchestra and choir.[52] The Saint Charles Theatre opened on November 26, but only for plays.[53] *Don Pasquale* was performed at the Théâtre d'Orléans on December 6, and Offenbach's operettas were there on December 22. Greuling supplied incidental music ("characteristic music") for the play *The Colleen Baun* by Boucicault at the Varieties Theater on the last day of 1863.[54]

One of the most interesting musical phenomena during the occupation was the presence in New Orleans of the most important military band conductor in America, Patrick Gilmore. Cooperation between the Union governors and local leaders could be visibly demonstrated by cooperation between Union musicians and local musicians. On January 26, 1864, there was a promenade concert at the new opera house, under the auspices of some of the most distinguished military gentlemen, assisted by leading citizens, both Creole and American. The musical portion was under the direction of Gilmore, who included his own works: marches, along with his new and popular song, "Johnny Comes Marching Home." Oliveira, accompanied by Greuling, performed a duo with orchestra arranged from the music of Mendelssohn, and local singers provided opera arias and songs.[55]

An opera season of sorts opened unusually late, on February 6, 1864, at the Saint Charles Theatre[56] and the next evening at the Théâtre d'Orléans. Over the next few weeks, New Orleanians could rejoice in some favorite works: *The Barber of Seville, Robert le Diable, Martha,* and *Don Pasquale,* among others.[57] The new opera house did not experience opera until April, with *The Barber of Seville* and Adam's *Toreador.* Predigam conducted these as well as operas comiques, operettas bouffes, and vaudevilles (one by Offenbach).[58]

The spring concerts included a musical soiree at the Opera House, with Mme L. Loening assisted by Oliveira, Mayer, and others on March 15, 1864; a grand complimentary concert at the Opera House given to Minnie Hauk, prior to her departure for Europe, with assisting artists Curto, Oliveira, Greuling and Louis Mayer on April 15; an evening of Italian opera selections sung by Miss Teresa Contoli at the Academy of Music on April 18; a benefit for M Durieu with scenes from opéra comiques and vaudevilles on April 24; and a grand concert by Auguste Davis at the Opera House with the assistance of Oliveira on May 7.[59] Minnie "Howe" was probably Minnie Hauk (1851–1929), then living in New Orleans as a pupil of Curto and later to become a famous American opera singer. Other musicians continued to perform in small locales in order to eke out a living. Such was the case when John Hosch announced on May 12 that he was sponsoring concerts for violin and piano in his salon and restaurant at rue Bienville No. 51, which served the best beer in the West. The concerts were performed by the Mayer (Meyer) brothers.[60] On June 16, at Saint Alphonse's Hall, there was a grande soiree musicale presented by La Hache, Oliveira, and Greuling and many women and men, distinguished amateurs of New Orleans. They performed major vocal works from operas; the instrumental works included duets for two pianos performed by unnamed female amateurs, and Souvenir de Bellini by Artôt played by Oliveira.[61] Another grand concert at Saint Alphonse's Hall was performed on July 7 for the benefit of the Church of Notre Dame de Bon Secours on Jackson Avenue. Oliveira, again, was on the program.[62]

On those occasions during the siege and occupation when complete operas were performed, clearly enough singers and the orchestra remained in the city so that such performances were feasible. During the siege it was difficult for anyone to leave the city, but once the Union conquered New Orleans, travel to places in the North like New York and to Europe was possible again. A small exodus began—at least of some of the singers, and Prévost did leave. But many were still in the city for the *La Favorite, The Barber of Seville,* and *Lucia* performances the winter of 1862–63 and remained for the various excerpts performed the next two years. In May 1864 Lewis Baker proposed establishing an Italian opera season and asked for subscribers,[63] but nothing seems to have come of it. The occupying forces used the Opera House for political purposes, such as for the concert on January 26, 1864, with Patrick Gilmore conducting,[64] but in general this magnificent new edifice was going to waste.

The final months of the occupation, comprising the fall and early spring season 1864–65, saw an increase in the number of concerts, with the appearance of two local musicians who had until then not figured prominently during the war. The four regulars—Oliveira, La Hache, Greuling, and Predigam—continued, but to them were added a number of others, especially Curto and, after several years of silence, Collignon. On Thursday, September 15, 1864, Jacques Oliveira tried to give a vocal and instrumental concert at the Opera House with distinguished unnamed amateurs, but because the hall was under the sheriff's seizure orders, the concert was postponed until September 19 and moved to Saint Alphonse's Hall, Saint Andrew Street. In advance the critic extolled, "The programme is enriched with splendid passages from the great masters. To lovers of the highest order of music the occasion appeals with special force."[65] Afterwards he stated, "This concert, given by Mr. Oliveira assisted by a number of accomplished amateurs, is conceded to have been a rare, rich and brilliant musical success. Correct instrumentation, artistic grace of execution, and splendid vocalization marked the performances." During the concert Oliveira, Louis Mayer, and Charles Mayer played a trio arrangement of a Weber overture and a Mayseder trio.

On October 11 and 29, 1864, there were two performances of Haydn's *Creation* at the Opera House, with a full orchestra and chorus directed by G. M. Loening. The orchestra was composed of artists and amateurs of the city and the chorus of a large number of amateurs from various church choirs. The second concert was for the benefit of the Louisiana Relief Lodge.[66] In honor of Sainte Cecilia's Day, Tuesday, November 22, 1864, Gustave Collignon, master of music at the Church of the Immaculate Conception, conducted the E-flat Solemn Mass of Weber. It was to benefit the poor of the Saint Vincent de Paul Society, and it took place at the Church of the Immaculate Conception.[67]

Miss Eva Brent sang three concerts at the Academy of Music on November 10 to 12, 1864, accompanied by the academy's orchestra under Oliveira.[68] An unnamed, young female pianist contributed a grand benefit concert on November 30 at the Opera House, during which various piano pieces and songs were performed. Most of her assisting performers were unnamed amateurs, but Auguste Davis also participated.[69] On Wednesday, December 14, 1864, there was a vocal and instrumental benefit concert at the French Opera House for Fourmestreau, first oboist of the Opera House Orchestra, with women and men, artists and amateurs of the city, assisting.[70] The fine soprano Anna Bishop appeared at the Academy of Music for two farewell concerts on December 23 and 24. She was accompanied by Mr. Charles Lascelles from the Royal Academy of Music in London. The program consisted of a grand opera aria, songs, and chansonettes, sung by both Bishop and the versatile Lascelles (accompanied by Charles Mayer), and piano pieces performed by Lascelles. Attendance was not too good owing to the bitter cold on the first evening and the competition of Christmas Eve events on the second.[71] A "musical and classical soiree" was held at the Locquet Institute on Camp Street on December 23, and another soiree musicale was given in the salons of Madame Boyer a week later.[72] Following the last soiree the critic of *L'Abeille* used this event as evidence of the musical depth of New Orleans:

> If New Orleans is to be noted among all other cities for the number of its excellent musicians, that fact is because of the happy musical organization of our young creoles and the zeal of the teachers of merit who have imported and still perpetuate among us the pure taste and good traditions taught by the grand masters. We have proof of it in the musical soiree that took place last Friday, in the salons of Mme Boyer, a society composed of the elite of our dilettanti. This charming reunion appeared to us to be an echo of the musical matinees of past times, and has procured for us, while we tend to forget it by our present preoccupations, some agreeable impressions. We have heard at this recital many generations of Boyer's students, from her young female pupils who already reveal their talent, to the oldest of them who, in turn, are mature artists who have taken their place among our most eminent professors. Above all, we have observed how, besides their natural and very happy dispositions, they show the fruits of excellent training and of elevated musical taste in their studies.[73]

Rumors circulated in New Orleans that Gottschalk would be giving a recital, but he did not come and was never to perform in his hometown again.[74] The first concert of the new year was a solemn high mass (the Mass for Peace) on Sunday, January 8, 1865, at Sainte Theresa's Church, under the direction of La

Hache, with orchestral accompaniment, to benefit the Female Orphan Asylum.[75] This was followed two days later by a charity concert at Saint Alphonse's Hall directed by Mr. Dubos, chapel master at Saint Louis Cathedral. "The varied and well selected programme includes the "Hymn of the Night," the poetry of Lamartine set to music by Neukomm. Participants included La Hache, Charles Mayer, Mr. Bremer, and the violinist Henri Page.[76] Both amateurs and professionals participated, and there was a full choir. On January 18, Oliveira announced that he would be giving a vocal and instrumental concert at the French Opera House "soon,"[77] but he did not appear again in concert in New Orleans until December and then, after only a few chamber music concerts, disappeared completely from the chronicles of the city. Considering how active he was during the war, his sudden death from cholera in 1867 was a tragedy not only for his family and friends but for the history of music in New Orleans. Henri Page, though not as well appreciated, quickly took his place as the premier professional violinist in the city.

Curto organized two sacred concerts this spring. On Thursday, February 23, 1865, he directed a sacred vocal and instrumental concert at the Church of Sainte Anne in order to help pay for the new organ.[78] The second one, on March 19, was a major event in honor of Saint Joseph's Day. He spearheaded a sacred concert at the Théâtre de l'Opéra in a program that included his own *Stabat Mater,* parts 1 and 2 (solos, chorus, and orchestra), Mercadante's Overture to Rossini's *Stabat Mater,* and a complete performance of Beethoven's oratorio *Christ on the Mount of Olives.*[79]

5

Recovery of the Postwar Years
1865–1872

When the war ended on April 9, 1865, the city, which had suffered virtually no physical damage, was in financial ruin, and yet concert life was quick to recover. On Sunday, April 16, 1865, there was a grand sacred concert at the Opera House by Miss Eva Brent, a favorite New Orleans artist, to raise money for the poor families of the city. A complete orchestra was engaged.[1] The next evening violinist Page gave an instrumental and vocal concert at the Saint Charles Theatre, with M Flandry and a group of amateur singers. Page performed his new, brilliant waltz, "Hommage aux Louisianais," the music for which could be purchased at local venders and the proceeds from which were donated to the poor of the city.[2]

Increasingly, the exiled musicians returned. There was a bustling of musical activity in May that far surpassed that of the previous four years and that resembled that of any year in the 1840s or 1850s. What adds to the impression of sudden renewal is that May previously was the time when the season began to wind down because of the onset of extreme heat and humidity, yet here the season suddenly came alive. Leon Prévost, son of Eugène, announced on May 1 that he was back to conduct the orchestra of the French Opera House in a special farewell concert on Saturday, May 6, 1865, for Miss A. Fleury, the well-known local singer who was going to Paris to study at the conservatory.[3] They were assisted by artists of the city. Prévost conducted an orchestra in another grand concert on May 24, 1865, again with Miss Fleury as soloist.[4] Meanwhile, on May 4, Fannie Melmer, joined by Luccia Bordesi and many amateurs under the direction of Harry Melmer, gave a grand vocal and instrumental concert at the Saint Charles Opera House;[5] the pupils of Theodore von la Hache gave a grand concert at Saint Alphonse's Hall on May 17 in a program that included Donizetti's *Les Martyrs* and various German, French, and English romances;[6] and on May 31 Leon Prévost conducted a grand charity concert offered by the women of New Orleans, including both amateurs and artists as soloists (Miss A. Fleury is the only one named), with a grand orchestra performing the overtures to Aimé Louis Maillart's *Les Dragons de Villars* and Hérold's *Zampa*.[7] In a review of this last concert, the critic waxed sentimental on returning, at last, to the prewar glory of the French Opera House after four long years of suffering. One further concert during the month occurred on May 22, in commemoration of the second anniversary of the Deutsche Company, which gave a grand vocal and instrumental concert and dramatic entertainment at the Opera House for the benefit of Jewish widows and orphans.[8]

Other signs of rebirth were evident. Beginning on May 20 the intermèdes returned to the Opera House between dramas and vaudevilles.[9] One of the city's most important voice teachers, Mme Charles Boudousquié, having returned to New Orleans, announced on May 30 to her former students, and to those families she had impressed, that she was again teaching voice. Mme Boudousquié, now married to the former director of the opera, Charles Boudousquié, had starred at the opera as Julie Calvé.[10]

Band concerts began to increase in popularity. On June 4, Jaeger's Wind Orchestra (the Jaeger Band) performed a grand sacred concert in the gardens of Cedre Magnolia, next to the Bayou Bridge, with illuminations.[11] Throughout June, Joseph V. Gessner's band performed musical soirees each Wednesday and Thursday.[12] School concerts again became festive occasions. On June 8 there was the concert and prize distribution of the Saint Louis Institute under Madame C. Deron. The institute, at 275 Dauphine Street, between Ursulines and Hospital streets, was an old and well-approved school for young women.[13] Not to be left behind, Mme Boyer's École de Musique announced that there would be monthly exercises (recitals) where one could hear the children sing in choir and play the piano.[14] Mme Magioni joined Boyer as an instructor.

This sudden upsurge in musical activity was a good sign of recovery. Nonetheless, it would take a few years for the city to fully reach its prewar eminence as a major center of classical music. While many musicians, both professionals and amateurs, either stayed in the city throughout the war or returned shortly thereafter, the steady flow of fresh musicians from Europe and the rest of America and the European education of many native children had been greatly curtailed. It would take a few years to restore this flow, but by the return of the Classic Music Series in 1871, the musical life of New Orleans approached its prewar status. The problem after that was maintaining, let alone enlarging, that status.

Reintroduction of a regular opera season was paramount to the restitution of a strong concert life in New Orleans. At the end of the war, the Academy of

Music was the only regular theater open for theater.[15] The French Opera was the center of classical music in the city for the first sixty years of the century, and the citizens depended on it and the many musical activities it spawned for a European style of concert life. Charles Boudousquié, who managed the Opera House when it opened in 1859, returned to New Orleans by the end of May after having served in the Confederate Army and took a job with an auction house. This was probably meant as a temporary position to keep bread on the table while he prepared for the reorganization of the opera.[16] However, the new owners of the theater passed over the management that had been running the theater before the war and opted for new talent. The result was an unsteady leadership in the city's opera arena for the rest of the nineteenth century, and despite some great successes during the thirty-five years following the end of the Civil War, it was nowhere as significant as before the war.

In order to begin an operatic season in the winter of 1865–66, Gustave Ostermann, the gifted manager of the German Theatre, which was using the French Opera House, was given authority to hire Max Strakosch's Italian Opera Company to perform fifteen operas.[17] The theater opened with German drama on October 27, 1865, while the opera enthusiasts waited two months longer for Strakosch's group.[18] Originating in New York, this company was traveling in the South and included among other stars Strakosch's daughter-in-law, his son Maurice's soprano wife, Amalia Patti. The performances, including a full orchestra, were to start on December 20 but did not actually begin until the following evening.[19] The highlight of their performances was the New Orleans premier on January 11, 1866, of Gounod's opera *Faust* which at once became one of the most popular operas in New Orleans. It also presented Verdi's *The Masked Ball* for the first time in the city.[20] The critic of the *New Orleans Daily Crescent* found that "the orchestra and chorus were superb" and that "the orchestra and chorus could not be excelled."[21] Solo singers, however, were not yet up to snuff.

The concert life in the city during the season 1865–66 included a few benefits. On December 29, 1865, there was a benefit concert for war victims (widows and orphans), performed by twenty-four women on twelve pianos, conducted by Mlle Octavie Romey. It took place in Odd Fellows' Hall. This concert was followed by another on Monday, April 30, 1866. Once again Mlle Octavie Romey was musical director; T. von la Hache was conductor of choruses. In addition to four grand opera overtures played by the twenty-four women, Oliveira performed two violin pieces, in one case accompanied by Greuling. There were several vocal pieces, including several sung by Miss Annie McLean ("who sings every Sunday at Trinity Church"). Romey played a few piano solos.[22] These two benefits netted $1,867.40. The beneficiary was Les Enfans de Marie, which distributed food, fuel, and clothing to the widows and orphans of those Louisianans who died in the Civil War. Mme Leonce Boudousquié, probably a relative of Mme Julie (Charles) Boudousquié, was president.[23] In addition there was a benefit concert on Thursday, May 10, 1866, for Mme Fleury Urban, with Oliveira on violin. She sang arias by Mercadante, Meyerbeer, and Campana.[24]

Two young pianists were the stars of the 1865–66 season: Marguerite Elie and Carlotta Shaw. (The former is discussed at length in book I.) In mid-January 1866, Miss Carlotta Shaw, a niece of Mrs. Harry Watkins (alias Mrs. Charles Howard), was playing at Odd Fellows' Hall in a pair of concerts featuring Mrs. Watkins, and a critic noted that she "surprised the audience with the power and expression with which she executed some very difficult and elaborate pieces."[25] A few days later, on January 20, she was playing at the Olympic Theatre, between acts of an Irish play. Miss Shaw, pianist, "challenge[s] the highest admiration. She is a player whose equal is rarely heard."[26] On May 12 Shaw was back at the Olympic Theatre and, for her own benefit, played several pieces between the two dramatic productions.[27]

Also a sign of recovery was the return of at least one of the major music publishers. A. E. Blackmar announced on January 16, 1866, that he had just published new music by Professor A. Cardona, C. Blamphin, and the "Grand Concert Fantasia upon 'La Marseillaise and Bonnie Blue Flag,' as performed with great applause, at her late concerts at Odd Fellows' Hall, by its composer, M'lle Romey."[28]

With the return of nightly opera performances, New Orleanians were getting back in stride with their cultural life, and now it was possible for the entire classical music scene to begin to grow. So successful were these performances that Strakosch agreed to stay on another few weeks for a second round of operas, and he arranged to return the following fall to the old Saint Charles Theatre; the new season began on November 5, 1866, with *Il Trovatore*.[29] That venue was chosen because the officers and management of the French Opera House decided that it was time to restore their own opera company, and in that case there would be no room for a visiting company.

The owners of the French Opera House hired a new manager who was French and who had experience in French theater. Marcelin Alhaiza set about creating a French drama group and a new French repertory opera. Alhaiza had been performing in Mexico and was part of a French theater group that opened at the Opera House on March 22, 1866. When chosen to be manager, he gave his concept of how he expected to run the hall. Opera and drama were to have equal time. There was to be a six-month season, during which each week would consist of five performances of opera, opéra comique, drama, comedy, and vaudeville. Sundays were free for whatever would come up.[30]

First he recreated the theater company. Repertory French drama returned to the Opera House after Strakosch's troupe left it in February 1866. The drama troupe was formed by Alhaiza himself; he and his brother Paul often appeared in it as actors.[31] Creating a new repertory opera company was more difficult, since, as was customary, many new singers had to be imported from France. During the summer of 1866, Marcelin went to France to recruit a new troupe for the French Opera House, but an unexpected disaster prevented this from happening. The boat Evening Star, with the opera troupe on it, sank in the Atlantic.[32] Marcelin Alhaiza and the entire European cast were drowned at sea as it neared America, and another plan had to be enacted. Strakosch did move his company over to the French Opera House on November 7, 1866, for a few performances to help the hall meet expenses and in sympathy for the many lost lives.[33] Under the baton of Sig. Nicolao, Strakosch's troupe performed six operas: *Fra Diavolo, The Barber of Seville, Faust, Martha, Ione* and *L'Africaine.*

The theater owners then appointed Paul Alhaiza as manager, who was able to reopen the drama season on November 16, 1866.[34] He arranged for musical intermèdes between acts of the plays, which kept the orchestra busy. A combination of French drama and benefit concerts enabled the Opera House to be active in the fall of 1866 until Alhaiza could recruit a new opera company. One such benefit was for Alhaiza himself, on November 15, 1866.[35] When the Théâtre d'Orléans burned, Alhaiza offered the French Opera House to help his comrades who had suffered such an unexpected catastrophe.[36] On January 11, 1867, however, Alhaiza's new troupe—a visiting Italian company known as the Roncari Italian Opera Troupe—opened an abbreviated season with Verdi's *Ernani.*[37] Jaime Nuno was conductor, and L. Donizetti was administrator.[38] Between January 11 and January 25 the Roncari Troupe performed *Ernani, La Traviata, La Favorite, Elisir d'Amore, Lucia di Lammermoor, Lucrezia Borgia, Norma, The Barber of Seville,* and *Don Pasquale.*

Meanwhile the city was not without opera during the fall of 1866. Besides Strakosch's troupe performing at the Saint Charles Theatre, Ostermann's group was endowed by the German community of New Orleans with its own theater, the new National Theater in the American sector of the city (on Baronne and Perdido streets). It opened on November 22, 1866.[39] For the official opening ceremony the conductor, Robert Meyer, composed a march and, in addition, the overture to *Yelva* by Reissinger was on the program. There is no mention of an orchestra in the newspaper accounts, but Robert Meyer was a conductor, and subsequently the operas performed there would have required an orchestra.[40] The new hall seated 1,500 to 1,600 persons and was the home from this point on of drama and operas in the German language.[41] At first Ostermann brought in Italian opera, which he took over from Alhaiza's French Opera House.[42] Except for a week-long hiatus (March 30–April 5), the Roncari Italian Opera Troupe was in residence from February 15 until late in April 1867.[43] Nonetheless, during this time Offenbach's *Orphée aux Enfers,* sung in German, experienced a long run. Over the next few years the performance of German-language opera added diversity and strength to the overall opera season of the city. In November 1867, both *Der Freischütz* and Lortzing's *Czar und Zimmermann* opened at the National Theater for sizeable runs.[44] On February 5, 1868, the Grande Troupe d'Opera Allemand began a run at the National Theater. The operas performed were *Martha, Faust, Die Zauberflötte, Der Freischütz, Fra Diavolo, The Daughter of the Regiment, Fidelio,* and others. German vaudevilles also were regular features at the National Theater.[45]

Since Alhaiza was not an expert in opera, he teamed up with Eduoard Calabrési during the summer of 1867 and returned with a new French troupe in time for the opening on November 21, 1867, with *La Favorite.*[46] Opera in Italian and opera in German may have satisfied some members of the New Orleans community, but the large number of French-speaking citizens desired their dramas and operas in French. It mattered little whether the operas were originally in German or French or Italian; for the French Opera House, Gounod, Verdi, and Weber were performed in French; and for the National Theater, Offenbach, Auber, and Lortzing were performed in German. This, then, was the first real repertory company at the French Opera House since the Civil War; the other repertory companies there were visiting temporarily. Strakosch's troupe and the Italian company hired by Paul Alhaiza did a great deal to lift the spirits of New Orleanians after the war and Evening Star disaster and to bring opera back to the city.[47] A sign of their importance for opera-loving citizens was that Strakosch's Italian opera season at the Saint Charles Theatre encouraged M A. Elie to start selling opera music again in his music store.[48] From the fall of 1867, however, the restoration of the prewar tradition of French opera began in earnest, and New Orleans was once again the opera capital of America.

But all was not yet healthy in the city since the economy had not yet rebounded. One observer marveled that Calabrési put together both the orchestra and the opera chorus in a week's time, and the opera performances at the French Opera House got lavish reviews daily in both *L'Abeille* and *The Bee.* Yet attendance was not good.[49] Although the quality of the performances was high, there were small audiences because of the economy—"by reason of the unwonted and extraordinary depression in monetary affairs which affects alike all classes and conditions of our people."[50]

Important, too, for the recovery of orchestral and chamber music was the restoration of Odd Fellows' Hall. The Union Army abandoned the hall once the war was over, and it left the place in shambles.[51] It was important for the orchestral and chamber music life of the city that it be available, especially since, with the revival of operas and dramas at the French Opera House, that hall would seldom be open to outside events. During the summer of 1865, Odd Fellows' Hall was renovated and new furniture and other appurtenances were provided. It reopened on October 16 with the first of a series of balls.[52] The first postwar concert there was on December 7, 1865, under the direction of La Hache.[53] It was a fund-raiser for Trinity Church and consisted of piano works and vocal works. The first recital there was that of eighteen-year-old Marguerite Elie on December 27. She had returned from her studies in Paris[54] on November 17 and gave her first public recital with Oliveira and Greuling at the Opera House on December 19,[55] but once Strakosch's Italian Opera Troupe took over the Opera House, Elie and her new friends presented her three subsequent recitals at Odd Fellows' Hall. Her collaboration with Oliveira and Greuling was important for the future of chamber music in the city, since it no doubt planted a seed in her head. When she returned from Europe in 1876 to settle permanently in New Orleans, she spearheaded the chamber music revival in the city through her work with the best local violinists and other top instrumentalists. On January 5, 1866, Marguerite Elie, Oliveira, and Meyer performed a Mendelssohn trio.[56] Subsequently, on February 9 and April 17, the Harmonic Association of New Orleans gave two concerts at Odd Fellows' Hall.[57]

As we have seen, benefit concerts continued after the end of the war since this was a type of concert that had proven useful for musicians for well over a hundred years throughout Europe as well as America. In the immediate aftermath of the war, the city was full of needy people—orphans and widows, injured soldiers, musicians who had not had full employment, among others—and benefits were a major source for raising money for charities to aid these people. For example, Eva Brent gave a benefit for "Familles pauvres de cette ville at the French Opera House on April 17, 1865";[58] and there was the benefit for Jewish widows and orphans that took place on May 22, 1865, also in the French Opera House.[59] Luccia Bordesi sang opera excerpts during a benefit for Fannie Melmes at the Saint Charles Opera House on May 4, 1865.[60] One week later was the charity concert at the French Opera House offered by the women of New Orleans.[61]

Two years later, the benefit concerts were still important, but, as before the war, usually for the benefit of the performer rather than for charities. On Saturday, May 4, 1867, a benefit was held at the French Opera House for M Prioré, chef d'orchestre, who often at a moment's notice had to arrange pieces for his incomplete orchestra.[62] Exactly what "incomplete" meant is uncertain, but since Prioré often conducted vaudevilles between acts of an opera or after an opera performance, it is possible that he had only a fraction of the opera orchestra at his disposal. He conducted two vaudevilles on this occasion. An orchestral benefit was held three days later, on May 7, at the National Theater as a tribute to Carlo Patti, the accomplished musician and leader of the orchestra at the Varieties Theater.[63] Those performing and thereby honoring Patti were Collignon, Miss Lora Rolff (German Theatre), Mr. Kaps (German Theatre), Auguste Davis, John Jacobs (Varieties Theater Orchestra), and Mr. S. Grillo (French Opera House), with sixty of the "best instrumental performers," the whole being under the direction of Collignon and Carlo Patti. A new work was written for the occasion, the Railroad Galop, by Mr. H. Goetzel.[64]

Only a handful of concerts with orchestra were not advertised as benefits. On Monday, April 29, 1867, Henri Page, first violinist of the French Opera House orchestra, gave a recital at the Opera House to a small audience.[65] He was an excellent violinist but apparently did not have the charm of Oliveira and received an indifferent response from the audience. The program, accompanied by "tous les artistes de l'orchestre,"[66] included opera excerpts performed on the violin, songs sung by M Fernando, a duo for flutes (performed by the pupils of Carrière, also a member of the house orchestra), a piece for two pianos from *Norma,* and so forth. There were separate pieces for clarinet and trombone. The orchestra played the overture to *Les Diamants de la Couronne* and the waltz *Les Soeurs de Charité* composed by Page. The concert had good parts, but some pieces dragged. Eleven-year-old Mark Kaiser made his debut in the National Theater on December 19, 1867, playing the Viotti Violin Concerto No. 5 with full orchestra. The orchestra also performed overtures.[67] A soiree was given on Saturday, January 18, 1868, at the German Hall on Bienville, during which the orchestra played some pieces, and there was some chamber music for violin and piano, and some vocal music.[68]

Besides the orchestras at the main opera houses (French Opera House, National Theater, Saint Charles Theatre) some of the other theaters maintained orchestras as they had during the prewar years. This was especially true of the Varieties Theater and the Academy of Music, where Professor Younkers was chef d'orchestra during the 1867–68 season.[69] On the other hand, the number of concerts in churches also grew after the war, and orchestras borrowed from the theaters were involved.[70]

As usual, little went on in concert life in New Orleans from summer until the late fall of 1867 when theaters and music schools reopened. The German National Theater was particularly active from November 3 on, with performances of Lortzing's *Czar and Zimmerman* and Weber's *Der Freischütz* heading the slate.[71] On November 21 the French Opera House reopened with a troupe recruited from France, in *La Favorite,* with Edouard Calabrési making his New Orleans conducting debut. The orchestra was deemed excellent.[72] And on December 7, 1867, the Academy of Music reopened, also with a new conductor, Professor Younkers.[73] With the economy in bad shape, however, people were finding it difficult to afford tickets, and the critic of *The Bee* noted poor attendance at the opera.[74] Meanwhile, Mmes Boyer and Magioni reopened their music school for young children and girls on November 4; Eugène Prévost, former orchestral conductor in New Orleans, arrived from New York on November 7 to teach at the Locquet Institute; Mme Cambier announced on November 17 that she was resuming teaching singing on Mondays, Wednesdays, and Fridays; and Mr. A Flandry also opened his piano studio on the same day.[75]

Eugène Prévost had plans beyond just teaching privately at an institute. On December 8, he announced that he had created the Orphéon Louisianais, which would meet for the first time on January 14, 1868. He opened special music classes for adult men and young men and boys from seven to fourteen years old. He expected that such a society would contribute to the development of musical taste among young people and help nurture instrumentalists and singers.[76] Eventually this organization would play a major role in the concert life of the city as a vital performing society.

The opening of the 1867–68 concert season occurred on December 10, 1867, with the recital of Madame Petipas, who arrived from Brazil, Cuba, and the Antilles with a great reputation and who had scored successes on the lyric stages of France and Belgium. The concert at the National Theater was not well attended, however.[77] She returned on Friday, January 3, 1868, in a grand vocal and instrumental concert at Masonic Hall. The piano used in the concert was a Steinway, which was provided by Grunewald.[78] As already mentioned, Mark Kaiser performed a grand concert at the National Theater on December 14 or 19. The orchestra played an unnamed overture, and Kaiser played the Viotti Violin Concerto No. 5 with full orchestra.[79] This was the official debut of Kaiser, then eleven years old, before he studied in Paris and became one of the most significant members of the concert scene in *fin de siècle* New Orleans.[80]

The concerts in the spring 1868 season were back on track. On Thursday, January 16, 1868, at the National Theater, there was a concert de dames, a soiree musicale et patriotique, for the benefit of the widows and orphans of southern soldiers at the Hôpital des Invalides du Sud under Abbé Turgis. Mlle Romey directed amateur men and women; she was known locally as a pianist and composer. One piece was for twelve pianos, twenty-four hands; another was a piece performed by the young Kaiser; other pieces were performed by M. and C. and R.[81] Then on January 17 Josephine Filomeno, just arrived from Paris where she had great success as pianist and violinist, proposed to give a concert soon with the assistance of amateurs. She was a native of Chile, and just fifteen years old. She performed privately at Collignon's home, where she played Gottschalk's *Fantasie* and two fantasies by Liszt—all on the piano; then she picked up the violin and performed a caprice by Vieuxtemps and a fantasy on a theme from Nabucco. She was a young artist but with mature style and taste—so wrote A. F. Lutton in a letter to the paper dated January 27, 1868.[82] During the next four months she lived in New Orleans and participated in a number of concerts. On February 6, Filomeno gave a grand vocal and instrumental concert in the German Hall. She was assisted by Jules Météyé, Auguste Davis, Gustave Smith, and some amateurs.[83] The reviewer showered praise on her: "She plays the violin really remarkably well, with a delicate Expression and a taste that is elitist and that shows excellent musical education. The audience of connoisseurs at her concert applauded her with enthusiasm."

On Friday, February 21, Filomeno gave a concert at the National Theater. She played piano works by Liszt, Gottschalk, Thalberg, and so forth; she also played the Mendelssohn Violin Concerto and other violin works by Paganini and Vieuxtemps.[84] On March 6, she participated in a concert again as both pianist and violinist. Her colleagues were La Hache, Braun, Dubos, and at least one amateur; La Hache arranged the concert.[85] She performed two concerts on Saturday, March 27. One was at Lyceum Hall accompanied by A. Graff (baritone of the German Opera), August Couderc (first oboist of the French Opera), and Greuling, accompanist.[86] The second was a grande soiree musicale at the French Opera House to benefit the famine sufferers of Prussia. Performers, besides Filomeno (violin), were Antoinette Fehriager (piano), solo singers, and a choir.[87] During the week of April 12 to 18 she performed "her choicest pieces" on both violin and piano during intermèdes at the Varieties Theater between magic shows and tableaux. Mr. Robert Meyer was leader of the orchestra.[88] Then on April 13 she was a participant in the first of a new series of chamber concerts in New Orleans referred to as parlor concerts. The main movers behind this series were the Mendelssohn Quartet (a singing group), Louis Mayer, and Philip Greuling. This concert was at Lyceum Hall.[89] She also participated in a benefit for the Orphans Home given by the Orleans Literary and Debating Society on April 24. It took place at the National Theater, and other performers included Greuling and several talented amateurs (Miss G., Miss W., and MM Météyé and Prévost).[90] Filomeno's final program during this season seems to have been on May 7 when she performed as part of a grand vocal and instrumental concert at the Lyceum Hall for the benefit of the rector of Saint Peters Protestant Episcopal Church. The Mendelssohn Quartet also participated.[91]

There were concerts where Filomeno did not participate. On January 18, 1868, there was a soiree musicale at the Salle Allemande, Rue Bienville. It was a varied program including orchestral works, pieces for violin and piano, and some vocal works.[92] Eugène Prévost, accompanied by distinguished artists, gave a concert of his own on January 22 to aid the Dames de la Providence.[93] On Wednesday, January 29, Oscar Pfeiffer, pianist, and his singer wife announced that they were disposed to give three concerts in New Orleans if there were enough subscribers. Louis Grunewald was in charge of getting the subscriptions.[94] Pfeiffer had already been acclaimed on two continents, but there is no evidence that he ever raised enough interest in New Orleans to perform there.

On Wednesday, February 5, 1868, there was a concert at the German Hall for the benefit of Mount Olivet Episcopal Church in Algiers. The performers were Mrs. Roach (the former Annie McLean), her sister Ms. McLean, Miss Romez, Mrs. Prudhomme, Mr. Cheeler, Mr. Meytier (probably Météyé), H. Braun, and "the young master of the violin" Mark Kaiser, directed by La Hache. Since not enough money was raised, however, a second concert was planned for February 24.[95] Collignon directed another grand sacred concert at the Church of Saint Vincent de Paul on March 15; it was in honor of Saint Joseph's Day, which was four days later. He performed works of Rossini, Haydn, Stradella, and Verdi.[96] Gustave Smith, pianist and organist, assisted by MM Picot and Le Chevalier, Mmes Audibert and Seguin, and Mmes Locquet and Loening (pianists), H. Braun (violoncello), and Page (violinist), gave his farewell concert on March 22; Smith was returning to his native Canada.[97] On April 1 there was a soiree of the Deutsche Company at the National Theater. Performers included Mrs. J. Schwartz, Météyé, Signor Palochi, Fanny Kreeger, Mrs. Wulff, Mrs. Mary Charpaux, Renzo Grunewald, and Mr. Cassard. There were orchestral overtures, pieces for piano four-hands, and singers. "Some of the musical selections, both vocal and instrumental, were rendered in most unexceptionably artistic style." The evening concluded with dancing.[98]

The second of the series of four parlor concerts at Lyceum (City) Hall by the Mendelssohn Quartet, with Josephine Filomeno, took place on Monday, April 20. Others on the program included her father, Miguel Filomeno (violoncello), Mme Marietta Sohiavoni Buck (soprano) in her New Orleans debut, and Greuling, accompanist. The program included songs and chamber music for violin, vocal quartet, piano, violoncello and piano duet.[99] The third parlor concert by the Mendelssohn Quartet at the Lyceum Hall was on April 27. "The attendance was very large, with more women than men, and every seat in the Lyceum Hall was taken."[100] The fourth and last of the series was given on May 4.[101] The Parlor Series was so popular that for the next several years it was repeated.

On April 22, 1868, there was a benefit concert at the Varieties Theater for John S. Bernard, the leader of the orchestra, and J. W. Thorpe, stage manager,[102] and on April 28 there were tableaux and a concert for the benefit of the Sainte Anna Asylum at the National Theater.[103] A grand promenade concert and rustic festival at Bloomingdale Garden on the line of the Carrollton Railroad took place on May 3 at 2 p.m. A band was provided for music and dancing.[104] In competition, the Grand May Festival of the New Orleans Turner Society went on for two days, May 3–4. Jaeger's Silver Cornet Band provided much of the music, but also concert music was under the direction of A. Bothe.[105] There were songs with orchestra, sung by the singers' section of the Turner Society. Two bands (ensembles) were in constant attendance: one for operatic arrangements and the other for dance music.[106] Then there was the concert on May 5 for the benefit of the First Baptist Church under the direction of Adolphe De Pelchia, organist of the Lafayette Presbyterian Church. Performers included E. Groenevelt (organist at Christ Church but playing the violin here), Ch. T. Urev (piano), Louis Mayer of the French Opera (violoncello), Greuling of the Varieties Theater (accompanist), singers S. Chase, J. Météyé, C. Tracy, C. Bremer (all members of the Mendelssohn Quartet), and others. Blackmar offered a grand Knabe for the event free, and Werlein offered a pedal organ, melodeon, manufactured by Cahart and Needham.[107]

A farewell concert was tendered for the benefit of young Mark Kaiser, at the Deutsche Company Hall on May 6, 1868,[108] and that same day there was a grand sacred concert, under the patronage of the women of the congregation of the cathedral, at the cathedral with organ music, opera arias and choruses (from Verdi's *Jérusalem*), a flute solo (Carrière of the French Opera), a violin solo (Page), and violoncello music (Damiani of the French Opera). Curto and others participated as well.[109] On May 8 the Opera House feted Calabrési, who conducted the fifth act of *L'Africaine,* the third act of *Faust,* and other pieces.[110]

On Sunday, May 17, there was a grand musical matinee and farewell concert for Carlo Patti and Jules Cartier, performed by leading artists of the French Opera, including chorus and orchestra.[111] Finally, on June 10, 1868, there was a grand vocal and instrumental concert at Saint Alphonse's Hall to benefit Sainte Mary's Church at Carrollton. The choir of Sainte Mary's Church was joined by artists and amateurs of New Orleans.[112]

In John Dwight's famous *Journal* of February 29, 1868, there appeared a comment by Viator on the state of music in New Orleans. It captures much of the feeling of New Orleanians toward their music less than three years after "foreign" occupation.

The French Opera in New Orleans

New Orleans, Feb. 18. From all that one sees in the musical or other journals of this country, one would never suspect the existence of a permanent and well sustained Opera in this far away Southern metropolis; much less would one suppose that here, even in these depressing times, the "stock" Opera establishment is one that, in the judgment of any impartial but cultivated, nay fastidious critic, would take the palm from any of the "Star" companies of the Northern cities, about which so much noise is made. And yet I am convinced that this is the case, and, that opera-goers of New York and Boston, Philadelphia and Chicago might know that this is no mere provincial boasting, as they will doubtless take it to be, I wish they might only be here on any of the grand opera nights and hear and judge for themselves. If they did not come away, feeling that, amid all the financial, civil, social distress of this city, amid all the breaking up and general dilapidation and positive ruin of its grand career of wealth and prosperity in times past, there is still left to New Orleans a native treasure, which no other city in the Union can boast, then I am no judge.

"Art is long!" I never felt the force of this adage as I did last night, while I sat at the French Opera, witnessing the production of "Le Prophète."

Here in the midst of a city groaning under a financial and political depression never felt before, where care, and anxiety, and dreary forebodings cast their gloom over the out-door world—here is this temple of musical art, beautiful to the eye, and ever ready to lift the mind up to the fair, fresh and peaceful world of poesy and harmony. And here the people come; come as of old; come because they love Art, and look to it in times of outward depression as a sure and blessed means of relief and refreshment. It is not as a new sensation, or as the fashion of the hour, that the public—that is, the old musical public of New Orleans, now patronize their opera. It is their old friend, their friend of palmy, bright days gone by, their friend now. It is their love for Art that makes their opera live in these days, when everything else is going over the board. Not that the season is a prosperous one financially; not that the house is nightly crowded; but that the demand for a high-toned, well sustained opera is one of the popular demands here, and consequently, while there is money left the people will give it, rather than have their cherished institutions go down. And what is the result? We have here for the whole season, which means here what it means in Europe, a season of months, not as in northern handbills a "season" of "four" nights or "two weeks," a beautiful, well appointed opera house, where a succession of operas of the highest order are brought out by a stock company, the grand opera nights alternating with those devoted to light opera, bouffe and the like, or the French drama.[113]

The fall 1868 season was typical. Institutions began to reopen all fall, and the Locquent School had its first student soiree on November 7.[114] The Carnatz Institute, along with poetical recitations in English and French, had musical entertainment on its first soiree on November 13.[115] Its second soiree was on December 30.[116] The first concert of this fall was on Thursday, November 12, at Odd Fellows' Hall. It was a concert organized by Leo Wheat, organist at Trinity Church, assisted by Mr. Farmer (flutist), Mr. Braun (violoncellist), Carlo Patti (violinist) and several amateurs. Wheat, pianist, came from the conservatories of Paris and Leipzig and was used to the highest level of concert programs. On this occasion his program was *The Barber of Seville* overture (French Opera Orchestra), a four-part song sung by the Mendelssohn Quartet, Wheat's own Grand Concerto in F Major, and a grand trio for piano, violin, and violoncello, and other works. There was a big house, and Wheat was buoyed by the thought of reviving the initial chamber series of Collignon. He "proposes to give a series of six concerts in our city, which he has made his home." In fact, he took over the Parlor Series and made it his own.[117] The French Opera season opened with *William Tell* on November 19.[118]

On November 13, 1868, the Deutsche Company gave a soiree dansante and promenade concert at their hall on Bienville Street, this evening under the leadership of Carlo Patti. The opera orchestra performed "choice music."[119] On November 30 Theresa Cannon, assisted by a large number of women and men, presented a grand vocal and instrumental concert at Odd Fellows' Hall for the benefit of the Saint Vincent de Paul Society for the Poor.[120] Theresa Cannon (later Buckley), it will be recalled, was an important singer and conductor of religious music during the rest of the century and in her later years was music director at Saint Louis Cathedral.

The spring 1869 concert season was very active. It began on Wednesday, January 6, with a benefit at the Opera House for the Société Charitable des Pompiers. The program consisted of the first and second acts of *Lucia*; the final scene of the third act of *Scene de la Folie* performed by Mlle M. Hasselman, M Peront, and the choir; the fourth act of Verdi's *I Lombardi (Jérusalem)*; and the fourth act of Offenbach's *Barbe-Bleue*. There were no reserved seats.[121] On January 11–12, 1869, the women of the Société de Bienfaisance de la Louisiane gave two grand soirees at Odd Fellows' Hall. They included a concert promenade, dancing, and refreshments.[122] Also on January 11 there was a soiree musicale at the Saint Louis Institute by the young girl students, who performed on the piano. They were students of Mme E. Lavillebeuvre. Also, there were some vocal students of Mme Boudousquié.[123] Edouard Groenevelt gave a vocal and instrumental concert at Odd Fellows' Hall on January 15, assisted by Mme S. G., Mme B, Louis Mayer, Greuling, and the German Quartet Club. The program had concertos by Moscheles and Vieuxtemps; vocal ensemble pieces by Abt, Fischer, Kucker, and Dunnen; Variations for Violin on a Theme by Mozart by Ferdinand David; a trio for piano, violin, and violoncello by Mageedes, and an aria from *Der Freischütz*.[124] On Sunday, January 17, at 1 p.m., there was a grand concert in the Hall of the Parfait Union Lodge on Rampart Street, as part of a fair that was held there by the women of the Children of Mary Society for the benefit of the widows and orphans in the Turgis Asylum. Performers included artists of the French Opera.[125]

February began with a complimentary concert at Lyceum Hall on the second given by the Central Hancock Club to Leo Wheat and Mr. Farmer, assisted by Mme Bourgeois, Carlo Patti, and the Mendelssohn Quartet Club.[126] Through much of February there were free concerts nightly from 7 p.m. to midnight, at Salle Napoléon, the beer hall on Royal Street.[127] On Sunday, February 7, 1869, at 12:30 p.m., there was a matinee musicale, vocale et instrumentale, to benefit the poor, given by the Ladies of the Society of the Poor, at the German Hall, Bienville Street.[128]

On March 11, 1869, the Silver Cornet Band performed as part of a minstrel show at the National Theater.[129] The principal vocalists and the orchestra of the French Opera performed a grand vocal and instrumental concert in Lyceum Hall on March 12. The orchestra performed an overture, an operatic finale, and an operatic potpourri; Carlo Patti played a violin solo; Leo Wheat played a piano piece; H. Braun played a violoncello solo; a Mendelssohn piano trio was performed; and the singers Gaston P., A. Bourgeois, Nardin, Uranie Cambier, and Picot sang mostly opera arias.[130] This may have been the same concert as that by the Italian Society on the same day.[131] On Friday, March 19, there was a concert to benefit the rebuilding of Spring Hill College in Mobile, performed at the Church of the Immaculate Conception under the direction of Calabrési and Collignon. The program had many religious and classical pieces, featuring Rossini's *Stabat Mater* complete and Meyerbeer's "Marche aux Flambeaux."[132]

From March 29 to April 3 there was a bazaar, which included concerts each evening featuring Sipp (pianist), Von Collam (violoncellist), and many singers under the direction of one of the Prévosts. On April 4, Sunday, at noon, Calabrési and members of the French Opera gave a concert to culminate the bazaar. Jaeger's band was also engaged for the occasion.[133] One hour later on that same April 4, there was another matinee concert by the Opera Orchestra under Carlo Patti with artists from the French Opera, to benefit the orphans of Saint Vincent, at Batisses Blaffer, 201 and 203 Canal Street. The program was marked by an overture and a grand finale by the orchestra, and various airs and songs by Gounod, Boildieu, Halévy, Gluck, Flotow, and others.[134] A series of four concerts de salon at Odd Fellows' Hall was held during April and May by the Mendelssohn Quartet, several professional and amateur singers, Carlo Patti (violin), H. Braun (violoncellist), and under the direction of pianist Leo Wheat. "These concerts are popular and still growing in favor with the lovers of fine music." They were a continuation of the parlor concerts of a year before. The first was on April 17, 1869, the second on April 23, the third on April 30, and the fourth on May 10. After the second concert, the critic in *The Bee* noted that it "drew a crowded audience to Odd Fellows' Hall Friday night and was in every respect a gratifying success."[135] M A. Duquesnay and his pupils gave a recital at the home of Mme E. Morphy, Esplanade Street, on April 23.[136] On April 25, Fourmestreau, first oboist of the French Opera and one of the oldest members of the orchestra there, gave a grand concert at the French Opera House. He was assisted by Uranie Cambier, Lambelé Alhaiza (wife of Paul),[137] Picot, Van Cauwelaert (violoncellist), Charles Bothe (clarinetist), Eckert (first hornist), Carlo Patti (first violinist), and the whole orchestra.[138] Three days later, on April 28, Edward Groenevelt, violinist, gave a concert at Odd Fellows' Hall. He was assisted by many singers, artists, and amateurs.[139]

May 1869 was much more active than in previous years. On May 2 there was a concert in the foyer of the Opera House to benefit the Targis Asylum. Principal artists and instrumentalists of the French Opera assisted.[140] A grand vocal and instrumental concert at the Varieties Theater to benefit La Hache took place on Friday, May 7. La Hache was assisted by Sipp (piano), Carlo Patti, and Herman Braun.[141] The next day a musical entertainment was given at the Church of Saint Vincent de Paul on Dauphine Street, for their benefit,[142] and the day after that, May 9, there was another grand vocal and instrumental concert at the Opera House to benefit the Turgis Asylum, with singers and instrumentalists from the French Opera including van Hufflen, Carlo Patti, and Cartier, along with Mmes Cambier, Lambéle-Alhaiza, and others. The program was mostly opera arias and songs, with Carlo Patti playing a violin fantasia on *Il Trovatore*.[143] The following Sunday, Mlle Marie Hasselman, first singer of the French Opera, gave a matinee musicale and farewell concert in the German Hall, with the assistance of other artists from the French Opera.[144] Two days later, on May 19, there was a benefit for E. Calabrési at the Opera House. The program consisted of the third and fourth acts of *Le Prophète,* the first act of *Roméo et Juliette,* Grand March and Chorus from *Tannhäuser,* and the third act from *Faust.*[145] To honor M Normaudin, controller of the French Opera, a grand vocal and instrumental concert was given at the Opera House on May 21 by members of the French Opera. Carlo Patti, Van Cauwelaert, and Greuling played a piano trio, Patti played a violin solo, and various singers sang airs and romances.[146] M Engel gave a concert on May 27 at Odd Fellows' Hall, with the assistance of other artists.[147] On May 30, the Jaeger Band played at the Fair Grounds for the Festa Dello Statuto held by the Italian Club of New Orleans.[148] Finally, the young and talented artist J. A. Dawson, a native of New Orleans, gave a concert at Odd Fellows' Hall on June 3 with the assistance of Auguste Davis, Carlo Patti, Herman Braun, Philip Greuling, and an amateur singer.[149]

Concerts began earlier than usual in the fall of 1869. There was a concert by the Jesuit Choir under Collignon on September 25, the first of several. The choir had seventeen members, both women and men, most of the men from the German community. The program included Cherubini's Mass, and some Mozart works including *Ave Verum Corpus.*[150] On October 2 the German Turner Singers, Gesang Section of the New Orleans Turngemeinde, once again gave a vocal and instrumental concert at the Turner Hall (corner of Lafayette and Dryades streets), assisted by an orchestra of thirty-two musicians from the theaters of the city, under the direction of Charles Bothe and Louis Mayer, to benefit their hall. Pieces on the program were by Reissiger, Kuecken, David, Ant. Thomas, Kornburger, Louis Mayer, Haydn, Hanser, Suppé, Lortzing, Levi, and Meyerbeer.[151] There was a fete champètre at the Fair Grounds October 2–4, to raise money for the erection of a church of Sainte Rose de Lima. The main attraction was sporting events, but there was also music by Jaeger's Silver Cornet Band.[152] All these events took place before the opening of the fall and winter season of the Varieties Theater[153] and before Calabrési had even left France with his new opera troupe of forty-two musicians for the French Opera.[154] Incidentally, Calabrési not only recruited singers in Paris but "also brought twelve [instrumental] musicians from Paris to add strength and talent to his orchestra."

The next concert was on October 23 at Odd Fellows' Hall by the pupils of Eugène Prévost for his benefit. He was now old and needy, but he was still held in high regard in the city since he was the triumphant leader of the French Opera during its golden years.[155] The next day Jaeger's Silver Cornet Band gave a grand free concert at the Magnolia Garden, Bayou Bridge, beginning at 9 a.m. The best of wines, liquors, and cold meals were served by attentive waiters.[156] On October 28, 1869, during a performance by the Chapman sisters, C. B. Bishop and their Great Burlesque Troupe at the Saint Charles Theatre, Mr. W. Withers played a violin solo.[157] The pupils of Leopold Carrière, first flutist of the French Opera, gave a grand vocal and instrumental concert at Lyceum Hall on October 30. A large number of amateurs and artists performed free; the concert ticket cost one dollar, and the proceeds went to Carrière. The program consisted of opera arias or variations on arias, performed not only by the pupils but also by the old pianist Norès and the pianists (Leon) Prévost and Carpenter, and the singer van Hufflen, among others.[158]

The opera season opened on Thursday, November 4, 1869. As *The Times* reported, "We are requested to state that the interval, on the opening night, between the second and third acts will be some twenty minutes in duration, in order to afford women an opportunity of visiting; the Grand Foyer, and the saloons which are to be specially reserved to them. Owing to the length of the performance, the curtain will rise at 7 o'clock."[159] In his brief review, the critic of the *Times* noted, "In this connection, it is our pleasant duty to congratulate M Calabrési upon the well appointed orchestra (forty-two persons) over which he presided with that rare taste, which has gained him the heartfelt appreciation of our citizens. No better *chef* has administered in our city the melodies of the great masters than Mr. Calabrési."[160] When the second grand opera production of the season opened on November 9 with Verdi's *Il Trovatore*, "perhaps, the most popular of operas with the musical amateurs of our city," the reviewer continued his praise: "The orchestra, under M Calabrési, was perfectly managed, and achieved a success of its own."[161] Meanwhile on November 8, 1869, the English Opera opened at the Academy of Music with Susan Galton's English Comic Opera Troupe.[162]

The second performance by the Jesuit Choir at the Jesuit Church occurred on Sunday, November 7, 1869. Collignon conducted a Haydn mass, the first performance of this piece since the war.[163] On November 12, there was a soiree musicale et littéraire at the Carnatz Institute. The program included piano works and songs performed by children at the school.[164] The third performance by the Jesuit Choir at the Jesuit Church took place during mass on Sunday, November 14, with Collignon conducting. An amateur woman sang the solos to Weber's Gloria and Credo, and Collignon played the Offertory on the organ.[165] There was a dramatic concert given November 21 by the friends and pupils of Saint Joseph's Convent, in Sainte Anne's Church, for the enlargement of the chapel.[166] Mlle A. Aron, "an intelligent and emotional young girl," gave a vocal and instrumental concert at the German Theatre on Bienville and Passage da la Bourse streets on December 15, 1869. Aron played the piano and sang. She was assisted by Mr. J. Ginet, first violinist of the French Opera, whom she accompanied in two pieces.[167] The following Monday, December 20, Miss Melanie May, pianist, assisted by "favorite" amateur vocalists, gave her first concert at Lyceum Hall. She had come to New Orleans recently from Baltimore and previously had given a "private" concert.[168]

The spring 1870 season was just as active as that in 1869. It began on January 3 with a grand vocal and instrumental concert by Mlle O. Romey, Van Hufflen, and Page plus Mlle Zeiss (contralto of the French Opera), to benefit L'Asile du Bon Pasteur (the Asylum of the Good Shepherd). It was held at Odd Fellows' Hall.[169] Then came the Franko family, which had left New Orleans for Europe at the outbreak of the War and was now returning with its incredible children: Nahan (seven), Rachel (nine), Sam (ten), Jeannette (twelve) and Selma (fourteen). Their first concert was on February 3 at Odd Fellows' Hall[170] and the second on February 9.[171]

Grand Concert d'Introduction
Le 3 FEVRIER 1870

Programme

I

1—Il Trovatore, Fantaisie Brillante, pour violon
    Joué par Sam, accompagné sur le piano par Jeannette
    ALARD

2—L'Invitation à la Danse, Ronde Brilliant
    Arrangé pour deux pianos par F. W. Bauer
    Joué par Selma et Jeannette
    WEBER

3—Ave Maria
   Joué par Nahan, Rachel, Sam, Jeannette, accompané par Selma
   GOUNOD

4—Helmaths Lange, pour deux violins
   Joué par Selma et Jeannette, accompagné par Sam
   GUNG'L

5—L'Oiseau sur l'Arbre, Grand Caprice Burlesque, pour violon
   Joué par Sam, accompagné par Selma
   HAUSER

II
1—Souvenir de Bellini, Fantaisie Brillante pour violon
   Joué par Jeannette, accompagné par Sam
   ARTÔT

2—Solo de Piano, Joyful & Sorrowful
   Pour la MAIN GAUCHE, Joué par Selma
   WILMERS

3—Tarentella, Morceau de Salon, pour violon
   Joué par Sam, accompagné Jeannette
   VIEUXTEMPS

4—Variations pour Quatre Violons, "God Save the Queen"
   Joué par Nahan, Rachel, Sam, Jeannette, accompagné par Selma
   SAM FRANKO

The musical successes of these five musicians were legendary by the end of the nineteenth century, when they were at the top of the professional musical circles of New York.[172]

On Friday, February 4, an oratorio was performed at Odd Fellows' Hall under Eugène Prévost; it was organized by the women of New Orleans for charity.[173] The same concert seems to have been repeated on February 10.[174] Then on February 14, Carlotta Patti, younger sister of Amalia and Adelina, presented the first of five concerts in New Orleans, accompanied by pianist Theo Ritter, violinist M Prume, American tenor Henry Squires, bass Joseph Hermans, and

M Colby, musical director. Subsequent concerts were on February 15, 17, 18, and 19 (matinee).[175] After her first concert, the critic of *L'Abeille* wrote, "The first concert of Carlotta Patti, given yesterday evening in Odd Fellows' Hall before a large and brilliant assemblage, was for this singer an immense success. She has fully justified by her talent the reputation that preceded her here. She has a soprano voice with a melodic timbre and a grand freshness. The vocalizes and the passage work are of a pure and irreproachable intonation. Finally Mlle Carlotta Patti posses that indefinable quality that is called 'charm.' She captivates and fascinates her audience. The bravos, the shouts, and the encores bear witness to the satisfaction of the public."

After an absence of two years Josephine Filomeno returned to New Orleans on February 18, 1870, where she intended to give a new series of concerts.[176] Her first appearance was in a grand concert to benefit Maison du Bon Pasteur, on February 23, 1870, at Odd Fellows' Hall, directed by M Emile La Hache.[177] Mlle Filomeno, the young Chilean pianist and violinist; M Braugh (Braud), violoncellist; and M Ginet, first violinist of the French Opera, were the performers.[178] Her second appearance was at Lyceum Hall on March 3, with Juan S. Salcedo, cornet à piston; M Filomeno, violoncellist; Julian O. Schultze, tenor; a group of amateurs; and Philip Greuling, piano. A benefit concert for Mlle Filomeno was on April 27, 1870, at Odd Fellows' Hall. She performed the Mendelssohn G Minor Piano Concerto No. 1 with full orchestra on May 18, 1870. Also on the program were the Overture to *Zampa* by Hérold and works by Filomeno herself. Other spring concerts included a soiree musicale et dansante on March 12 by the German Society;[179] a recital on March 19 at Mrs. Stamps' Academy at 404 Carondelet Street, where about twenty female students of Professor Sipp, Sipp himself, and Van Hufflen sang "difficult" choruses from Mozart's Mass No. 12 and Haydn's *Creation*;[180] and a performance of Rossini's *Stabat Mater* on April 11, 1870, at the French Opera House by musicians of the French Opera, on the occasion of Holy Week.[181]

Meanwhile the opera season was in full bloom. Not only was the French Opera thrilling audiences with *Faust, William Tell,* Gounod's *Roméo et Juliette,* and other favorites, but the German opera company led by Maurice Grau opened in New Orleans on January 24 with full chorus and orchestra. It had formerly appeared in New York, Philadelphia, Cincinnati, and Louisville. Operas in its New Orleans repertory were *The Magic Flute, Der Freischütz, Martha, La Dame Blanche, La Juive, Don Giovanni,* and *Fidelio.*[182] A few weeks later the English opera troupe of Richings announced that it would appear in New Orleans. It was a company of forty-eight persons, thirty-five in the mixed chorus; it was accompanied by a full orchestra led by Mr. S. Behrens. The operas to be performed were *Les Diamants de la Couronne* (Auber), *The Bohemian Girl, Maritana, Martha, La Traviata, Doctor of Alcántara, Norma, Faust, Les Huguenots, Il Trovatore, La Sonnambula,* and others.[183]

Cabaret concerts continued as well. On February 28, 1870, M S. Reemes, formerly owner of the Kossuth House on Royal Street at the Saint Louis Hotel, opened a new Café Royal. She served beers and wines, and "the excellent and new band of musicians 'Germania' has been engaged to play each evening some concert pieces chosen from among the newest and most pleasant there are."[184] At the same time Jaeger's popular band played on the streets of the French Quarter and provided open-air concerts.[185]

After a summer's hiatus, regular concerts resumed on Sunday, October 9, 1870. M Dubos, maître de chapelle, directed a sacred concert at the cathedral with the assistance of many professionals and amateurs (Auguste Davis, Krep, Mlle Wagner). M Caulier, a graduate of the Paris Conservatoire and first violin of the French Opera, performed Vieuxtemps's *Fantasie,* which the reviewer in *L'Abeille* found remarkable in style and beautiful in tone in the French violinistic school. Adolphe Duquesnay accompanied the program.[186] A group of professional musicians from the French Opera, who called themselves Chateau des Fleurs, had been giving some concerts during the summer and fall and gave their last concert of the season on October 23, 1870. As usual they sang excerpts from operettes, comique duos, romances, and chansonnettes.[187] The principal artistic attention was focused not on concerts but, as usual, on opera. The opera season opened on November 17 with *La Juive*; the orchestra got an ovation.[188] Yet there was a handful of concerts. La Société de Bienfaisance des Jeunes Gens sponsored a grand bal paré et concert promenade on December 7 at the Opera House to assist in the construction of the Robert E. Lee monument (which still stands at Lee Circle in New Orleans).[189] Once again the pupils of Professor Sipp (pianist), who had performed many times in New Orleans, presented a soiree musicale by children seven–twelve years in the Salle des Dames in the Saint Charles Hotel. They played classic and modern works.[190] On December 15 was the first of five concerts presented in connection with a grand French bazaar to benefit the French victims of the Civil War. The program of the first concert was "La Marseillaise" (solo piano) performed by Mlle O. Romey, a Halévy aria, a violin solo by M Caulier, a duet, an air from *Les Huguenots* (Mlle Aaron), another violin solo by M Caulier, a song by Prévost, a scene from Thomas's *Hamlet* sung by Mme L. M. (Henriette) Comès (daughter of Collignon), a fantasie de concert on *La Dame Blanche* composed and performed by Mlle Romey, and an aria from Verdi's *Jérusalem*.[191] Subsequent concerts with many of the same performers were performed on December 16, 21, and 23.[192] The final concert at the bazaar was a matinee on Sunday, December 25, by all the musicians of the opera orchestra led by Calabrési.[193]

The spring concert season of 1871 was even more active than those before. On January 16, 17, and 18 (both matinee and evening), Adelaide Phillips presented four concerts at Odd Fellows' Hall, assisted by M J. Levy, "the leading cornet à piston player of the world"; Edward Hoffman, pianist and composer; and M Jules Dasler, baritone.[194] On January 20 there was a musical and literary entertainment at Odd Fellows' Hall, a testimonial to benefit Lewis Baker.[195] A promenade concert followed on January 24 at Odd Fellows' Hall for Aetna No. 15, possibly related to the frigate of that name. It was the third annual grand mask and dress ball.[196] M Alfonso Miari, flutist, assisted by Mlle Zeiss and many artists and professors, as well as the orchestra of the National Theater, gave a grand vocal and instrumental concert at the Masonic Hall on January 26.[197] The music publisher Blackmar held a fair at his Temple of Music on Canal Street on February 6, 1871. It concluded with a grand concert given by Van Hufflen with the assistance of many artists and amateurs.[198]

An unusual series of concerts in February involved, first, at the Académie de Musique, the Royal Japanese Troupe of Satsuma consisting of twenty artists of both sexes.[199] Then, at the National Theater, there was a series of concerts of Russian music and other Russian ethnography on February 27, March 1 and 4.[200]

Back to more traditional concerts, a matinee concert at the Church of Sainte Rose de Lima, under the direction of M Dubos, chapel master at the cathedral, with the assistance of M Miari, M Caulier, and Adolphe Duquesnay, and a large number of others, took place on February 20. It was designed to raise funds for a new building.[201] Young female pupils at the Institut St-Louis gave a soiree musicale on March 17, 1871.[202] On March 22, Emma Fairex, assisted by some of the best artists and amateurs of the city, presented a grand concert at Odd Fellows' Hall.[203] There was a concert of sacred music, offered by the French Opera on April 4. It included Rossini's *Stabat Mater* and the orchestral march from *Tannhäuser*. The performers were artists, the chorus, and orchestra of the French Opera.[204] On Easter Sunday, April 9, in mid-afternoon there was a grand outdoor concert at the Château des Fleurs, consisting of songs, comic routines, dances and pantomimes, followed in the evening by illuminations accompanied by the Jackson Barracks Band.[205] During services that morning at Sainte Anne Church, there was a performance of Curto's *Sainte Cécile Mass*. A thirty-voice choir was conducted by Curto with Theresa Cannon, organist of the church, accompanying. Also featured was Mlle Fairex, who had sung at Odd Fellows' Hall a few years prior, and Mme Charles Witham.[206] The next day, April 10, the French Opera had its second spiritual concert, this time to benefit Mme Naddi, who among other things sang an aria from *Les Amours du Diable* by Grisar.[207]

The French Opera was operating at full force during the entire spring, and Calabrési was demonstrating to the audiences the superb orchestra of the theater that he had personally recruited. One highlight occurred on April 18 with a performance of Mozart's *Don Giovanni.* "Don Juan est peut-être le grand succès de l'année; à coup sûr," according to *L'Abeille.*[208] The season lasted all the way to May 16, when it concluded with *Mignon.*[209] Besides French opera, however, there was also English opera at the Academy of Music. On February 13, 1871, Mrs. Oates' Opera Bouffe Troupe started its run in New Orleans.[210] The pieces, forgotten today, included Offenbach's *Prima Donna of a Night, Flower Girls of Paris, The King's Secret, Little Faust* and *Big Mephisto,* and a *Daughter of the Regiment* that seemingly had nothing to do with Donizetti. In addition, intermèdes continued at the older theaters and at the new Théâtre de Vaudéville.[211]

Regular concerts continued in April. The pupils of Professor Rod. Sipp gave a testimonial concert at the Saint Charles Hotel at 8 p.m. While there was some vocal music, the piano was featured.[212] Alfonso Miari, distinguished artist, with the assistance of Mlle Zeiss and many other artists and professors, gave a vocal and instrumental concert in Lyceum Hall on Saturday, April 22,[213] and M Théry, first baritone of the opéra comique, at the Opera House, had his grand concert matinee benefit on April 30.[214] Miss Lydia Thompson and her troupe, on April 26 at the Academy of Music, gave a benefit concert for French artists caught in the Franco-Prussian War.[215] On May 17 the artists of the French Opera gave a farewell concert at the Hôtel St-Louis to benefit M Bénédick, régisseur de la scene de l'opera,[216] and the following day they gave a représentation extraordinaire at the Opera House, once again to benefit the Association des Artistes Dramatiques de France, victims of the Franco-Prussian War. The concert was patronized by all the friends of France and included the Overture and the Second Act of *Mignon,* the Second Act Trio and Finale of *William Tell,* the divertissement *Pas des Bouquets,* the second act of *Charles VI,* and the Third Act (garden scene) of *Faust.*[217] And finally Mlle Philippine Von Edelsberg, who thrilled audiences at the opera the past season, assisted by Mlle Zeiss, Mme Pollak, and Hermann Braun, gave a grand concert at the Salle du Lycée.[218]

Meanwhile preparations were made for some summer cabaret and outdoor concerts. On Sunday, April 30, 1871, the Grand Pavillon Denéchaud at Lake Pontchartrain opened with Charles Jaeger's band performing every evening for free. Every Saturday evening was a grand bal after the departure of the train and lasting all night.[219] These concerts were a prelude to the popular Lake Pontchartrain concerts that became regular from 1879 on. Similarly, according to *L'Abeille*, "Musical amateurs will learn with pleasure that starting next Saturday, May 20, [1871], some concerts will be given every evening at Café Bismark by a group of good professionals."[220] At Magnolia Garden at Bayou Bridge, opposite the Esplanade train station, concerts began on May 21. A "celebrated brass band" that arrived from Europe on the steamer *Frankfort* performed such programs as Wagner, Rossini, Verdi, Strauss, Suppé, Donizetti, Mendelssohn, and Wildeman.[221]

It was not until the season of 1871–72, however, that the orchestral life of the city at last returned to the glory days of the late 1850s. At this time the Classic Music Series was reborn with Collignon at the helm, and the season was not confined to a mere six concerts but rather to fourteen from fall through spring. At the first "open rehearsal" (séance) on Sunday, October 8, 1871, at half past noon, thirty-six of the best instrumental performers of the city presented Beethoven's *Pastoral* Symphony No. 6 and the Overture to Weber's *Oberon*.[222] The event took place in the foyer of the National Theater and was highly successful. Nearly three hundred subscribers were reported, though this large number of patrons was barely able to underwrite the expense of such a large and professional ensemble.[223] Although these were billed usually as rehearsals, they nonetheless provided New Orleanians the opportunity to hear the finest orchestral music by the great masters played by professionals. By the third concert the orchestra had been enlarged to a "complete orchestra."[224] The season included many full symphonies and numerous individual movements of symphonies, many overtures, and other important symphonic compositions. (See the list of Collignon's concerts after the Civil War on page 84.) German composers dominated. No concertos were performed. So enthusiastically were these concerts received that writer "X" in *L'Abeille* hoped that they would continue throughout the summer,[225] but alas, the season was over and not to be repeated.

Meanwhile, the Theodore Thomas Orchestra came to New Orleans during the 1871 to 1872 season (see page 47). This ensemble of fifty to sixty musicians, led by Thomas, was assisted by a solo pianist, Mlle Marie Krebs (in Chopin and Mendelssohn concertos); a solo violinist, Bernard Lestemann (Paganini's Violin Concerto No. 1); a solo cornetist, Louis Schreiber; and a solo harpist, Luigi Rocco.[226] They performed four grand concerts in Odd Fellows' Hall on February 19, 20, 21, and 23, 1872, a fifth concert at the German National Theater on February 22, a sixth, matinee concert at Odd Fellows' Hall on February 24, and a seventh concert at the Varieties Theater on February 25. Among the works performed were Beethoven's Symphony No. 5, piano concertos of Mendelssohn and Chopin, the overtures to *Lohengrin* and *Tannhäuser* by Wagner, *Der Freischütz* and *Oberon* by Weber, *A Midsummer Night's Dream* by Mendelssohn, *Prometheus* by Beethoven, Schubert's D Minor String Quartet (arranged for orchestra?), and other pieces.

Chamber music had a resurgence in New Orleans at this time. In February, a resident string quartet was formed by three members of the French Opera Orchestra—MM Auber, Comtat, and Raoul—joined by a "distinguished amateur" M Wapler. They inaugurated a new series devoted to the string quartets of Haydn, Mozart, Beethoven, and Mendelssohn.[227] Concerts were to take place at noon on Sundays. Then on April 12 the first of the new season's four parlor concerts, termed "concerts de salon," took place at Odd Fellows' Hall. The artists involved this time were Mme Zeiss-Dennis, Mlle Liberman, MM Van Hufflen, J. Météyé, Chase, Specht, and C. O. Weber.

By the spring of 1872, New Orleans seemed to have recovered completely from the musical hiatus caused by the Civil War. Opera, symphony, chamber music, and a host of other concerts were thriving just as in the years prior to 1861. The city was bustling with musicians of all sorts. The promise for future growth seemed strong.

The shock of the Civil War, however, broke the steady path of New Orleans to ever greater artistic achievement. It was not simply an interruption in the continual growth of classical musical institutions and the rise of the city as an international center for concert music that had occurred from 1800 to 1861. It caused a change in the direction because of economic factors from which the city has never recovered. Opera, the center of this musical life, now had a precarious existence because the people could no longer support it in the lavish way they had before the war. The French Opera continued, often in spurts, sometimes not at all, until it was destroyed in 1919. New Orleans was perhaps the most significant center for classical music in the United States during the 1840s and 1850s because it had a coterie of resident artists of the first class who performed, taught, and demanded the best. Foreign artists came to the city because it had an audience that was well informed, musically educated, and expectant of the highest standards in technique and musicality. In the immediate postwar years the city gradually renewed much of this local atmosphere for music, but without the financial resources to satisfy their tastes, there was frustration and gradual decline. There would always be a sizeable following for opera and concert music in New Orleans, but the dominance of these kinds of art were waning. The seeds for this ebbing of the great concert life of New Orleans were sown in the years 1872 to 1880.

6

From the City to the Lake and the Great Exposition
1872–1886

Unfortunately, the classical music scene took a nosedive during the season beginning in the fall of 1872, and the rest of the 1870s was largely a disappointment. The economy of the city remained bad, and the creditors once again stalked the Opera House and put a damper on all performances. The Opera House opened the 1872–73 season without grand opera, and few concerts were given.[1] From then until 1880 the city was often without its own grand opera company, and without a resident opera company there was no need to maintain a high-quality orchestra. When the orchestra was allowed to disintegrate, the number of chamber concerts, as well as orchestral concerts outside the opera, declined noticeably. There would be visiting opera companies, so that New Orleanians would on occasion be able to enjoy their favorite pastime, and these would usually be at venues other than the French Opera House—such as at the Varieties Theater[2] or the Saint Charles Theatre. Those theaters, as well as the more popular ones (especially the Academy of Music) maintained their own orchestras to play for vaudevilles, opéra comiques, circuses, and minstrel shows, but the level of playing there was apparently less rigorous than at the French Opera.

The failure of grand opera was offset only by the first concerts by world-famous artists since before the Civil War. The harbinger of things to come had been the Theodore Thomas concerts the previous season.[3] The fall–winter 1872–73 season was full of distinguished concerts, but the best were by visitors, not residents. Camelia Urso arrived at the end of October for concerts, which began at the end of November.[4] She performed evening concerts on November 26 and 28 and a matinee on November 3; all were at the fifteen-hundred-seat Salle de la Batisse de l'Exposition, Camp Street.[5] For her concerts, Urso was joined by a number of distinguished local musicians: Mme Comès (soprano),

Mlle Pauline Le Blanc (contralto), Jules Météyé (tenor), Van Hufflen (basso), the pianists Mlles Octavie Romey and LeBlanc, and the flutist Gustave D'Aquin. The concerts were directed by Collignon. For the first concert, Urso performed Vieuxtemps's *Caprice* and Paganini's *Danse des Sorcières.* For the second concert she played the *La Folia* variations in D Minor of Corelli and Paganini's *Carnaval de Venise.* D'Aquin also performed a solo. For her third concert, Urso played Leclair's *Sarabande et Tambourin* and her own *Le Reve.* Before coming to New Orleans, Urso had made a big hit in London playing in and leading Beethoven's Opus 59 string quartets; when she left New Orleans on December 10, 1872, she headed for Boston.

On December 16, 1872, Max Strakosch brought a group to New Orleans that included Carlotta Patti, the tenor Mario, the pianist Teresa Carreño (her New Orleans debut), the French violinist Emile Sauret (nineteen years old), and several other singers. There were initially three concerts: December 17 (Tuesday), 18, and 19 in the Salle de l'Exposition. On the first concert, Sauret played Ernst's Fantasy on *Otello.* On the second concert, Sauret and Carreño played a Beethoven sonata for violin and piano. Carreño also played a Chopin ballade and her own composition, *Le Printemps,* and Sauret played a fantasy by Paganini and another by Ernst. A matinee concert was added on Saturday, December 21. Max Strakosch's group then went to Galveston to fulfill prior engagements, and it returned to New Orleans for additional concerts on December 27 and 29. On December 27, Carreño and Sauret played De Bériot's Duo Fantasie on themes from *William Tell*; Carreño played Chopin and Gottschalk, Sauret played Wieniawski, and the singers sang Mozart, among other things.[6]

Before Max Strakosch was finished, Ole Bull returned to Odd Fellows' Hall for three evening concerts on December 23, 24, and 27, 1872. He was accompanied by John Nelson Pattison (1845–1905) on the first program and by Joseph Harte Denek (pianist and composer) on the second and third; he was assisted, as well, by several singers on all evenings. At the first concert, he played six pieces, including the allegro maestoso of a Paganini violin concerto, and received a rave review. On the second concert he played variations on a theme from Bellini's *Roméo et Juliette,* his own *Nightingale* and *El Saterbesok,* Paganini's *Di Tanti Palpiti,* and some others. On the third concert he played his own *Cantabile Doloroso e Rondo Giocoso* and Paganini's *Danse des Sorcières.* Then Bull added a matinee concert on December 28, again at Odd Fellows' Hall, where he played Paganini's Fantasy on *Non Più Mesta* (from Rossini's *La Cenerentola*) and the *Mother's Prayer,* and some of his own variations on *Carnaval de Venise.* As in the earlier concerts, he was accompanied by Denek on piano and assisted by several singers (M Ferranti and Miss Graziella Ridgeway).[7]

The most famous visiting artists, however, were Anton Rubinstein and Henri Wieniawski, who arrived in New Orleans on January 27, 1873, and although scheduled to give three concerts and a matinee, ended up giving eight concerts. Attendance was good, but apparently not as good as had been anticipated owing to the pecuniary difficulties of so many New Orleanians. No orchestras were involved, and the two virtuosi played no sonatas together and no other chamber music. Except for the final concert, the two played at the French Opera House under the aegis of Maurice Grau. At the first concert, Rubinstein played pieces by Beethoven (*Egmont,* "Turkish March"), Liszt (a rondo and variations on a Schubert song), Handel (gigue), Mendelssohn (*Wedding March*), Field (a nocturne), and Chopin (a ballade, a berceuse, and a polonaise), and Wieniawski played his own fantasy on *Faust* and Paganini's *Carnaval de Venise.* At the second concert, on January 31, Rubinstein played Robert Schumann's *Symphonic Etudes,* a Weber sonata, and several of his own pieces; Wieiniawski played an air of Vieuxtemps, his own *Legende et Airs Russes,* and the *Carnaval de Venise.* At the third concert, on February 1, Rubinstein played some pieces by Handel, Mendelssohn, Chopin, Liszt, Schubert, and a barcarole and an etude of his own, and Wieniawski played Ernst's *Le Pirate* and his own *Legende* and a waltz caprice. Rubinstein, who felt a rapport with the audience in New Orleans that he did not feel elsewhere in America, agreed to three more concerts and, eventually, to a fourth, final concert at the Varieties Theater on Sunday at 8 p.m. The appearances of Rubinstein and Wieniawski reminded New Orleanians of those of Vieuxtemps and Thalberg back in 1856 and 1857, and debate raged over who was the king of the piano and whose piano was better (Rubinstein used Steinways).[8] The reviewer of *L'Abeille* believed that Rubinstein surpassed Thalberg and that Wieniawski surpassed Bull.

Local musicians, despite the failure of the opera and the end of regular orchestral series but perhaps spurred on by the excitement of such world-class visitors, performed their own share of concerts during the 1872–73 season. On October 7, 1872, at 7 p.m., there was a concert benefiting the parochial school of Sainte Anne given by the men and women of this church. They performed Racine's three-act tragedy *Esther,* with incidental choruses by Curto, and followed this by a concert of vocal and instrumental (flute) music.[9] On Thursday, December 11, Gustave D'Aquin, the young flutist, performed with his teacher Carrière at Lyceum Hall. They were assisted by many professionals and amateurs and a Jewish choir. The concert raised money for D'Aquin to go to Paris to study further.[10] In January 1873, there were intermèdes at the Academy of Music, whose orchestra was conducted by the American William Withers (b. 1836). Withers, primarily a military band leader, was traveling with the entourage of Lydia Thompson and performed violin solos; according to *L'Abeille,* he "possesses a *coup d'archet* to reign in those who would be pretentious while playing charming obligatos."[11]

Following Carnival in February, Mr. Van Ghele, who was chef d'orchestra at the Varieties Theater, performed at the theater with orchestra during opéra comiques.[12] On March 8 there was a grand concert at Exposition Hall on Saint Charles Avenue for the benefit of fire victims. Octavie Romey (pianist), who was supervisor of the Haute-École of the Central District, was in charge and was assisted by Mme Zeiss-Denis, M Van Hufflen, and M Caulier (violinist), with a choir of a hundred young girls. Romey brought her students to this performance.[13] Meanwhile there were regular vocal and instrumental concerts at Café Bismarck, 42 de la Rue Royale, every evening at 7 p.m. Families were encouraged to attend. In December, the Imperial and Royal Troupe under Seppl' G'Ochwandner played there; beginning in January, there was a Parisian troupe under the direction of Mlle Thérésa, leading chanteuse of the Parisian cafés; and by March, a new group of performers, the Roche family, presented ballet and theater in French, English, and German.[14]

The vicissitudes of the French Opera in the 1870s must have been difficult for the members of the orchestra. The opera was revived by the fall of 1873,[15] but between 1876 and the middle of 1880 there was a four-year hiatus in which only visiting troupes performed full-scale opera. The orchestra was used for vaudeville, ballet, operettas, and an occasional concert, but the infrequency of full-scale operas with visiting conductors and singers would have inhibited the preservation of the quality of performance that a steady conductor and singers would have brought. There apparently was much more turnover in the personnel of the orchestra at this time, for something appeared in the newspapers at the end of the spring 1874 season that had not happened since the 1820s: advertisements for positions in the orchestra.[16]

The temporary return of the local opera during the fall of 1873 helped revive the music scene for the new season. On November 7, local violinist Mark Kaiser returned from Europe after studying there for five years. He was now, at age eighteen or nineteen, a first-class artist, and his presence in the city for nearly all of the next fifty-five years signaled a revived concert life.[17] On December 9, Kaiser played for invited guests at his father's house,[18] and on Wednesday,

December 17, he gave a single recital at Grunewald Hall. As is often the case in recitals by young virtuosi, the program consisted of bravura-type pieces. He was accompanied by Greuling and Pothonier at the piano.[19]

On November 9, the opera season opened at the French Opera with a performance of *Les Huguenots*. The reviewer A.M. in *L'Abeille* concluded his review with two paragraphs about the orchestra:

> There is another large voice which we must not forget to mention, that about which we end this musical essay. This voice is the orchestra, a voice that is a mixture of all the instruments. It is, so to speak, the mother voice about which all the other voices group and find their places. M Momas, in charge of directing all these sonorous waves into a harmonious whole, acquits himself skillfully and conscienciously [sic].
>
> He is regarded as one of the best conductors in France, and one can see why from the way he draws from the elements at his disposal. These musicians are of different nationalities, and some of them he did not know before his arrival in New Orleans, but he created an ensemble which, after some rehearsals, leaves little to be desired. He has done much in a short time, and we sincerely rejoice in it.[20]

The orchestra was fully appreciated at the time, which made its loss in subsequent years all the more painful.

There were two sacred concerts at the end of 1873. On November 26 there was a grand vocal and instrumental concert at the Lyceum Hall to benefit Central Congregational Church.[21] On Friday, December 12, Collignon conducted a concert at the Church of the Immaculate Conception on Baronne Street, with the assistance of many professionals and amateurs, especially Mme Comès (his daughter), Auguste Davis, M Gueymard, and Mlle Denain, besides the usual choir and soloists of the church. Collignon announced, in the paper, that the dress rehearsal would be on December 10 for the concert on December 12.[22] At the beginning of the new year, on January 8, 1874, there was another sacred concert at Coliseum Place Baptist Church, performed by the children of the church.[23]

In spring 1874 Louis Grunewald saw the position of the musicians as desperate and so, in order to save them, he created a spring festival of twelve concerts in his store on Baronne Street. Thirty members of the orchestra were hired.[24] These spring concerts, entitled Concerts Populaires, were given on Mondays, Wednesdays, and Fridays, and Robert Meyer was conductor. To ensure maximum returns for the players, musician-businessman Grunewald would earn something only if the musicians were fully paid. Admission was by subscription only, and it cost five dollars for tickets to all twelve concerts. The concerts extended from May 18 to June 13. The restaurant that abutted the concert hall was transformed into a parlor of ice creams and other refreshments. Smoking was permitted (for gentlemen only) in a room leading to the gallery. There were ten- to fifteen-minute intermissions for promenades, conversation, and refreshments. The programs, which were supposed to be different on each occasion, consisted of overtures and potpourris from operas, parts of classical masterpieces, dances (including the latest Strauss waltzes from Vienna), some instrumental solos with the accompaniment of piano or orchestra, some vocal solos, and so forth. A typical program was that on May 22: Wagner (*Tannhäuser* March), Hérold (Overture to *Zampa*), Rossini (excerpts from *William Tell*), Kalliwoda (Adagio and Scherzo from Symphony in A Minor), Strauss (*Wiener Woods*), Lindpaintner (Overture to *Jocko*), Robert Schumann (*Träumerei*), Meyerbeer (Air from *Robert le Diable*), waltzes, and a polka. On May 27 the program was the *Der Freischütz* Overture, different Strauss waltzes, Auber's Overture to *La Sirène*, and other pieces, but they did repeat Robert Schumann's *Träumerei* owing to popular demand, and the full Kalliwoda symphony.

As a result of the need of local musicians to perform outside opera, there were many more concerts by the resident musicians of New Orleans than usual. On January 8 and 10, there were performances by the German Quartet Club. On Sunday, January 11, 1874, the singer Theresa Cannon gave a concert at Grunewald Hall to benefit the orphans at Saint Vincent's. She was assisted by many local amateurs.[25] On February 4, there was a concert at Harmonie Hall on Bienville Street.[26] On February 6, there was a benefit concert at Grunewald Hall for the widow of Theodore von La Hache. La Hache, who had been so important for concert life in New Orleans in the 1850s and 1860s, had died poor in 1869. For the occasion, Grunewald supplied two Steinway grand pianos.[27]

On February 9 there was a benefit at the French Opera for its conductor, Eugène Momas, who conducted *Le Prophète*.[28] One month later, on March 9, there was a benefit concert at Grunewald Hall for the Immaculate Conception Asylum, in which several singers sang, Professor C. T. Frey played piano solos, and Mark Kaiser performed solo Alard's Fantasie sur *La Traviata* and, with Frey and Louis Grunewald, Gounod's Trio for piano, organ, and violin. There was no orchestra.[29] On Tuesday, March 24, Otto Weber directed a grand concert, at Grunewald Hall, given by the women of New Orleans to benefit the elderly and disabled at the Société des Servantes des Pauvres. There were works for piano and voice, performed by unnamed amateurs.[30] On the following Sunday, March 29, Collignon directed the Grand Mass by Gounod at the Immaculate Conception Church for the Festival of Rameaux. Mme Comès also sang Rossini's "Adoro Te."[31]

On April 6, Kaiser gave a concert at Grunewald Hall before returning to the American East and North and then to Paris to resume his studies. Kaiser had already received acclaim in the North and West, so it behooved his native city to hear him. He played four pieces and was assisted by pianists and singers on the program, but there was no chamber music and no orchestra.[32] On April 9–10, the women of the Church of New Jerusalem gave a promenade and concert at Odd Fellows' Hall, performed by one of the best bands of musicians in the city. People came in at 7:00, and the dancing started at 8:30 p.m. According to the advertisement, this event followed the English model of promenade concerts.[33] On Sunday, April 12, Mlle Arthurine Moreau, organist and singer at the Church of Notre Dame du Sacre Coeur (corner of Annette and Claiborne avenues), gave a concert. This all-women concert included singers from the French Opera, the violinist Gardner, and other amateurs.[34] Collignon was asked to conduct a concert at the Jesuit Church on April 15, but instead it occurred at Grunewald Hall.[35] The singers were led by Mme Devoyod-Acs, and Joubert performed four violin solos, including a Romance by Page. There was no orchestra. On Thursday, April 17, M D. Delcroix, Louisiana pianist, played a concert at Grunewald Hall with the assistance of the French Opera Orchestra under Momas and several singers (Devoyod-Acs and van Hufflen). The concert also included the violinist Madier de Montjau, concertmaster of the French Opera Orchestra and assistant conductor there, and the violoncellist Mayer.[36]

The friends of Collignon gathered on April 22, 1874, to honor him with a concert. It took place at the Jesuit Church and included amateur singers in Berlioz's "The Flight to Egypt" (from *L'Enfance du Christ*), for solo, chorus, and orchestra. Henriette Comès sang along with others, and Collignon conducted. The program also included the Gloria from Weber's Mass in E-flat, some Rossini, the andante of a trio by Beethoven played by organ, violin, and violoncello, and short pieces by Mercadante, Boulenger, Hummel, Gounod, Stradella, and Meyerbeer.[37]

On April 24, 1874, pianist Madame Herr, who had played a benefit for wounded Confederate soldiers in 1863 and subsequently limited her appearances to charity events, now played at her own benefit at Grunewald Hall.[38] She was assisted by Madier de Montjau and by some amateur women and men of talent.[39] Madier de Montjau performed De Bériot's Violin Concerto No. 7, and an andante and rondo in D major (from the Violin Concerto?) by Beethoven. Mme Herr's daughter Mlle Marie Herr also performed.

On April 29, Van Hufflen and Mme Nelville Mercier-Bier gave a concert at the Varieties Theater. Madier de Montjau and M Delcroix also participated; they played the Andante and Allegro from Mendelssohn's B-flat Minor Sonata and some solos. Mercier-Bier, a native Creole, was the pupil of Van Hufflen and was about to embark on her European experience (to Italy). Kate Thayer, a local singer, also sang on the program. Thayer, too, was a pupil of Van Hufflen, with a pretty, young voice. M Cartier was the accompanist.[40] On Friday, singers Mercier-Bier and Le Blanc were joined by Van Hufflen and the instrumentalists Gustave D'Aquin, Henri Joubert, and Cartier in a concert at Grunewald Hall for the benefit of Saint Augustin Church. The program consisted of the celebrated "Christmas Song" by Adam, arranged for trio and played on organ, piano, and violin (Schafter, Joubert, and Cartier); Van Hufflen sang an aria from *The Marriage of Figaro* by Mozart, and Joubert played *Elegie* by Page and *Romance without Words* by Sivori.[41]

A group of amateurs gave a concert at Grunewald Hall on May 7, 1874, for the benefit of the First Baptist Church (Magazine and Second streets), directed by F. Schaffer Jr., organist of Christ Church. It included opera singers, plus Auguste Davis, Joubert, and D'Aquin, with Cartier as accompanist. Nearly everything was songs, but there was one solo by D'Aquin and one by Joubert (who also played obbligato in a song).[42] Theresa Cannon directed a sacred concert on Sunday, May 10, at Sainte Anne's Church for the flood victims of Pointe Coupée Parish. The musicians performed sacred choruses and solo arias, including two each by Curto and Mozart, and one secular, nonvocal piece: Vieuxtemps's *Souvenir d'Haydn* was performed by Joubert.[43] The next day, D'Aquin and Joubert, assisted by both Devoyods, Madier de Montjau, and Mercier-Bier, gave a concert at the French Opera House. This was the tenth performance in one week at the French Opera. Momas conducted the orchestra.[44]

Another benefit took place on May 14 at Grunewald Hall for Mlle Lena Little. It consisted of vocal and instrumental music.[45] A week later Octavie Romey organized a concert at Grunewald Hall for the victims of the flood. With the assistance of Louis Grunewald, there were twenty-four pianists sitting at twelve pianos.[46]

The situation at the French Opera continued to deteriorate the following fall, however, since people were not coming in enough numbers to keep the house open. The fall season opened promisingly on November 5, 1874, with *Le Trouvère,* with Canonge in charge, and the rest of the proposed season looked very exciting for any opera enthusiast: *Lucia, La Juive, Rigoletto, The Daughter of the Regiment, William Tell, Les Huguenots, La Favorite, Jérusalem,* among others, were scheduled.[47] The season also was to include numerous opéra-comiques.[48]

But the promise cost money, and money was not coming in. Prices were slashed in December to try to encourage better attendance through the economic difficulties that the entire city faced,[49] but it did not work. By January 4, 1875, the French Opera was closed down and Canonge resigned (he thereupon launched a new career as the city's foremost music critic). The musicians of the French Opera House, desperate to continue to earn their livelihood, took over the house, under the leadership of the conductor Momas,[50] and reopened on Saturday, January 6, with a performance of *Robert le Diable.* They called on the subscribers to renew their subscriptions by February 1 and new patrons to come on board so that the operas could continue until the end of the season. "The Opera is an amusement that our people cannot well do without, and now they have an opportunity to do something towards the maintenance of the institution," maintained *L'Abeille.*[51] Meanwhile, on Sunday, March 28, 1875, Miss Emily Soldene's troupe opened at the Saint Charles Theatre by presenting Offenbach's *Geneviéve de Brabant.*[52] This began a series of performances of Offenbach's operettas so that, even after a threat of no opera, New Orleanians in fact had an abundance of opera in the spring of 1875.

While the professional musicians were struggling to survive, a new, small, young group of native New Orleanian performers was beginning to be heard, and within a few years they would be the ones to take over the concerts of both orchestral and chamber music. Principal among these were Theodore Curant, Guillaume Ricci, Mark Kaiser, and Henri Joubert, violinists; Borchert; and Gustave D'Aquin, flutist. Kaiser's and D'Aquin's lives and careers are described in book I.

During most of 1874, D'Aquin and Joubert played concerts in the hope of gaining financial backing so that they could travel to Paris to continue their studies. They were inseparable friends, and most often they played on the same program. Since their teachers were members of the French Opera Orchestra (D'Aquin studied flute with Leopold Carrière, and Joubert violin with Caulier), they had the sympathy of both the orchestral musicians and the singers. After their initial concert on February 8, 1874, they won the support of *L'Abeille* and the financial backing of the two leading singers at the opera, the husband-and-wife duo of M and Mme Devoyod.[53] *L'Abeille* stressed that, if New Orleans was to be the lyric capital of America, it must support its native talent.[54] Usually D'Aquin and Joubert each played a few solos on a mixed program of vocal and instrumental music, and occasionally each played on a concert without the other.[55] On May 1, 1874, they joined in a concert at Grunewald Hall for the benefit of Saint Augustin Church,[56] and a major benefit concert for the two young musicians was held on May 11, 1874, at the French Opera.[57] What was a rare occurrence at this time, the boys were accompanied by the French Opera Orchestra conducted by its leader, Monsieur Momas.[58] That fall D'Aquin and Joubert were in Paris, and on November 29 word reached New Orleans that they had been admitted to the Paris Conservatoire.[59]

After what seemed an interminable summer, recitals resumed in New Orleans at the end of November 1874. M E. Groenevelt, with the best professionals and amateurs of the city, presented a concert at Grunewald Hall on Baronne Street on Wednesday, November 25, 1874, for the benefit of the German-American Upper School. Among others, violinist V. Caulier played Paganini's *Carnival de Paris* and Ernst's "Hungarian Air" on the violin.[60] "It is a long time since we have had any concerts; this concert which inaugurates the season cannot fail to attract everyone."[61]

New Orleanians enjoyed balls instead. There were two on December 5, for example. One was given at the French Opera House with an excellent orchestra and for an entrance fee of two dollars, while the other, a grand masked ball at Grunewald Hall, drew only a small crowd because of the wind and rain. Yet everyone had a great time, according to *L'Abeille*: "The lady and gentleman dancers let themselves be carried away by the swirl of the dance and the harmony of the orchestra, and thereby showed their fearlessness."[62] Balls were a feature throughout the year and helped musicians by providing employment.

Wind chamber music was also a part of the 1874–75 season. On December 16, 1874, two wind quintets by Onslow were performed by soloists from the French Opera Orchestra: Suitaner, Gibot-Rivandon, Gonnet, Schnecgans, and Tilleux.[63] M Livain, who won first prize in flute from the Brussels Conservatory, was flute soloist on Wednesday, December 23, 1874, at a grand concert given for the opening of Saint Patrick's newly constructed hall (the largest hall then in the city, at Camp Street in Lafayette Square). The concert was sponsored by the women of New Orleans for the benefit of the orphans of Saint Vincent (corner of Race and Magazine streets). It was directed by M Cartier, principal flutist of the French Opera Orchestra. A brass band assisted.[64]

A variety of concerts continued in January 1875. On January 17, the annual session of the District Grand Lodge No. 7 of B'nai B'rith met and, accompanied by Robert Meyer's orchestral band, adjourned in a body to attend the anniversary celebration of the Jewish Widows and Orphans Home. They marched in the street, ultimately arriving at the home on Jackson and Chippewa streets.[65] On January 22 there was a grand concert by amateurs at Grunewald Hall to benefit the Sabbath School of the First Presbyterian Church. Featured was vocal and piano music, but there was also a violin obbligato, and Gibot Rivaudon performed two oboe solos by Verronet.[66] On January 27, professionals of the opera performed a grand charity concert at Saint Patrick's Hall. The music was mostly vocal, but Mrs. Vercken and Mr. Giannini played an unnamed work for violin and piano, Giannini added a solo violin piece, and Mr. Livain performed a flute solo.[67]

On Friday, February 5, 1875, there was a grand vocal and instrumental concert at Grunewald Hall to benefit the Saint Bernard Steam Engine (Compagnie de Pompiers) Fire Co. No. 1. It was directed by M J. Cartier, assisted by amateurs and artists and by flutist Livain.[68] There were two concerts on Monday, February 8. One was a concert at Grunewald Hall by the Club d'Euterpe to benefit the Asylum of the Immaculate Conception. The Club d'Euterpe was organized by the young Mme Louis Grunewald and consisted of persons of both sexes belonging to distinguished families. On this occasion the soloists were all amateurs: Mlles Julia T., Armantine M., Ida R, MM William S., Edmund T., and George R. Ida R. probably was Ida Riemann.[69] The other concert on the eighth was at Grunewald Hall by M Delcroix, professor of piano. The program included some opera transcriptions, and Delcroix was joined for two-piano works by amateurs Mlles A.G. and L.G., who were his pupils.[70] One more concert occurred in February, on the fifteenth. It was a solemn concert at Temple Sinai under Rabbi Leucht, a baritone, with amateurs Mmes Gustave B. and Mercier-Bier, professionals Feitlinger and Chelli, and a chorus of forty voices. They performed opera excerpts with Jewish content: "Moses' Prayer" and the prayer from *Aïda,* as well as a chorus from *Charles VI.* Works represented were by Mendelssohn, Verdi, Halévy, Vogel, Rossini, Méhul, and others. A special cantata, *Storm to Peace,* with words by Rabbi James K. Gutheim and set to music by Otto Weber (a local music professor) was premiered.[71]

In March, Mlle Ilma de Murska appeared in numerous operas in New Orleans at the French Opera. She debuted in the title role of *Lucia* on March 1. De Murska appeared under the aegis of M D. de Vivo, who also brought Mme Carreño-Sauret (a beautiful young woman from Venezuela and a strong pianist who had appeared earlier with Max Strakosch's troupe), M Ferranti (baritone), M Sauret (violinist and Carreño's husband at the time) and M Gaetano Braga (violoncellist). In addition to singing opera, De Murska and de Vivo's other artists gave two concerts at Grunewald Hall on Friday and Saturday, March 5 and 6. On March 10 De Murska interrupted her performance in *Robert le Diable,* the second and fourth acts, with a song as well as an aria from *The Magic Flute,* and in the intermède Braga executed an aria from *La Sonnambula* on the violoncello and scored a big success. On Friday, March 12, the de Vivo Troupe (de Murska, Carreño, Sauret, Braga, and Charles Pratt) gave another concert at Grunewald Hall. The group also gave a matinee concert at Grunewald Hall on the thirteenth, where an excerpt from *The Magic Flute* was especially well received. It gave "the idea, the grace and the delicateness of the thoughts of this divine genius." The group performed further concerts on March 20 and 28 and then traveled to Texas to fulfill an obligation. Immediately thereafter it returned to New Orleans for two more concerts on April 5 and 7 (a matinee). On one occasion the reviewer of *L'Abeille* compared De Murska's voice with the beautiful tones of Camile Urso's violin.[72]

While De Murska and her colleagues dominated the concert stage in March, there were other concerts as well. On March 19, 1875, Saint Joseph's Day, the Young Men's Benevolent Association gave a grand bal and masque as well as a concert promenade in the Grand Exposition Hall.[73] A sacred concert occurred on March 28 at Sainte Theresa's Church. M Heichelheim directed Weber's Mass; Eckert was at the organ. Mlle Grunewald sang the "Haec Dies" by Kapp.[74] There were two concerts on Wednesday, March 31. One was a concert of Ye Old Folk at Saint Patrick's Hall, by the Petites Soeurs des Pauvres, directed by Professor Watts, to benefit the poor elderly and infirm.[75] The other was a concert by Madame Zeiss-Dennis at Grunewald Hall, with the assistance of Mme Vercken of the opera and many other artists and distinguished amateurs. Included in the program was Mozart's "O Joy" from *The Magic Flute* for bass solo and chorus. Greuling accompanied.[76]

April 1875 was a particularly fruitful month for concerts in addition to the two by De Murska. There was a concert on April 1 by the artists of the French Opera to benefit the Society of the Servants of the Poor.[77] The next evening there was a concert at Saint Patrick's to benefit the family of the late Charles Brulard (d. September 14, 1874), under the direction of Collignon and consisting mostly of opera arias sung by artists of the French Opera and Mme Henriette Comès, Collignon's daughter. Grunewald donated Steinway pianos.[78] On the seventh Curto led a concert in Grunewald Hall featuring his own music (especially his *Requiem Oratorio*). Members of the Opera Orchestra and many amateurs and artists, some of whom were Curto pupils, assisted. The singer Theresa Cannon was singled out as charming. Mlle Mouton, a pupil of Hubert Rolling, performed on the piano Rolling's *La Mélodie Sacrée*.[79] On April 9 there was a matinee concert at Grunewald Hall by eleven-year-old Gustave Daussin, pianist, assisted by MM C. Hasse and A. Hasse (violinists), Mlle Hasse (pianist), Mlle Wagner, Bertha Parlongue and Eve Dablestten (singers) and M Météyé.[80]

There was another matinee concert on April 11 at Grunewald Hall to benefit the Société des Servantes des Pauvres (Little Sisters), given by artists of the French Opera. They raised more than twelve hundred dollars. A surprise party followed the concert.[81] Another concert of Vieilles Gens at Saint Patrick's was given to benefit Centenaire College of Louisiana, one of the best schools in the state.[82]

During the week of April 19, 1875, there was a benefit at the French Opera for the musicians in the orchestra. The musicians suffered much during the season and had real needs, yet they were loyal to the citizens of New Orleans by continually performing. They deserved this benefit.[83] On April 21, Curto and his pupils performed at Grunewald Hall in order to raise money to pay for the orchestra used at the April 7 concert (the Requiem). This program included songs and arias by Curto, Verdi, Weber, Auber, Méhul, and Meyerbeer. Among the performers were Mlle Marie Mouton, M Rolling Jr., Mlle Gruneberg, Mlle Reiman, M Cassard, Ida Rieman(n), and Mme Wilhem.[84] M Gaston Miral, former artist of the French Opera and comic singer, gave a matinee concert at Grunewald Hall on Saturday, April 24, assisted by many of his former colleagues of the French Opera.[85] There was yet another concert at Grunewald Hall, on Wednesday, April 28, by Mlle Corinne Bouligny, a strong singer, with the assistance of the leading amateurs of the city. "This concert was given under the auspices of a committee of distinguished ladies," reported *L'Abeille.* It included piano pieces, arias, a violin solo, and choruses. The piano accompanist was Mlle M. Laudamoy.[86]

May continued to be a very active month for concerts. On Sunday, May 2, 1875, M Laurent, light tenor, with Mmes Vercken, Teoni, Dumoulin, and MM Van Hufflen, Miral, Giannini, and Livain, gave a matinee concert at noon at Grunewald Hall.[87] Later that day some of the same singers—Mmes Vercken, Teoni and Dumoulin and MM Laurent, Miral, Giannini and Van Hufflen—gave a concert at 6 p.m. at the Hotel Carrollton in the Town of Carrollton (now a part of the City of New Orleans).[88] The next day the opera season came to a sudden close, and all the personnel lost their last two-and-a-half-months salary. To recoup this, the French Opera Troupe (some fifty persons), with its worthy conductor Momas, arranged to perform in Mexico. Still, this left some persons behind (mainly the orchestra), and they gave a benefit concert at the Opera House, including soloists and chorus and the orchestra conducted by M Momas.[89]

Two days later, on Wednesday, May 5, Curto conducted another benefit concert with the assistance of his most distinguished pupils and other amateurs of talent, at Grunewald Hall. This was to benefit the parish of the newly built Episcopal Church of Sainte Anna on Esplanade.[90] The program included vocal works by Hérold, Méhul, Meyerbeer, Donizetti, Halévy, Rossini, and Bellini.[91] On May 9, M Paulin Dardignac, baritone of the French Opera, gave a benefit concert in Economy Hall. The piano was played by M Basile, and others on the program were probably amateurs since only their initials are given. Since Barès was one of the most distinguished Creoles of color among the professional musicians, it is possible that some or all of the other performers were Creoles, too. The program included a trio (three persons' names are given, but the program lists only violin and piano), songs, and piano pieces.[92]

On Sunday, May 16, 1875, Mme Pauline Blache played a concert at Grunewald Hall, assisted by numerous local persons. Blache was a native Louisianan who excelled as pianist and singer and who had many pupils in the city. The program for Blache's concert included works by Halévy, Liszt, Gounod, Thalberg, Donizetti, David, and Rossini. Most performers were amateurs (only initials given), but also Mme U. Laroussini, Mme A. Schwartz, and M A. Cassard participated. M Cartier was at the piano.[93] On the same evening was the second concert at Economy Hall by Mlle le Liugier and M Miral, with M Dardignac.[94] A rare concert of early music—vielle musique—under the direction of Professeur T. R. Watts, took place on May 17 at Saint Patrick's. The performers played on old instruments.[95] The next day was the first performance in New Orleans of Gustave D'Aquin's new work, *Lamentation et Prière*, at the cathedral, for violin (Hayen), organ (Cartier), and flute (Livain). D'Aquin had then been studying in Paris for a year, and the work was written to commemorate the catastrophe that his uncle, Dr. H. Bayon, had experienced the previous January.[96] A critic for *L'Abeille* had the audacity to compare D'Aquin to Mozart![97]

There was a grand concert (May 21) and matinee (May 22) to benefit Sainte Elizabeth's Asylum, at Saint Patrick's under the direction of Theresa Cannon. It was performed by amateurs.[98] On Saturday May 22 there was a benefit concert at Saint Patrick's to help the musicians of the opera earn enough money to return to France.[99] They had gone to Mexico, but the returns were insufficient. Works were by Thomas, Meyerbeer, Alard (performed by violinist Giannini), Bellini, Seniet, Fauré, Aubert, and Henri. On Sunday, May 23, 1875, there was a grand concert at Grunewald Hall given to benefit Rev. Maumus of the cathedral. Performers included Mmes Blanche, Schwarz, U. Laroussini, Mlle H. Dolhonde, Mlle H. M, J. W. H. Eckert, W. N. Grunewald, MM les Professeurs Davis, Reich, Greuling, and Valades. Composers included Ketterer, Louis, David, De Bériot (violin solo), Meyerbeer, Donizetti (part of the opera *Don Pasquale*), Singelee, Massé, Gario, and Rossini.[100] Also on May 23 was another spectacle concert at Economy Hall, to benefit an unnamed society.[101] By

June regular concerts were over, but during a picnic at the Fair Grounds by the Société Francaise on June 6, Jaeger's band gave a grand concert.[102]

The fall 1875 season was average. A visiting Viennese orchestra performed at the Globe Theater from October 18 to 23. The orchestra consisted of thirteen young and beautiful women from Austria, who played both classical and popular music. They were artists who regrettably found themselves in a hall where the auditors drank, smoked, and in other ways relaxed and enjoyed themselves.[103] On Thursday, October 28, this Orchestre des Dames Viennoises, together with M Livain (flute), and Mr. L. Pascalis (baritone), performed in a regular setting at Grunewald Hall in a grand vocal and instrumental concert to benefit the German Protestant Orphan Asylum. The program included the *Poet and Peasant* Overture by von Suppé, works of Verdi, Thomas, Stradella, Strauss, Boehm, and Demersmann, and a "Spring Concerto" by Bach.[104] Meanwhile the Café Bismarck, in competition with the Globe Theater, rehired MM Rossi and Sig. Repetto of the Grand Opera and Miss Rostto to sing airs.[105]

In November 1875, M D. Delcroix, well-known pianist in New Orleans, gave the first of three recitals in Grunewald Hall. The other two were in December and January 1876. He was assisted by M Resch (violin solo) and by a quartet composed of MM Dantonnet and Bonivard (violins), Resch (viola) and L. Mayer (violoncello). It was by subscription. If there was no opera this season, at least there was some good music. But there was, nonetheless, operetta scheduled at the Varieties Theater, under the direction of Maurice Grau and Chizzola.[106] The operetta season opened at the Varieties on November 1 with a French comic troupe with a full chorus and orchestra. It was Lecocq's *Girofle-Girofla* in its first New Orleans performance.[107] On November 6 the Young Men's Violet Social Club gave a concert and an evening of dance at Exposition Hall.[108] For three evenings, November 23, 24, and 25, 1875 (Tuesday through Thursday), there were grand soiree concerts at Grunewald Hall to benefit the Church of New Jerusalem. The programs included chamber music, vocal works, and musical tableaux by Fesca, Mayseder, and others.[109]

There were a number of concerts in December 1875. These started on December 1 with a grand vocal and instrumental concert given to Mme Henriette Comès by the women of the Church of the Immaculate Conception. It was at Grunewald Hall and was directed by her father, Collignon. The instrumental part consisted of two violin solos by Mr. Caulier, a trio for piano, violin, and violoncello by MM Collignon, Caulier, and Monna, and a grand improvisation by Mr. Collignon on the piano celeste. The vocal pieces were sung by Madame Henriette Comès and Mlle Marie Collignon (Henriette's sister), MM Météyé and Cassard, and others.[110] On December 12 the Dramatic Club of Louisiana gave a benefit concert at the Opera House to benefit the Sisters of the House of Bon Pasteur. The composer Octavie Romey wrote a mass that she conducted at Saint Louis Cathedral on December 18 (performed by the Bouquet Musical Club), and she donated the money collected at the service to the same charity.[111] On December 17, during the performance of a comedy at the Opera House, there was a musical intermède in which Mr. Ludovic sang the "Romance Adieu Mignonne" (possibly from the opera *Mignon*), Mlle Duparc sang the "Romance Lettre of a Girl Cousin to Her Boy Cousin," Madame Geuffroy sang an air from *Faust,* and three other named singers sang a chansonette, a ballade, and another song.[112] There was a benefit grand concert at Economy Hall on December 20.[113] Music at the cathedral for Christmas Eve and Christmas Day was especially ornate. Midnight mass was sung by one of the best bass voices in New Orleans,[114] and the mass *Enfants de Marie* was chanted for the second time by the Bouquet Musical Club, directed by Romey.[115] Meanwhile, the French Comic Opera under Grau and Chizzola returned to New Orleans on December 12, after touring Texas and before touring Mexico.[116]

The decade from 1876 to 1886 saw a return of New Orleans as a stopover for international stars. Rubinstein and Wieniawski had tested the waters in 1873. Now in February 1876 one of the most important pianist/conductors in Europe came to the Crescent City. Hans von Bülow began a series of seven concerts at Grunewald Hall on February 15, with the young soprano, Lizzie Cronyn, with whom he was traveling throughout his first American tour.[117] He also scheduled concerts for Wednesday, February 16; Friday, February 18; and a matinee on Saturday, February 19, and because of the success of these four he added another two regular concerts on February 21 and 22 and a matinee on February 23. As in his other concerts in America, his programs emphasized the German and Austrian classics but were not limited to them. They included Bach, Beethoven (several sonatas including the *Pathétique),* Mendelssohn, Chopin, Liszt, Scarlatti, Gluck, Mozart, Schubert, and Rubinstein.[118]

The rest of the spring season was surprisingly short on concerts. On February 15, 1876, a new Philharmonic Society (recently organized by Louis Grunewald) and the Germania Quartette Club gave a vocal and instrumental concert which featured Mendelssohn's oratorio *Elijah*.[119] On February 25, Gruneberg directed a concert at Grunewald Hall featuring the singer Van Hufflen with some professionals and amateurs.[120] The widow Mme Charles Boudousquié's students gave a concert in her honor on March 15. They were assisted by the professionals Météyé, Cassard, and Caulier, and the program included two pieces for violin and piano performed by Caulier and Cartier.[121] There was a vocal and instrumental concert on March 21 at La Parfaite Union (Rampart Street) for the benefit of the amateur Mme Courtade, followed by a dance.[122] There was another benefit concert at Grunewald Hall, this time on March 23, to raise money for a monument to Robert E. Lee. Professor Adolphe Duquesnay was in charge. Most of the eighteen pieces on the program were for voice and/or piano played by Duquesnay and his pupils, with some professionals.[123] On April 21, Mark Kaiser gave a concert in Saint Patrick's Hall, for the benefit of the Royal Guards. The "Grande Marche" from Meyerbeer's *Le Prophète* was performed by the Euterpean Society. After the concert, the band of the Royal Guards under the direction of Professor Duquesnay played dance music, to which the audience danced.[124] On April 25 the Centennial of the United States was celebrated at the French Opera House.

The following fall had the usual dearth of concerts. F. W. Eckert led a concert at Grunewald Hall on November 14, 1876, with many amateurs to benefit the orphanage at the corner of Camp and Prytania streets.[125] Mme Herr and her daughter performed a concert of vocal and instrumental music at Grunewald Hall on December 27; the concert had been postponed from earlier in the month owing to the death of Mr. Herr.[126] An unusual advertisement appeared in *L'Abeille* on December 15–17 seeking sponsorship of a concert under the auspices of the Atheneum at either Grunewald Hall or the French Opera House, with full orchestra, featuring and promoting D'Aquin.[127] Nothing seems to have come of this request, though within a few years D'Aquin had established himself as one of the most popular performers in New Orleans.

Meanwhile, the opera season began with what seems to be counter to prevailing assumptions at the time about women: all three principal companies coming to town were directed and managed by women. The Varieties Theater announced on November 14 the upcoming season which included two of these: Clara Louisa Kellogg's opera troupe of eighty persons and Mlle Aimée's operetta company of fifty.[128] No record of the Kellogg performances is known. The Aimée Operetta Troupe, after performances in Havana, debuted at the Varieties Theater on December 23 with *Jolie Parfumeuse*.[129] At the same time, on December 14, Caroline Riching-Bernard's troupe of fifty artists opened at the French Opera House with *Maritana* followed by *Il Trovatore* and *Martha* and, on the Saturday matinee, *The Bohemian Girl*.[130] But all these were visitors; the city no longer had its resident company. It was hoped that at least an Italian opera company would come for a long stay since having a winter opera season was important in attracting visitors to the city.[131]

The spring 1877 season was reasonably full of concerts. On January 3, the Louisiana singer Pauline Blache gave a concert in Grunewald Hall, assisted by both amateur and professional musicians. Most of the program was sung, but it included a duet for violin and piano by Liszt, and Hermant's *Le Carnaval de Paris* performed by Caulier.[132] Mark Kaiser and A. Livain played a grand concert at Grunewald Hall on February 4. Among the pieces on the program was a trio by Reissiger for violin (Kaiser), piano (Cartier), and violoncello (Monna), some arias, and a work performed by a ten-year-old pupil of Livain.[133] The concert apparently was repeated on February 7.[134] On February 18, at Grunewald Hall, Mlle Louise Dorel of the Comedie Française of Paris and New York, performed concert versions of two vaudevilles and then an opera bouffe by Offenbach. She had the assistance of Louis Chauchon, tenor and professeur au Conservatoire de Musique and other distinguished professionals.[135] The Philharmonic Society had its fifth public concert at Grunewald Hall on Wednesday, February 28, 1877;[136] its first concert was a year earlier (see above and book I, part I, chapter 3), and it continued to give concerts into the 1890s.

On March 25 there was a grand sacred concert at Saint Louis Cathedral in honor of Father Maumas. J. Cartier directed sacred vocal works, with organ, piano, and a few other instruments accompanying. In addition, Caulier played Wieniawski's *Legende* and Monna played Sivori's *Romance sans Parole*. Van Hufflen was one of the vocal soloists.[137] There was a concert at Grunewald Hall under the auspices of the Société de Lévéque (Bishop) Polk on April 10. The highlight of the program was a Beethoven piano-violin sonata performed by Mlle M. Wilson and Caulier.[138] The next day there was a concert at Grunewald Hall in honor of the tenor Angelo Torriani, with professional and amateur musicians assisting. Mlle Mercier, Van Hufflen, Livain, J. W. H. Eckert, and W. N. Grunewald (pianist) performed works for voice, flute, and piano by various composers including Mozart, Bellini, Verdi, Auber, Donizetti, Morel, and Reichardt. Fred N. Thayer, a dealer in buggies, read recitations.[139]

A vocal and instrumental concert was held on April 12 at the French Opera to benefit Saint Joseph's Asylum.[140] On May 12, 1877, at 7:30 p.m., there was a sacred concert at Saint Louis Cathedral, under Jules Cartier, chapel master and organist of the cathedral, with Van Hufflen and the choir performing Rossini's Solemn Mass and other sacred vocal music. Caulier also performed a violin solo.[141] On May 15, Mlle Bouligny, having had successes in Paris and New York, returned to her home, New Orleans, to sing at Grunewald Hall. The unusual program included band music by the Thirteenth Infantry Regiment stationed in the city, opera arias (Van Hufflen again), Cartier accompanying at the piano, plus A. Livain and Mueller playing both solo and obbligato. An important work heard was Rolling's *Le Réveil du Sud*.[142] It was announced on February 22 that Fleury-Urban was performing in Havana in *Il Trouvère* and *La Favorite* and would be coming to New Orleans at the end of April for a concert, but she had to leave for France via New York in a hurry so she forfeited her concert in New Orleans.[143] But there were other recitals. Mme T. E. Broaddus gave a concert at Grunewald Hall on May 17.[144] There was a concert in the foyer at the Opera House on May 27 to benefit M A. Flandry, assisted by Cartier and other professional and amateur musicians. Flandry was one of the best pianists and teachers in New Orleans.[145]

Then, on June 1, the women of the choir of the Immaculate Conception Church, with the assistance of professional and amateur male musicians, offered a sacred vocal and instrumental concert in honor of Collignon. The program opened with an organ piece composed by Collignon, and later Collignon's composition *Sursum Corda,* an adagio de concert for piano, violin, and violoncello, was performed by M Rech (violinist), Monna (violoncellist), and Collignon (pianist). Mmes Comès and Dunn, Fred Kitziger, then organist at Saint Alphonse's, and Caulier assisted. Cartier, originally scheduled to participate, withdrew because of an accident.[146]

Mlle Bouligny offered a charity concert on June 5 to benefit the Lady Servants of the Poor. At first scheduled at the French Opera House, it was moved to Grunewald Hall. The soprano donated all her fees to the charity. Bouligny was assisted by Mme Schwartz and others. A military band played an overture and a march.[147] Mark Kaiser gave a concert on June 7, 1877, at the Opera House.[148] The final concert of the season was a special one at Grunewald Hall on June 15 in honor of Auguste Davis. Davis lost his voice, probably owing to throat cancer, and he was forced to step down as singer at the Immaculate Conception Church. He also had to stop teaching. The proceeds from this concert were to enable him to go to Virginia to a spa.[149] He died just two years later, on November 10, 1879, at the age of forty-one.[150]

With the scarcity of opera performances, the house instrumentalists and some of the singers kept busy, not only with incidental music at the theaters and these few concerts, but also in accompanying dances. For example, a brilliant wind orchestra accompanied the "grand bal paré et masqué, soirée du mardi gras à l'opéra" on February 14, 1877,[151] and the excellent music of A. Cunniot was hired for the fourth annual grand ball of the Saint Maurice Mutual Aid Society in Grunewald Hall on March 9.[152]

The fall 1877 season was slightly more active than past fall seasons. Kaiser and Marguerite Elie Samuel, newly returned for good from Paris, joined the Philharmonic Society in a concert at Grunewald Hall on October 21.[153] Four days later, at the same venue, there was a concert and amateur minstrel show for the benefit of the orphans of Sainte Therese, under the direction of J. W. H. Eckert. Besides some songs and piano pieces, the program included a cornet solo performed by George Pritchard and a violin solo performed by Mr. A. Gugenheim.[154] On November 13, there was a concert at Grunewald Hall to benefit the widow of Captain John Wilson; it was directed by Edward Groenevelt and included only professional performers: two choirs of a hundred voices, two vocal quartets, the flutist Livain, two pianists M Tyler and Mlle M. Wolf, and vocal soloists Mlle L. Little and M Bremer.[155] A German military band, led by Carl Beyer, began performing at Grunewald Hall on November 18. The *L'Abeille* critic considered this band, along with the Theodore Thomas band, one of the two best in the United States.[156] By equating these two bands, was the critic asserting that Thomas's group was not an orchestra?

When J. C. Fryer brought his Italian and German Opera Company to the Varieties Theater, he not only restored serious opera to the city but also brought in artists for concerts. Fresh from successes in Philadelphia, Cincinnati, and Chicago, and beginning on November 28, 1877, Fryer featured Mme Eugénie Pappenheim (prima donna) and Charles Adams (tenor), with a grand chorus and orchestra directed by Max Maretzek. The first week, through December 4, included *Il Trovatore, The Flying Dutchman* (New Orleans premier), *Les Huguenots, La Favorite, Lohengrin,* and *La Muette* (Masaniello).[157] *L'Abeille*'s critic concluded, after this week,[158] "When one realizes that the company played the very day of the arrival of the artists and each evening a new opera, which hardly allows time to connect with the work, the results obtained were astonishing. The orchestra is sufficiently staffed and well disciplined, and the choirs are better than we dared hope." The second week repeated some and added others: *Il Trovatore, Lohengrin, Les Huguenots, Lucia, Fidelio,* and *Tannhäuser.*[159] *Der Freischütz* was added on December 15.[160] Apparently, by the third week, it seems, they had moved over to the Opera House, where, for the first time in almost three years, high-level opera was performed. It started with Gounod's *Faust,* followed on consecutive evenings by *Rigoletto, La Favorite,* and *La Traviata.* The immense size of Fryer's chorus and orchestra, conducted by Maretzek, impressed the critic of *L'Abeille,* and with a heavy dose of Wagner, the French Opera House had moved into a new, modern era.[161]

Since Fryer's troupe was in town, occasions quickly presented themselves for concerts. On December 10, 1877, members of Fryer's troupe presented an all-vocal sacred concert at the Varieties Theater.[162] On December 22 they joined the Philharmonic Society in a performance of Mendelssohn's *Elijah* at the French

Opera House, with Pappenheim, Adams, and other stars from the troupe in the solo parts. Groenvelt conducted.[163]

Meanwhile there were other concerts at the end of the fall 1877 season. On November 20, Jules Cartier directed a vocal and instrumental concert at Odd Fellows' Hall to benefit the Methodist Church of Algiers,[164] and from December 9 on, J. H. Bonham conducted a grand orchestra at the Academy of Music between comic routines by the Rice Troupe.[165] Finally, the Société Musicale d'Euterpe tendered a soiree musicale at Grunewald Hall on December 20. Mlle I. Locquet, M E. Tyler, and one of the Eckerts led the performers.[166]

The spring 1878 season was reasonably active. On January 4 Mme Charles Boudousquié, with many of her pupils, performed a soiree musicale in the foyer of the French Opera House to benefit orphans.[167] She was, of course, training the young in one of the main social purposes for concerts, namely, assisting the needy through charity raised by musical performances. Marguerite Samuel and her pupils followed suit with a soiree musicale at Grunewald Hall on February 8. There were twelve pieces on the program, all for piano, and as a finale Samuel herself performed *Les Hirondelles.*[168] On February 26, Mme Alice Schwartz, singer at the synagogue on Rampart Street, gave a vocal and instrumental concert at Grunewald Hall. She was joined by Mme Pauline Blache, first soprano at Trinity Church, and Mlles Reiman, Pokorny, Parra and Lily Dreyfois, as well as MM Cartier, Curant, Keith, Salomon, and Krebs, amateurs and professionals.[169] This is the first known appearance of Theodore Curant, who, as violinist and conductor, had a large influence on concert life in New Orleans over the next fifteen years. Wenger Garden, 11 and 13 Bourbon Street, had light concerts throughout the spring of 1878; it had "the grandest orchestra in the world," executing airs from 11 a.m. to midnight.[170] Intermèdes between acts of plays continued at the various theaters. At the National Theater on March 8, for example, Mme Antoinette von Bader performed on the piano and also read a literary piece. The others who played during intermission were Mme Stamwitz, Mme Kuster, Curant, and M Gaevert, corniste.[171]

Marguerite Samuel returned to Grunewald Hall on Thursday, March 28, 1878. She performed two duos with Curant. The rest of the program was songs by various unnamed women, and piano pieces. J. C. Cartier was accompanist in the vocal music.[172] On April 4, Ida Riemann gave a grand concert at Grunewald Hall, directed by Ed. Groenevelt and with other friends. J. W. H. Eckert was at the piano. Riemann, who needed the proceeds of the concert to go to Italy to study, sang two songs; in addition, there were piano solos and other vocal music. When she returned from abroad, Riemann married Kaiser's brother and became a fixture in the concert life of the city.[173] The de Vivo Troupe, starring Ilma de Murska, gave its first of five concerts at the Varieties Theater on April 6. Subsequent concerts were on April 9, 10, 12, and 13 (matinee). The concerts included songs, arias, and several piano works. The flutist Livain joined in on the fourth concert.[174] Organist and pianist J. Cartier directed a concert at Saint Louis Cathedral on April 11. Cartier opened and closed the concert; the rest of the performances were opera arias and sacred music, including choral pieces.[175]

There was a cathedral concert, including Gounod's Mass and the quartet from Verdi's Mass, on April 18, 1878.[176] Four days later Miss Kate Thayer, daughter of New Orleanian Fred N. Thayer—the buggy maker—was home visiting her family and decided to give a recital at Grunewald Hall. She had been the pupil of Van Hufflen, and was now singing with great success in New York and Baltimore. She sang arias and a duet with Van Hufflen. On the program Curant performed Viotti's A Minor Violin Concerto No. 22 and A. Bazzini's Opus 42, D-Minor Military Concerto, with Cartier at the piano. Also, Borchert of the German military band played some flute music, and several singers sang arias, mostly by Verdi.[177] On May 2 at Grunewald Hall, Jules Cartier was honored in a concert by members of the cathedral choir under the patronage of the Sainte Cecile Society. Marguerite Samuel and V. Caulier also performed. Caulier played Wieniawski's *Legend,* and Larman's *Le Carnaval de Paris.* Samuel played Liszt's Andante and Sextet from *Lucia,* the rest being vocal arias and ensembles.[178] The final concert of the spring was on May 6 at the French Opera House and was in honor of Miss Corinne Bouligny before she headed for Europe. Curant performed works by Artôt and Kreuger, and Samuel performed pieces by Thalberg and Chopin (*Grande Valse en la Bémol*); Cartier was accompanist. The rest of the program consisted of vocals.[179]

There was only one concert, apparently, in the fall of 1878. It was a charity concert at Grunewald Hall on Thursday, November 28, to benefit the orphans at Sainte Theresa's. Eckert directed the program.[180] Without its own opera, the city relied on Adah Richmond's Opera Bouffe Troupe at the Saint Charles Theatre beginning on December 15, with operettas by Offenbach, Planquette, and Lecocq.[181] And on January 20, 1879, the Hess Troupe started at the Varieties Theater, "accompanied by a chorus and complete orchestra." During the first week it presented *Faust, Mignon,* and *The Bohemian Girl,* and during the second week it presented *Fra Diavolo, Les Cloches, Martha, La Rose de Castille* (by Balfé), and *Maritana.* It also gave a new opera, *Paul et Virginie,* by Victor Massé.[182] The opéra comique of the Varieties Theater, with its sizeable orchestra, gave the New Orleans premier of *H.M.S. Pinafore* on March 5, 1879.[183]

On January 18, 1879, there was a literary and musical meeting at Grunewald Hall. The program consisted of a mixture of readings and musical performances by H. Rolling fils.[184] A concert was presented to benefit Curto, given by his pupils, on February 4 at Grunewald Hall. Curto had just retired as chapel master at St. Patrick's Church. Two pieces by Curto were on the program: Trio (Curto was one of the singers) and Grand Choeur; Curant performed a violin solo, and W. H. Bischoff performed a guitar solo.[185] Then, the internationally famous violinist Wilhelmj came to New Orleans and performed three concerts at Grunewald Hall on February 17, 18, and 19. The fine pianist Carreño was also a participant. On the first two programs, Wilhelmj performed a fantasy of his own, a concerto by Paganini, a Chopin nocturne, a romance by Robert Schumann, "Hungarian Airs" by Ernst, the Mendelssohn Concerto, and Ernst's Fantasie on *Otello*. All these works are extremely difficult virtuoso pieces designed to excite the lay audience, and the critics had to compare Wilhelmj to Vieuxtemps and Paganini.[186]

On March 2, 1879, at the Saint Charles Theatre, there was a concert of the all-women vocal Swedish Quartet, with harp performed by Alexandre Freygang.[187] The following Sunday, March 9, Les Minstrels d'Emerson, with a grand orchestra and brass band, appeared at the Academy of Music.[188] A soiree musicale by pupils of the Saint Louis Institute, whose director was Mme Mathey, occurred on March 29.[189] There was a concert directed by Cartier at the cathedral on March 31. The program consisted of vocal, piano, and organ pieces.[190] There was a sacred concert at Saint Etienne's Church on Napoleon Avenue on April 13, with singers and instrumentalists.[191] Mlle Cora Roig, accompanied by J. W. H. Eckert, gave a grand concert at Grunewald Hall on April 14. For this occasion, Marguerite Samuel played Beethoven's *Moonlight* Sonata and Chopin's *Grande Polonaise Brillante,* Opus 3, in C Major. The rest of the program was songs.[192] On April 14, Curant directed a concert in which he played the Beethoven Violin Concerto with orchestra, Samuel played the Mendelssohn G Minor Piano Concerto No. 1 with orchestra, and Curant, Kitziger, Cartier, and Mueller performed a string quartet by Haydn.[193] Livain, who also performed a flute solo, conducted an orchestra of thirty of the best musicians of the city; as well as accompanying Curant and Samuel, he led the orchestra in the overtures to Wallace's *Maritana* and Weber's *Jubel.*

Cartier directed a concert on April 29, 1879, at Odd Fellows' Hall for the benefit of the Methodist Church.[194] The program was devoted to pieces for piano and voice, with one violin solo played by Albert Heichelheim: *Larghetto de Mozart* by Vieuxtemps. Mlles Arthurine Maureau and Jeanne Malochée, piano pupils of Le Mercier Duquesnay, with the aid of some of his better pupils, gave a matinee musicale at Grunewald Hall on May 3.[195] The program was mostly piano pieces and a few arias, with Gounod's "Ave Maria" arranged for violin, piano, and organ. The performers included also pupils of Bremer and some amateurs. Marguerite Samuel gave her concert on May 14.[196] The program, under the direction of Greuling and Cartier, included once again the Mendelssohn G Minor Concerto No. 1 with orchestra, Beethoven's *Moonlight* Sonata, and works by Chopin, Samuel herself, and others. Most of the evening was taken up with piano music, a few songs, and the overture to Reissiger's *Felsenmühle* by the orchestra. Despite the lateness of the season, there were still a few more concerts.

On May 27 Mme Henriette Comès, soloist for sixteen years at the Immaculate Conception Church and daughter of Collignon, gave a concert at Grunewald Hall.[197] She was assisted by Mme F. Dunn, Mlle Marie Collignon (Comès's sister), Curant, Livain, Mueller (violoncellist), Cassard, J. C. Broadley, and Jules L. de Barjac. Collignon directed the concert. The Sixth Annual Musical Festival, given by the musicians' union at the Fair Grounds, took place on June 1 and 2.[198] On the first there was a grand promenade concert by fifty musicians under the direction of Professor J. Eckert. Dances followed the concert. On Monday, June 2, there was a concert on the platform at 3 p.m., and at 5 p.m. a grand concert in the batisse principale by fifty musicians under the direction of Robert Meyer. At this last concert Collignon conducted an overture of his own composition in what was apparently his last public appearance in New Orleans before he emigrated back to Paris, where shortly thereafter he died. A dance followed this performance as well.

Summer concerts were now becoming a fixture in New Orleans. In July there were regular orchestral concerts at Magnolia Gardens conducted by Eckert and Robert Meyer. At one of these, Collignon had a work of his performed as part of the annual festival of the musician's benevolent society and union.[199] Curant and Robert Meyer appeared as soloists with an elite orchestra. But historically, the most significant summer event was the creation of the first regular concert series at Spanish Fort on Lake Pontchartrain. It was customary for local citizens of the city who remained in New Orleans during the summer to spend evenings on the shores of the lake in order to escape the heat and the epidemics. Concerts would often be played there, but not on a sustained, regular basis. One such evening concert occurred on May 29, 1879, when the Harmony Club gave a promenade concert for an "immense" number of guests.[200] But on Wednesday, July 9, there began a series of promenade concerts that lasted until September 20. Professor B. Moses, formerly conductor of the Fourth Louisiana Regiment Band, led a band of twenty-five "of the best artists of the city."[201] The opening concert, which began at 6 p.m., included works by Mendelssohn, Planquette, Strauss, Bellini, Meyerbeer, Heinicke, Sullivan, Offenbach, and Beyer. The concert on Tuesday, September 9, included works by Schoner, Wagner, Nolbig, Verdi, Heinicke, Weber, Suppé, Behr, Gounod, Donizetti, Planquerte, and Hamm. The following evening, the band played a charity concert, the proceeds to go to the flood children's fund. A reporter for the *Picayune* was impressed with the growing popularity of these concerts.

> The Lake Ends have of late become immensely popular places of resort. The evening concerts inaugurated at the Spanish Fort, and subsequently at the New Lake End, have added greatly to the attractiveness of those places. A more appropriate and euphemistic name might be given to the latter locality. It was once proposed to convert a portion of the swampy ground lying near the canal into a garden, and it is to be hoped that this plan will be carried out. The enterprise manufactured by the Mssrs. Schwartz in improving Spanish Fort and its surroundings is to be highly commended. We have too few enterprises of this character. If carried out with the proper spirit and determination they will always meet with public favor and support.[202]

From now on, series of summer concerts on the lake were a regular feature of the concert life of New Orleans.

The fall 1879 season had few concerts but did have the return of opera on a regular basis—albeit with a visiting company. On November 24, Max Strakosch's opera company opened in New Orleans after traveling through Baltimore, Chicago, Cincinnati, and Saint Louis.[203] Placide Canonge, who had managed the last regular New Orleans opera company, served as Strakosch's agent in the city. How sorry things in New Orleans were is revealed in an announcement on November 7 by Canonge that he still needed first and second violins, violas, and a second trumpet for the orchestra for Strakosch.[204] If these were not forthcoming within four or five days, Canonge would inform Strakosch who would then hire these musicians in Cincinnati and/or Saint Louis to come to New Orleans. While extras were often brought in at the beginning of opera seasons from Europe to supplement the French Opera Orchestra, the great center of music in the middle South of the country now could no longer supply even the basic instrumentalists. This city was renowned for opera before the war and for only seven or eight years between the end of the war and 1879, but Reconstruction had destroyed the ability of New Orleans to pay for opera.

A critic in *L'Abeille* suggested that maybe New Orleans should join one or two other cities in creating a company that would have a permanent orchestra and chorus and ensemble. In any case, Strakosch gave the city a month of great opera again, opening with *Il Trovatore* on November 24 and including the New Orleans premier of *Aïda* on December 6, 1879. Reviewing the second week of Strakosch's stand, the critic of *L'Abeille* stated, "What is left is for us to compliment the choir, which in general is very satisfying, and the orchestra, which acquits itself successfully in a really arduous task. It is wonderful that they realize fine ensemble playing when they must execute each evening a new score. The two leaders of Mr. Strakosch's orchestra, Behrens and Novelli, deserve much of the honor for the beautiful concerts that the public of New Orleans has heard and appreciated."[205] Interestingly, tenor Gaston Gottschalk, youngest brother of Louis Moreau and a native of New Orleans, was part of Strakosch's troupe at the French Opera House. In all, Strakosch's company performed thirty-five times in a month and five days, on average one performance per day.

Among the concerts this fall was that by M Hahnebohm, cithara player, on December 11 in Grunewald Hall.[206] It was an unusual mixture of early music (pre-1700) and modern music (mid-nineteenth century). Hahnebohm was assisted by M H. Baethge, violinist from South America, two vocalists, and Mr. J. Bremer, basso continuo. Baethge and Hahnebohm performed two duos for violin and lute, Bremer performed two solos, and Baethge performed two solos for violin. Pianist Mme De Lassichère played Liszt's fantasy on *Rigoletto*. On Friday, December 26, and on Saturday, December 27, Kate Thayer returned to New Orleans to perform at Grunewald Hall with Carreño.[207] On Saturday, Carreño played Liszt's Polonaise. MM Arbuckle (cornetist) and C. E. Pratt (accompanist) were also on the programs. And on the last day of the year, there was an important intermède at the Opera House. Between the second and third acts of *Il Trovatore* performed by Strakosch's troupe, the orchestra played the world premiere of *Harmonies of Nature,* a suite for orchestra by Hubert Rolling.[208] S. Behrens was the conductor.

The 1880s was a time of much musical activity and nostalgia for the good old days before the Civil War. It is true that the city would never recapture its supremacy in music, especially in opera, that it enjoyed in the 1840s and 1850s, but the city still hosted some fine concert musicians, and there were probably as many concerts given as before. But what was clearly dying in the city was its strong French culture, including the language, and its ties to Parisian music. More and more, English was the spoken language on the streets of the city, and American musical culture was getting more attention. One institution that was created to preserve French culture was the Louisiana Atheneum Club, which, among other things, awarded literary prizes each year for the best local works in French.[209] During the prize ceremonies, music was an important component, such as on Saturday, January 3, 1880, at the Opera House, when the orchestra participated with a fanfare, then the "Priests' March" from *Le Prophète*; in the second half the orchestra played an andante and then concluded the affair with Hubert Rolling's *Marche Triomphale* (Rolling was a member of the Atheneum Club). The rest of the program was speeches.[210]

An unusually large number of opera and operetta companies visited the city during the spring of 1880. Maurcie Grau's company, which included a grand orchestra, began a run of French opera at the Grand Opera House on Canal Street at Dauphine Street on January 6.[211] On February 9 the Emma Abbott Opera Company opened at the Grand Opera House with Balfé's *Bohemian Girl* and followed with *Paul et Virginie, Les Cloches de Corneville, Martha,* and other works, over the next two weeks. It, too, included a grand chorus and orchestra.[212] The King of Carnival came to the opera on the ninth, and when he arrived, the performance stopped and the orchestra played the national anthem.[213] The Colville Burlesque Company at the Saint Charles Theatre presented spoofs on operas in New Orleans, beginning on March 15.[214] On March 24, 1880, the D'Oyley Carte brought *The Pirates of Penzance* to the Grand Opera House (Dauphine and Canal streets).[215] Finally, for one week, starting on April 5, the Haverly Opera Company from New York performed *H.M.S. Pinafore* at the Academie de Musique.[216] All this time the French Opera House was in need of repair, and a major renovation was planned. It was hoped, then, a new French Opera Company would emerge, and plans were also made to budget salaries for forty persons in the orchestra, forty in the chorus, eighteen opera singers, ten actors, seventeen dancers, and seven administrators.[217]

On March 13 and April 7, 1880, there were two concerts of Irish music at the French Opera House. These were directed by Blake.[218] Kitziger, with the assistance of many professional and amateur musicians, directed the choir of Saint Louis Cathedral in a concert at the cathedral on March 20. The same day, Marguerite Samuel gave a concert at Grunewald Hall. On March 30, Theodore Curant directed a concert at Grunewald Hall, with singers Alice Schwartz, Annie Seawell, F. Bremer, D. Delcroix, and Eckert, and a complete orchestra of forty of the best musicians in the city.[219] It was by subscription only. There was a soiree littéraire et musicale on April 2, and on the same day, during a play, there was a musical intermède featuring the romance from Thomas's *Mignon* and an excerpt from *The Daughter of the Regiment*.[220] Mme Charles Boudousquié had a recital for her pupils at the home of Mme Olivier Carrière on April 5,[221] and Mme L. De Lassichère, pianist and organist, directed a grand concert for the benefit of the New Church of the Sacred Heart.[222] Everything on the program was vocal except for a piece by Gottschalk. On April 10, there was a recital by fifteen-year-old Henriette Collin at Grunewald Hall. Proceeds from this recital enabled her to go to Paris for further study.[223] Rolling had a recital for his students at Grunewald Hall on April 17.[224] Mme Courtade, a Louisiana soprano, held her benefit concert at Grunewald Hall on April 18.[225] She was assisted by professional and amateur musicians, among whom were Henriette Collin (violin), Albert Eichelheim (piano), and voices, all under the direction of Kitziger. There was no orchestra.

As the hot weather of summer approached, the second year of regular concerts began at Spanish Fort on May 1 with an orchestral program, conducted by Moses and featuring solo cornetist Rudolphe Gewert.[226] Still, at the end of September and into October, there were wonderful concerts at Spanish Fort every Tuesday, Thursday, and Saturday evening, directed by W. Borchert, with Gewert and Richard Kohl, clarinetist. The trains ran regularly from Canal Street to West End.[227] The last fireworks display for the season at Spanish Fort was on October 9, but concerts continued another week. Typical programs contained works by Flotow, Rivière, Strauss, Suppé, Meyerbeer, Mendelssohn, Verdi, and Legendre.[228] The performance level was high, and the critic of *L'Abeille* praised the precision of this band and its vast repertory.

The main musical event of the fall 1880 season was the restoration of French Opera at the Opera House. M de Beauplan sailed from Le Havre on October 29 with 128 persons bound for the New Orleans Opera House.[229] John Davis, who apparently was running the Opera House, was the brother of the late Auguste Davis, composer. Momas, De Lestrac, and Bonivard shared conducting duties.[230] There were 45 musicians in the orchestra, including D'Aquin and Joubert, who had just finished their studies in France. The French Opera season opened on Monday, November 8, with *Robert le Diable.* There were ballets during the intermèdes.[231] Meanwhile the other theaters offered stiff competition to the French Opera and gave the city, once again, a multifaceted opera season. On October 25–31, 1880, the Emma Abbott Troupe de Grand Opéra returned to the Grand Opera House with such operas as *Maritana, Paul et Virginie, Carmen, Lucia, Il Trovatore, Roméo et Juliette, Faust,* and *La Bohémienne*—all performed in English.[232] Not to be outdone, the Italian Opera Troupe of Tagliapietra, with 60 artists including a grand chorus and orchestra, opened on Sunday, October 31, at Bidwell's New Saint Charles Theatre. Their operas included *Lucia, Faust,*

La Favorite, Il Trovatore, Lucrezia Borgia, William Tell (twice), and *Martha*.[233] Into January 1881 there were operas simultaneously at the French Opera House and at the Saint Charles Theatre.

In the fall, as usual, there were only a few concerts. "Sometime soon . . . a Liedertafel concert for our friends from Texas" was announced on October 2, 1880, but there is no evidence when or if it took place.[234] Cabaret concerts continued to entertain local audiences. The beginning of the season at Wenger Gardens (on Bourbon Street) was on Saturday, October 2, by the Women's Orchestra of Berlin, which continued well into the new year.[235] This orchestra gave nightly concerts at Jardin Wenger, where one ate as well as listened. The orchestra was conducted by Mlle Kate Liebold. On Sunday, November 7, Mme E. Ambre, who sang Violetta on Tuesday evening at the French Opera, sang during the Offertory of the mass in Saint Louis Cathedral the "Ave Maria" by Bach-Gounod.[236] Perhaps this was not a concert but part of the regular liturgy. On Wednesday, November 17, Mme Zeiss-Dennis, prima donna contralto, sang a benefit for herself at the Théâtre California, before her return to France.[237]

The spring of 1881 was rich in concerts with the new generation of musicians leading the way. Collignon had gone to France, Curto was a very old man, and many of the earlier musicians were either dead or retired. The new generation included Samuel, Kaiser, D'Aquin, and Joubert as virtuosi and leaders. On January 9, 1881, Italian pianist Ernesto Pacini gave a grand concert with the assistance of Joubert and D'Aquin. Joubert played *Souvenir* by D'Hayn (solo violin) and D'Aquin played two flute solos. Pacini, for his part, played Liszt and Gottschalk.[238] Four days later, on January 13, D'Aquin conducted some musicians from the French Opera House in a performance of his Symphony in F in the salon of M le Dr. Bayon. The piece was dedicated to Mme Bayon. It was preceded by a prayer composed by D'Aquin, and seventeen-year-old Miss Haddie T. Tidd of Saint Louis played some excerpts from *Il Trovatore* on the violin.[239] Adolphe Duquesnay directed a grand vocal and instrumental concert at Grunewald Hall on January 14.[240] On January 26 there was a grand concert at Grunewald Hall which included C. M. von Weber's Trio for piano, flute, and violoncello (Auber, Pacini, and Schneider) and various piano pieces (mostly arrangements) for piano or flute and piano or violoncello and piano.[241] A symphony orchestra performed between the first and second acts of Victor Massé's opera *Paul et Virginie* at the Grand Opera House on February 1.[242]

There were more operas in the spring. On January 17, 1881, Max Strakosch and Marie Roze began performances of operas at the Saint Charles Theatre. This was now called the Strakosch-Hess Opera Company, with opera in English

(*Carmen, Mefistofele, Il Trovatore, William Tell, The Bohemian Girl,* and *Fra Diavolo*).[243] Meanwhile, operas continued at the French Opera House. In his review of two different performances, Mercier compared De Lestrac (*The Daughter of the Regiment*) as conductor with Momas (*La Muette*); he found the first wanting and the second exciting.[244] In a performance of *William Tell* conducted by Momas on February 8, Mercier was especially impressed by the conductor's handling of the overture.[245] But the big cultural event this spring was the arrival in New Orleans of the most famous actress in the world, Sarah Bernhardt. She opened at the Grand Opera House on February 6, arriving late.[246]

Concerts, nonetheless, continued. De Beauplan, head of the opera troupe at the French Opera House, offered a concert on February 13 to benefit flood victims. All the artists took part, and Momas conducted the orchestra once again in the *William Tell* overture.[247] A lottery was held, and the winner, M Clayette, received as his prize his appearance as trumpet soloist in the French Opera Orchestra on February 11.[248] On February 15, 1881, there was a grand concert at Grunewald Hall offered to Mlles A. J. Mercier and Alice Potter, with the assistance of Bremer, Broadley, Eckert, Tyler, Barsehide, Shield, and others.[249] The Philharmonic Society, too, gave a concert at Grunewald Hall on February 17 to benefit the flood victims.[250] The Frankos (Sam, Jeanne, Rachel, and Nahan) performed at Grunewald Hall on February 23 and March 6 (matinee).[251] On February 27 the band of the Seventy-first Regiment performed a sacred concert.[252] This spring's awards ceremony by the Atheneum Club of Louisiana took place on Sunday, March 27. There was a concert interspersed with orations. D'Aquin performed a flute solo, the thirteen-year-old pianist G. Paoletti played Gottschalk, and the young Mlle Berthe Pemberton played Chopin.[253] As an adult, Paoletti was one of the most important musicians in New Orleans in the ensuing decades.

On April 7, the young Brazilian violinist Maurice Dengremont gave a recital at Grunewald Opera House; it had originally been scheduled for March 31. He was touring America after having studied in Paris.[254] Unfortunately he died young, at twenty-five, in 1893. Samuel played Chopin, Mendelssohn, and Bach; Annie Seawell sang an air from *Le Prophète*; and Dengremont played one of the two Beethoven Romances for violin, Sivori's fantasy on *Il Trovatore*, a Nocturne of Chopin, and a piece by his Parisian teacher, Léonard. Mr. E. Tyler accompanied. On April 1 he gave a private recital at the home of Mr. and Mrs. Von Meyenberg, on Thalia Street. This time Samuel accompanied him. He got a rave review.[255] On May 19, there was a concert at Grunewald Hall, with Jeanne and Beth Dengremont.[256] Dengremont gave two more regular concerts in New

Orleans, on May 23, once again with Samuel, who played Brahms,[257] and on May 29 with Jeanne Franko,[258] but he was so popular that he appeared at Lake concerts and at the Jockey Club.

Theodore Curant, assisted by Alice Schwartz, Jeanne Franko, Robert Meyer, J. W. H. Eckert and his complete orchestra of forty, gave a grand concert at Grunewald Hall on April 27, 1881.[259] Curant performed the Beethoven Violin Concerto with orchestra; Franko played the Mendelssohn F Minor Concerto No. 2 with orchestra; they teamed up for the Andante from A. Rubinstein's Sonata Opus 13 in G Major; and a string quartet played a Robert Schumann quartet. The orchestra performed Leutner's *Festival Overture* and the March from Wagner's *Tannhäuser.* On May 12, the French Mutual Aid Society had a grand festival at the Fair Grounds, which included a concert and a ball.[260] The Rollings, father and son, offered a concert of their pupils on Saturday, May 14.[261] D'Aquin held a grand vocal and instrumental concert at Grunewald Hall on May 15, 1881. He was joined by Jeanne Franko, Mme Pauline Blache (singer), Curant (violinist), with Mme H. Bayon accompanist. D'Aquin also composed some of the music, and the second half of the concert was devoted to his Symphony in F Major, for which a grand orchestra was hired. Other works included works by Rossini, Demersemann, Chopin, and others.[262] From May 15 to 16 there was a grand German Folk Festival at the Fair Grounds, inaugurated by a concert at noon on the first day. The program was composed of operatic pieces executed by a double orchestra, with a Liedertafel and with speeches.[263]

Summers were now a different matter from before 1879. The Lake Pontchartrain shore offered a cool respite from the oppressive heat and humidity of the city, and by 1881 two major resorts were open: Spanish Fort and West End; the third, Milneburg, would open soon. Each had hotels, restaurants, dance halls, and concerts, and the railroad companies ran special trains from downtown New Orleans (Canal and Rampart streets) to the lake. Spanish Fort offered grand promenade concerts nightly from May 1 to October 5. Generally, W. Borchert conducted a forty-piece orchestra (probably wind band), featuring Rudolphe Gevert, cornetist, on each program, and other members of the orchestra: D'Aquin (solo flute), O. John (solo clarinet), and Professor Weifenbach (tambour major).[264] On special occasions, however, there would be guests, as on May 27 when Curant conducted the band and included pieces by Wallace, Vieuxtemps, and Strauss;[265] on May 31 when Dengremont played, assisted by the orchestra and by Jeanne Franko; on June 1 when Samuel was heard;[266] on June 19 when Pauline Blache performed the piano arrangement of the Beethoven Violin Concerto during a matinee concert without orchestra that also included Mme D'Aquin and Alice Schwartz singing and M Jules D'Aquin playing a flute solo;[267] and June 23 when Henri Joubert, Samuel, and Gustave D'Aquin performed.[268] The program for this last concert was as follows:

Spanish Fort Grand Concert

6:30–8 p.m.: Orchestra led by W. Borchert (Piefke's Parma March; Nicolai's *Merry Wives of Windsor* Overture; Waldteufel's Chantilly Waltz; Weber's *Der Freischütz* Scene and Aria; Hoch, *Nachklänge aus dem Zillerthal*).

8 p.m.: Overture *William Tell,* then solos for piano or violin or flute, including Samuel, Joubert (violin) and Gustave d'Aquin (flute).

After this, the orchestra returns: Doering's *Salut au Lointain* March, Weifenbach's Solo for 16 drums, Suppé's *Poet and Peasant* Overture, Strauss' *Toujours Fidèle* Waltz, and Daniels' *A la Turk* Galop.[269]

Likewise, there were concerts at West End each evening, featuring a large orchestra conducted by Moses and illuminated by electric lights.[270] William Rickel was cornet soloist; the cornet was considered a treat at the West End concerts. In addition to the big lake concerts, open to any paying guests, there were regular promenade concerts at the Jockey Club, for invited guests only, that sometimes featured outstanding soloists. For example, on May 30, 1881, an orchestra accompanied Maurice Dengremont, and the next day Samuel played.[271] As at Spanish Fort, there were two "orchestras": in the garden (probably winds) and in the dance hall (probably mostly strings).

The fall 1881 season began with the end of the summer lake concerts and other outdoor performances. There was a promenade concert at Washington Place on September 2, and on September 6 Jeanne Franko, G. D'Aquin, and Henri Joubert performed again.[272] Rolling, who often played in nearby parishes and on the Mississippi Coast, performed on September 10 at Bayou Saint Louis, playing a Chopin polonaise and one of his own works.[273] As in past years when opera flourished, the main musical events of fall were centered on the reestablishment of the French Opera. Since the previous March, plans were underway for the next season.[274] There had been talk of combining the local opera with troupes in Cincinnati and Chicago and even New York, but this did not pan out.[275] It was decided that Strakosch would run the French Opera, Momas would be rehired, and they would have an enlarged orchestra with a raise in salary for all.[276] Finally, on December 12 the opera season in New Orleans opened with *Tales of Hoffmann, Le Tribut de Zamora, La Sonnambula, Lucia, Rigoletto, Les Puritans, The Magic Flute, Dinorah, Faust, Linda di Chamounix, Martha, Don Pasquale, Aïda, Il Trovatore, La Favorite, Carmen, Mefistofele,* and others. Besides Momas, the conductors were S. Behrens and Sig. De Novellis.[277] Before Strakosch opened, however, another opera company, the Hess Opera Troupe, now named Acme Opera Company, opened in New Orleans on October 16 and continued for a few weeks.[278]

There were only two concerts in the fall. The first, on November 13, 1881, was a grand vocal and instrumental matinee concert at the French Union Hall for charity. Among the soloists were Météyé, D'Aquin, L. Heidingsfelder, Joubert, and Mme D'Aquin. Mme H. Bayon was the accompanist.[279] The second, on December 17, was a grand concert at Odd Fellows' Hall given to the restaurant waiters of New Orleans. It was performed by Borchert and his band.[280]

There were few concerts during the spring 1882 season, but at least one caused a stir. On January 17, Adelina Patti returned to the city for the first time since 1861. She gave a concert with a "grand orchestra," which performed the overture to *William Tell,* and Mlle T. Castellan performed De Bériot's *Seventh Grand Concert* for violin and orchestra.[281] The Philharmonic Society performed with orchestra on April 5.[282] Once Spanish Fort opened, Borchert conducted the orchestra of twenty-three in "choice pieces of music."[283] Herr Theodore Hoch was the featured horn player.[284] One highlight of the season was the concert and ball on June 17 by the Orphéon Français at the grand pavilion at Spanish Fort. A full orchestra accompanied arias by Mercadante, Offenbach, Thomas, and Rillé.[285] West End had events as well from May through September, and the Jockey Club, with its "hidden orchestra," also had performances during this time.[286] On May 13, there was a grand concert in honor of Miss Fannie Hunt (soprano) at Grunewald Hall. Assisting her were Météyé, Anton Strelenzki, W. W. Sumner, Charles Tracy and J. W. H. Eckert.[287] The next afternoon there was a concert at the French Union Hall, on Rampart near Dumaine Street, in honor of Isidore Nennig, "le doyen des choristes de l'Opéra," who had been there a long time.[288] On May 26 there was a performance of Gilbert and Sullivan's *Patience* at the French Opera House to benefit flood victims.[289]

There were three concerts during the fall of 1882. On November 2, Kaiser gave a major concert at Grunewald Hall. He performed the Robert Schumann Piano Quintet with Jeanne Franko, Curant, Mueller, and Emil Seifert. "The quintette was played with a great deal of vim and in a most correct manner, but lacked the delicacy and pure intonation which are so necessary in the performance of chamber music. Insufficient rehearsal was probably the cause of this," reported the *Picayune*. Seifert replaced Joubert at the last minute because of illness. Kaiser also played the Mendelssohn Violin Concerto, apparently with piano accompaniment.[290] Gustave Satter gave a grand matinee concert on November 9, which included the Overture to Rossini's *William Tell*.[291] On December 15, the Philharmonic Society gave a concert.[292]

The spring 1883 season was more active than most. Throughout January the Vienna Ladies Orchestra performed every evening, with matinees on Sunday afternoons, at Wenger's Garden.[293] Opera was back on track in the French Opera House. *Les Huguenots* on January 4 was the thirty-fifth subscription performance of the season.[294] Christine Nilsson, the latest Swedish nightingale, brought her company to the Saint Charles Theatre during January for three concerts: January 9, 11, and 13 (matinee). She performed with the renowned Mendelssohn Quintette Club of Boston, who for their part presented some serious chamber music. The program on January 9 included the Allegro Vivace from Mendelssohn's Quintet in B flat, Opus 87, and Boccherini's famous Minuet for quintet; Isidore Schnitzler played Sarasate's "Spanish Dance" on the violin. The program on January 11 included the Allegro con Moto from Mendelssohn's Quintet in A, Opus 18, and Theme and Variations from Schubert's Quartet in D Minor; Schnitzler performed a solo, and cellist Frederick Giese performed a solo. On January 13, the Mendelssohn Quintette Club performed the Allegro Moderato from Beethoven's Quintet in C, Opus 29, and the finale from Svendsen's Quintet in C, Opus 5; William Schade played Demersemann's fantasia for flute on a melody by Chopin.[295]

There was a vocal and instrumental concert at Grunewald Hall on Saturday, March 17, 1883, in honor of Oscar Reine, oboist in the French Opera Orchestra. Four violinists (Joubert, Kaiser, Curant, and Bayon), several singers, flutist Gustave D'Aquin, and a few others assisted.[296] The Philharmonic Society presented its twenty-seventh "rehearsal" at Grunewald Hall on March 21. It was a concert of sacred music.[297] On March 29 the Mexican Typical Orchestra, under Antonio Figueroa, a distinguished violinist, gave a grand concert,[298] and two nights later the French Orpheons held a grand concert and ball in Grunewald Hall.[299] A second concert, on March 31, was the soiree musicale given by the piano pupils of H. and W. Rolling: Mlles Kauffman, Sciaccaluga, Levert, G. Salle, L. Vignaud, B. Mollo, E. Vignaud, Abraham, Adler, Romain (two sisters), and MM F. Viavant, J. Liado, and Marinoni.[300]

The month of April was a very busy one for concerts. The French Union had a concert in honor of Mlle Régina Frémaux (mezzo soprano) at Grunewald Hall on April 1. It was mostly vocal, but flutist D'Aquin, violinist Joubert, pianist

W. H. Rolling, as well as instrumentalists Mme L. W. Fournier and Mlle Marie Fournier, assisted.[301] During April, the Louisiana Field Artillery and Louisiana Women held a charity festival with a symphony executed by forty amateur instrumentalists.[302]

West End opened its season of concerts a month earlier than in previous years, on April 1, 1883, but with a difference. The concerts ran from 4:00 to 7:00 p.m., with its new orchestral conductor, Gustave D'Aquin, conducting its new orchestra, carefully chosen from the best professionals who lived in New Orleans during the summer.[303] These Sunday concerts, however, were not part of the regular popular series at West End that began on May 3. Spanish Fort was not to be outdone, so they, too, began on April 1 with the grand orchestra under Professor Bochert. Also, on April 1, there was a grand vocal and instrumental concert at the Grand Opera House given by the Liedertafel of New Orleans to benefit Charity Hospital. The orchestra played the overture to Gluck's *Iphigenia in Aulis,* the Andante from Beethoven's Symphony No. 5, the "Swedish Wedding March" by Soedermann, and the Bacchanale from *Philomène et Baucis* by Gounod; Alice Schwartz sang an aria by Auber; Mlles Marie Wannack and Cécile Marx played Alard's *Fantaisie de Concert on Faust*; and, for the second half of the program, the grand chorus joined the orchestra in Romberg's setting of *Das Lied von der Blocke* by Schiller.[304]

The annual Athénée Louisianaise ceremony at Grunewald Hall, with music and speeches, took place on April 8. It included an homage to science, composed by Francis Navone, which was sung by a contralto, a baritone, and the choir accompanied by flute, violin, violoncello, piano, and organ; a solo piano piece played by Mlle Aménaide Blanchard; and a duo concertant for two violins by De Bériot (three movements) performed by Mlle Marie Wannack and M Henry Bayon.[305] On April 11, the Aeolian Harp Circle gave its second concert at Grunewald Hall.[306] This was a choral society of some eighteen to twenty young singers (not very well disciplined), conducted by George L. O'Connell. The pupils of Rolling gave another grand soiree at Grunewald Hall on April 14.[307] William Henry Pilcher, scion of a famous organ-building family and now a resident of New Orleans, played what may have been his first recital in New Orleans by performing on the organ at the cathedral on April 16.[308] The fifth concert at the Conservatoire de Musique (located at the corner of Royal and Quartier streets) occurred on April 18. It included literary readings, dancing, and music.[309]

There was a benefit concert for Joseph Durel by the Aeolian Harp Circle, at Grunewald Hall on April 22. The program included works by Gounod, Concome, Lecocq, Bellini, Varney, and Verdi. Performers included the whole group plus soloists Joseph Durel, Miss U. Magner, MM Alf. Théard and A. B. Lacoste, Miss Corinne Fairex, M Félix Cohen, and Miss Régina Frémeaux. M Hy. Bayon played a violin solo, a fantasy.[310] On April 27, there was a concert in honor of Mlle Eloise Hufft at Grunewald Hall.[311] The Southern Silk Industrial Association held a matinee benefit concert on April 29 at Grunewald Hall. The program consisted of songs and piano pieces, plus a De Bériot duo for two violins (Wannack and Henri Bayon), the Braga *Sérénade* (Mme G. D'Aquin accompanied by H. Bayon on violin), and two pieces for flute (G. D'Aquin); Mme H. Bayon was the accompanist.[312] Throughout the month, on top of all these concerts, the French Opera had regular stagings, and the Hess Opera Company, too, was performing in New Orleans.[313]

On May 4, the Washington Artillery Battalion gave a promenade concert and ball for children at its armory.[314] This was followed the next day by a concert at the conservatory by Marguerite Samuel and Pauline Blache, and on May 6 Mme D'Aquin held a benefit matinee concert at Grunewald Hall. The program for the last included arias and instrumental music performed by Joubert, Gustave D'Aquin, Bayon, C. Ziegler, and Mlles L. Rouan and E. Parra. Joubert played Wieniawski's *Légende*.[315]

During the summer of 1883, from May to September, the West End concerts took place every evening, under the direction of D'Aquin, with the engagement of the celebrated cornetist Signor A. Liberati, from May 15 to 29.[316] Thanks to D'Aquin, ever since West End opened it was distinguished by the composition of its orchestra and the choice of its programs.[317] For one week, September 3–10, West End had an enlarged orchestra (or band), which played grand overtures and, with a chorus, other opera excerpts. Also, M A. Lefebre (solo saxophone) and Charles Lowe (solo xylophone) were featured.[318] Meanwhile, during the summer, Spanish Fort had the grand orchestra of twenty-five led by Borchert; there were concerts every evening, and extra concerts on Tuesdays, Thursdays, and Saturdays. A typical concert was on June 9, consisting of works by Strassy, Auber, Strauss, Suppé, Keler-Bela, Gounod, Faust, and Schasa.[319] Furthermore, throughout the summer, as throughout the rest of the year, Wenger's Gardens continued with an orchestra of Viennese women.

The 1883–84 opera season was prepared to open on Monday, November 12, with a performance of *Faust*,[320] but it was not to be an entirely successful season. Hopes to get the great conductor Eugène Momas to return to New Orleans from Europe were dashed by his illness and death on November 13 in Rouen.[321] Défossez worked hard to secure sufficient funds to build a strong ensemble.[322] His orchestra alone had forty-six musicians altogether, some eighteen or twenty already residing in New Orleans, seven more than in the preceding season. The inability of New Orleanians to fully support him, however, drove Canonge to compare New Orleans to New York, with all its rich millionaires who throw money at everything. New Orleans had its opera, its rich jewel, which the world was about to see when the Cotton Exposition opened at the end of 1884.[323] Since performances lacked luster, audiences began to dwindle. People were going to light opera performances of Gilbert and Sullivan and other operettas at West End during the end of August, where the celebrated orchestra of Professor G. D'Aquin played many pieces of music before and after each opera.[324] And they continued to enjoy light opera when Duff's English and Italian Opera Company opened at the Saint Charles Theatre on November 4.[325] But Duff went beyond opéra comique by presenting *Faust* on November 9, and, during its last week, beginning on Sunday, November 11, by outdoing Défossez's opera with Défossez's own repertory: Lakmé, *Patience, Le Coeur et la Main, Faust, Mignon,* and *Carrie Swaine.*[326] As if that were not enough, from December 23 to 30 the Emma Abbott English Grand Opera Troupe performed *Il Trovatore, King for a Day, The Bohemian Girl, Lucia, Rigoletto, Mignon, Linda di Chamounix,* and *La Sonnambula* at the Grand Opera House, with complete orchestra and chorus.[327]

For a fall concert season, however, 1883 was fairly busy. On Saturday, September 1, there was the celebration, at Odd Fellows' Hall, by the Young Men's Gymnastic Club of its eleventh anniversary, preceded by a brass band. Hubert J. Rolling Jr. was an instructor's aide at the club, which may explain why over the next few years concerts occurred in connection with YMGC.[328] On Saturday, September 8, A. Vulliet led L'Orphéon Français in a concert of choruses and solo vocals.[329] During the Fête de Saint Maurice at the Catholic Saint Maurice Church in Saint Bernard Parish, on Sunday, September 23, Mlles Gildemestre, Corrine and Stella Kilshaw, Saulet, Mmes Oscar Gelpi and Kelly, MM Caesard, Daboval, Robert, and Cohen sang.[330] The renovated Wenger Gardens, renowned for its liquors, reopened on September 29 and featured again the female orchestra from Vienna.[331] The first program in the two-hundredth jubilee of German settlement in America opened on October 7 at Spanish Fort. All sorts of instrumental, vocal, and choral music were performed during the first part of the celebration.[332] The Sainte Agnes Club, with the assistance of artists and amateurs, gave a concert at Grunewald Hall on October 10 for a charitable purpose. Theodore Curant played the violin, Miss M. Fournier the piano, baritone Ed. Lacy Jones made his amateur debut singing "Non più andrai" from Mozart's *The Marriage of Figaro,* and the evening ended with a quartet "Ave Verum" (Mozart's?) by the members of the Sainte Agnes Club.[333] L'Orphéon

Français held another concert and ball in Grunewald Hall on Saturday, October 20. The Orphéon Français, which was organized in December 1881, with thirty members, now had over a hundred members.[334] Grand entertainments at the Opera House for the benefit of the Mount Carmel Asylum took place on October 27–28. Performers included L'Orphéon Français, D'Aquin, Joubert, the New Orleans Quartette Club, and an orchestra led by D'Aquin.[335]

There was a Grand Military Musical and Vocal Entertainment, with fencing, tableaux, and other activities, given on November 2–3 at the Opera House on Bourbon Street for the benefit of the Dreux Monumental Fund. Veterans of the late war assisted.[336] On Thursday, November 8, there was a vocal and instrumental concert by Van Hufflen at Grunewald Hall. Other performers included the Aeoleon Harp Circle, Marguerite Samuel, Mme E. D'Aquin, M Joubert (including a Beethoven sonata), G. D'Aquin, and E. Déjan.[337] During an intermède between acts of *Les Huguenots* at the Opera House on Monday, November 19, "Monseurs [sic] D'Aquin and Joubert played their solos with talent; the audience honored them with warm and long bravos."[338] To celebrate Sainte Cécile's Day at the cathedral on Thursday, November 22, there was a performance of D'Aquin's Solemn Mass. Mlle Varelli, contralto of the French Opera, with the violin accompaniment of Joubert, sang Gounod's "Ave Maria" during the Offertory; the young artist Paolo Giorza sang an "O Salutaris"; and the choir sang Goeb's "Tantum Ergo."[339]

In December 1883, Curant presented a vocal and instrumental concert by his pupils at Grunewald Hall. Local amateurs spontaneously offered to help, including Mme Ida Rieman-Kaiser, Mme Samuel, Miss Alice Afflick, and the New Orleans Quartette Club.[340] On December 14, pupils of H. A. Blake did the same.[341] The Spanish Choral Society held a concert, tableaux, and ball at Grunewald Hall.[342] Then on Christmas Day, the choir of Saint Augustin Church—directed by J. Hanno Deiler, organist—sang the first two Christmas masses with G. D'Aquin playing flute. D'Aquin was also the composer of several pieces. Mme D'Aquin sang, Joubert and Bayon played the violin, Leleu played the cor d'harmonie, and Reine played oboe. At 10 a.m., the choir also sang the Grand Mass in E Minor by Weber.[343]

The spring 1884 season was very active, both with opera and with concerts. Both occurred simultaneously on January 1. A performance of *The Barber of Seville* at the French Opera House, to benefit both the families of shipwrecked sailors and the French Union, was followed by a concert of arias and songs with a trio by François Beër performed by Mme Jourbet, MM Jourbet, and D'Aquin, which in turn was followed (part 3) by a ballet.[344] Just as it had the previous spring, the C. D. Hess Opera Troupe was performing operettas (including Gilbert and Sullivan) throughout January at the Saint Charles Theatre, with a chorus of thirty. At the end of March, Bidwell started a short season of Italian opera at the Grand Opera House, with *Don Pasquale.*[345]

The opera season at the French Opera House under Défossez ended early on January 23 with a performance of *Les Huguenots.* The company, under the directorship of Maurice Grau with Défossez as assistant, then intended to move to Havana, where it hoped for more financial support. While one critic thought the combination of these two men with Grau in charge was a good thing, Défoussez was not a good financial manager and personally was destitute by the end of the short opera season in New Orleans.[346] But the Havana tour did not materialize. A performance of *Les Huguenots* was held at the French Opera House on February 3 for the benefit of those musicians and choristers who were not going to Havana, and the Etudiants Espagnols held a benefit concert on February 13 to help Défossez himself.[347] La Estudiantina apparently was an organization formed by Défossez after the tour to Cuba was cancelled, and it continued to perform in New Orleans. The program on February 13 consisted of songs and readings, including Gounod's "L'Hymne à la Nuit" and Fauré's "La Charité."[348] La Estudiantina performed concerts subsequently at Spanish Fort on February 14, 16, 17, 19, 21, and 24, the last a matinee at 4:00 p.m.[349] Défossez, for his part, quickly reformed his opera troupe and presented *La Grande Duchesse de Gérolstein* (Offenbach) at Werlein Hall on Thursday, February 14, and at a special matinee at Spanish Fort Opera House the following Sunday.[350]

On March 2, the Etudiants Espagnols performed *La Grande Duchesse* at the French Opera House, but with a concert added. The program began with three orchestral works by Rossini, Granados, and Waldteufel, followed by the first act of the Offenbach, then more orchestral music by Arditi, Wagner, and Schubert, then the second and third acts of the Offenbach, followed by more orchestral music by Gounod, Verdi, and anonymous.[351] By the third week in March, Défossez's opera company had collapsed, and forty members of the chorus and others were in desperate need. Many wanted to return to France but had no means to do so. Two final performances of the Défossez Opera Troupe were arranged on March 22 at the French Opera House, the proceeds of which went to the chorus for their assistance. The matinee was *La Belle Hélène,* and the evening was *Orphée aux Enfers.*[352] On the same day, the Etudiants Espagnols performed a grand concert sacré at Saint Louis Cathedral, including sacred and secular works by Verdi, Schubert, Arditi, Gounod, Suppé, Mozart, Flotow, and anonymous.[353] At the same time, Charles Amstutz, one of the violinists in the orchestra of Défossez's troupe, gave a concert to raise money for his return to France. Nine other musicians from the troupe were destitute and joined in.[354]

There were many other concerts as well. On January 23, 1884, Jules Météyé gave an instrumental concert at Grunewald Hall with other players.[355] Also, throughout January, the Pavillon Faranta, a dime-entertainment spot on the corner of Bourbon and Orléans streets, boasted "the best orchestra in New Orleans."[356] Grunewald Hall announced on February 12 that it was sponsoring grands concerts de salons by the most celebrated professional musicians of the day.[357] The Aeoleon Harp Circle had an instrumental and vocal concert at the French Union Hall on February 15, with J. J. Sarrazin and Bayon (violinists) playing a duo and solos.[358] Three nights later, Mme Raisin also performed at the French Union Hall, with singers and instrumentalists, including the violinist Charles Amstutz in Singer's *Carnival de Venise* and Paganini's *Themes and Variations*.[359] A brass band of fourteen was hired to play a fanfare at a gathering at M Antoine Chastel's home at the corner of Saint Peter and Royal streets on February 23; the ensemble later played for the Ball of the French Benevolent and Mutual Aid Society of New Orleans at the French Opera House.[360] On March 5, Amy Fay presented a solo recital at Werlein Hall; this may have been the first time that a single artist presented an entire concert by herself. Her program was not printed; she played eleven pieces which were announced from the stage, including works by Gluck, Bach, Beethoven, Liszt, and Chopin.[361] The combination of a solo recital and the program announced from the stage remained a concert practice well into the twentieth century.

Mme J. Boudousquié, after conquering even New York and Paris with her singing, had now conquered New Orleans as a professor and presented her pupils in concert on March 22, 1884.[362] On March 23 there was a three-part performance at Spanish Fort: a concert of eight compositions, an operetta by Offenbach (*Les Deux Aveugles*), and a ballet comique by Mmes Gossi and Watson. According to one source, the concert began at 1:30 and the spectacle at 4:30, but another source stated that the spectacle consisted of three parts: the concert, the operetta, and the ballet, and all of this started at 4:30.[363] The Spanish Choral Society of New Orleans held its first anniversary meeting on April 6. One of the members of the orchestra of La Estudiantina, Mr. Ramiro Martinez, decided to stay in New Orleans and played some guitar pieces.[364] On April 19, the students of the Institute Locquet gave a concert.[365] The annual meeting of the Atheneum Club at the French Union Hall on April 20, as customary, was mixed with readings and music. Mlle Amélie Buck, pupil of her mother, played a piece by Ketterer; Mr. Edouard Déjan played two Chopin pieces and a piece by Mr. Basilère Reuen; and C. Van Hufflen sang an aria by Sacchini.[366]

On Wednesday, April 23, three singers from New Orleans—Mmes Sholia and Roux and M Puget—gave a concert at Spanish Fort, on behalf of the Dames Servantes des Pauvres for the benefit of those who needed to return to France: part 1: the operetta *Lischen et Fritzchen* (Offenbach), part 2: songs, part 3: *Le Piano de Berthe* (one-act comedy). Greuling played the piano. There were also monologues, romances, and chansonnettes.[367] By May 2 the New Louisiana Jockey Club had a concert by an orchestra of the best musicians and another orchestra to accompany the dancing.[368] Orchestral music had by now permeated almost all aspects of the city's life, and even at a communion ball for little children there was orchestral accompaniment.[369] These were mostly dance orchestras made up of the musicians who also played in the theater orchestras. On May 23, 1884, there was a soiree musicale given by Mme Mandevilla Prévost and her pupils at the French Union Hall, and simultaneously a concert and ball were given by the French Orphéon Society at Grunewald Hall.[370]

By the beginning of May, the summer resorts were now open. This included in 1884 not only Spanish Fort and West End but also Milneburg. On May 11, there was a concert promenade at West End, with D'Aquin conducting an excellent orchestra of eighteen to twenty which he formed, according to *L'Abeille,* "from the most popular musicians who have proven themselves a thousand times over." An operetta troupe was formed from New York singers. "Before and after the operetta, the orchestra, led by Mr. D'Aquin, executed, in the Pavillion, an entire program so that those who would not participate in the spectacle, would also have their own treat. . . . The orchestra under the baton of Professor D'Aquin will play the principal opera overtures before and after each show."[371] The "celebrated band of West End, under the direction of Professor D'Aquin and with the cornetist Fred C. Bryant," played most of the summer.[372] On July 4, Spanish Fort celebrated its fifteenth annual July 4 festival with fireworks and an orchestral concert which Professor Borchert conducted from 5:00 to 11:00 p.m. A grand ball followed in the concert hall.[373] Meanwhile, Milneburg, another resort on Lake Pontchartrain, specialized in vaudeville, with concerts surrounding these performances. The season started with a grand evening of amusements featuring the Grande Compagnie de Vaudeville. Vogel's orchestra played before and after a display of balloons. On July 7 the Milneburg Opera House had a "grand orchestre of winds and strings led by Professor J. B. Vogel."[374]

While all this was going on at the lake, in the city there were concerts at Jackson Square. M Moses, who formerly conducted the concerts at Spanish Fort and West End, directed concerts at Jackson Square at 7 p.m. every Friday from May until the beginning of winter. The repertory was dances and overtures to operas. On June 11, Borchert led a concert at Jackson Square with the overtures to *Poet and Peasant* (Suppé) and *Martha* (Flotow).[375]

In fall 1884 there were a few concerts in the city as well as a few at the lake. On September 13 the Aeolian Harp Circle held a soiree at Grunewald Hall. The program included works for violin by Rillé, Haydn, and Raff played by Bayon, as well as vocal compositions. One of the singers was the tenor F. Cohen, who for a short time appeared in many concerts.[376] A military band played at West End under G. D'Aquin on September 14, and there was a grand ball and concert at Spanish Fort on September 27.[377] Another literary and musical festival took place at the Institute des Orphelins (corner of Dauphine and Union) on October 5. The first matinee concert by the Association of Mutual Aid of Louisiana Women was held on November 9 at the French Union Hall.[378] On December 7, there was a performance of a Haydn mass at Saint Louis Cathedral, with participation by the Mexican military band under Encarnacion Payen.[379] This is the first appearance of the Mexicans who spent the greater part of 1885 in New Orleans as part of the Cotton Exposition (see page 61). They came to dominate concert life there and had a lasting effect on the popular music of the city, with rhythms and sonorities that influenced the development of ragtime and jazz. The pupils of Theodore Curant gave a concert at Werlein Hall on December 11, with J. W. H. Eckert as accompanist. Curant himself performed De Bériot's Concerto No. 7 and some Wieniawski pieces.[380] On December 22, Joubert and D'Aquin had a benefit at the French Opera House. Participants were Mmes Pemberton-Hincks, G. D'Aquin, H. Joubert, Mlle B. Pemberton, MM H. Joubert, G. D'Aquin, Lefebvre, Henri Bayon, and Auguste Dufilho. Part of the program had already been heard at the benefit for Henri Bayon and was "well-chosen for repetition."[381]

Meanwhile the French Opera, which had failed financially early in 1884, was taken over by new management, and hopes were raised for a brilliant new season beginning on December 1, 1884. There were fundraisers, and L. Emile Richard, the new director, drew up a sizeable list of personnel for the upcoming season. Specifically named among orchestral musicians were Mr. Le Chevallier A. Vianesi, first conductor (from the Italian orchestra at Covent Garden, the Metropolitan in New York, and the Saint Petersburg Opera); A. Martin, second conductor; Georges Hesse, répétiteur pianist (from Paris); Ernesto Giovi, concertmaster and solo violinist (from the Pasdeloup and Colonne in Paris and Metropolitan in New York), Harndorff, first violin soloist; Theon, piano accompanist; Pomero, viola soloist; Bernsortes, contrabassist; Cordelas, harpist; Pirotta, first flute soloist; Carrana, clarinet soloist; Ravenalli, oboe soloist; France, first bassoonist; Dornast, horn soloist; Domange, trumpet soloist; Cornai, timpanist—in all forty-four orchestral players.[382] The presence in New Orleans of such a new corps of top professional players meant that there was new blood for the formation of concert performances. A special effort by Richard to stage two operas by Massenet during the season and to bring the famous composer to New Orleans for the event ultimately failed.[383] Meanwhile the Vraie Troupe d'Opéra Comique opened a season of light opera on November 2 at Grunewald Opera House, with a performance of Lecocq's *Le Petit Duc.* Among its performers was a complete orchestra under the direction of Philip Greuling.[384]

The opening of the opera on December 1, 1884, coincided with the beginning of the Cotton Exposition at what is today Audubon Park. Performers and performing groups came from several countries and performed not only at the park but also in other venues in the city. As a result of the exposition, the city enjoyed one of its most bountiful concert seasons. The German Imperial Band played at the lake during January, and on Thursday, Friday, and Sunday, January 15, 16, and 18, 1885, they performed for the benefit of Touro Hospital.[385] Also on the eighteenth, Bode played his cornet at Washington Artillery Hall.[386] The Mexican Cavalry Band under Escarnacion Payen gave its first concert at the Music Hall in the exposition on that same Sunday, January 18. On January 21, Mlle Kate E. Bridewell gave a benefit recital at Odd Fellows' Hall.[387] On January 22, there was a concert at Werlein Hall to benefit the "Woman's Department of the World's Exposition," featuring Mmes Hincks and D'Aquin, Mlle Pemberton, Mmes Bayon and Lejeune, and MM D'Aquin, Joubert, Bayon, Knoll, and Siebrant.[388] Mapleson's opera troupe, starring Adelina Patti, opened at the Saint Charles Theatre on January 26 with *La Sonnambula.* They also performed *La Traviata, Il Trovatore, Murielle, Sémiramide, Lucia,* and *Ernani.* Signor Arditi, who led the complete chorus and orchestra, was also the composer of a lighter show, *The American Countess,* which was performed on February 1 with Mlle Rhéa as lead singer. Before their departure for California, the troupe, with Patti, gave some performances at the French Opera House.[389]

On Thursday, February 5, there was another concert by the Mexican band (which had already been performing benefits in New Orleans for two months), this time at Upper Bethel Church, Fulton Street near Jackson Street, for the benefit of the church.[390] The next day the same band gave another benefit concert for the "Woman's Department of the Exposition" featuring the Overture to *Sémiramide,* Mexican National Airs, and a fantasia on *Boccace* (Suppé). The program also had numerous arias ("Madamina, il catalogo" from Mozart's *Don Giovanni,* arias by Meyerbeer, and others), and a solo harp piece by Sacconi.[391] On the thirteenth the band played again.[392] The Kempa Ladies Orchestra led by the celebrated pianist and composer Piecsonka Kempa, performed at Grunewald Opera House on February 13 and 14.[393] A more local concert occurred on February 28 with the first concert of the year by the pupils of Corinne Nott at the Locquet-Leroy Institute.[394]

During the month of March the Mexican ensembles monopolized the concert scene in New Orleans, and not only at the exposition. The Typical Mexican Orchestra performed a complimentary concert on March 3 at 4:00 p.m. at Spanish Fort. A special train left Rampart Street at 3:30 to accommodate concertgoers.[395] On March 16 the Mexican orchestra performed an evening concert at Saint Louis Cathedral, about which Canonge gave a rave notice. The same group also performed at West End on the eighteenth.[396]

Only two concerts during March were not performed by the Mexicans. On Sunday, March 15, the Aeolian Harp Circle, under the direction of George O'Connell, which had not performed in some time, gave a concert in their hall on Royal Street. The program included: a trio for violin, flute, and piano by Behr entitled *Nocturne,* performed by H. Bayon, J. Gueringer, and George O'Connell; *Airs de Ballet* by De Bériot performed by Bayon; several songs; and a choral work by Curto from his *La Mort de Jeanne d'Arc.*[397] The other concert, on March 30, was unique: a Swiss clock concert at Werlein Hall.[398]

April was more balanced between local performers and the Mexicans. On Thursday, April 2, 1885, there was a concert at the exposition at 5:00 p.m. by the Mexican musicians. They played a Mexican national hymn, an American national hymn, *Cloches du Carnaval Valse* by Miss Blackman, Schubert's "Serenade," and works by Erkel, Verdi, Legner, Avilos, Rossi, Sturte, De Bériot, and Waldteufel.[399] The next day, two local orchestras played promenade concerts at the ninth annual Fête Champêtre at the Fair Grounds, followed by fireworks.[400] Also on April 3, Curto conducted his *Stabat Mater* at Sainte Anne's Church. The choir was made up of young women trained well at the Institution Curto by Curto and directed by Mme Curto.[401] Then, on April 4, the Typical Mexican Orchestra played at the Music Hall in the exposition: "Hail Columbia," a Mexican national hymn, *Cloches du Carnaval Valse,* and works by Rossi, Schubert, Sturte, De Bériot, Waldteufel, Erkel, Verdi, Legner, and Avilos.[402]

During Holy Weekend, D'Aquin provided sacred music at the cathedral. On Thursday evening, after the sermon, Mme D'Aquin chanted a grand piece with the accompaniment of organ, violin, and flute performed by MM Deiler, D'Aquin, and Joubert. On Friday evening, after the sermon, H. Eiler performed d'Allegri's *Miserere*. On Sunday, at the grand mass at 10:00 a.m., the choir performed the Mass of Weber. At the Offertory, Mme D'Aquin sang "Ave Maria" by Fauré with the accompaniment of organ, violin, and flute. At the Offertory, once again the trio of organ, violin, and flute performed.[403] After forty long years, on April 6, Mme E.B., "a charming lady," opened her salon on Bourbon Street to the public with a soiree performed by members of the Mexican orchestra and local amateurs.[404] On Tuesday, April 21, Miss Jeanne Faure, a pupil of Mme James Nott, played a benefit concert at the French Opera House to raise money for her travel to Dresden for further study.[405]

May and June were much more eventful than usual, but not owing to the exposition. The West End resort opened on May 3, and the concerts started on May 24. The wind orchestra remained under the direction of D'Aquin. His orchestra, a military fanfare, consisted of fifty professionals, featuring the celebrated cornetist A. H. Knoll, cornetist O. Schuchardt, trombonist George Sontag, D'Aquin himself on flute, and A. Renz, clarinetist. Concerts were at 5:00 p.m. on Sundays, at 6:00 p.m. other days. Not only were the soloists excellent, but also the ensemble.[406] In June, Milneburg's New Opera House opened for the summer season, with an orchestra of the first order directed by Thomas F. Weldon.[407] On May 25, the Jockey Club had its usual concert promenade and dance,[408] and on June 8, 1885, the club honored M Eduardo E. Zarate, Mexican commissioner general, with another promenade and dance, this time with the Mexican orchestra providing the music.[409]

On May 2, Mlle Mamie G. Preis, a pupil of Gregorio Curto, gave a vocal and instrumental concert at Werlein Hall.[410] On May 5, Mlle Baumann, another pupil of Curto, presented a vocal and instrumental concert at the French Opera House. She was accompanied by Mme H. Bayon. In addition to Baumann singing (Donizetti, Verdi, and Weber), Mlle M. Preis, M L. E. Crusel, Mlle F. Duffour, M A. H. Kernion, and M M. T. Mulledy also sang. Wannack played a violin solo, a fantasia on *Il Trouvère* by Alard.[411] Mlle Rachel Chandler played a complimentary vocal and instrumental concert on May 6 at Grunewald Hall.[412] Two charity concerts for the diocese of New Orleans were given at Washington Artillery Hall on May 6–7. The first concert was directed by the very busy Mme H. Bayon, with Mmes D'Aquin, C. Bayon, and others assisting.[413] On May 12, there was the third rehearsal of the Sainte Cecilia Society, conducted by Mme G. F. Locquet, well known for years in New Orleans. Mme G. F. Locquet, Mlles Marie Wannack, F. Grunewald, E. Roehl, I. Moore, A. Boissonneau, J. Boissonneau, and L. Espenan, and MM Van Hufflen, Henri Joubert, Henri Bayon, Eckert, Mueller, and a choir sang and presented piano music.[414] On May 14, there were intermèdes in the theater, and the Mexican orchestra continued to give concerts.[415] MM H. and W. H. Rolling and their pupils gave a soiree musicale at Grunewald Hall on May 18, assisted by Mlle Alice Pérat and MM Jules Météyé and Bremer. The program included a new piece by W. H. Rolling and works by Saint-Saëns, Ravina, Mendelssohn, G. Satter, Jaël, Henri Herz, Chopin, Goria, Strakosch, de Vilbac, H. Rolling, and Rossini.[416]

The benevolent society Young Sons of Louisiana started its festival at the Fair Grounds on May 17 with baseball and various activities to honor the month of May, and included a promenade concert.[417] The second concert of Nott's pupils, with Henry Bayon, was given on May 25.[418] The students of Mme Charles Boudousquié gave their matinee musical on May 27.[419] Mmes Pemberton-Hincks and J. Pinekney-Smith, Mlles Varelli-Jauquet, Berthe Pemberton, MM J. Météyé, Henri Bayon, and Auguste Dufilho presented a vocal and instrumental concert at Werlein Hall to benefit the Y.M.C.A. Mme Bayon and Mlle Berthe Pemberton accompanied.[420] A concert-rehearsal of the Aeolian Harp Circle took place at Grunewald Hall on May 30.[421] Carrie Baumann gave another vocal and instrumental concert at Grunewald Hall on June 1.[422] She was assisted by Marguerite Samuel, Carrie Baumann, and M Henri Joubert. The concert was sponsored by the press of New Orleans. On June 5, there was a soiree musicale by the young female vocal and piano pupils of Mme M. Prévost, piano professor, in the French Union Hall.[423] The Ladies Benevolent Society of Louisiana offered a recital to M L. Emile Crusel at the French Opera House on June 12. The varied program included Beethoven's Opus 13 Piano Sonata (Mlle Lilly Hauler), a *Faust* melody (M Emile Crusel), a Rossini *Barber of Seville* aria (Carrie Baumann), a duet from *La Favorite* (Mlle Varelli Jauquet and M Crusel), other arias, a Chopin waltz (Hauler), and the *Rigoletto* Quartet. Mme H. Bayon and M George O'Connell accompanied on piano.[424] There were also concerts by the Etudiants Espagnols in mid-June.

The last day of the first year of the Cotton Exhibition was on May 31.[425] The Mexicans performed right up to the end, their last concert in the exhibition on May 29 when they concentrated on Mexican music.[426] They continued to play in New Orleans, however, after that. On June 2, 1885, the Typical Mexican Orchestra, under Payen, played at Carrollton Gardens to help raise money for a school for the poor.[427] The next day they did a benefit at the French Opera House for Charity Hospital. They performed pieces by Bizet, Viderique, Strauss, Hernandez, Avilles, Suppé, Navarro, Wagner, Donizetti, and H.D.[428]

They returned to the Exhibition Grounds on the fifth for a free concert led by Payen and his assistant, Lt. Paris. The program consisted of works by Aguirré, Wagner, Tito Mattei, Verdi, Martin, Viderique, Suppé, Avilles, Rossini, Ravaro, Schubert, Strauss, and Menesacs.[429] What New Orleanians found remarkable was that this band played sometimes as many as three concerts a day, often for charity, without showing any signs of weariness. On June 7, the Mexican orchestra under Payen gave two final concerts at the Exhibition Grounds before moving on to Saint Louis and a U.S. tour; they left New Orleans on June 9.[430]

Beginning in October 1885 New Orleans experienced its most active concert season to date. It started on October 4 with a sacred concert by the Aeolian Harp Circle at Notre Dame of the Rosary in nearby Saint Charles Parish.[431] Two days later there was a soiree musicale et littéraire at the French Union Hall, at 1:00 p.m. Among the speeches were the following musical works: Fauré's "Charité" (sung by Charles Richard), Sarasate's *Habañera* for solo violin (performed by M Delisle), a Donizetti aria, a polka, Szermanowski's *Chanson Tzigane* for violin (performed by M Delisle), and many songs.[432] There was a benefit for Mme Faye-Grand at Grunewald Opera House on October 17, which had a concert as intermède between vaudevilles.[433] The Orphéon Français gave a concert, followed by a ball, on October 24.[434] On October 27 there was a concert at the French Opera House to aid Charles Richard. He was a promising tenor but temporarily lost his voice owing to a sickness; later he resumed his career, but as a baritone.[435] Mlle Marie Wannack, violinist, assisted by members of the Sainte Cecila Society (four pianos and two organs), presented a concert at the Grunewald Opera House on November 14, 1885. She played works by Alard, De Bériot, and Ravina. Wannack was from New Orleans, was trained in New Orleans, and was living in New Orleans.[436] A. G. Gardner directed a concert to benefit the poor on December 29 at Saint Alphonse's Church, on Saint Andrew Street at Magazine.[437]

D'Aquin, however, proved to be the most important musician during the entire fall. He first appeared in a performance at the reopening of the exhibition on October 11. For the occasion he organized a choir of all ages and both sexes, probably the largest ever to perform in New Orleans.[438] He reactivated the choir on January 8, 1886, for the opening of the Creole exhibit at the continuing exposition. D'Aquin had earlier invited all the inhabitants of New Orleans to meet at the Washington Armory to rehearse the choral pieces.[439] The program included the overture to *Sémiramide,* a "Gloria in Excelsis" by D'Aquin himself, Creole songs, Curto's solo and choir "Le Reveil de la Louisiane" with words by Canonge, Handel's *"Hallelujah"* Chorus and many speeches.

Back in November 1885, he had organized an orchestra which replaced the Mexican ensembles as the most prolific musical organization at the Cotton Exhibition. While playing at the exhibition was his first priority, he also took his orchestra into the city proper. On Monday, November 16, 1885, under the auspices of the Ladies' Committee of the American Exposition, D'Aquin and his orchestra joined the Shakespeare Club in a soiree at the French Opera House. The orchestra played the overture to Weber's *Der Freischütz,* a transcription of themes from *Faust,* Berlioz/Weber's *Invitation to the Dance,* Boccherini's Minuet, a Waldteufel "Polka de Minuet," and, at the end, Meyerbeer's "Marche aux Flambeaux."[440] Beginning on November 18, D'Aquin led his orchestra in four afternoon concerts (1:00, 2:15, 4:00, and 5.15) at the exhibition three to five times a week, with music by Adam, Arditi, Auber, Audran, Bach, Balfé, Beyer, Bizet, Boieldieu, Canterno, Coote, D'Aquin, Donizetti, Farbach, Faust, Fieso, Flotow, Gounod, Gung'l, Halévy, Hérold, Keler-Bela, Lecocq, Leutner Meissler, Mendelssohn, Metra, Meyerbeer, Mibloker, Michaelis, Navarro, Offenbach, Reisch, Rossini, Luigi Schneider (the clarinetist), Scylulka, Sonderman, Stassny (Johann?), Strauss, Sullivan, Suppé, Verdi, R. Wagner, Waldteuffel, Weber, Weiss, Zaniehelli (the cornetist), and Zikoff. This lasted until January 12.[441] His orchestra also participated in official ceremonies at the exposition, such as the Grande Fête Populaire, Jour de l'Emancipation, program on January 1, 1886, which began with the overture to *William Tell* and included some songs and too many speeches. This was followed later in the day by three concerts in the Music Hall.[442] On January 12, D'Aquin's orchestra continued with the same repertoire but with a new conductor, John Stoss, former conductor of the Imperial German Military Orchestra.[443] D'Aquin, for his part, had left New Orleans for good (see book I, part II, chapter 11).[444]

There were many other concerts during the spring 1886 season. On January 12 the Etudiants Espanols performed at Robinson's Dime Arcade on Canal Street.[445] A Japanese troupe opened at the French Opera House January 17. There was a concert on behalf of the Benevolent Society of Louisiana Women on January 22, with songs (one duet), violin pieces (Wannack), and piano pieces by Mme Henri Bayon and M George O'Connell.[446] The concert included a solo cornet à piston performance by A. Claverie as well as the violin solo. Mme Chatterton-Bohrer, English harpist, gave a concert at Grunewald Hall on January 28, assisted by MM Mark Kaiser and F. C. Richmond and Mlles Bridewell, Bessie Brunsun, and Alice Afflick.[447] Carrie Baumann gave a concert of sacred music at Saint John the Baptist Church, on Dryades between Clio and Calliope streets, on Sunday, January 31.[448] On February 1, an orchestra played dance music in the foyer of the French Opera House during the entr'actes; this was a benefit for the exposition under the auspices of the Ladies Committee.[449] Beginning on February 7, W. T. Francis directed *The Mikado* at the Grunewald Opera House, with subsequent performances over the next two weeks. It used a "full orchestra."[450] The National Club presented a vocal and instrumental fete musicale on Sunday, February 28. Performers included L. Dermigny, Dr. Formento, David, Gonthier, Gellé, Wehrman, Schmutz, and Lanos.[451] This was the first time that we know that the young violinist Henri Wehrmann (Henry Wehrman) appeared in a program, and it is the beginning of one of the most celebrated careers of any New Orleans musician.

On March 2, 1886, Woman's Day was celebrated at the New Orleans Exposition. It was a two-part program, with Japanese music as an intermède. The regular concerts included orchestra, voices, harp (Mme Chatterton-Bohrer); a trio of violin, piano, and organ; a solo violin (Claus Bogel); and solo piano (W. T. Francis and Max Gutheim). Also, there was music by the French Marine Orchestra.[452] The Orphéon Français, including members of the French Opera, presented a grand concert followed by a bal paré at Grunewald Hall on Wednesday, March 3.[453] On March 5 a number of singers at the French Opera House, with complete orchestra, offered a concert-spectacle (also referred to as a soiree) in honor of Mlle Varelli-Jauquet.[454] The newspaper noted that tourists were now in Louisiana in great number, and one reason they came was to experience the musical life of the city.[455] Then on Wednesday, March 10, Marguerite Samuel presented the first of a series of four Musique de Chambre concerts or recitals at Grunewald Hall.[456] The second, on March 17, included works by Robert Schumann (Piano Quintet), Mendelssohn (*Variations Concertantes* and his entire Trio No. 2), Schubert (*Trout* Quintet) and Handel. Greuling and Dantonnet participated.[457] The third, on March 24, included the Mozart Piano Quartet No. 4; the finale of Haydn's Symphony No. 16 arranged for piano, violin, and viola; Mendelssohn's *Rondo Capricioso*; Beethoven's Piano Trio No. 7 [sic], and Weber's Grand Sonata. Assisting Samuel were MM Monna, Kaiser, Dantonnet, and Greuling.[458] The fourth recital, originally scheduled for March 31, was actually postponed to April 3 to avoid a conflict with the French Opera. The program included Robert Schumann's Piano Quartet, Chopin's *Grand Scherzo*, and Beethoven's Septet arranged for piano, violin, viola, and violoncello.[459]

Clara Louise Kellogg came to New Orleans for a pair of concerts at the Opera House on March 10 and 11, 1886. She was assisted by Mlles Pauline Montegriffo, Ollie Torbett (violin); and MM Adolph Glose (piano), Francis H. Noyes, and Ross David. In the second concert she and her group performed works by Chopin, Flotow, De Bériot, Verdi, Schubert, Donizetti, Gottschalk, Mattei, Foster, Léonard, and others.[460] On Sunday, March 14, at 11:00 a.m., artists of the French Opera held a grande fete de charitie to benefit the Mt. Carmel Asylum.[461] There was a farewell concert by M and Mme Reine at the Opera House on Thursday, April 8.[462] A major grand concert sacré took place at Saint Louis Cathedral on Sunday, April 17. The program included a vocal work by Kaiser; a quartet for flute, oboe, violin, and violoncello performed by O. Reine, Meert, Monna, and Dantonnet; a solo by Rossini; a chorus by Kitziger, "Venez Dirin Messie"; an andante by Mozart performed by the same instrumental quartet; and other pieces. Additional participants included Mlles Frémaux and Pérat, Mmes Witham and Lejeune, and MM Vulliet, Van Hufflen, Rossi, and Kitziger, and the cathedral choir directed by Kitziger.[463]

On Friday, April 30, the pupils of Mme Charles Boudousquié held a soiree musicale at the French Union Hall.[464] On May 1, there was a vocal and instrumental concert offered to Mme C. V. Labarre (sister of Mme James Nott) at the Locquet-Leroy Institute, which had been postponed from April 17.[465] On May 6, the pupils of W. H. Rolling had their annual concert at Grunewald Hall.[466] The pupils of Hubert Rolling, the father of W. H. Rolling, held a soiree musicale of their own at Grunewald Hall on May 14. Assisting the students were Mme Henry Rolling, Mlles. J. and V. Trapolin, K. Kelly, G. Roux, Casanova, Relly, and Alain.[467]

About May 1, the citizens of New Orleans offered a medal to General Beauregard; the ceremony included several musical numbers by Verdi, Liszt, H. Herz, and Donizetti.[468] The fifth concert by the Musical Society of Sainte Cecilia took place at Grunewald Hall on May 4.[469] On Wednesday, May 5, Mme James Nott, who preferred to live in New Orleans rather than in Paris, offered a vocal and instrumental concert to Mlle Amélie Buck, a young Louisiana pianist. Buck was a pupil of Mme Charles Boudousquié, and had later studied at the Paris Conservatoire under Carvalho. This was her first concert in New Orleans, which was at the Grunewald Opera House. She was assisted by Kaiser, who played a fantasia on motives from *The Masked Ball* by Verdi. Also assisting were Van Hufflen, Eckert, and others.[470] The Battalion at Washington Artillery performed a concert promenade at its arsenal, followed by a free children's ball, on May 7.[471]

The Aeoleon Harp Circle, a musical society, held a soiree musicale at the Opera House on Saturday, May 22.[472] With O'Connell at the piano, it performed various choral works by Gounod, Dufilho, Félix Cohen, Schubert, Altès, Hérold, and others.[473] Despite the heat of late spring, concerts continued into June. There was a grand entertainment by the Lady Friends of Crescent

Encampment, No. 1, Knights of Temperance, at Odd Fellows' Hall on June 8. It included songs (one by Félix Cohen), a violin solo (Curant), and more, accompanied by Eckert.[474] There were religious services that concluded the religious year. For Confirmation at Touro Synagogue on June 10, Mark Kaiser played the violin and Kitziger the organ. On the previous evening, Kitziger supplied his own music for the entire service. Choir members were Mme LeJeune, Mrs. Witham, Mrs. Alice Schwartz, and Messrs Rossi and Dubos.[475] On June 18 there was an all-vocal concert for the benefit of the Ladies' Bethel Association, at the Upper Bethel. Eckert was the accompanist.[476]

Meanwhile the lake band concerts had started with pre-season events. There were open-air concerts at Spanish Fort by mid-May by the Spanish Fort Orchestra under Professor George Sontag (c. 1842–87), director and grand solo trombonist, assisted by J. Meert, piccolo, and a complete corps of artists. The concerts ran from 5:00 to 10:00 p.m.[477] West End, too, had its concerts by mid-May, at the same time. J. B. Vogel conducted the corps of musicians at West End.[478] The official opening of the season at West End, however, occurred only on May 23,[479] and that of Spanish Fort on May 30. Featured at the latter were Sontag's Military Orchestra (thirty musicians), Mr. Fred N. Innes ("the world's greatest trombonist"), and Miss Ida Clark (the wonderful child solo cornetist). Concerts were held every evening at 6:00 p.m. and on Sundays at 5:00 p.m. Conange considered George Sontag better than Patrick Gilmore.[480] At the end of the summer, West End engaged, for one week only, Spanish Fort's Military Orchestra with George Sontag, Armand Veazey (cornet), Oscar Reine (oboe), Jean Meert (piccolo), Victor Einhorn (baritone), and Sontag (trombone).[481] Spanish Fort, in turn, put on a concert of the Orphéon Français, followed by a ball, on Saturday, September 11, with eleven works on the program—choruses with orchestra. It also had a two-part intermède.[482] And then it got Sontag back for two concerts, on the eighteenth for a vocal and instrumental concert with the Orphéon Français to benefit a charity and on the nineteenth for a final concert.[483]

On June 5 the Milneburg Opera House opened for the summer, "with the most powerful Company of Vaudeville Artists [and] Grand concerts between the acts by Professor Schindler's Famous Orchestra."[484] The Jockey Club continued with its concerts, and the Continental Guard Band concerts at Jackson Square took place occasionally.[485] The Ladies Social at the Elks Club on June 3 included readings and music: a violin solo by Master Leopold; a song, "The Bugle Horn" (Durel, Cohen and Beër, accompanied by W. T. Francis); other songs; whistles; and so forth.[486] As for the city itself, during the summer, there apparently were many unlicensed music halls on Royal Street and elsewhere in the French Quarter (such as at the corner of Chartres and Conti), and some citizens complained that their proliferation caused too much noise.[487] What went on there, however, was not purely concert music.

The regular fall season began on September 8, 1886, with a soiree musicale by the pupils of Mme Marguerite Capo at the Club Centro Español Hispano-Americano, which was crowded despite the extreme heat. The year before, the Capo soiree was in a smaller hall, but since the audience had expanded so much, the critic recommended that next year she should consider either the much larger Opera House or Grunewald Hall.[488] The Eagle Brass Band gave its third Festival de Nuit on Saturday, September 18.[489] The entire week beginning September 22, there were grand concerts each evening at the Theatre Eden, 40–42 Royal Street, modeled after the café concerts in Paris. Each evening the program was in two parts: I: Putti Bishop, Kittie Randolph, Alfred Wagner, Lea Talvar, Fernande, and Perez; II: Annetie Gerfesch, Mamie McEvoy, Mr. Delaur, Jeanne Bardou, Mlle Debrimond, M Sablon, Mlle Lillie Lease, May Wilson, and Mlle et M Delord Debrimond. On Saturday, M B. Armand, heroic tenor, made his debut.[490] The pupils of Mlle A. Perat gave a soiree musicale on September 24. Although Perat was one of the city's best piano teachers, this was only the first public recital her pupils had given. The pupils ranged in age from eight or nine to eighteen.[491]

The Continental Quartette Club, assisted by the Crescent City Amateur Orchestra, gave a free concert at Grunewald Hall on October 11 to benefit M T. Mellody; the soloists were Mlles F. Duffour and Afflecle, Mme Roach, and MM Mellody, Rossi, and Cohen, and they were joined by the choir of Sainte Theresa's Church.[492] There were vocal and instrumental promenade concerts at the new school on Carrollton Avenue on October 16–17, followed by a lottery drawing.[493] Mlles Moise and C. Durrive organized a concert at the Locquet-Leroy Institute on October 19 to benefit the victims of the earthquake at Charleston. Performers included Ida Riemann, Mark Kaiser, Mme James Nott, Mme Alice Schwartz, Mme Clement Labarre, pianist Mlle P. Pitot, and the Continental Quartette. They performed works by Victor Massé, Raff, Gounod, Alard, Donizetti, Crozen and Verdi.[494] George L. O'Connell directed a soiree musicale to benefit the choir of Sainte Anne's Chapel, at the home of P. M. Schneidan, 201 Esplanade Avenue, between Marais and Villere streets. Entry was ten cents. Piano and vocal works were performed.[495]

On Tuesday, November 2, violinist Theodore Curant gave an instrumental and vocal concert at Grunewald Opera House. He was joined by Mme Ida Riemann, Katie Bridewell, Kaiser, van Hufflen, Salomon, B. Bruenn, and others, with piano accompaniment by J. W. H. Eckert.[496] There was a benefit for Félix Cohen at Grunewald Opera House on Wednesday, November 10, with the assistance of M L. Delpech, opéra-comique baritone of the French Opera. Cohen was a top amateur singer in New Orleans. Among the performers was S. Cohen, but we do not know if he was related to Félix.[497] On November 15, Mlle Florence Huberwald assisted at a Woman's Club soiree musicale et littéraire, where she sang several songs, one by Eugène Chassaignac.[498] Huberwald became a prominent singer in New Orleans and later, in 1895, was a national leader of the women's movement.[499] Curant, Hincks, Sumner, Yuille, Berthe Pemberton, and the Continental Quartette presented a soiree musicale et littéraire to raise money for Christ Church on or about November 18.[500] And at the end of November, the 1886–87 opera season at the French Opera House under Maugé began.

On Wednesday, December 8, 1886, there was a vocal and instrumental concert scheduled by the Woman's Club, a benefit at Grunewald Hall. Performers included Mlle Berthe Pemberton (pianist), her sister Mme Pemberton-Hincks, and Mark Kaiser. It is uncertain, however, if the concert actually took place on that date.[501] Mrs. Boudousquié's students, as well as amateurs and artists, gave a much-heralded concert on December 10 at the French Opera House. Among the artists were Marguerite Samuel, Mme Pemberton-Hincks, Mme Lejeune, and Mme Katzenberger (soprano).[502] On December 19 there was a concert to benefit the Benevolent Society of Louisiana Women at Grunewald Hall, with the assistance of Maugé and his artists from the French Opera House.[503] The preChristmas concerts were led by Adelina Patti, who returned to New Orleans for a grand concert at the Saint Charles Theatre on December 20, 1886. It included a few other singers in the second act of *Sémiramide*. There was "a large orchestra of fifty select musicians under the direction of Sig. Luigi Arditi."[504] The Orphéon Français gave a concert on December 22 at the French Union Hall.[505]

The fourteen years from 1872 to 1886 began with one of the worst periods in the concert life of the city and ended with a large renewal, thanks largely to the Cotton Exposition and its accompanying cultural events. A coterie of local musicians of high caliber gave concerts, as their predecessors had before the Civil War, and local amateurs, including students, continued to give many recitals. But there were changes. The opera was in economic trouble, and as a result the quality of the local theater orchestras diminished, leaving the city without the musicians needed for an orchestral concert season. In general, visiting artists came for short stopovers rather than for long residences, and clearly New York and other cities were eclipsing New Orleans as the most desired American concert destination. Some of the best musicians among native New Orleanians—such as D'Aquin and the Frankos—deserted the city in order to make their careers elsewhere. Yet, from 1887 on, there was still much activity, resulting in a temporary renewal of classical concert life.

7

The Grand Old City
1887–1897

The years after 1886 found the concert situation in New Orleans in a static mode. Without the excitement of the innovative *Lake Pontchartrain* concerts and without the stimulus of a world exposition, the pattern of concerts settled into a mold that would carry well into the twentieth century. There continued to be lake concerts, and there continued to be many student concerts. Home concerts, church concerts, and benefit concerts continued in increasing number. Famous artists arrived, now usually for only one or two performances rather than the month-long residencies heretofore. Local professionals were busier than ever, and many amateurs enriched the concert scene as before. Yet, the classical concert situation in New Orleans could no longer compete with that in New York and other American cities that were much faster growing and wealthier. The decline, anticipated in the 1870s, now set in with more clarity.

Without the help of a major exposition, the spring 1887 season was much less active than in the preceding two years. It began on January 14, in the salons of Mme John Augustin, with a soiree musicale by Marguerite Samuel and her students.[1] Augustin's daughter Helena was one of Samuel's most gifted students. On Thursday, January 27, William H. Pilcher, assisted by amateurs of distinction and accompanied by O'Connell, presented a concert sacré at Sainte Anne's Chapel on Esplanade Avenue. They performed works by Rossini, Weber, and Fauré.[2] The pupils of Mme James Nott gave a recital at the Picard Institute on January 28.[3] When the visiting artist, Emma Romeldi, American soprano, sang at Grunewald Opera House on January 31 (postponed from January 28), she continued past practices of including several outstanding local musicians on the program. She was assisted here by Ida Riemann-Kaiser, Mark Kaiser (*Fantasie on Tannhäuser*), and J. W. H. Eckert, who directed the program. Emma Romeldi and her sister Lillie, violinist, who was also on the program, arrived in the city from Chicago.[4]

On February 4, 1887, Mme and M Henri Bayon gave a soiree musicale. The program included a violin duet by Godard (Henri Bayon and Marie Wannack), two other violin solos by Bayon, and various other works performed by various singers and instrumentalists.[5] There was a sacred concert on February 6 at Sainte Anne's Church by its choir. The feature was a Mozart mass. M Van Loo sang a prayer by Gounod with violoncello obbligato by M I'empesti, and Theresa Cannon-Buckley, regular organist at Sainte Anne, accompanied.[6] Miss Fanny Hunt d'Alma presented a concert at Grunewald Hall on February 9. The program consisted of popular songs, banjo pieces, opera arias, and other works.[7] The month of February ended with another sacred concert, this one at Saint-Jean-Baptiste Church on Dryades Street, between Clio and Calliope streets. Maugé, director of the French Opera, and principal artists of his troupe performed with the assistance of many distinguished local musicians.[8]

The French Opera season ended on March 10, 1887. The troupe—sixty people—then sailed for Havana and Mexico.[9] It returned to New Orleans in June to disband, and then Maugé went to Paris to engage people for the next season. The 1886–87 season, which included many favorites like *La Favorite, Norma,* and *Tales of Hoffmann,* was an artistic success but not so successful financially.[10]

Concerts continued after the Opera House closed. On March 17, Saint Patrick's Day, there was a concert of Irish music at Saenger Hall. The program included several overtures and selections by an orchestra, plus vocalists, the Continental Quartette Club, and recitations. Eckert was the accompanist.[11] A testimonial concert was tendered to Gregorio Curto on March 18 by his former students and artists of the city, to raise money for him in his old age (he was also ill).[12] Curto, who had been a force on the concert scene since the 1830s, died later that year, on November 19, 1887, at age eighty-two.[13] Marguerite Samuel gave another recital on March 24 at Grunewald Hall, with the assistance of Corinne Castellanos, Mrs. James Nott, Mrs. Katzenberger, and Helena Augustin. The program included various French and English songs, *Danse Macabre* by Saint-Saëns arranged for two pianos (Samuel and Augustin), Beethoven's Sonata No. 58 [*sic*], an etude and ballade of Chopin (Samuel alone), and a prelude by Mendelssohn.[14]

At the beginning of April, there was a soiree musicale to benefit the Barbarin girls, given at the home of Mme Crawford (on Royal Street) and directed by Mme James Nott.[15] The Gounod Society of New Orleans, O'Connell director, was founded on January 23, 1887. It planned to give soirees musicales in various salons, featuring young men and women.[16] Its first was on April 1, 1887, at O'Connell's home, which included only the works of Gounod.[17] A literary, artistic, and musical festival was held at Grunewald Hall on April 2 to benefit Saint Louis Cathedral. The program included piano pieces (Mlle Berthe Pemberton), violin and piano duets (M and Mme Bayon), a piano duet (Samuel and Augustin), and other pieces played by Samuel.[18] On April 11 there was another grand concert at the French Opera House tendered to Mrs. James Nott by her pupils. The program included piano and vocal works by basic composers: Meyerbeer, Chopin, Tosti, Verdi, Donizetti, Gounod, Flotow, Weber, Glinka, and others. Samuel performed two movements of Weber's Sonata in B-flat Minor.[19]

On April 18 and 29, Borchert conducted two grand symphony concerts at the Grand Opera House with a new orchestra of sixty musicians, the New Orleans Symphony Orchestra. As early as 1883, Borchert had his own "band" at the lake, but this new ensemble was different. Following in the footsteps of Collignon, he now had a symphony orchestra that could play the best classics. The program for the first has not yet been found, but the second had Mendelssohn's *Ruy Blas* Overture, Swendsen's *Concert Andante,* the introduction to *Lohengrin,* Beethoven's *Namensfeuer* Overture, the Overture to Mozart's *Don Giovanni, Träumerei* by Robert Schumann, Weber's *Oberon* Overture, and selections by (Johann?) Strauss. A fine audience attended, and Borchert hoped to present other concerts by the orchestra in the future with such pieces as *Danse Macabre* by Saint-Saëns, Beethoven's Symphony No. 7, and the Overture to *Tannhäuser.*[20] According to the critic of the *Picayune,* this was the first time since the Thomas concerts that such a good program was heard in New Orleans, but he must have been absent during Collignon's concerts. In any case, symphonic music had a revival.

Meanwhile, on April 20, there was a concert tendered to Miss Berthe Pemberton at Grunewald Hall, with Miss Pemberton assisted by her sister (Mrs. Pemberton-Hincks), Theodore Curant, and Mrs. Yuille. Mr. Sybrandt was scheduled to appear but, in fact, was sick and didn't show up. The program included a violin solo performed by Curant, Liszt's *Faust* performed by Miss Pemberton, pieces by Robert Schumann and Meyerbeer performed by Mrs. Pemberton-Hincks, plus additional works by Gounod, Chopin, and Verdi.[21] This was the last appearance in New Orleans of Miss Pemberton and Mme Pemberton-Hincks, who moved to New York by September 1888.[22] There is no mistaking the significance of the two to concert life in New Orleans in the 1880s. Their frequent appearances in concerts performing the greatest European music helped keep the standards high in New Orleans, and their talents were as much appreciated in New York as in New Orleans. Their loss to New Orleans was symptomatic of the new state of affairs whereby the Crescent City was losing out to the Big Apple.

Nonetheless, some excellent musicians still made New Orleans their home. New Orleans native and resident Mark Kaiser presented a concert sponsored by his friends on April 26.[23] The program consisted of Chopin's *Grande Polonaise Brillante* (W. T. Francis), a violin solo (Master Alfred Holt), arias (Ida Riemann-Kaiser), De Bériot's Violin Concerto No. 9 (Kaiser), violin solos (Master Joe Leopold), and Mozart's "Ave Verum Corpus" performed by nineteen violin students of Kaiser. Curant also participated. On May 3, Mme M. Prévost's students performed at the French Union Hall.[24]

The lake concerts began earlier than usual. On Sunday, March 13, 1887, Spanish Fort jumped the gun with a public concert by the New Orleans Symphony Orchestra (grown to sixty-five musicians) under the direction of Borchert.[25] The official opening was not celebrated until June 13. At this time and subsequently, garden concerts were at 5:00–8:00 p.m., followed by operettas under W. T. Francis. On June 13, Francis led a fine orchestra with a grand chorus of thirty in a performance of Gilbert and Sullivan's *Iolanthe*.[26] The reviewer stated that "the orchestra was increased [over earlier performances] and while not numerous was efficient." Opera started at West End on May 5, and there was music every evening at Milneburg throughout May.[27] West End officially opened for the season on Sunday, May 22. Sontag's band of forty musicians performed nightly.[28] And the private New Louisiana Jockey Club hired both Sontag and Borchert with their bands (the latter's band of thirty) to perform for promenade concerts.[29] Clearly, Borchert's lake band, half the size of his symphony orchestra, was a different ensemble from the latter, but it is possible some players were carried over from one to the other. On a concert at the New Jockey Club on June 15, 1887, Borchert conducted, among many other works, a march by Sousa, who was just emerging as a favorite in New Orleans.

An alternative to concerts at Lake Pontchartrain were concerts on the Mississippi River. On May 10, the Steamboat *Oliver Beirne* had an evening cruise, and on the boat were the sixty-five musicians of the New Orleans Symphony Orchestra.[30] Borchert's next concert with the Symphony Orchestra was on May 19, this time on the steamer *E. J. Gay*.[31] Further cruises took place on May 22, May 24, and every Tuesday, Thursday, and Sunday at 7:00 p.m., from Canal Street and the landing at Jackson Street.[32] A typical program was the *Tannhäuser* March, Robert Schumann's *Träumerei*, the Overture to *Don Giovanni*, and selections from *Mignon, Faust* and other popular operas.

In the city, the Lafayette Square concerts by the Continental Guards Band, J. B. Wunsch leader, continued at least through June. On May 31, 1887, the program included works by L. Cursh, J. H. Wadsworth, F. J. Navarro (Mexican band), Waldteufel, George Wiegand, Sullivan (from *Mikado*), D. Braham, and L. Conterno.[33] On June 7, a week before the Jockey Club concert, the Lafayette Square concert included a Sousa march, which may be the first time that such a work by this soon-to-become-famous composer was heard in the city.[34]

In addition, there were a few regular, indoor concerts. William H. Pilcher gave a grand organ recital and sacred concert at Coliseum Place Baptist Church on May 23.[35] Master Isidore Jacobs, assisted by J. W. H. Eckert and Ida Riemann-Kaiser, presented a grand concert at Grunewald Hall on May 25. Jacobs played M Hoeffner's Grand Violin Concerto in the style of Paganini, Beethoven's Romance in F, the Adagio and *Rondo Brilliant* from a De Bériot concerto, and Ernst's *Carnival de Venise.* His accompanist, Lily Hauler, also played Beethoven's *Pathétique* Sonata, Opus 13.[36] The two leading Reform Jewish congregations, Sinai and Touro, each had confirmation services on May 30. J. W. H. Eckert was director of music at Sinai and had a good choir; Touro had Kitziger, who got Kaiser, Curant, Moses, and others to assist with the music.[37]

Two new societies were organized in spring. On May 22 and June 1 and 4 the Oratorio Society held organizational meetings with J. W. H. Eckert in charge. There were one hundred active (singing) members (sixty-one females including Nott, Riemann-Kaiser, and Mrs. W. H. Pilcher, and thirty-nine males including three Pilchers) and a group of inactive members including Mme G. F. Locquet, Samuel, Boudousquié, J. W. H. Eckert, Louis Grunewald, and Mark Kaiser.[38] In addition, a New Orleans Mendelssohn Society was founded which was primarily a singing group.[39]

June concerts included a recital by Pilcher's students on the second at his studio at 239 Carondelet Street. Pilcher opened with one of his own works and played several other pieces. Mr. C. H. Pilcher sang, Mr. and Mrs. W. H. Pilcher played *Fantasie on Norma,* a piece for two pianos, and Mr. J. B. Bassich played a violin obbligato.[40] While the Pilcher affair was a family concert, a pseudo concert en famille was presented at the hall of the Orphéon Français on June 5 by Eugene Medal, Paul Brunet, William Anglade, and August Vidondez, assisted by several friends. Medal and Brunet performed several duets for violin and piano; Misses A. and R. Bihli played solos and duets on the piano; Vidondez sang some comic songs; and Medal, Brunet, and Anglade performed a trio for violin, cornet, and piano.[41] On Tuesday, June 14, Sam Franko, assisted by Kaiser, Curant, and one or two vocalists, gave a violin recital at Grunewald Hall. The three violinists played together a capriccio by T. Hermann. Franko, by himself, played works by Corelli, B. Godard, and Sarasate.[42] In addition to the recitals at Pilcher's institute, there were other schools which presented music as part of graduation exercises. For the graduation of Professor Lecher's school at Grunewald Hall on June 16, 1887, for example, an orchestral overture introduced the customary recitations by the students.[43]

The fall seasons were now becoming more prolific with concerts. On October 3, 1887, there was the first vocal and instrumental concert of the second year of the Pilcher Studio. Along with his best students, Pilcher himself performed pieces by Beethoven, Verdi, Gounod, Rossini, Auber, and others, along with his own compositions. It was a long concert with high standards and medals for the best student performers.[44] For the name-day celebration at the Church of Sainte Theresa on October 15, there was a concert of sacred vocal music,[45] and on October 19–20 there were concerts of vocal and instrumental music at Grunewald Hall to benefit the children of Our Lady of Good Council.[46] The Harngard Männerchor (male singing society) and the Germania Lodge performed at Masonic Hall on October 24. The program, along with recitations, included music by a fine orchestra, the singing group, and two zitherists.[47] On October 27, the Orphéon Française under O'Connell entertained a crowded house at Grunewald Hall.[48] The final concert in October took place on the thirtieth at noon at the Grand Opera House. It was a benefit for the family of Professor George Sontag, who organized and led the Sontag Military Orchestra. W. T. Francis and others participated.[49]

On November 1, 1887, the celebrated women's orchestra, under the direction of Mlle Cora Zanita from Boston, was featured at L'Académie de Musique Impériale, at the corner of Chartres and Conti streets.[50] The artistic society I.O.B.B. (International Order of B'nai B'rith) gave a literary and musical performance at Grunewald Hall on November 9 to help raise money for the building of Grace Church. The performers were the singer Mlle Holland, a young pianist Mlle A. Dufilho in a polonaise, her brother (a singer), and Paul Bayon.[51] On Wednesday, November 30, Mlle Jeanne Faure gave a grand concert at Grunewald Hall. She had just returned from two years in Germany, where she studied to prepare for a career in music. She was assisted by her New Orleans teacher, Mme James Nott, by Mlle B. McCoard, and by Mark Kaiser. The program consisted of thirteen pieces, of which three were for piano and two for violin. Faure sang arias by Rubinstein, Massenet, Tosti, Wagner, Saint-Saëns, and Gastaldon.[52]

The friends and pupils of Mme H. H. Wulff, piano professor, gave a concert on December 2 at Grunewald Hall. Among the pieces performed were works by Verdi, Bellini, Auber, Gounod, and Curto ("Juxta Crucem"). Assisting Wulff were Mmes Theresa Cannon-Buckley and C. Witham, Mlles F. Duffour, L. Montaguet, H. Bridwell, and G. Hardell; MM Rossi, Kernion, Guesnon, and Cassard, and a choir from different churches conducted by William Pilcher. George O'Connell and W. E. Eckert served as accompanists.[53] On December 7, the Spanish and Hispanic-American Circle gave a soiree musicale et dramatique at its locale on Canal Street; there was instrumental music between theater and opéra-comique scenes.[54] The Gounod Circle, under the direction of O'Connell, gave its third soiree musicale in the salons of Dr. Henri Bayon, 125 Bourbon Street, between Toulouse and Saint Peters streets, on December 14.[55] The first concert of the new Mendelssohn Society took place at Grunewald Opera House on December 19; Kaiser, among others, participated. The newly arrived young Swedish piano virtuoso Hermann Dahlberg-Wenzel performed an afternoon soiree at the Grunewall Hall parlors on December 30. He played piano selections by Beethoven, Chopin, Jaell, and Robert Schumann, among others.[56]

Meanwhile, along with this thriving concert life, the 1887–88 French Opera season opened on November 12 with *Les Huguenots*.[57] It was joined, on February 21, 1888, by Grau's opera company performing opéra comiques at the Avenue Theater, including *Mikado*.[58] With a healthy opera, a successful concert season extending into 1888 seemed assured.

On New Years Day, Saint Stephen's Church on Napoleon Avenue was dedicated. "The organ loft, the largest in the city, contains a $10,000 organ built by the Pilcher Brothers.... The choir, conducted by Professor P. J. Guth, organist, and composed of Mrs. Charles H. Pilcher, Mrs. J. E. Richard and the Misses Mattingly, sopranos; Mrs. Dunn and Miss Melancon, altos; Mr. Charles H. Pilcher, tenor, and Mr. J. E. Richard, Basso, sang Goeb's 'Tantum Ergo' and Weber's 'Benedictus.' . . . Mrs. Pilcher's sweet soprano, Mr. Pilcher's pleasing tenor."[59] Marguerite Samuel inaugurated a series of piano recitals and chamber music at Grunewald Hall on January 8, 1888.[60] On Wednesday, January 18, there was a grand sacred concert at Sainte Ann's church under the musical direction of Theresa Cannon-Buckley for the benefit of the organ fund. The singers came from the French Opera and joined with some amateurs in sacred works by Gounod and Fauré.[61] At the end of January 1888, there was a benefit concert at Grunewald Hall for the German Protestant Home for the Aged. The performers included Mark Kaiser on piano [sic], and Misses Josephine and Rosa Frantz played Gottschalk's grand waltz and other works.[62]

The *Pilcher Conservatory Catalogue* for 1887–88 describes the Beethoven Society, whose purpose was to introduce students and the community to the works of ancient and modern masters. It held weekly rehearsals for pupils at no additional fees. This group formed the nucleus for a concert on February 1, 1888, at Grunewald Hall; it was a pupils' recital to benefit Saint Joseph's Orphan Asylum, by the Beethoven Instrumental Association and the Handel and Haydn Oratorio Society, comprising students of Pilcher's Studio of Music under the direction of William H. Pilcher. Pieces were performed on pianos or sung solo or in choir (including excerpts from Haydn's *Creation*). The program included Haydn's Symphony No. 7 performed by five pianists (one of whom was Mrs. William H. Pilcher), Beethoven's Symphony No. 5 performed by four pianists on two pianos (including both Mr. and Mrs. Pilcher), and works of Liszt, Gottschalk, and others. The concert must have lasted three hours.[63]

Two days later, on February 3, there was a concert at Grunewald Hall for the benefit of Saint Joseph's new church, under the direction of E. J. Newman, organist at Saint Joseph's. The program consisted of a chorus; "Theodore Curant, the skillful violinist, played a pretty solo," and later another piece; and a vocal quartet sang a work by Mozart; Eckert was the accompanist.[64] On the same day, the vocal class of the Woman's Club gave a concert at the club. Mrs. Samuel, "among the foremost of our American pianists," gave a concert for her students at Grunewald Hall on February 6. Every seat was occupied. Mostly students performed, but the program ended with Samuel playing Hummel's Concerto in B Minor, "accompanied by an orchestra of strings and wood-wind." Other composers represented on the program were Mozart, Beethoven, Moskowski, Chopin, Heller, Bizet, and Schubert. Guillaume Ricci played a violin solo.[65]

Members of Maugé's French Opera Troupe, accompanied by O'Connell, performed a concert on February 17 at Grunewald Hall to benefit the Dames Hospitalieres Charitable Association. Once again, Ricci played a violin solo.[66] On February 28, at Odd Fellows' Hall, there was a grand charity concert offered by the King's Daughters, with the cooperation of Maugé's French artists. It included several violin works played by Ricci, some piano works, and arias.[67]

The Mendelssohn Club of Boston came to Grunewald Opera House on February 28 and 29, 1888. The *Picayune* critic recognized that the audience for this kind of string music by the masters was "rare, special" or, in other words, not large. The club was founded in 1849 and by 1888 was probably the most prestigious chamber society in America. Its personnel consisted of two violins, viola or clarinet, violoncello, and soprano. Spurred on by Theodore Curant, their local producer, enough interest was generated in New Orleans for their concerts featuring primarily quartets and quintets. The program on February 28 was Mendelssohn's Quintet in B-flat, Opus 87, a flute solo, the quartetto *The Miller's*

Pretty Daughter by Raff, a violin solo, a clarinet solo, a violoncello solo, a song, and the andante from one of Beethoven's Opus 18 quartets.[68]

The second free concert of the Mendelssohn Society of New Orleans was on March 1, 1888. This was not the same as the Mendelssohn Club of Boston; it was, as mentioned above, a vocal group. At this concert, the group sang three choral works (two choruses from Mendelssohn's *Saint Paul* and a Latin drinking song for male chorus), and the rest of the program was sung by members of the French Opera Troupe; there were also violin solos by Theodore Curant, accompanied by Ella Grunewald.[69] The students of Pilcher's Studio of Music gave their eleventh recital at the studio on March 10. Pilcher himself performed Liszt's arrangement of Paganini's *La Campanella,* and the remainder of the program was performed by students (Mrs. Pilcher also chipping in). This included Beethoven's Symphony No. 1 arranged for four pianists on two pianos, Pilcher's *Grand Valse de Concert,* Opus 7, and so on.[70]

On March 12, the orchestra of the Cercle Gounod and the Orphéon Français, directed by O'Connell, performed at Grunewald Hall. The Cercle Gounod was a string quintet in one piece, a group of string instruments in another, and an orchestra in a third.[71] A sacred service, honoring the late Emperor Wilhelm I of Germany, took place at the Saint Charles Theatre on March 15. It included several orchestral works: an arrangement of Chopin's "Funeral March," Beethoven's chorus "The Heav'ns Proclaim," the German national anthem, and a German hymn by Martin Luther for male chorus and orchestra. The orchestra played Wagner's "Pilgrim's Chorus" "with delightful ensemble and brilliancy."[72] Samuel gave a recital at Grunewald Hall on March 15. She played one of Chopin's polonaises, the *Andante Spianato,* and the Mendelssohn G Minor Concerto No. 1 with orchestra; other Mendelssohn, Chopin, Liszt, and Stamaty were also on the program. Ricci played violin in a duet with Bayon.[73]

Easter was a wonderful occasion for the churches to show off their musical forces in what amounted to concerts as much as ritual. On Easter Sunday, April 1, 1888, there were musical services at numerous churches: the Jesuit Church (morning service: Hummel's Mass in E-flat, Beethoven's "Veni Creator" arranged by Meyerbeer, and more Hummel; evening service: Gounod, Hummel, Donizetti; the chorus directed and accompanied on organ by Pilcher with Mrs. Pilcher in the choir); Trinity Church (Dudley Buck, H. P. Danks, Mercadante; director and organist: Philip Dreuding); Church of the Annunciation (Danks, Burnap, and others; organist: Herbert Palfrey); Saint John the Baptist Church on Dryades (Weber's Mass in G); Sainte Anna's Episcopal Church on Esplanade (musical service under the direction of William H. Pilcher); and others.[74]

The next day, the assembly of the Creole Dramatique Franco-Louisianais was held, in which Ricci played his violin and several singers sang.[75] Helena Augustin performed a concert on April 3 at Grunewald Hall with the assistance of Ricci, Bayon, and the Cercle Gounod, under the leadership of O'Connell. Mrs. Bayon and Eckert were accompanists. Augustin, a pupil of Samuel, was the daughter of the late Major John Augustin of New Orleans, at whose home Samuel had given concerts the previous year. Helena played a duet with Samuel (*Danse Macabre* of Saint-Saëns) and solo works by Rubinstein, Chopin, and Bach, and, with orchestra, Hummel's Concerto No. 2 (Allegro only). Ricci played a Brahms Hungarian Dance. The orchestra, by itself, played a few additional works.[76]

There was an open rehearsal by the pupils of Mme Devrient at Grunewald Hall on April 5. Devrient arrived in New Orleans five or six months previously, so many of her pupils were just at the beginning stages. Included also were a violin and piano duet performed by Mrs. Greaud on the piano and Ricci on the violin, and a concerto for violin and piano performed by Master Isidore Jacobs, the young and talented violinist, and Corinne Vaught.[77] Mozart's Mass No. 1 in C and a work by La Hache were sung at Saint John the Baptist Church on Dryades Street on April 8.[78] Theodore Curant directed a grand orchestral concert with forty of the best players at Grunewald Opera House on April 10.[79] On this occasion, the orchestra played Beethoven's *Egmont* Overture, Robert Schumann's *Träumerei,* Weber's *Jubel* Overture, and "Prière d'une Vierge" from Massenet's oratorio *Marie Madeleine.* Pilcher played the Beethoven C Minor Piano Concerto No. 3, and Curant performed Godard's *Concerto Romantique,* both with orchestra. Mlle Valerie-Jauque sang some songs.

There were two concerts on April 24. The first was a musicale given by the Church Decorative Society at Prytania Street Presbyterian Church. Works on the program were by Donizetti, Rossini, Gounod, Bizet, and others. Mrs. Marie Wannack played some violin solos.[80] The other concert was the third of the season by the Mendelssohn Society of New Orleans. Ida Riemann-Kaiser sang a solo with chorus, Mlle Valerie Jauquet also sang a solo, there were additional choruses and songs by Benedict and Gounod, and there were solo piano works by Mendelssohn and Chopin.[81] For the sixty-ninth anniversary of the Odd Fellows' Order in America, celebrated at New Orleans' Odd Fellows' Hall on April 26, music was a central part of the program. After a brass band played an introductory overture, Master Isidore Jacobs rendered a solo by Sonta "and exhibited remarkable proficiency on that king of instruments, the violin."[82]

May 1888 got off to a fine start. On the first, William H. Pilcher had a grand orchestral concert at Grunewald Opera House with Curant as violin soloist. Orchestral works were interspersed with vocal works. Among the orchestral works were Rossini's Overture to *Sémiramide*; the Mendelssohn G Minor Piano Concerto No. 1 (performed by Pilcher with orchestra); a new work, *Unique Marche di Bravoura,* opus 8, by Pilcher, dedicated to Eckert; Beethoven's E-flat *Emperor* Piano Concerto No. 5 (performed by Pilcher with orchestra); Curant playing Bazzini's *Concerto Militaire* for violin and orchestra; and the Grand March and Pilgrim's Chorus from *Tannhäuser*.[83] The next day, Professor Rolling and his pupils gave a recital at Grunewald Hall, assisted by Curant, Eckert, and Mrs. G. Witham. One of the singers sang a song by Rolling, and Ms. A. Sucola, Ms. E. Noll, and Curant performed a *Sonato Andante* [sic] by Beethoven.[84] During a concert as part of the entertainment for the benefit of the building fund of the Protestant Orphans Home, on Magazine Street between Sixth and Seventh streets, several musicians performed a piano solo, vocal solos, and violin solos.[85] Joseph Miller Jr., organist and director at the church of Saint John the Baptist, led a concert there of sacred music to benefit the choir fund. The program included Curto's "Regina Terra." Once again, Ricci played violin.[86]

On May 10, 1888, Patrick Gilmore's Great Jubilee Band gave the first of five performances in New Orleans at the Saint Charles Theatre. Advertised as the "finest brass and reed organization in the country," its repertoire included classical works by Mendelssohn, Wagner, Liszt, and Rubinstein, and many popular pieces like "Dixie" and "Carry Me Back to Ole Virginny." Many in the audience recalled Gilmore's more modest jubilee twenty-four years earlier while he was stationed in New Orleans. The use of new artillery to be used in the concerts was reminiscent of Beethoven and Tchaikovsky, only here the bronze cannon were hooked electronically to a keyboard which was played in synchronization with the band and chorus. The actual cannons were outside the theater. According to the *Picayune,* "Gilmore fires one gun on the first beat of each measure in the sixteen-measure finale of the anvil chorus and in other choruses, and the effect of such punctuation when the band is playing, the chorus singing, anvils ringing and the special artists assisting, is electrical. It is a majestic and sublime climax."[87] At least it was noisy!

On Saturday, May 19, Victoria Hervey, prima donna of the opera, gave a grand concert at Grunewald Opera House. Ricci played the violin, and Eckert accompanied.[88] There was a soiree musicale and piano recital by the pupils of Miss Louise Malie at her home, 250 Bayou Road, near Villere Street, on June 1.[89]

Meanwhile, the lake concerts resumed, but with one important new face. Professor George A. Paoletti's band of forty first-class artists opened the summer season at West End on May 20.[90] D'Aquin and Sontag were now gone, and Paoletti was emerging as a major force in new music that would by the end of the nineteenth century and early twentieth century change the reputation of New Orleans. Toward the end of the summer, Mlle Alice Raymond and M V. Einhorn performed at West End with the orchestra of Paoletti.[91] The last concert for the season was on Sunday, September 2, with a Mexican band added for the occasion.[92] During September, there were other bands at West End; on the sixteenth Ricci, just returned from a summer vacation in Paris, gave a concert at West End, with M Messina directing thirty instrumentalists in Italian military music. Morales, Renaud, Butat, Mme Faye-Grand, Mlle Cora Samuel (Marguerite's daughter), and others sang. Mme Breaud and Mme Noiret played piano. The concert was followed by a ball.[93] Meanwhile, Paoletti and his band went on tour. In October he was performing for fifteen days in Rome, Georgia.[94]

The fall 1888 season of indoor concerts began on September 2 at the Gouthier Hotel in Covington on the other side of the lake, where the Orphéon Français gave a matinee concert under George O'Connell. Performers included E. Médal, Henry Wehrman Jr., J. Voorhies, H. Vallé, E. Dussé, L. H. Barbey, O. Legendre, A. Brunet, and P. E. Carrière.[95] The concert was so successful that they returned to Covington on October 7.[96] Back in the city, the Orphéon Français, O'Connell director, had a public rehearsal on Friday, September 21, at its location on Royal and Orleans streets. Pieces were by Suppé, Planquette, Spirti (performed by Ricci), Bruant, Verdi, Tito Mattei (sung by S. Cohen), Coen (performed by the orchestra), Massé, De Bériot (played by Ricci), Paulus (played by G. Oliver), Lecocq, Bumbert, and Waldteufel.[97] They performed another concert on October 25 with the addition of a children's chorus.[98]

On Friday, September 14, there was an outdoor promenade concert by the Continental Guards at Washington Square organized by the businesses there. Unfortunately, it rained, so attendance was meager.[99] Hubert Rolling returned to New Orleans at the end of September and gave his first concert of the season on Monday, October 1.[100] The German society Frohsinn held a musical and dramatic soiree at Grunewald Hall on October 23, but its gathering on the twenty-eighth was primarily a dramatic performance.[101] On November 23, at its entertainment at Odd Fellows' Hall, however, there were choruses and solos.[102] On the twenty-sixth the Women's Club gave a concert (soiree musicale et dramatique) at Grunewald Hall to raise money to support an atelier where the women could sew. Performers included Emilie de Lassus, August James, Pauline Blache accompanied by Ricci on violin, Bisland, Braud, Kernion, and Despommier.[103] The Spanish and Hispanic-American Circle held a soiree dramatique at its home (203 Canal Street), which included a piano piece as well as three short dramatic presentations, followed by a ball.[104] On October 29, the

New Orleans Quartette Club gave a soiree musicale at Grunewald Hall.[105] The Democratic French Club, which featured members of the Orphéon Français, sponsored a concert on November 5, as well as a conference directed by the eminent Alcée Fortier.[106]

Pilcher's recitals now were a fixture in New Orleans concert life and continued to be such into the first decade of the twentieth century. On November 14, 1888, there was a concert of Pilcher's students at his studio. Pilcher played extensively both organ and piano. A large number of students won medals. On December 12, there was another recital by Pilcher's students.[107] Other teachers held similar musicales, as they had done for most of the century. The musicale by Miss Jeanne Faure for her pupils was on November 30 at Grunewald Hall. Besides students, professional singers included Faure and Mrs. E. Pilcher, among others. "Faure is a young lady of great accomplishment as a singer."[108] Mrs. James Nott's musicale at Grunewald Hall on December 17, to an overflowing crowd, featured thirteen pieces, most by her students, but Ricci also played. The accompanist was Miss K. Dessommes.[109]

A number of artists gave a concert on November 26, 1888, at Grunewald Hall to benefit the church of Our Lady of Good Counsel. The Continental Band, singers from the French Opera House, and Kaiser performed.[110] A Masonic concert at Masonic Hall (Saint Charles Avenue at Perdido Street) consisted mostly of vocal music and a violin solo by Ricci.[111] Besides regular concerts, the fall had its share of other concert events. The café concerts at the Eden and the Palais Royal finally received permits to stay open between midnight and 1:00 a.m., provided that they did not serve liquor during those hours and that the sandwiches they did serve were not such as to confuse them with restaurants.[112] The French Opera opened its 1888–89 season on November 8 with *La Juive,*[113] and it flourished well into the new year with such operas as *Rigoletto, Der Freischütz, L'Africaine, Carmen, Faust,* and *Le Prophète.* Finances were still sketchy, and so, on February 20, a group of sixty citizens organized to buy the French Opera House, renovate it, and become the financial support for opera in New Orleans.[114] The group was not prepared to run the opera but would rent out the hall and maintain it. At the same time, Grau's company was doing operettas in English at the Saint Charles Theatre.

The spring 1889 concert season was typical. There was a benefit on January 14 at Grunewald Hall for the Shakespear Almshouse (named after mayor Shakespear and not the British playwright); Marguerite Samuel performed a *Valse Caprice* by Rubinstein, and several singers sang.[115] This concert was followed on January 23 by a vocal and instrumental recital presented by the students of Miss Kate Dykers.[116] On February 4, the New Orleans Quartette Club performed at Grunewald Hall. The program included Spohr's Concerto No. 10, performed by Mrs. Horace Peters (a native of New Orleans and daughter of Fred Peters, president of the Metropolitan Bank) and Mrs. Professor Sharp; both were graduates of the Leipzig Conservatory. Also on the program were piano works (including Weber's *Concertstück in F*) performed by various pianists including Miss Esther Levy, and vocal works sung by the chorus under J. Hanno Deiler. A dance followed the concert.[117] There was a concert on February 11 at the French Opera House to benefit the popular Ricci, who was a graduate of the "French Conservatory" (Paris?) and formerly first violinist of the New Orleans Opera Orchestra.[118] It was a typically varied program. The French Opera Orchestra performed the Overture to *William Tell* and ended the concert with Ricci's own *Les Etoiles Waltz.* Mlle Giraldine played a harp solo, a chorus of forty young women from New Orleans sang pieces by Rossini and Verdi, Mr. Sergysels of the French Opera played a clarinet solo, Grisai played LeBlair's Romance for violoncello with orchestra, and Ricci, of course, played violin solos and obbligatos.

On February 15, there was a concert at Grunewald Hall to benefit the German Protestant Home for the Aged. This was a remarkable event because, during a period of intense Jim Crow laws, whites and blacks could not perform on the same stage at the same time, yet here they did. Performers included Misses Emily and Katie Kundert, Minerva Adams, Etta Roehl, Mrs. Ida Riemann-Kaiser, MM Louis Fuhr and O. G. Keller, the Sixth District Singing Society under Professor J. Engel, the Oak City Quartette, the Colored Songsters from North Carolina accompanied by Eckert, and the Evangelical Singing Society of Carrollton under Mr. H. Haverkamp.[119] There was a grand instrumental and vocal concert at Grunewald Opera House on February 24 for the benefit of the young violinist Isidore Jacobs, whom we met the previous two years and who wished to go abroad for further studies. On the program, besides Jacobs himself, were Misses Amelia and Annie Jacobs, Lilly Hauler, Mmes Blache, Breard and B. Barnett, M T. Mulledy, and Dr. E. Ludwig. Jacobs played the *Saltarelle* by Alard, *Le Striche* by Paganini, a grand concerto by Mr. Hoeffner, and a violin solo by Pechatschek.[120] On February 25, a grand concert was held for the benefit of Florence Huberwald, at Grunewald Hall, by the Boston Symphony Orchestral Club ("who are delightful performers of a high class of music"). The program included flute, viola d'amour, and violoncello solos, singers, and the Boston Club playing five pieces. There were many encores,[121] so that the group was encouraged to return to New Orleans, which it did at the end of the year.

The month ended when Ricci presented a Spectacular Concert, with orchestra, chorus and soloists, at the French Opera House on February 29.[122]

On Sunday, March 10, 1889, the new French Opera Association, which had purchased the Opera House, published its official articles of incorporation. The *Picayune* praised the new association and its promise to make New Orleans a great center of musical culture. Central to this would be the creation of a New Orleans Conservatory "in vocal and instrumental music, so that the native talent could be developed, a competent chorus created and an orchestra trained."[123] By March 17, the French Opera Association was fully subscribed, and its leadership stated that the first object of the charter would be carried out: renovation of the French Opera House.[124]

Meanwhile, once Carnival was over, concert life continued unabated. There was a testimonial concert to Emmanuel Lafarge, tenor of the French Opera, at Grunewald Hall on March 13. Gaston Lematte, leader of the orchestra, played a piano solo, Ricci played several numbers, and several opera singers sang arias, including one by Mozart.[125] On March 14, J. W. H. Eckert announced that his music store, at 141–143 Camp Street, was presenting parlor concerts by competent pianists every evening from 5:00 to 8:00.[126] Also, on the afternoon of March 14, artists of the French Opera sang arias to the women at the Cotton Palace.[127] The next day, Misses A. Seybold, D. Hoper, R. Falls, C. Philip, and M. Deuchert, and MM Seelman, Engel, Baeher, Veith, Guth, Rogers, and the Carrollton and Sixth District singing societies gave a benefit concert for the German Evangelical School at Saenger Hall in the Sixth District; there were songs, choruses, recitations, and instrumental duets.[128] The pupils of Mme Charles Boudousquié gave a recital on March 24 in the "cosy parlors" of Mr. L. Placide Canonge on Saint Philip Street. Although she retired from the French Opera some forty years before, Boudousquié still was "certainly one of the most noted figures in the art of vocal music in New Orleans." The program consisted of works by Gounod, Godard, Cherubini, Saint-Saëns, Lepneveu, and Thome. Several of the works were choral.[129] Later that week, on Thursday, March 27, 1889, Mrs. Samuel performed her recital at Grunewald Hall. She played works by Chopin, Joseffy, Beethoven (*Appassionata*), and Liszt. She also performed in a duet by Robert Schumann; Kaiser played Sarrazat's (Pablo Sarasate's) *Fantasia of Faust* and Raff's *Scherzo;* and there also were songs.[130]

The array of classical concerts continued. Mlle Jauquet presented a concert at Grunewald Hall on April 13.[131] As was usual on Monday nights, there was a concert of classical music at the Upper Bethel on April 22, by lesser-known, probably amateur musicians under the management of Miss L. A. Colleti.[132] A benefit vocal and instrumental concert for Saint Louis Cathedral occurred on the same night at Washington Artillery Hall; it was a promenade concert that featured music by the Nippert Orchestra under the direction of M Lenfant, leader of the French Opera. The varied fare involved a military band playing the Overture to *Les Diamants de la Couronne,* and other selections. There were also songs by Mendelssohn, Saint-Saëns, and others sung by various singers, including Mlle Varelli-Jauquet.[133] Another benefit, to aid the Louisiana Society for the Prevention of Cruelty to Animals, took place on April 23 at the Grand Opera House. Ricci, Jauquet, and more participated in the concert; there was a comedy as well.[134] Mark Kaiser produced a grand orchestral concert at Grunewald Hall on April 25, to a sellout crowd. The orchestra, composed of thirty leading professional musicians and conducted by Curant and Bernard Bruenn, played works by Litolff, Gounod, Verdi, and Meyerbeer. Samuel contributed a Chopin concerto, and Kaiser proffered a De Bériot concerto and the Mendelssohn, all with orchestra. In addition, fifteen pupils of Kaiser together played a Handel arrangement, and Mrs. James Nott and Ida Riemann-Kaiser sang.[135]

A patriotic program at Grunewald Opera House on April 27, 1889, involved speeches, pantomimes, and music by pianists, singers, the Continental Guards, the Oak City Quartette under Eckert, and Ricci on violin. The ceremony was followed by dancing.[136] On April 28, there was a sacred concert at Saint John the Baptist Church to benefit its choir fund; Joseph Miller Jr. was organist and director. The program included pieces by Curto, Gounod, and Rossini. On the same evening there was also a sacred concert at Saint Stephen's Church under P. J. Guth and an organ recital at Saint Vincent de Paul's Church under W. H. Pilcher.[137] Works by Meyerbeer, Suppé, Waldteufel, Schulhof, Léo Delibes, Rossini, O. Maher, Weber, Marenge, Tuerner, Wagner, C. Faust, and others were on a concert at the Jockey Club on May 1.[138] On the same evening, at a meeting of the D. H. Holmes Literary Association at its hall at 163 Camp Street, there were vocal, piano, cornet, and other solos by amateurs sprinkled among recitations, a dialogue, and a comedy.[139] The old policy of not naming amateur musicians was no longer observed, and thus we have the names of Miss Derbes, Miss Molony, Mrs. West, Mr. G. W. Medus, Master Paul Doussan, and Mr. J. B. Fallaize, all of whom performed for the association.

At Grunewald Hall on May 3, Mrs. James Nott's pupils held a concert. In what had become a common practice of the time, a few of Nott's professional friends also appeared on the program, perhaps to draw a wider audience than what would be expected at a normal students' recital. Thus, on May 3, "Kaiser, the big, handsome violinist, played a ballad from Moskowski." Mrs. Samuel, "a pupil of Listz [sic]," also played. Gounod's "Ave Maria" was sung by twenty voice pupils accompanied by ten violins, organ, and piano. The violinists were Curant, Kaiser, Ricci, Becker, Thomson, Burke, Gonsenheim, C. and L. Hase, and Specht.[140] Unfortunately, this was the last public appearance of Curant, the very gifted young violinist and conductor, who died the following August 23 at age forty-two.

The New Orleans Choral Society gave a concert at Grunewald Hall on May 4. It performed choruses by Wagner, Saint-Saëns, and Rossini, and individual members sang solo songs. Henry Breaud sang a comic song, and "Miss Augusta H. James, with big, appealing blue eyes, gave a correct interpretation to *Mignon*'s aria *Je Suis Titania.*"[141] Ricci played obbligato, as well as solo, and with Heichelheim and Gernhauser in a trio from Gounod's *Colombe.* Entertainment for the benefit of the Creole Exchange at Grunewald Hall on May 8 found a military band playing several works, plus vocal solos, and Ricci, accompanied by Mrs. E. Breaud. Also part of the entertainment were a lantern show, tableaux, and other events.[142] The meetings of the Teacher's Benevolent Association at Grunewald Hall on May 10–12 included some music (violin and piano pieces, songs).[143] Little Minerva Adams gave a concert on May 15 at the Avenue Theater, assisted by well-known artists under the direction of W. T. Francis. She sang opera arias in four languages. Also on the program, Henry Wehrman Jr. made a hit in a violin solo.[144] The New Louisiana Jockey Club threw a promenade concert on May 17 from 6:00 to 11:00 p.m., "complimentary to the American Library Association" then meeting in the city.[145] The final public rehearsal of the Orphéon Français took place on May 31 at a hall on the corner of Royal and Orleans streets.[146] The orchestra of the society played Hasselmann's march, and the choir sang choruses from Gounod, Rupes, Lacombe, and Waldteuffel. In addition, there were solo songs and violin pieces by Ricci. Ricci was the musical director and Mr. M. Heichelheim the accompanist. The final concert of the season was on Saturday, June 1, 1889, at Grunewald Opera House. It was a grand instrumental and vocal concert tendered to Mrs. A. T. Vaurigaud by her pupils and assisted by the New Orleans Choral Society under the direction of Professor Ricci, with Mrs. Blache at the piano. Minerva Adams sang an aria; Eckert was also involved.[147]

By this time, the concerts at West End had begun. The official opening of the concert season there was on May 19. The West End Military Orchestra (band) was composed of selected artists and led by Maestro H. Lenfant of Paris.[148] "Mr. Victor Nippert, righthand man of Mr. Maugé of the French Opera House, hit upon the idea of forming a military orchestra, which would at least equal that of the lamented Mr. Sontag. Mr. Lenfant, the leader of the opera orchestra, was retained for the season here.... The band consists of thirty-five musicians, many of whom are excellent soloists." The most notable members of the band were Armand Veazy (cornet, a native of New Orleans), J. B. Meert (piccolo), and A. Doucet (oboe). This band probably was the one that played on June 4 for a promenade concert at the Southern Yacht Club.[149]

By the end of October, the regulars were back in town and the fall season was ready to begin. It started on October 24, 1889, at a gathering of the New Orleans Swiss Society at 79 Customhouse Street. Music and dramas were presented. The musicians were Mr. E. Brunner (piano), Mr. J. Corriveau (singer), Mrs. H. Ernst (singer), Mr. R. Hartmann (singer), Mrs. E. Malmquest (singer), the chorus of the Swiss Society, and a few others.[150] The first rehearsal by the Orphéon Français on Orleans and Royal streets took place on October 25. The Orpheon Orchestra performed an overture entitled *Promotion,* Henry Wehrman performed on the violin, and there were songs and choruses by the society.[151] Pilcher's Studio of Music, at 259 Carondelet Street, gave its first concert the same day as part of its fourth annual commencement. Mrs. William H. Pilcher (piano), William H. Pilcher (organist and pianist), and Professor Mark Kaiser (violin) also performed on what Pilcher noted was the forty-sixth recital at his place.[152] The memorial concert for Theodore Curant was held at the Grunewald Opera House on October 29, 1889.[153] Performers included Mr. Horace Peters, former student of Curant and recent graduate of the Leipzig Conservatory, Mrs. Samuel, Mrs. James Nott, Mark Kaiser, M. Rossi, and J. W. H. Eckert as accompanist. The program consisted of pieces by Mendelssohn, Beethoven (violin-piano-organ trio), Ernst, Bizet, Gounod, and others. Twelve hundred dollars after expenses was raised for the Curant family. On November 4 there was a grand concert and entertainment at the Union Français (North Rampart Street) by the Altar Chapter of Sainte Anna's Church.[154]

Kinzer reported that, sometime in the 1880s, before November 2, 1889, the Tio brothers helped form the Lyre Club, which in 1897 became the Lyre Club Symphony Orchestra.[155]

The French Opera season of 1889–90 opened on November 5, with, once again, *La Juive.* The choruses were enlarged, and they sang with good ensemble. "The women have not been beautified, some of the 'old times' still holding fast, but there is much improvement with the men. The orchestra, under the leadership of Monsieur Lenfant, did creditably," the *Picayune* reported.[156] Among the grand operas planned for the season were *Les Huguenots, La Juive, William Tell, Le Prophète, Aïda, Il Trovatore, La Favorite, L'Africaine, Ballo in Maschera, Moïse,*

La Muette de Portici, La Reine de Chypre, Les Vepres Siciliennes, Faust, Roméo et Juliette, Mignon, and *Carmen,* though only a few of these were actually performed. New Orleans premiers this season were *Le Roi d'Ys* (Lalo) and *Le Cid* (Massenet). By November 1, seats for the French Opera were auctioned off. After a week of rehearsals, Frederic Maugé found that not all the singers recruited in France were good enough, so a few new ones were recruited in a hurry from France. Ten days later, the citric of the *Picayune* wrote in a review of *La Favorite,* "The choruses, ballet and orchestra furnish no ground for complaint."[157]

At the performance of *Faust,* on November 23, an old custom at the French Opera was restored: during the intermission between the first and second acts, visiting from one box to another was permitted. However, "It is not designed for stockholders and managers to hold business meetings."[158] As for the performance itself, "The performance was somewhat smoother than that given last Saturday night [November 23] but likewise lacked brilliancy. The choruses, ballet and orchestra were, however, redeeming features and afforded the spectators some pleasure."[159] A rival opera company came to the city but did no better. On November 25 the Thompson Opera Company performed *Said Pasha* at the Grand Opera House; "The orchestra is still a little off; but it will come back and be sociable with the singers before the week is over," opined the *Picayune.*[160] Then in spring (February 26 to March 9), the Boston Ideal Opera Company performed at the Grand Opera House in direct competition to the French Opera. Their repertory, all in English, was impressive: *Rigoletto* (twice), *Faust* (twice), *Carmen* (thrice), *Il Trovatore, Lucia di Lammermoor, Norma,* and *Martha.*[161] The star of the company, Emma Romeldi, returning to the city after three years, scored a major triumph in the role of Norma.

November had some other musical events of importance. On November 6, 1889, the phonograph was introduced to New Orleans. The *Picayune* reported: "Messrs. Robinson & Underwood, the real estate agents, last evening entertained a large party of prominent gentlemen at their office, No. 164 Common street by affording them an opportunity of witnessing the working of the Edison phonograph, which invention these enterprising young business men desire to introduce in this market."[162] During the week beginning November 11, William J. Gilmore's *The Twelve Temptations,* a spectacular production from San Francisco and en route to New York, played in New Orleans with an "augmented orchestra."[163]

The Musicians' Guild of New Orleans reported, on November 17, that it had grown with many women, but men were invited, too.[164] The conservatory idea was too costly, so they were concentrating on developing local talent and taste by holding weekly meetings for the enjoyment of "perfect music works," concerted or solo, contributed by the members of the association under the superior direction of the musical leader, Mme Marguerite E. Samuel. They appreciated the assistance from Mr. Werlein, Mr. D. H. Holmes, and other prominent Orleanians.

During the next ten days, there was a variety of concerts. Pilcher's students gave their forty-eighth concert on November 20.[165] That same day, the Orphéon Français Orchestra, under the direction of Albert Heichelheim, volunteered its valuable services to a meeting of the Camera Club at Grunewald Opera House. They "opened the programme with a selection beautifully rendered." They sang songs, and "Mr. H. Wehrmann, a very clever young violinist, played a charming polonaise." Mr. C. W. Vogel played a violin obbligato, and Wehrman and Mr. George W. Weingart, accompanied by Mr. Paul Brunet, played a duet.[166] Not all the concerts featured European-type music. Thus, the Spanish-American Club, No. 144 Gravier Street, sponsored, on November 21, a concert of three Guatemalan Indians playing marimbas.[167] On Friday, November 29, at the Locquet-Leroy Institute, the King's Daughters provided literary and musical entertainment for the benefit of Soldiers' Home, Camp Nicholls. Among the various participants were Mrs. Nott and Mr. Dubuclet.[168] There was a private performance for the D. H. Holmes Literary Association on December 2 at the hall on Camp Street. Piano and vocal pieces were performed by amateurs, plus a comedy and recitations.[169] There was even a concert, on December 5, to benefit an athlete's widow, that of Professor Peynaud. It was given by members of various theaters including the French Opera House.[170]

As the decade drew to a close, the nature of the concerts continued as before. On December 6, 1889, there was an entertainment at Grunewald Hall for the benefit of the Unitarian Church on Saint Charles Avenue. There were songs and a piano sonata performed by Miss Crawford.[171] Gilmore's band returned to the city on December 8 and 9 and performed many arrangements of classical pieces by such composers as Mozart, Beethoven, Haydn, Wagner, Robert Schumann, Verdi, Gounod, Weber, and Liszt.[172] It also performed Schubert's *Unfinished* Symphony No. 8 in a band arrangement. The pupils of Jeanne Faure, vocal professor, gave a soiree musicale at Grunewald Hall on December 9. In addition to the vocal students, one student played a violin solo.[173] The Musicians' Guild decided it must go ahead with its benefit concert on December 11 despite the recent death of the former president of the Confederacy, Jefferson Davis.[174] The concert included members of the guild with the assistance of pupils of Mrs. Charles Boudousquié and Mr. H. Baeckley. They performed a Beethoven symphony on four pianos, songs, and a trio for piano, organ, and violin. Miss Ella Grunewald gave a piano selection by Liszt.

On Christmas Day, at High Mass at 10 a.m. at Saint Louis Cathedral, the choir performed Haydn's Mass No. 1 in B Flat, "Noël" by Adolphe Adam, "O Salutaris" by A. Lefebvre, and other pieces with soloists. The organist was Miss Bessie O'Cavanagh.[175] At the same time, at services at the Church of Our Lady of Good Counsel (Louisiana Avenue at Chestnut Street), the full choir and soloists (all amateurs) performed Haydn's Mass No. 3 in D, accompanied by a violin, and other pieces.[176] Mme J. F. Locquet's young pupils—both singers and instrumentalists—gave a recital on December 27 at her Prytania Street studio.[177] There was a grand sacred concert at Rayne Memorial Church on Saint Charles Avenue on Saturday, December 28, to raise money for the newly installed organ. J. W. H. Eckert was the organist.[178] Finally, on December 29, 30, and 31, 1889, the Boston Symphony Orchestral Club, some of whose members "were either former soloists of the Theodore Thomas Orchestra of New York, or the Boston Symphony Orchestra, or of Gilmore's Band," returned to New Orleans for three concerts. They performed works by Hoffmann, Verdi, Paganini, Mozart, Stoelzer, Langey, Brahms, Gernsheim, Lax, Gounod, De Seve, Langey, Popper, Arthur Foote, Sarasate, Braga, Krahl, and Rossini.[179]

At the beginning of 1890, the well-known composer William Taylor Francis, who had lived in New Orleans and was now back visiting the city, expressed his view on how music in New Orleans differed from music in Boston. In Boston "everything runs to classical music . . . oratorios, sonatas and pieces which are marked by skillful harmonic work and by superb orchestration. In New Orleans the most popular music is that which is marked by melody. As a result, every new song and dance which appears in Paris, Madrid, Florence, Vienna or Berlin appears in the latter city anywhere from six months to two years before it is heard in the Athens of America [Boston]."[180] "Spanish music" (by which Francis means, probably, music of the Spanish Caribbean as well as of Spain) was heard in New Orleans but was barely known in New York. Music was a necessity in the South, and therefore the financial rewards were not so great; music was a luxury in the North and therefore the financial rewards were much greater. Eventually the North, in his prescient view, would catch on to the music of the South and take over from the South its hegemony in lyrical music. Within twenty years, Francis was proven right.

On January 6, 1890, there was a major concert at the French Opera House. Marguerite Samuel, Mark Kaiser, Mr. A. Guillé, tenor of the French Opera, and others performed at a Philharmonic Concert to benefit the Home of the

Convalescents with the "enlarged Opera House Orchestra under the leadership of Sig. Julius A. Bona of Her Majesty's Opera, London." Bona was just visiting in New Orleans and was persuaded to lead the concert as a guest conductor. Samuel played Liszt's Hungarian Fantasy and two solo encores without the orchestra, and Guillé sang arias by Ponchielli and Flotow.[181]

Pilcher's students gave their fifty-third studio recital on Friday, January 10, 1890.[182] In line with its aim to educate New Orleanians in the great European musical tradition, the Musicians' Guild of New Orleans presented the distinguished Professor Louis C. Elson, of the New England Conservatory, on January 15, 1890, in the first of four lectures at the French Opera House on the genealogy of music.[183] The guild then followed on February 1 with its first annual meeting, where they elected Samuel officially "Musical Director."[184] Ovide Musin made his debut in a grand concert at the French Opera House with full orchestra on January 24. As the *Picayune* reported, "Mr. Ovide Musin, the violinist, was the feature of the evening. He played a caprice de concert of his own composition with much taste and finish. His execution was not only skillful, he played with profound feeling and caused his instrument to sing. In Wagner's 'Meistersinger,' Musin's 'Mazurka de Concert' and the 'Prière de Moïse' and 'Variations de Bravoure' as played by Paganini and executed on one string, he showed himself master of his violin. He received an ovation."[185] The orchestra played the Overture to *Le Roi d'Ys* and an orchestral selection from *La Muette de Portici*. Baritone Clemento Bologna and soprano Annie Louise Tanner (soon to become Mrs. Musin) sang arias by Verdi and Mozart, and pianist Edward Scharf played a *"mazourka"* by Godard and a *regaudon* by Raff.

The highlight of February 1890, was the national *Sängerfest* convention in New Orleans. This was the national umbrella organization to which several German musical groups in the city belonged. The *Deutscher Maenner Gesangeverein*, organized sixteen years earlier, was the oldest German singing society of New Orleans. Seven years after that came the New Orleans Quartette Club, whose president was J. Hanno Deiler. Back in March 1889, when the local German societies agreed to host the *Sängerfest,* Professor Deiler was put in charge of concerts.[186] They put on six of them during the convention—evening and matinee, all at the Saenger Halle (Saint Charles Avenue, near Howard Avenue), of which the first was on February 12, the second and third on February 13, the fourth and fifth on February 14, and the final, sixth, on February 15.[187] The programs included orchestral, choral, solo instrumental, and solo vocal music. Pieces on the first matinee (Thursday, February 13) were orchestral works by Wagner, Handel, Robert Schumann, A. Rubinstein, and songs by Brahms, C. J. Brambach, Spicker, Rossini, Alb. Dietrich, Méhul, Liebe, Wagner, and Bruch. That same evening the orchestra performed Beethoven's *Leonore* Overture No. 3 and the Symphony No. 5, and Liszt's Hungarian Rhapsody in C Minor No. 2. The next afternoon the program consisted of Weber's *Oberon* Overture, Schubert's *Unfinished* Symphony No. 8, Wagner's *Ride of the Valkyries* and Overture from *Rienzi,* Moszkowski's *Airs from Other Lands,* and Haydn's Symphony in G Major No. 6. There were also choruses and arias by Taubert, Alberto Sartori, Mozart, Wagner, Sachs, Saint-Saëns, Franz, Haertel, Gluck, Goldmark, Gounod, Kreutzer, Abt, and others. The last program (February 15) consisted of J. C. Bach's *Jubilee* Overture, Goldmark's Overture to *Sakuntala,* Hugo Kaun's symphonic poem *Vineta,* and additional orchestral selections from Berlioz's *Damnation de Faust,* with vocal music by Haydn, Arditi, Kogel, Weber, and Mozart. Samuel played Liszt's Hungarian Fantasy. This is one of the rare occasions when Berlioz's music was performed in New Orleans—a strange fact given the importance of Berlioz to French music during much of the nineteenth century.

There were other concerts in February. On February 3, 1890, members of the French Opera performed a charity soiree as an intermède to benefit Saint Vincent de Paul.[188] The New Orleans Choral Society gave its first complimentary vocal and instrumental concert at Grunewald Hall on Friday the sixth.[189] The next day there was a benefit concert at Grunewald Hall for George L. O'Connell. In two parts, the program consisted of the West End Orchestra directed by Lenfant, with several different choral groups (including a children's chorus), the orchestra and chorus of the Orphéon Français, Gustave Joubert, and others. There were some piano pieces, some songs, and other works.[190] On February 10 there was a conférence-concert-bal at the French Union Hall. Poetry and prose readings were intermingled with piano works and songs, a fantasia for oboe, and some other pieces.[191]

A week after Mardi Gras, which in 1890 fell on February 18, Ovide Musin gave another concert. He played the Mendelssohn Violin Concerto, and the orchestra performed several symphonies.[192] Three weeks later (March 18–21) he performed recitals with his entourage at Grunewald Hall (March 18 and 20), in Baton Rouge (March 19) and in Mobile (March 21). On March 18 Samuel joined Musin in the Beethoven Sonata in C Minor for piano and violin.[193] Also on this program were works by Kermesse, Saint-Saëns, Wagner, Wieniawski, and Mozart (an aria from *The Abduction from the Seraglio*). The program on March 20 included works by Liszt, Verdi, Felicien David, Gounod, Ferdinand Ries, Chopin, Raff, Johann Strauss, and Musin himself. On March 2, the entire personnel of artists and chorus of the French Opera and the full orchestra, under

Mr. Lenfant, gave a grand sacred concert which featured the premiere of *Harmonies de la Nature* by Hubert Rolling. They also performed Rossini's *Stabat Mater* and concluded with three acts of Verdi's *Jérusalem*.[194] The same performers repeated Rolling's piece on Saturday, March 8, and this time preceded it with a complete *La Traviata* and followed it with the Overture to *Le Roi d'Ys*, and a ballet.[195] Mme Dauriac and M Furst gave a soiree at the Opera House on March 4. They performed three acts of *Le Pre aux Clercs*, the second act of *Aïda*, an air from *Der Freischütz*, and the Ballet from *Le Cid*.[196]

The French Opera season was supposed to end on March 8 but was extended to March 11. This season stood out for the rancor which the audience held toward the establishment, despite the presence of excellent singers. Many singers left for other companies in other cities, and even members of the orchestra left New Orleans for New York and Europe. After eight months of stagnation, the audiences demanded new management.[197]

But concert life continued. On Monday, March 10, 1890, Miss Lena Little, who made a hit during the *Sängerfest*, gave a free concert at Grunewald Hall, and on April 10 she gave her farewell concert.[198] Mrs. James Nott and her pupils (all young girls) gave a concert at her home on Saturday, March 15. They all wanted to remain anonymous in *L'Abeille*'s review, but Canonge found he could not review anonymous performers, so—breaking with long-standing tradition—he gave all their names and what they played.[199] Mme Charles Boudousquié's voice pupils gave a concert for charity on March 22 at Grunewald Hall. She selected only those students who showed real promise.[200] On March 28, the Orphéon Français circle, under the direction of O'Connell, presented a concert by twenty students, accompanied by O'Connell and Paul Brunet.[201]

At the French Opera House there was a pair of vocal and instrumental concerts by amateurs of the city, on April 7 and 8, to benefit Saint Louis Cathedral. They performed works by Schlepegreli, Enfanta, Meyerbeer (March from *Le Prophète*), Fauré, Massenet, and Victor Massé. The Orpheon Orchestra performed on both occasions; on April 8 they were assisted by Kaiser and the singer Mme E. Lejeune.[202] There was a benefit at Grunewald Hall on Sunday, April 13, 1890, for Mme E. Breaud, whose illness had now deprived her of her only livelihood: teaching music. Participating were such important artists as Mme Julia Dargy, whose own benefit closed out the opera season; other singers; violinist Georges Weingart; and violoncellist Grisai of the French Opera. Two works were played by the French Opera Orchestra under the direction of O'Connell, and two choruses were performed by the Société Chorale of New Orleans. Eckert donated the piano for the occasion.[203] The pupils of Mlle Marie Roubion held a soiree musicale in Grunewald Hall on April 21,[204] and two days later, on April 23, Mme E. Lejeune, vocalist, gave her vocal and instrumental concert at the same hall. The latter was assisted by Grisai, Kaiser, several vocalists, and Eckert at the piano.[205] Mlle Santini gave a complimentary concert at Mme Gauthier's salons, 265 Dauphine Street, on April 26.[206] There was a benefit concert for Mlle Hortense Carver on April 30, at Grunewald Opera House. Performers included Mlles Varelli-Jauquet, Woulf, S. Mueller, and Eva Rochi; MM Grisai, Kaiser, Durel, and J. W. H. Eckert. Carver was a pupil of Varelli-Jauquet.[207]

Student recitals continued to be a feature of the end of the season. The pupils of both Rollings, of Mme Devrient, Mlle Leonie de Varenne, and of Mlle Louise Mahé got extensive reviews in the newspapers. Programs, in which music was part but not the main event, continued. There were more substantial concerts by J. W. H. Eckert on May 14, 1890, in New Iberia's elegant opera house, and on May 21 at Grunewald Hall. A sextet was performed on both occasions; it was comprised of Eckert (piano), Mme Pauline Blache (soprano), M Houmane (baritone), Armand Veazey (cornet), M Pomero (first violinist of the New Orleans Opera Orchestra) and Grisai (first violoncellist of the same theatre orchestra). This six-person ensemble visited other Louisiana cities, beginning next with Lafayette.[208] On May 15 the Orphéon Français gave an orchestral, choral, solo instrumental, and vocal concert, and on May 27, the Orphéon Français Orchestra, conducted by George O'Connell, participated in another tribute to Eckert.[209] This program included chamber music played by Kaiser, Wehrman, Armand Veasey, and Grisai. There was a concert on May 23 at Washington Artillery Hall by many amateurs and artists, including Mlles H. Seibeck, Picard, and Aron, MM Grisai and Veazey, Mme Pauline Blache (singing something from *Carmen*), and other performances. The concert was presented by Batterie B of the Louisiana Light Artillery.[210]

By May 7, 1890, concerts were being held again at West End. On this date, O'Connell brought the Orphéon Français, the Choral Society of New Orleans, the New Orleans Quartette Club, and various church choirs to the lake for a soiree complimentaire, assisted by the new orchestra of West End directed by Lenfant and managed by Victor Nippert. The vocal soloist was Mme F. Bourgeois, a pupil of Curto.[211] Lenfant directed a military orchestral concert at West End on May 11 and repeated the program for the official opening on May 18.[212] The orchestra (band) consisted of five cornets á piston, two flutes, one oboe, one small clarinet and ten large clarinets, two saxophones (alto and soprano), two bassoons, four horns, two baritones, three trombones, three basses, one contrabass, one timalier and xylophone, and two drums (one a bass drum). Most of the musicians came from the French Opera Orchestra. For the concert on May 24, the program included W. T. Francis's *Trades Assembly March, Colombe* by Gounod, *La Valse Je T'Aime* by Waldteufel, Fantasie on *La Fille du Tambour Major*, the Overture to Verdi's *Nabucco, Reminiscences* by Meyerbeer, a solo saxophone piece by Vizcarra, a polka for two cornets played by Clayette and Wangler, and a grand *Marche-Polka* by Chassaigne.[213] On June 1, the program was different, including, besides the above pieces, works by Suppé, E. Bach (probably C. P. E. Bach), Stradella, Liszt, and an otherwise unknown bit of racially insulting music: *Negromania, Pay Day on the Plantation* by Puerner.[214] The musicians at West End had so far outstripped those at Spanish Fort and Milneburg that, whereas there are frequent reviews in the newspapers of the first, the other two are basically ignored. The last few concerts included, as soloists, Grisai (September 3) and Clayette and Barro on cornet and trombone (September 6). The season ended on September 7.[215]

The fall 1890 season opened early, on September 8, with the young Eddie Moore, a prodigy on the piano, performing at the Saint Charles Theatre. His program included works by Gottschalk and "Home Sweet Home."[216] Then there was a hiatus until Thursday, October 23, when Werlein sponsored a chamber concert by the New Orleans Musical Society in memory of Franz Liszt, who had died four years earlier.[217] The next day, the Orphéon Français performed at their headquarters, on the corner of Orleans Street at Royal Street.[218] On Saturday, November 8, Le Société Musicale (Conservatoire de Musique de la Nouvelle-Orléans) offered its second concert at Werlein's store, 135 Canal Street. The musical director was Emile Malmquist.[219] The Musicians' Guild gave a concert on Wednesday, November 26, at Werlein's,[220] and Carrie Baumann returned for another grand vocal and orchestral concert at Grunewald Hall on December 17.[221] There was a special requiem mass at Saint Louis Cathedral on December 8 for Mme Placide Canonge, who died on December 7, 1885.[222] Her husband, a former director of the French Opera, was the outspoken critic for *L'Abeille* often cited here. On December 19, 1890, there was an entertainment by the Sainte Cecilia Circle at Saint Michael's Hall, including recitations, tableaux, and music. Mr. and Mrs. Eckert played a piano duet, Misses M. and V. Gauche played another piano duet, and Mr. Berthe Dee sang.[223]

Before the French Opera had a chance to open, the Académie de Musique gave the New Orleans premiere, on Sunday, October 26, of the operetta comique *Gondoliers* by Gilbert and Sullivan.[224] The piece was well received, though the critic of the *Picayune* was not ready to commit full endorsement of an as-yet-unknown score. As for the French Opera in New Orleans, New Orleanians regarded it as second only to the opera in Paris.[225] That did not always mean unqualified support for the local performers, as in the following review of *William Tell* on November 24, 1890.

> We come now to *William Tell* and once again we compliment the artists of the orchestra. Yes, they seem to me to play this overture with love; the spirit was everywhere, and M Lenfant did not have to do more than move his bow across the measures and the diverse movements all were successful.
>
> Let us say too that, in certain parts, the chorus sang with real ensemble and brought out the details and the nuances of the piece.[226]

While the orchestra, chorus, and conductor did admirably, the solo voices did not do so. One more operetta group came to the city before the end of the year. On December 21, 1890, the Heinrich Conreid Troupe performed *The Gypsy Baron* at the Grand Opera House. Other buffa operas followed on subsequent days. The Conreid Troupe had already performed in New York, Saint Louis, Boston, and Pittsburg.[227]

As usual, there were student recitals with faculty participating. Pilcher had a recital at his studio on December 8, Mlle Jeanne Faure gave her annual students' recital at Grunewald Hall on December 15, and the Guillot Institute had its annual scholars' festival at Grunewald Hall on December 23.

Sometime around 1890, Marguerite Samuel helped form a chamber music society in New Orleans. It was reported "that among the musicians who will take part in these recitals is Mr. Marks [sic] Kaiser, whose talent as a musician and a violinist is recognized here as foremost. Mrs. Samuel could not have secured a better auxiliary, for his German nature has inclined him to the study of the sort of music, which he knows well and plays with all the ardor of a lover and the correctness of a scientist."[228] At about the same time, Kaiser helped organize the New Symphony Quartette, with the purpose of performing all season. Its members were Kaiser and Wehrman, violins; Grisai, violoncello; and Emile Malmquist, viola. It gave its initial concert, informally, at Mark Kaiser's home on Saint Charles Avenue, and performed Beethoven's Opus 18, no. 4; Carl Schuberth's Opus 34; and a few other works.[229]

On January 15, 1891, at a Musicians' Guild Meeting, Kaiser and Ms. Blanche McGraw performed Beethoven's *Kreutzer* Sonata. The *Times-Democrat* reported, "The interest of the audience, which had been worked up to the highest point, reached its climax as the remarkable 'Kreutzer Sonata' progressed. From the first chord struck the most profound attention reigned throughout the large assembly, and this was kept up with breathless attention to the end. Not less remarkable was the enthusiasm manifested by the performers themselves. Miss Blanche McGraw and Mr. Marks [sic] Kaiser from the opening to the close of this arduous effort showed no sign of fatigue nor faltered throughout." The program included some songs and the first movement of Beethoven's Symphony No. 3 performed by five pianists. A lecture by Professor Weiss explained the symphony to the audience.[230] The next regular concert by the Musicians' Guild was not held until Wednesday, May 13, at 133 Canal Street, its home locale.[231]

The Orphéon Français presented a grand vocal and instrumental concert at Grunewald Hall on Friday, January 23, 1891, and later, on April 11, they held their concert and ball at the same place. On this latter occasion, both the orchestra and chorus performed works by Schubert and Bizet, among others. Charles Maillet was violin soloist, and there were some vocal solos as well.[232] Ovide Musin, with a visiting troupe (Mme Annie Louise Tanner [Mrs. Musin, soprano], M Edward Scharf [piano], Mme Inez Parmater, and M Karl Storr), returned for three concerts on February 13–15 at Grunewald Hall. On the second concert, Marguerite Samuel once again joined Musin in Beethoven's *Kreutzer* Sonata. On the fifteenth, a matinee, Musin and Eduard Scharf played the Rubinstein Sonata for piano and violin in G Major, Musin's own *Caprice,* and the Wilhelmj/Wagner Prelude from *Die Meistersinger.*[233] Helena Augustin, Samuel's star pupil who had just returned from two-years' study in Europe, gave her inaugural recital at Grunewald Hall on February 16. It was a vocal and instrumental concert offered to Augustin by the women of New Orleans. Assisting her were Mlles Martini, Varelli-Jauquet, and Mark Kaiser. Canonge noted that Augustin had acquired a German style because she studied in Germany; she had already acquired the French style from Marguerite Samuel.[234] Tenor Berger gave a benefit the same evening at the Opera House, but it was poorly attended because of the competing concert by Helena Augustin. This was deemed by the critic as unfair to Berger, who was a great tenor.[235]

The opera season closed early, on February 17, 1891. In what had become a routine situation, it had been an artistic but not especially a financial success. The régisseur, Seguier, was often attacked, so he decided to leave; a benefit was held in his honor on February 26 with soloists from the French Opera accompanied by Mme Meffre, official piano accompanist of the French Opera. On Sunday, March 1, a farewell concert was given by artists of the French Opera to benefit themselves. The season had been very short because of financial troubles, and the artists needed money so they could leave New Orleans.[236]

Marguerite Martini gave an instrumental and vocal concert on Monday, March 9, at Grunewald Hall. She was assisted by Marguerite Samuel, Mlles Jeanne Bermudez, Ella Sinnott, Bessie Rowan-Brunson, M Monna (violoncello), and Mme Meffre (piano accompanist).[237] The Musical Society of New Orleans, together with the Conservatoire de Musique under M Emile Malmquist, presented a new concert at 8:00 p.m. on March 10 at Werlein Hall.[238] Ten days later the Mendelssohn Quintette Club of Boston, sponsored by Frohsinn, gave a concert at Grunewald Hall.[239] Frohsinn had its own soiree musicale, littéraire, et dramatique at Grunewald Hall on April 5.[240] Meanwhile, there was a concert on April 3, 1891, at Grunewald Hall, offered by friends to the young Henry Wehrman, violinist and composer.[241] Sometime prior to April 5, three soirees, including young men and women in tableaux and in concert, were performed at the French Opera House to benefit Saint Louis Cathedral.[242]

Another new musical society was organized on April 7, 1891, at the home of Mme J. Mailhas, corner of Royal and Saint Louis streets. Called *La Lyre d'Orphée,* it was composed exclusively of young women and girls. This group was a choral group that would sing only in French.[243] Its first concert was not until the following October 28. (See book I, part I, chapter 3 for more information on this society.)

On April 10, Mlle Florence Huberwald, the young singer already applauded in New Orleans in the late 1880s, gave an audition to the press from 8:00 a.m. to 4:00 p.m. at Grunewald Hall to prepare the critics for her upcoming grand concert at the Hall on April 22. She had studied in Paris since she had last appeared in the city, and she wanted the people of New Orleans to know of her progress as a singer. For her appearance on the twenty-second, she was assisted by Mlle M. Santini, Mme William Evans, Grisai, and Maumus.[244] There were other concerts as well. On Saturday and Sunday, April 11–12, at the Audubon Park Festival, Herr S. B. Vogel conducted the Audubon Park Orchestra, which was made up of dilettantes.[245] Curto's pupil Carrie Baumann sang a few pieces at a grand orchestral concert on April 15 conducted by Sig. Bona at the French Opera House.[246] When the American Pharmaceutical Association held its annual meeting in New Orleans on April 27 and 28, two concerts were included. On April 27 there was a concert-promenade at Washington Artillery Hall, and on April 28 there was a vocal and instrumental concert at Grunewald Hall.[247] A month later, on May 26, the new group Mi-Sol-Ut performed at Werlein Hall. It was a musical circle composed of young girls under the direction of their professor, Mme D. Delcroix, widow of the well-known eminent musician Desiré

Delcroix. The girls performed works by Rossini, Decouvielles, Garia, Holtz, Fauré, Wallace, Czerny, and Hérold. They were assisted by Henry Wehrman (who played his own gavotte) and P. Brunet.[248]

A month after that, on Thursday, June 18, two male singers, Monna and Rossi, who had been faithful members of the French Opera since 1873, gave a vocal and instrumental concert at Grunewald Hall. They sang works by Adam, Granier, Alard, Gounod, Mendelssohn, Mattei, Léo Delibes, Verdi, and Porte. They were assisted by Salomon, Mlle Hermaize, H. Wehrman, Maumus, Ida Kaiser, Mme Witham, M Viavant, Samuel, Mme E. Lejeune, and Mme Werth. O'Connell and J. W. H. Eckert were piano accompanists.[249]

Once again, the season was peppered with student recitals, often with the teachers participating. On February 18, 1891, Marguerite Samuel and her best pupils gave their annual concert. A month later, on March 5, Mlle Jeanne Faure and her pupils, with the assistance of Samuel, Heinrich Kraus (violoncellist), Joseph Durel (baritone), and the Choral Society of the New Orleans [Frohsinn] under Professor C. Weiss, gave their grand benefit at Grunewald Hall. The program consisted of De Bériot, Shelly, Brahms, Raff, Schubert, Gounod, and others. A recital by nine pupils of Mme Charles Boudousquié, whose voices were "musical, full of sympathy, taste and style," took place on Sunday, April 12. On April 15 came the turn of the pupils of Mrs. T. Russell in voice and piano.

A grand benefit for the Foundes de Secours de l'Association de Bienfaisance des Professeurs took place on April 24–25 at the Grand Opera House. It included violin solos by the pupils at McDonough 17 School and vocal solos by Mrs. Warren Easton. The pupils of Mme Lafosse, piano professor, assisted by some pupils of Mme Boudousquié, gave their soiree musicale on April 25 at the Picard and Markey Institute. On April 26, the pupils of Mlle Marie Roubion, assisted by her sister, Marguerite Roubion, gave a recital at Grunewald Hall; tableaux were mixed with the musical program. A dance followed the concert. The pupils of Mme Devrient and artist friends held a soiree musicale on May 7 at Werlein Hall. They were assisted by Minnie Eckert, Emile Malmquist, Henry Wehrman, Pauline Blache, Helene Wright, Henrietta Selleck, Stella Levy, Belle Picard, and Marie Adams. Mme Devrient played the piano. On May 28, the pupils of Pauline Blache joined the Chorale Society of New Orleans at Werlein's Salons for a concert. The instrumental portions were performed by J. W. H. Eckert, who played his own work on the piano-harpe; George Weingart played the violoncello. On Wednesday, June 10, 1891, Mlle Louise Mahé and her pupils held their recital. A young, fiery teacher, Mahé organized a long program that seemed short. Finally, at the end of the summer, on August 29, Misses Mollie F. Reames and Henrietta Heichelheim performed at a pupil's recital at the Pilcher Studio.

The planned summer programs at West End for 1891 caused a furor. The sixty-piece Mexican band under Encarnacion Payen, which was so popular during the Cotton Exposition, was hired to play for the summer of 1891 at West End.[250] This was arranged by the New Orleans City and Lake Railroad Company, which was now sponsoring the series. The railroad earned a lot of money by transporting people from Canal Street (downtown) to the lake, and everything at West End and en route from Claiborne Avenue was decorated to make people want to travel by this railroad. The brilliant Mexicans were sure to draw a large crowd from the city, especially those who might have tired of the same musicians year after year in what had become Lenfant and his West End Orchestra. Indeed, as many as twenty-five thousand persons now came on a single evening, and the crowds gathering on the neutral ground on Canal Street, three or four hours before the train left for West End, was proof enough of the popularity of the Mexicans. Even the weather cooperated, initially at least.

A few prominent citizens (including W. N. Grunewald, Isidore Newman, Louis V. Eckert, Marguerite Samuel, and Mark Kaiser) did complain about the repertory, that it should contain more operatic music and more Mexican works, but the overwhelming majority of citizens were very happy with the Mexicans as they were.[251] Payon, however, did listen and changed his repertory slightly to accommodate the "prominent citizens."[252] The real problem, however, was that, by hiring foreign musicians, New Orleans musicians would not be employed. At first, the railroad said the Mexicans would play for only two weeks, but since the money was coming in so fast, they stayed the entire summer. Yet, the audiences at the lake the previous two seasons had been sizeable enough, the railroad had made a handsome profit then, and, most crucially, New Orleans musicians had a summer income. Without summer employment locally, New Orleans stood to lose a considerable number of its best instrumentalists, especially wind players. It was too late for 1891, but in the future the railroad—having learned that its greed ultimately harmed the musical life of the city—hired local musicians to do the job.

The Mexicans ended their stay on August 2, and on August 3 the Great Southern Military Band under Paoletti, a native New Orleanian, replaced the Mexicans at West End.[253] They played nightly and drew a good and appreciative audience. The point was that now local musicians were eking out a living while staying in New Orleans. The Great Southern Military Band performed operatic and popular selections which appealed not only to the general public but also to "prominent citizens."[254] For example, on August 6 the band under Paoletti, whose late father had been an orchestral leader, too, performed music by Waldteufel, Vivière, Planquette, Rossini (*Sémiramide*), Halévy, Verdi, Victor Einhorn, Godfrey, J. B. Claus, and Eilenberg.[255] The band finished its concerts at West End on September 6, 1891, so that Paoletti and his musicians could shift to their regular jobs with the orchestra of the Grand Opera House, which Paoletti and Nippert organized. Paoletti and the theater were happy that the thirty-eight to forty instrumental members had returned, despite not having jobs during the summer at West End because of the Mexican band (except for a few weeks during August).[256] The Mexicans, in turn, came back to New Orleans in the fall for a single, final concert. On November 11 they played at Grunewall Hall to benefit Sainte Mary's Catholic School in Carrollton.[257]

There were two concerts at West End during the summer that had nothing to do with the Mexican band. On July 9 there was a spectacle concert at Lake View Park (at West End) to benefit Mme Meffre, pianist of the French Opera. Economic life for many such persons was difficult, and she was therefore assisted by various singers also in serious straits.[258] At the same Lake View Park, Frohsinn held a dramatic, musical, and literary performance on August 5.[259]

Meanwhile, there were a few events at Spanish Fort. On Sunday, July 26, the Ramblers' Club sponsored a concert-promenade and ball there. Each person who assisted at the concert had a chance to win a lottery.[260] At the end of the summer, on September 27, the Red Men's Brass Band performed at Spanish Fort.[261] On the other side of the Lake, Mme Corinne (Mrs. James) Nott, together with other artists and amateurs, performed a vocal and instrumental concert sometime in August in Covington.[262]

The fall 1891 concert season began slowly, with only a minor intermède on September 18 at the Saint Charles Theatre. At the same time, during a benefit for the Newsboys' Home, featuring a comedy performed by capable amateurs, several songs and a duet were added.[263] On October 5, the Woman's Club took formal possession of their new quarters in the building formerly known as the Loquet-Leroy Institute on Camp Street. At the ceremony, "some delightful music [was] performed by members of the club. Miss Eugénie Points sang and Miss Delphine Points played a violin obligato."[264] Pilcher, never still very long, had his first fall recital on October 10 and followed it with another on October 29. His sister-in-law, Mrs. Charles H. Pilcher, who taught at her residence, had her fifth musical review on November 30 at the residence of Mrs. D. Edwards, 404 Saint Andrew Street.

A sacred music concert was held on October 17 at the Memorial Church, corner of Euterpe and Franklin streets. The performers were mostly young persons of the church singing, reciting, and playing violin and piano solos and a piano duet.[265] Also on Friday, October 17, Herr Josef Heine and his company of musicians performed at the Peoples Theatre. A native German, Heine played several violin works; Mrs. Heine, a pupil of Liszt, played a work by Liszt; and Miss Evelyn Heine sang. During the entr'actes the theater orchestra, under Signor Bona, gave the New Orleans premier of the Intermezzo from *Cavalleria Rusticana*. They were assisted by other musicians as well.[266] On October 28, there was a house concert at the home of Mrs. Moore, 188 Race Street, to benefit the orphans of Mount Carmel. Music and recitations alternated. Mr. Vivant played a piano solo, and Mrs. Nott sang a solo, accompanied by Madame Locquet.[267] La Lyre d'Orphée, the new musical society composed exclusively of young women, gave a soiree musicale at the French Union on October 28.[268]

There was a concert by "prominent artists" at Sainte Anna's Hall (186 Esplanade Avenue between Tremé and Marais streets) on Tuesday, November 10, 1891.[269] While minstrels technically performed concerts, often with magnificent bands and orchestras, as in the case of the Barlow Brothers at Peoples Theatre on November 15, their repertory was rarely "classical."[270] On the other hand, entertainments at church usually did include the concert repertory. Typical is the high tea on November 20 to benefit Trinity Church, under the auspices of the Woman's Guild, in the basement of Trinity Church. It was a concert with a violin solo (Master M. Hart, accompanied by Miss Shriever), a select reading, a piano solo (Mrs. Eckert), a violin duet (Mrs. Wehrman and Master Garmand), a soprano solo (Mrs. A. Roach), a baritone solo (Mr. J. O'Reardon), another piano solo (Miss Shriever), a tenor solo (Mr. C. Van Benthuysen), a vocal duet (Mrs. Roach and Mrs. Buckley), a mandolin solo (Henry Wehrman), and a piece by the orchestra.[271] There was a dramatic entertainment on November 21 at Saints Peter and Paul's Hall on Marigny Street for the relief fund of the Ladies' Benevolent Association. The music performed was Mendelssohn's *Rondo Capricioso* (Miss M. Molony), a vocal solo (Mr. Geo. W. Medus), an instrumental duet (James Carreas and Henry Wehrman), a comic song (Mr. H. J. Smith), jigs and reels for Irish pipes, a mandolin gavotte (Wehrman), and banjo pieces (Mr. Medus).[272] The Liederkreis Singing Society of the Fourth District held a soiree on November 25 at Sainte Mary's Hall (corner of Constance and Jackson streets). Interspersed with some plays, the chorus sang, and there were some banjo pieces.[273]

On December 2, 1891, there was a concert of sacred music in the German Protestant Church of the Fourth District, by the organist of the church, Joseph Engel, and members of the Young People's Aid Association. They performed choruses and vocal solos; a trio for soprano, violoncello, and violin (Misses E. Kostmeyer and L. Vahlmann and MM Schrenk and Grabau); and a cornet solo (Mr. Stumpf).[274] The international classical music world was commemorating the hundredth anniversary of the death of Mozart, but New Orleans had only a big article on Mozart in the *Picayune,* an intended performance by the New Orleans Quartette Club, and a recital of Mozart's works by the pupils of Pilcher's Studio of Music on December 5.[275] The Elite Parlor Orchestra was formed at the beginning of December, with O'Connell as leader and Henry Wehrman as assistant leader.[276] The Young Ladies and Gentlemen's Aid Association of the Fourth District gave a complimentary soiree on Thursday, December 10.[277]

Meanwhile, the French Opera season opened, as often before, with *La Juive,* on Saturday, October 31, 1891. The critics noted that what made this company strong was the orchestra and the chorus, which gave them hope for a successful season.[278] When a performance of *William Tell* was deemed weak on November 26, what carried the evening was the celebrated overture performed to perfection, and the choruses, showing careful training, divided honors with the orchestra.[279] The same held true two nights later in a performance of Meyerbeer's *Les Huguenots* and in December for *Faust.*[280] Both the Saint Charles Theatre and the Grand Opera House attempted to compete with the French Opera at the beginning of November. The former featured the William J. Gilmore Opera Company in opéra comiques, with an orchestra of eighteen, and the latter presented the Conried Opera Company, which combined the house orchestra with the traveling one, all under the direction of Maurice Gould.[281]

The concerts in December continued with a grand vocal and instrumental concert at Saint Michael's Hall on the eleventh to benefit the church. Performers included Johnnie Carroll, George McQueen, Willie Norton, Ed McCarthy, J. Keiffer, Master James McGowen (piano), J. Roan, Frank Porter, Thomas A. Haggerty, and the La Vine brothers (gymnasts).[282] At the same time there was a literary and musical entertainment for the benefit of Memorial Presbyterian Church by the Young People's Society of Christian Endeavor. The program started with a piece played on a phonograph (which at the time no doubt preempted everything else), and continued with a piano solo (Miss C. Hayen), songs, piano duets (MM Tudury and Voges), a violin solo (E. Gainard), another piano solo (this one by Miss A. Helkelheimer), and so forth.[283] Another musical and literary entertainment, now under auspices of the Ladies' Auxiliary of the

Spiritualistic Association at 59 Camp Street, was held on December 17.[284] Much more substantial was the musical matinee on December 19 by Miss Grace A. Kellogg, pianist, at the Woman's Club Rooms, 280 Camp Street. The program consisted of Hungarian Rhapsody No. 12 (Liszt); *Scherzo in B Flat* (Chopin); *Marche d'Nuit* (Gottschalk), *Pathétique* Sonata, Opus 13 (Beethoven); *L'Adieu* (Manning), and *Caprice,* Opus 91 (Raff).[285]

On December 21 the Seamen's Bethel, under management of Captain Amey and the other officers of the steamer *Cyrene,* presented a concert with Mrs. Mellune, Misses Fischer and Peillaler, and MM Sirby, Caruthers, Telemadon, and Medus in solo and choral selections.[286] Over the next few years the concerts at the Seamen's Bethel were regular features of the concert life of the city, although the level of performance was never at the highest. The Home Institute gave a Christmas concert at Grunewald Opera House on Tuesday, December 22. There was an instrumental trio (Misses A. Oden, D. Richardson, and R. Michaelis), piano solos by Miss R. Michaelis and Miss A. Oden, and other pieces.[287] Finally performers from the French Opera, the best church choirs, and some excellent instrumental soloists gave a grand vocal and instrumental concert at Saint Alphonse's Hall on December 30 to benefit the French Church of Notre Dame de Bon Secours.[288]

January 1892 had a plethora of concert and opera activities. January 1 began with an amateur concert at the Y.M.C.A. by its Ladies Auxiliary. Some three hundred guests heard several instrumental and vocal performances by the young women.[289] They gave a second performance on February 12. Meanwhile, a literary and musical entertainment at the same venue on January 4 was by serious local professionals: Mrs. Ida Riemann-Kaiser, Cesar Grisai, Mark Kaiser, and others.[290] On January 8, at Grunewald Opera House, the Boston Symphony Orchestral Club performed two movements from Haydn's Symphony in G Minor (No. 39 or 83), a flute solo, works by Bach and Bizet (orchestra), two violoncello solos, excerpts for orchestra by Delibes and Mascagni, a De Bériot violin solo, a Brahms Hungarian Dance, and vocal pieces.[291] On or about January 14 there was a fund-raiser for the Saint Vincent de Paul's School, in which Charles Dirmeyer, Mrs. A. J. Thilberger, and others performed pieces for piano, voice, and banjo interspersed with recitations.[292]

The opera continued into the New Year with its usual fare. On January 10 there was a benefit for the Union Française by artists of the opera troupe under Maugé. Besides several light operas, there was a musical intermède,[293] and the next evening the performance of *Les Huguenots* benefited the Eye, Ear, Nose and Throat Hospital.[294] The regular season of the French Opera closed with *Les*

Huguenots on March 3, 1892,[295] but the musicians of the troupe were hardly ready to retire so soon. A number of the leading singers united in a matinee concert at Grunewald Hall on January 5 for the benefit of Miss Ida Payton, whose photography gallery and art possessions were destroyed by a fire. Payton accompanied the performers on the piano.[296] That same evening two of the stars, Mr. and Mrs. Guillemot, made their last appearance in concert.[297] The next noon the musicians of the French Opera orchestra gave a benefit at the Opera House, opening with the third act of *Rigoletto* (Guillemot in the title role); followed by a grand concert by the orchestra of the opera under the leadership of Leps, musical director of the Frohsinn; then ending with a one-act operetta, *Les Charbonniers,* by Offenbach.[298] Three days later, panicked by the threatened loss of the French Opera, the Board of Directors of the French Opera met to try to secure an 1892–93 season. One solution was to raise the price of tickets, lowest in the nation for opera.[299]

For those who preferred their opera in English, the Emma Juch Grand Opera Company appeared at the Grand Opera House from January 3 to 12 with such works as *Cavalleria Rusticana, Lohengrin,* and *Faust.*[300] Signor G. Galloni, who came with Emma Juch's Opera Company, stayed on to give a concert on February 5 at Grunewald Hall.[301] A two-week season of Spanish opera at the Grand Opera House was announced to begin on March 27, 1892, but was subsequently cancelled.[302]

The attention of New Orleanians from February 7 to 13, 1892, was focused on the extraordinary theatrical performances of Sarah Bernhardt at the Grand Opera House.[303] There were virtually no concerts competing with her for audiences; these were either before or after her stay. The Frohsinn, for example, performed both before and after her presence in the city, on February 1 and 25 at the Grunewald Opera House. On February 1 William Leps conducted German works and one of his own pieces; his performers were Mme Elizabeth Abt, Xavier Soetens (first violinist of the French Opera), Charles Ludwig, Julius Maier, and Louis Grunewald, with members of the French Opera Orchestra. The musical program on February 25 was very short since the main entertainment was a masquerade ball.[304] At this time, members of Frohsinn presented their fifth annual concert at Grunewald Hall to benefit the German Protestant home for the aged and infirm. Vocal and instrumental solos were by Cesar Grisai, Henry Wehrman, Xavier Soetens, and a few others.[305]

There were several church concerts that were fund-raisers and not particularly religious. On February 2, 1892, the Knights of America held a variety entertainment at Saint Alphonse's Hall with vocal soloists, a zither quartet, a

Liederkreis singing association, and Henry Wehrman.[306] On February 24, there was a vocal and instrumental concert to benefit the choir of Saint Alphonse's Church, at the church hall on Sainte Mary and Constance streets. The program contained choir pieces, a violoncello piece played by Cesar Grisai, a violin solo by Xavier Soetens, vocal solos, and an ensemble work performed by Soetens, Grisai, and Welas. Miss M. Molony, a talented young musician, acted as accompanist.[307] The Carmelite fair, at Grunewald Hall on April 28, mixed recitations and musical numbers: *Valse Poetique* (Strakosch) performed by Miss Collette, vocal solos by Louis Fuhr, Mr. Olivier, and Miss Fuqua, and a violin obbligato by Wehrman. Miss Behan was piano accompanist.[308] The entertainment at Sainte Anna's Hall on May 6 included instrumental and vocal music, recitations, and the farce *Leave It to Me.*[309] None of the entertainments at the Seamen's Bethel could be called "religious." On the other hand, Sainte Cecilia's choir sang Mozart's Mass No. 12 at Saint Louis Cathedral on March 20, and, at the evening service on April 3, the congregation heard works by Beethoven, Barnby, and Niels Gade.[310]

There were other serious concerts during the spring of 1892, mostly by visitors. About February 5, at noon, Angelo Patricola, a graduate of the conservatory of Palermo, gave a piano recital at Werlein Hall. The recital was given complimentarily to the press and its friends.[311] Ovide Musin returned on March 12 and 13 to the French Opera House, with his colleague Eduard Scharf and a small group of other performers. According to the *Picayune*, "Upon his appearance last night [March 12], Mr. Musin received a magnificent ovation, and never appeared to better advantage in his brilliant display of skill. He is a masterful performer, and has a technique, an airiness, and a glitter, that are his own."[312] He performed Bazzini's *Fantaisie Characteristique*, a waltz by Wieniawski, and variations on a theme from Rossini's *Moïse* performed on one string. On March 18, there was a concert at Grunewald Hall by Patricola and Hector Gorjux, assisted by William Leps, Oscar G. Keller, Maumus, Grisai, and Wehrman. The audience was small because of cold weather.[313] Finally, Marguerite Samuel gave a matinee musicale with her advanced pupils at Grunewald Hall on March 20 at 1:00 o'clock.[314]

Of course, Samuel's pupils were not the only students to appear in concert this spring, though they may have been the best. Pilcher, as usual, was giving his recitals beginning on January 4, 1892—the 152nd studio performance by his pupils at his studio. Mrs. J. L. Vincent gave a complimentary musicale for pupils and friends at Grunewald Hall on March 16; various amateur performers and Henry Wehrman assisted her. On May 4, the pupils of Mrs. James Nott held a musical soiree at Grunewald Hall with the assistance of J. W. H. Eckert and Miss Marguerite Roubion. Mrs. Pilcher, on May 6, presented her student musicale and gypsy festival at her residence, 454 Saint Andrew Street, for the benefit of Trinity Chapel. On May 19, the general teachers of New Orleans received a benefit entertainment at Grunewald Opera House featuring a vocal solo by Mrs. Warren Easton.[315] The Carnatz Institute had its twenty-seventh graduation (solennité annuelle) on June 16, and included some musical portions by the students.

A handful of other benefit concerts occurred in April and May. On April 21, there was another grand musical and dramatic entertainment for the benefit of the Newsboys' Home at the Saint Charles Theatre. There was a concert in Jackson Square on May 3 to benefit the Fourteenth of September Fund, which aimed to erect a monument to commemorate the Crescent City White League insurrection against Reconstructionists on that day in 1874; the monument was eventually built and has been the center of controversy in New Orleans to the present day. And on May 18, Louis Grunewald sponsored a grand dramatic and musical entertainment to benefit the Louisiana Society for the Prevention of Cruelty to Animals, at Grunewald Opera House. Musicians included the musical section of the Frohsinn under William Leps and Mme E. Lejeune, Miss Socola, and Mr. H. Silverman (cantor of Temple Sinai).[316]

For the rest, there was a miscellany of concerts, beginning on March 2, at Grunewald Hall, with Hall's Old Guard Band of New York, consisting of thirty musicians under Professor H. A. Hall. As the *Picayune* put it, "Popular pieces will prevail."[317] Professor Paoletti's orchestra shaded, emphasized, and illustrated the theme, the tableaux, the marches, and the dances of *Lalla Rookh* at the French Opera House on April 22.[318] The next day, Le Luth, a society composed of the best amateur musical talent in the city, issued cards for a complimentary concert to be given at Grunewald Hall under its musical director, George O'Connell.[319] This was a men's chorus that would become more visible in the fall. The Orphéon Français, which used to give two series of concerts in their own hall and in Grunewald Hall, now relinquished the latter for good reason. It was too small an ensemble for the bigger hall, so the concert on May 28 was performed in the French Union Hall.[320] The orchestra, directed by Professeur P. A. Borge, had a dozen players: strings, woodwinds and brass. The ensemble was improved; especially effective was a piece by Léo Delibes. Henry Wehrman, who assisted, was exceptional in Sarasate's *Souvenirs de Faust,* and the choir did well. On June 4 there was one more soiree musicale et dramatique at Grunewald Hall for the dedication of the new Italian church, Saint Francois d'Assise.[321] Performers included Hubert Rolling, Marguerite Samuel, and Mme Charles Boudousquié (then in her late seventies), with Mlle Socola adding harmony to the compositions.

The summer of 1892 featured a new band at West End, the Edward Porte Great American Band, which began on May 17 and continued every evening. The band had fifty musicians, and Walter Rogers was the cornet virtuoso. The program, on June 2, was typical, with works by Hérold, Moskowski, Adam, Rossini, Reyer, Arbau, André, L. Valck, Meyerbeer, and Estrada; that on June 4 had pieces by Gounod, Balfé, Godfrey, Rossini, Doucet, Donizetti, and Lacome.[322] There is no sign of any concerts at Spanish Fort, but there were concerts each evening during the summer at Milneburg's Washington Hotel.[323] Meanwhile, back in the city, from June 12 there was of a run of *Cavalleria Rusticana,* in Italian, at the Academy of Music, performed by the Grand Lyric Company.[324] The New Louisiana Jockey Club sponsored a concert-promenade on June 15 from 6:00 to 11:00 p.m.[325] On June 18, the Crescent City Orchestra gave a concert followed by a ball at la Salle de la Parfaite Union on Rampart Street between Dumaine and Saint Philip streets.[326]

The fall 1892 season began with great expectations which were only partially realized. On October 19, Lyre d'Orphée, conducted by O'Connell, gave its initial soiree musicale at Grunewald Hall. The group consisted of fifty women. In addition to the choral music, the concert included solo songs and an instrumental quartet. The club was organized about a year and a half earlier for the purpose of cultivating an appreciation of higher classical music and developing such vocal and instrumental talent as was found to exist among the members. O'Connell hoped in a year's time to unite, in one grand orchestral chorus, Lyre de Orphée and Le Luth, an organization of gentlemen having the same object. The *Picayune* opined, "In time, it is hoped the organization will grow till New Orleans will have a grand choral oratorio such as exists in Boston, Saint Louis, Cincinnati and other cities. The members are very enthusiastic." Wehrman was an avid supporter of this endeavor. O'Connell's men's chorus, Le Luth, gave a reception and housewarming, on November 11, at 32 North Rampart Street, with choruses composed by Gounod, Wagner, and Bordese and solos performed by August Dufilho, Alfred Kernion, and S. Cohen.[327] The much-anticipated joint program by Le Luth and Lyre d'Orphée, in honor of their conductor, O'Connell, took place on December 12, 1892, at the Washington Artillery Hall.[328] The concert featured the New Orleans premiere of Gounod's cantata *Gallia.* Also on the program were Mozart's Overture to *The Abduction from the Seraglio,* some Mendelssohn vocal music, the Quartet from *Rigoletto,* Wehrman playing a piece by Alard, and other works. The choruses gave their second concert at Grunewald Hall on December 19.[329]

Another choral group, the New Orleans Oratorio Society, reported on October 23 that it had fifty singers and was preparing for a public singing of Haydn's *Creation.* Rehearsals were open at Grunewald Hall, and all singers were invited. "No expense is incurred."[330] If they gave the performance, no notice has been found.

Other musical organizations continued active in the fall of 1892. Frohsinn, whose membership was now about six hundred of the "best German citizens" of New Orleans, had an entertainment at Grunewald Hall on October 30 and another at Odd Fellows' Hall on December 9 (at the end of November, Grunewald Hall had burned down with all of Frohsinn's library). The concert on the ninth was a serious one with Grisai on violoncello; violin, and piano pieces; songs; and arias.[331] Albert Boulger, the young Swiss violinist, who met with much success in Cincinnati, Louisville, and Indianapolis, was in the city at the beginning of November and hoped to perform, but there is no evidence that he did.[332] Without proper backing it was difficult to hire a hall and assisting artists.

There was a concert on November 15 to benefit the Dryades Street Methodist Episcopal Church—at the church. Mr. Dirmeyer and others sang; there were piano duets and solos, a violin solo by Mr. B. Haag, and other performances.[333] The Metropolitan Club celebrated its third anniversary with a promenade concert and reception at Grunewald Hall on November 21.[334] On November 22, the Y.M.C.A. had its monthly entertainment of music and recitations, and probably on November 23 the Elite Parlor Orchestra under O'Connell and H. Wehrman gave an impromptu musicale at the residence of Henry Wehrman, 127 Saint Peter Street. They played the latest dance music and operettas.[335] The New Orleans Stenographers' Association held an entertainment with music on November 24.[336] The Seaman's Upper Bethel had concerts on November 24, December 1, and December 16.

On November 28, 29, and 30, 1892, the Josef Heine Concert Company performed three concerts for the Carrollton Woman's Social Industrial Association at their hall. Josef Heine was a blind violinist who performed the highest order of classical music; these programs included works by Haydn, Donizetti, Paderewski, Ernst, Dussec, Vieuxtemps, Chopin, and others.[337] P. A. Borge directed a grand vocal and instrumental concert on November 28 at Odd Fellows' Hall to benefit the Church of Saint John the Baptist. The musicians included the Orphéon Français Chorus, Mrs. H. Wehrman Jr., and Silverman in works by De Bériot, Chopin, and others.[338]

Whatever the plans were for the upcoming opera season, they were temporarily thwarted by a new situation. The orchestras of the Saint Charles Theatre, Grand Opera House, and Academy of Music went on strike on November 5, 1892.[339] Piano players substituted for them so the shows could go on. Fortunately, for the French Opera, the strike was over by November 12, but the musicians of the Grand Opera House remained on strike and in fact their services were not needed for a few weeks (piano accompaniment sufficed for one show, and one group came with its own orchestra). The season was in full swing when, on November 29, Louisiana Governor Murphy J. Foster and a party of his friends attended *Il Trovatore* at the French Opera House. The orchestra, at the conclusion of the first act, played "Hail Columbia" and "Dixie." Two days later Foster returned with Governor Fleming of Florida, Governor Kinney of Virginia, Senator Morgan of Alabama, and President Converse of Nicaragua for a performance of *Sigurd* in order to impress on his visitors the advanced cultural level of New Orleans.[340] Also in the repertory at this time were *Dinorah* and *Aïda*. Meanwhile the Mapleson Opera Company was at the Saint Charles Theatre from December 1892 to January 1893.

The only concert directly affected by the strike was the grand concert and bazaar to benefit the building of a new Saint George's Church, which was originally scheduled for November 15 and postponed to November 29 at Odd Fellows' Hall. November and December witnessed the usual spate of student recitals, starting, as always, with one on November 26 and another on November 28 at Pilcher's Studio of Music. Others followed there on December 3 (Miss Fannie L. Chase, of the graduating class of Pilcher's Studio, gave her first public vocal recital), December 17 (Miss Mamie P. Wayne, of the graduating class, gave her first recital at Pilcher's Studio), December 19 (pupils of Mrs. Eveline D. Pilcher), and December 26 (Pilcher himself gave an organ recital to inaugurate his studio's new organ). Miss Mollie F. Feames and the pupils of Mrs. Isabella M. Pilcher gave a concert on December 3 at Werlein Hall on Canal Street.

The remaining concerts for the fall of 1892 were a mix of fine recitals, sacred performances, and holiday events. On December 5, Marguerite Samuel entertained at a "very charming" musicale.[341] The celebrations surrounding the centennial of Saint Louis Cathedral on December 14–21 included a plethora of singing by artists of the French Opera as well as Creoles and local amateurs, orchestral music, a violin and piano duet (by Pomero, one of the first violins of the French Opera Orchestra, and Miss M. Cior), a piano duet (Miss V. De George and Miss E. Cior), and so on.[342] The Ladies' Auxiliary of the New Orleans Association of Spiritualists held a musical and literary entertainment at their Hall,

30 Camp Street, on December 14, and the Frances Willard Y.W.C.T.U. held one on December 27 at the Christian Church, corner of Melpomene and Camp streets, to benefit the Shakespear Almshouse.[343] A concert for the opening of the Saint Vincent Female Orphan Asylum Christmas Fair in Sainte Theresa's Hall, from December 19 to 26, was postponed one night because of bad weather, but the hired orchestra performed intermittently throughout the evening.[344] On the second evening young people performed piano duets and solos, a violin solo, and songs. On December 21, Emmanuel Lafarge, former tenor of the French Opera, gave a grand concert at the Washington Artillery Hall. He was assisted by some of his pupils and some of the most talented women and gentlemen of the city in solos, duets, and choruses from *Samson et Dalila* and *Esclarmonde*.[345] Christmas masses and services at all the churches boasted special music; exceptionally ornate were those at Grace Church (under Mrs. Isabella Pilcher) and Saint Louis Cathedral (under Gabrielle Tusson, organist).[346]

The concert highlight in spring 1893 was the three recitals by Marguerite Samuel in the foyer of the French Opera House on Saturday mornings. The first, on January 14, included a Beethoven sonata, plus works by Stamaty, Gluck, Saint-Saëns, Mendelssohn, Raff, Haydn, J. S. Bach, Chopin, and Liszt. The second was on February 18 and the third on March 11.[347] A concert was held on January 27, 1893, at the Opera House to raise money for the Chinchuba Institution. The program included works by Fauré, Massenet, Gluck, Gounod, Saint-Saëns, Holst, and others.[348] On the same day, William Leps led Frohsinn at their hall on Bourbon Street with the Grieg Piano Concerto, choruses by Weber, miscellaneous arias, Beethoven's *Leonora* Overture No. 3, a piece by Max Bruch, Schubert's "Der Erlkönig," *The Flying Dutchman* Overture, and other works.[349] Among the student recitals was one by Pilcher on January 2, Miss Delphine Points on January 17 at the Grand Opera House (Points came from one of the most prominent Creole and American families of the city), and Mlles Roubion on April 16.

On March 14 and 15, the Isabelle Bressler Concert Company featured Bressler, a child harpist, assisted by the artists of the French Opera Orchestra. On the second concert, Bressler, Grisai, and John Pomero played a trio for harp, violin, and violoncello by Carl von Oberthur.[350] Mlle Vincent, a pupil of Marguerite Samuel, played at Odd Fellows' Hall on March 15. She was assisted by Samuel herself, Varelli-Jauquet, Smittle, Anita Socola, Gonzales, H. Wehrman, Salomon, J. Durel, and some others.[351]

Le Luth Society gave a concert on March 21 at Odd Fellows' Hall. The varied program included the "Pilgrim's Chorus" from *Tannhäuser*, opera arias, and a bolero composed and played by Wehrman. O'Connell and Henry Jung were the accompanists.[352] Mme and M Shields give a soiree dramatique et lyrique at their salon, 440 Camp Street, on April 7. It included songs and instrumental pieces along with dramatic readings and tableaux.[353] The benefit offered to Mme Z. Lafosse by her friends and pupils, at the French Union Hall on Monday, April 10, 1893, included many arias and songs. Max Landry played a violin accompaniment. Lafosse was sick and exhausted after years of teaching, and this occasion provided her with some needed income.[354] The Orphéon Français offered a farewell concert to Bergé on April 20 at the French Union Hall. It included two young violinists, Charles Maillet and Paul Tosso, the clarinetist Ray Baud, singers, and others.[355] Yet, on May 7, Bergé was still around to lead the Orphéon Français in a concert at City Park.[356] On May 12 there was a grand concert at Odd Fellows' Hall by Grace A. Kellogg and Isidore Jacobs. They performed Beethoven's *Kreutzer* Sonata, Weber's *Concertstück* (Kellogg), vocal pieces, the Mendelssohn Violin Concerto (Jacobs), and other works. It was originally scheduled for May 9 but was postponed because of bad weather.[357]

Starting in November 1892, a formal committee met at Tulane Hall to learn about the musical aspects of the Columbian Exposition in Chicago the following year and to determine the Louisiana representatives for music. At a meeting of musicians on December 3 to organize the Louisiana delegation to the Columbian Exposition, Marguerite Samuel was elected president, Florence Huberwald vice-president, and Mark Kaiser to serve on the executive committee. On April 27, 1893, a benefit concert was held at Odd Fellows' Hall for the aspiring contralto Mathilde Bruguière, who was chosen by the leaders of the New Orleans committee to represent them at organizational meetings in Chicago. Performing participants in the exposition were to be Mlles Schmittle, Scola Cockery, and Cora M. Caruthers and MM Wehrman, Dalton, Williams, Grunewald and Leps and elite amateurs.[358]

The summer began early in 1893 with a concert promenade on Sunday, April 16, as part of a grand pique-nique complimentaire at Southern Park, by the New Orleans Brewing Association Society. The West End Orchestra was led by George A. Paoletti in a popular program.[359] The inaugural concert of the season at West End, "Le Coney Island du Sud," was on May 4 with George Paoletti in charge of an orchestra of fifty; Jules Levy was cornet soloist. The new owner of the City and Lake Railroad was committed to using local musicians in carrying on the great success of the past.[360] The season was supposed to end on September 4 but went to the twenty-fourth. On the concert on the fourth, M Lopez, a very young man, improvised on the cornet à piston, and it was marvelously received by his colleagues.[361] There were many virtuosi on this instrument and the trumpet á piston in New Orleans since 1838, and it remained an especially popular instrument among the masses of concertgoers.

The fall 1893 season began on October 6–9 with the music in a festival to raise money for the expansion of Sainte Rose de Lima Church. It included "choruses, duets, solos by skillful men and women singers, by excellent instrumentalists, pianists and violinists, very nice voices with irreproachable execution."[362] The Orphéon Français gave a free grand concert on October 14 in the presence of the French Consul. The program consisted of two halves, each beginning with an orchestral overture. Wehrman played a solo and a duo with O. Aubert Jr.[363] On October 21, there was a soiree musicale offered to Mme O. Vaurigaud at her home on Boulevard Champs-Elysées. It had been postponed from October 14 owing to the death of her uncle.[364]

The French Opera season opened on Thursday, October 26, with *Les Huguenots,* followed by *Faust, Carmen, La Juive, L'Africaine,* and others.[365] It was curtailed by February, however, owing to the usual economic constraints that were increasingly threatening all cultural life in the city.[366] Mme L. Arnauld sang at a wedding at Saint Louis Cathedral sometime before November 26; a critic for *L'Abeille* found that "She sings with intelligence and taste, has excellent diction, and can sing homogeniously in three registers."[367] On Sunday, December 10, Anita Lassen, who had been trained in France and England, sang a setting of "Ave Maria" by the Russian composer Alabieff, at the Offertory at Saint Louis Cathedral.[368] This was a small prelude to the grand concert offered to her at Odd Fellows' Hall on December 18, when she was assisted by Grace Kellogg (solo piano) and Henry Wehrman (solo violin). Also on the program, Henry Wehrman, M Duvigneaud, and Eugenia Wehrmann performed a trio for two violins and piano by Dancla. J. W. H. Eckert served as general accompanist.[369] So successful was Lassen that she decided to remain in the city, teaching and performing.

A highlight of the fall season was the return to the city of its native son, Edmond Dédé. On December 10, 1893, he gave his first concert at the hall Des Amis de l'Esperance, on Tremé Street, which had bad acoustics but, perhaps because of ever-present racial prejudice, he had to accept. He was accompanied on the piano by Basile Barès. Dédé was born in New Orleans in 1827, studied locally with Gabici, and, at the Paris Conservatoire, was taught composition by Halévy and violin by Alard. He had a distinguished forty-year career in France on the violin and as conductor, and was now coming home for the first time since leaving for France in the 1850s. He played mostly his own pieces and got a rave review.[370] His second concert was on December 17, 1893, in the France-Amis hall, on Robertson Street, between Saint Antoine and Bons-Enfants streets. Interestingly, on the program were two young girls, well-schooled girls "de race" (colored), who performed the Overture to *Les Diamants de la Couronne* for piano four hands. The critic assumed they were the daughters of Barès, who again assisted in the concert.[371] Dédé's farewell recital was back at the Amis de l'Esperance Hall on January 21, 1894. Besides the violin, he played guitar on this program.[372]

Among the remaining fall 1893 concerts were those given by Pilcher at Junius Hart's music store, starting on Tuesday, December 19, and continuing into 1894. Hart had recently died, and this concert was an attempt to support his widow in maintaining the store. Pilcher played primarily organ and piano works, and Carrie T. Pilcher and others sang.[373] The young harpist Bressler continued to awe the audiences in New Orleans; at her concert at the French Opera on December 24, she joined singers from the opera, Jules Nachtergaele on viola d'amour, and others. She proudly played on a prize-winning harp made by Lyon and Healy of Chicago.[374] On Christmas Day, the choir of Saint Louis Cathedral, with an orchestra of twenty and an organ performed by Jules Nachtergaele, performed a grand mass by Mazzo (Marzo, maestro of the pope's cappella?).[375] The Princeton Glee, Banjo, and Mandolin Club performed on December 26, 1893.[376] There was an active concert scene on the streets during the holiday season, though this was not legal and the street musicians were arrested and fined fifteen dollars each by Judge Adams.[377]

Pilcher continued his series at Junius Hart's store on January 2, 16, and 30, 1894.[378] There was a benefit, vocal and instrumental concert on January 10 for the children of the late August Dufilho. Participants included O'Connell, S. Cohen, Alfred Kernion, Walter Stauffer, C. Lopez, Henry Wehrman, Jules Sarrazin, Bressler, a chorus of the pupils of Mme Boudousquié, Grisai, and Bessie Shearer.[379] Rosa Frantz, a native New Orleans singer who had recently returned from studying in Germany, gave her introductory concert with other eminent artists (violinist Jacobs, pianist Grace Kellogg, and others), at Odd Fellows' Hall on Monday, January 15.[380]

Then, one of the most distinguished European violinists returned for a single concert. On January 22, the Hungarian Eduard Remenyi gave a violin recital in Odd Fellows' Hall; he had performed in New Orleans once before, in 1850. This time he performed several caprices of Paganini (which he called "fantasias"), Mendelssohn's *Allegro Appassionato,* and a waltz arranged from Delibes. There was also a singer, and the pianist was Signor de Riva Berni, who was especially successful playing Liszt's arrangement of a gavotte by Raff. The critic found Remenyi electrifying, which may explain why Brahms thought so highly of him.[381]

On January 24 there was the annual benefit for Chinchuba, an institution for the deaf and dumb, at Odd Fellows' Hall, performed by principals of the French Opera, including Mmes Tylda and Lassen.[382] Frohsinn celebrated its tenth anniversary in Washington Artillery Hall on January 28, and its only soiree musicale of the season was on March 25 at that hall.[383] The French Democratic Club presented a concert and ball on February 1. The concert had a mixture of works for violin (performed by Pomero), piano (De George), voice, harp (Bressler), and flute interspersed with monologues.[384] On Wednesday, February 14, 1894, there was a grand vocal and instrumental concert offered to the widow of William F. Reinecke, at the residence of George L. Wiltz, Washington Street near Esplanade Avenue. It included orchestral works, mandolin solos, songs, violin solos, piano duets, and pieces for banjo.[385] On Saturday, February 17, the French Opera presented a concert featuring Berlioz's complete *La Damnation de Faust* as a benefit for M E. Brunel, chef d'orchestre. This was one of two such concerts planned for the season; the other, Massenet's *Marie Madeleine,* was not performed.[386] There was a grand concert at the French Union Hall on February 26 to benefit M J. DeLeeuw, violoncellist, assisted by Tylda, Bressler, Dévries, Nachtergaele on the viola d'amore, and M Demeo on the violin.[387]

The Mexicans invaded again, this time beginning on Tuesday, February 27, at the French Union Hall, with a vocal and instrumental concert by José B. de Nava and Señora Virginia Galvan de Nava. Mrs. Nava was known as the Adelina Patti of Mexico. Both were excellent musicians and had traveled around the United States helping to raise money for charities. In New Orleans, the charity was the Maison du Pauvre, founded by the Société Hospitalière. She sang the "Mad Scene" from *Lucia* and, with her husband, a duet from *Aïda.* They were joined by local talent: Bressler (harpist), Brunel and Hesselberg (pianists), Pomero, Soubeyran, Devilliers, Montfort, Dévries, Grisai, and Mmes Tylda and Marsa.[388] So successful was this concert that Mr. and Mrs. de Nava sang five more concerts through April 29. On March 4, they performed with pianist Angel Lelo de Larrea, who played works of Paderewski and Chopin,[389] and, on March 29, they performed again at Odd Fellows' Hall.[390] On April 1 and 7, they gave matinees with Lelo de Larrea, and, on April 4, a regular evening concert. Mme de Nava preferred the old repertory, that is, Bellini, Donizetti, and Rossini, while Lelo de Larrea added works by contemporaries Grieg and Scharwenka on his last program.[391]

There was a smattering of other concerts as well. On February 27, Bressler gave a harp concert at the French Opera to benefit its pension fund. She was joined by Grisai and Pomero.[392] Mlles A. and J. Boissonneau and their pupils held a soiree musicale in early March.[393] Mlle Jennie Wolf, with the help of M E. Field, gave a concert at the Grand Opera House on March 31. Wolf, who was eighteen or nineteen years old, was about to depart for Europe. She played pieces by Beethoven (Sonata, Opus 53), Bach (a gigue), Chopin (*Valse Brillante*), Wagner, Raff, Henselt, and Mendelssohn.[394] On April 7, 1894, there was a concert of vocal and instrumental music at Odd Fellows' Hall featuring Wolf, Mme Tylda, M Fonteynes, several more from the French Opera, and Professor Hesselberg, with an orchestra. It was sponsored by B'nai B'rith in honor of Jacob Furth of Saint Louis.[395]

Marguerite Samuel was a high-profile concert artist in New Orleans, and this spring was one of her most prolific seasons. On Saturday, February 10, 1894, she and some of her pupils gave a soiree musicale at Odd Fellows' Hall. The next day she gave a solo recital in the back part of Odd Fellows' Hall, where she believed the acoustics were a bit better than on the regular stage. She played *Rigadon* by Balfé, Andante and Minuet from Weber's B Minor Sonata, and works by Rubinstein, Chopin, and Mendelssohn. Then on April 7, 14, and 21, she gave a series of three recitals at Werlein's.[396] On April 14 she performed the "Pilgrim's March" (Wagner), a polonaise (Liszt), several pieces by Chopin, the *Moonlight* Sonata (Beethoven), and *Twilight* (her own piece). The other programs have not been found.

On April 7, there was a grand soiree at the French Opera offered to Eugène Field by the elite society of New Orleans and many literary and artistic clubs. Performers included M L. Fonteynes, Mme Tylda, Mlles Jennie Wolf, and Etta Roehl.[397] On April 15, Mlles Roubion and their pupils held a soiree musicale et dansante at Union Hall.[398] Wehrman played a piece at the Offertory at Mass at Saint Augustine's Church on April 15, its patron saint's day.[399] The Orphéon Français held its annual general meeting on April 18, and on April 24, at the installation of new officers, MM Fonteynes, Maumus, and Alexander Lazare sang a small concert.[400] On Friday, April 27, at a service at Temple Sinai, Mme Tylda sang her last public performance in New Orleans before returning to Paris.[401] On May 5, 1894, there was a grand vocal and instrumental concert, performed by artists and well-known amateurs, to profit the school of Saint Joseph Academy.[402] The festival of the Society of Women Servants of the Poor on May 9 was a concert of vocal and instrumental music, recitations in French and English, and some piano works.[403] On Saturday, May 19, there was a soiree musicale at the Institute of Mmes Markey and Picard by the pupils of Mme Z. LaFosse.[404]

By the beginning of May, the concerts at West End started up again. The band had at least forty musicians, twenty-one or twenty-two of whom played the past season at the French Opera. As *L'Abeille*'s critic pointed out, "The concert at West End is composed of the best ensembles of the symphonic repertory or dramatic lyric and solos executed by the best artists who have ever come to New Orleans. Includes the first desk players of the Opera orchestra of the past season.... [T]he orchestra at West End is without weakness, rare in America. And the soloists are exceptional: Paoletti, M Chevre (piccolo), M Valck (flute), M Doucet (oboe), M Cuevas and M Reybaud (2 among 9 clarinetists), Fabian (cornetist flanked by 3 others), Vizcarra (saxhorn), Becker (saxophone), Barra (trombone)."[405] Paoletti, one of the most distinguished conductors in the history of concert music in New Orleans, had been leading bands at the lake since 1888. The amenities at the pavilion were upgraded during the winter, and after a fire destroyed the pavilion and the music library of the orchestra in May, concerts continued unabated as the facilities were rebuilt with a new platform. A typical program was that on May 2, with works by Doring, Jacobowsky, Thomas Benids, D'Arcy, Jacque, Verdi, Renaud, Bugalossi, Weiss, Liszt, Fohrbach, Escher, and Kennedy. Occasionally classical artists from the city performed, such as Grisai on June 9.

While nothing more is heard from Spanish Fort and Milneburg at this time, there were a few concerts in the city. On June 26, 1894, there was another festival by the students of Institution E. Robert at their French Quarter place. It included choruses, vocal and piano solos, as well as recitations.[406] And at Audubon Park, opposite Tulane University on Saint Charles Avenue, there were concerts by Le Corps de Musiciens Continental in June. Delicious refreshments were served. New Orleanians from the city—that is, the older populated areas of the French Quartet and English Sector—got to the park by electric "chars" (the famous Saint Charles Street Car).[407]

The most significant musical event in the fall 1894 season was the establishment of the Mark Kaiser String Quartet, the first resident quartet in the city since before the war, which was announced in the papers at the beginning of October.[408] Besides Kaiser, first violin, the members were Henry Wehrman, second violin; Emile Malmquist, viola; and Cesar Grisai, violoncello. A large audience attended their first public concert on Monday, November 26, 1894, at Odd Fellows' Hall, when they played Beethoven's Opus 18, no. 4; Carl Schuberth's Opus 34; Robert Schumann's Piano Quintet with Marguerite Samuel; and some arias.[409] Their next concert was on March 9, when, assisted by Samuel, they played a Mozart piano quartet, a Haydn quartet movement, and Raff's Sonata Opus 78 (Kaiser and Samuel).[410]

There was an unusually high number of other concerts this fall. On October 4 the Sainte Anne Festival had a concert directed by O'Connell.[411] A grand divertissement musical et varié was offered to Professor Lucius Lescale by his friends and pupils on October 12–13 at the French Union Hall. These friends included H. Kronengold (bass of the Boston Ideal Opera Company), A. Reser (bass of the Imperial Opera of Saint Petersburg), A. Barra (trombone), Grisai, C. Maillet (violinist), P. Roetiers (horn), C. P. Terranova (cornet), Thomas J. Omès (comedian), Mme H. Bosse (soprano), Mlle I. Ludwig (soprano), and the piano class of M F. N. Poché (tenor).[412] Another concert at the French Union Hall on October 18 featured Léon Fonteynes, ex-baritone of the French Opera, assisted by numerous amateurs and artists and some from the Orphéon (Maumus, Lazare, Gaillard, and Rutily), M Renaud, Grisai, Chèvre (piccolo player both at the French Opera and West End) and Henry Wehrman.[413]

A new Orchestre d'Euterpe, under the direction of Grisai, made its debut at the Parfaite Union on October 24. It was comprised of forty amateur musicians. Wehrman was also involved.[414] Mme Cassius Meye, with the help of many other women, presented a concert at the French Union Hall on October 26–27 to benefit the Women's Hospital Society. The concert was directed by Mme Louis Arnaud.[415] There was a grand concert on November 21 in the new Perseverance Hall, at the intersection of Saint Claude and Dumaine streets, given by the friends of M le Professor Joseph Durel for his benefit. Participants included O'Connell, H. Wehrman, Jules Gueringer, Junod, Mlles Eveline Lacoste, Ruby Sachs (sister of the Parisian singer), and Eugénie Wehrmann.[416] To celebrate Sainte Cecilia's Day at the cathedral on November 25, Gounod's *Messe du Couvent* was performed. Grisai led the orchestra which included forty string musicians (two violin sections and a viola section).[417]

Pilcher had two recitals at his studio in December: on the fourth with works by Robert Schumann, Richter, Handel, Rossini, Wagner, Beethoven, and Liszt, and on the seventeenth (program not yet found). The studio now had seventy-three vocal pupils, fifty-seven students in piano, forty-one in organ, seventeen in harmony and composition, plus a hundred in other branches of music.[418] O'Connell directed a musicale at the Young Men's Gymnastic Club on December 15, 1894, which included the March from *Tannhäuser,* vocal works, Grisai playing his own music, Wehrman playing a piece by Sivori, and other works.[419] A "well-known Symphony Orchestra," conducted by E. J. Bayle, performed at the

Catholic Club on December 16, about which we know nothing further.[420] The Philharmonic Society presented its first grand concert of the year on December 17 at Odd Fellows' Hall.[421]

Frank H. Simms gave an organ recital at Saint Paul's Church on December 18 and another one on March 11, 1895.[422] There was a musicale on December 19 at the home of Mr. Victor Despommier. The program included a trio from *William Tell* performed by MM Kernion, Despommiker, and Van Hufflen; Miss Kellog accompanied and H. Wehrman played a violin obbligato.[423] This fall's visiting college students were the Iowa State Band, playing daily at the Washington Artillery Hall from December 20, and the Vanderbilt University Glee, Banjo, Mandolin and Guitar Club at Odd Fellows' Hall on December 27.[424]

On Saturday afternoon, December 22, 1894, Grace Kellogg gave a "musical monologue" (illustrated lecture) at her rooms, 850 Camp Street. Her topic was Gottschalk, whom she discussed and whose music she performed.[425] On Christmas Day, there were noteworthy concerts at Sainte Theresa's Church, by the choir and Joseph A. Gernhauser, organist; at Saint Joseph's Church during High Mass at 4 p.m. when the musical portions included Haydn's *Imperial* Mass in D; and at Saint Stephen's Church, directed by William H. Pilcher, where Beethoven's Mass in C, Opus 86, was performed.[426] Then, on December 26 and 29, soprano Ellen Beach Yaw gave two concerts at Odd Fellows' Hall, assisted by Max Dick, violinist, and Georgiella Lay, pianist. On December 29, a Saturday matinee, she sang the "Mad Scene" from *Hamlet* and the "Laughing Song" from *Manon Lescaut*.[427]

As the 1895 spring season began, the French Opera seemed to be doing well. In December 1894, the troupe had traveled to Atlanta for a few days, and, back in New Orleans, *Le Prophète* on January 3 was followed a few days later by a premiere of *Richard III* on Saturday and the *Grande Duchess* on Sunday.[428] But danger signs were on the horizon. On February 14, the *Picayune* critic pleaded with visitors to the city to take in the French Opera, the only French opera troupe in the United States, and two days later he revealed publicly the sorry state of the finances of the company.[429] The performers continued, although the salaries were six weeks in arrears. By March it was all over. A concert was held on March 5 to raise funds to help the artists return home to France, and another for all the musicians of the theater on March 10.[430] All the time this was happening, the Tavary English Grand Opera Company presented operas at the Grand Opera House. Their repertory included *Il Trovatore, Martha, Carmen, The Bohemian Girl, Faust, Cavalleria Rusticana, Pagliacci* (New Orleans premier), *Tannhäuser, Lohengrin,* and *William Tell*.[431] The local thirst for opera was insatiable, even when economics made it nearly impossible. Yet, New Orleanians had reached a dilemma that would be an issue for at least the next century: how to balance all the expenditure on Carnival with the needs of other cultural attractions in the city.[432]

Most of the concerts after New Year's were benefits, as usual. On January 2, 1895, there was a grand vocal, instrumental, and boxing entertainment to benefit the widow of Andy Bowen, at the Olympic Club. Leading amateur and professional talents in both music and boxing appeared.[433] Frau Elizabeth Relehe, German pianist, performed a complimentary concert at Werlein's Music Parlors on January 3.[434] The next day there was a musicale and promenade concert at the Catholic Club.[435] The Society Saint Vincent de Paul, with Saint Louis Cathedral, sponsored a vocal and instrumental concert at the French Union Hall on Friday, January 18. The program started with an opéra comique, followed by a grand intermède featuring some songs, followed by another opéra comique.[436]

Of course many home concerts went unrecorded, and we can only guess about their number and content. But sometimes evidence of such happenings is revealed by ancillary stories in the papers. That rude behavior was a problem at such concerts was revealed in an article for women on how to behave at musicales; it appeared in the *Picayune* on February 3.[437] Such behavior, apparently, was not so much a problem at public concerts; it either did not occur or was more tolerated.

On February 10, 1895, Professor Joseph Pristia (cornetist) and his pupils gave a concert at the French Union Hall. He played some of his own compositions. "The singing of Miss Madeline Pristia was especially commendable," reported the *Picayune*.[438] Miss Rosa Frantz, an accomplished musician and vocalist, gave a benefit concert for the Leper's Home, at Odd Fellows' Hall on either February 10 or 19. She was assisted by Miss Corkery (alto), Mr. Byrd (tenor), Mr. Braunfield (baritone), Professor Borge (violin), Mr. Eckert (accompanist), and the Wells Banjo Quartet.[439] On February 12, the English baritone Herbert Wakefield sang and recited, with assistance from Mrs. Belle McLeod-Lewis, in the banquet room of the Grunewald Hotel.[440] There was a benefit for Miss Leona Ruiz, a young pianist, at Washington Artillery Hall, assisted by the Cahill-Wallace combination and Professor George Demonio.[441] On February 22, the women of the Church of the Annunciation held a high tea and musical entertainment with performers Mrs. Annie Roach, Miss Jennie Outlaw (harp), the Tulane Quartet, Grace A. Kellogg (pianist), Millie Cooke (violin), and Mr. J. Meres (cornet); it was postponed from February 15.[442] The women of Saint John's Episcopal Church gave a musicale with dancing and refreshments on Wednesday, February 20.[443] There was the annual concert to benefit the Chinchuba Charitable Deaf-Mute Institution, at French Union Hall on February 20, performed by several leading artists.[444] Musical excerpts were interspersed with recitations by the pupils of the elocution teacher Mrs. Annie S. Shields at their recital on February 22.[445] On Thursday, February 28, 1895, there was Carnival entertainment at the Young Men's Hebrew Association that included an orchestral overture; pieces for harmonica, piano, voices, violin (Carl H. Pinski); and recitations. Carl Pinski was a prominent violinist in New Orleans at the very end of the nineteenth century and during the first part of the twentieth.[446]

On March 1, there was an entertainment at Miss Sophie Wright's, No. 440 Camp Street, for the benefit of Mr. W. Garner of Osyka, Mississippi, an invalid. Refreshments and dancing followed the musical and literary part of the program.[447] A recital at 3:00 o'clock by the Musicians' Guild at Sophie Newcomb College took place on March 2.[448] On March 14 was the second complimentary entertainment and concert of the Young Men's Gymnastic Club at the clubhouse, directed by George L. O'Connell.[449]

The first public concert by Miss Sophie Blache, a young mezzo soprano, at the French Union Hall, prior to her departure for Europe, occurred on March 20. She was the daughter of Mme Pauline Blache, some of whose other students also appeared.[450] Several other student concerts were held on March 11 by the students of Emile Malmquist, director of the New Orleans Conservatory of Music, at Werlein's parlors, and on March 14 by the pupils of Florence Huberwald at Odd Fellows' Hall with the assistance of Samuel, Kaiser, and Henderson, with Huberwald herself singing "Der Erlkönig."

At the end of March through the next month or so, the city experienced the ultimate listening opportunity in American concert bands. Not only did New Orleanians hear its own bands, by Paoletti and others, but the three most famous East Coast bands played successively, followed by two other major American bands. It started on Sunday, March 31, 1895, when Gilmore's Famous Band, conducted by Victor Herbert, opened at the Grand Opera House. Herbert was assisted by Mme Louise Natali, prima donna soprano; Aldis J. Gery, autoharpist; Herbert L. Clarke, cornet; fifty other famous instrumentalists; and the child pianist Miss Frieda Simonson (age eleven).[451] The second concert was on April 2; the third, a matinee, on April 3; and the fourth on the evening of April 3. The performances were sold out, and the audiences heard not only the band but also Victor Herbert playing the violoncello.[452]

No sooner had Gilmore's band and Herbert left town when, on Friday, April 12, 1895, the United States Marine Band opened a series of concerts at the Grand

Opera House, under conductor Fancuilli. The ensemble had sixty musicians and was on its first southern tour in its hundred-year history. The noted prima donna soprano Mlle Roma sang at each concert.[453] Only a few days later, the Sousa band opened at the Academy of Music. Assisting Sousa were Miss Marie Barnard, soprano, and Miss Currie Duke, violinist. Duke studied with Josef Joachim and was a native of Kentucky. They performed in New Orleans from April 26 to 28.[454] Without catching a breath, the audiences then went on May 1 to the official opening of the West End summer season with a corps of musicians from Cincinnati led by M Littell. This was the military band Bellstedt Ballenburg, with Meran Bellstedt as cornet virtuoso. The cornetist Armand Veazey was exceptional, but after what they had just heard and in anticipation of Paoletti's summer season, the local listeners were a little disappointed in the Bellstedt band as a whole. New Orleans audiences differed from those in Cincinnati.[455] A few weeks later, the U.S. Marine Band of the Navire de Guerre, Trenton, under Cesare Torsiello, musical director, appeared at the Roof Garden of Hotel Grunewald.[456]

The rest of the spring 1895 concerts were mostly minor affairs. On March 31, Frohsinn presented a play at Washington Artillery Hall, wherein "the orchestra played some excellent music during the evening."[457] Ladies Bethel Association at the Bethel (Fulton near Jackson Street) gave a musicale and tea on April 5. Fred Lang sang, and other amateurs recited.[458] The *Saint Matthew Passion* was sung on Palm Sunday, April 7, at the Jesuit Church, but we do not know whose version (possibly Bach's). The choir had thirty voices and consisted of the regular choir augmented by the New Orleans Quartette Club.[459] The Mass was by Dechauer, the Offertory and "Inflammatus" by Rossini. The Viola String Band, Miss Bijou Evans (child singer), Mrs. M. M. Kennelly (singer), and the Kihneman brothers (mandolin and guitar) performed a vocal-instrumental benefit at Odd Fellows' Hall in April for the Convalescent Home.[460] At Saint Louis Cathedral on Easter Sunday, April 14, an elaborate musical program included "Regina Coeli" by Lambillotte and Eduardo Marzo's (1852–1929) celebrated mass with a full orchestra led by Grisai and Miss Ramonelta del Escobal at the organ. The final March was a composition by Miss del Escobal. The cathedral choir had nine sopranos, four altos, one tenor, and one bass.[461]

An editorial on April 3 in the *Picayune* denounced "concert saloons" in which any sort of entertainment (including music, concerts, wrestling, minstrels, boxing, and pornography) could be performed as long as liquor was served. This was licensed by the state for a fee of five thousand dollars.[462] While the music provided at these establishments might have been called "concerts," there is little connection between them and the other concerts described in this book.

The Ladies' Auxiliary of the Saint Vincent de Paul Society (Saint Augustin Parish) gave a grand entertainment for the benefit of the poor on April 15 at French Union Hall. The program included performers H. Wehrman, Castellanos, Joseph Durel, E. May, Laroussini, C. Gilbert, and D. C. Mellon.[463] At first communion, on April 18, at 7:00 a.m. and at 10:30 a.m. at Saint Louis Cathedral, the archbishop presided.[464] Mr. Callierd sang "Hosanna" and "Santa Maria," and MM Obert and Zeringer took part on the violin. On April 19, the Beasey children performed a concert at the Southern Academic Institute for the benefit of the Woman's Guild of Saint George's Church. As the *Picayune* reported, "The Beasey children are musical prodigies. Each evidences ability of the highest order and their performances are really remarkable. They interpret the fine masters with skill, grace and feeling that is rare in older musicians. The programme for this evening comprises solos, duets and quartettes for violins by the greatest composers, De Bériot, Schubert, Gottschalk, Verdi, Joseffy, Weiniaski [sic], Liszt and Ernst being among the number. . . . [R]efreshments and dancing afterwards. There will also be a matinée on Saturday noon."[465] Anita Lassen, Grace Kellogg (piano), Mr. L. Hochart (baritone), Eugene Lacoste ("the prince of whistlers"), Wehrman, and actors held a grand concert and dramatic performance at the Academy of Music on April 24 to benefit the waif's home of the Louisiana Society for the Prevention of Cruelty to Children.[466]

There was a musicale by the pupils of Miss Ella Todd, at the Coliseum Place Baptist Church on April 30. Mandolins, banjos, guitars, with violin and piano accompaniment, and vocal gems by Misses Rosa Frantz and Notie Price were on the program.[467] At a matinee musicale on May 4 at Odd Fellows' Hall on Camp Street, the Wehrman Trio (Henry Wehrman; Cesar Grisai; and Eugénie Wehrmann, niece of Henry), assisted by Theodore Hochart, baritone, and P. Duvigneaud, violin, performed works by Haydn (his last trio), Beethoven, Mendelssohn, Servain Rolla, and Fauré.[468] The trio performed again at Odd Fellows' Hall on June 15.[469] On Sunday, May 5, the Orchestre Euterpe, directed by M Octave Aubert Jr., and the Orphéon Français, directed by Professor H. Richard, gave a vocal and instrumental concert at Jackson Barracks Park for the benefit of Saint Maurice's Church.[470] The première conférence les heroines françaises, on May 12 at the French Union Hall, was performed by Henry Dubes assisted by many amateurs and artists. The program included a trio for piano, violin, and violoncello (E. Wehrmann, H. Wehrman, and Grisai), a song (Mlle Ponjol), a violoncello solo from *Lucia* (Grisai), and a duet for violoncello and violin.[471] The Gymnastic Club gave another concert on May 16. Faust directed it in the Overture to *The Abduction from the Seraglio* (Mozart), the "Soldiers' Chorus" from *Faust* (Gounod), and other vocal works accompanied by the orchestra. Grisai and H. Wehrman were also there.[472] On June 14, 1895, the Carnatz Institute celebrated its thirtieth anniversary with a concert that included piano solos, vocal music, and an original composition.[473]

New Orleanians were thrilled when, on May 1, West End officially opened for the season. Improvements had been made to West End and to the railway tracks from the city, and the new proprietors—MM Tranchina and Olivieri—took an interest in the resort that assured its prominence until well into the twentieth century.[474] A corps of musicians from Cincinnati had been brought in, which was a miscalculation by the railroad officials and not Tranchina and Olivieri. So at the beginning of June, Paoletti and his orchestra of fifty were in command in City Park and in Audubon Park, not on the lake. After the Cincinnati group had departed, Paoletti and his West End Band ended the season at West End on September 12 and 15 and showed that they were better than the Cincinnati band. The railroad executives learned their lesson in their pocketbooks, as City Park, Audubon Park and even Southern Park—where a French Women's Society festival took place on September 8, assisted by the Orphéon Français—drew away some of their clientele.[475]

The full 1895–96 season was a disappointment because of the failure to have a full-time opera. The operas the past two seasons had been cheap, both in cost and, as a result, in quality. Some lessons learned from this, they hoped during the year, would lead to a better situation in the fall of 1896.[476] But the city was not without opera in the meantime. Lillian Russell was in New Orleans on December 9, 1895, at the Grand Opera House in the title role of *The Grand Duchess of Gérolstein*.[477] She had an orchestra of twenty-two (including oboes, bassoons, and French horns) and a brass band on the stage. On Monday, December 16, 1895, the Damrosch Opera Company opened its Wagner opera week with *Lohengrin* at the Saint Charles Theatre.[478] To help his audience understand this relatively new music, Damrosch lectured on the Wagner operas at Sophie Newcomb Hall on Tuesday, Wednesday, and Friday at 3:30 p.m., under the auspices of the Quarante Club,[479] but the audience remained small for *Die Walküre* on December 17.[480] The *Picayune* asked Damrosch to perform a concert with his pit symphony orchestra of seventy-five—each one an artist; a concert with such an orchestra had never been given in New Orleans before. Instead, Damrosch's opera performed an extra matinee: *Fidelio*.[481] The result of this visit was that New Orleanians heard a kind of opera—late Wagner—to which they were unaccustomed, preparing them for better discernment when their French opera would resume the following year.

An isolated concert in September, on the twenty-first, was sponsored by the League of Cuban-American Ladies at Odd Fellows' Hall.[482] Florence Huberwald was supposed to sing Schubert's "Der Erlkönig," but she was sick. Instead, Grace Kellogg played Schubert's *Marche Militaire* in Tausig's arrangement. During the fall, O'Connell presented a series of four "impromptu" concerts at the Young Men's Gymnastic Club every Friday from October 11 to November 8. He performed music of the great masters, he said, rather than pandering to the general masses.[483] Later, on November 28, O'Connell directed another program at the Young Men's Gymnastic Club, this time including the Quartet of the Y.M.G.C., a choir of young persons, and the Spasm Band.[484] Sousa's Peerless Band appeared for two concerts on November 5 at Washington Artillery Hall, a matinee at 1:30 and an evening concert at 8:00, and he would return for more concerts in a little over a year. On this occasion he was assisted by Mlle Myrta French (soprano) and Mlle Currie Duke (violinist).[485] On November 9–10, 1895, the Ladies' Guibet Mutual Benevolent Association presented its first grand fair, concert, and dance at the French Union Hall. The music was led by Professor L. Fonteynes, ex-baritone of the French Opera.[486] Mme Bailey, who had sung such roles as Marguerite in *Faust* and Philine in *Mignon*, gave a concert at Washington Artillery Hall on November 15, assisted by the talented pianist Cecilia Eppinghousen.[487]

On November 30, at a gathering of the Musicians' Guild at Newcomb College Assembly Hall, Professor Frank Simms of Saint Paul's Church, musical director of the guild, conducted Mendelssohn's *Scottish* Symphony No. 3 (two movements) and Robert Schumann's B-flat Symphony No. 1 (several movements), performed by four pianists as well as a chorus.[488] Simms then presented an organ recital at Saint Paul's Church on December 2; it included works by Rheinberger, Spohr, Guilmant, F. B. Calkin, Merkel, and Batiste.[489] When the new Helme Auditorium opened at the Y.M.C.A., the inaugural concert was conducted by Mrs. Robert Abbott, and the performers were Miss De Gruy, Miss Outlaw, Mr. Sumner, Mr. Despommier, Mr. Norton, Mr. Abbott, and Mrs. Borges, leading soprano of the Bostonians for several seasons.[490] The Werlein Concert Company performed an entertainment at Saint Joseph's Hall on December 4 to help pay for a stained-glass window there.[491]

The next day there was a charity concert at Sainte Mary's Hall on Constance and Jackson streets for homeless persons after a big fire in Algiers, a part of the city located just across the Mississippi River. Included were various skits and songs.[492] On December 6 the Women's Guild of Saint George's Church had a birthday party concert for the benefit of the guild fund, performed by amateurs,[493] and the Keeley Help Club gave the first of a series of social musicales, including piano and violin solos, vocal works, and recitations.[494] The Arlington Quartette Club, talented amateurs, and the Philip Werlein Concert Company presented a vocal and instrumental musical entertainment at Lafayette Presbyterian Church on December 9 for the benefit of the Ladies' Bethel Association.[495] The Battalion Louisiana Field Artillery had recently upgraded its orchestra of twenty-five pieces and, on December 13, gave a complimentary musical and variety entertainment at its armory, Washington Artillery Hall.[496] The thirty-voice choir of Sainte Anna's Church—"the grandest probably in the city"—was augmented by some men and accompanied by a fine orchestra of some ten or twelve instruments for a concert on Christmas Day.[497] The existence of street concerts is attested to by the arrest on December 9 of two Italian organ grinders from New York for performing on the street.[498] This was a repetition of the arrests made during the Christmas season two years before.

Of course, with such an active musical scene in New Orleans, student recitals were always a part of it. On December 20, 1895, the pupils of the Music Department of the Home Institute, under the direction of Miss K. H. Shepard, gave a recital assisted by Misses Allie White, Gertrude Seligman, Sallie Murtagh, Eloise Cazentre, and Stella Lengsfield. The same day, there was a matinee concert by the juvenile orchestra and the Ideal Orchestra under Professor Francis L. Kirst for the benefit of the Female Orphan Asylum, at Odd Fellows' Hall.[499] The pupils of Grace A. Kellogg gave a piano recital at 848 Camp Street on January 22, 1896, featuring the music of Schubert, Gounod, Mendelssohn, and others. University students also participated. The Tulane University Glee, Banjo, and Mandolin Club performed at the French Opera House on December 21, 1895. They were followed on Christmas Day by the Princeton Glee, Banjo, and Mandolin Club, and three days later by the Yale Glee Club, both also at the French Opera House. The mandolin was in vogue at the time. Henry Wehrman took off time from his violin to play and teach the instrument, and Mr. S. Hernandez, professor of mandolin and guitar, opened a new studio at the warerooms of the Dunning-Medine Music Company on January 1, 1896. The following March 3, Mr. R. E. Wells, at Werlein's Music House, announced a rehearsal of a new mandolin and guitar orchestra,[500] and they gave a concert on April 23 at the Academy of Music.

Concerts continued unabated at the Seaman's Upper Bethel on Saint Thomas Street near Jackson Avenue. From December 1, 1894, to December 1, 1895,

4,634 people had attended. There was one concert on December 27, 1895, and others followed on January 2, March 9, March 30, and April 14, 1896.[501] The Philip Werlein Concert Troupe assisted on one occasion. Because of debt, the Seaman's Upper Bethel announced in April that it would close for the summer, so a concert was organized immediately, at the Y.M.C.A. auditorium, to raise money for it, with Jauquet and other singers, Mrs. Robert Sharp at the piano, and Wehrman on violin.

Several famous stars concertized in New Orleans during the spring season. The first was Signorina Nice Moreska, a dramatic soprano, born in Milan, who arrived in New Orleans on December 16, 1895, and immediately gave a rehearsal for selected guests (critics and the press) at the Hotel Royal. She was accompanied by Sig. Alfredo Gore, pianist, and Miss Charlotte Samuels, violinist.[502] She gave four regular concerts beginning on January 2, 1896, and continuing on January 14, 30, and February 21. The first was at the Dunning-Medine Music Company, the next two at the new Helme Memorial Hall of the Y.M.C.A., for the benefit of the Y.M.C.A., and the last at Odd Fellows' Hall. At the second and third concerts, she was accompanied by the Hernandez Mexican Orchestra rather than by Gore. At the last concert, played before a large audience, Gore played his own *Spanish Fantasy,* a Beethoven Sonata in C Minor, Chopin's Polonaise in A-flat, and, with Miss Eckert, a minuet and polka by Grieg. Moreska sang her grand aria from *Norma,* an aria from *L'Africaine,* and an aria from *Vespri Siciliani,* plus encores after each aria, including a Creole song.

After Moreska came Paderewski. On January 27 at the Academy of Music he performed Schubert's Impromptu in B-flat, Beethoven's Sonata Opus 53; the Mendelssohn-Liszt Fantasia on *A Mid-Summer Night's Dream*; Chopin's Nocturne Opus 37, no. 2, *Berceuse* Opus 57, Etudes Opus 25, nos. 3 and 9, Waltz Opus 34 in A-flat, and Mazurka in B Minor; Paderewski's Caprice and Minuet Opus 11; and Liszt's Hungarian Rhapsody No. 2.[503] In what seems to be a first for New Orleans since Herz's appearance in 1847, Paderewski played the entire recital by himself, by heart, without the assistance of any other artists. On January 29, he performed Beethoven Opus 57, Robert Schumann's *Papillons,* Schubert songs in Liszt arrangements (including "Der Erlkönig"), five pieces by Chopin, other pieces by Paderewski himself, and three works by Liszt.[504] For the matinee on January 30, he performed Beethoven's Opus 31, no. 3, a piece by Mendelssohn, Brahms's Variations on a Theme by Paganini, Robert Schumann, Chopin, Liszt, and Paderewski. He left the city immediately after the matinee.[505] While still in America, Paderewski took the time to listen to Celeste Groenevelt, a native New Orleanian and the daughter of Professor Edouard F. Groenevelt and Mrs. Groenevelt, who was herself an accomplished pianist. Celeste studied in New Orleans and New York and, by March 1896, was in Europe at Paderewski's suggestion studying with Leschetizky and Nikisch.[506]

Local pianists also gave concerts this spring, but in the traditional manner with assisting artists. Grace Kellogg, pianist, and her accomplished pupil Miss Stella Jacobs, played at Werlein's parlors on January 8.[507] Mr. Byrd sang some tenor songs by Kellogg. On January 20, 1896, the gifted young pianist Anita Socola played the premier of her new "charming" piece *Nocturne* at Odd Fellows' Hall for the benefit of the Cuban cause.[508] Miss Evelyn Lacoste sang, Henry Wehrman played violin solos, Grace Kellogg played the piano, and several other vocalists sang. The accompanists were Mrs. Leonice Vincent and Miss Eugénie Wehrmann. Miss Elizabeth Reiche, a student pianist, performed a concert at the Academy of Music on February 28 at 2:00 p.m.[509] Reiche performed Beethoven, Chopin, Paderewski, and Liszt. The cantor of Temple Sinai also sang. On March 19, in the auditorium of the Y.M.C.A., Mrs. Samuel played in a benefit for an almshouse given by the women in charge. Mrs. Mabel Munro Langan (the "Scottish Nightingale") sang.[510] Hubert Rolling played some of his own works when he hosted a gathering at his home to hear Henri Dubos, one of the editors of the *Bee,* talk about Wagner.[511]

There were fewer violin concerts this spring. On Saturday, March 7, 1896, Mark Kaiser played at the Catholic Winter School of America at Tulane Hall. He performed "two of his magnificent solos," before and after lectures.[512] Then the violinist, Miss Ollie Torbett, came to town, on March 11–12, together with Miss Frida de Tersmeden (pianist) and the Lutteman Swedish Sextette (male voices), to benefit the building fund of the Y.M.C.A. They performed works by Grieg, Wieniawski, Robert Schumann, Liszt, Gounod, and lesser-known persons.[513]

The singers gave concerts, too, though none of them was especially distinguished. On Sunday, February 16, Mrs. E. Chaillot gave a vocal and instrumental concert to her pupils at the Perfect Union Hall at 7:30 p.m. There was a dance after the concert.[514] Mrs. Mable Munro Langan performed twice, the first on March 17 at the Woman's Social Industrial Hall (Saint Charles Avenue and Hillary Street) for the benefit of the association, and the second on March 20 at the Elks Hall in an entertainment by the Scottish Club. In both cases she was assisted by local talent. She was scheduled to appear, as well, on March 23 at the Bethel, assisted by George G. McHardy on bagpipes and Miss Helen Pitkinon on harp, but she became ill, and the others performed without her.[515] A number of local singers sang with the Orphéon Français on April 5 at Tulane Hall.[516] Florence Huberwald and her pupils, along with Mme Samuel, MM Henderson, and Wehrman held a grand vocal and instrumental concert at Odd Fellows' Hall on April 8, and the next evening Miss Varelli-Jauquet, assisted by members of the Singers' Club, of which she was the leader, gave a concert at the Y.M.C.A. auditorium.[517]

There were three sacred concerts worthy of mention. On Sunday, February 2, 1896, there was a benefit for Sainte Theresa's Conference of the Saint Vincent de Paul Society, at Sainte Theresa's Church (Camp and Erato streets).[518] We do not know the program. On Palm Sunday, March 29, the priests at the Jesuit Church sang the "Passion of Our Lord" in Gregorian chant.[519] And on Sunday, April 12, at Saint Augustine's Church (corner of Saint Claude and Bayou Road), the choir sang Gounod's *Sainte Cecilia's Mass* and Mr. Frenclie (?) sang "Charité" by Fauré.[520]

Other concerts, mostly of a very local nature, were performed sporadically throughout the spring. There was a concert at the new Y.M.C.A. building on January 7 by Mrs. Diboll, Mrs. Borjes, Misses de Gruy, Bailen, Outlaw, and Kaufman; MM Despommier, Norton, Sumner, and Abbott.[521] There was another one on January 17, at the French Union Hall, for the benefit of the Chinchuba Deaf Mute Institution; it was performed by the "best amateur talent."[522] Paoletti led his famous orchestra from the balcony inside the Washington Artillery on February 1.[523] The Musicians' Guild held a recital at Sophe Newcomb College on February 8 and again on March 21.[524] At the second event, Frank Simms presented a Mozart and a Beethoven symphony (played by four women), various vocal pieces including one by Weber, and a grand overture by Mendelssohn. The Cahill-Wallace Combination, an orchestra organized in 1891, gave performances under Willie Messersmith, cornetist, on April 4–5 at the Church of the Assisi.[525] Mr. and Mrs. W. W. Summer gave a musicale, on March 16, in Mrs. Nixon's School Hall, 2722 Saint Charles Avenue, for the benefit of the Society for the Prevention of Cruelty to Animals. They were assisted by Corinne Bailey, Jeanne Outlaw, Anita Socola, Varelli-Jauquet, Mrs. C. C. Diboll, Victor Despommier, Henry Wehrman, Thomas B. Norton, Robert Abbott, and Bernard C. Shields.[526]

At a program sponsored by the New Orleans Stenographers' Association, on March 26, members of the association performed vocal and instrumental selections.[527] They had done the same thing in 1892. Both Eckert and Alice Hufft participated in a musical, literary, and dramatic celebration of the twentieth anniversary of the Orleans Pythians on April 10.[528] An attractive program was performed at "an enjoyable musicale" at the residence of Mrs. F. Choppin on April 11, 1896, to raise funds for the repair of Saint Patrick's Church. As the

Picayune reported, "A large audience filled the cozy parlors, which had been tastefully decorated for the occasion. Professor George O'Connell had charge of the musicale, and the select programme rendered was due to his untiring efforts and ability of the artists who contributed their talent."[529] The program included vocal solos and ensembles by Kreutzer, Massenet, Gounod, Verdi, and Robardi. Mr. George Blanchin provided violin obbligatos.

On April 12 there was a concert of Italian music at Tulane Hall rendered to Mlle Anna Rinaldi by the Gircolo Filodrammatico Italiano Pablo Ferrari. It included an orchestra, singers, and the violinist Durel.[530] There was a grand entertainment (songs, arias, monologues, a violin solo) performed at the French Union Hall on April 18 for the benefit of the poor under the patronage of the Ladies' Auxiliary of the Saint Vincent de Paul Society, Saint Augustin's Church. Admission was twenty-five cents. The event was marred by an unruly crowd that always was found in Congo Square.[531] On April 22, the students of the Matthey-Ricard Institute held a musical fete.[532] In early May 1896, there was a benefit concert for the very young musician and composer Walter Lee Therman at the Y.M.C.A. Hall.[533] But overshadowing all these minor concerts was the reappearance, in April, of the most famous actress in the world, Sarah Bernhardt.[534]

The summer concerts were once again dominated by Paoletti and his band at West End. From May until the first week of September they were the main source for concerts in New Orleans.[535]

The first fall concert was on September 10, 1896, at Perseverance Hall (Saint Claude and Dumaine streets). It was a fete by the Club des Acacias, and the performers included Mlles Michet and Pujol, MM Fonteynes, Gaillard, Maumus, Ronede, and Bellecourt; the Orphéon Français under George O'Connell; and piano by Mlles Wehrmann, Ruel, Mme Gaillard, Professor O'Connell, and others.[536] The Seamen's Bethel, under musical director Miss Delphine Steele (the pastor of the church was Rev. Steele) inaugurated its regular Monday night concerts of the 1896–97 season on October 5, 1896. Miss Steel was honored at a concert there on January 14, 1897.[537] On Monday, October 12, there was a concert at the Union Français that opened its newly rebuilt concert hall. Performers included Professor Fonteynes, Miss Adele Rivière, Mr. René Galliard, MM H. Wehrman, Durel, Miss Amelie Poujoul, Miss A. Ruel (piano), and the chorus of the Union Français.[538] The Concordia Young People's Association ran an entertainment at Saint Paul's Church on October 16 with selections by the choir, songs, and an overture, as well as tableaux and dramatic recitations.[539]

Mario Sanches, young Mexican violinist, pupil of Ovide Musin, gave a recital at the Dunning-Medine parlors on Thursday, October 22, assisted by

Grace Kellogg and Perival Doublass Byrd.[540] He performed pieces by Wieniawski, Musin, and others. They repeated the performance on October 29. On October 22 was also the first concert of the year by the Orphéon Français at French Union Hall, directed by O'Connell. It included an accompanied violin solo by Henry Wehrman and Miss Eugénie Wehrmann but was mostly choral works.[541] An entertainment at Washington Artillery, on October 23, to benefit Trinity Chapel involved female performers on mandolin, guitar, and piano.[542] The first concert of the Tulane Glee, Banjo, and Mandolin Club for the season occurred on October 24.[543] The Trilby Social and Musical Club gave a grand soiree complimentaire et dansante on Saturday, October 31, at Olympic Hall.[544] Forty hours of devotion at Saint Stephen's Church on Napoleon and Camp streets, on Thursday, November 19, featured music by various composers such as Verdi, Chickering, Millard, Curto, and Weber, performed by Gernhauser, a choir, and others.[545] On Friday, November 20, the Metropolitan Concert Series at the brand new Athenaeum Theater gave its first concert featuring the great Nordica and Linde, assisted by Riegn, Dempsay, and De Macchi.[546] This was a new kind of concert series for the city, since each event on the series was a single concert by a different international celebrity. The second concert featured Maud Powell on December 23. Concert series of this nature soon came to dominate the concert life of New Orleans.

As early as the beginning of March, the leaders of the Opera House, with the input of prominent citizens, brought in Mr. F. Charley, an impresario from Buenos Aires and Paris, with the purpose of reviving the French Opera in the fall of 1896. Opera was economically and culturally important to the city, and, despite a bad economy and the distraction of the presidential election in the fall of 1896, it could serve as the city's main attraction to bring in tourists. Charley went to France during the summer and recruited some fine singers, including tenor Prévost, bass Javid, baritone Albers, and contralto Mlle Marthe Combes, "a beautiful woman gifted with a wonderful voice." The opera season finally opened, after a lapse of almost two years, on November 24 with *Les Huguenots*. At last, New Orleans had its favorite type of music available nightly for a whole season—the only American city outside New York that in 1896 could make that claim.[547] In addition to the regular season at the French Opera, on October 11, 1896, the Whitney Opera Company performed the opéra comique *Rob Roy*, by DeKoven and Smith, at the Grand Opera House.[548] The French Opera season lasted only until the beginning of March, however, when it went on tour to San Francisco.[549]

Whereas the spring 1896 season, with only a few exceptions, had weak talent, the end of the year 1896 and the beginning of 1897 brought to the local concert stage some very fine, even great talent, both local artists and visitors. While most of the pupils of Marguerite Samuel who performed on Friday, December 4, at the Dunning-Medine Music Store were amateurs, the mere presence of this great artist was worthy of attention.[550] On the other hand, the concerts of the Frohsinn on the fourth and by Tulane's Glee, Mandolin and Banjo Club at old Tulane Hall on the eleventh were minor events, as was the singing of Gounod's "Ave Maria" by opera singer Mme Frémaux-Benatti and a "Crucifix" duet with M Fonteynes, formerly of the French Opera, at the 11:00 o'clock mass at the Cathedral on the twentieth.[551] The announcement, on December 19, 1896, of the formation of the New Orleans String Quartet by Henry Wehrman (first violin), J. Voorheis (second violin), J. Pomero (viola) and C. Grisai (violoncello), however, was a major event in the history of concert life in New Orleans.[552] The city once again would have a resident professional string quartet.[553] In one guise or another, this quartet lasted well into the twentieth century. Also significant was the performance on Christmas Day of Haydn's Mass No. 1 at Saint Louis Cathedral, accompanied by organ (J. Pomero) and orchestra. Paoletti conducted, and, given the high standards this conductor evinced before, the performance must have been first rate.[554]

Then, on Wednesday, December 23, Maud Powell presented a concert in the Athénée (Atheneum) with tenor Xanten of the Damrosch Troupe, Marthe Garrison Minor, Di Bassini baritone of Milan, and Jacques Friedberger pianist. This was the second concert of the Metropolitan Series at the Athénée. Powell played pieces by Mendelssohn, Chopin, Leoncavallo, Liszt, Meyerbeer, Wienawski, and Mozart, and showed why she was one of the greatest violinists of her time.[555] This concert demonstrated another trend in the concert life of the city after 1886. In the past, visiting virtuosi came for at least a few days and performed a number of times, often increasing the number as their reception proved warm. There were a few exceptions, such as Remenyi. But Powell came for one performance only, and this became the trend for future visitors. These single performances were part of a series of concerts lasting over the entire season.

The main events in January 1897 were the five concerts by the Sousa band on the fourteenth, fifteenth, sixteenth (matinee and evening) and seventeenth at the Saint Charles Theatre and the Academy of Music. Sousa brought Miss Martina Johnstone as violin soloist, Arthur Pryer as trombone soloist, a soprano, and several others. They played works by Suppé, Sousa, Nessler, Lalo, MacDowell, Gounod, Sgambati, Holman-Bizet, Wagner, Arnold, Liszt, Donizetti, Vieuxtemps, Godfrey, Rimsky-Korsakov (*Scheherazade*), and Eilenberg.[556]

Most of the rest of the concerts in January were routine. On January 15, 1897, there was a musical and literary entertainment at the rooms of the Keeley Institute, corner Aline and Magazine streets.[557] A musical and dramatic entertainment at the Y.M.H.A., by amateur performers on January 25, is notable for one unfortunate work on the program, "Negro Pastimes" sung by B. C. Casanos.[558] Between an operetta in three acts and a ballet at the French Opera on January 27, a musical intermède consisted of nine arias or ensembles by members of the French Opera company, accompanied by concertmaster Nicosias and by Paoletti.[559] M San Remo Souola directed a grande fete dramatique et musicale to benefit the Dominican Convent on January 29 and 30.[560] More significant was the grand concert by the pupils of Professor Adolphe Duquesnay, at Dunning's Concert Hall on Camp Street on January 25, 1897. There were choruses, solos on piano, and vocal selections by Mozart, Gottschalk, Rossini, Bellini, Verdi, and Thomas.[561]

The famous singer Yvette Guilbert and her concert opera troupe appeared in four concerts at the Academy of Music on January 31 and February 1–3, 1897.[562] Another famous singer, Eilen Beach Yaw, gave two concerts at the French Opera on March 15–16, to benefit the Y.M.C.A. Assisting her were the American Max Dick, violinist and pupil of Wieniawski, and Miss Georgiella Lay, American piano virtuoso.[563] Otherwise, the concerts were minor. There was a benefit for MM Alessandri and Lespinasse and Mme Lafauillade at the French Union on February 25,[564] and on March 21 Mme Clément Labarre, one of the most intelligent music teachers in the city, had some of her pupils perform—violin, piano, voice—in the salons of Mme H. C. Landry.[565]

By the middle of 1897, concert life in New Orleans had changed. While concerts proliferated from 1876 on, even surpassing the number of concerts from before the Civil War, New Orleans slipped during this period vis-à-vis New York into an inferior position. Whereas before the war the city boasted many significant artists who resided in New Orleans and then toured elsewhere, by the last three decades of the nineteenth century many local artists had moved to New York to carry on their careers. Most notable were the Frankos, the Pembertons, W. T. Francis, and D'Aquin—natives and leaders in the concert life of New Orleans at one time or another—who eventually made New York their home. Economics was a major factor. Whereas New Orleans was the leading city in America for opera before the war, it had a hard time keeping opera afterwards because of the expense. The number of concerts in New York and elsewhere in the major cities of the East Coast surpassed that in New Orleans, and increasingly New Orleans was off the beaten track for great European touring artists. Fortunately, there was a coterie of distinguished performers who remained in the city and kept it viable for at least another quarter-century—most notably Kaiser, Wehrman, Samuel, Grisai, and Paoletti. Others, however, no longer regarded the city as the musical jewel of American cities, as had, for example, Herz, Rubinstein, and Vieuxtemps. The Grand Old City of opera and classical concerts was preparing to move in a different musical direction.

NOTES

PREFACE

1. Henry A. Kmen's *Music in New Orleans: the Formative Years, 1791–1841* (Baton Rouge: Louisiana State University Press, 1966) remains a valuable study. Its focus, however, is different; it covers all aspects of the music of New Orleans, not just the concert life. I go into much greater detail on the concert life, including the personalities and the institutions. Also, Kmen stops at 1841, just as New Orleans was reaching its greatest years, while I continue to 1897 and include those great years, the Civil War, Reconstruction, and the gradual decline of the city in the late nineteenth century.

2. The essays on Paul Emile Johns and Jeanne Franko, though now updated, were originally published elsewhere.

INTRODUCTION

1. For an excellent scholarly discussion of the political and cultural origins of New Orleans, see Lawrence N. Powell, *The Accidental City: Improvising New Orleans* (Cambridge, Mass.: Harvard University Press, 2012). See also Ned Sublette, *The World That Made New Orleans: From Spanish Silver to Congo Square* (Chicago: Lawrence Hill Books, 2008).

Book I, Part I

CHAPTER ONE

1. An important early private venue for concerts took place at the home of Madame Herries on Chartres Street (see page 294). See also the private house concert described in Henry Didimus, *New Orleans As I Found It* (New York: Harper and Brothers, 1845), 54–60.

2. Winston C. Babb, "French Refugees from Saint-Domingue to the Southern United States, 1791–1810," Ph.D. diss., University of Virginia, 1954, 210.

3. Grétry's *Silvain* was performed frequently in Haiti from 1770 on. Jean Fouchard, *Artistes et Répertoire des scenes de Saint-Domingue* (Port-au-Prince: Imprimerie de l'État, 1955).

4. Kmen, *Music in New Orleans*, 47, 64, 67.

5. *Moniteur de la Louisiana*, Jan. 28, 1807, p. 2, col. 4; Jan. 31, 1807, p. 2, col. 4.

6. Ibid., Dec. 26, 1807, p. 2, col. 3.

7. Ibid., Oct. 22, 1808, p. 3, col. 1.

8. Ibid., May 24, 1806, 3 pages.

9. Kmen, *Music in New Orleans,* 67. The term "Chinoise" meant that it was decorated in a manner suggesting Chinese art.

10. *Moniteur de la Louisiana,* Mar. 4, 1809, p. 3, col. 2.

11. John Smith Kendall, *The Golden Age of New Orleans Theater* (Baton Rouge: Louisiana State University Press, 1952), 2–3.

12. *The Telegraphe,* Apr. 5, 1808, p. 3.

13. On Dec. 22, 1819, a French citizen of New Orleans went to the American Theatre which was occupying the St. Philippe Street Theatre. Instead of the artistic, subtle sounds of famous French operas he heard "Yankee Doodle" and other low-class things. He found a few laudable things to say, but basically he looked down on the Americans in the audience who seemed to thoroughly enjoy the entertainment (*Gazette de la Louisiana,* Dec. 22, 1819, p. 1, col. 5). At the same time, an American went to the same theatre on the same evening. He was much more sympathetic to the Americans and was basically opposed to the sneering view of the French citizen (*Louisiana Gazette,* Dec. 22, 1819, p. 2, col. 1). On Jan. 8, 1820, however, to commemorate the end of the War of 1812 (1815) the Théâtre d'Orléans united both the French and American troupes, to great acclaim.

14. *New Orleans Directory for 1842* (New Orleans: Pitts and Clarke, 1842), vol. 2: 53.

15. Kendall, *The Golden Age,* 2. See John Davis's announcement for the building of the second theater in *Courier,* Nov. 13, 1816, p. 2, col. 3.

16. *Tribune de la N.-Orleans,* Dec. 8, 1866, p. 1, col. 4; *L'Abeille de la Nouvell-Orléans,* Dec. 9, 1866, p. 1, col. 2.

17. Albert A. Fossier, *New Orleans, the Glamour Period, 1800–1840* (New Orleans: Pelican Publishing Co., 1957), 469.

18. *The Bee,* Nov. 7, 1837, p. 2, col. 2, and *L'Abeille,* Nov. 9, 1837.

19. *The Bee,* Dec. 12, 1866, p. 1, col. 2; Dec. 17, 1866, p. 1, col. 5; Dec. 24, 1866, p. 1, col. 1.

20. Concerts were held on Jan. 28, 1808; Mar. 29, 1808; Oct. 22, 1808; Nov. 18, 1808; Jan. 3, 13, 1809; Feb. 18, 1809; Dec. 8, 1809; Feb. 11, 1810; Mar. 9, 1810; Nov. 26, 1810; Dec. 6, 11, 12, 1810; and Mar. 2, 1811.

21. Jan. 27, 1812; Mar. 9, 19, 1813; Dec. 7, 10, 20, 1813; Mar. 9, 1814; Apr. 11, 1814; Jan. 10, 15, 22, 26, 1816; Feb. 5, 16, 1816; May 11, 1816; Dec. 30, 1816; Jan. 21, 1817; Feb. 4, 8, 25, 1817; Jan. 1, 1818.

22. Dec. 9, 1817 (the announcement states that this was the first concert at this theater); Dec. 31, 1817; Jan. 12, 17, 1818; Feb. 19, 1818; Apr. 7, 1818; Nov. 23, 25, 1818; Dec. 4, 1818; Jan. 18, 1819; Feb. 3, 10, 17, 1819.

23. Mar. 7, 13, 1811; Jan. 16, 1812; Feb. 20, 1813; Mar. 9, 1814; Feb. 27, 1819; Mar. 9, 1819; Apr. 1, 1819; May 6, 1819; Dec. 22, 1819.

24. Apr. 23, 1818; Feb. 10, 1819.

25. Such as on Nov. 4, 1817.

26. Kmen, *Music in New Orleans,* 6.

27. These are mentioned in the account of the 1866 fire in *L'Abeille,* Dec. 9, 1866, p. 1, col. 2. The description that follows is from *New-Orleans Directory for 1842* (New Orleans: Pitts & Clarke, 1842).

28. Kendall, *The Golden Age,* 18.

29. Ibid., 35–36.

30. Ibid., 167–68.

31. *New Orleans Directory for 1842* 2: 54.

32. After 1899 there was a third St. Charles Theater that became a movie house and was demolished in 1965. See Alex Alkire, "The St. Charles Theater" (a student paper, in Tulane University, Southern Architectural Archive, MSS 190 [215]).

33. Kendall, *The Golden Age*, 214 and 267.

34. Ibid., 214 and 253.

35. *New Orleans Directory for 1842*, 57.

36. Ibid., 54.

37. *L'Abeille*, Mar. 23, 1863, p. 1, col. 7.

38. *Harper's Weekly* (Aug. 25, 1866), 537. See review of James G. Hollandsworth Jr., *An Absolute Massacre: the New Orleans Race Riot of July 30, 1866*, in *Journal of Southern History* (Nov. 1, 2002).

39. *Library Journal* (Feb. 1997): 89, and William Kerr, "The Fisk Free and Public Library of New Orleans," 32.

40. *Daily Delta*, Sunday, Dec. 23, 1849, p. 1: plans for the hall.

41. *The Bee*, Dec. 4, 1865, p. 3, col. 1.

42. *Picayune*, Nov. 11, 1868, p. 2, col. 1.

43. Ibid., cols. 1–2.

44. *L'Abeille*, Feb. 13, 1894, p. 4, cols. 1–2.

45. Kendall, *The Golden Age*, 351ff and 472.

46. John E. Land, *Pen Illustrations of New Orleans* (New Orleans: published by the author, 1882), 117.

47. *The Bee*, Apr. 9, 1862, p. 1, col. 6.

48. Ibid., Apr. 16, 1864, p. 1, col. 6; Apr. 18, p. 1, cols. 1 and 5.

49. Jan. 1857; Apr. 1862; Dec. 1862; Oct. 1863; Nov. 1863; Apr. 1864; summer 1864; Nov. 1864; Dec. 1864; Apr. 1865; Oct. 1866; Feb. 1867; Dec. 1867; May 1868; Nov. 1869; Nov. 1870; Feb. 1871; Apr. 1871; Sept. 1872; Jan. 1873; Apr. 1876; Dec. 1877; Mar. 1879; Sept. 1879; Feb. 1882; Jan. 1889; Oct. 1889; Feb. 1892; Apr. 1895; Jan. 1896 (Paderewski); Feb. 1896; Apr. 1896; Jan.–Feb. 1897.

50. *The Life of P. T. Barnum, Written by Himself* (New York: Redfield, 1855).

51. *Picayune*, Dec. 2, 1859, p. 2, cols. 3–4.

52. Note that the *Picayune* critic considered the viewing of the audience more important than the viewing of the stage. Richard Wagner and Denkmar Adler would later call foul at this style of opera house in a democratic society, but the perverse horseshoe design lingers on in such recent major halls as that in Dallas. *The Bee* critic was far more astute.

53. *The Bee*, Dec. 2, 1859, p. 3, col. 4.

54. A letter to the paper by "Nemo" complains that the opera is uncomfortable, and that unless someone does something about it, the average citizen will not attend and it will fold. This elicited responses criticizing Nemo for going public and not going through proper channels to get things improved (*Picayune*, Jan. 28, 1875, p. 2, col. 5; rebuttal Jan. 31, 1875, p. 2, col. 5).

55. For a history of the French Opera House from 1859 to 1873, see *L'Abeille*, Feb. 23, 1873, p. 2, col. 1.

56. Nathaniel Curtis, *New Orleans, Its Old Houses, Shops, and Public Buildings* (Philadelphia: J. B. Lippincott Co., 1933), 199.

57. Lorelle Causey Bender, "The French Opera House of New Orleans 1859–1890," M.A. thesis, Louisiana State University, 1940, 8–11. Bender has based her description on *The New Orleans Delta*, May 3, 1859, p. 11.

58. *The Bee*, Nov. 22, 1866, p. 1, col. 1.

59. *New Orleans Times*, Apr. 11, 1868, p. 3, col. 2.

60. J. Curtis Waldo, a local publisher and photo-engraver, issued his *Illustrated Visitors' Guide to New Orleans* in 1879. The guide features tourist highlights in the Crescent City along with promi-

nent businesses (and businessmen), institutions, and organizations of the day. It is well illustrated with photo-engraved views of buildings and portraits of New Orleanians. There is considerable similarity between this work and the earlier Edwin Jewell's *Crescent City Illustrated* (New Orleans: published by the author, 1873) as well as similarities with such later guides such as Land's *Pen Illustrations,* William H. Coleman's *Historical Sketch Book and Guide to New Orleans* (1885), and Andrew Morrison's *Industries of New Orleans* (1885). We present here a sample of Waldo's building views, a glimpse of New Orleans 125 years ago.

61. *L'Abeille,* Feb. 1, 1874, p. 1, col. 2.

62. Ibid., Oct. 25, 1895, p. 3, col. 1.

63. New Orleans Public Library, Louisiana Division, City Archives, City Engineer's Office Records.

64. *L'Abeille,* Oct. 17, 1894, p. 4, col. 1; Oct. 21, 1894, p. 1, col. 8; p. 4, col. 2; Oct. 24, 1894, p. 4, col. 5; Oct. 25, 1894, p. 4, col. 1.

65. Ibid., May 23, 1884, p. 1, col. 3.

66. Andrew Morrison, *The Industries of New Orleans* (New Orleans: J. M. Elstner & Co., 1885), 19.

67. A third hall, People's Theatre on Magazine between Washington and Sixth streets, does not seem to have served any concerts. A detailed description of the hall, seating normally 1,400, can be found in *Picayune,* Sept. 18, 1891, p. 3, col. 6.

68. *Picayune,* Nov. 18, 1896, p. 9, cols. 1–4.

69. Ibid., Dec. 1, 1895, p. 15, col. 5.

70. *L'Abeille,* Nov. 22, 1864, p. 1, col. 5.

71. Ibid., Feb. 22, 1865, p. 1, col. 6.

72. *The Bee,* Jan. 8, 1865, p. 1, col. 1.

73. *L'Abeille,* Nov. 23, 1837, p. 3, col. 1.

74. Ibid., Dec. 6, 1851, p. 1, col. 1. Review: Dec. 8, 1851, p. 1, col. 2.

75. Ibid., Mar. 30, 1872, p. 1, col. 2.

76. Ibid., Dec. 19, 1875, p. 4, col. 1.

77. Ibid., Oct. 22, 1882, p. 4, col. 3.

78. *Picayune,* Apr. 4, 1876, p. 1, col. 5.

79. *L'Abeille,* May 2, 1877, p. 2, col. 3, May 6, 1877, p. 1, col. 2, and May 12, 1877, p. 1, col. 2. Review of a rehearsal: May 9, 1877, p. 1, col. 2. Review: May 15, 1877, p. 1, col. 2.

80. *L'Abeille,* Dec. 24, 1882, p. 1, col. 3.

81. Ibid., Dec. 7, 1884, p. 4, col. 3. Reviewed by Conange (he didn't like it), Dec. 9, 1884, p. 4, col. 2.

82. *Picayune,* Dec. 24, 1889, p. 6, col. 3.

83. Ibid., Mar. 21, 1892, p. 3, col. 4.

84. *L'Abeille,* Dec. 25, 1896, p. 3, col. 5.

85. Ibid., Mar. 24, 1877, p. 2, col. 4; Mar. 25, 1877, p. 1, col. 2.

86. Ibid., Apr. 12, 1878, p. 1, col. 3, and corrected Apr. 14, 1878, p. 1, col. 3.

87. Ibid., May 1, 1863, p. 1, col. 7.

88. Alecia P. Long, *The Great Southern Babylon: Sex, Race, and Respectability in New Orleans, 1865–1920* (Baton Rouge: Louisiana State University Press, 2005), chap. 2.

89. *L'Abeille,* June 2, 1894, p. 4, col. 1; June 6, 1894, p. 4, col. 1.

90. Fatima Shaik, "An Age of Men," in progress, communication from author.

91. *L'Abeille,* May 6, 1875, p. 1, col. 2; May 16, 1875, p. 2, col. 4.

92. Ibid., May 11, 1875, p. 1, col. 3.

93. Ibid., May 22, 1875, p. 1, col. 2.

94. Ibid., Dec. 19, 1875, p. 3, col. 2.

95. Ann Woodruff, "Society Halls in New Orleans: A Survey of Jazz Landmarks, Part I," *The Jazz Archivist* 20 (2007): 16–17.

96. Long, *The Great Southern Babylon,* 136.

97. Sister Mary Francis Borgia Hart, "Violets in the King's Garden: a History of the Sisters of the Holy Family of New Orleans," reproduced typescript, New Orleans, 1976, pp. 26, 33–35, and 111. Available in Loyola University Library, New Orleans.

CHAPTER TWO

1. Such uses of the "pit" orchestra were not, of course, unique to New Orleans; for example, they were the same in Charleston, South Carolina (Nicholas Michael Butler, *Votaries of Apollo* [Columbia: University of South Carolina Press, 2007], 176.

2. *Moniteur de la Louisiana,* Feb. 14, 1807, p. 3, col. 1.

3. *New Orleans Daily Creole* 1, no. 129ff., p. 3, col. 3.

4. Ibid., no. 121, Nov. 5, 1856, p. 3, col. 3.

5. *New Orleans Daily Creole,* Dec. 20, 1856, p. 2, col. 1.

6. *Picayune,* Dec. 8, 1859, supplement, p. 1, col. 3.

7. *The Bee,* Feb. 15, 1854, p. 1, col. 1, and *L'Abeille,* Feb. 15, 1854, p. 2, col. 2.

8. *The Bee,* Mar. 7, 1854, p. 1, col. 9.

9. Most of this biography of Collignon is taken directly from Jewell, *Crescent City Illustrated,* 172.

10. *Picayune,* Feb. 8, 1856, p. 2, col. 1.

11. Ibid., Apr. 4, 1856, p. 4, col. 1.

12. Ibid., Mar. 7, 1856, p. 4, col. 1.

13. *New Orleans Daily Creole* 1, no. 150, Dec. 8, 1856, p. 2, col. 3.

14. *Picayune,* Jan. 8, 1857, p. 5, col. 3.

15. Ibid., Jan. 29, 1857, p. 4, col. 1.

16. Ibid., Jan. 17, 1858, afternoon ed., p. 1, col. 4.

17. Ibid., Feb. 28, 1858, p. 4, col. 1.

18. Ibid., Apr. 3, 1859, p. 6, col. 1.

19. Ibid., May 17, 1860, p. 1, col. 3, and May 12, 1860, p. 1, col. 4.

20. *The Bee,* Jan. 24, 1856, p. 1, col. 10.

21. *Picayune,* Nov. 28, 1857, p. 4, col. 2, reports that at the opening of the season there were 223 subscribers.

22. Ibid., May 1, 1858, afternoon ed., p. 2, col. 2.

23. Ibid., Nov. 27, 1858, p. 2, col. 2.

24. Ibid., Dec. 1, 1859, p. 6, col. 1. How large the list of subscribers was at this point is not revealed in specific numbers.

25. Ibid., Nov. 18, 1860, p. 6, col. 1.

26. Ibid., Nov. 20, 1860, p. 2, col. 4. See also *Picayune,* Nov. 25, 1860, p. 8, col. 1.

27. Ibid., Dec. 23, 1860, p. 6, col. 1.

28. *The Bee,* Feb. 4, 1861, p. 1, col. 3.

29. *L'Abeille,* Mar. 11, 1858, p. 2, col. 2.

30. *Picayune,* Feb. 23, 1859, p. 1, col. 2.

31. Ibid.

32. *L'Abeille,* July 21, 1862, p. 1, col. 3.

33. Ibid., July 28, 1862, p. 1, col. 2.

34. A complete performance of *La Dame Blanche* along with the Confederate song "Guerre aux Yankees"—the Union forces had not yet entered the city (*L'Abeille,* Jan. 3, 1862, p. 1, col. 3).

35. *L'Abeille,* June 21, 1862, p. 1, col. 2.

36. Ibid., July 5, 1862, p. 1, col. 2.

37. This included a full orchestra for an overture and for accompaniment of singing (*L'Abeille,* July 26, 1862, p. 1, col. 2; July 21, p. 1, col. 3; July 22, p. 1, col. 1). Review, *L'Abeille,* July 28, 1862, p. 1, col. 2.

38. The fourth act of Donizetti's *La Favorite* (*L'Abeille,* Feb. 12, 1863, p. 1, col. 1).

39. A complete performance of *The Barber of Seville*—the first complete opera heard in New Orleans for nearly two years, laments the writer in *L'Abeille,* Feb. 28, 1863.

40. A complete performance of *Lucia di Lammermoor* (*L'Abeille,* Mar. 23, 1863, p. 1, col. 7, and Mar. 27, 1863, p. 1, col. 2).

41. *L'Abeille,* May 1, 1863, p. 1, col. 2, and *The Bee,* May 5, 1863, p. 1, col. 1.

42. *L'Abeille,* Oct. 3, 1863, p. 1, col. 2, and Sept. 30, 1863, p. 1, col. 6.

43. A complete performance of *The Barber of Seville* (*L'Abeille,* Mar. 29, 1864, p. 2, col. 3).

44. *L'Abeille,* Apr. 9, 1864, p. 1, cols. 2 and 5.

45. *The Bee,* Apr. 14, 1864, p. 1, cols. 1 and 6.

46. *L'Abeille,* Apr. 22, 1864, p. 1, col. 3.

47. In 1864, Lewis Baker proposed establishing an Italian opera season and asked for subscribers, but nothing seems to have come of it (*L'Abeille,* May 7, 1864, p. 1, col. 7).

48. *The Bee,* July 18, 1864, p. 1, col. 1.

49. *Picayune,* Apr. 15, 1859, p. 1, col. 2.

50. *The Bee,* Oct. 2, 1864, p. 1, col. 3.

51. *L'Abeille,* Oct. 6, 1864, p. 1, col. 7; *The Bee,* Oct. 20, 1864, p. 1, col. 6, and Oct. 28, 1864, p. 1, col. 6.

52. Some of the non-orchestral concerts at the Opera House at this time are recorded in *The Bee,* Nov. 28, 1864, p. 1, col. 1; *L'Abeille,* Nov. 29, 1864, p. 1, col. 2; review in *L'Abeille,* Dec. 2, 1864, p. 1, col. 2; and *L'Abeille,* Dec. 14, 1864, p. 1, col. 6.

53. For the fall 1865 season which opened on Oct. 27, see *L'Abeille,* Oct. 26, 1865, p. 2, col. 3.

54. *L'Abeille,* May 7, 1862, p. 1, col. 2.

55. *The Bee,* Apr. 9, 1862, p. 1, col. 6.

56. Ibid., Apr. 16, 1864, p. 1, col. 6, and Apr. 18, p. 1, cols. 1 and 5.

57. *L'Abeille,* Mar. 23, 1863, p. 1, col. 7.

58. Ibid., Feb. 9, 1863, p. 1, col. 7; Feb. 10, 1863, p. 1, col. 1.

59. *The Bee,* Apr. 1, 1863, p. 1, col. 7.

60. *L'Abeille,* Nov. 13, 1863, p. 1, col. 2.

61. Ibid., July 5, 1862, p. 1, col. 2.

62. *The Bee,* Mar. 23, 1863, p. 1, col. 9.

63. *L'Abeille,* Mar. 27, 1863, p. 1, col. 2.

64. Reviewers were amazed that such a serious actor who starred in the tragedies at the theater could also on occasion enact a role in a comedy (*The Bee,* Mar. 16, 1864, p. 1, col. 3).

65. *L'Abeille,* Sept. 12, 1863, p. 1, col. 2.

66. Ibid., Nov. 22, 1864, p. 1, col. 5.

67. Ibid., Feb. 22, 1865, p. 1, col. 6; *The Bee,* Jan. 8, 1865, p. 1, col. 1.

68. It was not unusual then for individuals to be professionally involved in more than one theater. The scenic designer of the French Opera House, M Develle, likewise served more than one

theater; he furnished drop curtains at both the Varieties and the Academy of Music (*The Bee,* Sept. 5, 1864, p. 1, col. 1).

69. *The Bee,* Nov. 11, 1864, p. 1, col. 1. Gabici, who was the most important violinist in the city before the war, died sometime before 1865, possibly as early as 1860 when he is last heard of.

70. *L'Abeille,* May 1, 1863, p. 1, col. 7.

71. Ibid., Mar. 14, 1865, p. 2, col. 3. The concert was originally scheduled for Mar. 19 but was postponed to Mar. 26.

72. For a biography of Oliveira, see Brian C. Thompson, "Journeys of an Immigrant Violinist," *Journal of the Society for American Music* 6 (2012): 51–82.

73. *The Bee,* Mar. 16, 1863, p. 1, col. 8; reviewed Mar. 18, p. 1, col. 1, and Mar. 20, p. 1, col. 1. At this point Greuling was the regular conductor of the orchestra at the Varieties Theater.

74. *L'Abeille,* Mar. 23, 1863, p. 1, col. 7.

75. *The Bee,* Apr. 8, 1865, p. 1, col. 1; *L'Abeille,* Apr. 14, 1865, p. 1, col. 7; and *L'Abeille,* Apr. 19, 1865, p. 1, col. 1.

76. *The Bee,* Jan. 15, 1863, p. 1, col. 7.

77. *L'Abeille,* June 5, 1863, p. 1, col. 5.

78. *The Bee,* Apr. 7, 1865, p. 1, col. 1, and Apr. 10, 1865, p. 1, col. 3.

79. Gustave Chouquet, "Prévost," in *Grove's Dictionary of Music and Musicians,* ed. J. A. Fuller Maitland (Philadelphia: Theodore Presser, 1926), vol. 3: 812.

80. *L'Abeille,* May 1, 1865, p. 1, col. 8.

81. Ibid., May 17, 1865, p. 1, col. 2; May 26, 1865, p. 1, col. 2; *The Bee,* May 17, 1865, p. 1, col. 1.

82. *L'Abeille,* Apr. 14, 1865, p. 1, col. 7.

83. Ibid., May 1, 1865, p. 1, col. 8.

84. *The Bee,* May 16, 1865, p. 1, col. 8.

85. For a few of the others, see *L'Abeille,* May 29, 1865, p. 1, col. 8; May 30, 1865, p. 1, col. 2; and June 3, 1865, p. 1, col. 2.

86. *L'Abeille,* May 3, 1867, p. 1, col. 2; *L'Abeille,* Apr. 26, 1867, p. 2, col. 3, May 1, 1867, p. 2, col. 3, and May 2, p. 1, col. 2; *The Bee,* May 2, 1867, p. 1, col. 1.

87. *L'Abeille,* May 1, 1867, p. 1, col. 2.

88. Ibid., Apr. 26, 1867, p. 2, col. 3; Apr. 28, 1867, p. 1, col. 2.

89. Ibid., Dec. 15, 1867, p. 1, col. 3 and p. 2, col. 3; *The Bee,* Dec. 21, 1867, p. 1, col. 1. Another non-benefit concert is recorded in *L'Abeille,* Jan. 18, 1868, p. 1, col. 1.

90. For example, see *L'Abeille,* Dec. 7, 1867, p. 2, col. 4.

91. *L'Abeille,* Feb. 11, 1867, p. 1, col. 1. The new Salle d'Orléâns was erected on the site of the old theater and opened on Mar. 5, 1867, with balls.

92. Ibid., Jan. 11, 1868, p. 1, col. 4; Jan. 22, 1868, p. 2, col. 3; and Jan. 26, 1868, p. 2, col. 2.

93. Ibid., Mar. 12, 1866, p. 1, col. 1, and Mar. 15, 1866, p. 1, col. 2.

94. Ibid., Nov. 22, 1866, p. 1, col. 3, and p. 2, col. 3.

95. Ibid., Nov. 23, 1866, p. 2, col. 2.

96. Ibid., Oct. 6, 1871, p. 1, cols. 2 and 6.

97. *Picayune,* Dec. 24, 1871, p. 2, col. 1.

98. *L'Abeille,* Nov. 3, 1871, p. 1, col. 2.

99. Ibid., Feb. 18, 1872, p. 2, col. 1: the orchestra consisted of 16 violins, 5 violas, 4 cellos, 4 basses, 1 harp, 1 piccolo, 2 flutes, 2 oboes, 1 English horn, 2 clarinets, 2 bassoons, 4 French horns, 2 trumpets, 3 trombones, 1 "saxhorn basse," and percussion.

100. Ibid., Feb. 21, 1872, p. 1, col. 2, and Feb. 25, 1872, p. 2, col. 2.

101. Ibid., Feb. 11, 1872, p. 2, col. 1.

102. Ibid., Nov. 9, 1873, p. 3, col. 2.

103. Ibid., May 21, 1874, p. 1, col. 2, advertises that the French Opera Orchestra has openings for first and second violins and violas for the 1874–75 season.

104. Ibid., May 6, 1874, p. 1, col. 3; May 16, 1874, p. 1, col. 2; and May 10, 1874, p. 1, col. 3. A review of the first concert of May 18 appears in *L'Abeille,* May 19, 1874, p. 1, col. 3.

105. Momas, who had proven to be a strong leader during the preceding season, spearheaded an effort for the musicians to keep the season going. There was a benefit for him on Monday, Feb. 9, 1874, when for the occasion he conducted *Le Prophète*; see *L'Abeille,* Feb. 8, 1874, p. 1, col. 3. See also *Picayune,* Jan. 5, 1875, p. 1, col. 3.

106. *L'Abeille,* Mar. 27, 1874, p. 1, col. 2, and Apr. 5, 1874, p. 2, col. 3. See also *L'Abeille,* Apr. 10, 1874, p. 2, col. 3, and Apr. 16, 1874, p. 1, col. 3. See also erratum in *L'Abeille,* Apr. 9, 1874, p. 1, col. 2.

107. Ibid., Mar. 21, 1874, p. 1, col. 2.

108. Ibid., Dec. 4, 1874, p. 1, col. 2, and Dec. 6, 1874, p. 4, col. 1. Entrance for the Opera House ball was two dollars.

109. Ibid., Feb. 14, 1877, p. 2, col. 4.

110. Ibid., Mar. 11, 1877, p. 1, col. 2.

111. *Picayune,* Jan. 18, 1875, p. 2, col. 5.

112. *L'Abeille,* Dec. 7, 1873, p. 1, col. 3, and Mar. 31, 1874, p. 1, col. 2. Review of the first concert: Dec. 13, 1873, p. 3, col. 2.

113. Ibid., Apr. 9, 1874, p. 1, col. 2; Apr. 12, 1874, p. 2, col. 3; Apr. 19, 1874, p. 1, col. 3; and Apr. 24, 1874, p. 1, col. 2. The program also included the Gloria from Weber's Mass in E-flat; Rossini, the Andante of a trio by Beethoven played by organ, violin, and cello; short pieces by Mercadante, Boulenger, Hummel, Gounod, Stradella, Meyerbeer; and the Berlioz.

114. Ibid., Apr. 2, 1880, p. 2, col. 1.

115. Ibid., Nov. 7, 1879, p. 1, col. 2, and Oct. 31, 1879, p. 1, col. 2.

116. Ibid., Nov. 16, 1879, p. 3, col. 1. Actually, five different opera companies visited New Orleans during the four seasons before Strakosch arrived: Clara Louisa Kellogg's opera troupe (1876), Aimée's Opera Company (Dec. 1876), Caroline Riching-Bernard's opera troupe (1876), Fryer's Opera Troupe (Max Maretzek, conductor, Nov.–Dec. 1877), Adah Richmond's Opera Troupe (Dec. 1878), and the Hess Opera Troupe (Jan. 1879). In addition there were light opera troupes, both local and traveling, that performed on occasion in the city. (*L'Abeille,* Nov. 12, 1876, p. 1, col. 3; Dec. 12, 1876, p. 2, col. 3; Dec. 17, 1876, p. 3, col. 3; Dec. 21, 1876, p. 1, col. 2; Nov. 18, 1877, p. 1, col. 4; Nov. 27, 1877; Dec. 2, 1877, p. 2, cols. 1–2; Dec. 7, 1877, p. 2, col. 2; and Dec. 9, 1877, p. 1, col. 3; Dec. 13, 1877, p. 2, col. 2; Dec. 18, 1877, p. 1, col. 2; Dec. 18, 1877, p. 2, col. 2; Dec. 23, 1877, p. 3, col. 1; Dec. 15, 1878, p. 2, col. 4; Jan. 12, 1879, p. 1, col. 3; and Jan. 14, 1879, p. 2, col. 1; Jan. 28, 1879, p. 2, col. 2, Feb. 6, 1879.)

117. Ibid., Oct. 31, 1879, p. 1, col. 2; Nov. 16, 1879, p. 3, col. 1; and Nov. 23, 1879, p. 3, col. 1. Reviewed Nov. 30, 1879, p. 3, cols. 1–3. Gaston Gottschalk, brother of Louis Moreau, was a member of Strakosch's troupe at French Opera House.

118. In the review of the second week of the Strakosch opera in New Orleans, the critic stated: "Il nous rest à complimenter les choeurs qui sont généralement satisfaisants, et l'orchestre qui s'acquitte avec succès d'une tâche réellement ardue. C'est merveille que d'arriver à de pareils résultats d'ensemble quand il faut excécuter presque chaque soir une partition nouvelle. aux deux chefs d'orchestre de M. Strakosch, à MM. Behrens et de Novelli, revient donc une grande partie de l'honneur des belles soirées que le public de la Nouvelle-Orléans a entendues et appréciées" (*L'Abeille,* Dec. 7, 1879, p. 3, cols. 1–3). In all Strakosch's company performed thirty-five times in a month and five days, on average one performance per day (*L'Abeille,* Dec. 28, 1879, p. 3, col. 1).

119. *L'Abeille,* Dec. 31, 1879, p. 1, col. 5.

120. Ibid., Mar. 5, 1879, p. 2, col. 2; Dec. 28, 1879, p. 1, col. 4; Feb. 1, 1880, p. 2, col. 4; and Mar. 29, 1880, p. 2, col. 2.

121. Ibid., Mar. 16, 1880, p. 2, col. 3.

122. Before 1880 these theaters often presented French and English operetta with orchestras. For example, following Carnival in Feb. 1873, Mr. Van Ghele, chef d'orchestre at the Varieties Theater, led the orchestra during an opéra comique. The operettas, though not as heavy works as the grand operas at the French Opera House, were significant productions and required significant orchestras. Some of the operettas performed at the Varieties Theater during the spring of 1873 were *La Belle Hélène, La Périchole, Le Petit Faust,* and *Geneviéve de Brabant.* Even minstrel shows required orchestras. The Kelley and Leon Minstrel Troupe, for example, appeared at the Academy of Music with a grand orchestra on Feb. 22, 1876. On Dec. 9 and following, in 1877, a grand orchestra conducted by J. H. Bonham performed nightly at the Academy of Music along with comic routines by the Rice Troupe, and on Sunday, Mar. 9, 1879, Les Minstrels d'Emerson, with *Grand Orchestre et Brass Band,* played at the Academy of Music.

123. *L'Abeille,* Apr. 17, 1880, p. 2, col. 1.

124. Ibid., Feb. 17, 1878, p. 2, col. 3; Mar. 21, 1878, p. 2, col. 2; and ongoing.

125. Ibid., Jan. 1, 1881, p. 2, col. 5.

126. *Daily States,* Jan. 3, 1883, p. 4, col. 7, and Jan. 7, 1883, p. 8, col. 3.

127. *L'Abeille,* Nov. 21, 1876, p. 1, col. 2.

128. Ibid., Feb. 18, 1877, p. 2, col. 4.

129. Ibid., Apr. 8, 1879, p. 2, col. 1, and Apr. 11, 1879, p. 1, col. 2. Review: Apr. 16, 1879, p. 1, col. 2.

130. Ibid., May 4, 1879, p. 1, col. 2; May 4, 1979, p. 2, col. 3; and May 11, 1879, p. 1, col. 2.

131. Ibid., May 18, 1879, p. 2, col. 3. The concerts were originally scheduled for June 1 and 2 at the Fair Grounds.

132. Ibid., July 2, 1879, p. 1, col. 2.

133. Ibid., Dec. 27, 1879, p. 2, col. 2. For a detailed program of Rolling's piece, see *L'Abeille,* Dec. 28, 1879, p. 3, col. 2.

134. Ibid., Mar. 7, 1880, p. 2, col. 2.

135. The concert was originally scheduled at the French Opera House (*L'Abeille,* May 27, 1877, p. 1, col. 2). Mlle. Bouligny wrote a letter to the paper indicating that she was donating all her fees to the charity (*L'Abeille,* June 1, 1877, p. 1, col. 3, and June 3, 1877, p. 1, col. 2). The program is published in *L'Abeille,* June 3, 1877, p. 2, col. 3.

136. *L'Abeille,* Nov. 17, 1877, p. 1, col. 2.

137. The last concert took place on May 27, 1879, at Grunewald Hall, featuring Madame Henriette Comès, who had been soloist for sixteen years at the Immaculate Conception Church (*L'Abeille,* May 11, 1879, p. 1, col. 2; May 18, 1879, p. 1, col. 2; and May 27, 1879, p. 1, col. 2). She was assisted by Mme F Dunn, Mlle Marie Collignon (Comes's sister), M. Theo. Curant, violinist; M. A. Livain, flutist; M. Mueller, violoncellist; MM Ad. Cassard, J. C. Broadley, and Jules L. de Barjac. Collignon directed (*L'Abeille,* May 18, 1879, p. 1, col. 2, and p. 2, col. 3). *L'Abeille,* Feb. 27, 1880, p. 1, col. 2, reported that the rumor that Mme Comès was dead was false. She was singing in concerts in Paris and was about to perform in a concert with the violin professor Dancla. Collignon, in turn, was preparing a second edition of his father-in-law's treatise (the father-in-law died the previous year).

138. *L'Abeille,* Apr. 29, 1880, p. 1, col. 5.

139. Ibid., Oct. 1, 1881, p. 2, col. 1, and Oct. 4, 1881, p. 2, col. 2.

140. Ibid., Apr. 30, 1881, p. 3, col. 1, and May 29, 1881, p. 2, col. 1.

141. Ibid., May 27, 1881, p. 2, col. 1.

142. Ibid., June 3, 1881, p. 2, col. 1.

143. Ibid., May 31, 1881, p. 1, col. 3, and June 1, 1881, p. 1, col. 5.

144. Ibid., June 14, 1881, p. 2, col. 1; June 19, 1881, p. 1, col. 2; June 21, 1881, p. 2, col. 1; June 22, 1881, p. 1, col. 2; and Sept. 6, 1881, p. 2, col. 2.

145. Ibid., May 11, 1882, p. 2, col. 1.

146. Ibid., May 23, 1882, p. 2, col. 2; May 23–June 6, 1882.

147. Ibid., May 1, 1881, p. 1, col. 3; June 5, 1881, p. 2, col. 1; and June 12, 1881, p. 1, col. 3.

148. Ibid., Apr. 1, 1883, p. 1, col. 3. Review: Apr. 3, 1883, p. 1, col. 2.

149. "L'orchestre sous le báton du professeur D'Aquin, jouera les ouvertures des principaux Opéras avant et après chaque représentation," *L'Abeille*, May 11, 1884, p. 1, col. 3; May 31, 1884, p. 1, col. 2; and May 31, 1884, p. 2, col. 1.

150. *L'Abeille*, Mar. 1, 1883, p. 3, col. 1.

151. Ibid., June 9, 1883, p. 1, col. 9. While Faust is listed under composers, it is possible that the ad meant additional excerpts from Gounod's opera *Faust*.

152. Ibid., Mar. 22, 1884, p. 1, col. 3. But another article states that the spectacle consisted of three parts: the concert, the operetta, and the ballet, and that all of this started at 4:30 (*L'Abeille*, Mar. 20, 1884, p. 1, col. 2).

153. Ibid., Apr. 18, 1884, p. 1, col. 2; Apr. 20, 1884, p. 1, col. 2; and Apr. 22, 1884, p. 1, col. 2.

154. Ibid., June 6, 1884, p. 1, col. 6.

155. Ibid., July 6, 1884, p. 1, col. 6, and p. 4, col. 2.

156. Ibid., May 28, 1884, p. 4, col. 2, and May 30, 1884, p. 4, col. 2.

157. Ibid., June 11, 1884, p. 2, col. 3.

158. The city leaders recognized the importance of an opera season for the economic health of the city (see *L'Abeille*, Mar. 8, 1881, p. 1, col. 2).

159. The budget was to include a chorus of forty, eighteen solo singers, ten actors, seventeen dancers, and seven administrators (*L'Abeille*, Mar. 25, 1880, p. 1 cols. 2–3).

160. Max Strakosch and Marie Roze, who ran the Strakosch-Hess Opera Company, began their New Orleans opera season at the St. Charles Theatre with English performances of *Carmen*, *Mefistofele*, *Il Trovatore*, *William Tell*, *The Bohemian Girl*, and *Fra Diavolo*. *L'Abeille*, Jan. 7, 1881, p. 1, col. 2; Jan. 18, 1881, p. 2, col. 2; and Jan. 13, 1881, p. 1, col. 5.

161. In a review of two different performances at the French Opera House, Alfred Mercier compared De Lestrac (*The Daughter of the Regiment*) as conductor with Momas (*La Muette*); he found the first wanting and the second exciting (*L'Abeille*, Jan. 25, 1881, p. 1, col. 2).

162. *L'Abeille*, Feb. 9, 1881, p. 1, col. 3.

163. Ibid., Feb. 11, 1881, p. 1, col. 3.

164. Ibid., Feb. 2, 1881, p. 1, col. 2.

165. Ibid., Feb. 11, 1881, p. 1, col. 3; Mar. 12, 1881, p. 1, col. 3; and Mar. 15, 1883, p. 1, col. 2.

166. Ibid., Mar. 30, 1881, p. 1, col. 2.

167. Seventeen-year-old Miss Haddie T. Tidd of St. Louis also played some excerpts from *Il Trovatore* on the violin (review by Alfred Mercier, Jan. 16, 1881, p. 2, col. 2). For notice of the world premier in Paris, see Apr. 25, 1880, p. 3, col. 1.

168. *L'Abeille*, Apr. 27, 1881, p. 12, col. 6; reviewed Apr. 28, 1881, p. 1, col. 4.

169. Ibid., May 8, 1881, p. 1, cols. 2–3, and May 13, 1881, p. 1, col. 3; review: May 18, 1881, p. 1, col. 3.

170. Ibid., Saturday, Mar. 17, 1883; Mar. 15, 1883, p. 1, col. 2; and Mar. 17, 1883, p. 1, col. 2.

171. Ibid., Oct. 23, 1881, p. 1, col. 2.

172. Ibid., May 11, 1881, p. 1, col. 2; May 24, 1881, p. 1, col. 2; and May 24, 1881, p. 1, col. 2.

173. Names of all the singers are in *L'Abeille*, Sept. 16, 1881, p. 1, col. 2.

174. *L'Abeille*, Nov. 13, 1881, p. 1, col. 4.

175. Ibid., Oct. 2, 1881, p. 1, col. 3.

176. Ibid., July 10, 1881, p. 1, col. 2, and July 29, 1881, p. 1, col. 2.

177. Ibid., Sept. 1, 1881, p. 1, col. 2, and Oct. 14, 1881, p. 1, col. 6.

178. Ibid., May 11, 1881, p. 1, col. 6.

179. Ibid., Mar. 13, 1883, p. 1, col. 2.

180. Ibid., May 31, 1881, p. 1, col. 3; June 2, 1881, p. 1, col. 3; June 16, 1881, p. 1, col. 2; May 28, 1882, p. 1, col. 3.

181. Ibid., June 11, 1882, p. 1, col. 6.

182. Ibid., Mar. 25, 1883, p. 2, col. 3.

183. Ibid., Apr. 1, 1883, p. 1, col. 4; Apr. 6, 1883, p. 1, col. 3.

184. An article in *L'Abeille,* Mar. 30, 1884, p. 4, outlined the finances of the failed 1883–84 opera season.

185. *L'Abeille,* Jan. 24, 1884, p. 1, col. 3. Défoussez was not a good financial manager.

186. Ibid., Feb. 2, 1884, p. 1, col. 5.

187. Ibid., Feb. 12, 1884, p. 2, col. 2.

188. Ibid., Mar. 26, 1884, p. 1, col. 4.

189. Ibid., Mar. 20, 1884, p. 4, col. 1, and Mar. 22, 1884, p. 1, col. 3.

190. A detailed financial and personnel account of the opera for the 1883–84 season, including details about singers and dancers, appears in *L'Abeille,* Mar. 2, 1883, p. 1, col. 2.

191. La Estudiantina performed at Spanish Fort on Feb. 14, 16, 17 (on Tuesday, Thursday and Sunday) and again on Feb. 21, 23, and 24 at 4 p.m. (*L'Abeille,* Feb. 14, 1884, p. 1, col. 4).

192. *L'Abeille,* Feb. 10, 1884, p. 4, col. 4; Feb. 12, 1884, p. 2, col. 2; and Feb. 14, 1884, p. 1, col. 4. The program consisted of songs and readings, including Gounod's *L'Hymne è la Nuit* and Fauré's *La Charité.* Review: Feb. 14, 1884, p. 1, col. 4.

193. *L'Abeille,* Mar. 2, 1884, p. 1, col. 4.

194. Ibid., Mar. 16, 1884, p. 1, cols. 1 and 5; Mar. 20, 1884, p. 1, col. 4; Mar. 21, 1884, p. 1, col. 4; and Mar. 22, 1884, p. 1, col. 3.

195. Ibid., Apr. 8, 1884, p. 1, col. 2. There was additional opera during the spring of 1884. On Mar. 26, Bidwell began a short season of Italian opera at the Grand Opera House (*L'Abeille,* Mar. 20, 1884, p. 1, col. 4).

196. Ibid., Jan. 23, 1884, p. 2, col. 2.

197. Ibid., Feb. 2, 1884, p. 1, col. 5.

198. Ibid., May 2, 1884, p. 1, col. 3; May 11, 1884, p. 1, col. 3.

199. Ibid., May 2, 1884, p. 1, col. 3.

200. Ibid., May 23, 1884, p. 1, col. 3.

201. Ibid., Mar. 15, 1884, p. 1, col. 4, and Apr. 20, 1884, p. 1, col. 2.

202. Ibid., Oct. 11, 1884, p. 4. In *L'Abeille,* Oct. 12, 1884, p. 1, col. 5, the names of specific new orchestral musicians were given: A. Martin, second conductor; Georges Hesse, répétiteur pianist, from Paris; Ernesto Giovi, concertmaster and solo violin (from the Pasdeloup and Colonne in Paris and Metropolitan in New York), Harndorff, first violin solo; Theon, piano accompanist; Pomero, viola soloist; Bernsortes, contrabass; Cordelas, harpist; Pirotta, first flute soloist; Carrana, clarinet solo; Ravenalli, oboe soloist; France, first bassoon; Dornast, horn solo; Domange, trumpet solo; Cornai, timpani.

203. Ibid., Aug. 13, 1884, p. 1, col. 3.

204. Ibid., Oct. 30, 1884, p. 2, col. 1.

205. In a review of the Mar. 11 concert, Placide Canonge describes the Mexican musicians in *L'Abeille,* Mar. 18, 1885, p. 4, cols. 1–2. There are two groups: the military band conducted by Encarnacion Payen and consisting of woodwinds and brass, and the typical Mexican Orchestra, consisting mostly of strings (eighteen players), conducted by Carlos Curti. He raves about Figueroa.

206. *L'Abeille,* Jan. 18, 1885, p. 4, col. 1.

207. Ibid., Mar. 3, 1885, p. 4, col. 2.
208. Ibid., Mar. 3, 1885, p. 4, col. 2; Mar. 4, 1885, p. 4, col. 1; Mar. 7, 1885, p. 2, col. 1.
209. Ibid., Mar. 8, 1885, p. 4, col. 3.
210. Ibid., Mar. 11, 1885, p. 4, col. 1.
211. Ibid., Mar. 13, 1885, p. 4, col. 2.
212. Ibid., May 24, 1885, p. 1, col. 1; May 31, 1885, p. 4, col. 5; and May 31, 1885, p. 4, col. 1.
213. Ibid., Mar. 15, 1885, p. 4, cols. 3–4.
214. Ibid., Mar. 23, 1885, p. 4, col. 3, and Mar. 25, 1885, p. 4, col. 2.
215. Ibid., Mar. 13, 1885, p. 4, col. 2.
216. Ibid., Dec. 7, 1884, p. 4, col. 3. Reviewed by Canonge (he didn't like it) *L'Abeille,* Dec. 9, 1884, p. 4, col. 2.
217. Ibid., Dec. 5, 1884, p. 4, col. 2, and Dec. 9, 1884, p. 4, col. 3. Canonge was disappointed because there were so many people there that he had to stand at the door and couldn't hear well (*L'Abeille,* Dec. 10, 1884, p. 4, col. 1, with printing error saying it is Dec. 9).
218. Ibid., Mar. 13, 1885, p. 4, col. 1.
219. Ibid., Mar. 19, 1885, p. 4, col. 1.
220. Ibid., June 3, 1885, p. 1, col. 6; June 3, 1885, p. 4, col. 1; June 4, 1885, p. 4, col. 1; and June 5, 1885, p. 1, col. 6.
221. Ibid., May 25, 1885, p. 4, col. 4; May 30, 1885, p. 4, col. 1; June 3, 1885, p. 1, col. 6.
222. Ibid., June 6, 1885, p. 4, col. 2; June 7, 1885, p. 4, col. 4.
223. Ibid., June 7, 1885, p. 4, col. 4; June 9, 1885, p. 4, col. 1.
224. Ibid., May 17, 1885, p. 4, col. 4. Grunewald announced new music, including another arrangement of *Serenade Boccaccio* as played by the Mexican Orchestra (*L'Abeille,* May 24, 1885, p. 4, col. 4). A month later Grunewald also published a Mexican piece by Edouard Déjan (*L'Abeille,* June 7, 1885, p. 4, col. 4).
225. Ibid., May 24, 1885, p. 4, col. 4; May 26, 1885, p. 1, col. 6; May 30, 1885, p. 4, col. 1; and June 4, 1885, p. 4, col. 1.
226. *L'Abeille,* Nov. 29, 1885, p. 4, col. 5, and Dec. 17, 1885, p. 4, col. 3.
227. Ibid., Nov. 14, 1885, p. 4, col. 1, and Nov. 15, 1885, p. 4, col. 4.
228. Ibid., Jan. 1, 1886, p. 3, col. 4.
229. Ibid., Jan. 5, 1886, p. 4, col. 4.
230. D'Aquin was still conducting on Jan. 10 (*L'Abeille,* Jan. 10, 1886, p. 4, cols. 4–5), but by Jan. 12, John Strauss was conductor (*L'Abeille,* Jan. 12, 1886, p. 4, col. 4, and Jan. 13, 1886, p. 4, col. 3). For d'Aquin's career after this date, see chapter 11.
231. On Feb. 1, 1886, an orchestra played dance music in the foyer of the French Opera House during the entr'actes for the benefit of the Ladies Committee of the Exposition (*Picayune,* Feb. 2, 1886, p. 4, col. 3). On Feb. 7, 1886, W. T. Francis directed the beginning of a run of the *Mikado* at Grunewald Opera House; it used a "full orchestra" (*Picayune,* Feb. 7, 1886, p. 3, col. 3, and p. 16, col. 6).
232. *Picayune,* Mar. 12, 1887, p. 5, col. 3, and Mar. 13, 1887, p. 8, col. 3.
233. Ibid., Apr. 17, 1887, p. 8, col. 2.
234. Ibid., Apr. 23, 1887, p. 5, col. 2; Apr. 29, 1887, p. 8, col. 6; and Apr. 30, 1887, p. 6, col. 2.
235. Ibid., May 5, 1887, p. 5, col. 2, and May 15, 1887, p. 5, col. 2.
236. Ibid., May 21, 1887, p. 5, col. 2; May 23, 1887, p. 5, col. 2; May 26, 1887, p. 5, col. 2; and May 27, 1887, p. 4, col. 5.
237. Professor Bruesle was leader of the orchestra accompanying the dancing (*Picayune,* June 13, 1887, p. 5, col. 2, and June 16, 1887, p. 4, col. 5).
238. *Picayune,* May 19, 1887, p. 5, col. 2.

239. Ibid., May 21, 1887, p. 5, col. 2; May 22, 1887, p. 6, col. 2; June 7, 1887, p. 8, col. 5; and June 5, 1887, p. 6, col. 4.

240. *L'Abeille,* Dec. 5, 1886, p. 1, col. 8, and Dec. 5, 1886, p. 4, col. 4.

241. *Picayune,* Feb. 25, 1889, p. 5, col. 3, and Jan. 8, 1892, p. 5, col. 2.

242. Ibid., Apr. 26, 1889, p. 4, col. 4.

CHAPTER THREE

1. Charleston, South Carolina, had a Philharmonic Society 1809–12 whose impetus was the presence of many musicians from Santo Domingo (Butler, *Votaries of Apollo,* 194), but it took New Orleans, with the same ethnic group, more than two decades longer to form such a group.

2. *Courier de la Louisiane,* Feb. 3, 1825, p. 3, col. 4. See below, page 292, for more details.

3. Ibid., May 24, 1827, p. 3, col. 4.

4. Ibid., June 20, 1827, p. 2, col. 4.

5. Ibid., Dec. 11, 1827, p. 2, col. 3.

6. The word "harmonie" usually refers to wind music performed in ensemble.

7. "We think it would not be difficult to project and effect a Philharmonic society; and to have occasionally concerts and oratorios as there is now a large number of excellent vocal and instrumental performers: Italian, French, English and American. But there is very little spirit of union or energy among the heterogeneous classes of our population in any matter of taste or refinement, belles lettres or music or fine arts" (*The Bee,* Dec. 5, 1835, p. 2, col. 2).

8. *L'Abeille,* Nov. 4, 1839, p. 3, col. 4.

9. "A une assemblée tenu samedi 12 du courant, part une majorité des anciens members, il a été ésolu, qu'à partir de cette date, la société Philharmonique serait considédée de nouveau en activité et qu'à l'avenir, elle reprendrait ses séances, conformément aux réglemenst. R. P. Gaillard, Secret. pro. tem" (*L'Abeille,* Nov. 15, 1836, p. 3, col. 5).

10. *L'Abeille,* Nov. 23, 1837, p. 3, col. 1.

11. *The Bee,* Nov. 13, 1838, p. 2, col. 5; *L'Abeille,* Nov. 22, 1838, p. 3, col. 5.

12. "The members of the philharmonic Society are requested to meet in the meeting room to rehearse some music and to discuss important business. Lehmann, leader of the orchestra of the Philharmonic Society" (*The Bee,* Nov. 28, 1838, p. 2, col. 6). *L'Abeille,* Oct. 3, 1866, p. 1, cols. 1 and 5; *Picayune,* Oct. 5, 1866, p. 4, col. 1.

13. *L'Abeille,* Nov. 23, 1838, p. 3, col. 1.

14. Ibid., Nov. 28, 1838, p. 3, cols. 3–4.

15. *The Bee,* Feb. 22, 1839, p. 2, col. 6; Feb. 24, 1839; Feb. 27, 1839, p. 2, col. 6; *L'Abeille,* Feb. 27, 1839, p. 3, col. 1.

16. *L'Abeille,* Nov. 6, 1839, p. 3, col. 4; *The Bee,* Nov. 6, 1839, p. 2, col. 4, and Nov. 7, 1839, p. 2, col. 6.

17. *L'Abeille,* Apr. 8, 1840, p. 3, col. 6, and Apr. 10, 1840, p. 3, col. 2. This embodiment of a philharmonic society may actually refer to an African American society; see below.

18. Ibid., Jan. 30, 1846, p. 2, col. 5. A bal paré is a ball in which the dancers are costumed.

19. *The Bee,* Oct. 11, 1847, p. 1, col. 5; Oct. 18, 1847, p. 1, col. 6, and Oct. 18, 1847, p. 1, col. 4; review: *L'Abeille,* Oct. 22, 1847, p. 1, col. 1; *L'Abeille,* Nov. 9, 1847, p. 1, col. 1, and Nov. 9, 1847, p. 1, col. 9.

20. *The Bee,* Oct. 18, 1847, p. 1, col. 4. This was an ensemble of 50 wind players—in other words, a concert band (*L'Abeille,* Nov. 9, 1847, p. 1, col. 9).

21. Especially his *Grand Danse Infernale* with the accompaniment of pistols, raras, hootings, gongs, tamtams, chains, castanets, whistlings, rattles, bells, etc.

22. *L'Abeille,* Dec. 9, 1844, p. 2, col. 4; p. 2, col. 5; Dec. 30, 1844, p. 2, col. 5.

23. A large collection of Lehmann's keyboard music is in the Coralie Leblond Collection, in Baton Rouge, Louisiana State University, Hill Library, 65 (3) 2204.

24. *The Bee,* Mar. 14, 1846, p. 1, col. 2; Mar. 24, 1846, p. 1, col. 2, Mar. 24, 1846, p. 1, col. 6, and Mar. 30, 1846, p. 1, col. 1, and *L'Abeille,* Mar. 30, 1846, p. 1, col. 2.

25. *L'Abeille,* Apr. 1, 1846, p. 1, col. 2, and *The Bee,* Apr. 1, 1846, p. 1, col. 1.

26. *Picayune,* Jan. 9, 1852, p. 2, col. 4.

27. Ibid., Feb. 15, 1852, p. 4, col. 1. St. Patrick's Cathedral was not the official cathedral of New Orleans; that was, instead, St. Louis Cathedral. In this volume, any reference to "cathedral" is to St. Louis Cathedral, unless clearly titled "St. Patrick's Cathedral." The latter was reclassified as a church by the end of the century.

28. *L'Abeille,* May 18, 1852, p. 1.

29. Ibid., May 20, 1852, p. 1; May 24, 1852; May 26, 1852, p. 1.

30. *New Orleans Deutsche Zeitung,* Oct. 14, 1853, p. 3, col. 2.

31. *L'Abeille,* Sept. 30, 1853, p. 1, col. 2; Oct. 6, 1853, p. 1, col. 3; Oct. 14, 1853, p. 1, col. 3; Oct. 18, 1853, p. 1, col. 3; *The Bee,* Oct. 3, 1853, p. 3, col. 8.

32. *L'Abeille,* Oct. 20, 1853, p. 1, col. 8.

33. James Monroe Trotter, *Music and Some Highly Musical People* (1878; rpt. New York: Johnson Reprint Corp., 1968), 351–52; *Cohen's New Orleans Directory* (New Orleans: Picayune, 1852–57).

34. *The Bee,* Apr. 8, 1840, p. 3, col. 6.

35. Trotter, *Music and Some Highly Musical People,* 188.

36. *Picayune,* Apr. 8, 1866, p. 6, col. 2; Apr. 11, 1866, p. 1, col. 4.

37. Described in the death notice of M. Kroll, distinguished clarinetist, at age seventy-eight on Mar. 7, 1885. Born in Mirecourt, Vosges, France, he spent most of his life in New Orleans. He won first prize for clarinet at the Paris Conservatoire, served as first clarinetist in the Théâtre d'Orléans, in the French Opera House, and in the Société de Philharmoniques. Then he retired and started teaching in Donaldsonville and at the Sacred Heart Convent in St. James Parish (*L'Abeille,* Mar. 17, 1885, p. 4, col. 2).

38. This may or may not have been related to the Germania Society discussed by Nancy Newman, "Good Music for a Free People: The Germania Musical Society and Transatlantic Musical Culture of the Mid-Nineteenth Century," Ph.D. diss., Brown University, 2002.

39. *L'Abeille,* Feb. 15, 1876, p. 1, col. 2; *Picayune,* Feb. 15, 1876, p. 2, col. 1.

40. *Picayune,* Mar. 26, 1876, p. 2, col. 7.

41. *L'Abeille,* Feb. 24, 1877, p. 1, col. 2.

42. Ibid., Oct. 21, 1877, p. 1, col.2.

43. *L'Abeille,* Dec. 13, 1877, p. 2, col. 2. Review: Dec. 23, 1877, p. 4, col. 2; *Picayune,* Dec. 22, 1877, p. 5, col. 6.

44. *Picayune,* Apr. 9, 1878, p. 1, col. 3.

45. *L'Abeille,* Feb. 15, 1881, p. 2, col. 1; *Picayune,* Feb. 17, 1881, p. 3, col. 6.

46. *States,* Apr. 5, 1882, p. 4, col. 1.

47. *Picayune,* Dec. 15, 1882, p. 5, col. 7.

48. *L'Abeille,* Mar. 21, 1883, p. 1, col. 2.

49. *Picayune,* Dec. 16, 1889, p. 5, col. 3; Dec. 22, 1889, p. 6, col. 6; Jan. 5, 1890, p. 7, cols. 4–5; Jan. 6, 1890, p. 3, col. 3, Jan. 6, 1890, p. 5, col. 2; and Jan. 7, 1890, p. 4, col. 5. *Times Democrat,* Jan. 6, 1890, p. 3, col. 3; Jan. 7, 1890, p. 2, col. 3; Feb. 24, 1890, p. 2, col. 3. Review: *Picayune,* Jan. 7, 1890, p. 4, col. 5. The concert was originally scheduled for Dec. 27, 1889.

50. *Times-Democrat,* Jan. 7, 1890, p. 2, col. 3.

51. *Picayune,* Dec. 2, 1894, p. 3, col. 3; Dec. 5, 1894, p. 5, col. 2; Dec. 17, 1894, p. 10, col. 2. Review: Dec. 18, 1894, p. 12, col. 6.

52. Kaiser scrapbook, Louisiana State Museum, 1/1 RG 136. Undated, probably 1890s, p. 59.

53. New Orleans Public Library Concert lists, 1896.

54. Tulane University Vertical File, Philharmonic Society, Symphony Orchestra Association of New Orleans, Ernest E. Schuyten, conductor, 1917–18 season.

55. *L'Abeille,* Nov. 16, 1848, p. 1, col. 1.

56. Ibid., Dec. 4, 1848, p. 1.

57. Ibid., Oct. 17, 1850, p. 3, col. 2; *L'Abeille,* Dec. 1850, p. 1, col. 3.

58. Ibid., Apr. 23, 1851, p. 1, col. 9.

59. Ibid., Feb. 17, 1854; Mar. 11, 1854, p. 1, col. 2.

60. Trotter, *Music and Some Highly Musical People,* 188, was correct that the Classical Music Society was enlarged in 1858, but not by adding to the number of concerts; rather the ensemble was enlarged from chamber to orchestral. He also mistook Collignon's name as George Collignan.

61. *The Bee,* Apr. 27, 1857.

62. The neglect of Berlioz, whom we today regard as the greatest French composer of the 1850s, is probably owing to his position in Paris as a rebel and an outsider. A composer like Ambroise Thomas, on the other hand, was much more popular both in France and New Orleans because he was part of the establishment and taught many of the performers there.

63. *Picayune,* Nov. 23, 1857, p. 4, col. 2; Nov. 26, 1857, p. 4, col. 1; Nov. 27, 1857, p. 2, col. 2.

64. *The Bee,* Feb. 4, 1861, p. 1, col. 3.

65. See *The Bee,* Jan. 24, 1856, p. 1, col. 10.

66. *L'Abeille,* Nov. 22, 1864, p. 1, col. 5.

67. Ibid., Nov. 21, 1866, p. 1, col. 4; Nov. 22, 1866, p. 1, col. 3.

68. Ibid., Nov. 23, 1866, p. 2, col. 2. Despite the title, much of the music was clearly not sacred.

69. Other participants included Mlle Lora Rolff and M Kaps of the German Theatre, M. A. Davis of New Orleans, M. John Jacobs of the orchestra of the Variety Theatre, and M. S. Grillo of the French Opera (*L'Abeille,* Apr. 26, 1867, p. 2, col. 3; Apr. 28, 1867, p. 2, col. 3; May 1, 1867, p. 2, col. 3; May 2, 1867, p. 1, col. 2; May 7, 1867, p. 1, col. 1. *The Bee,* May 2, 1867, p. 3, col. 1.)

70. *L'Abeille,* May 3, 1867, p. 1, col. 2; May 7, 1867, p. 1, col. 1; May 8, 1867, p. 1, col. 2 and p. 2, col. 3. *The Bee,* May 3, 1867, p. 3, col. 1; May 8, 1867, p. 3, col. 1. Review: *L'Abeille,* May 9, 1867, p. 1, col. 2.

71. *L'Abeille,* May 19, 1867, p. 1, col. 2; May 21, 1867, p. 1, col. 3. Program: *L'Abeille,* May 24, 1867, p. 1, col. 2. Review: *The Bee,* May 25, 1867, p. 3, col. 1; *L'Abeille,* May 29, 1867, p. 1, col. 2.

72. Ibid., Feb. 27, 1868, p. 2, col. 3; Mar. 4, 1868, p. 2, col. 2.

73. Ibid., Mar. 14, 1869, p. 1, col. 2; Mar. 16, 1869, p. 2, col. 4; Mar. 19, 1969, p. 1, col. 2. Review: Mar. 20, 1869, p. 1, col. 3.

74. *Times,* Oct. 1, 1869, p. 4, col. 4.

75. Ibid., Nov. 6, 1869, p. 1, col. 5.

76. Ibid., Nov. 17, 1869, p. 10, col. 2.

77. *L'Abeille,* Apr. 27, 1872, p. 1, col. 3, May 5, 1872, p. 2, col. 1.

78. When Urso performed three concerts in New Orleans at the end of Nov. 1872, Collignon conducted the orchestral accompaniment (*L'Abeille,* Nov. 9, 1872, p. 1, col. 2; Nov. 17, 1872, p. 2, col. 6, and p. 1, col. 2; Nov. 24, 1872, p. 1, col. 2; Nov. 26, 1872, p. 1, col. 2; Nov. 29, 1872, p. 1, col. 3; and Nov. 30, 1872, p. 1, col. 2).

79. These concerts and their reviews appeared in the local newspapers: *L'Abeille,* Dec. 7, 1873, p. 1, col. 3 and col. 2; Dec. 13, 1873, p. 3, col. 2; Mar. 31, 1874, p. 1, col. 2; Apr. 12, 1874, p. 2, col. 3; Apr. 16, 1874, p. 1, col. 3; Dec. 16, 1874, p. 2, col. 4, and Dec. 23, 1874, p. 2, col. 4; Feb. 24, 1875, p. 1, col. 3; Mar. 14, 1875, p. 1, col. 2; Mar. 21, 1875, p. 1, col. 1; Mar. 24, 1875, p. 2, col. 5; Mar. 28, 1875, p. 1, col. 2; Mar. 31, 1875, p. 2, col. 5 (program); Apr. 1, 1875, p. 1, col. 3; Apr. 2, 1875, p. 1, col. 2; Apr. 4, 1875, p. 1, col. 2; Apr. 4, 1875, p. 3, cols. 1–2; Nov. 21, 1875, p. 2, col. 4; Nov. 24,

1875, p. 2, col. 2; Dec. 1, 1875, p. 1, col. 1; Dec. 2, 1875, p. 1, col. 2; Jan. 16, 1876, p. 2, col. 4; Jan. 19, 1876, p. 1, col. 1. *Picayune,* Apr. 9, 1876, p. 10, col. 1; Apr. 16, 1876, p. 2, col. 6; Apr. 17, 1876 p.m., p. 1, col. 2; Apr. 19, 1876, p. 5, col. 7; May 11, 1879, p. 1, col. 2, May 18, 1879, p. 1, col. 2, and May 27, 1879, p. 1, col. 2; May 18, 1879, p. 1, col. 2, and p. 2, col. 3.

80. *L'Abeille,* May 25, 1876, p. 2, col. 3; May 28, 1876, p. 1, col. 2.

81. Collignon's composition *Sursum Corda,* an adagio de concert for piano, violin, and cello, was performed on June 1, 1877, at the Immaculate Conception Church by M. Rech (violinist), Mona (cellist), and Collignon (pianist) (*L'Abeille,* June 3, 1877, p. 1, col. 2). He also wrote an overture (*L'Abeille,* May 18, 1879, p. 2, col. 3). In July 1879, Collignon had a work performed in an orchestral concert at Magnolia Gardens as part of the annual festival of the Musician's Benevolent Society and Union (*L'Abeille,* July 2, 1879, p. 1, col. 2).

82. *L'Abeille,* Dec. 9, 1877, p. 1, col. 2.

83. Ibid., Feb. 27, 1880, p. 1, col. 2.

84. Ibid., Sept. 13, 1884, p. 1, col. 5.

85. Ibid., Dec. 8, 1867, p. 1, col. 2.

86. Ibid., Sept. 30, 1883, p. 1, col. 3; p. 1, col. 4. *Picayune,* Oct. 21, 1883, p. 2, col. 5.

87. *L'Abeille,* Dec. 18, 1886, p. 4, col. 1; Dec. 21, 1886, p. 1, col. 8; Dec. 22, 1886, p. 4, col. 2.

88. Ibid., Mar. 24, 1882, p. 1, col. 3.

89. Ibid., Apr. 1, 1882, p. 1, col. 2; Apr. 9, 1882, p. 1, col. 6; Apr. 11, 1882, p. 1, col. 2; p. 2, col. 1; Apr. 14, 1882, p. 1, col. 2. Review: Apr. 16, 1882, p. 1, col. 3.

90. Ibid., June 11, 1882, p. 1, col. 6.

91. Ibid., Oct. 15, 1882, p. 1, col. 3.

92. Ibid., Oct. 18, 1882, p. 1, col. 2.

93. Ibid., Mar. 25, 1883, p. 2, col. 3.

94. Ibid., Sept. 5, 1886, p. 4, col. 3; Sept. 8, 1886, p. 4, col. 1; Sept. 11, 1886, p. 4, col. 1; Sept. 15, 1886, p. 4, col. 1; Sept. 18, 1886, p. 4, col. 1.

95. Ibid., Sept. 8, 1883, p. 1, col. 4; *Picayune,* Oct. 21, 1883, p. 2, col. 5.

96. *Picayune,* Oct. 20, 1883, afternoon, p. 1, col. 3; Oct. 28, 1883, p. 11, col. 5.

97. *L'Abeille,* May 23, 1884, p. 1, col. 3.

98. *Picayune,* Oct. 28, 1887, p. 8, col. 4.

99. *L'Abeille,* Nov. 15, 1885, p. 4, col. 4.

100. *Picayune,* June 7, 1887, p. 8, col. 8.

101. Louisiana State Museum, concert program.

102. *L'Abeille,* Sept. 2, 1888, p. 4, col. 1; Sept. 6, 1888, p. 4, col. 1.

103. *L'Abeille,* Sept. 19, 1888, p. 4, col. 1; Sept. 21, 1888, p. 4, col. 1; Sept. 22, 1888, p. 4, col. 1; big review (includes a description of S. Cohen as singer, also M. Lazare): Sept. 23, 1888, p. 4, col. 1.

104. Ibid., Oct. 6, 1888, p. 4, col. 1; Oct. 9, 1888, p. 4, col. 1.

105. Ibid., Oct. 21, 1888, p. 4, col. 1; Oct. 24, 1888, p. 4, col. 1; Oct. 25, 1888, p. 4, col. 1. Review: Oct. 26, 1888, p. 4, col. 1; Oct. 28, 1888, p. 4, col. 2.

106. Ibid., Nov. 4, 1888, p. 4, col. 2.

107. *Picayune,* June 1, 1889, p. 2, col. 5.

108. *L'Abeille,* Sept. 2, 1889, p. 3, col. 1.

109. Ibid., Sept. 4, 1889, p. 4, col. 1; Sept. 6, 1889, p. 4, col. 1 (long description); Sept. 7, 1889, p. 1, col. 4; p. 4, col. 2.

110. *Picayune,* Oct. 26, 1889, p. 4, col. 5.

111. Ibid., Nov. 21, 1889, p. 8, col. 2.

112. *L'Abeille,* Feb. 7, 1890, p. 4, col. 1, col. 2. Review: Feb. 9, 1890, p. 4, col. 1.

113. Ibid., Mar. 28, 1890, p. 4, col. 1. Review: Mar. 30, 1890, p. 4, col. 1.

114. Ibid., Mar. 21, 1890, p. 1, col. 8; Apr. 6, 1890, p. 1, col. 9; Apr. 6, 1890, p. 4, col. 2; Apr. 8, 1890, p. 4, col. 1. Review: Apr. 9, 1890, p. 4, col. 1.

115. Ibid., April 20, 1890, p. 4, col. 1; May 2, 1890, p. 4, col. 1; May 4, 1890, p. 4, col. 2; May 6, 1890, p. 4, col. 1. Review: May 9, 1890, p. 4, col. 2; May 9, 1890, p. 4, col. 1–2.

116. Ibid., May 4, 1890, p. 4, col. 3; May 15, 1890, p. 4, col. 1. Lengthy review: May 16, 1890, p. 4, col. 2.

117. Ibid., May 11, 1890, p. 1, col. 8; May 11, 1890, p. 4, col. 2; May 15, 1890, p. 1, col. 8; May 18, 1890, p. 1, col. 9; May 18, 1890, p. 4, col. 2; May 20, 1890, p. 4, col. 1. Review: May 22, 1890, p. 4, col. 2; May 23, 1890, p. 4, col. 2.

118. Ibid., Oct. 18, 1890, p. 4, col. 1; Oct. 25, 1890, p. 4, col. 1.

119. Ibid., Nov. 29, 1890, p. 4, col. 4; Nov. 30, 1890, p. 4, col. 2 (commentary).

120. Ibid., Dec. 14, 1890, p. 4, col. 1.

121. Ibid., Dec. 28, 1890, p. 4, col. 1.

122. Ibid., Apr. 5, 1891, p. 4, col. 2; Apr. 9, 1891, p. 4, col. 2; Apr. 10, 1891, p. 4, col. 1; Apr. 11, 1891, p. 4, col. 1. Reviews: Apr. 12, 1891, p. 4, col. 2; Apr. 14, 1891, p. 4, col. 1.

123. Ibid., June 1, 1892, p. 4, col. 1.

124. Ibid., Apr. 16, 1893, p. 4, col. 2; Apr. 21, 1893, p. 4, col. 1.

125. Ibid., May 7, 1893, p. 4, col. 1.

126. Ibid., Sept. 17, 1893, p. 4, col. 1; Sept. 24, 1893, p. 4, col. 2; Oct. 1, 1893, p. 4, col. 1; Oct. 8, 1893, p. 4, col. 1; Oct. 11, 1893, p. 4, col. 1; Oct. 13, 1893, p. 4, col. 1; Oct. 15, 1893, p. 4, col. 2.

127. Ibid., Apr. 19, 1894, p. 4, col. 1.

128. Ibid., Apr. 25, 1894, p. 4, col. 1.

129. Ibid., Oct. 1, 1894, p. 4, col. 1; Oct. 18, 1894, p. 1, col. 8; Oct. 19, 1894, p. 1, col. 3.

130. Ibid., Jan. 12, 1895, p. 4, col. 2.

131. Ibid., May 2, 1895, p. 3, col. 2; p. 4, col. 4.

132. Ibid., Sept. 1, 1895, p. 2, col. 3.

133. *Picayune,* Mar. 22, 1896, p. 3, col. 5.

134. Ibid., Apr. 5, 1896, p. 5, col. 2.

135. The Historic New Orleans Collection owns most of the documents of the German clubs of New Orleans, and the information about them in this discussion comes from those documents as presented by Alfred Lemmon, a curator of the HNOC archives.

136. *Picayune,* July 9, 1893, p. 6, col. 1.

137. For the best history of Frohsinn, see Mary Sue Morrow, "Singing and Drinking in New Orleans: The Social and Musical Functions of Nineteenth-Century German Männerchöre," *Southern Quarterly* 27, no. 2 (Winter 1989): 17–21.

138. *Picayune,* Nov. 30, 1891, p. 3, col. 3.

139. Ibid., Apr. 1, 1895, p. 3, col. 5.

140. Ibid., Mar. 28, 1892, p. 3, col. 4.

141. Ibid., Oct. 31, 1892, p. 3, col. 2.

142. Ibid., Nov. 24, 1888, p. 6, col. 1.

143. *L'Abeille,* Feb. 22, 1891, p. 1, col. 9; p. 4, col. 1; Mar. 1, 1891, p. 1, col. 8; p. 4, col. 3; Mar. 3, 1891, p. 4, col. 1; Mar. 4, 1891, p. 4, col. 1.

144. *Picayune,* Feb. 2, 1892, p. 4, col. 2.

145. Wilhelm (also William) Leps was active in New Orleans from 1892 to 1895. He conducted a benefit at the French Opera on Mar. 6, 1892, at which time he is referred to as the musical director of Frohsinn (*Picayune,* Mar. 4, 1892, p. 8, col. 2, and Mar. 5, 1892, p. 5, col. 2 and p. 8, col. 3). He appears in the city directories for 1892 and 1893 as a teacher of "voice culture." He resigned from Frohsinn in Apr. 1894 because his salary was cut (Morrow, "Singing and Drinking in New Orleans,"

20). On Jan. 2, 1895, his father, Wilhelm Leps Sr., died in Russia, where he was a prominent musician (*Picayune*, Jan. 27, 1895, p. 4, col. 6).

146. *Picayune*, Feb. 18, 1892, p. 5, col. 3, and Feb. 19, 1892, p. 3, col. 4.

147. Ibid., May 15, 1892, p. 8, col. 6.

148. Ibid., Dec. 10, 1892, p. 2, col. 6.

149. Ibid., Feb. 26, 1892, p. 3, col. 3.

150. Ibid., Feb. 10, 1893, p. 6, col. 2; Feb. 3, 1894, p. 6, col. 5.

151. *L'Abeille*, Apr. 4, 1891, p. 4, col. 1; Apr. 5, 1891, p. 4, col. 1.

152. Ibid., Aug. 5, 1891, p. 4, col. 1.

153. Ibid., Jan. 25, 1894, p. 4, col. 3.

154. Ibid., Mar. 25, 1894, p. 4, col. 2.

155. *Picayune*, Sept. 23, 1894, p. 7, cols. 6–7.

156. Ibid., July 14, 1893, p. 10, col. 7. The all-male New Orleans Quartette Club and the smaller Harugari Maenner Chor also were at the fest (*Picayune*, July 5, 1893, p. 10, col. 6).

157. On this occasion the Frohsinn chorus consisted of twenty tenors, nineteen basses, and fourteen (female) altos (*Picayune*, May 9, 1894, p. 15, col. 7).

158. *L'Abeille*, Mar. 18, 1891, p. 4, col. 1; Mar. 20, 1891, p. 4, col. 2.

159. Ibid., Nov. 23, 1840, p. 3, col. 2, and *The Bee*, Nov. 21, 1840, p. 2, col. 2.

160. *L'Abeille*, Nov. 14, 1842, p. 2, col. 1.

161. *The Bee*, Jan. 20, 1843, p. 2, col. 2 and col. 6.

162. *L'Abeille*, Nov. 20, 1840, p. 3, col. 7, and *The Bee*, Nov. 21, 1840, p. 2, col. 7.

163. *L'Abeille*, Apr. 9, 1891, p. 4, col. 1.

164. *Picayune*, Oct. 25, 1891, p. 2, col. 6.

165. Ibid., Oct. 20, 1892, p. 3, col. 4.

166. Ibid., Nov. 20, 1892, p. 3, col. 3; Dec. 4, 1892, p. 2, col. 2; Dec. 11, 1892, p. 6, col. 6. A sizeable review appears in Dec. 13, 1892, p. 9, col. 8; another review, Dec. 13, 1892, p. 2, col. 5.

167. Ibid., Dec. 19, 1892, p. 6, col. 7.

168. *L'Abeille*, Nov. 29, 1890, p. 4, col. 4; Nov. 30, 1890, p. 4, col. 2.

169. Ibid., Feb. 15, 1884, p. 1, col. 4.

170. Ibid., Nov. 25, 1887, p. 4, col. 1.

171. *Picayune*, Apr. 1, 1888, p. 8, col. 6; Apr. 2, 1888, p. 4, col. 3; Apr. 3, 1888, p. 4, col. 5; and Apr. 4, 1888, p. 8, col. 4. Augustin was the daughter of the late Major John Augustine of New Orleans and a pupil of eminent pianist Marguerite Samuel. Also on the program were Samuel, Ricci, Mr. and Mrs. Bayon, and Eckert. Ricci played a Brahms Hungarian Dance.

172. *L'Abeille*, Apr. 15, 1869, p. 2, col. 4; Apr. 17, 1869, p. 1, col.5; *The Bee*, Apr. 15, 1869, p. 3, col. 1. The four men were M. C. C. Tracy (tenor), M. M. Meteye (tenor), M. J. G. Wheeler (baritone), M. A. G. Wheeler (bass).

173. Kaiser scrapbook, Louisiana State Museum, 1/1 RG 136, p. 59.

174. *Picayune*, Sept. 18, 1887, p. 11, col. 4.

175. Ibid., Feb. 19, 1888, p. 14, col. 2, and Mar. 2, 1888, p. 8, col. 2.

CHAPTER FOUR

1. See Joseph G. Treble Jr., "Creoles and Americans," in Arnold R. Hirsch and Joseph Logsdon, eds., *Creole New Orleans: Race and Americanization* (Baton Rouge: Louisiana State University, 1992), chap. 4, for the best analysis of the terms "Creole" and "Creole of color."

2. Jerah Johnson, "Colonial New Orleans: A Fragment of the Eighteenth-Century French Ethos," in Hirsch and Logsdon, eds., *Creole New Orleans,* 12–57. Just those refugees from Haiti alone included various ethnicities; see Babb, "French Refugees."

3. Specifically in music, many African slaves from Santo Domingo were well trained in European instruments (Jean Fouchard, *Le Théâtre à Saint-Domingue* [Port-au-Prince: Henri Duchamps, 1988], 61). In turn, some white or mulatto plantation owners from Haiti, when arriving in the United States without wealth and position, became professional musicians (Butler, *Votaries of Apollo,* 190).

4. Paul F. Lachance, "The Foreign French," in Hirsch and Logsdon, eds., *Creole New Orleans,* 130.

5. "Auguste Tessier a l'honneur de prévenir le Public qu'il est Locataire de la Maison en Ville, appurtenant à M. Bernard Coquet, & de la Salle de Bal, depuis le premier du courant. Il donnera BAL tous les Mercredi & Samedi aux femmes de couleur libres, comme il l'a annoncé; & il oso se flatter, quelque satisfait qu'on ait été au premier Bal, qu'on le sera encore plus aux autres. On y trouvera toutes sortes de Rafraichissemens, Consommés, Vins, &c&c, & meme de quoi y faire des soupers & déjeuners. Sa maison est, & continuera d'être ouverre à toutes les personnes, qui voudront, dans la journée, prendre des Rafraichissemens & faire une parie à des jeux permis. Il y sera server des Repas, en étant prévenu a tems, & louera la Salle à qui voudra donner une Fête particulière. Ce sera aux personnes qui l'honoreront de leur presence, à juger de la propreté & de la diligence qu'on meura en les servant" (*Moniteur,* Nov. 30, 1805, p. 2, col. 3). New research by Emily Clark suggests that these free women of color were not from older quadroon families but from the newer Haitian immigrant families.

6. *L'Abeille,* July 3, 1830, p. 2, col. 4.

7. Ibid., Apr. 8, 1847, p. 2, col. 2.

8. Ibid., Apr. 7, 1853, p. 1, col. 10.

9. Charles Edwards O'Neill, "Fine Arts and Literature: Nineteenth Century Louisiana Black Artists and Authors," in Robert R. Macdonald, John R. Kemp, and Edward F. Haas, eds., *Louisiana's Black Heritage* (New Orleans: Louisiana State Museum, 1979), 79.

10. *L'Abeille,* Jan. 5, 1829, p. 3, col. 4.

11. *The Bee,* Jan. 27, 1831, p. 2, col. 4.

12. Ibid., Jan. 10, 1835, p. 2, col. 5.

13. Ibid., Mar. 19, 1836, p. 2, col. 1.

14. Henri Herz, *My Travels in America,* trans. Henry Bertram Hill (Madison: State Historical Society of Wisconsin, 1963), 82–93.

15. Trotter, *Music and Some Highly Musical People,* 351–52.

16. Charles Kinzer, "The Tio Family and Its Role in the Creole-of-Color Musical Traditions of New Orleans," *Second Line,* 43 (1991): 19.

17. *L'Abeille,* Dec. 11, 1861, p. 1, col. 7.

18. *Le Menestrel,* Jan. 24, 1864, p. 63.

19. *Times,* May 7, 1865, p. 5, col. 4; *Black Republican,* Saturday, May 13, 1865, p. 3, col. 3. See Dale A. Somers, "Black and White in New Orleans: a Study in Urban Race Relations, 1865–1900," *Journal of Southern History* 40 (Feb. 1974): 32.

20. *New Orleans Daily Crescent,* Apr. 13, 1866, p. 2, col. 3.

21. *Picayune,* Apr. 4, 1866, p. 6, col. 2; Apr. 5, 1866, p. 3, col. 1; and Apr. 11, 1866, p. 9, col. 1.

22. John W. Blassingame, *Black New Orleans: 1860–1880* (Chicago: University of Chicago Press, 1973), 173, 183, 185.

23. *The Bee,* May 16, 1869, p. 3, col. 1; *L'Abeille,* Dec. 22, 1869, p. 1, col. 2, and Dec. 23, 1869, p. 1, col. 2.

24. The case is discussed in Blassingame, *Black New Orleans*, 185–87.

25. Somers, "Black and White in New Orleans," 26.

26. Blassingame, *Black New Orleans*, 189.

27. Somers, "Black and White in New Orleans," 29.

28. *L'Abeille*, May 6, 1875, p. 1, col. 2; p. 2, col. 4.

29. For example, *L'Abeille*, Feb. 8, 1890, p. 1, col. 8; May 15, 1890, p. 1, col. 8.

30. *L'Abeille*, May 11, 1875, p. 1, col. 3; May 22, 1875, p. 1, col. 2; Dec. 19, 1875, p. 3, col. 2.

31. Blassingame, *Black New Orleans*, 124–25; Charles Edwin Robert, *Negro Civilization in the South* (Nashville: Wheeler Brothers, 1880), 131–35; New Orleans University, *Seventy-five Years of Service* (New Orleans: 1935), 75–86.

32. *The Only Original New Orleans University Singers* (Philadelphia, 1881), 9–10.

33. Blassingame, *Black New Orleans*, 120.

34. *New Orleans Louisianian*, Oct. 29, 1877, as cited in Blassingame, *Black New Orleans*, 140–41.

35. Blassingame, *Black New Orleans*, 142.

36. *Picayune*, Feb. 16, 1889, p. 4, col. 4.

37. Somers, "Black and White in New Orleans," 33.

38. Ibid., 41–42.

39. *L'Abeille*, June 1, 1890, p. 4, col. 1.

40. *Times-Democrat*, Apr. 25, 1897, p. 8, col. 2.

41. *Picayune*, Dec. 10, 1893, p. 12, col. 7.

42. *L'Abeille*, Dec. 9, 1893, p. 4, col. 1; Dec. 10, 1893, p. 4, col. 2; Dec. 12, 1893, p. 4, col. 1; Dec. 16, 1893, p. 4, col. 2; Dec. 17, 1893, p. 4, col. 2; Dec. 19, 1893, p. 4, col. 1; Jan. 21, 1894, p. 4, col. 2; Jan. 23, 1894, p. 4, col. 1.

43. Ibid., Feb. 1, 1894, p. 4, col. 1.

44. For the biography of Dédé, see Lester Sullivan and Richard Rosenberg, *Edmond Dédé*, Naxos 8.559038 (2000), liner notes; Kwame Anthony Appiah and Henry Louis Gates Jr., eds., *Africana: The Encyclopedia of the African and African American Experience*, (New York: Basic Civitas Books, 1999).

45. *L'Abeille*, Sept. 10, 1896, p. 4, col. 3; Sept. 28, 1896, p. 8, col. 3.

CHAPTER FIVE

1. *Moniteur de la Louisiana*, Dec. 4, 1802, p. 1.

2. Ibid., Feb. 5, 1803, p. 1.

3. Ibid., Dec. 11, 1805, p. 2, col. 3. This is probably the Mr. Le Brun whose one-act opéra comique *Rossignol* was performed in one of John Davis's theaters; Babb, "French Refugees," 216.

4. *Le Telegraphe*, Oct. 13, 1807, p. 2, col. 3.

5. *Moniteur de la Louisiana*, Nov. 21, 1810, p. 3, col. 1; Dec. 1, 1810, p. 2, col. 2.; and Dec. 5, 1810, p. 2, col. 4.

6. *Courier de la Louisiane*, Nov. 9, 1910, p. 2, col. 3.

7. *Moniteur de la Louisiana*, Nov. 21, 1810, p. 3, col. 1; Dec. 1, 1810, p. 2, col. 2.; and Dec. 5, 1810, p. 2, col. 4.

8. Ibid., Mar. 5, 1811, p. 3, col. 4, and Mar. 7, 1811, p. 3, col. 2.

9. Ibid., Feb. 18, 1813, p. 3, col. 1; *Courrier de la Louisiane*, Feb. 17, 1813, p. 2, col. 3.

10. For example, see *Moniteur de la Louisiana*, Dec. 4, 1813, p. 3, col. 1; Dec. 9, 1813, p. 3, col. 2.

11. *Louisiana Courier,* Feb. 7, 1816, p. 2, col. 3. Charles Gilfert was a prominent musical and theatrical figure in Charleston from at least 1807 to 1825 when he moved to New York (Butler, *Votaries of Apollo,* 196–201).

12. *Louisiana Courier,* Nov. 10, 1820, p. 3, col. 5. He may be the same Le Roy who was from Santo Domingo and active as a musician in Charleston (Butler, *Votaries of Apollo,* 185 and 189).

13. *Courier de la Louisiane,* Mar. 18, 1824, p. 2, col. 4.

14. Ibid., Nov. 22, 1830.

15. Ibid., Dec. 13, 1830, p. 2, col. 4.

16. *L'Abeille,* May 2, 1834, p. 3, col. 5.

17. *The Bee,* Mar. 31, 1835, p. 2, col. 2.

18. Ibid., Jan. 13, 1837, p. 1, col. 4.

19. Ibid., Apr. 24, 1838, p. 2, cols. 2–3; *L'Abeille,* Apr. 23, 1838, p. 3, col. 2; Nov. 19, 1839, p. 3, col. 6.

20. *The Bee,* Dec. 31, 1839, p. 2, col. 7. Interested persons should "apply at Mrs. Eversahd."

21. S. Frederick Starr, *Bamboula: The Life and Times of Louis Moreau Gottschalk* (New York: Oxford University Press, 1995), 34.

22. *L'Abeille,* Nov. 1843.

23. Ibid., Dec. 15, 1851, p. 1, col. 2; Nov. 23, 1854, p. 1, col. 2.

24. *The Bee,* Mar. 7, 1855, p. 1, col. 1.

25. *L'Abeille,* Oct. 17, 1850, p. 3, col. 2.

26. *The Bee,* Mar. 2, 1855, p. 1, col. 1.

27. *Moniteur de la Louisiana,* Mar. 1, 1814, p. 2, col. 4; Mar. 5, 1814, p. 3, col. 2; Mar. 8, 1814, p. 3, col. 1; and Mar. 10, 1814, p. 3, col. 1.

28. *Louisiana Courier,* Apr. 26, 1816, p. 3, col. 2.

29. *The Bee,* Oct. 28, 1834, p. 1, col. 2; Nov. 13, 1834, p. 2, col. 2.

30. Ibid., Dec. 31, 1856, p. 3, col. 1; p. 1, col. 3.

31. *L'Abeille,* June 19, 1832, p. 3.

32. *Courier,* Dec. 3, 1830, p. 2, col. 3.

33. *The Bee,* June 11, 1857, p. 3, col. 2.

34. *Moniteur de la Louisiana,* Mar. 4, 1813, p. 3, col. 3; *Courrier de la Louisiane,* Mar. 4, 1813, p. 2, col. 2.

35. Ibid., Apr. 7, 1814, p. 3, col. 1.

36. *Courier de la Louisiane,* Nov. 25, 1817, p. 3, col. 3.

37. Ibid., Feb. 13, 1824, p. 3, col. 3, and Feb. 19, 1824, p. 2, col. 4.

38. *L'Abeille,* Nov. 26, 1830, p. 2, col. 4.

39. Starr, *Bamboula,* 35.

40. *L'Abeille,* May 22, 1843, p. 2, col. 3.

41. Ibid., Nov. 11, 1847, p. 1, col. 6. *The Bee,* Feb. 3, 1848, p. 1, col. 2. *L'Abeille,* May 2, 1849, p.1, col. 7.

42. *Moniteur de la Louisiana,* Feb. 5, 1803, p. 1.

43. Ibid., Dec. 11, 1819.

44. *The Bee,* May 22, 1839, p. 2, col. 7. *L'Abeille,* May 24, 1839, p. 3, col. 4; May 25, 1839, p. 3, col. 2.

45. *L'Abeille,* Apr. 13, 1863, p. 1, col. 2.

46. See the Curto biography below. One of Curto's pupils during the war sang as the city was being liberated; *The Bee,* Apr. 5, 1865, p. 1, col. 1; *L'Abeille,* Apr. 14, 1865, p. 1, col. 7. Review: *L'Abeille,* Apr. 19, 1865, p. 1, col. 1.

47. *L'Abeille,* May 30, 1865, p. 1, col. 6.

48. Ibid., July 29, 1865, p. 1, col. 3.

49. Ibid., June 6, 1867, p. 1, col. 2; June 8, 1867, p. 1, col. 2; June 9, 1867, p. 1, col. 2; June 11, 1867, p. 1, col. 1; Apr. 23, 1869, p. 1, col. 5; Mar. 24, 1876, p. 1, col. 2; Jan. 1, 1879, p. 1, col. 1; Oct. 31, 1879, p. 1, col. 3.

50. Ibid., Dec. 8, 1867, p. 1, col. 2.

51. *Times,* Nov. 7, 1869, p. 9, col. 4.

52. *L'Abeille,* Feb. 5, 1879, p. 1, col. 1.

53. Ibid., Mar. 28, 1872, p. 1, col. 2.

54. See *L'Abeille,* Mar. 7, 1875, p. 1, col. 3; Mar. 14, 1875, p. 1, col. 2; Apr. 2, 1875, p. 1, col. 2; Apr. 4, 1875, p. 3, cols 1–2; Apr. 6, 1875, p. 1, col. 2; Apr. 7, 1875, p. 1, col. 2; Apr. 8, 1875, p. 1, col. 2; Apr. 11, 1875, p. 3, cols. 1–2; Apr. 18, 1875, p. 1, col. 2; Apr. 20, 1875, p. 2, col. 4: Apr. 21, 1875, p. 1, col. 2; Apr. 22, 1875, p. 1, col. 2; Apr. 25, 1875, p. 3, cols 1–2; May 2, 1875, p. 1, col. 2, p. 2, col. 5; May 6, 1875, p. 1, col. 2; Feb. 5, 1879, p. 1, col. 1;

55. *L'Abeille,* Apr. 19, 1885, p. 4, col. 4, and May 2, 1885, p. 4, col. 1. Review: May 25, 1885, p. 4, col. 1.

56. Ibid., Apr. 10, 1885, p. 4, col. 3; Apr. 29, 1885, p. 4, col. 1; May 2, 1885, p. 4, col. 1; May 3, 1885, p. 2, col. 4; and May 5, 1885, p. 4, col. 2. Brief review: May 6, 1885, p. 4, col. 1, and extensive review: May 7, 1885, p. 4, col. 1.

57. *Picayune,* Mar. 18, 1887, p. 8, col. 3.

58. *L'Abeille,* Feb. 6, 1881, p. 1, col. 4.

59. Ibid., Jan. 13, 1869, p. 1, col. 2; Apr. 24, 1872, p. 1, col. 2.

60. Ibid., Mar. 11, 1876, p. 2, col. 3; Mar. 16, 1876, p. 1, col. 3; Apr. 6, 1880, p. 1, col. 2; May 28, 1885, p. 4, col. 1; May 30, 1885, p. 4, col. 1; Dec. 3, 1886, p. 4, col. 1; Dec. 4, 1886, p. 4, col. 1; Dec. 5, 1886, p. 4, col. 4, Dec. 9, 1886, p. 4, cols. 1–3 and Dec. 10, 1886, p. 4, col. 1; Dec. 1, 1886, p. 4, col. 1; Mar. 19, 1890, p. 4, col. 2; Mar. 20, 1890, p. 4, col. 1; Mar. 22, 1890, p. 4, col. 1; Mar. 26, 1890, p. 4, cols. 1–2; *Picayune,* Mar. 25, 1889, p. 8, col. 5; *Picayune,* Dec. 12, 1889, p. 4, col. 4.

61. *L'Abeille,* Dec. 30, 1877, p. 1, col. 2.

62. Ibid., Mar. 23, 1884, p. 1, col. 3

63. *Picayune,* Apr. 1, 1889, p. 4, col. 3.

64. *L'Abeille,* Mar. 21, 1890, p. 4, col. 1.

65. Ibid., Mar. 20, 1890, p. 4, col. 1.

66. *Picayune,* Apr. 15, 1876, p. 1, col. 7; Apr. 19, 1876, p. 5, col. 7.

67. *L'Abeille,* Apr. 17, 1878, p. 2, col. 2.

68. Ibid., Mar. 1, 1885, p. 4, col. 1.

69. Some of her concerts are highlighted in *L'Abeille,* Mar. 11, 1885, p. 4, col. 1, and Mar. 14, 1885, p. 4, cols. 1–2; May 26, 1885, p. 1, col. 1; Mar. 18, 1890, p. 4, col. 1; *Picayune,* Apr. 10, 1887, p. 5, col. 2; Apr. 12, 1887, p. 4, col. 4; Dec. 18, 1888, p. 8, col. 3; May 4, 1889, p. 8, col. 4; Apr. 27, 1889; Apr. 30, 1892, p. 8, col. 1; May 1, 1892, p. 8, col. 5; May 5, 1892, p. 3, col. 4.

70. *L'Abeille,* Jan. 27, 1887, p. 4, col. 1; Jan. 28, 1887, p. 4, col. 2.

71. Ibid., Apr. 5, 1885, p. 4, col. 3.May 27, 1885; May 28, 1885, p. 4, col. 1; May 30, 1885, p. 4, col. 1; Nov. 19, 1887, p. 1, col. 9; Nov. 24, 1887, p. 3, col. 2.

72. *Picayune,* Dec. 1, 1888, p. 4, col. 5; Dec. 10, 1889, p. 2, col.

73. *L'Abeille,* Oct. 27, 1877, p. 1, col. 2.

74. Ibid., Feb. 8, 1878, p. 1, col. 2.

75. Ibid., Mar. 7, 1875, p. 1, col. 3; Mar. 14, 1875, p. 1, col. 2; Apr. 2, 1875, p. 1, col. 2; Apr. 4, 1875, p. 3, cols 1–2; Apr. 6, 1875, p. 1, col. 2; Apr. 7, 1875, p. 1, col. 2; Apr. 8, 1875, p. 1, col. 2; Apr. 11, 1875, p. 3, cols. 1–2; Apr. 10, 1880, p. 1, col. 2; Apr. 1, 1883, p. 1, col. 3; Apr. 12, 1883, p. 1, col. 3; Apr. 15, 1883, p. 4, col. 1; Apr. 17, 1883, p. 1, col. 5; *Picayune,* May 3, 1888, p. 3, col. 3.

76. For example, see *L'Abeille,* May 17, 1881, p. 1, col. 4; Apr. 1, 1883, p. 1, col. 3; May 16, 1885, p. 4, col. 1; May 19, 1885, p. 4, cols. 1–2; Apr. 27, 1890, p. 4, col. 1.

77. *Picayune,* Apr. 24, 1887, p. 5, col. 2; Apr. 14, 1889, p. 5, col. 2; p. 8, col. 2; Apr. 21, 1889, p. 8, col. 2.

78. Ibid., Oct. 27, 1889, p. 8, col. 1; Oct. 30, 1889, p. 8, col. 5; Oct. 31, 1889, p. 8, col. 5.

79. *L'Abeille,* Oct. 5, 1873, p. 2, col. 4.

80. Ibid., May 23, 1884, p. 1, col. 3; June 4, 1885, p. 4, col. 1; June 6, 1885, p. 4, col. 2; *Picayune,* May 4, 1887, p. 3, col. 1.

81. For some additional information on Locquet see *L'Abeille,* Apr. 26, 1867, p. 2, col. 3; Apr. 28, 1867, p. 1, col. 2

82. *L'Abeille,* May 31, 1872, p. 4, col. 5.

83. Ibid., May 31, 1873, p. 1, col. 5; Apr. 10, 1884, p. 1, col. 2; June 23, 1885, p. 4, col. 3; Mar. 1, 1885, p. 4, col. 1; *Picayune,* Dec. 28, 1889, p. 4, col. 6.

84. It is listed in the *City Directory* only in 1872. *Morning Star,* Sept. 10, 1871, p. 4, col. 5; Sept. 17, 1871, p. 4, col. 6; May 26, 1872, p. 5, col. 3.

85. *L'Abeille,* May 1, 1872, p. 1, col. 2.

86. *Morning Star,* Sept. 22, 1872, p. 8, col. 2; Dec. 8, 1872, p. 5, col. 4.

87. Specifically his wife, Mrs. Isabella M. Pilcher; his father, William Pilcher; his mother, Julia Pilcher; his brother, Charles Pilcher; and his sister, Carrie Pilcher.

88. *Pilcher Conservatory Catalogue,* Tulane University, Howard-Tilton Library, Louisiana Collection, Vertical Files, 1887–88, p. 17.

89. *Picayune,* Oct. 4, 1887, p. 8, col. 1.

90. *L'Abeille,* Mar. 28, 1890, p. 4, col. 1; Mar. 30, 1890, p. 4, col. 1.

91. For example, see the graduation of Professor Lecher's School at Grunewald Hall on June 16, 1887, where recitations were each introduced by an orchestral overture (*Picayune,* June 17, 1887, p. 3, col. 4).

92. *The Bee,* Mar. 20, 1870, p. 1, col. 1.

93. *The Weekly Louisianian,* June 29, 1872, p. 2, col. 3.

94. *L'Abeille,* Mar. 6, 1873, p. 1, col. 2, and Mar. 8, 1873, p. 2, col. 4.

95. It is "Mathey" in 1879 and "Matthey in 1896."

96. *Morning Star,* Dec. 20, 1868, p. 5, col. 1.

97. Ibid., Jan. 17, 1870, p. 4, col. 1.

98. Ibid., June 9, 1872, p. 5, col. 1.

99. Ibid., June 9, 1872, p. 5, col. 2; June 16, 1872, p. 5, col. 2.

100. Ibid., June 30, 1872, p. 5, col. 2; July 7, 1872, p. 5, col. 2; July 14, 1872, p. 5, col. 1; July 21, 1872, p. 5, col. 1.

101. *Picayune,* June 21, 1896, p. 3, col. 5.

102. Ibid., Jan. 29, 1889, p. 4, col. 3.

103. Ibid., Nov. 17, 1889, p. 16, col. 6.

104. Ibid., Dec. 8, 1889, p. 8, cols. 2–3; Dec. 12, 1889, p. 4, col. 4.

105. Ibid., Jan. 16, 1890, p. 6, col. 4; Jan. 17, 1890, p. 8, col. 4; Jan. 18, 1890, p. 4, col. 5; and Jan. 19, 1890, p. 8, col. 3.

106. Ibid., Feb. 2, 1890, p. 8, col. 4.

107. Ibid., Apr. 6, 1890, p. 7, col. 3.

108. Ibid., Oct. 2, 1890, p. 8, col. 2.

109. Ibid., Nov. 27, 1890, p. 3, col. 2.

110. Ibid., Jan. 4, 1891, p. 3, col. 6.

111. Ibid., Feb. 26, 1891, p. 3, col. 7.

112. Ibid., Apr. 9, 1891, p. 3, col. 6; June 18, 1891, p. 3, col. 4.
113. Ibid., Jan. 28, 1894, p. 9, col. 4.
114. Ibid., Jan. 22, 1893, p. 6, col. 4.
115. Ibid., Jan. 27, 1895, p. 10, col. 4.
116. Ibid., Apr. 21, 1895, p. 8, col. 1.

CHAPTER SIX

1. The Capuchin monks established a school for boys two years earlier, in 1725, and included music in the curriculum. The school no longer exists.

2. Copy in the Bibliothèque de l'Arsenal, Paris. The manuscript is now in the possession of the Historic New Orleans Collection, New Orleans. See Alfred E. Lemmon (director, Williams Research Center, Historic New Orleans Collection), liner notes to the CD *Henry Desmarest, Manuscrit des Ursulines de la Nouvelle Orléans*.

3. Roger Baudier, *The Catholic Church in Louisiana* (New Orleans: [A.W. Hyatt Stationery Mfg. Co.], 1939), 395–402, gives an overview of the development of the education of women in New Orleans during much of the nineteenth century.

4. Baudier, *The Catholic Church in Louisiana,* 394

5. *L'Abeille,* Mar. 5, 1851, p. 1.

6. A list of the charities and the amount donated are given in *L'Abeille,* Mar. 3, 1851, p. 1.

7. *L'Abeille,* Mar. 8, 1851, p. 1.

8. Ibid., Feb. 14, 1854, p. 1, col. 2.

9. Nicolas Slonimsky, *The Concise Baker's Biographical Dictionary of Musicians,* 8th ed. (New York: Schirmer, 1994), 957.

10. Herman Klein, *The Reign of Patti* (1920; rpt. New York: Da Capo, 1978), 28–29 and 32–33. See John Frederick Cone, *Adelina Patti, Queen of Hearts* (Portland, OR: Amadeus Press, 1993), 29–31; John Dizikes, *Opera in America, a Cultural History* (New Haven: Yale University Press, 1993), 181.

11. "Le jeune Adeline Patti a marché dans cette soirée de succès en succès et a conquis la sympathie de son auditoire" (*L'Abeille,* Mar. 3, 1853, p. 1, col. 2).

12. *L'Abeille,* Feb. 15, 1854, p. 1, col. 2.

13. See Jack Belsom, "En Route to Stardom: Adelina Patti at the French Opera House, New Orleans, 1860–1861," *Opera Quarterly* 10 (1994): 113–30.

14. *Picayune,* Feb. 7, 1904, p. 11, col. 1.

15. Davis and his son were the impresarios of the Théâtre d'Orléans from 1819 until 1853, when Charles Boudousquié took over (Robert C. Reinders, *End of an Era: New Orleans 1850–1860* [New Orleans: Pelican, 1964], 183).

16. The boat ride could be perilous. On Oct. 3, 1866, the entire opera company was drowned near Tybee Island, Georgia, during a hurricane. See Belsom, *Opera in New Orleans* (New Orleans: New Orleans Opera Association, 1993), 5.

17. Jack Belsom, "Calve, Julie Rose," in *A Dictionary of Louisiana Biography* (Lafayette: Louisiana Historical Association, 1988), vol. 1: 147.

18. The New Orleans opera also visited Philadelphia; see Robert A. Gerson, *Music in Philadelphia* (Westport, CT: Greenwood Press, 1970), 70 and 372.

19. Vera Brodsky Lawrence, *Strong on Music 1: Resonances 1836–1850* (New York: Oxford University Press, 1988), 213–15.

20. Lawrence, *Strong on Music* 1: 329–35.

21. *L'Abeille,* Dec. 22, 1838, p. 3.

22. Ibid., Apr. 23, 1840, p. 2.

23. For example, for a special concert conducted by Curto at St. Patrick's Church on June 29, 1841, and at the Théâtre d'Orléans on May 17, 1845, for the benefit of three other singers of the opera company: MM. Arnaud, Douvry, and Garry.

24. Posters of Thayer's Company (copy in the Library of Congress) show portraits of Thayer and her assisting artists but give no further information on her or the tour.

25. *L'Abeille,* Dec. 23, 1879, p. 4, col. 1.

26. *Picayune,* Dec. 25, 1879, p. 2, col. 7.

27. *L'Abeille,* Dec. 21, 1879, p. 3, col. 3, and *Picayune,* Dec. 23, 1879, p. 3, col. 2. The tour included Charleston the week before Christmas; the concert was performed at the Charleston Academy of Music and had an overflow audience.

28. *Picayune,* Dec. 27, 1879, p. 2, col. 7.

29. "Elle a une voix de soprano qu'elle module avec une aisance qui indique un méthode de bonne école. Un peu émotionnée au début, la jeune virtuose est tout de suite entrée en possession de ses moyens et a chanté en véritable artiste son grand air hérissé de difficultés. Mademoiselle Thayer a un gosier perlé comparable à une flûte enchantée" (*L'Abeille,* Dec. 27, 1879, p. 1, col. 2).

30. Singer was active in Parma and was famous particularly for the major roles sung in New Orleans, especially from *Mephistophe* and *Norma.*

31. Litta (an assumed stage name) was born and buried in Bloomington, Illinois. Her brief career took her to London and to the White House where she performed for President Grant.

32. *L'Abeille,* Dec. 27, 1879, p. 1, col. 2. Gaston Gottschalk was the younger brother of Louis Moreau Gottschalk. He sang the role of Escamilo in *Carmen* on Dec. 18 and elicited from *L'Abeille's* reviewer on Dec. 21 (p. 3, col. 5): "Gottschalk is a superb toreador."

33. John Dwight gave her wonderful reviews and referred to her as "one of the purest manifestations of genius that ever seemed to come to us so straight from heaven" (*Journal* 2 [Oct. 16, 1852]: 15; see also 6–7).

34. Newman, "Good Music for a Free People," 491–96 and 499.

35. *The Bee,* Feb. 14, 1854, p. 1, col. 2.

36. *L'Abeille,* Apr. 18, 1854.

37. Ibid., May 3, 1854. According to the city directories, Mrs. Deron operated her institute from at least 1850 to 1866.

38. The New York Public Library for the Performing Arts, Music Division, possesses the flyer for an Urso concert of 1877 and the library comments accordingly:

> Camilla Urso's Concert Company featured French-born violinist Urso, pianist Auguste Sauret, and singers J. C. Bartlett, tenor; Clara Poole, contralto; Gaston Gottschalk, basso; and Louise Oliver, soprano. In the mid-nineteenth century, when Urso was a young girl, orchestral instruments were played by boys and men. After persuading her parents to let her take up the violin, and considerable practice, she became the first girl admitted to the Paris Conservatoire, where she graduated with first prize in the final examinations. Urso made her first American tour at the age of ten, and became one of America's foremost performers and music educators, as well as a spokeswoman for the cause of women as orchestral players. In 1867, more than 60 professional musicians in Boston signed and published a testimonial which characterized her playing as having a "complete repose of manner, largeness of style, broad, full and vigorous attacking of difficulties, utmost delicacy of sentiment and feeling, wonderful staccato, [and a] remarkable finish in trills, with an intonation as nearly perfect as the human ear will allow. . . . When to these are added a comprehensive mind, with a warm musical soul vibrating to its work, we have an artist who may nearly be called a phenomenon in the womanly form of Camilla Urso."

39. *L'Abeille,* Jan. 28, 1868, p. 1, col. 3.

40. Ibid., Feb. 6, 1868, p. 1, col. 3, and Feb. 8, 1868, p. 1, col. 2.

41. Ibid., Feb. 18, 1868, p. 2, col. 2.

42. Review in *L'Abeille,* Feb. 22, 1868, p. 1, col. 2.

43. *L'Abeille,* Mar. 4, 1868, p. 2, col. 2, and review, Mar. 8, 1868, p. 1, col. 2.

44. Ibid., Mar. 27, 1868, p. 1, col. 2.

45. *Picayune,* Jan. 18, 1882, p. 2, col. 3.

46. Ibid., Jan. 20, 1882, p. 2, col. 1.

47. *States,* Dec. 28, 1896, p. 5, col. 4.

48. *Picayune,* Dec. 17, 1872, p. 2, col. 7.

49. Ibid., Dec. 26, 1879, p. 5, col. 4.

50. Ibid., Dec. 18, 1872, afternoon ed., p. 2, col. 1.

51. Ibid., Dec. 27, 1879, p. 2, col. 7.

52. Ibid., Jan. 27, 1860, p. 1, col. 3.

53. Ibid., Mar. 14, 1908, p. 9, col. 1.

54. *Gazette musicale de Paris* 9: (1842): 15. See also *Journal des demoiselles,* May 1845, p. 160, where she writes a "mosaique."

55. For newspaper accounts of her activities see *L'Abeille,* July 21, 1862, p. 1, col. 3; July 22, 1862, p. 1, col. 1; and July 26, 1862, p. 1, col. 2. Review: *L'Abeille,* July 28, 1862, p. 1, cols. 2–3, and correction: July 29, 1862, p. 1, col. 2. *The Bee,* Dec. 27, 1865, p. 1, col. 1. *L'Abeille,* Dec. 29, 1865, p. 2, col. 3. *Times,* Apr. 27, 1866, p. 14, col. 4; Apr. 28, 1866, p. 10, col. 4; May 1, 1866, p. 3, col. 6. Review: *Times Auctioners' Supplement,* May 2, 1866, p. 1, col. 2. *L'Abeille,* Nov. 23, 1866, p. 1, col. 2. *L'Abeille,* Jan. 12, 1868, p. 1, col. 3; Jan. 16, 1868, p. 1, col. 3; Jan. 5, 1868, p. 1, col. 2. *The Bee,* Jan. 14, 1868, p. 1, col. 1. Concert de Dames de Providence postponed. *L'Abeille,* Jan. 19, 1868, p. 1, col. 2. *Times,* Oct. 10, 1869, p. 1, col. 4. *L'Abeille,* Dec. 30, 1869, p. 2, col. 4; Jan. 2, 1870, p. 2, col. 4; Dec. 16, 1870, p. 2, col. 4; lengthy review: Dec. 17, 1870, p. 1, col. 1; Nov. 17, 1872, p. 2, col. 6, and p. 1, col. 2; Mar. 6, 1873, p. 1, col. 2, and Mar. 8, 1873, p. 2, col. 4; May 6, 1874, p. 2, col. 2; program: May 20, 1874, p. 2, col. 2; Dec. 19, 1875, p. 4, col. 1; Dec. 22, 1875, p. 1, col. 2; May 4, 1876, p. 1, col. 2; May 7, 1876, p. 1, col. 2; May 10, 1876, p. 1, col. 5; May 17, 1876, p. 1, col. 2.

56. She appears in all but one of the directories from 1871 to 1880. Her name appears in the U.S. Census for 1870 but not for 1860 or 1880.

57. *L'Abeille,* Dec. 15, 1870, p. 2, col. 4. A copy is in the Library of Congress.

58. Ibid., Dec. 1875.

59. *Picayune,* Mar. 14, 1893, p. 5, col. 3.

60. Ibid., Mar. 15, 1893, p. 2, col. 7.

61. *Morning Star,* Feb. 20, 1870, p. 5, col. 1; Aug. 14, 1870, p. 4, col. 1. *Picayune,* Oct. 21, 1893, p. 4, col. 5. Many of these biographical facts are from her obituary in the *Times-Picayune,* June 30, 1930, p. 2, col. 4.

62. *Morning Star,* May 26, 1872, p. 5, col. 1.

63. Ibid., Dec. 28, 1873, p. 5, col. 2; Jan. 1, 1874, p. 4, col. 2; Jan. 11, 1873, p. 4, col. 1; p. 5, col. 2; Jan. 18, 1874, p. 4, col. 5.

64. Baton Rouge, Louisiana Archives, *Orleans Parish Brides Marriage Index 1800–1899* (Aug. 2004).

65. *Picayune,* Nov. 21, 1891, p. 6, col. 3; Aug. 11, 1895, p. 5, col. 6; May 11, 1899, p. 8, col. 5.

66. Ibid., May 20, 1894, p. 3, col. 2.

67. Ibid., Oct. 10, 1886, p. 4, col. 4; Sept. 18, 1887, p. 11, col. 4.

68. Marguerite Beugnot Wogan, "Mother's Book, May 1952," Tulane Rare Book Room, typescript 504 (98) (1), 28–30. From 1867 to 1879, Josephine lived in Paris, where she charmed Vieuxtemps and Ysaye with her beautiful piano playing.

69. Her music collection ca. 1850s–1860s, including her own *Louisa Polka,* is at Louisiana State University in Baton Rouge.

70. *L'Abeille,* May 3, 1867, p. 1, col. 2; May 8, 1867, p. 2, cols. 1 and 3; May 9, 1867, p. 1, col. 2.
71. Ibid., Nov. 16, 1866, p. 1, col. 2, and p. 2, col. 3; Nov. 19, p. 1, col. 3.
72. Ibid., Jan. 5, 1868, p. 1, col. 2.
73. Ibid., Jan. 16, 1868, p. 1, col. 3.
74. Ibid., Dec. 7, 1866, p. 1, col. 2.
75. *Courier de la Louisiane,* Dec. 3, 1830, p. 2, col. 3.
76. *Louisiana Advertiser,* Apr. 20, 1840, p. 2, col. 1.
77. *City Directory,* 1869, p. 401.
78. She was a private music teacher from 1868 to 1870 and again in 1878 (city directories). In 1872 she was a teacher at the Locquet Institute for Young Ladies, 253 Saint Charles Avenue, and in 1874 she was professor of vocal music at Saint Louis Institute for Young Ladies, 275 Dauphine Street.
79. *L'Abeille,* Dec. 12, 1876, p. 2, col. 3.
80. Ibid., Sunday, Dec. 17, 1876, p. 3, col. 3; and Dec. 21, 1876, p. 1, col. 2. *Picayune,* Dec. 12, 1876, p. 5, col. 7; and Dec. 21, 1876, p. 5, col. 6.
81. *Picayune,* Jan. 22, 1877, p. 3, col. 5.
82. Ibid., Dec. 21, 1876, p. 5, col. 7.
83. From the Wehrmann Family Papers in the Louisiana Collection, Howard-Tilton Library, Tulane University.
84. Facsimiles of some of these engravings can be seen in John H. Baron, *Piano Music from New Orleans 1851–1898* (New York: Da Capo, 1980).

Book I, Part II

CHAPTER ONE

1. He later changed his name to Louis Hus Desforges, or simply L. H. Desforges Sr. He is not to be confused with Pierre Louis Hus-Desforges (1773–1838) who seems never to have traveled to America (see François-Joseph Fétis, *Biographie Universelle des Musiciens* [2nd ed., Paris: Librairie de Firmin Didot Frères, Fils et Cie, 1864]).
2. See *Sacramental Records of the Roman Catholic Church of the Archdiocese of New Orleans* 6 (1991): 152–53, and vol. 7 (1992): 171. Louis H. Desforges fils was married to Marie Aminthe Bossiere, from whom he separated in 1830 (*L'Abeille,* Mar. 24, 1830, p. 8, col. 2).
3. *Moniteur,* Dec. 14, 1805, p. 2, col. 3.
4. Ibid., Jan. 17, 1807, p. 3, col. 1.
5. Ibid., Jan. 28, 1807, p. 2, col. 4.
6. Ibid., Feb. 18, 1807, p. 2, col. 4.
7. Ibid., Oct. 13, 1807, p. 2, col. 3. It is uncertain if it was performed only on Oct. 17 or on both Oct. 10 and 17.
8. Ibid., Dec. 26, 1807, p. 2, col. 3.
9. Ibid., Mar. 5, 1808, p. 3, col. 2. This work was probably the Violin Concerto Opus 6 by Joseph Fodor (1752–1828).
10. Ibid., Mar. 12, 1808, p. 3, col. 2.
11. Ibid., Sept. 21, 1808, p. 3, col. 3.
12. Ibid., Dec. 21, 1808, p. 3, col. 1.
13. Ibid., Dec. 31, 1808, p. 3, col. 2; and Jan. 11, 1809, p. 3, col. 1.
14. Ibid., Feb. 18, 1809, p. 3, col. 2.

15. Ibid., Mar. 8, 1809, p. 2, col. 4.

16. Ibid., Nov. 2, 1809, p. 3, col. 3.

17. The other two performers are not mentioned.

18. Why this is a sextet and not a quartet is not clear. The concert was originally scheduled for Feb. 5 (*Moniteur,* Jan. 31, 1810, p. 3, col. 3; Feb. 14, 1810, p. 3, col. 4).

19. *Moniteur,* Feb. 13, 1810, p. 3, col. 2.

20. *Courier de la Louisiane,* Nov. 9, 1910, p. 2, col. 3.

21. *Moniteur,* Jan. 14, 1812, p. 3, cols. 2–3.

22. *Courier de la Louisiane,* Mar. 4, 1813, p. 2, col. 2; *Moniteur,* Mar. 4, 1813, p. 3, col. 3.

23. *Moniteur,* Mar. 16, 1813, p. 3, col. 1; *Courier de la Louisiane,* Mar. 17, 1813, p. 2, col. 3.

24. *Moniteur,* Dec. 16, 1813, p. 3, col. 2.

25. Ibid., Apr. 7, 1814, p. 3, col. 1.

26. *Courier de la Louisiane,* Feb. 5, 1816, p. 2, col. 2.

27. Ibid., Dec. 27, 1816, p. 3, col. 4.

28. Ibid., Feb. 19, 1817, p. 2, col. 3.

29. Ibid., Dec. 5, 1817, p. 2, col. 3.

30. Ibid., Jan. 9, 1818, p. 3, col. 2; *La Gazette de la Louisiane,* Jan. 10, 1818, p. 3, col. 2, and Jan. 13, 1818, p. 1, col. 4.

31. *Courier de la Louisiane,* Nov. 10, 1818, p. 2, col. 3; Nov. 20, 1818, p. 2, col. 3.

32. *Gazette de la Louisiane,* Dec. 4, 1818, p. 1, col. 3.

33. *Courier de la Louisiane,* Feb. 17, 1819, p. 2, col. 4, and p. 3, col. 4.

34. Ibid., Feb. 4, 1820, p. 2, col. 4.

35. Ibid., Apr. 23, 1827, p. 2, col. 4.

36. *Louisiana Advertiser,* Apr. 25, 1827, p. 2, col. 4.

37. *Picayune,* Sept. 27, 1838, p. 2, col. 5.

38. Henry C. Castellanos, *New Orleans As It Was: Episodes of Louisiana Life* (New Orleans: L. Graham and Son, 1895, reprint Louisiana State University Press, 1978/2006), p. 224–226.

39. *Courier de la Louisiane,* Feb. 4, 1820, p. 2, col. 4.

40. There is no further mention of Desforges junior being musical. He was a customhouse officer in New Orleans, living at 353 Dauphine Street most of his adult life. In addition to Louis, junior, the elder Desforges and his wife Isavel had other children: Adolphe (born Dec. 27, 1803), Clara (born Aug. 20, 1805), Victor (born June 11, 1809, died from an accident—he fell from the tower of the Cathedral on Oct. 7, 1826), an unnamed infant who died at birth in 1812, Juana Eugenia Silvania (born July 13, 1814), Cipriano (born Dec. 28, 1818), and Maria Luisa Ysavel (born Feb. 15, 1819). Clara married Andres Dussumier on Apr. 20, 1822; Adolphe married Maria Eliza Blanchette on Dec. 24, 1825. For details on Desforges' family see *Sacramental Records of the Roman Catholic Church of the Archdiocese of New Orleans,* volumes 6–19 (1991–2004), the City Directories from 1834 to 1860, and the U.S. Census reports from 1820 to 1860.

CHAPTER TWO

1. The best biographical account of Curto, written during his lifetime, is Jewell's *Crescent City Illustrated.* See also his obituary in *The New Orleans Times Democrat,* Nov. 20, 1887, p. 3, col. 7: "On Saturday, Nov. 19, 1887, Gregorio Curto, aged eighty two years, a native of Tortoso, Spain and a resident of New Orleans for the last fifty-five years. His friends and acquaintances, also his pupils and the members of the Musical and Literary Societies, are invited to attend his funeral which will take place this evening, Nov. 21, at 4 p.m. from his residence, corner of St. Philip and Prieur Streets." His death was noted in newspapers as far away as New England.

2. *Picayune,* Jan. 26, 1882, p. 9, col. 3.

3. On the title page of his collection of masses in 1855, Curto refers to himself as "Ancien Maitre de Chapelle du Chapitre de la Cathèdrale de Soissons, et Professeur de Chant à l'Institution Royale de Musique Religieuse dirigée par A. Choron."

4. *L'Abeille,* Nov. 11, 1830. John Davis, with Curto in his entourage, arrived from Baltimore to set up his Théâtre d'Orléans.

5. *L'Abeille,* Nov. 12, 1830; Nov. 16, 1830.

6. Ibid., Nov. 17, 1830; Nov. 19, 1830.

7. Jewell lists *Les Huguenots* as one of the operas in which Curto appeared, but the opera had not yet been composed by 1832.

8. Jewell, *Crescent City Illustrated.*

9. St. Louis Cathedral archives, B36, B46; F14, F50.

10. The relationship between Curto and Closel (Clozel) can be gleaned from the city directories and U.S. Census reports. *City Directory,* 1830, has Mde. Delphine Closel as a comedian at the Théâtre d'Orléans and residing at 216 Dauphin. The 1830 U.S. Census (Orleans Parish, p. 186) lists her as Widow Closel, between twenty and thirty years old. *City Directory,* 1832, lists A. Curto as a comedian, residing at 93 St. Anne, and John G. Courto residing at 299 Bon Enfans (he disappears). *City Directory,* 1834: Antoine Curto, professor and composer of music, resides on St. Anne between Villeré and Robertson. Clozel is a comedian at the Théâtre d'Orléans, and Madame Clozel resides on St. Ann between Robertson and Villeré. *City Directory,* 1836: M. Curtaud is parish organist and resides on St. Ann Street between Villeré and Robertson. Mrs. Clozel is an artist at the Théâtre d'Orléans, residing at the corner of Orleans and Royal streets, while Mrs. Clozel widow lives on St. Ann between Marais and Villeré streets. *City Directory,* 1840: Gregorio Curto is a professor of music who lives on St. Ann between Villeré and Robertson. Clozel is an artist at the Théâtre d'Orléans, and Mrs. Clozel, artist, lives on St. Ann between Villeré and Robertson. *City Directory,* 1842: Gregoire Curto is a professor of music and resides on St. Ann between Villeré and Robertson. Mrs. Delphine Clozel, artist, lives on St. Ann between Robertson and Villeré streets and is an artist of the Théâtre d'Orléans.

11. The regular actors, signed in Havre, who had departed from there on Sept. 27, had not yet appeared in New Orleans, so Davis had to sign any local actors he could find.

12. There may be some remote connection with the comédien Clozet (Clausele) active in Saint Domingue in 1766–69 (Fouchard, *Artistes et Répertoire,* 13). Since many performers active in Haiti until the Revolution of 1791 emigrated to Charleston (Babb, "French Refugees," and "Miss La Roque's Concert" in *Charleston City Gazette* [Apr. 11, 1805]), this connection may not be so far fetched.

13. Canonge, son of a refugee from Santo Domingo, became one of the most important musical personalities in New Orleans during the second half of the nineteenth century (Babb, "French Refugees," 215).

14. Mrs. Delphin Curto dies at age seventy-five on Dec. 19, 1870. (*Commercial Bulletin,* Dec. 22, 1870, p. 1, col. 4) That would place her birth year at 1795, so she was ten years older than Curto. This is seconded by the 1840 U.S. census (Orleans Parish, p. 218) that lists Delphine Curto at between forty and fifty years old and Gregorio at between thirty and forty.

15. In the city directories of 1895 and 1897, there are listings for "Curto, Eugénie, wid. Gregora, r. 922 North Broad." The directories from 1884 to 1894 list the Mrs. Eugenia School. The 1896 directory lists "Curto, E. Mrs., teacher University School, 1923 Coliseum Street," which suggests that she closed her school by then and had joined the faculty of the new University School.

16. I have found no opera by this title authored by Curto or anyone else in New Orleans.

17. *Picayune,* Oct. 12, 1864, p. 4, col. 1. Thanks to Jack Belsom for pointing this out.

18. There are several varying listings of Curto's operas. Jewell lists them as: *Le Nouvel Ermite,* three acts, performed in 1832; *Amour et Folie,* three acts (1834); *Sardanapale,* two acts and three

tableaux (1838); *L'Héritière,* two acts; *La Mort d'Abel,* oratorio, composed in 1866. Louis Panzeri, *Louisiana Composers* (New Orleans: Dinstuhl, 1972), 17–18, based primarily on Jewell, lists them as: *Le Nouvel Ermite,* three acts, performed in 1832; *Amour et Folie,* three acts, performed in 1834; *Sardanapale,* two acts, performed in 1838; *L'Héritière,* two acts; *La Mort de Jeanne d'Arc,* two acts; and two oratorios: *Le Pepreu,* a dramatic scene to Placide Canonge lyrics 1845; and *La Mort d'Abel,* composed in 1866.

19. *L'Abeille,* May 3, 1834, p. 3, col. 4.

20. Ibid., May 5, 1834, p. 3, col. 1.

21. "[L]es inspirations du compositeur l'ont revêtue d'une musique oú la mélodie et la grâce le disputent à l'énergie" (*L'Abeille,* May 8, 1845, p. 1, col. 2). The writer gives a synopsis of the story of *Le Lépreux,* a tragedy.

22. *L'Abeille,* May 17, 1845, p. 1, col. 2.

23. Ibid., May 4, 1846, p. 1.

24. Ibid., May 9, 1849, p. 1.

25. *City Directory,* 1832: "A. Curto is a comedian, residing 93 St. Anne, and John G. Courto resides at 299 Bon Enfans (after this date he disappears)."

26. Alfred Lemmon, "*Te Deum Laudamus:* Music in St. Louis Cathedral from 1725 to 1844," in Glenn R. Conrad, ed., *Cross Crozier and Crucible: A Volume Celebrating the Bicentennial of a Catholic Diocese in Louisiana* (New Orleans: Archdiocese of New Orleans in cooperation with the Center for Louisiana Studies, 1993), 494–95.

27. Lemmon, "*Te Deum Laudamus,*" 496; Starr, *Bamboula,* 34. F. J. Narcisse Letellier is generally acknowledged as Gottschalk's teacher when he was a child in New Orleans.

28. The parish financial records from Sainte Theresa's Church are lost.

29. La Hache's *Messe de Ste Thérèse,* which is dedicated to Curto, was published in New Orleans by both Grunewald and Werlein in 1855. On the Werlein copies, which must be earlier than the Grunewald copies, La Hache refers to himself as from Dresden and simply an organist in New Orleans. On the Grunewald copies, however, La Hache lists himself as *presently* maître de chapelle de Ste Thérèse and Curto as "Maître de Chapelle de L'Eglise St. Patrick NO"—the insertion of the word "*presently*" suggests that these positions were very recently acquired.

30. Thereafter for the next few years these concerts continued but without Curto taking part. Rather William Furst directed them. Later, in 1845, Furst was director of the New Orleans Sacred Music Society at Rev. Theodore Clapp's Church, where with orchestra, soloists from the opera, and chorus he performed once or twice a year major concerts including Haydn's *Creation,* Rossini's *Stabat Mater,* and his own compositions.

31. Lemmon, "*Te Deum Laudamus,*" 494.

32. *The Bee,* Dec. 8, 1851; *Louisiana Courier,* Dec. 8, 1851; *Picayune,* Dec. 8, 1851; *Courier de la Louisiana,* Dec. 8, 1851.

33. Jan. 8, 1851. See *L'Abeille,* Jan. 8, 1851, p. 1.

34. *The Bee,* Jan. 10, 1851, p. 1, col. 1.

35. *Picayune,* Jan 9, 1852, p. 2, col. 4.

36. *L'Abeille,* May 18, 1852, p. 1; May 19, 1852, p. 1.

37. Ibid., May 19, 1852, p. 1.

38. Gottschalk's performances were on Apr. 5, 8, 13, 18, 25, 29, and May 11, 13, and 17, 1853, and in Feb. and Mar. 1854.

39. Son of Max Strakosch, Maurice made his New Orleans debut as a pianist on Mar. 9, 1849, at the Armory Hall.

40. Feb. 6, 1854.

41. *The Bee,* May 12, 1858, p. 1, col. 2, and p. 2, col. 2; *L'Abeille,* May 14, 1858, p. 1, col. 3.

42. *L'Abeille,* Nov. 12, 1866, p. 2, col. 2.

43. Review in *L'Abeille,* Nov. 13, 1866, p. 1, col. 2.

44. Rév. Père Halbedl, "Vicaire à l'Eglise de la Ste Trinité New Orleans, Louisiana," according to the city directories, served Trinity Church in New Orleans only during 1870 and 1871. His name does not occur before 1870, and by 1872 he was at a church in nearby Gretna, Louisiana.

45. The catalogue listing at the archive of Louisiana State University, Baton Rouge, has several errors in the title and in the date. There is also a copy of this mass at Tulane University, Louisiana Sheet Music Collection.

46. The printed copy in the Louisiana Sheet Music Collection, Tulane University Library, has penciled rubrics throughout the score indicating when the chants are to be inserted into the services.

47. The copy in the Louisiana Sheet Music Collection, Tulane University Library, has Curto's inked-in signature and a special dedication to Mlle James. There is another copy in the archives of Louisiana State University in Baton Rouge.

48. Ambre was at the French Opera House in 1880 to 1881. As in most cases of music published by Curto, the music is engraved by Mme. Henri Wehrmann.

49. English translation by Miss E. C. Wingate, dedicated to Professor Van Hufflen.

50. Sacred duet for alto and tenor with organ.

51. The city directories for 1880 and 1882–83 indicate that Curto was teaching at Peabody High School, Mrs. Kate R. Shaw, principal, at 304 St. Andrew Street. In 1884 Gregorio Curto is still a teacher at Peabody High School, but in that same year Mrs. Gregorio Curto opened a school at 299 St. Philip, in or adjacent to where the Curtos were residing. The 1886 directory indicates that Curto was a music teacher at Mrs. Eugénie Curto's private school, St. Philip Street near the corner of Prieur Street. The directory for 1887 has the confusing reference to the James Curto School, 301 St. Philip; there is no other reference anywhere to a James Curto, and the school in question is at the address of Mrs. Curto's school.

52. Minnie Hauk (Amalia Mignon Hauk) made her operatic debut in 1866 in Brooklyn and then toured America with Maretzek's company. Afterwards she studied with Maurice Strakosch in Paris and had a successful opera career in Europe as well as America. She later toured America with Mapleson's troupe and was especially well known for her roles as Carmen and Manon.

53. Minnie Hauk, *Memories of a Singer* (1925; rpt. New York: Arno Press, 1977), 23–24. As befits an opera singer, she lied about her age; she was eleven, not nine, when the war would have produced wounded in New Orleans.

54. Hauk, *Memories of a Singer,* 30.

55. Jewell, *Crescent City Illustrated*; and *Picayune,* Jan. 26, 1882, p. 9, col. 3.

56. Eugene H. Crosby, *Crosby's Opera House: Symbol of Chicago's Cultural Awakening* (Madison, NJ: Fairleigh Dickinson University Press, 1999), 227–78. Marie-Louise Durand, *Tribune* Oct 3, 1868; July 9, 1869.

57. *L'Abeille,* Oct. 30, 1861, p. 1, col. 1.

58. *Picayune,* Apr. 4, 1866. The concert was the following Apr. 9.

59. *The New Orleans Times Democrat,* Nov. 20, 1887, p. 3, col. 7. The newspaper incorrectly says that Curto was a resident of New Orleans for fifty-five years.

60. I would guess that the mistake is in the year of the census: 1830, not 1820.

61. New Orleans Public Library, Scrapbook # 1, 976.3L, pp. 34–35. This is a clipping, the source of which is unknown.

CHAPTER THREE

1. His death certificate states his age as sixty-two, which is probably more accurate than the age sixty in newspaper obituaries and on his gravestone.

2. New Orleans, St. Louis Cathedral Archives, Marriage Book III (1820), Act 945, p. 238. His stepmother was Carolina Yunker. In Marriage Book IV (1836), Act 166, and Baptismal Book XVI (1837), p. 415, written by a more careful scribe, Johns is called a native of Cracow and his real mother's name is given. He visited his relatives in Vienna in 1830; *Auszüge aus Briefen aus Nord-Amerika, geschrieben von zwei aus Ulm an der Donau gebürtigen, nun in Staat Louisiana ansäß Geschwistern* (Ulm: E. Rübling, 1833), p. 188.

3. Louisiana Work Projects Administration, "Passenger Lists Taken from Manifests of the Custom Service Port of New Orleans" (typewritten at Tulane University, 1940–41), II: 58, III: 219, IV: 112 and 213, which accounts for foreign trips in 1835, 1844, 1852, and 1857. For trips in 1830 and 1832, see below.

4. He married Anna Zoe Fauri of Baltimore (1801–May 15, 1833) on Feb. 20, 1820 (Marriage Book III, Act 945, p. 238); Jeanne Emma Favre D'aunoy (d. Jan. 23, 1851) on Jan. 11, 1836 (Marriage Book VI, Act 166); and Marie Celeste Rose D'aunoy on May 1, 1852 (Marriage Book X, Act 164, p. 466). He adopted a son, Paul Edouard Johns, in 1823 (b. Apr. 27, 1823; Baptismal Book X, Act 233, p. 42), and both Albert F. Johns and Jsidonée Johns may have been legitimate sons (Marriage Book XI [1860], f. 75). The daughters were Mari Elisabeth Leontine (b. Dec. 14, 1837; Baptismal Book XVI, p. 415), Luia Baselice (b. Sept. 2, 1847; Baptismal Book XIX, p. 440), Mathilde (see below), Marie Celestine Coralie Georgina (1839–1840; buried in St. Louis Cemeter No. 2), and Marie Filomene Alice (b. July 7, 1853; St. Mary Italian Archives, Baptismal Book III, p. 304).

5. *New Orleans Argus,* Mar. 28, 1826.

6. Harold Earle Johnson, *First Performances in America to 1900: Works with Orchestra* (Detroit: Published for the College Music society, 1979), xiii.

7. *Paxton's New Orleans Directory* (New Orleans, 1822), and *Louisiana Courier,* Feb. 28, 1823.

8. *L'Abeille,* Jan. 26, 1828. Review in *New Orleans Argus,* Jan. 30, 1828.

9. *L'ami des lois,* Jan. 31, 1824.

10. Ibid., Feb. 4, 1824.

11. *Louisiana Courier,* Feb. 4, 1824.

12. Ibid., Feb. 13, 1824.

13. *L'ami des lois,* Feb. 17, 1824.

14. *New Orleans Argus,* May 30 and 31, 1827.

15. *L'Abeille,* June 6, 1850, p. 1.

16. A. E. Lemmon: "Footnotes to History: Emile Johns," *Historic New Orleans Collection Quarterly* 10, no. 3 (1992): 5; and Lemmon, "*Te Deum Laudamus,*" 498–99.

17. Copies of Johns's collection are owned by the Historic New Orleans Collection.

18. This includes an introduction, five pieces, and a coda.

19. Lemmon, "Footnotes to History," 5.

20. *New Orleans Argus,* Jan. 23, 1826.

21. On his visit to Vienna to visit relatives and procure pianos, see *Auszüge aus Briefen aus Nord-Amerika,* 188.

22. John S. Kendall, "The Friend of Chopin and Some Other New Orleans Musical Celebrities," *Louisiana Historical Quarterly* (Oct. 1948): 860; *Boston Evening Transcript,* Nov. 19, 1927, part III, p. 8.

23. *Louisiana Courier,* Sept. 1831.

24. Ibid., Apr. 21 and 22, 1837, and Nov. 3, 1837. See J. Hanno Deiler, *Geschichte der New Orleans Deutschen Presse* (New Orleans: published by the author, 1901), 3–4.

25. It is not known for certain if the child prodigy Gottschalk knew or was known to Johns, but it seems likely that the two families were acquainted: the city was small, they both lived in the French Quarter, they attended the same church, they both were interested in music, and both Johns's and Gottschalk's father were in the same profession (printing).

26. Frederick Niecks, *Frederick Chopin as a Man and Musician* (1888; rpt. New York: Cooper Square Publishers, 1973), vol. 1: 249–50.
27. The works are in Tulane University Howard-Tilton Library.
28. *Cohen's New Orleans and Lafayette Directory* (New Orleans, 1851), 98 and facing page.
29. *Le Peuple,* Oct. 3, 1848, and *Cohen's New Orleans Directory* (New Orleans: Picayune, 1860).
30. St. Louis Cathedral, Marriage Book XI (1960), f. 75. A grandson Robert Christ was in possession of Emile Johns' documents in 1912.
31. *Picayune,* Sept. 1, 1860, and *L'Abeille,* Sept. 1, 1860. See note 1, above.

CHAPTER FOUR

1. *L'Abeille,* Feb. 10, 1862, p. 1, col. 5.
2. Ibid., July 25, 1883, p. 1, col. 5. Caroline was survived not only by her son C. L. Gabici but also by another son, A. B. Dantonet, from a previous marriage and by her son-in-law, E. Forestier, husband of Louise Amélie.
3. Ibid., Apr. 4 and 6, 1837. Kmen falsely assumes the "L. Gabici" is "Luigi" Gabici. As far as we know, there was no Luigi Gabici who conducted in New Orleans.
4. *Picayune,* June 22, 1838, p. 3, col. 1.
5. Ibid., Dec. 11, 1838, p. 2, col. 4; Dec. 14, 1838, p. 1, col. 3. The second item is dated Nov. 13, 1838, when the notice was given to the newspaper.
6. Ibid., Apr. 19, 1840, p. 3, col. 3. A second concert or the postponement of the first was on Apr. 27, 1840. Earlier, on Jan. 11, 1840, p. 2, col. 2, the *Picayune* advertises Gabici's new composition *Jackson's Grand March* for sale at Johns & Co., but this does not necessarily mean that he was already a resident of the city.
7. *Picayune,* Oct. 28, 1840, p. 2, col. 6.
8. Ibid., May 9, 1841, p. 2, col. 6, and May 16, 1841, p. 3, col. 2.
9. Ibid., Feb. 16, 1842, p. 2, col. 2.
10. Ibid., Apr. 28, 1842, p. 2, col. 5.
11. Ibid., May 18, 1842, p. 2, cols. 2 and 5.
12. Ibid., June 4, 1842, p. 2, col. 5.
13. Ibid., June 2, 1842, p. 2, col. 1.
14. *City Directory* for 1843.
15. *Picayune,* Apr. 9, 1843, p. 2, col. 6.
16. Ibid., May 14, 1843, p. 2, cols. 1 and 6.
17. Ibid., May 21, 1843, p. 2, col. 6.
18. Ibid., Aug. 27, 1844, p. 2, col. 2.
19. *L'Abeille,* Dec. 30, 1844, p. 2, col. 5. The program was a grand concert given by cellist Adrien Garreau, who joined Gabici and pianist Norès in the trio.
20. *The Bee,* Apr. 30, 1845, p. 1, col. 2; *Picayune,* May 1, 1845, p. 2, cols. 1 and 5.
21. The original French: "qui a voulu l'émoigner ainsi à cet excellent violon sa gratitude des services qu'elle en a reçus" (*L'Abeille,* Apr. 30, 1845, p. 1, col. 2).
22. *L'Abeille,* May 15, 1846, p. 2, col. 3; May 28, 1846, p. 1, col. 7; *The Jeffersonian,* May 16, 1846, p. 2, col. 5.
23. *The Bee,* May 28, 1846, p. 1, col. 7; *Picayune,* May 28, 1846, p. 2, col. 1.
24. *L'Abeille,* Nov. 17, 1846, p. 1, col. 8.
25. He continued to list his music store as a place where one could purchase all the scores for the pieces performed at the concerts (*L'Abeille,* Nov. 12, 1847, p. 1, col. 7).

26. *Picayune,* Dec. 18, 1847, p. 4, col. 2.

27. *L'Abeille,* Jan. 31, 1848, p. 1, col. 9.

28. *Picayune,* Mar. 9, 1849, p. 3, col. 4.

29. *L'Abeille,* May 2, 1849, p. 1, col. 9; *Picayune,* Apr. 29, 1849, p. 2, col. 1, and May 1, 1849, p. 3, col. 4.

30. Gerber supposedly left for Europe shortly afterwards, but he was back in New Orleans less than a year later when he appeared in a grand concert at Lyceum Hall with the young female pianist Désirée Delcroix (*L'Abeille,* Apr. 9, 1850, p. 1, col. 9).

31. *L'Abeille,* May 2, 1849, p. 1, col. 2.

32. Ibid., May 4, 1849, p. 1, col. 1.

33. *Picayune,* May 4, 1849, p. 2, col. 6.

34. See Gabici's *Grand Triumphal March,* discussed below.

35. *L'Abeille,* Dec. 7, 1849, p. 1, col. 9. *Picayune,* Dec. 7, 1849, p. 3, col. 2; Jan. 11, 1850, p. 2, col. 2.

36. *The Bee,* Apr. 10, 1850, p. 1, col. 9.

37. "A splendid orchestra led by the great Gabici" (*Picayune,* Dec. 3, 1950, p. 2, col. 4).

38. *L'Abeille,* Mar. 21, 1851, p. 1, col. 9. Gabici is not mentioned on the full program, but in the pre-concert advertisements he is listed as conductor of the orchestra for this event.

39. Ibid., Apr. 23, 1851, p. 1, cols. 1 and 9.

40. *Picayune,* Sept. 24, 1851, p. 3, col. 2.

41. Ibid., Oct. 28, 1852, p. 2, col. 1; Oct. 29, 1852, p. 2, col. 4.

42. Ibid., Apr. 14, 1853, p. 2, col. 1.

43. Ibid., June 19, 1853, p. 3, col. 2.

44. *New Orleans Daily Creole,* Oct. 11, 1856, p. 1, cols. 3–4; Nov. 12, 1856, p. 2, col. 5.

45. *L'Abeille,* Feb. 29, 1856, p. 2, col. 2.

46. *City Directory,* 1858.

47. *Picayune,* May 22, 1857, p. 3, col. 6.

48. This information is first mentioned by Trotter, *Music and Some Highly Musical People,* 340. See Lester Sullivan, "Composers of Color of Nineteenth-Century New Orleans: The History Behind the Music," *Black Music Research Journal* 8, no. 1 (1988): 54–58.

49. Kinzer, "The Tio Family," 21. Trotter, *Music and Some Highly Musical People,* 344, incorrectly gives his name as Maurice J. B. Doublet, born in New Orleans in 1831.

50. Kinzer, "The Tio Family," 22. Kinzer gives the name Anthony for one of the sons, but the only sons mentioned in the yearly city directories are Charles and Joseph M. or Joseph E. Doublet. All lived at one time at the father's address, 426 St. Ann Street, and Charles and Joseph are usually listed as musicians. Kinzer, "The Tio Family," 21, shows that J. B. M. Doublet was the son of Pamela Hazeur, youngest sister of Louis Hazeur, whose other sister was married to Thomas Tio and was the mother of Lorenzo Tio Sr. and Louis Tio.

CHAPTER FIVE

1. For his life and career in Paris, see Jean Mongrédien and Hervé Lacombe, "Prévost," in Grove Music Online (Oxford University Press, 2004).

2. In May 1850, the writer for *Picayune* states that Prévost had already been conductor of the French Opera for twelve years (May 18, 1850, p. 2, col. 1).

3. *L'Abeille,* Jan. 4, 1839, p. 3, cols. 1 and 7.

4. *Picayune,* Apr. 30, 1840, p. 3, col. 3; May 8, 1840, p. 3, col. 3.

5. It was repeated in May 1855 (*Picayune,* May 17, 1855, p. 2, col. 4).

6. *Picayune,* Sunday, Apr. 13, 1845, p. 2, col. 1.

7. Ibid., May 25, 1847, p. 2, col. 1.
8. Ibid., May 10, 1854, p. 2, col. 1; May 11, 1854, p. 2, col. 1.
9. Ibid., May 13, 1854, p. 2, col. 1; May 23, 1854, p. 2, col. 1.
10. It is termed an "operetta" in *Picayune*, May 8, 1854, p. 1, col. 7.
11. *Picayune*, May 13, 1854, p. 2, col. 1; May 23, 1854, p. 1, col. 2.
12. Ibid., May 17, 1855, p. 2, col. 4.
13. Ibid., Jan. 8, 1842, p. 3, col. 2.
14. Ibid., Jan. 8, 1845, p. 2, col. 5.
15. Ibid., Feb. 28, 1844, p. 3, col. 3.
16. Ibid., June 12, 1846, p. 2, col. 7.
17. Ibid., Oct. 1, 1846, p. 2, col. 1.
18. Ibid., Apr. 3, 1861, p. 4, col. 1.
19. Ibid., Apr. 13, 1844, p. 2, col. 2.
20. Ibid., Apr. 29, 1859, p. 2, col. 7.
21. *The Sunday Delta*, Nov. 11, 1859, p. 1, col. 6.
22. *Picayune*, May 4, 1844, p. 2, col. 5.
23. Ibid., Apr. 28, 1847, p. 2, col. 3.
24. Ibid., Mar. 13, 1850, p. 2, col. 1.
25. For example, besides those for 1847 and 1850, see *Picayune*, Apr. 5, 1848, p. 3, col. 7; Apr. 22, 1849, p. 3, col. 4; May 10, 1854, p. 2, col. 1; May 17, 1855, p. 2, col. 4; Apr. 9, 1856, p. 4, col. 1; Feb. 4, 1857, p. 4, col. 1.
26. *Picayune*, Mar. 29, 1856, p. 2, col. 3.
27. Ibid., Apr. 11, 1956, p. 3, col. 7.
28. Ibid., Apr. 17, 1861, p. 1, col. 5.
29. Ibid., July 26, 1862, p. 2, col. 1.
30. Ibid., Aug. 17, 1862, p. 2, col. 1.
31. In a "Letter from Gamma," which included opera news from Paris (*Picayune*, Dec. 21, 1863, p. 5, col. 4).
32. *Picayune*, Sept. 25, 1866, p. 4, col. 1.
33. Ibid.
34. *Picayune*, Apr. 24, 1868, p. 2, col. 1; Mar. 30, 1869, p. 4, col. 6; Aug. 29, 1869, p. 3, col. 1; Oct. 22, 1869, p. 10, col. 1.
35. Ibid., Feb. 5, 1870, p. 12, col. 6.
36. Ibid., Apr. 5, 1872, p. 1, col. 2.
37. Ibid., June 10, 1855, p. 3, col. 7. He taught in Pass Christian from June 1 to Nov. 1; see *Picayune*, Nov. 24, 1858, p. 2, col. 7.
38. Ibid., Aug. 20, 1872, p. 1, col. 2.
39. *Orleans Parish Death Certificates* 55, folio 413. Identified by Jack Belsom.
40. *Picayune*, July 4, 1872, p. 4, col. 6.
41. Ibid., Oct. 7, 1872, p. 1, col. 3.
42. *New Orleans Daily Creole*, Oct. 20, 1856, p. 3, col. 2.
43. *The Daily True Delta*, Feb. 16, 1862, p. 1, col. 4.
44. *Picayune*, Mar. 5, 1865, p. 1, col. 4; *Times*, Apr. 30, 1865, p. 1, col. 3.

CHAPTER SIX

An excellent, detailed biography and evaluation of La Hache is Warren Carl Fields, "Theodore La Hache and Music in New Orleans 1846–1869," *American Music* 8 (1990): 326–50.

1. Reissiger, 1798–1859, was Carl Maria von Weber's successor as conductor of the German opera at Dresden.

2. According to his obituaries in 1869, he had lived in New Orleans for twenty-seven years (*L'Abeille*, Nov. 23, 1869, p. 1, col. 3; *Times*, Nov. 23, 1869, p. 6, col. 2).

3. *Picayune*, May 23, 1854, p. 2, col. 4.

4. *The Bee*, Feb. 2, 1847, p. 1, col. 9, and p. 1, col. 5; *L'Abeille*, Feb. 2, 1847, p. 2, col. 3.

5. I am indebted to Harald Henrysson for information on Hammarskold.

6. *L'Abeille*, Nov. 9, 1847, p. 1, col. 1, and p. 1, col. 9.

7. *The Bee*, Mar. 1, 1848, p. 1, cols. 2 and 9; and Mar. 2, 1848, p. 1, col. 9.

8. Ibid., Jan. 1, 1862, p. 1, col. 7, and Jan. 3, 1862, p. 1, col. 3.

9. *L'Abeille*, Mar. 8, 1868, p. 1, col. 2.

10. That he had achieved a high stature in the community is attested to by his position among other highly regarded musicians whose recommendations were sought in the musical world. For example, in Dec. 1852, the piano firm of Schneider *frère* advertised that La Hache, as well as Gabici, Johns, and others vouched for their pianos (*L'Abeille*, Dec. 14, 1852, p. 2, col. 7).

11. *Picayune*, Nov. 20, 1851, p. 3, col. 2.

12. *The Bee*, Nov. 29, 1851, p. 3, col. 1.

13. How much beloved he was in New Orleans is affirmed by a letter from the editor of *The Musical World and Musical Times* of New York to La Hache's editor, on Mar. 13, 1853: "I find in your old contributor, La Hache, a most capital fellow and a thorough musician full of enthusiasm for his art. He has a great facility in composition and arrangement, and fine taste; he is exceedingly industrious, devoid of conceit, cares little for emoluments of his profession, and is a perfect devotee of music. He is much liked here; having a large circle of pupils and a still larger circle of friends."

14. *Picayune*, Jan. 13, 1854, p. 1, col. 6; p. 5, col. 2; Jan. 15, 1854, p. 4, col. 4. For information on the asylum, see *Picayune*, Jan. 15, 1854, p. 4, col. 4. Apparently there was an orchestra organized at Odd Fellows' Hall in Jan. 1854, that was to give a series of twelve concerts on subscription; see *Picayune*, Jan. 13, 1854, p. 5, col. 2. Collignon was the overall conductor of the orchestra. (See book I, part II, chapter 12.)

15. *L'Abeille*, Feb. 5, 1857, p. 2, col. 2. *The Bee*, Feb. 11, 1857, p. 3, col. 1. St. Patrick's Church was called St. Patrick's Cathedral during much of the nineteenth century.

16. *The Bee*, Oct. 14, 1862, p. 1, col. 1. Review: Oct. 21, 1862, p. 1, col. 1.

17. *L'Abeille*, June 15, 1864, p. 1, col. 2. Review: June 18, 1864, p. 1, col. 3.

18. *The Bee*, Jan. 8, 1865, p. 1, col. 1.

19. Ibid., May 16, 1865, p. 1, col. 8; *Picayune*, May 10, 1865, p. 5, col. 3; *Times*, May 25, 1865, p. 5, col. 4.

20. *L'Abeille*, Dec. 5, 1865, p. 1, col. 4; Dec. 7, 1865, p. 1, col. 1; *The Bee*, Dec. 5, 1865, p. 3, col. 1; review: Dec. 9, 1865, p. 1, col. 1.

21. *The Bee*, Feb. 9, 1866, p. 1, col. 1.

22. *Times*, Apr. 27, 1866, p. 14, col. 4; Apr. 28, 1866, p. 10, col. 4; May 1, 1866, p. 3, col. 6. Review: *Times Auctioners' Supplement*, May 2, 1866, p. 1, col. 2.

23. *Times*, May 6, 1866, p. 10, col. 6; *Times Supplement*, May 6, 1866, p. 10, cols. 5–6.

24. *L'Abeille*, Nov. 22, 1866, p. 1, col. 3; Nov. 23, 1866, p. 2, col. 2.

25. *The Bee*, Feb. 4, 1867, p. 3, col. 1; Feb. 6, 1867, p. 3, cols. 3 and 8; *L'Abeille*, Feb. 6, 1867, p. 1, col. 2.

26. *L'Abeille*, Mar. 23, 1867, p. 2, col. 1.

27. Ibid., May 19, 1867, p. 1, col. 2; May 21, 1867, p. 1, col. 3. Program: May 24, 1867, p. 1, col. 2. Review: *The Bee*, May 25, 1867, p. 3, col. 1; *L'Abeille*, May 29, 1867, p. 1, col. 2.

28. *The Bee*, Feb. 4, 1868, p. 1, col. 1; Feb. 20, 1868, p. 1, col. 1.

29. *L'Abeille,* May 6, 1869, p. 2, col. 2.

30. For example, the *Bee* on February 17, 1862, and *L'Abeille* on September 13, 1863. Grunewald issued new "spirited" and "pretty music" by La Hache: "I Would Like to Change My Name" (*The Bee,* Feb. 17, 1862, p. 1, col. 1. May 12, 1862). New music by La Hache was announced by the publisher Hart (*The Bee,* May 12, 1862, p. 1, col. 1). A new march by La Hache was published by V. Wiss, rue Conti No. 50 (*L'Abeille,* Nov. 13, 1863, p. 1, col. 2). A new piano piece by La Hache, "Elegy on the death of Mrs. G. T. Beauregard," was published (*L'Abeille,* Apr. 23, 1864, p. 1, col. 1). New vocal piece by La Hache, "Conquer la Demande" (*L'Abeille,* Apr. 29, 1864, p. 1, col. 1). New music at Grunewald included works by Theodore von La Hache (*Times,* May 7, 1865, p. 1, col. 3). Wehrmann announced publication of new works by Theod. von La Hache and Auguste Davis (*L'Abeille,* May 25, 1867, p. 1, col. 1).

31. *L'Union,* Mar. 3, 1857, p. 3, col. 2; *The Bee,* Mar. 5, 1857, p. 3, col. 7.

32. *The Bee,* May 25, 1854, p. 3, col. 1; *Picayune,* May 23, 1854, p. 2, col. 4. See also *L'Abeille,* Sept. 12, 1863, p. 1, col. 2.

33. *The Bee,* Mar. 10, 1872, p. 1, col. 8. Review: *L'Abeille,* Mar. 12, 1872, p. 1, col. 3.

34. *Picayune,* Apr. 8, 1888, p. 8, col. 4.

35. Ibid., Jan. 9, 1852, p. 2, col. 4.

36. *L'Abeille,* May 18, 1852, p. 1.

37. *Picayune,* Apr. 2, 1856, p. 6, col. 3.

38. *Times,* Oct. 7, 1866, p. 3, col. 5.

39. The above citation mentions only three concerts, but four seem to have taken place. First concert: Feb. 8; see *Picayune,* Feb. 11, 1866, p. 12, col. 2. Second concert: Apr. 12; see *Picayune,* Apr. 11, 1866, p. 1, col. 4. Third concert: May 30; *Times,* see May 29, 1866, p. 10, col. 1; May 31, 1866, p. 6, col. 3. Fourth concert: July 19; see *Picayune,* July 20, 1866, p. 2, col. 1.

40. *Picayune,* Feb. 11, 1866, p. 12, col. 2.

41. Ibid., Apr. 13, 1866, p. 12, col. 1.

42. *New Orleans Daily Crescent,* July 20, 1866, p. 4, col. 1.

43. *Picayune,* Nov. 24, 1869, p. 1, col. 4; *Times,* Nov. 24, 1869, p. 2, col. 1.

44. Emile La Hache was a conductor whose name appeared several times during the early 1870s. For example, on Wednesday, Feb. 23, 1870, there was a grand concert to benefit Maison du Bon Pasteur, at Odd Fellows' Hall, directed by M. Emile La Hache, with Mlle Josefina Filomeno, violinist, M. Braugh cellist, and M. Ginet, first violinist of the French Opera (*L'Abeille,* Feb. 20, 1870, p. 2, col. 2; Feb. 23, 1870, p. 1, col. 2). Other concerts by this La Hache occurred on Apr. 23, 1871 (*Morning Star,* Apr. 9, 1871, p. 4, col. 1; Apr. 23, 1871, p. 4, col. 1; reviews Apr. 30, 1871, p. 4, col. 1; and May 7, 1871, p. 4, col. 4); Aug. 27, 1871 (*Morning Star,* Aug. 27, 1871, p. 4, col. 1); July 7, 1872 (*Morning Star,* June 30, 1872, p. 5, col. 3; July 14, 1872 (review); July 21, 1872); and Feb. 20, 1873 (*Morning Star,* Feb. 16, 1873, p. 5, cols. 2 and 4; Feb. 23, 1873, p. 1, col. 6).

45. *Morning Star,* May 10, 1868, p. 4, col. 1; May 24, 1868, p. 5, col. 1; review May 31, 1868, p. 4, col. 1; June 21, 1868, p. 4, col. 2; June 28, 1868, p. 4, col. 2.

46. The *Times* had an advertisement section called "Musical," under which were listed the stores: Grunewalds, Theo von la Hache with Geo W. Doll, Reinike and Sons, and A. E. Blackmar (*Times,* Apr. 27, 1866, p. 12, col. 5).

47. *Picayune,* Nov. 24, 1869, p. 1, col. 4.

48. *Times,* Nov. 23, 1869, p. 6, col. 2.

49. *Morning Star,* June 23, 1872, p. 4, col. 1; p. 5, col. 5.

50. Ibid., Jan. 1, 1874, p. 4, col. 2; *L'Abeille,* Feb.1, 1874, p. 1, col. 4; and p. 1, col. 2.

51. In 1851 he completed his first religious work: *Grand Jubilee Mass,* a composition dedicated to the "Boston Händel & Haydn Society." In *The Daily Crescent,* June 21, 1851, La Hache was given a glowing review:

We hail with pleasure and pride every new production of art creditable to our city, and therefore we feel happy to have on record a new musical work, of M T. La Hache, which deserves the highest praise. This composer is already known to the public by various publications, such as Polkas, Variations and Fantasies; he is, besides, one of the most popular contributors to the leading musical periodicals of this country.

Now he has brought out a Grand Jubilee Mass for four voices, dedicated to the Boston Händel and Haydn Society. By placing his work under the patronage of a society bearing such a name, the author indicates on the very title page what are his musical predilections—in what taste and upon what principles he composed his Mass. He has remained true to the German school—he adheres strictly to it, and lays aside all the spurious embellishments which do not belong to that elevated style. It is, perhaps, for this that M. La Hache deserves most credit: he has produced an excellent composition without going beyond the limits of his subject; it is real sacred music, from the beginning to end, without any foreign admixture; and thus to compose requires genius, talent and study. . . .

We cannot but wish further success to the composer. Now that he has tried his wings in the sacred regions, he ought to soar a little higher still, and give us next an Oratorio. We would like, also, to hear his Mass performed in this city by an efficient choir, and we have no doubt it is the wish also of a great many who have not heard it yet, and only admired it from the score.

52. The *Mass for Peace* was first performed on Palm Sunday, Apr. 9, 1865, and repeated on Tuesday, Apr. 11, in the Church of Sainte Theresa. Offertory proceeds went to the Girls' Orphanage in Camp Street.

53. This song was based on Abram J. Ryan's poem "The Conquered Banner," also known as "Requiem for a Lost Cause." On Feb. 2, 1866, it was sung by a distinguished amateur after an oration on Stonewall Jackson at Odd Fellows' Hall (*New Orleans Daily Crescent*, Feb. 1, 1866, p. 4, col. 1).

CHAPTER SEVEN

1. Much of the biography of Rolling is in his obituary in the *Picayune*, May 15, 1898, section 1, p. 10, cols. 4–6.

2. Rolling often spent his summers elsewhere, most notably in Asheville, North Carolina, and in Waukesha, Wisconsin. He also spent time on the Mississippi Gulf Coast.

3. *The Bee*, Mar. 20, 1843, p. 2, col. 6. The concert was originally scheduled for Mar. 22.

4. *L'Abeille*, Apr. 3, 1873, p. 1, col. 2; Apr. 4, 1873, p. 1, col. 7; Apr. 5, 1873, p. 1, col. 2.

5. Ibid., Sept. 10, 1881, p. 1, col. 2. Reviewed Sept. 13, 1881, p. 1, col. 2.

6. Ibid., Mar. 25, 1883, p. 1, col. 2, Mar. 25, 1883, p. 2, col. 3, and Apr. 1, 1883, p. 1, col. 3. Semi-review: Apr. 3, 1883, p. 1, col. 2.

7. *Picayune*, Mar. 30, 1896, p. 10, col. 5.

8. *L'Abeille*, May 20, 1853, p. 1, col. 2.

9. As quoted in *L'Abeille*, Apr. 14, 1867, p. 1, col. 3.

10. As reprinted in *L'Abeille*, Dec. 27, 1868, p. 2, col. 2; and again Dec. 28, 1879, p. 3, col. 2, which also has a detailed program of Rolling's piece.

11. *L'Abeille*, Dec. 31, 1879, p. 1, col. 5.

12. *Picayune*, Feb. 28, 1890, p. 5, col. 2. *L'Abeille*, Mar. 1, 1890, p. 4, col. 1 (end); Mar. 2, 1890, p. 1, col. 9; review: Mar. 2, 1890, p. 4, col. 1; Mar. 8, 1890, p. 4, col. 1.

13. For example, see *L'Abeille*, Dec. 7, 1884, p. 4, cols. 1–2.

14. *L'Abeille*, Mar. 11, 1890, p. 4, cols. 1–3.

15. Ibid., Mar. 19, 1890, p. 4, col. 3.

16. "On se rappellera le success qu'elle [*L'Harmonie de la Nature*] obtint, sous la direction Maugé, alors qu'elle fut execute par l'orchestre de l'Opéra, que conduisait M. Lenfant. Quoique le morceau ait de grands développements, il fut bissé, et on dut le jouer entièrement une second fois" (*L'Abeille,* Mar. 15, 1891, p. 4, col. 1).

17. The critic, who heard the piece at the French Opera in the French Quarter, referred here to a performance at the Camp Street Theatre in the American Quarter.

18. *L'Abeille,* Nov. 26, 1869, p. 1, col. 2; Feb. 10, 1870, p. 1, col. 2.

19. Ibid., Mar. 4, 1870, p. 1, col. 2.

20. Ibid., May 6, 1877, p. 1, col. 2.

21. Ibid., Dec. 27, 1879, p. 2, col. 2.

22. Ibid., Mar. 30, 1872, p. 1, col. 2.

23. Ibid., Oct. 31, 1875, p. 1, col. 2.

24. *Picayune,* Apr. 11, 1876, p. 8, col. 7.

25. *L'Abeille,* Jan. 11, 1881, p. 1, col. 3.

26. Ibid., Mar. 7, 1875, p. 1, col. 3; Mar. 14, 1875, p. 1, col. 2; Apr. 2, 1875, p. 1, col. 2; Apr. 4, 1875, p. 3, cols 1–2; Apr. 6, 1875, p. 1, col. 2; Apr. 7, 1875, p. 1, col. 2; Apr. 8, 1875, p. 1, col. 2; Apr. 11, 1875, p. 3, cols. 1–2.

27. Ibid., Apr. 10, 1880, p. 1, col. 2.

28. Ibid., May 17, 1881, p. 1, col. 4.

29. Ibid., Apr. 1, 1883, p. 1, col. 3, and Apr. 12, 1883, p. 1, col. 3 (long article). Review by Canonge: Apr. 15, 1883, p. 4, col. 1. Addendum: Apr. 17, 1883, p. 1, col. 5.

30. Ibid., May 16, 1885, p. 4, col. 1; May 19, 1885, p. 4, cols. 1–2.

31. Ibid., Apr. 27, 1890, p. 4, col. 1. Review: May 3, 1890, p. 4, col. 1; May 4, 1890, p. 4, cols. 1–3; May 6, 1890, p. 4, col. 1.

32. Ibid., Mar. 19, 1882, p. 3, col. 1.

33. Ibid., May 11, 1886, p. 4, col. 1; May 14, 1886, p. 4, col. 1. Review: May 15, 1886, p. 4, col. 1; May 16, 1886, p. 4, cols. 2–4.

34. Ibid., Apr. 18, 1875, p. 1, col. 2; Apr. 20, 1875, p. 2, col. 4: Apr. 21, 1875, p. 1, col. 2. Reviews: Apr. 22, 1875, p. 1, col. 2; Apr. 25, 1875, p. 3, cols 1–2 (3 parts).

35. Ibid., Jan. 8, 1876, p. 1, col. 1.

36. Ibid., Mar. 14, 1880, p. 1, col. 4.

37. Ibid., Jan. 14, 1879, p. 1, col. 5.

38. Ibid., Oct. 22, 1882, p. 4, col. 3.

39. Ibid., Sept. 2, 1883, p. 4, col. 2.

40. Ibid., Apr. 13, 1881, p. 1, col. 2.

41. Ibid., Sept. 10, 1881, p. 1, col. 2; Sept. 13, 1881, p. 1, col. 2.

CHAPTER EIGHT

1. From Sam Franko, *Chords and Discords* (New York: Viking Press, 1938), and scrapbooks of programs and newspaper clippings, 5 vols., New York Public Library, Music Division, *ZAN-*M28, reel 46. See also clipping files of Jeanne Franko and Nahan Franko in the New York Public Library, Music Division, and scrapbooks of Nahan, *ZAN-*M28, reel 14.

2. Hamman Holländer changed his name to Franko in 1848. See Kirby Reid Jolly, "Edwin Franko Goldman and the Goldman Band," Ph.D. diss., New York University, 1971, 13.

3. *Picayune,* Feb. 23, 1886, p. 7, col. 3.

4. *L'Abeille,* Jan. 28, 1870, p. 1, col. 2; Jan. 30, 1870, p. 2, col. 4; Feb. 3, 1870, p. 1, col. 2. Program: Feb. 2, 1870, p. 2, col. 4. Note that the newspapers listed the children as two or three years younger than they actually were.

5. Ibid., Feb. 9, 1870, p. 1, col. 2.

6. Ibid., Feb. 24, 1881, p. 2, col. 1; p. 1, col. 2.

7. Ibid., Mar. 6, 1881, p. 1, col. 3.

8. Ibid., Apr. 27, 1881, p. 12, col. 6; reviewed Apr. 28, 1881, p. 1, col. 4. *Picayune,* Apr. 27, 1881, p. 5, col. 7.

9. *L'Abeille,* May 8, 1881, p. 1, cols. 2–3, and May 13, 1881, p. 1, col. 3. Review: May 18, 1881, p. 1, col. 3.

10. Ibid., May 27, 1881, p. 2, col. 1.

11. Ibid., May 28, 1881, p. 1, col. 6. Review: May 29, 1881, p. 1, col. 4.

12. Ibid., May 31, 1881, p. 1, col. 3; p. 2, col. 1; June 1, 1881, p. 1, col. 5.

13. Ibid., June 3, 1881, p. 2, col. 1.

14. Ibid., June 5, 1881, p. 2, col. 1.

15. Ibid., Sept. 6, 1881, p. 2, col. 2.

16. Ibid., Sept. 9, 1881, p. 2, col. 2.

17. "On sait quelle habile violoniste elle est. Elle s'est conquis ici, à ce titre, une juste renommée, et elle s'est fait estimer et aimer dans bien des families" (*L'Abeille,* Mar. 28, 1882, p. 2, col. 1; Mar. 30, 1882, p. 4, col. 4).

18. *L'Abeille,* Apr. 1, 1882, p. 1, col. 2; Apr. 9, 1882, p. 1, col. 6; Apr. 11, 1882, p. 1, col. 2; p. 2, col. 1; Apr. 14, 1882, p. 1, col. 2.

19. Ibid., Apr. 16, 1882, p. 1, col. 3.

20. *Picayune,* Nov. 3, 1882, afternoon ed., p. 1, col. 1; p. 2, col. 2; Nov. 2, 1882, p. 5, col. 7. *L'Abeille,* Oct. 29, 1882, p. 2, col. 4; Oct. 29, 1882, p. 4, col. 3.

21. *Picayune,* June 5, 1887, p. 5, col. 2; p. 6, col. 4; and June 14, 1887, p. 4, col. 4. Review: June 15, 1887, p. 8, col. 4.

22. *L'Abeille,* Jan. 12, 1884, p. 1, col. 4.

23. For example, on Mar. 7, 1911; see *Musical America* 13, no. 19 (Mar. 18, 1911), p. 37.

24. See New York Public Library, MBD (uncataloged) program.

25. For example, on Jan. 9, 1895; *The Musical Courier* 14, no. 2, p. 39; vol. 24, no. 9 (Mar. 2, 1892), p. 15; vol. 24, no. 11 (Mar. 16, 1892), p. 10; vol. 24, no. 13 (Mar. 30, 1892), p. 9; vol. 30 (Jan. 9, 1895), p. 34; vol. 34 (Jan. 13, 1897), p. 27; vol. 34 (Jan. 27, 1897), pp. 23 and 34; vol. 34, no. 9 (Mar. 3, 1897), p. 35; vol. 34, no. 12 (Mar. 24, 1897), p. 17; vol. 35, no. 13 (Sept. 29, 1897), p. 39; vol. 84, no. 3 (1940), p. 32; vol. 9 (July 27, 1907); vol. 9 (Oct. 5, 1907), p. 5; vol. 13, no. 19 (Mar. 18, 1911), p. 37; vol. 13 (Apr. 29, 1911), p. 26; vol. 35 (1940), no. 13, p. 47, are full of Jeanne's advice for students and announcements of her teaching and concerts.

26. See her obituary in *The New York Times,* Dec. 4, 1940, section A, p. 27, col. 3.

CHAPTER NINE

1. See John H. Baron, *Intimate Music: a History of the Idea of Chamber Music* (Stuyvesant, NY: Pendragon Press, 1998), 321.

2. *Orleans Parish Births* 9, p. 796. May W. Mount's assertion (*Some Notables of New Orleans* [New Orleans: the author, 1896], 146) that she was born in Paris is clearly false. See also Marguerite's obituary in the *Picayune,* Oct. 30, 1912, p. 6.

3. Adolphe Elie was the dedicatee of an important work by the Belgian violinist Henri Vieux-

temps—the oldest surviving African American music from New Orleans. For the tale of this roundabout composition, see John H. Baron, "Vieuxtemps (and Ole Bull) in New Orleans," *American Music* 8 (1990): 210–26. Adolphe is buried in New Orleans St. Louis Cemetery No. 2 (Square 1, Aisle 1, East). Marie's grave (Metairie Cemetery, Section 106, Lot 159–60) gives her birth and death dates and indicates that she is the widow of Adolphe Elie.

4. Louise married Rudolph Woeste (1832–1890), a German immigrant, and they had four children: Carl Woeste (1877–1931), Rudolph Woeste (d. 1931), Louise (Mrs. John M.) Huger (d. 1959), and Herman Woeste (d. 1960). These names appear in the obituaries of Marguerite and her daughter Margot.

5. *Picayune,* Apr. 25, 1856, p. 5, col. 3.

6. According to Mount's unreliable account, Marguerite was a cousin of Halévy. The only connection between the two that I have found is through the name "Elie," which was Fromenthal Halévy's father's first name. If indeed they were cousins, then it is likely that Adolphe Elie was Jewish by birth, and it is also possible that Leopold Samuel was Jewish. Although all Elies in New Orleans were Catholic, the name (French for Elijah) is usually Jewish, and there were many Jews in New Orleans and France with the surname Samuel. Where this leaves Marguerite is uncertain.

7. Marguerite's obituary in the *Picayune,* Wednesday, Oct. 30, 1912, p. 6, col. 6.

8. *Le Menestrel,* Jan. 24, 1864, p. 63.

9. Ibid., May 11, 1864, p. 199.

10. Ibid., Sept. 17, 1865, 332–33.

11. *Picayune,* Dec. 19, 1865, p. 1, col. 4.

12. The concert was originally scheduled for Dec. 27, 1865, but was postponed to Jan. 4.

13. *Picayune,* Dec. 15, 1865, p. 1, col. 4.

14. The program is given in the *Picayune,* Dec. 10, 1865, p. 1, col. 3.

15. *L'Abeille,* English ed., Dec. 20, 1865, p. 1, col. 1.

16. Ibid., French ed., Dec. 20, 1865, p. 1, col. 2.

17. *Picayune,* Dec. 20, 1865, p. 4, col. 1.

18. Ibid., Jan. 6, 1866, p. 4, col. 1. Other critics were more positive, e.g., in the *Daily Crescent,* Jan. 5, 1866, p. 4, col. 1.

19. *The Daily True Delta,* Jan. 13, 1866, p. 2, col. 1.

20. *The Daily Star,* Jan. 12, 1866, p. 2, col. 1.

21. *Daily Crescent,* Apr. 2, 1866, p. 6, col. 1.

22. *L'Étoile du Sud,* Apr. 10, 1866, p. 2, col. 2.

23. The reviewer in the *Picayune,* Jan. 11, 1866, p. 6, col. 2, stated: "M'lle Elie's last concert established her reputation here; she may now go on, conquering and to conquer."

24. *Picayune,* Feb. 11, 1866, p. 5, col. 1: "The musical world of New Orleans will join with us in expressing regret at the news that M'lle M. Elie is shortly to return to Paris, to make it her home."

25. One daughter was Margot Samuel (ca. 1868–1941), a piano teacher in New Orleans, who never married. See her obituary, *Times-Picayune,* Jan. 5, 1941, p. 2. The other daughter was Mrs. Charles Abnen De Lima, who moved to Florence, Italy. See Marguerite's obituary.

26. *Picayune,* Mar. 20, 1898, p. 4, col. 6.

27. Louisiana State Museum Historical Center, Accession No. 10778, RG 136, p. 84. Moszkowski moved to Paris in 1897.

28. After years of study in Europe, Helena Augustin returned to New Orleans, where she performed in the French Opera House on Apr. 3, 1902—a parallel to Marguerite's debut thirty-six years earlier. See *Picayune,* Mar. 23, 1902, part I, p. 10; part III, p. 8; Mar. 27, 1902, p. 3; Mar. 30, 1902, part II, p. 5; Apr. 3, 1902, p. 3 (which gives her program: works by Bach, Mozart, Weber, Schubert, Chopin, Moszkowski, and Liszt—clearly she had Marguerite's taste); and Apr. 4, 1902,

p. 9. Before her return to New Orleans in Mar. 1902, she made her debuts in Berlin and New York. It is curious that nowhere in the articles of 1902 is Mrs. Samuel mentioned. Meanwhile, Carreño herself performed at least twice in New Orleans: in a solo recital at the Athenaeum on Feb. 4, 1901, and in Grunewald Hall in conjunction with the famous violinist August Wilhelmj (date unknown). See Tulane University Louisiana Collection, vertical file "New Orleans Entertainment Theatres, Athenaeum" and "Grunewald Hall."

29. Program preserved in Tulane University Louisiana Collection, vertical file "New Orleans Entertainment Theatres, Grunewald Hall."

30. Henri Wehrmann and his wife were famous engravers of music, and their son and Eugénie's cousin Henry Wehrman (1871–1956) was one of the most important violinists in the city from the late nineteenth century until his death. See *Picayune,* Mar. 1, 1903, part III, p. 5, col. 5.

31. Louisiana State Museum Historical Center, RG# SB #10.

32. Published by M. Elie in New Orleans in 1879. A copy is in the Tulane University, Howard Tilton Memorial Library, Louisiana Collection. A certain ambiguity exists when the publisher is given as M. Elie; is this Marie Elie or Monsieur Elie? Usually from 1878 on Adolphe is identified clearly as such (he was basically retired by then and worked occasionally in the store run by his wife Marie), and we assume that M. Elie refers to Marie. During the 1850s and 1860s Adolph stamps all music sold at his store as "A. Elie."

33. A copy of the piece is in the University of Alabama Library, and a modern edition is in Baron, *Piano Music from New Orleans,* 85–91.

34. Published in New Orleans by Philip Werlein, 1885. Two copies of the piece are in the Tulane University, Howard Tilton Memorial Library, Louisiana Collection.

35. *Werlein's Musical Journal* 1, no. 1 (June 1, 1884), p. 2. The citation from the *New Orleans Times Democrat* is printed here.

36. The playbill is in Louisiana State Museum Historical Center, RG# SB #10. This was also printed in the *Picayune,* June 13, 1881, and the review appeared the next day (p. 2, col. 1).

37. Probably Rudolf Piefke (1835–1900). The other three remain unidentified.

38. "Madame Elie-Samuels was, as usual, most graceful in the rendering of "Third Ballad of Chopin," and "Septuor of Lucia," which awoke unbounded enthusiasm" (*Picayune,* June 24, 1881, p. 2, col. 1). The reviewer continued, "Altogether the concert may be said to have been a great success. It attracted connoisseurs, which fact is compliment enough, and beside had for audience our best society [sic]. The garden ablaze with light and beauty was a picture to behold, and long did it remain alive with visitors after the concert in the hall. The trains went and came on time, with ample room for all, bringing everybody home safe and satisfied after a delightful evening at the Fort."

39. Undated, without source, in a Mark Kaiser scrapbook in the M. Chapella Collection, Louisiana State Museum Historical Center, Accession No. 10778, RG 136, p. 49.

40. Louisiana State Museum Historical Center, RG# SB #10. The Grunewald Opera House (or Grunewald Hall) burned down in the 1892 and was replaced on the same site by the Grunewald Hotel (later Roosevelt, then Fairmont, now once again Roosevelt Hotel) with a new, small auditorium (known for the past seventy years as the Blue Room).

41. Probably William Mason's (1829–1908) "Romance-Idyl," opus 42. See Kenneth Graber, *William Mason (1829–1908): An Annotated Bibliography and Catalog of Works* (Warren, MI: Harmonie Park Press, 1989), 264.

42. *L'Abeille.* The program is in Tulane University Louisiana Collection, vertical file "Music, Mendelssohn Society." This file also contains the constitution and bylaws of the society.

43. Louisiana State Museum Historical Center, Accession No. 10778, RG 136, p. 59. Among the other gentlemen are Louis Grunewald and Philip Werlein, two of the city's most prominent

businessmen in the music industry. Despite Mark Kaiser's influence on the group, he and other musicians are excluded from the list of officers and directors of the Mendelssohn Society.

44. *Picayune,* Apr. 26, 1889, p. 4, col. 4.

45. The concert took place at Grunewald's Opera House, May 3, 1889. Others on the program were Miss A. Bouligny, Miss K. Dessommes, Mark Kaiser, T. Curant, William H. Rolling, and Nott's pupils (*Picayune,* Apr. 28, 1889, p. 5, col. 3).

46. *Picayune,* Apr. 28, 1889, p. 7, col. 4.

47. *Times-Democrat,* Mar. 18, 1890, p. 4, col. 4.

48. Review of a concert sponsored by the New Orleans Philharmonic Society on Mar. 12, 1898, in a Mark Kaiser scrapbook in the M. Chapella Collection, Louisiana State Museum Historical Center, Accession No. 10778, RG 136.

49. An undated newspaper clipping in English in the Louisiana State Museum Historical Center, Accession No. 10778, RG 136, p. 57.

50. *Picayune,* Mar. 18, 1890, p. 4, col. 5.

51. *The Times-Democrat,* Mar. 19, 1890, p. 3, col. 3.

52. *Daily States,* Mar. 19, 1890, p. 2, col. 1.

53. Ibid., Mar. 21, 1890, p. 2, col. 5.

54. An unidentified newspaper clipping in the Mark Kaiser Collection in the M. Chapella Collection, Louisiana State Museum Historical Center, Accession No. 10068, RG 131, Box 2/4.

55. Sometime in the 1880s or 1890s, Mme. Samuel printed a *Collection of Pieces Played by Memory by Mme Elie-Samuel,* of which a copy is in the Louisiana State Museum Historical Center, RG# SB #10. Seventy-nine works are listed on three pages, but the list cuts off in the beginning of the works of Schumann, and apparently a fourth or even a fifth page is missing. There are twenty-six works of Chopin, thirteen works of Mendelssohn (including the *Songs Without Words*), four movements by Bach, three Beethoven sonatas, two works of Liszt, various works by Alkan, Gottschalk, Schulhoff, Ketten, Ravina, and single works by Handel, Field, Heller, Hiller, Henselt, Mozart, T. Lack, Lavignac, Leschetizky, Brahms, Massenet, Scarlatti, and Mathias. Her programs include works by composers not on this list, such as Schubert, Grieg and Chabrier, that appear in the late 1890s, so we may presume the list dates from no later than 1897. This would match the serious repertory of any European pianist of the time.

56. From two unidentified newspaper clippings in a Mark Kaiser scrapbook in the M. Chapella Collection, Louisiana State Museum Historical Center, Accession No. 10068, RG 131, Box 2/4.

57. The original Athenaeum Theatre was built by the Young Men's Hebrew Association in 1896 and is where Marguerite performed. It burned down in 1905 and was replaced on the same site by the new Athenaeum Theatre in 1907, which in turn burned down in 1937. See *New Orleans States,* Feb. 16, 1896, p. 6, and *Times-Picayune,* Apr. 15, 1995. Information supplied by Jack Belsom. See also *Picayune's Guide to New Orleans,* 1904 ed., 209.

58. Tulane University Louisiana Collection, vertical file "Music New Orleans Musicians Guild."

59. An undated newspaper clipping in English describing the program is in a Mark Kaiser scrapbook in the M. Chapella Collection, Louisiana State Museum Historical Center, Accession No. 10778, RG 136, p. 54.

60. The printed program is in the M. Chapella Collection, Louisiana State Museum Historical Center, Accession No. 10068, RG 131, Box 2.

61. Parlor concerts were frequent in New Orleans in the nineteenth and early twentieth centuries. While most were by amateurs and not announced, occasionally the best musicians in town would announce theirs, as in the *Picayune,* Sunday, Mar. 1, 1903, part III, p. 5, col. 5, announcement of a chamber music concert by the Mark Kaiser Quartet in a private home.

62. *Picayune,* Mar. 17, 1901, p. 12, col. 4.

63. Ibid., Mar. 8, 1903, p. 13, col. 3.

64. Ibid., obituary of Marguerite Samuel.

65. *Time-Picayune,* obituary of Margot Samuel, refers to Marguerite Samuel, "who was famed as a pianist and a promoter of music in Louisiana."

CHAPTER TEN

1. *Picayune,* Dec. 14, 1867, p. 5, col. 4; repeated on Dec. 19.

2. Ibid., Dec. 19, 1867, p. 2, col. 1.

3. Ibid., Saturday, Dec. 21, 1867, p. 2, col. 1.

4. Emile and Mathilde, Baron and Baroness d'Erlanger, were the parents of four sons, of whom Rudolphe-Françoise (1872–1932) was once renowned as a pioneer musicologist of Arabic music and Frédéric (1868–1943) was a minor composer. Kaiser, meanwhile, while he was on the ship on the Atlantic Ocean, played a recital.

5. *Condinunilat Gazette,* Paris, as preserved in Louisiana State Museum Historical Center, Kaiser scrapbook. Ernest refers to Ernst.

6. For a little more on Garcin, see Françoise Michel, François Lesure, and Vladimir Fédorov, eds., *Encyclopédie de la Musique* (Paris: Fasquelle, 1959), vol. 2: 228.

7. Letter from Charles Dancla to Kaiser, dated Oct. 22, 1881, in Louisiana State Museum Historical Center, Kaiser scrapbook.

8. Letter from Ambroise Thomas to the United States Minister in Paris, dated June 19, 1873, in Louisiana State Museum Historical Center, Kaiser scrapbook.

9. Kaiser's scrapbooks include clippings of newspaper reviews of his concerts, but he did not date any of them, and in a few cases the city where the concert took place is not indicated.

10. He was a music teacher in New Orleans from at least 1873 to 1879. See city directories.

11. Probably Mme Pauline Le Blanc, who appears as a music teacher in New Orleans in the 1880s. See city directories.

12. *L'Abeille,* Dec. 20, 1973, p. 3, cols. 1–2. The concert is advertised in the same newspaper on Dec. 17, 1873, p. 2, col. 2, and an initial review occurred there on Dec. 18, 1873, p. 1, col. 3.

13. George T. Ferris, *Great Singers,* Second Series: *Malibran to Titiens* (New York: D. Appleton & Co., 1888), 234–48, gives Tietjens's dates as 1834 to 1879.

14. He may have toured with Coreño as well.

15. John Dwight was not very pleased with Tietjens's voice ("Titiens' voice is old and worn out" (*Journal* 35–36 [1875–77]: 148]) and does not mention Kaiser.

16. *Picayune,* Saturday morning, Apr. 22, 1876, p. 5, col. 7.

17. Ibid., Feb. 8, 1876, p. 8, col. 6. See also *Picayune,* Feb. 7, 1877, p. 5, col. 5. Obéron has not been identified.

18. *The Mapleson Memoires: the Career of an Operatic Impresario 1858–1888,* ed. Harold Rosenthal (New York: Appleton-Century, 1966), p. 328 and ad passim. She married Mapleson's son Henry.

19. *Detroit Free Press,* Nov. 24, 1878. Louisiana State Museum Historical Center, R6 136 acc #10778.

20. Copy of the review in Louisiana State Museum Historical Center, Kaiser scrapbooks.

21. Clippings from all these concerts are in the Kaiser scrapbooks, Louisiana State Museum Historical Center, R6 136 acc #10778. Many are undated and without the source newspaper.

22. Hamerik (1843–1923) was a Danish conductor and composer who headed the Peabody Institute (Conservatory) from 1871 to 1898 and the Peabody Orchestra from 1871 to 1896. The cellist of the quartet was "Louis Blumenberg, brother of Mark Blumenberg, of the Musical Courier." See Theodore Roehl, "Who's Who in Music," *The New Orleans States Item,* Sunday ([day and year not given], clipping in Louisiana State Museum Historical Center RG 136, acc # 10778).

23. "Mr. Mark Kaiser, a New Orleans violinist, is now in Chicago" (*Grunewald's Musical Journal* 4, no. 7 [Aug. 1882]: 1). However, his name does not appear in the Chicago city directories, and no sources in Chicago verify his presence there.

24. Newspaper accounts often refer to Kaiser as Marks rather than Mark.

25. No date or source given. Clipping in Louisiana State Museum Historical Center RG 136, acc # 10778. There is another clipping that refers to Kaiser's returning from a stay in the West; when, where, or how long this was is not indicated anywhere.

26. While Gaston Gottschalk remained a teacher in Chicago until his death in 1912, his school seems to have failed since there is no mention of it in the Chicago city directories after 1886.

27. *Picayune,* Nov. 3, 1882, p. 2, col. 2. The concert was announced as a Grand Concert of Mr. Mark Kaiser (*Picayune,* Nov. 2, 1882, p. 5, col. 7, and in the afternoon ed., p. 1, col. 1).

28. There is no "Mullen" listed as a musician in the 1880s in New Orleans. Louis Muller or Mueller, on the other hand, was a professor of music and director of the Louisiana Conservatory of Music from 1878 to 1880, and Albert Muller was a professor of music in New Orleans from 1882 to 1883. See city directories.

29. Emil Seifert was head of the Music School of Grunewald Hall in 1883. See city directory.

30. *Picayune,* Apr. 28, 1889, p. 5, col. 3. A review without source is preserved in Louisiana State Museum Historical Center, RG 136, pp. 54 and 58.

31. Apr. 25, but no year given. Louisiana State Museum Historical Center, RG 136 acc. #10778.

32. She died Feb. 24, 1935. She was the wife of Kaiser's brother Esmar, who died Mar. 7, 1924, at age sixty-five. While Mark and Hattie Kaiser had no descendants, Esmar and Ida did.

33. *Times-Democrat,* Jan. 7, 1890, p. 2, col. 3.

34. "Musique de Chambre," unmarked clipping, in Louisiana State Museum Historical Center, R6 136, acc. # 10778.

35. Theodore Roehl states that there was a series of recitals by Kaiser's group at Howard's home.

36. *Chicago Herald,* Aug. 11, 1893, p. 9, col. 1. *Chicago Tribune,* Aug. 11, p. 3, reviews only the playing by Samuel.

37. J. Cesar Grisai was born in Mantua, studied at the Conservatory of Parma, was first cellist of the Grand Opera Theatre at Marseilles, the Theatro Sociale of Mantua, the Theatre de Verme at Milan, and the Mapleson Italian Opera Company. Apparently he met Kaiser during the Mapleson tour and settled in New Orleans by 1891. During the Chicago Fair of 1893 he was a member of Theodore Thomas's Magnum Orchestra and the Rosenbecker Classic Orchestra in Chicago. Emile Malmquist was born in Stockholm in 1857, studied at the conservatory in Stockholm, toured through Europe and South America, and settled in New Orleans in 1882, where he organized the New Orleans Conservatory of Music. See *Picayune,* Tuesday, Nov. 27, 1894, p. 3, cols. 2–3.

38. *Times-Picayune,* Nov. 27, 1894, p. 3, cols. 2–3.

39. Louisiana State Museum Historical Center, RG 131, Box 2/4.

40. For example, the Newcomb String Quartet consisted of René Salomon and Adrian Freische, violins; Henry Wehrmann, viola; and Otto Finck, cello, when they performed Mozart's K. 387 Quartet and the first movement of Schubert's A Minor Quartet in a concert at Gibson Hall on Mar. 22, 1915. On Apr. 13 that same year the same ensemble performed at Grunewald Convention Hall, with Mme. Eugénie Wehrmann Schaffner, Henry's sister, as pianist.

41. The director of this conservatory was Ernest E. Schuyten, who also was head of the Violin Department of the Newcomb School of Music in 1913. About 1920 one of Kaiser's pupils was Harby Kreeger, who later studied at the New York Institute of Musical Art and later took over his family business, the prominent department store in New Orleans that bore his name.

42. This medal was still being given in 1953 but has not been known for the past fifty years.

43. The members of the Kaiser Quartet were Gladys Pope and Florence Hiteshaw, violins; Erin Black, viola; and Sara Lob, cello. See *Times-Picayune,* Nov. 30, 1927.

44. The Ysaye concert programs are in the New Orleans Public Library Concert Lists.

CHAPTER ELEVEN

1. *L'Abeille,* Nov. 17, 1872, p. 2, col. 6; Nov. 29, 1872, p. 1, col. 3.

2. Ibid., Nov. 30, 1872, p. 1, col. 2; Dec. 8, 1872, p. 2, col. 1.

3. Ibid., Apr. 15, 1873, p. 2, col. 5; Apr. 16, 1873, p. 2, col. 4.

4. Ibid., Oct. 5, 1873, p. 2, col. 4; Nov. 5, 1873, p. 1, col. 2.

5. Ibid., Apr. 30, 1874, p. 1, col. 3, and p. 2, col. 2; May 3, 1874, p. 1, col. 3.

6. Ibid., May 7, 1874, p. 2, col. 2; and May 8, p. 2, col. 2.

7. Ibid., Feb. 8, 1874, p. 1, col. 3.

8. Ibid., Mar. 1, 1874, p. 1, col. 2; Mar. 15, 1874, p. 1, col. 2.

9. Ibid., May 3, 1874, p. 1, col. 3; May 8, 1874, p. 1, col. 3; May 9, 1874, p. 2, col. 2; May 13, 1874, p. 1, col. 3.

10. Ibid., Nov. 29, 1874, p. 2, col. 2.

11. Ibid., May 15, 1875, p. 1, col. 1; May 16, 1875, p. 1, col. 2; May 30, 1875, p. 3, col. 1.

12. *Picayune,* Apr. 15, 1876, p. 1, col. 7; Apr. 19, 1876, p. 5, col. 7.

13. *L'Abeille,* Nov. 21, 1876, p. 1, col. 2.

14. Ibid., Sept. 30, 1877, p. 2, col. 3; Oct. 2, 1877, p. 1, col. 1.

15. Ibid., Apr. 25, 1880, p. 3, col. 1.

16. Ibid., Oct. 22, 1880, p. 1, col. 3; Oct. 26, 1880, p. 1, col. 3.

17. Ibid., Jan. 4, 1881, p. 2, col. 1; Jan. 8, 1881, p. 1, col. 2.

18. Ibid., Jan. 16, 1881, p. 2, col. 2.

19. Ibid., Mar. 27, 1881, p. 1, col. 3; Mar. 29, 1881, p. 1, col. 1.

20. Ibid., May 8, 1881, p. 1, cols. 2–3, and May 13, 1881, p. 1, col. 3. Review: May 18, 1881, p. 1, col. 3.

21. Ibid., May 29, 1881, p. 2, col. 1.

22. Ibid., June 14, 1881, p. 2, col. 1, and June 19, 1881, p. 1, col. 2.

23. Ibid., June 21, 1881, p. 2, col. 1; and June 22, 1881, p. 1, col. 2. *Picayune,* June 24, 1881, p. 2, col. 1. A copy of the program handed out at the performance is at Louisiana State Museum.

24. *L'Abeille,* Sept. 6, 1881, p. 2, col. 2.

25. Ibid., Nov. 12, 1881, p. 2, col. 1.

26. Ibid., Feb. 18, 1882, p. 2, col. 2. This may be the same concert mentioned by Canonge, Feb. 10, 1882, p. 1, cols. 4–5.

27. Ibid., Mar. 28, 1882, p. 4, col. 1; Mar. 30, 1882, p. 4, col. 4.

28. Ibid., Mar. 31, 1882, p. 1, col. 5; Apr. 1, 1882, p. 1, col. 2.

29. Ibid., Apr. 1, 1882, p. 2, col. 2.

30. Ibid., Apr. 3, 1882, p. 1, col. 4; Apr. 11, 1882, p. 2, col. 2; Apr. 12, 1882, p. 1, col. 3; Apr. 16, 1882, p. 1, col. 3.

31. Ibid., Apr. 11, 1882, p. 2, col. 2.

32. Ibid., Nov. 14, 1882, p. 4, col. 2; Nov. 22, 1882, p. 1, col. 2. Review: Nov. 23, 1882, p. 1, col. 2.

33. Ibid., Dec. 24, 1882, p. 1, col. 3.

34. Ibid., Mar. 15, 1883, p. 1, col. 2, and Mar. 17, 1883, p. 1, col. 2.

35. Ibid., Mar. 25, 1883, p. 1, col. 2; Mar. 25, 1883, p. 2, col. 3; and Apr. 1, 1883, p. 1, col. 3. Semi-review: Apr. 3, 1883, p. 1, col. 2.

36. Ibid., Apr. 1, 1883, p. 1, col. 3. Review: Apr. 3, 1883, p. 1, col. 2.

37. Ibid., June 9, 1883, p. 1, col. 8.

38. Ibid., Sept. 1883, p. 3, col. 7.

39. Ibid., Apr. 26, 1883, p. 2, col. 1; Apr. 29, 1883, p. 4, col. 2, and p. 2, col. 4.

40. Ibid., Apr. 29, 1883, p. 4, col. 2; Apr. 29, 1883, p. 2, col. 3.

41. *Picayune,* Oct. 20, 1883, afternoon, p. 1, col. 3; Oct. 28, 1883, p. 11, col. 5.

42. *L'Abeille,* Nov. 6, 1883, p. 1, col. 4; Nov. 7, 1883, p. 1, col. 4; Nov. 8, 1883, p. 1, col. 6; p. 1, col. 4. Review: Nov. 9, 1883, p. 1, col. 4.

43. Ibid., Mar. 15, 1883, p. 1, col. 2; *Picayune,* Nov. 1, 1883, p. 2, col. 3.

44. *L'Abeille,* Nov. 21, 1883, p. 1, cols. 4–6.

45. Ibid., Dec. 28, 1883, p. 1, col. 3; Dec. 29, 1883, p. 1, col. 5; Dec. 30, 1883, p. 4, cols. 1–4; Jan. 1, 1884, p. 2, col. 1.

46. Ibid., Nov. 18, 1883, p. 1, col. 2; Nov. 22, 1883, p. 1, col. 3. Review: Nov. 23, 1883, p. 1, col. 2.

47. Ibid., Dec. 23, 1883, p. 1, col. 2.

48. Ibid., May 11, 1884, p. 1, col. 3; May 31, 1884, p. 1, col. 2; May 31, 1884, p. 2, col. 1.

49. Ibid., July 25, 1884, p. 1, col. 7, and Aug. 20, 1884, p. 1, col. 3.

50. Ibid., Sept. 14, 1884, p. 2, col. 3.

51. Ibid., Dec. 20, 1884, p. 2, col. 1; Dec. 23, 1884, p. 4, col. 2.

52. Ibid., Jan. 23, 1885, p. 4, col. 1.

53. Ibid., Mar. 29, 1885, p. 1, col. 2.

54. Ibid., May 6, 1885, p. 1, col. 6; May 7, 1885, p. 4, col. 2.

55. Ibid., May 24, 1885, p. 4, col. 4; May 26, 1885, p. 1, col. 6; May 30, 1885, p. 4, col. 1; and June 4, 1885, p. 4, col. 1.

56. Ibid., Oct. 11, 1885, p. 4, col. 4.

57. Ibid., Nov. 14, 1885, p. 4, col. 1, and Nov. 15, 1885, p. 4, col. 4.

58. Ibid., Nov. 22, 1885, p. 4, col. 3.

59. For example, see *L'Abeille,* Nov. 19, 1885, p. 4, col. 5; Dec. 16, 1885, p. 4, col. 4; Jan. 1, 1886, p. 3, col. 4; Jan. 6, 1886, p. 4, col. 4; Jan. 7, 1886, p. 4, col. 4; Jan. 10, 1886, p. 4, cols. 4–5.

60. *L'Abeille,* Jan. 5, 1886, p. 4, col. 4.

61. Ibid., Apr. 21, 1886, p. 4, col. 1.

62. Ibid., Tuesday, Aug. 5, 1913, p. 5, col. 2

63. *New York Times,* Sept. 30, 1886, p. 5, col. 2.

64. Ibid., Apr. 6, 1890, p. 20, col. 5; Dec. 27, 1890, p. 7, col. 2.

65. Ibid., Feb. 22, 1891, p. 11, col. 3.

66. Ibid., Sept. 27, 1892, p. 5, col. 1.

67. Ibid., May 7, 1893, p. 16, col. 6.

68. Ibid., May 14, 1895, p. 7.

69. Ibid., Oct. 29, 1895, p. 8. The piece was published in the *New York Times,* Oct. 27, 1895, p. 29.

70. *House Furnishing Review* 26, no. 9 (Sept. 1906): 693–95.

71. *New York Times,* May 26, 1893, p. 9, col. 2.

72. Ibid., June 13, 1895, p. 13. Other such concerts are reported in the *New York Times,* July 30, 1893, p. 16, col. 2; June 1, 1894, p. 2, col. 3; July 15, 1894, p. 20, col. 6.

73. *New York City Department of Parks, Annual Report,* 1915, p. 129.

74. *New York Times,* June 17, 1917, Real Estate, p. 7.
75. Ibid., July 19, 1916, p. 7
76. Ibid., July 14, 1918, special section, p. 36.
77. Ibid., Aug. 2, 1918, p. 9.
78. Ibid., Aug. 29, 1926, p. X16, col. 1.
79. For example, see *New York Times,* Dec. 19, 1926, p. X11, col. 3; Jan. 16, 1928, p. 11, cols. 4–5; Jan. 29, 1928, p. 114, col. 2.
80. *New York Times,* Dec. 19, 1932, p. 15, col. 7.

CHAPTER TWELVE

1. According to his obituary he was a member of Johann Strauss II's orchestra. See *Picayune,* Wednesday, Oct. 30, 1889, p. 8, col. 5.
2. *Picayune,* Sunday, Nov. 11, 1888, p. 10, col. 3.
3. He spent a short time in Mexico City in 1885.
4. *L'Abeille,* Feb. 10, 1878, Sunday, p. 1, col. 3, and Feb. 17, 1878, p. 1, col. 2. Program: Feb. 17, 1878, p. 2, col. 3.
5. Ibid., Mar. 9, 1878, 1878, p. 1, col. 2.
6. Ibid., Apr. 17, 1878, p. 2, col. 2.
7. Ibid., May 1, 1878, p. 1, col. 2, and May 5, 1878, p. 2, col. 3.
8. Ibid., Feb. 5, 1879, p. 1, col. 1.
9. Ibid., Apr. 8, 1879, p. 2, col. 1, and Apr. 11, 1879, p. 1, col. 2.
10. Ibid., Apr. 16, 1879, p. 1, col. 2. Marguerite Samuel was scheduled to accompany Curant, but she was ill.
11. Ibid., Mar. 7, 1880, p. 2, col. 2.
12. Ibid., Apr. 27, 1881, p. 12, col. 6.
13. Ibid., Apr. 28, 1881, p. 1, col. 4.
14. Ibid., May 8, 1881, p. 1, cols. 2–3; May 13, 1881, p. 1, col. 3; and May 18, 1881, p. 1, col. 3.
15. Ibid., May 27, 1881, p. 2, col. 1.
16. Ibid., Mar. 28, 1882, p. 4, col. 1; Mar. 30, 1882, p. 4, col. 4.
17. *Picayune,* Nov. 3, 1882, afternoon ed., p. 1, col. 1; p. 2, col. 2.
18. *L'Abeille,* Mar. 15, 1883, p. 1, col. 2; Mar. 17, 1883, p. 1, col. 2.
19. *Picayune,* Oct. 9, 1883, p. 5, col. 1; Oct. 11, 1883, p. 2, col. 2.
20. *L'Abeille,* Dec. 5, 1884, p. 4, col. 2, and Dec. 7, 1884, p. 4, col. 3.
21. Ibid., Oct. 30, 1886, p. 4, col. 1; Nov. 2, 1886, p. 4, col. 1.
22. Ibid., Nov. 17, 1886, p. 4, col. 1.
23. *Picayune,* May 30, 1887, p. 2, col. 1.
24. Ibid., Feb. 4, 1888, p. 4, col. 5.
25. Ibid., Apr. 20 1887, p. 5, col. 2; Apr. 21, 1887, p. 4, col. 6.
26. Ibid., Mar. 13, 1887, p. 8, col. 1; Apr. 10, 1887, p. 5, col. 2; and Apr. 24, 1887, p. 5, col. 2.
27. Ibid., June 5, 1887, p. 6, col. 4; June 14, 1887, p. 4, col. 4.
28. Ibid., Jan. 22, 1888, p. 10, col. 5; Feb. 19, 1888, p. 7, col. 4; Feb. 19, 1888, p. 8, col. 5; Feb. 29, 1888, p. 8, col. 2.
29. Ibid., Mar. 11, 1888, p. 5, col. 2; Mar. 18, 1888, p. 12, col. 3; and Apr. 10, 1888, p. 8, col. 3.
30. Ibid., Apr. 15, 1888, p. 5, col. 3; Apr. 22. 1888, p. 5, col. 2; and May 2, 1888, p. 4, col. 6.
31. Ibid., May 3, 1888, p. 3, col. 3.

32. Ibid., Apr. 26, 1889, p. 4, col. 4; *L'Abeille,* Apr. 25, 1889. Review: *Picayune,* Apr. 26, 1889, p. 4, col. 4.

33. *Picayune,* May 4, 1889, p. 8, col. 4.

34. Ibid., Aug. 24, 1889, p. 3, col. 2; p. 4, col. 5; Sept. 1, 1889, p. 4, col. 5.

35. *L'Abeille,* Sept. 11, 1889, p. 4, col. 1. *Picayune,* Oct. 6, 1889, p. 8, col. 4; Oct. 13, 1889, p. 6, col. 5; Oct. 27, 1889, p. 8, col. 1; Oct. 28, 1889, p. 5, col. 2; p. 8, col. 4. After expenses, $1,200 were raised for the Curant family (*Picayune,* Oct. 31, 1889, p. 8, col. 5).

36. *Picayune,* Oct. 30, 1889, p. 8, col. 5.

CHAPTER THIRTEEN

1. *L'Abeille,* Sept. 2, 1888, p. 4, col. 1; Sept. 6, 1888, p. 4, col. 1.

2. Ibid., Oct. 6, 1888, p. 4, col. 1; Oct. 9, 1888, p. 4, col. 1.

3. Ibid., Oct. 21, 1888, p. 4, col. 1; Oct. 25, 1888, p. 4, col. 1; Oct. 26, 1888, p. 4, col. 1; Oct. 28, 1888, p. 4, col. 2.

4. *Picayune,* Nov. 21, 1889, p. 8, col. 2.

5. *L'Abeille,* Mar. 28, 1890, p. 4, col. 1. Review: Mar. 30, 1890, p. 4, col. 1.

6. The others were J. Voorhies (violin 2), J. Wiegel (viola), J. Wortmann (string bass), F. Ramos (flute), and P. Brunet, piano.

7. *L'Abeille,* May 15, 1890, p. 4, col. 2.

8. Ibid., May 18, 1890, p. 1, col. 9; May 18, 1890, p. 4, col. 2; May 20, 1890, p. 4, col. 1; and May 23, 1890, p. 4, col. 2. Some of the advertisements give the false date of May 27, 1890.

9. Ibid., Mar. 15, 1891, p. 4, col. 1.

10. Ibid., Apr. 4, 1891, p. 4, col. 1.

11. Ibid., May 17, 1891, p. 4, col. 2; May 24, 1891, p. 4, col. 3; May 26, 1891, p. 4, col. 1. Reviews: May 27, 1891, p. 4, col. 1; May 28, 1891, p. 4, col. 1.

12. Ibid., June 7, 1891, p. 4, col. 2; June 11, 1891, p. 1, col. 8; June 14, 1891, p. 4, col. 1.

13. *Picayune,* Dec. 6, 1891, p. 8, col. 5.

14. Ibid., Nov. 24, 1892, p. 4, col. 6. The home was that of the senior Henri Wehrmann.

15. Ibid., Mar. 17, 1892, p. 3, col. 6.

16. Ibid., Mar. 19, 1892, p. 2, col. 2.

17. Ibid., Apr. 29, 1892, p. 6, col. 4; May 1, 1892, p. 6, col. 7.

18. *L'Abeille,* June 1, 1892, p. 4, col. 1.

19. *Picayune,* Oct. 20, 1892, p. 3, col. 4. This Lyre d'Orphée Society seems to be separate from the Lyre Club that was founded by the Tio brothers and flourished during the late 1880s to 1897. See Kinzer, "The Tio Family," 18–27.

20. *Picayune,* Nov. 20, 1892, p. 3, col. 3, Dec. 4, 1892, p. 2, col. 2, Dec. 11, 1892, p. 6, col. 6; Dec. 13, 1892, p. 9, col. 8; Dec. 13, 1892, p. 2, col. 5.

21. Ibid., Nov. 27, 1892, p. 9, col. 4, and p. 7, col. 7

22. Ibid., Nov. 29, 1892, p. 3, col. 3.

23. *L'Abeille,* Mar. 15, 1893, p. 1, col. 9; p. 4, col. 1; Mar. 16, 1893, p. 4, col. 1.

24. Ibid., Mar. 22, 1893, p. 4, col. 1.

25. *L'Abeille,* Apr. 21, 1893, p. 4, col. 1; Apr. 23, 1893, p. 1, col. 9; p. 4, col. 2; Apr. 27, 1891, p. 1, col. 8; Apr. 27, 1893, p. 4, col. 1; Apr. 28, 1893, p. 4, col. 1. What Bruguière (d. 1951) did in Chicago is uncertain. Unlike others, Canonge preferred to call her a mezzo soprano.

26. *Picayune,* Dec. 7, 1893, p. 12, col. 1; Dec. 12, 1893, p. 5, col. 2; Dec. 13, 1893, p. 5, col. 2;

Dec. 17, 1893, p. 6, col. 5; p. 2, col. 6; Dec. 18, 1893, p. 9, col. 2. *L'Abeille,* Dec. 12, 1893, p. 1, col. 8; Dec. 13, 1893, p. 1, col. 8; Dec. 16, 1893, p. 4, col. 1; Dec. 17, 1893, p. 1, col. 8. Review: *L'Abeille,* Dec. 19, 1893, p. 4, col. 1. *Times-Democrat,* Dec. 17, 1893, p. 7, col. 7. *States,* Dec. 19, 1893, p. 4, col. 6. *Picayune,* Dec. 19, 1893, p. 3, col. 2. Eugénie was the daughter of Henry Wehrman's deceased older brother Valentine.

27. *States,* Dec. 17, 1893, p. 17, col. 4.

28. *Picayune,* Dec. 20, 1893, p. 11, col. 1.

29. *L'Abeille,* Apr. 13, 1894, p. 4, col. 1.

30. Ibid., Oct. 1, 1894, p. 4, col. 1; Oct. 18, 1894, p. 1, col. 8; Oct. 19, 1894, p. 1, col. 3.

31. Ibid., Oct. 17, 1894, p. 4, col. 1; Oct. 21, 1894, p. 1, col. 8; p. 4, col. 2; Oct. 24, 1894, p. 4, col. 5. Review and detailed description of this club: Oct. 25, 1894, p. 4, col. 1.

32. Ibid., Nov. 21, 1894, p. 4, col. 4.

33. *Picayune,* Apr. 15, 1895, p. 5, col. 3.

34. Ibid., Apr. 21, 1895, p. 8, cols. 4–5; Apr. 24, 1895, p. 12, col. 1.

35. *L'Abeille,* May 5, 1895, p. 3, col. 4; May 12, 1895, p. 2, col. 3. Review: May 17, 1895, p. 2, col. 3.

36. *Picayune,* Jan. 15, 1896, p. 7, col. 5; Jan. 19, 1896, p. 7, col. 4; Jan. 20, 1896, p. 8, col. 6. Review: Jan. 21, 1896, p. 3, col. 7.

37. Ibid., Mar. 13, 1896, p. 3, col. 4. Review: Mar. 17, 1896, p. 8, col. 4.

38. Ibid., Mar. 29, 1896, p. 12, cols. 5–6, 2 parts; Apr. 5, 1896, p. 5, col. 1–2; Apr. 8, 1896, p. 14, col. 3. Lengthy review: Apr. 9, 1896, p. 5, col. 7.

39. Ibid., Apr. 14, 1896, p. 3, col. 3. Review: Apr. 15, 1896, p. 3, col. 4.

40. Ibid., Oct. 11, 1896, p. 7, col. 6. Review: Oct. 13, 1896, p. 3, col. 3.

41. Ibid., Oct. 18, 1896, p. 3, col. 6. Review: Oct. 23, 1896, p. 2, col. 6.

42. *Times-Democrat,* Mar. 16, 1897, p. 6, col. 6; Mar. 23, 1897, p. 5, col. 3; Mar. 25, 1897, p. 3, col. 2; Mar. 26, 1897, p. 7, col. 2.

43. Ibid., Apr. 18, 1897, p. 12, col. 2; Apr. 22, 1897, p. 5, col. 3; p. 3, col. 2. Lengthy review: Apr. 23, 1897, p. 3, col. 3.

44. Tulane University Manuscript and Rare Books, Wehrmann Papers, Coll. 873, Box 2.

45. Ibid. On one occasion Frank and Wehrmann conducted a concert that included Rossini's *Tancredi* Overture, a Tchaikovsky piano concerto, and a Haydn symphony.

46. Louisiana State Museum Historical Center, R6 136, acc #10778. The document is undated.

47. Ibid., Mark Kaiser Collection. Undated document.

48. *L'Abeille,* Nov. 4, 1894, p. 4, col. 3; Nov. 18, 1894, p. 1, col. 8; Nov. 25, 1894, p. 1, col. 8; Nov. 27, 1894, p. 1, cols. 2–3. *Picayune,* Nov. 26, 1894, p. 3, cols. 2–3. See also Tulane University, Manuscripts and Rare Books, Wehrmann papers coll. 873, box 2.

49. *L'Abeille,* Nov. 27, 1894, p. 1, cols. 2–3.

50. Ibid., Dec. 19, 1896, p. 2, col. 8. See also Wehrmann papers, Tulane, coll. 873, Box 2.

51. Wehrmann papers, Tulane, coll. 873, box 2.

52. Tulane University, Manuscripts and Rare Books, Wehrmann Papers, Coll. 873, Box 2. Notice of the new quartet appeared in *The Violinist* 6, no. 6 (Mar. 1909): 41: "The Beethoven Quartet of New Orleans will give their first concert March 13. Those who compose the quartet are MM Henry Wehrman, René Salomon, violins; M. L. Barzin, viola; and M. A. Faget, 'cello."

53. *Item,* Apr. 16, 1911, p. 14.

54. *Picayune,* Apr. 28, 1895, p. 7, col. 7. *L'Abeille,* May 3, 1895, p. 2, col. 6. Review: *L'Abeille,* May 7, 1895, p. 2, col. 5. See also Tulane University Manuscripts and Rare Books, Wehrmann Papers, Coll. 873, Box 2.

55. *L'Abeille,* May 10, 1895, p. 2, col. 8; May 12, 1895, p. 2, col. 8.

56. Ibid., June 9, 1895, p. 3, col. 4.

57. *Times-Democrat,* Mar. 28, 1897, p. 3, col. 6; Apr. 18, 1897, p. 12, cols. 2–3; Apr. 20, 1897, p. 4, col. 7; Apr. 21, 1897, p. 4, col. 7.

58. Ibid., Apr. 30, 1897, p. 2, col. 3.

59. *Picayune,* Dec. 17, 1893, p. 6, col. 6. For more on Shields, elocutionist, see Dec. 12, 1893, p. 6, col. 4.

60. Ibid., Dec. 13, 1891, p. 7, col. 3. Louis Grunewald published the work the following year; see Oct. 23, 1892, p. 6, col. 4.

61. *L'Abeille,* May 20, 1894, p. 4, col. 1.

62. *Picayune,* Dec. 23, 1894, p. 7, col. 7.

63. A copy is in the Duke University Library.

CHAPTER FOURTEEN

This chapter was originally a speech delivered at the U.S. Mint, New Orleans, Apr. 12, 2002.

1. The importance of European opera for such greats as Tony Jackson, Jelly Roll Morton, and Louis Armstrong is affirmed in interviews and memoirs. See Alan Lomax's recorded interview of Jelly Roll Morton at the Library of Congress in 1938, and Joshua Berrett, "Louis Armstrong and Opera," in *Musical Quarterly* 76 (1992): 216–41.

2. For brief discussion of the New Orleans Conservatory founded in 1871, see above, page 114.

3. Ostensibly, the Hamman Franko family left New Orleans for Europe in 1862 in order to escape the economic hardships of the Civil War imposed by the Union occupation of the city, but they took full advantage of the situation to have their numerous children study with important European musicians; among them Jeanne worked with Vieuxtemps, Sam with Joachim, and Nahan with Joachim and Wilhelmj.

4. The following information on the Pilcher family comes from obituaries in the local New Orleans newspapers (copies of which are on microfilm in the New Orleans Division, New Orleans Public Library, and in the microforms reading room, Howard Tilton Memorial Library, Tulane University, New Orleans): William Pilcher (*Picayune,* Sept. 9, 1912, p. 6, col. 4), Julia Wendover Pilcher (*Picayune,* June 1, 1917, p. 2, col. 8), William Henry Pilcher (*Picayune,* Sept. 16, 1910, p. 8, col. 5), Charles Pilcher (*Picayune,* June 2, 1912, p. 8, col. 4), and Mrs. William H. (Isabella Stevenson) Pilcher (*Times Picayune,* Sept. 19, 1935, p. 2, col. 8). There is also an extensive biography of William Henry Pilcher by an unknown author written during his lifetime that gives much information on his family: *Biographical and Historical Memoirs of Louisiana* (1892; rpt. Baton Rouge: Claitor's Publishing Division, 1975), vol. 2: 310–11.

5. Many members of the family had similar names, so that Barbara Owen, in her otherwise excellent entry on Pilcher in H. Wiley Hitchcock and Stanley Sadie, eds., *The New Grove Dictionary of American Music* (New York: Oxford University Press, 2002), vol. 3: 568, is led astray.

6. Owen states that Henry Pilcher settled in New Jersey, but the documents cited in note 4 above state that he settled in New York.

7. *Picayune* obituary gives the date as Dec. 29, 1854, but the more likely date of Dec. 29, 1855 is given in the *Biographical and Historical Memoirs.*

8. Page 26 of the 1926 edition; this is repeated in the 1946 Grove's *American Supplement,* p. 328.

9. There is no evidence that William Henry ever showed interest in the business of building organs, whereas at least three of his brothers were later intimately involved in that profession.

10. The factory was located at 6201–6213 Tchoupitoulas Street and 300–312 Henry Clay, with the main office at 6022 Laurel Street, which, according to New Orleans city directories, is where William and Julia Pilcher lived. This places the factory in Uptown (western) New Orleans, the fashionable English-speaking area, and close to the Mississippi River.

11. See John H. Baron, "Werlein," in Hitchcock and Sadie, eds., *The New Grove Dictionary of American Music* 4: 510.

12. Note that Owen has mistaken this organ for a Louisville Pilcher organ.

13. The church was razed in 1927 and a new building erected at the same location, apparently with the Pilcher organ transferred to the second building.

14. For information on this organ, see Alan M. Laufman, ed., *Organ Handbook 1989,* published by the Organ Historical Society for its 34th Annual National Convention in New Orleans, 19–24 June 1989, 43.

15. Despite Pilcher's claim that he studied and received a doctorate in music in Europe and repetition of that claim with more details in the *Biographical and Historical Memoirs,* I have not been able to verify it.

16. An anonymous critic reported in the *Picayune* (Wednesday, Apr. 11, 1888, p. 2, col. 6): "Professor Wm. H. Pilcher, as the pianist of the evening, gave a very acceptable and, in fact, quite artistic rendition of Beethoven's C minor concerto. He entered fully with the intention of the composition, invested the entire presentation with a very musicianly effectiveness, and fully delivered himself of the rather arduous as well as responsible task with very good results."

17. At that time Temple Sinai was located on Carondelet Street near Lee Circle, which was close to downtown New Orleans and was the heart of the Jewish neighborhood.

18. I am grateful to Joseph M. Pilcher, grandson of Joseph Felix Mendelssohn Pilcher, for some of this genealogy and much more than is included here.

19. A mass, entitled *Hesse [sic] Solennelle in D Major,* was published in Boston by Oliver Ditson & Co. and in New York by C. P. Ditson & Co. in 1888. Copies are at the Library of Congress and the New York Public Library.

20. The only other work by Pilcher I have located is his "Bedouin Love Song," from *Six Songs,* Opus 34 (1893), which is listed in the British Library Public Catalogue online.

21. George MacDonald (1824–1905) was a Scottish preacher and teacher as well as an author of thirty novels, numerous fairy tales, poetry, essays, and sermons. See www.tayloru.edu/upland/programs/lewis/macdonald.

22. A second copy is in the Historic New Orleans Collection.

23. A half-dozen catalogs of the conservatory survive in the vertical files under "music" in the Louisiana Division, Tulane University Library. These catalogs not only list in detail all the requirements for admission and graduation (specific composers and compositions are mentioned), fees, and faculty, but give the names and hometowns of the students and the concert programs of the previous year.

24. See John H. Baron, "Blackmar," in Hitchcock and Sadie, eds., *The New Grove Dictionary of American Music* 1: 226–27.

25. In 1909, for example, Isabel was residing at 8126 Plum Street, Uptown, while William Henry was living at 6022 Laurel Street, about two miles apart. When Isabella died in 1935, she was living across Lake Pontchartrain in Covington, Louisiana, far from the other surviving Pilchers.

26. For a history of the Tulane University Music Department, see John H. Baron, *Newcomb-Tulane Music Department 1909–2009* (New Orleans: Tulane University, 2009).

27. The dates for the founding of conservatories in these cities come from various articles on the cities themselves and from the article "Conservatories" in *The New Grove Dictionary.*

Book II

CHAPTER ONE

1. *Moniteur de la Louisiana,* Dec. 11, 1805, p. 3, col. 3, and Dec. 18, 1805, p. 2, col. 3.

2. Jean Fouchard, *Plaisirs de Saint-Domingue: Notes sur la Vie Sociale, Litteraire et Artisque* (Port-au-Prince: Éditions Henri Deschamps, 1988), 104–5.

3. The elder Fleury may have been the comedienne Mme. Fleury who performed in Saint-Domingue 1775–1783 (Fouchard, *Artistes et Répertoire,* 27).

4. Probably Philip Laroque of New Orleans, who was leader of the orchestra at the Spectacle Theater (*Moniteur de la Louisiana,* May 7, 1812, p. 3, col. 1).

5. Kmen, *Music in New Orleans,* 58.

6. Fouchard mentions specific Santo Domingo musicians who left Haiti to perform in New Orleans, such as the soprano Mme Clairville, her husband, and seven or eight other artists who signed with Lafond at a theater in New Orleans in May 1797 (*Artistes et Répertoire,* 12 and 41). *Sylvain* was a standard in the repertory of Haitian theaters and had been performed in Jan. and Mar. 1791, just before the beginning of the revolution (189 and 192).

7. *Moniteur de la Louisiana,* Jan. 11, 1806, p. 3, cols. 1–2.

8. Ibid., Feb. 1, 1806, p. 3, col. 2.

9. Ibid., Jan. 15, 1807, p. 2, col. 4.

10. Probably the setting by Luigi Cherubini.

11. *Moniteur de la Louisiana,* Jan. 17, 1807, p. 3, col. 1.

12. Ibid., Jan. 28, 1807, p. 2, col. 4, and Jan. 31, 1807, p. 2, col. 4.

13. Ibid., Feb. 14, 1807, p. 3, col. 1, and Feb. 18, 1807, p. 2, col. 4.

14. Ibid., Feb. 14, 1807, p. 3, col. 1.

15. Ibid., Apr. 5, 1808, p. 3, col. 2.

16. Ibid., May 9, 1807, p. 2, col. 1. "Cimanosa" is probably "Cimarosa."

17. *Le Telegraphe,* Oct. 13, 1807, p. 3, and Oct. 17, 1807, p. 3, col. 2.

18. *Moniteur de la Louisiana,* Aug. 24, 1808, p. 3, col. 4.

19. Ibid., Apr. 15, 1807, p. 3, col. 2.

20. "Les personnes de couleur libres, qui désireront y assister, sont prevenues que la galerie, dans laquelle elles ont coutume de venir, est arrangée de la maniere la plus commede, & qu'aucun esclave ne peut y parvenu. Il y a un endroit particulier pour les domestiques. M. Remondet ose esperer de la bonté du Public, qu'instruit de la position tacheuse ou le jette un accident, qui lui enleve pour longetems les movens d'exercet son état, il dangnera seconder & encourager les intentions bienfailantes, ainsi que les talens des artistes qui veulent bien donner ce concert a son benéfice" (*Moniteur de la Louisiana,* Oct. 2, 1807, p. 2, col. 3; Oct. 10, 1807, p. 2, col. 4). *Le Telegraphe,* Oct. 13, 1807, p. 2, col. 3.

21. Jane Labat and her two daughters were also active performers in Charleston 1807–1812; see Butler, *Votaries of Apollo,* 193–94.

22. *Moniteur de la Louisiana,* Dec. 26, 1807, p. 2, col. 3.

23. Ibid., Jan. 27, 1808, 3, col. 1.

24. Probably the Violin Concerto, Opus 6, by Joseph Fodor (1752–1828).

25. *Moniteur de la Louisiana,* Mar. 5, 1808, p. 3, col. 2.

26. Ibid., Mar. 12, 1808, p. 3, col. 2.

27. Ibid., Mar. 23, 1808, p. 3, col. 2.

28. The performances of Jadin's *Coin du Feu* as late as June 29 and the opera *The Angry Lover,*

at the theater, interspersed with plays, the following Aug. 31, both in 1806, were very rare (*Moniteur de la Louisiana,* June 29, 1806, Supplement no. 627, p. 1; *The Telegraph,* Aug. 30, 1806, p. 3).

29. Either Anton Wranitzky (1761–1820) or his brother Paul (1756–1808).

30. The notice in *Moniteur de la Louisiana* has *"la bouche."* This probably refers to the Jew's harp.

31. *Moniteur de la Louisiana,* Nov. 16, 1808, p. 3, col. 1.

32. Ibid., Dec. 21, 1808, p. 3, col. 1.

33. Ibid., Dec. 24, 1808, p. 3, col. 3.

34. This may be Jean-Jacques Miniere, active in Charleston (Butler, *Votaries of Apollo,* 183 and 190).

35. *Moniteur de la Louisiana,* Dec. 31, 1808, p. 3, col. 2; Jan. 4, 1809, p. 3, col. 3; and Jan. 7, 1809, p. 2, col. 3.

36. In the nineteenth century there was no standard numbering of the Haydn symphonies. The *Surprise* Symphony (today No. 94) is therefore given in this book only with its title. The other frequently performed Haydn symphonies are cited as Nos. 3 and 4, and we do not know for certain to which works they would correspond today. Of course, the "unnamed" symphony could be any one of the 104.

37. *Moniteur de la Louisiana,* Feb. 11, 1809, p. 3, col. 2; Feb. 18, 1809; Feb. 18, 1809, p. 3, col. 2. The concert was originally scheduled for Feb. 17 and postponed to the next day because of bad weather.

38. Ibid., Mar. 8, 1809, p. 2, col. 4.

39. Ibid., Sept. 21, 1808, p. 3, col. 3.

40. Ibid., Oct. 22, 1808, p. 3, col. 1.

41. Ibid., Nov. 2, 1809, p. 3, col. 3; Dec. 23, 1809, p. 3, col. 2; Jan. 31, 1810, p. 3, col. 3, and Feb. 14, 1810, p. 3, col. 4; Feb. 24, 1810, p. 3, col. 2; and Mar. (?), 1810 (Mercredi), no. 1018, p. 3, col. 3.

42. *Courier de la Louisiane,* Nov. 9, 1810, and *Moniteur de la Louisiana,* Nov. 10, 1810, p. 3, col. 2, and Nov. 14, 1810, p. 3, col. 4. *Courier de la Louisiane,* Nov. 20, 1810. *Moniteur de la Louisiana,* Nov. 21, 1810, p. 3, col. 1; Dec. 1, 1810, p. 2, col. 2.; Dec. 5, 1810, p. 2, col. 4; Dec. 8, 1810, p. 2, col. 4; Dec. 12, 1810, p. 2, col. 2; Dec. 15, 1810, p. 3, col. 2; Dec. 18, 1810, p. 3, col. 2; Dec. 25, 1810, p. 3, col. 1; Mar. 2, 1811, p. 3, col. 1; Mar. 5, 1811, p. 3, col. 4, Mar. 7, 1811, p. 3, col. 2; Mar. 12, 1811. p. 3, col. 2; Mar. 21, 1811, p. 3, col. 2.

43. *Moniteur de la Louisiana,* Feb. 5, 1811, p. 3, col. 3; Feb. 9, 1811, p. 3, col. 2. *Gazette de la Louisiane,* Feb. 1818; Dec. 10, 1819, p. 2, col. 4.

44. Jo Ann Carrigan, *The Saffron Scourge: a History of Yellow Fever in Louisiana, 1796–1905* (Lafayette: University of Southwestern Louisiana, 1994), 55.

45. See the benefit concert for Chéry on Feb. 20, 1813.

46. *Moniteur de la Louisiana,* Jan. 14, 1812, p. 3, cols. 2–3.

47. Ibid., Jan. 23, 1812, p. 3, col. 1.

48. Ibid., Feb. 18, 1813, p. 3, col. 1.

49. Ibid., Mar. 4, 1813, p. 3, col. 3.

50. Ibid., Mar. 16, 1813, p. 3, col. 1.

51. Probably Grétry's version rather than Rameau's.

52. This could be an arrangement of the Double Concerto for two violins by Ignaz Fränzl (1736–1811).

53. *Moniteur de la Louisiana,* Dec. 4, 1813, p. 3, col. 1, and Dec. 9, 1813, p. 3, col. 2.

54. In 1815 one piaster was worth five francs, and adjusted in 2012 one piaster was worth approximately twenty-three euros.

55. The escalin was the principal Haitian currency. It was worth .75 francs around 1721–1815 or approximately U.S. $17.25 in 2012 currency.

56. *Moniteur de la Louisiana,* Dec. 16, 1813, p. 3, col. 2.

57. Ibid., Jan. 8, 1814, p. 3, col.3.

58. Ibid., Feb. 10, 1814, p. 4, col. 3.

59. Ibid., Mar. 5, 1814, p. 3, col. 1.

60. Ibid., Mar. 1, 1814, p. 2, col. 4; Mar. 5, 1814, p. 3, col. 2; Mar. 8, 1814, p. 3, col. 1; and Mar. 10, 1814, p. 3, col. 1. The concert was originally scheduled for Mar. 9, 1814.

61. Ibid., Apr. 7, 1814, p. 3, col. 1.

62. *Louisiana Courier,* Jan. 19, 1816, p. 3, col. 3.

63. There is no opera by that name by any of the Bertons, but Boieldieu did write one in 1798.

64. *Louisiana Courier,* Jan. 10, 1816, p. 3, col. 2, Jan. 15, 1816, p. 3, col. 2.

65. Ibid., Jan. 10, 1816, p. 2, col. 2.

66. Ibid., Feb. 7, 1816, p. 2, col. 3.

67. By Julie Candeille (?).

68. The opera probably is that by Stanislas Champein (*Louisiana Courier,* Feb. 14, 1816, p. 2, col. 2).

69. *Louisiana Courier,* Apr. 26, 1816, p. 3, col. 2; May 6, 1816, p. 3, col. 2.

70. Ibid., Oct. 25, 1816, p. 2, col. 3.

71. Ibid., Dec. 9, 1816, p. 3, col. 2.

72. The earliest intermède in New Orleans, as a part of a larger dramatic evening, was performed.

73. *Louisiana Courier,* Dec. 27, 1816, p. 3, col. 4.

74. Ibid., Jan. 20, 1817, p. 2, col. 3.

75. Ibid., Feb. 3, 1817, p. 2, col. 2.

76. Ibid., Feb. 7, 1817, p. 3, col. 3; Feb. 14, 1817, p. 3, col. 3; and Feb. 19, 1817, p. 2, col. 3.

77. Ibid., Oct. 24, 1817, p. 2, col. 3.

78. Ibid., Dec. 5, 1817, p. 2, col. 3.

79. Ibid., Dec. 29, 1817, p. 2, col. 3, and Dec. 31, 1817, p. 2, col. 4.

80. *Louisiana Gazette,* Jan. 1, 1818, p. 2, col. 4.

81. *Louisiana Courier,* Jan. 9, 1818, p. 2, col. 2, and Jan. 14, 1818, p. 2, col. 3; *Louisiana Gazette,* Jan. 10, 1818, p. 2, col. 4, and Jan. 13, 1818, p. 1, col. 4.

82. *Louisiana Gazette,* Feb. 6, 1818, p. 2, col. 3.

83. *Louisiana Courier,* Feb. 16, 1818, p. 2, col. 3.

84. *Gazette de la Louisiane,* Apr. 3, 1818, p. 1, col. 2.

85. Ibid., Apr. 23, 1818, p. 1, col. 2.

86. *Louisiana Courier,* Nov. 20, 1818, p. 2, col. 3, and *Gazette de la Louisiana,* Nov. 19, 1818, p. 1, col. 3.

87. *Gazette de la Louisiane,* Dec. 4, 1818, p. 1, col. 3.

88. *Louisiana Courier,* Jan. 15, 1819, p. 3, col. 2; Feb. 3, 1819, p. 3, col. 4.

89. Ibid., Feb. 2, 1819, p. 3, col. 4.

90. *Louisiana Gazette,* Feb. 8, 1819, p. 2, col. 4. Kmen, *Music in New Orleans,* 222.

91. Probably Louis-Sébastien Lebrun (1764–1829).

92. *Louisiana Courier,* Feb. 17, 1819, p. 3, col. 4.

93. *Gazette de la Louisiane,* Feb. 27, 1819, p. 2, col. 5.

94. Ibid., Mar. 6, 1819, p. 2, col. 4.

95. *L'Ami des lois et journal du commerce,* Mar. 29, 1819, p. 2, col. 4, and *Louisiana Gazette,* Mar. 30, 1819, p. 2, col. 3.

96. *The Friend of the Law and Commercial Journal,* May 4, 1819, p. 2, col. 5, and *Gazette de la Louisiane,* May 5, 1819, p. 1, col. 23.

97. *L'Ami des lois et journal du commerce,* Aug. 28, 1819, p. 2, col. 5.

98. At this time there were two different theatres with "Orleans" in the title: American Theatre on Orleans and Théâtre d'Orléans (Orleans Theater). Competition was keen, so Davis, proprietor of the Théâtre d'Orléans, advertised that he would provide four carriages to bring ladies to a play or a ball. If they lived in the city, it would cost fifty cents; if they lived in the suburbs it would cost seventy-five cents (*Louisiana Gazette,* Dec. 22, 1819, p. 1, col. 6). But despite this, he would not or could not break racial divides that would have increased his audience. On Jan. 8, 1820, he announced at the Théâtre d'Orléans "L'entrée des esclaves est supprimée" (*Courier de la Louisiane,* Jan. 8, 1820, p. 2, col. 3).

99. Probably Charles Bochsa (d. 1821), father of the better-known Robert-Nicholas-Charles Bochsa.

100. *Louisiana Courier,* Dec. 8, 1819, p. 3, col. 4; Dec. 10, 1819, p. 3, col. 4.

101. Ibid., Dec. 24, 1819, p. 2, col. 3.

102. Ibid., Dec. 31, 1819, p. 3, col. 3. *Felix* may be the opera *Agnès et Félix* by François Devienne or the opera *Félicie* by Gioseffo Catrufo.

103. *Gazette de la Louisiana,* Dec. 22, 1819, p. 1, col. 5.

104. *Louisiana Gazette,* Dec. 22, 1819, p. 2, col. 1.

105. *The Bee,* Mar. 2, 1835, p. 2, col. 1.

106. Ibid., Apr. 1, 1835, p. 2, col. 1.

107. *Courier de la Louisiane,* Jan. 26, 1820, p. 3, col. 5.

108. Ibid., Feb. 4, 1820, p. 2, col. 4.

109. In 1820 there were opera performances during May through Aug. at Théâtre d'Orléans, at least one per week. In 1821 operas were performed throughout the summer, at least one per week. In 1822, operas and vaudevilles were performed during the summer but ended by Sept.

110. *Courier de la Louisiane,* Dec. 27, 1820, p. 3, col. 4.

111. Ibid., Jan. 24, 1821, p. 2, col. 3.

112. Ibid., Jan. 29, 1821, p. 2, col. 2.

113. Ibid.

114. Ibid., Feb. 2, 1821, p. 2, col. 3.

115. Ibid., Feb. 5, 1821, p. 2, col. 3.

116. Ibid., Feb. 7, 1821, p. 2, col. 3.

117. Note that while the pianist's name here and in some earlier citations is given as "Mr. Jones," in the English version of the *Courier* it is "Mr. Johns," whose identity is well establshed (*Courier de la Louisiane,* Mar. 14, 1821, p. 2, col. 4).

118. *Courier de la Louisiane,* Apr. 2, 1821, p. 3, col. 3; Apr. 6, 1821, p. 3, col. 3.

119. Ibid., Apr. 25, 1821, p. 2, col. 4.

120. *L'Ami des lois et journal du commerce,* Jan. 2, 1822, p. 2, col. 4.

121. *Courier de la Louisiane,* Dec. 16, 1822, p. 2, col. 3.

122. Ibid., Mar. 15, 1823, p. 2, col. 3.

123. Ibid., Mar. 12, 1823, p. 2, col. 4; Mar. 17, 1823, p. 2, col. 3.

124. Ibid., Mar. 27, 1824, p. 3, col. 3; Apr. 1, 1824, p. 2, col. 3; Apr. 6, 1824, p. 3, col. 2.

125. Ibid., Apr. 30, 1823, p. 3, col. 4; June 6, 1823, p. 2, col. 4.

126. Ibid., June 23, 1823, p. 2, col. 5.

127. *L'Amis des Lois,* Jan. 31 and Feb. 4, 1824.

128. Subsequently the concerts were dropped from Carnival season but not the balls, which continue to the present day.

129. *L'Amis des Lois,* Feb. 17, 1824. The author of the *L'Amis* article is challenging the author of another, as yet unknown article who finds the combination of a full concert and a lavish ball—each in its own right charming—as too much amusement.

130. The "Grand Military March" and *A Warlike Symphony* were two distinct pieces. Neither is known to survive.

131. Either Giovanni Gambaro (1785–1828) or Vincent Gambaro (1785–1824).

132. Postponed from Feb. 18 (*Courier de la Louisiane,* Feb. 13, 1824, p. 3, col. 3, and Feb. 19, 1824, p. 2, col. 4).

133. *Courier de la Louisiane,* Mar. 30, 1824, p. 2, col. 3.

134. Ibid., May 7, 1824, p. 2, col. 2, and May 13, 1824, p. 2, col. 3.

135. Ibid., May 21, 1824, p. 3, col. 4.

136. Ibid., June 1, 1824, p. 3, col. 2.

137. "Tous les artistes et les amateurs les plus distingués de cette ville, . . . et l'on aura rarement vu à la Nouvelle-Orléans un orchestre aussi complet et aussi choisi" (*Courier de la Louisiane,* June 17, 1824, p. 2, col. 2).

138. *Courier de la Louisiane,* Dec. 9, 1824, p. 2, col. 4.

139. Ibid., Dec. 21, 1824, p. 2, col. 4; Dec. 22, 1824, p. 3, col. 4; and Dec. 23, 1824, p. 2, col. 3.

140. Ibid., Feb. 3, 1825, p. 3, col. 4.

141. Ibid., Feb. 3, 1825, p. 3, col. 4, and Feb. 4, 1825, p. 2, col. 4.

142. Ibid., Apr. 11, 1825, p. 2, col. 4.

143. Ibid., Dec. 15, 1826, p. 2, col. 3.

144. Ibid., Dec. 15, 1826, p. 2, col. 3.

145. Ibid., Jan. 27, 1827, p. 2, col. 4.

146. Ibid., Apr. 23, 1827, p. 2, col. 4.

147. An instrument invented ca. 1805 by Johann Nepomuk Maelzel (1772–1838). It was some sort of robot that performed military tunes.

148. *Louisiana Courier,* May 3, 1827, p. 3, col. 2.

149. Ibid., May 16, 1827, and May 18, 1827, p. 3, col. 4. *L'Amis des Lois,* May 18, 1827.

150. *L'Amis des lois,* May 30, 1827.

151. *Courier de la Louisiane,* May 24, 1827, p. 3, col. 4.

152. Ibid., June 20, 1827, p. 2, col. 4.

153. Ibid., June 11, 1827, p. 2, col. 2.

154. Such as on May 31, 1827. *Courier de la Louisiane,* May 31, 1827, p. 3, col. 4.

155. *Courier de la Louisiane,* Dec. 11, 1827, p. 2, col. 3.

156. *L'Abeille,* Jan. 26, 1828, p. 2, col. 3; and *L'Amis des Lois.*

157. *L'Abeille,* Feb. 5, 1828, p. 2, col. 4.

158. *The Bee,* Feb. 25, 1828, p. 2, col. 1.

159. *L'Abeille,* Feb. 8, 1828, p. 2, col. 5.

160. Ibid., Jan. 3, 1829, p. 2, col. 4, and Jan. 7, 1829, p. 2, col. 4.

161. Ibid., Jan. 24, 1829, p. 2, col. 5; Feb. 7, 1829, p. 4, col. 4.

162. Ibid., Jan. 29, 1829, p. 2, col. 5.

163. Ibid., Feb. 5, 1829, p. 2, col. 4.

164. Ibid., Feb. 14, 1829, p. 2, col. 4.

165. Ibid., Feb. 18, 1829, p. 2, col. 4, and Feb. 23, 1829, p. 2, col. 5.

166. Ibid., Mar. 3, 1829, p. 2, col. 4.

167. Ibid., Mar. 27, 1829, p. 2, col. 4.

168. Ibid., Jan. 21, 1829, p. 2, col. 4.

169. Ibid., Jan. 21, 1829, p. 2, col. 4; Jan. 26, 1830, p. 3, col. 3.

170. Ibid., Apr. 22, 1829, p. 2, col. 4.

171. Ibid., May 24, 1830, p. 2, col. 4; May 29, 1830, p. 4, col. 4.

172. *The Bee,* May 18, 1831, p. 2, col. 4.

173. Ibid., June 3, 1831, p. 2, col. 4.
174. *L'Abeille,* June 6, 1831, p. 2, col. 5.
175. *The Bee,* Feb. 20, 1832, p. 2, col. 3.
176. *L'Abeille,* Mar. 13, 1832, p. 3, col. 4. See *The Bee,* Apr. 16, 1832, p. 2, col. 4.
177. *The Bee,* May 18, 1832, p. 2, col. 3.
178. *L'Abeille,* Dec. 10, 1832, p. 3, col. 3.
179. Ibid., Jan. 3, 1833, p. 3, col. 3.
180. Ibid., Jan. 6, 1837, p. 3, col. 5.
181. *The Bee,* June 8, 1832, p. 2, col. 4.
182. Ibid., Apr. 26, 1833, p. 2, col. 5.
183. Ibid., May 21, 1833, p. 2, col. 4.
184. *L'Abeille,* Mar. 17, 1834, p. 3, col. 6.
185. Ibid., Feb. 24, 1834, p. 3, col. 5.
186. Ibid., Mar. 10, 1834, p. 3, col. 3.
187. *The Bee,* May 21, 1834, p. 2, col. 4.
188. Ibid., Dec. 11, 1834, p. 2, col. 3; Dec. 15, 1834, p. 2, col. 5.
189. Ibid., Nov. 10, 1834, p. 2, col. 1, and *L'Abeille,* Nov. 10, 1834, p. 3, col. 1.
190. *The Bee,* Jan. 21, 1835, p. 2, col. 5.
191. Ibid., Feb. 10, 1835, p. 2, col. 4; *L'Abeille,* Jan. 31, 1835, p. 3, col. 1.
192. *L'Abeille,* Jan. 8, 1835, p. 3, col. 5.
193. Ibid., Feb. 24, 1835, p. 3, col. 5.
194. *The Bee,* Mar. 10, 1835, p. 2, col. 1; Mar. 12, 1835, p. 2, col. 4; Mar. 14, 1835, p. 2, col. 4; Mar. 17, 1835, p. 2, col. 5.
195. A letter to *The Bee* criticizing the American Theatre's quality of performance (Dec. 11, 1834, p. 2, col. 2). The paper is full of the kinds of entertainment at the American Theatre: fencing, balloonists, circuses.
196. *The Bee,* p. 2, col. 4.
197. *L'Abeille,* May 1, 1835, p. 3, col. 4. Review of the opening: *The Bee,* p. 2, col. 1.
198. *L'Abeille,* Dec. 7, 1835, p. 3, col. 5. The St. Charles Theatre opened on Nov. 30, 1835.
199. *The Bee,* Dec. 9, 1835, p. 2, col. 1, and *L'Abeille,* Dec. 9, 1835, p. 3, col. 4.
200. *The Bee,* Dec. 11, 1835, p. 2, col. 6.
201. Ibid., Dec. 12, 1835, p. 2, col. 1.
202. On Tuesday, Dec. 15, 1835, at the American Theatre (Camp Street) between two dramas, Gambatti performed the same piece of music played at the trial of skill between Mr. Norton and himself in New York (*The Bee,* Dec. 15, 1835, p. 2, col. 5).
203. *The Bee,* Dec. 1, 2835, p. 2, col. 2.
204. Ibid., Dec. 7, 1835, p. 2, cols. 2–3. Review of his concert: *L'Abeille,* Dec. 8, 1835, p. 3, col. 1.
205. One of the most important reviews of the two major opera houses—the French and the American—appeared earlier in 1835. "Robert le Diable will shortly be performed at the French theatre [Théâtre d'Orléans], and Massaniello at the American. A shrewd discerner of public taste would conclude that operas suit the wishes of our playgoing community better than any other dramatic performance" (*The Bee,* Apr. 23, 1835, p. 2, col. 1; May 12, 1835, Tuesday). The performance of *Robert le Diable* at the French theater, once it opened, was then compared to a rendition of the same work a few weeks before at the American Theatre. At the former, "the orchestral arrangements and accompaniments were in general very efficient; yet too often there appeared a deficiency of wind and bass instruments. We can with safety give the preference to the French representation over the American only as regards the orchestra, the choruses and [especially the choruses of] nuns." The critic preferred the soloists and scenery at the American but expects subsequent performances at the

French to be better (*The Bee*, May 13, 1835, p. 2, col. 1). This does indeed happen (*L'Abeille*, May 14, 1835, p. 3, col. 1). Subsequently he gave rave reviews of the opera and its production at the Théâtre d'Orléans: *L'Abeille*, June 4, 1835, p. 3, col. 1, etc.

206. *The Bee*, Dec. 17, 1835, p. 2, cols. 2–3.

207. For a few citations that describe dance orchestras, see *Moniteur de la Louisiana*, Nov. 16, 1805, p. 2, col. 3; Nov. 20, 1805, p. 2, col. 3; Nov. 30, 1805, Sunday; Dec. 7, 1808, p. 3, col. 2; Jan. 11, 1809, p. 3, col. 1; Dec. 3, 1812, p. 4, col. 1. *Louisiana Gazette*, Dec. 20, 1805, p. 3, col. 3. *L'Abeille*, Jan. 28, 1828, p. 2, col. 4; Feb. 8, 1828, p. 2, col. 5; Mar. 19, 1829, p. 2, col. 4; Feb. 18, 1833, p. 3, col. 5.

CHAPTER TWO

1. This editor, who served from Feb. 22, 1835, resigned from *The Bee* on June 22, 1836 in order to start a new newspaper, *The Standard*, which dealt primarily with business news. During his first year he toed the traditional *Bee* line, but during his last six months he made dramatic changes at the paper (*The Bee*, June 18, 1836, p. 2, col. 2).

2. *The Bee*, Jan. 20, 1838, p. 2, col. 2.

3. Ibid., Feb. 15, 1853, p. 1, col. 2.

4. Ibid., Jan. 18, 1836, p. 2, col. 2; *L'Abeille*, Jan. 15, 1836, p. 3, col. 6.

5. *The Bee*, Feb. 15, 1836, p. 2, col. 2.

6. Ibid., Feb. 24, 1836, p. 2, col. 1.

7. *L'Abeille*, Feb. 24, 1836, p. 3, col. 1, and Feb. 27, 1836, p. 2, col. 1.

8. *The Bee*, Mar. 7, 1836, p. 2, col. 3.

9. *L'Abeille*, Mar. 25, 1836, p. 3, col. 1; Mar. 31, p. 2, col. 6; Apr. 1, 1836, p. 2, col. 6; *The Bee*, Apr. 5, 1836, p. 2, col. 6.

10. *The Bee*, Apr. 9, 1836, p. 2, col. 2.

11. *L'Abeille*, Apr. 12, 1836, p. 3, col. 1. Bailly, who died in the summer of 1839, was the most prominent basso at the French Opera during his tenure in New Orleans.

12. *The Bee*, Apr. 28, 1836, p. 2, col. 2.

13. Ibid., Apr. 26, 1836, p. 2, col. 1.

14. *L'Abeille*, May 3, 1836, p. 3, col. 4.

15. *The Bee*, May 11, 1836, p. 2, col. 5.

16. *L'Abeille*, May 13, 1836, p. 3, col. 4.

17. *The Bee*, May 18, 1836, p. 2, cols. 1 and 3.

18. The paper has a misprint: "viooa" for viola (*L'Abeille*, May 18, 1836, p. 3, col. 5).

19. *L'Abeille*, Jan. 4, 1836, p. 3, col. 6; *The Bee*, Jan. 8, 1836, p. 2, col. 1.

20. *The Bee*, Jan. 12, 1836, p. 2, col. 1.

21. Ibid., Jan. 28, 1836, p. 2, col. 1.

22. Ibid., Feb. 18, 1836, p. 2, col. 1.

23. Ibid., Mar. 17, 1836, p. 2, col. 1.

24. *L'Abeille*, Apr. 1, 1836, p. 2, col. 6; Apr. 5, 1836, p. 2, col. 1.

25. Ibid., May 10, 1836, p. 3, col. 4; May 12, 1836, p. 3, col. 1.

26. *The Bee*, Feb. 10, 1836, p. 2, col. 1.

27. The opening was on Mar. 6, 1836 (*L'Abeille*, Feb. 26, 1836, p. 3, col. 2). The first reviews were not favorable: too much instrumentation and noise (*The Bee*, Mar. 7, 1836, p. 2, col. 3), and some good, some bad singers; the orchestra was okay but too much drumming (*The Bee*, Mar. 8, 1836). A few days later the critic added: "Spectacle and operas appear to delight our citizens more

than any other species of public amusement—ex balls.... Caldwell is however determined to unite all at this theatre. He has an Italian company, an excellent orchestra, a tolerable operatic company, a pretty fair specimen of tragedians, and now he is resolved to add the equestrian to his histrionic company—in order to represent *Timor the Tartar, Mazeppa,* etc." He had special criticism for the singer Reynoldson, who was hissed off the New York stage; he can't sing and "let him direct the orchestra as he pleases" (*The Bee,* Mar. 19, 1836, p. 2, cols. 2–3). The last performance was on May 27.

28. *L'Abeille,* Apr. 13, 1836, p. 2, col. 1; *The Bee,* Apr. 23, 1836, p. 2, col. 2; Mar. 18, 1836. Concerning the sixth performance of *Il Pirata* at the St. Charles Theatre, the critic recommended that French citizens of New Orleans should go so that they can compare this opera with *Norma* since only at the Italian Opera can they hear this particular Bellini opera.

29. "The orchestra at this theatre [the St. Charles Theatre] is excellent, and alone merited unqualified praise." The singers did not do so well (*The Bee,* Apr. 12, 1836, p. 2, col. 2).

30. *The Bee,* May 23, 1836, p. 2, cols. 2–3. Actually many wanted Caldwell to repeat his opera season the next year, but with some changes, such as mixing English and Italian operas (*L'Abeille,* May 31, 1836, p. 3, col. 1; *The Bee,* June 7, 1836, p. 2, col. 2).

31. *The Bee,* May 12, 1836, p. 2, cols. 1–2.

32. *L'Abeille,* May 13, 1836, p. 3, col. 4.

33. *The Bee,* May 16, 1836, p. 2, col. 1; May 21, 1836, p. 2, col. 5.

34. Ibid., May 25, 1836, p. 2, col. 1.

35. *L'Abeille,* May 3, 1836, p. 3, col. 3. *The Bee,* Nov. 8, 1837, p. 2, col. 2.

36. *The Bee,* Nov. 22, 1836, p. 2, col. 5.

37. Ibid., Dec. 1, 1836, p. 2, col. 1.

38. Also on Dec. 8 and 12; Dec. 5, 1836, p. 2, col. 5.

39. Ibid., Dec. 9, 1836, p. 2, col. 1.

40. Ibid., Dec. 23, 1836, p. 2, col. 6.

41. Ibid., Dec. 26, 1836, p. 2, col. 4.

42. *L'Abeille,* Jan. 13, 1837, p. 3, col. 5.

43. *The Bee,* Jan. 24, 1837, p. 2, col. 5.

44. Ibid., Feb. 13, 1837, p. 2, col. 7.

45. *L'Abeille,* Feb. 28, 1837, p. 3; Mar. 4, 1837, p. 3, col. 5; *The Bee,* Mar. 9, 1837, p. 2, col. 1.

46. *The Bee,* Mar. 27, 1837, p. 2, col. 3.

47. Ibid., Apr. 6, 1837, p. 2, col. 6.

48. *L'Abeille,* Apr. 4, 1837, p. 3, col. 6; Apr. 4, 1837, p. 2, col. 3; Apr. 6, 1837, p. 3, col. 5; and *The Bee,* Apr. 6, 1837, p. 2, col. 2.

49. *The Bee,* Apr. 13, 1837, p. 2, col. 4.

50. Ibid., Nov. 8, 1837, p. 2, col. 2.

51. *L'Abeille,* Nov. 23, 1837, p. 3, col. 1.

52. Ibid., Dec. 4, 1837, p. 3, col. 1.

53. He was conductor of the orchestra at the Salle St. Louis (*L'Abeille,* Dec. 20, 1839).

54. *The Bee,* Jan. 10, 1838, p. 2, col. 8. Pre-view: *L'Abeille,* Jan. 12, 1838, p. 3, col. 1.

55. *The Bee,* Jan. 16, 1838, p. 2, col. 7.

56. Ibid., Jan. 20, 1838, p. 2, col. 7.

57. *L'Abeille,* Dec. 20, 1837, p. 3, col. 1.

58. *The Bee,* Jan. 27, 1838, p. 2, col. 7; Jan. 29, 1838, p. 2, col. 7; and Jan. 29, 1838, p. 2, col. 2.

59. *L'Abeille,* Jan. 15, 1838, p. 3, col. 1; review: Jan. 16, 1838, p. 2, col. 1.

60. *The Bee,* Jan. 20, 1838, p. 2, col. 7; Jan. 22, 1838, p. 2, col. 3. *L'Abeille,* Jan. 20, 1838, p. 3, col. 1.

61. *The Bee,* Jan. 25, 1838, p. 2, col. 7, and Jan. 27, 1838, p. 2, col. 7. *Commercial Bulletin,* Jan. 27, 1838, p. 2, col. 8.

62. *The Bee,* Feb. 10, 1838, p. 2, col. 3.
63. Ibid., Feb. 28, 1838, p. 2, col. 7.
64. Ibid., Feb. 28, 1838, p. 2, col. 7, and Mar. 1, 1838, p. 2, col. 7.
65. Ibid., Mar. 12, 1838, p. 2, col. 2.
66. Ibid., Mar. 17, 1838, p. 2, col. 3.
67. Ibid., Mar. 6, 1838, p. 2, col. 7, and Mar. 7, 1838, p. 2, col. 6.
68. Ibid., Apr. 24, 1838, p. 2, cols. 2–3, and *L'Abeille,* Apr. 23, 1838, p. 3, col. 2.
69. *L'Abeille,* Apr. 23, 1838, p. 3, col. 2; *The Bee,* May 1, 1838, p. 2, col. 3.
70. *L'Abeille,* May 4, 1838, p. 3, col. 6. Preview: *The Bee,* May 5, 1838, p. 2, col. 3.
71. *L'Abeille,* May 12, 1838, p. 2, col. 6.
72. Ibid., May 12, 1838, p. 2, col. 6, and May 14, 1838, p. 3, col. 7; review: May 18, 1838, p. 3, col. 4.
73. Ibid., June 13, 1838, p. 3, col. 6.
74. *The Bee,* Nov. 7, 1837, p. 2, col. 2, and *L'Abeille,* Nov. 9, 1837.
75. *The Bee,* Nov. 14, 1837, p. 2, col. 3.
76. *L'Abeille,* Apr. 27, 1838, p. 3, col. 5.
77. Ibid., May 7, 1838, p. 3, col. 5; May 19, 1838, p. 3, col. 6.
78. Ibid., May 28, 1838, p. 3, col. 7.
79. The tributes to her poured in over the next few years, and because of her genius she was able to carry the whole company when otherwise there were problems. See the lengthy tribute to Calvé—the only great thing about the opera season 1838–39 (*L'Abeille,* Apr. 20, 1839, p. 3, col. 1).
80. *L'Abeille,* May 3, 1838, p. 3, col. 6.
81. Another argument centered on the supposedly secrecy of the Philharmonic Society. See above, book I, part 1, chapter 3.
82. *L'Abeille,* Oct. 27, 1838, p. 3, col. 1.
83. Ibid., Nov. 9, 1838, p. 3, col. 3; letter by B.G., Nov. 20, 1838, p. 3, col. 3; Nov. 22, 1838, p. 3, col. 2. An English review of the French Opera was prefaced by a backhanded complement to the orchestra. *The Bee,* Dec. 4, 1838, p. 2, col. 1.
84. *L'Abeille,* Nov. 14, 1838, p. 3.
85. *The Bee,* Nov. 17, 1838, p. 1, col. 1.
86. *L'Abeille,* Nov. 28, 1838, p. 3, col. 2; Jan. 17, 1839, p. 3, col. 3.
87. *The Bee,* Nov. 13, 1838, p. 2, col. 5; *L'Abeille,* Nov. 22, 1838, p. 3, col. 5.
88. *The Bee,* Dec. 17, 1838, p. 2, col. 7.
89. Ibid., Dec. 15, 1838, p. 2, col. 7.
90. Ibid., Dec. 22, 1838, p. 2, col. 1.
91. Ibid., Dec. 24, 1838, p. 2, col. 7; and *L'Abeille,* Dec. 24, 1838, p. 3, col. 1.
92. *The Bee,* Jan. 3, 1839, p. 2, col. 6.
93. Ibid., Feb. 27, 1839, p. 2, col. 6.
94. Ibid., Feb. 25, 1839, p. 2, col. 6.
95. Ibid., Mar. 4, 1839, p. 2, col. 5; pre-review: Mar. 6, 1839, p. 2, col. 1.
96. Ibid., Mar. 9, 1839, p. 2, col. 3; and *L'Abeille,* Mar. 15, 1839, p. 3, col. 2. *The Bee,* Apr. 3, 1839, p. 2, col. 4.
97. *The Bee,* Nov. 18, 1837, p. 2, col. 3.
98. Ibid., Feb. 22, 1839, p. 2, col. 6. *L'Abeille,* Feb. 27, 1839, p. 3, col. 1.
99. *The Bee,* Mar. 6, 1839, p. 2, col. 7, and Mar. 9, 1839, p. 2, col. 3; pre-review: Mar. 9, 1839, p. 2, col. 2; review: Mar. 11, 1839, p. 2, col. 3, and *L'Abeille,* Mar. 11, 1839, p. 3, col. 3.
100. *L'Abeille,* Apr. 3, 1839, p. 3, col. 2.
101. This is apart from benefit performances of full operas at the French Opera, such as for Curto on June 4, 1839.

102. *L'Abeille,* Apr. 1, 1839, p. 3, col. 7; review: Apr. 3, 1839, p. 3, col. 2.
103. *The Bee,* Apr. 3, 1839, p. 2, col. 4, and Apr. 8, 1839, p. 2, col. 6.
104. *L'Abeille,* Apr. 18, 1839, p. 3, col. 6.
105. Ibid., May 2, 1839, p. 3, col. 6.
106. *L'Abeille,* May 24, 1839, p. 3, col. 4.
107. *The Bee,* May 22, 1839, p. 2, col. 7. Tribute to Cioffi: *L'Abeille,* May 25, 1839, p. 3, col. 2.
108. *L'Abeille,* Oct. 5, 1839, p. 3, col. 1, and *The Bee,* Oct. 3, 1839, p. 2, col. 1.
109. *L'Abeille,* Oct. 8, 1839, p. 3, col. 1, and *The Bee,* Oct. 8, 1839, p. 2, col. 2. The German Theatre was a fairly large company and had an orchestra of well-known local musicians, whose conductor was Bruns (*L'Abeille,* Dec. 17, 1839, p. 3, col. 6; Dec. 20, 1839; and *The Bee,* Dec. 20, 1839, p. 2, col. 1).
110. *L'Abeille,* Nov. 5, 1839, p. 3, col. 1, and Nov. 7, 1839, p. 3, col. 1.
111. *The Bee,* Dec. 25, 1839, p. 2, col. 2.
112. Ibid., Nov. 4, 1839, p. 2, col. 4.
113. *L'Abeille,* Dec. 16, 1839, p. 3, col. 7.
114. *The Bee,* Dec. 25, 1839, p. 2, col. 7.
115. *L'Abeille,* Nov. 6, 1839, p. 3, col. 4; *The Bee,* Nov. 6, 1839, p. 2, col. 4, and Nov. 7, 1839, p. 2, col. 6.
116. *The Bee,* Jan. 8, 1840.
117. Ibid., Mar. 2, 1840, p. 3, col. 7.
118. Ibid., Apr. 8, 1840, p. 3, col. 6. Exactly who M. Constantin was is discussed above, book I, part I, chapter 4.
119. *L'Abeille,* Apr. 20, 1840; Apr. 27, 1840.
120. *The Bee,* Nov. 20, 1836, p. 2, col. 7; Dec. 8, 1840, p. 2, col. 2. *L'Abeille,* Dec. 18, 1840, p. 2, col. 1.
121. *L'Abeille,* Nov. 23, 1840, p. 3, col. 7.
122. *The Bee,* Dec. 18, 1840, p. 2, col. 6.
123. Ibid., Nov. 7, 1840, p. 2, col. 5; Nov. 10, 1840, p. 2, col. 7; Nov. 11, 1840, p. 2, col. 2; Nov. 23, 1840, p. 2, col. 7. *L'Abeille,* Nov. 10, 1840, p. 3, col. 7; Nov. 10, 1840, p. 3, col. 2.
124. *L'Abeille,* Nov. 23, 1840, p. 3, col. 2, and *The Bee,* Nov. 21, 1840, p. 2, col. 2.
125. *L'Abeille,* Apr. 5, 1841, p. 3, col. 7.
126. Ibid., June 28, 1841, p. 3, col. 6.
127. Ibid., Nov. 22, 1841, p. 3, col. 1.
128. *The Bee,* Nov. 24, 1841, p. 2, col. 6.
129. Ibid., Nov. 9, 1841, p. 2, col. 2.
130. Ibid., Nov. 10, 1841, p. 2, col. 2. This may have been a wind band or an orchestra.
131. Ibid., Nov. 19, 1841, p. 2, col. 6; Nov. 20, 1841, p. 2, col. 2; Nov. 22, 1841, p. 2, col. 1.
132. Ibid., Dec. 18, 1841, p. 2, col. 6.
133. *L'Abeille,* Nov. 30, 1841, p. 3, col. 6.
134. *The Bee,* Dec. 5, 1841, p. 2, col. 6.
135. Ibid., Jan. 21, 1842, p. 3, col. 6. The *Picayune* gave the overture to *Le Cheval de Bronze* in place of *Les Deux Journées* (Jan. 21, 1842, p. 3, col. 2).
136. *The Bee,* Feb. 11, 1842, p. 3, col. 6.
137. *L'Abeille,* Apr. 27, 1842, p. 3, col. 5.
138. *The Bee,* Oct. 26, 1842, p. 2, col. 2.
139. Ibid., Jan. 9, 1843, p. 2, col. 2.
140. Ibid., Jan. 19, 1843, p. 2, col. 3.
141. *L'Abeille,* Oct. 20, 1842, p. 2, col. 1.
142. Ibid., Nov. 14, 1842, p. 2, col. 1.

143. "Of the performance of the opera, we have less to say [after a lengthy description of the opera itself]. The chorus and orchestra, for a first representation, were uncommonly good. The former was very full, and apparently well disciplined,—the latter, with the exception of an exceedingly vile horn, did justice to the partition. . . . In fine, the managers of the Théâtre d'Orléans brought out their opera as well as the limited stock of musical talent which they possess enabled them to do. Its execution, so far as it depended on the orchestra and choruses, was admirable" (*The Bee*, Dec. 15, 1842, p. 2, col. 3).

144. See all issues of *L'Abeille* during Nov. and Dec. Balls were held every Sunday, Tuesday, and Thursday at the Conti Street Ball Room. *The Bee* reported, "The orchestra in number and talent, is unrivalled in this city and will execute all the latest waltz and quadrilles. Several original pieces of music composed by members of the orchestra will be introduced" (Nov. 8, 1842, p. 2, col. 5, and Dec. 1, 1842, p. 2, col. 6).

145. *L'Abeille*, Oct. 21, 1842, p. 2, col. 4; Oct. 24, 1842, p. 2, col. 1. *The Bee*, Oct. 28, 1842, p. 2, col. 2.

146. *L'Abeille*, Nov. 14, 1842, p. 2, col. 1.

147. Ibid., Oct. 29, 1842, p. 2, col. 1, *The Bee*, Dec. 1, 1842, p. 2, col. 6, and Dec. 1, 1842, p. 2, col. 3.

148. *L'Abeille*, Jan. 28, 1843, p. 3, col. 7, and Feb. 1. 1843.

149. *The Bee*, Mar. 20, 1843, p. 2, col. 6, p. 3, col. 2; Mar. 28, 1843, p. 2, col. 2; and Mar. 31, 1843, p. 3, col. 1.

150. Ibid., Feb. 11, 1843, p. 2, col. 2.

151. Ibid., Feb. 8, 1843, p. 2, col. 6.

152. Ibid., Mar. 7, 1843, p. 2, col. 6; Apr. 10, 1843, p. 2, col. 6; Apr. 21, 1843, p. 2, col. 2.

153. Ibid., May 9, 1843, p. 1, col. 4.

154. *L'Abeille*, May 13, 1843, p. 1, col. 6.

155. *The Bee*, Mar. 29, 1843, p. 2, col. 6, and p. 2, col. 2.

156. Originally scheduled for Apr. 5 (*The Bee*, Apr. 4, 1843, p. 2, col. 6, and p. 3, col. 1). Review: *L'Abeille*, Apr. 10, 1843, p. 5, cols. 1–2.

157. *The Bee*, Apr. 18, 1843, p. 2, col. 6, and Apr. 18, 1843, p. 3, col. 1.

158. *L'Abeille*, May 4, 1843, p. 1, col. 6, and May 5, 1843, p. 2, col. 4. Review: May 8, 1843, p. 1, col. 6.

159. Review of her second concert: *The Bee*, Apr. 29, 1843, p. 2, col. 2 (or in French, *L'Abeille*, Apr. 29, 1843, p. 1, col. 1).

160. *The Bee*, Apr. 18, 1843, p. 2, col. 6, and Apr. 21, 1843, p. 2, col. 2; Apr. 25, 1843, p. 2, col. 8; May 4, 1843, p. 1, col. 6.

161. *L'Abeille*, May 10, 1843, p. 2, col. 3.

162. Ibid., May 22, 1843, p. 2, col. 3.

163. Ibid., June 2, 1843, p. 2, col. 3.

164. *The Bee*, Jan. 20, 1843, p. 2, col. 2 and col. 6.

165. Ibid., Feb. 2, 1843, p. 2, col. 6; Feb. 4, 1843, p. 3, cols. 1–2; Feb. 6, 1843, p. 3, col. 7; Feb. 11, 1843, p. 3, col. 1; Mar. 7, 1843, p. 2, col. 6.

166. Ibid., Dec. 5, 1843, p. 1, col. 4; *L'Abeille*, Dec. 5, 1843, p. 1, col. 6.

167. For a more detailed account of the visits of Vieuxtemps, Bull, and Artôt to New Orleans, see Baron, "Vieuxtemps (and Ole Bull)," 210–26; Baron, "Vieuxtemps," 211.

168. The announcement that Madame Damoreau and the violinist Artôt left Havre for New Orleans, not New York, where they will make their American debuts, has not been corroborated (*L'Abeille*, Oct. 16, 1843, p. 1, col. 6).

169. *L'Abeille*, Apr. 30, 1844, p. 2, col. 6; *The Bee*, May 2, 1844, p. 3, col. 3.

170. *L'Abeille*, May 20, 1844, p. 1, col. 3; May 21, 1844, p. 1, col. 5 and p. 2, col. 6.

171. Ibid., May 23, 1844, p. 1, col. 3.

172. Ibid., May 22, 1844, p. 2, col. 6; p. 1, col. 3.
173. Ibid., Dec. 30, 1844, p. 2, col. 5.
174. Ibid., Dec. 30, 1844, p. 2, col. 5.
175. *The Bee,* Jan. 29, 1845, p. 3, col. 2; Jan. 31, 1845, p. 4, col. 6.
176. *L'Abeille,* Feb. 12, 1845, p. 2, col. 6.
177. Ibid., Feb. 17, 1845, p. 2, col. 6.
178. *The Bee,* Feb. 21, 1845, p. 4, col. 6.
179. Ibid., Feb. 26, 1845, p. 4, col. 6.
180. *L'Abeille,* Mar. 10, 1845, p. 2, col. 8; p. 1, col. 2; Mar. 13, 1845, p. 2, col. 7.
181. *The Bee,* Feb. 24, 1845, p. 4, col. 6; Feb. 26, 1845, p. 4, col. 6.
182. *L'Abeille,* Mar. 17, 1845, p. 2, col. 7; Apr. 16, 1845, p. 4, col. 5.
183. Ibid., Mar. 25, 1845, p. 2, col. 6.
184. Ibid., Mar. 28, 1845, p. 1, col. 2.
185. *The Bee,* Mar. 29, 1845, p. 2, col. 5; p. 3, col. 4; Apr. 2, 1845, p. 4, col. 2. *L'Abeille,* Apr. 4, 1845, p. 1, col. 2; Apr. 5, 1845, p. 1, col. 2.
186. *L'Abeille,* Apr. 22, 1845, p. 2, col. 6; p. 3, col. 2; Apr. 25, 1845, p. 1, col. 2.
187. *The Bee,* Apr. 24, 1845, p. 4, col. 5; Apr. 25, 1845, p. 2, col. 6.
188. *L'Abeille,* Apr. 29, 1845, p. 2, col. 6.
189. Ibid., Apr. 25, 1845, p. 2, col. 6; Apr. 30, 1845, p. 1, col. 2.
190. Ibid., May 5, 1845, p. 2.
191. Ibid., May 16, 1845, p. 2, col. 4.
192. *The Bee,* Nov. 7, 1845, p. 1, col. 2.
193. Ibid., Nov. 21, 1845, p. 2, col. 5; Nov. 22, 1845, p. 1, col. 2.
194. Ibid., Nov. 10, 1845, p. 1, col. 6.
195. Ibid., Nov. 22, 1845, p. 1, col. 2.
196. The original French: "exécutées avec la perfection ordinaire d'un orchestre où les artistes de talent se coudoient" (*L'Abeille,* Nov. 25, 1845, p. 1, col. 3).
197. The original French: "Il y a entre l'orchestre du Théâtre d'Orléans et le public, une sympathie établie, et les artistes du dehors qui ont le désir de se faire entendre, auraient tort de croire que ce soit chose facile à obtenir" (*L'Abeille,* Dec. 27, 1845, p. 3, cols. 2 and 5).
198. *The Bee,* Dec. 8, 1845, p. 2, col. 3.
199. Ibid., Nov. 25, 1845, p. 1, col. 4.
200. Ibid., Dec. 9, 1845, p. 4, col. 3; Dec. 12, 1845, p. 1, col. 2; *L'Abeille,* Dec. 10, 1845, p. 3, col. 2.
201. *L'Abeille,* Dec. 15, 1845, p. 3, col. 4.
202. Ibid., Jan. 27, 1846, p. 1, col. 2.
203. *The Bee,* Jan. 10, 1846, p. 1, col. 4; Jan. 21, 1846, p. 1, col. 3.
204. Ibid., Jan. 31, 1846, p. 1, col. 4.
205. Ibid., Feb. 26, 1846, p. 1, col. 6, and Feb. 28, 1846, p. 1, col. 3.
206. *Picayune,* Mar. 15, 1846, p. 3, col. 2. *The Bee,* Mar. 14, 1846, p. 1, col. 2; Mar. 24, 1846, p. 1, col. 2; Mar. 24, 1846, p. 1, col. 6; and Mar. 30, 1846, p. 1, col. 1. *L'Abeille,* Mar. 30, 1846, p. 1, col. 2; review: Apr. 1, 1846, p. 1, col. 2. *The Bee,* Apr. 1, 1846, p. 1, col. 1.
207. *The Bee,* Mar. 17, 1846, p. 1, col. 2, and Mar. 20, 1846, p. 1, col. 3.
208. *L'Abeille,* Apr. 7, 1846, p. 2, col. 3.
209. *The Bee,* Apr. 7, 1846, p. 1, col. 2. *L'Abeille,* Apr. 15, 1846, p. 2, col. 4; Apr. 16, 1846, p. 1, col. 3; and Apr. 16, 1846, p. 1, col. 2; review: Apr. 17, 1846, p. 1, col. 2. *The Bee,* Apr. 18, 1846, p. 1, col. 2.
210. *The Bee,* Apr. 18, 1846, p. 1, col. 7. Review: *L'Abeille,* Apr. 21, 1846, p. 1, col. 2. *The Bee* reported on Apr. 23, 1846, p. 1, col. 7, that Meyer was to give his second and last concert on Apr. 24, but this seems to have been the newspaper's error.

211. *The Bee,* Apr. 23, 1846, p. 1, col. 7; Apr. 25, 1846, p. 1, col. 7; May 10, 1846, p. 1, col. 4. *L'Abeille,* May 5, 1846, p. 2, col. 3; May 8, 1846, p. 2, col. 3.

212. *L'Abeille,* Apr. 13, 1846, p. 1, col. 2.

213. Ibid., May 4, 1846, p. 1, cols. 3–4.

214. *The Bee,* May 16, 1846, p. 1, col. 7; *L'Abeille,* May 22, 1846, p. 2, col. 3, and May 23, 1846, p. 1, col. 4.

215. *L'Abeille,* May 15, 1846, p. 2, col. 3. *The Bee,* May 23, 1846, p. 1, col. 4. *L'Abeille,* May 21, 1846, p. 1, co. 4; May 27, 1846, p. 3, col. 3.

216. *L'Abeille,* Oct. 27, 1846, p. 1, col. 8.

217. *The Bee,* Oct. 29, 1846, p. 1, col. 6.

218. *L'Abeille,* Apr. 8, 1847, p. 2, col. 2.

219. Ibid., Oct. 30, 1846, p. 1, col. 3, and Nov. 6, 1846, p. 1, col. 3.

220. Ibid., Nov. 17, 1846, p. 1, col. 8.

221. *The Bee,* Feb. 2, 1847, p. 1, col. 9. *L'Abeille,* Feb. 2, 1847, p. 2, col. 3. *The Bee,* Feb. 2, 1847, p. 1, col. 5.

222. *L'Abeille,* Feb. 9, 1847, p. 1, col. 2.

223. Ibid., Feb. 10, 1847, p. 2, col. 2, and Feb. 10, 1847, p. 1, col. 1. *Picayune,* Feb. 10, 1847, p. 3, col. 2. See also *L'Abeille,* Oct. 23, 1846, p. 1, col. 3.

224. *L'Abeille,* Feb. 12, 1847, p. 2, col. 2. *Picayune,* Feb. 11, 1847, p. 3, col. 3. See also *L'Abeille,* Feb. 25, 1847, p. 1, cols. 1–2, for an evaluation of Sivori.

225. *The Bee,* Feb. 20, 1847, p. 1, col. 9. Review: *L'Abeille,* Feb. 24, 1847, p. 1, col. 2.

226. *The Bee,* Feb. 24, 1847, p. 1, col. 9. Review: *L'Abeille,* Feb. 25, 1847, p. 1, col. 1.

227. *L'Abeille,* Feb. 26, 1847, p. 2, col. 2; Mar. 3, 1847, p. 1, col. 3; Mar. 4, 1847, p. 2, col. 2; Mar. 6, 1847, p. 1, col. 1; Mar. 8, 1847, p. 1, col. 3. *Picayune,* Feb. 26, 1847. *The Bee,* Mar. 1, 1847, p. 1, col. 9.

228. Herz, *My Travels in America,* 83.

229. *L'Abeille,* Mar. 11, 1847, p. 2, col. 2; Mar. 15, 1847, p. 2, col. 2. *The Bee,* Mar. 16, 1847, p. 1, col. 2. *L'Abeille,* Mar. 16, 1847, p. 2, col. 2, and Mar. 17, 1847, p. 1, col. 2; lengthy review: Mar. 19, 1847, p. 1, col. 2.

230. Mme. L, "who has overcome the repugnance natural to her sex, and consented to display her eminent talent in a duet with Herz."

231. *The Bee,* Mar. 20, 1847, p. 1, col. 4. The armory concert was originally scheduled for Mar. 23 (*L'Abeille,* Mar. 19, 1847, p. 2, col. 2, and Mar. 20, 1847, p. 2, col. 2). Review: *L'Abeille,* Mar. 26, 1847, p. 2, col. 2.

232. *L'Abeille,* Mar. 29, 1847, p. 1, col. 7; Mar. 30, 1847, p. 1, col. 2; Apr. 8, 1847, p. 1, col. 2; Apr. 8, 1847, p. 2, col. 2; Apr. 10, 1847, p. 2, col. 2; Apr. 12, 1847, p. 1, col. 1; and Apr. 14, 1847, p. 1, col. 1; review: Apr. 1, 1847, p. 1, col. 1; Apr. 8, 1847, p. 2, col. 2; Apr. 10, 1847, p. 2, col. 2; Apr. 12, 1847, p. 1, col. 1; and Apr. 14, 1847, p. 1, col. 1.

233. *Picayune,* Mar. 30, 1847, p. 5, col. 3.

234. *L'Abeille,* Apr. 14, 1847, p. 2, col. 2.

235. *The Bee,* Apr. 14, 1847, p. 1, col. 4, and *L'Abeille,* Apr. 14, 1847, p. 1, col. 1, and p. 2, col. 2.

236. *The Bee,* May 6, 1847, p. 1, col. 5.

237. *L'Abeille,* Apr. 27, 1847, p. 1, col. 1; May 27, 1847, p. 2, col. 1. See Mar. 22, 1843.

238. Ibid., Sept. 2, 1847, p. 1, col. 5.

239. *The Bee,* Oct. 11, 1847, p. 1, col. 5; Oct. 18, 1847, p. 1, col. 6, and Oct. 18, 1847, p. 1, col. 4. Review: *L'Abeille,* Oct. 22, 1847, p. 1, col. 1. *L'Abeille,* Nov. 9, 1847, p. 1, col. 1, and Nov. 9, 1847, p. 1, col. 9.

240. The opera season opened on Nov. 19 at the Théâtre d'Orléans with *La Dame Blanche.*

241. *L'Abeille,* Nov. 11, 1847, p. 1, col. 6; Nov. 12, 1847, p. 1, col. 7.

242. Ibid., Nov. 23, 1847, p. 1, col. 2; Dec. 2, 1847, p. 1, col. 6.

243. Ibid., Jan. 24, 1848, p. 1, cols. 4 and 9; Jan. 26, 1848, p. 1, col. 9; review: Jan. 29, 1848, p. 1, col. 1, and *The Bee*, Jan. 29, 1848, p. 1, col. 3.

244. *L'Abeille*, Jan. 29, 1848, p. 1, col. 9; Feb. 3, 1848, p. 1, col. 9; Feb. 8, 1848, Feb. 10, 1848, p. 1, col. 1, and Feb. 12, 1848, p. 1, col. 2. *The Bee*, Feb. 4, 1848, p. 1, col. 3; review: Feb. 3, 1848, p. 1, col. 2; Feb. 7, 1848, p. 1, col. 3. *L'Abeille*, Feb. 3, 1848, p. 1, cols. 1–2.

245. *L'Abeille*, Jan. 13, 1848, p. 1, col. 9; Jan. 29, 1848, p. 1, col. 1.

246. Ibid., Feb. 24, 1848, p. 1, col. 9, and Feb. 26, 1848, p. 1, col. 1. *The Bee*, Feb. 26, 1848, p. 1, col. 4. See advertisement for the Catalan Band in most newspapers, e.g., *The Bee*, Apr. 28, 1848, p. 1, col. 9.

247. *The Bee*, Mar. 1, 1848, p. 1, cols. 2 and 9, and Mar. 2, 1848, p. 1, col. 9.

248. *L'Abeille*, Apr. 1, 1848, p. 1, col. 9; Apr. 6, 1848, p. 1, cols. 2 and 9; Apr. 8, 1848, p. 1, col. 9; Apr. 10, 1848, p. 1, col. 9; Apr. 11, 1848, p. 1, col. 9; Apr. 12, 1848, p. 1, col. 1. For more on the Steyermarkische Orchester see Newman, "Good Music for a Free People."

249. *L'Abeille*, Apr. 5, 1848, p. 1, col. 1; Apr. 7, 1848, p. 1, col. 1; Apr. 12, 1848, p. 1, col. 9; Apr. 13, 1848, p. 1, col. 2; Apr. 15, 1848, p. 1, col. 2; Apr. 17, 1848, p. 1, col. 9; Apr. 27, 1848, p. 1, col. 2, and Apr. 28, 1848, p. 1, col. 1. Lengthy review: Apr. 17, 1848, p. 1, cols. 1–2.

250. Ibid., Apr. 5, 1848, p. 1, col. 1; review: Apr. 6, 1848, p. 1, cols. 1–2.

251. Ibid., Mar. 17, 1848, p. 1, col. 9, Mar. 20, 1848, p. 1, col. 2; May 2, 1848, p. 1, col. 1; May 4, 1848, p. 1, col. 9. *The Bee*, Apr. 28, 1848, p. 1, col. 9.

252. *The Bee*, Aug. 23, 1848, p. 1, col. 9. This was probably a string "band" or string ensemble.

253. *L'Abeille*, Oct. 5, 1848, p. 1, col. 4; Nov. 8, 1848, p. 1, col. 1; Nov. 11, 1848, p. 1, col. 2.

254. *The Bee*, Nov. 1, 1848, p. 1, col. 8; Nov. 16, 1848, p. 1, col. 1.

255. *L'Abeille*, Nov. 16, 1848, p. 1, col. 1.

256. Ibid., Dec. 4, 1848, p. 1.

257. *Picayune*, Mar. 6, 1849, p. 3, col. 4. *L'Abeille*, Mar. 6, 1849, p. 1, col. 9.

258. *L'Abeille*, Mar. 9, 1849, p. 1, col. 9; Mar. 12, 1849, p. 1, col. 8. *The Bee*, Mar. 7, 1849, p. 1, cols. 1 and 8; Mar. 13, 1849, p. 1, col. 2.

259. *L'Abeille*, Mar. 7, 1849, p. 1, col. 8; p. 1, col. 1; Mar. 13, 1849, p. 1, col. 2; Mar. 22, 1849, p. 1, col. 1; Mar. 24, 1849, p. 1, col. 1; Mar. 28, 1849, p. 1, col. 8. *The Bee*, Mar. 12, 1849, p. 1, col. 8; Mar. 14, 1849, p. 2, col. 1; Mar. 16, 1849, p. 1, col. 8; Mar. 21, 1849, p. 1, col. 8; Mar. 28, 1849, p. 1, col. 8; Mar. 29, 1849, p. 1, col. 1.

260. *The Bee*, Mar. 16, 1849, p. 2, col. 1. See *L'Abeille*, Mar. 6, 1849, p. 1, col. 9.

261. *L'Abeille*, Apr. 12, 1849, p. 1, col. 8.

262. Ibid., Apr. 24, 1849, p. 1, col. 8; Apr. 26, 1849, p. 1, col. 8; Apr. 27, 1849, p. 1, col. 2; May 1, 1849, p. 1, col. 1; May 3, 1849, p. 1, col. 8; May 4, 1849, p. 1, col. 1; p. 1, col. 9. *The Bee*, May 4, 1849, p. 1, col. 7.

263. *The Bee*, Mar. 19, 1849, p. 1, col. 8; Mar. 21, 1849, p. 1, col. 8; Mar. 28, 1849, p. 1, col. 8.

264. *L'Abeille*, Apr. 26, 1849, p. 1, col. 8; May 2, 1849, p.1, col. 7.

265. Ibid., Dec. 7, 1849, p. 1, col. 9.

266. Ibid., Nov. 8, 1849, p. 1, col. 2; *The Bee*, Nov. 9, 1849, p. 1, col. 1; p. 1, col. 6.

267. *Tagliche Deutsche Zeitung*, Dec. 16, 1849, p. 3, col. 2; Dec. 23, 1849, p. 2, cols. 3–4.

CHAPTER THREE

1. *The Bee*, Jan. 3, 1850, p. 1, col. 2; p. 3, col. 9. *L'Abeille*, Jan. 5, 1850, p. 1, col. 3; p. 3, col. 2.

2. *L'Abeille*, Jan. 5, 1850, p. 1, col. 9. *The Bee*, Jan. 7, 1850, p. 3, col. 2; Jan. 10, 1850, p. 1, col. 2.

3. *L'Abeille*, Jan. 11, 1850, p. 3, col. 9; Jan. 12, 1850, p. 1, col. 9. *The Bee*, Jan. 14, 1850, p. 3, col. 1.

4. *The Bee,* Jan. 15, 1850, p. 3, col. 1; Jan. 16, 1850, p. 3, col. 1.

5. *L'Abeille,* Jan. 28, 1850, p. 1, col. 9.

6. *The Bee,* Feb. 16, 1850, p. 3, col. 2; Feb. 21, 1850, p. 3, col. 1; *L'Abeille,* Feb. 18, 1850, p. 1, col. 9.

7. *The Bee,* Mar. 12, 1850, p. 1, col. 9; see Mar. 1, 1850, p. 3, col. 1, and *L'Abeille,* Feb. 26, 1850, p. 1, col. 1.

8. *L'Abeille,* Apr. 9, 1850, p. 1, col. 9.

9. *The Bee,* Apr. 10, 1850, p. 1, col. 9.

10. *Tagliche Deutsche Zeitung,* Apr. 16, 1850, p. 3, col. 5.

11. *L'Abeille,* May 1, 1850, p. 1, col. 10.

12. *Picayune,* May 10, 1850, p. 3, col. 2; *L'Abeille,* May 8, 1850, p. 1, col. 9.

13. *L'Abeille,* May 17, 1850, p. 1, col. 10.

14. Ibid., May 18, 1850, p. 1, col. 9.

15. Ibid., May 25, 1850, p. 1, col. 10.

16. Ibid., May 22, 1850, p. 1, col. 10.

17. *Picayune,* May 24, 1850, p. 3, col. 2.

18. Ibid., June 14, 1850, p. 3, col. 2.

19. Ibid., July 6, 1850, p. 3, col. 3.

20. *L'Abeille,* Nov. 14, 1850, p. 1, col. 2; Nov. 26, 1850, p. 1, col. 2.

21. Ibid., Oct. 17, 1850, p. 3, col. 2.

22. Ibid., Oct. 22, 1850, p. 3, col. 2.

23. Ibid., Nov. 13, 1850, p. 1, col. 1.

24. Ibid., Nov. 19, 1850, p. 1, col. 2; and *The Bee,* Nov. 19, 1850, p. 1, col. 2. "M. Placide, le Directeur des Variétés, a généreusement retardé l'ouverture de son theatre pour permettre à M. Gabici, son habile che[f] d'orchestre, de diriger une seconde fois l'exécution du Stabat" (*L'Abeille,* Nov. 20, 1850, p. 1, col. 1).

25. *L'Abeille,* Nov. 18, 1850, p. 1, col. 1; Nov. 30, 1850, p. 1, col. 8.

26. Ibid., Jan. 8, 1851, p. 1, col. 2.

27. "Un excellent orchestre composé des principaux instrumentistes de New York et de la Nouvelle Orleans a été engagé et sera conduit par M. Joseph Burke" (*L'Abeille,* Feb. 13, 1851, p. 1, col. 8).

28. *L'Orleanais,* Feb. 11, 1851, p. 1, col. 2.

29. Parodi (b. 1827 in Genoa, Italy) was the favorite pupil of Giuditta Pasta, the famous nineteenth-century diva for whom Bellini wrote *Norma.* Parodi was singing in Bergamo in 1845 and at Covent Garden in 1850. Max Maretzek went to London and bought out her contract so he could have a star to compete with Barnum's star attraction, Jennie Lind. Parodi made her American debut under the direction of Maretzek in New York at the Astor Place Opera House on Nov. 4, 1850, in the role of Norma, and she scored great success during the 1850–51 season. Parodi remained in the United States until 1853 when she went to sing for a season at the Paris Opera. She was featured again in both Maretzek's and Strakosch's opera troupes in 1857. Meanwhile she toured the United States and Canada, first with Strakosch in 1851 and 1852 and again in 1855 and 1856 and then with her own Italian opera company in 1859–60. She sang with the Germania Musical Society Orchestra of Boston in Baltimore; Washington, D.C.; Richmond; and Petersburg in Mar. 1851; see Newman, "Good Music for a Free People," 481. Her fame in America was such that at least a dozen songs were published between 1851 and 1856 that advertised that they were sung by Parodi. Max Maretzek composed a romance, *La Tradita,* for her (Philadelphia: Edward L. Walker, 1951), and Maurice Strakosch himself wrote an opera, *Giovanna Prima di Napoli,* dedicated to her, from which six songs survive. There were also piano dances where her name was attached to the title: "Parodi Polka" by Charles Mueller (New York: Kerksieg and Breusing, 1851) and "Parodi Schottisch" by E. Gleffer (New York: Wm. E. Millet, 1851). John Dwight (*Journal* 8 [Oct. 20, 1855]: 22; and vol. 10

[Oct. 4, 1856]: 7, [Oct. 11, 1856]: 15, and [Oct. 18, 1856]: 22) found her voice powerful and rich but unrefined, and thought she scored her great popularity because she appealed to the most shallow elements of the musical audience. Indeed, in the last cited review he couldn't even remember what she sang, surely nothing "new or noticeable." Nothing is known about her after 1860. See Katherine K. Preston, *Opera on the Road: Traveling Opera Troupes in the United States, 1825–1860* (Urbana: University of Illinois Press, 1993).

30. *The Bee*, Apr. 19, 1851, p. 1, col. 9; Apr. 23, 1851, p. 1, col. 1; *L'Abeille*, Apr. 24, 1851, p. 1, col. 1.
31. *L'Abeille*, Apr. 22, 1851, p. 1, col. 9.
32. *The Bee*, Apr. 29, 1851, p. 1, col. 9; May 1, 1851, p. 1, col. 9.
33. Ibid., May 5, 1851, p. 1, col. 9.
34. *L'Abeille*, May 10, 1851, p. 1, col. 9; May 16, 1851, p. 1, col. 9; May 26, 1851, p. 1, col. 9.
35. Ibid., Mar. 21, 1851, p. 1, col. 9.
36. *The Bee*, Apr. 4, 1851, p. 1, col. 9.
37. *L'Abeille*, Apr. 21, 1851, p. 1, col. 9; Apr. 23, 1851, p. 1, col. 1; p. 1, col. 9.
38. Ibid., May 1, 1851, p. 1, col. 9.
39. *The Bee*, May 24, 1851, p. 1, col. 9.
40. Ibid., May 20, 1851, p. 1, col. 9. *L'Abeille*, May 21, 1851, p. 1, col. 9; May 28, 1851, p. 1, col. 9.
41. *L'Abeille*, May 26, 1851, p. 1, col. 9.
42. Ibid., May 29, 1851, p. 1, col. 9; June 3, 1851, p. 1, col. 2.
43. *The Bee*, June 4, 1851, p. 1, col. 9.
44. *L'Abeille*, June 7, 1851, p. 1, col. 9.
45. Ibid., Nov. 8, 1851, p. 1, col. 2; *The Bee*, Nov. 8, 1851, p. 3, col. 6.
46. *L'Abeille*, Nov. 21, 1851, p. 1, col. 2, and p. 1, col. 6.
47. *The Bee*, Nov. 29, 1851, p. 3, col. 1.
48. *L'Abeille*, Dec. 16, 1851, p. 1, col. 2.
49. Ibid., Dec. 6, 1851, p. 1, col. 1.
50. Ibid., Dec. 25, 1851, p. 1, col. 2.
51. Ibid., Dec. 27, 1851, p. 1, col. 2.
52. Born in Hanover, Germany, Bothe came to New Orleans in the 1840s and is listed as a musician in the city directories from 1851 on.
53. *The Bee*, Jan. 14, 1852, p. 1, col. 2; p. 1, col. 10. *L'Abeille*, Jan. 14, 1852, p. 1, col. 2; Jan. 20, 1852, p. 1, col. 1.
54. *Picayune*, Jan. 9, 1852, p. 2, col. 4.
55. Ibid., Feb. 15, 1852, p. 4, col. 1.
56. *L'Abeille*, May 18, 1852, p. 1.
57. Ibid., May 20, 1852, p. 1.
58. Ibid., May 24, 1852; May 26, 1852, p. 1.
59. Ibid., Feb. 2, 1852, p. 1, col. 8; Feb. 4, 1852, p. 1, col. 10; Feb. 5, 1852, p. 1, col. 10; p. 1, col. 1; Feb. 7, 1852, p. 1, col. 2.
60. Ibid., Feb. 4, 1852, p. 1, col. 10; Feb. 7, 1852, p 1, col. 2; Feb. 9, 1852, p. 1, col. 10.
61. Ibid., Apr. 6, 1852, p. 1, col. 2; Apr. 22, 1852, p. 1, col. 10; *The Bee*, Apr. 17, 1852, p. 1, col. 1.
62. *L'Abeille*, Apr. 26, 1852, p. 1, col. 10; Apr. 29, 1852, p. 1, col. 10.
63. Ibid,, Apr. 9, 1852, p. 1, col. 10.
64. Ibid., Apr. 21, 1852, p. 1, col. 2.
65. Ibid., May 6, 1852, p. 1, col. 10.
66. Ibid., Oct. 7, 1852, p. 1, col. 3; Oct. 16, 1852, p. 1, col. 2; and Oct. 18, 1852, p. 1, col. 10.
67. *The Bee*, Oct. 28, 1852, p. 1, col. 10; Nov. 10, 1852, p. 1, col. 10.
68. *L'Abeille*, Nov. 23, 1852, p. 1, col. 2.

69. Ibid., Nov. 23, 1852, p. 1, col. 2.

70. *The Bee*, Jan. 4, 1853.

71. *L'Abeille*, Jan. 29, 1853, p. 1, col. 2.

72. *The Bee*, Feb. 23, 1853, p. 1, col. 1.

73. *L'Abeille*, Jan. 31, 1853; Feb. 21, 1853, p. 1, col. 3. *The Bee*, Feb. 23, 1853, p. 1, col. 2. The concert was originally scheduled for Feb. 24, but Bull was too fatigued.

74. Not the more famous work by Gottschalk.

75. *L'Abeille*, Feb. 23, 1853, p. 1, col. 2. *The Bee*, Feb. 23, 1853, p. 1, col. 10.

76. Klein, *The Reign of Patti*, 28–29 and 32–33. See Cone, *Adelina Patti, Queen of Hearts*, 29–31; Dizikes, *Opera in America*, 181.

77. *L'Abeille*, Feb. 25, 1853, p. 1, cols. 1 and 10. *The Bee*, Feb. 26, 1853, p. 1, col. 1; review: Feb. 28, 1853, p. 1, col. 2.

78. *L'Abeille*, Mar. 3, 1853, p. 1, col. 2.

79. Ibid., Mar. 1, 1853, p. 1, col. 10. *The Bee*, Mar. 2, 1853, p. 1, col. 1; review: Mar. 3, 1853, p. 1, col. 2.

80. *L'Abeille*, Mar. 3, 1853, p. 1, col. 10; review: Mar. 5, 1853, p. 1, col. 1.

81. Ibid., Mar. 8, 1853, p. 1, col. 10.

82. Ibid., Mar. 10, 1853, p. 1, col. 10, and Mar. 11, 1853, p. 1, col. 2.

83. Ibid., Mar. 15, 1853, p. 1, col. 2.

84. Ibid., Mar. 22, 1853, p. 1, cols. 1 and 10.

85. *The Bee*, Mar. 24, 1853, p. 1, col. 1.

86. Ibid., Feb. 14, 1853, p. 1, col. 1. More details on her assistants: Feb. 14, 1853, p. 1, col. 10; *L'Abeille*, Feb. 14, 1853, p. 1, col. 10.

87. *The Bee*, Feb. 19, 1853, p. 1, col. 1.

88. Ibid., Mar. 1, 1853, p. 1, col. 5.

89. Ibid., Feb. 17, 1853, p. 1, col. 1; Feb. 22, 1853, p. 1, col. 10; Feb. 24, 1853, p. 1, col. 10; Mar. 7, 1853, p. 1, col. 10; Mar. 8, 1853, p. 1, col. 10; Mar. 9, 1853, p. 1, col. 1, and Mar. 11, 1853, p. 1, col. 2. *L'Abeille*, Feb. 21, 1853, p. 1, cols. 3 and 10; Feb. 25, 1853, p. 1, col. 1; Mar. 7, 1853, p. 1, col. 2. Reviews: *The Bee*, Feb. 22, 1853, p. 1, col. 2; Feb. 24, 1853, p. 1, col. 1.

90. *L'Abeille*, Mar. 7, 1853, p. 1, col. 2.

91. Ibid., Apr. 14, 1853, p. 1, col. 1.

92. Ibid., May 6, 1853, p. 1, col. 10; May 11, 1853, p. 1, col. 2.

93. *The Bee*, Mar. 9, 1853, p. 1, col. 1. *L'Abeille*, Mar. 22, 1853, p. 1, col. 10.

94. *The Bee*, Mar. 25, 1853, p. 1, cols. 1, 4, and 10.

95. *L'Abeille*, Mar. 2, 1853, p. 1, col. 2.

96. *The Bee*, May 13, 1853, p. 1, col. 10. Brief review: *L'Abeille*, May 14, 1853, p. 1, col. 3.

97. *The Bee*, May 21, 1853, p. 1, col. 1; May 23, 1853, p. 1, col. 1. *L'Abeille*, May 23, 1853, p. 1, col. 10.

98. *L'Abeille*, Jan. 12, 1853. *The Bee*, Feb. 5, 1853, p. 1, col. 3.

99. *L'Abeille*, Mar. 28, 1853, p. 1, col. 1.

100. *The Bee*, Apr. 22, 1847, p. 1, col. 1.

101. *L'Abeille*, Jan. 10, 1848, p. 1, col. 2.

102. Ibid., Apr. 20, 1848, p. 1, col. 1.

103. *The Bee*, Oct. 15, 1850, p. 1, col. 1. *L'Abeille*, Dec. 3, 1850, p. 1, col. 2.

104. *L'Abeille*, Apr. 4, 1853, p. 1, col. 3.

105. *The Bee*, Apr. 5, 1853, p. 1, col. 10. Review: *L'Abeille*, Apr. 7, 1853, p. 1, col. 3.

106. *The Bee*, Apr. 8, 1853, p. 1, col. 10; Apr. 13, 1853, p. 1, col. 10; Apr. 15, 1853, p. 1, col. 10; Apr. 18, 1853, p. 1, col. 10; Apr. 25, 1853, p. 1, col. 10; Apr. 28, 1853, p. 1, col. 10; May 4, 1853, p. 1,

col. 10; May 9, 1853, p. 1, col. 10. *Picayune,* Apr. 29, 1853. *L'Abeille,* May 17, 1853, p. 1, col. 2. Reviews: *The Bee,* Apr. 19, 1853, p. 1, col. 1; May 5, 1853, p. 1, col. 1; May 12, 1853, p. 1, col. 2; *L'Abeille,* May 5, 1853, p. 1, col. 3.

107. On the eighth program he performed De Bériot's *Le Trémolo.*

108. *L'Abeille,* May 16, 1853, p. 1, col. 4.

109. *The Bee,* May 17, 1853, p. 1, col. 10.

110. Ibid., May 16, 1853, p. 1, col. 1; Dec. 22, 1853, p. 1, col. 3. *L'Abeille,* May 16, 1853, p. 1, col. 4.

111. *L'Abeille,* June 1, 1853, p. 1, col. 2; *The Bee,* June 3, 1853, p. 1, col. 10. Review (secondhand): *The Bee,* June 7, 1853, p. 1, col. 1.

112. The concert was originally scheduled for July 11 but postponed to July 18 owing to the weather; likewise the concert for July 25 was postponed to Aug. 1.

113. *L'Abeille,* June 18, 1853, p. 1, col. 10, and June 20, 1853, p. 1, col. 2; June 27, 1853, p. 1, cols 2 and 6; July 11, 1853, p. 1, col. 5, and July 18, 1853, p. 1, col. 7; July 23, 1853, p. 1, col. 8, and July 25, 1853, p. 1, col. 8; Aug. 1, 1853; Aug. 8, 1853, p. 1, col. 7; Aug. 15, 1853, p. 1, col. 7.

114. Ibid., June 20, 1853, p. 1, col. 2; *The Bee,* June 22, 1853, p. 1, cols. 1 and 9.

115. *L'Abeille,* Aug. 26, 1853, p. 1, col. 1.

116. "Yellow Fever Epidemics of New Orleans 1796–1853," in *Cohen's New Orleans Directory . . . for 1854;* and Carrigan, *The Saffron Scourge,* 80.

117. *L'Abeille,* Aug. 29, 1853, p. 1, col. 4.

118. *The Bee,* Sept. 22, 1853, p. 1, col. 1.

119. *L'Abeille,* Nov. 7, 1853, p. 1, col. 6. *The Bee,* Nov. 26, 1853, p. 1, col. 10.

120. *The Bee,* Nov. 12, 1853, p. 1, col. 10.

121. Ibid., Nov. 14, 1853, p. 1, col. 8.

122. *L'Abeille,* Oct. 18, 1853, p. 1, col. 3, and Oct. 20, 1853, p. 1, col. 8. See above, page 73.

123. *L'Abeille,* Dec. 27, 1853, p. 2, col. 2.

124. *The Bee,* Jan. 14, 1854, p. 1, col. 1.

125. *L'Abeille,* Jan. 31, 1854, p. 1, col. 2; *The Bee,* Jan. 31, 1854, p. 1, col. 1. For a reprint, see Starr, *Bamboula,* 157.

126. *L'Abeille,* Feb. 12, 1854, p. 2, col. 2; Feb. 15, 1854, p. 2, col. 2.

127. Ibid., Feb. 15, 1854, p. 1, col. 2.

128. *The Bee,* Apr. 28, 1853, p. 1, col. 5.

129. Ibid., Feb. 15, 1854, p. 1.

130. *L'Abeille,* Feb. 16, 1854, p. 2, col. 2.

131. *The Bee,* Mar. 7, 1854, p. 1, col. 9. *L'Abeille,* Feb. 24, 1854, p. 2, col. 2; Mar. 8, 1854, p. 2, col. 2.

132. *L'Abeille,* Mar. 7, 1854, p. 2, col. 2; Mar. 8, 1854, p. 1, col. 2.

133. *The Bee,* Mar. 21, 1854, p. 3, col. 10; Mar. 23, 1854, p. 3, col. 1.

134. *L'Abeille,* Feb. 14, 1854, p. 1, col. 2. See also *The Bee,* Feb. 17, 1854, p. 1, col. 1.

135. *The Bee,* Feb. 18, 1854, p. 1, col. 1.

136. Ibid., Dec. 13, 1852, p. 1, col. 4.

137. Slonimsky, *Concise Baker's Biographical Dictionary of Musicians,* 957. A *New York Times* article compared Sontag and Marietta Alboni: "Alboni sings in tune and Sontag is often sharp" (*L'Abeille,* Jan. 31, 1853, p. 1, col. 5). Critics in New Orleans found Alboni to be a serious singer more musical and less ornate than Sontag or Lind (*L'Abeille,* p. 1, col. 3, and Oct. 19, 1852, p. 1, col. 2).

138. *L'Abeille,* Feb. 15, 1854, p. 2, col. 2.

139. *The Bee,* Feb. 18, 1854, p. 1, col. 1.

140. Ibid., Feb. 18, 1854, p. 1, col. 1.

141. *L'Abeille,* May 2, 1854, p. 2, col. 2; May 8, 1854, p. 2, col. 2. *The Bee,* May 4, 1854, p. 2, col. 2.

142. *The Bee,* Nov. 18, 1854, p. 3, col. 1.

143. *L'Abeille,* Dec. 15, 1854, p. 4, col. 2; Dec. 18, 1854, p. 2, col. 2.

144. Ibid., Feb. 12, 1855, p. 1, col. 2. This is supposed to be her first concert in New Orleans, but no subsequent concerts are found. Also, the appearances of ads up to two days after her concert are either mistakes or postponements, perhaps because of weather.

145. The Théatre Pélican was in what was formerly Dan Rice's Amphitheater and continued programs that had originally been scheduled for the Varieties Theater (*The Bee,* Jan. 8, 1855, p. 1, col. 1).

146. *L'Abeille,* Feb. 28, 1855, p. 1, col. 2.

147. *The Bee,* Mar. 2, 1855, p. 1, col. 1.

148. Ibid., Mar. 10, 1855, p. 1, col. 3; Mar. 12, 1855, p. 1, col. 1; and Mar. 13, 1855, p. 1, col. 4; and *L'Abeille,* Mar. 10, 1855, p. 2, col. 2. Génibrel was sick, so Laget sang an extra aria. *The Bee,* Mar. 14, 1855, p. 1, col. 4. Review: *L'Abeille,* Mar. 15, 1855, p. 1, col. 3.

149. *L'Abeille,* Mar. 20, 1855, p. 2, col. 2.

150. Ibid., Mar. 20, 1855, p. 2, col. 2; *The Bee,* Mar. 27, 1855, p. 1, col. 10.

151. *The Bee,* May 5, 1855, p. 1, col. 1; *L'Abeille,* May 7, 1855, p. 1, col. 4; *Picayune,* May 6, 1855, p. 4, col. 2 and p. 7, col. 2.

152. *Picayune,* May 10, 1855, p. 3, col. 1; May 11, 1855, p. 2, col. 1; p. 3, col. 2.

153. *The Bee,* Mar. 8, 1855, p. 1, col. 10; review: still a favorite in New Orleans: Mar. 10, 1855, p. 1, col. 3; Mar. 12, 1855, p. 1, col. 4.

154. Ibid., Mar. 10, 1855, p. 1, col. 10, and Mar. 12, 1855, p. 1, col. 4; review: Mar. 13, 1855, p. 1, col. 4.

155. Ibid., Mar. 13, 1855, p. 1, col. 4; *L'Abeille,* Mar. 14, 1855, p. 2, col. 2.

156. *The Bee,* Mar. 24, 1855, p. 1, col. 4.

157. Ibid., Apr. 9, 1855, p. 1, col. 2; *L'Abeille,* Apr. 11, 1855, p. 2, col. 2. Review: *The Bee,* Apr. 12, 1855, p. 1, col. 4.

158. *L'Abeille,* May 22, 1855, p. 1, col. 3.

159. Ibid., May 22, 1855, p. 1, col. 3.

160. Trotter, *Music and Some Highly Musical People,* 188, confused some of his facts concerning the Classical Music Society. It was in rehearsal in 1855 but the first concert was on Jan. 16, 1856. The enlarged ensemble (the orchestra) appeared already in Nov. 1857.

161. *The Bee,* Jan. 15, 1856, p. 1, col. 10.

162. Ibid., Jan. 24, 1856, p. 1, col. 10.

163. *Picayune,* Feb. 20, 1856, p. 6, col. 1.

164. *L'Abeille,* Feb. 29, 1856, p. 2, col. 2. *Picayune,* Feb. 28, 1856, afternoon ed., p. 3, col. 1; Feb. 29, 1856. The advertisement in *L'Abeille* asserted that the program would include the choicest masterpieces of Haydn, Mozart, Beethoven, Weber, Gluck, Hummel, Mendelssohn, Spohr, Onslow, Rossini, Meyerbeer, and so forth, but this did not mean that works by all these composers would be performed on a single concert.

165. *Picayune,* Mar. 7, 1856, p. 4, col. 1.

166. *L'Abeille,* Apr. 4, 1856, p. 1, col. 1; *Picayune,* Apr. 4,1856, p. 4, col. 1.

167. *Picayune,* Jan. 2, 1856, p. 4, col. 1.

168. Ibid., Jan. 3, 1856, p. 4, col. 1.

169. *The Bee,* Jan. 5, 1856, p. 2, col. 2; Jan. 16, 1856, p.1, cols. 1 and 10. *L'Abeille,* Jan. 7, 1856, p. 1, col. 3; Jan. 11, 1856, p. 2, col. 2; Jan. 12, 1856, p. 1, col. 3; Jan. 14, 1856, p. 1, col. 4; Jan. 15, 1856, p. 1, col. 3; Jan. 16, 1856, p. 2, col. 2; Jan. 18, 1856, p. 2, col. 2; Feb. 8, 1856, p. 2, col. 2; Feb. 11, 1856, p. 1, col. 3; Feb. 12, 1856, p. 2, col. 2.; Feb. 14, 1856, p. 2, col. 2; Feb. 18, 1856, p. 2, col. 2; Feb. 20, 1856, p. 1, col. 2; p. 2, col. 2; Feb. 22, 1856, p. 2, col. 2.

170. *The Bee,* Feb. 7, 1856, p. 1, col. 2.

171. *Picayune,* Jan. 5, 1856, p. 4, col. 1.

172. *The Bee,* Mar. 20, 1856, p. 1, col. 8; Mar. 24, 1856, p. 1, col. 8; Mar. 29, 1856, p. 1, col. 8; Mar. 31, 1856, p. 1, col. 1; p. 2, col. 2; Apr. 1, 1856, p. 2, col. 2. *L'Abeille,* Mar. 31, 1856, p. 1, col. 2; Mar. 31, 1856, p. 2, col. 2.

173. Ibid., Mar. 31, 1856, p. 1, col. 1.

174. Ibid., Mar. 20, 1856, p. 1, col. 8; Mar. 31, 1856, p. 2, col. 2; Apr. 1, 1856, p. 1, col. 8. *L'Abeille,* Apr. 1, 1856, p. 2, col. 2; Apr. 2, 1856, p. 1, col. 2.

175. *Picayune,* Apr. 25, 1856, p. 5, col. 3.

176. Ibid., Apr. 2, 1856. *L'Abeille,* Apr. 2, 1856, p. 1, col. 2.

177. *The Bee,* Apr. 10, 1856, p. 1, col. 8.

178. Ibid., Apr. 23, 1856, p. 1, col. 8.

179. *L'Abeille,* May 12, 1856, p. 2, col. 2.

180. *New Orleans Daily Creole,* Nov. 5, 1856, p. 3, col. 3; Nov. 28, 1856, p. 2, col. 1; p. 3, col. 3.

181. Ibid., Dec. 12, 1856, p. 2, col. 1; Dec. 20, 1856, p. 2, col. 1.

182. For some description of the operas at the Gaiety Theater, see *The Bee,* Apr. 8, 1857, p. 3, col. 1; Apr. 14, 1857, p. 3, col. 1; Apr. 17, 1857, p. 3, col. 5; Apr. 18, 1857, p. 3, col. 1; May 6, 1857, p. 3, col. 1; May 19, 1857, p. 3, col. 1; May 20, 1857, p. 3, col. 1; May 26, 1857, p. 3, col. 1; May 30, 1857, p. 3, col. 1. *L'Abeille,* Apr. 11, 1857, p. 2, col. 3; Apr. 20, 1857, p. 1, col. 2; May 18, 1857, p. 3, col. 1; May 19, 1857, p. 2, col. 2. For a comparison of Verdi's *Il Trovatore* at the Théâtre d'Orléans and the Gaiety Theater, see *The Bee,* Apr. 17, 1857, p. 3, col. 1.

183. *Picayune,* Jan. 29, 1857, p. 4, col. 1.

184. *L'Abeille,* Feb. 7, 1857, p. 2, col. 2.

185. Ibid., Feb. 5, 1857, p. 2, col. 2. *The Bee,* Feb. 11, 1857, p. 3, col. 1.

186. *The Bee,* Feb. 20, 1857, p. 3, col. 1; Feb. 25, 1857, p. 1, col. 10.

187. *L'Union,* Feb. 25, 1857, p. 2, col. 4.

188. Ibid., Feb. 28, 1857, p. 2, col. 4.

189. *The Bee,* Feb. 27, 1857, p. 1, col. 10.

190. *L'Union,* Mar. 1, 1857, p. 1, col. 6. *The Bee,* Mar. 2, 1857, p. 1, col. 10.

191. *L'Union,* Mar. 6, 1857, p. 3, col. 2. *The Bee,* Mar. 5, 1857, p. 1, col. 7.

192. *L'Abeille,* Mar. 10, 1857, p. 1, col. 2; Mar. 12, 1857, p. 2, col. 2.

193. Ibid., Apr. 2, 1857, p. 3, col. 2. *The Bee,* Apr. 3, 1857, p. 3, col. 1.

194. *L'Abeille,* Mar. 12, 1857, p. 1, col. 2; Mar. 16, 1857, p. 2, col. 2; Mar. 18, 1857, p. 2, col. 2; *The Bee,* Mar. 19, 1857, p. 3, col. 1. There is an extensive review of LaGrange's performances by A[lbert] F[abre] in *L'Abeille,* Mar. 23, 1857, p. 1, col. 5.

195. *The Bee,* Apr. 22, 1857, p. 3, col. 9.

196. Ibid., June 22, 1857, p. 3, col. 1.

197. Ibid., Apr. 27, 1857. *L'Abeille,* Apr. 28, 1857, p. 1, col. 3; Apr. 29, 1857, p. 1, col. 4; Apr. 30, 1857, p. 3, col. 4; May 4, 1857, p. 1, cols 4–5.

198. *Picayune,* Nov. 23, 1857, p. 4, col. 2; Nov. 27, 1857, p. 2, col. 2.

199. Ibid., Jan. 17, 1858, p. 1, col. 4.

200. *L'Abeille,* Feb. 22, 1858, p. 2, col. 2.

201. Ibid., Feb. 19, 1858, p. 1, col. 2.

202. Ibid., Feb. 2, 1858, p. 2, col. 2. Data on the first concert is missing.

203. Ibid., Mar. 11, 1858, p. 2, col. 2.

204. *The Bee,* Mar. 13, 1858, p. 2, col. 2.

205. *Picayune,* Mar. 31, 1858, afternoon ed., p. 1, col. 3.

206. *The Bee,* May 12, 1858, p. 2, col. 2; May 14, 1858, p. 1, col. 1; *L'Abeille,* May 12, 1858, p. 2, col. 2.

207. *L'Abeille,* May 14, 1858, p. 1, col. 3.

208. The review appeared in the *Picayune,* Dec. 9, 1858, afternoon ed., p. 1, col. 5.

209. *The Bee,* Feb. 14, 1859, p. 1, col. 10.

210. Ibid., Feb. 19, 1859, p. 1, col. 10; Feb. 22, 1859, p. 1, col. 10; Feb. 22, 1859, p. 1, col. 10. *Picayune,* Feb. 23, 1859, p. 1, col. 2.

211. *The Bee,* Feb. 19, 1859, p. 1, col. 10; Feb. 25, 1859, p. 1, col. 10; Feb. 26, 1859, p. 1, col. 10.

212. *L'Abeille,* Feb. 21, 1859, p. 2, col. 2.

213. Ibid., Mar. 12, 1859, p. 2, col. 2.

214. *The Bee,* Mar. 8, 1859, p. 1, col. 10; Mar. 9, 1859, p. 1, col. 10.

215. Ibid., Feb. 14, 1859, p. 1, col. 10; Mar. 9, 1859, p. 1, col. 10. *L'Abeille,* Mar. 12, 1859, p. 2, col. 2.

216. *The Bee,* Mar. 9, 1859, p. 1, col. 10.

217. Ibid., Apr. 5, 1859, p. 1, col. 10; Apr. 14, 1859, p. 1, col. 2; p. 1, col. 10; Apr. 19, 1859, p. 1, col. 1. Reviews: Apr. 20, 1859, p. 1, col. 1; Apr. 22, 1859, p. 1, col. 1.

218. Ibid., Apr. 21, 1859, p. 1, col. 10; Apr. 25, 1859, p. 1, col. 1; Apr. 26, 1859, p. 1, col. 9; Apr. 28, 1859, p. 1, col. 9.

219. *Picayune,* Mar. 1, 1859, p. 1, col. 3.

220. Ibid., Apr. 15, 1859, p. 1, col. 3.

221. *The Bee,* Apr. 14, 1859, p. 1, col. 1; p. 1, col. 10; Apr. 18, 1859, p. 1, col. 2. *L'Abeille,* Apr. 19, 1859, p. 1, col. 2.

222. *The Bee,* Apr. 23, 1859, p. 1, col. 1.

223. Ibid., Feb. 25, 1859, p. 1, col. 7.

224. Ibid., Apr. 23, 1859, p. 1, col. 1.

225. *Picayune,* Jan. 11, 1860.

226. Ibid., Dec. 1, 1859, p. 1, col. 2.

227. Ibid., Nov. 30, 1859, p. 1, col. 2 and p. 6, col. 1.

228. Ibid., Dec. 7, 1859, p. 1, col. 2; Dec. 8, 1859, supplement, p. (?) col. 3.

229. *L'Abeille,* Jan. 25, 1860, p. 2, col. 3. *The Bee,* Jan. 20, 1860, p. 2, col. 10; Jan. 27, 1860, p. 1, col. 1.

230. *L'Abeille,* Feb. 2, 1860, p. 2, col. 2; Feb. 9, 1860, p. 2, col. 2; Feb. 10, 1860, p. 2, col. 4; Feb. 13, 1860, p. 2, col. 3; Feb. 15, 1860, p. 2, col. 2; Feb. 16, 1860, p. 2, col. 2.

231. Ibid., Mar. 5, 1860, p. 1, col. 3; p. 2, col. 2; Mar. 10, 1860, p. 2, col. 3. *The Bee,* Mar. 5, 1860, p. 3, col. 2; Mar. 7, 1860, p. 3, col. 1.

232. Thomas Wiggins, 1849–1908. See *John Davis Plays Blind Tom The Eighth Wunder,* compact disc, Newport Classic NPD 85660 (Newport, RI, 1999). Tom was "owned" for most of his life by the Bethune family.

233. *L'Abeille,* Mar. 5, 1860, p. 1, col. 3; p. 2, col. 2.

234. Ibid., Mar. 22, 1860, p. 2, col. 3.

235. Ibid., Mar. 23, 1860, p. 1, col. 1; p. 2, col. 2; Mar. 31, 1860, p. 2, col. 3; Apr. 10, 1860, p. 2, col. 2; Apr. 11, 1860, p. 2, col. 3.

236. Verdi wrote the title role of *Luisa Miller* for her. It is unknown whether she is descended from Giuseppe Gazzaniga, the eighteenth-century opera composer.

237. *L'Abeille,* Mar. 31, 1860, p. 2, col. 3.

238. *The Bee,* Apr. 2, 1860, p. 3, col. 1; Apr. 3, 1860, p. 3, col. 1; Apr. 4, 1860, p. 3, col. 1. *L'Abeille,* Apr. 3, 1860, p. 2, col. 3.

239. *L'Abeille,* Apr. 6, 1860, p. 1, col. 1.

240. Ibid., Apr. 9, 1860, p. 1, col. 1; p. 2, col. 2.

241. Ibid., Apr. 11, 1860, p. 2, col. 3.

242. *Drapeau de l'Ascension,* Apr. 14, 1860, as cited in *L'Abeille,* Apr. 17, 1860, p. 1, col. 3.

243. *L'Abeille,* Apr. 21, 1860, p. 2, col. 3; *Picayune,* Apr. 29, 1860, third section, p. 1, col. 2.
244. Ibid., Apr. 17, 1860, p. 1, col. 2.
245. *Picayune,* Nov. 18, 1860, p. 6, col. 1; Nov. 20, 1860, p. 2, col. 4.
246. Ibid., Nov. 25, 1860, p. 8, col. 1. See also *L'Abeille,* Oct. 25, 1860.
247. *L'Abeille,* Nov. 19, 1860.
248. See Belsom, "Enroute to Stardom," 113–30.

CHAPTER FOUR

1. *The Bee,* Feb. 4, 1861, p. 1, col. 3.
2. *L'Abeille,* May 15, 1861.
3. *Picayune,* May 2, 1861, p. 2, col. 5.
4. *L'Abeille,* Oct. 21, 1861, p. 1, col. 7.
5. Ibid., Oct. 29, 1861, p. 1, col. 6; review: Oct. 30, 1861, p. 1, col. 1.
6. Ibid., Nov. 7, 1861, p. 1, col. 9.
7. Ibid., Dec. 4, 1861, p. 1, col. 2.
8. Ibid., Dec. 9, 1861, p. 2, col. 4; review: Dec. 19, 1861, p. 1, col. 2.
9. Ibid., Dec. 21, 1861, p. 1, col. 7; review: Dec. 25, 1861, p. 1, col. 3.
10. Ibid., Dec. 15, 1861, p. 1, col. 2.
11. *The Bee,* Jan. 1, 1862, p. 1, col. 7, and Jan. 3, 1862, p. 1, col. 3.
12. *L'Abeille,* Jan. 20,1862, p. 1, col. 2. *The Bee,* Jan. 30, 1862, p. 1, col. 3.
13. *The Bee,* Apr. 9, 1862, p. 1, col. 6.
14. *L'Abeille,* Aug. 12, 1862, p. 1, col. 4.
15. Ibid., May 30, 1862, p. 1, col. 1.
16. Ibid., June 4, 1862, p. 1, col. 2.
17. Ibid., June 21, 1862, p. 1, col. 2.
18. Ibid., July 5, 1862, p. 1, col. 2.
19. Ibid., July 21, 1862, p. 1, col. 3; July 22, 1862, p. 1, col. 1; and July 26, 1862, p. 1, col. 2; review: July 28, 1862, p. 1, cols. 2–3, and correction: July 29, 1862, p. 1, col. 2.
20. *The Bee,* Aug. 14, 1862, p. 1, col. 1. Review: *L'Abeille,* Aug. 16, 1862, p. 1, col. 2.
21. *The Bee,* Oct. 14, 1862, p. 1, col. 1. Review: Oct. 21, 1862, p. 1, col. 1.
22. *L'Abeille,* Oct. 30, 1862, p. 1, cols 1 and 6.
23. Ibid., Nov. 15, 1862, p. 1, col. 2; review: Nov. 18, 1862, p. 1, col. 2.
24. Ibid., Dec. 1, 1862, p. 1, col. 2.
25. Ibid., Dec. 16, 1862, p. 1, cols. 3 and 7; *The Bee,* Dec. 24, 1862, p. 1, col. 1.
26. *L'Abeille,* Dec. 27, 1862, p. 1, col. 2.
27. *The Bee,* Jan. 15, 1862, p. 1, col. 7.
28. Ibid., Jan. 24, 1863, p. 1, col. 7, and Jan. 27, 1863, p. 1, col. 4.
29. For example, the second ball of the season took place on Friday, Feb. 6, 1862: "the complete orchestra of the Theatre d'Orleans will execute the newest dances" under the direction of Predigam (*L'Abeille,* Feb. 6, 1863, p. 1, col. 7).
30. *The Bee,* Apr. 1, 1863, p. 1, col. 7.
31. *L'Abeille,* Feb. 9, 1863, p. 1, col. 7, and *The Bee,* Feb. 12, 1863, p. 1, col. 1.
32. *The Bee,* Feb. 14, 1863, p. 1, col. 1.
33. Ibid., Feb. 16, 1863, p. 1, col. 1, and Feb. 17, 1863, p. 1, col. 1; *L'Abeille,* Feb. 18, 1863, p. 1, col. 1.
34. *The Bee,* Mar. 9, 1863, p. 1, col. 8.
35. Ibid., Mar. 16, 1863, p. 1, col. 8.

36. *L'Abeille,* Feb. 28, 1863.
37. *The Bee,* Mar. 23, 1863, p. 1, col. 9.
38. *L'Abeille,* Mar. 23, 1863, p. 1, col. 7, and Mar. 27, 1863, p. 1, col. 2.
39. *The Bee,* Apr. 1, 1863, p. 1, col. 7.
40. Ibid., Apr. 9, 1863, p. 1, col. 1.
41. *L'Abeille,* Apr. 29, 1863, p. 1, col. 2, and *The Bee,* Apr. 30, 1863, p. 1, col. 1.
42. *The Bee,* Apr. 29, 1863, p. 1, col. 1. French version: *L'Abeille,* Apr. 29, 1863, p. 1, col. 2, and May 1, 1863, p. 1, col. 2. *The Bee,* May 5, 1863, p. 1, col. 1. There is no indication of the fifth performer in the quintet.
43. *The Bee,* Apr. 20, 1863, p. 1, col. 1; Apr. 30, 1863, p. 1, cols. 1 and 5. *L'Abeille,* May 1, 1863, p. 1, col. 7.
44. *L'Abeille,* June 5, 1863, p. 1, col. 5.
45. Ibid., June 9, 1863, p. 1, col. 7.
46. Ibid., Sept. 12, 1863, p. 1, col. 2.
47. Ibid., Sept. 24, 1863, p. 1, col. 7.
48. Ibid., Sept. 30, 1863, p. 1, col. 6, and Oct. 3, 1863, p. 1, col. 2.
49. *The Bee,* Sept. 29, 1863, p. 1, col. 1. *L'Abeille,* Oct. 7, 1863, p. 1, col. 5; review: Oct. 8, 1863, p. 1, col. 3.
50. *L'Abeille,* Oct. 10, 1863, p. 1, col. 8.
51. Ibid., Oct. 24, 1863, p. 1, col. 8.
52. Ibid., Nov. 13, 1863, p. 1, col. 2.
53. Ibid., Nov. 26, 1863, p. 1, col. 3.
54. *The Bee,* Dec. 31, 1863, p. 1, col. 6.
55. Ibid., Jan. 22, 1864, p. 1, col. 1, and Jan. 26, 1864, p. 1, col. 6.
56. During Mar. the St. Charles Theater had impressive theater. On Mar. 16, 1864, John Wilkes Booth began a run in *Richard III* and other plays by other playwrights (*The Bee,* Mar. 16, 1864, p. 1, col. 3).
57. *L'Abeille,* Feb. 5, 1864, p. 2, col. 3.
58. Ibid., Mar. 29, 1864, p. 2, col. 3; Apr. 9, 1864, p. 1, cols. 2 and 5; Apr. 22, 1864, p. 1, col. 3.
59. Ibid., Mar. 15, 1864, p. 1, col. 2; Apr. 22, 1864, p. 1, col. 3; May 7, 1864, p. 1, col. 2. *The Bee,* Apr. 14, 1864, p. 1, cols. 1 and 6; Apr. 16, 1864, p. 1, col. 6, Apr. 18, 1864, p. 1, cols. 1 and 5.
60. *L'Abeille,* May 12, 1864, p. 1, col. 7.
61. Ibid., June 15, 1864, p. 1, col. 2; review: June 18, 1864, p. 1, col. 3.
62. *The Bee,* July 7, 1864, p. 1, col. 1.
63. *L'Abeille,* May 7, 1864, p. 1, col. 7.
64. *The Bee,* Jan. 22, 1864, p. 1, col. 1, and Jan. 26, p. 1, col. 6.
65. *L'Abeille,* Sept. 9, 1864, p. 1, col. 2; Sept. 11, 1864, p. 1, col. 2. *The Bee,* Sept. 15, 1864, p. 1, col. 1; Sept. 16, 1864, p. 1, col. 5; and Sept. 19, 1864, p. 1, col. 1; review: Sept. 14, 1864, p. 1, col. 3; Sept. 21, 1864, p. 1, col. 3. *L'Abeille,* Sept. 21, 1864, p. 1, cols. 1–2.
66. *L'Abeille,* Oct. 6, 1864, p. 1, col. 7. *The Bee,* Oct. 20, 1864, p. 1, col. 6; Oct. 29, 1864, p. 1, col. 6. The second performance was originally scheduled for Oct. 27.
67. *L'Abeille,* Nov. 22, 1864, p. 1, col. 5.
68. *The Bee,* Nov. 11, 1864, p. 1, col. 1.
69. Ibid., Nov. 28, 1864, p. 1, col. 1. Review *L'Abeille,* Dec. 2, 1864, p. 1, col. 2.
70. *L'Abeille,* Dec. 14, 1864, p. 1, col. 6.
71. *The Bee,* Dec. 24, 1864, p. 1, col. 1. *L'Abeille,* Dec. 26, 1864, p. 1, col. 2.
72. *The Bee,* Dec. 23, 1864, p. 1, col. 1. *L'Abeille,* Jan. 1, 1864, p. 1, col. 2.
73. *L'Abeille,* Jan. 1, 1865, p. 1, col. 2.

74. Ibid., Nov. 4, 1864, p. 1, col. 2.

75. *The Bee,* Jan. 8, 1865, p. 1, col. 1.

76. Ibid., Jan. 8, 1865, p. 1, col. 1.

77. Ibid., Jan. 18, 1865, p. 1, col. 3.

78. *L'Abeille,* Feb. 22, 1865, p. 1, col. 6.

79. Ibid., Mar. 14, 1865, p. 2, col. 3, and *The Bee,* Apr. 7, 1865, p. 1, col. 1, and Apr. 10, 1865, p. 1, col. 3. See page 43 for more details on this concert.

CHAPTER FIVE

1. *L'Abeille,* Apr. 14, 1865, p. 1, col. 7.

2. *The Bee,* Apr. 5, 1865, p. 1, col. 1. *L'Abeille,* Apr. 14, 1865, p. 1, col. 7; review: Apr. 19, 1865, p. 1, col. 1.

3. *L'Abeille,* Apr. 19, 1865, p. 1, col. 1; May 1, 1865, p. 1, col. 1; May 1, 1865, p. 1, col. 8; *The Bee,* May 4, 1865, p. 1, col. 1.

4. *L'Abeille,* May 17, 1865, p. 1, col. 2; May 26, 1865, p. 1, col. 2; *The Bee,* May 17, 1865, p. 1, col. 1. Review: *L'Abeille,* May 26, 1865, p. 1, col. 2.

5. *L'Abeille,* May 1, 1865, p. 1, col. 8.

6. *The Bee,* May 16, 1865, p. 1, col. 8.

7. *L'Abeille,* May 29, 1865, p. 1, col. 8, and May 30, 1865, p. 1, col. 2. The newspaper ad gives the composer as Paillant. Long review: *L'Abeille,* June 3, 1865, p. 1, col. 2.

8. *The Bee,* May 16, 1865, p. 1, col. 8, and *L'Abeille,* May 22, 1865, p. 1, col. 2.

9. *L'Abeille,* May 19, 1865, p. 1, col. 3.

10. Ibid., May 30, 1865, p. 1, col. 6. Charles died the following year.

11. Ibid., June 5, 1865, p. 1, col. 8.

12. Ibid., June 6, 1865, p. 1, col. 6. Gessner was born ca. 1828 and died in New Orleans in 1869 (*Picayune,* Oct. 29, 1869, p. 4, col. 3; Oct. 31, 1869, p. 12, col. 3). See city directories, 1849–68.

13. *The Bee,* June 6, 1865, p. 1, col. 1. Review: *L'Abeille,* June 10, 1865, p. 1, col. 3.

14. *L'Abeille,* June 20, 1865, p. 1, col. 2.

15. *The Bee,* Apr. 24, 1865, p. 1, col. 1.

16. Ibid., June 27, 1865, p. 1, col. 1. However, Charles died in 1866.

17. *L'Abeille,* Dec. 11, 1865, p. 1, col. 2.

18. Ibid., Oct. 26, 1865, p. 1, col. 3.

19. Ibid., Dec. 18, 1865, p. 1, col. 1.

20. Ibid., Jan. 9, 1866, p. 1, col. 2; Jan. 14, 1866, p. 4, col. 2.

21. *New Orleans Daily Crescent,* Jan. 14, 1866, p. 4, col. 2; Jan. 19, 1866, p. 4, col. 1.

22. *Times,* Apr. 27, 1866, p. 14, col. 4; Apr. 28, 1866, p. 10, col. 4; May 1, 1866, p. 3, col. 6. Review: *Times Auctioners' Supplement,* May 2, 1866, p. 1, col. 2.

23. *The Bee,* Dec. 27, 1865, p. 1, col. 1; *L'Abeille,* Dec. 29, 1865, p. 2, col. 3. *Daily Crescent,* May 16, 1866, p. 4, col. 1.

24. *Times,* May 5, 1866, p. 3, col. 5; May 6, 1866, p. 10, col. 5; May 9, 1866, p. 10, cols. 1 and 6; May 10, 1866, p. 10, col. 1; May 11, 1866, p. 10, col. 2; May 12, 1866, p. 3, col. 2. *Daily Crescent,* May 9, 1866, p. 4, col. 1.

25. *Daily Crescent,* Jan. 16, 1866, p. 4, col. 1.

26. Ibid., Jan. 20, 1866, p. 4, col. 1.

27. *Times,* May 12, 1866, p. 3, col. 2. *Daily Crescent,* May 12, 1866, p. 4, col. 1.

28. *Daily Crescent,* Jan. 16, 1866, p. 4, col. 4.

29. *L'Abeille,* Nov. 2, 1866, p. 2, col. 2.

30. Ibid., Mar. 21, 1866, p. 2, col. 2.

31. Ibid., Nov. 16, 1866, p. 1, col. 2.

32. Ibid., Nov. 2, 1866, p. 2, col. 2; Nov. 5, 1866, p. 1, col. 1; and Nov. 8, 1866, p. 1, col. 2.

33. Ibid., Nov. 16, 1866, p. 1, col. 2. Review of *L'Africaine*: Nov. 19, 1866, p. 1, col. 3 and especially col. 5.

34. A detailed history of the French Opera House from its inception to 1873 can be found in *L'Abeille*, Feb. 23, 1873, p. 2, col. 1.

35. *L'Abeille*, Nov. 12, 1866, p. 2, col. 2, and Nov. 16, p. 2, col. 3.

36. Ibid., Dec. 9, 1866, p. 1, col. 2.

37. Ibid., Nov. 16, 1866, p. 1, col. 2; Nov. 29, p. 1, col. 2; and Jan. 8, 1867, p. 1, col. 1.

38. Ibid., Jan. 9, 1867, p. 1, col. 2.

39. *The Bee,* Nov. 22, 1866, p. 1, col. 1.

40. *L'Abeille*, Nov. 22, 1866, p. 2, col. 3.

41. Ibid., Dec. 4, 1866, p. 1, col. 1.

42. *L'Abeille*, Feb. 15, 1867, p. 1, col. 2. The operas performed at the National Theater included *La Traviata, La Favorita, Norma, Il Trovatore, Ione, Martha,* and *Rigoletto.*

43. Ibid., Mar. 27, 1867, p. 1, col. 2.

44. Ibid., Nov. 2, 1867, p. 1, col. 10, and Nov. 14, 1867, p. 2, col. 3.

45. Ibid., Dec. 18, 1866, p. 2, col. 2.

46. Ibid., Nov. 15, 1867, p. 1, col. 3; Nov. 17, 1867, p. 1, col. 2; and Nov. 22, 1867, p. 1, col. 2. See also *The Bee,* Nov. 22, 1867, p. 1, col. 1, and Nov. 23, 1867, p. 1, col. 1.

47. For an appraisal of the short season and its value to rejuvenating opera in the city, see *The Bee,* Feb. 2, 1866, p. 1, col. 1, and *L'Abeille,* Feb. 3, 1866, p. 1, col. 2. The Italian opera season of Strakosch ended on Feb. 1, 1866, and the troupe was off to Mobile.

48. *L'Abeille,* Nov. 8, 1866, p. 1, col. 2.

49. *The Bee,* Nov. 26, 1867, p. 1, col. 2.

50. Ibid., Dec. 24, 1867, p. 1, col. 1.

51. A description of the hall after the war is given in *The Bee,* Dec. 4, 1865, p. 1, col. 1, written upon completion of the renovation.

52. *L'Abeille,* Oct. 10, 1865, p. 1, col. 10.

53. Ibid., Dec. 5, 1865, p. 1, col. 4, and Dec. 7, 1865, p. 1, col. 1.

54. *The Bee,* Nov. 18, 1865, p. 1, col. 1.

55. *L'Abeille,* Dec. 13, 1865, p. 1, col. 2.

56. *Picayune,* Jan. 4, 1866, p. 6, col. 3; *Daily Crescent,* Jan. 5, 1866, p. 4, col. 1.

57. *Times,* Feb. 9, 1866, p. 2, col. 2. *Picayune,* Feb. 11, 1866, p. 12, col. 2; Apr. 8, 1866. *Daily Crescent,* Apr. 17, 1866, p. 4, col. 4.

58. *L'Abeille,* Apr. 14, 1865, p. 1, col. 7.

59. *The Bee,* May 16, 1865, p. 1, col. 8.

60. *L'Abeille,* May 1, 1865, p. 1, col. 8.

61. Ibid., May 29, 1865, p. 1, col. 8; May 30, 1865, p. 1, col. 2; and June 3, 1865, p. 1, col. 2.

62. Ibid., May 3, 1867, p. 1, col. 2.

63. Ibid., Apr. 26, 1867, p. 2, col. 3; May 1, 1867, p. 2, col. 3; and May 2, p. 1, col. 2. *The Bee,* May 2, 1867, p. 1, col. 1.

64. This may be the publisher S. H. Goetzel of Mobile, who spent some time in New Orleans.

65. *L'Abeille,* May 1, 1867, p. 1, col. 2.

66. Ibid., Apr. 26, 1867, p. 2, col. 3; Apr. 28, 1867, p. 1, col. 2.

67. Ibid., Dec. 15, 1867, p. 1, col. 3 and p. 2, col. 3; *The Bee,* Dec. 21, 1867, p. 1, col. 1; *Picayune,* Dec. 14, 1867, p. 5, col. 4.

68. *L'Abeille,* Jan. 18, 1868, p. 1, col. 1.

69. For example, see *L'Abeille,* Dec. 7, 1867, p. 2, col. 4.

70. For example, on Wednesday, May 27, 1868, at St. Alphonse's Hall to benefit the sisters of St. Elizabeth and repeated the following June 29 at St. Patrick's Church in honor of the Pope, members of the French Opera Orchestra joined all the church choirs of the city combined and many other amateur singers, totaling one hundred voices, in a performance of Mozart's Mass No. 12. La Hache conducted. (*Morning Star,* May 10, 1868, p. 4, col. 1; May 24, 1868, p. 5, col. 1; review May 31, 1868, p. 4, col. 1; June 21, 1868, p. 4, col. 2; June 28, 1868, p. 4, col. 2.)

71. *L'Abeille,* Nov. 2, 1867, p. 1, col. 10; Nov. 14, 1867, p. 2, col. 3.

72. Ibid., Nov. 15, 1867, p. 1, col. 3; review: Nov. 22, 1867, p. 1, col. 2. *The Bee,* Nov. 22, 1867, p. 3, col. 1; Nov. 23, 1867, p. 3, col. 1.

73. *L'Abeille,* Dec. 7, 1867, p. 2, col. 4.

74. *The Bee,* Nov. 26, 1867, p. 1, col. 2.

75. *L'Abeille,* Oct. 26, 1867, p. 1, col. 2; Nov. 7, 1867, p. 1, col. 2; Nov. 10, 1867, p. 1, col. 1; Nov. 17, 1867, p. 1, col. 2.

76. Ibid., Dec. 8, 1867, p. 1, col. 2.

77. Ibid., Nov. 6, 1867, p. 1, col. 1; review: Dec. 11, 1867, p. 1, col. 2.

78. Ibid., Jan. 1, 1868, p. 2, col. 3.

79. *Picayune,* Dec. 14, 1867, p. 5, col. 4.

80. *L'Abeille,* Dec. 15, 1867, p. 1, col. 3. Or Dec. 14 (?). Review: *The Bee,* Dec. 21, 1867, p. 1, col. 1.

81. *L'Abeille,* Jan. 12, 1868, p. 1, col. 3; Jan. 16, 1868, p. 1, col. 3; Jan. 5, 1868, p. 1, col. 2; Jan. 19, 1868, p. 1, col. 2. *The Bee,* Jan. 14, 1868, p. 1, col. 1.

82. *L'Abeille,* Jan. 17, 1868, p. 2, col. 2; Jan. 28, 1868, p. 1, col. 3.

83. Ibid., Jan. 28, 1868, p. 1, col. 3; Feb. 6, 1868, p. 1, col. 3; review: Feb. 8, 1868, p. 1, col. 2.

84. Ibid., Feb. 18, 1868, p. 2, col. 2; Feb. 21, 1868, p. 2, col. 2; Feb. 22, 1868, p. 1, col. 2; *The Bee,* Feb. 21, 1868, p. 1, col. 1.

85. *L'Abeille,* Mar. 8, 1868, p. 1, col. 2.

86. Ibid., Mar. 27, 1868, p. 1, col. 2.

87. *Times,* Apr. 2, 1868, p. 2, col. 4.

88. Ibid., Apr. 11, 1868, p. 4, col. 5; Apr. 12, 1868, p. 2, col. 2 and p. 5, col. 6.

89. Ibid., Apr. 11, 1868, p. 4, col. 5; Apr. 11, 1868, p. 4, col. 5; Apr. 12, 1868, p. 5, col. 6.

90. Ibid., Apr. 8, 1868, p. 1, col. 3; Apr. 19, 1868, p. 2, col. 4; Apr. 24, 1868, p. 2, col. 1. Review: Apr. 25, 1868, p. 1, col. 3.

91. Ibid., May 7, 1868, p. 5, col. 6.

92. *L'Abeille,* Jan. 18, 1868, p. 1, col. 1.

93. Ibid., Jan. 5, 1868, p. 1, col. 2.

94. Ibid., Jan. 29, 1868, p. 1, col. 2.

95. *The Bee,* Feb. 4, 1868, p. 1, col. 1; Feb. 20, 1868, p. 1, col. 1. *L'Abeille,* Feb. 22, 1868, p. 1, col. 2.

96. *L'Abeille,* Mar. 15, 1868, p. 2, col. 3; concert originally (?) slated for Mar. 19: Feb. 27, 1868, p. 2, col. 3; Mar. 4, 1868, p. 2, col. 2.

97. Ibid., Mar. 21, 1868, p. 1, col. 2.

98. *Times,* Apr. 3, 1868, p. 4, col. 3.

99. Ibid., Apr. 19, 1868, p. 5, col. 6; p. 10, col. 2; review: Apr. 21, 1868, p. 4, col. 3.

100. Ibid., Apr. 28, 1868, p. 2, col. 3.

101. Review: *Times,* May 5, 1868, p. 8, col. 1.

102. *Times,* Apr. 19, 1868, p. 5, col. 6.

103. Ibid., Apr. 21, 1868, p. 3, col. 6.

104. Ibid., Apr. 29, 1868, p. 2, col. 5; May 2, 1868, p. 3, col. 5. (A dance band<<?>>)

105. Probably Charles Bothe. There was no known musician A. Bothe at any time during the nineteenth century in New Orleans.

106. *Times,* May 2, 1868, p. 3, col. 4.
107. Ibid., Apr. 12, 1868, p. 2, col. 2; program: May 3, 1868, p. 3, col. 5; May 5, 1868, p. 5, col. 6.
108. Ibid., Apr. 26, 1868, p. 1, col. 6.
109. Ibid., Apr. 30, 1868, p. 1, col. 3; May 2, 1868, p. 1, col. 3; May 3, 1868, p. 3, col. 5.
110. Ibid., May 5, 1868, p. 8, col. 1; May 7, 1868, p. 5, col. 6; May 8, 1868, p. 4, col. 4.
111. Ibid., May 6, 1868, p. 1, col. 5.
112. *Morning Star,* June 7, 1868; p. 4, col. 1; p. 5, col. 5.
113. *Dwight's Journal,* Feb. 29, 1868, quoted in Irving Sablosky, *What They Heard in America 1852–1881* (Baton Rouge: Louisiana State University Press, 1986), 159. Full text: *Times,* May 7, 1868, p. 2, cols. 4–5.
114. *L'Abeille,* Nov. 10, 1868, p. 1, col. 2.
115. *The Bee,* Nov. 14, 1868, p. 1, col. 1.
116. *L'Abeille,* Dec. 30, 1868, p. 1, col. 2.
117. *The Bee,* Nov. 14, 1868, p. 1, col. 1; *L'Abeille,* Nov. 12, 1868, p. 2, col. 4.
118. *The Bee,* Nov. 13, 1868, p. 1, col. 1. Opening postponed because the lead tenor got sick.
119. Ibid., Nov. 13, 1868, p. 1, col. 1.
120. *L'Abeille,* Nov. 22, 1868, p. 2, col. 4 and p. 1, col. 3; *Morning Star,* Nov. 22, 1868, p. 4, col. 4.
121. *L'Abeille,* Jan. 1, 1869, p. 2, col. 4.
122. Ibid., Jan. 9, 1869, p. 3, col. 1.
123. Ibid., Jan. 13, 1869, p. 1, col. 2.
124. Ibid., Jan. 13, 1869, p. 2, col. 4.
125. *The Bee,* Jan. 15, 1869, p. 1, col. 1. Review: *L'Abeille,* Jan. 20, 1869, p. 1, col. 3.
126. *The Bee,* Feb. 2, 1869, p. 1, col. 9.
127. *L'Abeille,* Feb. 3, 1869, p. 2, col. 4.
128. Ibid., Feb. 4, 1869, p. 2, col. 4; review: Feb. 9, 1869, p. 1, col. 2.
129. *The Bee,* Mar. 11, 1869, p. 3, col. 7.
130. *L'Abeille,* Mar. 2, 1869, p. 2, col. 4; Mar. 7, 1869, p. 2, col. 5.
131. Ibid., Mar. 14, 1869, p. 1, col. 2.
132. Ibid., Mar. 14, 1869, p. 1, col. 2; Mar. 16, 1869, p. 2, col. 4; Mar. 19, 1869, p. 1, col. 2; review: Mar. 20, 1869, p. 1, col. 3.
133. *The Bee,* Mar. 30, 1869, p. 2, col. 4.
134. *L'Abeille,* Apr. 4, 1869, p. 1, col. 7.
135. *The Bee,* Apr. 15, 1869, p. 3, col. 1; Apr. 15, 1869, p. 2, col. 4; p. 3, col. 1; Apr. 25, 1869, p. 3, col. 2; Apr. 30, 1869, p. 3, col. 1; May 9, 1869, p. 3, col. 2.
136. *L'Abeille,* Apr. 23, 1869, p. 1, col. 5.
137. "She was one of our best light singers—pretty voice, facile, good style, charming, as well as a real nice woman" (*L'Abeille,* Mar. 3, 1891, p. 4, col. 1).
138. *L'Abeille,* Apr. 23, 1869, p. 1, col. 5.
139. Ibid., Apr. 28, 1869, p. 1, col. 2.
140. Ibid., Apr. 25, 1869, p. 1, col. 1; May 1, 1869, p. 1, col. 1.
141. Ibid., May 6, 1869, p. 2, col. 2.
142. *The Bee,* May 3, 1869, p. 3, col. 2.
143. Ibid., May 2, 1869, p. 2, col. 5; May 6, 1869, p. 3, col. 2. *Morning Star,* May 9, 1869, p. 4, col. 3.
144. *L'Abeille,* May 8, 1869, p. 1, col. 2.
145. *The Bee,* May 18, 1869, p. 3, col. 1.
146. *L'Abeille,* May 21, 1869, p. 1, col. 3. *The Bee,* May 21, 1869, p. 3, col. 3.
147. *L'Abeille,* May 23, 1869, p. 1, col.
148. Ibid., May 30, 1869, p. 1, col. 2.

149. Originally scheduled for May 28, 1869 (*L'Abeille,* May 24, 1869, p. 1, col. 2; May 26, 1869, p. 2, col. 4; May 27, 1869, p. 1, col. 2; May 28, 1869, p. 1, col. 2; May 30, 1869, p. 1, col. 3).

150. *Times,* Oct. 1, 1869, p. 4, col. 4.

151. Ibid., Oct. 1, 1869, p. 2, col. 5.

152. Ibid., Oct. 1, 1869, p. 2, col. 6.

153. Ibid., Oct. 1, 1869, p. 2, col. 6.

154. Ibid., Oct. 17, 1869, p. 11, col. 1; Oct. 27, 1869, p. 1, col. 3.

155. Ibid., Oct. 17, 1869, p. 7, col. 3; Oct. 17, 1869, p. 3, col. 4; Oct. 23, 1869, p. 1, col. 5.

156. Ibid., Oct. 23, 1869, p. 3, col. 5.

157. Ibid., Oct. 28, 1869, p. 2, col. 5.

158. Ibid., Oct. 23, 1869, p. 3, col. 4; Oct. 29, 1869, p. 1, col. 5; Oct. 30, 1869, p. 1, col. 5; Nov. 2, 1869, p. 1, col. 5.

159. Ibid., Nov. 4, 1869, p. 1, col. 6.

160. Ibid., Nov. 9, 1869, p. 2, col. 4.

161. Ibid., Nov. 13, 1869, p. 1, col. 3.

162. Ibid., Nov. 9, 1869, p. 3, col. 2; Nov. 17, 1869, p. 2, col. 5.

163. Ibid., Nov. 6, 1869, p. 1, col. 5.

164. Ibid., Nov. 13, 1869, p. 10, col. 2.

165. Ibid., Nov. 17, 1869, p. 10, col. 2.

166. Ibid., Nov. 17, 1869, p. 2, col. 5.

167. *L'Abeille,* Dec. 2, 1869, p. 1, col. 2; Dec. 12, 1869, p. 1, cols. 2 and 5.

168. *The Bee,* Dec. 17, 1869, p. 3, col. 1; *L'Abeille,* Dec. 17, 1869, p. 1, col. 2.

169. *L'Abeille,* Dec. 30, 1869, p. 2, col. 4; Jan. 2, 1870, p. 2, col. 4.

170. Franko Family concert, with Odd Fellows' Hall (*L'Abeille,* Jan. 28, 1870, p. 1, col. 2; Jan. 30, 1870, p. 2, col. 4; Feb. 3, 1870, p. 1, col. 2). Program: *L'Abeille,* Feb. 2, 1870, p. 2, col. 4. Review: *L'Abeille,* Feb. 3, 1870, p. 1, col. 2.

171. *L'Abeille,* Feb. 9, 1870, p. 1, col. 2.

172. For a brief account of the career of Jeanne Franko and her siblings, see John H. Baron, "Franko, Jeanne," in *Jewish Women in America: An Historical Encyclopedia,* ed. Paula Hyman and Deborah Dash Moore (New York: Carlson Publishers, Inc., 1997), 472–73.

173. *L'Abeille,* Feb. 2, 1870, p. 1, col. 2, p. 2, col. 4; Feb. 3, 1870, p. 1, col. 2; Feb. 5, 1870, p. 2, col. 4.

174. Ibid., Feb. 3, 1870, p. 1, col. 2; Feb. 9, 1870, p. 1, col. 2.

175. Ibid., Feb. 5, 1870, p. 1, col. 2; p. 2, col. 4; Feb. 9, 1870, p. 1, col. 2; Feb. 10, 1870, p. 1, col. 1; Feb. 11, 1870, p. 1, col. 2; Feb. 15, 1870, p. 1, col. 2; Feb. 19 1870, p. 1, col. 2. *The Bee,* Feb. 19, 1870, p. 3, col. 3. Reviews: *L'Abeille,* Feb. 15, 1870, p. 1, col. 2; *The Bee,* Feb. 15, 1870, p. 3, col. 2; Feb. 16, 1870, p. 1, col. 2; Feb. 18, 1870, p. 1, col. 3; Feb. 19 1870, p. 1, col. 2.

176. *L'Abeille,* Feb. 2, 1870, p. 2, col. 4; Feb. 19 1870, p. 1, col. 2; Mar. 2, 1870, p. 1, col. 1; Apr. 1, 1870, p. 1, col. 2. *Picayune,* May 18, 1870, p. 5, col. 6. Review: *L'Abeille,* Mar. 4, 1870, p. 1, col. 2.

177. Emile's father, Theodore, had recently died, and the son, though never equaling his father's stature, was a significant musician in New Orleans over the next few decades.

178. *L'Abeille,* Feb. 20, 1870, p. 2, col. 2; Feb. 23, 1870, p. 1, col. 2.

179. Ibid., Mar. 11, 1870, p. 1, col. 2.

180. *The Bee,* Mar. 20, 1870, p. 1, col. 1.

181. *L'Abeille,* Apr. 7, 1870, p. 1, col. 4.

182. *The Bee,* Jan. 16, 1870, p. 3, cols 2 and 8; Jan. 25, p. 3, col. 8. *L'Abeille,* Jan. 22, 1870, p. 1, col. 2; Jan. 30, 1870, p. 2, col. 4; Feb. 2, 1870, p. 2, col. 4.

183. *The Bee,* Feb. 19, 1870, p. 3, col. 2; Feb. 25, 1870, p. 3, col. 1.

184. *L'Abeille,* Feb. 27, 1870, p. 1, col. 1.

185. Ibid., Mar. 4, 1870, p. 1, col. 2.

186. Ibid., Oct. 11, 1870, p. 1, col. 2.
187. Ibid., Oct. 2, 1870, p. 2, col. 6.
188. Ibid., Nov. 15, 1870, p. 1, col. 2, and p. 2, col. 4; review: Nov. 20, 1870, p. 2, col. 1.
189. Ibid., Nov. 6, 1870, p. 2, col. 5.
190. Ibid., Dec. 13, 1870, p. 1, col. 2.
191. Ibid., Dec. 15, 1870, p. 2, col. 4.
192. Ibid., Dec. 16, 1870, p. 2, col. 4; Dec. 22, 1870, p. 1, col. 1; Dec. 23, 1870, p. 2, col. 4; review: Dec. 17, 1870, p. 1, col. 1; Dec. 24, 1870, p. 1, col. 3.
193. Ibid., Dec. 22, 1870, p. 1, col. 1; Dec. 23, 1870, p. 1, col. 2; p. 2, col. 4; Dec. 24, 1870, p. 2, col. 4; Dec. 25, 1870, p. 1, col. 2; Dec. 25, 1870, p. 3, col. 2; Dec. 27, 1870, p. 1, cols. 1–2.
194. Ibid., Jan. 11, 1871, p. 2, col. 4; Jan. 12, 1871, p. 1, col. 2. *The Bee,* Jan. 12, 1871, p. 3, col. 2.
195. *The Bee,* Jan. 19, 1871, p. 3, col. 7. Review: *L'Abeille,* Jan. 23, 1871, p. 1, col. 2.
196. *The Bee,* Dec. 6, 1870, p. 3, col. 9.
197. *L'Abeille,* Jan. 22, 1871, p. 2, col. 6.
198. Ibid., Feb. 5, 1871, p. 1, col. 7.
199. Ibid., Feb. 9, 1871, p. 2, col. 4. *The Bee,* Feb. 17, 1871, p. 3, col. 2.
200. *L'Abeille,* Feb. 25, 1871, p. 2, col. 4; *The Bee,* Feb. 28, 1871, p. 1, col. 2.
201. *L'Abeille,* Feb. 9, 1871, p. 1, col. 2; p. 2, col. 4; Feb. 15, 1871, p. 2, col. 4.
202. Ibid., Mar. 17, 1871, p. 1, col. 2; Mar. 19, 1871, p. 1, col. 1.
203. Ibid., Mar. 8, 1871, p. 2, col. 4, Wednesday; Mar. 22, 1871, p. 1, col. 2.
204. Ibid., Mar. 28, 1871, p. 2, col. 4; Mar. 29, 1871, p. 1, col. 3; Mar. 30, 1871, p. 1, col. 2; Apr. 2, 1871, p. 2, col. 8; Apr. 4, 1871, p. 1, col. 3; lengthy review: Apr. 9, 1871, p. 1, col. 1, 2 pts.
205. Ibid., Apr. 7, 1871, p. 2, col. 4.
206. Ibid., Apr. 9, 1871; Apr. 11, 1871, p. 1, col. 2.
207. Ibid., Apr. 2, 1871, p. 2, col. 8; Apr. 4, 1871, p. 1, col. 3; Apr. 9, 1871, p. 1, col. 1.
208. Ibid., Apr. 15, 1871, p. 1, col. 2; Apr. 18, 1871, p. 2, col. 4; review: Apr. 19, 1871, p. 1, col. 1; Apr. 22, 1871, p. 1, col. 2; Apr. 23, 1871, p. 2, cols. 1–2.
209. Ibid., May 16, 1871, p. 1, col. 2.
210. *The Bee,* Feb. 14, 1871, p. 3, col. 5; Feb. 28, 1871, p. 3, col. 2. *L'Abeille,* Feb. 15, 1871, p. 2, col. 4.
211. *L'Abeille,* Apr. 23, 1871, p. 2, col. 5.
212. *The Bee,* Apr. 18, 1871, p. 3, col. 2; *L'Abeille,* Apr. 19, 1871, p. 1, col. 1.
213. *L'Abeille,* Apr. 20, 1871, p. 1, col. 2.
214. Ibid., Apr. 23, 1871, p. 2, col. 5; Apr. 26, 1871, p. 2, col. 3. It was postponed from Apr. 23.
215. *The Bee,* Apr. 21, 1871, p. 1, col. 1.
216. *L'Abeille,* May 14, 1871, p. 2, col. 6; May 16, 1871, p. 1, col. 2; May 19, 1871, p. 1, col. 1.
217. Ibid., May 13, 1871, p. 2, col. 3; *The Bee,* May 13, 1871, p. 3, col. 1. Review: *L'Abeille,* May 19, 1871, p. 1, col. 1.
218. *L'Abeille,* May 26, 1871, p. 1, col. 1.
219. Ibid., May 24, 1871, p. 2, col. 3.
220. Ibid., May 14, 1871, p. 2, col. 3.
221. Ibid., May 16, 1871, p. 2, col. 4; May 20, 1871, p. 1, col. 2. *The Bee,* May 16, 1871, p. 3, col. 2.
222. Ibid., Oct. 6, 1871, p. 1, cols. 2 and 6.
223. *Picayune,* Dec. 24, 1871, p. 2, col. 1.
224. *L'Abeille,* Nov. 3, 1871, p. 1, col. 2.
225. Ibid., May 5, 1872, p. 2, col. 1.
226. Ibid., Feb. 18, 1872, p. 2, col. 1: the orchestra consisted of sixteen violins, five violas, four cellos, four basses, one harp, one piccolo, two flutes, two oboes, one English horn, two clarinets, two bassoons, four French horns, two trumpets, three trombones, one "saxhorn basse," and percussion.
227. Ibid., Feb. 11, 1872, p. 2, col. 1.

CHAPTER SIX

1. Canonge hired some singers for the season but not the leading women (*L'Abeille,* Sept. 22, 1872, p. 1, col. 2; Oct. 6, 1872, p. 1, col. 1). The dramatic season for 1872–73 opened Nov. 7, 1872, and a list of all actors at the theater for the season was given in *L'Abeille,* Oct. 13, 1872, p. 2, col. 2. But the opera season never happened.

2. Offenbach's *La Belle Hélène, La Périchole, Le Petit Faust,* and *Geneviéve de Brabant* were performed during the season at the Varieties Theater.

3. *Picayune,* Feb. 19, 1872, p. 8, col. 6.

4. *L'Abeille,* Oct. 25, 1872, p. 1, col. 2.

5. Ibid., Nov. 9, 1872, p. 1, col. 2; Nov. 10, 1872, p. 1, col. 2; Nov. 17, 1872, p. 2, col. 6, and p. 1, col. 2; Nov. 24, 1872, p. 1, col. 2; Nov. 26, 1872, p. 1, col. 2; Nov. 29, 1872, p. 1, col. 3; Nov. 30, 1872, p. 1, col. 2; Dec. 10, 1872, p. 1, col. 3.

6. Ibid., Nov. 26, 1872, p. 1, col. 2; Nov. 29, 1872, p. 1, col. 3; Dec. 5, 1872, p. 1, col. 2; Dec. 8, 1872, p. 2, col. 1; Dec. 12, 1872, p. 2, col. 5; Dec. 15, 1872, p. 2, col. 1; Dec. 17, 1872, p. 1, col. 2; Dec. 20; Dec. 21, 1872; Dec. 27, 1872; Dec. 27, 1872, p. 1, col. 2. Reviews: Dec. 18, 1872, p. 1, col. 3; Dec. 19, 1872, p. 1, col. 3.

7. Ibid., Dec. 17, 1872, p. 1, col. 2; Dec. 22, 1872, p. 2, col. 1; Dec. 25, 1872, p. 1, col. 2; Dec. 27, 1872, p. 1, col. 2; Dec. 28, 1872, p. 1, col. 2. Review: Dec. 24, 1872, p. 3, col. 1.

8. *Picayune,* Jan. 29, 1873, p. 2, col. 6. *L'Abeille,* Jan. 19, 1873, p. 2, col. 2; Jan. 23, p. 1, col. 3; Jan. 28, 1873, p. 1, col. 2; Jan. 29, 1873, p. 1, col. 3; Jan. 31, 1873, p. 2, col. 1; Jan. 30, 1873, p. 1, col. 3; Feb. 1, 1873, p. 1, col. 3; Feb. 2, 1873, p. 2, col. 1; Feb. 4, 1873, p. 2, col. 5; Feb. 7, 1873, p. 1, col. 5; Feb. 9, 1873, p. 1, col. 4. Extensive review and comparison: *L'Abeille,* Feb. 4, 1873, p. 2, col. 1; Feb. 9, 1873, p. 2, col.2.

9. *L'Abeille,* Oct. 6, 1872, p. 2, col. 7 and p. 1, col. 1.

10. Ibid., Nov. 30, 1872, p. 1, col. 2; Dec. 8, 1872, p. 2, col. 1.

11. Ibid., Jan. 18, 1873, p. 1, col. 4. Withers was conductor at Ford's Theater in Washington, D.C., the night that President Lincoln was shot.

12. Ibid., Feb. 11, 1873, p. 2, col. 4.

13. Ibid., Mar. 6, 1873, p. 1, col. 2, and Mar. 8, 1873, p. 2, col. 4.

14. Ibid., Dec. 12, 1872, p. 2, col. 5; Jan. 23, 1873, p. 2, col. 4; Mar. 8, 1873, p. 2, col. 4.

15. Canonge announced that he fully intended to open a new season in 1873–74 with both opera and drama. There were four evenings per week of opera (Monday, Tuesday, Thursday, and Saturday), and Sunday evenings were reserved for operetta, drama, comedy, or vaudeville. The French Opera House was probably going to be sold, but he hoped it would remain open for its original intention: opera (*L'Abeille,* Mar. 14, 1873, p. 1, col. 2).

16. *L'Abeille,* May 21, 1874, p. 1, col. 2, advertises that the French Opera Orchestra has openings for first and second violins and violas for the 1874–75 season.

17. Ibid., Nov. 8, 1873, p. 1, col. 2.

18. Ibid., Dec. 9, 1873, p. 1, col. 2.

19. Ibid., Dec. 15, 1873, p. 1, col. 2; Dec. 17, 1873, p. 1, col. 2. Reviews: Dec. 18, 1973, p. 1, col. 3; Dec. 21, 1873, p. 3, col. 2.

20. Ibid., Nov. 9, 1873, p. 3, col. 2.

21. Ibid., Nov. 26, 1873, p. 1, col. 2.

22. Ibid., Dec. 7, 1873, p. 1, col. 2; Dec. 7, 1873, p. 1, col. 3. Review: Dec. 13, 1873, p. 3, col. 2.

23. *Picayune,* Jan. 9, 1874, p. 3, col. 7.

24. *L'Abeille,* May 6, 1874, p. 1, col. 3; May 16, 1874, p. 1, col. 2; and May 10, 1874, p. 1, col. 3. Review of the first concert of May 18: May 19, 1874, p. 1, col. 3.

25. Ibid., Jan. 11, 1874, p. 2, col. 3.

26. Ibid., Jan. 22, 1874, p. 1, col. 2.

27. Ibid., Feb. 1, 1874, p. 1, col. 4; Feb. 1, 1874, p. 1, col. 2. For a detailed study of the life and music of La Hache see Fields, "Theodore La Hache and Music in New Orleans," 326–50.

28. *L'Abeille,* Feb. 8, 1874, p. 1, col. 3. Momas (1821–1883) was a very popular conductor at the French Opera from 1873 to 1875 and again in 1880–81.

29. Ibid., Mar. 8, 1874, p. 2, col. 3.

30. Ibid., Mar. 20, 1874, p. 2, col. 2. Review: Mar. 26, 1874, p. 1, col. 2. Weber (b. Karlsruhe ca. 1847; d. New Orleans 1901) was music director at Temple Sinai and the Jesuit Church.

31. Ibid., Mar. 31, 1874, p. 1, col. 2.

32. Ibid., Mar. 1, 1874, p. 1, col. 2; Mar. 24, 1874, p. 1, col. 2; Apr. 5, 1874, p. 1, col. 3; Apr. 5, 1874, p. 2, col. 3. Review: Apr. 9, 1874, p. 1, col. 2.

33. Ibid., Mar. 21, 1874, p. 1, col. 2.

34. Ibid., Apr. 5, 1874, p. 1, col. 2; p. 2, col. 3; Apr. 10, 1874, p. 2, col. 3; Apr. 12, 1874, p. 2, col. 3.

35. Ibid., Mar. 31, 1874, p. 1, col. 2; Apr. 12, 1874, p. 2, col. 3. Review: Apr. 16, 1874, p. 1, col. 3.

36. Ibid., Mar. 27, 1874, p. 1, col. 2; Apr. 5, 1874, p. 2, col. 3; Apr. 10, 1874, p. 2, col. 3; Apr. 16, 1874, p. 1, col. 3. See also erratum, Apr. 9, 1874, p. 1, col. 2.

37. Ibid., Apr. 9, 1874, p. 1, col. 2; Apr. 12, 1874, p. 2, col. 3; Apr. 19, 1874, p. 1, col. 3; Apr. 24, 1874, p. 1, col. 2.

38. Ibid., Apr. 5, 1874, p. 1, col. 2. It was originally scheduled for Apr. 29.

39. Ibid., Apr. 9, 1874, p. 1, col. 2; Apr. 22, 1874, p. 1, col. 2, p. 2, col. 3; Apr. 24, 1874, p. 1, col. 2; and Apr. 25, 1874, p. 1, col. 3. Greuling accompanied.

40. Ibid., Apr. 9, 1874, p. 1, col. 2; Apr. 21, 1874, p. 2, col. 2; Apr. 25, 1874, p. 2, col. 2; Apr. 26, 1874, p. 1, col. 2. Review: Apr. 26, 1874, p. 3, cols. 1–2.

41. Ibid., Apr. 30, 1874, p. 1, col. 3; p. 2, col. 2. Review: May 3, 1874, p. 1, col. 3.

42. Ibid., May 3, 1874, p. 1, col. 3; May 6, 1874, p. 2, col. 2; May 7, 1874, p. 2, col. 2; May 8, p. 2, col. 2.

43. Ibid., May 8, 1874, p. 2, col. 2; May 9, 1874, p. 1, col. 2.

44. Ibid., May 3, 1874, p. 1, col. 3; May 8, 1874, p. 1, col. 3; May 9, 1874, p. 2, col. 2; Feb. 8, 1874, p. 1, col. 3; p. 3, col. 2; Mar. 15, 1874, p. 1, col. 2. Mar. 1, 1874; Mar. 1, 1874, p. 1, col. 2. Review: May 13, 1874, p. 1, col. 3.

45. Ibid., May 14, 1874.

46. Ibid., Apr. 22, 1874, p. 1, col. 2; May 6, 1874, p. 2, col. 2; May 20, 1874, p. 2, col. 2.

47. Review of the opening in *L'Abeille,* Nov. 8, 1874, p. 2, col. 1.

48. The opéra-comique season opened on Nov. 8, 1874; see *L'Abeille,* Nov. 7, 1874, p. 1, col. 3.

49. *L'Abeille,* Dec. 22, 1874, p. 2, col. 4, and Dec. 23, 1874, p. 2, col. 4.

50. Momas had proven a strong leader during the preceding season and probably spear-headed the effort for the musicians to keep the season going. There was a benefit for him on Monday, Feb. 9, 1874, when he conducted *Le Prophète;* see *L'Abeille,* Feb. 8, 1874, p. 1, col. 3.

51. *Picayune,* Jan. 5, 1875, p. 1, col. 3.

52. *L'Abeille,* Mar. 23, 1875, p. 1, col. 4; Mar. 26, 1875, p. 1, col. 3.

53. Ibid., Mar. 1, 1874, p. 1, col. 2.

54. Ibid., Feb. 8, 1874, p. 1, col. 3, and p. 3, col. 2, and Mar. 15, 1874, p. 1, col. 2.

55. Such as on Apr. 15, 1874, at a concert for the benefit of the Jesuit Church (Immaculate Conception) conducted by Collignon and performed at Grunewald Hall, led by Mme Devoyod'-Acs. Although there was mostly singing, Joubert played four violin solos, including a romance by Page (*L'Abeille,* Apr. 12, 1874, p. 2, col. 3). Review: *L'Abeille,* Apr. 16, 1874, p. 1, col. 3, which deals especially with Joubert. Another was on Sunday, May 10, 1874, a sacred concert for the flood victims

of Pointe Coupée Parish, performed at St. Anne's Church and directed by Mlle Theresa Cannon. Joubert performed Vieuxtemps's *Souvenir d'Haydn* (*L'Abeille,* May 8, 1874, p. 2, col. 2).

56. *L'Abeille,* Apr. 30, 1874, p. 1, col. 3, and p. 2, col. 2. Review: May 3, 1874, p. 1, col. 3. There were other concerts such as on May 8, 1874 at Grunewald Hall (*L'Abeille,* May 3, 1874, p. 1, col. 3; May 6, 1874, p. 2, col. 2; May 7, 1874, p. 2, col. 2; and May 8, p. 2, col. 2).

57. *L'Abeille,* May 3, 1874, p. 1, col. 3.

58. Ibid., May 8, 1874, p. 1, col. 3.

59. Ibid., Nov. 29, 1874, p. 2, col. 2.

60. "Il y a bien longtemps que nous n'avons eu de concert; celui-ci qui est le concert inaugurateur de la saison ne peut manquer d'attirer beaucoup de monde" (*L'Abeille,* Nov. 22, 1874, p. 1, col. 1). Program: *L'Abeille,* Nov. 23, 1874, p. 2, col. 3.

61. *L'Abeille,* Nov. 22, 1874, p. 1, col. 1. Program: Nov. 23, 1874, p. 2, col. 3.

62. Ibid., Dec. 4, 1874, p. 1, col. 2; Dec. 6, 1874, p. 4, col. 1.

63. Ibid., Dec. 16, 1874, p. 1, col. 3. Program: Dec. 16, 1874, p. 2, col. 4.

64. Ibid., Dec. 16, 1874, p. 2, col. 4, and Dec. 23, 1874, p. 2, col. 4.

65. *Picayune,* Jan. 18, 1875, p. 2, col. 5.

66. Ibid., Jan. 22, 1875, p. 1, col. 1.

67. Ibid., Jan. 24, 1875, p. 3, col. 7.

68. *L'Abeille,* Feb. 1, 1875, p. 2, col. 4. There is some confusion on the actual date; it was originally scheduled for Feb. 1; Feb. 2, 1875, p. 1, col. 2.

69. Ibid., Feb. 6, 1875, p. 1, col. 3; Feb. 7, 1875, p. 2, col. 1.

70. Ibid., Feb. 7, 1865, p. 2, col. 1.

71. Ibid., Feb. 7, 1875, p. 2, cols. 1–2; Feb. 13, 1875, p. 2, col. 4; p. 1, col. 2; Feb. 14, 1875, p. 3, col. 1–2. Review: Feb. 21, 1875, p. 3, cols. 1–2.

72. Ibid., Feb. 20, 1875, p. 1, col. 2; Feb. 21, 1875, p. 1, col. 3; p. 2, col. 5; Feb. 23, 1875, p. 1, col. 4; Feb. 25, 1875, p. 1, col. 4; p. 2, col. 4; Feb. 28, 1875, p. 3, cols. 1–2; Feb. 28, 1875, p. 2, col. 5; Mar. 3, 1875, p. 1, col. 2; Mar. 4, 1875, p. 1, col. 2; Mar. 5, 1875, p. 2, col. 5; Mar. 7, 1875, p. 3, col. 1; Mar. 9, 1875, p. 1, col. 2; Mar. 10, 1875, p. 1, col. 3; Mar. 11, 1875, p. 2, col. 5; Mar. 12, 1875, p. 1, col. 2; Mar. 12, 1875, p. 1, col. 2; Mar. 13, 1875, p. 2, col. 5; Mar. 14, 1875, p. 1, cols. 1–2; Mar. 20, 1875, p. 1, col. 2; Mar. 20, 1875, p. 2, col. 5; Mar. 24, 1875, p. 2, col. 5; Mar. 27, 1875, p. 1, col. 2; Mar. 31, 1875, p. 1, col. 6; Apr. 1, 1875, p. 1, col. 3; Apr. 3, 1875, p. 1, col. 2; Apr. 4, 1875, p. 4, col. 1; Mar. 31, 1875, p. 1, col. 6; Apr. 6, 1875, p. 1, col. 2; Apr. 7, 1875, p. 1, col. 2; Apr. 8, 1875, p. 1, col. 2. Reviews: Mar. 6, 1875, p. 1, col. 3; Mar. 7, 1875, p. 1, col. 3; Mar. 13, 1875, p. 1, col. 3; Mar. 14, 1875, p. 1, col. 2; Mar. 21, 1875, p. 1, col. 2; Apr. 6, 1875, p. 1, col. 2; Apr. 11, 1875, p. 3, cols. 1–2.

73. Ibid., Mar. 14, 1875, p. 4, col. 1.

74. Ibid., Mar. 28, 1875, p. 1, col. 2.

75. Ibid., Mar. 11, 1875, p. 2, col. 5; Mar. 16, 1875, p. 2, col. 2; Mar. 20, 1875, p. 2, col. 5; Mar. 21, 1875, p. 1, col. 2; Mar. 24, 1875, p. 1, col. 3; Mar. 28, 1875, p. 1, col. 2; p. 2, col. 6.

76. Ibid., Mar. 25, 1875, p. 1, col. 3; Mar. 28, 1875, p. 2, col. 5 (program); Mar. 31, 1875, p. 1, col. 3. Review: Apr. 1, 1875, p. 1, col. 3.

77. Ibid., Mar. 7, 1875, p. 1, col. 3; Mar. 24, 1875, p. 1, col. 3.

78. Ibid., Feb. 24, 1875, p. 1, col. 3; Mar. 14, 1875, p. 1, col. 2; Mar. 21, 1875, p. 1, col. 2; Mar. 24, 1875, p. 2, col. 5; Mar. 28, 1875, p. 1, col. 2; Mar. 31, 1875, p. 2, col. 5 (program); Apr. 1, 1875, p. 1, col. 3. Review: Apr. 2, 1875, p. 1, col. 2; Apr. 4, 1875, p. 1, col. 2; Apr. 4, 1875, p. 3, cols. 1–2.

79. Ibid., Mar. 7, 1875, p. 1, col. 3; Mar. 14, 1875, p. 1, col. 2; Apr. 2, 1875, p. 1, col. 2; Apr. 4, 1875, p. 3, cols 1–2; Apr. 6, 1875, p. 1, col. 2; Apr. 7, 1875, p. 1, col. 2; Apr. 8, 1875, p. 1, col. 2. Review: Apr. 11, 1875, p. 3, cols. 1–2.

80. Ibid., Apr. 9, 1875, p. 1, col. 3. Review: Apr. 10, 1875 p. 1, col. 3.

81. Ibid., Apr. 3, 1875, p. 1, col. 2; Apr. 8, 1875, p. 1, col. 2; Apr. 8, 1875, p. 1, col. 2; Apr. 9, 1875, p. 1, col. 3; Apr. 10, 1875, p. 1, col. 3; Apr. 11, 1875, p. 4, col. 1. Large review: Apr. 13, 1875, p. 1, col. 3; Apr. 17, 1875, p. 1, col. 3.

82. Ibid., Apr. 10, 1875 p. 1, col. 3.

83. Ibid., Apr. 18, 1875, p. 3, col. 2.

84. Ibid., Apr. 18, 1875, p. 1, col. 2; Apr. 20, 1875, p. 2, col. 4: Apr. 21, 1875, p. 1, col. 2. Reviews: Apr. 22, 1875, p. 1, col. 2; Apr. 25, 1875, p. 3, cols 1–2.

85. Ibid., Apr. 23, 1875, p. 1, col. 2.

86. Ibid., Apr. 8, 1875, p. 1, col. 2; Apr. 14, 1875, p. 2, col. 5; Apr. 23, 1875, p. 2, col. 5; Apr. 25, 1875, p. 1, col. 3; Apr. 28, 1875, p. 1, col. 3. Brief review: Apr. 29, 1875, p. 1, col. 1.

87. Ibid., Apr. 28, 1875, p. 1, col. 3; May 1, 1875, p. 1, col. 3; May 2, 1875, p. 1, col. 2, p. 2, col. 5.

88. Ibid., May 1, 1875, p. 1, col. 3; May 2, 1875, p. 1, col. 2.

89. Ibid., Apr. 27, 1875, p. 1, col. 2; May 1, 1875, p. 1, col. 3; May 2, 1875, p. 1, col. 2; May 6, 1875, p. 1, col. 2. Concert on Sunday, May 4 (?): Review: May 11, 1875, p. 1, col. 3.

90. Founded in 1846 as St. Peter's Seaman's Bethel, Sainte Anna's Church was built in 1875 and rebuilt in 1877.

91. Ibid., May 2, 1875, p. 1, col. 2, p. 2, col. 5. Review: May 6, 1875, p. 1, col. 2.

92. Ibid., May 6, 1875, p. 1, col. 2, p. 2, col. 4.

93. Ibid., May 2, 1875, p. 1, col. 1; May 9, 1875, p. 1, col. 2, p. 2, col. 5 (program); May 11, 1875, p. 2, col. 4; May 16, 1875, p. 1, col. 2.

94. Ibid., May 11, 1875, p. 1, col. 3.

95. Ibid., May 11, 1875, p. 1, col. 2; May 11, 1875, p. 2, col. 4.

96. Ibid., May 15, 1875, p. 1, col. 1; May 16, 1875, p. 1, col. 2.

97. Ibid., May 30, 1875, p. 3, col. l.

98. Ibid., May 20, 1875, p. 1, col. 2.

99. Ibid., May 18, 1875, p. 1, col. 2; May 20, 1875, p. 1, col. 2; May 20, 1875, p. 1, col. 6; May 22, 1875, p. 1, col. 2. Review: May 23, 1875, p. 3, col. 1.

100. Ibid., May 16, 1875, p. 2, col. 4; May 22, 1875, p. 2, col. 2. The concert was originally announced for Thursday, May 20.

101. Ibid., May 22, 1875, p. 1, col. 2.

102. Ibid., May 23, 1875, p. 3, col. 1.

103. Ibid., Oct. 17, 1875, p. 2, col. 4; Oct. 19, 1875, p. 1, col. 2; Oct. 22, 1875, p. 1, col. 2; Oct. 23, 1875, p. 1, col. 2. Review: Oct. 19, 1875, p. 1, col. 2. Although over, the concerts were still advertised: Oct. 24, 1875, p. 2, col. 5.

104. Ibid., Oct. 28, 1875, p. 2, col. 3.

105. Ibid., Oct. 31, 1875, p. 1, col. 3.

106. Ibid., Oct. 24, 1875, p. 1, col. 3.

107. Ibid., Oct. 24, 1875, p. 2, col. 4. Review: Nov. 2, 1875, p. 1, col. 3.

108. Ibid., Nov. 2, 1875, p. 1, col. 3.

109. Ibid., Oct. 26, 1875, p. 2, col. 2; Nov. 21, 1875, p. 2, col. 4; Nov. 23, 1875, p. 2, col. 2; Nov. 24, 1875, p. 2, col. 2.

110. Ibid., Nov. 21, 1875, p. 2, col. 4; Nov. 24, 1875, p. 2, col. 2; Dec. 1, 1875, p. 1, col. 1. Review: Dec. 2, 1875, p. 1, col. 2.

111. Ibid., Dec. 19, 1875, p. 4, col. 1.

112. Ibid., Dec. 17, 1875, p. 1, col. 2. Review (of the intermède): Dec. 18, 1875, p. 1, col. 3.

113. Ibid., Dec. 19, 1875, p. 3, col. 2.

114. Ibid., Dec. 22, 1875, p. 1, col. 2.

115. Ibid., Dec. 22, 1875, p. 1, col. 2.

116. Ibid., Dec. 5, 1875, p. 1, col. 2.

117. Alan Walker, *Hans von Bülow: A Life and Times* (Oxford, UK: Oxford University Press, 2010), 229–31.

118. *L'Abeille,* Feb. 8, 1876, p. 2, col. 4; Feb. 13, 1876, p. 1, col. 2; Feb. 22, 1876, p. 2, col. 3.

119. *Picayune,* Feb. 15, 1876, p. 2, col. 1. Compare to the Germania Society (see Newman, "Good Music for a Free People").

120. *L'Abeille,* Feb. 15, 1876, p. 1, col. 2, and Feb. 16, 1876, p. 1, col. 1.

121. Ibid., Feb. 20, 1876, p. 4, col. 1, and Mar. 11, 1876, p. 1, col. 2; Mar. 11, 1876, p. 2, col. 3. Review: Mar. 16, 1876, p. 1, col. 3.

122. Ibid., Mar. 14, 1876, p. 2, col. 2. It was originally scheduled for Mar. 19.

123. Ibid., Mar. 24, 1876, p. 1, col. 2.

124. *Picayune,* Apr. 21, 1876, p. 1, col. 3. Review: Apr. 22, 1876, p. 5, col. 7.

125. *L'Abeille,* Nov. 14, 1876, p. 1, col. 3. This, apparently, is not the same as J. W. H. Eckert.

126. Ibid., Dec. 5, 1876, p. 1, col. 3, and Dec. 17, 1876, p. 3, col. 3.

127. Ibid., Nov. 21, 1876, p. 1, col. 2.

128. Ibid., Nov. 12, 1876, p. 1, col. 3.

129. Ibid., Sunday, Dec. 17, 1876, p. 3, col. 3, and Dec. 21, 1876, p. 1, col. 2.

130. Ibid., Dec. 12, 1876, p. 2, col. 3.

131. Ibid., Dec. 21, 1876, p. 1, col. 2.

132. Ibid., Dec. 5, 1876, p. 1, col. 3; Dec. 17, 1876, p. 3, col. 1; Dec. 31, 1876, p. 2, col. 5.

133. Ibid., Feb. 4, 1877, p. 1, col. 2, and p. 2, col. 4.

134. *Picayune,* Feb. 7, 1877, p. 5, col. 5.

135. *L'Abeille,* Feb. 18, 1877, p. 2, col. 4.

136. Ibid., Feb. 24, 1877, p. 1, col. 2.

137. Ibid., Mar. 24, 1877, p. 2, col. 4; Mar. 25, 1877, p. 1, col. 2.

138. Ibid., Apr. 6, 1877, p. 1, col. 2; Apr. 12, 1877, p. 1, col. 1.

139. Ibid., Apr. 3, 1883, p. 2, col. 2; Apr. 8, 1877, p. 2, col. 3; and Apr. 11, 1877, p. 1, col. 2.

140. Ibid., Apr. 8, 1877, p. 2, col. 2, and Apr. 11, 1877, p. 1, col. 2.

141. Ibid., May 2, 1877, p. 2, col. 3; May 6, 1877, p. 1, col. 2; May 9, 1877, p. 1, col. 2; and May 12, 1877, p. 1, col. 2. Review: May 15, 1877, p. 1, col. 2.

142. Ibid., May 6, 1877, p. 1, col. 2; May 12, 1877, p. 1, col. 2; May 13, 1877, p. 1, col. 2; May 13, 1877, p. 2, col. 3; May 15, 1877, p. 1, col. 2. Review: May 17, 1877, p. 1, col. 3.

143. Ibid., Feb. 22, 1877, p. 1, col. 3; May 20, 1877, p. 1, col. 2.

144. Ibid., May 10, 1877, p. 1, col. 2.

145. Ibid., May 20, 1877, p. 1, col. 3; May 20, 1877, p. 2, col. 3; May 27, 1877, p. 1, col. 2. Review: May 29, 1877, p. 1, col. 2.

146. Ibid., May 30, 1877, p. 2, col. 2, and June 1, 1877, p. 1, col. 3. Review: June 2, 1877, p. 1, col. 2; June 3, 1877, p. 1, col. 2.

147. Ibid., May 27, 1877, p. 1, col. 2; June 1, 1877, p. 1, col. 3; June 3, 1877, p. 1, col. 2; June 3, 1877, p. 2, col. 3.

148. Louisiana State Museum, Kaiser Collection.

149. *L'Abeille,* June 3, 1877, p. 1, col. 2; June 8, 1877, col. 1.

150. Ibid., Nov. 11, 1879, p. 1, col. 2; p. 1, col. 4.

151. Ibid., Feb. 14, 1877, p. 2, col. 4.

152. Ibid., Mar. 11, 1877, p. 1, col. 2.

153. *L'Abeille* (?),Oct. 21, 1877, p. 1, col.2.

154. *L'Abeille,* Oct. 24, 1877, p. 2, col. 1.

155. Ibid., Nov. 11, 1877, p. 1, col. 3; p. 2, col. 3, Nov. 13, 1877, p. 1, col. 2; and Nov. 14, 1877, p. 1, col. 2.

156. Ibid., Nov. 17, 1877, p. 1, col. 2.

157. Ibid., Nov. 18, 1877, p. 1, col. 4; Nov. 27, 1877.

158. Ibid., Dec. 2, 1877, p. 2, cols. 1–2.

159. Ibid., Dec. 7, 1877, p. 2, col. 2; Dec. 9, 1877, p. 1, col. 3.

160. Ibid., Dec. 13, 1877, p. 2, col. 2.

161. Ibid., Dec. 18, 1877, p. 1, col. 2; Dec. 18, 1877, p. 2, col. 2; Dec. 23, 1877, p. 3, col. 1.

162. Ibid., Dec. 9, 1877, p. 1, col. 3.

163. Ibid., Dec. 13, 1877, p. 2, col. 2. Review: Dec. 23, 1877, p. 4, col. 2. The statement in the *Picayune,* Dec. 22, 1877, p. 5, col. 6, that this was the first full performance of *Elijah* may be true since we do not know if the earlier performance by the Philharmonic Society was a "full" performance.

164. *L'Abeille,* Nov. 20, 1877, p. 1, col. 2.

165. Ibid., Dec. 13, 1877, p. 2, col. 1.

166. Ibid., Dec. 23, 1877, p. 4, col. 2.

167. Ibid., Dec. 30, 1877, p. 1, col. 2.

168. Ibid., Feb. 8, 1878, p. 1, col. 2.

169. Ibid., Feb. 10, 1878, Sunday, p. 1, col. 3; Feb. 17, 1878, p. 1, col. 2; p. 2, col. 3.

170. Ibid., Feb. 17, 1878, p. 2, col. 3; Mar. 21, 1878, p. 2, col. 2.

171. Ibid., Mar. 9, 1878, 1878, p. 1, col. 2.

172. Ibid., Mar. 24, 1878, p. 2, col. 3; Mar. 26, 1878, p. 1, col. 2. Review: Mar. 30, 1878, p. 1, col. 2.

173. Ibid., Mar. 31, 1878, p. 2, col. 3; Apr. 4, 1878, p. 1, col. 2.

174. Ibid., Apr. 6, 1878, p. 1, col. 2; Apr. 9, 1878, p. 1, col. 2; Apr. 11, 1878, p. 1, col. 2. Review: Apr. 9, 1878, p. 1, col. 2; Apr. 12, 1878, p. 1, col. 3.

175. Ibid., Apr. 12, 1878, p. 1, col. 3, and corrected Apr. 14, 1878, p. 1, col. 3.

176. Ibid., Apr. 18, 1878, p. 1, col. 3.

177. Ibid., Apr. 17, 1878, p. 1, col. 2; p. 2, col. 2.

178. Ibid., Apr. 27, 1878, p. 1, col. 2; p. 2, col. 2.

179. Ibid., May 1, 1878, p. 1, col. 2, and May 5, 1878, p. 2, col. 3.

180. Ibid., Nov. 17, 1878, p. 1, col. 2.

181. Ibid., Dec. 15, 1878, p. 2, col. 4.

182. Ibid., Jan. 12, 1879, p. 1, col. 3; Jan. 14, 1879, p. 2, col. 1; Jan. 28, 1879, p. 2, col. 2; Feb. 6, 1879.

183. Ibid., Mar. 5, 1879, p. 2, col. 2.

184. Ibid., Jan. 14, 1879, p. 1, col. 5.

185. Ibid., Jan. 26, 1879, p. 1, col. 2; Feb. 2, 1879, p. 2, col. 2; and Feb. 4, 1879, p. 1, col. 2.; Feb. 5, 1879, p. 1, col. 1.

186. Ibid., Jan. 30, 1879, p. 1, col. 3; Feb. 18, 1879, p. 1, col. 2; Feb. 19, 1879, p. 1, col. 2; Feb. 20, 1879, p. 1, col. 2.

187. Ibid., Mar. 1, 1879, p. 2, col. 2.

188. Ibid., Mar. 5, 1879, p. 2, col. 2.

189. Ibid., Mar. 30, 1879, p. 1, col. 2.

190. Ibid., Mar. 27, 1879, p. 2, col. 1.

191. Ibid., Apr. 11, 1879, p. 1, col. 2.

192. Ibid., Apr. 5, 1879, p. 2, col. 1.

193. Ibid., Mar. 30, 1879, p. 2, col. 4; Apr. 7, 1879, p. 2, col. 1; Apr. 8, 1879, p. 2, col. 1; Apr. 11, 1879, p. 1, col. 2; Apr. 14, 1879, p. 1, col. 3. Review: Apr. 16, 1879, p. 1, col. 2.

194. Ibid., Apr. 29, 1879, p. 2, col. 2.

195. Ibid., Apr. 30, 1879, p. 1, col. 2; p. 2, col. 1. Review: May 4, 1879, p. 1, col. 2.

196. Ibid., May 4, 1879, p. 1, col. 2; p. 2, col. 3, and May 11, 1879, p. 1, col. 2. *Picayune,* May 14, 1879, p. 5, col. 6.

197. *L'Abeille,* May 11, 1879, p. 1, col. 2; May 18, 1879, p. 1, col. 2; p. 2, col. 3; May 27, 1879, p. 1, col. 2.

198. Ibid., May 18, 1879, p. 2, col. 3.

199. Ibid., July 2, 1879, p. 1, col. 2.

200. *Picayune,* May 31, 1879, p. 2.

201. Ibid., July 8, 1879, p. 4; Sept. 20, 1879, p. 1.

202. Ibid., July 27, 1879, p. 2.

203. *L'Abeille,* Oct. 31, 1879, p. 1, col. 2; Nov. 16, 1879, p. 3, col. 1; Nov. 23, 1879, p. 3, col. 1; Dec. 28, 1879, p. 3, col. 1. Review: Nov. 30, 1879, p. 3, cols. 1–3.

204. Ibid., Nov. 7, 1879, p. 1, col. 2.

205. Ibid., Dec. 7, 1879, p. 3, cols. 1–3.

206. Ibid., Dec. 10, 1879, p. 1, col. 2; Dec. 11, 1879, p. 1, col. 5.

207. Ibid., Dec. 21, 1879, p. 3, col. 3; Dec. 25, p. 4, col. 1. Review: Dec. 27, 1879, p. 1, col. 2.

208. Ibid., Dec. 31, 1879, p. 1, col. 5. For more on this piece, see Mar. 15, 1891, p. 4, col. 1.

209. See Alfred Mercier, "La musique à la nouvelle-Orléans: le grand opéra français, la troupe dramatique," in *L'Abeille,* Nov. 28, 1880, p. 2, cols. 1–2. All reviews in *L'Abeille* signed "A.M." are by Alfred Mercier.

210. *L'Abeille,* Dec. 27, 1879, p. 2, col. 2; Dec. 28, 1879, p. 3, col. 2.

211. Ibid., Dec. 28, 1879, p. 1, col. 4.

212. Ibid., Feb. 1, 1880, p. 2, col. 4.

213. Ibid., Feb. 10, 1880, p. 1, col. 2.

214. Ibid., Mar. 16, 1880, p. 2, col. 3.

215. Ibid., Mar. 29, 1880, p. 2, col. 2.

216. Ibid., Apr. 17, 1880, p. 2, col. 1.

217. Ibid., Mar. 23, 1880, p. 1, col. 2; Mar. 25, 1880, p. 1 cols. 2–3; Apr. 11, 1880, p. 3, col. 1.

218. Ibid., Mar. 13, 1880, p. 2, col. 1; Apr. 16, 1880, p. 2, col. 3; Mar. 23, 1880, p. 1, col. 2; Apr. 4, 1880, p. 1, col. 2; Apr. 7, 1880, p. 2, col. 1.

219. Ibid., Mar. 7, 1880, p. 2, col. 2.

220. Ibid., Apr. 2, 1880, p. 2, col. 1.

221. Ibid., Apr. 6, 1880, p. 1, col. 2.

222. Ibid., Apr. 5, 1880, p. 2, col. 1.

223. Ibid., Mar. 14, 1880, p. 1, col. 2; Apr. 4, 1880, p. 1, col. 2; Apr. 5, 1880, p. 2, col. 1; Apr. 9, 1880, p. 1, col. 2, and 4.

224. Ibid., Apr. 10, 1880, p. 1, col. 2.

225. The concert was originally scheduled as a matinee on Apr. 6 (*L'Abeille,* Apr. 4, 1880, p. 1, col. 2; Apr. 17, 1880, p. 2, col. 1).

226. *L'Abeille,* Apr. 29, 1880, p. 1, col.

227. Ibid., Oct. 1, 1880, p. 1, col. 9; p. 1, col. 3.

228. Ibid., Oct. 2, 1880, p. 1, col. 3; Oct. 5, 1880, p. 1, col. 3; Oct. 7, 1880, p. 1, col. 3; Oct. 8, 1880, p. 1, col. 3; Oct. 9, 1880, p. 1, col. 3; Oct. 10, 1880, p. 4, col. 1; Oct. 14, 1880, p. 1, col. 5; Oct. 16, 1880, p. 1, col. 9. Review: Oct. 3, 1880, p. 1, col. 3.

229. Ibid., Oct. 10, 1880, p. 4, col. 1.

230. Ibid., Oct. 19, 1880, p. 1, cols. 3–4; Oct. 20, 1880, p. 1, col. 2; Oct. 22, 1880, p. 1, col. 3; Oct. 26, 1880, p. 1, col. 3.

231. Ibid., Nov. 7, 1880, p. 1, col. 9. Review: Nov. 9, 1880, p. 1, col. 3.

232. Ibid., Oct. 23, 1880, p. 1, col. 9; Oct. 28, 1880, p. 1, col. 9. Review: Oct. 26, 1880, p. 1, col. 3.

233. Ibid., Oct. 24, 1880, p. 1, col. 9; Oct. 28, 1880, p. 1, col. 9.

234. Ibid., Oct. 2, 1880, p. 1, col. 3.

235. Ibid., Oct. 1, 1880, p. 1, col. 5; Oct. 2, 1880, p. 1, col. 2; Oct. 14, 1880, p. 1, col. 5; Oct. 16, 1880, p. 1, col. 9; Jan. 1, 1881, p. 2, col. 5.
236. Ibid., Nov. 9, 1880, p. 1, col. 3.
237. Ibid., Nov. 19, 1880, p. 1, col. 4.
238. Ibid., Jan. 4, 1881, p. 2, col. 1, and Jan. 8, 1881, p. 1, col. 2.
239. Ibid., Jan. 16, 1881, p. 2, col. 2.
240. Ibid., Jan. 14, 1881, p. 1, col. 2.
241. Ibid., Jan. 23, 1881, p. 1, col. 2; Jan. 26, 1881, p. 1, col. 3. Review: Jan. 27, 1881, p. 1, col. 3.
242. Ibid., Feb. 2, 1881, p. 1, col. 2.
243. Ibid., Jan. 7, 1881, p. 1, col. 2; Jan. 18, 1881, p. 2, col. 2; Jan. 13, 1881, p. 1, col. 5.
244. Ibid., Jan. 25, 1881, p. 1, col. 2.
245. Ibid., Feb. 9, 1881, p. 1, col. 3.
246. Ibid., Feb. 6, 1881, p. 1, col. 4.
247. Ibid., Feb. 11, 1881, p. 1, col. 3.
248. Ibid.
249. Ibid., Feb. 15, 1881, p. 2, col. 2; Feb. 16, 1881, p. 1, col. 4.
250. See above, page 75.
251. *L'Abeille,* Feb. 24, 1881, p. 2, col. 1; Mar. 6, 1881, p. 1, col. 3. Review: Feb. 24, Thursday, p. 1, col. 2.
252. Ibid., Feb. 27, 1881, p. 2, col. 3.
253. Ibid., Mar. 27, 1881, p. 1, col. 3; Mar. 29, 1881, p. 1, col. 1.
254. Ibid., Mar. 27, 1881, p. 1, col. 2; Apr. 7, 1881, p. 1, col. 3; p. 2, col. 1.
255. Ibid., Mar. 30, 1881, p. 1, col. 2. Review: Apr. 5, 1881, p. 1, col. 3.
256. Ibid., May 28, 1881. p. 1, col. 2.
257. Ibid., May 21, 1881, p. 1, col. 3; May 21, 1881, p. 1, col. 7. Review: May 24, 1881, p. 1, col. 1; May 25, 1881, p. 1, col. 3.
258. Ibid., May 28, 1881, p. 1, col. 6. Review: May 29, 1881, p. 1, col. 4.
259. Ibid., Apr. 27, 1881, p. 12, col. 6. *Picayune,* Apr. 27, 1881, p. 5, col. 7. Review: *L'Abeille,* Apr. 28, 1881, p. 1, col. 4.
260. *L'Abeille,* May 12, 1881.
261. Ibid., May 17, 1881, p. 1, col. 4.
262. Ibid., May 8, 1881, p. 1, cols. 2–3; May 13, 1881, p. 1, col. 3. Review: May 18, 1881, p. 1, col. 3.
263. Ibid., May 11, 1881, p. 1, col. 6.
264. Ibid., Apr. 30, 1881, p. 3, col. 1; May 29, 1881, p. 2, col. 1; Oct. 1, 1881, p. 2, col. 1, and Oct. 4, 1881, p. 2, col. 2.
265. Ibid., May 27, 1881, p. 2, col. 1.
266. Ibid., June 1, 1881, p. 1, col. 5.
267. Ibid., June 14, 1881, p. 2, col. 1, June 19, 1881, p. 1, col. 2.
268. Ibid., June 21, 1881, p. 2, col. 1; June 22, 1881, p. 1, col. 2.
269. *Picayune,* June 24, 1881, p. 2, col. 1.
270. *L'Abeille,* May 1, 1881, p. 1, col. 3; June 5, 1881, p. 2, col. 1; June 12, 1881, p. 1, col. 3.
271. Ibid., May 31, 1881, p. 1, col. 3; June 2, 1881, p. 1, col. 3; June 16, 1881, p. 1, col. 2.
272. Ibid., Sept. 3, 1881, p. 1, col. 2; Sept. 6, 1881, p. 2, col. 2.
273. Ibid., Sept. 10, 1881, p. 1, col. 2. Reviewed Sept. 13, 1881, p. 1, col. 2.
274. Ibid., Mar. 8, 1881, p. 1, col. 2; May 11, 1881, p. 1, col. 2; May 24, 1881, p. 1, col. 2; May 24, 1881, p. 1, col. 2.
275. Ibid., Mar. 30, 1881, p. 1, col. 2.
276. Ibid., Sept. 1, 1881, p. 1, col. 2; Nov. 13, 1881, p. 1, col. 4.

277. Ibid., July 10, 1881, p. 1, col. 2; July 29, 1881, p. 1, col. 2; Oct. 2, 1881, p. 1, col. 3.
278. Ibid., Oct. 9, 1881, p. 1, col. 2.
279. Ibid., Nov. 12, 1881, p. 2, col. 1.
280. Ibid., Oct. 23, 1881, p. 1, col. 2.
281. *Picayune,* Jan. 17, 1882, p. 5, col. 2.
282. *States,* Apr. 5, 1882, p. 4, col. 1.
283. *L'Abeille,* May 11, 1882, p. 2, col. 1.
284. Ibid., May 23, 1882, p. 2, col. 2.
285. Ibid., June 11, 1882, p. 1, col. 6.
286. Ibid., May 28, 1882, p. 1, col. 3.
287. Ibid., May 12, 1882, p. 1, col. 6.
288. Ibid., May 14, 1882, p. 1, col. 3.
289. Ibid., May 23, 1882, p. 2, col. 1.
290. *Picayune,* Nov. 2, 1882, p. 5, col. 7; Nov. 3, 1882, afternoon ed., p. 1, col. 1; p. 2, col. 2.
291. Ibid., Nov. 9, 1882, p. 4, col. 4.
292. Ibid., Dec. 15, 1882, p. 5, col. 7.
293. *Daily States,* Jan. 3, 1883, p. 4, col. 7; Jan. 7, 1883, p. 8, col. 3.
294. Ibid., Jan. 3, 1883, p. 4, col. 7.
295. Ibid., Jan. 7, 1883, p. 8, col. 3; Jan. 8, 1883, p. 4, col. 2; Jan. 9, 1883, p. 4, col. 3. *Picayune,* Jan. 11, 1883, p. 1, col. 5; Jan. 11, 1883, p. (?), col. 4; Jan. 13, 1883, p. 4, col. 7; p. 2, col. 2.
296. *L'Abeille,* Mar. 15, 1883, p. 1, col. 2; Mar. 17, 1883, p. 1, col. 2.
297. Ibid., Mar. 21, 1883, p. 1, col. 2.
298. *Picayune,* Mar. 29, 1885, p. 15, col. 2.
299. *L'Abeille,* Mar. 25, 1883, p. 2, col. 3.
300. Ibid., Apr. 1, 1883, p. 1, col. 3.
301. Ibid., Mar. 25, 1883, p. 1, col. 2; Mar. 25, 1883, p. 2, col. 3; Apr. 1, 1883, p. 1, col. 3. Review: Apr. 3, 1883, p. 1, col. 2.
302. Ibid., Mar. 13, 1883, p. 1, col. 2.
303. Ibid., Apr. 1, 1883, p. 1, col. 3. Review: Apr. 3, 1883, p. 1, col. 2.
304. Ibid., Apr. 1, 1883, p. 1, col. 4. Review: Apr. 6, 1883, p. 1, col. 3.
305. Ibid., Apr. 8, 1883, p. 1, col. 3.
306. Ibid., Apr. 3, 1883, p. 1, col. 2; Apr. 11, 1883, p. 1, col. 2.
307. Ibid., Apr. 1, 1883, p. 1, col. 3; Apr. 12, 1883, p. 1, col. 3. Review: Apr. 15, 1883, p. 4, col. 1; Apr. 17, 1883, p. 1, col. 5.
308. Ibid., Apr. 17, 1883, p. 1, col. 5.
309. Ibid., Apr. 17, 1883, p. 1, col. 5; Apr. 18, 1883, p. 1, col. 5.
310. Ibid., Apr. 18, 1883, p. 1, col. 6.
311. Ibid., Apr. 28, 1883, p. 1, col. 2.
312. Ibid., Apr. 26, 1883, p. 2, col. 1; Apr. 29, 1883, p. 4, col. 2; p. 2, col. 4.
313. Ibid., Apr. 1, 1883, p. 2, col. 3.
314. Ibid., Apr. 18, 1883, p. 1, col. 5.
315. Ibid., Apr. 29, 1883, p. 4, col. 2; Apr. 29, 1883, p. 2, col. 3.
316. Ibid., June 9, 1883, p. 1, col. 8; Sept. 9, 1883, p. 1, col. 3.
317. Ibid., Sept. 8, 1886, p. 1, col. 4.
318. Ibid., Mar. 1, 1883, p. 3, col. 1.
319. Ibid., June 9, 1883, p. 1, col. 9.
320. *Picayune,* Oct. 28, 1883, p. 11, col. 5. *L'Abeille,* Nov. 10, 1883, p. 2, col. 1.
321. *L'Abeille,* Nov. 30, 1883, p. 1, col. 4; Dec. 2, 1883, p. 4, col. 3; Dec. 8, 1883, p. 1, col. 4.

322. *L'Abeille,* Mar. 15, 1883, p. 1, col. 2. *Picayune,* Nov. 1, 1883, p. 2, col. 3.
323. *L'Abeille,* Dec. 2, 1883, p. 4, cols. 1–3.
324. Ibid., Sept. 1883, p. 3, col. 7.
325. *Picayune,* Oct. 1883, p. 4, col. 3.
326. *L'Abeille,* Nov. 10, 1883, p. 2, col. 3.
327. Ibid., Dec. 27, 1883, p. 2, col. 3.
328. Ibid., Sept. 2, 1883, p. 4, col. 2.
329. Ibid., Sept. 4, 1886, p. 1, col. 2; Sept. 8, 1883, p. 1, col. 4; Sept. 11, 1883, p. 1, col. 2.
330. Ibid., Sept. 25, 1883, p. 4, col. 2.
331. Ibid., Sept. 28, 1883 p. 1, col. 2.
332. Ibid., Sept. 30, 1883, p. 1, col. 4.
333. *Picayune,* Oct. 9, 1883, p. 5, col. 1; Oct. 11, 1883, p. 2, col. 2.
334. *L'Abeille,* Sept. 30, 1883, p. 1, col. 3; p. 1, col. 4; *Picayune,* Oct. 21, 1883, p. 2, col. 5.
335. *Picayune,* Oct. 20, 1883, afternoon, p. 1, col. 3; Oct. 28, 1883, p. 11, col. 5.
336. Ibid., Oct. 13, 1883, p. 1, col. 2. *L'Abeille,* Nov. 1, 1883, p. 1, col. 7; Nov. 2, 1883, p. 1, col. 2.
337. *L'Abeille,* Nov. 6, 1883, p. 1, col. 4; Nov. 7, 1883, p. 1, col. 4; Nov. 8, 1883, p. 1, col. 6; p. 1, col. 4. Review: Nov. 9, 1883, p. 1, col. 4.
338. Ibid., Nov. 21, 1883, p. 1, cols. 4–6.
339. Ibid., Nov. 18, 1883, p. 1, col. 2; Nov. 22, 1883, p. 1, col. 3. Review: Nov. 23, 1883, p. 1, col. 2.
340. Ibid., Dec. 9, 1883, p. 1, col. 2; p. 2, col. 3; Dec. 12, 1883, p. 1, col. 4.
341. Ibid., Dec. 13, 1883, p. 1, col. 3.
342. Ibid., Dec. 16, 1883, p. 1, col. 3; p. 4, col. 4; Dec. 20, 1883, p. 1, col. 4.
343. Ibid., Dec. 23, 1883, p. 1, col. 2.
344. Ibid., Jan. 1, 1884, p. 2, col. 1.
345. Ibid., Mar. 20, 1884, p. 1, col. 4.
346. Ibid., Jan. 24, 1884, p. 1, col. 3. For an outline of the bad financial situation of the French Opera, see Mar. 30, 1884, p. 4.
347. Ibid., Feb. 2, 1884, p. 1, col. 5; Feb. 10, 1884, p. 4, col. 4, Sunday; Feb. 12, 1884, p. 2, col. 2.
348. Ibid., Feb. 14, 1884, p. 1, col. 4. Review: Feb. 14, 1884, p. 1, col. 4.
349. Ibid., Feb. 14, 1884, p. 1, col. 4.
350. Ibid., Feb. 12, 1884, p. 2, col. 2.
351. Ibid., Mar. 2, 1884, p. 1, col. 4.
352. Ibid., Mar. 20, 1884, p. 4, col. 1; Mar. 22, 1884, p. 1, col. 3.
353. Ibid., Mar. 16, 1884, p. 1, cols. 1 and 5; Mar. 20, 1884, p. 1, col. 4; Mar. 21, 1884, p. 1, col. 4; Mar. 22, 1884, p. 1, col. 3.
354. Ibid., Mar. 26, 1884, p. 1, col. 4.
355. Ibid., Jan. 23, 1884, p. 1, col. 4; Jan. 24, 1884, p. 1, col. 3.
356. Ibid., Jan. 23, 1884, p. 2, col. 2.
357. Ibid., Feb. 12, 1884, p. 2, col. 2.
358. Ibid., Feb. 15, 1884, p. 1, col. 4.
359. Ibid., Feb. 15, 1884, p. 1, col. 4; Feb. 17, 1884, p. 4, col. 4.
360. Ibid., Feb. 2, 1884, p. 1, col. 5.
361. Ibid., Mar. 6, 1884, p. 1, col. 4.
362. Ibid., Mar. 23, 1884, p. 1, col. 3.
363. Ibid., Mar. 20, 1884, p. 1, col. 2; Mar. 22, 1884, p. 1, col. 3.
364. Ibid., Apr. 8, 1884, p. 1, col. 2.
365. Ibid., Apr. 10, 1884, p. 1, col. 2.
366. Ibid., Apr. 18, 1884, p. 1, col. 6.

367. Ibid., Apr. 18, 1884, p. 1, col. 2; Apr. 20, 1884, p. 1, col. 2; Apr. 22, 1884, p. 1, col. 2.
368. Ibid., May 2, 1884, p. 1, col. 3; May 11, 1884, p. 1, col. 3.
369. Ibid., May 2, 1884, p. 1, col. 3.
370. Ibid., May 23, 1884, p. 1, col. 3; May 23, 1884, p. 1, col. 3.
371. Ibid., May 3, 1884, p. 1, col. 6; May 11, 1884, p. 1, col. 3; May 31, 1884, p. 2, col. 1.
372. Ibid., July 25, 1884, p. 1, col. 7; Aug. 20, 1884, p. 1, col. 3.
373. Ibid., June 6, 1884, p. 1, col. 6.
374. Ibid., July 6, 1884, p. 1, col. 6, and p. 4, col. 2.
375. Ibid., June 11, 1884, p. 2, col. 3.
376. Ibid., Sept. 16, 1884, p. 4, cols. 1–2.
377. Ibid., Sept. 14, 1884, p. 2, col. 3.
378. Ibid., Oct. 26, 1884, p. 4, col. 2.
379. Ibid., Dec. 7, 1884, p. 4, col. 3. Review: Dec. 9, 1884, p. 4, col. 2.
380. Ibid., Dec. 5, 1884, p. 4, col. 2; Dec. 7, 1884, p. 4, col. 3.
381. Ibid., Dec. 20, 1884, p. 2, col. 1; Dec. 23, 1884, p. 4, col. 2.
382. Ibid., Oct. 11, 1884, p. 4; Oct. 12, 1884, p. 1, col. 5; Oct. 26, 1884, p. 4, col. 2; Oct. 30, 1884, p. 4, cols. 1–2.
383. Ibid., Mar. 15, 1884, p. 1, col. 4; Apr. 20, 1884, p. 1, col. 2; Aug. 13, 1884, p. 1, col. 3.
384. Ibid., Oct. 30, 1884, p. 2, col. 1.
385. Ibid., Jan. 15, 1885, p. 1, col. 2.
386. Ibid., Jan. 18, 1885, p. 1, col. 2.
387. Ibid., Jan. 23, 1885, p. 4, col. 1.
388. Ibid., Jan. 23, 1885, p. 4, col. 1.
389. Ibid., Jan. 20, 1885, p. 2, col. 1; Feb. 1, 1885, p. 4, col. 3. Review: Jan. 27, 1885, p. 2, cols. 1–2.
390. Ibid., Feb. 1, 1885, p. 4, col. 3.
391. Ibid., Feb. 6, 1885, p. 4, col. 1.
392. Ibid., Feb. 13, 1885, p. 4, col. 3.
393. Ibid., Sunday, Feb. 15, 1885, p. 2, col. 4.
394. Ibid., Mar. 1, 1885, p. 4, col. 1.
395. Ibid., Mar. 3, 1885, p. 4, col. 2; Mar. 4, 1885, p. 4, col. 1.
396. Ibid., Mar. 19, 1885, p. 4, col. 1.
397. Ibid., Mar. 13, 1885, p. 4, col. 1. Review: Mar. 17, 1885, p. 4, cols. 1–2, and correction: Mar. 19, 1885, p. 4, col. 1.
398. Ibid., Mar. 29, 1885, p. 4, col. 3.
399. Ibid., Apr. 2, 1885, p. 4, col. 4.
400. Ibid., Mar. 29, 1885, p. 1, col. 5.
401. Ibid., Apr. 5, 1885, p. 4, col. 4.
402. Ibid., Apr. 4, 1885, p. 4, col. 2.
403. Ibid., Mar. 29, 1885, p. 1, col. 2.
404. Ibid., Apr. 7, 1885, p. 4, col. 4.
405. Ibid., Apr. 5, 1885, p. 4, col. 3.
406. Ibid., May 24, 1885, p. 4, col. 4; May 26, 1885, p. 1, col. 6; May 30, 1885, p. 4, col. 1; June 4, 1885, p. 4, col. 1.
407. Ibid., June 5, 1885, p. 2, col. 1.
408. Ibid., May 20, 1885, p. 4, col. 1.
409. Ibid., June 6, 1885, p. 4, col. 2, and June 7, 1885, p. 4, col. 4.
410. Ibid., Apr. 19, 1885, p. 4, col. 4; May 2, 1885, p. 4, col. 1. Review: May 25, 1885, p. 4, col. 1.
411. Ibid., Apr. 10, 1885, p. 4, col. 3; Apr. 29, 1885, p. 4, col. 1; May 2, 1885, p. 4, col. 1; May 3, 1885, p. 2, col. 4; May 5, 1885, p. 4, col. 2. Review: May 6, 1885, p. 4, col. 1; May 7, 1885, p. 4, col. 1.

412. Ibid., May 6, 1885, p. 4, col. 1.

413. Ibid., May 6, 1885, p. 1, col. 6. Review of Wednesday concert: May 7, 1885, p. 4, col. 2.

414. Ibid., May 12, 1885, p. 4, col. 1.

415. Ibid., May 14, 1885, p. 4, col. 2.

416. Ibid., May 16, 1885, p. 4, col. 1. Review: May 19, 1885, p. 4, cols. 1–2.

417. Ibid., May 16, 1885, p. 4, col. 1.

418. Ibid., May 26, 1885, p. 1, col. 1.

419. Ibid., May 28, 1885, p. 4, col. 1. Review: May 30, 1885, p. 4, col. 1.

420. Ibid., May 24, 1885, p. 4, col. 4.

421. Ibid., May 17, 1885, p. 4, col. 4, May 20, 1885, p. 4, col. 1.

422. Ibid., May 21, 1885, p. 4, col. 1; May 26, 1885, p. 1, col. 1; May 30, 1885, p. 4, col. 1. Review: June 3, 1885, p. 4, col. 1.

423. Ibid., June 4, 1885, p. 4, col. 1, and June 6, 1885, p. 4, col. 2.

424. Ibid., June 19, 1885, p. 4, col. 1.

425. Ibid., May 24, 1885, p. 1, col. 1.

426. Ibid., May 28, 1885, p. 4, col. 2.

427. Ibid., May 25, 1885, p. 4, col. 4; May 30, 1885, p. 4, col. 1.

428. Ibid., June 3, 1885, p. 1, col. 6.

429. Ibid., June 3, 1885, p. 1, col. 6; June 3, 1885, p. 4, col. 1; June 4, 1885, p. 4, col. 1; June 5, 1885, p. 1, col. 6.

430. Ibid., June 7, 1885, p. 4, col. 4; June 9, 1885, p. 4, col. 1.

431. Ibid., Oct. 3, 1885, p. 4, col. 1.

432. Ibid., Oct. 6, 1885, p. 4, col. 1.

433. Ibid., Oct. 14, 1885, p. 4, col. 1; Oct. 16, 1885, p. 4, col. 1.

434. Ibid., Oct. 27, 1885, p. 4, col. 1.

435. Ibid., Oct. 18, 1885, p. 4, col. 2.

436. Ibid., Nov. 13, 1885, p. 4, col. 1; Nov. 14, 1885, p. 4, col. 1. Review: Nov. 17, 1885, p. 4, col. 1.

437. Ibid., Dec. 28, 1885, p. 4, col. 1.

438. Ibid., Oct. 11, 1885, p. 4, col. 4.

439. Ibid., Jan. 5, 1886, p. 4, col. 4.

440. Ibid., Nov. 14, 1885, p. 4, col. 1; Nov. 15, 1885, p. 4, col. 4.

441. Ibid., Nov. 18, 1881, p. 4, col. 5; Nov. 19, 1885, p. 4, col. 3; Nov. 22, 1885, p. 4, col. 3; Nov. 22, 1885, p. 4, col. 4; Nov. 25, 1885, p. 4, col. 3; Nov. 27, 1885, p. 4, col. 3; Nov. 28, 1885, p. 4, cols. 3–4; Nov. 19, 1885, p. 4, col. 5; Dec. 1, 1885, p. 4, col. 4; Dec. 2, 1885, p. 4, col. 3; Dec. 3, 1885, p. 4, col. 4; Dec. 4, 1885, p. 4, col. 3, Dec. 5, 1885, p. 4, col. 3; Dec. 9, 1885, p. 4, cols. 2–3; Dec. 1, 1885, p. 4, col. 3; Dec. 11, 1885, p. 4, col. 4; Dec. 16, 1885, p. 4, col. 4; Dec. 17, 1885, p. 4, col. 3; Dec. 19, 1885, p. 4, col. 2; Dec. 20, 1885, p. 4, cols. 4–5; Dec. 29, 1885, p. 4, col. 3; Jan. 6, 1886, p. 4, col. 4; Jan. 7, 1886, p. 4, col. 4; Jan. 10, 1886, p. 4, cols. 4–5.

442. Ibid., Jan. 1, 1886, p. 3, col. 4.

443. Ibid., Jan. 12, 1886, p. 4, col. 4; Jan. 13, 1886, p. 4, col. 3.

444. On Apr. 21 D'Aquin returned from Paris, where he had spent several weeks (*L'Abeille,* Apr. 21, 1886, p. 4, col. 1).

445. *L'Abeille,* Jan. 12, 1886, p. 1, col. 9.

446. Ibid., Jan. 20, 1886, p. 4, col. 1; Jan. 21, 1886, p. 4, col. 2; Jan. 23, 1886, p. 4, col. 1.

447. Ibid., Jan. 28, 1886, p. 4, col. 1.

448. Ibid., Jan. 29, 1886, p. 4, col. 1; Feb. 2, 1886, p. 4, col. 1.

449. *Picayune,* Feb. 2, 1886, p. 4, col. 3.

450. Ibid., Feb. 7, 1886, p. 3, col. 3; p. 16, col. 6.

451. *L'Abeille,* Mar. 2, 1886, p. 4, col. 1.

452. Ibid., Mar. 2, 1886, p. 4, cols. 3–4.

453. Ibid., Mar. 2, 1886, p. 1, col. 8; Mar. 3, 1886, p. 4, col. 1. Review: Mar. 4, 1886, p. 4, col. 1.

454. Ibid., Mar. 3, 1886, p. 4, col. 1; Mar. 4, 1886, p. 1, col. 9; p. 4, col. 1; Mar. 5, 1886, p. 4, col. 1. Review: Mar. 6, 1886, p. 4, col. 1.

455. Ibid., Mar. 10, 1886, p. 4, col. 1.

456. Ibid., Mar. 7, 1886, p. 1, col. 9; p. 4, col. 3.

457. Ibid., Mar. 14, 1886, p. 4, col. 4; Mar. 16, 1886, p. 4, col. 1. Review: Mar. 18, 1886, p. 4, col. 2; Mar. 21, 1886, p. 4, cols. 2–4.

458. Ibid., Mar. 21, 1886, p. 1, col. 8; Mar. 21, 1886, p. 4, cols 2–4; Mar. 23, 1886, p. 4, col. 1; Mar. 24, 1886, p. 4, col. 1.

459. Ibid., Mar. 25, 1886, p. 4, col. 1; Mar. 28, 1886, p. 4, col. 1; Mar. 30, 1886, p. 4, col. 4; Mar. 31, 1886, p. 4, col. 1; Apr. 3, 1886, p. 4, col. 1; Apr. 4, 1886, p. 4, col. 2.

460. Ibid., Mar. 10, 1886, p. 4, col. 1; Mar. 11, 1886, p. 4, col. 9; p. 4, col. 1. Review: Mar. 14, 1886, p. 4, cols. 1–3.

461. Ibid., Mar. 13, 1886, p. 1, col. 8; Mar. 14, 1886, p. 4, col. 4.

462. Ibid., Apr. 6, 1886, p. 4, col. 1.

463. Ibid., Apr. 11, 1886, p. 1, col. 8; p. 4, col. 3; Apr. 15, 1886, p. 4, col. 1; Apr. 17, 1886, p. 4, col. 1; Apr. 18, 1886, p. 4, col. 1.

464. Ibid., Apr. 21, 1886, p. 4, col. 1; Apr. 25, 1886, p. 4, col. 2; Apr. 27, 1886, p. 4, col. 2; Apr. 30, 1886, p. 4, col. 1.

465. Ibid., Apr. 11, 1886, p. 1, col. 9; Apr. 16, 1886, p. 4, col. 1; Apr. 25, 1886, p. 4, col. 3; Apr. 28, 1886, p. 4, col. 4; Apr. 30, 1886, p. 4, col. 1; May 1, 1886, p. 4, col. 1. Review: May 2, 1886, p. 4, col. 1; p. 4, col. 2.

466. Ibid., May 4, 1886, p. 4, col. 1; May 5, 1886, p. 4, col. 1; May 7, 1886, p. 4, col. 1. Review: May 9, 1886, p. 4, cols. 1–3.

467. Ibid., May 11, 1886, p. 4, col. 1; May 14, 1886, p. 4, col. 1. Review: May 15, 1886, p. 4, col. 1; May 16, 1886, p. 4, cols. 2–4.

468. Ibid., May 1, 1886, p. 1, col. 2.

469. Ibid., May 2, 1886, p. 4, col. 3.

470. Ibid., Apr. 15, 1886, p. 4, col. 1; Apr. 25, 1886, p. 1, col. 2; May 4, 1886, p. 4, col. 1; May 5, 1886, p. 4, col. 1. Review: May 9, 1886, p. 4.

471. Ibid., Apr. 23, 1886, p. 4, col. 1; May 2, 1886, p. 4, col. 3.

472. At its fall 1886 meeting, O'Donnell was named its director. It had ninety members (*L'Abeille*, Oct. 11, 1886, p. 4, col. 1).

473. *L'Abeille*, May 16, 1886, p. 4, cols. 2–4; May 19, 1886, p. 4, col. 1; May 21, 1886, p. 4, col. 1. Review: May 25, 1886, p. 4, cols. 1–2.

474. *Picayune*, June 6, 1886, p. 8, col. 6.

475. Ibid., June 10, 1886, p. 8, col. 5.

476. Ibid., June 18, 1886, p. 5, col. 3. Review: June 19, 1886, p. 4, col. 6.

477. *L'Abeille*, May 15, 1886, p. 1, col. 9; May 16, 1886, p. 4, col. 4; May 23, 1886, p. 1, col. 9.

478. Ibid., May 16, 1886, p. 1, col. 8; May 16, p. 4, col. 4.

479. Ibid., May 16, 1886, p. 1, col. 8; May 21, 1886, p. 4, col. 2; May 23, 1886, p. 1, col. 9.

480. *Picayune*, June 1, 1886, p. 5, col. 3; June 6, 1886, p. 3, col. 6; June 21, 1886, p. 5, col. 3, June 24, 1886, p. 3, col. 5; June 26, 1886, p. 8, col. 4; June 27, 1886, p. 11, col. 5; June 29, 1886, p. 4, col. 5.

481. *L'Abeille*, Sept. 2, 1886, p. 1, col. 9; p. 2, col. 3; Sept. 5, 1886, p. 4, col. 3; Sept. 11, 1886, p. 4, col. 1; Sept. 2, 1886 p. 2, col. 2. This last source lists all the members of the band.

482. Ibid., Sept. 5, 1886, p. 4, col. 3; Sept. 8, 1886, p. 4, col. 1; Sept. 11, 1886, p. 4, col. 1; Sept. 15, 1886, p. 4, col. 1.

483. Ibid., Sept. 18, 1886, p. 4, col. 1; Sept. 19, 1886, p. 1, col. 9.

484. *Picayune,* June 1, 1886, p. 5, col. 3; June 11, 1886, p. 5, col. 3. *L'Abeille,* Sept. 2, 1886, p. 1, col. 9; p. 2, col. 2.

485. *Picayune,* June 2, 1886, p. 3, col. 3; June 21, 1886, p. 5, col. 3; June 24, 1886, p. 3, col. 5.

486. Ibid., June 4, 1886, p. 4, col. 5.

487. Ibid., June 25, 1886, p. 4, col. 3.

488. *L'Abeille,* Sept. 9, 1886, p. 4, col. 1.

489. Ibid., Sept. 11, 1886, p. 4, col. 1.

490. Ibid., Sept. 22, 1886, p. 1, col. 9.

491. Ibid., Sept. 25, 1886, p. 4, col. 1.

492. Ibid., Oct. 12, 1886, p. 4, col. 1.

493. Ibid., Oct. 11, 1886, p. 4, col. 2.

494. Ibid., Oct. 10, 1886, p. 4, col. 3; Oct. 12, 1886, p. 4, col. 1; Oct. 19, 1886, p. 4, col. 1. Lengthy review: Oct. 21, 1886, p. 4, col. 1.

495. Ibid., Oct. 24, 1886, p. 4, col. 3; Oct. 27, 1886, p. 4, col. 1.

496. Ibid., Oct. 30, 1886, p. 4, col. 1; Nov. 2, 1886, p. 4, col. 1.

497. Ibid., Nov. 7, 1886, p. 4, col. 2; Nov. 9, 1886, p. 1, col. 8; p. 4, col. 2; Nov. 10, 1886, p. 4, col. 2.

498. Ibid., Nov. 16, 1886, p. 4, col. 1.

499. Florence Huberwald, a leader in the women's rights organization, wowed delegates in Atlanta when she started to sing at a national convention (*Picayune,* Feb. 5, 1895, p. 3, col. 6).

500. *L'Abeille,* Nov. 17, 1886, p. 4, col. 1.

501. Ibid., Dec. 4, 1886, p. 4, col. 1. See Dec. 5, 1886, p. 4, col. 4.

502. Ibid., Dec. 3, 1886, p. 4, col. 1; Dec. 4, 1886, p. 4, col. 1; Dec. 5, 1886, p. 4, col. 4 (very lengthy); Dec. 9, 1886, p. 4, cols. 1–3; and Dec. 10, 1886, p. 4, col. 1. Review: Dec. 1, 1886, p. 4, col. 1.

503. Ibid., Dec. 5, 1886, p. 4, col. 4.

504. Ibid., Dec. 5, 1886, p. 1, col. 8; Dec. 5, 1886, p. 4, col. 4.

505. Ibid., Dec. 4, 1886, p. 4, col. 1.

CHAPTER SEVEN

1. *L'Abeille,* Jan. 9, 1887, p. 4, col. 4; Jan. 13, 1887, p. 4, col. 1.

2. Ibid., Jan. 23, 1887, p. 4, col. 4; Jan. 26, 1887, p. 4, col. 2; Jan. 27, 1887, p. 4, col. 1.

3. Ibid., Jan. 27, 1887, p. 4, col. 1; Jan. 28, 1887, p. 4, col. 2.

4. Ibid., Jan. 26, 1887, p. 1, col. 9; Jan. 26, p. 4, col. 2; Jan. 27, 1887, p. 4, col. 1; Jan. 28, 1887, p. 4, col. 1; Feb. 1, 1887, p. 4, col. 2.

5. Ibid., Feb. 8, 1887, p. 4, col. 1.

6. Ibid., Feb. 5, 1887, p. 4, col. 1.

7. Ibid., Feb. 6, 1887, p. 1, col. 2.

8. Ibid., Feb. 13, 1887, p. 1, col. 8.

9. Maugé was so impressed with the New Orleans–Havana connection that he decided that the upcoming 1887–88 season would open in Havana in Nov. before moving to New Orleans around Dec. 1, 1887 (*Picayune,* May 17, 1887, p. 4, col. 5).

10. *Picayune,* Mar. 11, 1887, p. 8, col. 4.

11. Ibid., Mar. 18, 1887, p. 3, col. 2.

12. Ibid., Mar. 18, 1887, p. 8, col. 3.

13. *L'Abeille,* Nov. 20, 1887, p. 1, col. 3; p. 4, col. 3; Nov. 22, 1887, p. 4, cols. 1–2.

14. *Picayune,* Mar. 25, 1887, p. 4, col. 4.

15. *L'Abeille,* Apr. 1, 1887, p. 4, col. 1.

16. Ibid., Jan. 25, 1887, p. 4, col. 2.

17. Ibid., Apr. 1, 1887, p. 4, col. 1.

18. Ibid., Apr. 2, 1887, p. 4, col. 1.

19. *Picayune,* Apr. 10, 1887, p. 5, col. 2. Review: Apr. 12, 1887, p. 4, col. 4.

20. Ibid., Apr. 17, 1887, p. 8, col. 2; Apr. 23, 1887, p. 5, col. 2; Apr. 29, 1887, p. 8, col. 6; Apr. 30, 1887, p. 6, col. 2.

21. Ibid., Apr. 20, 1887, p. 5, col. 2. Review: Apr. 21, 1887, p. 4, col. 6.

22. "Mme. Pemberton Hincks, the singer, has left for New York, with her sister Mlle. Berthe Pemberton, the pianist whom we regret is no longer living in New Orleans. They will no doubt make a sensation in New York" (*L'Abeille,* Sept. 27, 1888, p. 4, col. 1). News came from New York that Mlle Berthe Pemberton, pianist who left New Orleans a year ago, was now teaching at New York's College of Music (*L'Abeille,* Oct. 14, 1888, p. 4, col. 1). Later the papers carried a long account of the success in New York, Boston, Lenox, and Philadelphia, of Mme. L. Pemberton Hincks, soprano from New Orleans (*L'Abeille,* Sept. 8, 1889, p. 4, col. 2; Sept. 22, 1889, p. 4, col. 2). In May 1891, Pemberton-Hincks was singing to great acclaim in London.

23. *Picayune,* Mar. 13, 1887, p. 8, col. 1; Apr. 10, 1887, p. 5, col. 2; Apr. 24, 1887, p. 5, col. 2.

24. Ibid., May 4, 1887, p. 3, col. 1.

25. Ibid., Mar. 12, 1887, p. 5, col. 3; Mar. 13, 1887, p. 8, col. 3.

26. Ibid., June 11, 1887, p. 5, col. 3; June 12, 1887, p. 5, col. 1; June 14, 1887, p. 4, col. 4.

27. Ibid., May 5, 1887, p. 4, col. 4.

28. Ibid., May 21, 1887, p. 5, col. 2; May 22, 1887, p. 6, col. 2; June 7, 1887, p. 8, col. 5; June 5, 1887, p. 6, col. 4.

29. Ibid., May 19, 1887, p. 5, col. 2; June 13, 1887, p. 5, col. 2; June 16, 1887, p. 4, col. 5.

30. Ibid., May 5, 1887, p. 5, col. 2.

31. Ibid., May 15, 1887, p. 5, col. 2.

32. Ibid., May 21, 1887, p. 5, col. 2; May 23, 1887, p. 5, col. 2; May 26, 1887, p. 5, col. 2; May 27, 1887, p. 4, col. 5.

33. Ibid., May 41, 1887, p. 4, col. 4.

34. Ibid., June 7, 1887, p. 8, col. 4.

35. Ibid., May 21, 1887, p. 5, col. 2; May 23, 1887, p. 5, col. 2.

36. Ibid., May 22, 1887, p. 5, col. 2; May 26, 1887, p. 8, col. 5.

37. Ibid., May 30, 1887, p. 2, col. 1.

38. Ibid., June 2, 1887, p. 8, col. 3.

39. *Constitution and By-Laws of the Mendelssohn Society* (New Orleans: Pelican Steam Book and Job Printing House, 1887). Copy at Tulane, Rare Books, Vertical File, under Musical Organizations.

40. *Picayune,* June 3, 1887, p. 8, col. 3.

41. Ibid., June 7, 1887, p. 8, col. 8.

42. Ibid., June 5, 1887, p. 5, col. 2; p. 6, col. 4; June 14, 1887, p. 4, col. 4. Review: June 15, 1887, p. 8, col. 4.

43. Ibid., June 17, 1887, p. 3, col. 4.

44. Review in *Picayune,* Oct. 4, 1887, p. 8, col. 1.

45. *Picayune,* Oct. 16, 1887, p. 9, col. 5.

46. Ibid., Oct. 16, 1887, p. 7, col. 2.

47. Ibid., Oct. 25, 1887, p. 4, col. 5.

48. Ibid., Oct. 28, 1887, p. 8, col. 4.

49. Ibid., Oct. 2, 1887, p. 11, col. 6; Oct. 23, 1887, p. 8, col. 3; Oct. 26, 1887, p. 4, col. 5; Oct. 28, 1887, p. 5, col. 2; Oct. 30, 1887, p. 8, col. 5. Review: Oct. 31, 1887, p. 4, col. 4.

50. *L'Abeille,* Nov. 1, 1887, p. 1, col. 9.

51. Ibid., Nov. 4, 1887, p. 4, col. 16. Review: Nov. 10, 1887, p. 6, col. 1.

52. Ibid., Nov. 19, 1887, p. 1, col. 9; Nov. 24, 1887, p. 3, col. 2; Nov. 26, 1887, p. 4, col. 1; Nov. 27, 1887, p. 1, col. 8; p. 4, col. 3; Nov. 30, 1887, p. 4, col. 2. Review: Dec. 1, 1887, p. 4, col. 1; Dec. 4, 1887, p. 4, col. 2.

53. Ibid., Nov. 19, 1887, p. 4, col. 2; Nov. 27, p. 4, col. 3; Dec. 1, 1887, p. 4, col. 1; Dec. 2, 1887, p. 4, col. 1. Review: Dec. 4, 1887, p. 4, col. 2.

54. Ibid., Dec. 3, 1887, p. 4, col. 2.

55. Ibid., Nov. 25, 1887, p. 4, col. 1.

56. *Picayune,* Jan. 1, 1888, p. 15, col. 2.

57. *L'Abeille,* Nov. 11, 1887, p. 4, col. 1; Nov. 13, 1887, p. 4, cols. 1–3.

58. *Picayune,* Feb. 21, 1888, p. 5, col. 2.

59. Ibid., Jan. 2, 1888, p. 2, col. 5.

60. Ibid., Jan. 8, 1888, p. 8, col. 2.

61. Ibid., Jan. 14, 1888, p. 8, col. 4.

62. Ibid., Feb. 1, 1888, p. 2, col. 5.

63. *Pilcher Conservatory Catalogue,* 1887–88, p. 17; *Picayune,* Feb. 1, 1888, p. 5, col. 2.

64. *Picayune,* Feb. 4, 1888, p. 4, col. 5.

65. Ibid., Feb. 7, 1888, p. 4, col. 4.

66. Ibid., Feb. 18, 1888, p. 8, col. 3.

67. Ibid., Feb. 28, 1888, p. 5, col. 3, and Feb. 29, 1888, p. 8, col. 2.

68. Ibid., Jan. 22, 1888, p. 10, col. 5; Feb. 19, 1888, p. 7, col. 4; Feb. 19, 1888, p. 8, col. 5; Feb. 28, 1888, p. 5, col. 2; Feb. 29, 1888, p. 8, col. 2.

69. Ibid., Feb. 19, 1888, p. 14, col. 2; Mar. 2, 1888, p. 8, col. 2.

70. Ibid., Mar. 11, 1888, p. 6, col. 7.

71. Louisiana State Museum, concert program.

72. *Picayune,* Mar. 14, 1888, p. 3, col. 3; Mar. 16, 1888, p. 8, col. 3.

73. Ibid., Friday, Mar. 16, 1888, p. 3, col. 2.

74. Ibid., Apr. 1, 1888, p. 3, col. 2.

75. Ibid., Apr. 3, 1888, p. 4, col. 4.

76. Ibid., Apr. 1, 1888, p. 8, col. 6; Apr. 2, 1888, p. 4, col. 3; Apr. 3, 1888, p. 4, col. 5; Apr. 4, 1888, p. 8, col. 4. The program is preserved at the Louisiana State Museum.

77. *Picayune,* Apr. 7, 1888, p. 4, col. 3.

78. Ibid., Apr. 8, 1888, p. 8, col. 4.

79. Ibid., Mar. 11, 1888, p. 5, col. 2; Mar. 18, 1888, p. 12, col. 3; Apr. 10, 1888, p. 8, col. 3; Apr. 11, 1888, p. 2, col. 6. The program is preserved in a Wehrmann scrapbook at the Louisiana State Museum.

80. *Picayune,* Apr. 22, 1888, p. 5, col. 2.

81. Ibid., Apr. 25, 1888, p. 4, col. 4.

82. Ibid., Apr. 27, 1888, p. 4, col. 6.

83. Ibid., Apr. 15, 1888, p. 5, col. 3; Apr. 22. 1888, p. 5, col. 2; May 2, 1888, p. 4, col. 6.

84. Ibid., May 3, 1888, p. 3, col. 3.

85. Ibid., May 3, 1888, p. 5, col. 2.

86. Ibid., May 7, 1888, p. 8, col. 3.

87. Ibid., Apr. 22, 1888, p. 9, col. 7; Apr. 25, 1888, p. 8, col. 3; May 6, 1888, p. 8, cols. 6–7; May 7, 1888, p. 8, col. 4.

88. Ibid., May 18, 1888, p. 5, col. 2; May 20, 1888, p. 7, col. 6.

89. Ibid., June 2, 1888, p. 4, col. 6.

90. Ibid., May 18, 1888, p. 5, col. 2.
91. *L'Abeille,* Aug. 31, 1888, p. 1, col. 1.
92. Ibid., Sept. 1, 1888, p. 2, col. 3; Sept. 2, 1888, p. 4, col. 1; Sept. 3, 1888, p. 4, col. 1.
93. Ibid., Sept. 14, 1988, p. 4, col. 1; Sept. 15, 1888, p. 4, col. 2; Sept. 16, 1888, p. 4, col. 2. Review: Sept. 23, 1888, p. 4, col. 1.
94. Ibid., Oct. 6, 1888, p. 4, col. 1.
95. Ibid., Sept. 2, 1888, p. 4, col. 1; Sept. 6, 1888, p. 4, col. 1.
96. Ibid., Oct. 6, 1888, p. 4, col. 1; Oct. 9, 1888, p. 4, col. 1.
97. Ibid., Sept. 19, 1888, p. 4, col. 1; Sept. 21, 1888, p. 4, col. 1. Review: Sept. 22, 1888, p. 4, col. 1; Sept. 23, 1888, p. 4, col. 1.
98. Ibid., Oct. 21, 1888, p. 4, col. 1; Oct. 24, 1888, p. 4, col. 1; Oct. 25, 1888, p. 4, col. 1. Review: Oct. 26, 1888, p. 4, col. 1; Oct. 28, 1888, p. 4, col. 2.
99. Ibid., Sept. 9, 1888, p. 4, col. 1; Sept. 13, 1888, p. 4, col. 2; Sept. 14, 1888, p. 4, col. 1. Review: Sept. 16, 1888, p. 4, col. 1.
100. Ibid., Sept. 27, 1888, p. 4, col. 1.
101. Ibid., Oct. 11, 1888, p. 4, col. 1; Oct. 30, 1888, p. 4, col. 2.
102. *Picayune,* Nov. 24, 1888, p. 6, col. 1.
103. *L'Abeille,* Oct. 21, 1888, p. 4, col. 1; Oct. 26, 1888, p. 4, col. 1. Review: Oct. 27, 1888, p. 4, col. 2; Oct. 28, 1888, p. 4, col. 2.
104. Ibid., Oct. 28, 1888, p. 4, col. 1.
105. Ibid., Oct. 28, 1888, p. 4, col. 3.
106. Ibid., Nov. 4, 1888, p. 4, col. 2.
107. *Picayune,* Nov. 15, 1888, p. 4, col. 5; Dec. 12, 1888, p. 3, col. 3.
108. Ibid., Dec. 1, 1888, p. 4, col. 5.
109. Ibid., Dec. 18, 1888, p. 8, col. 3.
110. Ibid., Nov. 27, 1888, p. 8, col. 6.
111. Ibid., Dec. 16, 1888, p. 5, col. 2; Dec. 20, 1888, p. 8, col. 4.
112. *L'Abeille,* Nov. 6, 1888, p. 4, col. 3.
113. Ibid., Oct. 24, 1888, p. 4, col. 1; Oct. 25, 1888, p. 4, col. 1; Oct. 7, 1888, p. 4, col. 1; Nov. 8, 1888, p. 4, col. 1.
114. *Picayune,* Feb. 21, 1889, p. 8, col. 3.
115. Ibid., Jan. 15, 1889, p. 3, col. 3.
116. Ibid., Jan. 24, 1889, p. 4, col. 3.
117. Ibid., Feb. 5, 1889, p. 8, col. 6.
118. Ibid., Feb. 10, 1889, p. 8, col. 2; p. 5, col. 2, Feb. 11, 1889, p. 3, col. 2, p. 5, col. 3 ; Feb. 12, 1889, p. 2, col. 2.
119. Ibid., Feb. 16, 1889, p. 4, col. 4.
120. Ibid., Feb. 24, 1889, p. 3, col. 4; Feb. 25, 1889, p. 3, col. 4.
121. Ibid., Feb. 24, 1889, p. 3, col. 4; Feb. 25, 1889, p. 3, col. 4; p. 5, col. 3; Feb. 26, 1889, p. 4, col. 5.
122. Ibid., Feb. 29, 1889, p. 5, col. 2.
123. Ibid., Mar. 10, 1889, p. 12, col. 7; Mar. 12, 1889, p. 4, col. 4.
124. Ibid., Mar. 17, 1889, p. 4, col. 4; Mar. 26, 1889, p. 8, col. 4.
125. Ibid., Mar. 14, 1889, p. 8, col. 2.
126. Ibid., Mar. 14, 1889, p. 3, col. 4.
127. Ibid., Mar. 14, 1889, p. 5, col. 2.
128. Ibid., Mar. 16, 1889, p. 8, col. 2.
129. Ibid., Mar. 25, 1889, p. 8, col. 5.
130. Ibid., Mar. 28, 1889, p. 8, col. 4.

Notes to Pages 495–500 | 645

131. Ibid., Mar. 31, 1889, p. 5, col. 2; Apr. 13, 1889, p. 5, col. 2.
132. Ibid., 1889, p. 5, col. 2.
133. Ibid., Apr. 22, 1889, p. 4, col. 3; Apr. 23, 1889, p. 8, col. 4.
134. Ibid., Apr. 24, 1889, p. 8, col. 4.
135. Ibid., Apr. 14, 1889, p. 5, col. 2; p. 8, col. 2; Apr. 21, 1889, p. 8, col. 2; Apr. 25, 1889. Review: Apr. 26, 1889, p. 4, col. 4.
136. Ibid., Feb. 27, 1889, p. 5, col. 3.
137. Ibid., Apr. 29, 1889, p. 8, col. 3.
138. Ibid., Apr. 28, 1889, p. 10, col. 6.
139. Ibid., May 5, 1889, p. 7, col. 5.
140. Ibid., May 4, 1889, p. 8, col. 4.
141. Ibid., May 5, 1889, p. 3, col. 3. While the aria is from *Mignon,* it is sung by Philine, not Mignon.
142. *Picayune,* May 5, 1889, p. 5, col. 2.
143. Ibid., May 10, 1889, p. 8, col. 5.
144. Ibid., May 12, 1889, p. 5, col. 3; May 16, 1889, p. 3, col. 2.
145. Ibid., May 16, 1889, p. 3, col. 2.
146. Ibid., June 1, 1889, p. 2, col. 5.
147. Ibid., May 26, 1889, p. 5, col. 2; June 2, 1889, p. 4, col. 5.
148. Ibid., May 18, 1889, p. 5, col. 2; May 20, 1889, p. 4, col. 6. Review: June 5, 1889, p. 8, col. 2.
149. Ibid., May 26, 1889, p. 5, col. 2.
150. Ibid., Oct. 25, 1889, p. 4, col. 4.
151. Ibid., Oct. 26, 1889, p. 4, col. 5.
152. Ibid., Oct. 26, 1889, p. 8, col. 3.
153. Ibid., Oct. 27, 1889, p. 8, col. 1; Oct. 30, 1889, p. 8, col. 5; Oct. 31, 1889, p. 8, col. 5.
154. Ibid., Nov. 4, 1889, p. 5, col. 2.
155. Kinzer, "The Tio Family," 22. See *New Orleans Weekly Pelican,* Nov. 2, 1889.
156. *Picayune,* Oct. 26, 1889, p. 8, col. 4; Oct. 27, 1889, p. 8, col. 1; Nov. 1, 1889, p. 3, col. 4; Nov. 4, 1889, p. 5, col. 2; Nov. 6, 1889, p. 2, col. 6; Nov. 9, 1889, p. 4, col. 5.
157. Ibid., Nov. 20, 1889, p. 2, col. 4.
158. Ibid., Nov. 23, 1889, p. 4, col. 6.
159. Ibid., Nov. 27, 1889, p. 1, col. 7.
160. Ibid., Nov. 26, 1889, p. 4, col. 4.
161. *L'Abeille,* Feb. 26, 1890, p. 1, cols. 8–9; p. 4, col. 2; Feb. 27, 1890, p. 4, col. 1; Mar. 2, 1890, p. 1, col. 8; Apr. 2, 1890, p. 4, col. 2; Mar. 8, 1890, p. 4, col. 1.
162. *Picayune,* Nov. 7, 1889, p. 7, col. 3.
163. Ibid., Nov. 10, 1889, p. 16.
164. Ibid., Nov. 17, 1889, p. 16, col. 6.
165. Ibid., Nov. 20, 1889, p. 2, col. 2 and 4.
166. Ibid., Nov. 21, 1889, p. 8, col. 2.
167. Ibid., Nov. 22, 1889, p. 8, col. 4.
168. Ibid., Nov. 28, 1889, p. 5, col. 2.
169. Ibid., Dec. 8, 1889, p. 7, col. 3.
170. Ibid., Dec. 6, 1889, p. 3, col. 2.
171. Ibid., Dec. 7, 1889, p. 4, col. 6.
172. Ibid., Dec. 17, 1889, p. 6, col. 3; Dec. 8, 1889, p. 8, col. 2; Dec. 9, 1889, p. 5, col. 2. Reviews: Dec. 9, 1889, p. 2, col. 3; Dec. 10, 1889, p. 7, col. 3.
173. Ibid., Dec. 10, 1889, p. 2, col. 7.

174. Ibid., Dec. 8, 1889, p. 8, cols. 2–3; Dec. 12, 1889, p. 4, col. 4.
175. Ibid., Dec. 24, 1889, p. 6, col. 3.
176. Ibid., Dec. 25, 1889, p. 4, col. 4.
177. Ibid., Dec. 28, 1889, p. 4, col. 6.
178. Ibid., Dec. 22, 1889, p. 6, col. 6.
179. Ibid., Dec. 25, 1889, p. 8, col. 3; Dec. 29, 1889, p. 7, col. 2; Dec. 30, 1889, p. 5, col. 2. Review: Dec. 30, 1889, p. 2, col. 2.
180. Ibid., Jan. 2, 1890, p. 3, col. 4.
181. See above, p. 75.
182. *Picayune,* Jan. 10, 1890, p. 4, col. 5.
183. Ibid., Jan. 14, 1890, p. 2, col. 3.
184. Ibid., Feb. 2, 1890, p. 8, col. 4.
185. Ibid., Jan. 25, 1890, p. 6, col. 6.
186. Ibid., Mar. 28, 1889, p. 8, col. 4; Nov. 4, 1889, p. 8, col. 6.
187. Ibid., Feb. 13, 1890, p. 6, cols. 5–6; Feb. 13, 1890, p. 6, cols. 5–6; Feb. 14, 1890, p. 8, col. 3; Feb. 15, 1890, p. 5, col. 2; p. 6, col. 2.
188. *L'Abeille,* Feb. 2, 1890, p. 4, col. 3.
189. Ibid., Feb. 5, 1890, p. 4, col. 1.
190. Ibid., Feb. 7, 1890, p. 4, col. 1, col. 2. Review: Feb. 9, 1890, p. 4, col. 1.
191. Ibid., Feb. 9, 1890, p. 4, col. 1.
192. *Picayune,* Feb. 25, 1890, p. 5, col. 3.
193. *Times-Democrat,* Mar. 18, 1890, p. 3, col. 3; *Picayune,* Mar. 18, 1890, p. 5, col. 2; *L'Abeille,* Mar. 20, 1890, p. 4, col. 2. Review: *Daily States,* Mar. 19, 1890, p. 2, col. 1. *L'Abeille,* Mar. 19, 1890, p. 4, col. 2.
194. *Picayune,* Feb. 28, 1890, p. 5, col. 2. *L'Abeille,* Mar. 1, 1890, p. 4, col. 1 (end); Mar. 2, 1890, p. 1, col. 9; review: Mar. 2, 1890, p. 4, col. 1.
195. *L'Abeille,* Mar. 8, 1890, p. 4, col. 1; Mar. 11, 1890, p. 4, cols. 1–3. See also Mar. 19, 1890, p. 4, col. 3.
196. Ibid., Mar. 4, 1890, p. 4, col. 1; Mar. 5, 1890, p. 4, col. 1; Mar. 7, 1890, p. 4, col. 1.
197. Ibid., Mar. 1, 1890, p. 4, col. 1; Mar. 8, 1890, p. 4, col. 1; Mar. 11, 1890, p. 4, col. 1–3; Mar. 13, 1890, p. 4, col. 1; Apr. 6, 1890, p. 4, col. 1; Apr. 12, 1890, p. 4, col. 1.
198. Ibid., Mar. 2, 1890, p. 4, col. 1; Mar. 7, 1890, p. 4, col. 2; Apr. 10, 1890, p. 4, col. 1.
199. Ibid., Mar. 18, 1890, p. 4, col. 1.
200. Ibid., Mar. 19, 1890, p. 4, col. 2; Mar. 20, 1890, p. 4, col. 1; Mar. 21, 1890, p. 4, col. 1; Mar. 22, 1890, p. 4, col. 1. Review: Mar. 26, 1890, p. 4, cols. 1–2.
201. Ibid., Mar. 28, 1890, p. 4, col. 1. Review: Mar. 30, 1890, p. 4, col. 1.
202. Ibid., Mar. 21, 1890, p. 1, col. 8; Apr. 6, 1890, p. 1, col. 9; Apr. 6, 1890, p. 4, col. 2; Apr. 8, 1890, p. 4, col. 1. Review: Apr. 9, 1890, p. 4, col. 1.
203. Ibid., Mar. 30, 1890, p. 4, col. 1; Apr. 6, 1890, p. 4, col. 2; Apr. 11, 890, p. 4, col. 1; Apr. 12, 1890, p. 4, col. 1; Apr. 13, 1890, p. 4, col. 2.
204. Ibid., Apr. 13, 1890, p. 4, col. 1; Apr. 19, 1890, p. 4, col. 1; Apr. 20, 1890, p. 4, col. 1. Review: Apr. 22, 1890, p. 4, col. 1; Apr. 23, 1890, p. 4, col. 1.
205. Ibid., Apr. 17, 1890, p. 4, col. 1; Apr. 20, 1890, p. 4, col. 1; Apr. 23, 1890, p. 4, col. 1. Review: Apr. 24, 1890, p. 4, cols. 1–2 ; Apr. 27, 1890, p. 4, col. 2.
206. Ibid., Apr. 27, 1890, p. 4, col. 2.
207. Ibid., Apr. 29, 1830, p. 1, col. 9; Apr. 30, 1890, p. 4, col. 1. Review: May 1, 1890, p. 4, col. 1.
208. Ibid., May 4, 1890, p. 4, col. 3; May 10, 1890, p. 4, col. 1.

209. Ibid., May 4, 1890, p. 4, col. 3; May 11, 1890, p. 1, col. 8; p. 4, col. 2; May 15, 1890, p. 1, col. 8; p. 4, col. 1; May 18, 1890, p. 1, col. 9; May 18, 1890, p. 4, col. 2; May 20, 1890, p. 4, col. 1. Review: May 16, 1890, p. 4, col. 2; May 22, 1890, p. 4, col. 2; May 23, 1890, p. 4, col. 2.

210. Ibid., May 24, 1890, p. 4, col. 2.

211. Ibid., Apr. 20, 1890, p. 4, col. 1; May 2, 1890, p. 4, col. 1; May 4, 1890, p. 4, col. 2; May 6, 1890, p. 4, col. 1. Review: May 9, 1890, p. 4, col. 2; May 9, 1890, p. 4, col. 1–2.

212. Ibid., Apr. 20, 1890, p. 4, col. 1; May 2, 1890, p. 4, col. 1; May 4, 1890, p. 4, col. 2; May 6, 1890, p. 4, col. 1; May 13, 1890, p. 4, col. 1; May 18, 1890, p. 1, col. 8; May 18, 1890, p. 4, col. 1. Review: May 9, 1890, p. 4, col. 2; May 9, 1890, p. 4, col. 1–2.

213. Ibid., May 24, 1890, p. 4, col. 2.

214. Ibid., June 1, 1890, p. 4, col. 1.

215. Ibid., Sept. 3, 1890, p. 4, col. 1; Sept. 4, 1890, p. 4, col. 2; Sept. 6, 1890, p. 4, col. 1; big article, Sept. 7, 1890, p. 4, col. 1. Review of season: Sept. 9, 1890, p. 4, col. 1.

216. Ibid., Sept. 7, 1890, p. 4, col. 1. Review: Sept. 9, 1890, p. 4, col. 1.

217. Ibid., Oct. 19, 1890, p. 4, col. 4.

218. Ibid., Oct. 18, 1890, p. 4, col. 1; Oct. 25, 1890, p. 4, col. 1.

219. Ibid., Nov. 7, 1890, p. 4, col. 1; Nov. 8, 1890, p. 4, col. 1.

220. Ibid., Nov. 11, 1890, p. 4, col. 2.

221. Ibid., Dec. 7, 1890, p. 1, col. 9; Dec. 10, 1890, p. 4, col. 1; Dec. 11, 1890, p. 4, col. 1; Dec. 16, 1890, p. 4, col. 1; Dec. 17, 1890, p. 4, col. 1. *Picayune,* Dec. 17, 1890, p. 5, col. 3. Review: *L'Abeille,* Dec. 19, 1890, p. 4, col. 1.

222. *L'Abeille,* Dec. 5, 1890, p. 1, col. 4.

223. *Picayune,* Dec. 20, 1890, p. 3, col. 6.

224. *L'Abeille,* Oct. 23, 1890, p. 4, col. 1; Oct. 28, 1890, p. 4, col. 1.

225. Ibid., Oct. 9, 1890, p. 4, col. 1.

226. Ibid., Nov. 26, 1890, p. 4, col. 2.

227. Ibid., Dec. 21, 1890, p. 4, col. 2.

228. Louisiana State Museum Historical Center, R6 136, acc #10778.

229. Ibid.

230. *Times-Democrat,* Jan. 15, 1891, p. 7, col. 5.

231. *L'Abeille,* May 9, 1891, p. 4, col. 1; May 13, 1891, p. 4, col. 1.

232. Ibid., Dec. 28, 1890, p. 4, col. 1; Apr. 5, 1891, p. 4, col. 2; Apr. 9, 1891, p. 4, col. 2; Apr. 10, 1891, p. 4, col. 1; Apr. 11, 1891, p. 4, col. 1. Reviews: Apr. 12, 1891, p. 4, col. 2; Apr. 14, 1891, p. 4, col. 1.

233. *Picayune,* Feb. 13–14, 1891, p. 5, col. 3. *L'Abeille,* Feb. 15, 1891, p. 4, col. 1; review: Feb. 15, 1891, p. 4, col. 1.

234. *L'Abeille,* Feb. 15, 1891, p. 4, col. 1. Review: Feb. 17, 1891, p. 4, col. 1; Mar. 1, 1891, p. 4, cols. 1–3.

235. Ibid., Feb. 17, 1891, p. 4, col. 1.

236. Ibid., Feb. 17, 1891, p. 4, col. 1; Feb. 28, 1891, p. 4, col. 1. Review: Feb. 27, 1891, p. 4, col. 1.

237. Ibid., Mar. 8, 1891, p. 1, col. 9; p. 4, col. 1; Mar. 11, 1891, p. 4, col. 1.

238. Ibid., Mar. 10, 1891, p. 4, col. 1.

239. Ibid., Mar. 18, 1891, p. 4, col. 1; Mar. 20, 1891, p. 4, col. 2.

240. Ibid., Apr. 4, 1891, p. 4, col. 1; Apr. 5, 1891, p. 4, col. 1.

241. Ibid., Mar. 15, 1891, p. 4, col. 1; Apr. 4, 1891, p. 4, col. 1.

242. Review: *L'Abeille,* Apr. 5, 1891, p. 4, col. 1.

243. *L'Abeille,* Apr. 9, 1891, p. 4, col. 1.

244. Ibid., Apr. 10, 1891, p. 4, col. 1; Apr. 19, 1891, p. 1, col. 9; p. 4, col. 1; Apr. 21, 1891, p. 4, col. 1; Apr. 22, 1891, p. 4, col. 1. Review: Apr. 23, 1891, p. 4, col. 1; Apr. 24, 1891, p. 4, col. 1.

245. Ibid., Apr. 9, 1891, p. 1, col. 9; Apr. 10, 1891, p. 4, col. 1.

246. Ibid., Apr. 10, 1891, p. 4, col. 1; Apr. 12, 1891, p. 1, col. 9; Apr. 14, 1891, p. 4, col. 1; Apr. 15, 1891, p. 4, col. 2. *Picayune,* Apr. 15, 1891, p. 5, col. 3. Review: *L'Abeille,* Apr. 17, 1891, p. 4, col. 1.

247. *L'Abeille,* Apr. 26, 1891, p. 4, col. 2. Review: Apr. 29, 1891, p. 4, col. 2.

248. Ibid., May 17, 1891, p. 4, col. 2; May 24, 1891, p. 4, col. 3; May 26, 1891, p. 4, col. 1. Reviews: May 27, 1891, p. 4, col. 1; May 28, 1891, p. 4, col. 1.

249. Ibid., June 7, 1891, p. 4, col. 2; June 11, 1891, p. 1, col. 8; June 14, 1891, p. 4, col. 1.

250. Ibid., May 12, 1891, p. 4, col. 1; May 17, 1801, p. 3, col. 2; May 20, 1891, p. 4, col. 1; May 21, 1891, p. 4, col. 1; May 23, 1891, p. 4, col. 1; p. 1, col. 9; May 24, 1891, p. 4, col. 3; May 26, 1891, p. 4, col. 1; May 27, 1891, p. 4, col. 1; May 28, 1891, p. 4, col. 1; May 29, 1891, p. 4, col. 2; May 30, 1891, p. 4, col. 1; May 31, 1891, p. 4, col. 1; June 2, 1891, p. 4, col. 1; June 3, 1891, p. 4, col. 1; June 5, 1891, p. 1, col. 8; p. 4, col. 1; June 6, 1891, p. 4, col. 1; June 7, 1891, p. 4, col. 1; June 11, 1891, p. 1, col. 8; June 13, 1891, p. 4, col. 1; July 2, 1891, p. 4, col. 1; July 5, 1891, p. 4, col. 4; July 8, 1891, p. 4, col. 1; July 17, 1891, p. 4, col. 1; July 19, 1891, p. 4, col. 2; July 31, 1891, p. 4, col. 1; Aug. 1, 1891, p. 4, col. 1; July 26, 1891, p. 4, col. 1; July 28, 1891, p. 4, col. 1.

251. Ibid., June 9, 1891, p. 4, col. 1.

252. Ibid., July 9, 1891, p. 4, col. 1.

253. Ibid., July 15, 1891, p. 4, col. 1; July 18, 1891, p. 4, col. 1; Aug. 4, 1891, p. 4, col. 1; Aug. 5, 1891, p. 4, col. 1.

254. *Picayune,* Aug. 23, 1891, p. 8, col. 5–6; Aug. 25, 1891, p. 3, col. 2; Aug. 29–91, p. 3, col. 6; Sept. 1, 1891.

255. Ibid., Aug. 6, 1891, p. 3, col. 3. *L'Abeille,* Aug. 6, 1891, p. 4, col. 1.

256. *Picayune,* Sept. 6, 1891, p. 8, col. 2; Sept. 7, 1891, p. 3, col. 4. *L'Abeille,* Aug. 2, 1891, p. 4, col. 2.

257. *Picayune,* Nov. 9, p. 5, col. 4.

258. *L'Abeille,* July 6, 1891, p. 4, col. 1; July 8, 1891, p. 4, col. 1.

259. Ibid., Aug. 5, 1891, p. 4, col. 1.

260. Ibid., July 19, 1891, p. 4, col. 2.

261. *Picayune,* Sept. 28, 1891, p. 3, col. 5.

262. *L'Abeille,* Aug. 6, 1891, p. 4, col. 1.

263. *Picayune,* Sept. 19, 1891, p. 3, col. 6.

264. Ibid., Oct. 6, 1891, p. 3, col. 4.

265. Ibid., Oct. 18, 1891, p. 7, col. 6.

266. Ibid., Oct. 17, 1891, p. 5, col. 3; Oct. 19, 1891, p. 3, col. 3.

267. Ibid., Oct. 25, 1891, p. 2, col. 6; Oct. 29, 1891, p. 8, col. 2.

268. Ibid., Oct. 25, 1891, p. 2, col. 6.

269. Ibid., Nov. 9, 1891, p. 5, col. 4.

270. Ibid., Nov. 20, 1891, p. 5, col. 2.

271. Ibid., Nov. 20, 1891, p. 5, col. 3.

272. Ibid., Nov. 22, 1891, p. 6, col. 3.

273. Ibid., Nov. 26, 1891, p. 3, col. 4.

274. Ibid., Dec. 3, 1891, p. 3, col. 2.

275. Ibid., Nov. 21, 1891, p. 4, cols. 3–4; Dec. 6, 1891, p. 8, col. 5.

276. Ibid., Dec. 6, 1891, p. 8, col. 5.

277. Ibid., Dec. 6, 1891, p. 8, col. 5.

278. Ibid., Sept. 27, 1891, p. 6, col. 4; Oct. 18, 1891, p. 7, col. 5; Nov. 4, 1891, p. 2, col. 3.

279. Ibid., Nov. 27, 1891, p. 2, col. 2.

280. Ibid., Nov. 29, 1891, p. 7, col. 5; Dec. 11, 1891, p. 3, col. 5.

281. Ibid., Nov. 4, 1891, p. 8, col. 1; Nov. 6, 1891, p. 5, col. 3.

282. Ibid., Dec. 11, 1891, p. 3, col. 5. Review: Dec. 12, 1891, p. 8, col. 5.
283. Ibid., Dec. 12, 1891, p. 8, col. 5.
284. Ibid., Dec. 17, 1891, p. 5, col. 2; Dec. 18, 1891, p. 6, col. 4.
285. Ibid., Dec. 20, 1891, p. 2, col. 5.
286. Ibid., Dec. 22, 1891, p. 3, col. 5.
287. Ibid., Dec. 23, 1891, p. 2, col. 4.
288. Ibid., Dec. 20, 1891, p. 2, col. 5.
289. Ibid., Jan. 2, 1892, p. 6, col. 3; Feb. 13, 1892, p. 3, col. 4.
290. Ibid., Jan. 4, 1892, p. 3, col. 4.
291. Ibid., Jan. 8, 1892, p. 5, cols. 2–3.
292. Ibid., Jan. 14, 1892, p. 5, col. 2.
293. Ibid., Jan. 8, 1892, p. 3, col. 2.
294. Ibid., Jan. 2, 1892, p. 2, col. 4.
295. Ibid., Mar. 4, 1892, p. 8, col. 2.
296. Ibid., Mar. 1, 1892, p. 2, col. 5; Mar. 3, 1892, p. 5, col. 3; Mar. 4, 1892, p. 8, col. 2; and Mar. 5, 1892, p. 5, col. 2 and p. 8, col. 3. Review: Mar. 6, 1892, p. 6, col. 3.
297. Ibid., Mar. 4, 1892, p. 8, col. 2.
298. Ibid., Mar. 4, 1892, p. 8, col. 2; Mar. 5, 1892, p. 5, col. 2 and p. 8, col. 3.
299. Ibid., Mar. 9, 1892, p. 4, col. 3, and Mar. 11, 1892, p. 3, col. 2.
300. Ibid., Dec. 28, 1891, p. 5, cols. 2–3; Jan. 2, 1892, p. 6, col. 3; Jan. 9, p. 6, col. 5.
301. Ibid., Feb. 5, 1892, p. 5, col. 3; Feb. 6, 1892, p. 2, col. 5.
302. Ibid., Mar. 3, 1892, p. 7, col. 3.
303. Ibid., Feb. 5, 1892, p. 5, col. 2.
304. Ibid., Feb. 2, 1892, p. 4, col. 2; Feb. 26, 1892, p. 3, col. 3.
305. Ibid., Feb. 18, 1892, p. 5, col. 3; Feb. 19, 1892, p. 3, col. 4.
306. Ibid., Feb. 3, 1892, p. 7, col. 4.
307. Ibid., Feb. 21, 1892, p. 8, col. 3; Feb. 25, 1892, p. 3, col. 7.
308. Ibid., Apr. 29, 1892, p 6, col. 4; May 1, 1892, p. 6, col. 7.
309. Ibid., May 6, 1892, p. 6, col. 2.
310. Ibid., Mar. 21, 1892, p. 3, col. 4; Apr. 3, 1892, p. 6, col. 3.
311. Ibid., Feb. 5, 1892, p. 8, col. 4.
312. Ibid., Mar. 12, 1892, p. 5, col. 3; Mar. 13, 1892, p. 8, col. 3.
313. Ibid., Mar. 19, 1892, p. 2, col. 2.
314. Ibid., Mar. 20, 1892, p. 6, col. 6. Review: Mar. 21, 1892, p. 3, col. 3.
315. Ibid., May 15, 1892, p. 8, col. 7.
316. Ibid., May 15, 1892, p. 8, col. 6.
317. Ibid., Feb. 29, 1892, p. 2, col. 5, Mar. 2, 1892, p. 6, col. 6; Mar. 3, 1892, p. 7, col. 3.
318. Ibid., Apr. 23, 1892, p. 3, col. 4.
319. Ibid., Apr. 17, 1892, p. 10, col. 2; Apr. 23, 1892, p. 3, col. 4.
320. *L'Abeille,* June 1, 1892, p. 4, col. 1.
321. Ibid., June 3, 1892, p. 4, col. 2; June 4, 1892, p. 4, col. 1.
322. *Picayune,* May 15, 1892, p. 6, col. 6 and p. 8, col. 7. *L'Abeille,* June 1, 1892, p. 1, col. 9; June 2, 1892, p. 4, col. 1; June 3, 1892, p. 4, col. 1; June 15, 1892, p. 1, col. 9; p. 4, col. 1; July 1, 1892, p. 1, col. 9.
323. *L'Abeille,* June 1, 1892, p. 4, col. 2; June 2, 1892, p. 4, col. 1; June 3, 1892, p. 4, col. 1.
324. Ibid., June 7, 1892, p. 4, col. 1; June 12, 1892, p. 4, col. 2; June 15, 1892, p. 1, col. 9; p. 4, col. 1.
325. Ibid., June 14, 1892, p. 4, col. 1.
326. Ibid., June 5, 1892, p. 4, col. 1.
327. *Picayune,* Nov. 6, 1892, p. 12, col. 2; Nov. 11, 1892, p. 4, col. 2.

328. Ibid., Nov. 20, 1892, p. 3, col. 3; Dec. 4, 1892, p. 2, col. 2; Dec. 11, 1892, p. 6, col. 6. Review: Dec. 13, 1892, p. 9, col. 8; Dec. 13, 1892, p. 2, col. 5.

329. Ibid., Oct. 20, 1892, p. 3, col. 4; Dec. 19, 1892, p. 6, col. 7.

330. Ibid., Oct. 23, 1892, p. 6, col. 3; Dec. 4, 1892, p. 2, col. 2.

331. Ibid., Oct. 31, 1892, p. 3, col. 2; Dec. 10, 1892, p. 2, col. 6.

332. Ibid., Nov. 2, 1892, p. 5, col. 3.

333. Ibid., Nov. 16, 1892, p. 3, col. 3.

334. Ibid., Oct. 29, 1892, p. 3, col. 4.

335. Ibid., Nov. 22, 1892, p. 3, col. 2; Nov. 24, 1892, p. 4, col. 6.

336. Ibid., Nov. 24, 1892, p. 4, col. 7.

337. Ibid., Nov. 20, 1892, p. 3, col. 3; Nov. 27, 1892, p. 9, col. 4; Nov. 27, 1892, p. 7, col. 7; Nov. 28, 1892, p. 3, col. 2; Nov. 30, 1892, p. 6, col. 5.

338. Ibid., Nov. 27, 1892, p. 9, col. 4; p. 7, col. 7. Review: Nov. 29, 1892, p. 3, col. 3.

339. Ibid., Nov. 5, 1892, p. 3, col. 3; Nov. 6, 1892, p. 12, col. 2; Nov. 7, 1892, p. 3, col. 4; p. 7, col. 5; Nov. 11, 1892, p. 4, col. 2; Nov. 12, 1892, p. 2, col. 7; Nov. 16, 1892, p. 3, col. 4.

340. Ibid., Nov. 25, 1892, p. 4, col. 3; Nov. 30, 1892, p. 6, col. 5; Dec. 1, 1892, p. 10, col. 2.

341. Ibid., Dec. 11, 1892, p. 13, col. 7.

342. Ibid., Dec. 8, 1892, p. 6, col. 5; Dec. 13, 1892, p. 5, col. 3; Dec. 17, 1892, p. 9, col. 4.

343. Ibid., Dec. 14, 1892, p. 5, col. 3; Dec. 20, 1892, p. 8, col. 2.

344. Ibid., Dec. 18, 1892, p. 7, col. 7; Dec. 20, 1892, p. 9, col. 4.

345. Ibid., Dec. 9, 1892, p. 9, col. 7; Dec. 11, 1892, p. 6, col. 6; Dec. 18, 1892, p. 6, col. 4 and p. 7, col. 7; Dec. 19, 1892, p. 3, col. 6; Dec. 20, 1892, p. 8, col. 2; and Dec. 21, 1892, p. 2, col. 2 and p. 5, col. 3. Review: Dec. 22, 1892, p. 6, col. 3.

346. Ibid., Dec. 24, 1892, p. 3, col. 4.

347. *L'Abeille,* Jan. 6, 1893, p. 4, col. 1; Jan. 8, 1893, p. 1, col. 8; Jan. 12, 1893, p. 4, col. 1; Jan. 14, 1893, p. 4, col. 1; Jan. 15, 1893, p. 4, col. 1.

348. Ibid., Jan. 26, 1893, p. 4, col. 1; Jan. 27, 1893, p. 4, col. 1. Review: Jan. 28, 1893, p. 4, col. 1.

349. Ibid., Jan. 28, 1893, p. 4, col. 1.

350. *Picayune,* Mar. 14, 1893, p. 5, col. 3; Mar. 15, 1893, p. 2, col. 7.

351. *L'Abeille,* Mar. 15, 1893, p. 1, col. 9; p. 4, col. 1. Review: Mar. 16, 1893, p. 4, col. 1.

352. Ibid., Mar. 22, 1893, p. 4, col. 1.

353. Ibid., Apr. 9, 1893, p. 4, col. 1.

354. Ibid., Mar. 11, 1893, p. 4, col. 1; Mar. 19, 1893, p. 4, col. 1; Apr. 1, 1893, p. 1, col. 9; Apr. 2, 1893, p. 4, col. 1; Apr. 4, 1893, p. 4, col. 1.

355. Ibid., Apr. 16, 1893, p. 4, col. 2; Apr. 21, 1893, p. 4, col. 1.

356. Ibid., May 7, 1893, p. 4, col. 1.

357. Ibid., May 7, 1893, p. 1, col. 9; p. 4, col. 2; May 10, 1893, p. 1, col. 9; p. 4, col. 1. Review: May 13, 1893, p. 4, col. 1.

358. Ibid., Nov. 20, 1892, p. 4, col. 3; Nov. 26, 1892, p. 3, col. 2; Dec. 4, 1892, p. 6, col. 7; Apr. 21, 1893, p. 4, col. 1; Apr. 23, 1893, p. 1, col. 9; p. 4, col. 2; Apr. 27, 1891, p. 1, col. 8; Apr. 27, 1893, p. 4, col. 1. Review: Apr. 28, 1893, p. 4, col. 1.

359. Ibid., Apr. 16, 1893, p. 1, col. 9; p. 4, col. 2; Apr. 18, 1893, p. 4, col. 2.

360. Ibid., Mar. 19, 1893, p. 4, col. 1; Apr. 2, 1893, p. 4, col. 2; Apr. 5, 1893, p. 1, col. 7; Apr. 23, 1893, p. 4, col. 2; May 2, 1893, p. 4, col. 1; May 3, 1893, p. 4; May 10, 1893, p. 4, cols. 1 and 9; May 11, 1893, p. 4, col. 1; May 12, 1893, p. 4, col. 1; May 13, 1893, p. 4, col. 1; May 20, 1893, p. 4, col. 1; May 28, 1893, p. 4, col. 2; May 30, 1893, p. 4, col. 1. Review: May 7, 1893, p. 4, col. 1; May 14, 1893, p. 4, col. 1; May 26, 1893, p. 4, col. 1.

361. Ibid., Sept. 2, 1893, p. 4, col. 1; Sept. 3, 1893, p. 4, col. 1; Sept. 5, 1893, p. 4, col. 1; Sept. 23, 1893, p. 4, col. 1; Sept. 24, 1893, p. 4, col. 2.

362. Ibid., Oct. 8, 1893, p. 4, col. 1.

363. Ibid., Sept. 17, 1893, p. 4, col. 1; Sept. 24, 1893, p. 4, col. 2; Oct. 1, 1893, p. 4, col. 1; Oct. 8, 1893, p. 4, col. 1; Oct. 11, 1893, p. 4, col. 1; Oct. 13, 1893, p. 4, col. 1; Oct. 15, 1893, p. 4, col. 2.

364. Ibid., Oct. 8, 1893, p. 4, col. 1; Oct. 17, 1893, p. 4, col. 1.

365. Ibid., Oct. 22, 1893, p. 1, col. 9.

366. Ibid., Feb. 28, 1894, p. 4, col. 1.

367. Ibid., Nov. 26, 1893, p. 4, col. 3.

368. Ibid., Dec. 9, 1893, p. 4, col. 1; Dec. 10, 1893, p. 4, col. 2.

369. Ibid., Dec. 12, 1893, p. 1, col. 8; Dec. 13, 1893, p. 1, col. 8; Dec. 16, 1893, p. 4, col. 1; Dec. 17, 1893, p. 1, col. 8. Review: Ibid., Dec. 19, 1893, p. 4, col. 1.

370. Ibid., Dec. 9, 1893, p. 4, col. 1; Dec. 10, 1893, p. 4, col. 2; Dec. 12, 1893, p. 4, col. 1.

371. Ibid., Dec. 16, 1893, p. 4, col. 2; Dec. 17, 1893, p. 4, col. 2. Review: Dec. 19, 1893, p. 4, col. 1.

372. Ibid., Jan. 21, 1894, p. 4, col. 2; Jan. 23, 1894, p. 4, col. 1.

373. Ibid., Dec. 12, 1893, p. 1, col. 8; Dec. 13, 1893, p. 1, col. 8; Dec. 17, 1893, p. 1, col. 9. Review: Dec. 20, 1893, p. 4, col. 1.

374. Ibid., Dec. 23, 1893, p. 4, col. 1.

375. Ibid., Dec. 23, 1893, p. 4, col. 1; Dec. 26, 1893, p. 4, col. 1.

376. Ibid., Dec. 16, 1893, p. 4, col. 1; Dec. 21, 1893, p. 1, col. 9.

377. Ibid., Dec. 30, 1893, p. 4, col. 2.

378. Ibid., Dec. 31, 1893, p. 1, col. 9; p. 4, col. 1; Jan. 16, 1894, p. 1, col. 8.

379. Ibid., Jan. 4, 1894, p. 4, col. 1; Jan. 9, 1894, p. 4, col. 2; Jan. 10, 1894, p. 4, col. 1. Review: Jan. 11, 1894, p. 4, col. 2.

380. Ibid., Jan. 7, 1894, p. 1, col. 8; p. 4, col. 2; Jan. 14, 1894, p. 4, col. 1; Jan. 16, 1894, p. 4, col. 1.

381. Ibid., Jan. 23, 1894, p. 4, col. 1; Jan. 24, p. 4, col. 2. Brahms and Remenyi concertized together in Europe.

382. *L'Abeille,* Jan. 14, 1894, p. 4, col. 1; Jan. 21, 1894, p. 4, col. 2; Jan. 23, 1894, p. 4, col. 1; Jan. 24, 1894, p. 4, col. 1. Review: Jan. 25, 1894, p. 4, col. 1.

383. Ibid., Jan. 25, 1894, p. 4, col. 3; Mar. 25, 1894, p. 4, col. 2.

384. Ibid., Jan. 30, 1894, p. 4, col. 2; Feb. 1, 1894, p. 4, col. 1; Feb. 2, 1894, p. 4, col. 1.

385. Ibid., Feb. 11, 1894, p. 1, col. 9; p. 4, col. 2.

386. Ibid., Jan. 20, 1894, p. 4, col. 1; Feb. 16, 1894, p. 4, col. 1; Feb. 17, 1894, p. 1, col. 8; Feb. 23, 1894, p. 4, col. 1; Feb. 25, 1894, p. 1, col. 8; Feb. 25, 1894, p. 4, col. 1. Review: Feb. 18, 1894, p. 4, cols. 1–2.

387. Ibid., Feb. 24, 1894, p. 4, col. 1; Feb. 25, 1894, p. 4, col. 1; Feb. 27, 1894, p. 4, col. 1.

388. Ibid., Feb. 20, 1894, p. 4, cols. 1–2; Feb. 23, 1894, p. 4, col. 2; Feb. 25, 1894, p. 4, col. 2.

389. Ibid., Mar. 3, 1894, p. 4, col. 1; Mar. 3, 1894, p. 1, col. 8; Mar. 4, 1894, p. 4, col. 1. Review: Mar. 6, 1894, p. 4, col. 1.

390. Ibid., Mar. 28, 1894, p. 1, col. 8; p. 4, col. 1; Mar. 29, 1894, p. 4, col. 1.

391. Ibid., Mar. 30, 1894, p. 4, col. 1; Apr. 1, 1894, p. 1, col. 9; p. 4, col. 2; Apr. 4, 1894, p. 1, col. 8; p. 4, col. 1; Apr. 6, 1894, p. 4, col. 1; Apr. 7, 1894, p. 1, col. 9; p. 4, col. 1. Review: Apr. 5, 1894, p. 4, col. 2; Apr. 8, 1894, p. 4, col. 1.

392. Ibid., Feb. 27, 1894, p. 4, col. 1.

393. Ibid., Mar. 3, 1894, p. 4, col. 1.

394. Ibid., Mar. 18, 1894, p. 4, col. 1; Mar. 25, 1894, p. 1, col. 8; p. 4, col. 1; Apr. 1, 1891, p. 4, col. 1.

395. Ibid., Apr. 7, 1894, p. 4, col. 1.

396. Ibid., Feb. 10, 1894, p. 4, col. 1; Feb. 13, 1894, p. 4, cols. 1–2; Apr. 1, 1894, p. 4, col. 1; Apr. 7, 1894, p. 4, col. 1. Review: Apr. 15, 1894, p. 4, col. 1.

397. Ibid., Apr. 7, 1894, p. 4, col. 1. Review: Apr. 8, 1894, p. 4, col. 2.

398. Ibid., Apr. 8, 1894, p. 4, col. 2.

399. Ibid., Apr. 13, 1894, p. 4, col. 1.
400. Ibid., Apr. 19, 1894, p. 4, col. 1; Apr. 25, 1894, p. 4, col. 1.
401. Ibid., Apr. 29, 1894, p. 4, col. 1.
402. Ibid., Apr. 22, 1894, p. 1, col. 8. Review: May 13, 1894, p. 4, col. 1.
403. Ibid., May 9, 1894, p. 4, col. 3.
404. Ibid., May 19, 1894, p. 4, col. 4; May 20, 1894, p. 4, col. 1. Review: May 22, 1894, p. 4, col. 1.
405. Ibid., Apr. 15, 1894, p. 4, col. 1; Apr. 23, 1894, p. 4, col. 1; Apr. 25, 1894, p. 4, col. 2; Apr. 27, 1894, p. 4, col. 1; May 13, 1894, p. 4, col. 2; May 20, 1894, p. 4, col. 1; May 23, 1894, p. 4, col. 1; May 24, 1894, p. 4, col. 1; May 26, 1894, p. 4, col. 1; May 31, 1894, p. 4, col. 1; June 2, 1894, p. 4, col. 1; June 6, 1894, p. 4, col. 1; June 10, 1894, p. 4, col. 1; June 15, 1894, p. 4, col. 1; June 16, 1894, p. 4, col. 1; June 24, 1894, p. 4, col. 2.
406. Ibid., June 27, 1894, p. 4, col. 1.
407. Ibid., June 27, 1894, p. 1, col. 9.
408. Ibid., Oct. 7, 1894, p. 4, cols. 2–3.
409. Ibid., Nov. 4, 1894, p. 4, col. 3; Nov. 18, 1894, p. 1, col. 8; Nov. 25, 1894, p. 1, col. 8; Nov. 27, 1894, p. 1, cols. 2–3. Review: *Picayune,* Nov. 27, 1894, p. 3, cols. 2–3. Tulane University, Manuscripts and Rare Books, Wehrmann Papers, Coll. 873, Box 2.
410. Louisiana State Museum, scrapbook Box 2/4 RG 131.
411. *L'Abeille,* Oct. 4, 1894, p. 4, col. 1; Oct. 5, 1894, p. 4, col. 1.
412. Ibid., Oct. 7, 1894, p. 1, col. 8; p. 4, col. 3; Oct. 10(?) 1894, p. 4, col. 2.
413. Ibid., Oct. 1, 1894, p. 4, col. 1; Oct. 18, 1894, p. 1, col. 8; Oct. 19, 1894, p. 1, col. 3.
414. Ibid., Oct. 17, 1894, p. 4, col. 1; Oct. 21, 1894, p. 1, col. 8; p. 4, col. 2; Oct. 24, 1894, p. 4, col. 5. Review: Oct. 25, 1894, p. 4, col. 1.
415. Ibid., Oct. 23, 1894, p. 1, col. 8.
416. Ibid., Nov. 21, 1894, p. 4, col. 4.
417. Ibid., Nov. 23, 1894, p. 4, col. 2; Nov. 24, 1894, p. 4, col. 2; Nov. 25, 1894, p. 4, col. 3; Nov. 27, 1894, p. 1, col. 3.
418. *Picayune,* Dec. 4, 1894, p. 3, col. 5; Dec. 16, 1894, p. 24, col. 3; Dec. 17, 1894, p. 10, col. 2.
419. Ibid., Dec. 2, 1894, p. 10, col. 4; Dec. 15, 1894, p. 4, col. 2.
420. Ibid., Dec. 16, 1894, p. 15, col. 4.
421. See page 76.
422. *Picayune,* Dec. 16, 1894, p. 15, col. 3; Mar. 10, 1895, p. 5.
423. Ibid., Dec. 21, 1894, p. 12, col. 6.
424. Ibid., Dec. 20, 1894, p. 5, col. 2; Dec. 23, 1894, p. 7, col. 6; Dec. 27, 1894, p. 3, col. 5.
425. Ibid., Dec. 24, 1894, p. 8, col. 2.
426. Ibid., Dec. 21, 1894, p. 12, col. 4; Dec. 26, 1894, p. 10, col. 2; Dec. 27, 1894, p. 12, col. 4.
427. Ibid., Dec. 20, 1894, p. 5, col. 2; p. 8, col. 4; Dec. 21, 1894, p. 8, col. 4; Dec. 23, 1894, p. 3, col. 2; Dec. 24, 1894, p. 10, col. 2; Dec. 25, 1894, p. 3, col. 4; p. 6, col. 6; Dec. 26, 1894, p. 8, col. 3; Dec. 27, 1894, p. 5, col. 2; Dec. 29, 1894, p. 12, col. 4. Review: Dec. 27, 1894, p. 7, col. 5.
428. *L'Abeille,* Jan. 3, 1895, p. 1, col. 5. *Picayune,* Dec. 20, 1894, p. 8, col. 4; Dec. 21, 1894, p. 8, col. 4.
429. *Picayune,* Feb. 14, 1895, p. 8, col. 6; Feb. 16, 1895, p. 14, col. 4; Feb. 17, 1895, p. 2, col. 6; Feb. 18, 1895, p. 10, col. 4; Feb. 19, 1895, p. 8, col. 5; Feb. 20, 1895, p. 12, col. 6; Feb. 21, 1895, p. 8, col. 4; Feb. 23, 1895, p. 7, col. 3; Mar. 3, 1895, p. 12, cols. 5–6; Mar. 4, 1895, p. 4, col. 4; p. 10, col. 6; Mar. 7, 1895, p. 12, col. 2.
430. Ibid., Mar. 4, 1895, p. 10, col. 6; Mar. 9, 1895, p. 5, col. 3.
431. Ibid., Jan. 31, 1895, p. 8, col. 6; Feb. 3, 1895, p. 7, col. 7; Feb. 6, 1895, p. 5, col. 3; Feb. 7, 1895, p. 11, col. 6; Feb. 8, 1895, p. 3, col. 2; Feb. 11, 1895, p. 8, col. 3; Feb. 17, 1895, p. 7, col. 5.
432. The *Picayune* did a study on an opera troupe for New Orleans versus Mardi Gras that appeared on Apr. 1, 1895. It looked to French models for some solutions (Apr. 1, 1895, p. 3, col. 5).

433. *Picayune,* Dec. 31, 1894, p. 5, col. 3.
434. Ibid., Dec. 30, 1894, p. 3, col. 4.
435. Ibid., Dec. 16, 1894, p. 15, col. 4.
436. *L'Abeille,* Jan. 17, 1895, p. 4, col. 2; Jan. 20, 1895, p. 4, cols. 4–5.
437. *Picayune,* Feb. 3, 1895, p. 3, cols. 5–6.
438. Ibid., Feb. 12, 1895, p. 8, col. 4.
439. Ibid., Feb. 3, 1895, p. 7, col. 4; Feb. 10, 1895, p. 3, col. 2; Feb. 19, 1895, p. 8, col. 5. Review: Feb. 20, 1895, p. 6, col. 2.
440. Ibid., Feb. 13, 1895, p. 6, col. 4.
441. Ibid., Feb. 3, 1895, p. 7, col. 4.
442. Ibid., Feb. 10, 1895, p. 3, col. 2; p. 5, col. 3. Review: Feb. 23, 1895, p. 6, col. 2.
443. *Picayune,* Feb. 17, 1895, p. 7, col. 5.
444. Ibid.
445. Ibid., Feb. 23, 1895, p. 7, col. 4.
446. Ibid., Feb. 24, 1895, p. 9, col. 6.
447. Ibid., Mar. 1, 1895, p. 12, col. 2. Review: Mar. 2, 1895, p. 12, col. 1.
448. Ibid., Mar. 2, 1895, p. 10, col. 1.
449. Ibid., Mar. 7, 1895, p. 12, col. 2; Mar. 10, 1895, p. 3, col. 7.
450. Ibid., Mar. 10, 1895, p. 5; Mar. 17, 1895, p. 12, col. 2.
451. Ibid., Mar. 24, 1895, p. 7, col. 4; p. 9, cols. 6–7; Mar. 27, 1895, p. 9, col. 3; Mar. 28, 1895, p. 11, col. 6. Review: Apr. 1, 1895, p. 8, col. 5.
452. Ibid., Apr. 3, 1895, p. 9, col. 5.
453. Ibid., Mar. 21, 1895, p. 3, col. 3; Apr. 10, 1895, p. 3, col. (?). Review: Apr. 13, 1895, p. 3, col. 2.
454. Ibid., Apr. 21, 1895, p. 8, col. 4; Apr. 24, 1895, p. 12, col. 1; Apr. 26, 1895, p. 12, col. 2.
455. *L'Abeille,* May 1, 1895, p. 4, col. 3; May 2, 1895, p. 3, col. 2; May 10, 1895, p. 2, col. 8. Review: June 1, 1895, p. 2, col. 6; June 5, 1895, p. 2, col. 8; p. 3, col. 1; June 6, 1895, p. 3, col. 1; June 7, 1895, p. 2, col. 6; Sept. 11, 1895, p. 3, col. 2.
456. Ibid., June 5, 1895, p. 2, col. 8; June 5, 1895, p. 3, col. 1; June 6, 1895, p. 3, col. 1; June 7, 1895, p. 2, col. 6.
457. *Picayune,* Apr. 1, 1895, p. 3, col. 5.
458. Ibid., Apr. 6, 1895, p. 12, col. 2.
459. Ibid., Apr. 8, 1895, p. 3, col. 4.
460. Ibid., Apr. 10, 1895, p. 6, col. 5.
461. Ibid., Apr. 14, 1895, p. 16, col. 6.
462. Ibid., Apr. 3, 1895, p. 4, col. 2.
463. Ibid., Apr. 15, 1895, p. 5, col. 3.
464. Ibid., Apr. 19, 1895, p. 11, col. 4.
465. Ibid., Apr. 19, 1895, p. 3, col. 4.
466. Ibid., Apr. 21, 1895, p. 8, cols. 4–5; Apr. 24, 1895, p. 12, col. 1.
467. Ibid., Apr. 24, 1895, p. 12, col. 1.
468. Ibid., Apr. 28, 1895, p. 7, col. 7; May 3, 1895, p. 2, col. 6. Review: *L'Abeille,* May 7, 1895, p. 2, col. 5.
469. *L'Abeille,* June 9, 1895, p. 3, col. 4.
470. Ibid., May 2, 1895, p. 3, col. 2; p. 4, col. 4.
471. Ibid., May 10, 1895, p. 2, col. 8; May 12, 1895, p. 2, col. 8.
472. Ibid., May 5, 1895, p. 3, col. 4; May 12, 1895, p. 2, col. 3. Review: May 17, 1895, p. 2, col. 3.
473. Ibid., June 15, 1895, p. 2, col. 6.
474. Ibid., Apr. 1, 1895, p. 7, col. 2; May 1, 1895, p. 2, col. 5.

475. Ibid., May 26, 1895, p. 2, col. 8; Sept. 1, 1895, p. 2, col. 3; Sept. 5, 1895, p. 3, col. 7; Sept. 7, 1895, p. 3, col. 3; Sept. 11, 1895, p. 3, col. 2.

476. *Picayune,* Mar. 8, 1896, p. 10, cols. 4–5.

477. Ibid., Dec. 1, 1895, p. 15, col. 4; Dec. 7, 1895, p. 11, col. 4; Dec. 10, 1895, p. 9, col. 2; Dec. 12, 1895, p. 5, col. 3; p. 4, col. 4 (long interview); Dec. 17, 1895, p. 3, col. 5.

478. *L'Abeille,* Nov. 10, 1895, p. 2, col. 4; Nov. 28, 1895, p. 3, col. 1. *Picayune,* Dec. 1, 1895, p. 15, cols. 4–5; Dec. 2, 1895, p. 5, cols. 2–3; Dec. 3, 1895, p. 2, col. 6; change of program to all Wagner: Dec. 6, 1895, p. 6, col. 3; Dec. 7, 1895, p. 11, col. 4; Dec. 8, 1895, p. 7, col. 3; Dec. 10, 1895, p. 9, col. 2; Dec. 11, 1895, p. 12, col. 2; Dec. 14, 1895, p. 6, col. 5; Dec. 15, 1895, p. 7, col. 6; p. 11, col. 3; Dec. 16, 1895, p. 10, col. 2; Dec. 17, 1895, p. 3, col. 4; Dec. 18, 1895, p. 6, cols. 3–4.

479. *Picayune,* Dec. 15, 1895, p. 7, col. 6.

480. Ibid., Dec. 18, 1895, p. 7, col. 4.

481. Ibid., Dec. 18, 1895, p. 7, col. 5; Dec. 19, 1895, p. 9, col. 4. Review: Dec. 23, 1895, p. 10, cols. 6–7.

482. *L'Abeille,* Sept. 24, 1895, p. 2, col. 6.

483. Ibid., Oct. 6, 1895, p. 2, col. 5; Oct. 25, 1895, p. 3, col. 1; Nov. 8, 1895, p. 2, col. 7.

484. Ibid., Nov. 29, 1895, p. 2, col. 7.

485. Ibid., Nov. 3, 1895, p. 8, col. 2; Nov. 5, 1895, p. 2, col. 3.

486. Ibid., Nov. 9, 1895, p. 4, col. 3.

487. Ibid., Nov. 11, 1895, p. 3, col. 2; Nov. 14, 1895, p. 4, col. 4; Nov. 15, 1895, p. 2, cols. 7–8.

488. *Picayune,* Dec. 1, 1895, p. 7, col. 3.

489. Ibid., Dec. 1, 1895, p. 15, col. 5.

490. Ibid., Dec. 1, 1895, p. 15, col. 5.

491. Ibid., Dec. 1, 1895, p. 15, col. 5; Dec. 6, 1895, p. 6, col. 2.

492. Ibid., Dec. 6, 1895, p. 3, col. 4.

493. Ibid., Dec. 6, 1895, p. 6, col. 3.

494. Ibid., Dec. 8, 1895, p. 14, col. 3.

495. Ibid., Dec. 10, 1895, p. 3, col. 4.

496. Ibid., Dec. 10, 1895, p. 3, col. 3.

497. Ibid., Dec. 26, 1895, p. 3, col. 4.

498. Ibid., Dec. 11, 1895, p. 11, col. 2.

499. Ibid., Dec. 20, 1895, p. 14, col. 2; Dec. 21, 1895, p. 6, col. 2.

500. Ibid., Mar. 1, 1896, p. 7, col. 2; Mar. 29, 1896, p. 7, col. 3; Apr. 19, 1896, p. 7, col. 6.

501. Ibid., Dec. 22, 1895, p. 8, col. 4; Dec. 29, 1895, p. 3, col. 3; Dec. 31, 1895, p. 5, col. 2; p. 3, col. 5; Mar. 8, 1896, p. 7, col. 7; Mar. 29, 1896, p. 7, col. 3; Apr. 14, 1896, p. 3, col. 3. Review: Apr. 15, 1896, p. 3, col. 4.

502. Ibid., Dec. 15, 1895, p. 11, col. 3; Dec. 17, 1895, p. 9, col. 3; Dec. 19, 1895, p. 5, col. 2; Dec. 29, 1895, p. 3, col. 3–4; Jan. 7, 1896, p. 7, col. 1 and 6; Jan. 15, 1896, p. 3, col. 3; Jan. 22, 1896, p. 3, col. 7; Feb. 22, 1896, p. 3, col. 3.

503. *L'Abeille,* Nov. 19, 1895, p. 1, col. 5. *Picayune,* Dec. 1, 1895, p. 1, col. 2; Dec. 27, 1895, p. 12, col. 6; Jan. 14, 1896, p. 3, col. 7; Jan. 20, 1896, p. 8, col. 6; Jan. 22, 1896, p. 9, col. 3; Jan. 23, 1896, p. 3, col. 4; Jan. 26, 1896, p. 22, cols. 3–4; Jan. 26, 1896, p. 10, col. 4; Jan. 27, 1896, p. 8, col. 3; review: Jan. 28, 1896, p. 9, cols. 5–6.

504. *Picayune,* Jan. 14, 1896, p. 3, col. 7; Jan. 28, 1896, p. 9, cols. 6–7; Jan. 31, 1896, p. 10, col. 6. Review: Jan. 30, 1896, p. 8, cols. 6–7.

505. Ibid., Jan. 28, 1896, p. 5, col. 2; Jan. 30, 1896, p. 8, col. 7; Jan. 31, 1896, p. 7, col. 4; p. 10, col. 6.

506. Ibid., Mar. 8, 1896, p. 16, cols. 3–4.

507. Ibid., Jan. 9, 1896, p. 12, col. 2.
508. Ibid., Jan. 15, 1896, p. 7, col. 5; Jan. 19, 1896, p. 7, col. 4; Jan. 20, 1896, p. 8, col. 6. Review: Jan. 21, 1896, p. 3, col. 7.
509. Ibid., Feb. 23, 1896, p. 2, col. 7. Review: Feb. 29, 1896, p. 6, col. 3.
510. Ibid., Mar. 19, 1896, p. 10, col. 6. Review: Mar. 20, 1896, p. 9, col. 6.
511. Ibid., Mar. 30, 1896, p. 10, col. 5.
512. Ibid., Mar. 7, 1896, p. 5, col. 2.
513. Ibid., Mar. 8, 1896, p. 7, col. 7. Review: Mar. 13, 1896, p. 6, col. 2.
514. Ibid., Feb. 16, 1896, p. 12, col. 2.
515. Ibid., Mar. 15, 1897, p. 7, col. 7; Mar. 16, 1896, p. 3, col. 3; Mar. 17, 1896, p. 5, col. 2; Mar. 21, 1896, p. 3, col. 4; p. 10, col. 2; Mar. 22, 1896, p. 12, col. 6; Mar. 24, 1896, p. 3, col. 5. Review: Mar. 18, 1896, p. 9, col. 5.
516. Ibid., Apr. 5, 1896, p. 5, col. 2.
517. Ibid., Mar. 22, 1896, p. 12, col. 2; Mar. 29, 1896, p. 12, cols. 5–6; Apr. 5, 1896, p. 5, col. 1–2; Apr. 8, 1896, p. 14, col. 3. Review: Apr. 9, 1896, p. 5, col. 7; Apr. 10, 1896, p. 3, col. 3.
518. Ibid., Jan. 28, 1896, p. 5, col. 2; Jan. 29, 1896, p. 5, col. 2.
519. Ibid., Mar. 28, 1896, p. 10, col. 4.
520. Ibid., Apr. 11, 1896, p. 3, col. 4.
521. Ibid., Jan. 6, 1896, p. 5, col. 2.
522. Ibid., Jan. 7, 1896, p. 7, col. 6; Jan. 12, 1896, p. 7, col. 7.
523. Ibid., Feb. 2, 1896, p. 11, col. 6.
524. Ibid., Feb. 2, 1896, p. 3, col. 6; Mar. 22, 1896, p. 3, col. 7.
525. Ibid., Mar. 22, 1896, p. 12, col. 2.
526. Ibid., Mar. 13, 1896, p. 3, col. 4. Review: Mar. 17, 1896, p. 8, col. 4.
527. Ibid., Mar. 25, 1896, p. 11, col. 4.
528. Ibid., Apr. 11, 1896, p. 6, col. 3.
529. Ibid., Apr. 5, 1896, p. 5, col. 2. Review: Apr. 12, 1896, p. 3, col. 3.
530. Ibid., Apr. 13, 1896, p. 9, col. 5.
531. Ibid., Apr. 16, 1896, p. 5, col. 3. Review: Apr. 19, 1896, p. 6, col. 7.
532. Ibid., Apr. 19, 1896, p. 6, col. 7.
533. Ibid., Apr. 19, 1896, p. 3, col. 6.
534. Ibid., Apr. 14, 1896, p. 3, col. 3; Apr. 16, 1896, p. 5, col. 3; p. 13, col. 7; Apr. 17, p. 5, col. 3; Apr. 19, p. 25, col. 4.
535. *L'Abeille,* Sept. 1, 1896, p. 5, col. 8.
536. Ibid., Sept. 11, 1896, p. 3, col. 1.
537. *Picayune,* Oct. 4, 1896, p. 3, col. 4; Oct. 18, 1896, p. 3, col. 6; Nov. 29, 1896, p. 3, col. 4; Jan. 10, 1897, p. 3, col. 4; Jan. 12, 1897, p. 5, col. 2. Review: Jan. 15, 1897, p. 7, col. 2; Jan. 26, 1897, p. 2, col. 5.
538. Ibid., Oct. 11, 1896, p. 7, col. 6. Review: Oct. 13, 1896, p. 3, col. 3.
539. Ibid., Oct. 17, 1896, p. 12, col. 2.
540. Ibid., Oct. 18, 1896, p. 3, col. 6; Oct. 25, 1896, p. 19, col. 2.
541. Ibid., Oct. 18, 1896, p. 3, col. 6. Review: Oct. 23, 1896, p. 2, col. 6.
542. Ibid., Oct. 24, 1896, p. 3, col. 7.
543. Ibid., Oct. 8, 1896, p. 6, col. 5.
544. Ibid., Oct. 25, 1896, p. 19, col. 2.
545. Ibid., Nov. 18, 1896, p. 7, col. 3.
546. Ibid., Nov. 17, 1896, p. 5, col. 2; p. 12, col. 1; Nov. 18, 1896, p. 3, col. 3; Nov. 19, 1896, p. 12, col. 6. Review: Nov. 21, 1896, p. 6, col. 6.

547. Ibid., Mar. 1, 1896, p. 4, col. 2; Mar. 5, 1896, p. 7, col. 3; Oct. 7, 1896, p. 3, col. 5; Oct. 11, 1896, p. 7, col. 6; Oct. 25, 1896, p. 13, col. 5; p. 20, cols. 2–5; Nov. 17, 1896, p. 6, col. 3; Nov. 22, 1896, p. 4, col. 4; Nov. 24, 1896, p. 4, col. 4; p. 7, col. 5. *L'Abeille,* Sept. 9, 1896, p. 3, col. 3; Sept. 20, 1896, p. 7, col. 1; Sept. 30, 1896, p. 3, col. 3.

548. *Picayune,* Oct. 5, 1896, p. 9, col. 6; Oct. 10, 1896, p. 6, col. 5.

549. *L'Abeille,* Mar. 6, 1897, p. 3, col. 5.

550. *Picayune,* Nov. 29, 1896, p. 3, col. 4.

551. Ibid., Nov. 28, 1896, p. 2, col. 4; Nov. 30, 1896, p. 2, col. 7. *L'Abeille,* Dec. 18, 1896, p. 2, col. 7.

552. *L'Abeille,* Dec. 19, 1896, p. 2, col. 8.

553. Kaiser seems to have formed his quartet earlier, with Wehrman as second violinist, but we have no dates for any of the clippings in which the Kaiser Quartet's concerts are mentioned.

554. *L'Abeille,* Dec. 25, 1896, p. 3, col. 5.

555. Ibid., Dec. 6, 1896, p. 4, cols. 1–2; Dec. 16, 1896, p. 3, col. 5; Dec. 18, 1896, p. 4, col. 3; Dec. 19, 1896, p. 2, col. 8; Dec. 23, 1896, p. 3, col. 4.

556. *Picayune,* Jan. 7, 1897, p. 12, col. 5; Jan. 8, 1897, p. 9, col. 5; Jan. 10, 1897, p. 3, cols. 3–4; Jan. 12, 1897, p. 5, col. 2; Jan. 14, 1897, p. 6, col. 1; Jan. 15, 1897, p. 7, col. 1; Jan. 16, 1897, p. 11, col. 5; Jan. 18, 1897, p. 3, col. 3. En route to Natchez on Jan. 18, one member of the Sousa band was arrested in New Orleans for smoking on a street car (*Picayune,* Jan. 19, 1897, p. 10, col. 5).

557. *Picayune,* Jan. 15, 1897, p. 7, col. 2.

558. Ibid., Jan. 24, 1897, p. 3, col. 5; Jan. 25, 1897, p. 8, col. 7.

559. *L'Abeille,* Jan. 17, 1897, p. 4, col. 5; Jan. 27, 1897, p. 4, col. 5; Jan. 28, 1897, p. 3, col. 3.

560. Ibid., Jan. 26, 1897, p. 4, col. 4.

561. *Picayune,* Jan. 26, 1897, p. 7, col. 4. Review: *L'Abeille,* Jan. 26, 1897, p. 3, col. 2.

562. *L'Abeille,* Jan. 29, 1897, p. 4, col. 4; Feb. 3, 1897, p. 3, col. 5.

563. Ibid., Mar. 11, 1897, p. 3, col. 4; p. 4, col. 4; Mar. 12, 1897, p. 3, col. 4; Mar. 14, 1897, p. 7, col. 6; Mar. 28, 1897, p. 7, col. 3; p. 6, col. 3.

564. Ibid., Feb. 21, 1897, p. 7, col. 5; Feb. 25, 1897, p. 3, col. 4.

565. Ibid., Mar. 23, 1897, p. 7, col. 5.

BIBLIOGRAPHY

I. NEWSPAPERS

L'Abeille de la Nouvell-Orléans. See also *The Bee.*
L'Ami des lois et journal du commerce / The Friend of the Law and Commercial Journal.
The Bee. Usually published in tandem with the French-language *L'Abeille* as its English version, but often the articles were not the same.
Black Republican.
Boston Evening Transcript.
Charleston City Gazette.
Chicago Herald.
Chicago Tribune.
Commercial Bulletin.
Courier de la Louisiane / Louisiana Courier.
Daily States.
Detroit Free Press.
Drapeau de l'Ascension.
L'Étoile du Sud.
Gazette de la Louisiana / Louisiana Gazette.
Gazette musicale de Paris 9 (1842).
Grunewald's Musical Journal, house journal of Grunewald's music business.
Harper's Weekly.
The House Furnishing Review.
The Jeffersonian.
Journal des demoiselles, May 1845, p. 160.
Louisiana Advertiser.
Le Menestrel (Paris).
Moniteur de la Louisiana.
Morning Star.
Musical America.
The Musical Courier.

New Orleans Argus.
New Orleans Daily Creole.
New Orleans Daily Crescent.
The New Orleans Daily Delta.
New Orleans Deutsche Zeitung / Tagliche Deutsche Zeitung,.
New Orleans Item.
New Orleans Louisianian.
New Orleans Times.
New Orleans Weekly Pelican.
The New York Times.
L'Orleanais.
Le Peuple.
Picayune. Mostly Daily Picayune. Founded in 1837, quickly became principal English-language newspaper and, as the Times-Picayune, remained only major newspaper in New Orleans, 1970s until 2012.
The Telegraphe.
Times Democrat.
Tribune de la N.–Orleans.
L'Union.
The Violinist.
The Weekly Louisianian.
Werlein's Musical Journal /House journal of Werlein's music business.

II. BOOKS AND ARTICLES

Appiah, Kwame Anthony, and Henry Louis Gates Jr., eds. *Africana: The Encyclopedia of the African and African American Experience.* 1999. Rpt. Oxford, UK: Oxford University Press, 2005.

Auszüge aus Briefen aus Nord-Amerika, geschrieben von zwei aus Ulm an der Donau gebürtigen, nun in Staat Louisiana ansäß Geschwistern. Ulm: E. Rübling, 1833.

Babb, Winston C. "French Refugees from Saint-Domingue to the Southern United States, 1791–1810." Ph.D. diss., University of Virginia, 1954.

Barnum, P. T. *The Life of P. T. Barnum, Written by Himself.* New York: Redfield, 1855.

Baron, John H. "Blackmar." In Hitchcock and Sadie, eds., *The New Grove Dictionary of American Music* 1: 226–27.

———. "Franko, Jeanne." In *Jewish Women in America: An Historical Encyclopedia,* ed. Paula Hyman and Deborah Dash Moore. New York: Carlson Publishers, Inc., 1997. 472–73.

———. *Intimate Music: A History of the Idea of Chamber Music.* Stuyvesant, NY: Pendragon Press, 1998.

———. "New Orleans." In *Die Musik in Geschichte und Gegenwart,* ed. Ludwig Finscher. 2nd ed. Kassel: Bärenreiter, 1994–2008. Vol. 7 (1997): 145–53.

———. *Newcomb-Tulane Music Department 1909–2009.* New Orleans: Tulane University, 2009.

———. "Paul Emile Johns of New Orleans: Tycoon, Musician, and Friend of Chopin." In *Report of the Eleventh Congress* [of the International Musicological Society] Copenhagen 1972. 246–50.

———. *Piano Music from New Orleans 1851–1898.* New York: Da Capo, 1980.

———. "Vieuxtemps (and Ole Bull) in New Orleans." *American Music* 8 (Summer 1990): 210–26.

———. "Werlein." In *The New Grove Dictionary of American Music,* ed. Hitchcock and Sadie. Vol. 4: 510.

Baudier, Roger. *The Catholic Church in Louisiana.* New Orleans: [A.W. Hyatt Stationery Mfg. Co.], 1939.

Belsom, Jack. "Calve, Julie Rose" In *A Dictionary of Louisiana Biography.* Lafayette: Louisiana Historical Association, 1988. 147.

———. "En Route to Stardom: Adelina Patti at the French Opera House, New Orleans, 1860–1861." *Opera Quarterly* 10 (1994): 113–30.

———. *Opera in New Orleans.* New Orleans: New Orleans Opera Association, 1993.

Bender, Lorelle Causey. "The French Opera House of New Orleans 1859–1890." Louisiana State University M.A. dissertation, 1940.

Berrett, Joshua. "Louis Armstrong and Opera." *Musical Quarterly* 76 (1992): 216–41.

Biographical and Historical Memoirs of Louisiana. 1892. Rpt. Baton Rouge: Claitor's Publishing Division, 1975.

Blassingame, John W. *Black New Orleans: 1860–1880.* Chicago: University of Chicago Press, 1973.

Bradford, T. G. *An Illustrated Atlas: Geographical, Statistical and Historical of the United States and the Adjacent Countries.* Philadelphia: E. S. Grant & Co., 1838.

Butler, Nicholas Michael. *Votaries of Apollo.* Columbia: University of South Carolina Press, 2007.

Carrigan, Jo Ann. *The Saffron Scourge: a History of Yellow Fever in Louisiana, 1796–1905.* Lafayette: University of Southwestern Louisiana, 1994.

Castellanos, Henry C. *New Orleans As It Was: Episodes of Louisiana Life.* New Orleans: L. Graham and Son, 1895. Reprint Baton Rouge: Louisiana State University Press, 1978/2006.

Chouquet, Gustave. "Prévost." *Grove's Dictionary of Music and Musicians,* ed. J. A. Fuller Maitland. Philadelphia: Theodore Presser, 1926. Vol. 3: 812.

Coleman, William H. *Historical Sketch Book and Guide to New Orleans.* New York: W. H. Coleman, 1885.

Cone, John Frederick. *Adelina Patti, Queen of Hearts.* Portland, OR: Amadeus Press, 1993.

Cooke, James Francis. *Great Pianists on Piano Playing.* Philadelphia: Theodore Presser, 1913.

Crosby, Eugene H. *Crosby's Opera House: Symbol of Chicago's Cultural Awakening.* Madison, NJ: Fairleigh Dickinson University Press, 1999.

Curtis, Nathaniel. *New Orleans, Its Old Houses, Shops, and Public Buildings.* Philadelphia: J. B. Lippincott Co., 1933.

Davis, John. *John Davis Plays Blind Tom The Eighth Wunder.* Compact disc. Newport Classic NPD 85660. Newport, RI, 1999.

Deiler, J. Hanno. *Geschichte der New Orleans Deutschen Presse.* New Orleans: published by the author, 1901.

Didimus, Henry. *New Orleans As I Found It.* New York: Harper and Brothers, 1845.

Dizikes, John. *Opera in America, a Cultural History.* New Haven: Yale University Press, 1993.

Dwight, John. *Journal.* 41 volumes. Boston: 1853–81.

Ferris, George T. *Great Singers,* Second Series: *Malibran to Titiens.* New York: D. Appleton & Co., 1888.

Fétis, François-Joseph. *Biographie Universelle des Musiciens.* Paris: Librairie de Firmin Didot Frères, Fils et Cie, 1864. Second edition. 8 volumes.

Fields, Warren Carl. "Theodore La Hache and Music in New Orleans 1846–1869." *American Music* 8 (1990): 326–50.

Gibson, John. *Gibson's Guide and Directory.* New Orleans: 1838.

Fossier, Albert A. *New Orleans, the Glamour Period, 1800–1840.* New Orleans: Pelican Publishing Co., 1957.

Fouchard, Jean. *Artistes et Répertoires des Scenes de Saint-Domingue.* 1955. Rpt. Port-au-Prince: Éditions Henri Deschamps, 1988.

———. *Le Théâtre à Saint-Domingue.* Port-au-Prince: Henri Duchamps, 1988.

———. *Plaisirs de Saint-Domingue: Notes sur la Vie Sociale, Littéraire et Artisque.* Port-au-Prince: Éditions Henri Deschamps, 1988.

Franko, Sam. *Chords and Discords.* New York: Viking Press, 1938.

Gerson, Robert A. *Music in Philadelphia.* Westport, CT: Greenwood Press, 1970.

Graber, Kenneth. *William Mason (1829–1908): An Annotated Bibliography and Catalog of Works.* Warren, MI: Harmonie Park Press, 1989.

Hammond, J. T. *Crescent City Business Directory for 1858–59 with Fine Engravings of the Most Conspicuous Public Buildings . . .* New Orleans: published by the author, 1858.

Hart, Sister Mary Francis Borgia. *Violets in the King's Garden: a History of the Sisters of the Holy Family of New Orleans.* Reproduced typescript. New Orleans, 1976. Copy in Loyola University of New Orleans Library.

Hauk, Minnie. *Memories of a Singer.* 1925. Rpt. New York: Arno Press, 1977.

Herz, Henri. *Mes Voyages en Amérique.* Paris: Achille Faure, 1866. Trans. Henry Bertram Hill. *My Travels in America.* Madison: State Historical Society of Wisconsin, 1963.

Hitchcock, H. Wiley, and Stanley Sadie, eds. *The New Grove Dictionary of American Music.* New York: Oxford University Press, 2002.

Hollandsworth, James G., Jr. *An Absolute Massacre: the New Orleans Race Riot of July 30, 1866* (Baton Rouge: Louisiana State University Press, 2001), review by Caryn Cossé Bell, *Journal of Southern History* 68 (Nov. 1, 2002): 980–81.

The Industries of New Orleans. New Orleans: J. M. Elstner & Co., 1885.

Jewell, Edwin. *Crescent City Illustrated.* New Orleans: published by the author, 1873.
Johnson, Harold Earle. *First Performances in America to 1900: Works with Orchestra.* Detroit: Published for the College Music Society, 1979.
Johnson, Jerah. "Colonial New Orleans: A Fragment of the Eighteenth-Century French Ethos," in Arnold R. Hirsch and Joseph Logsdon, editors, *Creole New Orleans: Race and Americanization* (Baton Rouge: Louisiana State University Press, 1992), pages 12–57.
Jolly, Kirby Reid. "Edwin Franko Goldman and the Goldman Band." Ph.D. diss., New York University, 1971.
Kendall, John Smith. "The Friend of Chopin and Some Other New Orleans Musical Celebrities." *Louisiana Historical Quarterly* (Oct. 1948): 860.
———. *The Golden Age of New Orleans Theater.* Baton Rouge: Louisiana State University Press, 1952.
Kerr, William. "The Fisk Free and Public Library of New Orleans." *Library Journal* (Feb. 1997): 32.
Kinzer, Charles. "The Tio Family and Its Role in the Creole-of-Color Musical Traditions of New Orleans." *Second Line,* 43 (1991): 18–27.
Klein, Herman. *The Reign of Patti.* 1920. Rpt. New York: Da Capo, 1978.
Kmen, Henry A. *Music in New Orleans: the Formative Years, 1791–1841.* Baton Rouge: Louisiana State University Press, 1966.
Lachance, Paul F. "The Foreign French." in Arnold R. Hirsch and Joseph Logsdon, eds., *Creole New Orleans: Race and Americanization.* Baton Rouge: Louisiana State University Press, 1992.
Lahee, Henry Charles. *Famous Violinists of To-day and Yesterday* Boston: L. C. Page & Co., 1899.
Land, John E. *Pen Illustrations of New Orleans.* New Orleans: published by the author, 1882.
Laufman, Alan M., ed. *Organ Handbook 1989.* New Orleans: Organ Historical Society, 1989.
Lawrence, Vera Brodsky. *Strong on Music.* Vol. 1. *Resonances 1836–1850.* New York: Oxford University Press, 1988.
Lemmon, Alfred E. "Footnotes to History: Emile Johns," in *Historic New Orleans Collection Quarterly* 10, no. 3 (1992): 5.
———. "*Te Deum Laudamus:* Music in St. Louis Cathedral from 1725 to 1844." In Glenn R. Conrad, ed., *Cross Crozier and Crucible: a Volume Celebrating the Bicentennial of a Catholic Diocese in Louisiana.* New Orleans: Archdiocese of New Orleans in cooperation with the Center for Louisiana Studies, 1993. 494–95.
———. *Henry Desmarest, Manuscrit des Ursulines de la Nouvelle Orléans.* Compact disc. Arles: Longeville Les Metz, 2003. Distributed by Harmonia Mundi. Liner notes.
Long, Alecia P. *The Great Southern Babylon: Sex, Race, and Respectability in New Orleans, 1865–1920.* Baton Rouge: Louisiana State University Press, 2005.
Michel, Françoise, François Lesure, and Vladimir Fédorov, eds. *Encyclopédie de la Musique.* Paris: Fasquelle, 1959.

Morrison, Andrew. *The Industries of New Orleans.* New Orleans: J. M. Elstner & Co., 1885.

Morrow, Mary Sue. "Singing and Drinking in New Orleans: The Social and Musical Functions of Nineteenth-Century German Männerchöre," *Southern Quarterly* 27, no. 2 (Winter 1989): 17–21.

Mount, May W. *Some Notables of New Orleans.* New Orleans: the author, 1896.

New Orleans University, Seventy-five Years of Service. New Orleans, 1935.

Newman, Nancy. "Good Music for a Free People: The Germania Musical Society and Transatlantic Musical Culture of the Mid-Nineteenth Century." Ph.D. diss., Brown University, 2002.

Niecks, Frederick. *Frederick Chopin as a Man and Musician.* Vol. 1. 1888. Rpt. New York: Cooper Square Publishers, 1973.

O'Neill, Charles Edwards. "Fine Arts and Literature: Nineteenth Century Louisiana Black Artists and Authors." In Robert R. Macdonald, John R. Kemp, and Edward F. Haas, eds., *Louisiana's Black Heritage.* New Orleans: Louisiana State Museum, 1979. 63–84.

The Only Original New Orleans University Singers. Philadelphia, 1881.

Panzeri, Louis. *Louisiana Composers.* New Orleans: 1972.

Picayune's Guide to New Orleans, 1904.

Powell, Lawrence N. *The Accidental City: Improvising New Orleans.* Cambridge, Mass.: Harvard University Press, 2012.

Pratt, Waldo Selden, and Charles N. Boyd, editors, *Grove's Dictionary of Music and Musicians, American Supplement.* Philadelphia: Theodore Presser Co., 1926.

Preston, Katherine K. *Opera on the Road: Traveling Opera Troupes in the United States, 1825–1860.* Urbana: University of Illinois Press, 1993.

Reinders, Robert C. *End of an Era: New Orleans 1850–1860.* New Orleans: Pelican Press, 1964.

Robert, Charles Edwin. *Negro Civilization in the South.* Nashville: Wheeler Brothers, 1880.

Rosenthal, Harold, editor. *The Mapleson Memoires: the Career of an Operatic Impresario 1858–1888.* New York: Appleton-Century, 1966.

Sablosky, Irving. *What They Heard: Music in America 1852–1881.* Baton Rouge: Louisiana State University Press, 1986.

Shaik, Fatima. "An Age of Men." In progress. Communication from author.

Slonimsky, Nicolas. *The Concise Baker's Biographical Dictionary of Musicians.* 8th ed. New York: Schirmer, 1994.

Somers, Dale A. "Black and White in New Orleans: a Study in Urban Race Relations, 1865–1900." *Journal of Southern History* 40 (Feb. 1974): 32.

Starr, S. Frederick. *Bamboula: The Life and Times of Louis Moreau Gottschalk.* New York: Oxford University Press, 1995.

Sublette, Ned. *The World That Made New Orleans: From Spanish Silver to Congo Square.* Chicago: Lawrence Hill Books, 2008.

Sullivan, Lester. "Composers of Color of Nineteenth-Century New Orleans: The History Behind the Music." *Black Music Research Journal* 8, no. 1 (1988): 54–58.

———, and Richard Rosenberg. *Edmond Dédé*. Compact disc. Naxos 8.559038 (2000). Liner notes.
Thompson, Brian C. "Gustave Smith's Louisiana Episode," in *Institute for Canadian Music Newsletter*, v, nos. 1–2 (2007), 8–13.
———. "Journeys of an Immigrant Violinist: Jacques Oliveira in Civil War–Era New York and New Orleans." *Journal of the Society for American Music* 6 (2012): 51–82.
Treble, Joseph G., Jr. "Creoles and Americans." In Arnold R. Hirsch and Joseph Logsdon, eds., *Creole New Orleans: Race and Americanization* (Baton Rouge: Louisiana State University Press, 1992).
Trotter, James Monroe. *Music and Some Highly Musical People*. 1878. Rpt. New York: Johnson Reprint Corp., 1968.
Waldo, J. Curtis. *Illustrated Visitors' Guide to New Orleans*. New Orleans: J. C. Waldo, 1879.
Walker, Alan. *Hans von Bülow: A Life and Times*. Oxford, UK: Oxford University Press, 2010.
Woodruff, Ann. "Society Halls in New Orleans: A Survey of Jazz Landmarks, Part I." *The Jazz Archivist* 20 (2007): 16–17.

III. MANUSCRIPT DIARIES, SCRAPBOOKS, AND OTHER MATERIALS

Baton Rouge, Louisiana Archives
 Orleans Parish Brides Marriage Index 1800–1899.

Baton Rouge, Louisiana State University, Hill Memorial Library, Special Collections
 Coralie LeBlond Music Collection, Mss. 2204, 2205, Louisiana and Lower Mississippi Valley Collections.

Cohen's New Orleans Directory. New Orleans: Picayune, 1852–60.

Historic New Orleans Collection
 John Magill, *Welcome Tuesday's Child.*
 Manuscrit des Ursulines de la Nouvelle Orléans. Cf. Alfred E. Lemmon (Director, Williams Research Center, Historic New Orleans Collection), liner notes to the CD "Henry Desmarest."

Louisiana State Museum Historical Center, New Orleans
 Concert programs.
 Samuel personal papers, Accession Box RG# SB #10.
 Mark Kaiser scrapbooks in the M. Chapella Collection, Accession Box RG 136 (includes a letter from Charles Dancla to Kaiser, dated Oct. 22, 1881, and a copy of *Condinunilat Gazette*).
 Accession Box RG 131.

New Orleans Directory for 1842. New Orleans: Pitts and Clarke, 1842.

New York City Department of Parks, Annual Report, 1915.

New York Public Library for the Performing Arts, Music Division
    Franko papers: scrapbooks of programs and newspaper clippings, 5 volumes *ZAN–*M28, reel 46.
    Clipping Files of Jeanne Franko and Nahan Franko.
    Scrapbooks of Nahan, *ZAN–*M28, reel 14.

New Orleans Public Library, The Louisiana Division
    City Archives, Obituary Files.
    City Engineer's Office Records.
    New Orleans Concert lists.
    Scrapbook # 1, 976.3L.
    Orleans Parish Death Certificates, vol. 40.
    Orleans Parish Births.

Paxton's New Orleans Directory. New Orleans, 1822.

Roman Catholic Church of the Archdiocese of New Orleans. Sacramental Records
    New Orleans, St. Louis Cathedral Archives, Marriage Book III.
    New Orleans, St. Louis Cathedral Archives, Baptismal Book XVI.

Tulane University, Howard-Tilton Library, Louisiana Collection
    Vertical Files: New Orleans Entertainment Theatres, Athenaeum, Philharmonic Society, *Pilcher Conservatory Catalogue,* Music New Orleans Musicians Guild, and Grunewald Hall.
    Marguerite Beugnot Wogan, "Mother's Book, May 1952": Tulane Rare Book Room, typescript 504 (98) (1).
    Wehrmann Family Papers, coll. 873.
    Louisiana Works Projects Administration, "Passenger Lists Taken from Manifests of the Custom Service Port of New Orleans" (typewritten at Tulane University, 1940–1941).
    Constitution and By-Laws of the Mendelssohn Society. New Orleans: Pelican Steam Book and Job Printing House, 1887. Copy at Tulane, Rare Books, Vertical File, under Musical Organizations.

Tulane University, Howard-Tilton Library, Southern Architectural Archive
    Alkire, Alex. "The St. Charles Theater" (student paper, MSS 190 [215]).

INDEX

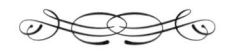

Aaron, Mlle, 422
Abbott, Emma, 52, 137, 453–54, 463
Abbott, Mary, 117
Abbott, Robert, 536, 540
Abbott, Robert, Mrs., 25, 536
Ablamowicz, Mme, 173, 343
Abraham, Mlle, 460
Abt, Elizabeth, 93, 516
Abt, Franz, 81, 85, 387, 415, 503
Adam, Adolphe, 26, 64, 87, 128, 135, 153, 162, 185, 190, 195, 234, 241, 328, 358, 386, 392, 396, 397, 434, 474, 501, 510, 519
Adams, Charles, 74, 446
Adams, Judge, 525
Adams, Marie, 510
Adams, Minerva, 103, 447, 494, 497
Adler, Mlle, 460
Afflecle, Mlle, 478
Afflick, Alice, 464, 474
Aguirré, 473
Aimé, 143, 285, 286–89, 290
Aimée, Marie, 137, 443
Alabieff, 524
Alaimo, 389
Alain, 476
Alard, Jean-Delphin, 59, 96, 104, 131, 132, 206, 211, 213, 225–29, 246, 252, 253, 362, 363, 385, 419, 432, 440, 461, 471, 473, 478, 494, 510, 520, 524
Albers, 542
Albert, Roch, 369
Albites, Lucianao, 388, 389
Alessandri, 544

Alexandre, Mr., 293, 294
Alexis, 289, 290
Alhaiza, Lambelé, 416–17
Alhaiza, Marcelin, 404–5
Alhaiza, Paul, 136, 405–6
Allard, 254, 327
Allison, E. M., 159
Altès, 476
Amat, 142
Ambre, Mme E., 158, 455, 577
Amédée, Leon, 299
Ammel, Charles, 73
Amstutz, Charles, 59, 465–66
Anderson, 270
Andran, 66
André, 519
Anglade, William, 485
Anoris, Elodie, 313
Anschutz, Carl, 38, 383
Antognini, Cerillo, 337
Appy, Henry, 362–63
Arbau, 519
Archer, 313
Ardavani, 382
Arditi, Luigi, 60, 66, 126, 131, 344, 370, 465, 469, 474, 479, 503
Armand, B., 478
Arnaud, Mme Louis, 529, 571
Arnaud, Angélique, 280
Arnaud, 150, 336, 339
Arne, Thomas, 33, 170, 297
Arnold, 543
Arnoldi, 359, 370

Aron, Mlle A., 419, 505
Artôt, Alexandre-Joseph, 206, 245, 328–29, 332–34, 336, 347, 363, 373, 396–97, 420, 448, 609
Auber, Daniel-François-Esprit, 33, 36, 37, 44, 47, 48, 50, 56, 59, 62, 64, 73, 80, 82, 85, 88, 124, 128, 150, 154–55, 174–75, 184, 210, 212, 225, 241, 296, 298, 304, 313–15, 317–20, 323–24, 327, 329–31, 333–35, 341–44, 346, 350–53, 356–58, 365–66, 369, 371, 376, 381–82, 386, 392, 394, 406, 422, 426, 432, 439–40, 444, 455, 461–62, 474, 486–87, 524, 534
Aubert, Octave, Jr., 92, 162
Aubry, 83
Audibert, Madame, 411
Audran, 474
Auglade, William, 89
Augustin, Helena, 96, 215–16, 218, 481–83, 490, 508, 564, 587
Augustin, Major John, 215–16, 490, 564
Augustin, Mme John, 481
Avignone, 354
Avilles, 472, 473
Avilos, 61, 470

Bach, C. P. E., 506
Bach, Johann Sebastian, 62, 66, 96, 132, 217, 220, 229, 255, 387–88, 441–42, 455–56, 466, 474, 490, 515, 522, 527, 533, 587, 589
Bach, Johann Christian, 66–67, 503
Bachholtz, 357
Bader, Antoinette von, 447
Baeckley, H., 500
Baeher, 495
Baethge, H., 452
Bailen, 540
Bailey, Corinne (Bailly), 149, 312–13, 536, 540
Bailey, Thomas H., 380
Baille, Pretti, 374
Bailliot, 316
Bainbridge, 283
Baker, Lewis, 398, 423, 552
Balfé, 52, 64, 339, 378, 382, 448, 453, 474, 519, 527
Bamberger, 70, 317, 323, 326
Baquerti, Paola, 358
Barabino, Nicolas, 295

Barbarin, 482
Barbereau, Mathurin-Auguste-Balthasar, 34
Barbey, L. H., 89, 492
Barbiere, 313
Bardou, Jeanne, 478
Barès, Basile, ix, 29, 102, 104, 303, 440, 524–25
Barili, Ettore, 377
Barjac, Jules L. de, 450, 555
Barlow Brothers, 513
Barnard, Marie, 533
Barnby, 517
Barnett, Mme B., 494
Barnett, 297
Barnum, P. T., 19, 124, 549, 613
Baron, Elizabeth, 174
Barra, A., 528–29
Barré, Pierre-Yves, 69, 165, 293
Barro, 506
Barsehide, 456
Barth, 215
Barthélemy, Mme, 305
Barthet, 314
Barton, 298, 309, 336
Bassich, J. B., 485
Bassompierre Sewrin, Charles-Augustin de, 280
Bastloul, 28, 42
Batiste, Antoine Edouard, 261, 536
Bauce, 329–33, 335, 386
Baud, Ray, 523
Bauer, F. W., 336, 419
Baumann, Carrie, 110, 471–72, 474, 506, 509
Bayersdorffer, Leonard, 46
Bayle, E. J., 288, 529
Bayon, Mme C., 208, 236, 237, 240, 471
Bayon, Mme H., 58, 235, 240, 246, 455, 457, 459, 469–70, 483, 490
Bayon, Henri, 58, 96, 142, 235, 236, 239–40, 440, 455, 461–62, 472, 474, 482–83, 487
Bayon, Hyman, 239, 246, 460, 462, 466, 468–70, 489–90
Bayon, Louis, 292–93, 295, 314
Bayon, Paul, 486
Bayon (widow), 277
Bazzini, A., 227, 245, 247, 448, 491, 517
Beasey children, 534
Beauce. *See* Bauce

Beaumarchais, 320
Beaumont, Joseph, 99
Beauplan, de, 58, 454, 456
Beauregard, 108, 143, 279
Beauregard, Gen. Pierre Gustave Toutant, 200, 204, 476, 583
Becker, 47, 83, 187, 248, 497, 528
Beër, François, 239, 300, 314, 316, 464, 477
Beethoven, 25, 33–38, 43, 47–48, 53, 55, 58–59, 62–63, 66–67, 71, 75, 77–85, 95, 119–20, 155, 164, 170, 173, 207, 213, 215–17, 219–20, 228, 230–31, 245–48, 254–56, 262, 264–65, 283, 289, 295, 297–98, 310, 321, 324, 330, 338, 344, 347, 351, 354–55, 359, 365, 369, 375–76, 378, 380–83, 387–89, 392, 400, 425–26, 428–29, 433, 442, 444, 449–50, 456–57, 460–61, 464, 466, 472, 475, 482–83, 485–91, 495, 498, 500, 503, 507–8, 515, 517, 522–23, 527–30, 534, 538–40, 554, 589, 596, 598, 617
Behr, 451, 470
Behrens, Siegfried, 52, 58, 199, 384, 422, 452, 459, 554
Beirne, Oliver, 66, 484
Bell, 109, 286–87, 290, 292
Bellecourt, 541
Belleti, 124
Bellini, V., 81, 85, 124, 126, 131, 161–62, 169–73, 206, 305–7, 310, 316–19, 326–27, 330, 332, 334–35, 339, 343–44, 347, 349–51, 361–63, 365–66, 368–69, 371, 373, 379, 382, 385, 387, 390, 392, 397, 420, 428, 440, 444, 451, 461, 487, 526, 544, 606, 613
Bellstedt, Meran, 533
Benachi, Marie, 178
Bender, Lorelle, 20, 549
Bénédick, 424
Benedict, 353–54, 490
Bengnot, Mrs., 119
Benicwsky, 280
Benids, Thomas, 528
Bergé, 92, 523
Berger, 66, 508
Berisi, 316
Berkal, 383–84
Berlioz, H., 36, 47, 51, 67, 78, 80–81, 84, 87, 155, 168, 179, 433, 474, 503, 526, 554, 561
Bermudez, Jeanne, 509

Bernadet, 152, 321–23
Bernard, John S., 412
Bernardi, Mme, 238
Bernhardt, Sarah, 456, 516, 541
Bernsortes, 469, 557
Berr, F., 235, 300, 304, 313, 318–19, 354
Berthal, 388
Bertin, Louise, 321
Bertini, Mme, 368
Berton, Henri-Montan, 275, 279
Berton, Mme, 151
Berton, 151, 201, 279, 285, 297, 350, 601
Bessin, 351
Best, William Thomas, 261
Betout, 368, 371
Beugnot, Josephine Schreiber, 135, 572
Beyer, Carl, 54, 64, 377, 446, 451, 474
Bianchi, 351, 355
Bibera, 344
Bidwell, David, 19, 137, 454, 465, 557
Bihli, Misses A. and R., 89, 485
Biscaccianti, E., 349
Bischoff, W. H., 449
Bishop, Anna, 345, 359, 362, 388, 399, 444
Bishop, C. B., 418
Bishop, Henry Rowley, 154, 288, 297, 339, 353
Bishop, Putti, 478
Bishop, T., 310–14, 323, 349
Bisland, Margaret C., 117, 492
Bizet, Georges, 62, 64, 66, 91, 211, 227, 248, 255, 298, 472, 474, 488, 490, 498, 508, 515, 543
Blache, Pauline, 113, 237, 440, 444, 447, 457, 462, 492, 494, 497, 505, 510, 532
Blache, Sophie, 532
Blache, 108, 141–42, 272, 275, 277
Blackman, Miss, 470
Blackmar, A. E., 134, 136, 192–93, 195–96, 264, 404, 412, 423, 583, 598
Blackmar, Henry C., 92, 263
Blake, H. A., 453, 464
Blamphin, C., 404
Blanc, Ad., 211
Blanchard, Aménaide, 461, 507
Blanchin, George, 541
Blès, 331
Blum, Alouin, 74

Boccherini, L., 65–66, 241, 460, 474
Bochsa, C., 68, 165, 285, 290, 297, 310, 327, 602
Bode, 469
Boehm, 235, 336, 441
Boeschhorn, 366
Bogel, Claus, 475
Bohm, 119
Bohrer, M, 326
Boieldieu, François-Adrien, 69, 144, 147, 162, 241, 279, 281, 284–86, 290, 323, 331, 354, 387, 392, 474, 601
Boissonneau, Mlle A., 471, 527
Boissonneau, Mlle J., 471, 527
Boito, 127, 130
Bologna, Clemento, 502
Bona, Julius A., 75, 229, 502, 509, 513
Bonart, N., 280
Bonham, J. H., 447, 555
Boniquet, Joseph Antoine, 12, 276
Bonivard, 441, 454
Bont, 61
Bontempo, 279
Booth family, 337, 352
Booth, Edwin, 352
Booth, John Wilkes, 42, 621
Borchert, William, 56–58, 65–66, 237, 435, 448, 454, 457–59, 462, 467–68, 483–84
Bordas, 364
Bordese, 519
Bordesi, Luccia, 45, 401, 407
Borge, P. A., 92, 251, 518, 520, 531
Borges, Mrs., 536
Borghèse, E., 336, 368
Borjes, Mrs., 540
Bosse, Mme H., 529
Bostwick, E. G., 529
Botesini, 344, 368
Bothe, A., 412, 624
Bothe, Charles, 115, 357, 416–17, 614, 624
Bottesini, 244, 369
Bouchardy, 148
Boucher, Alfred, 304
Boudousquié, Mrs. Charles, *See* Calvé (Boudousquié), Julie
Boudousquié, Charles, viii, 20, 40, 128, 180, 367, 382, 402–3, 570
Boudousquié, Julie. *See* Calvé (Boudousquié), Julie

Boudousquié, Leonce, 404
Boudre, Mme, 43
Boudro, 378, 395
Boulanger, E., 357–59
Boulenger, 433, 554
Boulger, Albert, 520
Bouligny, A., 589
Bouligny, Corinne, 54, 245, 439, 444–45, 448, 555
Bounivard, Adolphe, 109, 171, 327
Bourary, 174
Bourgeois, A., 416
Bourgeois, Mme F., 91, 415, 505
Bourgeois, Leon, 10, 271
Bourgeois, Lucien, 386
Bournos, Emma, 40, 395
Bousquet, 64
Bowen, Andy, 531
Bowers, Vining, 395
Boyer, Mme G., 107, 109, 137, 313, 399, 402, 409
Bradford, Miss A., 118
Braga, Gaetano, 437–38, 462, 501
Braham, D., 485
Braham, J., 288, 297, 310
Brahms, J., 66, 255, 457, 490, 501–2, 510, 515, 526, 538, 564, 589, 651
Braud (Braugh, Breaud), Henry, 421, 492, 497, 583
Braun, Herman, 185–87, 359, 363, 365, 368, 371, 379, 382–83, 410–11, 414–17, 424
Braunfeld (Braunfield), Jules (Julius), 76, 265, 531
Braunfels, 321
Brawn, 328
Brazier, 298
Breard, Mme, 494
Breaud, Mrs. E., 492, 497, 504
Bremer, C., 25, 208, 400, 412, 446, 450, 456, 472
Bremer, F., 54, 245
Bremer, J., 452–53
Brenan, Joseph, 380
Brent, Eva, 45, 398, 401, 407
Bressler, Isabelle, 134, 256, 522, 525–27
Brichta, Mme, 299
Bridewell, Kate E., 469, 474, 479
Bridwell, Mlle H., 487
Brighta, Mme, 344

Brighta, Sr., 344
Brignoli, 161
Broaddus, Mme T. E., 445
Broadley, J. C., 450, 456, 555
Brocard, A., 341
Brod, Henri, 300, 307, 311, 314
Brooks, Reuben R., 242
Brosset, 108, 143, 279
Brough, W. F., 325, 364–65, 383
Broun, Hermann. *See* Braun, Herman
Brown, Eddy, 76
Brown, Herman, 372
Browska, Hedwig, 133, 136, 386–87
Bruant, 89, 492
Bruch, Max, 255, 503, 522
Bruenn, Bernard, 218, 221, 248, 479, 496
Brugriera, 318
Bruguière, Mathilde, 127, 252, 523, 595
Brulard, Charles, 438
Brun, B., 141, 269, 271, 285, 288, 608
Brunel, M. E., 526
Brunet, A., 89, 492
Brunet, Paul, 89–90, 106, 115, 250, 485, 500, 504, 510, 595
Brunner, E., 498
Brunsun, Bessie, 474
Bryant, Fred C., 56, 240, 467
Brzowskia, Hedwige. *See* Browska, Hedwig
Buccholz, 79, 175, 375
Buch, 287, 314
Buci, 335
Buck, Amélie, 466, 476
Buck, Dudley, 489
Buck, Marietta Sohiavoni, 412
Buck, Mme, 113
Buck, 286, 293
Buckley, Denis Henry, 135
Buckley, Teresa. *See* Cannon, Theresa
Buffalo Bill, 130
Bugalossi, 66, 528
Bull, Ole, 125, 132, 154, 171, 328–32, 335–36, 341, 354, 359–62, 367–68, 371, 377, 428–29, 587, 615
Bülow, Hans von, 22, 261, 442
Bumbert, 89, 492
Burden, Rose. *See* Franko, Rose
Burecci, G., 310
Burke, Joseph, 124, 184, 248, 340, 353, 497, 613

Burke, Mme, 288
Burke, Master, 298
Burnap, 489
Burr, Mlle, 113
Butat, 492
Butler, General, 205
Byrd, Perival Doublass, 531, 539, 542
Byron, Lord, 69, 150–51

Caesard, 463
Cahill, 531, 540
Cailly, Mme T., 173, 346–47
Cairoli, 384–85
Calabrési, Eduoard, 101, 406, 409, 412, 416–18, 423–24
Calcaterra, 336
Caldwell, J., 10–15, 128, 145, 297–98, 307–10, 323, 325, 392, 606
Calkin, F. B., 536
Call, L. von, 285
Callierd, 534
Calvé, Emma, 128
Calvé (Boudousquié), Julie, 107, 110–12, 114, 118, 128–30, 136, 182, 203, 237, 303, 314–15, 319, 321–23, 327, 402, 404, 415, 442, 447, 453, 466, 472, 479, 485, 495, 500, 504, 510, 519, 525, 607
Cambiaso, John, 27
Cambier, Uranie, 110, 113, 372–74, 380, 409, 416–17
Camillier, 377
Cammack, Amelia, 117
Camp, Alderman, 102
Campana, 404
Campiglio, Paolo F., 241
Campra, André, 122
Candereen, 295
Candi, 336
Cannon, Mary, 135
Cannon, Theresa, 134–35, 414, 423, 432, 434, 438, 440, 482, 487, 630
Canonge, Mme Placide, 506
Canonge, Placide, 50–51, 58, 62, 65, 71, 88, 91, 111, 148, 151, 158–60, 182, 199, 202, 238–39, 336, 351, 356, 434–35, 451, 463, 470, 473, 495, 504, 506, 508, 557–58, 575–76, 592, 595, 628
Canterno, 474
Capo, Marguerite, 478

Caradori Allan, Mme, 317, 343
Caraffa, 53, 314, 327
Cardon, J.-B., 277
Cardona, A., 404
Cargill, 281–82
Carnatz, 115, 414, 419, 518, 535
Caroline, Mlle, 150
Carrana, 469, 557
Carreas, James, 513
Carreño, Maria Teresa, 130, 133, 215, 428, 437–38, 449, 452, 588
Carrière, Leopold Charles Augustin, 45, 109, 113, 173, 233, 235, 303, 323, 343, 346, 350–52, 355–58, 364, 394, 408, 412, 418, 429, 435
Carrière, Mme Olivier, 454
Carrière, P. E., 89, 492
Carroll, Johnnie, 514
Cartier, Jules, 26, 53–54, 113, 197, 227, 233–35, 245, 413, 417, 434, 436–37, 440, 443–45, 447–50
Caruthers, Cora M., 515, 523
Carver, Hortense, 505
Casanos, B. C., 544
Casanova, 476
Casey, 335
Caspar, Hattie, 231
Cassard, M. A., 411, 439–40, 442, 450, 487, 555
Cassini, 336, 341, 346, 349–51
Cassolani, 308
Castellan, Mme A., 326–27
Castellan, Mrs., 325
Castellan, Mme T., 171, 325
Castellan, Mlle T., 132, 459
Castellanos, Corinne, 482, 534
Castellanos, Henry, 144–45
Castello, Miss, 166
Castil Blaze, 297
Castillon, G., 255
Castro, Ricardo, 62
Catalani, 288, 298
Catani, 359
Catrufo, G., 282, 286, 602
Caulier, Vieter, 54, 115, 233, 422–23, 430, 435–36, 441–42, 444–45, 448
Cazentre, Eloise, 537
Ceresa, 379
Certel, 175

Chabrier, 220, 589
Chaillot, Mrs. E., 113, 539
Chambers, 283
Chandler, Rachel, 471
Chapman sisters, 418
Chapman, Luela, 117
Charles, J. S., 149, 347, 393
Charleton, 328
Charley, F., 542
Charlton, J., 28, 42
Charpaux, Mrs. Mary, 411
Charpeaux, Mlle, 43
Charpeaux, Mme, 107, 357
Charpentier, B., 293
Chase, Fannie L., 521
Chase, S., 412, 426
Chassaignac, A., 391
Chassaignac, Eugène, 108, 173, 346–47, 350–52, 377, 479
Chassaigne, 506
Chastel, Antoine, 60, 466
Chatterton-Bohrer, Mme, 474–75
Chauchon, Louis, 444
Chavenet, 272–73
Chazotto, E., 70, 317
Cheeler, 187, 411
Chelli, 437
Chenal, C., 382
Cherbuliez, 382
Chéret, 165, 285, 287–90, 292
Cherubini, L., 83, 135, 322, 395, 417, 495, 599
Chéry, 106, 276–77, 600
Chèvre, 92, 528–29
Chickering, 241, 335, 542
Chizzola, 441–42
Chopin, F., 47, 75, 96, 119, 133, 164, 166–67, 197, 202, 207, 209, 212, 215–21, 229, 254, 351, 357, 382, 387–88, 425–26, 428–29, 442, 448–50, 456–58, 460, 466–67, 472, 475–76, 482–84, 487–90, 495–96, 503, 515, 520, 522, 526, 538–39, 543, 587–89
Choppin, Mrs. F., 540
Choron, Alexandre, 146, 149, 160, 575
Christ, Leopold, 158
Christiani, 289–90
Christy, George W., 177
Cimanosa, 271, 599
Cioffi, 70, 109, 170, 301, 303, 305–14, 317, 322, 325, 327, 608

Cior, Miss E., 521
Cior, Miss M., 521
Claiborne, 87, 433, 511
Clapp, T., 95, 170, 327, 334–36, 342, 576
Clark, Ida, 477
Clark, Isidora, 371
Clarke, Herbert L., 532
Claus, J. B., 512
Claverie, A., 474
Clayette, 58, 456, 506
Clement, 328
Clementi, M., 270, 272, 276
Clérambault, Louis-Nicolas, 122
Closel, 148, 575
Clozel, Delphine, 147–49, 319, 575
Clozel, Jean Joseph Eduard, 147
Clozel, Modeste Henri, 147
Clozel, Mr., 148
Coastes, 328
Cobini, F., 71, 95, 303, 311, 316, 322, 335, 340
Cockery, Scola, 523
Coen, 89, 492
Coeur de Roi, 279
Cohen, Félix, 462–63, 468, 476–79,
Cohen, S., 89–90, 492, 519, 525, 562
Colby, M., 421
Coleridge-Taylor, 256
Collam, Von, 416
Colleti, L. A., Miss, 495
Collette, Miss, 517
Collignon, Gustave, 25, 34–37, 42, 45–47, 51, 54, 76–87, 107, 132, 135, 155, 174–75, 187, 189–90, 198, 233, 303, 345, 352, 375–76, 380–81, 383, 387, 389, 391–92, 398, 408, 410–11, 414, 416–19, 422, 425, 428, 431, 433, 438, 441, 445, 450, 455, 483, 551, 555, 561–62, 582, 629
Collignon, Henriette. See Comès, Henriette (Mrs. L. M.)
Collignon, Marie, 441, 555
Collin, Henriette, 454
Colon, Eléonore, 179
Colson, Mme, 80, 376–78
Combes, Marthe, 542
Comès, Henriette (Mrs. L. M.), 35, 54, 87, 197, 422, 427, 431, 433, 438, 441, 445, 450, 555
Comtat, 48, 426

Concome, 461
Conduit, 312
Conioli, Teresa, 19, 41
Conreid, Heinrich, 507
Constantin, M., 70, 73, 320, 608
Constantin (Deberque). See Deberque, Constantin
Conterno, L., 485
Contoli, Teresa, 397
Converse (president of Nicaragua), 521
Cooke, Millie, 531
Coote, 64, 474
Coppola, 310
Coquet, Bernardo, 10, 98, 565
Cordelas, 469, 557
Cordier, Angèle, 180, 386
Corelli, A., 208, 428, 486
Corkery, Miss, 531
Cornai, 469, 557
Corneille, 147
Corradi, 351
Corral, 318
Corriveau, J., 498
Cossas, 321
Coudere, August, 132
Couperin, François, 122
Courtade, Mme, 443, 454
Covas, Mrs. S., (née Miss E. Tremoulet), 177
Cowen, 120
Cramer, J. B., 273, 275–76, 286
Cramer-Plumer, Mr., 297
Cramer-Plumer, Mrs., 297
Crawford, Mme, 482, 500
Cripps, 313, 385, 391
Croce, L. 232, 321
Cronyn, Lizzie, 442
Crossman, Mayor, 19
Crozen, 478
Crusel, L. E., 471–72
Crusell, B. H., 284
Cuevas, 528
Cunniot, A., 51, 445
Curant, Théodore, 53–55, 58, 67, 96, 113, 203, 207–8, 216, 229, 237, 244–48, 263, 344, 435, 447–50, 453, 457, 459–60, 463–64, 468, 477–79, 483–85, 488–91, 496–98, 555, 589, 594–95
Curei, 328
Cursh, L., 485

Curtaud, 152, 575
Curti, Carlos, 61–63, 549, 557
Curto, Mrs. Eugénie Gregorio, 148, 470, 577
Curto, Gregorio, 25, 43–44, 54, 65, 70, 72–73, 77, 88, 91, 107–12, 122, 134–35, 138, 146–63, 172–73, 180, 185, 188–89, 203, 214, 245, 299–300, 303, 305, 311, 321–22, 327, 333, 337, 339, 341–42, 345, 352–53, 357–58, 382, 392, 397–98, 400, 412, 423, 429, 434, 438–39, 449, 455, 470–71, 473, 482, 487, 491, 496, 505, 509, 542, 567, 571, 574, 607
Czepek, 344
Czerny, 72, 510

d'Alma, Fanny Hunt, 482
D'Aquin, Mme Eugénie, 208, 237–41, 458, 462, 464, 469–71
D'Aquin, Gustave, 53–56, 58, 64–65, 197, 207–8, 217, 233–43, 246, 428–30, 434–36, 440, 443, 454–64, 467–71, 473–74, 480, 491, 544, 556, 558, 639
D'Aquin, Jeanette and Yvonne, 243
D'Arcy, 528
D'Erlanger, 255
D'Hayn, 236, 455
d'Ozy, E., 287
Dablestten, Eve, 438
Daboval, 463
Dacosta, I-F., 284, 287
Dahlberg-Wenzel, Hermann, 487
Dakin, Charles B., 15, 26
Dakin, James, 26
Dalayrac, N., 271, 276–77, 286, 290, 295
Dalmont-Messmaker, Mme, 82
Dalton, 523
Damiani, 412
Damoreau, L. C-., 328–29, 332–34, 343, 609
Damrosch, Walter, 535, 543
Dancla, Charles, 132, 225–26, 252, 386, 524, 555, 590
Daniels, 217, 458
Danks, H. P., 489
Dantonnet, A., 28, 42
Dantonnet, C., 28, 42
Dantonnet, Mrs., 320
Dantonnet (violinist), 441
Dantonnet (violoncellist), 170, 296, 299–300, 314, 393, 395, 475–76

Dapeuty, 149
Dardignac, Paulin, 29, 102, 440
Dargy, Julia, 504
Dasler, Jules, 423
Dauriac, Mme, 504
Daussin, Gustave, 438
David, Felicien, 395, 503
David, Ferdinand, 371, 385, 415, 417, 440, 475
David, Ross, 475
Davies, J. A., 102
Davis (flutist), 336
Davis, Auguste, 132, 136, 397, 399, 408, 410, 417, 422, 431, 434, 440, 445, 454, 561, 583
Davis, Jefferson, 118, 500
Davis, John, 11, 13, 34, 68, 98, 128, 147, 154, 160, 292, 295, 306, 340, 345, 347, 454, 548, 566, 570, 575, 602
Davis, Pierre, 34, 337, 570
Dawson, J. A., 417
De Ahna, Heinrich, 205
De Bar, 313
De Beauplan, 58, 456
De Bériot, Charles, 66–67, 71, 94, 124, 132, 171, 173–74, 229, 246, 248, 252, 297, 300, 312, 314, 316, 318, 324, 327, 329–36, 339, 345–46, 352–54, 357–58, 363, 371, 373–74, 385, 387, 389, 393, 395–96, 428, 433, 440, 459, 461–62, 468, 470, 473, 476, 484–85, 492, 496, 510, 515, 520, 534, 616
de Brueys, 275–76
de Fotz, 277
De George, Miss V., 521, 526
De Gruy, Miss, 536
De Lassichère, Mme, 452, 454,
De Latournerie, Mme, 40–41
De Lestrac, 57, 454, 456
De Lille, 343
De Lima, Mrs. Charles Abnon, 222, 587
De Macchi, 542
de Meyer, L., 184, 193, 339–40, 363
De Montfort, 387
De Murska, Ilma, 22, 437–38
de Nava, José B., 526
de Nava, Virginia Galvan, 526
De Novellis, 58, 459
De Pelchia, Adolphe, 412
de Riva Berni, 525
de Rosa, 305, 308, 314, 316
De Seve, 501

de Tote, 274
De Vernay, Mme, 131, 386–87
de Vilbac, 202, 472
Deberque, Constantin, 73, 100
Debrimond, M et Mlle Delord, 478
Debrinay, 380
Debussy, C., 298
Dechauer, 533
Decouvielles, 510
Dédé, Edmond, ix, 29–30, 39, 101, 103–4, 109, 176, 303, 524–25, 566
Dee, Berthe, Mr., 506
Défossez, 59, 88, 462–63, 465–66
Deiler, A., 257
Deiler, J. Hanno, 239–40, 464, 471, 494, 502
Déjan, Edouard, 237, 239, 464, 467, 558
DeKoven, 542
del Escobal, Ramonelta, 533
Delagrave, 79–81, 375–78, 380, 382, 386
Delatournerie, 391, 393–95
Delaur, Mr., 478
Delcroix, Désiré, Mme, 250, 509, 580
Delcroix, Désiré, 50, 54, 113, 181, 245, 250, 350, 378–79, 433–34, 437, 441, 453, 509
DeLeeuw, J., 526
Delibes, Léo, 66, 168, 243, 496, 510, 515, 518, 525
Delisle, M, 473
Delpech, L., 479
Delrat, 238
Delserte, 80, 376
Demeo, 526
Demersemann, 237–38, 457, 460
Demonio, George, 531
Dempsay, 542
Dempster, 312–13
Denain, Mlle, 431
Denek, Joseph Harte, 428–29
Dengremont, Beth, 456
Dengremont, Jeanne, 456–58
Dengremont, Maurice, 56, 207, 246, 456
Deninger, Caroline, 169
Depass, Mme, 69, 294
Derbes, Miss, 496
Dermigny, L., 475
Deron, Mme C., 131, 394, 402, 571
Deschamps, Mr., 296
DeSeve, 231
Desfontaines, 69, 293

Desforges, Louis Hus, Jr., 108, 141, 145
Desforges, Louis Hus, 10, 106, 108–9, 141–45, 197, 269–84, 286, 293, 573–74
Desforges, Marie Louise Willamine Irma, 145, 197, 204
Desmarest, Henry, 122
Desnoueties, Gen. Lefebvre, 143
Despommier, Victor, 492, 530, 536, 540
Despommiker, 530
Desrayaux, Mme, 107, 182
Dessommes, Miss K., 493, 589
Dessommes, Mme, 237
Dessonville, 336
Destroup, 108–9, 282
Desvernine, 344
Deuchert, Miss M., 495
Develle, 552
Devienne, 273, 281, 602
Devilliers, 526
Devisme, 393
Devoyod, M, 434–35
Devoyod-Acs, 50, 433–35, 629
Devrient, Mme, 113, 250, 490, 505, 510
Devries, Rosa, 303, 351–52, 355–56, 367, 370, 373–74, 526
Di Bassini, 543
Diboll, Mrs. C. C., 540
Dick, Max, 530, 544
Dietrich, Alb, 503
Diguet, 154, 357, 364
Dimitry, 392
Dirmeyer, Charles, 515, 520
Dits, 295–96
Dobbels, 388
Doering, 217, 458
Dofilho, August, 240
Dolhonde, Mlle H., 440
Doll, George W., 191, 583
Domange, 469, 557
Domenico, 384
Donizetti, G., 43, 51, 55, 62, 64, 88, 126, 128–31, 135, 147, 149–50, 154, 171–74, 181, 184–86, 190, 213, 217, 223, 241, 300, 310, 316–19, 321, 323–24, 327, 334–34, 343–44, 346, 350–51, 354, 358–59, 362–63, 365, 368–69, 371, 373, 378–79, 382, 385, 388–90, 392–94, 401, 424–25, 440, 444, 451, 471–74, 476, 478, 483, 489–90, 519–20, 526, 543, 552

Donizetti, L., 405
Doppler, 237, 241
Dorel, Louise, 53, 444
Doring, 528
Dornast, 469, 557
Doublet, Anthony (or Joseph E.), 177, 580
Doublet, Charles, 177, 580
Doublet, John B., 100, 176–77, 580
Doucet, 498, 519, 528
Doussan, Paul, 496
Douvillier, 105–6, 109
Douvry, 150, 571
Downes, 301, 306, 308
Doyle, 288
Dresher, 354
Dreuding, Philip, 489
Dreyfois, Lily, 447
Drouet, L. F-P., 296–97
Dubos, Henri, 25, 185, 198, 395, 400, 410, 422–23, 477, 539
Dubos, Mme, 201
Dubreuil, 341
Dubuclet, 500
Ducange, Victor, 148
Ducatel, H., 317
Duclos, 352
Duff, 463
Duffield, Mrs., 177
Duffour, Mlle F., 471, 478, 487
Dufilho, Mlle A., 486
Dufilho, Auguste, 468, 472, 476, 519, 525
Duke, Currie, 533, 536
Duluc, 151, 351, 355, 373–74
Dumagene, Mme L., 99
Dumas, Alexander, 147–48, 314
Dumersan, 297
Dumoulin, 439
Dunn, Mrs., 445, 450, 487, 555
Dunnen, 415
Dunning, 92, 220, 537–38, 541, 543–44
Duparc, Mlle, 442
Dupeire, Mme, 185, 392
Duport, J-L., 275
Dupre, Isavel Victoria, 141
Duprez, 161, 395
Dupuis, Ms., 300
Duquesnay, A., 110, 416, 422–23, 443, 450, 455, 544

Duquesne, Mme S., 76
Durand, Marie-Louise, 161, 163, 577
Durel, Joseph, 93, 250, 253, 461–62, 477, 505, 510, 522, 529, 534, 541
Durieu, 40, 397
Durrivé, Miss C., 118–19, 478
Durutti, 335
Dussé, E., 89, 492
Dussek, J. L., 143, 165–66, 273, 276, 280, 283, 286, 290, 520
Duvigneaud, P., 252–53, 256, 524, 534
Dwight, John, 413, 571, 590, 613
Dykers, Kate, 113, 494

Easton, Mrs. Warren, 510, 518
Eberhardt, F., 28, 42
Eckert, F. W., 416, 443, 447
Eckert, J. W. H., 53–54, 58, 75, 91, 94, 96, 103, 207–8, 245, 247–48, 250, 252, 374, 438, 440, 444, 446–50, 453, 456–57, 459, 468, 472, 476–77, 479, 481–82, 485, 487–88, 490–91, 494–98, 501, 504–6, 510, 518, 524, 531, 540, 564
Eckert, John, 115
Eckert, Louis V., 511
Eckert, Minnie, 510, 538
Eckert, Mrs., 506, 513
Ede, 328
Edelsberg, Mlle Ph. De, 159, 424
Edmonston, C. L., 392
Edmonston, Mrs. C., 159
Edwards, Mrs. D., 512
Eichelheim, Albert, 454
Eilenberg, 512, 543
Eiler, H., 471
Einhorn, Victor, 477, 492, 512
El Dora Lonie, 363
Elie (Paul) Adolphe, 32, 109, 130, 176, 210, 215, 292–93, 295–97, 300, 310, 321, 377, 406, 586–88
Elie, Louise, 210, 587
Elie, Marguerite. *See* Samuel, Marguerite Elie
Elie, Marie Waller, 137, 210, 216, 588
Ellene, 291
Ellermann, 129
Elliot, Charles, 389
Elson, Louis C., 118, 502
Elwart, 199, 201–4

Emerson, Billy, 101, 449, 555
Enfanta, 91, 504
Engel, J., 103, 417, 494–95, 514
English, Master, 363
Eppinghousen, Cecilia, 536
Erard, 175, 339
Erkel, 470
Erlanger, Emile von, 225, 255, 590
Ernst, Mrs. H., 498
Ernst, 248, 351, 359, 371, 428–29, 436, 449, 485, 498, 520, 534, 590
Escarraguell, 318
Escher, 528
Esembau, 364–66
Espeinhelm, 321
Espenan, Mlle L., 472
Esterbrook, 20
Estrada, 519
Eugénie, Mme, 315, 336
Eustis, Lydia, 221
Evans, Bijou, Miss, 533
Evans, Mrs. William R., 114, 509
Even, 283–84, 286–88, 293
Eziha, F., 345

Fabian, 528
Faby, 346
Fairex, Corinne, 462
Fairex, Emma, 155, 187, 423–24
Faivre, 27, 356–57, 364
Fallaize, J. B., 496
Fallon, 314
Falls, Miss R., 495
Fancuilli, 533
Farbach, 64, 474
Farinelli, 290
Farmer, 414–15
Farragut, David, 39
Fastman, 373
Faucheux, 250
Fauconier, 90, 115
Fauré, G., 66, 91, 127, 221, 240, 247, 256, 440, 465, 471, 473, 481, 487, 504, 510, 522, 534, 540, 557
Faure, Jeanne, 93, 112, 218–19, 471, 486, 493, 500, 507, 510
Faust, C., 55–56, 241, 462, 474, 496, 535, 556
Faye-Grand, Mme, 473, 492

Feames, Mollie F., 521
Fehriager, Antoinette, 410
Feitlinger, 365–66, 387, 437
Fenellen, Eugene, 174, 390
Ferguson, R., 282
Fernande, 478
Fernando, 45, 136, 408
Feron, Mme, 297–98
Ferranti, 429, 437
Ferrata, Giuseppe, 222, 232, 255, 266
Fesca, 153, 185, 379, 441
Fétis, 300
Fiedler, 384
Field, Eugène, 427, 527
Field, J., 297, 429, 589
Field, Mr. and Mrs., 338
Fiersteman, 366
Fieso, 474
Figueroa, Antonio, 62–63, 460, 557
Fillmore, M, 345
Filomeno, Josephine, 132, 185, 410–12, 421, 583
Filomeno, Miguel, 412, 421
Finck, Otto, 256, 591
Fioravante, 297
Fiot, 150, 184
Fischer, Miss, 515
Fischer, 344, 415
Fitch, Annie Lee, 219
Fitch, Mrs. John, 259, 262
Flandry, Alexandre, 43, 382, 387, 401, 409, 445
Fleming, Francis P. (governor of Florida), 521
Fleming, William L., 19
Flemings, T., 28, 42
Fleury Jolly, Mme, 154, 161, 269, 271–73, 329, 334, 355–56, 365
Fleury, Alice, 160–61, 401–2
Fleury, Laurette, 142, 274–75, 277, 279, 281–82, 284–85, 290, 293, 327
Fleury, Eugénie, 278–79
Fleury, Hermilie, 280
Fleury-Urban, Mme, 136, 161, 269, 271–73, 404, 445, 499
Florenza, 383
Flotow, 39, 57, 60, 62–64, 75, 82, 85, 126–27, 175, 241, 250, 366, 383, 390, 396, 416, 454, 465, 468, 474, 476, 483, 502

Fodor, 141, 273, 573, 599
Fohrbach, 528
Fonteynes, Léon, 92, 253, 527, 529, 536, 541, 543
Foote, Arthur, 501
Formento, Dr., 300, 475
Formes, Carl, 383–84
Fornasari, 311
Fortier, Alcée, 90, 493
Fortier, 142, 273, 277, 279, 282
Foster, Murphy J., 521
Foster, Stephen, 130, 476
Fourmestreau, 72, 109, 154, 170, 189, 321, 323, 325, 327, 333, 341–42, 357–58, 365–66, 374, 399, 416
Fournier, L. W., Mme, 246, 461
Fournier, Mlle Marie, 461, 463
Fourrier, Henri, 194
Fourrier, J. A., 92
Framery, N. E., 270
France, 469, 557
Francis, W. T., 92, 475, 477, 484, 486, 497, 501, 506, 544, 558
Frank, 255, 596
Franklin, 101
Franko family, 132, 258, 419, 456, 480, 544
Franko, Hamman, 205, 585, 597
Franko, Helene Bergman, 205
Franko, Jeanne, 56, 58, 88, 132, 205–9, 229, 237, 245–46, 420, 457–59
Franko, Nahan, 205–9, 420
Franko, Rachel, 205–9, 420
Franko, Rose, 209
Franko, Sam, 205–9, 247, 420, 485
Franko, Selma, 132, 205–9, 420
Frantz, Josephine, 487
Frantz, Rosa, 525, 531, 534
Franz, 503
Fränzl, 278, 286, 600
Freghe, Gilbert, 388
Freische, Adrian, 256, 591
Frémaux, Régina, 197, 238, 460, 476
Frémaux-Benatti, Mme, 543
French, Myrta, 536
Frenclie, 540
Freret, James, 23
Frey, C. T., 432
Freygang, Alexandre, 449

Frezzolini, E., 382
Friedberger, Jacques, 543
Frigerio, 357
Fryer, J. C., 74–75, 446, 554
Fuhr, Louis, 103, 494, 517
Fumagalli, A., 236
Fuqua, Miss, 251, 517
Furatenan, 175
Furst, William, 72, 95, 324, 326–27, 334–36, 338–39, 504, 576
Furth, Jacob, 527

G'Ochwandner, Seppl', 430
Gabi, Mme, 107, 109
Gabici, Charles L., 169, 579
Gabici, Louise Amélie, 169
Gabici, Ludovico, 35, 54, 77, 79, 104, 109, 169–178, 303, 310–15, 320, 323–25, 327, 335–37, 339–40, 343, 346–47, 353–55, 360, 365–67, 371, 375, 378, 524, 553, 579–80, 582, 613
Gade, Niels, 120, 517
Gaevert, 447
Gaillard, Mme, 92, 253, 529, 541
Gaillard, René, 148
Gainard, E., 514
Galarza, Adrian V., 62
Galdsane, Mrs. W. C., 41
Galine, 287
Galinier, Mme, 351
Gallegher, Mrs. M. S., 118
Gallier, James, 17, 20, 27
Galloni, G., 516
Galton, Susan, 418
Galvani, 355
Gambaro, 290, 294, 603
Gambatti, 301, 303–7, 309, 310, 604
Garcia Ruíz, Mme, 316
García, 62, 316
Garcin, Jules, 225–26
Gardner, A. G., 433, 473
Garia, 510
Gariboldi, 382
Gario, 440
Garmand, 513
Garner, W., 532
Garreau, A., 335, 579
Garrison, Marthe, 543

Garry, 150, 336, 571
Gasmann, V., 374
Gast, 55
Gastaldon, 486
Gauche, Misses M. and V., 506
Gaussin, 285
Gauthier, Mme, 505
Gauthier, 10, 165, 270–71, 274, 290–94, 297
Gaveaux, P., 277, 280, 297
Gazzaniga, Marietta, 388–89, 619
Gebauer, 297
Gebel, F-X., 287
Gelinek, J., 289
Gellé, 475
Gelpi, Mme Oscar, 463
Geme, Sie, 108
Générali, P., 291
Génibrel, 154, 355–58, 364–65, 372–73, 387, 393, 617
Gérard, A., 391
Gerber, V., 109, 173, 176, 343, 346–47, 350, 371, 580
Gerber (violoncellist), 374
Geresini, 316
Gerfesch, Annetie, 478
Gernhauser, Joseph A., 497, 530, 542
Gernsheim, 501
Gervartes, 54
Gery, Aldis J., 532
Gessner, Joseph V., 402, 622
Geuffroy, Madame, 442
Gewert, Rudolphe, 55, 454
Ghidni, 384
Giannini, 437, 439–40
Gibot-Rivandon, 436
Giese, Frederick, 460
Gilbert, C., 534
Gilbert, W., 52, 137, 238, 459, 463, 465, 484, 506
Gildemestre, Mlle, 463
Gilfert, Charles, 106, 280, 567
Gilles, 314, 343, 356
Gilmore, Patrick, 24, 28, 230, 396–98, 477, 491, 500–501, 532
Gilmore, William J., 499, 514
Ginet, J., 419, 421, 583
Giorza, Paolo, 464

Giovi, Ernesto, 468, 557
Giraldine, Mlle, 494
Giraud, T. E., 27, 310
Girault, A., 143, 280
Gladstane, Mrs. W. C., 395
Glatigny, E., 40, 393
Glose, Adolph, 475
Gluck, Alma, 76
Gluck, C. W., 34, 46–47, 59, 80–85, 153, 185, 187, 195, 269, 273, 276–77, 416, 442, 461, 466, 503, 522, 617
Gnone, 389
Gockel, A., 377
Godard, B., 207–8, 247, 482, 486, 490, 495, 502
Goddard, Arabella, 225–26
Godefroid, 134
Godefroy, 273
Godfrey, 233, 512, 519, 543
Goeb, 464, 487
Goethe, J., 170, 323
Goetzel, H., 408, 623
Goez, J., 274–75
Goldbeck, 261
Goldman, David, 209
Goldman, Edwin, 585
Goldmark, K., 67, 503
Goldsmith, 298
Gomes, 92
Gomez, Mme Valery, 372
Goni, 334
Gonnet, 436
Gonsenheim, 248, 497
Gonthier, 249, 293, 475
Gonzales, 522
Gore, Alfredo, 25, 538
Goria, 202, 472
Gorjux, Hector, 251, 517
Gorman, 101
Gossi, Mme, 57, 466
Gottschalk, Gaston, 130, 452, 554, 571, 591
Gottschalk, L. M., ix, 16, 62, 83, 107, 109, 124, 132–33, 136, 138, 152, 154, 167, 175, 202, 210–11, 213–14, 228, 230, 236–37, 258, 303, 321, 358, 364, 367, 370, 372–73, 399, 410, 428, 454–56, 476, 487–88, 506, 515, 530, 534, 544, 576, 578, 589
Gould, Maurice, 514

Gounod, C., 4, 51, 54, 56, 59–60, 62–64, 66, 83, 87–91, 96, 119, 135, 206, 230, 241–43, 246, 248, 403, 406, 416, 420–21, 432–33, 440, 446, 448, 450, 451, 455, 461–62, 464–65, 474, 476, 478, 482–83, 486–87, 489–90, 495–98, 500–501, 503, 506, 510, 519, 522, 529, 535, 537, 539–41, 543, 554, 556–57
Graat, 351, 356–58
Grabau, 514
Graff, A., 132, 410
Granados, 60, 465
Granier, 91, 510
Grant, Ulysses S., 44, 571
Grasi, 357
Grau, E., 187
Grau, Maurice, 52, 59, 421, 429, 441–42, 453, 465, 487, 493
Gray, Mrs., 289
Greaud, Mrs., 490
Grétry, 9, 269–71, 273, 278, 351, 547, 600
Greuling, Philip, 28, 42–43, 53, 57, 61, 132, 186–87, 211, 226, 393–98, 403, 407, 410–12, 415, 417, 421, 431, 438, 440, 450, 467, 469, 475, 553, 629
Grieg, E., 119, 220–21, 522, 526, 538–39, 589
Grillo, S., 408, 561
Grisai, Caesar, 91–92, 94, 230–31, 253, 255–56, 494, 504–7, 509, 515–17, 520, 522, 525–29, 533–35, 543, 545, 591
Grisar, 131, 323, 346, 424
Groenevelt, Celeste, 538–39
Groenevelt, Edward (Edouard), 74–75, 174, 354, 373, 412, 415–16, 436, 446–47, 538
Groschoff, 366
Grosdidier, 324
Grosseth, 329–31, 333–34
Gruenevelt, Mrs., 74, 118
Grüneberg, Mlle, 234, 439, 442
Grunewald, Ella, 96, 489, 501
Grunewald, Mlle F., 438, 471
Grunewald, Mme Louis, 437
Grunewald, Louis, 17, 22, 25, 49–51, 53, 64, 74, 92, 94, 138, 156, 158–59, 188, 191, 201, 248, 262, 411, 431–32, 434, 442, 485, 516, 518, 558, 576, 583, 588
Grunewald, Renzo, 411, 523
Grunewald, W. N., 440, 444, 511
Guardot, Mme, 149

Guasdingi, 328
Gucht, Vender, 136
Guébauer, F., 296
Gueringer, Jules, 470, 529
Guesnon, 487
Gueymard, 431
Gugenheim, A., 446
Guilbert, Yvette, 544
Guillé, A., 75, 199, 501–2
Guillemot, Mr. and Mrs., 516
Guillon, 234
Guillot, 507
Guilmant, 507
Guilmette, O., 339
Guilmotto, 335
Guion, Miss L., 187
Guiraud, Mme A., 298, 309–11, 318
Guiraud, Ernest, 106, 210–11, 221, 258, 298, 303, 306–7, 319, 339, 356–57, 363
Guitry, Mlle, 201
Gumbert, 379
Gung'l, J., 64, 175, 206, 344, 366, 420, 474
Gustano, D., 316
Guth, P. J., 28, 42, 395, 487, 495–96
Gutheim, Rabbi James K., 437
Gutheim, Max, 475
Gyrowetz, A., 270–71

Haag, B., 520
Habeneck, F-A., 290
Hackney, Carrie J., 92
Haertel, 503
Haffner, H., 394
Haggerty, Thomas A., 514
Hahnebohm, 452
Hai-Hanan-Bal Hakan, 322
Halbedl, Father, 156, 577
Halévy, Fromenthal (Jacques), 54, 64, 88, 104, 127–29, 150, 155, 210, 314, 319, 321, 334, 343–44, 350, 360, 382, 389, 391, 416, 422, 437, 440, 474, 512, 524, 587
Hall, Foley, 192
Hall, H. A., 518
Hamerick, Oscar, 228
Hamm, 351
Hamma, B., 194
Hammarskold, Mme, 184, 335, 340–42, 582
Hammel, 72–73, 154

Handel, G. F., 62, 65, 73, 95, 154, 170, 194, 220, 264, 304, 313, 324, 327, 353, 358, 363, 429, 473, 475, 488, 496, 502, 529, 583–84, 589
Hansen, E. R., 371
Hanser, Miska, 132, 417
Hansett, 234
Hardell, Mlle G., 487
Harndorff, 469, 557
Harris, Mr., 298
Harrison, Gen., 143, 278
Hart, Junius, 92, 101, 138, 525, 583
Hart, M, 513
Hartmann, R., 498
Hase, C. and L., 248, 497
Hasse, A., 438
Hasse, C., 438
Hasse, Mlle, 438
Hasse, 366
Hasselman, Marie, 415, 417
Hasselmens, A., 90, 134, 497
Hauk, Minnie, 40, 109–10, 160–61, 396–97, 577
Hauler, Lilly, 472, 485, 494
Hauser, M., 206, 354, 359, 420
Haverkamp, H., 103, 494
Haydn, J., 26, 34–36, 40, 47–48, 53, 63, 66–67, 76–84, 86, 95, 115, 119, 149, 153, 170, 180, 185, 187, 194–95, 217, 221, 231, 238, 245, 256, 264, 275–777, 279–81, 287–88, 290, 304, 313, 316, 324, 327, 334–36, 353, 369, 375, 381, 383, 398, 411, 417, 418, 421, 426, 434, 449, 468, 475, 488, 500–501, 503, 515, 520, 522, 529–30, 534, 543, 576, 596, 600, 617
Hayen, Miss C., 235, 440, 514
Hayes, C., 83, 358
Hedge, 385
Hegeland, 335
Heichelheim, Albert, 90, 250, 438, 449, 497, 500
Heichelheim, Henrietta, 511
Heichelheim, L., 158
Heichelheim, M, 90, 497
Heidingsfelder, L., 459
Heifetz, Jascha, 76
Heine, Miss Evelyn, 513
Heine, Josef, 513, 520

Heine, Mrs., 459
Heinicke, 451
Heinmeyer, 234
Hélène, Mr., 295
Helkelheimer, Miss A., 514
Heller, S., 220, 488, 589
Henderson, Miss, 119
Henderson, E., 256, 532, 539
Henings, 70, 299, 317, 319, 327
Henselt, 220, 527, 589
Heph, 395
Herbert, Victor, 209, 532
Hermaize, Mlle, 510
Herman, L., 293, 316
Hermann, T., 208, 247, 485
Hermans, Joseph, 420
Hermant, 444
Hernandez, S., 25, 472, 537–38
Hérold, 36–37, 50, 80, 82, 86, 128, 150, 180, 234, 321, 330, 344, 354, 366, 378, 381, 402, 421, 432, 440, 474, 476, 510, 519
Heron, Matilda, 33
Herr, M, 443
Herr, Mme, 433, 443
Herr, Mlle Marie, 75, 433, 443
Herries, Mme, 69, 294, 297, 547
Herve, Florimond, 137
Hervey, Victoria, 491
Herz, C., 68, 109, 143, 145, 285–88, 290, 292, 295–96, 352
Herz, Henri, ix, 99, 107, 149, 202, 211, 285–86, 296, 300, 305, 309, 326, 330, 340–42, 356, 377, 472, 476, 538, 545, 611
Herzog, 366
Hess, C. D., 448, 455, 459, 462, 465, 554, 556
Hesse, Georges, 468, 557
Hesselberg, 526–27
Hessing, 328
Hewitt, H. D., 154, 166, 189
Heymann, 149, 300, 309, 311, 314
Heywood, 384–85
Hickinson, Marie Durand. *See* Durand, Marie-Louise
Hilariet, Mlle A., 174
Hiller, Ferdinand, 167, 220, 589
Hillyer, 22
Hincks, 240, 247, 468–69, 472, 479, 483, 642
Hitchcock, C. M., 344

Hitchcock, Marie Durand, 161, 163
Hoch, Theodore, 56, 217, 458–59
Hochart, L., 534
Hochart, Theodore, 256, 534
Hodges, 305
Hoeffner, Michael, 35, 185, 223, 351, 355, 371, 378, 380, 385, 392, 485, 494
Hoffman, Edward, 423, 501
Holland, G., 312, 316, 328
Holland, Mlle, 486
Holländer, Gustav, 205
Holländer, Victor, 205
Holman, 543
Holmes, D. H., 117, 496, 500
Holt, Alfred, 484
Holtz, 510
Hölzel, 80, 376
Hoper, Miss D., 495
Hopf, C., 28, 42, 342
Horn, C. E., 310, 332
Horst, 180
Horton, Miss, 310
Hosch, John, 397
Hoseler, 321
Hostie, 278
Houmane, 505
Howard, Mrs. C., 349, 355, 358, 364, 404
Howard, Harry T., 230
Howard, Henry, 17
Howard, Mrs., 177, 352
Huberwald, Florence, 18, 66, 113, 127, 254, 256, 257, 479, 494, 509, 523, 532, 536, 539, 641
Hufft, Alice, 540
Hufft, Eloise, 462
Hughes, 368
Hugo, Victor, 148, 308
Hulhan, 237
Hummel, J. N., 35, 72, 77, 79–80, 96, 153–54, 166, 185, 195, 293, 350, 359–60, 375–76, 433, 488–90, 554, 617
Hunt, Fannie, 459, 482

Ibañez, 336
Icard, J., 62, 295
Innes, Fred N., 477
Isai, 46
Isouard, Nicolo, 128, 279, 293

Jackson, A., 279–80, 288, 320, 337
Jackson, Stonewall, 186, 584
Jacob, 366
Jacobowsky, 528
Jacobs, Amelia and Annie, 494
Jacobs, Isidore, 485, 490, 494, 523, 525
Jacobs, John, 408, 561
Jacobs, Stella, 539
Jacque, 166, 528
Jacquet, Miss, 197
Jaeger, Charles, 44, 46, 83, 187, 192, 200–201, 204, 396, 402, 412, 416–18, 422, 424, 441
Jaël, 202, 377, 472, 487
Jahn, 72, 154, 189, 355–58
James, August, 492
James, Mlle Augusta, 497, 577
Jandot (father and son), 109, 165, 294, 296–99, 314, 317–18
Janes, 81
Jauquet, Mlle Varelli-, 113, 472, 475, 495–96, 505, 508, 522, 538, 540
Javid, 542
Joachim, Josef, 225, 533, 597
Jobert, A., 386
John, 40
John, O., 55, 457
Johns, Mme E., 166
Johns, Frederic, 164
Johns, Paul Emile, 69, 106, 143, 164–68, 283–84, 286–90, 293–94, 298, 578, 582, 602
Johnson, 328
Johnston, Maria Emilia, 184
Johnstone, Martina, 543
Jones, Ed. Lacy, 463
Joseffy, Rafael, 219, 495, 534
Joubert, Gustave, 90
Joubert, Mme H., 239
Joubert, Henri, 54, 56, 58, 197, 206, 208, 217, 233–40, 246, 433–36, 454–55, 458–60, 462, 464, 468–69, 471–72, 503, 629–30
Juch, Emma, 516
Juette, 365
Julia, A., 106, 270
Julian, 394
Julien, Paul, 66, 126, 155, 377
Jullien, Louis, 33–34, 77, 367–70
Junca, 79–80, 375–78, 380, 382
Jung, Henry, 523

Jungnickel, 345
Junod, 529
Juré, 277

Kaiser, Ida Riemann. *See* Riemann-Kaiser, Ida, Mrs.
Kaiser, Maria, 223
Kaiser, Mark, 45, 54, 58, 67, 74–75, 91, 96, 113, 118–19, 136, 187, 208, 218, 220–32, 246–48, 255–56, 263, 266, 408–12, 430, 432–33, 435, 443–45, 447, 455, 459–60, 464, 474–779, 481, 484–87, 490, 493, 495–98, 501, 504–5, 507–8, 510–11, 515, 523, 528–29, 532, 539, 545, 589–92, 596, 656
Kaiser, Samuel, 223
Kalkbrenner, F., 284, 286, 309, 314
Kalliwoda, 50, 335, 366, 371, 432
Kane, E. K., 380
Kappell, Mrs., 306
Kaps, 408, 561
Katzenberger, Mme, 479, 482
Kauffman, Mlle, 460
Kaufman, 540
Kaun, Hugo, 67, 503
Keckel, F., 28, 43
Keene, A. F., 299–300
Keiffer, J., 514
Keith, 447
Keler, Bela, 56, 64, 66, 462, 474
Keller, C., 170
Keller, Miss E. C., 263
Keller, O. G., 103, 494, 517
Kelley, 555
Kellogg, Clara Louisa, 127, 443, 475, 554
Kellogg, Grace A., 113, 515, 523–25, 530–31, 534, 536–37, 539, 542
Kelly, Mme K., 463, 476
Kempa, Piecsonka, 470
Kendall, E., 367
Kendall, G., 367
Kendall (clarinetist), 301, 306, 308
Kennedy, Mrs. T. S., 117
Kennedy, 528
Kennelly, Mr. and Mrs., 533
Kent, 313
Kerker, Gustav, 242
Kermesse, 503
Kern, Jerome, 209

Kernion, Alfred H., 471, 487, 492, 519, 525, 530
Ketten, Henri, 75, 216, 589
Ketterer, 440
Kihneman brothers, 533
Kilshaw, Corrine and Stella, 463
Kinen, Anita, 111
King, 208, 282–83
Kinney (governor of Virginia), 521
Kirst, Francis L., 537
Kitziger, E. Frederick, 53, 87, 237, 245, 247, 263, 445, 449, 453–54, 476–77, 485
Knight, Mme, 296–97
Knittel, Madame, 284
Knoll, A. H., 62, 64, 240, 311, 469, 471
Knoop, G. G. E., 334
Koenig, 368–69
Kogel, 503
Kohl, Richard, 454
Kohn, 318
Kornburger, 417
Kost, 328
Kostmeyer, Miss E., 514
Kraemer, Hugo, 209
Krahl, 501
Krakamp, 309
Kraus, Heinrich, 93, 510
Krebs, L., 187, 447
Krebs, Marie, 425
Kreeger, Fanny, 411
Kreeger, Harby, 592
Krep, 422
Kreuger, 245, 448
Kreutzer, Conradin, 46–47, 80, 83, 86, 187, 503, 541
Kreutzer, Rodolph, 108, 130, 292, 295–96, 321
Kroll, F., 74, 109, 288, 300, 303–5, 307, 309–10, 313–14, 318, 320–22, 560
Kroll, P., 344
Krollman, 343
Kronengold, H., 529
Kronold, Hans, 209
Krug, Arnhold, 66
Kucker, 415
Kuecken, 417
Kuffner, G., 35, 77, 80, 290, 357, 371, 376
Kuffner, J., 284

Kuhlau, Fr., 153, 185
Kullak, 119
Kundert, Emily and Katie, 103, 494
Kuster, Mme, 447

La Hache, Emile, 421, 583
La Hache, T., 25, 46–47, 72–74, 83, 135, 138, 152–55, 176, 181, 184–96, 303, 343–44, 357–57, 377, 379, 385–86, 391–94, 396–98, 400, 407, 410–11, 416, 421, 432, 490, 576, 582–84, 624
La Hache, Theodore, Jr., 191
La Manna, C., 171, 337
La Vine brothers, 514
Labadie, Mme, 106, 280
Labadie, 271, 278–80
Labarre, Mme Clement V., 476, 478, 544
Labarre, 323, 351
Labat, 142, 273, 283, 286, 294, 296
Labat, Constance, 286–87, 291, 294–96, 599
Labat, Mme, 141, 272–74, 283, 286, 294, 296, 599
Labat, Ursula, 276, 283–84, 286, 291, 294, 296, 599
Labau, Ernestine, 178
Labavre, 304
Labitzky, 344, 366
Laborde, 383
Lachmund, Carl V., 209
Lachnilh, 106
Laciotte, 10
Lacome, 519
Lacoste, A. B., 462
Lacoste, Eugene, 534
Lacoste, Eveline (Evelyn), 529, 539
Lacroix (bassoonist), 327
Lacroix (singer), 373–74
Ladombe, 90
Lafarge, Emmanuel, 113, 495, 522
Lafargue, Miss P., 211, 214
Lafauillade, Mme, 544
Lafayette, Gen., 292
Lafont, 296, 330, 352
Lafontaine, 299
LaFosse, Mme Z., 528
Lafranque, 386
Laget-Planterre, 372–74
LaGrange, 188, 379–80, 618

Lairis, Mme, 182
Lalo, E., 255, 499, 543
Lamartine, 25, 400
Lambert, Charles, 39, 73, 104, 109
Lambert, Michel, 122
Lambert, Richard, 73, 100, 303
Lambillotte, 135, 533
Lamothe, J. H., 373, 380
Lamotte, A., 88
Landry, H. C., Mme, 544
Landry, Max, 523
Lands, 344
Lang, Fred, 533
Langan, Mabel Munro, 539
Langey, 66, 501
Lanner, 344, 366
Lanos, 475
Lanuer, 175
Laporte, Mr. and Miss, 107, 109, 280–81
Larman, 448
Laroque, Philip, 142–43, 269, 271, 273–74, 277, 279–82, 284, 599
Laroussini, Mme U., 440, 534
Larseneur, 300
Larseur, 299
Lascelles, Charles, 399
Lassen, Anita, 252, 524, 526
Lassus, Emilie de, 492
Lathan, 308
Latour, Lacariere, 11
Latournerie, 40–41
Laudamoy, Mlle M., 439
Laudumiez, Mlle, 110
Laudumley, 357
Laurent, 439
Lavenant, 337
Lavillebeuvre, Mme E., 111, 415
Lawrence, George C., 19
Lax, 501
Lay, Georgiella, 530, 544
Lazare, Alex, 90, 92, 253, 527, 529
Lazare, Martin, 373–74, 562
Le Blanc, Mrs. Pauline, 226, 233, 246, 328, 434, 590
Le Chevalier, 411
Le Roy, 106, 567
Le Sueur, Fr., 179
Lease, Lillie, 478

Leati, 350, 355
Lebeman, 298
LeBlair, 494
Lebouc, 100
Lebrun, 128, 284, 286, 332, 601
Lecher, 486, 569
Leclair, 428
Lecocq, 61, 89, 137, 441, 448, 461, 469, 474, 492
Lecourt, 331
Lee, 345
Lee, Robert E., 44, 422, 443
Lefaucheur, 12, 270
Lefebre, A., 56, 240, 277, 462, 468, 501
Lefèvre, J. X., 284
Legendre, F. A., 340, 384, 454
Legendre, O., 89, 492
Legner, 470
Lehmann, H. E., 53, 70–71, 95, 149, 184, 299, 300, 309–10, 314–15, 322, 327, 340, 342–43, 355–56, 374, 559
Lehmann, Mlle E., 216
Lejeune, Mme E., 91, 240, 469, 476, 479, 504–5, 510, 518
Leleu, 464
Lelo de Larrea, Angel, 526
Lematte, Gaston, 495
Lenfant, H., 90–91, 199–200, 496–98, 503–5, 507, 585
Lengsfield, Stella, 537
Leon, 555
Léonard, Hubert, 54, 56, 245, 456, 476
Leonardi, 376
Leoncavallo, 543
Leopoldo, Joe, 113
Lepage, 109, 285–87, 290, 293
Lepneveu, 495
Leprutre, 108
Leps, William (Wilhelm), 94, 516–18, 522–23, 563–64
Leriche, 11
Leroy, Prof., 72, 154
Leroy, Ms., 112–13, 154, 231, 470, 476, 478, 500, 512
Lescale, Lucius, 529
Leschetizky (Leshytiski), 220, 539, 589
Lespinasse, 544
Lestemann, Bernard, 425

LeSueur, 281
Letellier, F. J. Narcisse, 107, 130, 314, 321, 576
Letellier, Mme, 136
Letelliox, M and Mme, 108
Leucht, Rabbi I. L., 248, 437
Leutner, 64, 207, 457, 474
Levert, Mlle, 460
Levy, Esther, 494
Levy, Jules, 423, 523
Levy, Stella, 510
Lewis family, 68, 289
Lewis, P., 68, 292
Liado, J., 460
Liberati, A., 56, 462
Liberman, Mlle, 426
Liebe, 503
Liebling, 220
Liebold, Kate, 53, 455
Lincoln, A., 39, 44, 628
Lind, Jenny, 124–25, 127, 155, 186, 352–53, 355, 362, 368, 370, 613, 616
Linde, 542
Lindpaintner, 50, 191, 432
Liogier, Mlle, 102
Lise, Miss, 279
Liszt, Franz, 56, 67, 75–76, 119, 132–33, 207–9, 213, 217–18, 220, 229, 236, 254, 261, 266, 344, 385, 387–88, 410, 429, 440, 442, 444, 448, 452, 455, 466, 476, 483, 488–89, 491, 495, 500–503, 506, 513, 515, 522–29, 534, 538–39, 543, 587, 589
Litolff, 496
Litta, Maria, 130, 571
Littell, 533
Little, Lena, 53, 434, 446, 504
Liugier, Mlle le, 29, 440
Livain, A., 53–54, 113, 227, 235, 436–37, 439–41, 444, 446, 448–50, 555
Locquet, J. F. (G. F.), Mme, 112–14, 136–37, 182, 231, 399, 409, 411, 447, 466, 470–72, 476, 478, 485, 500–501, 513, 573
Loening, G. M., (J. M.) 40, 187, 398
Loening, Mme L., 397, 411
Loffing, M., 300, 305–6, 314
Loo, Van, 482
Lopez, C., 523, 525
Lorenzia, 279
Lorenziti, Bernard, 143

Loss, 270
Louis, N., 385
Lovenberg, 103
Lowe, Charles, 56, 462
Luciani, P., 358
Ludlam, 365
Ludlow, Noah, 14–15, 283
Ludovic, 442
Ludwig, Charles, 93, 516
Ludwig, E., 494
Ludwig, Mlle I., 529
Lully, Jean-Baptiste, 122, 277
Lumbye, 366
Luther, J., 372
Luther, M., 313, 489
Lutton, A. F., 410

Macarty, Amedie, 159
Macchi, 382–83, 542
Macdonald, George, 263
MacDowell, 543
Mace, 392
Macmurdo, Mrs. R. L., 118
Madier, 433–34
Maelzel, J. N., 298, 603
Mageedes, 415
Maggiobotti, 384
Magin, 174
Magioni, 402, 409
Magner, Mme E. R., 160
Magner, Ms. U., 462
Mahé, Louise, 510
Maher, O., 496, 505
Maier, Julius, 94, 516
Mailhas, Mme J., 95, 509
Maillard, 87
Maillart, Aimé Louis, 402
Maillet, Charles, 91–92, 508, 523, 529
Maillet, Mlle, 40
Majocchi-Valtellina, L., 337
Malie, Louise, 113, 491
Malmquist, Emile, 114, 220, 230–31, 255, 265, 506–7, 509–10, 528, 532, 591
Malmquist, Mme E. Marie, 230
Malochée, Jeanne, 449
Malone, Miss, 349
Manalmi, Guillaume, 382
Manouvrier, G. P., 160, 166–67, 317

Mapleson, 227–28, 469, 521, 577, 590–91
Marais, Marin, 122
Marchand, Louis, 122
Marchat, 321
Marchesi, Mathilde, 127
Marenge, 496
Maretzek, Max, 75, 161, 352, 446, 554, 577, 613
Maria, Mlle, 315
Mariage, Mlle, 296–97
Marinoni, 460
Marliani, 83, 323, 326
Marmontel, Antoine-François, 203
Marozzi, 308
Marquis, A., 318
Marsa, Mme, 526
Marschner, 299, 355
Marshall, 373
Martellini, de, 363
Martin y Soler's, 284
Martin, A., 468, 473, 557
Martin, Louis, 62, 103
Martinez, Ramiro, 60, 313–14, 321, 466
Martini, Marguerite, 219, 508–9
Marx, Cécile, 59, 461
Mary, Aristide, 103
Mary, Baron, 62
Marzo, Eduardo, 194, 525, 533
Masac, Theophilus, 114
Mascagni, 66, 515
Mason and Hamlin, 175
Mason, L., 313
Mason, W., 588
Maspero, P., 12, 281
Massach, 175, 366
Massart, Lambert, 131
Massé, Victor, 58, 87, 89, 91–92, 440, 448, 455, 478, 492, 504
Massenet, 61, 75, 91, 247, 469, 486, 490, 499, 504, 522, 526, 541, 589
Masson, W., 217
Mathey, Mme, 115, 449, 541, 569
Mathias, Georges, 216, 589
Mattei, Tito, 89, 473, 476, 492, 510
Matthey. *See* Mathey, Mme
Mattingly, Miss, 487
Maugé, Frederic, 200, 479, 482, 488, 497, 499, 515, 585, 641
Maugin, 174

Maumus, 92, 253, 440, 509–10, 517, 527, 529, 541
Maureau, Arthurine, 449
Maurer, L., 173, 296
Maurise, 143, 280–83
Maxwell, Leon, 266
May, E., 534
May, Melanie, 419
Mayer, Charles, 25, 187, 398–400
Mayer, Louis, 28, 42, 187, 211, 213, 393, 395–98, 411–12, 415, 417, 433, 441
Mayer, Miss, 119
Mayer, 298, 357
Mayo, William T., 154, 168, 173, 177, 180
Mayseder, Joseph, 35, 46, 79, 165, 169, 290, 296, 318, 343, 375, 382, 396, 398, 441
Mazzo, 525
McCabe, James S., 92
McCarthy, Ed, 514
McCarty, Victor Eugene, 101–2
McCoard, Mlle B., 117, 486
McDowell, E., 221
McEvoy, Mamie, 478
McGowen, James, 514
McGraw, Blanche, 507–8
McHardy, George G., 539
McKeon, 177
McLean, Annie (Mrs. Roach), 187, 403, 411
McLean, Jessi, 382
McLean, Ms. (sister of Annie), 411
McLeod-Lewis, Belle, 531
McNairy, Sue V., 195
McQueen, George, 514
McVicker, Mary, 387
Meader, J. G., 307
Medal, Eugene, 89, 485, 492
Medine, 92, 220, 537–38, 541, 543
Medus, Geo. W., 496, 513, 515
Meert, Jean, 476–77, 498
Meffre, Mme, 508–9, 512
Méhul, 68, 81, 86, 153–54, 185, 273, 276–78, 282, 285, 292–93, 295–96, 299, 322, 327, 332, 353, 382, 437, 439–40, 503
Meissler, 241, 474
Meitzel, J., 278
Melancon, Miss, 487
Melchisedec, 387
Mellon, D. C., 534

Mellune, Mrs., 515
Melmer, Fannie, 401
Melmer, Harry, 401
Melmes, Fannie, 45, 407
Melville, Miss, 177
Mendelssohn, Felix, 4, 34–38, 47–48, 53, 58, 64–65, 67, 74–86, 95–96, 119–20, 123, 132–33, 135, 155, 187, 190, 202, 207–8, 211, 213, 216–20, 229–30, 245, 247–48, 256, 344, 351, 353–54, 359, 369, 375–76, 380–82, 384–88, 397, 407, 410–12, 419–26, 421, 425–26, 429, 434, 437, 442, 446, 449–51, 454, 456–57, 460, 472, 474–75, 482–83, 485, 487–91, 496, 498, 503, 509–10, 513, 520, 522–23, 525, 527, 534, 536–38, 540, 543, 589, 617
Menehand, 351
Menesacs, 473
Menny, J. B., 178
Menol, 363
Mercadante, S., 88, 95, 290, 298, 299, 310, 312, 324, 350, 356, 378, 400, 404, 433, 459, 489, 554
Mercier du Quesnay, Le. See Duquesnay, A.
Mercier, Mlle A. J., 456
Mercier, Alfred, 159, 226, 235–36, 456, 556, 634
Mercier-Bier, Mme Nelville, 233, 434, 437, 444
Meres, J., 531
Merkel, 536
Merle, 298
Messersmith, Willie, 540
Messina, 492
Messmaker, Dalmont, 82, 388
Messmer, J. M., 334, 347
Météyé, Jules, 87, 132, 182, 410–12, 426, 428, 438, 441–42, 459, 466, 472, 564. See also Meytier
Metra, 474
Meye, Mme Cassius, 529
Meyenberg, Von, 456
Meyer, Fred, 153
Meyer, Leopold de, 184, 193, 339–40, 610
Meyer, Louis. See Mayer, Louis
Meyer, Robert, 155, 33, 43–45, 49, 51, 53, 58, 77, 207, 405, 407, 431, 436, 450, 457
Meyer, Rudolph, 35, 79, 376, 378

Meyer, 297, 352, 366, 396–97
Meyerbeer, 33, 39, 47, 50–51, 54, 65–66, 81–84, 86–87, 91, 95, 124, 126, 129, 131, 135, 147–48, 154–55, 162, 170, 187, 238, 241, 296–97, 316, 321–22, 326, 344, 346, 351–52, 358, 361, 363, 369, 371, 373–73, 379, 382, 385, 387–88, 390, 392, 404, 416–17, 432–33, 436, 440, 443, 451, 454, 470, 474, 483, 489, 496, 504, 506, 514, 519, 543, 554, 617
Meyers (drummer), 321
Meyreto, Mme, 311
Meytier, 187, 411
Miari, Alfonso, 114, 423–24
Miaulan, 316
Mibloker, 474
Michaelis, Miss R., 515
Michaelis, 64, 474
Michel, C., 371
Michel, J. W., 270, 273, 277, 280–81, 292, 295
Michet, Mlle, 541
Miguel, 337
Milan, 130
Millard, 542
Miller, Joseph, Jr., 184, 491, 496
Milon, Charles, 108–9, 293–94, 296–97
Milon, 293
Miniere, 106, 142, 273, 275–76, 600
Miolan, 70, 317–18, 320–21, 327–28, 334–35
Miral, Gaston, 29, 102, 439–40
Missud, 66
Moehring, 62
Moise, Mlle, 478
Molet, 321
Mollenhauer, 368–69
Mollo, Mlle B., 460
Molony, Miss M., 496, 513, 517
Momas, Eugène, 48–50, 57–58, 234, 431–36, 439, 454, 456, 458–59, 462, 554, 556, 629
Mondelli, 14
Mongin, Miss, 291
Monna, G., 250–51, 441, 444–45, 475–76, 509–10
Montaguet, Mlle L., 487
Montegriffo, Mlle Pauline, 475
Monteri, G., 28, 43
Montes, 360

Montfort, 387, 526
Montgomery brothers, 14
Montilly, 108
Montjau, Madier de, 433–34
Montressor, 308
Moore, 256, 313
Moore, Eddie, 506
Moore, Mlle I., 471
Moore, Mrs., 513
Morales, 492
Morand, 108, 143, 279
Moreau, Arthurine, 433
Morel, 444
Moreno, 318
Moreska, Nice, 25, 538
Morgan, 283
Morgan (senator of Alabama), 521
Morino, 373–74
Morley, 310
Morphy, E., 318, 416
Morrelli, 344
Mosche, S., 45
Moscheles, I., 291, 318, 415
Moses, B., 55–57, 247, 450, 454, 458, 468, 485
Moszkowski, Moritz, 66–67, 215, 229, 503, 587
Mouton, Marie, 202, 438–39
Mozart, L., 316
Mozart, W. A., 25–26, 35–38, 46–48, 60, 66, 72, 77–86, 95–96, 115, 119–20, 123–24, 135, 151, 153–54, 165, 170, 175, 181, 185, 187, 189–90, 195, 203, 217, 219–20, 231, 255–56, 265, 270, 272, 276, 281, 288–91, 294–95, 297–98, 304, 309, 320, 324, 327–28, 330, 335, 339, 344, 354–55, 357, 363, 365, 369, 373–75, 377, 379, 381, 383, 387–89, 391, 415, 417, 421, 424, 426, 428, 434, 438, 440, 442, 444, 449, 463, 465, 470, 475–76, 482–84, 488, 490, 495, 500–503, 514, 517, 519, 529, 535, 540, 543–44, 587, 589, 591, 617, 624
Mueller, 53, 444, 449–50, 459, 472, 555
Mueller, C. M., 321–22, 613
Mueller, F. F., 153, 245, 334, 342–44
Mueller, Louis. *See* Muller, A.
Mueller, Mlle S., 505
Mulledy, T., 471, 478, 494

Mullen, 208, 229, 246, 591
Muller, A., 591
Munios, 149
Murphy, René, 237
Murr, Mrs. J. D., 113
Murtagh, Sallie, 537
Musard, F., 39, 316, 356, 372, 383–84
Musin, Ovide, Mrs. *See* Tanner, Annie Louise
Musin, Ovide, 219, 230, 253, 502–3, 508, 517, 541–42
Myner, 321

Nachtergaele, Jules, 525–26
Naddi, 424
Nagel, 322–23
Napoleon, Arthur, 384–85, 388
Nardin, 416
Natali, Louise, 532
Navarro, F. J., 64, 472, 474, 485
Navone, Francis, 461
Navoro, 241
Nay, Mme, 107
Neal, L., 363
Nenning, Isidore, 40, 395
Nessler, 543
Neukomm, 25, 342, 400
Nevada, Emma, 127
Néveu, 272, 275, 277, 315
Newman, E. J., 488
Newman, Isidore, 511
Nichols, Francis P. (governor), 201, 204
Nicholson, 219
Nicolai, Mme, 141, 270, 273, 278
Nicolai, Otto, 39, 217, 383, 458
Nicolai (clarinetist), 106, 269–70, 272–73, 277–78
Nicolo, 69
Nicosias, 544
Niecks, 167
Niedermeyer, Louis, 214
Nikisch, 539
Nilsson, Christine, 127, 460
Nippert, Victor, 91, 496–97, 505, 512
Nixon, Mrs., 253, 540
Noiret, Mme, 492
Nolbig, 451
Noll, Miss E., 248, 491
Nordica, Lillian, 127, 542

Norès, J., 106, 136, 149, 297, 299–300, 303, 305, 307, 311, 313–14, 318–19, 323, 327, 335, 341–44, 346, 350, 356, 418, 579
Norès, Mme, 304
Normaudin, 417
Norton, Thomas B., 540
Norton, Willie, 514
Norton (trumpet player), 301, 305, 536, 540, 604
Nott, James (Corinne), Mrs., 112, 114, 218, 229, 248, 254, 470–72, 476, 478, 481–83, 485–86, 493, 496, 498, 500, 504, 512–13, 517, 589
Nourrit, A., 152, 320–23
Novelli (Novellis), de, 58, 452, 459, 554
Novello, 153, 185
Noyes, Francis H., 475
Nuno, Jaime, 405
Nyers, 328

O'Cavanagh, Bessie, 501
O'Connell, George L., 23, 29, 89–91, 95–96, 114, 249–54, 257, 461, 470, 472, 474, 476, 478, 481–83, 486–90, 492, 503–5, 510, 514, 518–20, 523, 525, 529, 532, 536, 541–42
O'Guilmotte, 335
O'Reardon, J., 513
Oates, Mrs. Alice, 137, 424
Obert, 534
Oberthur, Carl von, 134, 522
Octave, 40, 92
Oden, Miss A., 515
Oertl, 35, 79, 136, 375
Offenbach, Jacques, 53, 57, 60, 64, 88, 100, 137, 181, 241, 396–97, 406, 415, 424, 435, 444, 448, 451, 459, 465–68, 474, 516, 628
Oldham, P., 345
Oliveira, Jacques, 28, 40, 42–43, 45, 54, 186–87, 211, 213–14, 223, 393–98, 400, 403–4, 407–8
Oliver, Annie, 362–63
Oliver, G., 89, 492
Olivier, Louise, 571
Olivieri, 535
Omès, Thomas J., 529
Onslow, 297, 386, 436, 617
Ordy, 318

Orphenan family, 337
Osborn, Doehler, 384–85
Osborne, 318, 358
Ostermann, Gustave, 187, 403, 405–6
Outlaw, Jennie (Jeanne), 531, 536, 540

Pacini, Ernesto, 236, 455
Pacini, G., 293, 298
Paderewski, 520, 526, 538–39, 549
Paër, F., 190, 286, 291, 294–96
Paganini, N., 47, 132, 224, 322–24, 329–32, 335, 341, 347, 351, 356, 359–62, 368, 374, 377, 383, 410, 425, 428–29, 436, 449, 466, 485, 489, 494, 501–2, 525, 538
Page, Henri C., 25, 43, 45, 135–36, 165, 173, 234, 347, 388, 400–401, 408, 411–12, 419, 433–34, 629
Paini, V., 310
Palagiz, 338
Palaoni, 135
Palfrey, Herbert, 489
Panisack, 153
Panoska, 323
Panzeri, Louis, 155
Paola, 364–65
Paoletti, George, 237, 243, 456, 491–92, 511–12, 518, 523, 528, 532–33, 535, 540–41, 543–45
Pappenheim, Eugénie, 74, 446–47
Paquetti, 364
Paradol, 285, 288, 296–97, 305
Parent, Mme, 108
Paris, Lt., 63, 473
Paris, 279
Parker, Dick, 101
Parlongue, Bertha, 438
Parlow, 66
Parmater, Mme Inez, 508
Parodi, Theresa, 125–26, 154, 352, 354, 359, 376–77, 389, 613
Parra, Mlle E., 239, 447, 462
Pascalis, L., 441
Patricola, Angelo, 251, 517
Patterson, D. T., 281
Patterson(flutist), 319
Patti, Adelina, ix, 39, 66, 83, 125–27, 132, 154–55, 360–61, 366–68, 377, 390, 459, 469, 479, 526, 570

Patti, Amalie, 125, 127, 154, 354, 359–62, 368–69, 376, 382, 403
Patti, Carla, 136
Patti, Carlo, 45–46, 83, 187, 408, 413–117
Patti, Carlotta, 127, 133, 420–21, 428
Pattison, John Nelson, 428
Patton, 12
Pauer, 373
Paulsackel, G., 36, 81, 359, 365–66, 368, 371
Paulus, 89, 492
Payen, Encarnacion, 61–63, 468–69, 472–73, 511, 557
Payne, J. H., 308, 380
Pazarelli, 373–74
Peabody, George, 158, 160, 577
Peak family, 372
Pearman, 297
Pechatschek, 494
Peillaler, Miss, 515
Pemberton, Berthe, 240, 247, 456, 468–69, 472, 479, 483, 544, 642
Pemberton-Hincks, Mme, 240, 468, 479, 483, 544, 642
Pena, Ignacio, 106, 108
Pérat, Alice, 87, 472, 476, 478
Perez, 478
Pergolesi, 95, 324, 384
Peront, M, 415
Perozzi, 336
Perrin, 300, 307
Perring, 384
Perry, 190
Peters, Fred, 494
Peters, Horace, 113, 248, 498
Peters, Mrs. Horace, 494
Petipas, Mme, 409
Petrie, Miss, 352
Peynaud (professor), 500
Pfeiffer, Oscar, 411
Philip, Miss C., 495
Philippe, 388
Phillips, Adelaide, 74, 127, 423
Phillips, H., 335
Picard, Belle, 112, 481, 505, 510, 528
Picco, R., 337
Piccolomini, 384
Picot, 411, 416
Piefke, 217, 458, 588

Pierné, 231, 255
Pike, Mme J., 159
Pilcher, Albert, 260, 263
Pilcher, Carrie (Mrs. Albiades W. Broussard), 263, 525, 569
Pilcher, Charles H., 260, 262–63, 485, 487, 569
Pilcher, Mrs. Charles H., 487, 512, 514, 517–18
Pilcher, Elizabeth (Mrs. J. N. Bond), 262
Pilcher, Eveline D., 265
Pilcher, George Washington Doan, 262
Pilcher, Henry, Jr., 259
Pilcher, Henry, Sr., 259
Pilcher, Isabella M., (Mrs. E.), 493, 521–22
Pilcher, Isabella Mamie Stevenson (Mrs. William Henry), 137, 262, 265, 569
Pilcher, James A., 262
Pilcher, Joseph Felix Mendelssohn, 262
Pilcher, Rosa (Rosie, Mrs. John B. Fitch), 262
Pilcher, Mrs. W. H., 114, 485, 488–89, 498
Pilcher, Mrs. W. T., 265, 569, 598
Pilcher, William Henry, 62, 114, 137, 247, 258, 461, 481, 485–91, 493, 496, 500, 502, 507, 512, 521, 525, 529, 530
Pilcher, William, 259, 265, 569, 598
Pilcher family, 124, 487, 597
Pilfe, 55
Pilié, 284
Pilot, 357
Pinparé, Mlle E., 159
Pinski, Carl H., 532
Pirotta, 469, 557
Pitkin, J. R. G., 257
Pitkin, Nellie, 257
Pitkinon, Miss Helen, 539
Pitot, Mlle P., 478
Piukney-Smith, J., 472
Placide, H., 338
Placide, J., 174, 177, 352, 613
Placide, L., 282
Placide, Tom, 19
Planquette, 89, 243, 448, 451, 492, 512
Plauché, Major, 144
Pleyel, Camille, 167, 175, 211
Pleyel, Ignaz, 106, 141–42, 144, 166–67, 273–75, 279, 293, 296
Poché, M. F. N., 529

Poinsof, 383
Points, Delphine, 113, 265, 512, 522
Points, Eugénie, 512
Pokorny, 447
Pomero, John, 94, 255, 469, 505, 521–22, 526–27, 543, 557
Ponchielli, 75, 502
Ponjol, Mlle, 534
Ponton, 12
Popper, 255, 501
Porpera, 273
Porte, Edward, 510, 519
Porter, Frank, 514
Pothonier, F., 113, 226, 354–56, 374, 385, 431
Potter, Alice, 456
Poujoul, Amelie, 541
Powell, Maud, 133, 225, 542–43
Poznanski, L., 374
Praechelt, 296
Pratt, Charles, 438, 452
Predigam, 40–42, 388, 393–98, 620
Preis, Mamie G., 110, 471
Pretti, Marie, 79, 375, 387
Prévost, Aimée, 179, 183
Prévost, Eugène, 32–33, 39–42, 54, 87, 104, 110, 128, 130, 156, 170, 176, 179–83, 189, 303, 311, 316–18, 320–21, 323–24, 329, 333–34, 337, 342–44, 351, 363–64, 371, 374, 377–78, 386–88, 393, 398, 409, 411, 416, 418, 420, 422
Prevost, Eugène *fils*, 183
Prévost, Leon, 44, 106, 113, 183, 351, 401, 411, 416, 418, 580
Prévost, M. (tenor), 542
Prévost, Mme Mandevilla, 89, 113, 467, 472, 484
Price, Notie, 534
Prioré, 408
Pristia, Joseph, 531
Pristia, Madeline, 531
Pritchard, George, 446
Privat, Mr., 296–97
Proch, 175, 366
Prudent, 365
Prudhomme, Mrs., 187, 411
Prume, 420
Pruschell, 296
Pryer, Arthur, 543

Pucci, 281
Puerner, 103, 506
Puget, Louise, 80, 376
Puget, 57, 467
Pugno, Raoul, 220
Pujet, 332
Pujol, Mlle. *See* Poujoul, Amelie

Queen Sisters, 19, 41, 392
Queyrouze, Léona, 62

Racine, 147–48, 429
Radet, Jean-Baptiste, 165
Raff, Joachim, 119, 217, 220–21, 231, 254, 468, 478, 489, 495, 502–3, 510, 515, 522, 526–27, 529
Raisin, Mme, 37, 466
Rakemann, L., 326
Ramati, Capt., 293
Ramos, F., 90, 115, 595
Randolph, Kittie, 478
Raoul, 48, 426
Rash, 69, 294
Ravaglia, 305, 308, 310
Ravaro, 473
Ravenalli, 469, 557
Ravina, Jean-Henri, 202, 214, 472–73, 589
Raybaud, 92
Raymond, Alice, 492
Rayner, 253
Reames, Mollie F., 511
Rebandi, 250
Reber, 228
Rech, 445, 562
Reemes, S., 422
Reeves, 355
Reghini, 170
Reich, 440
Reichard, 62
Reichardt, 444
Reiche, Elizabeth, 539
Reine, Mme, 476
Reine, Oscar, 58, 238, 246, 460, 464, 476–77
Reinecke, William F., 526
Reines, 313
Reisch, 474
Reissiger, Karl Gottlieb, 53, 171, 227, 335, 352, 417, 444, 450, 582

Reiter, 43, 393, 395
Reiter, Mme, 393
Relehe, Elizabeth, 531
Relly, 476
Remenyi, E., 351, 525–26, 543, 651
Remondet, 106, 141, 270, 272, 599
Renaud, 92, 253, 492, 528–29
Rentier, L., 62
Renz, A., 64, 240, 471
Repetto, 441
Resch, 441
Reser, A., 529
Reuen, Basilère, 467
Reybaud, 528
Reyer, 519
Rhéa, Mlle, 469
Rheinberger, 536
Ribas, 109, 328
Ricard, 115, 541
Ricau, Edna Flotte, 215
Ricci, A., 336
Ricci, Guillaume, 89–90, 217–18, 248, 250, 310, 318, 435, 488–97, 564, 564
Ricci, Luigi and Federico, 126
Rice, Dan, 19, 360, 447, 555, 617
Richard, Charles, 473
Richard, Hans, 92, 534
Richard, J. E., 487
Richard, L. Emile, 113, 468–69
Richard, Mr., 293–94
Richard, Mrs. J. E., 487
Richardson, Miss D., 515
Riching-Bernard, Caroline, 137, 421, 443, 554
Richmond, Adah, 448, 554
Richmond, F. C., 474
Richter, Hans, 244, 529
Rickel, William, 56, 458
Ridgeway, Graziella, 429
Riegn, 542
Riemann-Kaiser, Mrs. Ida, 103, 247, 437, 447–48, 481, 484–85, 490, 494, 496, 515
Ries, F., 286, 297, 503
Rifaux, 12
Rillé, L. de, 88, 459, 468
Rimsky-Korsakov, N., 543
Rinaldi, Anna, 541
Rink, 95, 327
Rion, T., 279–80

Ripley, Gen., 281
Ritter, Theo, 420
Rivaudon, Gibot, 437
Rivers, Pearl, 219
Rivière, Adel, 454, 541
Roach, Mrs. *See* McLean, Annie (Mrs. Roach)
Roan, J., 514
Robardi, 541
Robert, 43
Robertson, Mr., 293
Robinson, 474, 499
Robyn, 321
Rocco, Luigi, 370, 425
Roche family, 430
Rochefort, 107, 142, 149, 277, 279, 281, 284–85
Rochi, Eva, 505
Roclisa, 345
Roda, 319
Rode, 142–43, 277, 280, 282–83, 285–87, 290, 296, 333, 363, 379
Rodriguez, Rebecca, 177
Rodwell, G., 316
Roehl, Etta, 103, 471, 494, 527
Roemer, 226
Roetiers, P., 529
Rogers, Walter, 495, 519
Roig, Cora, 449
Rolff, Lora, 408, 561
Rolla, Servain, 256, 534
Rolling, Mme H., 197
Rolling, Hubert, 26, 52, 54, 113, 134–35, 145, 197–204, 229, 247, 263, 323, 438, 445, 452–54, 457–58, 463, 472, 476, 491–92, 504–5, 519, 539, 584
Rolling, William Hubert, Jr., 26, 113, 197, 202–4, 229, 439, 449, 457, 460–61, 463, 472, 476, 505, 589
Roma, Mlle, 533
Roman, A. B. (governor), 317
Romain, Mlle, 460
Romanie, 324
Romberg, B., 37, 59, 82, 86, 296, 304, 323, 326, 461
Romeldi, Emma, 127, 132, 481, 499
Romeldi, Lillie, 132
Romey, Octavie, 26, 115, 133–34, 136, 187, 403–4, 410, 419, 422, 428, 430, 434, 442

Romez, Mlle, 411
Roneberg sisters, 337
Ronede, 541
Roseberger, 338
Rossi, J., 88, 248, 251, 510
Rossini, G., 25–26, 34–38, 43, 47, 50, 54, 56, 60, 62–64, 69–70, 72, 78, 80–84, 86, 95, 124–28, 130–31, 134–35, 146–47, 149–51, 153–55, 162, 165–66, 172, 174, 180, 185, 187, 195, 198, 202, 210–11, 217, 246, 288, 290–91, 293–94, 296–300, 304, 306–7, 309–12, 314–21, 323–24, 326–27, 329, 331–37, 339, 341–43, 350, 352–53, 357, 359, 361, 365–66, 370, 373–74, 377–79, 381–82, 386, 389–90, 392, 395, 400, 411, 416, 421, 423, 425, 428, 432–33, 437, 440–41, 444, 457, 460, 465, 470, 472–74, 476–78, 481, 486–87, 490–91, 494, 496–98, 501, 503–4, 510, 512, 517, 519, 526, 529, 533, 544
Rostto, Miss, 441
Roth, F., 377
Rouan, Mlle L., 239, 462
Roubion, Marguerite, 510, 518, 522, 527
Roubion, Marie, 113, 504, 510, 522, 527
Rouquette, 166, 378
Roux, G., 476
Roux, Mme Helene le, 57, 233, 467
Rowan-Brunson, Bessie, 509
Roze, Marie, 227–28, 455, 556
Rubinstein, Anton, ix, 67, 76, 94, 96, 119, 133, 207, 218, 220–21, 229, 245, 255, 387, 429, 442, 457, 486, 490–91, 493, 502, 508, 527, 545
Rudophson, F., 388
Ruel, Miss A., 541
Ruffier, 360
Ruhl, P., 81, 387
Ruiz, Leona, 316, 531
Rupes, 90, 497
Rushton, 101
Russell, H., 339
Russell, Lillian, 535
Russell, Miss (pianist), 107, 305
Russell, Mrs. T., 510
Rust, 247
Rutily, 92, 253, 529
Ryer, George, 394

Sablon, 478
Sacchini, A., 275, 467
Sacconi, 470
Sachs, Ruby, 503, 529
Saetens, Xavier, 93–94
Saint-Saëns, 66, 202, 215, 220, 230, 243, 252, 255, 472, 482–83, 486, 490, 495–97, 503, 522
Salle, Mlle G., 460
Salomon, René, 230–31, 247, 255, 447, 479, 510, 522, 591, 596
Samuel, Mlle Cora, 492
Samuel, Leopold, 136, 214, 587
Samuel, Margot, 587
Samuel, Marguerite Elie, 18, 22, 25, 53–54, 56, 62, 64, 67, 74–75, 93, 112, 117–18, 133, 136, 138, 198, 210–22, 229–32, 237, 239, 248, 252, 255–56, 263, 292, 445, 447–50, 453, 455–58, 462, 464, 472, 475, 479, 481–83, 485, 487–90, 493, 495–96, 498, 500–503, 507–11, 517, 519, 521–23, 527–29, 532, 539, 543, 545, 564, 588–90, 591
Samuels, Charlotte, 538
San Remo Souola, 544
Sanches, Mario, 541
Sanderson, Harry, 388–89
Sanford, 41, 396
Sansor, 314
Santangelo, Mary de A., 136
Santini, Mlle M., 505, 509
Santini, R., 72, 318–19, 339
Sapignoli, 305, 308, 312, 314
Sarasate, P. de, 55, 92, 208, 251, 460, 473, 486, 495, 501, 518
Sarrazin, Jules J., 96, 466, 525
Sartori, Alberto, 503
Satter, Gustave, 202, 383, 460, 472
Saubert, 99
Saulet, Mlle, 463
Sauret, Emile, 428, 437–38, 571
Sbriglia, 389
Scarlatti, D., 220, 442, 589
Schade, William, 460
Schafter, F., 434
Schank, 83
Scharwenka, 526
Scharf, Eduard, 219, 502, 508, 517
Schasa, 462

Schetky, Christophe, 142
Schiller, Celia, 209
Schiller, Friedrich, 59, 196, 461
Schindler, Aloise, 153, 477
Schlepegreli, 91, 504
Schmidt, Charles P., 209, 346
Schmitz (horn player), 384
Schmutz, 475
Schnecgans, 436
Schneici, 314
Schneidan, P. M., 478
Schneider, F., 186, 379
Schneider, Luigi, 241, 455, 474
Schnell (trombonist), 321
Schnitzler, Isidore, 460
Schoenfeld, Mrs. Arthur J., 265
Schoenheit, Theodore, 72, 338
Schoenheit, Thomas, 356
Scholtz, 215
Schönbrunner, A., 347
Schoner, 451
Schramm, Charles, 187
Schreiber, Louis, 135, 377, 425
Schrenk, 514
Schroeder, 385
Schubert, F. P., 25, 33–34, 36, 47, 60, 62–63, 67, 78, 81, 83–84, 86–87, 91, 119–20, 130, 187, 220, 234, 256, 323, 369, 379, 384, 426, 429, 442, 460, 465, 470, 473, 475–76, 488, 500, 503, 508, 510, 522, 534, 536–38, 587, 589, 591
Schuberth, Carl, 220, 230–31, 255, 507, 528
Schubey, Mrs., 118
Schuchardt, O., 64, 240, 471
Schulhof, Julius, 62, 211–13, 215, 378, 496, 589
Schultze, Julian O., 421
Schumann, Clara, 36, 81, 87
Schumann, Robert, 34, 47, 50, 66, 76, 78, 85, 87, 119, 207–8, 217, 220–21, 229, 231, 246, 247, 255, 359, 429, 432, 449, 457, 475, 483–84, 487, 490, 495, 500, 502, 528–29, 536, 538–39, 589
Schuyten, Ernest E., 255, 561, 592
Schwartz, Alice, 54, 56, 207, 440, 445, 447, 453, 457–58, 461, 477–78
Schwartz, J., 451
Schwartz, Mrs. J., 411

Sciaccaluga, Mlle, 460
Scott, Mrs. Ike, 118
Scott, Mary, 117–18, 355
Scribe, 150
Scylulka, 474
Seawell, Annie, 54, 245, 453, 456
Seelman, 495
Seguier, 508
Seguin, 411
Segura, 69, 165, 293–94
Seibeck, Mlle H., 505
Seidl, Anton, 209, 242
Seifert, Emil, 208, 229, 246, 459–60, 591
Selanit, 314
Seligman, Gertrude, 537
Selleck, Henrietta, 510
Seniet, 440
Sergysels, Mr., 494
Seybold, Miss A., 495
Sgambati, 543
Shakespear (mayor), 493, 522
Shakespeare, W., 16, 19, 41–42, 64, 241, 301, 308, 338, 394, 474
Sharp, Mrs. Robert, 494, 538
Shaw, Carlotta, 404
Shaw family, 320
Shaw, Kate, 117, 158, 577
Shearer, Bessie, 525
Shelly, 510
Shepard, Miss K. H., 537
Sheppard, E., 171, 324
Sheppard, R., 324
Sheridan, 309
Shield, 456
Shields, Annie S., 257, 532
Shields, Bernard C., 540, 597
Shields, Mme and M, 523
Sholia, Mme, 57, 467
Shriever, Miss, 513
Siebrant, 240, 469
Siede, 359, 62
Siedenburg, 370, 379
Silverman, H., (cantor), 518, 520
Simms, Frank H., 119–20, 530, 536, 540
Simon (cure de St Eustache), 156
Simonson, Frieda, 532
Singelée, Jean-Baptiste, 249, 440
Singer, Teresina, 130

Sinnott, Ella, 509
Sipp, 115, 187, 416, 421–22, 424
Sirby, 515
Sivori, C., 26, 234, 340–42, 344, 434, 444, 456, 529
Slidell, John, 225
Sloman family, 339
Smith, Gustave, 46, 83, 132, 135–36, 187, 410–11
Smith, H. J., 513
Smith (opera composer), 542
Smith, Mrs. Pinekney, 117, 472
Smith, Sol, 14–15
Smittle, 522
Snaer, Samuel, Jr., 101–2
Socola, Anita, 119, 215, 220, 248, 518–19, 522, 539–40
Soedermann, 59, 461
Soetens, Xavier, 516–17
Soldene, Emily, 137, 435
Soler, 270, 281, 284
Sonderman, 241, 474
Sontag, G., 64, 66, 240, 471, 477, 484, 486, 491, 498
Sontag, Henrietta, ix, 124–25, 127, 131, 155, 367, 370–71, 373, 616
Sotto, 388
Soubeyran, 526
Sousa, John Philip, 66, 205, 209, 230, 243, 484–85, 533, 536, 543, 656
Spear, 177
Specht, 248, 426, 497
Spicker, 503
Spinola, A., 377
Spirti, 89, 492
Spohr, L., 36, 77, 81–82, 87, 120, 153, 185, 195, 379, 383, 494, 536, 617
Spontini, G., 280–81, 298, 323
Sporer, J., 201
Sprecht, Anita Socola. *See* Socola, Anita
Squires, Henry, 387–88, 420
Stamaty, Camille-Marie, 211–13, 220, 489, 522
Stamps, Mrs., 115, 421
Stamwitz, Mme, 447
Stassny, 474
Stauffer, Walter, 525
Steele, Delphine, 541

Steele, Rev., 541
Steibelt, 165, 270–71, 273–78, 286, 290
Steinway, 175, 191, 205, 209, 409, 429, 432, 438
Stella, A., 311–12, 314, 316, 319, 463
Stendhal, 168
Stevens, Miss Nealy, 119
Stoelzer, 501
Stopel, R., 33, 378
Storr, Karl, 508
Stoss. *See* Strauss, John
Stradella, 135, 411, 433, 441, 506, 554
Strakosch, Maurice, 19, 38, 125–26, 154, 193, 202, 345–46, 349–51, 354, 359–62, 367–68, 376–77, 382, 388, 517, 576, 577
Strakosch, Mrs. Maurice. *See* Patti, Amalie
Strakosch, Max, 51–52, 58, 130, 133, 199, 226, 403–7, 428, 437, 451–52, 455, 458–59, 472, 554, 556, 576, 613, 623
Strassy, 56, 462
Strauss, J. (family), 28, 42, 50, 54–56, 66, 166, 217, 312, 316, 320, 333, 344, 366, 396, 425, 432, 441, 451, 454, 457–58, 462, 472–74, 483, 503
Strauss, John, 65, 558
Strelenzki, Anton, 459
Stross. John Strauss, John
Stumpf, 514
Sturte, 470
Stutz, 87
Sucola, Ms. A., 491
Suitaner, 436
Sullivan, Arthur, 52, 64, 120, 127, 137, 238, 241, 451, 459, 463, 465, 474, 484–85, 506
Sumner, Mr. and Mrs. W. W., 247, 459, 479, 536, 540
Suppé, 56–57, 60–62, 64, 66, 89, 216–17, 230, 417, 425, 441, 451, 454, 458, 462, 465, 468, 470, 472–74, 492, 496, 506, 543
Svendsen, 65, 460
Syr, C., 70, 72–73
Szermanowski, 473

Tabary, Louis, 9–10
Taffanelli, 379
Talvar, Lea, 478
Tamaro, 388–89
Tanner, Annie Louise, 502, 508
Tarrut, Miss, 197

Tasca, Taccani, 79, 375–76
Tasse, Victor, 211
Taste, 386
Taubert, 503
Tausig, 536
Taylor, G., 328
Taylor, Gen. Zachary, 172–74, 177, 180, 193, 340, 342–43, 345
Taylor, 288
Tchaikovsky, P. I., 255, 491, 596
Tcheszka, Barbara, 164
Telemadon, 515
Teltow, 321
Templeton, 338
Teoni, 439
Terranova, C. P., 529
Tersmeden, Frida de, 539
Tessier, August, 12, 98, 565
Thalberg, S., ix, 43, 132–33, 190, 212–13, 318, 326, 330–31, 335–36, 344, 350, 352, 378, 381–82, 386–88, 391, 395, 410, 429, 440, 448
Thayer, Fred N., 112, 130, 448
Thayer, Kate, 112, 130, 133, 137, 245, 434, 444, 448, 452, 571
Théard, Alfred, 462
Théaulon, 297
Theon, 469, 557
Thérésa, Mlle (chanteuse), 430
Therman, Walter Lee, 541
Thibaut, Jacques, 215
Thiedepape, 346
Thilberger, Mrs. A. J., 515
Thilow, 362–63
Thomas, Ambroise, 51, 63, 75, 80, 88, 182, 201, 210, 221, 225, 356, 376, 422, 440–41, 453, 459, 544, 561
Thomas, Theodore, 47–48, 54, 65–66, 209, 244, 383, 425, 427, 446, 483, 501, 591
Thome, 63, 495
Thompson, Lydia, 424, 430, 499
Thompson, 62
Thomson, 248, 497
Thorne, Mr., 299
Thorpe, J. W., 412
Tidd, Haddie T., 455, 556
Tietjens, Therese, 226–27, 590
Tilden, Belle T., 262
Tilleux, 436

Tio family, 39, 100, 580, 595
Tio, Lorenzo, Sr., 177, 498
Tio, Louis, 177, 498
Titl, E., 344
Tobey, 300, 307, 313–116
Todd, Ella, 534
Tolou, 165
Tom, Blind, 388
Torbett, Ollie, Mlle, 475, 539
Torriani, Angelo, 444
Torsiello, Cesare, 533
Tosso, Paul, 92, 279, 523
Tosti, 483, 486
Tournié, 58, 238
Townsend, Cora A., 159
Tracy, Charles, 412, 459, 564
Tranchina, 535
Trapolin, Mlles J. and V., 119, 476
Trastour, 373
Traub, 286–87
Trotter, 73, 561, 517
Trust, A. (harpist), 72, 107, 109, 154, 169–70, 186, 189, 309–14, 318, 323, 335, 357–58, 374, 379
Trust, H., 311–112
Tudury, 514
Tuerner, 496
Tulou, J-L., 233–35, 294, 296, 356
Tusson, Gabrielle, 522
Tylda, Mme, 526–27
Tyler, E., 446–47, 456

Uberwall, Mme, 201
Ullman, 38
Underwood, 499
Urban. See Fleury-Urban, Mme
Urev, Ch. T., 412
Urso, Camille, 125, 131, 155, 233, 370–71, 427, 438, 561, 571

Vahlmann, L., 514
Vail, A., 377
Valades, 440
Valck, L., 519, 528
Valentine, J., 339
Vallé, H., 89, 492
Valles, H. (dancer), 174
Vallière (oboist), 149, 299–300, 303–5, 307, 309–11, 313–14, 316, 318

Valois, 274–75, 282
Valtellina, A., 337
Van Benthuysen, C., 513
Van Cauwelaert, 416–17
Van Den Daelen, 94
Van Ghele, 430, 555
Van Hufflen, 50, 87, 112, 113–15, 201, 233, 239, 247, 419, 421, 423, 426, 428, 430, 434, 439, 442, 444, 448, 464, 467, 472, 476, 530, 577
Vanloo, 374
Varelli, Mlle, 113, 464, 472, 475, 496, 505, 508, 522, 540
Varenne, Leonie de, 505
Varnay, A., 149, 171, 180
Vasseur, Léon, 137
Vaughan, 283
Vaurigaud, Mrs. A. T., 113, 497
Vaurigaud, Mme O., 524
Vay, F., 310
Veazey, Armand, 477, 505, 533
Vegas, 174
Veith, 495
Vêque, Charles, 102
Verbrugghen, Henri, 232
Vercken, Mrs., 437–39
Verdi, G., 60–62, 64, 66, 75, 81, 83, 87–89, 126–27, 130, 135, 153, 162, 185, 190, 199, 225, 238, 244, 343, 349–51, 358, 361, 366, 368, 371, 374, 378–79, 385, 388–90, 392, 403, 405–6, 411–12, 415, 418, 423, 425, 437, 439, 441, 444, 448, 451, 454, 461, 465, 470–71, 473–74, 476, 478, 483, 486–87, 492, 494, 496, 500–504, 506, 510, 512, 528, 534, 541–42, 544, 618–19
Verronet, 437
Vestvali, 382
Vianesi, Le Chevallier A., 61, 468
Viavant, F., 460, 510
Victor, Mr., 290, 327
Videnqué, 61
Vidondez, August, 89, 485
Vieuxtemps, H., ix, 88, 120, 131–32, 205–6, 208–9, 225, 227, 233–34, 238, 246–47, 328–31, 333–34, 346, 341, 344, 347, 351, 356, 363, 371, 373–74, 381–82, 394, 410, 415, 420, 422, 428–29, 434, 449, 457, 520, 543, 545, 572, 597, 630
Vignaud, Mlles E. and L., 460

Vigule, 27, 310
Vilbac, de, 202, 472
Villaprado, 62
Villère, J. (governor), 143, 278, 281, 286
Vincent, Mrs. J. L., 113, 251, 517
Vincent, Léonice, 252, 522, 539
Viotti, G. B., 45, 68, 108–9, 142–43, 223, 245, 276, 279–80, 282, 286, 288, 290, 292–93, 408–9, 448
Vivant, 513
Vivière, 512
Vizcarra, 506, 528
Vogel, C. W., 90, 500
Vogel, J. B., 57, 467, 477
Vogel, J. C., 290, 437
Vogel, S. B., 509
Voges, 92, 514
Volanges, 288
Voltaire, 71, 148
Von Edelsberg, Philippine, 424
Voorhies, J., 89–90, 115, 492, 595

Waddel, W. W., 166
Wadsworth, J. H., 485
Wagner, Alfred, 478,
Wagner, Mlle, 422, 438
Wagner, R., 48, 50, 53, 60–62, 64–67, 75, 127, 198, 219, 366, 425–26, 432, 446, 451, 457, 465, 472–74, 486, 489, 491, 496–97, 500, 502–3, 508, 519, 527, 529, 535, 539, 543, 549, 654
Wakefield, Herbert, 531
Walcher, J., 201
Waldauer, A., 72, 339
Waldo, J. Curtis, 22, 549–50
Waldteufel, 55, 60–62, 64–65, 89, 217, 241, 458, 465, 470, 474, 485, 492, 496, 506, 512
Walkiers, 318
Wall (harpist), 184
Wallace, William V., 53, 170–71, 197, 324–25, 336–37, 344, 350–51, 363, 449, 457, 510, 531, 540
Walsh, 296
Walther, 344
Wangler, 506
Wannack, Marie, 59, 461–62, 471, 473–74, 482, 490
Wapler, 48, 426

Ward, Cabot, 243
Warren, 328
Watkins. *See* Howard, Mrs. C.
Watson, 313
Watson, Mme, 57, 312–13, 466
Watts, T. R., 230, 438, 440
Wayne, Mamie P., 521
Weber, Carl Maria von, 25, 34–37, 42, 47–48, 53–54, 61, 65–67, 71, 77–85, 87, 119, 132–33, 155, 175, 187, 190, 206, 212, 217, 220, 240–41, 247, 295, 297, 299, 331, 333, 335–37, 339, 344, 347, 351, 354, 357, 365, 369, 371, 375–76, 380–83, 387, 391–92, 398, 406, 409, 419, 425–26, 429, 433, 438–39, 449, 451, 455, 458, 464, 471, 474–75, 481, 483, 487, 489, 490, 494, 496, 500, 503, 522–23, 527, 540, 542, 554, 582, 587, 617
Weber, C. Otto, 426, 432, 437, 629
Weber (violoncellist), 321
Webster, 278–79
Wehrman, Henry, Jr., 89–92, 94, 96, 113–15, 138, 220, 222, 230–31, 249–57, 263, 266, 475, 492, 497–98, 500, 505, 507, 509–10, 513–14, 516–20, 522–25, 527–30, 534–35, 537–43, 545, 588, 591, 596, 656
Wehrman, Mrs. (Renzo?), 510
Wehrmann, Mrs. H., Jr., 520
Wehrmann, Henri, Sr., 104, 138, 177–78, 588
Wehrmann, Charlotte (Mme Henri, Sr.), 138, 216, 249, 262–63, 577, 588
Wehrmann, Valentine, 138
Wehrmann-Moore, Mrs., 256
Wehrmann-Schaffner, Eugénie, 76, 138, 215, 222, 253, 255–56, 524, 529, 534, 539–42, 588
Weifenbach, 55, 457–58
Weigl, J., 153, 185
Weingart, George W., 90, 250, 500, 504, 510
Weiss, Carl, 93, 118–19, 241, 257, 474, 508, 510, 528
Wekerlin, 88
Welas, 517
Welch, 148, 311
Weldon, Thomas F., 471
Wells, R., E., 113, 531, 537
Wely, 83, 135, 378
Wendover, Harriet, 259–60
Wendover, Julia, 259–60, 597

Werlein, Philip, 22, 59, 64, 92, 110, 113, 117, 119, 138, 168, 176, 192–93, 195, 204, 216, 240, 250, 257, 260, 263, 412, 465, 466, 468–72, 500, 506, 509–10, 517, 521, 527, 531–32, 536–39, 576, 588
Werth, Mme, 510
West, Mrs., 496
Wheat, Leo, 414–16
Whitaker, J., 379
White, Allie, 537
White, José Silvestre, 100, 211
White, 382
Whitfield, Mrs. and Miss, 117, 119
Wickliffe, G. M., 196
Wideman, 358, 364–65
Widerkehr, J., 393
Widor, 111
Wiede, 363
Wiedemann, Mme A., 151, 154, 160
Wiegand, George, 485
Wiegel, J., 90, 115, 595
Wieniawski, Henri, 26, 209, 239, 246–47, 249, 252, 428–29, 442, 444, 448, 462, 468, 503, 517, 539, 544
Wildeman, 425
Wilhelm I (emperor of Germany), 489
Wilhelmj, 22, 449, 508, 588, 597
Wilhem, Mme, 439
Willard, Frances, 522
Williams, Arthur P., 102, 115, 523
Williers, 64
Willig, George, 166
Willis, H., 306, 308
Willoughby, Grace, 389
Wills, Mr., 306
Wilmers, 206, 420
Wilson, John, 446
Wilson, Mary, 117–18
Wilson, Mlle May, 444, 478
Wilson, Mr. (of London), 347
Wiltz, George L., 526
Wingate, Miss E. C., 158, 577
Winter, 190, 195
Wirth, Mrs., 119
Witham, Mme Charles, 424, 476–77, 487

Witham, Mrs. G., 491, 510
Withers, William, 418, 430, 628
Wittriz, 382
Wjille, 368
Woelfl, J., 286
Wogt, 304
Wohlein, T., 36, 81
Wolf, Jennie, 527
Wolf, Mlle M., 446
Wolf, O., 344
Wortmann, J. (string bassist), 90, 115, 595
Woulf, Mlle, 505
Wranitsky, 247
Wright, Helene, 510
Wright, Sophie, 532
Wuille, 369
Wulff, Mme H. H., 113, 235, 411, 486–87
Wunch, 103
Wunsch, J. B., 485
Wynen, Charles, 174, 354–56

Xanten, 543

Yaw, Ellen Beach, 127, 530, 544
Yenssen, 221
Younkers (chef d'orchestre), 46, 408–10
Ysaye, Eugene, 232, 572
Yuille, Mrs., 118–19, 247, 479, 483

Zamila, Roza, 132
Zaniehelli (cornetist), 474
Zanita, Cora, 486
Zapucci, V., 291
Zarate, Eduardo E., 63, 471
Zarzycki, 255
Zeisler, Fannie Bloomfield, 133
Zeiss-Denis, Mme, 115, 226, 419, 423–24, 426, 430, 438, 455
Zeringer, 534
Zerr, A., 368–69
Ziegler, C., 239, 462
Zikoff, 474
Zimmer, Mme, 107, 109, 300, 304
Zimmerman, Pierre-Joseph-Guillaume, 34
Zuberier, Mme M., 208